7th International Conference on Reliability of Electrical Products and Electrical Contacts (ICREPEC 2019)

Suzhou, China
4-6 November 2019

Editors:

Jingqin Wang
Jingying Zhao

ISBN: 978-1-5108-9802-8

Printed from e-media with permission by:

Curran Associates, Inc.
57 Morehouse Lane
Red Hook, NY 12571

Some format issues inherent in the e-media version may also appear in this print version.

Printed with permission by Curran Associates, Inc. (2020)

For permission requests, please contact International Academic Publishers
at the address below.

International Academic Publishers
137 Chaonei Dajie
Beijing 100010 China

Additional copies of this publication are available from:

Curran Associates, Inc.
57 Morehouse Lane
Red Hook, NY 12571 USA
Phone: 845-758-0400
Fax: 845-758-2633
Email: curran@proceedings.com
Web: www.proceedings.com

Proceedings of the 7th International Conference on Reliability of Electrical Products and Electrical Contacts

November 4-6, 2019
Lakeside Hotel, Suzhou, China

ICREPEC 7th 2019

Edited by
Jingqin Wang   Jingying Zhao

Organized by
Electrical Products Reliability Professional Committee of Chinese Electrotechnical Society

Sponsored by
Suzhou Future Electrical Appliances Co., Ltd.
Provincial and Ministerial Co-construction Collaborative Innovation Center on Reliability Technology of Electrical Products
Harbin Institute of Technology

International Academic Publishers Ltd.

International Academic Publishers Ltd.
E-mail: iap-bj@hotmail.com

Edited by Jingqin Wang, Jingying Zhao

Proceedings of the 7th International Conference on Reliability of Electrical Products and Electrical Contact

Preface

Welcome to the 7th International Conference on Reliability of Electrical Products and Electrical Contacts. It is a great pleasure and my distinct privilege as Chairman of the conference to welcome you to Suzhou, China. The 7th International Conference on Reliability of Electrical Products and Electrical Contacts will be held in Lakeside Hotel, Suzhou, China, from November 4 to 6, 2019. Besides the planned activities, the conference includes some technical visits. It is organized by Electrical Products Reliability Professional Committee of Chinese Electrotechnical Society, and sponsored by Suzhou Future Electrical Appliances Co., Ltd., Provincial and Ministerial Co-construction Collaborative Innovation Center on Reliability Technology of Electrical Products and Harbin Institute of Technology.

Persons who attended the conference are engineers, scientists, managers of various companies and professors of the universities abroad and home.

The proceedings of the conference include more than 70 papers contributed by authors from different countries after peer reviewing. The papers presented authoritative comments on Reliability Design, Statistics of Reliability, Reliability Management, Reliability Manufacture, Failure Modes and Mechanism, Reliability Analysis, System and Software Reliability, Reliability Test Method and Test Device, Quality Management and Assurance, Reliability of Electrical Products and Equipment, Electrical Contact Phenomenon, Electrical Contact Failure and Testing, Environmental Effect on Electrical Contact, Contact Material, Contact Failure Simulation and Prediction, Safety Device and Other Related Topics.

In closing, please let me express my special thanks to the authors and presenters, our Conference Co-Chairman, Conference Honorary Chairman, Technical Program Committee, Organization Committee, International Advisory Committee, as well as the individuals, sponsors and organizations, who worked so hard to prepare the 7th International Conference on Reliability of Electrical Products and Electrical Contacts. As chairman of this conference, please allow me to express my gratitude for having had this unique opportunity to closely work with such a fine group of professional people. I am looking forward to continue my support of the International Conference on Reliability of Electrical Products and Electrical Contacts.

Jiaomin Liu
Chairman

CONFERENCE ORGANIZATION

CONFERENCE CHAIRMAN

Jiaomin Liu

CONFERENCE CO-CHAIRMAN

Jianguo Lu Manjin Guo Chunchao Tang

CONFERENCE HONORARY CHAIRMAN

Yansun Lu Werner Johler (Switzerland)

TECHNICAL PROGRAM COMMITTEE

Chairman:	Jingqin Wang
Vice Chairman:	Youtong Fang Zhenbiao Li Guofu Zhai Guichu Wu

ORGANIZATION COMMITTEE

Chairman:	Jingying Zhao
Vice Chairman:	Jianping Mo Xuerong Ye

INTERNATIONAL COMMITTEE

Chairman:	Yanyan Luo
Vice Chairman:	Chi H. Leung（America） Zhihong Xu Jinchun Gao

PROCEEDINGS EDITORAL BOARD

Chief Editors:	Jingqin Wang Jingying Zhao

Contents

Session 1:

Session 2:

Session 3:

Session 4:

Session 5:

Session 6:

Session 7:

7th International Conference on Reliability of
Electrical Products and Electrical Contacts,
November 04-06, 2019 **(Invited Paper)**

Novel Design Approach for Cantilever of Relay Contact Using the Preference Set-based Design (PSD) Method

Hiroshi Inoue[1], Yoshiki Kayano[1], Kazuaki Miyanaga[2]
[1]The University of Electro-Communications, Chofu-shi, 182-8585, Japan
[2]Fujitsu Component Limited
E-mail: inoue-hirosi@rouge.plala.or.jp,ykayano@uec.ac.jp

***Abstract*—A new design concept of Preference Set-based Design (PSD) Method was proposed to apply for designing a shape of cantilever in relay contacts. PSD method was developed as a useful method for implementing designer's intention especially in the field of mechanical design. Examples of design for nine design parameters and four required performances are illustrated successfully. Introducing of PSD method in designing a part of relay will possibly expand the margin of designer.**

***Index Terms*—Preference Set-based Design (PSD) Method, Electrical contact, Cantilever, Relay.**

I. INTRODUCTION

The technology of the electrical circuit switches, relays and connectors are still necessary and important in the information society with high performances but small size. Especially, as the electro-mechanical devices are useful for power delivery system of information and power system, the contact failure occurred along with the opening and the closing operations [1] are mainly originated by the arc discharge, welding or erosion of contacts, which are thermal problem.

Breaking of the electrical contacts in relay devices is generally drove by the mechanical movement using electrical magnetic drive that is supported by mechanical spring or cantilever. Design of the mechanical drive part in the design of electrical contacts device, should be satisfied simultaneous multi-objective (electrical, mechanical, and thermal) performances that are including conflicting requirements. So, multi-objective or concurrent design approach should be introduced for the future design methodology of the contact devices, such as in relay products, which are becoming small size but high power, high function and small housing.

Design methodologies should have advantages to reduce time and cost in product development. One of typical techniques of concurrent design approach is Fuzzy Set-based Design (FSD) method [2]. FSD method has been proposed as a method for multi- objective-satisfactory design. FSD has innovated on the concept of "traditional" point based design method. The Point Based Design (PBD) method is based on a point-to-point fitting process between parameters and required performances of specification, basically using simulation software, like Finite Element Method (FEM), and/or experiments. Therefore, PBD method usually requires long calculation time and/or a lot of experiments for cut-and-try design.

In FSD method, design parameters and required performances are expressed in set theory, and narrowing the sets of design parameters could lead to the common set satisfied with a lot of the required performances. This means that FSD method [2] is one of the candidates for new approach to design part of mechanical driven contact.

Preference Set-based Design (PSD) has been proposed as practical procedure of the FSD method [3], [4]. So far PSD method has been successfully applied to an automotive field, and the application of PSD to electrical design is being attempted [5]–[8]. As "Preference" means not only importance of the parameter but also idea of the designer, expand of the margin in the results of design would be expected. Application of PSD method to contact driver in relay would be new and future approach for relay design [9]-[10].

This paper attempts to describe a concurrent design method technique by PSD applied to electrical contact, specifically design of cantilever as a preliminary and case study. Conceptional outline of the PSD method is given in Section II. In Section III, the cantilever geometries and some conditions used in this study are described. In Section IV, designing of parameters and validity and possibility of the proposed method are discussed. Some conclusive remarks are expressed in Section V.

II. PREFERENCE SET-BASED DESIGN (PSD) METHOD

Figure 1 shows the flow of the design process of PSD method. "Preference" is expressed by "set or range" and "preference number", which reflect designer's idea and/or preference or choice. Figure 2 shows an example of preference set of parameters and performances when a trapezoid function form is given as preference function. Abscissa axis indicates region of the design parameter or required performance, and vertical axis is preference number (PN, dimensionless).

PN is set as number of 0 to 1. PN = 0 is lowest number of PN which is the allowable interval of design parameter. And PN = 1 corresponds to the most proper region meeting with designer's demand and wish, i.e. preference. Range of parameter on PN>0 indicate allowable range of the parameter.

In the "Preliminary Phase" in Fig 1, preparation of calculation models regarding the relationship between design parameters and required performances is necessary for searching of design parameters, which have possibility to satisfy design requirements. In PSD, the meta-modeling is used as an approximate calculation model. A response surface methodology (RSM) [11] is used as a meta-modeling in this paper. Firstly, the involved performance is calculated by combining discrete points for each design parameters. Then, the approximate formulation is derived from discrete data obtained from calculation, simulation such as FEM or experiment.

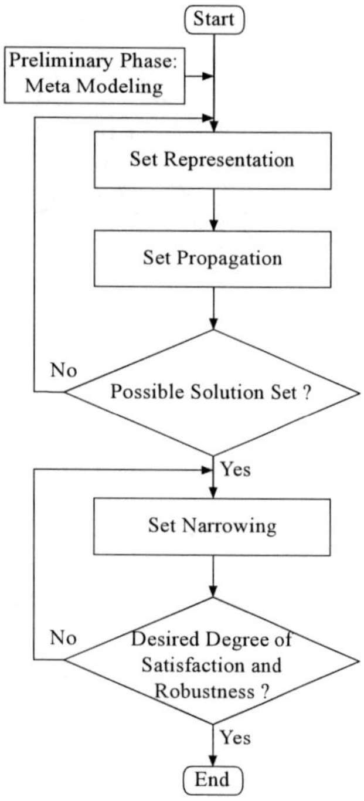

Fig.1Process flow of PSD

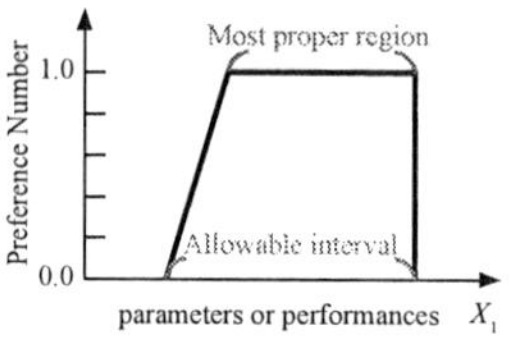

Fig.2Preference Number vs. parameters or performances

Main body of the PSD consists of three phases [3], [4].

1) Set Representation: set the region or range of the design parameters and the required performances using Preference Number as shown in Fig.2. Representations of design concepts, experiences and /or idea are included as PN.

2) Set Propagation: calculation searching sets of possible regions, where the performances are put into practice, are visualized as shown in Fig. 3 (a).

3) Set Narrowing: narrowing the set by removing non-available partial sets from the sets of the design parameters, as shown in Fig. 3(b).

In the PSD method, when all the performances meet with the required specifications, the allowable ranges of design parameters are able to decide finally with those in the highest level of their indexes of satisfaction and robustness. PSD procedure is described in Refs. [3], [4], [7], and programed at The University of Electro-Communications, Japan.

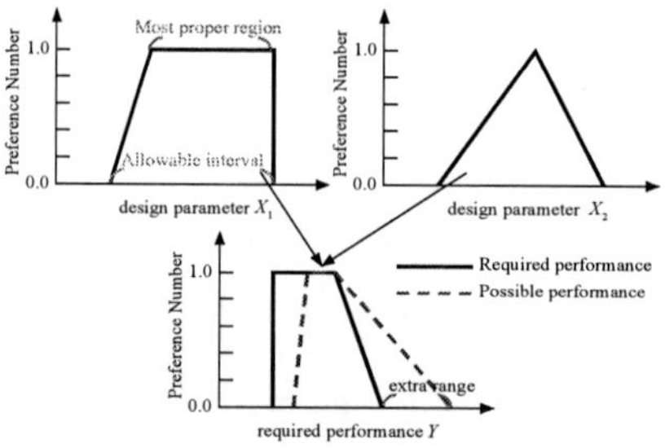

(a) Possible set obtained by set propagation

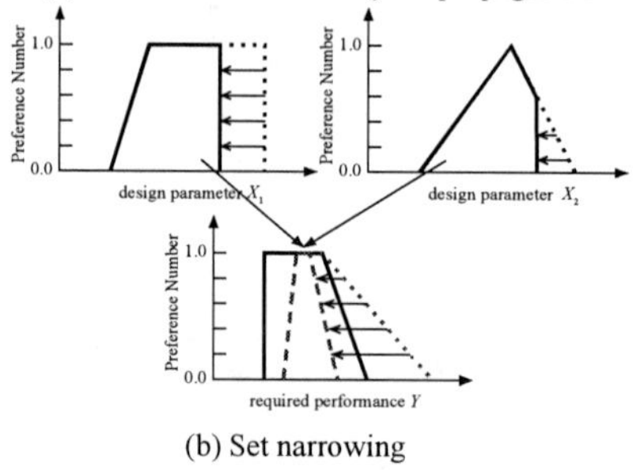

(b) Set narrowing

Fig. 3 Example illustrations of PSD procedure

III. EXAMPLE GEOMETRIES UNDER STUDY

Examples understudy are simplified models on the geometries of the cantilever for electrical contact in small typical relays that are illustrated in Fig. 4. (a), (b) and (c), respectively. At first, PSD method was applied for "example 1" shown in Fig. 4 (a) and (b). (a) is almost real configuration of cantilever and (b) is simplified structure. PSD method has been used for design W and L with almost same result for both structure of examples[12].

This paper mainly describes for "example 2" shown in Fig. 4 (c) [13]. Magnetic driver pulls two points of "force application point", and the deflection bending occurs as shown in Fig. 4 (d) like complex spring, then at the contact load point, electrode is going to make/break electrically.

The thickness T of the cantilever is 0.14 mm, and material is copper with E=125GPaof Young's modulus.

The design of stiffnesses$S_{k1,2}$and $S_{s1,2}$ are considered for a preliminary study, when the load P_k is applied on the tip of the cantilever as shown in Fig. 4 (d). Requested design parameters are nine that are five lengths (L_1 to L_5) and four widths (W_1 to W_4). We set 4 requirements for design, as the followings.

1)When weight load P_k is applied to card position, Stiffness related with amount of deflection at card position:

$0.530 \leq S_{k1} \leq 0.647$[N/mm]

2)When weight load P_k is applied to card position, Stiffness related with amount of deflection at contact position:

$1.192 \leq S_{s2} \leq 1.456$[N/mm]

3)When weight load Ps is applied to contact position, Stiffness related with amount of deflection at contact position:

$0.676 \leq S_{s1} \leq 0.827$[N/mm]

4)When weight load Ps is applied to contact position, Stiffness related with amount of deflection at card position:

$1.087 \leq S_{k2} \leq 1.329$[N/mm]

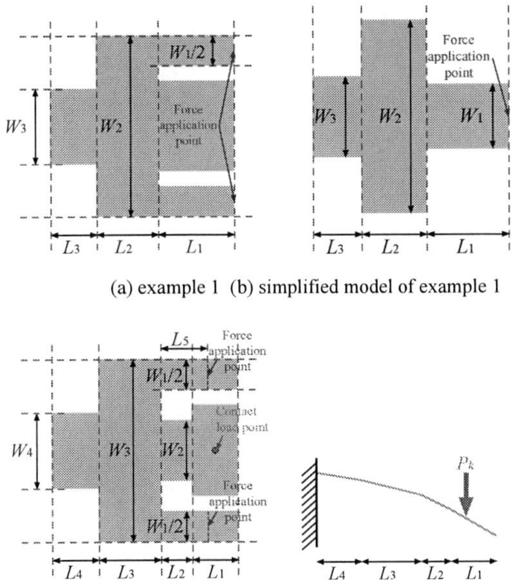

(a) example 1 (b) simplified model of example 1

(c) complex example 2 (d) deflection with load P_k

Fig. 4 geometries of sample under consideration

Data for searching the values of design parameters, which satisfy required performances, were created by the response surface method [9], [10], [11]. Initial data can be made using experiment, or simulation, or theoretical approaches. In this paper, initial data of required performances were created by theoretical calculations [12], as reduction of the calculation coast.

IV. DESIGN OF CANTILEVER BY PSD

A. Meta Modeling

Meta modeling is possible and important process to reflect designer's preference which base on accumulated techniques and knowledge. When designer have no accumulation of technological data or qualitative requirement is unclear, equal interval 3 level can be set arbitrary as initial data. As one of examples of this study, design parameters of 3 levels were set as Table I. After comparison of numerical analysis had been checked for all combination in Table I, which is 19,683 (3^9) cases, second order meta-modeling polynomial equation (1) was used.

$$y = \beta_0 + \sum_{i=1}^{n} \beta_{ixi} + \sum_{i=1}^{n} \beta_{ii} x_i^2 + \sum_{i,j=1}^{n} \beta_{ij} x_i x_j \qquad (1)$$

x_i and x_j correspond to nine design parameters, length L_1 to L_5, width W_1 to $W_4 y$ four required performances S_{k1}, S_{k2}, S_{s1} and S_{s2} and beta is coefficients of the parameters.

Table I Initial value for meta-modeling (response surface method)

para meter	initial 3 level in mm		
	1	2	3
L1	3.50	4.00	4.50
L2	0.20	0.70	1.20
L3	2.80	3.30	3.80
L4	1.80	2.30	2.80
L5	2.85	3.35	3.85
W1	2.90	3.40	3.90
W2	3.50	4.00	4.50
W3	8.50	9.00	9.50
W4	3.50	4.00	4.50

B. Result of Design

Figure 6 and 7 show results of the narrowing-down of the preference distributions on design parameters and required performances. Initial 3 levels, shown in Table I, were used. For each axes of abscissas in Fig. 6, minimum and maximum value of design parameter is initial value of level 1 and level 3 in Table I, respectively. At the peak of preference number, which is 1 at this time, design parameter corresponds to level 2 in Table I. Shape of the preference function is set to the isosceles triangle. In Fig. 6, regions surrounded by black dot lines indicate preference number of the design parameters set up by "Set Representation" in Fig.1. Regions surrounded by red lines are the solution ranges of design parameters where satisfy all of the required performances obtained in "Set Narrowing" of PSD method.

In Fig. 7, regions surrounded by black dot lines indicate preference number of the required performances set up by "Set Representation". Regions surrounded by blue lines are the possible distributions obtained at "Set Propagation". Regions surrounded by red lines are the results of "Set Narrowing" of PSD method. The solution ranges exist in the overlapped areas of possible distributions and required performances.

Obtained range of solution for design parameters, which were narrowed down, is listed in the column of solution range 1 of Table II.

Verification of the designed parameters in Table II was performed by 10,000 times, where the design parameters set by uniform randomly in solution ranges. Figure 8 are the results as the frequency distributions of required performances. All of the required performances satisfies the requirements of 1) to 4) in section III.

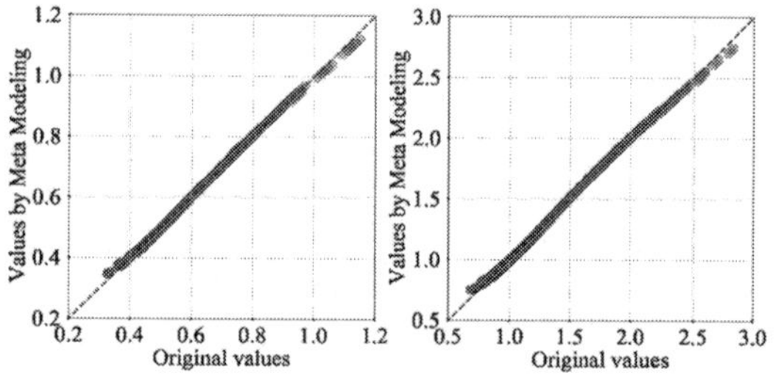

(a) S_{k1} (b) S_{s2}

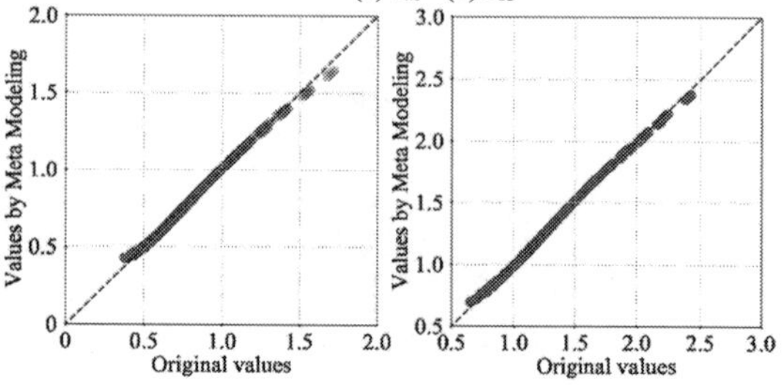

(c) S_{s1} (d) S_{k2}

Fig. 5 Scatter diagram theoretical vs. meta-modeling of Stiffness (calculated)

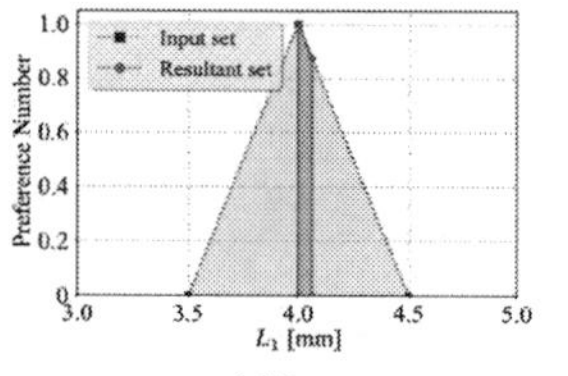

(a)L_1

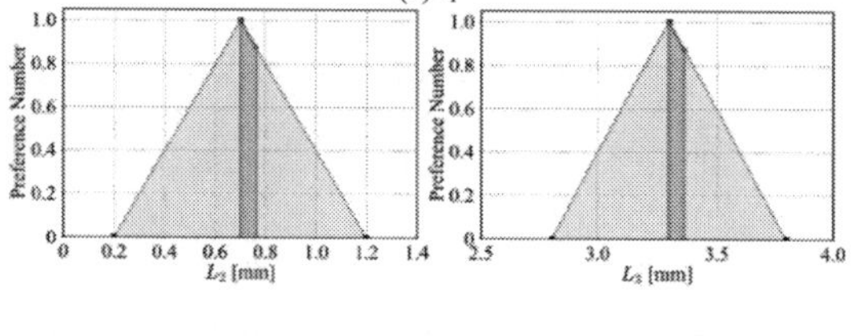

(b) L_2 (c)L_3

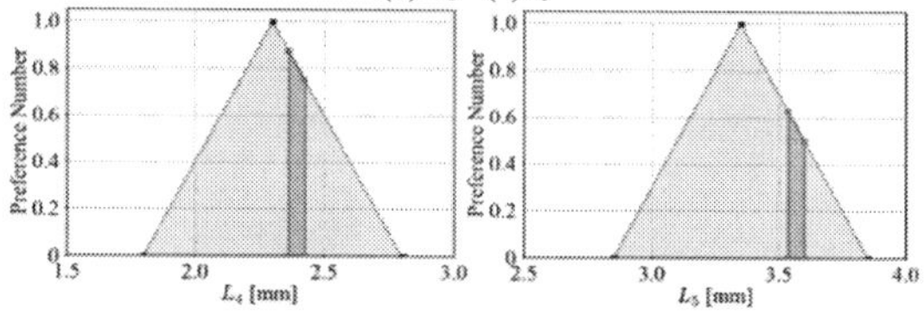

(d) L_4 (e)L_5

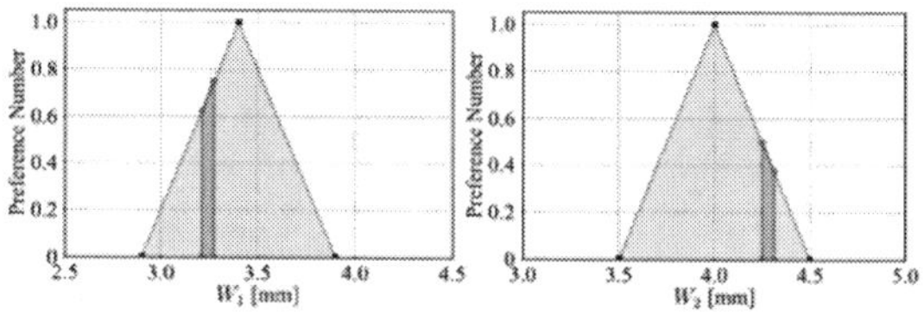

(f)W_1 (g)W_2

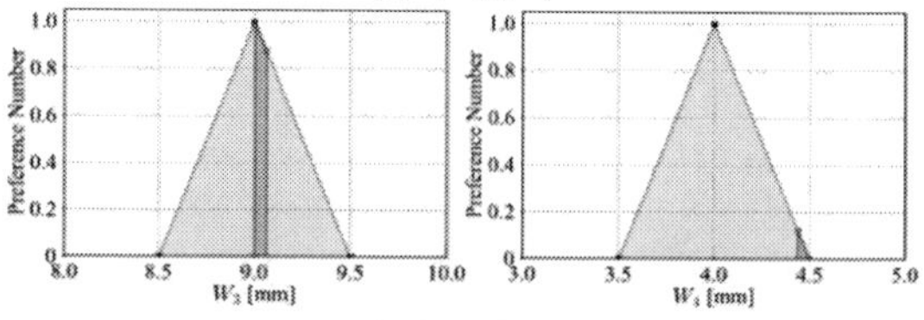

(h) W_3 (i)W_4

Fig. 6 Results of narrowing down of design parameters by PSD

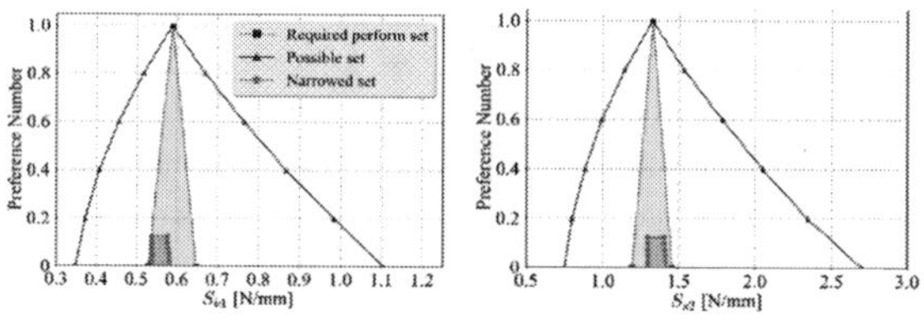

(a) S_{k1} (b)S_{s2}

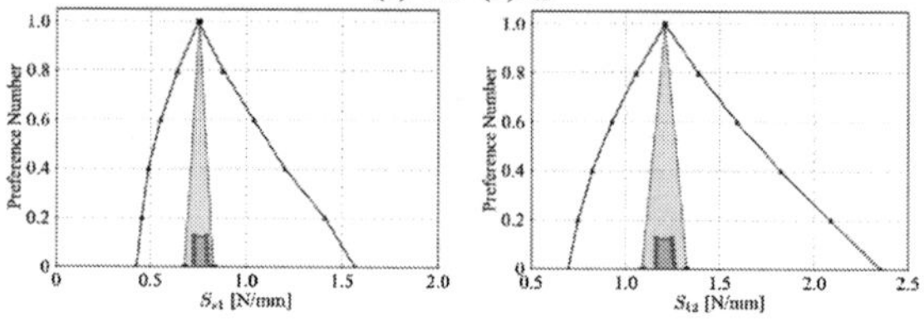

(c) S_{s1}(d)S_{k2}

Fig. 7 Results of narrowing down of required performances by PSD

Table II Initial values and solution values (in mm)

para-meter	initial range	solution range 1 by eq. (1)	solution range 2 by DoE
L1	3.50~4.50	4.00~4.06	4.46~4.50
L2	0.20~1.20	0.70~0.76	0.20~0.23
L3	2.80~3.80	3.30~3.36	3.36~3.39
L4	1.80~2.80	2.36~2.43	2.30~2.33
L5	2.85~3.85	3.54~3.60	3.07~3.10
W1	2.90~3.90	3.21~3.28	3.55~3.59
W2	3.50~4.50	4.25~4.31	3.90~3.94
W3	8.50~9.50	9.00~9.06	8.60~8.65
W4	3.50~4.50	4.44~4.50	3.94~3.97

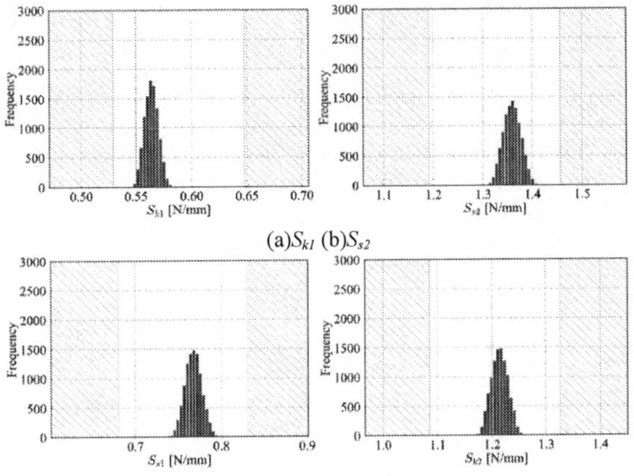

(a)S_{k1} (b)S_{s2}

(c) S_{s1} (d)S_{k2}

Fig. 8 Results of the feasibility verification of solution ranges of required performances.

C. Discussion

Case study of designing cantilever in relay with nine design parameters and four required performances was performed using PSD method. The results indicted that design parameters have solution ranges in which parameters can be chosen accordingly by designer's preference. Validity of the results was checked by 10,000 times verification. Practical remaining problem would be that the manufacturing tolerance could be satisfied in the range made by PSD method. Results by PSD have advantage that design parameters are not the pin-point values but the set of the values of parameters.

When the number of the design parameters and requirements, nine parameters and four requirements in this paper, are increased, the costs and time for calculation of the meta-modeling would increase dramatically. Decreasing of the data for meta-modeling is practical problem.

One of approach for decreasing the data of meta-modeling efficiently is to use "Design of Experiments method (DoE)" [11], [14], [15]. Application of so called "typical L27(3^{13})orthogonal table for 3 levels system" can be replaced for finding response curves. It is not by second order orthogonal terms of Eq. (1), but 27 initial data can be replaced for finding meta-modeling. The decrease of the initial data is theoretically 27/19683=1/279.

Then, eq. (1) can be decrease as eq. (2) for ignored cross term of the equation.

$$y = \beta_0 + \sum_{i=1}^{n} \beta_i x_i + \sum_{i=1}^{n} \beta_{ii} x_i^2 \qquad (2)$$

Examples of stiffness on theoretical and meta-modeling are shown in Fig. 9 (a), (b), which is comparable as Fig. 5 (a) S_{k1} and (b) S_{s2}, respectively. Figures of results on S_{s1} and S_{k2}, in which correspond to Fig. 5 (c) and (d), are omitted here because of multiplex explanation. As correlation coefficientsof scatter diagrams for S_{k1}, S_{k2}, S_{s1} and S_{s2}were over 0.98, respectively, DoE and eq. (2) can be considered to apply for PSD design. The narrowing downs of design parameters and required parameters and the feasibility verification of solution rage of required performances like Fig. 8 had been confirmed, but these figures are omitted here. Results of design parameters obtained by PSD design using DoE for meta-modeling is listed in Table II, column of "solution range 2 by DoE".

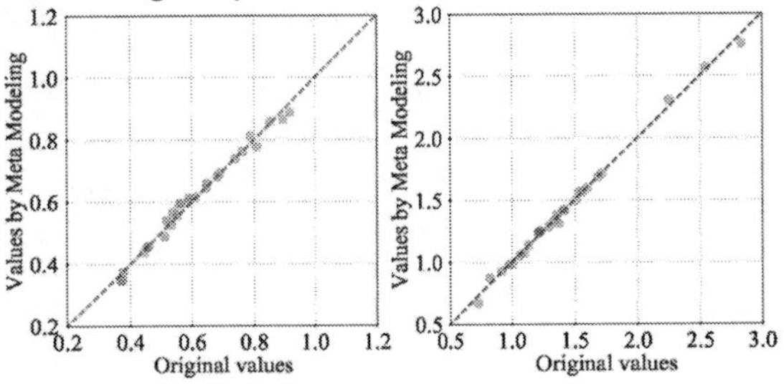

(a) S_{k1} (b) S_{s2}

Fig. 9 Scatter diagrams of theoretical vs. meta-modeling by DoE

Looking at the results of solution range1 and 2in Table II, both are in the limits of initial ranges, but range 2 by DoE is narrower than range 1. For meta-modeling of range 2, the used data was reduced to 1/729 compered for range 1. It is an advantage of calculation cost. Both results setting of the meta-modeling, without and with DoE,suggest important process to make good design resultsby PSD method, especially when increasing the number of the design parameters and required performances and considering the design cost.

Proposal of novel and robust design methodology would be possible solution for innovative design. PSD method is still on the development, but it has possibility to spread preference of the designer to the shape of the molding and/or contact construction.

V. CONCLUSION

Challenging study on the novel approach of the design methodology for relay device is described. Not only concurrent phenomena and requirements, which include mechanical, thermal and geometrical, but also preference idea of the designer are expected to satisfy by proposed "Preference Set-base Design Method". A case study for the relay contact was shown successfully. As many requirements like thermal condition are still remained, we expect the progress of the robust design methodology and also the point-to-point simulation method with supplementing the disadvantages.

ACKNOWLEDGMENT

The authors wish deeply to appreciate Emeritus Professors Haruo Ishikawa and Yoshio Kami and Professor Feng chao Xiao in The University of Electro-

Communications who have helped for conducting PSD method, and Fujitsu Component Limited for discussion.

REFERENCES

[1] T.Takagi, *Arc Discharge Phenomenain Electric Contacts(in Japanese)*, Corona Publishing Co., LTD., 1995.

[2] A.Ward, J.K.Likker, J.J.Cristiano and D.K.Sobek, "The Second Toyota Paradox: How Delaying Decisions Can Make Better Cars Faster", *Sloan management review*, pp.43–61, 1995.

[3] Y.E. Nahm and H. Ishikawa, "A New 3D-CAD system for set-based parametric design", *The International Journal of Advanced Manufacturing Technology*, vol.29, pp.137–150, May 2006.

[4] H. Ishikawa, *Multi-Objective optimum Design –Multi-Objective Satisfactory Design by Preference Set-Based Design Approach–*, Corona Publishing Co., LTD., 2010.

[5] M. Kawakami, H. Ishikawa, Y. Kami and F. Xiao, "An Application of the Preference Set-based Design Method to Filter Designs", in *Proc.2015 IEEE Int. Symp. EMC*, pp.1315–1318, Aug. Dresden, 2015.

[6] M. Kawakami, Y. Kami, H. Ishikawa and F. Xiao, "Application of the Preference Set-based Design Method to Filter Design", *IEEJ Trans. Fundamentals and Materials*, vol.136, no.10, pp.621–628, 2016.

[7] Y.Kami, Y.Kayano, H.Ishikawaand F.Xiao, "On Technique of Preference Set-based Design", *IEICE Tech. Report (in Japanese)*, EMCJ2017- 59, Nov. 2017.

[8] Y. Kayano, Y. Kami, H. Ishikawa, F. Xiao and H. Inoue, "Application of the Preference Set-based Design Method to Bent Differential-Paired Lines", *IEICE Trans. Electron. (Japanese Ed.)*, vol.J101-C, no.5, pp.233- 244, May 2018.

[9] R.H.Myers, D.C.Montgomery and C.M.Anderson-Cook, *Response Surface Methodology –Process and Product Optimization Using Designed Experiments, Wiley*, 2008.

[10] A.I. Khuri and S. Mukhopadhyay, "Response Surface Methodology", *Wiley Interdisciplinary Reviews: Computational Statistics*, vol.2, no.2, pp.128–149, 2010.

[11] D.C. Montgomery, *Design and Analysis of Experiments, Wiley*, 2012.

[12] Y. Kayano, K. Miyanaga and H. Inoue, Application of the Preference Set-based Design Method to Cantilever for Electrical Contact", *Proceedings of International Conference on Electrical Contacts, ICEC 2018*, pp.143-149, Oct. 2018.

[13] Y. Kayano, K. Miyanaga, H. Inoue and Y.Kami, "Multi-Objective Design of Cantilever for Electrical Contact by Preference Set-base Design", *IEICE Tech. Report (in Japanese)*, EMD2019-3, May, 2019.

[14] Shu Yamada, *Design of Experiments-methodology- (in Japanese), JUSE Press, Ltd.* 2004.

[15] M. Yoshino and K. Nishina, *Simulation and SQC (JSQC selections) (in Japanese), Japanese Standards Association*, 2009

Hiroshi Inoue received B.E., M.E. and Ph.D. in Electronics from Tohoku University, Japan, in 1969, 1971 and 1978, respectively. He had worked for Tohoku University and Akita University from 1975 to 2012. He was a vice director of Akita prefectural Resource Technology Development Organization for 1 year. And He was a designated Professor and director of Akita study center, The open University of Japan for 4 years. He is currently an emeritus professor of Akita University and a visiting professor of The University of Electro-Communications. His research interests are electromagnetic noise, electromagnetic compatibility, electrical contact phenomena, ultrasonic and applications to biomedical engineering. He is a member of Academic Institutions of Japan and IEEE.

Yoshiki Kayano graduated from Kisarazu National College of Technology, Kisarazu, Japan in 1999.He received B.E., M.E., and Ph.D. in Electrical and Electronic Engineering from Akita University, Japan in 2001, 2003, and 2006, respectively. He had worked for Akita University from 2006 to 2016.He is currently an associate professor of the Graduate School of Informatics and Engineering of The University of Electro-Communications from 2016.His research interests are the electromagnetic interference problem and contact phenomena. He is a member of the IEICE Japan and IEEE. He is a recipient of the 2002 ICEP Best Paper Award, the EMC' 04/Sendai Student Award, the 2011 Young Researchers' Award of the IEICE Japan, and the IEICE EST Best Presentation Award for Young Researcher in FY2014.

Kazuaki Miyanaga graduated from Salesian Polytechnic, Tokyo, Japan, in 2003. He received B.E. and M.E. Ph.D. in Electrical and Electronic Engineering from Akita University, Japan, in 2005, 2007 and 2010, respectively. He was a Post-doctoral Research Fellow (Central Research Institute Research Fellow) of Akita University from 2010 to 2012. In 2012, he joined Fujitsu Component Ltd. His research interest is electrical contact phenomena. He is a member of the JSAP, the IEEJ and the IEEE. Heis a recipient of the 2009 Young Researchers' Award of the IEICE Japan.

7th International Conference on Reliability of Electrical Products and Electrical Contacts, November 04-06, 2019 **(Invited Paper)**

Silver Layer on AgW, AgMo and AgWC Electric Contacts for Circuit Breakers

Chi H. Leung
Electric Contact Material Consultant
Export, Pennsylvania, USA
cleung1@yahoo.com

***Abstract*—AgW, AgMo and AgWC powder metal composite contacts are commonly used in UL approved residential and commercial circuit breakers. Unacceptable contact resistance and temperature rise in closed contacts can develop after more than a few hundred switching cycles if contact material selection is not proper. It is a careful balance of contact material properties of weld resistance, contact erosion and switched contact interface resistance. To reduce surface resistance, there are methods to produce a functional silver layer of 5-25µm on the contact surface. This includes the processes such as (a) electrochemical etching of W, LT (Low Temperature); and (b) thermos-chemical oxidation of W, LR (Low Resistance); and (c) Ag electroplating. The pros and cons of different ways to produce this silver layer are discussed and their implementation in production.**

***Index Terms*— Silver refractory contact, Circuit breaker, Rsistance, Heat rise, Millivolt drop, Silver layer**

I. INTRODUCTION

Molded case circuit breakers under UL certification are required to pass XYZ electrical tests including overload (X), switching endurance (Y), short circuit interruption (Z). The performance criteria are anti-welding, temperature rise, arc erosion and erosion integrity. The successful contacts used are always a powder metal composite of high conductivity element (Ag) and a refractory material (W, Mo or WC) made by sintering and infiltration methods. These include moving/fixed contact pairs such as AgW/AgW, AgW/AgWC, AgW/AgC, AgW/AgWCC, and to a lesser extent AgW/AgCdO or AgW/AgSnO2. The popular contact combinations of interest here are as shown in Table I.

High refractory (W, WC) content is better for anti-welding and arc erosion and high silver content is good for contact resistance, the final composition is usually also skewed to have the minimum silver content to reduce cost. The requirement for low contact resistance or heat rise is particularly important in Switch Duty Class of circuit breakers.

Table I Common UL circuit breaker contact combinations

Rated Current (A)	*Fixed Contact*	*Moving Contact*
15-50	35Ag65W	35Ag65W
50-70	35Ag65W, 50Ag50W	35Ag65W
70-120	50Ag50W, 60Ag40WC	35Ag65W, 50Ag50WC

For many years, it is desirable to have only a minimum layer of silver, less than 2µm, referenced as "natural finish" on the finished contact surface just to preserve the shelf life of the contacts from atmospheric corrosion and the formation of tungsten oxides. A thicker layer of surface silver layer is considered harmful to the assembly line productivity where the contacts are welded to a copper terminal because of occasional contact sticking to the welding electrode. Contacts were generally larger for erosion and heat transfer so this silver layer is not so much a functional parameter. Cost reduction has contacts now designed with minimum dimensions that arc erosion and thermal considerations are requiring better use of all material and process options to pass UL tests.

Heat rise tests are particularly challenging at the overload and switching duty test where arc erosion and oxidation products of silver, tungsten oxides and tungstates are formed on the contact surface. A low amount of elemental silver left on the surface will result in high contact resistance and temperature rise. The interface contact resistance is dependent on silver composition, tungsten particles size, distribution and manufacturing methods. It was also found that a thicker silver layer on the new contact can enrich the amount of silver left on the arc eroded contact surface affecting welding properties [1,2].

Similar to the electrical contact industry, the cutting tool industry uses Co-WC inserts made by powder metal processes. The metal composites of Co-WC inserts are made of 3-10%Co binder, balance WC. A binder rich layer of Co is necessary to have a wettable surface for braze adhesion. Toney [3] patented a molten salt process where barium chloride salt is heated to 1200C to oxidize the

surface layer tungsten carbide particles to tungsten oxides and then dissolved into the molten salt. This leave a porous Co layer that has better wettability with braze alloys. Thorsen [4] summarized 5 ways to improve wettability of CoWC cutting tool inserts:
1) mechanical cleaning: this only peen the Co soft phase
2) molten salt treatment of cemented carbide, Ishida[5]
3) electrolytic method: the carbide phase was dissolved anodically in an alkaline KOH solution leaving a 0.1-10μm of spongey cobalt layer;
4) coating of Ni or Co by electroplating showed poor adhesion; or PVD (physical vapor deposition) is expensive.
5) thermo-chemical treatment by air oxidation at 900C and then pickling in boiling NaOH solution at 140C.

The electrical contact industry has used the molten salt and electrolytic method to create the silver layer that is functionally required to solve heat rise problems. Some process control problems persist in achieving a uniform silver layer on AgW, AgMo and AgWC contacts.

In this paper is a review of the manufacturing methods to produce a functional silver surface layer of 5-25μm: (a) the electrochemical leaching method to preferentially remove surface tungsten particles, and (b) the thermal chemical method with molten salt oxidation.

II. BACKGROUND

A. Powder metal composite Ag/W, Ag/Mo and Ag/WC:

The various methods of press-sinter or press-sinter-infiltration have been described in previous papers. The process temperatures at 1100-1250C melt the silver metal to infiltrate a Ag and W powder mixture skeleton through capillary liquid flow. As a result, when the silver is molten, it can leak from the established silver and tungsten mixture skeleton to the outside surface of the contact. This is bound to happen when all the porosities inside the contact have been filled by the molten silver through capillary action. The control of this silver leak is dependent on composition, process time, temperature, furnace atmosphere, silver and tungsten particle size, final density, porosities etc. If leakage of this silver is excessive and usually non-uniform, the surface can become rough and the silver layer can cause contact welding in electrical switching.

A natural finish is just the as infiltrated amount of silver leaked to the contact surface, usually 0-2μm thick. Ideally, this layer is uniform for all parts at the exit of the infiltration furnace. A shinny surface with little roughness is achieved. Minor burnishing or peening with steel balls can make this acceptable for many applications. Some variations are:

- Under infiltrate to produce a part that is less than 97% dense with some residual porosities, surface is not shinny and silver layer = 0;
- Addition of alloying elements such as Ni and Cu to promote wetting and even spreading of the leaked silver layer = 0 to 3 micron;
- Protective coating on contact surface to keep silver leak to minimum, this allows the maximum infiltration density, silver layer = 0 micron;

A functional Ag layer of 2-7μm, 7-12μm, or 12-25μm requires a controlled preparation method.

B. Surface silver layer after infiltration

Figure 1 shows some infiltrated 35Ag65W powder metal contacts from the same production batch as an example of the Ag content variations on the surface. This variation is a result of the various amounts of molten silver leaked to the surface and this can affect the circuit breaker performance especially if the design has no safety margins such as contact force to compensate for it. Table II shows the x-ray surface composition and show a variation of more than 10% of exposed tungsten to atmospheric oxidation and arc oxidation. This can result in variations in heat rise tests in marginal designs.

C. Surface silver layer preparation methods

In order to have a functional silver layer thickness on the contact surface, several methods can be used. This included:

(1) Silver plating after infiltration: This is seldom used in the contact manufacturing step because of the added cyanide waste treatment, and poor adhesion quality of the Ag plating which can cause sticking to the welding electrode in the spot welding assembly line. However, sometimes, the brazed assemblies are silver plated to prolong shelf life of the contact as well as the copper terminals. This is more difficult to optimize because the silver plating thickness adequate for corrosion protection of copper can be too much for contact electrical performance.

(2) Electrochemical etching of AgW, AgMo and AgWC contacts in a NaOH solution. This is quite efficient once the electrochemical principal and reactions are understood. This is later referred as the LT (low temperature) process.

(3) Thermal chemical oxidation of W, Mo or WC with common heat treatment molten salts such as a eutectic mixture of 60% $NaNO_3$ and 40% KNO_3 in a molten salt bath at 300-500C to remove W, Mo or WC. This is later referred to as the LR (low resistance) process.

III. LT PROCESS

In this electrochemical etching of a Ag/W composite material, the anodic oxidation of Ag and W in an alkaline solution such as KOH or NaOH must be understood.

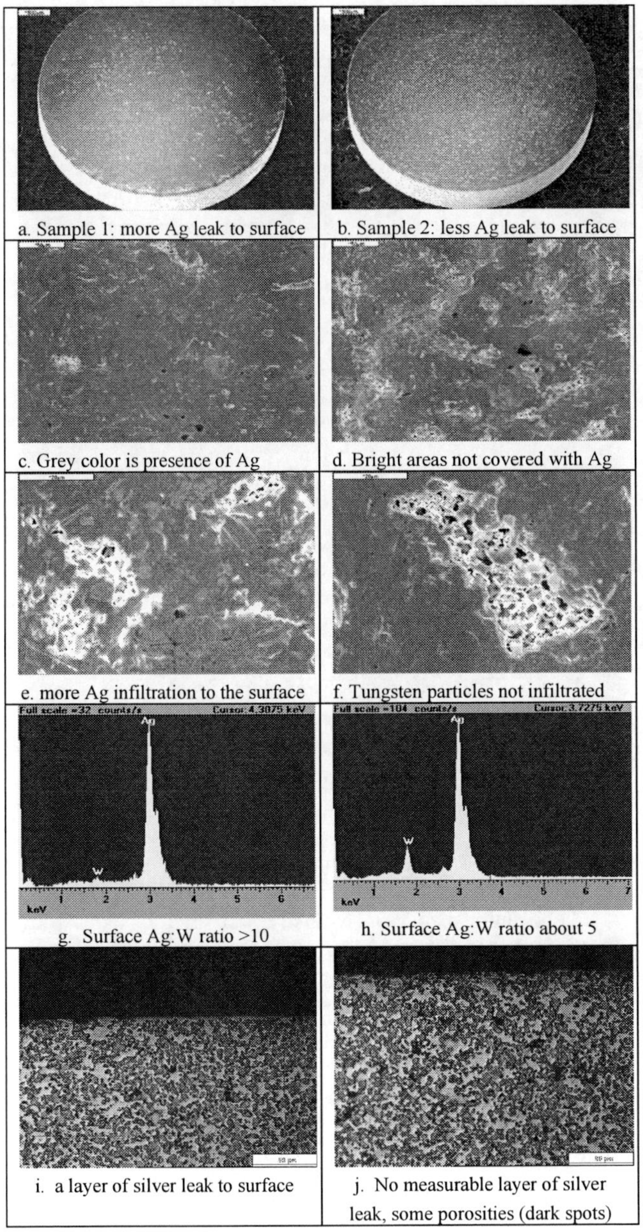

a. Sample 1: more Ag leak to surface
b. Sample 2: less Ag leak to surface
c. Grey color is presence of Ag
d. Bright areas not covered with Ag
e. more Ag infiltration to the surface
f. Tungsten particles not infiltrated
g. Surface Ag:W ratio >10
h. Surface Ag:W ratio about 5
i. a layer of silver leak to surface
j. No measurable layer of silver leak, some porosities (dark spots)

Fig. 1 Natural finish: Surface variations 35Ag65W contact

Table II – Surface Ag and W composition variation

EDAX Ag:W peak ratio	Calculated Exposed W %
2 : 1	12.8 -16.0
2.5 : 1	13.0 : 16.2
5 : 1	3.9 : 8.6
6 : 1	4.7 : 10.6

A. *Silver anodic oxidation*

Early work was done by Dignam [6] in the development of Ag/AgO electrode used in batteries in a KOH solution. A silver anode reaction at current densities of .04-.77mA/cm^2 was studied. As shown in figure 2, they found that bare Ag metal first formed Ag_2O, followed by the conversion of the Ag_2O to AgO. Upon conversion of all the Ag_2O to AgO, oxygen is evolved. The surface of the Ag will turn black with AgO and passivates. The AgO is insoluble in the alkaline electrolyte and a hydrolysis of water takes over, presumably as:

$$4OH^- \leftrightarrow 2H_2O + O_2 \uparrow$$

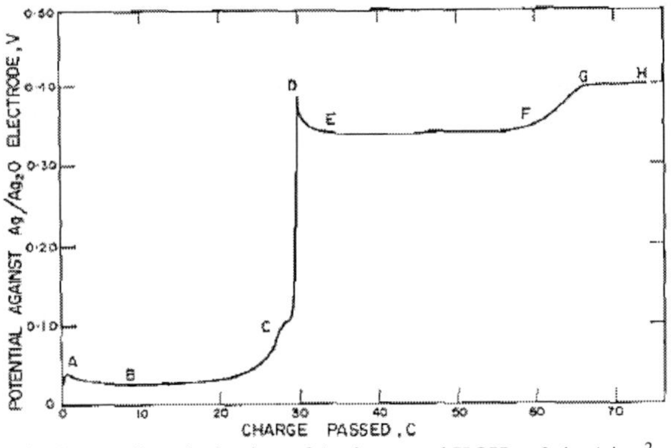

Fig. 2 Anodic polarization of Ag in normal KOH at 0.4mA/cm^2. Regions of Ag_2O formation (A to D); AgO formation (E-F), and oxygen evolution (G-H)

The significance of the current density is the voltage variation in region A to C because of the rate of Ag_2O formation on the metal surface. The current density will determine the time it takes to transfer the necessary amount of charge.

B. *Tungsten anodic oxidation*

The electrochemical etching of tungsten anode in NaOH solution is similar to that of silver except the reaction of the so formed tungsten oxide is readily soluble in the NaOH solution. So the etching away of tungsten can continue for hours un-inhibited.

Cathode $2H_2O + 2e^- \Leftrightarrow H_2(gas) + 2OH$

Anode $W + 6OH^- \Rightarrow WO_3^{2} + 3H_2O + 6e^-$ (1)

Overall $W + 2H_2O + 2NaOH \Rightarrow 3H_2(gas) + Na_2WO_4$

Using Faraday's constant (F=96485 Coulomb/mol), and its relation to the Avogadro's constant N_A 6.02x1023 mol^{-1}, and the electron charge e=1.6x10^{-16}C, it was possible to approximately calculate the charge passed to affect the amount of tungsten oxidized at 6 electrons per atom. The final formula is:

$$d = 9.84 \times 10^{-4} \times J_w \times t \quad (2)$$

where d (cm) is thickness, J_w is current density (A/cm^2) of tungsten area, and it is time in minutes.

Recent publications [7,8] on the electrochemical etching of tungsten in NaOH electrolyte discussed the results of developing fabrication technique of sharp tungsten tips suitable for field ion microscopy and scanning tunneling microscopy. 25 micron tungsten wires were thinned to a needle point of 50nm tip radius. The operation parameters of NaOH electrolyte, dc voltage (2.5-9V), current and time were reported and the fast etching of tungsten metal is easily reproduced.

C. *Silver/Tungsten composite anodic oxidation*

In the electrochemical etching of Ag/W composite, with 25 to 50 wt.% Ag balance W, a setup with a horizontal rotating plating barrel, an electrolyte of a 1N NaOH solution, a large stainless steel plate as cathode and the contacts as anode can be etched at 5-10 V in 10-20 minutes to a silver layer of 8-12 microns. The silver phase went through the transition from Ag to Ag_2O and AgO with eventual evolution of O; and the tungsten portion is oxidized and dissolved into the NaOH. Three stages of the etching can be observed:

1. Tungsten dissolution: the contacts lose shine and no gas evolution at the anode parts; the stainless steel cathode has some gas evolution, likely hydrogen. This is the important stage when the bulk of the surface tungsten particles are removed and open channels are available to allow dissolution of some sub-surface particles.
2. Transition: when most of the tungsten particles are etched away, the surface is very rich in Ag and the oxidation of Ag takes over. The contacts turn brown then black. This is when further etching will not increase the silver layer thickness at the same rate.
3. Contacts turn black when AgO covered the surface.

With high current densities, the Ag/W contacts may pass through stages 1 and 2 very quickly and enter stage 3. Then these parts will have very shallow silver layer and longer etching times do not increase the Ag layer thickness. At the same time, if the contact surface already has too much silver leak out at infiltration, this can hinder with the underlying tungsten particles from the electrolyte and result in uneven etched Ag layer.

A series of experiments determined that a current density of .015 to .03 A/cm^2 can etch properly in the stage 1 condition for roughly 40 and 180 minutes respectively. This allows the calculation of etch time relationship with current, tungsten content and etch thickness according to equation 2. The total anode surface area equals (number of parts) x (surface area) x (volume percent of tungsten in the part). An anode current density of .02 A/cm^2 is a good start assuming normal and 100% efficient etching. Some equipment calibration can get this to be a reliable process control method.

This LT procedure can also be used with AgMo contacts but not so successful with AgWC contacts. After etching, the contacts are heated in a reducing atmosphere at around 750C for 20 minutes to clean any residue tungsten oxide and silver oxide. This silver layer is rather porous and is peened with some media, such as steel balls to densify. This peening may take only15 to 30 minutes. Figures 3 and 4 are some photos of the silver layer after LT or LR process.

IV. LR PROCESS

The LR (low resistance) process is a thermo-chemical molten salt process used to oxidize and remove the refractory phase (W, Mo or WC) from the contact surface and leave a silver layer of control thickness in the 3-25μm range. The LR process is mainly used on AgWC because WC is not easily removed by the NaOH anodic oxidation method. The molten salt method uses a commercial heat treat salt mixture of 60% $NaNO_3$ and 40% KNO_3 and operated at 300-500C for15-30 minutes. This is a powerful oxidizer and reacts rapidly with an exothermic reaction. Proper safety guidelines in regard to molten salt baths must be observed. The reaction is even more rigorous when AgW and AgMo contacts are dipped into the molten salt and the best way to moderate the reaction is by lowering the salt bath temperature. In the reaction, WC is oxidized as follows:

$$WC + 3NaNO_3 + \tfrac{1}{4}\,O_2 \Rightarrow Na_2WO_4 + \tfrac{1}{2}\,Na_2O + 3NO + CO_2$$

$$WC\ (powder) + Na_2O + 2O_2 \Rightarrow Na_2WO_4 + CO$$

The reaction product is mostly sodium tungstate solid left as sludge in the salt bath. The parts are quenched in water to dissolve the residual salt on the surface, and then heated in a reducing atmosphere to reduce any surface silver and tungsten oxides. The porous silver layer is then peened to densify.

Both LT and LR processes generated Ag layers that can be measured with a Kocour meter, X-ray fluorescence, or micro-section.

V. ELECTRICAL PERFORMANCE OF AG LAYER

Switch duty tests at 120VAC 20A resistive load were performed on several batches of 35Ag65W infiltrated contacts in a model circuit breaker as described [1984]. Table 3 shows six samples with variations of tungsten particle size combinations (medium, medium+fine, and fine) and LT Ag thickness layer. These are 4mm diameter contacts used in 20A residential circuit breakers in USA and Canada. The changes of millivolt drop vs switching cycles from 0 to 3000 operations are shown in figure 5. Usually, a larger tungsten particle contact are softer and has better millivolt or heat rise properties but may be inadequate in erosion and anti-welding. So combinations of Ag content and tungsten particle size are part of material design and performance optimization.

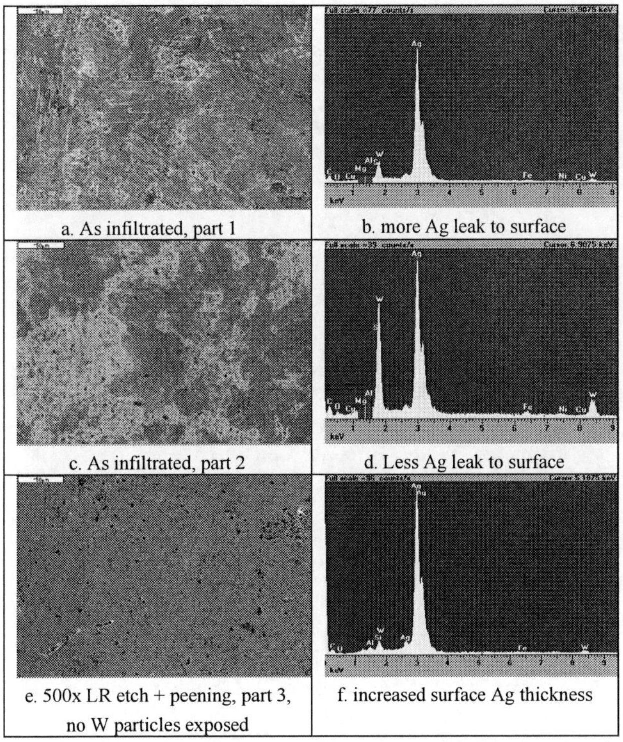

a. As infiltrated, part 1 | b. more Ag leak to surface | c. As infiltrated, part 2 | d. Less Ag leak to surface | e. 500x LR etch + peening, part 3, no W particles exposed | f. increased surface Ag thickness

Fig. 3 35Ag65W surface comparison of natural finish parts 1 and 2; and after complete LR process part 3

The high rates of millivolt increase are reduced from A to B band, to C band and D band with various tungsten side and LT thickness samples.

(a). Sample A (medium + fine) has 0μm silver layer in natural finish condition and the millivolt increased rapidly to a stable level of 500mv. Sample C is same material but processed by LT process to a silver layer of 25μm. This has the millivolt reduced to the values of C band. This is often useful to meet the overload test temperature rise validation.

(b). Samples B1, B2 and D (medium tungsten) show similar millivolt drop reduction from band B to band D, because of thicker Ag layer in Sample D.

(c) Samples B3 (fine) and B1 (medium + fine) are processed to have similar millivolt drop properties in spite of differences in tungsten particle size. This is with modifications to the silver thickness. Therefore a thinner Ag layer of 2.5-7.5μm in B1 can have similar low millivolt drop as in B3 with 25μm. Some benefits of the fine tungsten in B3 can be increased hardness and better anti-welding. So the millivolt deficiency is improved with the silver layer.

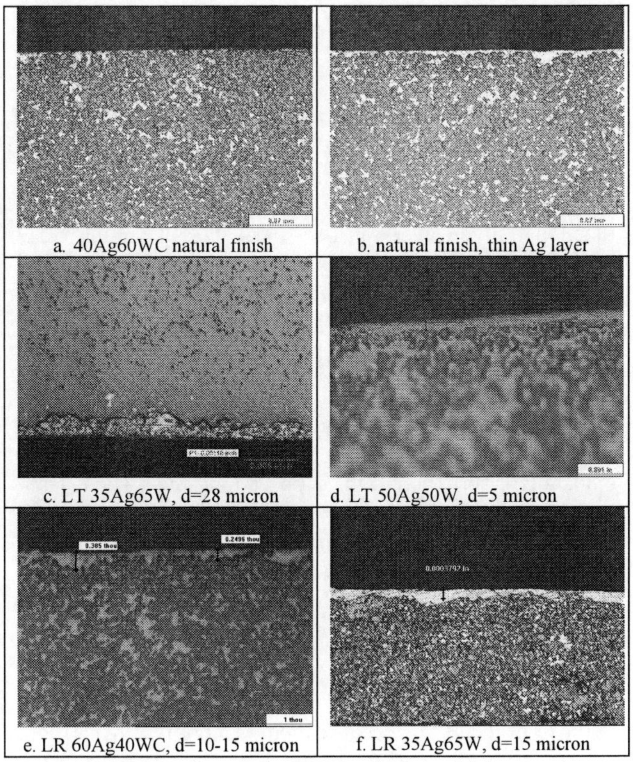

a. 40Ag60WC natural finish | b. natural finish, thin Ag layer | c. LT 35Ag65W, d=28 micron | d. LT 50Ag50W, d=5 micron | e. LR 60Ag40WC, d=10-15 micron | f. LR 35Ag65W, d=15 micron

Fig. 4 some examples of LT and LR Ag thickness

Table 3 35Ag65W contact material used in switching duty test

Sample #	Material	Tungsten size	LT Ag thk (μm)
A	W13 (043)	Medium + fine	0
B1	W1302	Medium	2.5
B2	W1302	Medium	7.5
B3	W1310	Fine	25
C	W13(043)	Medium + fine	25
D	W1302	Medium	25

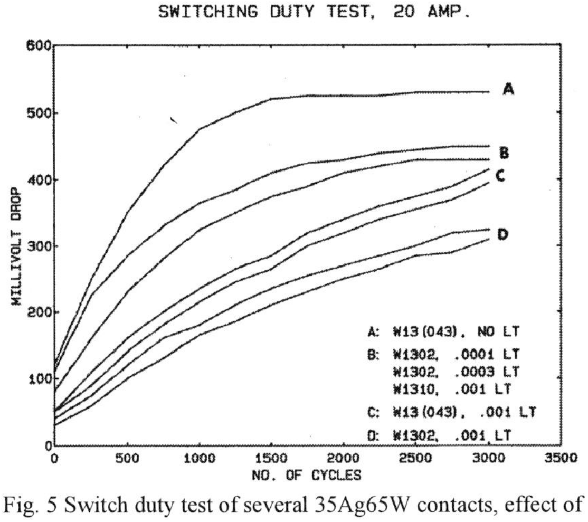

Fig. 5 Switch duty test of several 35Ag65W contacts, effect of tungsten particle size and Ag layer thickness on millivolt drop

VI. DISCUSSIONS

In UL certification tests of circuit breakers, millivolt drop or temperature rise is required after overload, endurance and interruption tests. The common contact materials of AgW and AgWC are first optimized for composition to survive the erosion and anti-welding. Heat rise is often the final hurdle after the arc erosion tests and a functional silver layer can help meet the temperature rise tests. This is done by the LT and LR processes as described in the previous sections. Some pros and cons of this silver layer are list below:

1 Natural finish is defined as no prepared silver thickness enhancement. This can result in some variations in Ag:W ratios from part to part because of the infiltration process limitations. This condition can result in atmospheric oxidation or corrosion of the exposed tungsten particles and cause calibration problems in the circuit breaker assembly line. So it is common that a chemical or mechanical cleaning is done to remove the surface tungsten. This is not considered to be a functional silver thickness requirement. This surface condition also makes contact sticking to the welding electrode very infrequent.

2 Functional silver layer 5-25μm: this can definitely improve heat rise test because there is more residual Ag on the contact surface after arc erosion. The control of this thickness is necessary with various acceptable ranges. If this layer gets too thick, then (a) sticking to the welding electrode can occur; (b) tack welding or low level fault sticking at the 500-1000A range when the magnetic tripping is not very effective at this lower currents.

SUMMARY

The benefits of a silver layer of 5-25μm on AgW, AgMo and AgWC contacts are shown with improved millivolt drop or temperature test results. The LT (anodic oxidation) process in a NaOH solution requires proper current density to remove the surface and embedded tungsten particle before passivation of the Ag phase. When AgO is formed on the anode, this stops further removal of tungsten. The LR (molten salt oxidation) processes is an exothermic reaction that is preferred in etching of AgWC contacts. Proper safety precautions must be observed for all molten salt heat treatment procedures.

REFERENCES

[1] Leung etal,"A comparison of Ag/W, Ag/WC and Ag/Mo electrical contacts". IEEE Transactions CHMT, vol. CHMT-7, no.1, March 1984.

[2] Leung etal, "Microstructure effects on dynamic welding of Ag-W contacts", IEEE Holm conference 1987.

[3] US Patent 2979811. Cemented Carbide Body Having Wettable Surface and Method of Producing Same, L. Toney et al, 1961

[4] K. Thorsen etal, "An Explanation of Wettability Problems When Brazing Cemented Carbides", 15th International AWS-WRC Brazing and Soldering Conference, 1984.

[5] T. Ishida et al, "Development of Technologies for Recycling Cemented Carbide Scrap and Reducing Tungsten Use in Cemented Carbide Tools", SEI Technial Review, No.75, Octomer 2012

[6] M. Dignam, H, Barrett, G. Nagy, "Anodic behavior of Silver in alkaline solutions", Canadian Journal of Chemistry, vol. 47, 1969.

[7] Y. Kamimoto etal, "Electrochemical Leaching of Tungsten from Hard metal Alloy Using Molten Sodium Hydroxide", Materials Transactions, v56, n5, 2015, p733-737

[8] T. Duong, "Electrochemical etching techniqure for tungsten electrode", International journal of precision engineering and manufacturing, June 2015

7th International Conference on Reliability of
Electrical Products and Electrical Contacts,
November 04-06, 2019 (Invited Paper)

Detection and Characterization of Intermittent Shortsand Opensin Permanent Magnet AC Machines

Elias G. Strangas
Department of Electrical and Computer Engineering
Michigan State University
East Lansing, MI 48824, USA
email: strangas@egr.msu.edu

***Abstract*—Intermittent faults in equipment, especially in electrical machines in the field, are generally difficult to recognize and identify, until they have become well established, if not permanent. Detecting them cannot be based on the steady-state performance of the faulted machine, since steady state may not be reached. It is proposed that instead the inception and clearing of the fault be identified, using a multi-step process, shift-invariant feature extraction, Undecimated Discrete Wavelet Transform) and linear discriminant analysis. The technique is applied for different fault characteristics, and controller speeds.**

***Index Terms*—Permanent Magnet AC machines, Intermittent fault, Wavelet analysis, Fault Diagnosis**

I. INTRODUCTION

Intermittent faults in PMAC stator windings come primarily through mechanical stresses. Shorts (turn-to-turn and turn to ground) are often due to vibrations and insulation degradation caused by the combination of chafing and thermal aging. Opens are caused by either soldering, crimping or brazing of windings or by deterioration of contacts in connectors due to contamination and movement. Since they do not present themselves during tests, these faults may not last long enough as intermittent to affect performance until it is too late, and cannot be easily mitigated.It is therefore important to detect them early.

Intermittent faults have certain characteristics, which require careful monitoring and identification and specialized handling of the relevant signals; They do not fall within the typical categories of steady faults, even under transient operating conditions. The duration of the fault is random and may be very brief, so the fault cannot be identified from the characteristics of steady operation. Instead, here it is identified from the inception and/or termination performance. This leads to the requirement of identifying the presence and characteristics of transients. These transients are determined by the characteristics of the fault and of the circuit.

A large portion of the related research has been dedicated to the identification of faults in ;ow-power circuits, with very interesting results [1]. For Permanent Magnet AC machines the circuit characteristics (on both sides of the fault) can be considered dominant during steady state operation, while the fault characteristics can be considered of a time scale which is much faster than the machine electrical dynamics and

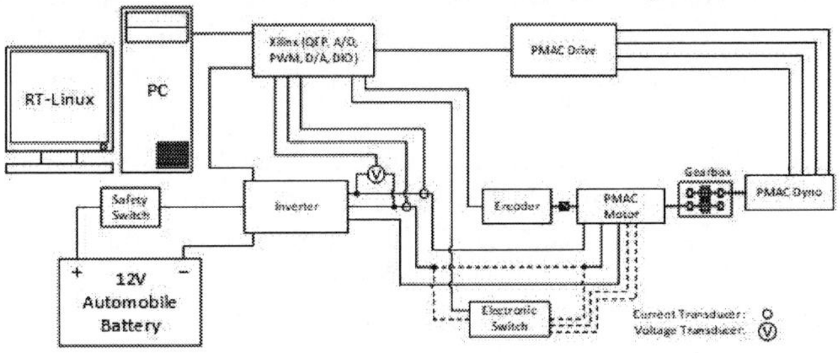

Fig. 1. The experimental setup representing typical connections of a PMAC machine

hence should be used for the detection of the fault. [2] The time scale of the signal is significant, since PMAC machines are controlled often by a current-controlled voltage-source inverter, which can have a time constant similar to those of the periods of the frequencies associated with the fault.

Modeling of the circuits analytically in order to determine the behavior under fault has not been proven feasible, due to the complexity of the systems, and the requirement for the detection of fast transients. Things are a little simpler in detection of intermittent faults in cables [3], where the transmission characteristics have been well studied, understood, and to some degree, well modeled.

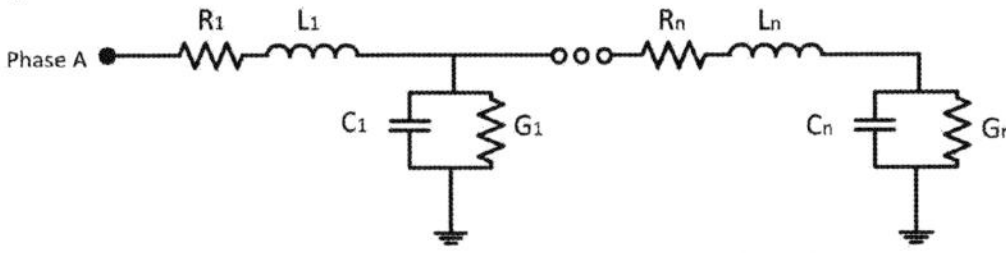

Fig. 2. A lumped parameter model of a winding for the purposes of fault signature analysis

In our previous work, [4] [5] we introduced methods to identify intermittent faults in PMAC machines, open and short circuits, and related them only to the data collected and not the equivalent circuit of the machine. Wavelets were used to characterize the faults, and a shift-invariant version was introduced. On the same problem, more recently in [5], the authors used a similar technique by employing adaptive wavelets to identify an intermittent short circuit.

A number of concerns remain for the process of intermittent fault identification and characterization: Can the characteristics of the supply affect the detection of the fault, i.e. can the speed of the inverter mask the fault characteristics to the point that it may be misdiagnosed?

Switching of an inverter can produce a signal that can be confused with the intermittent fault, so techniques have to be developed to separate these.

II. FAULT CHARACTERISTICS

As stated in the introduction, the characteristics of the fault and hence its signature and detection method, are defined by a number of parameters:

- The load, in our case the resistance, inductance, speed, and back emf of the electrical machine.
- The source characteristics. Here they are primarily the voltage of the DC link. and possibly it impedance,
- The characteristics of the contact, e.g. the impedance of the contact and arcing etc.
- The current transients resulting from the fault can be sensed in the inverter, with the sensors available for the control of the drive.

The fault time scale then can be defined by the initial transient during and immediately after the open or short, dominated by the parameters discussed above, and in particular the possible arc or resistance, and the capacitance and inductance in the immediate proximity of the fault, the transient corresponding to the response of the system to the disturbance in its own time constant, and the steady state response. The duration of this last one is not easily determined, and usually does not participate in the detection. The steady state operation then is characterized by the presence of the shorted winding (with unknown number of turns), which has been studied extensively, e.g. [6].

The different time scales, and the characteristics of the faults, correspond to different modes and signals. One case, the open or close at a cable, leads to analysis of deflections in the cable, and the recognition of the resulting chaotic signals [3]. [7] models both the connector and the cable characteristics. A similar approach for a stator winding [8], emulating it as a network of lumped inductances and capacitances, although attempted with acceptable results, only leads to an understanding of the phenomena, rather than a robust detection technique.

Looking at the power flow [9] again would work for cables, but it would present implementation difficulties in terms of time scale. A detailed model of the intermittent short circuit in one phase was presented by Obeid et al. [10]. It was based on the characteristics of the power circuit and lead to the determination of the location of the fault.

A the major concern of the detection of an intermittent fault is the need to process voltage or current sampled data continuously. This is expensive as it requires the continuous processing of the data. An alternative is to sample data from a rolling window, detect any possible variation (e.g. exceeding of a threshold) and then perform time-frequency analysis for feature extraction. This requires the the use of a shift invariant transformation. Among the possible alternatives is the Undecimated Discrete Waveform Transoform, 3.

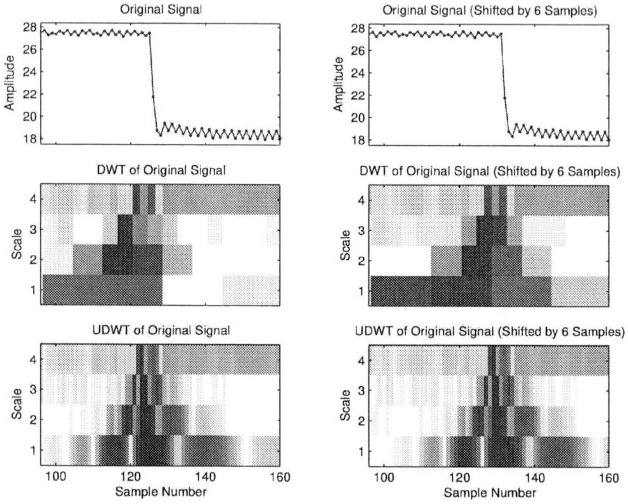

Fig. 3. Typical Results

III. CATEGORIZATION

In this work, the currents in the drive are analyzed using time-frequency analysis tools including Discrete Wavelet Transform. When the presence of a fault in the drive is detected, the signal is sampled and analysis coefficients are categorized, with the possible categories corresponding to one of several known fault types.

To accomplish this categorization, a variety of techniques are available. At the onset of this work, the nearest neighbor rule was used. Further refinement of the algorithms led to the use of linear discriminant analysis, which added a training procedure to improve the design of the classification algorithm.

Finally, the coefficients corresponding only to either the inception or the clearing of a fault were classified separately from each other.

A. Nearest Neighbor Rule

In order to categorize a sample point in d-dimensional space into a set of previously classified points, one technique is the nearest neighbor rule (1-NN). It is assumed that observations which are close to each other will have the same classification. This problem can be approached in two different ways, first, by assuming that some statistical distribution is given for the data, and second, by assuming no knowledge of a distribution except for what can be concluded from the samples. In this work, the focus is on the second method, where no probabilistic model of a distribution is assumed.

In calculating the minimum distance, some appropriate measure needs to be used. Any dissimilarity measure (1) would be applicable, however the most commonly used dissimilarity measures are the Minkowski p metrics, where d is the dimensionality of the vectors$\mathbf{X}_m$ and $\mathbf{X}_n$.

$$d(\mathbf{X}_m, \mathbf{X}_n) = g\left[\sum_{i=1}^{d} f_i(X_{im}, X_{in})\right] \quad (1)$$

$$d(\mathbf{X}_m, \mathbf{X}_n) = \left[\sum_{i=1}^{d} |X_{im} - X_{in}|^p \right]^{\frac{1}{p}} \quad (p \geq 1) \qquad (2)$$

The three most often used Minkowski metrics are the taxi-cab distance (3) where $p = 1$, the Euclidean metric (4) for which $p = 2$ and the maximum coordinate distance (5) where $p = \infty$.

$$d(\mathbf{X}_m, \mathbf{X}_n) = \sum_{i=1}^{d} |X_{im} - X_{in}| \qquad (3)$$

$$d(\mathbf{X}_m, \mathbf{X}_n) = \left[\sum_{i=1}^{d} (X_{im} - X_{in})^2 \right]^{\frac{1}{2}} \qquad (4)$$

$$d(\mathbf{X}_m, \mathbf{X}_n) = \max_{1 \leq i \leq d} \{|X_{im} - X_{in}|\} \qquad (5)$$

B. Linear Discriminant Analysis

A second approach to categorizing points in a d-dimensional space relies on the use of discriminant functions. In the implementation of discriminant functions, no prior knowledge of a probability distribution among the sample points is assumed. The space is divided into K regions, each having its own weighting coefficients. In this work, linear discriminant functions (6) [11] are used,

$$D_k(\mathbf{x}) = x_1\alpha_{1k} + x_2\alpha_{2k} +, \ldots, + x_N\alpha_{Nk} + \alpha_{N+1,k} \quad k = 1, 2, \ldots, K \qquad (6)$$

where x is the N-dimensional sample vector and α are the normalized weighting coefficients for the k-th class. Linear discriminant functions were chosen for the algorithm since they are the most computationally efficient form. A sample vector belongs to a particular class if its discriminant function is greater for that class than for any other class, i.e., $\mathbf{x}_i$ belongs to class C_j if

$$D_j(\mathbf{x}) > D_k(\mathbf{x}) \quad \text{for every } k \neq j.$$

The weighting coefficients are adjusted from their initial guess through a training procedure using sample vectors which the proper classification is known. The algorithm for this procedure makes adjustments to the weighting coefficients until each sample vector is correctly classified.

Young and Calvert [11] show that this training algorithm will converge in a finite number of steps. When a sample vector is correctly classified, no adjustment to the weighting coefficients is made. When a sample vectors is incorrectly classified, or

$$D_j(\mathbf{x}) \leq D_l(\mathbf{x}),$$

where

$$D_l(\mathbf{x}) = \max_{l \neq j} \left[D_1(\mathbf{x}), \ldots, D_K(\mathbf{x}) \right],$$

adjustments are made to $\boldsymbol{\alpha}_j$ (7) and $\boldsymbol{\alpha}_l$ (8) only,

$$\boldsymbol{\alpha}_j(i+1) = \boldsymbol{\alpha}_j(i) + a\mathbf{x}_i \qquad (7)$$

$$\boldsymbol{\alpha}_l(i+1) = \boldsymbol{\alpha}_l(i) - a\mathbf{x}_i, \qquad (8)$$

where a is a gain constant.

IV. TRANSFORM DISCRIMINATION STRENGTH

The Fisher ratio is used as figure of merit to measure the discriminative strength of the features generated by the distributions. It compares the within class spread of features of the same category and between class scatter of features from different categories. Ideally, the within class spread should be as low as possible and the between class scatter should be as high as possible. The Fisher ratio is computed for all the four candidate transforms. From 20 sampled currents signals, four meshing events were recorded for each class making at total samples size of eighty meshing events per class.

V. DETECTION AND CLASSIFICATION METHODS

A. Intermittent Increased Contact Resistance

The first fault explored in this work is an intermittent increased contact resistance between the motor and the controller. An experiment was designed to simulate this. The fault is achieved by adding the parallel combination of a normally closed switch, and a resistance in series with one of the motor phases as shown in Fig.

The fault is initiated by opening the switch for a short time interval, causing current to flow through the resistance. Various values for the contact resistance were used, including $2.14pu$, $2.80pu$, $4.03pu$, $6.33pu$, and $15.84pu$. The fault can be initiated at varying levels of the peak amplitude of the phase current command; 5%, 50%, and 95% were tried. Tests with fault durations of $5ms$ and $10ms$ have been performed to investigate invariance of the results with respect to this parameter as well.

B. Turn-Terminal Short

The second fault explored here is insulation failure in the stator windings of the motor. To simulate this fault in the experimental setup, at one point in a single strand of one of the windings, the insulation was removed, and a normally open switch was added between this point and the corresponding phase terminal of the motor. The fault was initiated by momentarily closing the switch, causing current to be split between the intended path and the switch.

C. Algorithm Based on the UDWT Applied to Electrical Faults with Separate Classification of Fault Inception and Clearing (Slow Controller Response)

The input to the algorithm developed in is 64 UDWT samples, or $3.2ms$, of the measured q-axis current, i_{qs}. This time interval is selected to capture the beginning and end of each fault separately. For this step, the Daubechies D4 mother wavelet was used and decomposition was performed to 6 levels. The algorithm has two parts; a detection phase and a classification phase. The detection phase of the algorithm is based on thresholding on the weighted energy in the UDWT. The threshold was set at 40% greater than the largest which was observed in all samples from the healthy machine data. If the weighted energy in new test data exceeds this threshold, a fault is considered to exist.

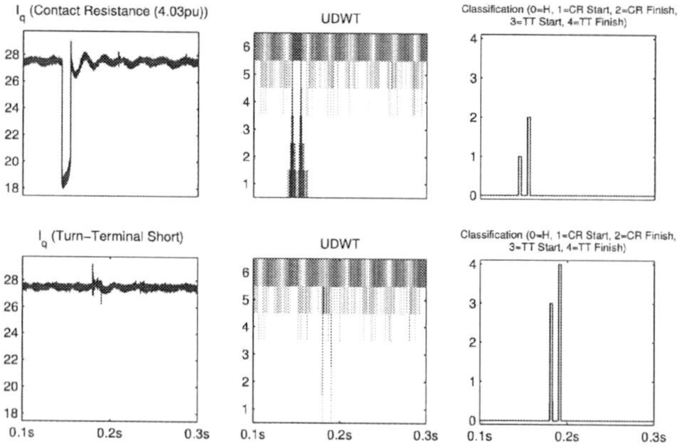

Fig. 4. Typical Results (Fault Inception and Clearing - Slow Controller)

The classification phase was based on linear discriminant analysis. This phase is implemented when the criterion for detection is met. Since the fault duration is random, two distinct events were assigned to each intermittent fault; one corresponding to the inception, and the other to the clearing of the fault. The advantage of havingtwo separate classes for each fault is invariance to the duration of the fault. Additionally, a postprocessing algorithm to verify that subsequent classification of the beginning and end of the same fault type would further confirm existence of the fault. To train the algorithm, thereby determining the weighting coefficients, data were used from eight experiments from each of the following operating conditions: Healthy, increased contact resistance ($5ms$ and $10ms$), and turn-terminal short ($5ms$ and $10ms$). The data used were the 64 samples in the UDWT corresponding to each event.

Following the training of the weighting coefficients, data that had not been used in the training algorithm were tested. Two data sets from each of the following operating conditions were tested: Healthy; $5ms$ increased contact resistance; $10ms$ increased contact resistance; $5ms$ turn-terminal short; and $10ms$ turn-terminal short.

The results from two typical test cases are shown in Fig. 4. The top row of Fig. 4has results from the increased contact resistance fault. The bottom row has results from the turn-terminal short. The left column shows the measured torque producing component of the current, i_{qs}, for each test case. The center column shows the spectrogram of the data to the left. The right column is the output of the detection and classification algorithm with 0=healthy, 1=beginning of increased contact resistance fault, 2=end of increased contact resistance fault, 3=beginning of turn-terminal short, and 4=end of turn-terminal short.

There it can be seen that the amplitude of the UDWT coefficients is increased at the points of inception and clearing of the faults. The increased energy at these points meets the criterion for detection, and the classification algorithm operates on the UDWT coefficients corresponding to $3.2ms$ of data at these points. The results shown indicate correct classification of the inception and clearing of both faults explored in this work.

The ten tests described above resulted in no false positives and one false negative. In the two healthy cases, no fault events were detected. In the four cases with the increased contact resistance fault, all fault inception and clearing events were identified correctly. In the four cases with the turn-terminal short, three of the four fault inception events were identified correctly, and the fourth did not meet the criterion for detection; all four fault clearing events were identified correctly.

D. Algorithm Based on the UDWT Applied to Electrical Faults with Separate Classification of Fault Inception and Clearing (Fast Controller Response)

The experimental data in this section was a result of faster controller response than the original experiments, giving improved transient response and less steady state error. While previous experiments have shown that the algorithms developed are generally invariant to fault duration and rotational speed, the emphasis of thethese experiments is to show invariance to the resistance value used in the increased contact resistance experiments.

The training data, fault resistance values, mother wavelet, threshold level for fault detection, classification method etc., were the same as for the slow-response controller. Again the technique using UDWT and STFT were compared.

Following the training of the weighting coefficients, data that had not been used in the training algorithm were tested. Two data sets from each of the following operating conditions were tested: Healthy, increased contact resistance ($2.14pu$, $2.80pu$, $4.03pu$, $6.33pu$, and $15.84pu$), and turn-terminal short.

The faster controller response has decreased the fault recovery times for both faults explored. In the case of the UDWT, it is possible to get both good time and frequency resolution in the same analysis. The performance of the UDWT algorithm was much better than the performance of the STFT algorithm under the same test conditions.

The results from two typical test cases are shown in Fig.5 The top row of Fig. 5 has results from one of the increased contact resistance faults. The bottom row has results from the turn-terminal short. The left column shows the measured torque producing component of the current, i_{qs}, for each test case. The center column shows the spectrogram of the data to the left. The right column is the output of the detection and classification algorithm with 0=healthy, 1=beginning of increased contact resistance fault, 2=end of increased contact resistance fault, 3=beginning of turn-terminal short, and 4=end of turn-terminal short.

There were no false detections. All fault events were detected and classified correctly except for the clearing of one of the $2.14pu$ increased contact resistance faults. The $2.14pu$ increased contact resistance fault, however, is outside of the range of values for which the algorithm was trained.

VI. FAULT DURATION AND SEPARATION

In the previous discussion we described how to differentiate between two intermittent faults, which translated in the

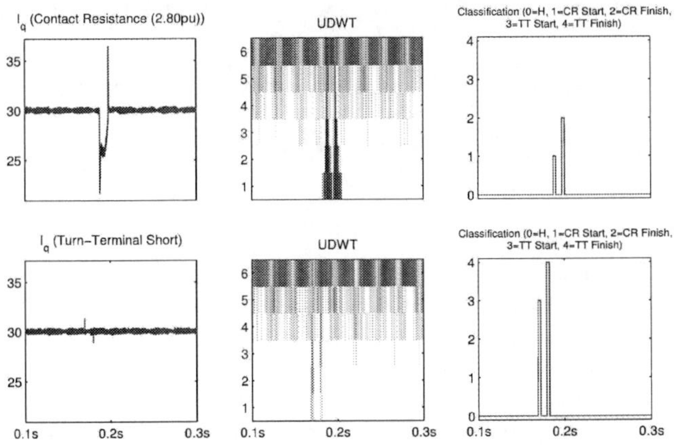

Fig. 5. Typical Results (Fault Inception and Clearing - Fast Controller)

identification of four separate events: inception of a short and of an open, and clearing of each of these faults. Other faults are also characterized by a short duration. Among them mechanical faults in gears and bearings, and switching of power electronics under both healthy and faulty conditions of the switch and of the insulation. Gear faults have been discussed in earlier work [4], and although they are of similar time scale, they can be separated from electrical faults, albeit through additional training of the algorithm. A plethora of studies exist for the detection of faults in bearings, and aside from the detection of early crater faults in the races, their signatures are distinct from the ones studied here.

Although transients due to switching of devices can be used to detect both insulation and power electronics faults, the time scales vary dramatically. In the cases discussed here, the phenomena as reported last a few ms, while the switching transients due to power electronics last a few hundreds of μs, and they cannot be confused.

It is important, though to train the algorithm for the time constant of the current controller, since it does affect the transient that is identified and can lead to false positives and false negatives if not accounted for.

VII. CONCLUSIONS

Intermittent faults present different characteristics than static or periodic faults in PMAC machines. What characterizes them is the random inception and duration. It is often the case that the fault is such that it cannot reach steady state, making classic detection methods unfeasible.

In this work we present a technique based on the detection and characterization of the inception and clearing of the fault, using decreased data storage requirements, fault detection, identification and characterization and independent of the machine characteristics.

REFERENCES

[1] W. A. Syed, S. Perinpanayagam, M. Samie, and I. Jennions, "A novel intermittent fault detection algorithm and health monitoring for electronic interconnections," *IEEE Transactions on Components, Packaging and Manufacturing Technology*, vol. 6, no. 3, pp. 400–406, March 2016.

[2] D. Zhou, Y. Zhao, Z. Wang, X. He, and M. Gao, "Review on diagnosis techniques for intermittent faults in dynamic systems," *IEEE Transactions on Industrial Electronics*, pp. 1–1, 2019.

[3] F. Auzanneau and C. Layer, "Microsecond intermittent fault detection for wire and connector defect prognostics," in *2017 IEEE SENSORS*, Oct 2017, pp. 1–3.

[4] W. G. Zanardelli, E. G. Strangas, and S. Aviyente, "Identification of intermittent electrical and mechanical faults in permanent-magnet AC drives based on timefrequency analysis," *IEEE Transactions on Industry Applications*, vol. 43, no. 4, pp. 971–980, July 2007.

[5] S. H. Zaidi, W. G. Zanardelli, S. Aviyente, and E. G. Strangas, "Comparative study of time-frequency methods for the detection and categorization of intermittent faults in electrical drives," in *2007 IEEE International Symposium on Diagnostics for Electric Machines, Power Electronics and Drives*, Sep. 2007, pp. 39–45.

[6] S. Huang, E. G. Strangas, A. Aggarwal, K. Li, and F. Niu, "Arobust interturn short-circuit detection in PMSMs with respect to current controller bandwidth," in *The Eleventh Annual Energy Conversion Congress and Exposition*, Oct 2019.

[7] Q. Shen, K. Lv, G. Liu, and J. Qiu, "Impact of electrical contact resistance on the high-speed transmission and on-line diagnosis of electrical connector intermittent faults," *IEEE Access*, vol. 5, pp. 4221–4232, 2017.

[8] W. R. Jensen, E. G. Strangas, and S. N. Foster, "A method for online stator insulation prognosis for inverter-driven machines," *IEEE Transactions on Industry Applications*, vol. 54, no. 6, pp. 5897–5906, Nov 2018.

[9] F. Xu, W. Huang, L. Zhou, N. Tai, J. Wen, and L. Cao, "An intermittent high-impedance fault identification method based on transient power direction detection and intermittency detection," in *2017 IEEE Power Energy Society General Meeting*, July 2017, pp. 1–5.

[10] N. H. Obeid, A. Battiston, T. Boileau, and B. Nahid-Mobarakeh, "Identification and localization of incipient intermittent inter-turn fault in the stator of a three phase permanent magnet synchronous motor," in *2017 IEEE 11th International Symposium on Diagnostics for Electrical Machines, Power Electronics and Drives (SDEMPED)*, Aug 2017, pp. 173–180.

[11] T. Y. Young and T. W. Calvert, *Classification, Estimation and Pattern Recognition*. American Elsevier Publishing Co., Inc., 1974.

Elias G. Strangas received the Dipl. Eng. degree in Electrical Engineering from the National Technical University of Greece, Athens, Greece, in 1975, and the Ph.D. in electrical engineering from the University of Pittsburgh, Pittsburgh, PA, USA, in 1980.He was with Schneider Electric, Athens, from 1981 to 1983 and with the University of Missouri, Rolla, MO, USA, from 1983 to 1986. Since 1986, he has been with the Department of Electrical and Computer Engineering, Michigan State University, East Lansing, MI, USA, where he heads the Electrical Machines and Drives Laboratory. His research interests include the design and control of electrical machines and drives, finite-element methods for electromagnetics, and failure prognosis and mitigation of electrical drive systems

7th International Conference on Reliability of Electrical Products and Electrical Contacts, November 04-06, 2019 **(Invited Paper)**

Arc Energy Calculation During Re-striking Phenomena in Break Operations of $AgSnO_2$ Contacts in Inductive DC Load Conditions up to 20V-17A with Different Contact Opening Speeds

Seika Tokumitsu *Makoto Hasegawa
Department of Opto-Electronic System Engineering
Chitose Institute of Science and Technology, Chitose, Hokkaido, 066-8655, Japan
*E-mail: hasegawa@photon.chitose.ac.jp Phone/Fax: +81-123-27-6059

***Abstract*— $AgSnO_2$ contacts were operated to break an inductive DC load circuit of 14V-7A, 14V-12A, 20V-7A, and 20V-17A with an applied external magnetic field of about B=120mT at contact opening speeds of 1mm/s to 200mm/s. Re-striking phenomena were likely to be observed with larger load current levels or faster contact opening speed levels. The number of re-strikes was sometimes two or more. The calculation results of arc energy revealed that the total arc energy from ignition to extinction reached almost the same level irrespective of re-striking incidents. Thus, occurrences of re-striking phenomena in break operations of inductive DC loads up to 20V-17A are influenced by the amount of energy that is supplied into and to be consumed at a contact gap. Even when arc is blown out of a contact gap due to an external magnetic field, re-striking may occur and repeat until the supplied energy is consumed.**

***Index Terms*— DC break arc, Re-striking, Re-ignition, $AgSnO_2$ contacts, Arc energy.**

I. INTRODUCTION

Upon switching of a load current by means of a mechanical switching device, re-striking or re-ignition phenomena of break arcs are sometimes observed. Several studies on such phenomena were previously reported.

For example, Hauer and Xin Zhou [1] studied re-ignition processes during standardized 10kA/600V single-phase short circuit interruption tests with Molded Case Circuit Breakers (MCCBs). They reported the two different re-ignition phenomena. The first category was "instantaneous re-ignition", in which an arc re-ignites immediately after the current-zero point and a short circuit current continues to flow in reverse polarity. The second category was "delayed re-ignition", in which re-ignition takes place with a certain time period after the current-zero point. Slade [2] described in detail about re-striking phenomena in capacitor switching with vacuum interrupters. Slade and Tayler [3] further investigated influences of emission currents from a cathode contact on occasional late or delayed re-strike after capacitor switching with vacuum interrupters.

In addition to the above-mentioned studies for AC switching, re-striking or re-ignition phenomena have been also reported in DC switching under application of an external magnetic field.

For example, Xue Zhou et al. [4] reported arc re-ignitions in a bridge-type Cu contact pair when breaking a DC resistive 270V-200A, based on arc current measurements and arc image observations. They suggested that a uniform magnetic field with a proper density would reduce arc re-ignitions. Xue Zhou et al. [5] further reported, based on arc voltage measurements and arc image observations during breaking experiments of a DC resistive 50A at 280-730V with a bridge-type Cu contact, occurrences of re-striking by multiple-arcs and re-ignition leading by swirl motion of arcs. Their investigations continued into the following researches [6] on re-strike phenomena during breaking experiments of a DC resistive 50A at 300-800V with a bridge-type Mo30%-Cu70% alloy contact pair based on arc voltage measurements and arc image observations. They reported that the arc re-strike phenomena can be categorized into two types (i.e., a contact-contact type and an arc-contact type) based on observed arc voltage waveforms. Multi-arcs striking phenomena were also reported by Ono et al. [7-8] when breaking a DC resistive 10A current at up to 450V with an Ag contact pair, although they called the phenomena as re-ignition.

In the authors' investigations [9-11] on switching of DC inductive loads with an $AgSnO_2$ contact pair under application of an external magnetic field, re-ignition or re-striking phenomena were also observed, even in smaller load conditions up to 20V-17A. Thus, re-striking or re-ignition phenomena of break arcs can be sometimes observed with an applied external magnetic field even at small or middle load levels. Studies of the phenomena in such load regions have not been done in detail. Their better understanding, for example on their occurrence conditions, will be advantageous for realizing better performances and reliabilities of mechanical relays.

In this paper, re-striking or re-ignition phenomena to be observed in break operations of $AgSnO_2$ contacts in an inductive DC load circuit up to 20V-17A with an applied external magnetic field of about 120mT at contact opening speeds of 1mm/s to 200mm/s were studied in view of arc energy levels.

II. EXPERIMENTAL CONDITIONS AND PROCEDURES

A. Experimental setup

The same experimental setup as that in the authors' recent studies [10-12] was also employed in this study. Fig.1 shows pairs of $AgSnO_2$ contacts (Ag88%-SnO212%, prepared by internal oxidation with no additives) used in this study. Both stationary (right in Fig.1) and movable (left in Fig.1) electrodes were of solid rivet-type with a head thickness of about 1mm and a head diameter of about 3mm. The head of the stationary electrode was attached onto a metal plate (18mm x 6mm), while the head of the movable electrode was attached onto a spring plate (also 18mm x 6mm) made of phosphor bronze.

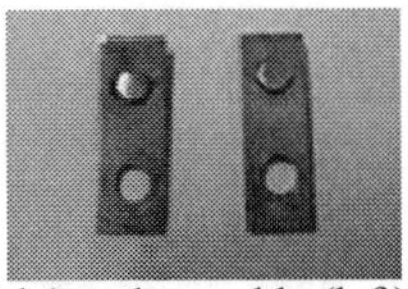

Fig. 1 Stationary (right) and movable (left) electrodes in this study [12].

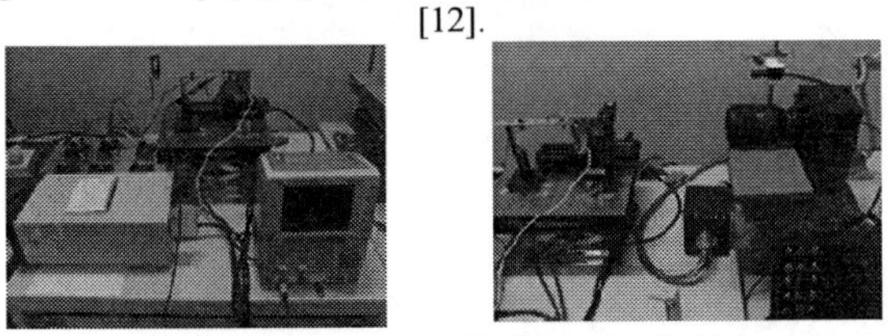

(a) overall view (b) placement of a high speed camera

Fig. 2 Photos of the experimental setup in this study [12].

The switching mechanism includes a motorized stage driven by an AC servo motor. The motorized stage is placed onto a stable metal platform on which one electrode of a contact pair is also fixed as a stationary electrode via a certain attachment jig. Another electrode is mounted onto the motorized stage as a movable electrode. Switching operations of the contact pair can be realized via movements of the motorized stage by controlling the AC servo motor through instructions from a PC program.

The inductive load circuit in this study included an inductive component of about 5.7 mH. It was not intended to realize any specific applications, but rather, it was intended to mitigate influences of unregulated inductive components in the circuit (e.g., stray inductance components due to wirings) by employing such an intentional inductive component. No specific control for the load current flow was employed during the switching operations and thus both break and make discharges were actually occurred. Among them, only break arc discharges were investigated in this study.

For application of an external magnetic field, a piece of neodymium magnet (with 0.5 cm in height and 1.5 cm in diameter) was placed at about 0.5 cm away from the contact gap position. With such a placement, the resultant magnetic flux density at the contact gap was measured to be about 120 mT, although it was not able to confirm whether or not the magnetic flux density was uniform in the contact gap.

In order to observe arc movements, a high-speed camera (Photron FASTCAM MiniAX200) was also placed as shown in Fig.2(b), and employed in some situations.

TABLE I
EXPERIMENTAL CONDITIONS

Contact material	Ag(88%)-SnO_2(12%)
Load circuit	DC inductive (L = 5.7 mH)
Load conditions	14V-7A, 14V-12A, 20V-7A, and 20V-17A
Ambient environment	laboratory air (no control)
Contact opening speed	1, 10, 50, 100, 200 mm/s
External magnetic field	about 120 mT @ contact gap

B. Measurement and observation procedures

Before the test, the surfaces of both electrodes of a test contact pair were polished with #1000 sandpaper and then wiped with methyl alcohol. Thereafter, the contact pair was mounted onto the switching mechanism with the movable electrode as an anode and the stationary electrode as a cathode.

At the closed position, the movable anode electrode was slightly pushed backward by the mating stationary cathode electrode, thereby resulting in slight bending of the spring plate (an electrode assembly arm for the movable anode electrode) due to its elasticity. This may cause some wiping between the electrode surfaces as is usual in commercial relays.

In each of the test conditions, four arc voltage waveforms across the separating contacts upon contact opening, as well as corresponding arc current waveforms, were recorded with a digital storage-scope (Yokogawa DL1620). In addition, simultaneously, arc movement was observed by means of a high-speed camera. Recorded movies of the arc movements, as well as the arc voltage/current waveforms, were later analyzed.

III. EXPERIMENTAL RESULTS AND DISCUSSIONS

A. Occurrence tendencies of arc re-striking phenomena

In the following descriptions, the term "re-strike" or "re-striking" will be used, and no specific distinctions will be done between "re-strike (re-striking)" and "re-ignition", different from the several other researchers' previous references as mentioned in the above.

Whether re-strike was occurred or not was determined based on the measured arc voltage waveforms. For example, Fig.3(a) shows exemplary arc voltage/current waveforms without re-strikes, while Fig.3(b) shows the waveforms with one re-strike. In both of the figures, blue traces represent the arc voltage waveforms, and orange traces represent the arc current waveforms. In addition, the gray-colored vertical line at around the timing of rapid increase in the arc voltage waveform before the final extinction corresponds to the arc blown-out timing, as determined from the respective corresponding high-speed movies. It should be noted that due to limitation of the measurement range of the digital storage-scope employed, the arc voltage waveforms are flattened at 80V in these figures.

From the waveforms as shown in Fig.3(a), without arc re-striking phenomena, the arc current was likely to rapidly decrease during arc blown-out. On the other hand, with arc re-strikes, decrease in the arc current during arc blown-out was likely to take a longer time period, as shown in Fig.3(b).

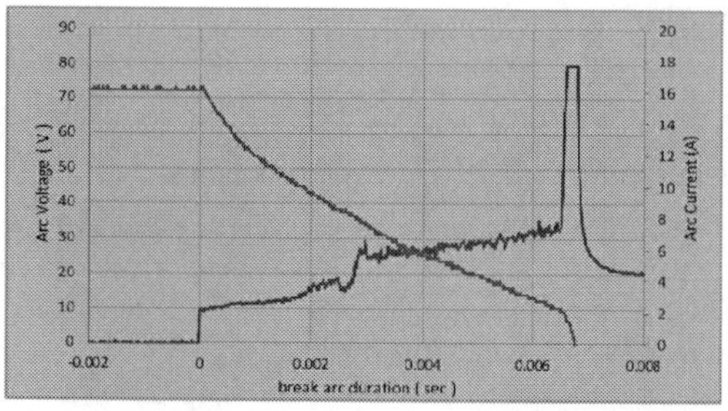

(a) without arc re-strikes (20V-17A@50mm/s)

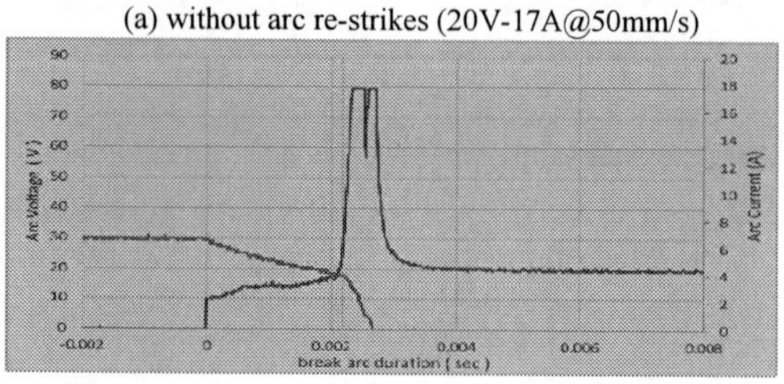

(b) with arc re-strikes (20V-7A@200mm/s)

Fig. 3 Exemplary arc voltage/current waveforms with/without arc re-strikes.

The observed results on occurrence tendencies of arc re-striking phenomena are summarized in Table II.

In this table, the mark "x" means that arc blown-out (and arc re-strikes) was not observed among the respective four observations. The number "0" means that although arc blown-out was observed, no arc re-strikes were observed among the four observations. The other numbers indicate the averages of observed re-striking phenomena among the four observations. For example, in the 14V-7A@50mm/sec condition, the number "0.25" means that only one re-strike was observed among the four observations.

These summarized results show that re-striking phenomena were likely to be observed with larger load current levels such as at 14V-12A and 20V-17A. Furthermore, in those conditions, multiple re-strikes were observed at faster contact opening speed levels. In the other two load conditions (14V-7A and 20V-7A), arc re-striking phenomena were likely to be observed at faster contact opening speeds.

In the following conditions, at least one re-strike was observed in each of the four observations:

- 14V-12A @ 50mm/s;
- 14V-12A @ 100mm/s;
- 14V-12A @ 200mm/s;
- 20V-17A @ 10mm/s; and
- 20V-17A @ 200mm/s.

TABLE II
OCCURRENCE TENDENCIES OF RE-STRIKING PHENOMENA

Contact opening speed	Load conditions			
	14V 7A	14V 12A	20V 7A	20V 17A
1mm/sec	×	×	×	0.25
10mm/sec	×	0.25	×	3
50mm/sec	0.25	2.75	0.25	2.25
100mm/sec	0.5	2.25	0	1.75
200mm/sec	0	2.5	0.25	2.5

B. Arc energy comparisons between the cases with/without arc re-strikes

For the purpose of make comparisons between the cases with/without arc re-strikes, the four operating conditions as shown in Table 3 below were picked up. In these four conditions, both of the cases with/without arc re-striking phenomena were observed among the respective four observations.

More specifically, as shown in Table 3, in the 20V-7A@200mm/s condition and in the 20V-17A@1mm/s condition, re-strike was observed only once among the four observations, respectively, and the number of observed re-strike was one for each case. In the 20V-17A@50mm/s condition, multiple re-strikes were observed in three out of four observations. Multiple re-strikes were also observed in some of the observations in the 20V-17A@100mm/s condition.

TABLE III
THE NUMBER OF OBSERVED RE-STRIKE PHENOMENA

	Operating conditions															
	20V-7A 200mm/sec				20V-17A 1mm/sec				20V-17A 50mm/sec				20V-17A 100mm/sec			
	1	2	3	4	1	2	3	4	1	2	3	4	1	2	3	4
Re-strike (yes:O no:×)	O	×	×	×	×	×	×	O	O	×	O	O	×	O	O	O
Number of observed re-strikes	1	/	/	/	/	/	/	1	2	/	4	3	/	4	1	2

Based on the measured arc voltage/current waveforms as shown in Fig.3, arc energy was calculated as the product of the arc voltage and the arc current. The thus-obtained exemplary arc energy waveforms are shown in Fig.4(a) and Fig.4(b), respectively. In both of these figures, the green-colored vertical line at around the timing of rapid increase before the final extinction indicates the arc blown-out timing corresponding to the gray-colored vertical line in Fig.3. Furthermore, the blue-colored vertical line corresponds to the arc extinction timing also determined from the respective corresponding high-speed movies.

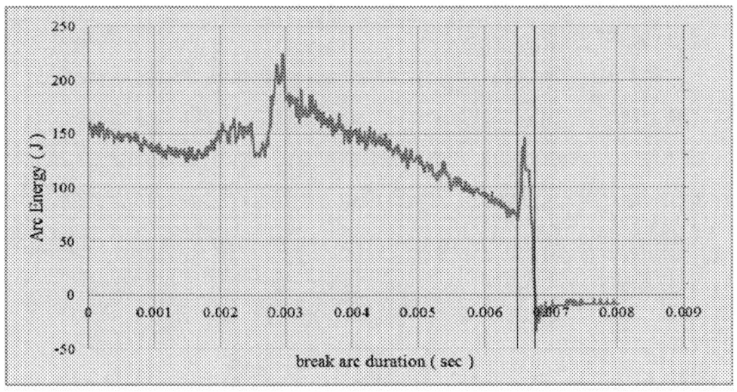

(a) without arc re-strikes (20V-17A@50mm/s)

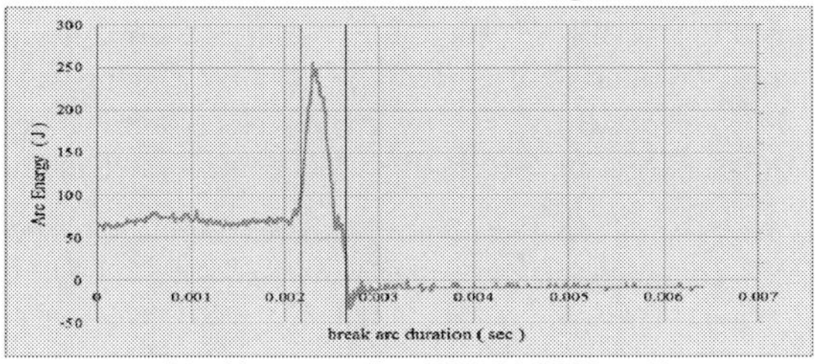

(b) with arc re-strikes (20V-7A@200mm/s)

Fig. 4 Exemplary arc energy waveforms with/without arc re-strikes.

Fig.5(a)-(d) shows the total arc energy values in the respective four observations for the operating conditions as shown in Table III where at least one arc re-strike was observed. Interestingly, in each of these operating conditions, the total arc energy for each of the four observations reaches almost the same level, irrespective of whether or not arc re-strike was observed, and irrespective of the number of actually observed re-strikes.

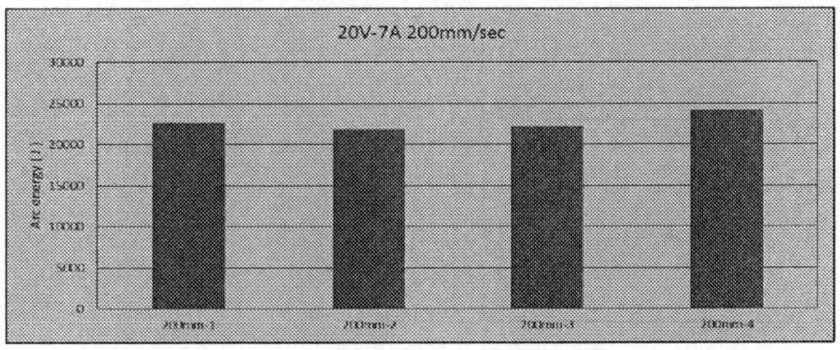

(a) 20V-7A@200mm/s

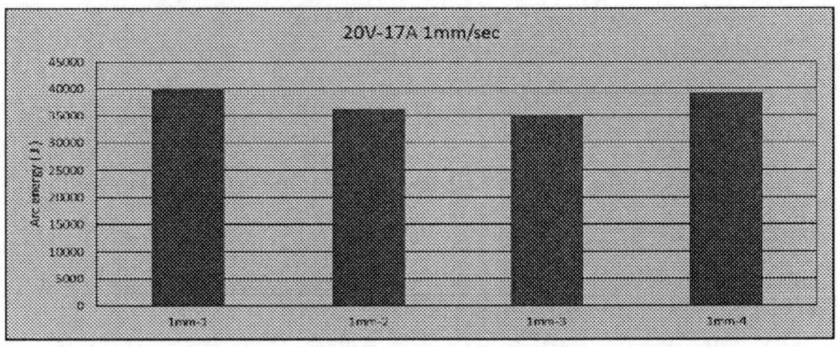

(b) 20V-17A@1mm/s

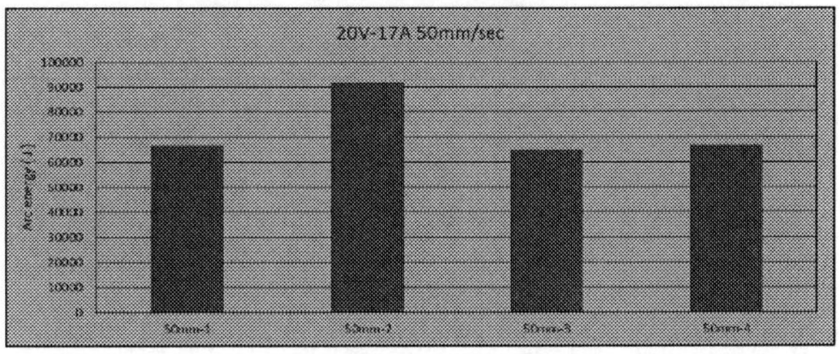

(c) 20V-17A@50mm/s

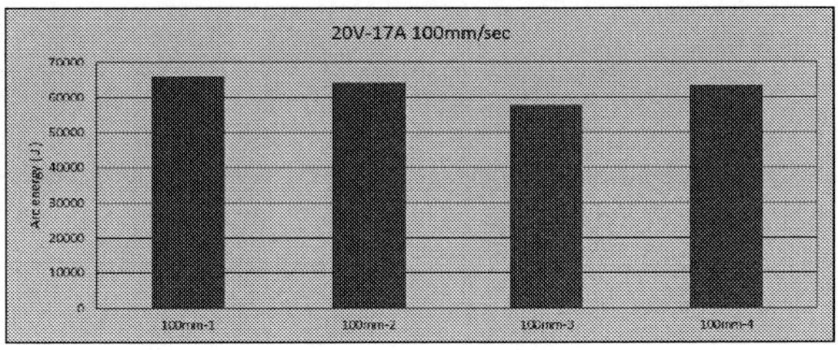

(d) 20V-17A@100mm/s

Fig. 5 The calculated total arc energy values in the respective four observations for the operating conditions where at least one arc re-strike was observed.

Thus, it may be possible to say that in the operating conditions investigated in this paper, even when a break arc is magnetically blown out, the arc will not completely extinguish until the energy supplied into the contact gap is finally consumed while experiencing one or more re-striking phenomena. Consumption of the supplied energy at the contact gap can be one of possible factors influencing occurrence of arc re-strikes.

IV. CONCLUSIONS

Re-striking or re-ignition phenomena in break operations of $AgSnO_2$ contacts in an inductive DC load circuit of 14V-7A, 14V-12A, 20V-7A, and 20V-17A with an applied external magnetic field of about 120mT at contact opening speeds of 1mm/s to 200mm/s were studied in view of arc energy levels. The calculation results of arc energy revealed that the total arc energy from ignition to extinction reached almost the same level irrespective of re-striking incidents.

Thus, occurrences of re-striking phenomena in break operations of inductive DC loads up to 20V-17A are influenced by the amount of energy that is supplied into and to be consumed at a contact gap. Even when arc is blown out of a contact gap due to an external magnetic field, re-striking may occur and sometimes repeat until the supplied energy is finally consumed.

ACKNOWLEDGMENT

The authors thank Tanaka Kikinzoku Kogyo Co., Ltd. for supplying contact samples used in this study. The authors also thank Photron Ltd., for their courtesy of letting us use their high-speed camera for this study.

REFERENCES

[1] W. Hauer, Xin Zhou, "Re-ignition and post arc current phenomena in low voltage circuit breaker", Proc. 27th Intl. Conf. on Electrical Contacts (ICEC2014), pp.398-403, June 2014.

[2] P. G. Slade, "The vacuum interrupter: Theory, Design, and Application" CRC Press, pp.363-372, 2008.

[3] P. G. Slade, E. D. Taylor, "Emission currents and late restrikes after switching capacitors using vacuum interrupters", Proc. 29th Intl. Conf. on Electrical Contacts (ICEC2018) and 64th IEEE Holm Conf. on Electrical Contacts (Holm2018), pp.229-234, October 2018.

[4] Xue Zhou, Xinglei Cui, Guofu Zhai, "Study on arc behaviors at opening a 270 V resistive circuit by bridge-type contacts under magnetic field", IEICE Trans. Electron., vol. E96-C, no.9, pp.1124-1131, September 2013.

[5] Xue Zhou, Xinglei Cui, Mo Chen, Guofu Zhai, "Experimental study on arc behaviors of a bridge-type contact when opening a resistive load in the range of from 280 VDC to 730 VDC", Proc. 60th IEEE Holm Conf. on Electrical Contacts (Holm2014), pp.341-347, October 2014.

[6] Xinglei Cui, Xue Zhou, Mo Chen, Kai Bo, Xiyuan Peng, "Experimental research on re-strike phenomenon occurring during high-voltage direct-current breaking process under transverse magnetic field", Proc. 61st IEEE Holm Conf. on Electrical Contacts (Holm2015), pp.187-190, October 2015.

[7] H. Ono, J. Sekikawa, T. Kubono, "Arc duration of break arcs magnetically blown-out in a DC 450 V resistive circuit", IEICE Trans. Electron., vol.E95-C, no.9, pp.1515-1521, September 2012.

[8] H. Ono, J. Sekikawa, "Arc length of break arcs magnetically blown-out at arc extinction in a DC450V/10A resistive circuit", IEICE Trans. Electron., vol.E96-C, no.9, pp.1132-1137, September 2013.

[9] M. Hasegawa, S. Tokumitsu, "Break arc duration characteristics of $AgSnO_2$ contacts under magnetic field application with contact opening speeds in the range up to 200mm/s in DC load conditions", Proc. 62nd IEEE Holm Conf. on Electrical Contacts (Holm2016), pp.119-124, October 2016.

[10] S. Tokumitsu, M. Hasegawa, "Effective shortening of break arc durations of Ag and several Ag-based contacts in DC load conditions with increased contact opening speeds and external magnetic field", Proc. 29th Intl. Conf. on Electrical Contacts (ICEC2018) and 64th IEEE Holm Conf. on Electrical Contacts (Holm2018), pp.87-94, October 2018.

[11] S. Tokumitsu, M. Hasegawa, "Influences of contact opening speeds and external magnetic field on shortening of break arc durations of $AgSnO_2$ in a DC inductive load circuit up to 20V-17A", IEICE Technical Report, EMD2018-52, January 2019 (in Japanese language).

[12] S. Tokumitsu, M. Hasegawa, "Arc movement investigations of break arcs of $AgSnO_2$ contacts under applied external magnetic field in inductive DC load conditions", to be included in Proc. 65th IEEE Holm Conf. on Electrical Contacts (Holm2019), September 2019.

Seika Tokumitsu received her Bachelor's degree of Science and Engineering and Master's degree of Science and Engineering, both in photonics science, from Chitose Institute of Science and Technology, Chitose, Japan, in 2017 and 2019, respectively. Her research subjects were related in photonics science as well as electrical contact phenomenon.

Makoto Hasegawa received his B.E., M.E. and Ph.D. degrees in electrical engineering from Keio University, Yokohama, Japan, in 1986, 1988 and 1991, respectively. After spending several years in industry, Dr. Hasegawa is now a Professor at the Department of Opto-Electronic System Engineering, Chitose Institute of Science and Technology, Japan. He is currently involved in research on electrical contact phenomenon and related measuring techniques, optical sensing techniques, as well as development of experiment and education programs on physics and engineering education.

7th International Conference on Reliability of
Electrical Products and Electrical Contacts,
November 04-06, 2019 **(Invited Paper)**

Availability Estimation of Repairable Parallel Load-sharing *k*-out-of-*n*: *G* Systems with Limited Repair Resource

Jian Zhang, Jinhao Shen, Xiaoyan Huang, Youtong Fang
College of Electrical Engineering, Zhejiang University, Hangzhou, China
E-mail:ShenJh@zju.edu.cn Tel: 86-571-87953134 Fax: 86-571-87953134

***Abstract*—The dependency among the units of repairable parallel load-sharing *k*-out-of-*n*:*G* systems is the biggest challenge confronting their availability evaluation. This paper focused on the state evolution of the investigated load-sharing system and then proposed its availability estimation method. A Markov process was adopted to describe the state evolution with the number of failed units increasing. First-fail-first-repair policy was utilized due to the limited repair resource. Capacity Flow Model was used as the link function mapping the relationship between unit lifetimes and load level.Finally, the Kolmogorov differential equations of each system state's probability at any time is established for further estimating system availability. A numeric example was presented to illustrate the result of this model.**

***Index Terms*—Load-sharing system, *k*-out-of-*n*:*G* system, Availability evaluation.**

I. INTRODUCTION

Load-sharing *k*-out-of-*n*:G system is a typical kind of multi-unit system and is widely applied in industrial practice. Electrical generators, servers in a distributed computer system, engines on an airplanes are all the typical examples of load-sharing systems [1],[2]. For multi-unit systems, it is often assumed that units work independently due to the convenient mathematical properties and computational efficiency. However, this independent assumption is not valid for load-sharing *k*-out-of-*n*:G systems, whose units are subject to a shared system workload [3]. Component failures will result in an increased workload for the remaining surviving units. It has been demonstrated that workload level is closely related to unit failure rate, and the increase of workload caused by the failed units will lead to an elevated failure rate of the surviving units [4]. How to describe the inherent dependencies among the units' availability in load-sharing *k*-out-of-*n*:G systems is a great challenge to reliability engineers.

To model a load-sharing *k*-out-of-*n*:G system, a proper baseline distribution for unit lifetimes and a link function mapping the relationship between unit lifetimes and load level are indispensable. The other key task is the description of system state evolution during system's lifecycle. The exponential distribution assumption for unit lifetimes is widely used in system reliability evaluation [5],[6]. It is consensus that failure rate escalates with the increase of load level. Singh assumed that the component lifetime under different stress levels follows an exponential distribution with different failure rate [7]. The relationship between work load level and failure rate is described in detail in literature [8].

Therefore, this paper focuses on the availability evaluation of a repairable parallel load-sharing system in which the identical units with limited repair resource. The rest of this paper is organized as follows. Section 2 describes the basic assumption and problem setting. Section 3 models the state evolution of system reliability with the increasing number of failed units. A simulation study is conducted in Section 4 to show the performance of the proposed model and a conclusion is provided in section 5.

II. PROBLEM STATEMENT AND DESCRIPTION

A. Assumption

Assumptions of repairable load-sharing systems are given as below.

(1) We focus on a repairable parallel load-sharing system with n identical units, and each unit has two states, working state and functional failure. The system fails when n-k+1units fail.

(2) When the system is just put into use, all units is perfectly in working state. The n units equally share the overall workload of the system and when unit failure occurs, the workload taken by the failed units will equally distributed to the surviving units.

(3) The essential condition to keep the system functional is that k units out of the total n units are in working state, which can also be described as a *k*-out-of-*n*:G system with n identical units.

(4) The lifetime of each unit follows an identical exponential distribution at the same workload level. The

failure rate of each unit will be monotonously elevated with in- creasing workload.

(5) Unit failure is self-announcing and repair action will be triggered immediately after the failure occurrence. The repair resource is limited and a unique repair crew is shared by all units. Hence, we adopt a first-fail-first-repair policy. This means that when more than one units are in the functional failure state, repair of the failed units can only be carried out in turn. The repair duration of each unit follows an identical exponential distribution.

B. State transition description

According to the above assumptions, the evolution of system state can be described as a Homogeneous Markov chain $X(t)=\{X_0,X_1,\cdots,X_{n-k}\}$, in which $X_i=i(i\le n-k)$, and i is the number of failed units. In the state set, X_0 means all the units are in working state; $X_{n\text{-}k}$ means that n-k units have already failed and the system cannot operate any more. Illustration of system state transition is shown in Fig.1.Here we suppose $S_{ij}(t)$ as the transition probability from state i to state $j$at time $t$and $\lambda_i$as the failure rate of each unit with i failed units in the system, in which $i<j<n\text{-}k$.

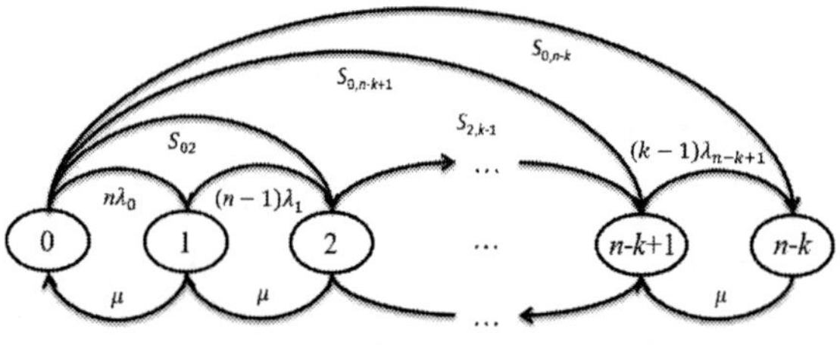

Fig.1System state transition

C. State transition probability under different load level

Here, we use the Power Law [7] to describe the relationship between load level , which is shown in Equation(2.1).

$$\lambda(l)=\left(\frac{l}{l_0}\right)^{\gamma}\lambda(l_0) \tag{2.1}$$

where $\lambda(l)$ denotes the failure rate at load level l, $l_0$is the baseline load level, , and λ is a constant load factor.

For a load-sharing system, after a large amount of theory and practice validation, VDI (German Engineer Institute) has demonstrated that the failure rate of individual unit in load-sharing systems will vary according to the following Capacity Flow Model[9,10], which is a particular case of the Power law, shown in (2.2).

$$\lambda_i=\left(\frac{n}{n-i}\right)^{\gamma}\lambda_0 \tag{2.2}$$

where n indicates the total number of the load-sharing system, i is the number of failed units and γ is a constant load factor.

It can be derived that

$$S_{i,i+k}(t)=\frac{C_{n-i}^{k}\lambda_i e^{-\lambda_i t}\left(1-e^{-\lambda_i t}\right)^{k-1}}{1-\left(1-e^{-\lambda_i t}\right)^{k}} \tag{2.3}$$

It should be noted that when k=1,$S_{i,i+1}(t)$ is a constant and can derived as

$$S_{i,i+1}(t)=(n-i)\lambda_i \tag{2.4}$$

III. SYSTEM AVAILABILITY MODELING

Suppose $p_i(t)$ as the probability when the system is in state i at time t and it can be expressed as

$$P_i(t)=\Pr\{X(t)=i\} \tag{3.1}$$

Therefore, the main task to describe the availability of the investigated load-sharing system is to model $p_i(t)$ evolution with time going.

If the repair time of one failed unit follows an identical exponential distribution with the parameterμ, the Kolmogorov differential equations of the probability of system state can be model as

$$\begin{cases}\dfrac{\mathrm{d}p_0(t)}{\mathrm{d}t}=\mu p_1(t)\text{-}p_0(t)\sum\limits_{e=1}^{n\text{-}k}S_{0.e}(t)\\ \dfrac{\mathrm{d}p_i(t)}{\mathrm{d}t}=\mu p_{i+1}(t)+\sum\limits_{e=0}^{i\text{-}1}S_{e.i}(t)p_e(t)\text{-}p_i(t)\sum\limits_{e=i+1}^{n\text{-}k}S_{i.e}(t)\\ \dfrac{\mathrm{d}p_{n\text{-}k}(t)}{\mathrm{d}t}=\sum\limits_{e=0}^{n\text{-}k\text{-}1}S_{e.n\text{-}k}(t)p_e(t)\text{-}p_{n\text{-}k}(t)\mu\end{cases}$$

$$\left(1\le i\le n\text{-}k\right) \tag{3.2}$$

Due to the fact that the probability thatmore than one units fail synchronously during a small interval is very slim, for computational simplicity, the description of system state transition can be reduced to a one-step transition Markov process, which is shown in Fig.2.

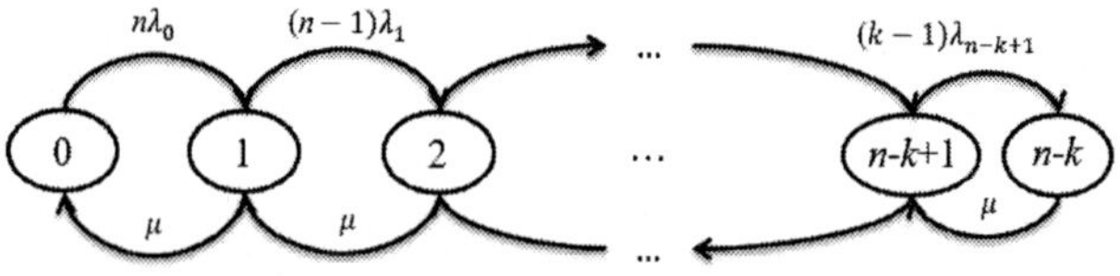

Fig.2One-step system state transition

Then the differential equations of the probability of system state can be simplified as

$$\begin{cases}\dfrac{\mathrm{d}p_0(t)}{\mathrm{d}t}=\mu p_1(t)\text{-}p_0(t)n\lambda_0\\ \dfrac{\mathrm{d}p_i(t)}{\mathrm{d}t}=\mu p_{i+1}(t)\text{-}p_i(t)(n\text{-}i)\lambda_i+(n\text{-}i+1)\lambda_{i\text{-}1}p_{i\text{-}1}(t)\\ \dfrac{\mathrm{d}p_{n\text{-}k}(t)}{\mathrm{d}t}=p_{n\text{-}k\text{-}1}(t)(k+1)\lambda_{n\text{-}k+1}\text{-}p_{n\text{-}k}(t)\mu\end{cases}$$

$$\left(1\le i<n\text{-}k\right) \tag{3.3}$$

The initial condition of (3.3) is $p_0(t)=1$, and $p_1(t)=p_2(t)=\cdots=p_{n-k}(t)=0$, which means at the beginning of the system's lifecycle, all the units are in working state. $p_i(t)(i=1,2,\cdots,n-k)$ can be obtained through solving (3.3).

The system availability at time t is the probability that the number of failed units is less than k and can be expressed as

$$A(t)=\sum_{n=0}^{n-k} p_i(t) \quad (3.4)$$

IV. NUMERICAL EXAMPLE

We consider a 2/4:G parallel repairable load-sharing system and at least two units arenecessarily workable to maintain the system operation. All units have two states, working state and functional failure. The baseline failure rate $\lambda_0=1/month$ and load factor is $\gamma=1$. The repair rate $\mu=5/month$. Then, the differential equations of the probability of system state can be expressed as:

$$\begin{cases} \frac{dp_0(t)}{dt}=5p_1(t)-4p_0(t) \\ \frac{dp_1(t)}{dt}=5p_2(t)+4p_0(t)-4p_1(t) \\ \frac{dp_2(t)}{dt}=4p_1(t)-5p_2(t) \end{cases} \quad (4.1)$$

By solving the above equations by the Laplace transform, we can get

$$\begin{cases} p_0(t)=\sum_{i=0}^{3} a_{0i}e^{-b_{0i}t} \\ p_1(t)=\sum_{i=0}^{3} a_{1i}e^{-b_{1i}t} \\ p_2(t)=\sum_{i=0}^{3} a_{2i}e^{-b_{2i}t} \end{cases} \quad (4.2)$$

Where

$$A=\{a_{ij}\}_{3\times4}=\begin{bmatrix} 1.285 & -0.892 & 0.048 & 7.579 \\ 0.805 & -0.944 & 0.139 & 0.000 \\ 0.282 & 4.839 & -0.121 & -5.000 \end{bmatrix}$$

$$B=\{b_{ij}\}_{3\times4}=\begin{bmatrix} -10.614 & -4.472 & 2.086 & -4.000 \\ -10.601 & -4.497 & 2.098 & 0.000 \\ -10.601 & -4.497 & 2.098 & -5.000 \end{bmatrix}$$

We can obtain the availability of system by substituting $p_0(t)$, $p_1(t)$ and $p_2(t)$ into (3.4)

V. CONCLUSION

A quantified availability evaluation model of repairable parallel load-sharing k-out-of-n:G systems with limited repair resource is established by combining capacity flow model and Markov process model, which are used to quantitatively describe the relationship between unit lifetimes and load level and system state transition respectively. A numeric example for a 2/4:G repairable parallel load-sharing system is presented as an illustrationfor its availability modeling.

ACKNOWLEDGEMENT

This work was jointly supported by the National Natural Science Foundation of China (No.51977192, 51637009), the Natural Science Foundation of Zhejiang Province (No. LY18E070002),and the Fundamental Research Funds for the Central Universities(No. 2018QNA4021).

REFERENCE

[1] P.S.Pundir, P.K.Gupta, "Reliability Estimation in Load-sharing System Model with Application to Real Data" inAnnals of Data Science, 2018,5(1): 69-91.

[2] Y. Kong, Z. Ye. "Interval estimation for k-out-of-n load-sharing systems"in IISE Transactions, 2017,49(3):- 344-353.

[3] Lisniansk A., Levitin G., "Multi-state system reliability: assessment, optimization and applications". Singa- pore: World Scientific, 2003.

[4] [4]Yu, H. Y., Chu, C. B., Chatelet, E. and Yalaoui, F., "Reliability optimization of a redundant system with failure dependencies" in Reliability Engineering and System Safety, 2007, 92, 1627-1634.

[5] Kong, Y. and Ye, Z., "A cumulative-exposure-based algorithm for failure data from a load-sharing system" in IEEE Transactions on Reliability, 2016, 65(2), 1001–1013.

[6] Park, C., "Parameter estimation for the reliability of load-sharing systems" in IIE Transactions, 2010, 42(10), 753–765.

[7] Singh, B., Sharma, K., Kumar, A., "A classical and Bayesian estimationof a k-components load-sharing parall- el system. ComputationalStatistics & Data Analysis" inComputational Statistics & Data Analysis, 2008, 52(12), 5175–5185.

[8] G.Levitin, S. Amari, "Optimal load distribution in series parallel systems" in Reliability engineering & system safety, 2009, 94:254-260.

[9] TANG Y.H., ZHANG J., "New model for load sharingk-out-of-n: G systems with different components" in Journal of Systems Engineering and Electronics, 2008,19(4): 748-751.

[10] AMARI S. V., BERGMAN R., "Reliability analysis ofk-out-of-n load-sharing systems"//The 54th AnnualReliability and Maintainability Symposium. Las Vegas:IEEE, 2008: 440-445.

7th International Conference on Reliability of
Electrical Products and Electrical Contacts,
November 04-06, 2019

Electromechanical Products Manufacturing Process Modeling Based on Approximate Model and Process Data

Xuerong Ye, Jun Tan, Yue Wang, Guofu Zhai
Reliability Institute for Electric Apparatus and Electronics
Harbin Institute of Technology, Harbin, 150001, China
E-mail: tanjun_ee@hit.edu.cn Tel: 86-451-86412976 Fax: 86-451-86412979

Abstract—**Manufacturing process contains many important information that affects the reliability of the product. How to fully utilize the process data to model the manufacturing process is the premise for effective monitoring, diagnosis, optimization and control of the manufacturing process, which is important for ensuring the quality of electromechanical products and production efficiency. The traditional manufacturing process modeling method has a large demand for process data and fewer influence factors having been considered, and it is difficult to solve the increasingly complex and diverse discrete manufacturing process modeling problems. Therefor this paper proposes a modeling method of electromechanical product manufacturing process based on approximate model and process data, which has little dependence on process data and can comprehensively consider the influencing factors of manufacturing process. Firstly, the finite element simulation method is used to establish the multi-physics simulation model of electromechanical products based on the manufacturing process data. Secondly, for the influencing factors of several types of manufacturing processes, the injection method of the characterization parameters in the simulation model is determined. Thirdly, based on the simulation model, the approximate model of manufacturing process parameters and performance parameters of electromechanical products are constructed. Finally, the key procedures are determined according to the established approximate model, which provides a basis for the monitoring of the manufacturing process of electromechanical products. Through the application of the proposed method, a certain type of aerospace electromagnetic relay is taken as an example to establish the manufacturing process modeling and determine key procedures, which further explains the specific application method of the proposed method and verify its effectiveness.**

Index Terms— **Approximate model, Process data, Electromechanical product, Manufacturing process, Key procedure**

I. INTRODUCTION

Manufacturing process is an important part of the product life cycle. Faced with increasingly complex and diverse discrete manufacturing processes, how to use the information to conduct effective process monitoring, diagnosis, control and optimization to improve product quality and core competition of enterprises has become a research hotspot recently[1,2].

Under the premise of good design, the normal fluctuation of the manufacturing process parameters within the tolerance range will not lead to failure of the final product performance parameters. Due to abnormal causes, such as tool wear, material performance degradation, manual adjustment deviations, etc., abnormal fluctuations in manufacturing process parameters will cause drift in the output characteristics of batch products, causing huge losses for the enterprise. Therefore, how to find out the key manufacturing procedure and monitor its characteristic parameters to ensure the normal operation of the production process is extremely important.

There are many factors influencing the final performance parameters of the product in the manufacturing process. Manufacturing process modeling refers to establishing the relationship between these influencing factors and product quality characteristics, and laying the foundation for manufacturing process monitoring and diagnosis. In general, there are two manufacturing process modeling methods: data-driven methods and model-based methods. The data-driven approach requires a large amount of historical and online monitoring data, but does not require much institutional understanding of the system, mainly through artificial intelligence algorithms; the model-based approach requires the storage of sufficient knowledge about the manufacturing process, which can be derived from physical mechanism and expert experience[3,4].

There are many parts for electromechanical products, and the manufacturing process includes heat treatment, welding, electroplating, assembly, debugging, packaging and other stages[5,6]. The complexity of the manufacturing process makes the model-based method difficult to implement; small batch customized production mode and the complexity of the product structure result in many processes still relying on manual debugging. Sensor technology and automation equipment are difficult to popularize. Real-time collection and monitoring of manufacturing process data is difficult to achieve, resulting in data-based methods that are difficult to implement.

With the development of computer simulation technology, the performance parameters of the product can be easily calculated by numerical methods such as finite element method, finite difference method, matrix method, etc. There are also many ways to inject the manufacturing process parameters into the model[7,8]. However, because the complexity of the simulation model requires a lot of computational cost, a good way to solve this problem is to use the approximate model instead of the simulation model. The approximation model can be understood as the "model of the model", which is a statistical model of the response surface of the simulation model, describing the relationship between system inputs (such as manufacturing process parameters) and outputs (product performance parameters). Training a precise approximation model requires enough simulation sample points, and an effective experimental design method can reduce the training sample points and thus shorten the simulation time[9,10].

This paper proposes a manufacturing process modeling method based on approximate model and small amount process data, which is difficult to achieve by traditional methods. Through the simulation model of the established product, the relationship between the input and output of the manufacturing process can be described to some extent, and the Monte Carlo method is used to expand the process database based on the approximate model and a small amount of measured data, which is used to determine the key procedures of the manufacturing process. This work provides a basis for monitoring and improvement of the manufacturing process.

II. MULTI-PHYSICS SIMULATION MODEL ESTABLISHMENT

The research object of this paper is a 1.5 cubic inch sealed DC power relay with a coil parameter of 28VDC/160Ω, 6 sets of transfer contacts, rated resistive load DC 10A/28VDC, and external dimensions 36.8mm×24.8mm×25.8mm.

Firstly, according to the design drawings, the whole relay model is established in UG, and then the electromagnetic system and the spring system are respectively introduced into the finite element simulation software such as FLUX and ADAMS to solve the static characteristics. The 3D model and FLUX simulation model are shown in Fig. 1 and Fig. 2.

According to the test data in actual production, the relative position of the components and the magnetic gap size in the established simulation model are corrected. The comparison between the electromagnetic system simulation

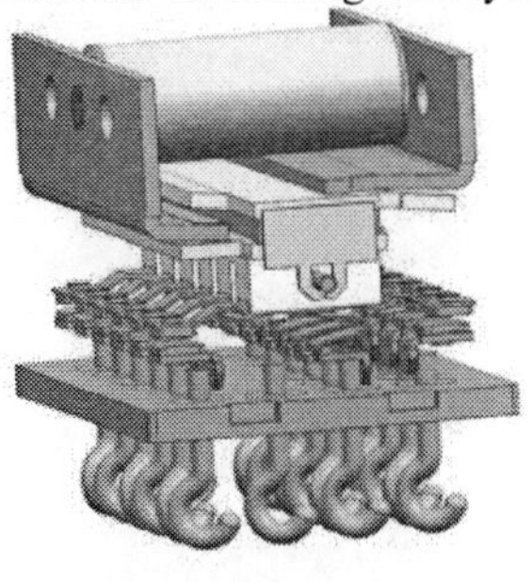

Fig. 1 UG model

Fig. 2 FLUX electromagnetic system simulation model

model and the measured results is shown in Fig. 3. The relative error is within 10%.

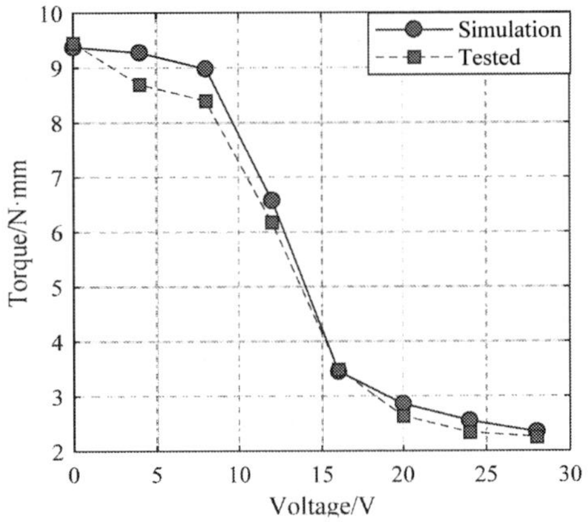

Fig. 3 Simulation model and measured results comparison

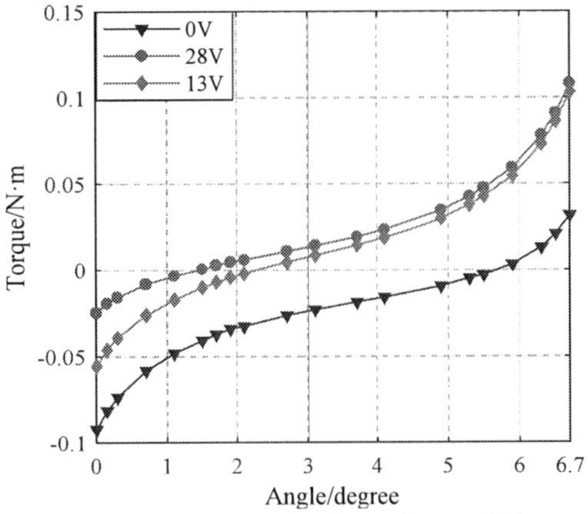

Fig. 4 Static attraction force characteristics

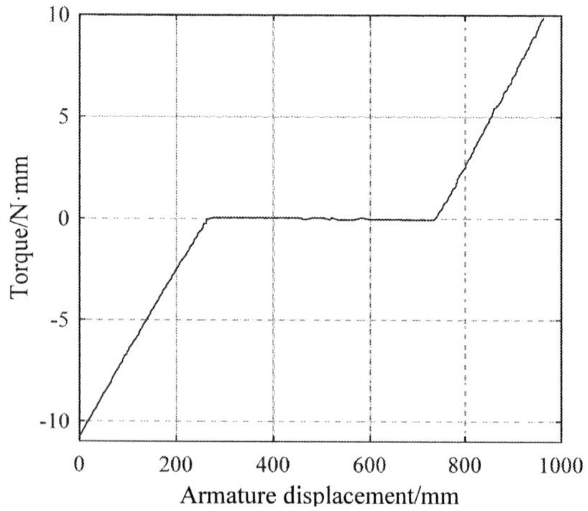

Fig. 5 Static reaction force characteristics

The static attraction and reaction force characteristics obtained in the final simulation model are shown in Fig. 4 and Fig. 5.

In order to further verify the accuracy of the multi-physics simulation model, the dynamic characteristics of the relay were solved by FLUX-ADAMS-MATLAB joint simulation. The comparison of the measured and simulated coil current waveforms is shown in Fig. 6. The waveforms are consistent, which is a good illustration of the correctness of the simulation model.

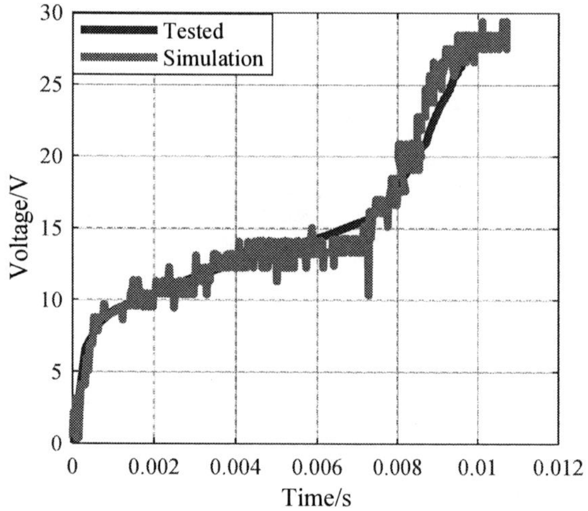

Fig. 6 Tested and simulated coil current waveforms comparison

III. MANUFACTURING PROCESS PARAMETERS SIMULATION INJECTION METHOD

A. Manufacturing process parameters classification

In the classic quality management theory, there are six main reasons for the fluctuation of product quality ("5M1E"):

1) Man: The operator's understanding of quality, technical proficiency, physical condition, etc.;
2) Machine: accuracy and maintenance status of machinery and equipment;
3) Material: the composition, physical properties and chemical properties of the material;
4) Method: processing technology, tooling selection, operating procedures, etc.;
5) Measurement: Whether the method adopted during measurement is standard and correct;
6) Environment: temperature, humidity, lighting and cleaning conditions at the workplace.

The latter three factors can be basically managed and controlled on mature production lines. The first three factors have the greatest impact on product quality uncertainty, and most likely cause abnormal fluctuations in product quality.

Combined with the specific manufacturing process and process flow of the relay, the manufacturing process factors and corresponding characterization parameters that affect the final performance parameters of the relay are classified, and the classification results are shown in Fig. 7.

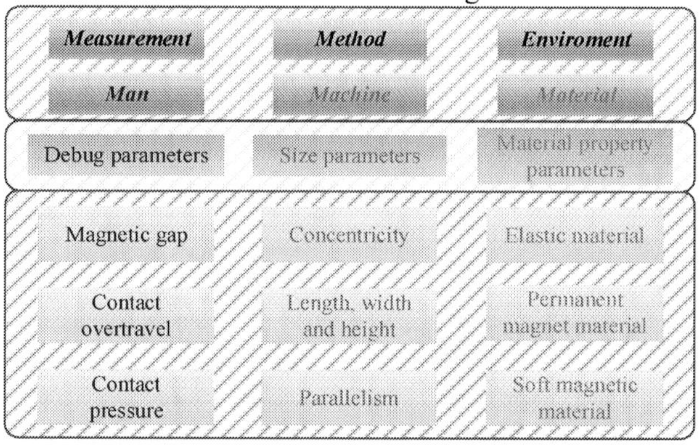

Fig. 7 Manufacturing process factors classification

As shown in the Fig. 7, the manufacturing process parameters can be divided into three categories:

1) Debug parameters. Corresponding to the impact of the debugging process that characterizes participation mainly by people;
2) Size parameters. Corresponding to characterizing the fluctuation of component size caused by abnormal conditions such as aging and wear of machine equipment;
3) Material property parameters. Corresponding to characterizing the influence of elasticity or magnetic material properties caused by differences in preparation processes, incoming materials, etc.

B. Manufacturing process parameters simulation injection method

The injection method of the three types of manufacturing process parameters in the simulation model is as shown in Fig. 8. The specific rules are as follows:

1) For most of the debug parameters, it is necessary to set the contact force, the kinematic pair, dumb objects, etc.

in the kinetic model to obtain the required values, and some parameters such as contact force can realize parametric modeling;

2) Part of the debug parameters, such as the magnetic gap, can be considered simultaneously with the size parameters. By parameterizing the size, the continuous change of the value can be realized. At the same time, the control of the magnetic gap can be transformed into controlling the corresponding armature and yoke size parameters;
3) For some parameters that can be directly modified in the simulation software, such as simple material property parameters (linear permanent magnet remanence, return line permeability, elastic material elastic modulus, etc.) can be directly modified;
4) For more complex permanent magnet or soft magnetic material models, material property models can be built according to their own needs, such as complex hysteresis loop models;
5) For some material properties of the actual test, sometimes it is necessary to extract the characteristic parameters of the relevant material properties, such as the knee point, for the characteristics of the curve or data.

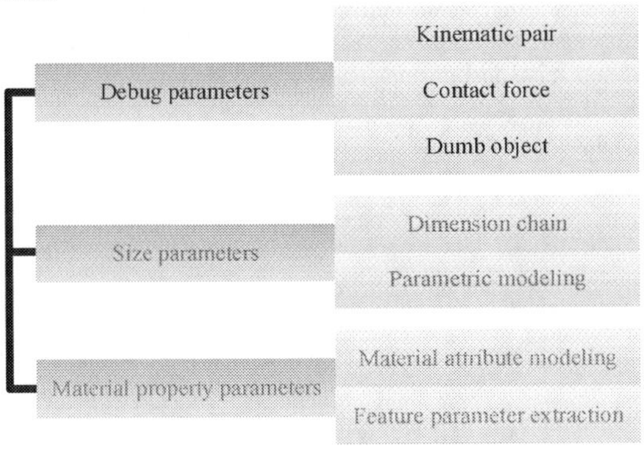

Fig. 8 Injection method of the three types of manufacturing process parameters

C. *Actual product analysis*

The relay mainly realizes the switching function by the cooperation of the electromagnetic system attraction force and the reaction force of the contact spring system. Therefore, the parameters in the manufacturing process that have great influence on the electromagnetic attraction force and the contact-spring reaction force should be selected.

Since the electromagnetic force is mainly affected by the air gap and the magnetic flux, the length, width and thickness of the armature and the yoke, core diameter, and permanent magnet remanence may affect the air gap and the magnetic flux. Through the electromagnetic system limit capability test, it is known that the length influence of the component is greater than the influence of the width and thickness on the electromagnetic force. Therefore, the length of the component is first considered when selecting parameters.

The contact pressure is used to match the cooperation of the attraction force and reaction force and is an important parameter affecting the mechanical properties at the later stage. If the contact pressure is too small, it is easy to shake the contact in the vibration experiment; if the contact pressure is too large, the corresponding over-travel will become larger, which will reduce the contact gap, causing the contact to be closed or even un-released. Therefore, the contact pressure should be within a reasonable range. The reed stiffness is the material parameter of the reed itself, which mainly affects the relationship between contact pressure and over-travel. The reaction force is mainly affected by the reed material and related debug parameters.

According to the above analysis, the preliminary selection of key manufacturing process parameters is shown in Tab. 1.

Tab. 1 Preliminary selection of key electromagnetic relay manufacturing process parameters

Parameter type	Manufacturing process parameter
Debug parameter	Contact pressure
Size parameter	Core diameter
	Length of release yoke
	Length of move armature
	Width of move armature
Material property parameter	Permanent magnet remanence
	Reed stiffness

Similarly, the manufacturing process parameters in the table are injected into the simulation model according to the above method.

IV. CONSTRUCTION OF THE APPROXIMATE MODEL

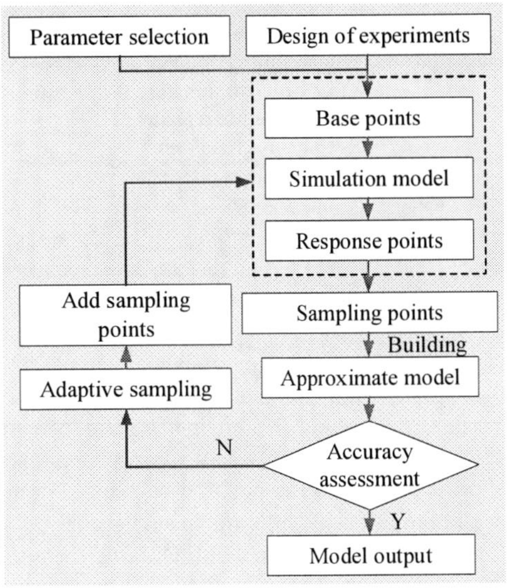

Fig. 9 Procedure of the approximate model construction

The procedure of the approximate model construction is shown in Fig. 9.

A. Parameter selection

Firstly, the input and output parameters of the approximate model are determined. For the modeling of the manufacturing process, the input parameters of the approximate model are the key manufacturing process parameters, and the output parameters are the key performance parameters of the product.

In the actual production process, the product has a very low pass rate in the mechanical screening test. and the low holding force under the state of pick-up and release is the main reason. Considering the cooperation of attraction and reaction, the holding force of the first inflection point of the reaction force is also an important parameter. The holding force at the inflection point determines the pull-in voltage of the relay, and the armature holding force in the state of pick-up and release determines the mechanical characteristic of the product. These three parameters directly affect the quality of the product.

Therefore, the key manufacturing process parameters determined in the previous section are selected as the input parameters of the approximate model, and the output parameters of the approximate model are determined as holding force at the 0V of the release, the 28V of the pick-up and the 13V of the inflection point as the output parameters of the approximate model. The range of parameters is shown in Tab. 2.

Tab. 2 Range of approximate model parameters

Type	Parameter name	Range
Output	$F\|_{U=0V/Angle=0^{\circ}}$	/
	$F\|_{U=28V/Angle=6.7^{\circ}}$	/
	$F\|_{U=13V/Angle=1.3^{\circ}}$	/
Input	Contact pressure	600~1100mN
	Core diameter	3.8~4.6mm
	Length of release yoke	4.95~7.23mm
	Length of move armature	1.97~5.64mm
	Width of move armature	16~20mm
	Permanent magnet remanence	0.535~0.654T
	Reed Young's modulus	53.6~80.4GPa

B. Data preparation

In approximate modeling techniques, the accuracy of the approximate model is affected by the choice of sample points. An excellent experimental design enables uniform and efficient sampling of the parameter space, with a comprehensive and appropriate number of sample points to ensure the accuracy of the model. Latin Hypercube Sampling (LHS) is an experimental design method for constraining random generation of uniform sample points. The essence of this method is to control the position of sample points and avoid overlapping of sample points in small areas.

The optimal Latin Hypercube Sampling design is an improvement of the LHS method. The objective of optimization is to make all sample points distribute as evenly as possible in the design space. It has very good space filling and balance. This method is adopted in this paper.

90 sets of input parameter combination data are extracted and brought into the simulation model to calculate the corresponding output parameters.

C. Approximation model construction

Based on the Kriging approximation modeling method, an approximate model between the manufacturing process parameters and the product performance parameters is constructed based on the prepared sample data.

The commonly used model accuracy evaluation index RMSE is selected to evaluate the model, and its calculation formula is shown in Formula (C.1).

$$\mathrm{RMSE} = \sqrt{\frac{1}{n_{test}} \sum_{s=1}^{n_{test}} (y_{is} - \hat{y}_{is})^2} \tag{4.1}$$

Where n_{test} is the number of selected test samples and y_{is} is the actual response value of the test sample points, that is, the simulation value. $\hat{y}_{is}$ is the predicted value of the surrogate model. A small RMSE reflects high model accuracy. When the model accuracy fails to meet the requirements, it can be increased by increasing the number of sample points.

10 sets of input parameter test sample point combinations are extracted for each of the three output parameters, and the corresponding output parameters are calculated by the simulation model and the constructed approximate model respectively, and the relative error distribution is as shown in Fig. 10.

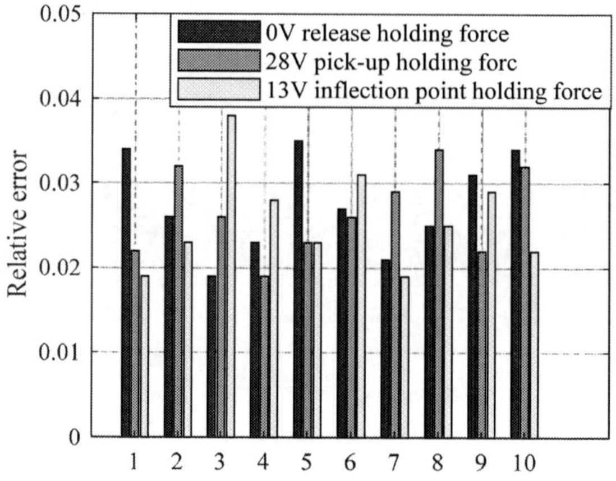

Fig. 10 Relative error distribution

Still, the calculated RMSE is:

$$\mathrm{RMSE} = \sqrt{\frac{1}{n_{test}} \sum_{s=1}^{n_{test}} (y_{is} - \hat{y}_{is})^2} = 0.037$$

Through the above calculation and analysis, the relative error of the approximate model and the simulation model is less than 4%, and the RMSE value is small. The accuracy of the approximate model is high.

V. KEY PROCEDURES DETERMINATION

A. Batch product quality performance calculation

From the measured data of key manufacturing process parameters, a small amount of data is expanded into batch product data by Monte Carlo method, and the manufacturing process parameters are randomly combined. The key output performance parameters of each individual are obtained through the established approximate model. The batch product output performance parameters are counted, and the batch product output quality characteristic parameters (mean, variance, pass rate, etc.) are obtained.

The calculation flow is shown in Fig. 11.

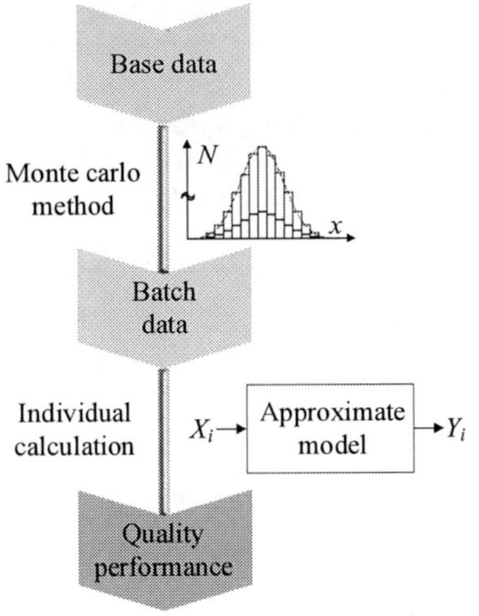

Fig. 11 Calculation flow of quality performance

B. Univariate analysis

Analysis of the single factor change corresponding to the output characteristic distribution can determine the significant effect of each input variable on the output characteristics within the tolerance range.

By analyzing the distribution trend of the output parameters corresponding to different input variables, the significant input variables corresponding to each output parameter are sorted, and the input variables with the saliency ranked are taken as shown in Tab. 3 to Tab. 5.

Tab. 3 $F|_{U=28V/Angle=6.7^{\circ}}$ input variable significant ordering

Rank	Parameter name	Standard deviation
1	Length of move armature	1.09N
2	Core diameter	0.87N
3	Length of release yoke	0.56N
4	Reed Young's modulus	0.42N
5	Contact pressure	0.34N
6	Width of move armature	0.31N
7	Permanent magnet remanence	0.25N

Tab. 4 $F|_{U=0V/Angle=0^{\circ}}$ input variable significant ordering

Rank	Parameter name	Standard deviation
1	Length of release yoke	0.86N
2	Contact pressure	0.81N
3	Length of move armature	0.71N
4	Reed Young's modulus	0.62N
5	Core diameter	0.45N
6	Permanent magnet remanence	0.32N
7	Width of move armature	0.23N

Tab. 5. $F|_{U=13V/Angle=1.3^{\circ}}$ input variable significant ordering

Rank	Parameter name	Standard deviation
1	Length of release yoke	0.19N
2	Permanent magnet remanence	0.12N
3	Width of move armature	0.10N
4	Core diameter	0.08N
5	Reed Young's modulus	0.05N
6	Length of move armature	0.02N
7	Contact pressure	0.01N

C. Key procedures analysis

From the above significant ranking results and related data analysis, we can see that:

1) The overall standard deviation of the holding force at the 13V inflection point is small, which is less affected by the manufacturing process parameters. But for the pull-in voltage, a small holding force influence may cause fluctuations of several volts, so it is also necessary to monitor release relevant parameters such as length of release yoke and permanent magnet remanence;
2) According to the debugging experience, the holding force fluctuation above 0.5N is the key parameter, then the length of release yoke, the length of move armature, and the reed Young's modulus are the key manufacturing process parameters.

VI. CONCLUSION

Modeling of electromechanical products manufacturing processes is the premise and basis for the later diagnosis and optimization of manufacturing processes. This paper proposes a manufacturing process modeling method based on approximate model for the modeling of small batch customized electromechanical products manufacturing processes. Influencing factors have been comprehensively analyzed and classified, and the key manufacturing procedures have been selected through analysis, which provides a basis for manufacturing processes monitoring. This is also useful for other products and can be widely used in the modeling of electromechanical products manufacturing process.

ACKNOWLEDGMENT

This work was supported by the National Key R&D Program of China [grant number 2017YFB1300800] and the National Natural Science Foundation of China [grant number 61671172].

REFERENCES

[1] L. Qiao, S. Kao, Y. Zhang, "Manufacturing process modelling using process specification language," *International Journal of Advanced Manufacturing Technology*, 55 (2011) 549-563.

[2] J.H. Yan, Y. Meng, L. Lu, L. Li, "Industrial Big Data in an Industry 4.0 Environment: Challenges, Schemes, and Applications for Predictive Maintenance," *Ieee Access*, 5 (2017) 23484-23491.

[3] Y. Xu, Y.M. Sun, J.F. Wan, X.L. Liu, Z.T. Song, "Industrial Big Data for Fault Diagnosis: Taxonomy, Review, and Applications", *Ieee Access*, 5 (2017) 17368-17380.

[4] M. Yu, C. Xiao, W. Jiang, S. Yang, H. Wang, "Fault Diagnosis for Electromechanical System via Extended Analytical Redundancy Relations", *Ieee Transactions on Industrial Informatics*, 14 (2018) 5233-5244.

[5] X. Ye, Y. Lin, Q. Wang, H. Niu, G. Zhai, "Manufacturing process-based storage degradation modelling and reliability assessment", *Microelectronics Reliability*, 88-90 (2018) 107-110.

[6] J. Deng, X. Ye, Y. Lin, Q. Li, G. Zhai, "A new robust tolerance design method for electromechanical device based on variable contribution rate coefficients", *Journal of Engineering Design*, 28 (2017) 532-548.

[7] B. Li, Y.B. Huang, L. Yang, Q.Z. Zhang, Z.S. Zheng, B.H. Li, H.P. Zhu, J.H. Bu, H.X. Yin, J.J. Luo, Z.S. Han, H.B. Wang, "Process variation dependence of total ionizing dose effects in bulk nFinFETs", *Microelectronics Reliability*, 88-90 (2018) 946-951.

[8] Z.P. Ye, J.W. Zhu, Q. Li, B. Mo, B.M. Lei, Y.Q. Li, C.H. Wang, C.M. Huang, "A novel method of reliability-centered process optimization for additive manufacturing", *Microelectronics Reliability*, 88-90 (2018) 1151-1156.

[9] K. Mao, H.S. Wang, Y. Yao, H. Nie, G. Chen, J. Zhou, Z. Chen, J. Du, "A 0.18-mu m LDMOS With Excellent Ronsp and Uniformity by Optimized Manufacture Process", *Ieee Transactions on Semiconductor Manufacturing*, 32 (2019) 129-133.

[10] D.-S. Liu, C.-J. Lu, C.-W. Hung, Y.-C. Huang, "Experimental Method and Finite-Element Simulation Model for Investigation Into Flip-Chip-on-Film Inner Lead Bonding Parameters", *Ieee Transactions on Device and Materials Reliability*, 16 (2016) 194-199.

7th International Conference on Reliability of
Electrical Products and Electrical Contacts,
November 04-06, 2019

Influence of Oxygen Partial Pressure and Fretting Amplitude onthe Lifetime of Electrical Contacts

Haomiao Yuan; Jian Song
Precision Engineering Laboratory
Ostwestfalen-Lippe University of Applied Sciences and Arts, Lemgo, 32657, Germany
E-mail: jian.song@th-owl.deTel: +49 5261 702 5028 Fax: +49 5261 70285028

***Abstract*—Electrical contacts are fundamental components which transfer the current and signals in electromechanical systems. The reliability of the electrical contacts influences the system reliability greatly, in the light of their large quantity. In order to improve the performance of electrical contacts, plating is generally applied on the base material. Tin plating is widely used due to its good solderability, corrosion resistance and low cost. Fretting corrosion is one of the most critical failure mechanisms of tin-plated electrical contacts enduring relative micro-motions. During operation, the tin plating is worn, generating wear debris. Since tin is a non-noble metal, its wear debris will be oxidized to form an insulating layer after long-term use. In many power semiconductor components, the housing is firstly pumped to a vacuum condition, and then filled with nitrogen, which leads to a reduced amount of oxygen, a lower oxygen partial pressure and a longer mean free path of oxygen molecules. This service condition influences the lifetime of the tin-plated electrical contacts significantly, since a longer mean free path of oxygen molecules corresponds to a lower collision possibility of oxygen molecules to the tin surface, which can retard the oxidation process. Moreover, the two parts of electrical contacts can experience different amplitude in relative micro-motion, which also has an effect on the lifetime. In order to investigate the influence of oxygen partial pressure and fretting amplitude on the lifetime of electrical contacts, measurements are conducted with a fretting corrosion test device under various vacuum degrees and fretting amplitudes. A theoretical model illustrating the relationship between the lifetime of electrical contacts and pressure is established and verified by the measured results. The lifetime of electrical contacts in fretting corrosion tests is prolonged with a lower pressure and larger fretting amplitude.**

***Index Terms*—Amplitude, electrical contacts, fretting corrosion, tin plating, vacuum**

I. INTRODUCTION

The development of the cyber-physical systems, such as the smart factories and autonomous vehicles, increases the demand on electrical contacts to transfer current and signals between terminals in these systems. Not only a large amount of electrical contactsbut also an excellent quality is required. In order to improve the performance of the electrical contacts, plating is generally applied on the base material. Tin is one of the most widely used plating materials because of its good corrosion resistance, low price and good solderability [1]-[3].

Since tin is a non-noble material, a thick oxide layer can be formed, if the relative motion between the two parts of electrical contacts is unavoidable. Therefore, under the operation with fretting, the lifetime of tin plated electrical contacts is short. Since the fretting corrosion of the tin plating is closely related to the oxidation, lifetime of tin plated electrical contacts is significantly influenced by the oxidation rate of the tin plating.

Electrical contacts can be applied in various environments, one of which is the application in the power semiconductor components. At first, the housing is pumped into a vacuum condition, and then filled with nitrogen. This procedure generates a low oxygen partial pressure environment in the housing, which leads to an increase in mean free path of oxygen and decreased collision possibility of the oxygen molecules to the tin surface. As a consequence, the lifetime of the tin plated electrical contacts is expected to be prolonged.

In this paper, in order to simulate this service condition, the electrical contacts with tin plating are tested with a wear and fretting corrosion test device in a vacuum chamber. The tests are conducted under the normal atmosphere and under various vacuum degrees. Different fretting amplitude is used to investigate its influence on the fretting behavior of the electrical contacts.

II. THEORY

A. Failure Mechanism of Tin Plated Electrical Contacts

Tin plating has a good corrosion resistance, because a thin air-tight oxide layer is built on the tin surface and protects the underlying fresh tin from further oxidation. However, the micro relative motion between the two sides of electrical contacts is difficult to avoid in many applications. The micro relative motion can be generated by the vibration during the operation, or when the contacts are held by materials with different thermal expansion coefficient. Typical holding materials are one side PCB enhanced with glass fibers with better thermal stability and the other side housing with a larger thermal expansion coefficient. When experiencing this relative motion, the thin oxide layer will be broken and the fresh tin will have access to the air, causing the further oxidation. This process is called fretting corrosion [4], [5], Fig. 1. The fretting corrosion is one of the most critical failure mechanisms for tin plated electrical contacts, when the relative motion is unavoidable.

B. *Oxidation Laws*

Since the fretting corrosion is related to the oxidition of tin plating, the oxidition laws should be reviewed. Some empirical oxidation laws are summazied in Fig. 2 [6]. If the tin plating does not experience fretting, the oxidation of tin plating can follow the logarithmic or linear rate law under different pressure [7], [8]. When the tin plating endures the fretting during operation, the periodic cracking attracts more attention. Oxide layer grows fast initially, but it slows down as the thickness increases. However, the oxide layer is cracked by the normal force and relative motions. Then the oxygen has access to the fresh metals again, and a new cycle of fast oxidation starts. This cycle repeats during the fretting of the tin plating. As a result, the curve averages out to a linear oxidation rate law [6], [9].

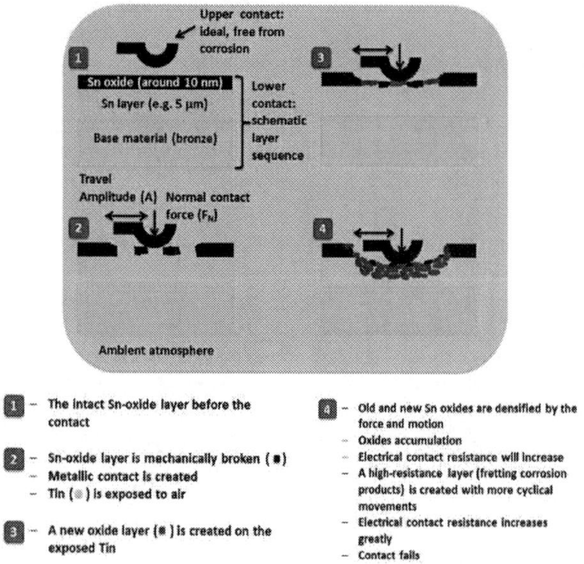

Fig. 1 Fretting corrosion of tin plated electrical contacts

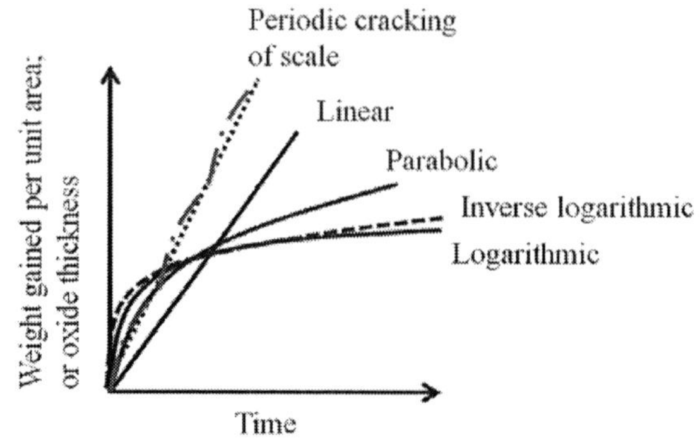

Fig. 2 Schametical illustion of empirical oxidation laws [6]

C. *Correlation between Oxidation Rate and Pressure*

Unlike the investigation of the correlation between oxidation rate and temperature, less study is conducted with regard to the correlation between oxidation rate and pressure. Boggs [7], [8], [10] studied the oxidation of tin foil, and found that below 1 mmHg (1.3 mbar) oxygen pressure, the initial oxidation rate shows a linear relation with the square root of oxygen pressure at 10^{-3}, 10^{-2} and 10^{-1} mmHg.Another researcher also has found the exponential relationship between the oxidation rate and the oxygen partial pressure, but with different exponential index, from 1/7 to 1/4, [11], [12].

D. *Correlation between Lifetime of Tin Plating in Electrical Contacts and the Oxygen Partial Pressure*

According to Section II.B. and Section II.C., if the oxidation rate of tin plating in electrical contacts follows the periodic cracking of scale, and the oxidation rate has an exponential relation with oxygen pressure, one can obtain:

$$x = k_{pc}t \tag{1}$$

where x is the oxide thickness under a certain test condition, t is time, and $k_{pc}$is the average linear oxidation rate of periodic cracking.

$$k_{pc} \propto P_{oxygen}{}^{\sigma} \tag{2}$$

where P_{oxygen} is the oxygen partial pressure, σ is the exponential index.

Substituting (2) into (1), one can obtain:

$$x = k'_{pc} \cdot P_{oxygen}{}^{\sigma} \cdot t \tag{3}$$

where k'_{pc} is a constant.

Then the correlation between the time to fail (lifetime) and the oxygen partial pressure follows:

$$LT \propto \cdot P_{oxygen}{}^{-\sigma} \tag{4}$$

where LT is the lifetime of tin plated electrical contacts.

In order to verify (4) the wear and fretting corrosion tests of tin plated electrical contacts are conducted in a vacuum chamber with different oxygen partial pressure and two fretting amplitudes are used.

III. EXPERIMENTAL

The base material of the contacts is copper and is deformed to the flat and spherical parts. Then tin is galvanic plated on the base material.

The wear and fretting corrosion tests are conducted in a vacuum chamber, Fig. 3. The air in the chamber is pumped out to create a reduced oxygen partial pressure. The oxygen partial pressure is calculated by multiplying 0.21 onto the pressure according to Dalton's law of partial pressures [13], [14].The test parameter is listed in Table I. During the test, the electrical contact resistance is measured by the four-point-method and recorded. The tests are run until the electrical contact resistance reaches 300 mΩ, and the corresponding fretting cycle is considered as the lifetime of electrical contacts in the test.

Fig. 3 Test rig in vacuum chamber

TABLE I
TEST PARAMETERS

Parameter	Values
Amplitude peak-peak	50, 100 µm
Normal force	2 N
Temperature	ambient temperature (20 °C ~ 23 °C)
Fretting frequency	1 Hz
Limit of contact resistance	300 mΩ
Relative humidity	35 ~ 45 %
Total pressure	50 µm amplitude: 0.3, 0.5,20, 1000 mbar 100 µm amplitude: 3, 5, 1000 mbar
Approximate oxygen partial pressure	50 µm amplitude:0.063, 0.105,4.2, 210 mbar 100 µm amplitude: 0.63, 1.05, 210 mbar

IV. RESULTS AND DISCUSSION

A. *Mean Free Path of Oxygen under Each Oxygen Partial Pressure*

The mean free path can be calculated according to [15]:

$$l = \frac{k_B T}{\sqrt{2}\pi d^2 p} \quad (5)$$

where l is mean free path, k_B is Bolzmann constant $1.38 \cdot 10^{-23}$ J/K, T is temperature in K, d is kinetic diameter of gas molecules, for oxygen, d is 3.46 Å [16], and p is pressure.

The mean free path of oxygen under each pressure is listed in Table II.

TABLE II
MEAN FREE PATH OF OXYGEN UNDER EACH OXYGEN PARTIAL PRESSURE

Oxygen partial pressure [mbar]	Mean free path [m]
0.063	$1.2 \cdot 10^{-3}$
0.105	$7.2 \cdot 10^{-4}$
0.63	$1.2 \cdot 10^{-4}$
1.05	$7.2 \cdot 10^{-5}$
4.2	$1.8 \cdot 10^{-5}$
210	$3.6 \cdot 10^{-7}$

B. *Wear Scar*

The size of the wear scar is measured after the wear and fretting corrosion tests. Examples of the wear scars from the tests with 50 µm and 100 µm peak-peak amplitudes are shown in Fig. 4.The wear scar is nearly an ellipse, with the major axis along the sliding direction. The size of wear scars along sliding direction under tests with 50 µm peak-peak amplitude varies from approx. 590 µm to 760 µm, size of wear scars perpendicular to the sliding direction is from approx. 430 µm to 590 µm. For the 100 µm peak-peak amplitude tests, the size along the sliding direction is from approx.790 µm to 1100 µm, and the size of wear scars perpendicular to the sliding direction is from approx. 660 µm to 880 µm. Compared with the values in Table II, the mean free path at oxygen partial pressure of 0.105 mbar is comparable to the size of wear scars. As a consequence, when changing the pressure, collisions of oxygen to the tin plating will be greatly influenced and the oxidation rate can change accordingly.

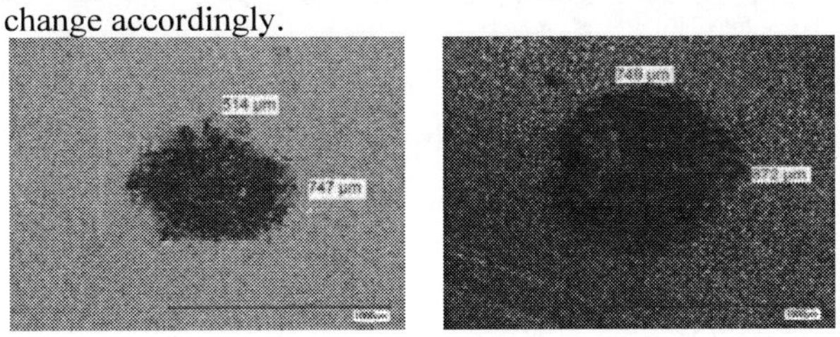

(a) (b)

Fig. 4 Size of wear scars, exemplary: (a) 50 µm peak-peak amplitude, 0.063 mbar oxygen partial pressure; (b) 100 µm peak-peak amplitude, 0.63 mbar oxygen partial pressure

C. *Oxygen Content in Contact Area*

The oxygen content in the contact area after the electrical failure of the samples is measured by energy-dispersive X-ray spectroscopy (EDS). The maximum oxygen content is listed in Table III and Table IV. The maximum oxygen content in all of the samples exceeds 50 at.% after the sample fails electrically, which has a good agreement with the failure criterion in the study by other researchers [17]. Moreover, the oxygen content in the contact area of samples experiencing 100 μm peak-peak amplitude is lower than that under 50 μm peak-peak amplitude tests.

TABLE III
MAXIMUM OXYGEN CONTENT IN CONTACT AREA, WITH 50 μM PEAK-PEAK AMPLITUDE

Oxygen partial pressure [mbar]	Maximum oxygen content in contact area [at.%]
0.063	66
0.105	61
4.2	60
210	67

TABLE IV
MAXIMUM OXYGEN CONTENT IN CONTACT AREA, WITH 100 μM PEAK-PEAK AMPLITUDE

Oxygen partial pressure [mbar]	Maximum oxygen content in contact area [at.%]
0.63	51
210	54

D. Lifetime in Wear and Fretting Corrosion Tests

The average lifetime of the electrical contacts with 50 μm peak-peak amplitude is listed in Table V.

TABLE V
AVERAGE LIFETIME UNDER 50 μM PEAK-PEAK AMPLITUDE

Oxygen partial pressure [mbar]	0.063	0.105	4.2	210
Mean value of lifetime [cycles]	20936	11495	2408	714

Under the peak-peak amplitude of 100 μm, the lifetime of samples under different oxygen partial pressure is listed in Table VI. According to the results, the lifetime is slightly longer when the samples are tested with larger fretting amplitude.

TABLE VI
AVERAGE LIFETIME UNDER 100 μM PEAK-PEAK AMPLITUDE

Oxygen partial pressure [mbar]	0.63	1.05	210
Mean value of lifetime [cycles]	10501	5648	1005

The reason for the improvement in lifetime can be attributed to the oxygen uptake under the different fretting amplitude. The contact area expands with larger fretting amplitude, so moreoxygen molecules will be consumed to build the oxygen layer with the same thickness, and it takes more time for the situation with 100 μm peak-peak amplitude. In this way, to accumulate the oxides that cause the electrical failure will need more time, and the lifetime of the electrical contacts is consequently prolonged.

E. Correlation between Lifetime and Oxygen Partial Pressure

The correlation between the lifetime of tin plated electrical contacts and the oxygen partial pressure is shown in Fig. 5. The correlation between lifetime and oxygen partial pressure obeys the exponential relation in (4). The exponential index is 0.4 and 0.36 for the tests under 50 μm peak-peak amplitude and 100 μm peak-peak amplitude, respectively.

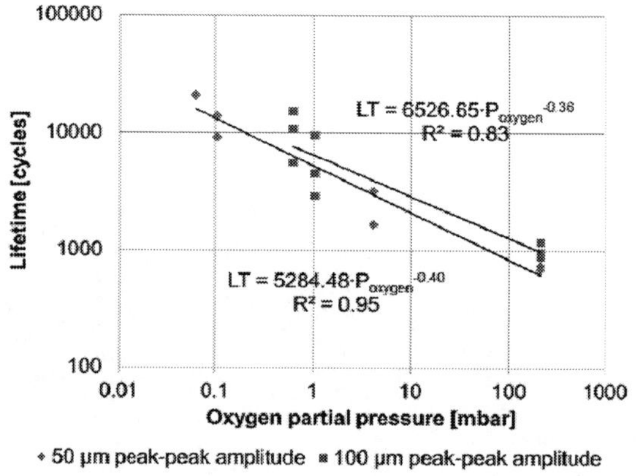

Fig. 5 Correlation between lifetime and oxygen partial pressure

V. CONCLUSION

In this paper, the fretting behavior of tin plated electrical contacts under a reduced oxygen partial pressure is investigated. Two peak-peak sliding amplitudes of 50 μm and 100 μm are used. According to the results, the lifetime is prolonged under lower oxygen partial pressure and at the larger sliding amplitude. The lifetime of the electrical contacts has an exponential relation with the oxygen partial pressure.

ACKNOWLEDGMENT

This study is financially supported by the German Federal Ministry for Economic Affairs and Energy (BMWi, IGF, 20139 N).

Gefördert durch:

Bundesministerium für Wirtschaft und Energie

aufgrund eines Beschlusses des Deutschen Bundestages

REFERENCES

[1] Y.W. Park, T.S.N.S. Narayanan, and K.Y. Lee, "Fretting corrosion of tin-plated contacts: evaluation of surface characteristics," Tribol. Int., vol. 40, 2007, pp. 548–559

[2] N.N., "Surface coating technologies," in*Data book of electrical contacts*, 3rd ed., E. Vinaricky and V. Behrens, Eds. Muehlacker: Stieglitz Verlag, 2012, pp. 283–284

[3] T.S.N.S. Narayanan, Y.W. Park, and K. Y. Lee, "Fretting-corrosion mapping of tin-plated copper alloy contacts," Wear, vol. 262, 2007, pp. 228–233

[4] E.M. Bock, J.H. Whitley, "Fretting corrosion in electric contacts", in: Proceedings of Twentieth Annual Holm Seminar on Electrical Contacts, Chicago, USA, 1974, pp. 128−138

[5] M. Antler, "Survey of contact fretting in electrical connectors", IEEE Trans. Compon. Hybrids Manuf. Technol., CHMT-8, 1985, pp. 87−104

[6] J. Song, H. Yuan, and V. Schinow, "Fretting corrosion behavior of electrical contacts with tin coating in atmosphere and vacuum," Wear, vols. 426–427, 2019, pp. 1439–1445

[7] W.E. Boggs, R.H. Kachik, and G.E. Pellissier, "The oxidation of tin I. The kinetics of oxidation of pure tin and the effects of temperature and oxygen pressure," J. Electrochem. Soc., vol. 108, 1961, pp. 6–12

[8] W.E. Boggs, "The oxidation of tin III. The mechanisms of oxidation of pure tin and their dependence on time and oxygen pressure," J. Electrochem. Soc., vol. 108, 1961, pp. 124–129

[9] S.A. Bradford, *Corrosion Control*, New York: Springer, 1993, pp. 296–303.

[10] W.E. Boggs, P.S. Trozzo, G.E. Pellissier, "The oxidation of tin II. The morphology and mode of growth of oxide films on pure tin," J. Electrochem. Soc., vol. 108, 1961,pp. 13−24

[11] M. Björck, R. Elger, "Oxidation kinetics of copper at reduced oxygen partial pressures," SKB document ID 1410172 version 1.0, Svensk Kärnbränslehantering AB, October 2013.

[12] S.K. Roy, S.K. Bose, S.C. Sircar, "Pressure dependencies of copper oxidation for low- and high-temperature parabolic laws," Oxid. Met.,vol. 35, 1991, pp. 1−17

[13] Z. Tan, *Air Pollution and Greenhouse Gases: From Basic Concepts to Engineering Applications for Air Emission Control*, Singapore: Springer Science+Business Media,2014, pp. 33−37

[14] J. Dalton, Essay IV. "On the expansion of elastic fluids by heat," Memoirs of the Literary and Philosophical Society of Manchester, vol.5, 1802,pp. 595–602

[15] W. Jitschin, "Gasgesetze und kinetische Gastheorie," in *Wutz Handbuch Vakuumtechnik*, 11th ed. K. Jousten, Ed.Wiesbaden: Springer Vieweg, 2012, pp. 48

[16] A.F. Ismail, K.C. Khulbe, T. Matsuura, *Gas Separation Membranes: Polymeric and Inorganic*, Basel: Springer International Publishing Switzerland, 2015, pp. 14

[17] O. Perrinet, J. Laporte, S. Fouvry, O. Alquier, "The electrical contact resistance endurance of heterogeneous Ag/Sn interfaces subjected to fretting wear," in 27th ICEC, 2014, pp. 114–119

Analysis and Improvement of a Wire Harness Terminal Connector with Insufficient Locking Force

Yilin Zhou, Junyu Yang, Xuxin Yin
Beijing University of Post and Telecommunication, Beijing, 100876, China
E-mail: ylzhou@bupt.edu.cn Tel: 86-10-62283173

Abstract—**Spring terminal is a kind of connector used for the electrical connection of wiring harness, which is convenient to install and has high reliability so as to reduce downtime and maintenance times. How to design its structural parameters to meet the locking force requirements of wire harnesses with different diameters is the key to the spring terminal design. In this paper, the stress analysis by finite element simulation was carried out on the problem of low locking force when a certain type of spring terminal was connected with wire harness with small diameter. It was found that plastic deformation of spring material caused by over-stress design was the main reason of insufficient locking force. The key structural parameters affecting the deformation of the spring terminal were found out by the Castigliano's theorem, and then the parameters of spring terminal were adjusted and checked by simulation. The locking wire force experiments showed that the performance of the improved spring was proved to be in accordance with the design requirements. Finally, the design method of spring terminal structure and the necessity of avoiding overstress were discussed.**

Index Terms— **harness connectors, spring terminals, physical design, finite element analysis**

I. INTRODUCTION

The connection methods often used for the wiring harness terminals are mainly bolted, crimped and the like. The bolted connection is a detachable connection, which is convenient for maintenance and disassembly. However, different standard torques are required for the different sizes of screws during installation, and the installation operation is complicated. The crimping connection mainly uses the crimping pliers to perform the crimping operation of the wire harness and the terminal, which is a permanent connection, and the connection reliability is high, but it is not convenient for maintenance [1].

The spring terminal connector overcomes the drawbacks of the first two. The common cage spring terminal structure is shown in Fig. 1. The spring terminal is easy to operate when it is connected to the wire harness. It only needs to press the spring, insert the wire, remove the pressure, and the spring can lock the wire harness, which saves the wiring time and reduces the labor cost. When one wire needs to be replaced, it does not affect other wires at all [2]. Moreover, the spring clamping force automatically compensates for the locking force after the vibration environment or the wire contact point is worn or corroded, effectively avoiding the looseness of the contact point, reducing the maintenance cost, and making the system have better running stability and reliability [3]. The design process of the spring terminal mainly satisfies the yield limit of the spring at the maximum deformation; the upper limit of the contact resistance is satisfied at the minimum deformation. When calculating the amount of spring deformation, Castigliano's theorem is mainly used to calculate the force and displacement of the spring in every segments, and then each segment is superimposed [4, 5].

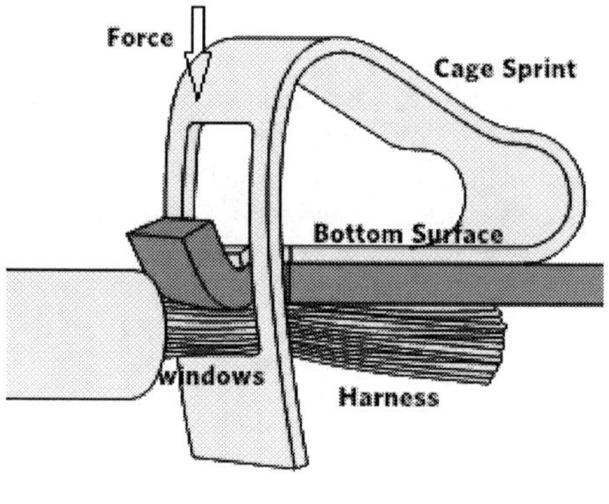

Fig. 1 Cage spring terminal structure

At present, a spring terminal connector designed by a connector manufacturer in China used in the control system has a problem that the wire locking force is low when connecting the small wire harness. This paper analyzed the possible failure causes of the existing products and used finite element modeling to determine the cause of failure. The stress analysis of the spring terminal was carried out by using the Castigliano's theorem, and the key structural parameters affecting the performance of the spring were obtained. Then by using finite element analysis, the key structural parameters of the spring terminal were adjusted and the stress was checked. The locking force of the improved spring terminal was verified by tests. Finally, the structural design method of the spring terminal and the precautions to prevent the overstress design were summarized.

II. MECHANISM ANALYSIS OF THE INSUFFICIENT LOCKING FORCE OF SPRING TERMINALS

The pull-out force experiment was used to analyze the phenomenon of insufficient lock force of spring terminal for wire harness, and the cause of failure was preliminarily judged. The finite element simulation was used to analyze the stress and strain of the terminal to determine the failure mechanism of insufficient lock force [6, 7].

A. Analysis of the Phenomenon of Insufficient Locking Force of Spring Terminals

The structure of spring terminal connector is shown in Fig. 2. According to the national standard GB17464-2012, the spring terminal of this type should be suitable for the wire harness connection with the cross-sectional area in the range of 0.2mm^2~ 2.5 mm^2. The corresponding locking force requirements are shown in Table 1.

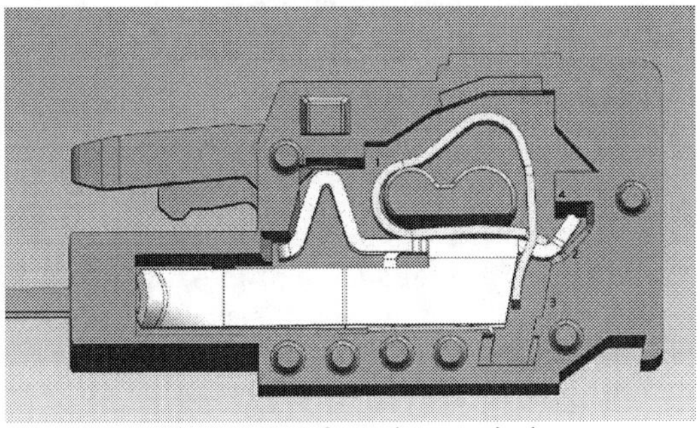

Fig. 2 Overall structure of a spring terminal connector

TABLE 1
RELATION BETWEEN SECTIONAL AREA OF WIRE HARNESS AND PULLING FORCE

Area (mm^2)	0.2	0.3	0.5	0.75	1.0	1.5	2.5
Single core diameter (mm)	0.51	0.63	0.9	1.0	1.2	1.5	1.9
Multi-core wire diameter (mm)	0.53	0.66	1.1	1.2	1.4	1.7	2.2
Pulling force (N)	10	15	20	30	35	40	50

For the spring terminal product No.1 with insufficient locking force, the tensile test was carried out by a computer tensile tester [8, 9], and the experimental method referred to the national standard GB17464-2012. The cross-sectional area of the wire harness is as shown in Table 1, and the pull-out force of 10 spring terminals was measured for each wire diameter, as shown in Fig. 3. It can be seen that the overall locking force of the spring terminal is low, and when the cross-sectional area of the harness is less than 1mm^2, the locking force does not increase significantly as the diameter of wire harness increases, and the pull-out force of the wire harness with the cross-sectional area of 0.75-1.5 mm^2 is lower than the standard requirement. Even the median value of locking force of samples for all wire harness with various diameters is not too much higher than the standard requirements.

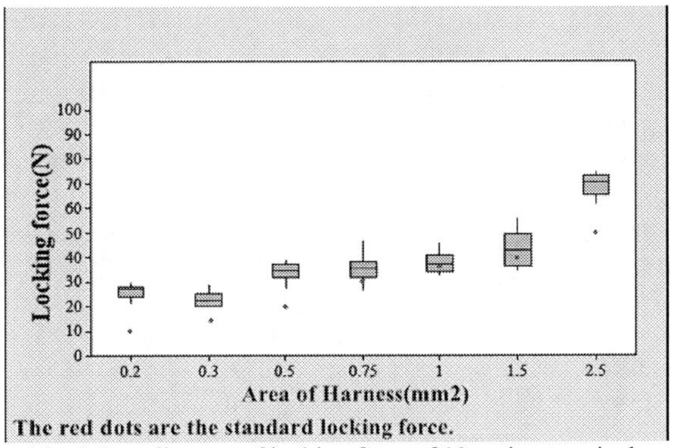

The red dots are the standard locking force.

Fig. 3 Box diagram of locking force of 10 spring terminals

According to the analysis of the low locking force of this spring terminal product, there are two possible reasons for common faults. One is that the overall stiffness of the spring terminal is not enough, the other is the deformation in the spring locking process is large, making the maximum stress exceed the yield strength of the material, and there is obvious plastic deformation, resulting in insufficient locking force. The failure reason can be judged by the stress and strain analysis of the finite element model of the product No.1.

B. Mechanism of Insufficient Locking Force of Spring Terminals

The stress and strain simulation analysis of spring terminals should be based on the size of the terminals at a free state. By cutting off the assembled spring terminals, the spring was restored to a free state. After obtaining the sizes of each section, ANSYS finite element software was used for simulation analysis [10]. The material parameters of the terminals are shown in Table 2.

TABLE 2
MATERIAL PARAMETERS OF SPRING TERMINALS

Material	Poisson's ratio	density	Young's modulus	Fracture strength	Yield strength
Stainless steel 14310 fd	0.3	7.9 g/cm^3	19700 kgf/mm^2	2400Mpa	2000Mpa

The locking force is directly related to the depression of the spring terminal, so the pressing process of the spring is used to simulate the locking state of the spring during the simulation. The amount of deformation of the spring is equivalent to the diameter of the wire harness of the locked wire harness. The process of pressing down the spring has two states: one is to apply pressure so that the spring reaches the initial assembled state, so that the bottom surface and the window in the spring are substantially flush; the second is to continue to apply pressure to open the window of the spring until a wire harness with a maximum wire diameter of 1.9 mm can be inserted.

By running the simulation model, it is concluded that the maximum stress value of the spring is 2211Mpa shown in Fig.4, which is close to the fracture strength limit of 2400Mpa, and the stress is close to 1000Mpa when the spring is at the initial assembly state. It indicates that the plastic deformation will occur in the spring clamping process, which indicates that the product has a problem because the spring terminal has formed large deformation and initial stress at the initial assembly state. In the subsequent locking process, the maximum spring stress far exceeds the yield strength of the material. However, the actual elastic clamping force of the spring terminal after plastic deformation is reduced, resulting in insufficient locking force.

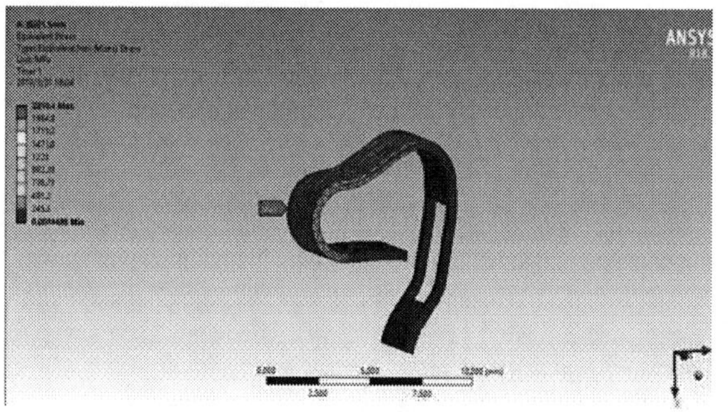

Fig. 4 Stress results by finite element simulation

A simulation experiment was designed for the case where the product No.1 spring terminal may be plastically deformed during service. The experiment used a special fixture to clamp the spring terminal to be tested. The contact was vertically loaded with positive pressure at the upper end of the spring terminal, and the sample is touched and deformed. The total deformation was set to be 1.9 mm, which corresponds to the maximum stroke when the harness is used. The profile of spring terminal was scanned and compared before and after the experiment, and the normal pressure change before and after loading and unloading was also measured.

The spring terminals showed significant plastic deformation before and after the loading experiment, as shown in Fig. 5. When the deformation was 1.9mm, the normal force reduced from 50.3N to 45.8N, about 9% decline. This also proves that the spring does undergo plastic deformation during the actual use, and the elastic force of the terminal reduces, which leads to the corresponding force for locking wire harness reduces.

In view of the case that spring deformation is too large to produce plastic deformation, it is necessary to analyze the key structural parameters that affect spring deformation, and then adjust the key parameters to improve the spring structural design, so that it can meet the design requirements of spring performance.

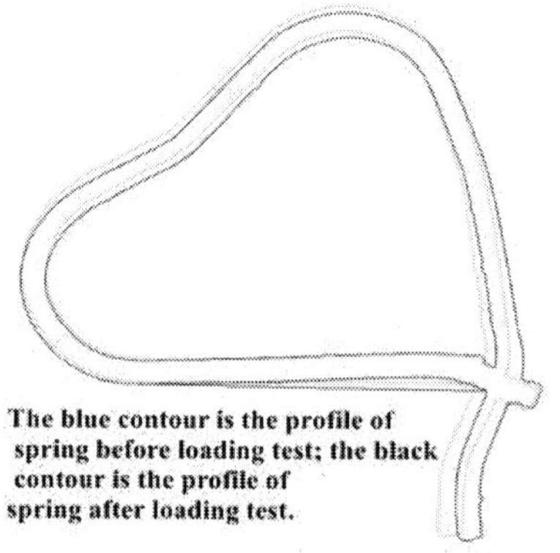

Fig. 5 Profile comparison of product No.1 before and after loading experiment

III. ANALYSIS OF KEY FACTORS AFFECTING ELASTIC DEFORMATION OF SPRING TERMINALS

The structural parameters of the spring terminal are processed in sections, and the elastic deformation of the terminal under the pressure of P is calculated by energy conservation and Castigliano's theorem [11]. The greater the deformation is, the greater the clamping force on the wire harness and the stronger the locking force is.

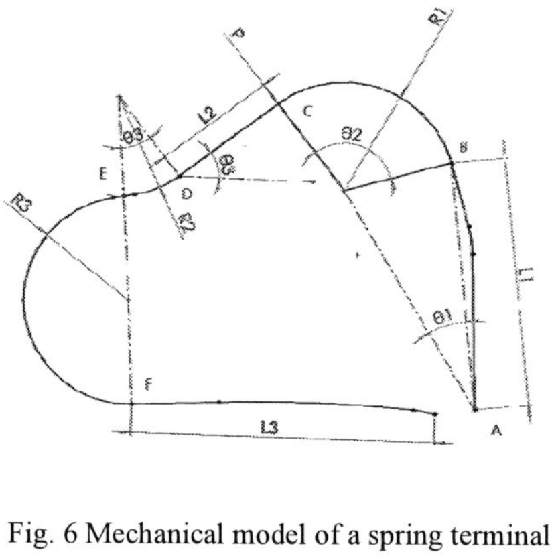

Fig. 6 Mechanical model of a spring terminal

A. Model Simplification of Spring Terminal

As shown in the Fig. 6, in order to facilitate calculation, the line segment L_1 between two points A and B is regarded as tangent to arc segment BC (radius R_1). Line segment L_2 is tangent to arc segments BC and DE (radius R_2), and θ_3 is at the horizontal line. Arc EF (radius R_3) is tangent to arc DE at an Angle of 180°. FA is a horizontal fixed segment L_3.

B. Analysis of the Force of Spring Terminals

When the connector product is assembled and the spring is in the equilibrium state, according to the equilibrium condition and the boundary condition of the spring, it can be determined that the end of the spring piece FA is tightly attached to the plastic part and no displacement occurs. Therefore, the spring can be regarded as a complex cantilever beam fixed at point F. When the wire harness is inserted, the spring will be deformed under the action of pressure, and the external force can be equivalent to the pressure P at the point C of the model. Due to the deformation of the spring, point A at the free end of the spring will move downward, and the wire harness will be inserted. As the spring bounces back, the wire harness will be clamped, forming a good contact. Under such a force condition, the key structural parameters which affect the spring deformation can be analyzed. Since there is an angle θ_1 from the direction of the pressure P to the actual deformation, the actual insertion of the wire diameter at point A is also related to the angle θ_1.

C. Theoretical Derivation of Spring Deformation

To find the unconstrained displacement of point A under the action of P, an imaginary force p_A needs to be added in the same direction as P, so that the displacement of point A under the action of P force can be gained by Castigliano's theorem. The bending moment M_i and deformation energy U_i of each section are as follows.

In section AB:

$$M_{AB}=P_A\sin\theta_1 x_1$$

$$U_{AB}=\int_0^{L_1}\frac{(P_A\sin\theta_1 x_1)^2}{2EJ}dx_1=\frac{P_A^2\sin^2\theta_1}{2EJ}\frac{L_1^3}{3}$$

In section BC:

$$M_{BC}=P_AR_1\sin\alpha_1$$

$$U_{AB}=\int_0^{\theta_2}\frac{(P_AR_1\sin\alpha_1)^2}{2EJ}R_1d\alpha_1=\frac{P_A^2R_1^3}{2EJ}\frac{(2\theta_2-\sin 2\theta_2)}{4}$$

In section CD:

$$M_{CD}=(P+P_A)x_2$$

$$M_{CD}=(P+P_A)x_2$$

In section DE:

$$M_{DE}=(P+P_A)(L_2+R_2\sin\alpha_2)$$

$$U_{DE}=\int_0^{\theta_3}\frac{[(P+P_A)(L_2+R_2\sin\alpha_2)]^2}{2EJ}R_2d\alpha_2$$

$$=\frac{(P+P_A)^2R_2}{2EJ}\begin{pmatrix}L_2^2\theta_3+\frac{1}{2}R_2^2\theta_3-\frac{R_2^2}{4}\sin 2\theta_3\\-2L_2R_2\cos\theta_3+2L_2R_2\end{pmatrix}$$

In section EF:

$$M_{EF}=(P+P_A)[(L_2+R_2\sin\theta_3)+R_3\sin(\alpha_3)]$$

$$U_{EF}=\int_0^{\pi}\frac{(P+P_A)^2[(L_2+R_2\sin\theta_3)+R_3\sin(\alpha_3)]^2}{2EJ}R_3d\alpha_3$$

$$=\frac{(P+P_A)^2R_3}{2EJ}*\begin{pmatrix}\pi L_2^2+\pi R_2^2\sin^2\theta_3+2\pi L_2R_2\sin\theta_3\\+\frac{1}{2}\pi R_3^2+4L_2R_3+4R_2R_3\sin\theta_3\end{pmatrix}$$

Then, the total deformation energy U and the deformation of point A is (1) and (2) respectively.

$$U=U_{AB}+U_{BC}+U_{CD}+U_{DE}+U_{EF} \quad (1)$$

$$\delta=\frac{\partial U}{\partial P_A}|_{P_A=0}=\frac{P}{EJ}\begin{bmatrix}\frac{L_2^3}{3}+R_2\begin{pmatrix}L_2^2\theta_3+\frac{1}{2}R_2^2\theta_3-\frac{R_2^2}{4}\sin 2\theta_3\\-2L_2R_2\cos\theta_3+2L_2R_2\end{pmatrix}+\\R_3\begin{pmatrix}\pi L_2^2+\pi R_2^2\sin^2\theta_3+2\pi L_2R_2\sin\theta_3\\+\frac{1}{2}\pi R_3^2+4L_2R_3+4R_2R_3\sin\theta_3\end{pmatrix}\end{bmatrix} \quad (2)$$

The relevant dimensions of the spring terminal model are as follows: L_1 = 3.0 mm, L_2 = 2.68 mm, R_1 = 1.8 mm, R_2 = 1.65 mm, R_3 = 1.78 mm, b= 3.8 mm, h= 0.37 mm, θ_3= 30 °, J_z is the moment of inertia of the spring section: $J_z=\frac{bh^3}{12}=0.016mm^4$, the young's modulus E of stainless steel 14310FD material = 19700 kg/mm^2.

D. Influence of Spring Structural Parameters on Deformation

It can be known that the spring deformation δ is inversely proportional to the moment of inertia of the shaft, as (2). The larger Jz is, the smaller the δ is. It is known that δ is also inversely proportional to b and h. The larger the width b and the height h, the smaller the deformation δ is. If b or h increases 10%, δ decreases 10% or 27.1% correspondingly. When the L_2, R_2, R_3 size changes by 10%, the effect on δ is 12%, 4%, and 14%, respectively. The effect of the key structural parameters of the spring L_2 R_2 R_3 on the deformation is shown in Fig. 7-9.

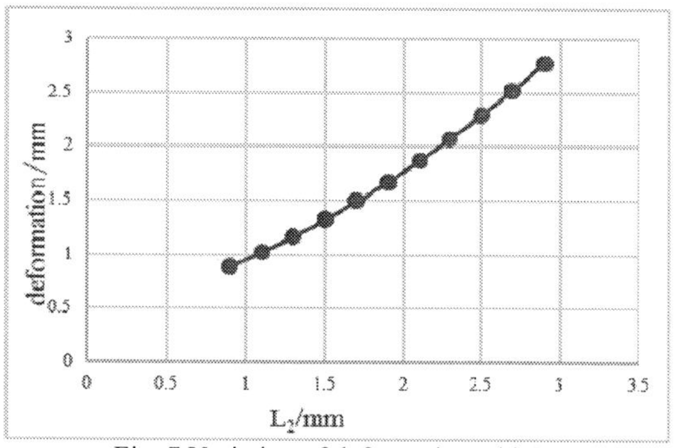

Fig. 7 Variation of deformation with L_2

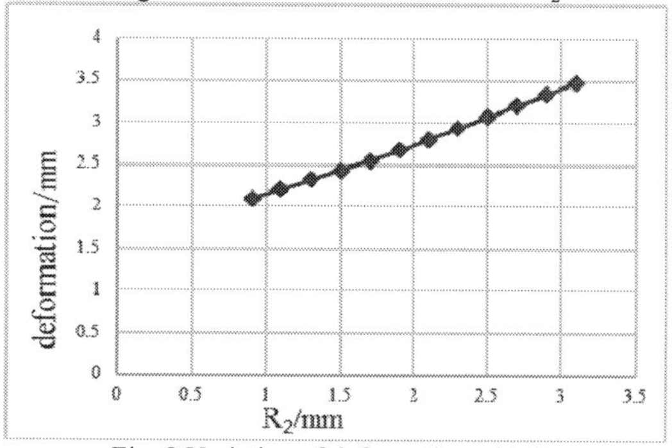

Fig. 8 Variation of deformation with R_2

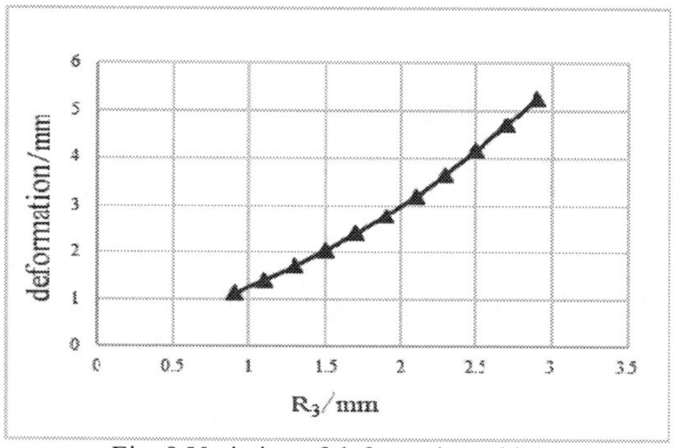

Fig. 9 Variation of deformation with R_3

Section size b, h, spring terminal structural parameters L_2 R_2 R_3 will affect δ to some degree. For b, h, L_2, R_3, when their dimension changes 10%, the effect on the deformation amount is greater than 10%. For L_2, R_2, R_3, the influence on the deformation is R_3, L_2, R_2 in order from large to small.

In the actual work, if the spring raw material is not replaced, the h and b parameters are unchanged, and the adjustment of R_3 and L_2 makes it easier to improve the spring performance.

IV. IMPROVEMENT SCHEME AND VERIFICATION OF SPRING TERMINAL

The key factors affecting the spring deformation are obtained through theoretical design, and the structure of the spring is adjusted according to the actual process and processing requirements, as shown in Table 3. Improved product 1 increases L_2 by 10%, and improved product 2 increases R_3 by 10%. It is expected that the pull-out force of the improvement 1 and the improvement 2 will increase, but the maximum stress will decrease to meet the product standard requirements.

TABLE 3
MAIN DIMENSIONS OF SPRING STRUCTURE

	L_1/ mm	L_2/ mm	R_1/ mm	R_2/ mm	R_3/ mm
Product 1	4.0	2.8	1.9	0.8	1.8
Improvement 1	4.0	3.1	1.9	1	1.8
Improvement 2	4.0	2.8	1.9	1	2.0

In order to verify the improvement scheme, the finite element analysis and locking force of wire harness experiment were carried out for the original product 1, improvement product 1 and 2 respectively. For the original spring terminal structure and the two improved schemes, the maximum stress was compared when the maximum wire harness was 1.9mm, as shown in Table 4. It can be seen from the simulation results that in the case where the connector product produces the same amount of deformation, the maximum stress generated by the improvement 1 and the improvement 2 is reduced by 10% and 16% respectively compared with the original product 1. It shows that changing the key parameters of the structure can improve the spring performance and thus improve the spring locking force for wire harness.

TABLE 4
MAXIMUM STRESS CORRESPONDING TO THE MAXIMUM DEFORMATION

Spring deformation namely line thickness (mm)	Maximum stress (MPa)		
	Product 1	Improvement 1	Improvement 2
1.9	2211	1976	1874

The pullout force of the improved products is shown in Fig. 10-11. According to the experimental data, it can be seen that the minimum, maximum and median values of the actual pullout force of the original products have been significantly improved by improvement 1 and 2. For the improvement 1, the minimum values of the actual pullout force are at least 28% above the standard requirements. For the improvement 2, the minimum values of the actual pulling force are at least 30% above the standard requirement. The median pullout force is 9%~52% higher than the minimum pullout force. Therefore, the possibility of unqualified pullout force appears in the two improved products reduces markedly. From the point of view of experiment, the correctness of the theory and the simulation model is verified, and it shows that the spring performance can meet the requirements through proper adjustment of key parameters in the case of poor performance. At the same time, it can be seen that the pullout force of the improvement 2 is better than that of the improvement 1.

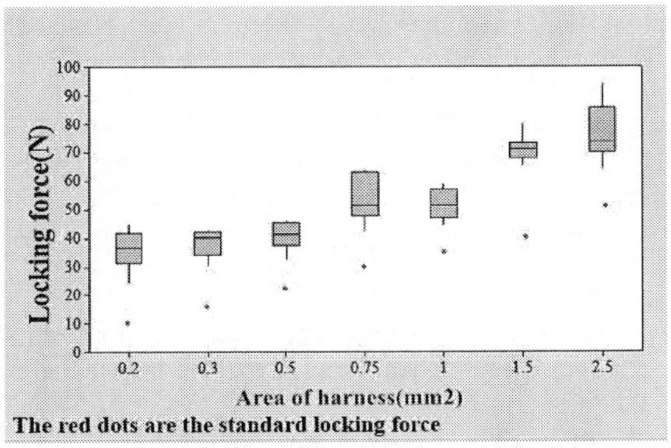

Fig. 10 Box diagram of improvement 1 pullout force

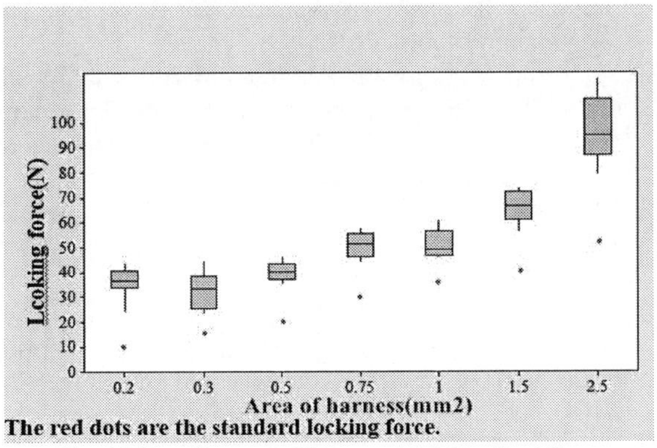

Fig. 11 Box diagram of improvement 2 pullout force

The profile of spring terminal after improvement was scanned and compared before and after the loading experiment, and the normal pressure change was also measured. The contours of the improved products 1 and 2 are compared before and after loading tests respectively, as shown in Fig. 12 and 13. The spring profile of both improvement product 1, improvement product 2 has no significant deformation before and after the loading experiments. The normal pressure of the improvement product 1 before and after the experiment is basically unchanged at around 45N, and that of the improvement product 2 is at around 48N; which also proves that the product does not appear plastic deformation after the structure improvement.

Considering that the decrease in elastic force after improvement may lead to an increase in contact resistance, the contact resistance is calculated by (3).

$$R_{\varepsilon}=0.89\rho\sqrt{\frac{H\xi}{F}} \quad (3)$$

By the theoretical estimation, the contact resistance of the improved product 1 is 0.57mΩ; that of the improved product 2 is 0.55mΩ, which still meets the design requirements.

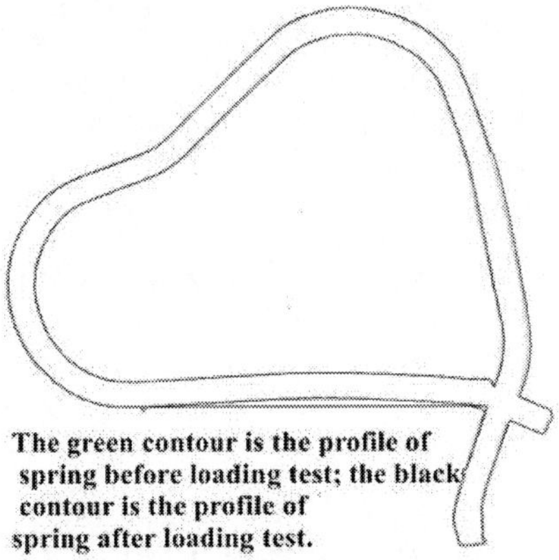

Fig. 12 Profile comparison of improvement product 1 before and after loading experiment

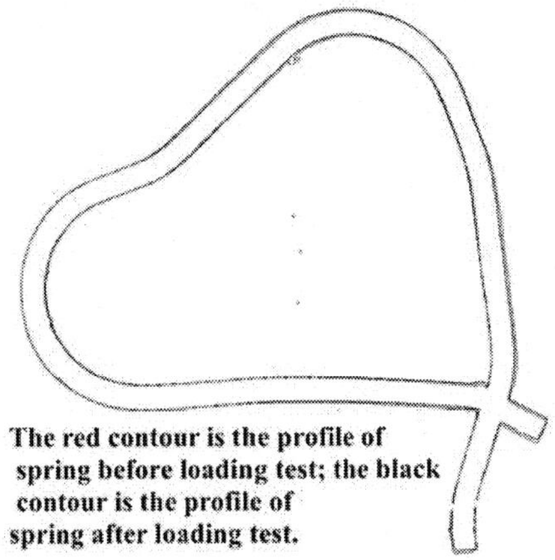

Fig. 13 Profile comparison of improvement product 2 before and after loading experiment

V. DISCUSSION

A. Over-stress Design of Elastic Elements

The main reasons for the overstress of elastic elements are as follows: in the initial stage of design, the scope of elastic force demand of elastic elements is not clear, which leads to the blind desire to increase the initial elastic force to improve the working capacity of elastic elements; as a result, the component is prone to plastic deformation during subsequent use, so that the normal pressure of the clamping spring during operation is reduced by about 9%, which leads to the decrease of the spring locking force.

B. Design Method of Elastic Element

In the design process of elastic element, the structure of elastic element can be simplified appropriately, so as to get the preliminary mechanical model easily. According to the mechanical model, the elastic element deformation is calculated and the theoretical formula of elastic element deformation is obtained. Further data processing and analysis are carried out for the formula to analyze the influence of structural parameters on deformation. Finally, the feasibility of each parameter adjustment is analyzed based on the processing technology and actual situation. For product 1, theoretical calculations show that the structural parameter width b, thickness h, L_2, R_2 R_3 have different degrees of influence on the deformation, and then two improvement measures are obtained according to the actual situation and the importance of the influence parameters. Improvement 1 mainly modifies L_2, and improvement 2 mainly modifies R_3. In the end, the pullout force of the connector products have been improved, and the requirements of the standard have been met. But at the same time, it can be seen that even if both the improvement 2 and the improvement 1 are modified by 10%, the pullout force of improvement 2 is higher than that of the improvement 1, indicating that R_3 is the most important factor and also the key factor in the design.

VI. CONCLUSION

In this paper, the main influencing factors of spring mechanical properties, structural adjustment and locking force of connectors for wire harness are discussed. The key factors affecting the spring performance are obtained, and the faults of specific products are analyzed and improved through the key factors, so as to guide the design process of elastic terminals. The main conclusions of this paper are as follows:

(1) In the design of elastic terminals, many design faults are caused by insufficient clamping force of spring terminals, so a large initial deformation and initial stress are applied to the spring, resulting in plastic deformation of the spring in the subsequent locking process for wire harness. But on the contrary, the actual clamping force becomes smaller. Therefore, the pre-deformation and prestress of the initial assembly should also be a measure index of the spring terminals in the factory.

(2) The structural parameter width b, thickness h, L_2, R_2 and R_3 of the spring terminals have different effects on the deformation. Considering the actual process, it is easier to change R_3, L_2, R_2 than to change the width b and thickness h. Order by the importance of parameter influence is $R_3 > L_2 > R_2$. Therefore, it is recommended to modify R_3 in the design.

(3) In the design of the spring terminals, it is necessary to focus on analyzing the influence of key parameters on the performance of the spring terminal; implementing the specific product design and adjusting the key parameters according to the specific specifications of the products can make the whole product design process dependable. After the design is completed, if the performance of spring terminal is not good, the spring performance can be satisfied by appropriately adjusting the key parameters of the spring.

ACKNOWLEDGMENT

The authors are thankful for the support of the National Natural Science Foundation of China (No. 61674017) to carry out this study.

REFERENCES

[1] Zhijun Xie. Terminal selection of signal products [J]. Railway communication signal engineering technology, 2006(06):31-32.

[2] Wenjing Han. Research and improvement of cage spring performance of two-core fast lock product [D]. Beijing: Beijing university of posts and telecommunications, 2012.

[3] PV Varde, M Agarwal, PP Marathe. The Reliability and life prediction for electronic connectors for control applications. The IEEE International Conference on Reliability, Safety & Hazard, 2010, (2):63-67.

[4] JIMA. B, 2713:2009. The design calculating formulas and the procedures of decision of specifications for Flat Springs[M]. Japan: JSA, 2009.

[5] Xiaoxuan Wang. Structural design and vibration impact immunity analysis for quick-contact leaf spring connector [D]. Shanghai: Shanghai jiao tong university, 2016.

[6] Zhenghao Tang, Tie Wang, Xuepeng Yan, Nonlinear finite element analysis of double-arched asymmetrical taper leaf springs [J]. Mechanery design and manufacture, 2019, (4):9-12, 16. (in Chinese).

[7] I Sawchyn, ES Sproles. Optimizing the force and geometry parameters in the design of reduced insertion force connectors [J]. IEEE the transactions on components, hybrid, and manunfacturing technology,1992, (6):1025-1033.

[8] GB 17464-2012, Connecting device-electrical copper conductors-safety requirements for screw-type and screwless-type clamping units for conductors from $0.2mm^2$ up to 35 mm^2 (included) [S].

[9] Jun Pan, FangJian Jin, Wenhua Chen, et al. Structural analysis of electrical connector contacts and insertion-extraction test [J]. China mechanical engineering, 2013, 24(12):1636-1641.

[10]Jianwei Zhang, Haibo Bai, Xin Li. ANSYS 14.0 super learning manual [M]. People's posts and telecommunications press, 2013.

[11]Jigao Zhang, Electrical contact theory and design technology[M], school of automation, Beijing university of posts and telecommunications, 2002, p76-90.

7th International Conference on Reliability of
Electrical Products and Electrical Contacts,
November 04-06, 2019

Research on Convolutional Neural Network Regression forContact Erosion Estimation of AC Contactors

Ziran Wu, Hechen Cui, Guichu Wu, Yingmin You
The Key Laboratory of Low-voltage Apparatus Intellectual Technology of ZhejiangWenzhou University
No. 276, Xueyuan Mid Road, Lucheng District, Wenzhou, Zhejiang Province, 325027, China
E-mail: nature.nano@gmail.com Tel: 86-577-88373126-8305 Fax: 86-577-88373127

***Abstract*—The paper proposes a contact erosion estimation method that models electrical signal data of breaking processes by Convolutional Neural Network Regression(CNNR) for AC contactors. Voltage and current waveform data of breaking operations is acquired during AC-4 tests, and meanwhile the contact mass loss of each phase is measured after every 600 operations. We apply voltage waveforms, current waveforms and voltage-current-combo waveforms as feature arrays, and label them by accumulated contact mass loss values via piecewise linear interpolation from the mass loss measurements. Thus the training and testing datasets for CNN are founded. The breaking waveforms are reformed to two-dimensional feature metrices and input them to a CNN model which consists of three convolution layers, three pooling layers and two full connection layers. For the training process, the model parameters are optimized by the mean square error (MSE) between the ground-truth mass loss labels and the CNN outputs. The test results show that the proposed method achieves a relatively high estimation precision of contact erosion of AC contactors when voltage waveforms are utilized as features.**

***Index Terms*—AC contactors, contact mass loss, convolutional neural networks, regression**

I. INTRODUCTION

A. Overview

For an alternating current (AC) contactor, the condition of the contacts is tightly related to its electrical endurance. On the other hand, the condition is reflected the mass loss of the silver-metal-oxide alloy on the contact. The alloy helps reducing the contact resistance and strengthening the capabilities of anti-welding and arc suppression. However, making and breaking operations erode the alloy. In other words, when the alloy is mostly eroded, the electrical endurance goes to the end. Therefore, estimation of the contact mass loss can help users to determine the electrical endurance of AC contactors, which makes them become 'smart'.

Contact erosion estimation is a difficultissue due to three main causes: firstly, the mass loss amount is very small (in milligrams for a contactor weighted several kilograms);Secondly, contacts are normally built inside contactors. Therefore, it is impractical that obtain the contact mass variation by direct measurement or observation;Thirdly, since the transient voltage and current condition varies since the making/breaking phase angles are nonconstant, the mass losses of two pairs of contacts can be significantly different. In order to resolve this issue, scholars and engineers have proposed a number of methods that estimate the mass loss by indirect measurement and modelling.

B. Previous Work

Multiple sensing methods are proposed to measure typical characteristics which can be mapped to the contact erosion condition. Some approaches are costly, e.g., Zhou et al. [1]estimated the contact mass loss via measuring the over-travel variation by a precise laser distance sensor; Berger et al. [2]acquired the sonogram of every operation by a piezoelectric stack attached on the contacts and achieved the change of the contact resistance. These approaches require modifying the structure of the AC contactor to build-in or embed sensors, which is not friendly to manufactures and users. The most practical approach is sensing the voltage between the contacts and the current through the contacts, and analyzing the change of signals to reflect the change of the contact condition. Kawakami et al. [3] modelled contact mass loss with the operation number and arcing energy which was computed from the voltage and current. The method was developed by Sawa et al. [4] who applied the arcing duration as an additional factor which is also determined by the voltage waveform. However, at present, proposed approaches are based on the historical data of operations, i.e., the running and operation process of the AC contactor must be traced all time, and the mass loss estimation is achieved by the tracing data. If given a used AC contactor without its historical operation data, these methods do no work.

Our previous paper presented a method that applied Conditional Density Estimation to predict the electrical endurance of AC contactors [5], which was our preliminary exploration of contact condition estimation. The method used the arcing characteristicscomputed from voltage and current signals, e.g., the arcing energy, duration, power, etc. However, the characteristics utilized were the average values within a number of operations, e.g., 100 operations, due to the nonconstant arcing phase angles (APAs) which led to significant value differences between different operations.

Therefore, a method that achieves real-time estimation of the contact mass loss without historical data is proposed. The method acquires voltage and current signals during breaking processes of AC-4 tests and inputs the reformed signal arrays into a Convolutional Neural Network Regression (CNNR) model. The mass loss values of each phase are used as the labels of the signals arrays. The CNNR model is trained by minimizing the mean square error (MSE) between the estimated mass loss values and the measured ones. The model can be used under such a situation: given a used AC contactor without any historical usage information, the user performs an AC-4 making-breaking operation on the contactor and collect the voltage and current waveforms which are then used as the input for the CNNR model. Thus, the mass loss condition can be automatically computed by the model.

II. DATA ACQUISITION AND PRE-PROCESSING

The data collection process is the same as that was introduced in our previous papers [6] that employed an endurance system for electrical apparatuses. We use the Schneider LC1D80 model (rated voltage: 220 V, 60 Hz, rated current: 80 A) as the testing specimens. The maximum operation count is set to 6000, according to the China GB standard[7]. The voltage and current waveforms of the three phases during every making-breaking process are recorded.

In this paper, the contacts of each phase are considered as a separate switch system, viz, an AC contactor has three switch systems. In the LC1D80 structure, the switch system of a phase consists of two stationary contacts and one moving contact with two contact points. Therefore, the moving contact works as a bridge to connect the two stationary contacts. During the test, we measure the mass of all contacts and compute the accumulated mass loss of each phase. The accumulated contact mass loss (ACML)of a phase, which can reflect the condition of the contacts, is defined as the sum of accumulated mass losses of the contacts in this phase. Therefore, with 6000 operations, 18000 examples of phase mass losses are obtained.

In practice, it is impossible to measure the contact masses of every operation. Therefore, we perform measurement after every 600 operations and apply piecewise linear interpolation to retrieve the ACMLs of the other operations. These ACMLs are used to define the contact condition of corresponding operations.

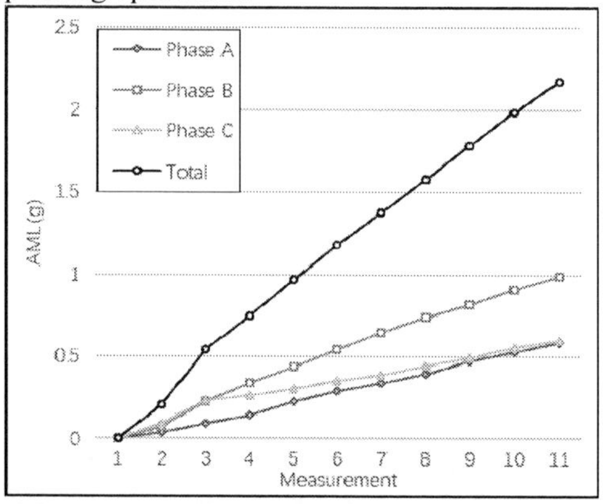

Fig. 1 Increasement of the accumulated mass loss of each phase

Voltage and current waveforms are acquired during the operations. For a voltage-and-current waveform pair of a phase, we select the period when the breaking arc occurs as the sample feature array. There are 1024 sampling points for both the voltage and current signals in a period, so the features of an operation are represented by an array with two channels (voltage and current channels), and each channel has 1024 features. Fig. 2 shows a period of breaking operation, in which t_0 is the starting moment of the period, t_a is the starting moment of the breaking arc. We acquire the waveforms within 20ms after t_0.

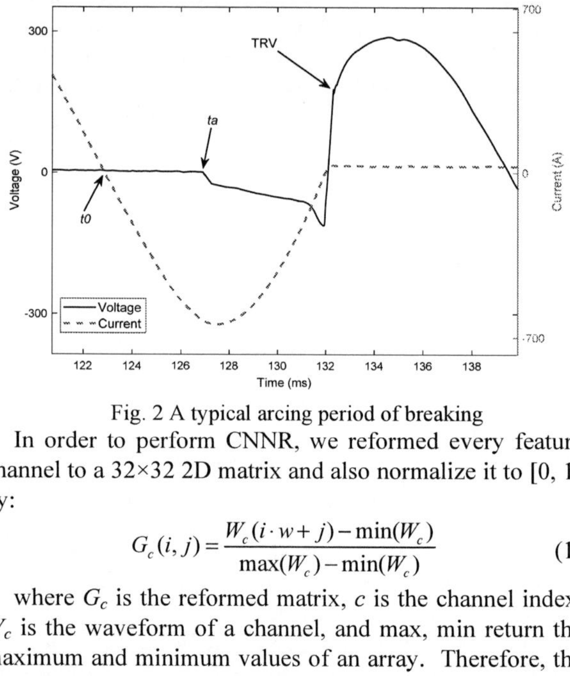

Fig. 2 A typical arcing period of breaking

In order to perform CNNR, we reformed every feature channel to a 32×32 2D matrix and also normalize it to [0, 1] by:

$$G_c(i,j) = \frac{W_c(i \cdot w + j) - \min(W_c)}{\max(W_c) - \min(W_c)} \tag{1}$$

where G_c is the reformed matrix, c is the channel index, W_c is the waveform of a channel, and max, min return the maximum and minimum values of an array. Therefore, the features are is reformed to 2×32×32 with the value range [0, 1]. An example for CNNR is thus composed by the features and the corresponding ACML of a phase after an operation.The ACML is utilized as the label. The aim of our CNNR modelling is to estimate the label from the features. Fig. 3 (firstly published in our previous paper[8]) indicates the reforming process.

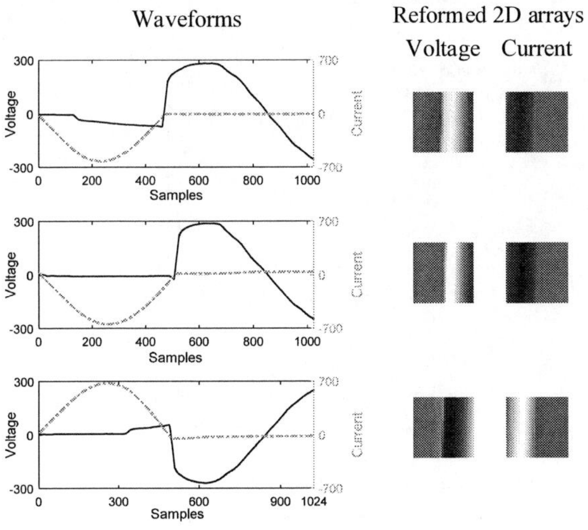

Fig. 3 Feature reforming process

III. NNR MODELING

The modeling process is illustrated in Fig.4

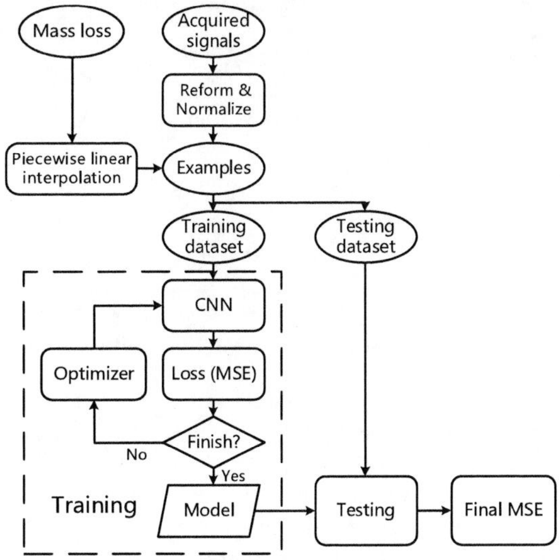

Fig. 4 Flowchart of CNNR modeling process

The structure diagram of the CNNR model is shown in Fig. 5.

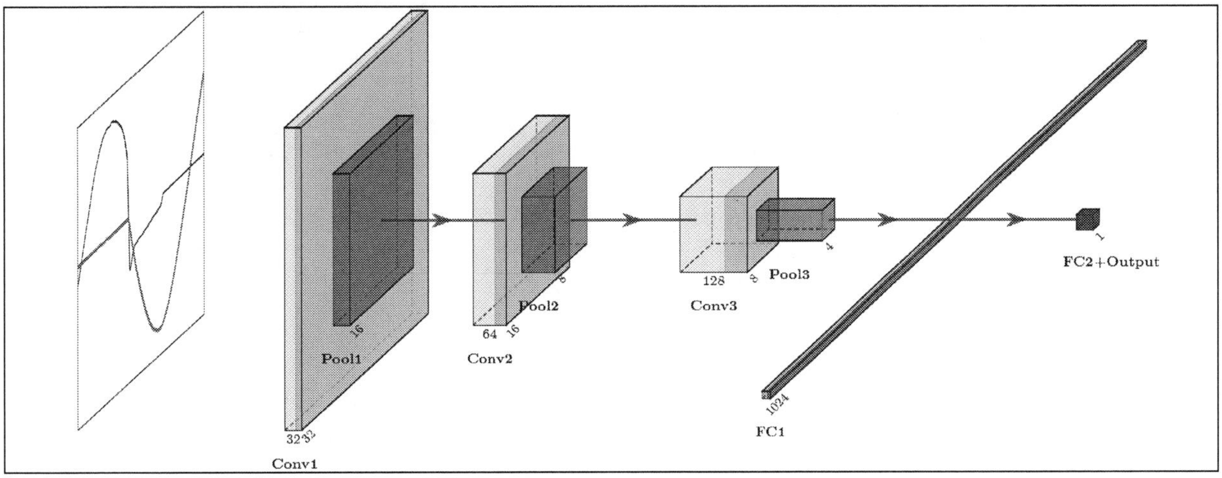

Fig. 5 Structure of the convolutional neural network regression model

The CNNR model consists of three convolution layers (Conv1, 2 and 3) and three pooling layers (Pool1, 2 and 3), see Fig. 2. After the third pooling layer, two full-connection layers (FC1 and 2) are applied, to finally get a single output which is the mass loss estimation. The dimensions of the layers are shown in Table I:

In Table I, the dimensions of the layers are represented by channels×height×width for convolution and pooling layers. We perform 2D convolution in the model, therefore, the kernel sizes of convolution layers are channels×5×5. Meanwhile, the 'SAME PADDING' mode is applied, so the height and width are kept the same as those before convolution. In every pooling layer, MaxPooling with a pooling size of 2×2 is executed, which means that every pooling process extract the maximum value from a 2×2 window, and thus the height and width are scaled to 1/2. For Conv1, the input can be one channel for voltage or current waveforms, or two channels for both. After every convolution layer, batch normalization [9] and ReLU[10] are performed, which are indicated by darker yellow in the convolution layer boxes.

TABLE I
DIMENSIONS OF THE LAYERS

Layer name	Input dims.	Output dims.	Kernel size	Num. of kernels
Conv1	?×32×32	32×32×32	2×5×5	32
Pool1	32×32×32	32×16×16		
Conv2	32×16×16	64×16×16	32×5×5	64
Pool2	64×16×16	64×8×8		
Conv3	64×8×8	128×8×8	64×5×5	128
Pool3	128×8×8	128×4×4		
FC1	2048	1024		
FC2	1024	1		

In the training stage, we used the mean square error (MSE) between the estimated ACML and the ground-truth ACML as the loss function. An Adam optimizer [11] is utilized to update the parameters to minimize the MSE. The initial learning rate of the optimizer is set to 10^{-4} and will be automatically altered during the training process. After the FC1 layers, a dropout operation is performed with a defined dropout rate to avoid over-fitting issues.

We test 3 AC contactor specimens with AC-4 18000 operations, so finally 54000 examples are obtained. In post processing, we discard some of the examples and get 47538 valid examples. The examples are divided into two sets: the training set and the testing set.The ratio between the training and testing examples is 4:1, i.e., 38030 training examples and 9508 testing examples. In the training stage, the batch size for every training loop is set to 100. Hence, the program runs approximately 380 loops to complete an epoch. Random permutation on the examples is performed every time when the training reaches the end of an epoch.

IV. EXPERIMENTS AND RESULTS

As described in Section III, three schemes are implemented in the experiments: using voltage features, using current features and using both (voltage-current-combo features). The CNNR model is constructed, trained and tested by TensorFlow[12]. An Nvidia Titan V Graphic Card[13] is utilized to accelerate the computation. In the training stage, 2×10^6 loops are executed, and loss curves are obtained. Meanwhile, the test examples are applied to the under-training model after every 1000 loops.

Fig. 6 shows the MSE curve of the training process along with the testing results when the dropout rate is 0.5.It is indicated that both training and testing MSEs reach minimum values when only voltage waveforms are used. The training loss curve falls quickly and finally reaches 0.00497. he final testing MSE reaches 0.0084, which means the average value of absolute errors is 0.0917 g. However, when only current waveforms are used, the result is much worse. The training loss reaches 0.0215 and the testing MSE reaches 0.0354, which are about four times of those using voltage waveforms. While using both voltage-current-combo waveforms, the final testing MSE is 0.0127.

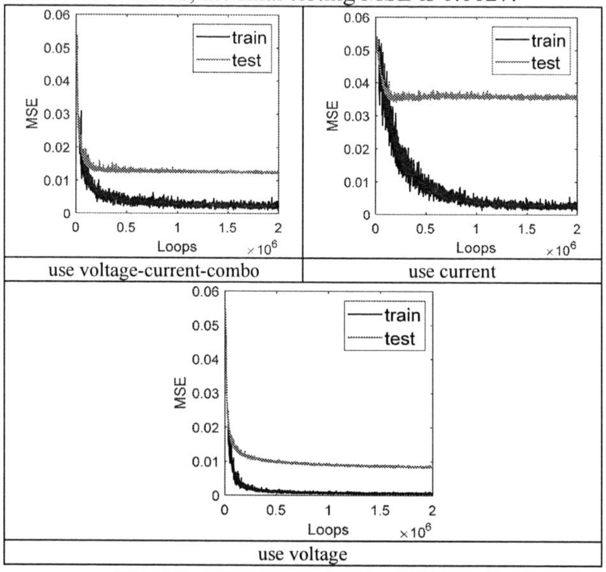

Fig. 6 Training processes using different data

Hence, it is proven that voltage waveforms contain more information relating to the contact endurance condition. Fig. 7 displays the 3-phase waveforms of two operations: the left column is acquired at the beginning of the AC-4 test, and the right column is acquired when the test number approaching 6000. It can be observed that during the arc duration, voltage waveformsof operation b contains more vibration than those of operation a.

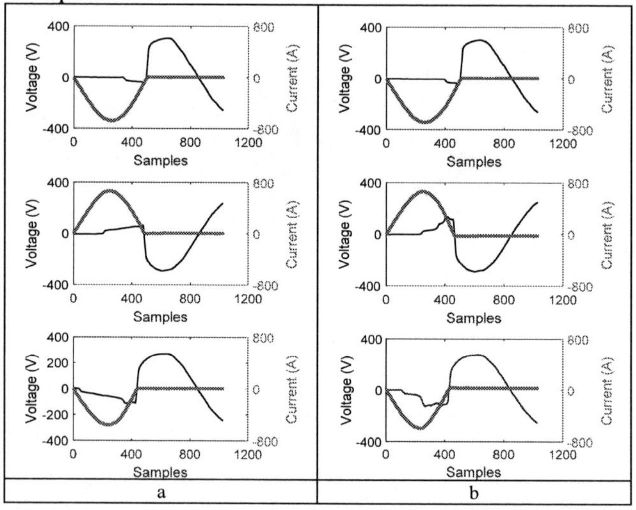

Fig. 7 Waveforms at the beginnin (a) and the end (b) of the AC-4 test

On another hand, current waveforms cannot provide sufficient information, and even cause negative effect when combined with voltage waveforms. We thus perform further investigation with voltage waveforms by adjusting the dropout rate to achieve a lower MSE. The dropout rate is set to 0, 0.25, 0.5 and 0.75, and the training processes are presented in Table II respectively.

TABLEII

TRAINING AND TESTING RESULTS USING VOLTAGE WAVEFORMS

Dropout rate	Training MSE	Testing MSE
0.00	0.00038	0.00958
0.25	0.00030	0.00773
0.50	0.00049	0.00842
0.75	0.00054	0.00763

According to Table II, the minimum testing MSE reaches 0.00773 when the dropout rate equals to 0.75. Therefore, averagely the absolute error in this situation is 0.88g. The maximum mass loss of a phase in Fig. 1 is 0.984g (phase B). Hence, the lowest average error rate is 8.93%.

V. CONCLUSION

The paper proposes a method that estimates the accumulated mass loss of the contacts of each phase by training a convolutional neural network regression model with voltage and current waveforms at breaking processes. The results indicate that using voltage waveforms as features reaches the lowest estimation error. The method provides an approach that achieve online contact condition estimation without historical data. The minimum estimation error is lower than 9%, which can be implemented in practical applications.

ACKNOWLEDGMENT

The work presented in the paper is supported in part by the National Natural Science Foundation of China through the Project entitled Research on Residual Electrical Endurance Prediction of AC Contactors based on Conditional Density Estimation under Grant 51507113, Natural Science Foundation of Zhejiang Province through the Project entitled Black-Box Modeling on Variable-Length Breaking Arcs in Low-Voltage Switching Apparatuses under Grant LQ16E070004.

REFERENCES

[1] X. Zhou, L. Zou, and R. J. Briggs, "Prognostic and Diagnostic Technology for DC Actuated Contactors and Motor Starters," IEICE Transactions on Electronics, vol. 92, no. 8, pp. 1045–1051, 2009.

[2] F. Berger, F. Schubert, and M. Gmbh, "Determination of Residual Lifetime of Electrical Contacts by Sonogram Analysis," in Proc. of 21st ICEC, 2002.

[3] Y. Kawakami, M. Hasegawa, Y. Watanabe, and K. Sawa, "An investigation for the method of lifetime prediction of Ag-Ni contacts for electromagnetic contactor," in Electrical Contacts, Proceedings of the Annual Holm Conference on Electrical Contacts, 2005, vol. 2005, pp. 151–155.

[4] K. Sawa, K. Yoshida, M. Watanabe, and K. Suzuki, "Arc characteristics and electrode mass change of AgNi Contacts for Electromagnetic Contactors," in Electrical Contacts, Proceedings of the Annual Holm Conference on Electrical Contacts, 2010, pp. 261–266.

[5] Z. Wu, G. Wu, H. Huang, and Y. You, "A novel residual electrical endurance prediction method for low-voltage electromagnetic alternating current contactors," IEEE Transactions on Components, Packaging and Manufacturing Technology, vol. 5, no. 4, pp. 465–473, 2015.

[6] Z. Wu, Y. You, G. Wu, and H. Huang, "Research on Arcing Characteristics of AC Contactor Breaking Processes based on Statistics," Proceedings of the 5th International Conference on Reliability of Electrical Products and Electrical Contacts, pp. 70–75, Nov. 2014.

[7] "GB 14048.4-2010 Low-voltage switchgear and controlgear - Part 4-1: Contactors and motor-starters - Electromechanical contactors and motor-starters (Including motor protector)." General Administration of Quality Supervision, Inspection and Quarantine of the People's Republic of China; Standardization Administration of the People's Republic of China, 2010.

[8] H. Cui, Z. Wu, G. Wu, X. Xu, Y. You, and Y. Fang, "Convolutional Neural Networks for Electrical Endurance Prediction of Alternating Current Contactors," IEEE Transactions on Components, Packaging and Manufacturing Technology, pp. 1–1, 2019.

[9] S. Ioffe and C. Szegedy, "Batch normalization: Accelerating deep network training by reducing internal covariate shift," 32nd International Conference on Machine Learning, ICML 2015, vol. 1, pp. 448–456, 2015.

[10] V. Nair and G. E. Hinton, "Rectified Linear Units Improve Restricted Boltzmann Machines," Proceedings of the 27th International Conference on Machine Learning, no. 3, pp. 807–814, 2010.

[11] D. Kingma and J. Ba, "Adam: A Method for Stochastic Optimization," in International Conference on Learning Representations (ICLR), 2014.

[12] TensorFlow, "TensorFlow is an Open Source Software Library for Machine Intelligence," 2016. [Online]. Available: https://www.tensorflow.org/.

[13] NVIDIA, "The World's Most Powerful Graphics Card | NVIDIA TITAN V," 2019. [Online]. Available: https://www.nvidia.com/en-us/titan/titan-v/.

BIOGRAPHIES

Ziran Wu, born in 1984, is the deputy director of the Key Laboratory of Low-voltage Apparatus Intellectual Technology of Zhejiang. He is also an associate researcher in the College of Electrical and Electronic Engineering of Wenzhou University. His research focuses on data analysis on electrical apparatuses by artificial intelligence methods, including arc modeling, reliability, endurance prediction, and fault detection. He also contributes to applications smart manufacturing, machine vision and cyber physical systems.

HechenCuiwas a research member of the Key Laboratory of Low-voltage Apparatus Intellectual Technology of Zhejiang, Wenzhou University. He was a MSc student and graduated in June 2019. He majored in Electrical Engineering. His research subject for the MSc degree focused on applying deep learning methods to electrical endurance prediction. His research interest covers machine learning, contact endurance and electrical reliability.

Guichu Wu is the director of the Key Laboratory of Low-voltage Apparatus Intellectual Technology of Zhejiang. He also works as a professor in the College of Electrical and Electronic Engineering of Wenzhou University. His educational and research interest covers electrical intellectualization, embedded systems, cyber physical systems and solar energy.

Yingmin You received the MSc degree from Chongqing University in 2009. He is currently an experimentalist with the Key Laboratory of Low-Voltage Apparatus Intellectual Technology of Zhejiang, Wenzhou University. His current research interests include intelligence and reliability of electrical apparatuses, and theories and experiments on electrical discharges and plasms.

7th International Conference on Reliability of
Electrical Products and Electrical Contacts,
November 04-06, 2019

The Influence of Over Travel of Contacts on Arc Erosion under DC Load

Lei Yi, Qiyan Wu, Guangxiang Yu, NingyiLu
Testing Center, Xiamen Hongfa Electroacoustic Co., Ltd., Xiamen 361021, China

***Abstract*—One fundamental reason for the failure of contact materials is because of the effect of arc in the process of electrical contact. In order to decrease the arc on the effect of erosion to contact materials as possible, it is very important to decrease the lasting time and bounce times of arc. In this paper, by using the apparatus built by self, the voltage, current, lasting time and bounce times of arc generated under DC Load with different over travel (O.T.) of contact were collected at every operation, and the data of these parameters collected during the whole electrical life were analyzed. The research results affirmed that the bounce times and the energy of arc decreased with increasing O.T. value of contact within a certain range, and it could be explained the function of O.T. value of contacts on the effect of arc erosion characteristic. By using the research result when the relay is designed and assembled, it will be beneficial to improve its electrical life level.**

***Index Terms*—Over Travel of Contact, Bounce, Arc Erosion, Contact Materials**

I. INTRODUCTION

Arc belongs to a kind of high temperature plasma, and it is one of the fundamental reason for the failure of electric contact materials. There are many factors that affect the generation and persistence of arc, which can be divided into three categories. One is the factors of product and part structure, such as contact breaking rate, contact gap, contact morphology and size. Another is contact material factors, such as material composition and organizational structure, and the other is the applied environmental factors , such as load conditions, environmental temperature and humidity, atmosphere, air flow and so on. How to reduce the bounce times and duration of arc, so as to reduce arc energy by optimizing or avoiding the above related factors, has been widely concerned by researchers in the field of electrical contact and electrical component manufacturers over the years.[1-3]

N.Y. Lu et al. [3] has researched the bounce between contacts on the effect of electrical life through patting electromagnetic relay, and it is pointed out qualitatively that he more the bounce is, the easier the contact is welded. Z. K. Chen and G. Witter [4] has reported the influence of breaking rate on the arc erosion characteristics, and it is found out that the bounce would increase with the decreasing rate of movable spring during make operation, there for, the welding and erosion probability of contact also would increase when arc acts on contacts. By using riveted contact, B.O. Ciocirlan et al.[5] has changed the design of axially symmetric surface into eccentric surface, according to the principle that eccentric impact converts the rebound motion of the contacts after the initial impact into rolling or sliding motions, and the bounce probability without load decreases obviously. Up to now, most evaluation and analysis on the arc erosion of contact have just stayed on the final results, while less attention has been paid to the procedural parameters, such as arc energy, arc lasting time, bounce times and so on, due to the lack of effective testing equipment, although the collection of arc energy and welding force during every operation have been realized by W.B. Ren et al.[6]

In this paper, data collection and monitoring system during every operation on arc energy, contact resistance, bounce and so on have been added based on the simulation apparatus designed by self [7]. The over travel of contacton the effect of arc erosion under DC load has been researched. The testing method and research results are expected to apply for the evaluation of contact material and the improvement of product.

II METHOD & EXPERIMENT

In order to meet the need of engineering application, some principles were followed when the simulation testing device was designed: (1) action characteristic was the same as that of relay as possible, (2) mechanical parameters were stable and adjustable, (3) installation and dis-assembly of contact samples were convenient. The stability and reliability of the simulation apparatus have been verified in details in the previous work [7]. Here, the introduction are focused on the new added function. As shown in Fig. 1, the typical waveform of voltage and current between the contacts during one operation obtained by oscilloscope are given in Fig.1(a), the synchronous acquisition collected by testing system developed by self are give in Fig. 1(b). The primary information includes bounce times, the lasting time

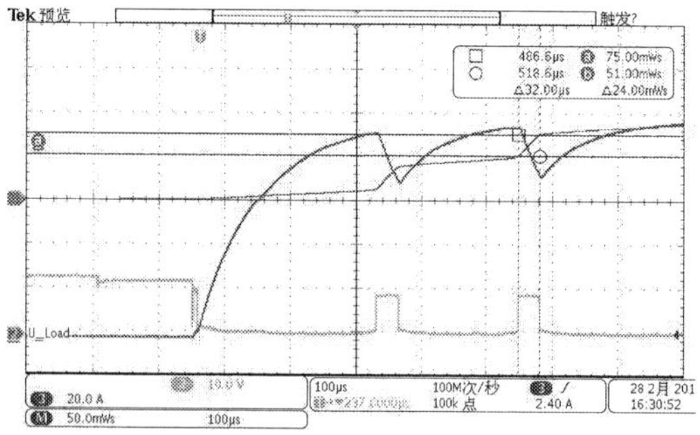

(a)

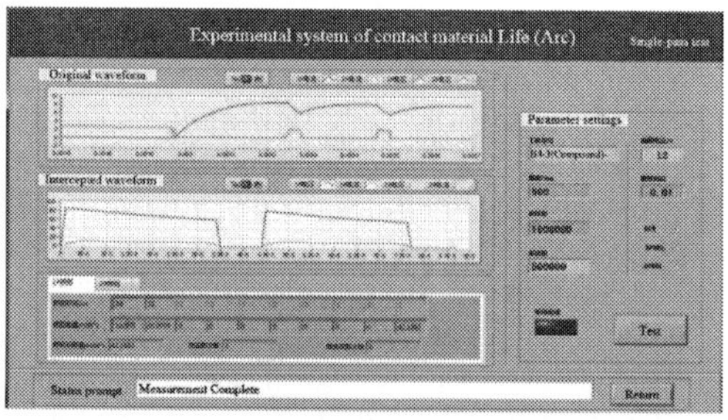

(b)

Fig. 1 Typical waveform of voltage and current between the contacts during operation of the simulation apparatus:
(a) obtained by oscilloscope;
(b) obtained by the testing system developed by self

Table I Comparison of the results between the testing system developed by self and the commercial precise devices

Parameter	Measured by testingsystem	Measured by precise devices
Steady current	29.7A	30V
Contact voltage drop	191mV	190 mV [a]
Bounce times	2	2
Arc lasting time	t_1=34 µs, t_2=32µs	t_1=33 µs, t_2=32µs
Arc energy	Arc_1=22.1mJ, Arc_2=20.0mJ	Arc_1=27.0mJ, Arc_2=24.0mJ

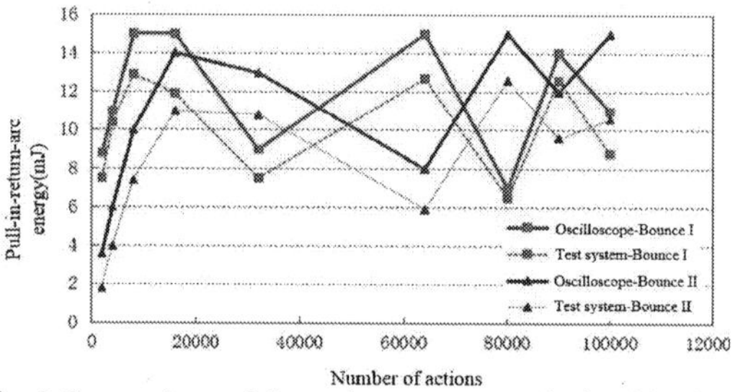

Fig. 2 Comparison of the make arc energy obtained by the testing system and oscilloscope after a certain time with the operation of the simulation apparatus

Table II The information of contact samples and experiment conditions

Contact materials	$Ag/SnO_2(10.5)/In_2O_3(4)$
Type of load	Analog lamp load
Class of load	13.5 VDC, Steady: 30 A, rush: 100A
Gap of contact	0.330mm
O.T. ofcontact	0.235 mm ~ 0.416mm

Table III The morphology of surface and longitudinal section of the contacts after experiment with different O.T. Values

O.T.		0.295mm	0.355mm	0.415mm	0.465mm
Movable contact	Morphology of surface		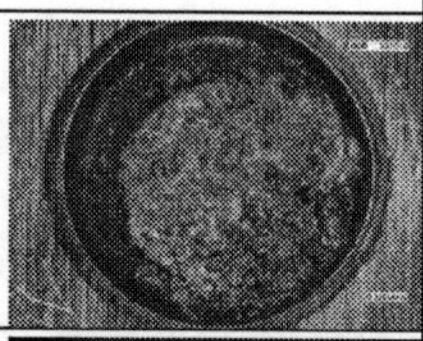	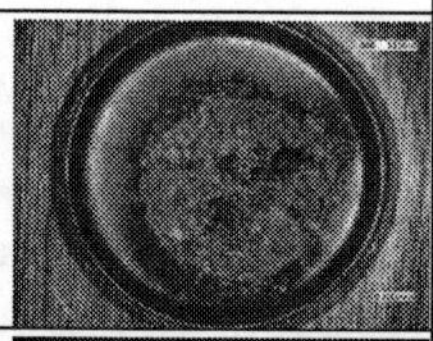	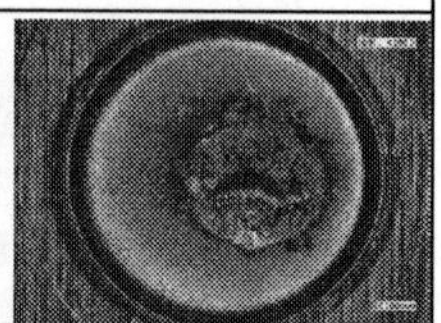
	Morphology of longitudinal section	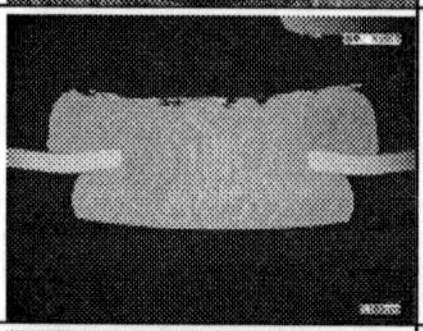	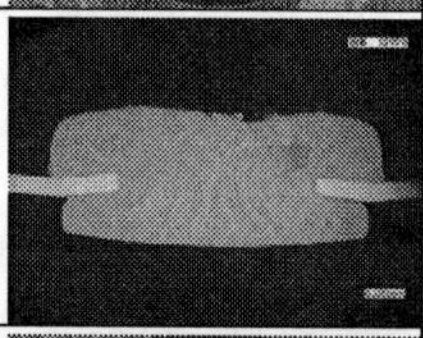	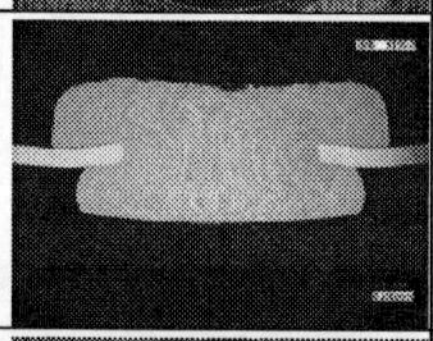	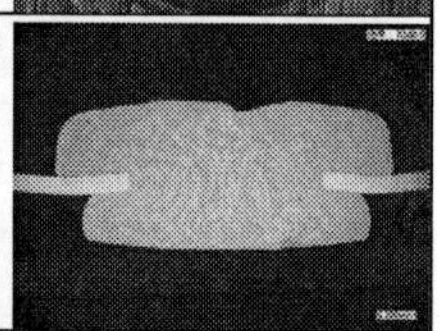
Static contact	Morphology of surface				
	Morphology of longitudinal section	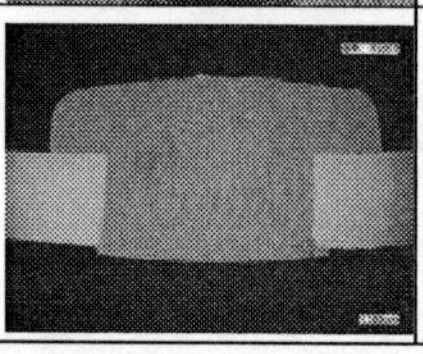	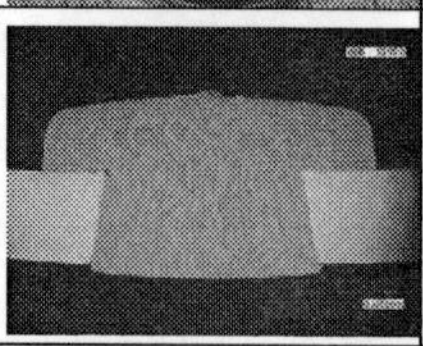	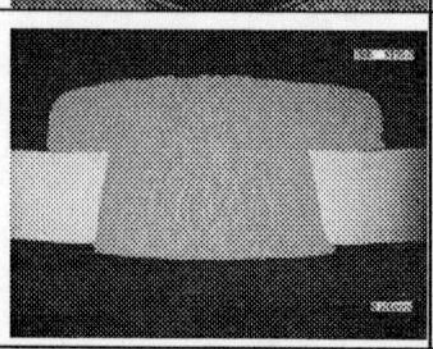	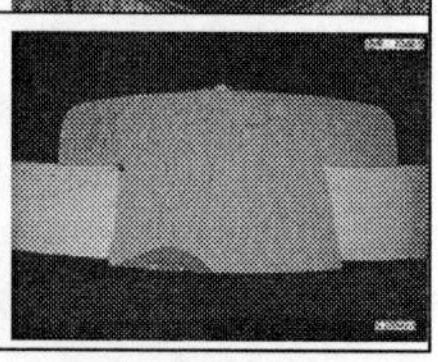

Of bounce, and arc energy. Here the arc energy Q is calculated using the resistance equivalent method, and it is shown as the following formula (1)

$$Q = \int UIdt \tag{1}$$

where, U, I, and t are the voltage, current and lasting time of arc, respectively.

Compared with oscilloscope, the testing system developed by self has the advantage in data collection and processing. That is, the parameters such as contact voltage drop, steady current, arc energy, lasting time of arc, bounce times and so on produced every operation during the whole electric life experiment can be automatically and continuously stored, and these procedural parameters will be useful for the evaluation of contact material and the improvement of product. In order to affirm the effectiveness of the testing system developed by self, the key output parameters has been compared with the results obtained by precision commercial instrument, such asoscill oscope(Mixed Domain Oscilloscope, MDO3014, Tektronix), tabletop multimeter (45 Dual Display Multimeter, FLUKE) and so on. The comparative results have been shown in TableI. Except for the arc energy, all the results match well. Though, there are some different on arc energy, the difference is relatively stable during the whole operation(See Fig. 2). This difference would be due to a kind of systematic error, which are needed to be further explored, but it would not have obvious influence on the relative value of arc energy. So, It can be considered that the testing system developed by self are effective.

The experiment procedure is almost the same as the introduction in the previous work[7]. In this work, it is noted that the O.T. of contact is variable, the sample information and test conditions are shown in TableII.

III. RESULTS &DISCUSSION

In the experiment, all the movable contacts are connected as anode pole, all the static contacts are connected as cathode pole. The weight of anode contact always shows obvious decrease, and the weight of cathode contact shows slight increase. This phenomenon is the same as the previous observation [7], and it can be associated with the mass transfer direction from anode to cathode in the case of metal phase arc. Because the weight of static contact increases not obvious (less than 0.5 mg), and the variation is disorder, the arc erosion on the effect of contact materials is described by the loss of movable contacts.

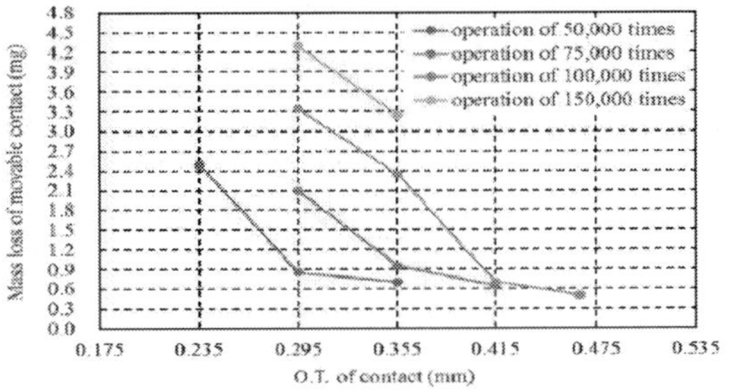

Fig. 3 The erosion of movable contact with different O. T.

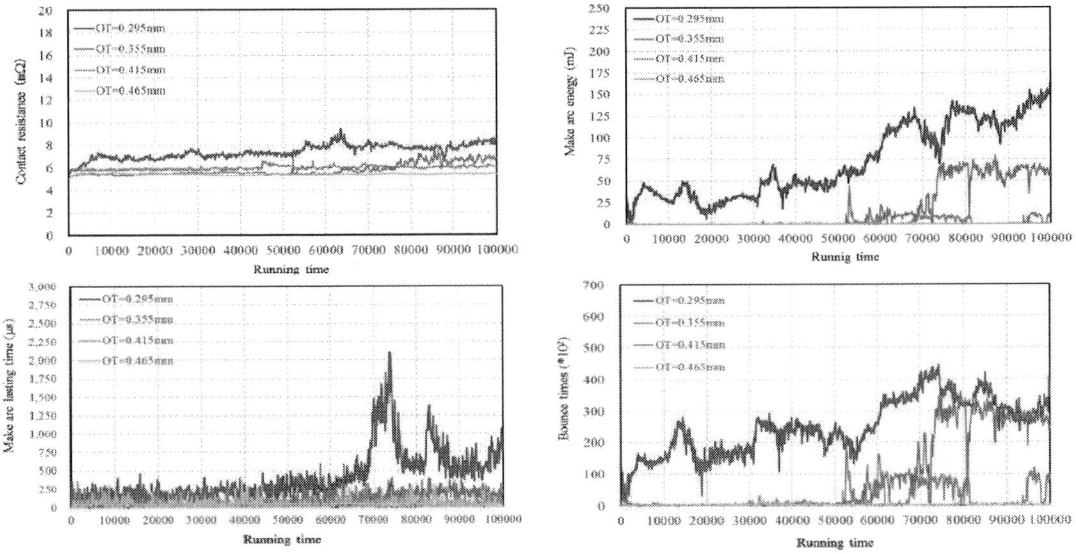

Fig. 4 The parameters during operation of the simulation apparatus with different O.T. values:
(a)contact resistance, (b) arc energy during make operation,
(c) arc time during make operation, (d) bounce times during make operation

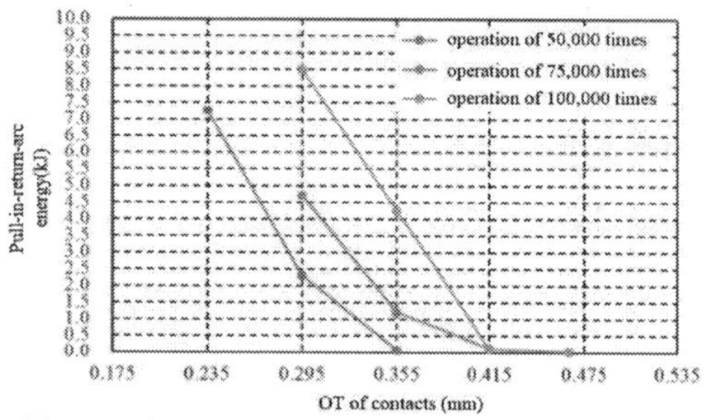

Fig. 5 The total arc energy during make operation withdifferentO.T.values

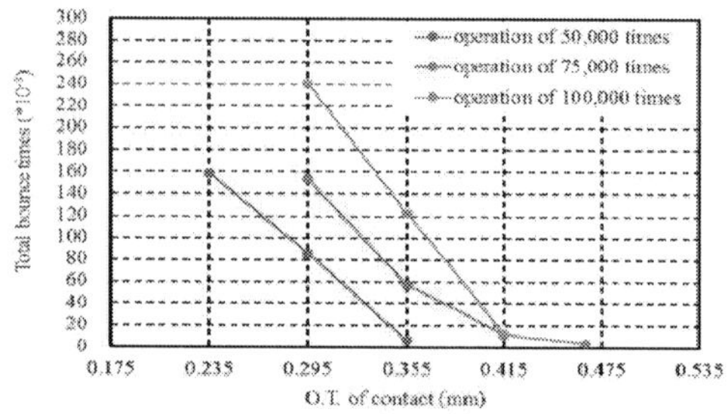

Fig. 6 The total bounce times during make operation withdifferentO.T.values

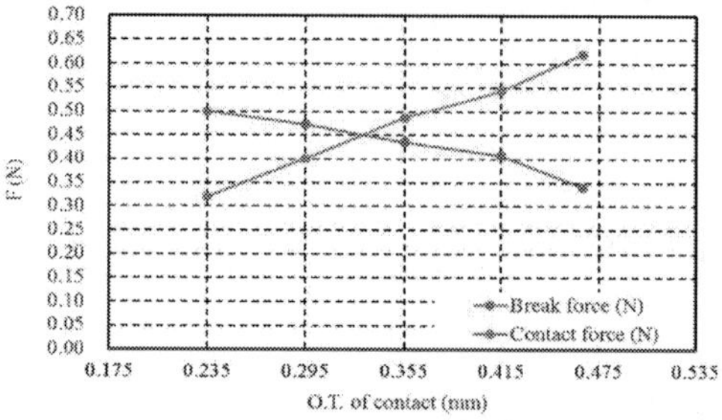

Fig. 7 Contact force and break force with different O.T. values

Fig. 3 gives the results of arc erosion on the effect of contact materials with different O.T. of contact. When the total operation time is the same, the weight of movable contact decreases obviously with the increasing O.T. (all the O.T. in this paper means over travel of contact). The morphology of surface and longitudinal section of the contacts after experiment (under 100,000 operation times) with different O.T. values are shown in Table III. With the increasing of O.T. values, the area and depth eroded by arc on the surface of contact decreases gradually. And this variation trend is associated with the consumption of the movable contact.

In order to explore the reason that the consumption of the movable contact decreases with increasing O.T., the data collected during every testing operation are analyzed. Fig.4givestheparametersofcontactresistance,arcenergy,lastin gtime of arc and bounce times as the variation of operation time. Here the average value of every 100 data is counted as one when plot for the former three parameters, while the sum value of every 100 data is counted as one for bounce times. All the contact resistance varied a little with different O.T. during the electric life operation, exceptfor O.T.=0.295mm. The variation of contact resistance would be associated with the uneven surface of the contact, the the distribution of oxides, and the aging of mechanical parameters. Within a long period, the arc energy for the O.T. of 0.335 mm, 0.415mm and 0.465mm is small. Whilefor O.T. of 0.295mm, the arc energy is large during the wholeo peration. Compared with the curve trend of arc lasting time and bounce times with operation times, the latter is closer to that of arc energy. It is proved that the bounce times can be used to predict the arc erosion of the contact. In order to verify this results further, arc energy and bounce times during the whole operation are accumulated, respectively (See Fig. 5 andFig.6). It is found that the variation trend of these two parameters almost the same with the change of O.T.. The reason that the consumption of the movable contact decreases with increasing O.T. can be due to the decrease of accumulated arc energy and bounce times. The bounce times are less when the O.T. value is larger, it can be associated with the contact force which can suppresses the production of bounce in a certain rang. Fig.7 gives the contact force and the break force of the movable spring before testing at different O.T. values. The former increases linearly with the increasing of O.T. values, while the latter varies oppositely. When O.T. increases, the contact force increases synchronously, the arc erosion on the effect of contact becomes weaker because of the decrease of bounce when make operation. Even in the case of break force reduced, the failure model of welding between contacts has not been found during the whole operation.

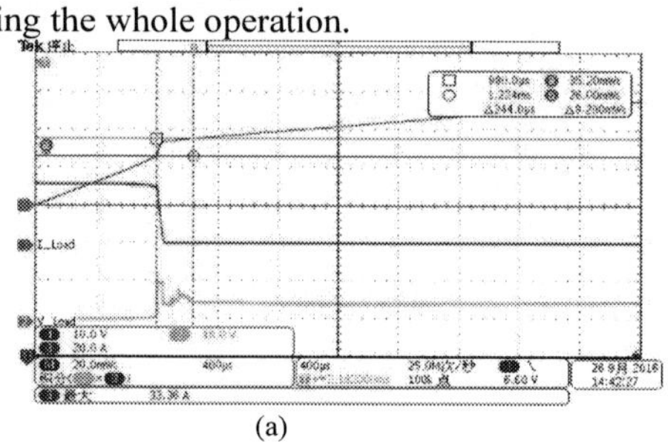

(a)

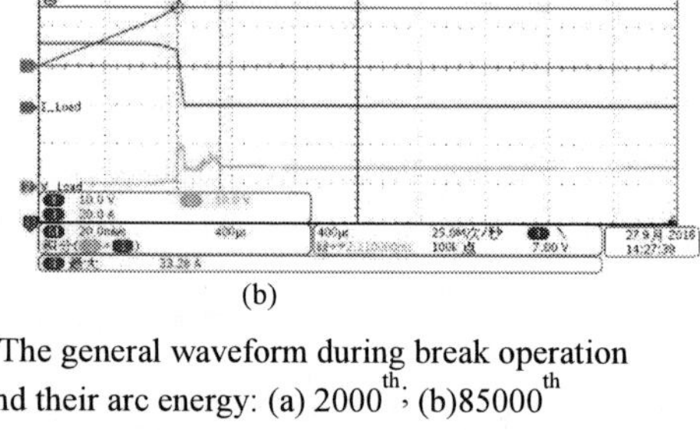

(b)

Fig. 8 The general waveform during break operation and their arc energy: (a) 2000th; (b)85000th

It is noted that the arc energy mentioned above happens at make operation, while the arc energy happens at break operation is due to the break of contact, there is no obvious bounce during every break operation, and it varies little(See Fig.8), so there is not too much discussion here.

CONCLUSIONS

The variation of key parameters during every operation, such as arc energy, lasting time of arc, bounce times and soon has been researched using the testing system developed by self. It is affirmed that the bounce times and arc energy decreases obviously with increasing O.T. of contact in a certain range. This result will be useful for the design and assembly of the relay. The testing system has the advantage in data collection and processing, it is expected to play an important role in the further study on the factors that affect the electrical life of relay, such as the hardness of contact, the size of the contact gap, the thermal stress characteristics of movable spring, and soon.

REFERENCES

[1] S. Tokumitsu and M. Hasegawa. Effective Shortening of Break Arc Durations of Ag and Several Ag-based Contacts in DC Load Conditions with Increased Contact Opening Speeds and External Magnetic Field. Proc. 64th IEEE Holm Conf. on Electrical Contacts, 2018, pp. 87-94.

[2] H.M. Liang, D.L. Liu, X. Zhou, and et. al.. Arc Behaviors of Three Kinds of Bridge-type Contacts when Opening a Resistive Load in Range of from 300VDC to th 750VDC. Proc. 64IEEE Holm Conf. on Electrical Contacts, 2018, pp. 81-93.

[3] Ningyi Lu, Fanbin Meng, and et al.. The Influence of Contacts Bounce on Relay Electric Life. Proc. 2 Int. Conf. on Reliability of Electrical Products and Electrical Contacts, 2007, pp. 179-182.

[4] Z.K. Chen and G. Witter. Evaluation of Contact nd Materials in Automotive Relay Applications. Proc. 2Int. Conf. on Reliability of Electrical Products and Electrical Contacts, 2007, pp. 73-78.

[5] B.O. Ciocirlan and H. Herrmann. Switching Contact th Bounce Reduction. Proc. 55IEEE Holm Conf. on Electrical Contacts, 2009, pp. 56-64.

[6] Xu Zhang, Zhe Zheng, and Wanbin Ren. An Experimental Investigation of Dynamic Welding Mechanism of Contacts Used in Low Current Switching th Devices. Proc. 64IEEE Holm Conf. on Electrical Contacts, 2018, pp. 488-495.

[7] Lei Yi and Ningyi Lu. Evaluation and Comparison of the Arc Erosion Characteristic of Ag/SnO2/In2O3 Contact Materials Used for An Automotive Relay. Proc. th 64IEEE Holm Conf. on Electrical Contacts, 2018, pp. 387-393.

7th International Conference on Reliability of
Electrical Products and Electrical Contacts,
November 04-06, 2019

Study on Closed Collision Bounce Characteristics and Contact Reliability of Contactors under Capacitive Load

Wenying Yang, Lanxiang Liu, Guofu Zhai
Institute of Reliability in Electrical Apparatus and Electronics
Harbin Institute of Technology, Harbin, 150001, China
E-mail: 18b906037@stu.hit.edu.cn Tel: 18845610982

***Abstract*— When the contactor is closed under capacitive load, a large surge current will be generated, which will aggravate the collision bounce of the contact and cause a large energy arc. The contact reliability of the contactor will be affected seriously in this case. At present, the studies on contact reliability under capacitive load currently are mainly conducted on the contact materials, contact resistance and arc behaviors. Few publications concerning the collision bounce parameters, dynamic contact process and mechanism of contactors can be found. Therefore, in this paper, the closed dynamic contact process of the contactor under surge current is analyzed firstly. Then, based on the impact function method, the intermittent collision model between the movable contact and the static contact is constructed, and the dynamic model of the contact closure collision bounce for the contactor under capacitive load is established. After that, the theoretical calculation and experimental verification of the bouncing time, amplitude and numbers of the contact closed collision under surge current are carried out. Finally, the changing regularity of the bouncing characteristics for the contactor under different operating voltages and capacitance is analyzed in detail. The research results are of great value to improve the surge handling capability and contact reliability of contactors.**

***Index Terms*— Contactor, Collision bounce, Capacitive load, Contact reliability, Surge current**

I. INTRODUCTION

The capacitive load in power network can cause overvoltage or overcurrent at the moment of contactor contact closure, and the contact will be damaged by transient arc ablation due to over electric stress. The process of contact arc ablation is often intertwined with contact collision bounce. The joint action of collision bounce and surge current can accelerate the degradation of contact resistance and the transfer of contact material, and aggravate the surface melting of moving and static contacts, which will lead to the failure of contactor adhesion and affect its reliability.

In recent years, many scholars have studied the contact dynamic characteristics of load circuits. Chen and Witter [1] found that the short-term and small-distance bounce causes high intensity contact fusion welding by studying the mechanical parameters of silver alloy contacts. Neuhaus et al. [2-3] used a two-mass three-spring mechanical-mathematical dynamic model to describe the relationship between welding force and contact dynamic parameters. It was found that the fusion welding force increases with the increment of arc, decreases with the increment of collision velocity, and was not affected by static contact force. However, they did not give the dynamic characteristics of contact bounce in the dynamic action process. Based on the experimental results, Rieder and Neuhaus [4] established the relationship between contact collision bounce and arc, and they found that short bounce arc produces stronger welding force. Haase and Berger [5] used MATLAB/Simulink to establish a switching simulation model of the contact system, and the current and arc-pressure curves of the collision bounce process under different electrical loads were calculated. Hotta and Inaguchi [6] designed experiments to investigate the contact welding mechanism between contact bounce and arc. It was found that the bounce arc provides electric energy to the contact surface and heats the contact to form melting spots. Ren et al. [7-9] simulated the dynamic contact process by means of simulation test. It was found that a strong fusion welding force appeared during the collision bounce time of the contact, and the welding process was closely related to the contact collision in the closing process [7]. Through the capacitance test of silver tin oxide contact material, the change rule of contact resistance and contact force with the operation period is analyzed. It was found that the anodic arc caused by contact impact bounce under capacitive load plays a leading role in contact corrosion [8]. The mechanical parameters of the switch contact were determined, and the contradiction between reducing the arc duration and the collision bounce time was solved to a certain extent [9]. Liang et al. [10] designed a load circuit and test program with adjustable surge current time behaviors, and the behaviors of contact breaking arc and closed bounce under surge load were analyzed. The above researches mainly focused on the contact material, contact resistance and arc characteristics to study the contact dynamics of the contact. Based on this, Kharin et al. [11] established a hybrid mathematical model of contact motion in contact area based on nonlinear equations of contact motion and experimental data such as current, voltage, contact resistance and contact distance. In reference [12-14], a new protection circuit against surge current is proposed, which plays an important role in suppressing collision bounce and arc under surge load.

Based on above analyses, the collision bounce process will increase the safety hazard of the contacts. Therefore, we hope to accurately describe this collision bounce process to ensure that collision bounce is suppressed as much as possible during load switching. At the same time, the contact stabilization time is reduced to the minimum, which can reduce the arc ablation and improve the reliability of the contactor. In this study, the influence of surge current on the dynamic behavior of the collision bounce for a certain type contactor is analyzed. Then, according to the working characteristics of the load loop, the contact dynamics model of the closed collision bounce of the contact under capacitive load is established. The dynamic behaviors of intermittent collision bounce between moving and static contacts are calculated based on the impact function. After that, the correctness of the bounce calculation results is verified by the design experiment. Finally, the effects of different loop voltages and capacitances on the collision bounce of the contact are analyzed. The research results in this study have guiding significance for improving the surge resistance of the contactor and suppressing the contact welding caused by the bounce arc.

II. CONTACT PROCESS AND MODEL EQUIVALENCE

Fig. 1 shows a typical contactor control load circuit. E_e is the power supply; C_{ts} and C_{to} are the static and moving contacts; E_s is a switch to control the on-off of the load circuit; C and R are the total equivalent capacitance and resistance; I, I_c and I_r are the main loop current, branch C current, and branch R current.

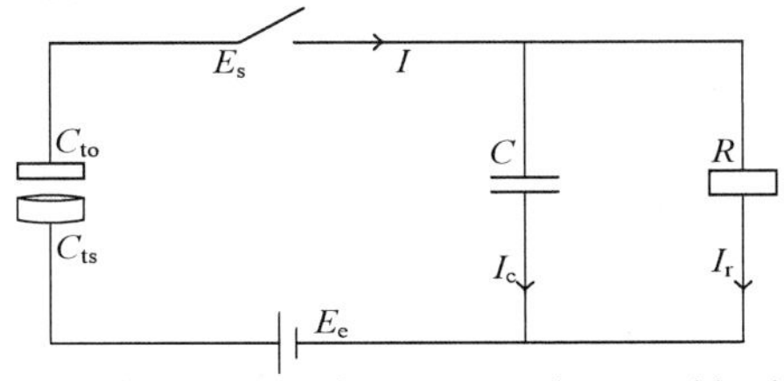

Fig. 1 Working circuit of contactor under capacitive load.

Power lines usually contain capacitance elements or other additional capacitors. When E_s is closed, the capacitor element needs to be charged through resistance and generate surge current in the circuit until the steady state voltage is reached. If the load resistance is small, the loop surge current will be very large. When the moving contact is closed, the capacitor connected to the contact starts to charge, and the surge current generates an electric repulsion between the moving and static contacts, which separates the moving and static contacts. Due to the existence of electromagnetic and elastic forces, the moving contact is forced to move to the static contact again, which increases the probability of collision bouncing and aggravates the contact environment.

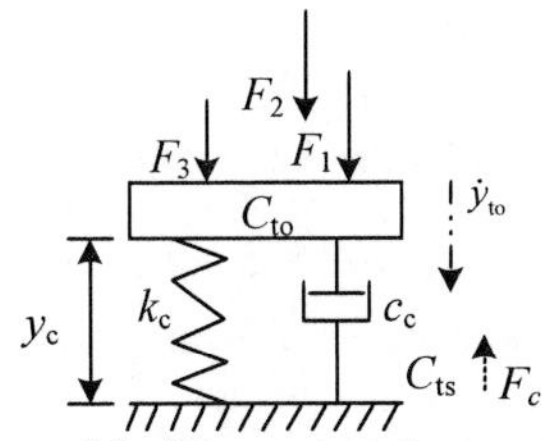

Fig. 2 Dynamic model of the contact closure collision bounce.

Fig. 2 shows the equivalent dynamic model of the contact closure collision bounce. In Fig. 2, k_c and c_c are the contact stiffness and damping coefficients; y_c is the distance between moving and static contacts; F_1 and F_2 denote the electric repulsive force and resultant force acting on the moving contact; and F_3 is the collision force. The mass of the moving contact is denoted by m_{to}; t_{to} is the moving time of the contact; y_{to} represents the displacement of the moving contact; and F_c denotes the spring force.

Under capacitive load, the resultant force F acting on the contact is changed due to the surge current flowing through the contact, which affects the collision bounce characteristics of the contact. In Fig.2, the collision between moving and static contacts is a rigid collision, and the static contact is a fixed structure. The moving contact moves towards the static contact at speed v_{to}. When the two contacts come into contact with each other, the contact surface begins to deform. In this process, the kinetic energy of the moving contact is mostly converted into the deformation energy of the contact material except for a part of the contact friction and the dielectric damping. When the surface of the contact reaches the maximum deformation x_b, the deformation energy of the contact reaches the maximum, and the kinetic energy of the moving contact becomes zero, that is, the motion stops. After that, the elastic deformation of the contact begins to recover, and the energy is released. The moving contact starts to move in the opposite direction with the speed v_{t2}, that is, the motion of the contact moves into the bounce stage. When the kinetic energy of the moving contact is completely transformed into the elastic potential energy of the overtravel spring, the moving contact stops moving in the opposite direction, and the moving contact bounce reaches the maximum value x_m. Afterwards, the moving contact starts to move towards the direction of the static contact under the action of F_1, and the second collision and bounce occur. Part of the energy is consumed during each cycle of the collision bounce process of the moving contact. When the maximum kinetic energy of the moving contact is less than the elastic potential energy stored by the overtravel spring due to the preload, the collision bounce of the moving contact no longer occurs, that is, the collision bounce process of the contact ends. In addition, when the bounce distance of the moving contact is smaller than the deformation of the contact, there is still a collision process between the moving and static contacts, but it is very weak. At this time, it is considered that moving and static contacts are no longer separated and the collision bounce process of the contact ends.

III. CONTACT FORCE AND COLLISION BOUNCE

A. Mathematical model of electric repulsion

When the contactor switches the capacitive load, the current passing through the contact is limited to a very small area, and the electric repulsive force is generated between the moving and static contacts, including the Holm force caused by the current contraction between the contacts and the Lorentz force generated by the conductive circuit. The Holm force exists for a short time on the overtravel stage of the contact. When the moving and static contacts are separated, it does not exist, and the Lorentz force exists until the arc is extinguished [15-16].

In this study, the contactor is a direct acting structure, and the electric repulsive force $F_1 = F_{holm}$ without considering the arc ablation. In order to obtain the electric repulsive force, the following assumptions are made:

1) All the conductive spots on the contact surface concentrate on the center to form a large conductive spot.
2) The conductive spot on the contact surface is an allotropic superconducting sphere.

Then the electric repulsive force F_1 between contacts can be calculated by the following formula [17]:

$$F_1 = 4.45\times10^{-7} I_m^2 \tag{1}$$

where I_m is surge current.

In Fig 1, the contactor control loop is connected to the capacitive load, and the circuit is in zero initial state before the switch E_s is closed, i.e. $U_c(0_-)=0$. At $t=0$, the switch E_s is closed and the circuit is connected to the DC voltage U_s. The circuit equation of the load loop can be expressed as

$$\begin{cases} E_e = U_c + IR_t \\ I = I_c + I_r \end{cases} \tag{2}$$

where R_t is the contact resistance.

B. Forced-force mathematical model

The force F_2 acting on the moving contact is the resultant force of the electromagnetic force F_m and spring force F_c. The basic equations for solving electromagnetic force are written as follows:

$$\begin{cases} \nabla\times\dfrac{1}{\mu}\nabla\times \boldsymbol{A} = \boldsymbol{J}_s + \boldsymbol{J}_e \\ \boldsymbol{J}_e = -\sigma\left(\dfrac{\partial \boldsymbol{A}}{\partial t} + \nabla\varphi\right) \\ \nabla\cdot \boldsymbol{J}_e = 0 \\ \boldsymbol{B} = \nabla\times\boldsymbol{A} \\ \boldsymbol{H} = \dfrac{1}{\mu}\boldsymbol{B} \end{cases} \tag{3}$$

where $\boldsymbol{A}$ is the magnetic potential vector; $\boldsymbol{J}_s$ and $\boldsymbol{J}_e$ are the current density and eddy current density; μ is the magnetic permeability; σ and φ are the conductivity and the electric potential; $\boldsymbol{B}$ is the magnetic flux density; and $\boldsymbol{H}$ is the magnetic field intensity.

$$\begin{cases} dW_m = \int_0^B \boldsymbol{H}d\boldsymbol{B} \\ W_m = \int_V (dW_m)dV \\ F_m = \dfrac{\partial W_m}{\partial y_1} \end{cases} \tag{4}$$

where W_m is the energy of magnetic field and V is the volume of the solution domain.

The magnetic field strength can be obtained by Eq. (3). Then, the relationship between magnetic field energy and flux density, magnetic field intensity and magnetic field energy density is obtained by Eq. (4), and then the F_m is obtained by the virtual work method. The spring force F_c can be expressed as

$$\begin{cases} f_c = f_{c1} + k_{c1}y & 0\le y < 2.7 \\ f_c = f_{c1} + f_{c2} + (k_{c1}+k_{c2})y & 1.7 \le y \le 2.7 \end{cases} \tag{5}$$

where f_{c1} and k_{c1} are the preload and stiffness of overtravel spring, f_{c2} and k_{c2} represent the preload and stiffness of return spring.

C. Mathematical model of collision bounce

To describe the intermittent state of the contact, the impact function is used to define the collision force, including the elastic force produced by the mutual cutting into each other and the damping force caused by the relative motion. When the contact is detected, the corresponding contact force element is added to the contact surface until the contact is separated. According to the penetration depth of the moving contact, the contact force F_p is given directly by the impact function. The equation of motion of the moving contact is established as:

$$M_{to}\ddot{y}_{to} + c_{c1}\dot{y}_{to} + k_{c1}y_{to} = F \tag{6}$$

where c_{c1} is the damping coefficient of the overtravel spring.

Since each collision contact of the moving and static contacts causes partial energy loss, the collision damping D is introduced to simulate the energy loss during the collision of the moving and static contacts. The impact force F_p is mainly determined by the stiffness coefficient k, the collision index n, the damping coefficient D and the penetration depth δ. It can be expressed as

$$F_p = \begin{cases} 0 & if\ q > q_0 \\ k\delta^n + D\dot{\delta} & if\ q \le q_0 \end{cases} \quad (7)$$

where q and q_0 are the actual and initial distances of the two colliding objects. The collision index n denotes the material nonlinear degree of the colliding object, which is related to the collision contact area. The coefficient D is simulated by the damping coefficient c and the motion function, and the variation range of c is determined by δ. When $\delta > d$, the value of the coefficient D is equal to c. When $0 < \delta < d$, the value of the coefficient D is determined by the motion function.

IV. CALCULATION OF COLLISION BOUNCE AND ANALYSIS OF INFLUENCING FACTORS

A. Surge current

By analyzing the working circuit of the contactor in Fig. 1, the main circuit current of the capacitive load C charging through the circuit resistance R_1 can be obtained and the surge current flowing through the contact can be calculated. The results are shown in Table 1. In the calculation, R_t = 0.32mΩ, R_2 = 22Ω, C = 220μF, and E_e = 1.5V.

Table 1 The surge currents flowing through the contact under different voltages.

E_e/(V)	2	4	6	8
I_{m1}/(A)	6250	12500	18750	25000

Table 2 The surge currents flowing through the contact under different contact resistances.

R_t/(mΩ)	0.07	0.21	0.42	0.63
I_{m3}/(A)	21430	7143	3571	2381

It can be noted from Tables 1 and 2 that the surge current is closely related to the power supply voltage and contact resistance. The surge current is positively correlated with circuit voltage, but it is negatively correlated with contact resistance. That is to say, the surge current increases with the increase of the circuit voltage, and it decreases with the increase of the contact resistance. Moreover, the surge current varies linearly with the change of the circuit voltage and contact resistance.

B. Moving contact displacement

The surge current flowing through the contact under different parameters can be obtained by changing the circuit voltage and contact resistance. Based on the electric repulsion model, the electric repulsion acting on the contacts under specific conditions can be calculated. The dynamic characteristics of the moving contact can be calculated by interacting with the electromagnetic force mathematical model and the collision bouncing model, and the bouncing status of the moving contact under the capacitive load can be obtained. The whole dynamic process is divided into several time periods, and the Runge-Kutta iterative calculation is preformed in each time period Δt until the calculation in the whole time t is completed. The specific calculation flow is shown in Fig 3.

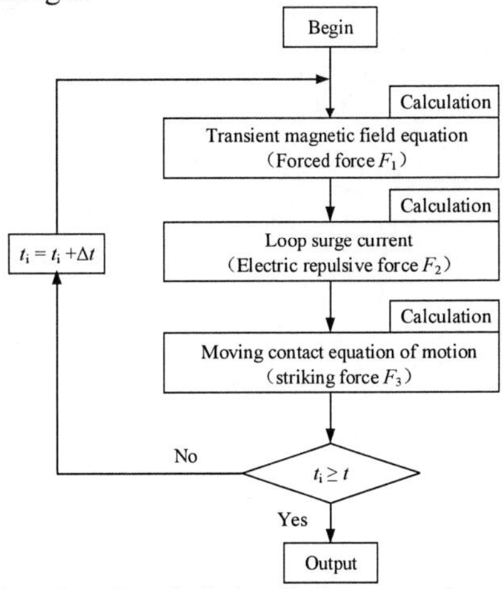

Fig. 3 Flow chart for calculating displacement of moving contact

Fig. 4 displays the time displacement curves of the moving contact obtained by the theoretical and experimental methods. In the calculation, the surge current is equal to 3.125kA. It can be found from the figure that the theoretical results are in good agreement with the experimental results. The experimental bounce time of the moving contact is 0.69 ms, and the bounce amplitude is 58μm. The theoretical calculation bounce time and amplitude are 0.63 ms and 62μm. The relative errors of the bounce time and amplitude between theoretical and experimental results are equal to 9% and 7%.

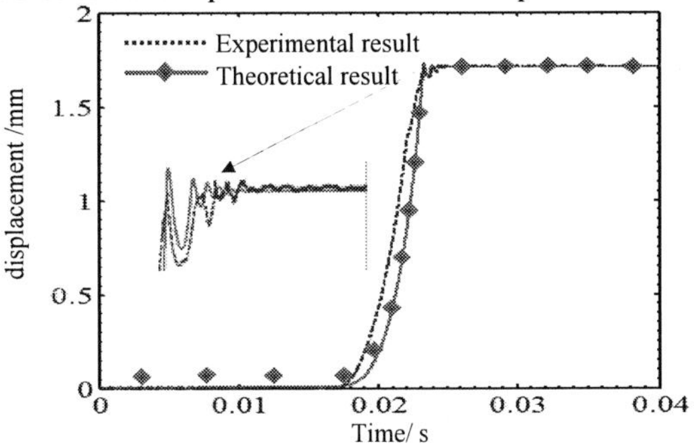

Fig. 4 Curve of displacement of moving contact with time

C. Effect of circuit voltage on contact bounce

Fig. 5 shows the displacement curves of the moving contact under different voltages. When the circuit voltage equals to 0, the bounce time and amplitude of the moving contact are equal to 0.56 ms and 63 μm. It is seen that, with the increase of the circuit voltage, the bounce amplitude and time of the moving contact increase. The relationship between the bounce amplitude and time of the moving contact and the circuit voltage is obtained and the results are shown in Fig. 6.

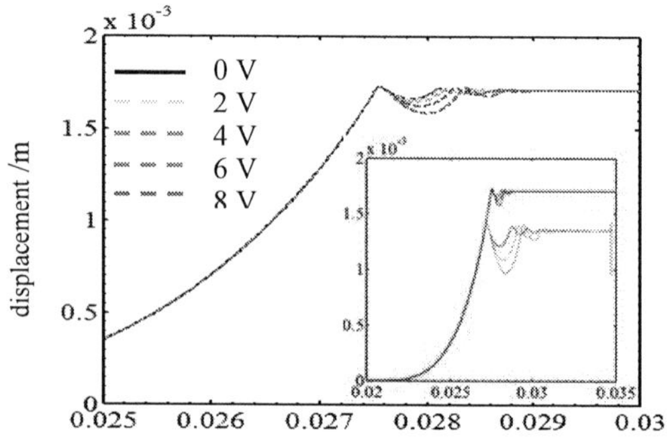

Fig. 5 Displacement curves of the moving contact under different voltages.

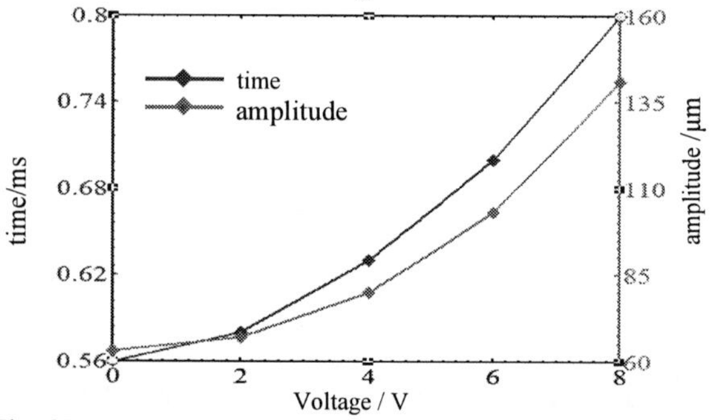

Fig. 6 Bounce characteristic curves of the moving contact under different circuit voltages.

It can be seen that the bounce amplitude and time of the moving contact increase approximately linearly with the increase of the circuit voltage. The surge current changes with the change of the circuit voltage, which will affect the resultant force acting on the moving contact and changes the dynamic characteristics of the moving contact. When the circuit voltage is small, the moving contact tends to be stable after several main bounces, and the moving and static contacts can be closed reliably. When the circuit voltage and current are large, the moving contact shows the stability time becomes longer after the main bouncing. Especially when the circuit voltage and surge current equal to 8 V and 2.5kA, the bounce amplitude and time of the moving contact are equal to 141μm and 0.8ms, which are about 2 and 1.5 times of the bounce amplitude and time for the contactor without the capacitive load. It can be seen from Fig. 5 and Fig. 6 that the bounce amplitude of the moving contact is strengthened in the later period of the bounce. If the circuit voltage is continuously increased, the moving contact will not work reliably because of the large electric repulsion force.

When the electric repulsive force generated by the surge current of the load circuit is small enough, the influence of the capacitive load on the bounce of the moving contact can be ignored. We assume that when the increase of the moving contact bounce amplitude with the surge current is less than 1% of that of the contactor without capacitive load, the influence of capacitive load on the contact bounce can be ignored. By calculation, when the loop current is equal to 2.33kA, the bounce amplitude of the moving contact is 63.63 μm, and the increase of the bounce amplitude relative to the zero loop voltage is equal to 1%. Therefore, when the surge current is less than 2.33kA, the influence of the capacitive load on the bounce of the moving contact can be ignored. At this time, the bounce time of the moving contact is approximately equal to that of the contactor with zero-loop voltage.

D. Effect of contact resistance on contact bounce

To study the effect of contact resistance on the contact bounce, the bounce amplitudes and time of the moving contact under different contact resistances are displayed in Table 3. In the table, a_b and t_b are the bounce amplitude and time of the moving contact.

Table 3 Bounce characteristics of the moving contact under different contact resistances

R_t/(mΩ)	0.63	0.42	0.21	0.07
a_b/(μm)	64	65	69	117
t_b/(ms)	0.56	0.57	0.59	0.74

When the contact resistance is changed, the bounce time and amplitude of the moving contact are also changed. It is found from Fig. 5 and Table 3 that the bounce characteristic of the moving contact with R_t= 0.63 mΩ are approximately the same as that of the contactor with zero loop voltage, and the bounce amplitudes and time are equal to 64 μm and 0.56 ms. In addition, when contact resistance is greater than 0.21 mΩ, the bounce characteristics of the moving contact do not change much. However, the bounce amplitude of the moving contact with R_t = 0.07mΩ is about 2 times as much as that of the moving contact with R_t=0.63mΩ. Therefore, under the same capacitive load and circuit voltage, the reduction of contact resistance will make the contact more conductive. Moreover, the increase of surge current leads to the increase of electric repulsion force between moving contact and static contact, which makes the bounce of the moving contact more severely.

V. CONCLUSION

In this study, the dynamic characteristics of the intermittent collision bounce between moving and static contacts are calculated based on the impact function. The following key observations can be obtained:

1) The model presented in this study can effectively simulate the contact bouncing process under capacitive load. The error between theoretical calculation and experimental

results can be controlled within 10%.

2) The circuit voltage and contact resistance have an important influence on the surge current flowing through the contact. The surge current is positively correlated with the circuit voltage and negatively correlated with the contact resistance.

3) The bounce characteristics of the moving contact are closely related to the circuit voltage and contact resistance. The bounce of the moving contact increases with the increase of the circuit voltage and decreases with the increase of the contact resistance.

ACKNOWLEDGMENT

This research was supported by the Youth Foundation Project of the National Natural Science Foundation of China (Project-No. 51507033).

REFERENCES

[1] Z. Chen and G. Witter, "Dynamic welding of silver contacts under different mechanical bounce conditions," IEEE 45th Holm Conference on Electrical Contacts, 1999, pp. 1-8.

[2] A. R. Neuhaus, W. F. Rieder and M. Hammerschmidt, "Influence of arc duration and current on contact welding in low power switches," IEEE 48th Holm Conference on Electrical Contacts, 2002, pp. 17-20.

[3] A. R. Neuhaus, W. F. Rieder and M. Hammerschmidt, "Influence of electrical and mechanical parameters on contact welding in low power switches, IEEE Transactions on Components and Packaging Technologies, vol. 27, no. 1, pp. 4-11, 2004.

[4] W. F. Rieder and A. R. Neuhaus, "Short arc modes determining both contact welding and material transfer," IEEE Transactions on Components and Packaging Technologies, vol. 30, no. 1, pp. 9-14, 2007.

[5] R. Haase and F. Berger, "Simulation of relay contact bouncing including a short arc model," The 27th International Conference on Electrical Contacts. Dresden, June 2014, pp. 540-545.

[6] K. Hotta and T. Inaguchi, "Dependence of contact weld force on arc energy supplied to contact surface in low voltage switches," IEEE 61th Holm Conference on Electrical Contacts, 2015, pp. 160-165.

[7] W. B. Ren, J. B. Jin, Y. H. Fu and C. Chang, "A novel test rig for in situ and real time measurement of welding force and impact force of contacts within electromagnetic relay," IEEE 60th Holm Conference on Electrical Contacts, 2014, pp. 1-7.

[8] W. B. Ren, J. M. Wei, X. Zhang et al., "Preliminary study on switching characteristics of silver tin oxide type contacts for capacitive load," IEEE Holm Conference on Electrical Contacts, 2017, pp. 63-68.

[9] W. B. Ren, S. J. Ma, G. F. Zhai, et al., "The effect of mechanical parameters of switch-type contact on relay operation characteristics," IEEE 57th Holm Conference on Electrical Contacts, 2011, pp. 1-5.

[10]H. M. Liang, H. D. Yu, G. C. Ma, et al., "Surge load experiment design and results analysis of relay," IEEE 61th Holm Conference on Electrical Contacts, 2015, pp. 107-110.

[11]S. N. Kharin, "Role of metallic vapor pressure in contact bouncing and welding at closure of electrical contacts in vacuum," IEEE 58th Holm Conference on Electrical Contacts, 2012, pp. 1-7.

[12]S. N. Kharin, H. Nouri and D. Amft, "Dynamics of arc phenomena at closure of electrical contacts in vacuum circuit breakers," IEEE Transactions on Plasma Science, vol. 33, no. 5, pp. 1576-1581, 2005.

[13]H. Honma, S. Kimura, K. Shoji, et al., "Arc discharge and surge suppression during a breaking operation of a magnetic relay," IEEE 53th Holm Conference on Electrical Contacts, 2007, pp. 280-283.

[14] N. Wakatsuki and Y. Yonezawa, "Relay contact of multi-electrodes with timely controlled operation for arc discharge suppression," IEEE 50th Holm Conference on Electric Contacts, 2004, pp. 474-479.

[15]W. Yang, M. Z. Rong, X. H. Wang, et al., "Dynamic simulation of high-voltage circuit breaker concerning electrodynamic force," Proceedings of the CSEE, 2003, 23(5): 103-107.

[16]X. W. Li, D. G. Chen, H. G. Xiang, et al., "3-D finite element nonlinear analysis and experimental investigation of electro-dynamic repulsion force in molded case circuit breakers. Proceedings of the CSEE, 2004, 24(2): 150-155.

[17]P. Slade, Electrical contacts: principles and applications, CRC Press, 2017.

Wenying Yang received the Ph.D. degree in Electrical Machinery and Apparatus from Harbin Institute of Technology, Harbin, China, in 2009. Presently, he is an Associate Professor at Harbin Institute of Technology, Harbin, China. His research interests include computational electromagnetics, electromagnetic capability, and digital simulation and optimization of electromagnetic devices.

Lanxiang Liu received the M.S. degree in Electrical Engineering from Harbin Institute of Technology, Harbin, China, in 2018. She is a Ph.D. Candidate in the Electrical Engineering Department at Harbin Institute of Technology. Her research interests include electrical numerical analysis, and digital simulation and electrical contact reliability design theory.

Guofu Zhai received the Ph.D. degree in Testing and Measuring Technology and Instruments from Harbin Institute of Technology, Harbin, China, in 1998. Presently, he is a Professor at Harbin Institute of Technology, Harbin, China. His research interests include electrical contacts and the reliability and testing technique of electrical apparatus.

Reliability Evaluation Method and Simulation of Sampling Test for Transient Electronic Products

Jingde Huang, Benfu Jiang, Yansheng Zhang
Zhuhai College of Jilin University, Zhuhai, 519041,China
E-mail: jdh925@sina.com Tel: 86-756-7626130 Fax: 86-756-7626130

***Abstract*—The electronic equipment with transient working sequence, its function is in a silent state for a long time, and there is no external excitation and working response, however, its working reliability is still affected by the storage environment factors (such as temperature, humidity, air pressure, etc.) and the technological level in the production process. In this paper, a sampling test scheme and simulation method for transient electronic products reliability are proposed. A prior distribution model before sampling inspection is established, then a sampling test scheme for reliability is designed and the reliability trend prediction model of the transient electronic products which is waiting to be used is established. Finally, the validity of the reliability sampling test scheme is verified by experiments.**

***Index Terms*—Transient electronic products, Working reliability, prior distribution, Trend prediction**

I. INTRODUCTION

Transient electronic products are mostly sophisticated control modules or instruments with high cost, integrated functions and complex structures, such as electronic startup modules for missiles, precision guided munitions, aircraft, etc.It has typical high reliability requirements, and its working reliability only has two states of success or failure. The reliability characteristic quantity is the number of success in the test. Transient electronic products must perform functions at a specified time when they receive requests, and when they do not perform functions, they are regarded as failures. Because of the improvement of system complexity and the limitation of test conditions, it is almost impossible to carry out reliability test for the whole system. Theoretically, the reliability of transient electronic products during the period of no work is mainly controlled by the failure mechanism of potential long-term dormancy storage and production process variables. The existing conventional sampling theory, test scheme, reliability evaluation method and accelerated life test theory and method can not meet the needs of technical maintenance. In order to ensure the reliability level of this kind of electronic equipment, reliability sampling test must be carried out to check whether the reliability of this kind of system meets the required requirements. This paper focuses on the reliability test verification scheme of transient electronic products during silence period, to solve the outstanding contradiction between the high reliability requirements of transient electronic products and silent failure, and to ensure the working performance of the system.

II. DETERMINATION OF PRIOR DISTRIBUTION OF SAMPLED OBJECTS

When sampling acceptance test of small sample reliability for transient electronic products is carried out, Firstly, Bayes method is used to determine the prior distribution of the sample.

Assuming that the probability of success of the batch sample test is p, then the probability of failure is $q=1-p$, the number of successful times Γ of corresponding n sampled products obeys binomial distribution

$$P(\Gamma \mid p)=\begin{bmatrix} n \\ \Gamma \end{bmatrix} p^{\Gamma}(1-p)^{n-\Gamma} \qquad (1)$$

In order to formulate reliability sampling test scheme by Bayes method, the products participating in the sampling test must be selected, the prior distribution of its success probability p is given. Consider choosing its conjugate distribution $\beta(a,b)$ as its prior distribution, i.e.

$$\pi(p)=\frac{1}{\beta(a,b)}p^{a-1}(1-p)^{b-1}, 0<p<1, a>0, b>0 \quad (2)$$

For different hyper parameters a and b, the probability density function curves of prior distribution $\beta(a,b)$ are different.

If $a>1$, $b>1$, then the probability density function curve is single peak, and when $\tilde{p}=\frac{a-1}{a+b-2}$, $\pi(\tilde{p})$ reaches the maximum.

If $a \geq b$, then $E(p) \leq \tilde{p}$, when the median p_m satisfies $E(p) \leq p_m \leq \tilde{p}$, then

$$P(p \geq E(p)) \geq P(p \geq p_m)=0.5 \qquad (3)$$

If $a>1$ and $b \leq 1$, the probability density function of their prior distribution $\beta(a,b)$ is singular and satisfies

$$P(p \geq E(p)) \geq 0.5 \tag{4}$$

Considering that the reliability sampling test of transient electronic products belongs to a typical small sample test, the estimation $\hat{p}$ of the average probability $E(p_{(1)})$ of product success can be obtained by making full use of the test information during the production and development of products. Considering that $\hat{p}$ is the estimate of $E(p_{(1)})$, the two estimates are not exactly equal, so the following assumptions can be made

$$P(p \geq \hat{p}) \geq 0.3 \tag{5}$$

Because transient electronic products are constantly eroded by environmental factors during storage, the reliability level of products after regular storage is reduced appropriately. The following assumptions are made

$$P(p \geq 0.3 p_1) \geq 0.9 \tag{6}$$

which p_1 is the indicator of success probability.

According to the above formulas, the simultaneous equations are solved.

$$\begin{cases} P(p \geq \hat{p}) \geq 0.3 \\ P(p \geq 0.3 p_1) \geq 0.9 \end{cases} \tag{7}$$

The parameters a and b in the prior distribution $\beta(a,b)$ are obtained, so $\beta(a,b)$ can be used as the prior distribution of p.

III. DESIGN OF SAMPLING TEST SCHEME

Assuming that the test data of transient electronic products to be sampled is (n,Γ), there are n products to be tested. If the number of successful products is Γ, the likelihood function is as follows:

$$l(p \mid \Gamma) = \begin{bmatrix} n \\ \Gamma \end{bmatrix} p^{\Gamma}(1-p)^{n-\Gamma} \tag{8}$$

So the posterior distribution of P is as follows:

$$h(p \mid \Gamma) = \pi(p) l(p \mid \Gamma) = \frac{1}{\beta(a+\Gamma, n+b-\Gamma)} p^{a+\Gamma-1}(1-p)^{n+b-\Gamma-1} \tag{9}$$

The posterior distribution of p is $\beta(a+\Gamma, n+b-\Gamma)$ distribution.

Assuming the probability of success $p \sim \beta(a,b)$ of the product test to be sampled, parameters $a > 0$ and $b > 0$, Success number of n pieces test products is Γ, the posterior distribution of p is $h(p \mid \Gamma)$, formula (9), if $p_1 < 1$ then

$$P(p \leq p_1 \mid \Gamma = r) \leq P(p \leq p_1 \mid \Gamma = r-1) \tag{10}$$

If the limit quality level of the product to be sampled is p_1. Assuming that the appraisal test scheme is (n,c), the number of products specified for the test is n, and the maximum allowable test failure number is c (the smallest test success number is $n-c$).

As can be seen from the above, the maximum posteriori risk that users are exposed to is

$$\max_{\Gamma \geq n-c} P(p < p_1 \mid \Gamma) = P(p < p_1 \mid \Gamma = n-c) \tag{11}$$

When accepting the sampled products according to the appraisal test plan (n,c), the product success probability p is less than the maximum posteriori probability of the limit quality level p_1. if given user risk β, there should be

$$P(p < p_1 \mid \Gamma = n-c) \leq \beta \tag{12}$$

To sum up, the Bayes sampling test scheme can be summed up as finding the n, c of $L(p_1) = p(p \leq p_1 | \Gamma = n-c) \leq \beta$ which satisfies the equation under given limit quality level A and use risk B. In the formula $L(R) = P(p \leq R \mid \Gamma = n-c)$, Because c is an integer, the sampling test scheme (n,c) make the equation approximated set up.

IV. RELIABILITY TREND PREDICTION MODEL

A. Linear trend prediction

The linear trend linear equation of least squares regression analysis is as follows:

$$\hat{Y}_t = \alpha + \beta \bullet t \tag{13}$$

In the formula, the fitting parameters are α and β.

$$a = \bar{y} - \bar{x}b, \quad b = \frac{\sum x_i y_i - \bar{x}\sum y_i}{\sum x_i^2 - \bar{x}\sum x_i},$$

$$\bar{x} = \frac{1}{n}\sum x_i, \bar{y} = \frac{1}{n}\sum y_i.$$

Here $\hat{Y}_t$ is the predicted value of t t period, and α is the intercept or invariant term of y. It is defined as a unit of time. β is the estimated value of this trend factor. Such trend prediction is most useful for medium and long term prediction.

B. Moving average method

Select a certain number of observations, calculate their average value, and take this average value as the next forecast value. The moving average can be generally defined as:

$$\hat{Y}_{t+1} = \frac{Y_t + Y_{t-1} + \cdots + Y_{t-N+1}}{N} \tag{14}$$

In the formula, $\hat{Y}_{t+1}$ — the predicted value of Y for a future period; $Y_t, Y_{t-1}, \cdots + Y_{t-N+1}$ —respectively, they are The observed values of Y in t, t-1, ··· t-N+1 period; N —The number of observations in the moving average.

If the number of observations N used in moving average method is larger, the smoothing effect is more obvious. With the increase of N, the weight ($1/N$) of each new observation is smaller. Therefore, the greater the randomness of the data sequence, the slower the change in the main patterns, and the better the prediction results using a relatively large number of past observations. Therefore, the selection of the best moving average should be based on the minimum mean square error.

C. *First-order exponential smoothing technique*

The exponential smoothing method can overcome this shortcoming if the most recent observations contain more useful information for current prediction than those of a longer time ago. Establish the following prediction models:

$$\hat{Y}_{t+1} = wY_t + (1-w)\hat{Y}_t \quad (15)$$

This model assigns the weight of the nearest observation value to w (a value between 0 and 1), and the weight of the past prediction value to (1 - w). A larger w denotes a greater weight on the most recent observations.

Predicting $\hat{Y}_t$ with the above formula can also be written as follows:

$$\hat{Y}_t = wY_{t-1} + (1-w)(\hat{Y}_t - 1) \quad (16)$$

Thus, it can be obtained that:

$$\hat{Y}_{t+1} = wY_t + w(1-w)Y_{t-1} + (1-w)^2\hat{Y}_{t-1} \quad (17)$$

After reciprocating substitution, a general formula is obtained:

$$\hat{Y}_{t+1} = wY_t + w(1-w)Y_{t-1} + w(1-w)^2\hat{Y}_{t-2} + w(1-w)^3Y_{t-3} + \cdots \quad (18)$$

The above formula shows that the general formula of an exponentially weighted moving average method is a weighted average of all the observed values in the past. The weight is defined by the following geometric series:

$$w;(1-w)w;(1-w)^2w;w(1-w)^3w;(1-w)^4w;(1-w)^5w;\cdots \quad (19)$$

If the initial value of w is high, the most recent observations are given a larger weight, and the earlier values are given a rapidly decreasing weight.

The general prediction model can be recorded as:

$$\hat{Y}_{t+1} = \hat{Y}_t + w(Y_t - \hat{Y}_t) \quad (20)$$

According to the two forecasting models mentioned above, the combination of linear regression and exponential sliding can be forecasted:

$$\hat{Y}_{t+1} = w_1\hat{Y}_{1(t+1)} + w_2\hat{Y}_{2(t+1)} \quad (21)$$

In the formula, $w_1 + w_2 = 1$.

V. ANALYSIS OF EXPERIMENTAL RESULTS

Assuming that the probability of success of a transient electronic product is not less than 0.9, the identification ratio D = 3, and the risk of use is not less than 0.2. According to the reasoning of the sampling test scheme, the sampling test scheme is (50,2). That is, sample product quantity is 50 pieces. If the number of failures is not more than 2, the sampling test can be carried out. The reliability trend of the four prediction methods is calculated by synthesizing all kinds of detection data information during the storage period of the product. The reliability trend of the four prediction methods is shown in Fig. 1, respectively, by formula (13), (14), (20), (21).

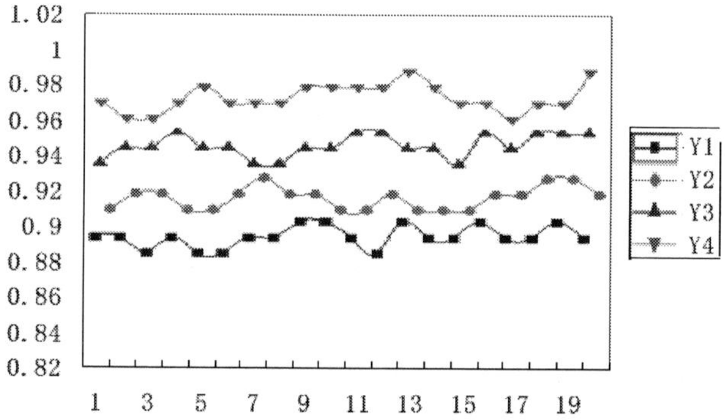

Fig. 1 Reliability Trend Prediction Chart

The above results show that when the product passes the sampling test, the probability that its quality level is lower than the limit quality level does not exceed β. In engineering practice, this is exactly the most concerned problem for users. The maximum posterior risk of sampling test scheme clearly reflects the product quality, which shows that it is reasonable to use the maximum posterior risk criterion to formulate sampling test scheme. The reliability trend in Fig. 1 also reflects the quality trend analysis by fully mining the existing data, which can reflect the past level and law of performance parameters. The more historical data of products, the higher reliability accuracy, the more stable trend development.

VI. CONCLUSION

In the long-term silent state of transient electronic products, the detection conditions are limited and the amount of available data is small. The reliability sampling test scheme mainly uses the detection data from various historical tests, but these test data are implemented at different module levels, under various environmental conditions and with different working objectives. When evaluating the reliability of sampling test, the prior distribution of products is determined firstly. Secondly, on this basis, the verification scheme of reliability sampling test for transient electronic products is established to evaluate the reliability level and use risk of such systems. Finally, the reliability trend prediction model and simulation method are studied in depth. The theoretical method has important theoretical significance for improving the reliability evaluation level of transient electronic products and ensuring that they fulfill their scheduled functions.

REFERENCES

[1] GJB450A-2004 General Requirements for Equipment Reliability Work

[2] Y. M. Tian, Z. H.Zhang. A Bayes reliability acceptance test scheme under binomial distribution [J]. Operations research and management science, 2004, 13(4)

[3] Y. Q. Zang, Q. Liu. Reliability Evaluation of Small Sample Performance Based on Bayes-Normal Model [J]. Journal of Aerocraft TT&C, 2006, 25(3)

[4] B. Z. Liu, T. C. Ding. Reliability Assessment Method for Small Sample Verification with High Reliability and Its Application [J]. Quality and reliability, 2004(1)

[5] J. D. Huang, W. Liu,Y. Huang. Design and Analysis of Reliability Test Scheme for Disposable Use System [J]. Journal of Dalian Jiaotong University, 2014(10)

3D Modeling and Characteristic Analysis of RCD

Weilong Su, Zhihong Xu
Fujian Province Key Laboratory of New Energy Generation and Power Conversion, College of Electrical Engineering and Automation, Fuzhou University, Fuzhou 350108 Fujian Province China
E-mail: 576737933@qq.com Tel: 13107685520

***Abstract*—The residual current circuit breaker with permanent magnet is the most widely used type of switchgear, which is small in size, cost-effective and flexible in operation. However, as the core component current release of the circuit breaker, the operational characteristics of the current release are affected by many factors such as magnetic material characteristics, processing technology, environment, etc., resulting in extremely unstable operation characteristics. In this paper, the overall motion performance and influencing factors are analyzed and simulated in detail through the establishment of 3D finite element model of current release with permanent magnet. Moreover, the key parameters affecting the process of holding, demagnetizing and tripping are sought, by changing the structural parameters, permanent magnet position and material properties. In the working current range, aiming at reducing the tripping time and expanding the adjustable range of the tripping force, the relationship between the key parameters of the release are explored, and the theory is provided to improve the performance index of the release.**

***Index Terms*—Current release, finite element analysis, permanent magnet, residual current circuit breaker**

I. INTRODUCTION

Residual current circuit breakers are widely used in low voltage distribution systems. The residual current circuit breaker with permanent magnet is widely used in domestic and foreign regions because of its small size, simple structure, flexible operation and the influence of operating voltage fluctuations. The authors in [1] have analyzed and studied the current-operating, current-separating and pulse-operated residual current protection technologies and devices, and it has been concluded that no residual current protection device has completely eliminated the dead zone and malfunction. The improvement and research direction of the structure and process of the release are proposed, through the comparative analysis of electromagnetic residual current release from several manufacturers in [2]. The action characteristics of the release are susceptible to the external environment, processing technology and material properties, resulting in poor operational stability. In this paper, the motion characteristics and influencing factors are analyzed and simulated in detail through the establishment of 3D finite element model of current release with permanent magnet based on Maxwell. It focuses on the influence of residual magnetism, coercive force, permanent magnet radius and permanent magnet mounting position on the dynamic characteristics of the release, which provides a theoretical basis for improving the performance of the release.

II. 3D SOLID MODELING OF CURRENT RELEASE

The entity model of the residual current release is shown in Fig. 1. It consists of permanent magnet, yoke, armature, coil and other components. When the power supply system works normally, the suction torque provided by the permanent magnet causes the armature to be held on the working surface of the yoke. When the power supply line leaks, the exciting coil generates a magnetic field opposite to the permanent magnet, which cancels the suction torque until the suction torque is less than the spring reaction torque, and the armature acts to push the circuit breaker by the pole.

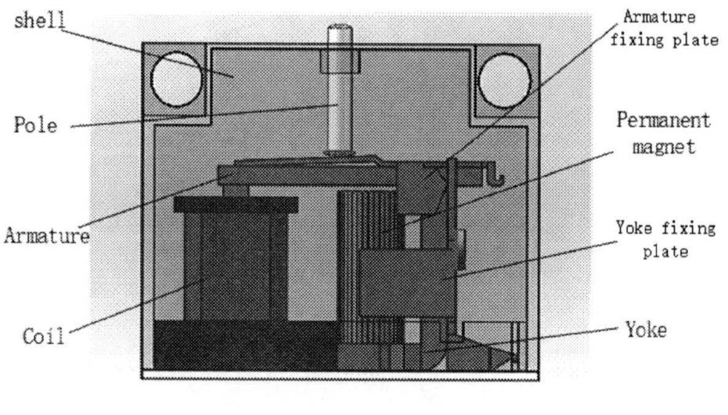

Fig. 1 Residual current release solid model

A. Calculation of dynamic characteristics of current release

The residual current release follows the voltage balance equation, Dalangbert equation and Maxwell equation, and its dynamic characteristics satisfy the equations:

$$\begin{cases} \dfrac{d\psi}{dt} = u - iR \\ \dfrac{d\omega}{dt} = \dfrac{T_1(\theta) - T_2(\theta, i) - T_f}{J} \\ -\dfrac{d\theta}{dt} = \omega \end{cases} \quad (2.1)$$

Where, θ is the angle between the armature and the yoke, T_1 is the suction torque generated by the permanent magnet, T_2 is the equivalent reaction torque of the reverse excitation coil, T_f is the reaction torque provided by the reaction spring, ω is the angular velocity of the armature, and J is the moment of inertia of the armature.

B. *Calculation of the reaction torque of the release*

The reasonable combination of the suction and reaction force of the release determines the sensitivity and reliability of the action characteristics. It is extremely important to accurately calculate the reaction torque. The spring force diagram is shown in Fig. 2. There, O is the rotation point of the armature action, F_1 is the spring force, F_1' is the spring force after the armature rotates θ, F_2 is the spring force perpendicular to the armature, and θ is the opening angle of the armature. The spring reaction torque characteristic curve during the opening of the release can be calculated by (2.2).

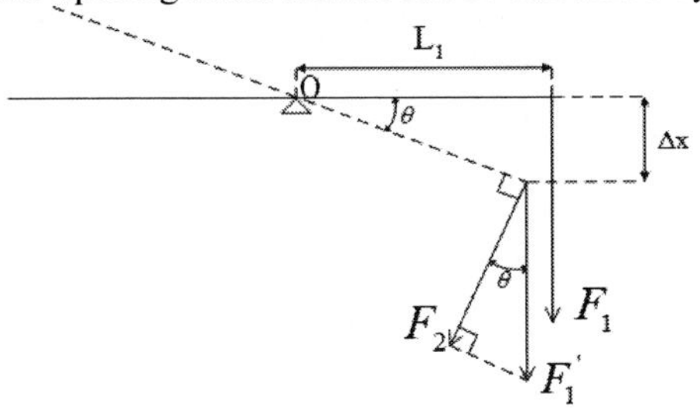

Fig. 2 Spring force diagram

$$\begin{cases} F_2 = (F_1 - k * \Delta x) * \cos\theta \\ \Delta x = L_1 * \sin\theta \\ T_f = F_2 * L_1 \end{cases} \quad (2.2)$$

L_1 is the force arm of the spring force, k is the spring stiffness coefficient, and Δx is the spring tensile displacement.

III. SIMULATION ANALYSIS AND EXPERIMENTAL VERIFICATION OF CURRENT RELEASE

A. *3D simulation analysis*

The 3D finite element model of the residual current release is shown in Fig. 3. The model is simplified to increase the speed of calculation. Since the armature fixing plate and the yoke fixing plate are made of stainless steel, they are not magnetized, and are omitted. The moment of inertia of the yoke fixing plate is equivalent to the armature.

Fig. 3 3D finite element model of the release

The release coil current, suction torque, reaction torque, and armature displacement characteristic curve is shown in Fig. 4. Its working characteristics can be divided into the suction retention phase (A), release phase (B), motion phase (C) and open retention phase (D). When the coil is energized, a magnetic field opposite to the permanent magnet is generated, and the weakening of the magnetic field causes the suction torque to decrease until the suction torque is equal to the reaction torque. Then, the suction torque is less than the reaction torque and the armature begins to move.

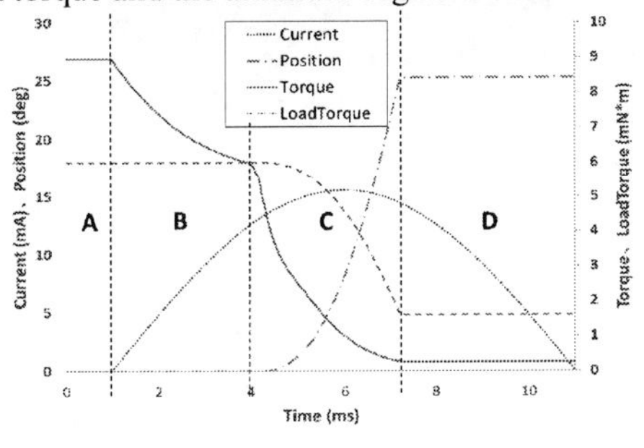

Fig. 4 Release dynamic characteristic curve

The magnetic density distribution of the components at different times during the movement of the release is shown in Fig. 5. After the coil is energized, the coil generates a magnetic field opposite to the permanent magnet, weakening the magnetic field of the left yoke. When the left yoke magnetic density is reduced such that the reaction torque is greater than the suction torque, the armature begins to move (Fig. 5(b)).

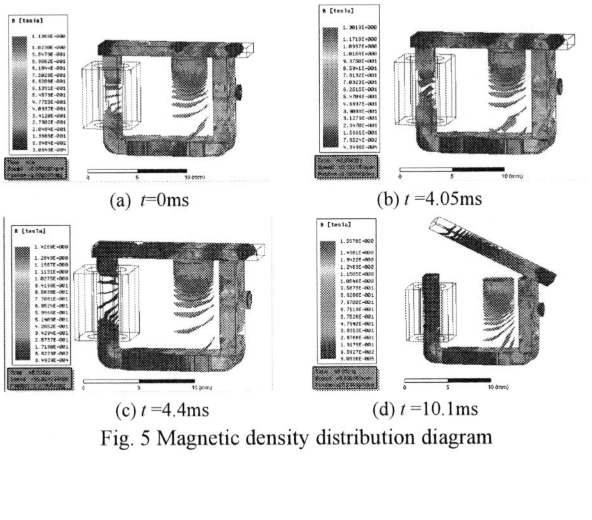

(a) t=0ms (b) t =4.05ms

(c) t =4.4ms (d) t =10.1ms

Fig. 5 Magnetic density distribution diagram

B. *Experimental verification*

In order to verify the accuracy of the model, the action characteristics test of the release was carried out in this paper. The current generated by the current generator acts as a residual current to the coil. The motion process of the marked point on the release is captured by the high speed camera, and the motion path curve of the armature is obtained through image analysis processing. The experimental site map is shown in Fig. 6.

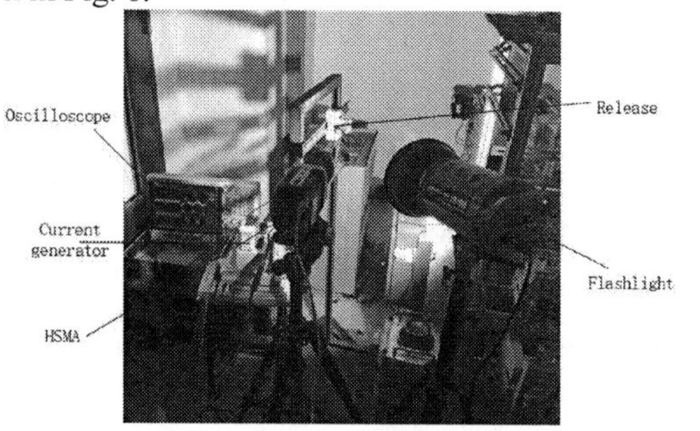

Fig. 6 Experimental site

The comparison of experimental test results of armature displacement with simulation results is shown in Fig. 7. Through comparative analysis, it is found that the two have a high degree of fit, which verifies the accuracy of the established model. The fluctuation of the experimental displacement curve is due to the collision between the armature and the outer shell.

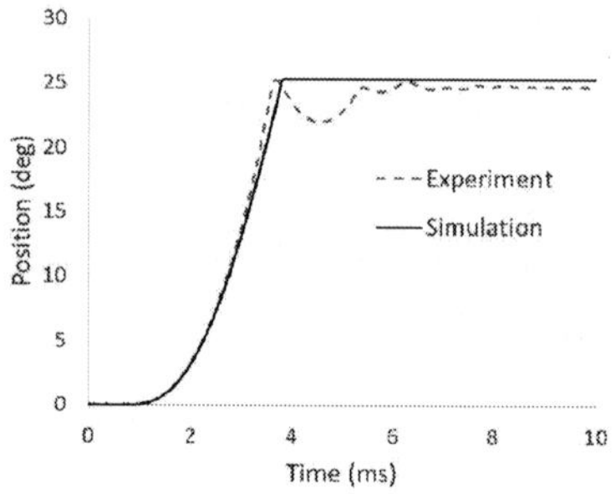

Fig. 7 Comparison of experiment and simulation results

IV. ANALYSIS OF PARAMETER CHARACTERISTICS OF CURRENT RELEASE

A. *Determination of key parameters*

The release is small in size and its operating characteristics are easily affected by machining processes, material properties and assembly errors. In order to improve its sensitivity and reliability, it is necessary to study the key parameters that have a great influence on the release's action performance, and obtain the optimal value of the relevant parameters, so that the action characteristics of the release are the slowest in the vicinity of the parameter value.

The key to improving the stability of the release is to properly control the matching relationship between the suction and reaction torques. First, the suction torque provided by the permanent magnet is less affected by the outside. Secondly, the adjustable range of the tripping reaction torque is expanded within the operating current range. The release operating current ranges from 9 mA to 11 mA. When the coil is connected to these two current levels, the difference in suction torque between the two is ΔT . In order to prevent the release from malfunctioning below 9mA, or not operating above 11mA, the spring reaction torque value must be set between the two. If ΔT is large, the adjustment range of the reaction torque will be made larger, thereby improving the operational stability of the release.

The permanent magnet material used herein is alumino-nickel-cobalt, with B_r being 0.857T and H_c being 1591.1A/m. The simplified diagram of the release magnetic circuit is shown in Fig. 8. The dynamic characteristics of the release are affected by the mounting position, height, diameter and material of the permanent magnet as expressed in (4.1).

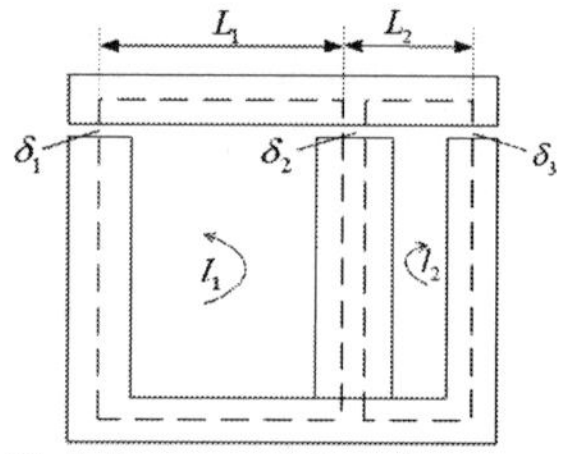

Fig. 8 Simplified diagram of the release magnetic circuit

$$\begin{cases} F_1 = \dfrac{1}{2\mu_0} B_{g_1}^2 S_{g_1} \\ F_2 = \dfrac{1}{2\mu_0} B_{g_2}^2 S_{g_2} \\ T_1 = (L_1 + L_2) * F_1 \\ T_2 = L_2 * F_2 \end{cases} \tag{4.1}$$

Where, F_1 is the electromagnetic attraction under δ_1, and F_2 is the electromagnetic suction under δ_2.

B. *Analysis of key parameters of release*

The demagnetization curve of the permanent magnet and the relationship between its magnetic flux and the magnetic potential are shown in Fig. 9. As the coercive force and the remanence increase, the magnetic potential of the permanent magnet F_c and the magnetic potential of outward magnetic circuit F_m increases (Fig. 9). The suction torque comparison and ΔT comparison for permanent magnets with different B_r and H_c is shown in Fig. 10-a. It can be seen that as B_r and H_c increase, the suction torque increases faster and ΔT is also increased. When B_r and H_c are not enough, the F_m is small, which allows the degaussing of the reverse excitation coil to have reached saturation when the current is small. A current of 11mA and 20mA was supplied to the release with a remanence of 0.514T. The release with a remanence of 0.771T is also treated this way. In the first case, the suction torque appears to be saturated during the reduction when 11mA is applied. Forward excitation occurs when the current is 20mA. However, the release with a remanence of 0.771T will not (Fig. 10-b).

When the suction torque increases, the reaction torque also increases, which shortens the action time of the release and improves its sensitivity (Fig. 10-c). This situation is also consistent with the analysis of other parameters, which will not be described later.

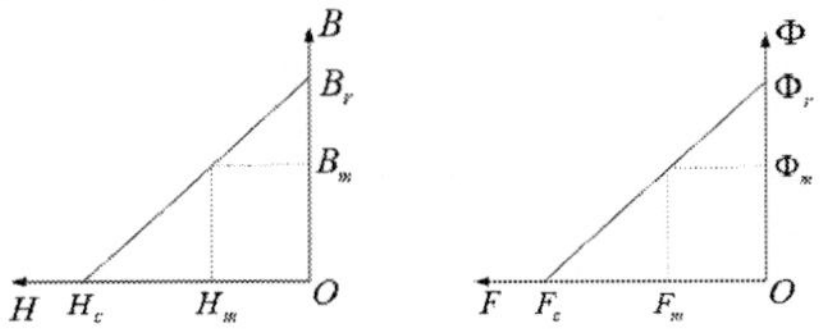

(a) $B=f(H)$ (b) $\Phi=f(F)$

Fig. 9 Permanent magnet material characteristic curve

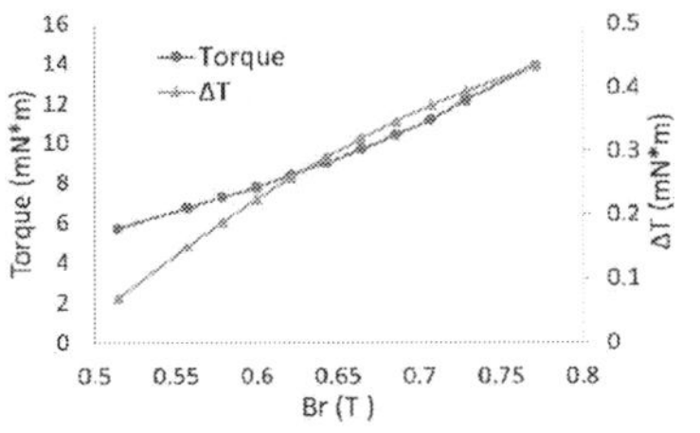

(a) Suction torque and ΔT under different permanent magnet materials

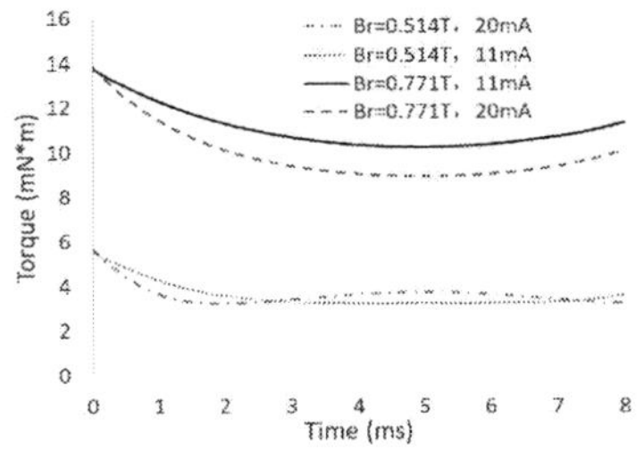

(b) Analysis of demagnetization saturation

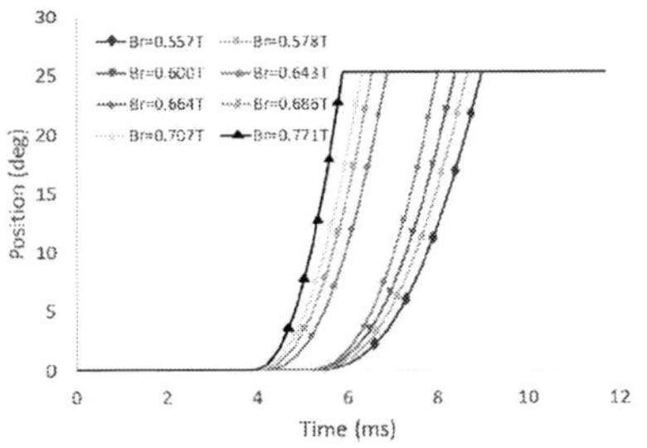

(c) Displacement curve of the release with different permanent magnet materials

Fig. 10 Analysis of the influence of different permanent magnet materials on the characteristics of the release

The suction torque comparison and ΔT comparison for permanent magnets with different permanent magnet diameters is shown in Fig. 11. When the diameter is 3.4-3.6mm, the range of variation of suction torque is the smallest. The reason is that the permanent magnet can be regarded as a series of magnetic potential and magnetic resistance. From (4.2) and (4.3), it is known that the magnetoresistance has a quadratic function relationship with the radius of the permanent magnet. When the radius is too small, the magnetoresistance increases rapidly, and the magnetic potential provided by the permanent magnet to the external magnetic circuit decreases rapidly. The suction torque has a quadratic function relationship with the radius of the permanent magnet as expressed in (4.1). When the radius of the permanent magnet is large, the suction torque increases rapidly with the increase of the radius. As the radius of the permanent magnet increases, ΔT also increases. Therefore, under the premise of ensuring the stability of the suction torque, the diameter of the permanent magnet should take a larger value to increase its stability.

$$R_m = \frac{h_m}{\pi \mu_r \mu_0 r_m^2} \tag{4.2}$$

Where, r_m is the radius of the permanent magnet, μ_r is the relative magnetic permeability of the permanent magnet material, h_m is the length of the magnetization direction of the permanent magnet.

$$F_m = F_C - \Phi_m R_m \tag{4.3}$$

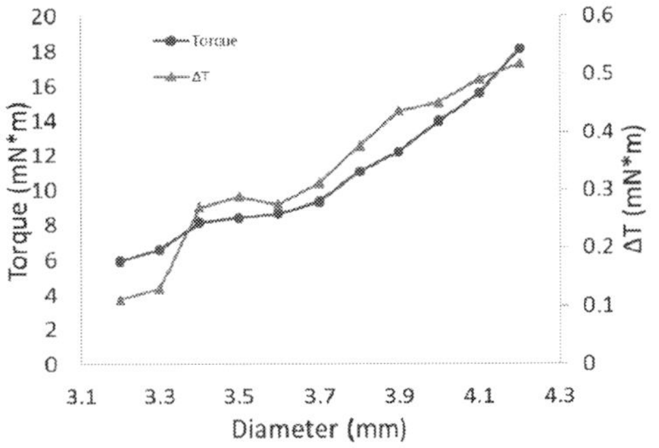

Fig. 11 Suction torque and ΔT under different permanent magnet diameter

The suction torque comparison and ΔT comparison for permanent magnets with different permanent magnet height is shown in Fig. 12. As the height of the permanent magnet increases, the change in suction torque becomes more pronounced. This is because when the air gap is small, the change of the air gap causes the air gap magnetoresistance to change greatly, so that the suction torque variation is also obvious. However, if the air gap is too large, the permanent magnets are not fully utilized, and the material is wasted. The ΔT also increases as the height of the permanent magnet increases. For this prototype, it take between 8.3-8.5mm.

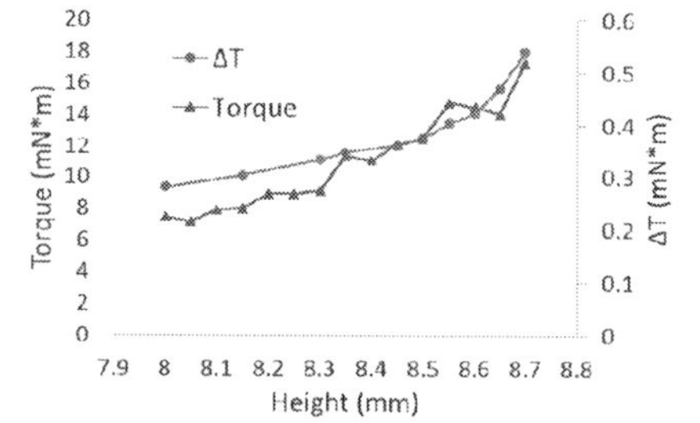

Fig. 12 Suction torque and ΔT under different permanent magnet height.

Release magnetic circuit simplified diagram is shown in Fig. 13. The suction torque comparison and ΔT comparison in the case where the permanent magnet mounting positions are different is shown in Fig. 14. It can be seen from the analysis of Figs. 13 and Fig. 14 that the range of variation of the suction torque is the smallest when the permanent magnet mounting position, i.e., L_2 is 1.9-2.9mm. When L_2 exceeds 2.9mm, from (4.1), Fig. 8 and Fig. 13, it is found that as L_2 increases, HL_1 decreases so that F_1 becomes larger, and therefore the suction torque fluctuates significantly with a change of L_2. On the contrary, when L_2 is less than 1.9 mm, the phenomenon is opposite to the above description.

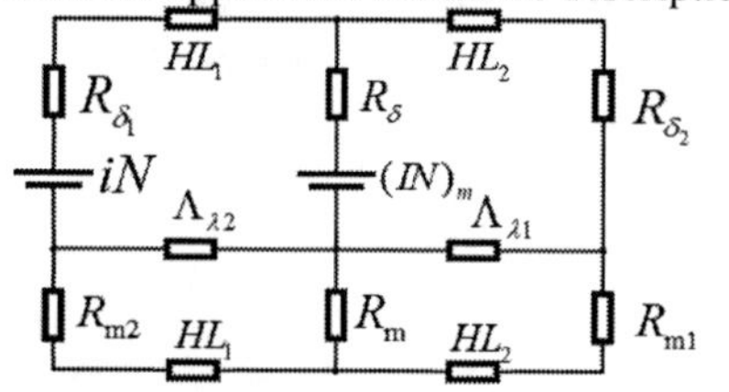

Fig. 13 Simplified magnetic circuit diagram of the release

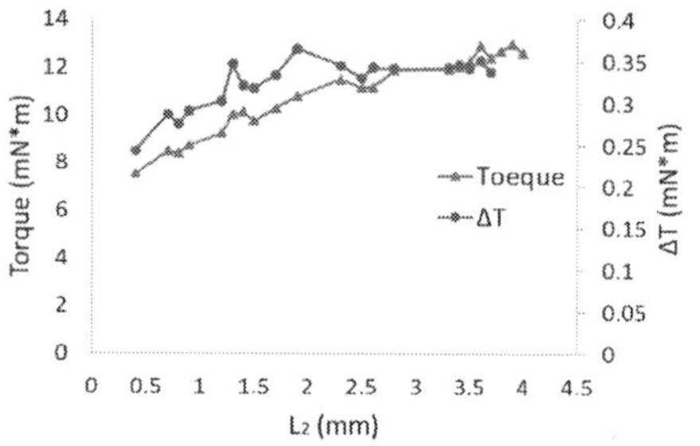

Fig. 14 Suction torque and ΔT under different permanent magnet mounting positions

C. *Comparison of overall performance indicators of releases*

According to the analysis in Section 4.2, the permanent magnet mounting position, height and diameter are used as key parameter variables. The permanent magnet mounting position is set to be 2.5mm from the right yoke iron with a tolerance of 0.1mm. The permanent magnet has a height of 8.35mm and a tolerance of 0.05mm. The permanent magnet has a diameter of 3.45mm and a tolerance of 0.05mm. An orthogonal test table of L_9 (3^3) is established. The permanent magnet mounting position of the original prototype is 1mm from the right yoke, the height of the permanent magnet is 8.35mm, and the diameter of the permanent magnet is 3.60mm. The same tolerance is used to establish the orthogonal test table of L_9 (3^3). As shown in Fig. 15, it can be seen that the suction torque of the optimized release changes with the relevant parameters of the permanent magnet, the fluctuation range becomes smaller, and the stability performance is improved. Since the set values of the reaction torques of the two are not much different, the sensitivity is basically the same.

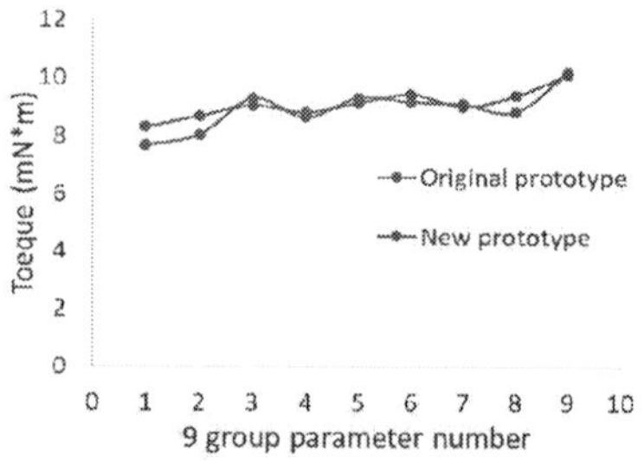

Fig. 15 Comparison of the original prototype and the optimized prototype

V. INTRODUCTION

In order to improve the sensitivity and stability of the residual current release, this paper establishes a three-dimensional model of the current release based on Maxwell, and combines the theory and simulation analysis to determine the key parameters affecting the action characteristics of the release. It is concluded that the reasonable value of the permanent magnet material, diameter, height and installation position can improve the working stability of the release. For this prototype, the diameter should be between 3.4-3.6mm, the height should be between 8.35-8.45mm, and the installation position should be between 2.3-2.5mm from the right yoke. Under the premise of ensuring that the suction torque provided by the permanent magnet is stable, simultaneously increasing the suction torque and the spring reaction torque can improve the working sensitivity of the release. Finally, according to the simulation analysis results, a set of optimized release parameters are selected and analyzed for its characteristics. The performance is higher and the stability is better than that of the original prototype.

ACKNOWLEDGMENT

This work was supported in part by the Funding program for leading talents in scientific and technological innovation of Fujian Province, and in part by the Research Development Fund of Ningde Normal University under Grant 2016FZ14.

REFERENCES

[1] Xia Yue, Du Songhuai, Li Chunlan, Su Juan, Zhang Junjie, Zhang Lie. Development tendency of residual current protection technology and device in China[J]. Transactions of the Chinese Society of Agricultural Engineering, 2010(S2):151-155.

[2] Zheng Yonggang, Su Yulin. Structural Analysis and Research of Electromagnetic Residual Current Release [J]. Electrical & Energy Management Technology, 2015(1): 24-28.

[3] Yu Xiang, Cuk, V., Cobben, J.F.G.. Impact of residual harmonic current on operation of residual current devices[P]. Environment and Electrical Engineering (EEEIC), 2011 10th International Conference on,2011.

[4] Yang Yizheng,Pang Wenyi.Optimized Design of RCBO Electromagnetic Release Device[J].Electric Power System Equipment,2015,(10):47-49.

[5] Hu Jianping, Li Peiqiang. Failure Analysis of Electromagnetic Residual Current Operated Circuit Breaker[J]. Electrotechnics Electric, 2015(7): 50-53.

[6] Z Erdei,M Horgos,C Lung,A Pop-Vadean,R Muresan. Frequency behavior of the residual current devices[J]. IOP Conference Series: Materials Science and Engineering, 2017,163(1).

[7] Qi Zhiping, Shu Guobiao. Study and Simulation of Permanent Magnetic Operating Mechanism Based on Software Ansoft[J]. Electrotechnics Electric, 2014(10): 24-27.

[8] Deng Jie,Tang Wei. Theory and Method of Eliminating Operating Dead Zone of Residual Current Protection [J]. Transactions of China Electrotechnical Society, 2016,36(5):7-10,48.

[9] Zhang Qing, Dong Xueling. Discussion on Residual Current Setting Method of Electromagnetic Circuit Breaker. Electrotechnics Electric, 2000(3): 41-43.

[10] Tang Renyuan. Modern Permanent Magnet Machines[M]. Beijing: Mechanical Industry Press, 1997.

First Author, Weilong Su(1996-) is currently pursuing the M.S degree in the College of Electrical Engineering and Automation, Fuzhou University, China. His research interests is in the Electrical Appliances and Intelligent Technology.

Corresponding Author, Zhihong Xu(1963-) received her B.S, M.S and Ph.D. degrees from Fuzhou University, China, all with electrical engineering major. Since 1983, She works as a teacher in College of Electrical Engineering and Automation, Fuzhou University. And Currently, she is a professor and a doctor tutor. She has involved in teach and research. Her research interests is in the Electrical Appliances and Intelligent Technology.

7th International Conference on Reliability of
Electrical Products and Electrical Contacts,
November 04-06, 2019

KeyTechnologies of the Operational Reliability Evaluation for the Large-scale Battery Energy Storage System

Lin Cheng[1], Yuxiang Wan[1], Yi Jiang[1], Zhidong Wang[2], Mei Liu[2]
[1]State Key Laboratory of Control and Simulation of Power Systems and Generation Equipment,Tsinghua University, Beijing 100084, China
[2]State Grid Economic and Technological Research Institute Corporation Limited,State Grid Corporation of China, Beijing 102209, China
E-mail: wyx17@mails.tsinghua.edu.cn

Abstract—**The large-scale battery energy storage system (BESS) can effectively meet the diversified needs of power grid dispatching. Therefore, the improvement of the BESS operational reliability is of great significance to ensure the operation safety of the grid. However, the BESS is composed of a large number of batteries. This fact suggests the BESS reliability depends not only on the battery operating state but also on the strategy of battery networking reconfiguration. In this paper, the analysis of the operational reliability research of large-scale BESS is carried out in-depth. The research status of reliability of large-scale BESS is investigated, and some thoughts on the obstacles to the BESS operational reliability evaluation are given. The promotion of the new technology of BESS and the development of the ubiquitous Internet of Things on BESS operation reliability are analyzed. In addition, the framework of the operational reliability evaluation of a large-scale BESS is proposed. Some key technologies such as failure mechanism, equipment reliability modeling, evaluation, and optimization are summarized, providing some suggestions for the application of large-scale BESS.**

Index Terms—**Operational Reliability, Battery Energy Storage System (BESS), Battery Networking Reconfiguration, Reliability Optimization**

I. INTRODUCTION

With the large-scale access of new energy sources such as wind power and photovoltaic, the randomness and volatility are introduced into the power grid, which brings great challenges to the safe, stable and efficient operation. The grid flexibility urgently needs to be increased[1].Compared with other regulatory means, the battery energy storage system (BESS) has the advantages of fast power response, dense energy storage, flexible and convenient deployment, etc. The large-scale BESS is expected to play an important role in some grid-level application scenarios such as peak shaving, frequency regulation, fluctuation stabilization, and emergency power support. However, the practical application shows that although the battery cell can reach nearly 10,000 times of full-filled cycle life, while the large-scale BESS composed of massive battery cells has a seriously reduced life [2]. Insufficient reliability has become a major barrier for the widespread use of large-scale BESS.

Due to the low voltage and capacity level of the batterycell, megawatt BESS typically string/parallel "millions" of cells in the form of fixed welding to increase voltage and current ratings. This physical rigid connection means that failure of any single cell might cause a system-level failure. In terms of reliability logic, this kind of BESS belongs to a series systemof which reliability is difficult to be improved. Redundancy is usually adopted in the design of large-scale BESS to improve the system margin. “Slow charge/discharge” is used to lower the charge/discharge rate and “shallow charge/discharge” to reduce the charge/discharge depth to reduce the operational risk [3]. Therefore, low capacity utilization of the BESS occurs which is characterized by insufficient economics.

Operational reliability evaluation typically requires consideration of changes in the state/performance of the product/system over time or conditions of use[4].Different from the conventional short-term reliability evaluation, the operational reliability needs to consider the impact of equipment's own health status, external environment, system operating conditions and system operating behavior on the component failure probability [5]. Operational evaluation of the BESS can provide the decision-making basis for operation personnel.With a reasonable control strategy to achieve active security prevention, the quantification of BESS utilization potential is beneficial to improve the safe operation level of the power system under the premise of ensuring the operational reliability[6]. This work can promote the widespread application of large-scale BESS in the power system, which is of great significance. In this paper, the existed researches and thoughts of the key technologies on the operational reliability of large-scale BESS are summarized and analyzed.

The paper is organized as follows. In Section II, the development and the problems in the implementation of BESS operational reliability are reviewed and analyzed. In Section III, the opportunity of the BESS operational reliability is discussed with the development of dynamic battery networking reconfiguration and IoT technology. In Section IV, the evaluation framework of the operational reliability is introduced. In SectionV, some key technologies of operational reliability are introduced. Finally,this paper is concluded in Section VI.

II. THE RESEARCH AND OBSTACLES OF THE BESS OPERATIONAL RELIABILITY

A. The Research Status of Large-scale BESS Reliability

In fact, the basis for the operational reliability evaluation of power systems is the condition-dependent outage model of various electrical equipment, which requires to reflect changes in the operating conditions [4]. The condition-dependent outage models of various types of power equipment have been widely concerned and studied in the power system [7]. The research results obtained so far cover many aspects of power system generation, transmission and distribution. Ref. [8] establishes a short-term reliability evaluation model as well as the corresponding unit control strategy. Ref. [9] analyzed the influence of the model parameter changes on the operational reliability of transmission lines. The influence of the ambient temperature, load rate and aging status on the transformer failure rate are discussed in [10].Similar to other devices in the power system, the BESS operational reliability is closely related to the battery's own health, real-time operating conditions and external environmental factors. However, the existed literature rarely evaluates the operational reliability of the large-scale BESS.

The existing reliability research of the energy storage systems still stays in the relatively simple conventional static reliability modeling. The basic idea is to divide the energy storage equipment into functional subsystems such as battery module and management module, and then use reliability block diagram, fault tree analysis, Markov model and other methods to evaluate the device reliability [11]. The statistical outage rate is usually used to characterize the reliability level of the energy storage equipment. The purpose is mainly to evaluate the reliability of wind and solar systems or power grids with energy storage devices [12][13]. This reliability model has good reference value for long-term scale planning work. However, in the actual operation, the failure rate of any equipment component has time-varying and uncertain.The simple modeling method is difficult to reflect the influence of uncertainty factors on reliability level in operation.

In addition, the large-scale BESS itself is a large complex system composed of a large number of battery cells connected organically. Meanwhile, some operation risks can also be avoided through operation control strategies such as equalization, reconfiguration and isolation. The reliability evaluation needs further combine with complex battery topologies. Many scholars have conducted researches on system-level reliability state analysis and quantitative calculation, such as dynamic fault tree, Monte Carlo simulation, Petri Net (PN), dynamic Bayesian Network (DBN). On the other hand, due to the large scale and high complexity of BESS, the system state modeling is usually complicated. Complex System Theory provides a BETTER solution for the modeling and optimization of the complex network structure with such characteristics as large-scale, high-dimensional, dynamic and nonlinear[14]. Now, it is widely used in various complex physical networks in reality, such as the Internet, transportation, and power networks [15].Therefore, the complex network theory can be considered to solve the complex problem of network state analysis in the reliability evaluation of large-scale BESS.

B. The Obstacles to the BESS Operational Reliability

The reliability of large-scale battery energy storage system is affected by the battery cell state, battery connection topology and complex operating conditions, simultaneously. The evaluation difficulty of its operational reliability mainly reflects the following points.

- The increased difference in battery cells can seriously affect the life and efficiency of the BESS. The BESS reliability is closely related to the state of the battery cell. Due to the complex and diverse battery failure mechanism, the differences between the battery cells are unavoidable. Batteries are connected to each other to form a network to meet the grid dispatching requirements, leading the expansion of the differences in operation.
- In actual operation, the battery health condition has time-varying characteristics due to operating conditions and environment. However, a fixedly connected battery network topology is utilized in the traditional energy storage system, which cannot flexibly isolate and protect the faulty unit. The BESS reliability is greatly affected by the operating state of the battery cells. At the same time, the existing reliability evaluation still stays in the long-term planning process, and the results cannot support the equipment reliability improvement during operation.
- The application mode of the energy storage system in the power grid is diversified. The same energy storage equipment plays different roles in the operation of the power system, and it is required to meet different requirements. However, the traditional energy storage system design can only adjust the

battery charge and discharge rate (slow charge and slow discharge) and charge and discharge depth (shallow charge and shallow discharge) to ensure that the energy storage system operates in a safe range. However, the traditional energy storage system can only be designed to ensure that the energy storage system operates within a safe range by adjusting the battery charge/discharge rate (slow charge/discharge) and depth (shallow charge/discharge), which cannot meet the requirements of multiple scenarios and result in a low equipment utilization and poor economy.

Therefore, to ensure the reliability and safety of the large-scale energy storage system during operation, it is necessary to consider the influence of different factors such as the cell differences, the operating conditions and the environment to evaluate the operational reliability of the BESS. And effective operational control strategies are also essential to accommodate diverse grid needs.

III. THE DEVELOPMENT OPPORTUNITY OF OPERATION RELIABILITY OF THE LARGE-SCALE BESS

A. The Promotion of the Ubiquitous IoT of Power System on BESS Operational Reliability

The assessment of operational reliability depends on the historical operating conditions and real-time operating conditions of the device. Thus, the operational reliability assessment of the BESS needs to include full life cycle data support from battery production to use.

Fortunately, the construction of the ubiquitous electric IoT is proposed by the State Grid Corporation of China in 2019 [16]. The ubiquitous electric IoT is essentially an Internet of Things. It refers to the interconnection and interworking of all electricity-related physical objects or equipment, including the transmission, distribution, transformation and utilization of the power and even the energy network. There is not only interconnection of electricity, but also theinterconnection of information[17].With its unique advantages, the Internet of Things can meet the requirements of real-time, accuracy and comprehensiveness of information acquisition for the intelligent grid in various occasions. Effective grid situational awareness and standardized management capability can be achieved.

Therefore, under the background of the development of the ubiquitous power Internet of Things, it will no longer be a technical barrier to build a battery-operated data sharing cloud platform, which might cover the entire life cycle of battery production, vehicle and energy storage applications.

B. The Promotion of the topology control strategy on BESS Reliability Optimization

In addition, with the deepening of battery network research, thebattery network topology of the BESS is able to be adjusted in the operation to meet the performance requirements of the power grid equipment in multi-application scenarios. From the perspective of safe operation, the outage rate of the BESS needs to be reduced or maintained at a reasonable level. Through the active safety control strategy, fault diagnosis and isolation can be realized. Theoperational reliability of the BESS can be improved.

The research of the battery network has attracted wide attention.Energy storage of hybrid heterogeneous batteries proposed in [3]applies the idea of "Everything within our capabilities" to the BESS reliability design. A modeling and hierarchical control method are proposed. The heterogeneous BESS compensates for the negative effect caused by the fixed connection of the battery to a certain extent. But the improvement of the BESS reliability cannot be achieved fundamentally.

In contrast, the reconfigurable battery network can flexibly adjust the battery connection structure to meet the differentiated requirements of grid scheduling in terms of the charge/discharge rate and depth. Therefore, the researchers proposed a battery topology network by means of a flexible grouping of battery cell or pack. The dynamic matching requirements, fault tolerance and balanced control can be realized [18].The general method used in the reconfiguration design of battery network topology isabstract modelingbased on graph theory. With adaptive battery topology, a battery network reconfigurable schemecan be designed [19]. From the perspective of optimal control of energy storage systems, Ci *et al.*[20] optimize the battery topology control architecture for multi-type and dynamic requirements, which compensates for the theoretical missing phenomenon in battery topology design. Kim*et al.*[21] propose a dynamic topology optimization control architecture combing the battery cell failure isolation to deal with the reliability risk of the BESS operation under sudden high load conditions.

A flexible topology control strategy of the battery network can change the status that the redundant design and the shallow charging/discharging working mode are adopted to ensure the operational reliability.

IV. THE FRAMEWORK OF OPERATIONAL RELIABILITY EVALUATION OF A LARGE-SCALE BESS

At present, many in-depth researches have been carried out on the theory of power system operation reliability, while the reliability evaluation of energy storage equipment itself is relatively small. The evaluation of its operational reliability has not been carried out yet, which is quite challenging.In fact, there are many similarities between the operational reliability evaluation of large-scale BESS and that of the power system, as shown in Table 1. It is technically feasible to evaluate the operational reliability of the energy storage system by referring to the idea of the power system operational reliability.

The technical framework for the operational reliability evaluation of the BESS proposed in this paper is shown in Fig. 1, which mainly includes the failure mechanism analysis, reliability assessment and reliability optimization. Among them, the failure mechanism analysis is mainly to provide the required battery safety boundary and operation status for reliability evaluation and optimization; the evaluation work can locate the reliability weak link of the system, thus providing a decision-making basis for the reliability enhancement strategy implementation such as battery network reconfiguration. Finally, the rolling evaluation and improvement of the BESS operational reliability of the energy storage system can be realized.

V. KEY TECHNOLOGIES ON THE OPERATIONAL RELIABILITY OF A LARGE-SCALE BESS

This section mainly summarizes key technologies involved in the operation reliability research of large-scale battery energy storage system, such as the battery failure mechanism, reliability modeling, reliability evaluation, and reliability optimization enhancement

A. Failure Mechanism Analysis and Operation Status Estimation of Battery Cell

There are many factors affecting battery failure. In different scenarios, due to the different degrees of battery aging, various failure modes might occur in such complex electrochemical systems.The battery operating state and safety boundary might change differently [22].

The analysis of the battery decay mechanism is the basis for the estimation of the operating state and safety boundary of the BESS. It is necessary to study the failure characteristics of the battery under different temperature, charge/discharge rate and depth.Usually, a parameter characterization model of external battery characteristics coupled by multiple factors should be constructed to realize the externalized characterization of internal failure characteristics, such as an equivalent circuit model of the battery [23]. Parameters such as capacitance and resistance of the equivalent circuit model can be identified to describe the external performance of the battery.

In addition, the accurate evaluation of the current and future operation status of the battery is the basis for the safe and reliable operation of the large-scale BESS. The existing evaluation research is mainly for battery off-state deployment. Based on the analysis of electrochemical reaction characteristics, Wang *et al.* [24]propose an analyzing method for the operational state space of battery pack based on the equivalent circuit model. By analyzing the SOC estimation error source, Zhang *et al.*[25] use the unscented Kalman filtering method to identify the SOC parameters of the battery pack operating state, achieving improvement on the online SOC estimation accuracy of the battery.In recent years, with the promotion and application of artificial intelligence in various fields, the machine learning method has also been introduced into the estimation of battery operation state. Hu *et al.*[26]propose a learning model based on fuzzy clustering for battery state estimation to predict future trends.

B. Condition-dependent Outage Model for Operational Reliability Evaluation

It is the basis for evaluating the BESS operational reliability to establish a condition-dependent outage model of the battery cell/pack, which is supposed to reflect the battery's own health status, real-time operating conditions, external operating environment, as shown in Fig. 2.

TABLE I COMPARISON OF THE OPERATIONAL RELIABILITY EVALUATION BETWEEN POWER SYSTEM AND BESS

	Operational Reliability of Power system	Operational Reliability of the BESS
Influence Factor	1) Health condition of electrical equipment 2) External environment 3) System operating conditions	1)Battery health condition 2) External operating environment 3) Real-time operating conditions
Components	Electrical equipment + Switching devices	Battery cells + Power electronic switches
Network Connections	Electrical equipment such as generators/transformers/lines is connected to the power system through switching devices.	Battery components such as cells/pack are connected to the BESS through power electronic switches.
Risk Strategies	1) Power flow balancing strategy such as active scheduling/reactive optimization 2) Fault detection and faulty equipment removal 3) Network reconfiguration and load transfer supply	1) Capacity/Voltage active balancing strategy 2) Vulnerability analysis and faulty battery isolation 3) Battery network reconfiguration and dynamic matching

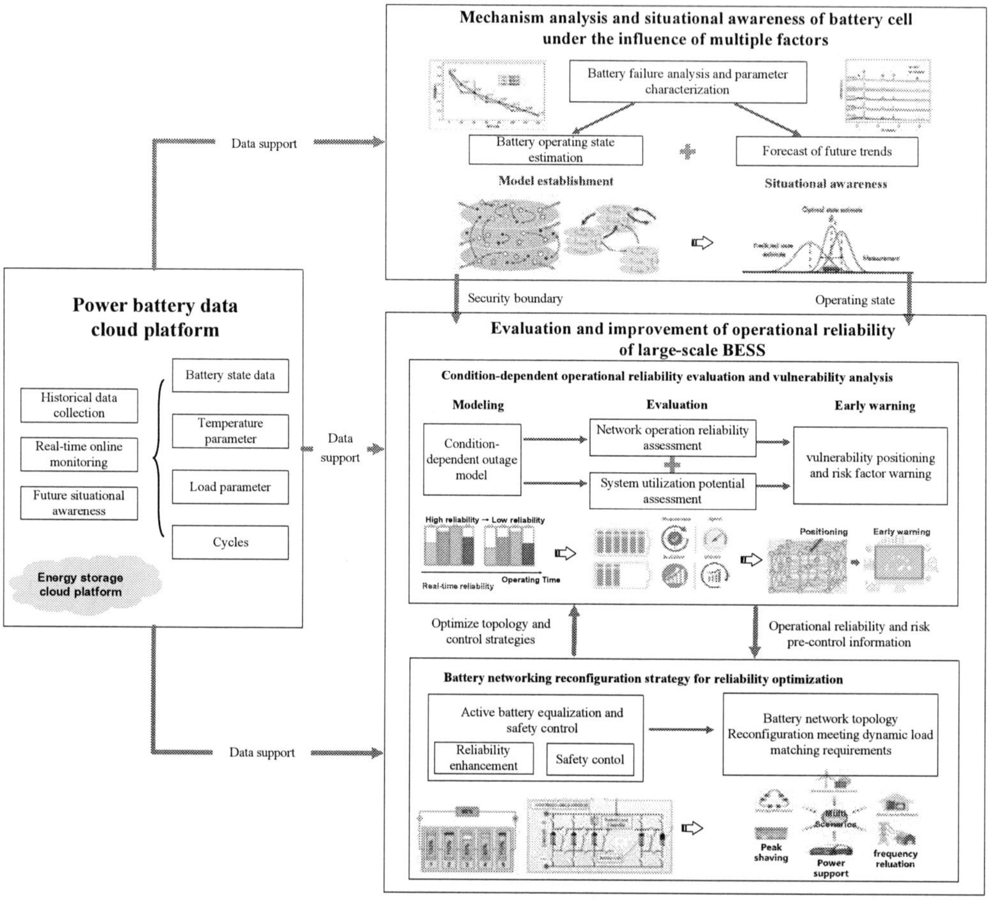

Fig. 1 The evaluation framework of the BESS operational reliability

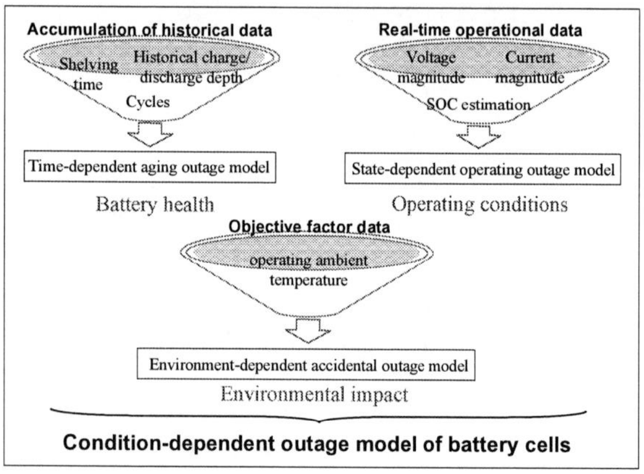

Fig. 2 The condition-dependent outage model

C. *Vulnerability Analysis of Large-scale BESS in Reliability Evaluation*

The core of the operational reliability evaluation of the BESS is to predict the short-term battery state under a specific topology strategy and obtain the reliability level change of the BESS in the future short-term operation time. The reasons for the reduced reliability need to be evaluated. The process of vulnerability analysis is shown in Fig. 3.

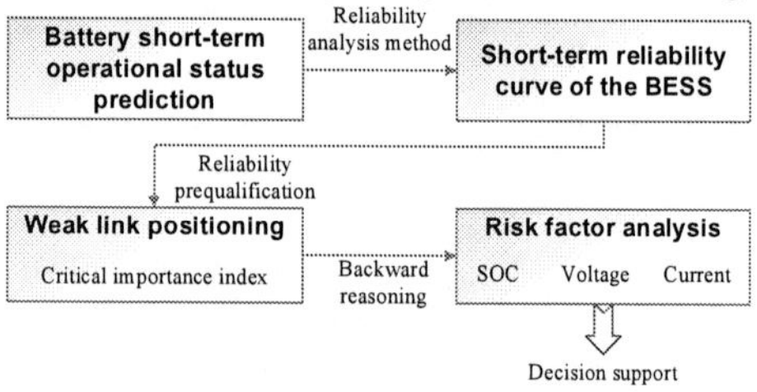

Fig. 3 Vulnerability analysis of the BESS

For the weak link positioning, the formula for calculating the critical importance of battery reliability should be derived to characterize the contribution of the cell to the unreliability of the system operation. Thus, the variation degree of system reliability index caused by the change of component outage probability can be worked out. By ranking the critical importance indexes, the precise positioning of the weak link of reliability can be achieved.

In addition, the battery condition-dependent outage model in the above can be used to calculate the expected reliability of the weak link to determine whether it can be repaired. For the repairable battery, the factors that reduce the cell reliability are derived backward, so that the safety protection strategies such as capacity balance and voltage balance can be adopted. The irreparable battery shall be timely isolated and replaced

The analysis of early warning weak links and potential risk factors can guide the reconfiguration of the battery network to improve the reliability of the energy storage system in practical operation. Under the premise of ensuring the reliability level, the utilization potential of the current BESS can be further evaluated such as power, duration, reliability, etc.

D. Battery Networking Reconfiguration Strategy for Operational Reliability Optimization

The reconfigurable battery network can reduce the difference between the cells through the active equalizationas well as effectively isolate the weak battery cells. A reasonable reconfiguration strategy should take into account both reliability improvement and load dynamic matching requirements, as shown in Fig. 4.

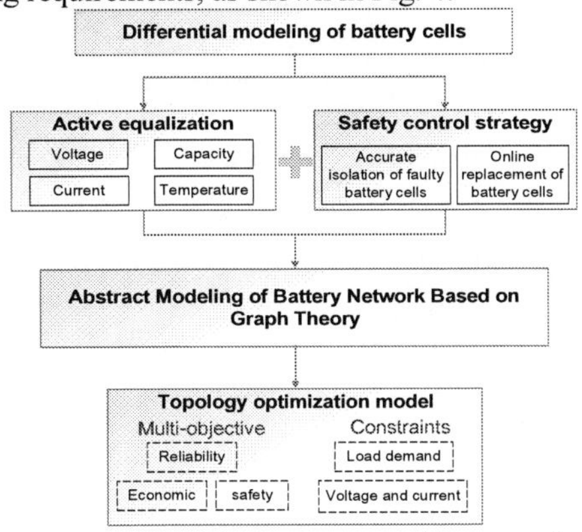

Fig.4The framework of the battery networking reconfiguration strategy

There are some differences in battery cell characteristics. The difference would be further expanded under different operating conditions and the external environment. For the weak reliability of energy storage system during operation, it is necessary to carry out active battery equalization and safety control for the energy storage system.

Active equalization and safety control are mainly to study the characteristics of battery cells inconsistency from the aspects of capacity, internal resistance, self-discharge rate, SOC and terminal voltage. Further, on the basis of data statistics and practical experience, the dispersion model of battery difference is established. Taking the battery SOC as an example, the dispersion model can be expressed to determine the dispersion boundary between the battery cells,

$$\xi = \sqrt{\sum_{i=1}^{n} \frac{\left(SOC_i - SOC_m\right)^2}{n}} \qquad (1)$$

For the battery cells in a reasonable safety interval, the voltage/current/capacity active equalization control strategies should be studied to delay the battery decay speed and prevent the battery cell difference from further expanding. For the battery cells outside the safety zone, the safety control strategies for accurate isolation and online replacement of battery cells should be made to improve the reliability of energy storage systems.

At the same time, the reconfigurable battery network can dynamically sense the operating state and utilization potential of the battery cells. The connection structure can be adjusted flexibly to match the appropriate battery cells for reconfiguration.It satisfies the differential demand of power grid dispatching for energy storage charge/discharge rate, depth, and times.

In this regard, the battery cells can be abstracted into a fully connected graph. For such a network composed of many individuals with different discrete units, the Hamilton graph theory can be used to abstract the battery network and transform it into a standard directed graph optimization problem, achieving fast processing of multidimensional data. Further, combing with the reliability enhancement such as the active equalization control strategies, a battery network optimization model needs to be established to meet the diversified dispatching requirements and constrained by the battery safety boundary.

VI. CONCLUSION

The traditional reliability evaluation method of energy storage systems havecertain defects. The evaluation results are usually different from the actual operation conditions. Meanwhile, the fixed topology design cannot meet the high-reliability and multi-scenario application requirements of the power grid, which is not conducive to the large-scale promotion and application of the BESS.

To carry out the operational reliability evaluation and optimization of large-scale BESS and quantify the utilization potential is beneficial to improving the safe operation level of the power system. Among them, the battery failure analysis and quantitative characterization under the influence of multi-factor coupling can effectively reflect the operation state and safe operation boundary, which can guarantee the accuracy of the operation state estimation and optimization control. Through the operational reliability of the BESS, the vulnerability analysis including positioning and warning is an important basis to realize the combination of large-scale BESS for operational risk prevention and control. Through the reconfiguration scheme of the battery topology, the risk link of the BESS can be avoided or isolated actively, which is conducive to improving the enthusiasm of energy storage system to participate in power grid dispatching operation.

ACKNOWLEDGMENT

This work is granted by State Grid Corporation of China "Research on Coordination Development Model and Reliability Evaluation Technology of Source, Network, Load and Storage Considering Intrinsic Safety Requirements of Power Grid" (B3440818K005)and National Natural Science Foundation of China (No. 51777105).

REFERENCES

[1] Ma, Z, Zhou, X, Shang, Y, et al. Form and development trend of futuredistribution system [J]. Proceeding CSEE, 2015, 35(6): 1289–1298

[2] Kim J, Shin K G, Chun C Y, et al. Stable configuration of a Li-ion series battery pack based process on screening process for improved voltage/SOC balancing [J]. IEEE Tran. Power Electronics, 2012, 27(1): 411-416.

[3] Xu Q, Wang P, Xiao J, et al. Modeling and stability analysis of hybrid energy storage system under hierarchical control [C]. Power and Energy Engineering Conference (APPEEC), 2015 IEEE PES Asia-Pacific. IEEE, 2015: 1-5.

[4] Zhang W, Han X, Song S, et al. Operational reliability evaluation of wind integrated power systems based on markov chain considering uncertainty factors of source-grid-load [J]. Power System Technology, 2018, 42(3): 762-771.

[5] Duan D, Wu X, Deng H. Reliability evaluation of distribution systems based on time-varying failure rate and service restoration time model [J]. Proceedings of the CSEE, 2011, 31(28): 57-64.

[6] Kim H, Shin K G. On dynamic reconfiguration of a large-scale battery system [C]. 15th IEEE Real-Time and Embedded Technology and Applications Symposium. IEEE, 2009: 87-96.

[7] Zhang T and Horigome M. Availability and reliability of system with dependent components and time-varying failure and repair rates [J]. IEEE Transactions on Reliability, 2001, 50(2): 151-158.

[8] Singh C and Lago-Gonzalez A. Improved algorithms for multi-area reliability evaluation using the decomposition-simulation approach [J]. IEEE Transactions on Power Systems, 1989, 4(1): 321-328.

[9] Wang J, Xiong X, Zhou N, et al. Time-varying failure rate simulation model of transmission lines and its application in power system risk assessment considering seasonal alternating meteorological disasters [J]. IET Generation, Transmission & Distribution, 2016, 10(7): 1582-1588.

[10] He J, Sun Y, Wang P, et al. A hybrid conditions-dependent outage model of a transformer in reliability evaluation [J]. IEEE Transactions on Power Delivery, 2009, 24(4): 2025-2033.

[11] Zhong Y, Huang M, Qiang D. Reliability modeling of battery energy storage system and its effect on the reliability of distribution system [J]. Power System Protection and Control, 2013, 41(19): 95-102.

[12] Xu Y and Singh C. Power system reliability impact of energy storage integration with intelligent operation strategy [J]. IEEE Transactions on Smart Grid, 2014, 5(2): 1129-1137.

[13] Liu M, Li W, Wang C, et al. Reliability evaluation of largescale battery energy storage systems [J]. IEEE Transactions on Smart Grid, 2017, 8(6): 2733-2743.

[14] Artyom N and Panos P. Adaptive dynamic cost updating procedure for solving fixed charge network flow problems [J]. Computational Optimization and Applications, 2008, 39(1): 37-50.

[15] Ana Q, Esteban G, McCalley J D, et al. A multiperiod generalized network flow model of the U.S. integrated energy system: Part I-Model description [J]. IEEE Transactions on Power Systems, 2007, 22(2): 829-836.

[16] Wang Y, Chen Q, Zhang N, et al. Fusion of the 5G communication and the ubiquitous electric Internet of Things:application analysis and research prospects [J]. Power System Technology, 2019(early access)

[17] Liu J, Zhao Z, Ji X. Research and application of Internet of things inpower transmission and distribution system [J]. Chinese Journal on Internet of Things, 2018, 2(3): 88-102.

[18] Ci S, Lin N, Wu D. Reconfigurable battery techniques and systems: A survey [J]. IEEE Access, 2016, 4: 1175-1189.

[19] He L, Kong L, Lin S, et al. Reconfiguration-assisted charging in large-scale Lithium-ion battery systems [C]. ICCPS'14: ACM/IEEE 5th International Conference on Cyber-Physical Systems (with CPS Week 2014). IEEE Computer Society, 2014: 60-71.

[20] Lin N, Ci S, Wu D, et al. An Optimization Framework for Dynamically Reconfigurable Battery Systems [J]. IEEE Transactions on Energy Conversion, 2018, 33(4): 1669-1676.

[21] Kim H, Shin K G. DESA: Dependable, efficient, scalable architecture for management of large-scale batteries [J]. IEEE transactions on Industrial Informatics, 2012, 8(2): 406-417.

[22] Neubauer J and Pesaran A. The ability of battery second use strategies to impact plug-in electric vehicle prices and serve utility energy storage applications [J]. Journal of Power Sources 2011, 196 (23), 10351-10358.

[23] Mukherjee N, Strickland D, Cross A, et al. Reliability estimation of second life battery system power electronic topologies for grid frequency response

applications [C]. The 6th IET International Conference on Power Electronics, Machines and Drives (PEMD 2012), Bristol, 2012, pp. 1-6.
[24] Wang S L, Fernandez C, Zou C Y, et al. Open circuit voltage and state of charge relationship functional optimization for the working state monitoring of the aerial lithium-ion battery pack [J]. Journal of Cleaner Production, 2018, 198: 1090-1104.
[25] Zhang X, Wang Y, Yang D, et al. An on-line estimation of battery pack parameters and state-of-charge using dual filters based on pack model [J]. Energy, 2016, 115: 219-229.
[26] Hu X, Li S E, Yang Y. Advanced machine learning approach for lithium-ion battery state estimation in electric vehicles [J]. IEEE Transactions on Transportation electrification, 2016, 2(2): 140-149.

7th International Conference on Reliability of Electrical Products and Electrical Contacts, November 04-06, 2019

A Study of Effect of Roughness on the Contact Surface Temperature of Coaxial Connector

Yuqi Zhou, Jinchun Gao, Qingya Li, Gang Xie
Beijing University of Posts and Telecommunications, Beijing 100876, China
E-mail: gjc@bupt.edu.cn

Abstract—**The coaxial connector, as a significant part of the communication system, has an important impact on the reliability of the communication system. In the engineering applications, when coaxial connector transmits high frequency signal, its contact surface has a temperature rise phenomenon, which affects the reliability of signal transmission. This paper analyzed and modeled this phenomenon theoretically and studied the effect of coaxial connector rough surface on temperature rise under the condition of high frequency signal. Besides, the temperature rise effect of different plating materials of coaxial connector was studied. This work could provide an important guidance on the connector design to some extent.**

***Index Terms*-Coaxial connector, roughness, temperature rise, high frequency**

I. INTRODUCTION

As a commonly used connecting device, the coaxial connector is widely used in communication systems, and it has an essential influence on the reliability of the RF circuit and the entire communication device [1]. From a microscopic point of view, all contact surfaces are uneven and composed of irregular "peaks" [2]. This indicates that the actual contact surface is composed of many contact points, and the real contact area is smaller than the visible contact area of the surface. The real contact conditions are different with different roughness, causing there exists a relationship between the distribution of current density and the surface structure. That means the distribution of resistance at contact points between contact surfaces is related to the structure of surface [3]. When high-frequency signals flow through the contact surface of coaxial connectors, due to the skin effect, resulting in the current flow only in the outermost layer of the contact surface, which indicates that the current distribution is closely related to the surface roughness.

With more and more advanced scientific instruments and simulation software, and more and more innovative electrical contact theory, many people at home and abroad use different mathematical methods to model the contact surface. Holm proposed a classical theoretical model of electrical contact in 1930s, which gives a method to calculate the contact resistance of a single point contact based on some assumptions[4]. Based on the statistical theory, Greenwood and Williamson established the famous GW model, which contains the calculations of the number of contact spots, real contact area, contact force, etc.[5]. Under the condition of low frequency, the calculation of contact resistance is a main research direction, Researchers are searching for an accurate method of calculation. Benoit b. Mandelbrot firstly proposed that fractal and multi-scale models can be used in the natural world [6], which promotes the modeling of contact surfaces. Using the fractal concept in Weierstrass-Mandelbrot equation, Ciavarella modeled the contact surface with self-imitation and calculated the contact resistance of the contact surface [7]. In addition, Jackson et al. used the ratio of wave peak and amplitude in the fractal concept to measure the fractal dimension [8]. Considering the plating of the contact surface, Malucci established a three-dimensional model, and calculated the contact resistance of the contact surface [9]. When the current passes through the contact surface from the contact point, the current contraction will lead to the temperature rise at the contact point, which affects the performance of the communication system. Under DC conditions, Timsit established a single-point contact model to study the temperature distribution of contact points [10].

In this paper, the contact model of N-type coaxial connector is established combing the surface profile data under the condition of low frequency and high frequency. The influences of connector roughness on temperature distribution of contact surface and temperature rise of connector under different metal coating conditions were studied. The roughness of connector is affected by machining process, this work provides some guidance for the design of connectors.

II. CONTACT MODEL

The research object of this paper is N-type coaxial connector, as shown in Figure 1. The connector, a kind of low-power connector, is widely used in the RF loop of microwave equipment and digital communication system, and its function is to connect the RF cable or microstrip line.

The base material of N-type coaxial connector is copper, the plating material of male is gold, but the plating material of female is silver. The contact of connector is actually the contact of coating material. This paper studies the contact resistance of contact surface and the temperature rise effect caused by electrical connection of contact surface.

Fig. 1 N-type coaxial connector

The cross section of male head and female head of N-type coaxial connector is shown in figure 2. It can be observed that the shape of the contact surface is composed of four identical sections. The total contact resistance can be considered as the parallel contact resistance of four small contact surfaces:

$$R_{total} = \frac{R_c}{4} \tag{1}$$

where R_{total} is the total contact resistance and R_c is the contact resistance of a single contact surface. At lower frequencies or DC conditions, the current is transmitted through the entire contact surface, while at higher frequencies, the current only distributes on the outermost surface of the connector, and flows only within the skin depth range of the contact surface when passing through the contact surface. The model is divided into two parts: low frequency contact model and high frequency contact model.

In this paper, N-type coaxial connector is selected as the test sample, and the roughness of the contact surface edge is measured with the surface profilometer, and the surface profile of connector is drawn, as shown in Figure 3.

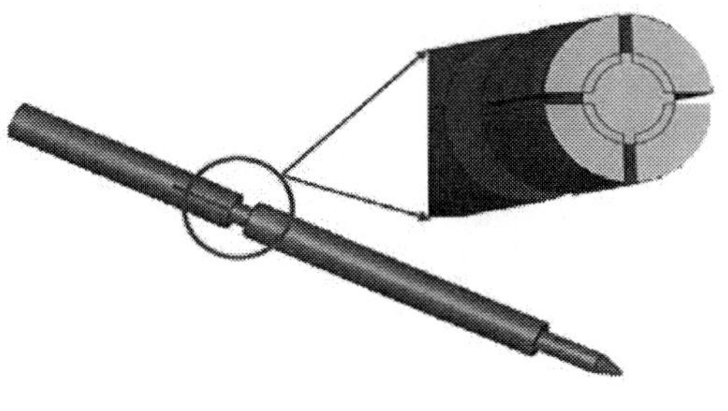

Fig. 2 Section of coaxial connector

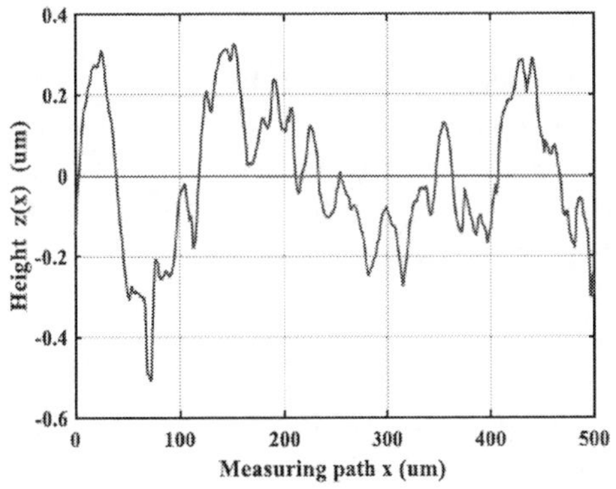

Fig. 3 profile of N-type coaxial connector surface

A. Low-frequency Contact Model

Under low frequency or DC conditions, the current passes through the contact surface at the contact point formed by the "peak". Under this condition, the contact resistance is related to the material, contact force, roughness and other factors of the contact surface [11]. In experience, the calculation of contact resistance under such conditions often uses the concept of probability theory to solve the problem of the number and size of electrical contact points [6-9]. N-type connectors are manufactured with production standards, and their surface roughness and surface topography are measurable. Multi-scale methods are used to model contact resistance [12].

Fast Fourier Transform(FFT) is used to calculate the surface contour data. For each scale:

$$a_i = \sqrt{\frac{A_i}{2\pi A_{i-1} f^2}} \tag{2}$$

where a_i is the radius of the contact point at scale i, a_i is the area of the contact point at scale i, and f is the frequency corresponding to the scale i. Based on the calculation method of single point contact resistance proposed by Holm [4], the total contact resistance in the multi-scale model is:

$$R_c = \sum_{i=1}^{i_{max}} \left(\frac{\rho_1 + \rho_2}{4a_i} \frac{1}{n_i} \right) \tag{3}$$

where ρ_1 and ρ_2 are the resistivity of the material on each side of the contact surface, n_i is the number of contact points on the i scale. The resistance at low frequency can be calculated by equations (1) and (3). The total heating power is determined by the contact resistance and the bulk resistance. This paper only considers the temperature rise generated by the contact surface, so the heating power of the contact surface of the N-type coaxial connector is:

$$P = \frac{I^2}{4} \sum_{i=1}^{i_{max}} \left(\frac{\rho_1 + \rho_2}{4a_i} \frac{1}{n_i} \right) \tag{4}$$

where I is the the current flowing through the N-type coaxial connection.

B. High-frequency Contact Model

Under high-frequency conditions, the current of N-type coaxial connector flows on the surface plating due to skin effect, and skin depth can be calculated by the following formula

$$\delta = \sqrt{\frac{\rho}{\pi f \mu_r \mu_0}} \tag{5}$$

where f is the signal frequency, μ_0 is the magnetic permeability of free space ($4\pi \times 10^{-7} H/m$), μ_r is the relative permeability of the conductor, and ρ is the resistivity of the conductor.

At high frequency, the flow path of current is shown in figure 4. When the current flows through the contact surface, skin effect limits the current to the "peak" at the edge of the contact surface, so the roughness of the edge of the contact surface has a great impact on the contact resistance.

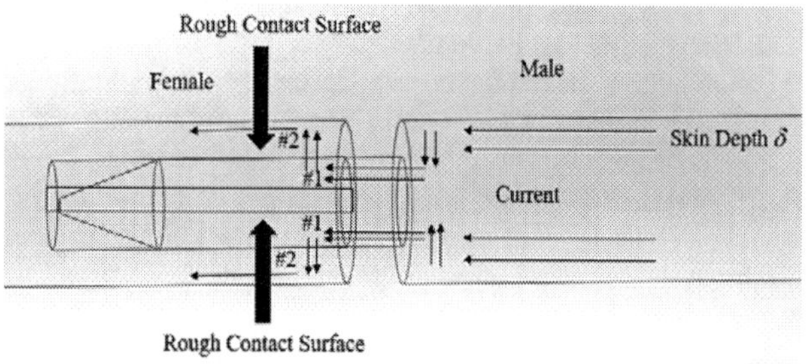

Fig. 4 Directions of current in coaxial connectors

This section models the actual connector surface profile. Under high frequency conditions, although the surface topography has a great influence on the contact performance of the connector, only the roughness of the edge portion of the contact surface is considered. The window function of the wavelet transform can be adjusted with the fluctuation of the surface contour, which can be used to study the influence of roughness on the contact surface of the N-type coaxial connector accurately. In this paper, the surface profile is processed by the one-dimensional wavelet transform method to calculate the contact resistance of the inner conductor of the N-type coaxial connector:

$$WT(a,\tau) = \frac{1}{\sqrt{a}} \int_0^{h_0} h(t) * \Psi\left(\frac{t-\tau}{a}\right) \tag{6}$$

where $h(t)$ is the contact surface profile, $\Psi(t)$ is the basic wavelet. The Daubechies wavelet db6 scale is chosen to process the edge profile , h_0 is the length of the edge profile, a is the wavelet scale, and τ is the translation. The value of the roughness is:

$$R_a = \frac{1}{h_0} \int_0^{h_0} h(t) - \bar{h}\, dt \tag{7}$$

$$\bar{h} = \frac{1}{h_0} \int_0^{h_0} h(t)\, dt \tag{8}$$

where $\bar{h}$ is the average height of edge profile, R_a is the roughness of the profile. This transformation has a 6-layer structure, and the higher-level low frequency profile contain smoother contact surfaces and fewer raised "peaks". However, the actual contact portion of the high-level contact surface is small, so only the first four layers are taken for the following analysis. Since the contact pressure and the roughness of the contact surface are constant, the spacing between the upper and lower surfaces is also determined [8]. The number of contact points and the radius of the contact point for each of the first four layers can be calculated:

(1) Solve the $h_1(t) + h_2(t) = H$ of each layer to get the solution set $x(i)$ and $i=1, 2, 3, ..., N$. And $h_1(t)$ 和 $h_2(t)$ are the profiles of the contact surface, and H is the average distance between the upper and lower contact faces.

(2) The radius of contact points are $a_j = x_{2j} - x_{2j-1}$, and $j=1, 2, 3, ..., N/2$.

(3) The resistance of each contact point is $R_j = \dfrac{\rho_1 + \rho_2}{4a_j}$, and all contact resistances are connected in parallel, the total contact resistance is $R_{total} = \rho_1 + \rho_2 \Big/ \sum_1^{\frac{N}{2}} 4a_j$.

(4) The total contact resistance R_c is composed of four layers in db6, and it is obtained by connecting four layers of R_{total} in parallel. The heating power at the contact surface can be obtained by using (4) in the low frequency model.

III. SIMULATION

In this paper, the finite element simulation model is used to study the temperature distribution of the surface of N-type coaxial connectors. As mentioned above, the base material of the N-type coaxial connector is copper, the surface plating of the male inner conductor is gold, the surface plating of the female is silver. Thus, the real contact surface is the contact of gold and silver plating, and the section of the model is shown in Figure 5. Tables 1 and 2 show the physical parameters associated with gold and silver plating, and the stress at the contact surface in the simulation model is 550 MPa. The value of surface roughness of n-type coaxial connector in the second part is 0.54, and the roughness of gold coating and silver coating is set as 0.54 in the simulation.

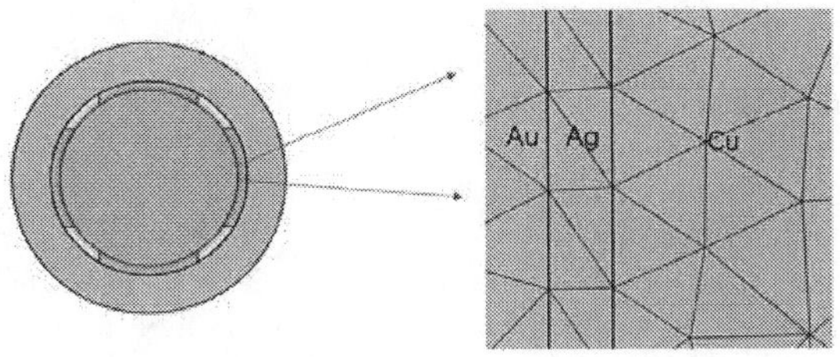

Fig. 5 Section and grid diagram of Connector

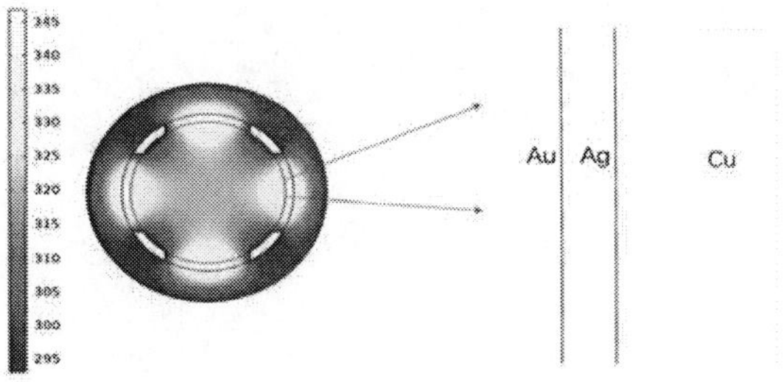

Fig. 6 Temperature distribution of N-type coaxial connector

Table 1. Related physical parameters of gold plating in the model

Model Properties	Value	Unit
Young's modulus	7×10^{10}	Pa
Thermal transmissivity of material	317 (373.15K)	W/m·K
Poisson ratio	0.44	1
Resistivity	2.4×10^{-8}(293.15K)	Ω·m

Table 2. Related physical parameters of silver plating in the model

Model Properties	Value	Unit
Young's modulus	8.3×10^{10}	Pa
Thermal transmissivity of material	429 (373.15K)	W/m·K
Poisson ratio	0.37	1
Resistivity	1.55×10^{-8}(293.15K)	Ω·m

A. The Temperature Distribution of N-type Coaxial Connector

The current and frequency are 50A and 10kHz in the simulation, respectively. The temperature distribution of N-type coaxial connector is shown in Figure 6.

The radial temperature distribution is shown in Figure 7. From the axis of the inner conductor of the N-type coaxial connector to the boundary, the temperature first rises and then decreases, and the highest point appears at the junction of gold coating and silver plating, which is 347.1K. It can be observed that there is also an obvious temperature change at the junction of the base copper and the plated metal. This is because the base metal and the plating material are different, resulting in changes in parameters such as resistivity. Accordingly, the heating power and the overall temperature variations of the connector are also different. By contrast, the temperature rise caused by the contact surface is higher than the heat generated by the metal itself.

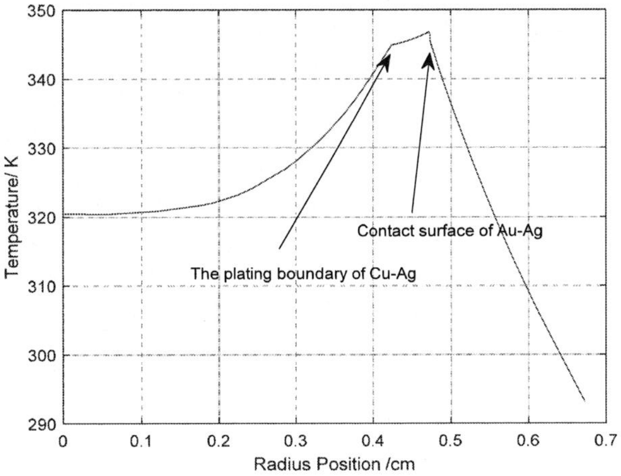

Fig. 7 Radial temperature distribution of the coaxial connector(Au-Ag)

B. The Temperature Distribution of N-type Coaxial Connector

In the following simulation, the contact pressure and current keep the constant, and the female plating material still set as the silver. Whereas the material of the male metal plating is changed from gold to nickel. The result of temperature distribution is shown in Figure 8.

As is shown in Figure 8, from the axis of the inner conductor of the N-type coaxial connector to the boundary, the temperature first rises and then decreases, and the highest temperature appears at the contact surface, which is 354K. The contact surface made of silver and nickel has a higher overall temperature and the highest temperature than the contact surface made of gold and silver, because the resistivity of nickel metal is greater than that of gold. Regarding the slope of the temperature rise, the contact interfaces between gold and silver are steeper than the contact surfaces between silver and nickel, which indicates that the temperature rise of the former is more pronounced in the case of the same roughness.

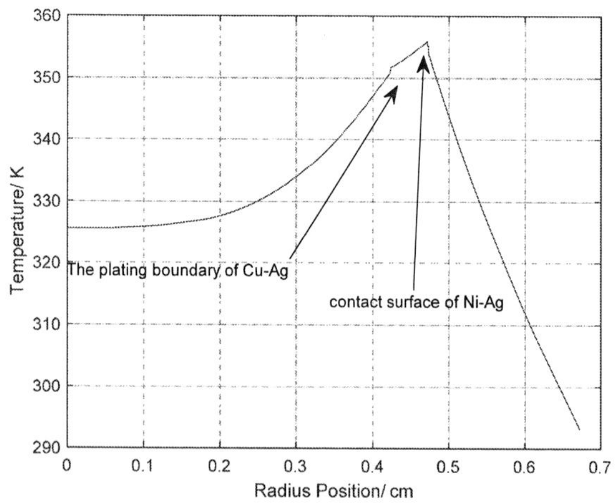

Fig. 8 Radial temperature distribution of the coaxial connector(Ni-Ag)

C. Relationship Between Roughness and Temperature

This simulation select the contact surface of gold and silver, and the contact pressure, contact area and current are the same as previous. the roughness of the contact surface range from 0 to 1.5, interval 0.1 for simulation, the temperature distribution of the N-type coaxial connector is shown in Figure 9.

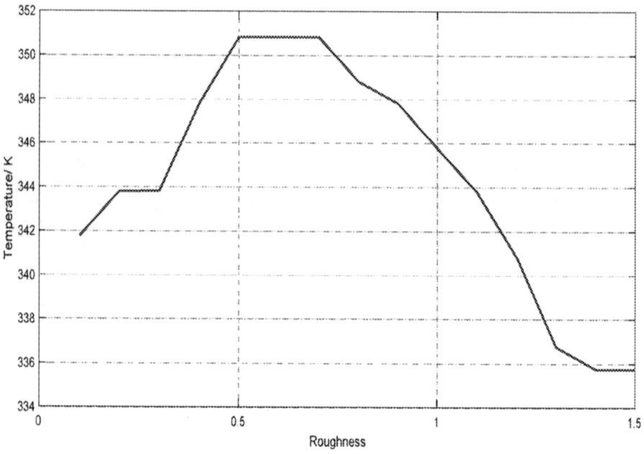

Fig. 9 The relationship of roughness and temperature

As shown in the figure, as the roughness increases, the temperature rises first and then decreases. When the roughness is in the range of 0.5 to 0.6, the temperature of the N-type coaxial connector contact point is the highest. That means when the roughness is small, as the surface roughness of the contact surface increases, the contact surface of the connector is in poor contact, the contact resistance increases, thus, the temperature rise is obvious. When the roughness is higher than 0.6, as the roughness increases, the "peaks" on the contact surface are sharper, but the contact situation is better. The reason may be that when the roughness is large, the contact area between the "peak" on the two surfaces is larger, resulting in better contact performance and lower temperature rise.

IV. CONCLUSION

In this paper, based on the surface profile of the actual contact surface, two mathematical models of contact resistance based on low frequency signal and high frequency signal were proposed. Both models involve the calculation of contact resistance by surface roughness, which visually analyzed the effect of roughness on contact resistance. This model is useful for evaluating the electrical performance of N-type coaxial connectors. On this basis, the finite element simulation software was used to study the temperature distribution of N-type coaxial connectors under working conditions and the influence of roughness on temperature rise. Furthermore, the effect of different metal coatings on the temperature rise of N-type coaxial connectors was also studied. This paper provides some guiding significance for the design of coaxial connector, including the choice of coating and processing mode.

V. ACKNOWLEDGEMENT

This work was supported in part by the National Natural Science Foundation of China (No. 51877010), in part by the Open Fund of State Key Laboratory of Information Photonics and Optical Communications, Beijing University of Posts and Telecommunications (BUPT), and in part by the Fundamental Research Funds for the Central Universities, BUPT (No.2019PTB-014).

REFERENCES

[1] R.Ji, J.C.Gao, G.Xie, et al. Fault Analysis and Diagnosis of Coaxial Connectors in RF Circuits[J]. IEICE Transactions on Electronics, 2017, 100(11): 1052-1060.

[2] P.G. Slade, "Electrical Contact Resistance: Fundamental Principles," in Electrical Contacts Principles and Applications. 2nd ed, New York: CRC Press, 2014, pp. 4-5.

[3] P.G. Slade, "Electrical Contact Resistance: Fundamental Principles," in Electrical Contacts Principles and Applications. 2nd ed, New York: CRC Press, 2014, pp. 89-90.

[4] R. Holm, Electrical Contacts. New York: Springer,1979.

[5] J. A. Greenwood and J. B. P. Williamson, "Contact of nominally flat surfaces", in Proceedings of the Royal Society A, pp.300–319, Dec. 1966.

[6] J. F. Archard, "Elastic Deformation and the Laws of Friction," Proc. R. Soc. Lond. A vol.243, pp. 190-205, 1957.

[7] M. Ciavarella, G. Murolo and G. Demelio, "The electrical/thermal conductance of rough surfaces—the Weierstrass-Archard multiscale model", International Journal of Solids and Structures, vol. 41, no. 15, pp.4107-4120, July. 2004.

[8] R. L. Jackson and J. L. Streator, "A multiscale model for contact between rough surfaces", Wear, vol. 261, no. 11-12, pp. 1337-1347, May. 2006,

[9] Robert D. Malucci. High Frequency Considerations for the Multi-Point Contact Interfaces. the 47th IEEE HOLM Conf. On Electrical Contacts, 2001:175-185.

[10] R. S. Timsit and A. Luttgen, "Temperature distribution in a constriction heated by a high frequency electrical current", in 28th International Conference on Electrical Contacts, pp. 3-8 , June. 2016.

[11] J. F. Archard. "Elastic deformation and the laws of friction", in Proceedings of the Royal Society A, pp.190-205, Dec. 1957.

[12] X. Zhang and R. L. Jackson, "The influence of multiscale roughness on the real contact area and contact resistance between real reference surfaces", in Proc. the 27th International Conference on Electrical Contacts ICEC, pp. 1–6,July.201.

Detection of Inter-turn Short-circuit Faults in PMSMsBased on Instantaneous Reactive Power

Shaopo Huang[1], Elias G. Strangas[2], Kui Li[1], Feng Niu[1]
[1]State Key Laboratory of EERI, Hebei University of Technology, Tianjin, 300130, China
[2]Electrical and Computer Engineering, Michigan State University, East Lansing, MI, 48824, USA
E-mail: shaaopo0303@163.com Tel: 86-18601920902

Abstract—**Reliable stator faults diagnosis is important for machine drives. This work presents an inter-turn short-circuit faults detection and faulty phase location method for PMSMs with neutral conductor, based on the percentage of the second harmonics in the three phase instantaneous reactive powers, defined in the *abc* frame of reference. A faulty PMSM model which is widely used for the detection of inter-turn short-circuits is used to build a simulation setup in MATLAB/Simulink. From the theoretical analysis and the simulations, the second harmonics in instantaneous reactive powers are proven to be the characteristic feature for fault detection. Simulations at different operating conditions show that the percentages of the second harmonics to their dc components in phase instantaneous reactive powers are more reliable than the second harmonic amplitudes themselves for the inter-turn short-circuits detection and location.**

***Index Terms*— faults detection, faults location, inter-turn short-circuit faults, the second harmonic, reactive powers.**

I. INTRODUCTION

Inter-turn Short-circuit (ITSC) is reported to be one of the most common faults in PMSMs, and always leads to a catastrophic failure in a short time [1], [2]. It is difficult to reduce the damage to the machine when there is an ITSC, because the magnets cannot be switch off and a high short-circuit current generates due to the induced voltage cross the shorted turns.

Machine currents and voltages signature analysis have proven to be efficient techniques for fault detection because of their non-invasive feature and easy to access. The currents measurements are essential for the machine control and the voltages can also be acquired from voltage sensors. As an alternative of the voltages measurement, the controller reference voltages have been proved to be applicable in faults detection [2]. In [3], the stator currents were used to detect ITSCs and the fault severity is determined by the amplitude of the side band components of the stator currents. In the synchronous frame of reference, the changes of the current vector magnitude and angle were used to detect the stator winding faults and distinguish them from demagnetization fault [4]. The relationship between the fault characteristics and the voltage drop of the winding with ITSC was analyzed in [5], and the faulty phase was detected by comparing the residual components in the three phase voltages. Besides, the third negative and positive harmonics in the space vectors of current and voltage in the *dq* frame [6], the Park's Vectors of current and voltage [3], the back induced electromotive forces (EMFs) and the impedance [7], [8] were also used for ITSCs detection.

Most of the above techniques are based on the analysis of one signal, such as voltages or currents. However, due to the weak fault characteristics in the signals, special for the incipient faults with low severity, it becomes a difficult task to recognize the fault. For ITSC with a few shorted turns, the fault information contained in voltages or currents are always not sufficient for detecting [2]. Therefore, researchers have been investigated alternative parameters for fault detection, such as instantaneous active power (IAP) or instantaneous reactive power (IRP) [1], [9].

The second harmonic in IRP, defined in the *dq* frame of reference, was reported to be an effective indicator for ITSCs detection in PMSMs under motoring mode [9]. This work presents an ITSC indicator based on the second harmonic in IRP, defined in the *abc* frame of reference. For a three-phase machine, the proposed indicator can not only detect the ITSC fault but also locate the faulty phase. The neutral conductor is required for the fault locating in PMSMs.

II. INSTANTANEOUS REACTIVE POWER SIGNATURE ANALYSIS

Different from the classical power definition based on the root mean square (RMS) and mean values of current and voltage, the instantaneous power is defined with their instant value. An advantage is that it is valid in the transient state, such as the load change in the case of a motor operating. Considering that the stator active power changes in a much wider range and in a faster way when compared to the reactive power, the analysis of the stator reactive power is used for fault diagnostic purposes [10].

A. *Instantaneous Reactive Power Definition*

The generalized IRP is defined as:

$$q(t)=\sqrt{q_a^2+q_b^2+q_c^2} \tag{1}$$

in which the phase IRPs, q_{abc}, are defined to be the cross-product of the voltage and current vectors, shown as:

$$q=v\times i=\begin{bmatrix}v_a\\v_b\\v_c\end{bmatrix}\times\begin{bmatrix}i_a\\i_b\\i_c\end{bmatrix}=\begin{bmatrix}q_a\\q_b\\q_c\end{bmatrix}$$

where

$$\begin{cases}q_a=v_bi_c-v_ci_b\\q_b=v_ci_a-v_ai_c\\q_c=v_ai_b-v_bi_a\end{cases} \tag{2}$$

This definition is valid for three-phase three-wire system, and the original authors introduced in [11] showed that many other definitions can be deducted from (1) using different transformations.

The objective of this work is detecting and locating the ITSCs in PMSMs, so the absolute value of the three phase IRPs, $|q_a|$, $|q_b|$ and $|q_c|$, are investigated, in order to show a different phase IRPs behavior between the three phases when an ITSC only happens in one of them.

B. *ITSC Characterization*

1) Case of Healthy PMSMs.

Assuming the healthy PMSM is powered from a balanced three-phase sinusoidal voltage source and driving a constant load, the expressions of stator voltages and currents are modeled by the following:

$$\begin{cases}v_a(t)=\sqrt{2}V\cos(\omega t)\\v_b(t)=\sqrt{2}V\cos(\omega t-2\pi/3)\\v_c(t)=\sqrt{2}V\cos(\omega t+2\pi/3)\end{cases} \tag{3}$$

$$\begin{cases}i_a(t)=\sqrt{2}I\cos(\omega t-\varphi)\\i_b(t)=\sqrt{2}I\cos(\omega t-\varphi-2\pi/3)\\i_c(t)=\sqrt{2}I\cos(\omega t-\varphi+2\pi/3)\end{cases} \tag{4}$$

The phase IRPs can be calculated by substituting (3) and (4) into (2), and derived the $q_i(t)$ in healthy case as:

$$|q_a(t)|=|q_b(t)|=|q_c(t)|=\sqrt{3}VI\sin\varphi \tag{5}$$

where φ is the power factor of the machine.

It is clear that phase IRPs only contain dc components in healthy condition.

2) Case of Faulty PMSMs.

In real applications, PMAC machines work together with controllers, and there will be no harmonics in currents if the current controllers are perfect. Even for the controllers with limited bandwidth, in ideal symmetric three-phase machines without neutral conductor, the third order harmonic currents are absent because they are in phase with each other and there is no return path. While, in the case of PMSMs with ITSCs, the third order harmonic voltages in three phases change both in magnitude and phase angle due to the unbalance caused by the machine faults, leading to the third order harmonics in phase voltages no longer in phase and the third harmonic currents generated [12]. These third harmonics in phase currents exist in a faulty PMSM no matter with neutral conductor or without. The phase currents and voltages with ITSC are expressed as:

$$\begin{cases}i_{vf}(t)=v_a(t)+\sqrt{2}V_{a3}\cos(3\omega t+\varphi_{av3})\\i_{vf}(t)=v_b(t)+\sqrt{2}V_{b3}\cos(3\omega t+\varphi_{bv3})\\i_{vf}(t)=v_c(t)+\sqrt{2}V_{c3}\cos(3\omega t+\varphi_{cv3})\end{cases} \tag{6}$$

$$\begin{cases}i_{af}(t)=i_a(t)+\sqrt{2}I_{a3}\cos(3\omega t+\varphi_{ai3})\\i_{bf}(t)=i_b(t)+\sqrt{2}I_{b3}\cos(3\omega t+\varphi_{bi3})\\i_{cf}(t)=i_c(t)+\sqrt{2}I_{c3}\cos(3\omega t+\varphi_{ci3})\end{cases} \tag{7}$$

According to the definitions in (2), the second, the fourth and the sixth harmonics will come out in spectra of the phase IRPs. Besides, the dc components are also effected by the faults. Comparing to the healthy condition, where only dc component is contained, these pulsations caused by fault are credible for ITCSs detection in PMSMs.

In this work, the percentages of the second harmonics to their dc components in phase IRPs are proposed as the indicators for ITSC detection and location. The effectiveness of the proposed indicator is validated through simulation in section IV.

III. FAULTY MODEL AND SIMULATION SETUP

In order to investigate the second harmonics behaviors in the phase IRPs, a faulty PMSM model was introduced and a simulation setup was established in MATLAB/Simulink.

A. *Voltage Equations of Faulty PMSM*

The circuit model of PMSM with ITSC, shown in Fig. 1, has been widely used to study the effects of ITSC [2].

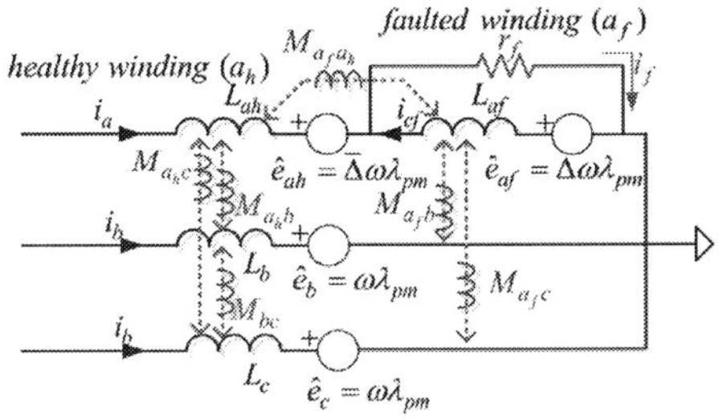

Fig. 1 Three phase electrical model for a PMSM with ITSC.

Each phase is modeled using its resistance (r_s), self and mutual inductance (L and M) and the EMFs (e_{abc}). The ITSC is introduced by shorting a portion ofhealthy windings with a resistor (r_f), which represents the insulation degradation between two shorted turns. Phase A is split into two separate windings, denoted as a_h for the healthy part and a_f for the shorted area. A faulted circulating current, i_f, is generated in the short-circuit path. The voltage equations for an PMSM with ITSC is given as [2]:

$$\begin{bmatrix} v_a \\ v_b \\ v_c \\ 0 \end{bmatrix} = \begin{bmatrix} r_s & 0 & 0 & -r_{a_f} \\ 0 & r_s & 0 & 0 \\ 0 & 0 & r_s & 0 \\ -r_{a_f} & 0 & 0 & r_{a_f} + r_f \end{bmatrix} \cdot \begin{bmatrix} i_a \\ i_b \\ i_c \\ i_f \end{bmatrix} + L_{sf} \frac{d}{dt} \begin{bmatrix} i_a \\ i_b \\ i_c \\ i_f \end{bmatrix} + \begin{bmatrix} e_a \\ e_b \\ e_c \\ -e_{a_f} \end{bmatrix} \quad (8)$$

where

$$M_{a_{h+f}b} = M_{a_h b} + M_{a_f b} M_{a_{h+f}c} = M_{a_h c} + M_{a_f c}$$

$$L_f = -\left(L_{a_f} + M_{a_h a_f}\right)$$

$$L_{sf} = \begin{bmatrix} L_a & M_{a_{h+f}b} & M_{a_{h+f}c} & L_f \\ M_{a_{h+f}b} & L_b & M_{bc} & -M_{a_f b} \\ M_{a_{h+f}c} & M_{bc} & L_c & -M_{a_f c} \\ L_f & -M_{a_f b} & -M_{a_f c} & L_{a_f} \end{bmatrix}$$

$$\begin{bmatrix} e_a \\ e_{a_f} \\ e_b \\ e_c \end{bmatrix} = \begin{bmatrix} \omega_e \lambda_{pm} \cos\theta_e \\ \Delta\omega_e \lambda_{pm} \cos\theta_e \\ \omega_e \lambda_{pm} \cos(\theta_e - 2\pi/3) \\ \omega_e \lambda_{pm} \cos(\theta_e + 2\pi/3) \end{bmatrix}$$

The number of turns involved in the ITSC is denoted as $N_f$and the total number of turns per phase is N_{total}. The ratio is defined as $\Delta = N_f/N_{total}$. Comparing with the equations in healthy condition, a fourth line, which shows the voltage relationship in the circling circuit, is added. And, the remaining healthy part (rows 1 to 3) are effected by the fault current.

TABLE I

MACHINE SPECIFICATION

Parameters	Value	Parameters	Value
Number of Phases	3	Number of Slots/Poles	12/10
$I_{rms\ max}$	18 A	Turns per Phase	300
$V_{rms\ max}$	480 V	Phase Resistance r_s	1.5 Ω
Base RPM	600	Phase Inductance L_s	112 mH
λ_{pm}	0.28 $V \cdot s$	Mutual Inductance M_s	≈ 0 mH

B. Machine Parameters and Simulink Model

A single-layer fractional-slot concentrated-winding PMSM is analyzed in this work. The main advantages of this configuration relating to decreasing the effect of winding fault is eliminating the possibility of overlapping between end windings of different phases, leading to low mutual inductance between phases, therefore reducing the effect of the short-circuit current in one phase has on others. For this winding configuration, all the mutual inductances between the healthy coil or the faulted coil in the faulty phase and the other two healthy phases can be neglected [2]. While the mutual inductance between the healthy coil and the faulted coil is not negligible as they share the same slot. The healthy machine specification is described in Table I. The self and mutual inductances regarding the ITSC are determined in a same way as that in [2].

Based on the faulty PMSM model in (8), a simulation setup is built in Simulink and shown in Fig. 2. The ITSC is introduced to phase A.

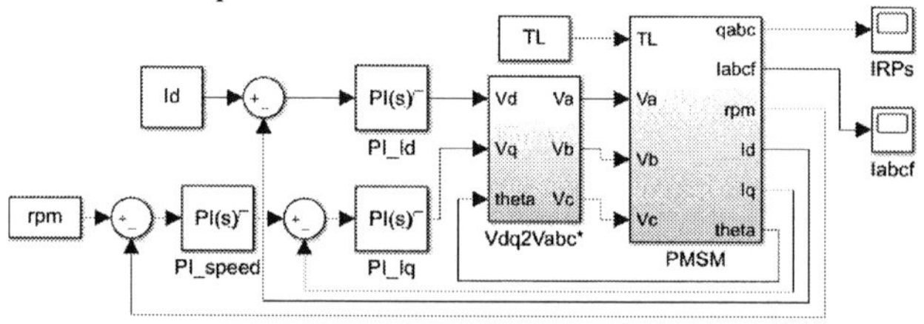

Fig. 2 Simulation setup in MATLAB/Simulink.

IV. SIMULATION RESULTS AND ANALYSIS

The advantages of the proposed ITSC indicator were validated through simulation and introduced in this section.

A. Fault Feature Analysis

The machine was operated in constant speed mode under FOC control, i_d was set to zero. Fig. 3 shows the phase currents and the short-circuit current, the neutral current and the phase IRPs before and after introducing ITSC at $t = 2$ s.

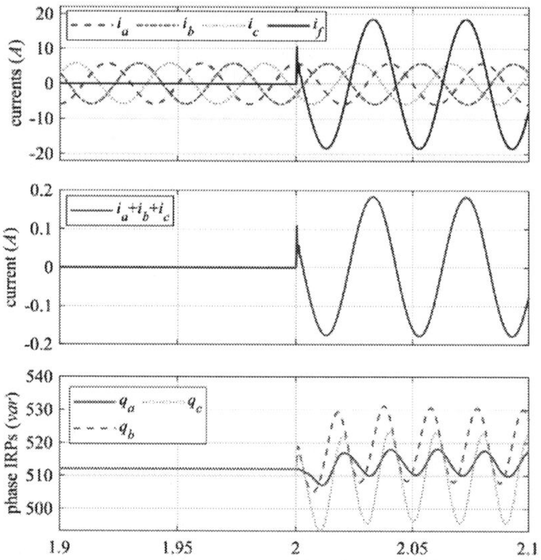

Fig. 3 The phase currents and short-circuit current (top), the neutral current (middle) and the phase IRPs (bottom) before and after ITSC. Operating conditions: machine speed $\omega_m = 300$ rpm and load torque $T_L = 10$ $N{\cdot}m$. fault severity: $\Delta = 0.01$, $r_f = 50$ $m\Omega$.

The ITSC generated circulating current, i_f, in the short-circuit path, and a small current in the same phase of i_f was introduced to the neutral conductor due to the fault. It was clear that the ITSC also caused dc component changes and the second harmonic pulsations in the three phase IRPs. Moreover, the second harmonic amplitude of q_a was smaller than that of q_b and q_c, which was reasonable because more disturbance was generated in the faulty phase (phase A) compared to the other two healthy phases. According to (2), the pulsations in q_b and q_c should be larger than that in q_a. Fig. 4 shows the spectra of currents, voltages and phase IRPs in healthy case and in faulty case, which are marked with H and F, separately. The fundamentals of currents and voltages in (a) and (b), and the dc components of phase IRPs in (c) are relatively high and don't have much changes after ITSC, hence they are not shown in Fig. 4.

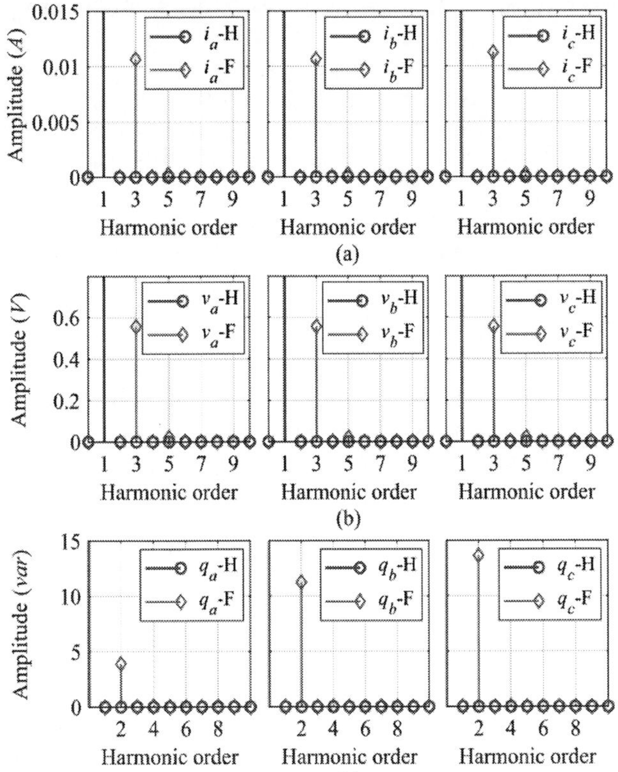

Fig. 4 The spectra of currents (a), voltages (b) and phase IRPs (b) in healthy and faulty cases. The same operating conditions and fault severity as Fig. 3.

Apparently, the third harmonics in currents and voltages, and the second harmonics in phase IRPs increase after ITSC. The percentages of the third harmonics to their fundamentals in currents and in voltages, and proposed indicators are compared in table II.

TABLE II

PERCENTAGES OF FAULT FEATURE (%)

Currents	$\frac{3^{rd}}{1^{st}} \times 100$	Voltages	$\frac{3^{rd}}{1^{st}} \times 100$	IPRs	$\frac{2^{nd}}{dc} \times 100$
i_a	0.19	v_a	0.5	q_a	0.76
i_b	0.18	v_b	0.51	q_b	2.17
i_c	0.18	v_c	0.53	q_c	2.68

The third harmonics in currents and in voltages, and the second harmonic phase IRPs are zero in healthy case.So the ITSCs can be detected by spectra analysis of currents, voltages or IRPs. While, from Table II it is clear that the percentages of the second harmonic phase IRPs are larger than that of the third harmonics in currents and in voltages, and the indicator of q_b and q_c are greater then q_a, which provides a method to locate the faulty phase.

B. *ITSCs Detection at Different Operating Conditions*

The effectiveness of the proposed indicator was validated under different operating conditions. The amplitudes of the second harmonic IRPs and the proposed indicators, at different speeds, are shown in Fig. 5, in which the fault severity is the same as that in Fig. 3.

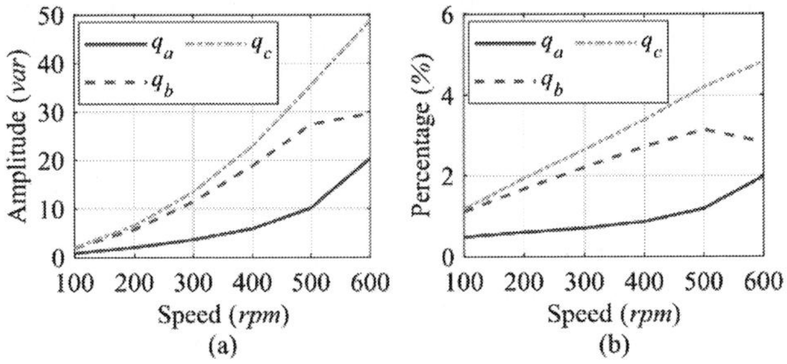

Fig. 5 The amplitudes of the second harmonics in IRPs (a) and the proposed indicators (b), with ITSC, at different speeds. T_L was fixed at 10 $N{\cdot}m$.

Both the amplitudes and the percentages increase as the speed increase, which is mainly caused by the increasing voltages due to the EMFs. As introduced in the previous section, the q_a indicator are always below that of q_b and q_c which makes it available for ITSC location. In Fig. 5 (a). the amplitudes of q_a also have the similar behavior, while the differences at low speeds is not obvious.

The machine was also tasted at different load torques with the same fault severity, and the results are shown in Fig. 6. At zero torque, there was no current inject to the machine, the amplitudes of the second harmonic IRPs are close to zero. Even though, the fault current due to the EMFs introduces more features to the faulty phase than the other two healthy phases. In this case, the percentages of q_b and q_c are 79.9% and 105.3%, respectively, which are very high caused by the small dc components of q_b and q_c.

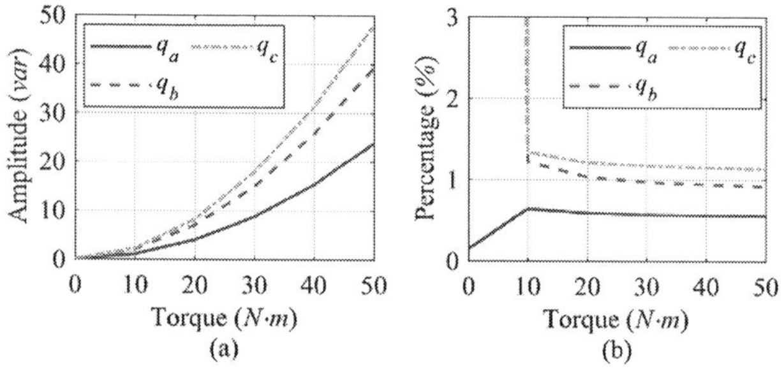

Fig. 6 The amplitudes of the second harmonics in IRPs (a) and the proposed indicators (b), with ITSC, at different torques. ω_m was fixed at 100 *rpm*.

The results from Fig. 6 (b) also confirm that the ITSC in phase A can be located because the q_a indicator are always below that of q_b and q_c at the whole torque range.

C. Discussion

Above, the proposed ITSCs indicator is valid for a three-phase PMSM with a neutral conductor. If the neutral is not connected, the fault still can be detected by this indicator, however, the faulty phase location is not available. Because the three phase currents add up to zero and the phase IRPs will have the same dc component changes and the same harmonic fluctuations, according to (2). In this case, the phase IRPs are shown is Fig. 7.

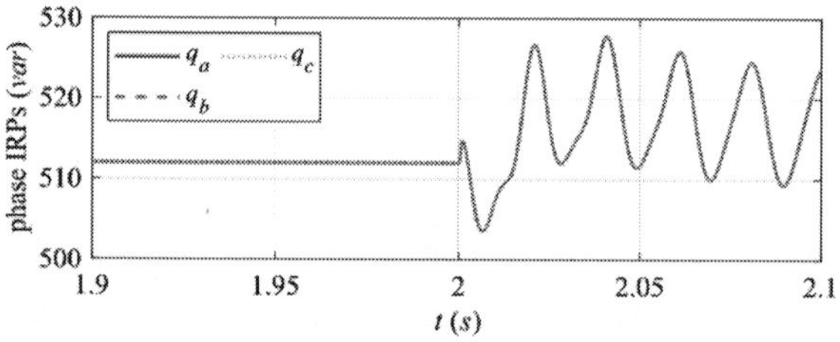

Fig. 7 The phase IRPs before and after ITSC, without neutral conductor. Operating conditions: machine speed ω_m = 300 *rpm* and load torque T_L = 10 *N·m*. fault severity: $\Delta = 0.01$, $r_f = 50\ m\Omega$.

V. CONCLUSION

ITSCs introduce imbalance to the machine, which generates the third harmonics in the phase currents and voltages. IRP provides a method to combine the fault features in voltages and in currents for fault diagnosis. The definition of phase IRPs in *abc* frame of reference makes it possible to not only detect the ITSCs but also locate them for the PMSMs with neutral conductor. Simulation results show that the percentages of the second harmonics in phase IRPs to their dc components are more appropriate for the faulty phase location than the amplitudes themselves. The results in this work are from steady state, and the proposed indicators can be used to detect ITSCs in PMSMs online by introducing harmonic extraction techniques to the drive systems.

ACKNOWLEDGMENT

This work was supported in part by the State Scholarship Fund of China under Grant 201606700009, and in part by the National Natural Science Foundation of China under Grant 51707174.

REFERENCES

[1] M. Drif and A. J. M. Cardoso, "Stator fault diagnostics in squirrel cage three-phase induction motor drives using the instantaneous active and reactive power signature analyses," *IEEE Transactions on Industrial Informatics*, vol. 10, no. 2, pp. 1348–1360, May 2014.

[2] S. N. Foster, J. G. Cintron-Rivera, and E. G. Strangas, "Detection of incipient stator winding faults in PMSMs with single-layer fractional slot concentrated windings," *Electric Power Systems Research*, vol. 131, pp. 231–243, Feb 2016.

[3] J. Faiz, A. H. Exiri, and H. Nejadi-Koti, "Current-based inter-turn short circuit fault modeling in permanent magnet synchronous machine using magnetic equivalent circuit model," in *2016 10th International Conference on Compatibility, Power Electronics and Power Engineering (CPE-POWERENG)*, June 2016, pp. 265–270.

[4] S. Moon, H. Jeong, H. Lee, and S. W. Kim, "Detection and classification of demagnetization and interturn short faults of IPMSMs," *IEEE Transactions on Industrial Electronics*, vol. 64, no. 12, pp. 9433–9441, Dec 2017.

[5] S. Moon, H. Jeong, H. Lee, and S. W. Kim, "Interturn short fault diagnosis in a PMSM by voltage and current residual analysis with the faulty winding model," *IEEE Transactions on Energy Conversion*, vol. 33, no. 1, pp. 190–198, March 2018.

[6] F. ira, M. Arkan, B. Gm, and T. Goktas, "Analysis of stator inter-turn short-circuit fault signatures for inverter-fed permanent magnet synchronous motors," in *IECON 2016 - 42nd Annual Conference of the IEEE Industrial Electronics Society*, Oct 2016, pp. 1453–1457.

[7] B. Du, S. Wu, S. Han, and S. Cui, "Interturn fault diagnosis strategy for interior permanent magnet synchronous motor of electric vehicles based on digital signal processor," *IEEE Transactions on Industrial Electronics*, vol. 63, no. 3, pp. 1694–1706, March 2016.

[8] Y. Qi, M. Zafarani, and B. Akin, "A diagnosis procedure in standstill mode for inter turn short circuit faults of PMSMs through modified self-commissioning," in *2016 IEEE Energy Conversion Congress and Exposition (ECCE)*, Sept 2016, pp. 1–7.

[9] B. Wang, J. Wang, A. Griffo, and B. Sen, "Stator turn fault detection by second harmonic in instantaneous power for a triple-redundant fault-tolerant PM drive," *IEEE Transactions on Industrial Electronics*, vol. 65,

no. 9, pp. 7279–7289, Sept 2018.

[10] M. B. Abadi, S. M. A. Cruz, A. P. Gonalves, P. F. C. Gonalves, A. M. S. Mendes, A. Ribeiro, and F. Silva, "Detection of stator and rotor faults in a dfig based on the stator reactive power analysis," in *IECON 2014-40th Annual Conference of the IEEE Industrial Electronics Society*, Oct 2014, pp. 2037–2043.

[11] M. Drif and A. J. M. Cardoso, "The use of the instantaneous-reactive-power signature analysis for rotor-cage-fault diagnostics in three-phase induction motors," *IEEE Transactions on Industrial Electronics*, vol. 56, no. 11, pp. 4606–4614, Nov 2009.

[12] S. Huang, E. G. Strangas, A. Aggarwal, K. Li, F. Niu, "Robust inter-curn short-circuit detection in PMSMs with respect to current controller bandwidth,'' in *2019 IEEE Energy Conversion Congress and Exposition (ECCE),* to be published.

Research on the Influence of Arc-iron Wall Interactions to Arc Volt-ampere Characteristics

Tiansheng Zhu[1,2], Hongwu Liu[2], Ruiliang Guan[2], Shenli Jia[1], Junxian Ma[2]
[1]State key laboratory of electrical insulation and power equipment, Xi'an Jiaotong University, Xi'an, Shanxi Province 710049, China
[2]Changshu Switchgear Mfg. Co., Ltd.,(Former Changshu Switchgear Plant)&Jiangsu Key Laboratory of Smart Grid Distribution and Utilization Technology Research, Changshu, Jiangsu, 215500, China
E-mail: zhutiansheng@aliyun.com

Abstract—**In this paper, the influence of air arc-iron wall interactions to the arc volt-ampere characteristics is studied experimentally. Under the experimental conditions, when the current is less than 220 A, arc-iron wall contacting has no significant effect on the volt-ampere characteristics of the arc; and when the current is greater than 220 A, the arc-iron wall contacting obviously increase the arc voltage. According to further analysis, when the current is greater than 220A, the iron vapor generated by the ablation of the iron wall changes the properties of the arc plasma, and the strong radiation of the air-Fe arc plasma decreases the arc temperature which increases the arc voltage; when the current is low, the amount of iron ablation is small and it has few effect on the volt-ampere characteristics of the arc.**

Index Terms—**Arc-iron wall interactions, volt-ampere characteristics, iron vapor.**

I. INTRODUCTION

Splitting long arcs into series short arcs with metal plates is widely used in interrupting process for modern air circuit breakers. The actions between the undivided long arc and the metal plates are important factors for whether the arc can be divided by the plates.

Lindmayer et al. carried out a lot of research on the process of arc splitting by a combination of simulation and experiments[1-4]. In their simulation model, the blocking effect of metal plates on arc bending, elongation, and extrusion are taken into account before the arc is divided.Yang et al. considered the influence of the magnetic field of the ferromagnetic plate to the arc motion[5]. However, the above studies did not consider the heat exchange and ablation of the metal plates. When the arc is in contact with the metal plates, the surface of the plates will melt and evaporate due to the conduction and radiation of the arc energy. On the one hand, the process will absorb the arc energy; on the other hand, the metal vapor generated by the evaporation will spread in arc chamber. The composition of arc plasma will be changed and it can affect the volt-ampere characteristics of arc column.So the interaction between air arc and iron plates must be considered.

In previous researches, many studies have been carried out on the effect of interactions between air arc and non-metallic materials, especially gas-producing materials[6–8], However, there are few studies on influence of arc-iron interactions to volt-ampere characteristics of arc column.

In this paper, the voltage-ampere characteristics of arc in contact with ceramic wall and iron wall are compared experimentally. The experimental current varies from 30A to 7500A. The special designed experimental model can greatly eliminate the difference of arc column length and magnetic field distribution in the arc chamber.

Under the experimental conditions, when the current is greater than 220 A, the voltage of arc in contact with iron wall is higher than that of arc in contact with ceramic wall; when the current is less than 220 A, there is no significant difference for arc voltage in above conditions.

II. EXPERIMENTSETUP

The arc experimental apparatus is shown in Figure 1(a), the test component upper wall is installed between two copper electrodes. In the experiment, a copper fuse was used for arc igniting.

After the arc was generated, it moved to the parallel upper segments of the copper electrode due to electromagnetic force and was in contact with the upper wall of the arc chamber. The distance between the parallel upper segments of the copper electrode is 45.5 mm, and the length of the arc column is approximately 45.5 mm by ignoring the difference of arc length in each experiments.

In order to avoid the arc being short-circuited by the iron wall in the experiment, the upper wall of the arc chamber cannot use a whole iron block. In this paper, as shown in Figure 1(b), a group of 3mm thick iron pieces is used, and ceramic(Al_2O_3) pieces are used to insulate adjacent iron pieces. One of the iron pieces is divided into halves, and the two halves are short connected outside the arc chamber. A

Rogowski coil is applied to measure the current that flows through the two halves. If arc column is short circuited by the two halves, the Rogowski coil can detect current signal, and it means that the iron pieces is too thick under the experimental conditions, it is needed to reduce the thickness of the iron pieces. The thickness is suitable if there is no current through the two halves, the measured arc voltage contains the arc column voltage and the near-pole voltage drop on two copper electrodes.

As shown in Figure1(b), a ceramic wall of 0.6mm thickness can be installed below the iron pieces group. When the ceramic wall is installed, the arc will contact with the ceramic wall. When the ceramic wall isn't installed, the arc column directly contacts with the iron piece wall. Ceramic material is inert to arc and almost has no effect on the physical properties of the arc plasma[6], and ceramic material was used as comparative material in manystudies on gas-producing material. Since the thickness of the ceramic wall is small, the magnetic field distribution of arc chamber with or without the ceramic wall is almost the same. In other words, the influence of difference of the magnetic field with or without the ceramic wall can be excluded.

In addition, one of the side walls and the bottom wall of the arc chamber is made of DMC(Dough Molding Compounds) which also inert to the arc. The other side wall of the arc chamber is made of silica glass. Then the arc can be observed on this side by using a high-speed camera. The frame rate of the high-speed camera is 10,000 frames/second.

In order to avoid excessive ablation of the iron wall and significant increase of the pressure in the arc chamber, larger arc chamber widths W is used in higher experimental currents. The detail values of widths and currents are described below.

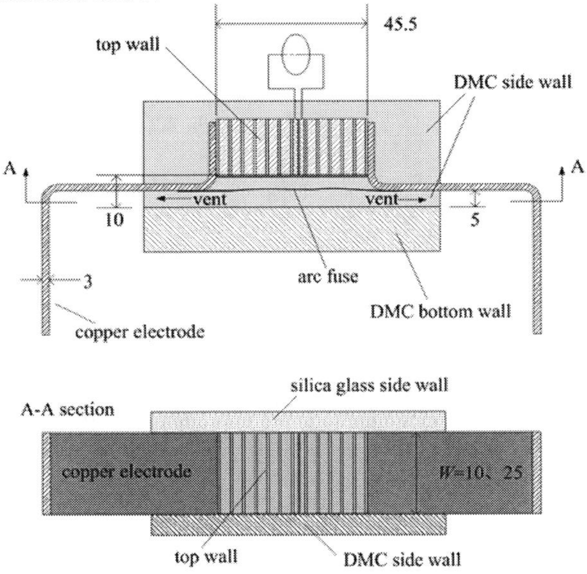

(a)

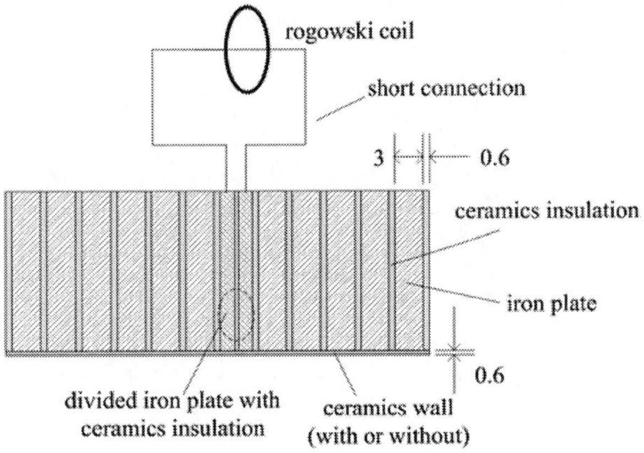

(b)

Fig. 1(a) Experimental set-up. (b)Top wall structure.

III. ARC CURRENTS

According to the experimental current value, the arc current is generated by two types of circuits. As shown in Figure 2, when the switch S1 is on and the switch S2 is off, DC640V power is supplied by the three-phase bridge rectifier circuit. When S2 is on and S1 is off, the oscillating current is supplied by the capacitor bank.

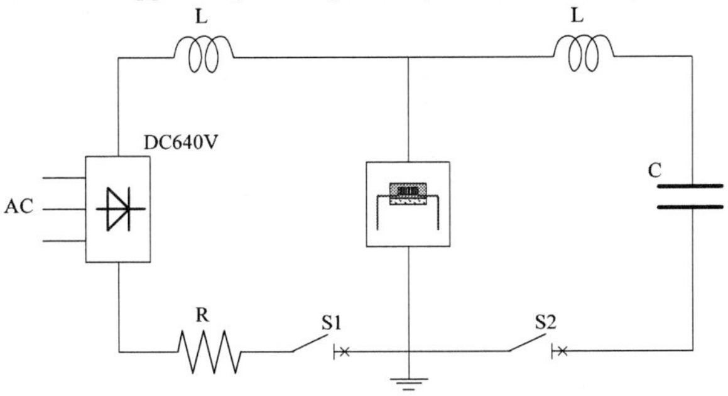

Fig. 2Current supply circuits.

A. Current from30A to 590 A

Arc chamber width W=10 mm. The arc current is supplied by the DC circuit and the power voltage is 640V. In order to make the arc have sufficient time to reach stability, the current duration time is 100ms. At least two tests are carried out for each current level.

The typical current and arc voltage waveforms are shown in Figure3.

The high-speed camera captured arc images at times t1, t2, and t3 are shown in Figure4. Time t1 is the fuse blowing moment, and the arc was ignited in the middle of the arc chamber. At the time t2, the arc root had transferred to upper parallel part of the copper electrode. The arc was closely contact with the top wall of the arc chamber and the arc length is approximately 45.5mm. At the time t3, arc position didn't change on the whole, but the arc voltage in time t3 is much higher than it in time t2.

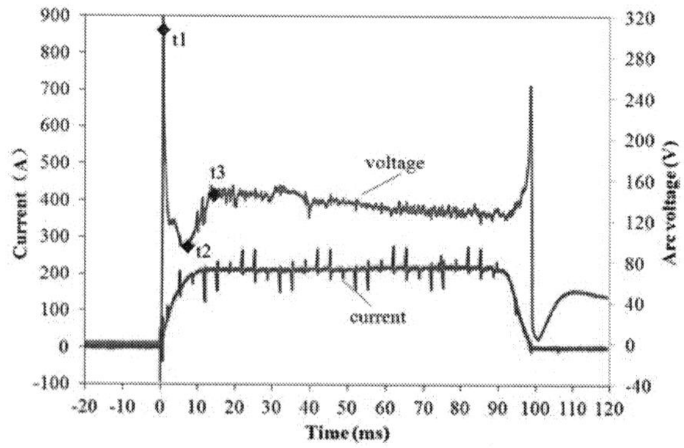

Fig. 3 Typicalwaveforms for dc current arc.

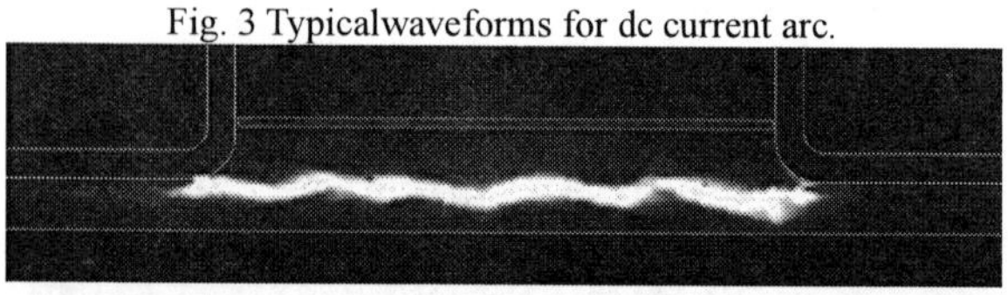

(a)

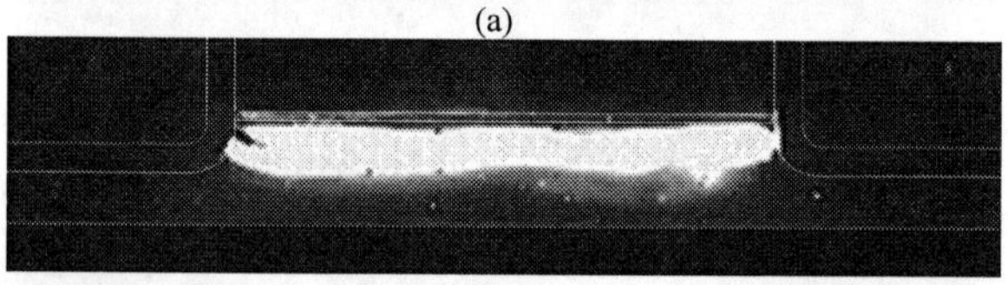

(b)

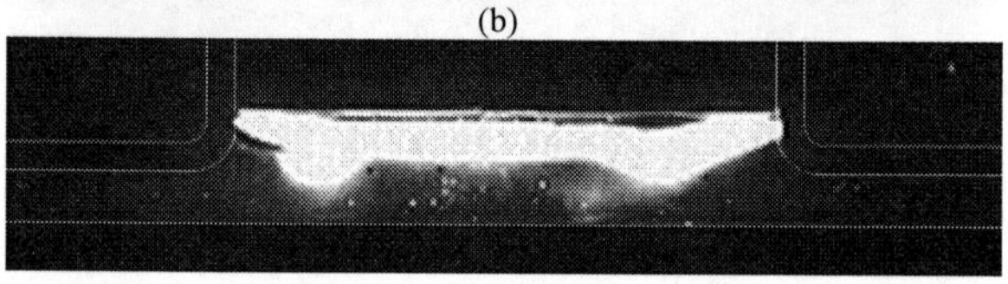

(c)

Fig. 4 Arc images (a) t1 =0.7ms. (b) t2 =7.4ms. (c) t3=14.5ms.

B. Current from 4000A to 7500A

Arc chamber width W = 25mm. Due to the large current, too long duration time of current will cause large ablation of the iron material wall. Here the duration of the current is adjusted to about 12ms. At least two tests are carried in each current level. The typical waveforms of arc current and voltage are shown in Figure 5. In experiment conditions with or without ceramic wall, the trends of arc current and voltage are similar and the corresponding values of current and voltage are different.

There is no current signal detected by the Rogowski coil in the above DC and oscillating current arc experiments. It means that the arc was not short circuited by the iron pieces.

IV. VOLT-AMPERE CHARACTERISTICS

A. Volt-ampere Characteristics of DC arc

After the arc was ignited for tens of milliseconds, the arc current and voltage tend to be stable in Figure3. After arc was ignited the average values of current and voltage in the time period of 70-80 ms are used as the volt-ampere characteristic data. The volt-ampere characteristics data in different experimental currents is shown in Figure 6. When the current is greater than 220 A, the arc voltage in the experiment conditions without ceramic wall is higher than it with ceramic wall. When the current is less than 220 A, there is no significant difference of arc voltage in experiments with or without the ceramic wall.

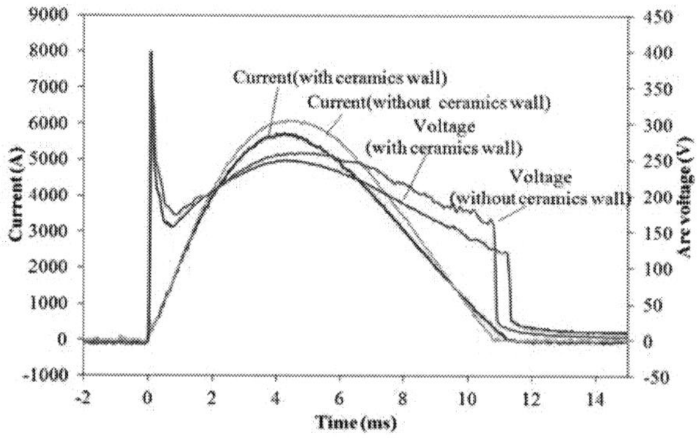

Fig. 5Typical waveforms for oscillating current arc.

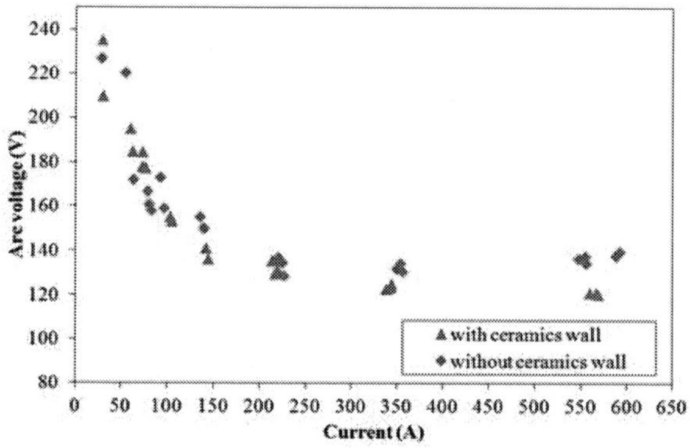

Fig. 6Volt-ampere CharacteristicofDC current arc.

B. Volt-ampere Characteristics of oscillating current arc

The volt-ampere curves in different current levels are shown in Figure 7.

In Figure7(a) when the current amplitude is about 4000 A, the volt-ampere curve of the arc contacted with the iron wall (without ceramic wall) is very close to that of the arc contacted with the ceramic wall. When the arc is going to extinguish, the volt-ampere curve of the arc contacted with the iron wall is slightly higher than that of the arc contacted with ceramic wall.

In Figure 7(b), the current peak is about 6000A, with the decrease of the current, the volt-ampere curve of the arc contacted with the iron wall is gradually higher than that of the arc contacted with the ceramic wall.

In Figure 7(c), the current peak is about 7500A. In the whole decreasing stage of arc current, the volt-ampere curve of the arc contacted with the iron wall is significantly higher than that of the arc contacted with the ceramic wall.

This shows that the higher the current, the higher the arc volt-ampere characteristics.

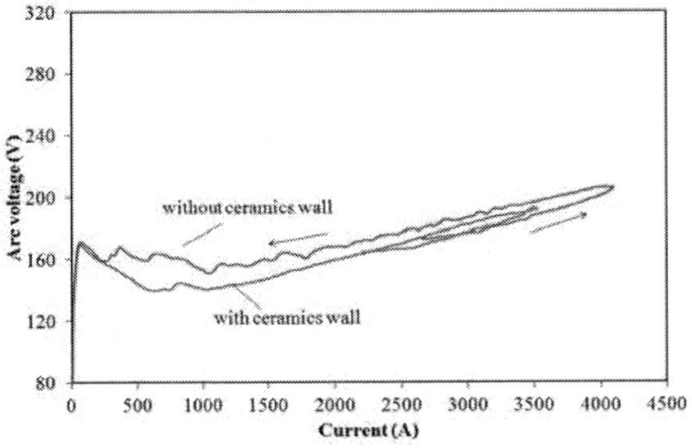

(a)

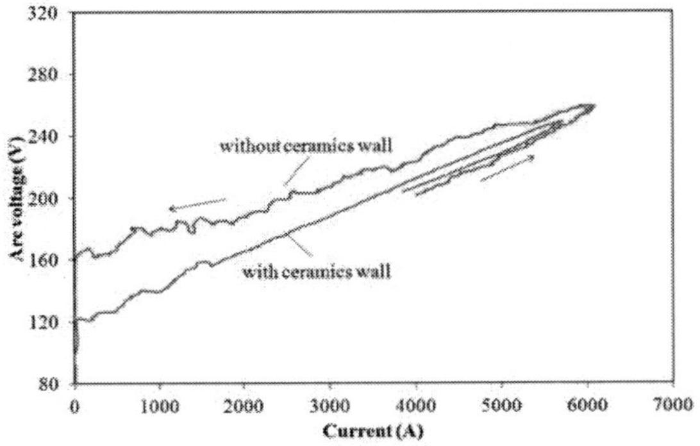

(b)

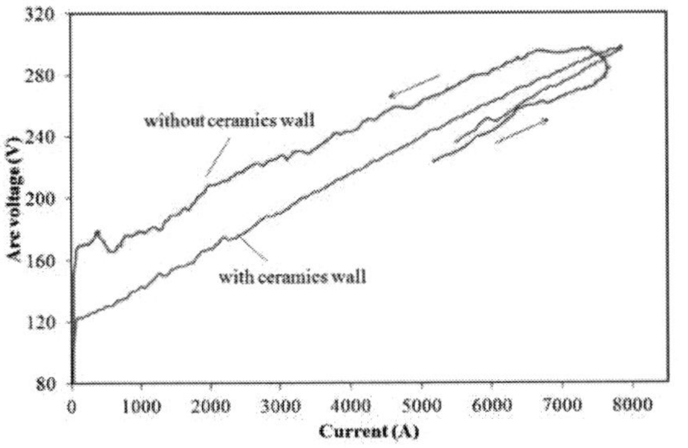

(c)

Fig. 7Volt-ampere Characteristic of oscillating current arc. (a) Current amplitude about 4000A. (b) Current amplitude about 6000A. (c) Current amplitude about 7500A.

V. ANALYSIS AND DISCUSSION

A. Numerical analysis

As shown in Figure 8(b),(c),(d), there is obvious ablation on the surfaces of the iron pieces after twice tests for each current. In Figure 8(a), the current is 60A, the arc energy is relatively low, in this condition the surfaces of the iron pieces has no obvious ablation, even the mass of the iron wall is slightly increased due to pollution and oxidation.

(a)

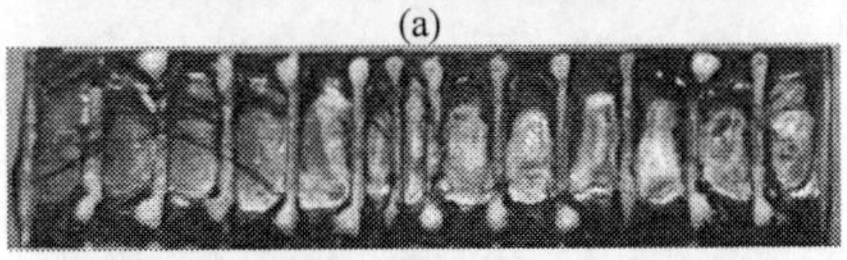

(b)

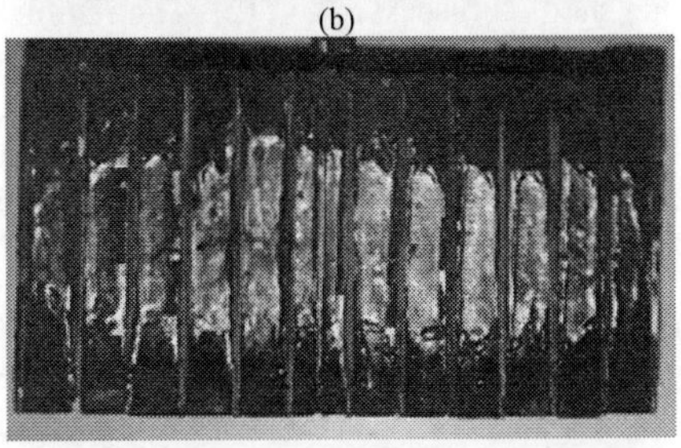

(c)

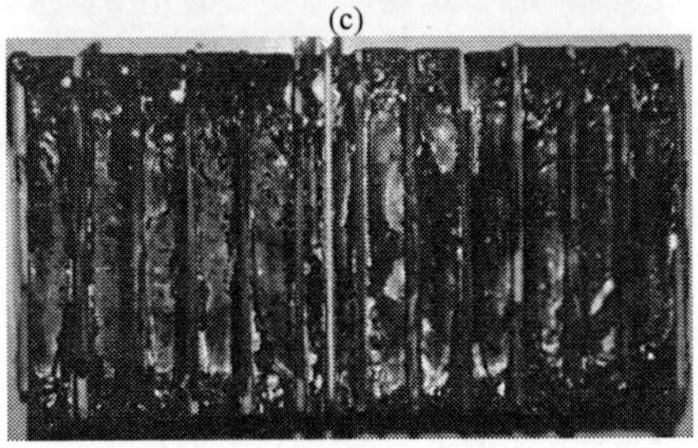

(d)

Fig. 8 Iron wall ablation. (a)DC 60A (mass increased 0.0017g).(b) DC 590A (mass reduced 0.0052g).(c) Current amplitude about 4000A (mass reduced0.2905g).(d) Current amplitude about 4000A(mass reduced 2.2358g).

The melting and evaporating process of the iron material absorbs the arc energy. The diffused metal vapor in arc chamber will cause changes of the physical properties of the arc plasma, which can affect the volt-ampere characteristics of the arc column.

In this paper, a steady-state wall stabilized arc model is adopted to investigate the influence of iron vapor to arc electric field intensity in qualitative analysis. The arc chamber is simplified as a cylinder with radius r. The concentration of iron vapor is assumed to be uniform in the arc chamber, and the temperature T only depends on the radial distance r. The energy balance equation is based on Ohm's law and can be represented as:[9]

$$\sigma E^2 = -\frac{1}{r}\frac{d}{dr}\left(rk\frac{dT}{dr}\right) + 4\pi\varepsilon_N \qquad (1)$$

Here σ is the conductivity, E is the electric field intensity, k is the thermal conductivity, and ε_N is the net emissivity coefficient. The electric field intensity E is assumed to be uniform in the radial direction of the arc column.

$$I = 2\pi E \int_0^R r\sigma dr \qquad (2)$$

The conductivity of pure air and different concentrations of iron vapor mixture are from [10] and [11], the thermal conductivity is from [12], and the net emissivity coefficient of plasma region radius $R = 2$ mm is from [12] and [13], the net emissivity coefficient of $R = 5$ mm is from [14]. When the iron vapor concentration is between the literature data, the physical property parameter is obtained by the molar interpolation method discussed in [12]. The region with the temperature higher than 4000K is regarded as plasma region. When the radius of the plasma region R is between 2mm and 5mm, interpolation is used to obtain the net emissivity coefficient. All iron vapor concentrations in this paper is mass fraction, and the calculated arc temperature is less than 30,000K.

Typical arc temperature and current density distribution are shown in Figure 9.

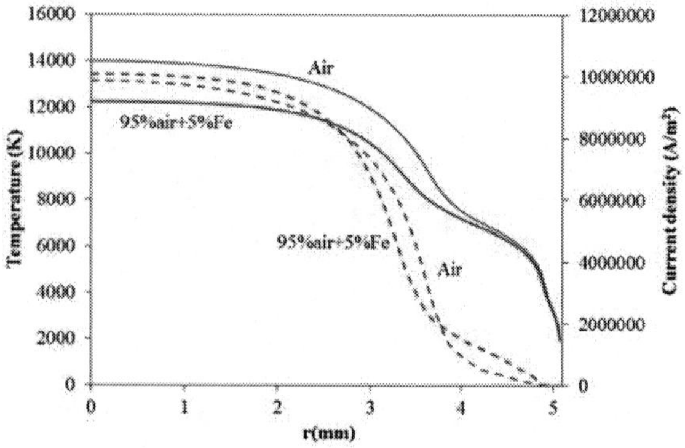

Fig. 9Radial temperature and current density distribution(i=350A, r=5.05mm).

Solid line: temperature; Dashed line: current density

The electric field intensity of the arc column in different currents is plotted in Figure 10.

As shown in Figure 10, there is a cross point between the E-I curves of the mixture gas arc and the pure air arc. When the current is greater than the cross point, the E-I curve of the mixture gas arc is higher than that of the pure air arc. The result is opposite when the current is less than the cross point.

As shown in Figure6,when the current is greater than 220A in the experiment, the volt-ampere data of arc mixed with iron vapor(without ceramics wall) is higher than that of pure air arc(with ceramics wall). The experiment results are consistent with the result of the simplified numerical model when the current is greater than 220A.

As shown in Figure7, when the experiment current is several thousand amperes, the voltage-ampere curves of arc mixed with iron vapor are higher than that of pure air arc. Although the width of arc chamber is larger than that in numerical model, however the cross point of current in Figure 10 isn't sensitive to the volume of arc chamber. So the experiment results can verify trend of the voltage-ampere curves in thousand amps current level.

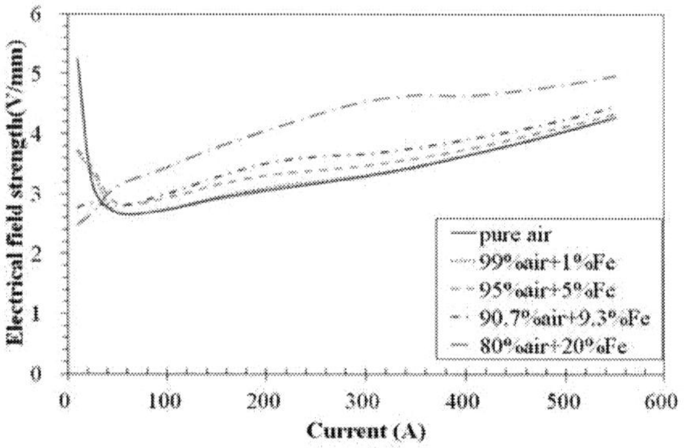

(a)

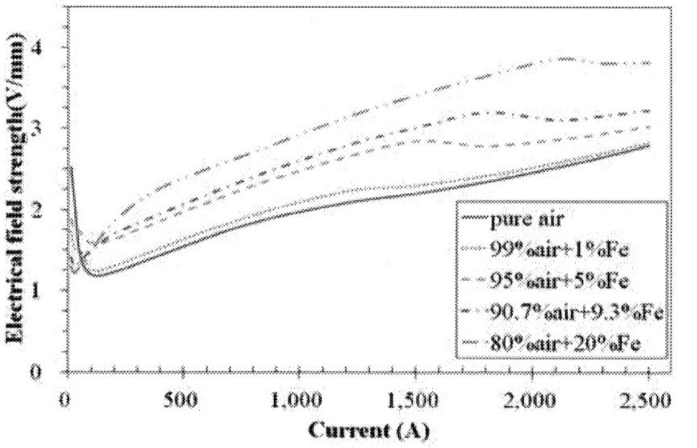

(b)

Fig. 10Electrical field intensity-Current curves.(a)r=2.5mm.(b) r=5.05mm.

Although when the current is lower than 220A, volt-ampere data of arc mixed with iron vapor and pure air arc are very close in experiments. The trend of E-I curves of numerical results are not consistent with experimental results. The reason of contradiction probably be that in experiment condition the iron pieces only have very little ablation in small current level,in small current condition there is very little iron vapor in the arc plasma and it can be considered as pure air arc.

B. Influencing factors

With the increase of iron vapor concentration, the net emissivity coefficient increases and the thermal conductivity decreases; When the temperature is lower than 10000K, the electrical conductivity increases; When the temperature is higher than 15000K, the electrical conductivity decreases; The temperature range from 10000K to 15000K is the transition region. In order to analyze the influence of each physical parameter to the electric field intensity, only single parameter is changed in each simulation model. And the corresponding calculation results are shown in Figure 11.

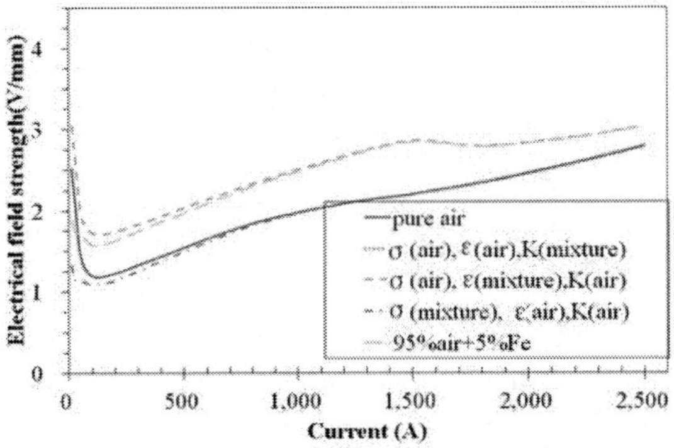

Fig. 11Pure air and 95%air+5%Fe arc electric field intensity.

As shown in Figure11, the thermal conductivity only can affect the electric field intensity slightly, that is because the thermal conductivity of 95%air+5%Fe is very close to that of pure air.

For low current arc plasma the conductivity of 95%air+5%Fe is obviously higher than that of pure air, so in low current level the conductivity can greatly affect the electric field intensity. For high current arc plasma the difference of conductivity of 95%air+5%Fe and pure air is small, the conductivity effect can be neglected.

As shown in Figure11, when the current is above dozens of amps, the thermal radiation has significant effect on the electric field intensity. In this current range (arc temperature is lower than 25000K), the net emissivity coefficient of 95%air+5%Fe is significantly higher than that of pure air.

Since the physical properties of arc plasma vary with arc temperature, the electric field intensity of the arc is essentially related to the temperature distribution in the arc chamber. As shown in Figure 12, the axial temperature of the arc mixed with iron vapor is lower than that of pure air arc.

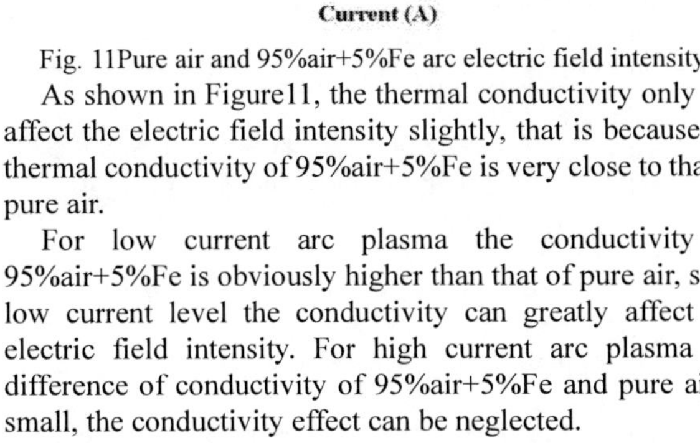

Fig. 12Axis temperature(r=5.05mm).

It can be concluded that, in high current level, the effect of radiation occupies the main influence on arc voltage.The strong radiation reduces the arc temperature,which increase the electric field intensity, so the volt-ampere curve of arc mixed with iron vapor is higher than of pure air arc.

C. Discussion

Yang simulated and analyzed the influence of iron vapor generated by electrode arc ablation on air arc voltage in [11]. The simulation results showed that the iron vapor reduces the arc voltage. Li established a numerical model to analyze the influence of 1% iron vapor on the moving speed of the arc and the arc voltage gradient in [15]. It showed that the iron vapor reduces electric field intensity of the air arc. Above literatures only focused on relatively low current level, and the influence of the conductivity of the mixture gas on the arc voltage under small current level was obtained.

In this paper, the influence of air arc-iron interactions to the arc volt-ampere characteristics is studied experimentally , anda simplified steady-state arc model is adopted for numerical calculation. In the numerical result, the iron vapor reduces the arc voltage in low current level mainly due to high conductivity, and the iron vapor raises the arc voltage in high current levelmainlydue to high emissivity. The experimental results verified the credibility of numerical calculation conclusion in high current level.

VI. CONCLUSIONS

1) In this paper, the influence of air arc contacted with iron to the arc voltage is studied experimentally. The experimental setup eliminates differences of arc length and magnetic field distribution in the arc chamber.
2) In our experimental conditions, when the current is greater than 220 A, the voltage of arc contacted with iron is higher than that of arc contacted with ceramic.According to theoretical analysis, in high current level, when arc contacts with the iron wall, the iron vapor generated by ablation changes physical properties of arc plasma. Then the strong radiation of mixture gas significantly reduces the arc temperature, which increases the arc voltage.
3) Under the experimental conditions herein, when the current is less than 220 A, there is no significant difference on arc voltage between arc contacted with iron or ceramic. The main reason probably is that the iron wall has no obvious ablation when the current is small, the arc is approximately pure air arc.

REFERENCES

[1] M. Lindmayer, E. Marzahn, A. Mutzke, T. Ruther, and M. Springstubbe, "The process of arc splitting between metal plates in low voltage arc chutes,"IEEETransactions on Components and Packaging technologies, vol. 29, no. 2, pp. 310-317, Jun. 2006.

[2] A. Mutzke, T. Ruther, M. Kurrat, M. Lindmayer, E. Wilkening,"Modeling the arc splitting process in low-voltage arc chutes," 53rd IEEE Holm

Conference on Electrical Contacts, pp. 175–182, 2007.
[3] J. Riss, M. Lindmayerand M. Kurrat, "Simplification of the arc splitting processinnumerical gas flow simulations," 26th International Conference on Electrical Contacts (ICEC2012), pp. 245–249, 2012.
[4] A.Mutzke, T. Ruther, M. lindmayer, and M. Kurrat, "Arc behavior in low-voltagearc chambers,"Eur.Phys.J.Appl.Phys, vol. 49, no. 2, 22910(6 pp.) Feb. 2010.
[5] Fei Yang, Mingzhe Rong, Yi Wu and etc., "Numerical analysis of arc characteristics of splitting process considering ferromagnetic plate in low voltage arc chamber," IEEE Transactions on Plasma Science, vol. 38, no. 11, pp. 3219-3225, Nov. 2010.
[6] P. Rodriguez, J. Didier, G.Bernard, and S. Rowe. "Arc contact insulating wall interactions in low voltage circuit breakers," IEEE Transactions on Power Delivery, vol.13, no.2, pp. 480-488, Apr. 1998.
[7] E.Domejean, P.Chevrier, C.Fievet, and P. petit, "Arc wall interaction modeling in a low voltage circuit breaker," Journal of Physics D: Applied Physics, vol. 30, no. 15, pp. 2132-2142, Aug. 1997.
[8] Toumazet,Jean-Pierre, Velleaud, etc., "Study of the influence of the wall' nature on the behavior of a low voltage arc breaker by means of an inverse method,"Journal of Physics D: Applied Physics, vol. 32, no. 2, pp. 121-127, Jan. 1999.
[9] A. Gleizes, J.J. Gonzalez, B. Liani, and G. Raynal, "Calculation of net emission coefficient of the thermal plasmas in mixtures of gas with metallic vapour," Journal of Physics D:AppliedPhysics, vol. 26, no. 11, pp. 1921-1927, Nov. 1993.
[10] Y. Cressault, R. Hannachi, P. Teulet, A. Gleizes, J.P. Gonnet, "Influence of metallic vapours on the properties of air thermal plasmas," Plasma Sources, Science and Technology, vol. 17, no. 3, 035016 (9 pp.), Aug. 2008.
[11] Fei Yang, Mingzhe Rong, Yi Wu etc., "Numerical analysis of the influence of splitter plate erosion on an air arc in the quenching chamber of a low voltage circuit breaker," Journal of Physics D: Applied Physics, vol. 43, no. 43, 434011 (12 pp.), Nov. 2010.
[12] A. Gleizes, Y. Cressault and P. Teulet, "Mixing rules for thermal plasma properties in mixtures of argon, air and metallic vapours," Plasma Sources, Science and Technology, vol. 19, no. 5, 055013 (13 pp.), Oct. 2010.
[13] A. Gleizes, Y. Cressault, "Effect of metal vapours on the radiation properties of thermal plasmas," Plasma Chemistry and Plasma Processing, vol. 37, no.3, pp.581-600, May 2017.
[14] Y. Cressault, A. Gleizes, G. Riquel, "Properties of air aluminum thermal plasmas," Journal of Physics D:AppliedPhysics, vol.43, no. 26, 265202(12pp.), Jul. 2012.
[15] Xingwen Li, Rui Li, Hao Sun, K. Tusongjiang, Degui Chen, "Ferromagnetic material effects on air arc behavior," IEEE Transactions on Plasma Science, vol. 37, no. 3, pp. 463-469, Mar. 2009.

First Author. Zhu Tiansheng was born in Hunan, China, in 1982. He received the B.S. and M.S. degrees in electrical engineering from Xi'an Jiaotong University, Xi'an, China, in2005 and 2008, where he is currently studying for the Ph.D. degree in electrical engineering. His research interests focus on low voltage apparatus

Contact Bounce Performance and Robust Optimization for Railway Relay

Jie Deng, Rui Tu, Guofu Zhai
Harbin Institute of Technology, Harbin, 150001,China
E-mail: 15776761615@163.com Tel:15776761615 Fax: 86-451-86413192

Abstract—**The overlong contact bounce time and poor consistency are common problems of railway relay series. Due to the low electromagnetic efficiency of the railway relay snap-on structure, the long reed size and the large number of contact sets, it is very difficult to design and optimize the contact bounce. Based on the concept of robust design, this paper proposes a reliability optimization method that reduces contact bounce time and improves its consistency at the same time. Firstly, an approximate mathematical model between the processing parameters and the contact bounce amplitude is established, combining with the simulation modeling method. On this basis, the objective function of reliability optimization is constructed with the purpose of simultaneously reducing the mean value and standard deviation. Finally, the correctness of optimization scheme is verified by prototype manufacturing and test.**

Index Terms— **Contact bounce, Performance optimization, Robust design, Electromechanical products.**

I. INTRODUCTION

The rebound phenomenon of the railway signal relay is a key factor affecting its normal operation when it is working. The arcing happens when it rebounds badly, which will lower efficiency of the relay and reduce its service life. Therefore, the analysis of bounce performance of the electromechanical device is important to the optimization of relay [1].

At present, the related research technology about electromagnetic relay mainly focuses on the optimization and design of electromagnetic and mechanical systems based on virtual prototype technology internationally, as well as the development of arcing theory and simulation technology [2]. In the field of automatic control, electromagnetic relays play an important role due to their unique advantages, but it is still unsuitable to many occasion due to the existence of contact bounce. Bounces is one of the main reasons for the premature failure of relay life at the same time [3].

In this paper, the fault recurrence method is used to determine the fault mechanism of the contact bounce overshoot for railway relay. Then the approximation modeling method is used to establish the mathematical function model between the relevant design parameters and the contact bounce characteristics. On this basis, aiming at reducing the mean and standard deviation simultaneously, the objective function of reliability optimization is constructed. Finally, the effectiveness of the optimization scheme is verified by prototype manufacturing and testing. The related methods and techniques in this paper can provide a complete analysis and optimization process for the reliability optimization of electromechanical devices.

II. SIMULATION ANALYSIS OF STATIC AND DYNAMIC CHARACTERISTICS

Static suction characteristics, static counterforce characteristics and dynamic characteristics of the S relay are simulated and analyzed through the virtual prototyping simulation technology, and the correctness of the simulation results is verified by the measured data.

A. Simulation analysis of electromagnetic property

Firstly, the finite element simulation software is used to simulate the electromagnetic system, and mesh model is shown in Figure1.

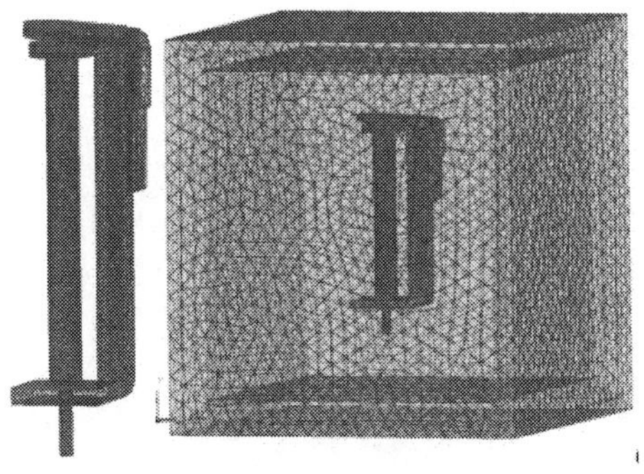

Fig. 1 FLUX finite element simulation model

The comparison between simulation results and measured electromagnetic suction curve is shown in Figure 2. It shows the comparison between the simulation and the measured results under different voltages such as the pull-in voltage, and shows the simulated electromagnetic suction amplitude and the variation trend are coincident with the measured basically.

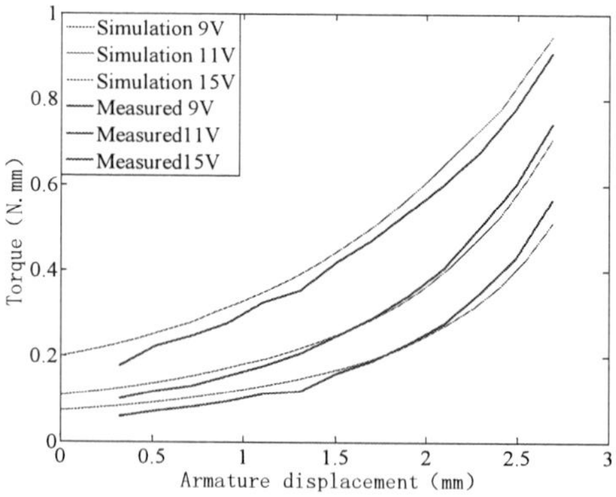

Fig. 2 Comparison of electromagnetic suction between measurement and simulation

B. *Simulation analysis of static counterforce*

A simulation model of the counterforce characteristics of the relay is established in the dynamic analysis software. The finite element model of the reed is built using finite element software, as shown in Figure 3. Then import it into the dynamic software for assembly and debugging of the whole machine. The simulation model is shown in Figure 4. The obtained counterforce curve and the measurement comparison chart are shown in Figure 5. It shows that the simulation is consistent with the measurement basically.

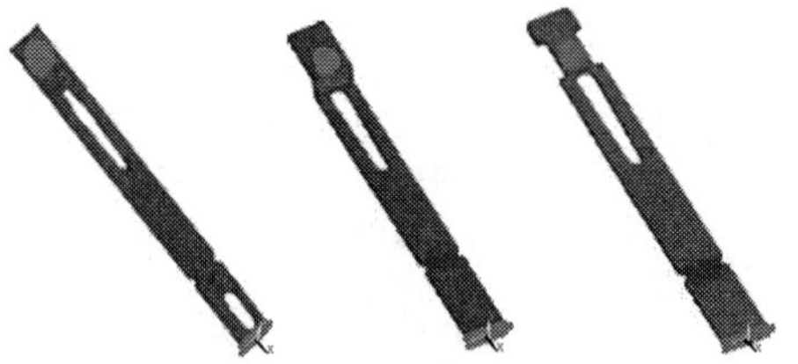
Fig. 3 Relay reed model

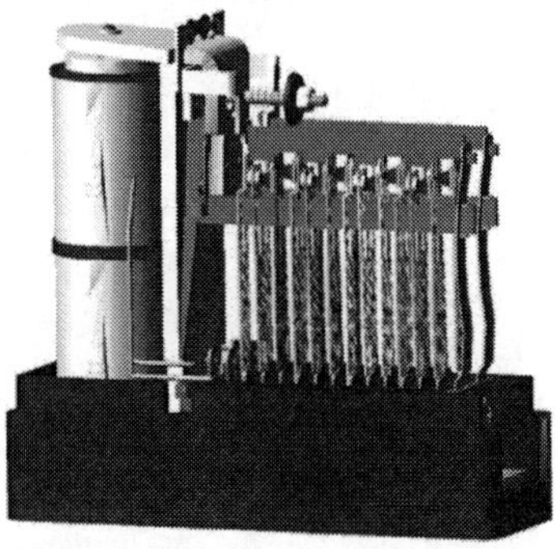
Fig. 4 Simulation model of static counterforce characteristics of the S relay

The simulation results of the suction force and the counterforce are matched to obtain the static suction-reaction force matching characteristic curve of the relay, as shown in Figure 6. It shows that the simulation results are consistent with the measured results basically and it can reflect the actual situation of the product. Next, the rebound phenomenon is simulated and reproduced with the proven simulation model. The simulation of the contact bounce is shown in Figure 7.

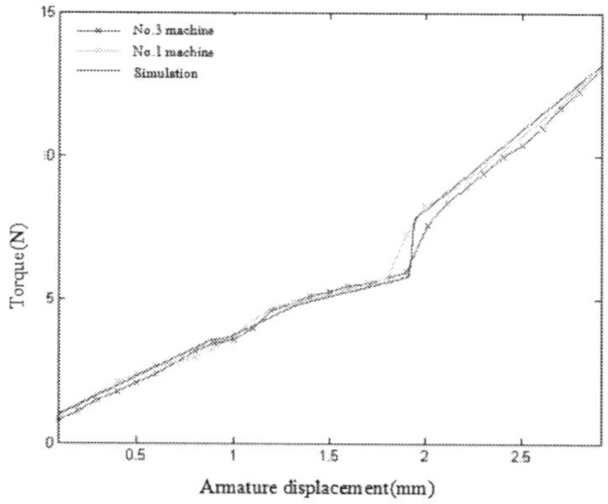

Fig. 5 Comparison of counterforce between measurement and simulation

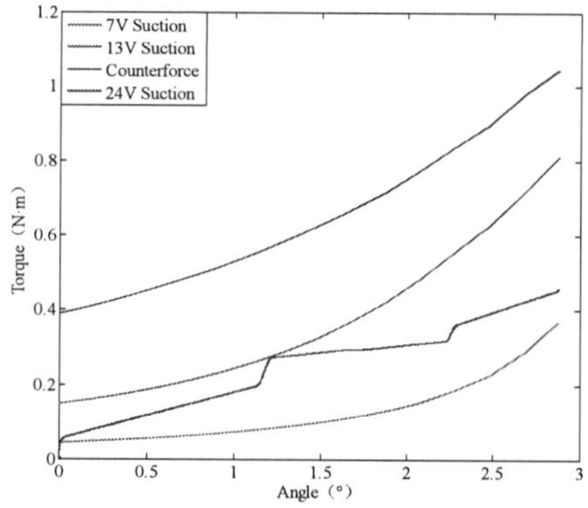

Fig. 6 Simulation results of static suction-reaction matching

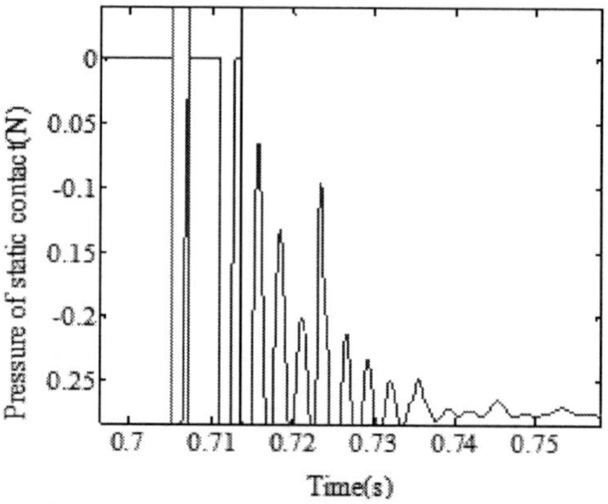

Fig. 7 Simulation results of static contact rebound

The bounce time of the static contact is 8.4ms which is small compared with the measured bounce time of 7.5ms. It can be considered that the simulation model can reflect the actual rebound phenomenon of the product.

C. *Simulation analysis of dynamic characteristics*

The dynamic characteristics can reflect the action of the relay over time truly, and it can be obtained through simulation. The simulation control diagram is shown in Figure 8.

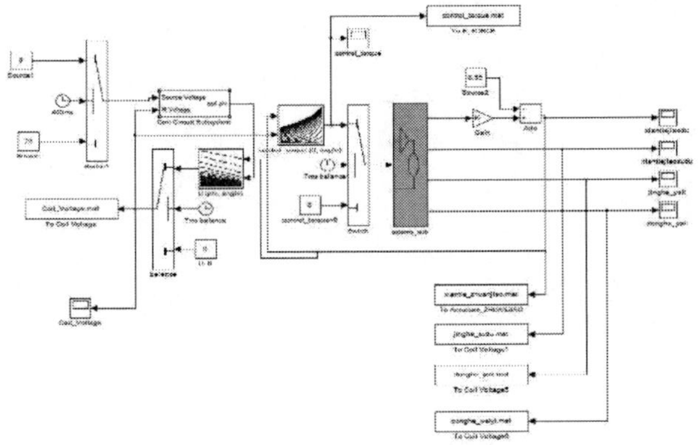

Fig. 8 Simulation control chart of dynamic characteristics

Through the simulation of dynamic characteristics, the pull-in time of the relay is calculated to be 283.1ms, and the release time is 5.1ms. The dynamic simulation results of the pull-in process and the release process are shown in Figure 9. The measured pull-in time is 264.5ms, the release time is 8.8ms, and the simulation is consistent with the actual measurement basically, which verifies the correctness of the simulation calculation exactly.

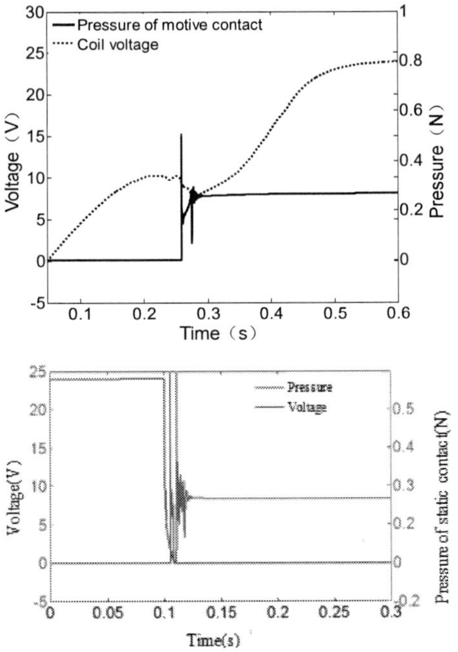

Fig. 9 Simulation results of dynamic characteristics

D. *Failure analysis*

From the static and dynamic simulation analysis of the original relay scheme above, it can be seen that the main problem of the current product design scheme is that the initial value of the counterforce is too low, so that the armature does not get enough holding force to maintain the release state after the armature released, and result serious bounce. Figure 10 shows that the angular velocity of the armature is substantially zero when the static contact is rebounded, and the armature does not rebound, indicating the bounce of static contact is caused by its own collision, not caused by the armature rebound; and the armature rebound after the finish of the static contact bounce, indicating that the armature bounce is caused by the bounce of the static contact.

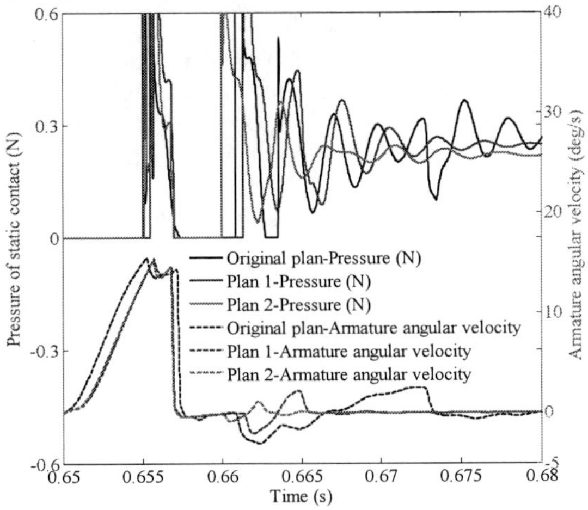

Fig. 10 Comparison of static contact pressure and armature angular velocity curve

III. APPROXIMATE MODELING

In the simulation study, three types of debugging parameters were selected for analysis, which are the spring, the back part, and the front part. The bounce amplitude is used as the objective function of the contact bounce characteristic, and the simulation results are used to fit the corresponding function relation which forms a function about the contact bounce characteristics to make it convenient for later debugging and analysis.

A. *Analysis of spring parameters*

The spring structure that provides the counterforce mainly includes two adjustable factors, namely spring stiffness and spring preload. In the case that the other setting parameters are invariant, the experimental design and simulation are performed by changing the two factors. The relationship between the spring stiffness and the spring pre-pressure with the bounce amplitude is shown in Figure 11.

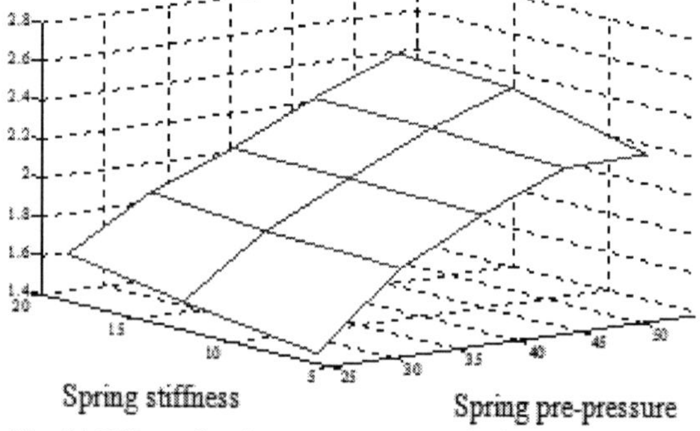

Fig. 11 Effect of spring parameters on the bounce amplitude

It can be seen from the figure that the spring stiffness and the spring preload show a positive correlation with the bounce amplitude. Then the existing simulation data is used to fit the functional relationship of the bounce amplitude by establishing a mathematical function model, and the relationship graph is used to analyze the data. The relationship between spring stiffness (x1) and spring preload (x2) as a function of bounce amplitude (y2) is:

$$y_1 = -0.388 + 0.015x_1 + 0.085x_2 \tag{1}$$

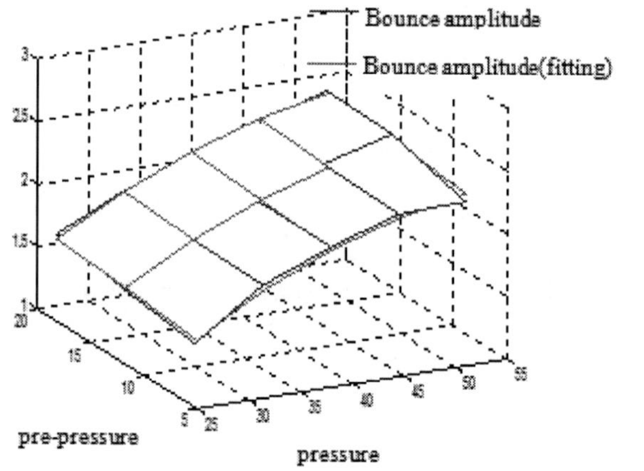

Fig. 12 The comparison between the measured and fitted data

It can be seen from Figure 12 that the simulation value obtained by the fitting function is consistent with the measured parameters, and it also shows that the spring stiffness and the spring pre-pressure have a greater influence on the bounce amplitude and the bigger factor is the spring preload.

B. Analysis of influence of the back contact parameters

The adjustable parameters of the back contact mainly include two factors, namely the back contact pressure and the pre-pressure. According to the simulation result, the relationship between the back contact pressure and the pre-pressure with the bounce amplitude is obtained as shown in Figure 13.

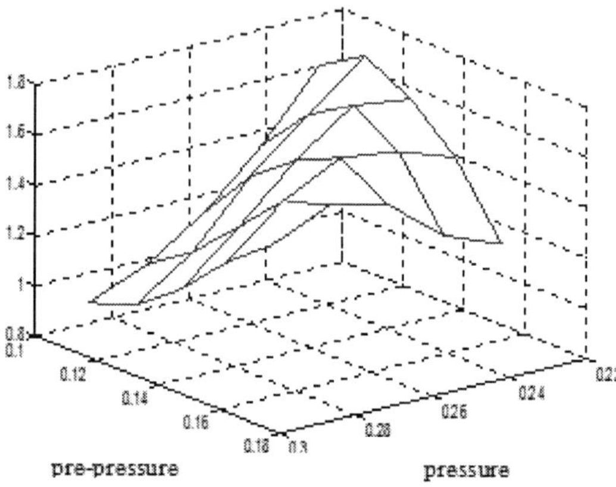

Fig. 13 Effect of the parameters of the back contact on the bounce amplitude

The obtained post-contact pre-pressure (x3) and post-contact pressure (x4) as a function of the bounce amplitude (y2) are:

$$\begin{aligned} y2 &= 4.121 - 27.762x3 - 1.455x4 - 163.175x_3^2 \\ &+ 286.667x3 * x4 - 83.175x_4^2 \end{aligned} \tag{2}$$

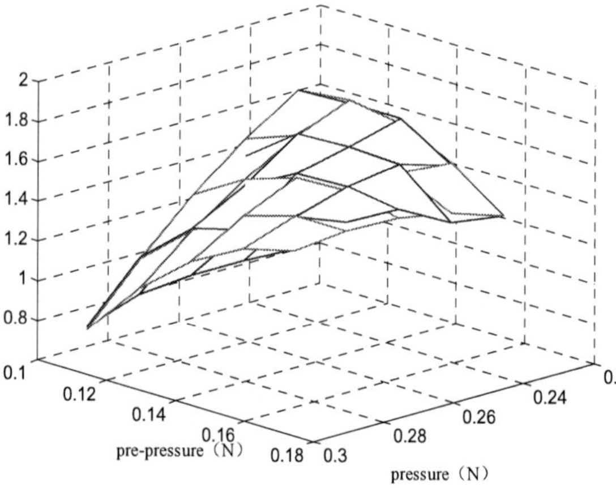

Fig. 14 The comparison between the measured and fitted data

It can be seen from Figure 14 that the back contact pressure and the pre-pressure have a great influence on the bounce amplitude, and have an interactive influence on the bounce amplitude.

C. Analysis of influence of the front contact parameters

There are two main factors in the analysis of the front contact, namely the front contact pressure and the pre-pressure. The relationship between the front contact pressure and the pre-pressure with the return jump value is shown in Figure 15. The impact of the front contact parameters is minimal and negligible.

Based on the above analysis, the total functional relationship for the influence of the bounce amplitude is (where x1 is the spring stiffness, x2 is the spring preload, x3 is the back contact pressure, and x4 is the back contact pressure):

$$y = 2.236 + 0.015x_1 + 0.085x_2 - 27.76x_3 - 1.455x_4 + 286.67x_3x_4 - 163.175x_3^2 - 83.175x_4^2 \quad (3)$$

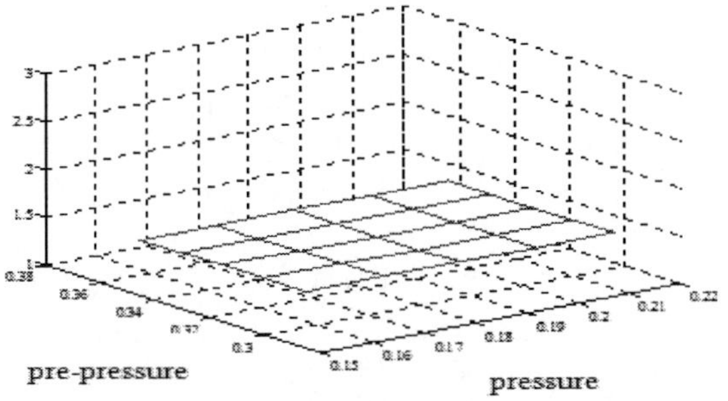

Fig. 15 Effect of the parameters of the front contact on the bounce amplitude

IV. PARAMETER OPTIMIZATION

This paper chose the evolution algorithm of AR-MOEA. Considering the uncertainty of each parameter, according to the original scheme: take the spring stiffness of 13N / mm, the spring pre-pressure is 26.3N, the back contact pre-pressure is 131mN, the back contact pressure is 257mN. According to the analysis of the spring parameters, the spring stiffness and the spring pre-pressure have a great influence on the rebound amplitude, and the larger factor is the spring pre-stress. Since that the spring stiffness is difficult to debug and is not beneficial to manufacturing, it is a fixed value here. Assuming that the remaining three parameters are subject to the normal distribution, the Monte Carlo method is used to simulate and analyze, and the mean and standard deviation are 1.357 and 1.056 when the original tolerances are 0.5, 0.05, and 0.05 respectively.

In order to improve the performance and robustness of the spring system, it is necessary to reduce the mean and standard deviation of the bounce amplitude at the same time. The established objective function is shown as Equation (4).

$$F = [\frac{|\delta - 0.264|}{0.339 - \mu}] \quad (4)$$

μ and δ means the mean and variance of the bounce amplitude respectively, and 0.264 and 0.339 are the optimization target values of the standard deviation and the mean. It can be known from the equation (4) that the minimum value of the function is necessary when searching. In summary, the bounce amplitude optimization model is:

$$\begin{cases} \min[F] \\ 20 \le x_2 \le 30 \\ 0.08 \le x_3 \le 0.20 \\ 0.2 \le x_4 \le 0.29 \\ 0.2 \le \Delta x_2 \le 0.5 \\ 0.01 \le \Delta x_3 \le 0.05 \\ 0.01 \le \Delta x_4 \le 0.05 \end{cases} \quad (5)$$

The AR-MOEA optimization algorithm is used to solve the model, and the combination of parameters that meet the requirements is shown in Table 1.

Table 1

COMPARISON OF PARAMETER VALUES BEFORE AND AFTER OPTIMIZATION

Parameter	X1 (mm/N)	X2 (N)	X3 (N)	X4 (N)	Y
Before	13	26.3	0.131	0.257	2.0135
After	13	20.0	0.081	0.290	0.1288

Table 2

COMPARISON OF TOLERANCE VALUES BEFORE AND AFTER OPTIMIZATION

Tolerance	ΔX2 (N)	ΔX3 (N)	ΔX4 (N)
Before	0.5	0.05	0.05
After	0.15	0.01	0.01

After the optimization, the mean value becomes 0.116 and standard deviation becomes 0.125. It can be seen that this optimization scheme is feasible.

V. PRODUCTION VERIFICATION

Applying the simulation analysis conclusion to the actual prototype production, the debugging range of post contact pressure is 280~300mN, and the debugging range of spring pre-pressure is 17~23N. The actual prototype's bounce is compared with the original product as shown below.

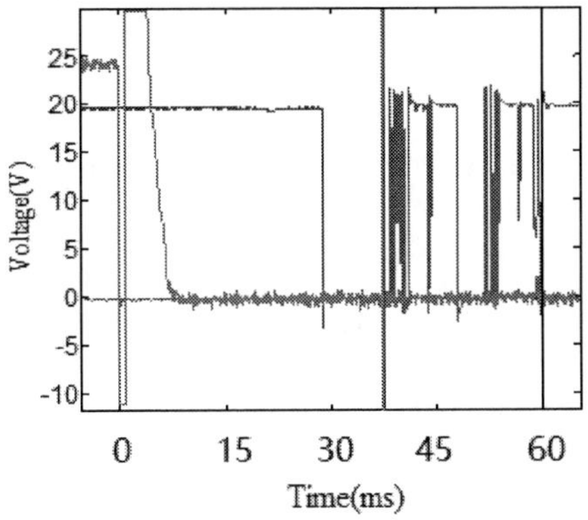

Fig. 16 Original product's bounce

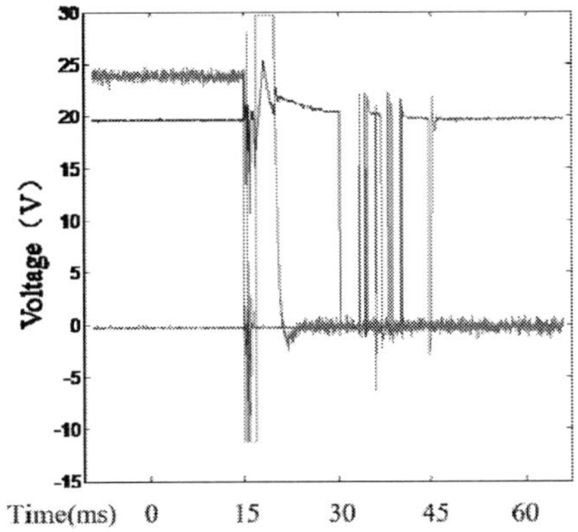

Fig. 17 Optimizing product's bounce

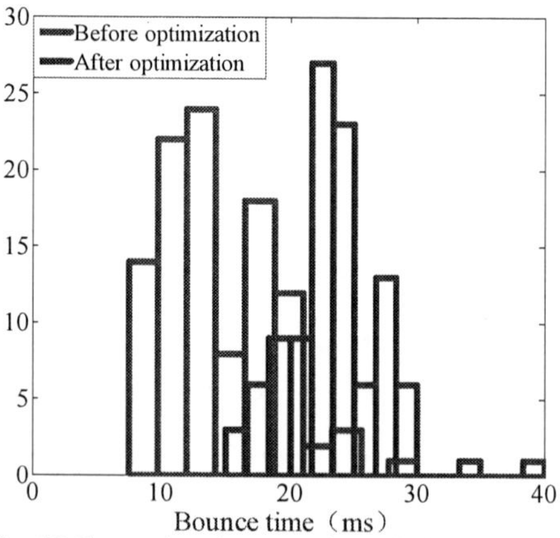

Fig. 18 Comparison between the optimization scheme with the original scheme

It can be seen from the comparison that the relay decreases the bounce time obviously from the original 22.5ms to 14.16ms after the optimization, which verifies the correctness of the simulation analysis. And from the distribution map of bounce time of batch product after optimization, it can be seen that the optimized rebound time reduced significantly too.

VI. CONCLUSION

This paper proposes a reliability optimization method that simultaneously reduces contact bounce time and improves its consistency, which has important research value.

1) Combining the simulation modeling method, an approximate mathematical model of processing parameters and contact amplitude is established.

2) With the goal of reducing the mean and standard deviation at the same time, the objective function of reliability optimization is constructed, and the reliability optimization scheme is determined by AR-MOEA evolutionary algorithm.

3) The correctness of optimization scheme is verified by prototype manufacturing and test.

ACKNOWLEDGMENT

This work was supported by the National Natural Science Foundation of China [grant numbers 51707044]; and the China Postdoctoral Science Foundation [grant number 2018M632377].

REFERENCES

[1] Gaolei Guan, Research on the Characteristics of Railway Signal Relay Machine [D]. Shenyang University of Technology, 2016.

[2] Guofu Zhai ,Xinglei Cui , Wenying Yang. Overview of Electromagnetic Relay Products and Research Technology Development[J]. Electrical Apparatus and Energy Efficiency Management Technology, 2016(2): 1-8.

[3] Yaojun Zhu. Analysis of Electromagnetic Relay Contact Jumpback[J]. Electromechanical Components, 2007(04): 17-23.

[4] Ye Tian. Solving Complex Multi-objective Optimization Problem by Evolutionary Algorithm [D]. Anhui University, 2018.

[5] Changming Yang, Shengqiu Duan. Robustness Analysis and Optimization of Vibration Absorption of Boring Bar[J]. Tool Technology, 2016, 50(05): 72-75.

[6] Huimin Liang, Guofu Zhai. Three Stages Design of Aerospace Electromagnetic Relay [M]. Harbin: Harbin Institute of Technology Press, 2014.

7th International Conference on Reliability of
Electrical Products and Electrical Contacts,
November 04-06, 2019

Simulation and Experimental Study of Dy Doped $AgSnO_2$ Contact Materials

Ying Zhang[1], Zhizhou Bao[2], Jingqin Wang[1], Guangzhi Zhang[3], Yancai Zhu[1]
[1]Laboratory of Reliability and Intelligence of Electrical Equipment, Hebei University of Technology, Tianjin 300130, China
[2]People's Electrical Appliance Group Zhejiang Co., Ltd., Zhejiang, 325000, China
[3]Shanghai Liangxin Electrical Appliance Co., Ltd., Shanghai, 200333, China
E-mail: 13512474229@163.com Tel: 13512474229

***Abstract*—SnO_2 in $AgSnO_2$ contact material is a high-hardness and nearly-insulated wide bandgap semiconductor material. During use, the contact resistance is large, the temperature rise is high, and cracks are easily formed, which reduces the reliability of contact and shortens the electrical life. In order to improve the comprehensive properties of $AgSnO_2$ contact material, based on the first principle of density functional theory, the simulation calculation of different ratios of Dy doped SnO_2 supercell models are carried out. By analyzing the energy band, density of states and elastic constant, the results show that when the doping ratio of Dy is 12.5%, the conductivity is the best, the hardness is reduced, and the microcrack is the hardest to form. Finally, in the experiment, SnO_2 powders with different doping ratios are prepared by sol-gel and $AgSnO_2$ contact materials with different doping ratios are prepared by powder metallurgy method. The arc energy, contact resistance, welding force and hardness are measured. The results show that the electrical conductivity of the doped $AgSnO_2$ contact material is increased, and the welding force and hardness are reduced. When the doping ratio of Dy is 12.5%, the comprehensive properties is the best. Finally, it is proved that the simulation and experimental results can match well.**

***Index Terms*—$AgSnO_2$ contact material, first principle, Dy-doped SnO_2, comprehensive properties**

I. INTRODUCTION

With the rapid development of various electrical-related devices towards intelligence, automation, and miniaturization, the requirements for electrical contact reliability of electrical systems are also increasing. The performance of the contact material directly affects the life and reliability of low-voltage electrical appliances. Research has shown that making better the electrical contact reliability by improving the material properties of the contact is the key to making the electrical equipment stable, reliable and accurate [1-4].

The environmentally friendly $AgSnO_2$ electrical contact material is the most potential metal composite material dispersed by the second phase SnO_2 in the Ag matrix [5-6]. However, the $AgSnO_2$ contact material is difficult to decompose because the decomposition temperature of the second phase SnO_2 is as high as 2373 C, which results in high resistivity of SnO_2 accumulating on the contact surface and increase the contact resistance of $AgSnO_2$ [7-8]. Moreover, SnO_2 in $AgSnO_2$ belongs to wide bandgap semiconductor material. SnO_2 material has large particle size, high hardness and brittleness, which makes $AgSnO_2$ contact material easy to form cracks during use, and has poor repetitive deformation ability, reducing electric wear resistance and life [9]. Therefore, the research of $AgSnO_2$ contact materials is urgently needed to find effective microstructure design and performance prediction to improve its defects in subsequent processing and electrical properties.

With the rapid development of computer technology, modern computer has established a good bridge between theory and experiment. Whether a theory is correct can be verified by computer simulation and quantitative comparison of experimental results, and the physical processes in the experiment can also be understood through simulation [10]. On the basis of various numerical calculation methods, combined with the results of experiments and theories, it has opened up a new method for humans to understand the natural world.

Microdoping has always been an important research direction in the research of $AgSnO_2$ contact material modification at home and abroad [11-15], especially the modification of element doped SnO_2 by computer simulation. The research group carried out several rare earth element doped contact materials and found that the rare earth element Dy-doped is better than that of other rare earth element doped $AgSnO_2$ contact materials. Therefore, this paper further studied the electrical and mechanical properties of different ratio of rare earth element Dy-doped $AgSnO_2$ contact materials to obtain better doping ratio.

II. SIMULATION CALCULATION AND ANALYSIS

In this paper, the CASTEP module in Materials Studio software is used for the first-principles calculation based on density functional theory. Using periodic boundary conditions, plane wave super-soft pseudopotential is selected to describe the interaction between Ion Reality and valence electrons and PBE method of the generalized gradient approximation (GGA) is used as an exchange correlation function [16-18]. The valence electron configurations considered in the calculation are: O $2s^2 2p^4$; Sn $5s^2 5p^2$; Dy $4f^{10} 5p^6 06s^2$.

A. Construction of supercell model

This paper constructs the SnO_2 cell model, as shown in Fig. 1(a). Three ratios of supercell models (8.3%, 12.5%, 16.7%) with Dy doped were constructed by atomic substitution method. The corresponding relationship between doping ratio and supercell is shown in Table 1. Taking the doping ratio of 8.3% as an example, the SnO_2 supercell model of 1×2×3 is established, and a Sn atom at the center position is replaced by the rare earth atom Dy, as shown in Fig. 1(b).

TABLE I

DOPING RATIO AND SUPERCELL CORRESPONDENCE

Supercell Models	Ratio
1×1×3	16.7%
1×2×2	12.5%
1×2×3	8.3%

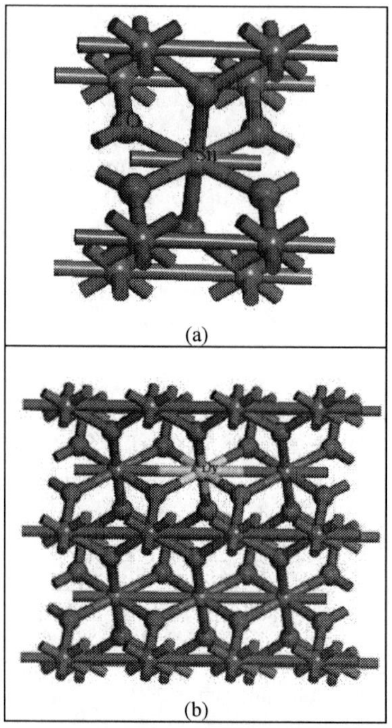

Fig.1 Cell model (a) SnO_2 (b) Dy Doped SnO_2

B. Energy Band and Density of States

The energy band of SnO_2 and SnO_2 doped with different proportions of rare earth element Dy is shown in Fig.2. Among them, (a) is the energy band of SnO_2, and (b), (c), and (d) are the energy band of SnO_2 with Dy doping ratios of 16.7%, 12.5%, and 8.3%, respectively. Select 0eV as the Fermi level. Above 0eV is the conduction band, and below 0eV is the valence band.

Density of States (DOS) is the visualization result of the energy band. Total Density of States (TDOS) represents the state of energy distribution of all electrons in the system. Partial Density of States (PDOS) represents the bonding of electrons in different orbits of different atoms. Fig.3 shows the density of states of SnO_2 and SnO_2 doped with different proportions of rare earth element Dy. (a) is a density of states of SnO_2, and (b), (c), and (d) are density of states of SnO_2 with Dy doping ratios of 16.7%, 12.5%, and 8.3%, respectively.

After several different doping ratios, the energy band of the conduction band and the valence band become dense, and the energy levels of the valence band are refined. Especially the valence band near the Fermi level, the number of bands increases significantly, and the valence band is stimulated, and the number of electrons transferred from valence band to conduction band increases, which improves the conductivity. Moreover, the fluctuations between the bands become gentle, indicating that the localization of the electrons is enhanced after doping. After doping, the conduction band moves toward the low energy end, and the valence band also moves slightly in the direction of the conduction band, and even passes through the Fermi level. It indicates that the doping of Dy element leads to the interaction between different atoms becoming stronger, and the distance from the excitation of the electrons to the conduction band is reduced, that is, the required energy becomes smaller, and the conductivity of the doped SnO_2 is enhanced.

The Partial Density of States can clearly see the details of each electron orbit of the atom.

It can be seen from Fig. 3(a) that the valence band at -20eV to -15eV is mainly the 2s state contribution of O. In the valence band portion of -10eV to 0eV, the density of states at the top of the valence band is mainly from the 2p state of O contribute, and in the conduction band portion of 0eV ~ 20eV, the density of states at the bottom of the conduction band is mainly contributed by the 5s and 5p states of Sn.

It can be seen from Fig. 3(b)-(d) that the new peaks in the region of -45eV are mainly caused by the 6s state of Dy, and the deep rail energy level contributes less to the conductivity, which is not discussed. In the valence band region of -20eV to -15eV, it contributes from the 5p state of the Dy atom and the 2s state of the O atom. Moreover, the peak of the s-orbital of the O atom decreases after doping, indicating that the O atom and Dy atom are bonded. The change in the O-orbital position of the valence band region tends to gradually move toward the Fermi level. In addition to the 2p state of O, 5S and 5p state of Sn, the 4f state of Dy contributes to the Fermi level region. The contribution of rare earth elements to the density of states near the Fermi level proves the contribution of rare earth elements to conductivity. The conduction band area is widened and may be a contribution of the Dy5p state.

C. *Electrical conductivity analysis*

The conductivity δ_i can be used to indicate the electrical conductivity of the material, the conductivity formula is [19]

$$\delta_i = n_i q \mu_i \tag{1}$$

Where q is the electron charge constant, n_i is the electron concentration, and μ_i is the electron mobility.

According to semiconductor theory, under certain temperature conditions, the electron mobility is proportional to the electron scattering relaxation time, inversely proportional to the electron effective mass, and the electron scattering relaxation time is inversely proportional to the doping concentration. Therefore, he relationship between electron mobility and the doping concentration and the electron effective mass is as shown in formula (2):

$$\mu_i \propto \frac{q}{m_e^* \cdot N_i} \tag{2}$$

The formula for the electron effective mass is as follows.

$$m_e^* = \frac{h^2}{4\pi^2 \frac{d^2E}{dk^2}} \tag{3}$$

Where h is Planck constant, k is the wave vector, and E is the electron energy at the wave vector.

According to the actual situation of the model in this paper, to compare the influence of different doping Dy atoms on the conductivity, the relative conductivity can be obtained by comparing them, as shown in Equation 4.

$$\frac{\delta_i}{\delta_j} = \frac{n_i \cdot m_{ej}^* . N_j}{n_j \cdot m_{ei}^* . N_i} \qquad \delta_i \propto \frac{n_i}{m_e^* . N_i} \tag{4}$$

The electronic concentration can be obtained by integrating the density of states with origin software, and the electrons effective mass can be obtained by second derivation of the energy band. The calculated data are shown in Table 2.

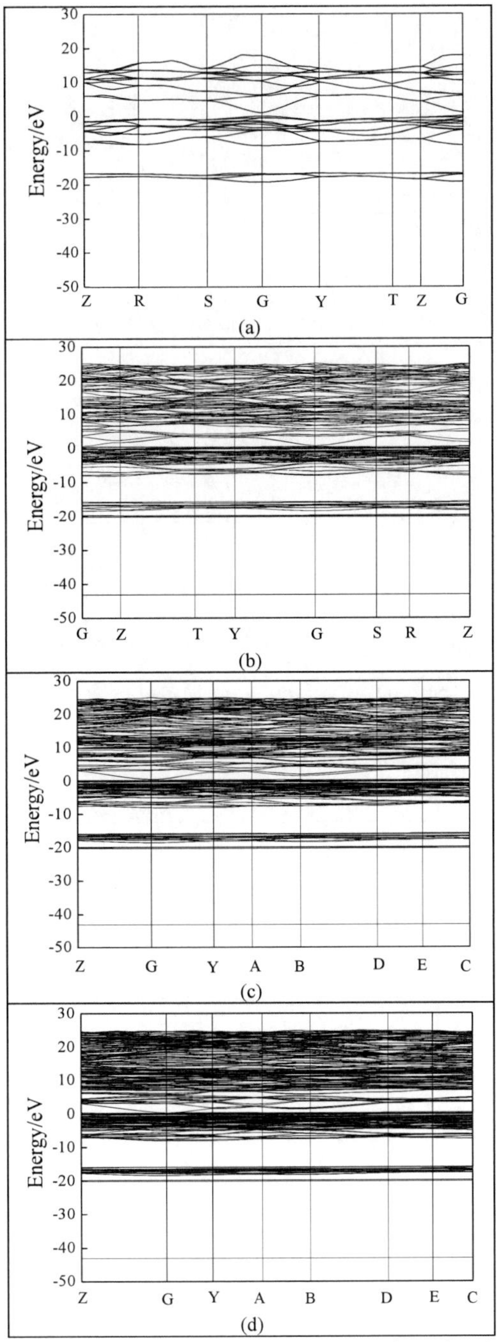

Fig. 3 Band structure (a) SnO_2 (b) 16.7% of Dy-doped (c) 12.5% of Dy -doped (d) 8.3% of Dy -doped

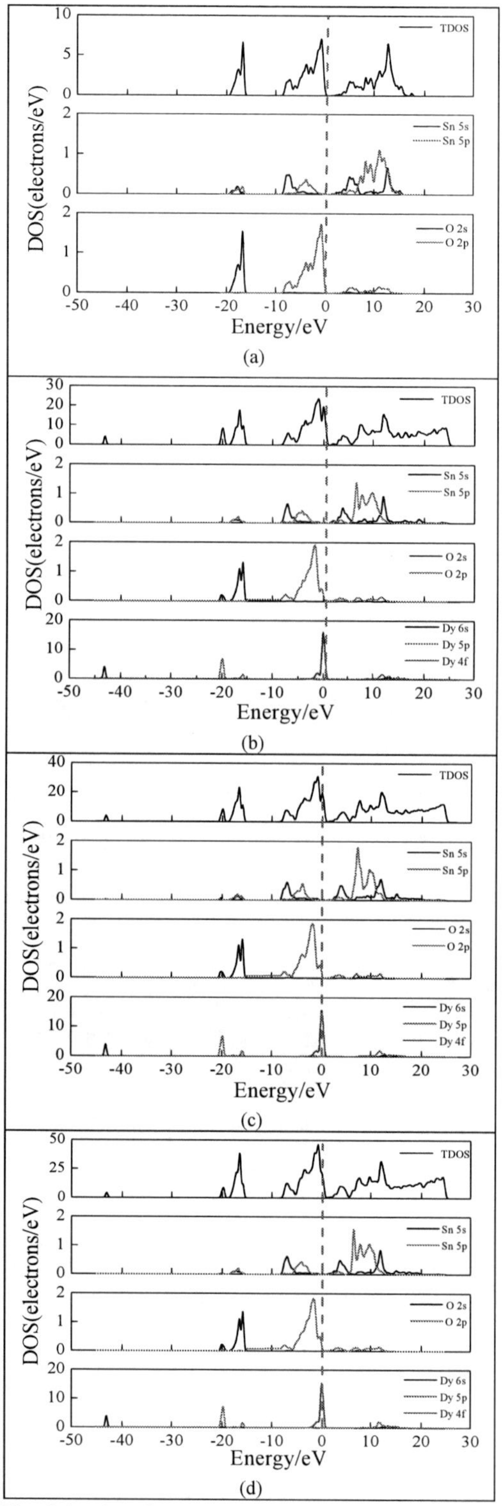

Fig. 4 density of states (a) SnO_2 (b) 16.7% of Dy-doped (c) 12.5% of Dy -doped (d) 8.3% of Dy –doped

TABLE II

RELATIVE CONDUCTIVITY

Ratio	16.7%	12.5%	8.3%
Two Derivation	512.8	391.1	258.9
Effective Electron Mass/10^{-32}kg	2.18	2.87	4.29
Relative Electron Number	3.1	3.3	2.9
Relative Electron Concentration/10^{22}cm^{-3}	3.82	4.09	3.54
Relative Conductivity	0.92	1	0.87

It can be seen from the relative conductivity of the doped SnO_2-Dy given in Table 2. The conductivity order is: 12.5%>16.7%>8.3%.

D. Elastic constants

The elastic constants were calculated for SnO_2 and different proportions of doped SnO_2-Dy to analyze mechanical properties. The universal elastic anisotropy index and hardness values are obtained in Table 3.

TABLE III

THE UNIVERSAL ELASTIC ANISOTROPY INDEX AND HARDNESS

Ratio	16.7%	12.5%	8.3%	0
B/GPa	145.9	154.9	127.9	145.6
G/GPa	69.6	76.7	68.7	80.6
HV/GPa	8.0	8.9	9.1	10.5
A^U	1.58	1.31	1.90	2.04

Through elastic calculation, the hardness value and the universal elastic anisotropy index A^U value are obtained, as shown in Table 3. It can be seen from Table 3 that the hardness of SnO_2 is the largest, and the hardness decreases with the increase of doping ratio. The universal elastic anisotropy index reflects the difference of bonding strength in different directions, and is closely related to the microcrack induction in materials [20]. The universal elastic anisotropy index A^U value is usually the decisive factor for cracking. As can be seen from Table 3, the AU value after doping is smaller than that of SnO_2, the universal elastic anisotropy index A^U value with doping.

III. EXPERIMENTAL VERIFICATION

A. Preparation of contact materials

In order to correspond to the theoretical calculation model in this paper, Dy doped SnO_2 powders containing different proportions were prepared by sol-gel method. Table 4 gives the atomic and mass ratios of the main raw materials.

TABLE IV

THE MAIN RAW MATERIAL RATIO

$SnCl_4 \cdot 5H_2O$: $DyCl_3 \cdot 6H_2O$	16.7%	12.5%	8.3%
Atomic ratio	83.3:16.7	87.5:12.5	91.7:8.3
Mass ratio	0.99:0.21	1.04:0.16	1.09:0.11

Firstly, the refined and substituted Dy doped SnO_2 powder was prepared by sol-gel method. On the basis of the above, the SnO_2 powder and the doped powder were mixed with Ag powder by a high energy ball milling process at a ratio of 1.2 g: 8.8 g, respectively. The $AgSnO_2$ contact materials were prepared by pressing, initial firing, recompression, reburning, polishing and cutting.

B. Experimental data results

The electrical contact properties of the test materials were tested using a JF04C electrical contact material tester. The simulated electrical contact environment was DC 24V, 13A. Each pair of contacts performed 25,000 on-off tests, and the contacts measured the arc energy, contact resistance and welding force every 100 times. The contact resistance, arc energy and welding force of $AgSnO_2$ and different proportions of Dy-doped $AgSnO_2$ are shown in Table 5.

TABLE V

ELECTRICAL CONTACT PERFORMANCE TEST PARAMETERS

Ratio	16.7%	12.5%	8.3%	0
Arc Energy (mJ)	146.9~ 181.2	150.3~ 174.9	143.7~1 94.2	159.0~ 235.3
Average Arc Energy (mJ)	158.3	160.2	161.3	192.9
Contact Resistance (mΩ)	0.49~ 1.08	0.25~ 0.87	0.49~ 1.22	0.35~ 8.93
Average contact resistance (mΩ)	0.61	0.43	0.77	1.83
welding force (cN)	1.14~ 3.11	0.72~ 3.14	1.87~ 3.50	1.31~ 34.53
Average welding force (cN)	1.91	1.32	2.35	15.24

From the average arc energy, contact resistance and welding force in Table 5, it can be seen that the average arc energy, contact resistance and welding force of the contact material after doping are both low, and from the viewpoint of the range, when the doping concentration is 12.5%, the average contact resistance and the welding force are reduced more. Although the arc energy is not the smallest, but it can be seen from the variation range that after doping, the maximum value of the arc energy is the smallest among the doping ratios, and the range of the arc energy is also the most stable. When the doping concentration is 12.5%, the electrical property is the best, and the second is 16.7%, which is consistent with the relative conductivity results obtained from the simulation.

C. Measurement of hardness

The hardness of the contact material was measured by HXD-1000TM digital microhardness tester. First, the test pressure is selected, and then turn the diamond indenter to the surface of the test sample. After holding for a few seconds, use the microscope to find and observe the diamond indentation on the surface of the sample, then adjust the grating position and place on both sides of the two diagonals of the diamond, the length of the diagonal is measured, and finally the hardness value is read. In order to improve the reliability of the calculation result, three positions are selected for each sample to be measured, and then the average of the three sets of data is taken.

Table 6 shows the hardness values of $AgSnO_2$ and different doping ratios of $AgSnO_2$-Dy.

TABLE VI

HARDNESS

Ratio	16.7%	12.5%	8.34%	0
Hardness (HV)	85.5	91.7	107.1	117.1

By comparing the theoretical and practical hardness values of Tables 3 and 6, it is found that simulation and experiment can match well.

IV. CONCLUSION

Based on the first principle of density functional theory, three kinds of (8.3%, 12.5%, 16.7%) Dy-doped supercell models were simulated and analyzed for energy band, density of states and elastic constants. The results show that:

1) The relative conductivity of the doping system is obtained by the energy band and density of states and using the origin software. When the Dy doping ratio is 0.125, the conductivity is the best.
2) By calculating the elastic constant, the doping system can reduce the hardness of the material. When the Dy doping ratio is 0.125, the probability of cracking is the smallest.

Finally, $AgSnO_2$ contact material with different doping ratios are prepared, and the arc energy, contact resistance, welding force and hardness are measured. The final simulation and experimental results are well matched.

ACKNOWLEDGMENT

This study was funded by the National Natural Science Foundation (51777057)

REFERENCES

[1] Y.G. Wang, X.Q. Cao, Y.P. Ni, Application of Electrical Contact Materials in Low Voltage Electrical Apparatus[J]. Low Voltage Apparatus, 2011, 10:58-61

[2] D.F. Cui, Analysis of the development of electric contact material market in China [J]. Electrical Materials, 2016, (02): 24-25

[3] F.Q. Dou, Application of silver-based electrical contact materials in relays [D]. Tianjin: Tianjin University, 2009
[4] H.Y. Chen, M. Xie, J. Wang, Research Status and Development Trend of Silver Tin Oxide Electrical Contact Materials [J]. Precious Metals, 2011, 2: 77-81X. M. Liu, Nano-doped $AgSnO_2$ study electrical contact materials [D]. Tianjin University, 2004.
[5] Y.C. Zhu, Preparation and properties of nano- $AgSnO_2$ electrical contact materials [D]. Hebei University of Technology, 2014.
[6] F. Q. Zhang, Application Research of Silver-based Electrical Contact Materials in Relays [D]. Tianjin University, 2009.
[7] Z. H. Ma, Research Organization electrical properties of silver tin oxide contact materials [D]. Kunming University of Science, 2002.
[8] H. T. Wang, Silver oxide research to improve the properties of the contact mechanism tin material [D]. Hebei University of Technology, 2007.
[9] D. X. Jian, Prepared by high energy ball milling AgSnO2 Study of electrical contact material [D]. Tianjin University, 2004.
[10] Z. Y. Liu, Calculation and research of nano-doped $AgSnO_2$ electrical contact materials [D]. Tianjin: Tianjin University, 2007.
[11] Brisson E, Carre P, Desplats H, Effective thermal and electrical conductivities of $AgSnO_2$ during sintering. Part I: Experimental characterization and mechanisms[J]. Metallurgical and Materials Transactions, 2016, 47(12):6304-6318
[12] Y.C. Zhu, J. Q. Wang, L. Q An, H. T. Wang, Novel $AgSnO_2/CeO_2$ Preparation and electrical properties of the electrical contact material. [J] Metal Materials and Engineering, 2015,44 (08): 2011-2014.
[13] Y.C. Zhu, Study of rare earth oxide added silver tin oxide contact material [D]. Hebei University of Technology, 2007.
[14] M. L. Ni, Effect of additives on microstructure and properties of $AgSnO_2$ electrical contact materials [D]. Zhejiang University, 2006.
[15] N. Liu, C. Fu, Y. H. Zhang, R. H. Chou, J. B. Wang, Y. L. Wang, Sb doping $AgSnO_2$ Preparation and Properties of Contact Materials [J]. Xi'an Polytechnic University, 2017,31 (05): 652 -656.
[16] Thangaraju. B. Structural and electrical studies on highly conducting spray deposited fluorine and antimony doped SnO_2 thin films from $SnCl_2$ precursor [J]. Thin Solid Films, 2002, 402(1): 71
[17] Godinho K G, Walsh A, Watson G W. Energetic and electronic structure analysis of intrinsic defects in SnO_2[J]. The Journal of Physical Chemistry C,2008,113(1): 439-448.
[18] X. Li, First-principles calculation and design of spintronic materials and photolysis water catalytic materials [D]. Anhui: University of Science and Technology of China, 2015
[19] Liu E K, Zhu B S, Luo J S .2003 Semiconductor Physics (6th Ed.) (Beijing: Publishing House of Electronics Industry) pp111,129.
[20] Bouhemadou A. Theoretical study of the structural, elastic and electronic properties of the GeX_2O_4 (X = Mg, Zn, Cd) compounds under pressure[J]. Modelling & Simulation in Materials Science & Engineering, 2008, 16(5):055007.

Ying Zhang was born in Baoding District, Hebei Province, in 1993. The author is a Master at Hebei University of Technology. Graduated from Hebei University of Technology in 2019, now a PHD is reading.

She has published five papers and applied for Hebei Provincial Graduate Innovation Funding Project.

Zhizhou Bao is an vice president of People's Electrical Appliance Group Zhejiang Co., Ltd.

Jingqin Wang was born in Hengshui District, Hebei Province, in 1964. The author received the B.S., M.S. and Ph.D. degrees in electrical engineering from Hebei University of Technology, Tianjin, P.R.China, in 1984, 1986 and 1997 respectively.

Since 1998, she has been a Professor. And she became Doctoral Tutor of Electrical Engineering College, Hebei University of Technology in 2003. She currently holds 21 patents and has written more than 110 journal articles.

Prof. Wang is the Secretary General of Electrical Products Reliability Association of China Electro Technical Society (CES). She was a recipient of the National Science and Technology Progress Award in 2000, 2002, 2008, Science and Technology Progress Award of Hebei Province in 1991, 2005, 2013.

She is currently deputy director of the Institute of Electrical Appliances of Hebei University of Technology. She is an expert on special allowances of the State Council, a national candidate for hundreds of millions of the talents project of the new century, and an outstanding expert of Hebei Province. Vice Chairman and Member of the Arc-electricity Contact Committee of China Electrotechnical Society, Member of the Low-voltage Electrical Appliances Committee of China Electrotechnical Society.

Guangzhi Zhang is an manager of Shanghai Liangxin Electric Appliance Co., Ltd.

Yancai Zhu published more than 10 papers on the preparation process of low-voltage electrical contact materials and the influence of additives on the properties of $AgSnO_2$ contact materials, and participated in 5 scientific research projects, one of which won the second prize of Hebei Province Science and Technology Progress and has strong scientific research ability.

7th International Conference on Reliability of
Electrical Products and Electrical Contacts,
November 04-06, 2019

Reliability Analysis of the Operating Mechanism of Molded Case Circuit Breaker

Changchun Chi, Zetao Wang, Yifan Tong
School of Electrical Engineering, Shanghai Dianji University, Shanghai, 201306, China
E-mail: chicc@sdju.edu.cn Tel: 13701608259

***Abstract*—Molded case circuit breakers are important protection devices in power distribution systems, and their reliability is of paramount importance. The flexible body finite element model of the circuit breaker operating mechanism components is established by Ansys, and the rigid-flexible coupling mechanism model is established in Adams for dynamic stress simulation. The simulation obtains the maximum stress value of the flexible body part in the free tripping action, outputs the load file of the force component in the simulation, and simulates the stress distribution cloud image in Ansys. According to the obtained data, the stress distribution and the cause of the maximum stress are analyzed, which lays a foundation for the reliability analysis and optimization design of the component. According to the stress-strength interference model, the reliability analysis of the components with the largest stress change is carried out, and the reliability of static strength and the reliability of fatigue strength are calculated respectively. The calculation results show that the research object has high reliability under static strength and fatigue strength, and the structural design and material selection meet the technical requirements.**

***Index Terms*—Molded case circuit breaker, operating mechanism, reliability analysis, stress-strength interference model**

I. INTRODUCTION

During the operation of the molded case circuit breaker, there are some collision relationships between the components, because the action time is shorter and the component action speed is higher. These high-speed collision forces can cause momentary changes in the stress on the component. When the maximum stress on the dangerous surface of the component exceeds the yield strength of the material used, the component will plastically deform and even break under long-term operation, resulting in the breaker not being able to be properly divided. Closing [1].

Currently, researchers in the circuit breaker operating mechanism during operation of the stress and reliability have been studied from various aspects. In literature [2], the flexible body model of the relevant components of the molded case circuit breaker was generated by Ansys, and the rigid-flexible coupling model was built into Adams for dynamic stress analysis. The components were optimized according to the simulation results. In literature [3], the finite element modeling of the high-voltage circuit breaker spring operating mechanism was firstly carried out by Hyper Mesh software, and the stress analysis was carried out by Ls-Dyna software. The influence of stress distribution and its dynamic changes on the dynamic performance of the circuit breaker was analyzed. In literature [4], the reliability calculation model of high-voltage circuit breaker energy storage spring considering strength degradation and stress relaxation is established, and the life expectancy of the spring is analyzed. In literature [5], Monte Carlo method was used to analyze the operational reliability and operational reliability sensitivity of the miniature circuit breaker operating mechanism. The above literatures use the simulation software to analyze the stress of the circuit breaker or establish the relevant mathematical model to calculate the reliability of the circuit breaker operating mechanism. The stress distribution obtained by the software simulation is not combined with the reliability analysis of the circuit breaker operating mechanism.

In this paper, by combining Adams and Ansys simulation software, the rigid-flexible coupling mechanism model of a molded case circuit breaker operating mechanism is established, and the dynamic stress simulation is carried out. The stress distribution of key components is analyzed according to the obtained data, and the reliability is calculated.

II. STRESS-STRENGTH INTERFERENCE MODEL

The stress-strength interference model is one of the main ideas in mechanical reliability analysis[6]. This model can clearly reveal the cause of failure of mechanical parts and the cause of certain failure rate and the nature of mechanical strength reliability design [1]. In mechanical design, strength and stress have the same dimensions, so their probability density curves can be represented in the same coordinate system. If the strength of the part is much higher than the working stress in the mechanical design, the two distribution curves do not intersect, as shown in the left figure of Fig. 1

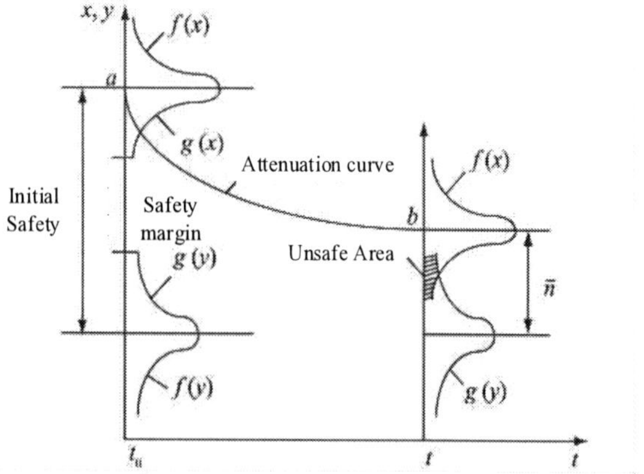

Fig. 1 Stress-strength curves and their relationship.

. Then the part is in the initial stage of work, under normal working conditions, the strength is always greater than the stress, no failure. However, due to the discreteness of the strength value and stress value of the part, the strength of the material deteriorates under the influence of factors such as environment and use conditions, so that the two probability-density function curves of stress and strength may intersect under certain conditions. As shown in the right image of Fig. 1 (shaded in the figure), this is the area where the part may fail, called the interference zone[7].

It can be seen from the figure that when the dispersion of the strength and stress of the part becomes larger, the interference area increases, and the unreliability of the part increases. When the material performance is good and the working stress is stable, the stress and When the dispersion of the intensity distribution is small, the interference portion will be correspondingly reduced, and the reliability of the part will increase[7]. If the probability distribution curve of stress and strength is known, the reliability of the part can be calculated from its interference model. As shown in the left figure of Figure 1, the stress-intensity probability distribution curve does not interfere, and there is enough safety margin, and the probability that the working stress is greater than the part strength is zero.That is:

$$P(S>\delta)=0 \tag{1}$$

In the formula： S —Working stress; δ —Material strength.

When the mechanical part has a stress-strength model such as formula(1), the part is safe and does not malfunction. When the stress-intensity probability distribution curve interferes, although the average value of the working stress μ_S is still much smaller than the average value of the ultimate stress (strength) μ_δ, it cannot be absolutely guaranteed that the working stress is not greater than the ultimate stress under any circumstances. That is, the probability that the working stress is greater than the strength of the part is greater than zero.

$$P(S>\delta)>0 \tag{2}$$

When the working stress exceeds the mechanical parts suffered a mechanical strength of the material, it will produce a malfunction or failure.

The probability that the stress is greater than the strength is the probability of failure, that is, the degree of unreliability, expressed as:

$$F=P(S>\delta)=P[(\delta-S<0)] \tag{3}$$

When the working stress is less than the strength of the part, the part does not malfunction or fail. The full probability that the stress is less than the intensity is the reliability, expressed as:

$$F=P(S<\delta)=P[(\delta-S>0)] \tag{4}$$

Since the strength δ and the working stress S of the part are random variables, the difference between the two, $Z=\delta-S$, is also a random variable called an interference random variable.

Since the size of z is directly related to the degree of security, the random variable z is sometimes referred to as a safety reserve in practical applications. When the stress and the strength are both normally distributed, the difference in the normal distribution is still a normal distribution, and the safety reserve is also a normal distribution.

$$f(Z)=\frac{1}{\sqrt{2\pi}\sigma_Z}e^{-\frac{1}{2}\left(\frac{Z-\mu_Z}{\partial_Z}\right)^2} \tag{5}$$

In the formula: $\mu_Z=\mu_\delta-\mu_S$； $\partial_Z=\left(\partial_\delta^2-\partial_S^2\right)^{\frac{1}{2}}$。

The reliability is:

$$R=P(Z>0)=\int_0^\infty\frac{1}{\sqrt{2\pi}\sigma_Z}e^{-\frac{1}{2}\left(\frac{Z-\mu_Z}{\partial_Z}\right)^2} \tag{6}$$

The above formula is converted into a standard normal distribution form:

$$R=\int_0^\infty f(Z)dZ=\int_{Z_0}^\infty\varphi(Z)dZ=1-\Phi(Z_0) \tag{7}$$

In the formula: $\varphi(Z)=\frac{1}{\sqrt{2\pi}}e^{-\frac{1}{2}z^2}$; $Z=\frac{Z-\mu_Z}{\partial_Z}$;

$$Z_0=-\frac{\mu_Z}{\partial_Z}=-\frac{\mu_\delta-\mu_S}{\left(\partial_\delta^2+\partial_S^2\right)^{\frac{1}{2}}}.$$

Take: $\beta=\frac{\mu_Z}{\partial_Z}=\frac{\mu_\delta-\mu_S}{\left(\partial_\delta^2+\partial_S^2\right)^{\frac{1}{2}}}$

When the strength and stress both satisfy the normal distribution, the reliability is calculated as:

$$R=1-\Phi(Z_0)=\Phi(\beta)=\Phi\left(\frac{\mu_\delta-\mu_S}{\left(\partial_\delta^2+\partial_S^2\right)^{\frac{1}{2}}}\right) \tag{8}$$

In the formula: μ_δ —Average strength; μ_S —Mean stress;

∂_δ—Sample standard deviation of μ_δ ; ∂_S—Sample standard deviation of μ_S 。

III. STRESS DISTRIBUTION OF KEY COMPONENTS OF THE OPERATING MECHANSIM

A. Finite element model of flexible body

In order to study the stress distribution of the key components of the circuit breaker operating mechanism, it is first necessary to establish a flexible body model of the relevant components, and then establish a rigid-flexible coupling mechanism model in Adams. There are many methods for flexible body modeling. This paper uses the finite element flexible body (Flex) method: using professional finite element software such as Ansys to set various parameters such as material properties, geometric properties, and partition properties. Generating a flexible body finite element model. The flexible body can then be used by outputting the specified modal neutral file (.mnf format) through the corresponding conversion interface. The related modeling process is shown in Fig. 2.

The material used for the operating mechanism components of this type of circuit breaker is quenched and tempered 40Cr steel, and the better mechanical properties can be obtained by the quenched and tempered steel.Yield strength σ_S is the limit of elastic deformation of metal materials[8],The stress when the circuit breaker operating mechanism lever exceeds the yield strength σ_S , deformed, or even break the lever long-term action, affecting the normal operation of the molded case circuit breaker[9-11].

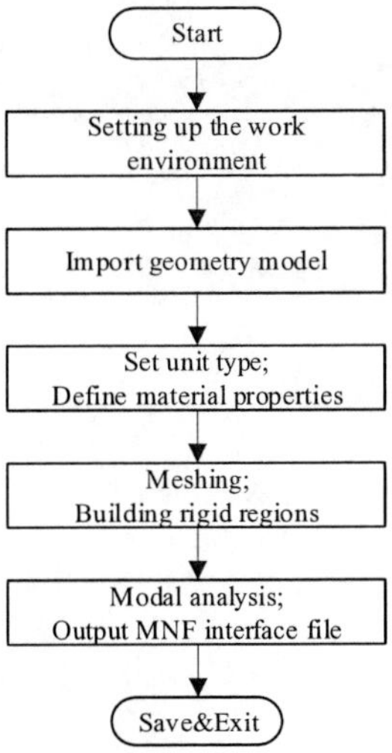

Fig. 2 ANSYS flexible body finite element modeling flow chart.

Open Ansys Apdl, first set the working environment: select the working directory, enter the task name, set the unit. The rigid body three dimensional model of the operating mechanism component is imported, and the mesh is divided by the command flow method according to the flow chart sequence shown in Fig. 2 to generate a modal neutral file of the flexible body[2]. The flexible body finite element model of the generated jump pin and lower link is shown in Fig. 3.

B. Establishment of a rigid-flexible coupling mechanism model

In Adams, the rigid body is replaced by the established flexible body model. The replacement of the rotation constraint on the component is also replaced at the same time, but the collision constraint cannot be automatically replaced. The collision type needs to be reset and the collision parameters are set. Fig.4 shows the rigid-flexible coupling model of the established circuit breaker operating mechanism[12~13]. Change the integrator in the Solver option to the SI2 integrator (Slabilized Index2 imegrator), which can be used to obtain higher simulation accuracy[8][12]. In the tools plugin manager, select the Durability plugin, which can view the stress hotspot table of the relevant flexible body and the stress history curve of the relevant nodes[11~13],and provide analytical data for analyzing the stress distribution and generation. Set the simulation parameters and run the simulation.

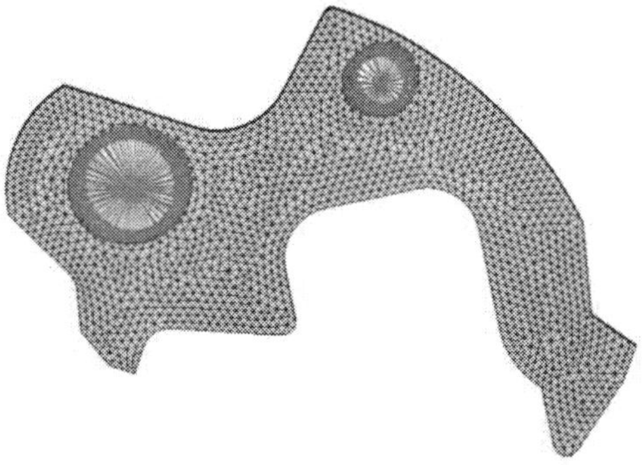

(a) Jump pin finite element model

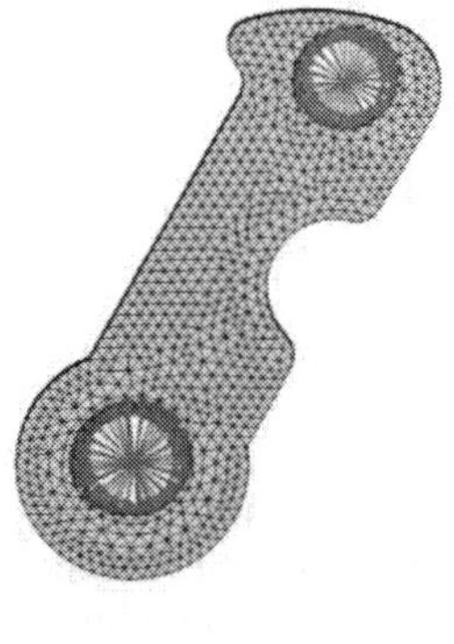

(b) Lower link finite element model

Fig. 3 Finite element model of jump pin and lower link generated by ANSYS.

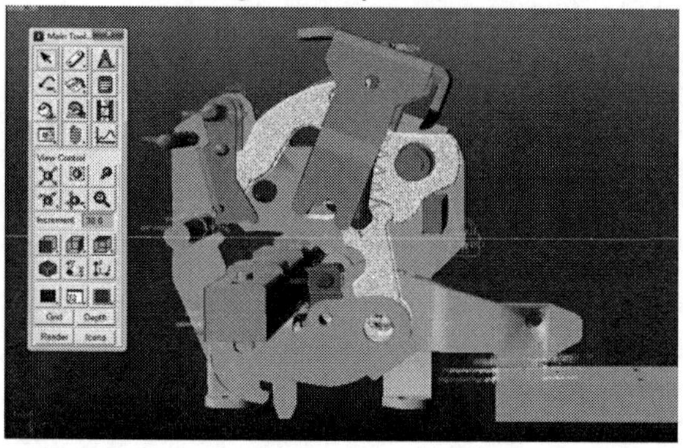

Fig. 4 Circuit breaker rigid-flexible coupling mechanism model assembly drawing.

C. Stress and analysis of levers

After the dynamic stress analysis is completed, click on the Hot Spots Table under the Durability module to view the stress level of the dangerous node and the time when the maximum stress occurs during the action. The flexible body is converted into a rigid body, and the load file of the jump pin and the lower link at 4.797ms in .lod format is output as a rigid body in Adams. Open the flexible finite element model established in Ansys, apply a load to the nodes at the center of the hole, and import the load file output from Adams. After solving the operation, the post processing module views and outputs the stress cloud diagram of the jump pin and the lower link at 4.797ms, as shown in Fig. 5.

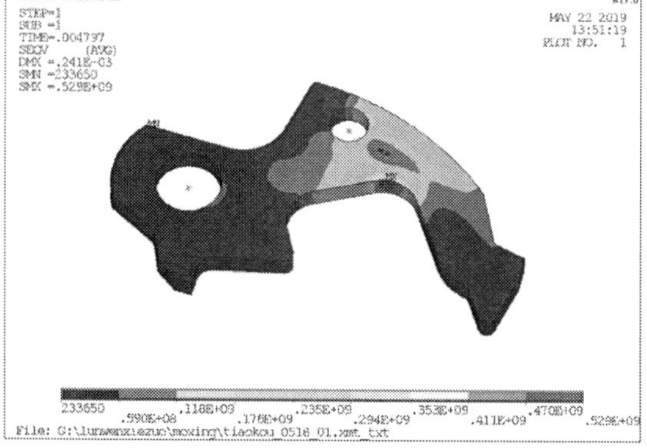

(a) Jump pin stress cloud

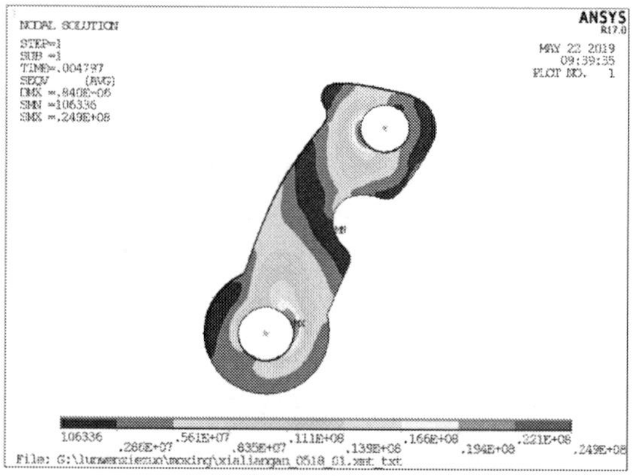

(b) Lower link stress cloud

Fig. 5 Jump pin and lower link stress distribution cloud map(t=0.004797s).

It can be seen from the stress distribution cloud diagram that when the circuit breaker operating mechanism is freely tripping, the jump pin is much more stressed than the lower link. And the maximum stress appears in the lower right bend of the jump pin and the upper link rotation axis, so the stress of the jump pin is mainly analyzed below, and the reliability calculation is performed.

Load the Durability module, click on the Hot Spots Table, and select and view the node stress table of the jump pin flexible body during the free trip action, as shown in Fig. 6. The figure shows the number of nodes, coordinates and time of the 10 maximum stress values during the breaking process. Enter the dangerous stress node number into the Nodal Plots command to view the stress history curve for the dangerous node. Select node number 4641 and generate the stress variation curve of the node in the 10ms simulation time in the Nodal Plots command, as shown in Fig. 7.

VON MISES Hot Spots for niaotouhuan_flex Date= 2019-05-22 13:43:05						
Model= .MODEL_1251		Analysis= Last_Run		Time = 0 to 0.01 sec		
Top 10 Hot Spots			Abs	Radius= 0.0 meter		
Hot Spot	Stress	Node	Time	Location wrt LPRF (meter)		
#	(newton/meter**2)	id	(sec)	X	Y	Z
1	5.21661e+008	4641	0.00479728	0.161054	0.106683	-0.0211261
2	5.19908e+008	4659	0.00479728	0.160876	0.105817	-0.0207699
3	5.16358e+008	1911	0.00479728	0.160835	0.1075	-0.0206789
4	5.12426e+008	4660	0.00479728	0.161284	0.105962	-0.0215169
5	5.10541e+008	4640	0.00479728	0.160672	0.106658	-0.0202643
6	5.06756e+008	1910	0.00479728	0.161279	0.1075	-0.0215091
7	4.97964e+008	4664	0.00479728	0.160863	0.104137	-0.0207402
8	4.94409e+008	1912	0.00479728	0.160527	0.1075	-0.0197895
9	4.89052e+008	4649	0.00479728	0.161048	0.103304	-0.0211165
10	4.88388e+008	4665	0.00479728	0.161277	0.104023	-0.0215058

Fig. 6 Jump pin flexible body dangerous node stress table.

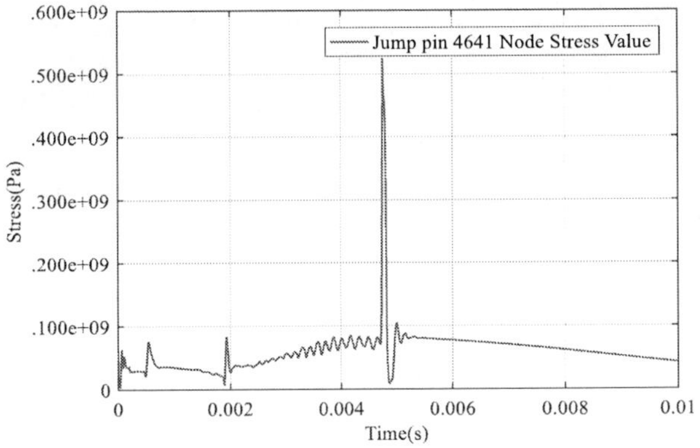

Fig. 7 Jump pin joint 4641 stress history curve.

It can be seen from the above figure that when the free tripping action of the circuit breaker is about 4.8ms, the maximum stress value of the jump pin is: σ=$0.529\times10^{9}\,Pa$, yield strength less than 40Cr steel.According to the stress history curve, it can be considered that the stress on the jump pin after 5.0ms hardly affects the performance of the member. Click to enter the Adams/Post Processor post-processing interface, and output the stress history curve of the flexible body jump pin No. 4641 and the impact force during the tripping action, as shown in Fig. 8.

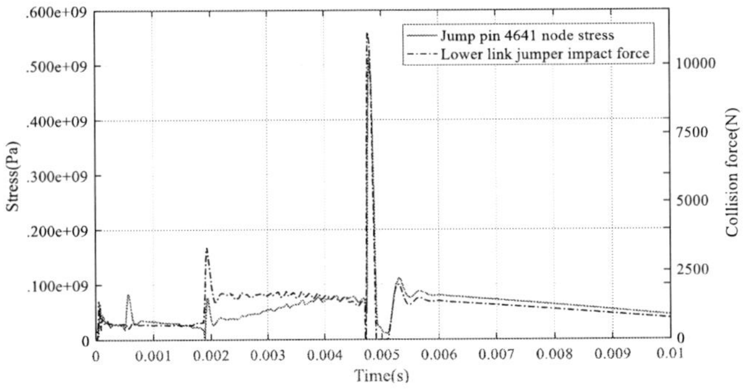

Fig. 8. Schematic diagram of the force of jump pin.

It can be seen from the figure that during the action, the collision force curve between the lower link and jump pin is similar to the maximum stress history curve of the jump pin, and the value is large. The collision force between the remaining bars and the jump pin is low (not shown) and can be ignored. It is inferred that during the free tripping process, the collision force between the jump pin and the lower link is the cause of the large stress on the jump pin.

It should be noted that the calculated stress values in Adams here are different from those of Ansys. This is because Adams also includes the influence of the rigid body in the analysis, and the exported load file will also appear incomplete data[14~15]. Therefore, before the load file is output, the jump pin of the flexible body is converted into a rigid body, and then the load file when the jump pin is a rigid body is output, which can effectively reduce the error. The stress values in this paper are based on the Ansys stress simulation values.

IV. RELIABILITY ANALYSIS OF KEY COMPONENTS OF OPERATING MECHANISM

A. *Jump pin stress distribution*

The coefficient of variation, also known as the "discrete coefficient", is a normalized measure of the degree of dispersion of the probability distribution, defined as the ratio of the standard deviation to the mean.

It is assumed that the stress S of the connecting rod is related to the load F, the thickness D of the connecting rod material, and the width B. If the mean and deviation of the load, the thickness and width of the connecting rod material are known, the standard deviation can be determined by the "3σ" rule [16].

40Cr quenched and tempered steel with material thickness $5.0\pm0.15mm$ of jump pin, common precision, width tolerance $\pm0.50mm$ .Let the coefficients of variation of stress S, load F, thickness D, and width B be C_S, C_F, C_D, and C_B, respectively, and calculate them as follows:

$$C_F = \frac{200}{1500\times3} = 0.0444$$

$$C_D = \frac{0.15}{5\times3} = 0.01$$

$$C_B = \frac{0.5}{46.5\times3} = 0.0036$$

Then the coefficient of variation of the stress S is:

$$C_S = \sqrt{C_F + C_D + C_B} = 0.046$$

According to the formula:

$$C_S = \frac{\partial_S}{\overline{S}} \tag{9}$$

Among them, the average stress $\bar{S}$ of the maximum stress of the jump pin is:

$$\bar{S} = \mu_S = 501.956MPa$$

Then from formula (9):

$$\partial_S = C_S \times \bar{S} = C_S \times \mu_S = 0.046 \times 501.956 = 23.09MPa$$

B. Jump pin static strength reliability calculation

According to a large amount of statistical data, the strength of the material, such as the yield strength σ_S and the tensile strength σ_b, basically obey the normal distribution.

According to the material used for the jump pin is 40Cr quenched and tempered steel, assuming that the strength of the jump pin follows a normal distribution, the hardness after quenching and tempering is between HRC32-36, and the data relationship between the hardness and the strength of the material is obtained from the relevant data. 1 shown [17]:

TABLE I

RELATIONSHIP BETWEEN HARDNESS AND STRENGTH OF 40CR STEEL

HRC	32	33	34	35	36
$\bar{\sigma}_b / MPa$	1060	1086	1113	1141	1170

Process the above data:

$$\bar{\sigma}_b = \frac{1}{n}\sum_{i=1}^{n}\sigma_{bi} = 1114 = \mu_\delta$$

$$S_{\sigma_b} = \sqrt{\frac{1}{n-1}\sum_{i=1}^{n}\left(\sigma_{bi} - \bar{\sigma}_b\right)^2} = 43.49MPa = \partial_\delta$$

Calculated by formula (8):

$$R = \Phi(\beta) = \Phi\left(\frac{\mu_\delta - \mu_S}{\left(\partial_\delta^2 + \partial_S^2\right)^{\frac{1}{2}}}\right) = \Phi\left(\frac{1114 - 501.956}{\left(43.49^2 + 23.09^2\right)^{\frac{1}{2}}}\right) = \Phi(12.4299)$$

Check the normal distribution table to know that the static strength reliability of the circuit breaker operating mechanism R>0.99999.

c. reliability calculation of jump pin fatigue strength

According to the stress intensity interference model, when the yield strength of the material is higher than the maximum working stress of the rod, no failure occurs, that is, the static strength requirement can be satisfied. However, as the number of circuit breakers increases, the jump pin will cause metal fatigue and the material strength will decrease as it is subjected to cyclic loads such as collisions and vibrations. When the yield strength is lower than the maximum working stress, the probability of failure of the jump pin will be greatly increased. Therefore, in addition to verifying the static strength, the calculation of the reliability of the fatigue strength needs to be considered [18].

Through a large number of fatigue tests, it is shown that when the number of operation steps of the circuit breaker reaches 10^3~10^5 times, the stress of the rod will reach an extreme value, which is called low cycle fatigue, during which fatigue failure may occur in the rod [19].

The distribution of material fatigue strength can also be approximated as a normal distribution, and the formula used for calculation is also mostly an empirical formula. The P-S-N and S-N curves are usually used to calculate the fatigue strength reliability. The former characterizes the relationship between failure rate (P), cycle number (N) and fatigue life (S), while the latter is stress-life curve [18].For the steel material, preferably the number of cycles $N_\infty = (1 \sim 10) \times 10^6$, usually take $N_\infty = 10^7$.

For 40Cr steel after quenching and tempering treatment, when $N_0 = 10^3$:

$$\bar{\delta}_{-1N_0} = 0.65\mu_\delta = 0.65 \times 1114 = 724.1MPa$$

When $N_0 = 10^7$, check the relevant data table available [1]:

$$\bar{\delta}_{-1} = 0.46\mu_\delta = 0.46 \times 1114 = 512.44MPa$$

Therefore, the S-N curve of the jump pin material can be obtained as shown in Fig. 9:

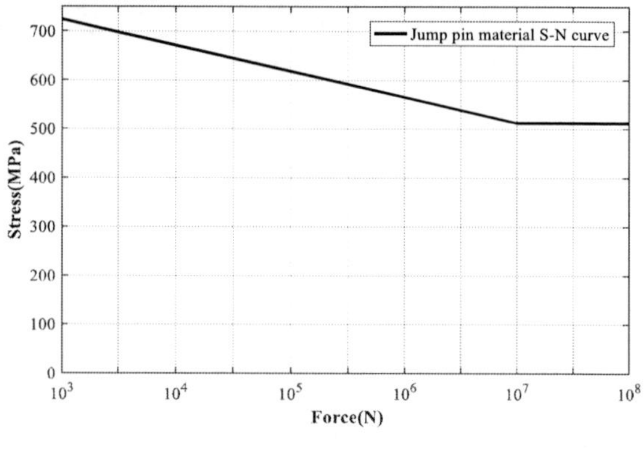

Fig. 9 Jump pin material S-N curve.

The design of this type of circuit breaker has a mechanical life of 20,000 times and an electrical life of 7000 times. When calculating the fatigue reliability of the jump pin under the specified number of operations, the fatigue strength corresponding to different operation times can be obtained through Fig. 9:

$$\bar{\delta}_{-1L(7000)} = 512.44 + (724.1 - 512.44) \times \frac{7 - \lg 7000}{7-3} = 679.38MPa$$

$$\bar{\delta}_{-1L(20000)} = 512.44 + (724.1 - 512.44) \times \frac{7 - \lg 20000}{7-3} = 655.26MPa$$

Analysis of the motion state of the circuit breaker operating mechanism shows that the jump pin is subjected to stress as a pulsating cycle during the action, and the fatigue strength value obtained by the SN curve is the fatigue strength value of the symmetric cycle, so the calculation is based on the empirical formula of the relevant data [20].

$$\delta_{0L(7000)} = 1.42\delta_{-1L(7000)} = 964.72MPa$$

$$\delta_{0L(20000)} = 1.42\delta_{-1L(20000)} = 930.47MPa$$

According to the data, the coefficient of variation of fatigue strength of steel is C=0.08, so:

$$\partial_{\delta_{0L(7000)}} = 0.08 \times \sigma_{0L(7000)} = 0.08 \times 964.72 = 77.18MPa$$

$$\partial_{\delta_{0L(20000)}} = 0.08 \times \sigma_{0L(20000)} = 0.08 \times 930.47 = 74.44MPa$$

Calculated according to formula (8):

$$R_{N(7000)} = \Phi\left(\frac{964.72 - 501.956}{\left(77.18^2 + 23.09^2\right)^{\frac{1}{2}}}\right) = \Phi(5.744)$$

$$R_{N(20000)} = \Phi\left(\frac{930.47 - 501.956}{\left(74.44^2 + 23.09^2\right)^{\frac{1}{2}}}\right) = \Phi(5.498)$$

Looking at the normal distribution table, it can be seen that the fatigue strength reliability R of the jump pin action 7000 times and 20,000 times is greater than 0.99999. Therefore, the design and material selection of the jump pin meets the strength requirements and the reliability is high.

V. CONCLUSION

In this paper, the rigid-flexible coupling model of the circuit breaker operating mechanism is constructed by combining Ansys and Adams software, and the dynamic stress simulation analysis of the free tripping action of the circuit breaker is carried out. According to the simulation data, the stress analysis of the rod was carried out and the reliability of the jump pin was calculated according to the stress-strength interference model. Main conclusions are as follows:

（1）When using Ansys and Adams to perform dynamic stress joint simulation of the rigid-flexible coupling mechanism model of the circuit breaker. The flexible body part can be converted into a rigid body, and then the load file when the part is a rigid body can be derived. This can effectively reduce the errors caused by rigid body or file transfer.

（2）In the reliability analysis of the circuit breaker operating mechanism components, not only the static strength reliability calculation of the components but also the fatigue strength calculation is required. The calculation results show that there must be sufficient safety margin when designing and selecting materials for the components of the circuit breaker operating mechanism.

REFERENCES

[1] Ren Junyong. Study on the reliability and optimum design of low-voltage circuit breaker operating mechanism[D]. Heibei University of Technology, 2011.

[2] Xu Dan, Wu Yi, Chen Qiaoxia, et al. Mechanism Optimization Based on MCCB Dynamic Stress Analysis[J]. Electrical & Energy Management Technology, 2017,(4):27-31.

[3] Liu Ronghai, Yang Yingchun, Cheng Lifeng, Guo Xinliang, Wan Shuting, He Zhihua, Zhang Xiong. Simulation and Stress Analysis for Spring Actuator of CT14 High-voltage Circuit Breaker Based on LS-DYNA[J]. High Voltage Apparatus, 2017,53(10): 29-35.

[4] Tian Tao, Zhang Zhaojun, Zhu Chao, Chen Hao, Wang Yangyingfu, Zhang Jianzhong. Reliability and Life Analysis of Energy-storing Spring for High Voltage Circuit Breaker[J]. Electric Power Engineering Technology, 2017,36(05):103-108.

[5] Chen Wenhua, Zhang Wen, Pan Jun, Zhang Tingxiu, Chen Lili. Action Reliability Analysis of Operating Mechanism in Miniature Circuit Breaker[J]. China Mechanical Engineering, 2015,26(21): 2918-2922.

[6] Rui Yannian, Fu Geyan, Pan. Modern Reliability Design[M]. Beijing: National Defense Industry Press, 2007.

[7] Cheng Wuyi. System Reliability Theory and Its Application[M].Beijing:Beijing University of Aeronautics and Astronautics Press, 2012 135

[8] Cheng Degui, Li Xingwen. Virtual Prototype Technology for Low Voltage Circuit Breakers[M]. Beijing: Mechanical Industry Press, 2009

[9] Virupaxayya Hiremath,Nithin Venkataram. Vibration Charecteristics of a High Speed Gearbox through Dynamic Analysis[J]. Materials Today: Proceedings, 2017,4(10).

[10] Zhang Wen. Reliability Analysis and Evaluation of Operating Mechanism in Miniature Circuit Breaker[D]. Zhejiang Sci-Tech University, 2015.

[11] P. Zarafshan,S. Ali A. Moosavian. Dynamics modelling and Hybrid Suppression Control of space robots performing cooperative object

manipulation[J]. Communications in Nonlinear Science and Numerical Simulation,2013,18(10).
[12] Zhao Xiangjie. Optimization of Rotary Handle of Low Voltage Switch Based on ADAMS and ANSYS[J]. Journal of Mechanical & Electrical Engineering, 2018,35(09):949-954.
[13] B. Siva kumar,P. Prasanna,J. Sushma,K.P. Srikanth. Stress Analysis And Design Optimization Of A Pressure Vessel Using Ansys Package[J]. Materials Today: Proceedings,2018,5(2).
[14] Li Zhen, Xu Wenliang. Application of Ansys Workbench Structural Analysis in Moulded Case Circuit Breaker[J]. Electrical & Energy Management Technology, 2013(03):17-21.
[15] Huang Jing,Shen Bing. Simulation analysis on dynamic protection characteristics of low voltage circuit molded case breakers based on PSCAD/EMTDC[P]. Control Conference (CCC), 2014 33rd Chinese,2014.
[16] Liu Hunju. Mechanical reliability design [M]. Beijing:Science Press, 2012
[17] Zhang Feng, Gu Le. Mechanical Design Course Design Manual[M]. Beijing:Higher Education Press, 2010
[18] Zhou Guangzhao. Optimal Design and Reliability of Double-breaker MCCB Contact Mechanism[D]. Wenzhou University, 2016.
[19] Gao Zhengtong, Xiong Junjiang. Fatigue Reliability [M]. Beijing:Beijing University of Aeronautics and Astronautics Press, 2000.12.
[20] Meng Xianyi. Mechanical reliability design [M].Beijing:Metallurgical Industry Press, 1992.

Shanghai University Students Innovation and Entrepreneurship Training Program (Project No.: 201911458027)

7th International Conference on Reliability of
Electrical Products and Electrical Contacts,
November 04-06, 2019

Study on the Structural Design and Test Verification of Composite Filter Electrical Connector

Guanghua Guo, Bin Lv, Jun Zhang, Yubin Chen, Kaiye Chai
Hangzhou Aerospace Electronic Technology Co., Ltd., Hangzhou, 310051, China
E-mail: eadison508@163.com Tel: 0571-88359384

Abstract—**The paper takes the models application as the background, by focusing on the interference situation of multi-core cable in different systems working at different frequencies, different filtering characteristic parameters are designed and integrated together to realize the performance optimization of systems under radiation interference and the signal transmission accuracy and anti-interference ability of the system are improved. Based on the structural design and prototype production of composite filter electrical connector, the reliability of the prototype structure and the effectiveness of shielding efficiency were verified by shielding effectiveness test, so as to establish a technology platform of R&D(research and development) and testing of special ani-interference electrical connector that can meet the urgent need of anti-radiation reinforcement of systems of models in China.**

Index Terms— **Composite filter electrical connector, Composite filter structural design, Structural design and test verification, Shielding effectiveness test, Application of model systems**

I. INTRODUCTION

In all types of models systems, electrical connectors are the basic components necessary to form a complete system. In recent years, with the rapid development of the space industry, it is faced with the macro situation of high-density launch and transformation development, which brings great opportunities and severe challenges to the development of space enterprises, and puts forward higher requirements for the performance and reliability of electrical connectors used in various systems of space models. Existing anti-interference technology of electrical connector mainly relies on shielding technology of shell and signal shielding technology of inner core wire. This technology has good application effect in small electrical connector, but it is difficult to meet the application requirements of large-area and multi-core electrical connector, especially separation electrical connector. The development of electrical connector with composite filter function, and the validity of its structure reliability and filter performance are verified by relevant tests, is of great significance to the development of aerospace models in the new situation.

II. ELECTRICAL CONNECTOR OVERVIEW

Electrical connector is widely used in rocket, satellite, spacecraft and other types of systems to achieve the connection and disconnect of electrical signals. According to the function and application of electric connector, electric connector can be divided into general electric connector and detached electric connector. The structure of general electric connector is relatively simple and it is widely used in various types of systems. The separated electrical connector is only used in special occasions such as interstate section, rocket-ground and so on, and its structure is relatively complex. It can realize automatic separation by unlocking the electrical signal, and then cut off the line signal remotely, so as to avoid the harm to human body caused by the electromagnetic environment caused by model emission.

Electrical connector including plug and socket, through the use of plug and socket pair to achieve the on and off of electrical signals. Figure 1 below shows a three-dimensional model of a type of separation electrical connector, with the socket on the left and the plug on the right

Fig. 1 3D model of a type of separated electrical connector

III. STRUCTURAL DESIGN OF COMPOSITE FILTER ELECTRICAL CONNECTOR

The structure of separated electrical connector is complex , and its composite filter structure design is more prospective and representative. In the actual use of separated electrical connector, the plug is usually left on the ground or burned down after the socket and plug are separated, and the socket generally flies with the model. Therefore, the filtering performance of the socket directly affects the anti-electromagnetic interference ability of the model, and the key to the design of the composite filtering structure of separated electrical connector lies in the socket.

According to the research on the development status of filter electrical connector in China, it is found that the large volume and high pressure sealed separated electrical connector does not have filtering function, and the design of filtering structure in this field is still blank.

Based on the mature technology and process foundation of the existing separated electrical connector, combined with the model requirements, a type of high pressure sealed electrical connector is taken as the prototype to design the composite filter structure. The prototype product is high and low frequency mixed electrical connector, with three kinds of low frequency contact parts with different diameters and the 8# double coaxial contact parts, a total of 186 cores, a large contact surface, a large number of cores, with high pressure sealing and flame protection performance, its composite filter structure design and shielding effect has a significant representative.

A. Prototype separated socket structure

In order to meet the performance of sealing and fire prevention, the separated socket is generally designed with a three-layer structure. The specific structure is shown in figure 2 below.

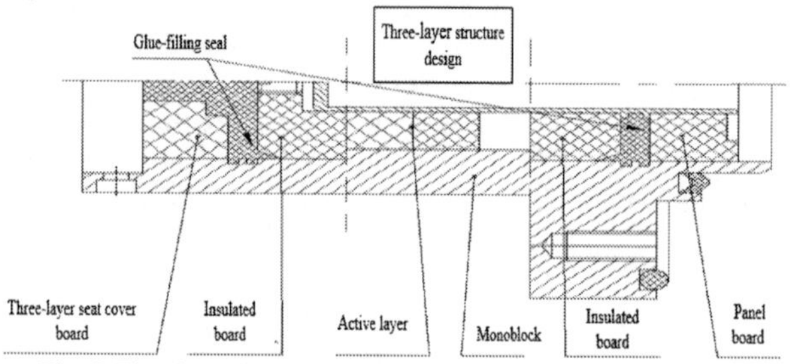

Fig. 2 The three-layer structure of prototype separated socket

The socket shell is machined with ribbed grooves, on the one hand to realize the insulator positioning, on the other hand to achieve the predetermined position because of the plug and socket is contacted earlier than the contact of pin and jack during the docking process; Insulators, face insulator, back insulator and movable layer are all made by insulation materials, whose function is to realize the precise positioning of contact parts and insulation between core wires, so as to ensure good interchangeability and insulation performance of products. The movable layer is composed of two pieces of insulators, which can move from side to side with the insertion and separation of the plug and socket, and it is mainly used to prevent flame. The main purpose of adhesive potting is to improve the environmental resistance of the product, on the one hand, to prevent the moisture in the air and rain from entering the product, on the other hand, to ensure the sealing performance of the product.

In the three-layer structure design, there are contact parts in each layer. With the left and right movement of the movable layer, the insertion and separation of both the internal contact parts in the socket and the contact parts in the plug and socket are realized synchronously.

B. The Difficulty of Composite Filter Structure Design

There are two main implementations of anti-electromagnetic shielding functions of the existing separated electrical connector: shell shielding and filter pin. After the plug and socket of electrical connector are inserted, a relatively sealed shielding structure is formed by "plug cable cover- plug shell- socket shell- socket cable cover", which can achieve a certain shielding effect. The filter pin is mainly designed for the core wire with higher shielding requirements, and the shielding performance is improved by adding filter tube at the appropriate position of the low-frequency pin.

The above two shielding structures have obvious shortcomings: when the size of cable cover outlet is large, the metal shielding effect is poor, the shielding efficiency is only about 50dB. In order to keep the shells of socket and plug fit closely, shielding reed is embedded in socket shell, and under the condition of existing technology, shielding reed processing quality is low, cause electrical connector products compatibility problems, lead to product quality to zero. Although the filter pin can improve the shielding effect of the product, it still cannot meet the requirements of the new model. On the other hand, the qualified rate of the filter needle production is very low, especially a large number of filter needles are scrapped due to the pressing process.

The design of composite filter structure should not only consider the reliability of product structure, economy of production and effectiveness of shielding effect, but also consider the complex structure of electrical connector separation and the mechanical environment inside the product when the socket and plug are inserted, which increases the design difficulty of composite filter structure.

C. Composite Filter Structure Design

Electromagnetic interference exists in two forms, namely radiant electromagnetic interference and conduction electromagnetic interference. Radiation electromagnetic interference can often be protected by metal shielding. For conducting electromagnetic interference, filtering is the most effective anti-interference method. For separated electrical connector, the shielding metal has certain electromagnetic shielding effect, and in a certain magnetic pulse field environment, shielding effectiveness can reach about 60 dB, but still cannot meet the requirements of models, so considering increase the filter element on separated electrical connector, through the shell shielding and filtering elements work together to achieve the shielding effectiveness is not less than 70 dB.

The filter element used in electrical connector in China is mainly c-type filter, as shown in Figure 3. This filter is composed of a penetrating capacitor, which is suitable for connecting high impedance source and high impedance load. This kind of filter is simple in structure, small in size, and will not have great influence on the overall structure of the product after assembling with contact parts, so it is easy to integrate into the product.

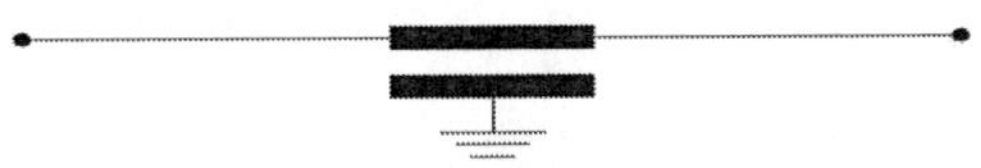

Fig. 3 The c-type filter

If the c-type filter is directly integrated into the contact ,the problem of low production qualification rate will also occur. Therefore, it is considered that the c-type filter is integrated into the ceramic dielectric plate according to the contact spectrum of the prototype product, and then the contact is welded to the contact position of the capacitor plate to form the filter capacitor plate element.

Since the capacitor plate is made of ceramic material, which is brittle material, and the prototype product requires a large size of the capacitor plate, the mechanical strength of the capacitor plate is insufficient, so sufficient protection should be carried out on the structure to avoid the damage of the capacitor plate and the failure of filtering. On the one hand, considering the large size of capacitor plate, in order to reduce the difficulty of protection, it can be divided into parts. The combination of several capacitor plates with small area can be used to realize large-area filtering. On the other hand, considering the high requirements of mechanical properties and other indicators of the prototype products, the commonly used measures to add rubber pads for protection cannot meet the requirements of product performance indicators, so the installation structure of filter plate is added. The filter plate is first installed on the metal bracket, and then integrated into the product structure of the separated electrical connector to ensure the effectiveness of protection.

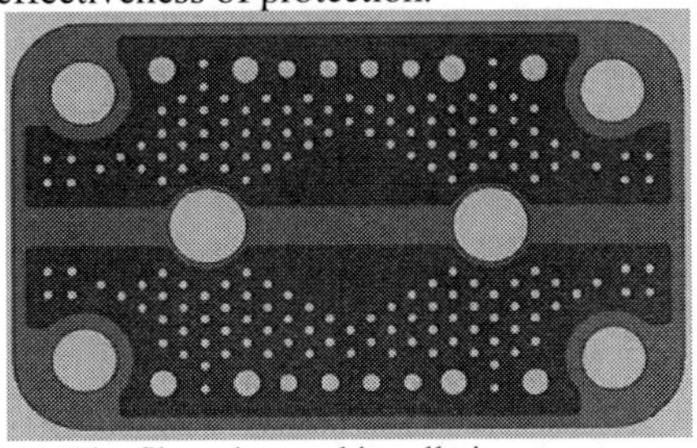

Fig. 4 The filter plate and installation structure

In order to retain the original product performance of the separated electrical connector, when integrating the designed filter board into the separated socket, it is not only necessary to consider the sealing and fire prevention performance of the product, but also to ensure the good shielding performance of the filter board. The movable layer is a movable component, it bears force with the cyclic movement of insertion and separation, integrating the filter plate into the active layer will undoubtedly increase the risk of protection and shorten its service life. Different from the face insulator, the signal still exists in the back insulator after the separation of the socket and plug. Therefore, integrating the filter plate into the back insulator has more application value.

The filter plate is integrated into the back insulator of the socket, as shown in Figure 5. The protection of the filter plate is increased through the metal mounting frame, and the good sealing performance of the integrated product is guaranteed by adhesive potting.

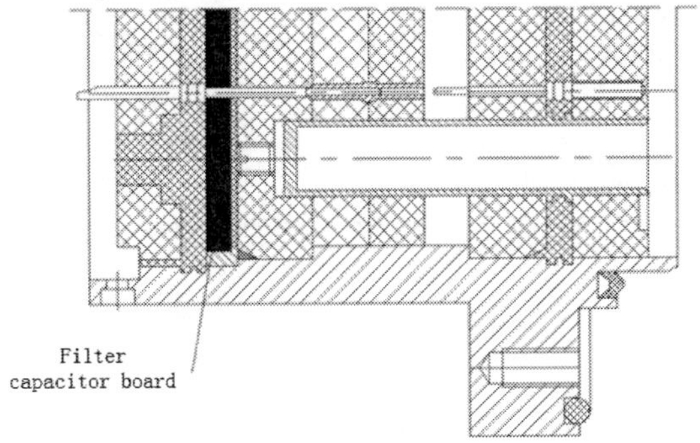

Fig.5 The structure of composite filter electrical connector

IV. COMPOSITE FILTER ELECTRICAL CONNECTOR TEST VERIFICATION

Whether the composite filtering structure is reliable and the filtering effect can meet the requirements of model type needs, test verification is needed to be design. The verification test in this paper is mainly conducted from two aspects: composite filter electrical connector performance test and electromagnetic pulse shielding effectiveness test.

A. *Composite filter electrical connector performance test*

The performance test of composite filter electrical connector is based on the performance indexes of prototype products. On the basis of the test items of prototype products, such as interchangeability, mechanical life, insulation withstand voltage, sinusoidal vibration, impact, etc., the test of filter characteristics of different frequency bands is added.

Through the performance test, the performance indexes of the composite filter electrical connector can meet the technical requirements of the prototype. Partial test results are shown in table 1 below.

B. *Electromagnetic pulse shielding effectiveness test*

The electromagnetic pulse shielding effectiveness test was carried out in accordance with the relevant provisions in

GJB 8848-2016 test method for system electromagnetic environment effect and GJB 4429-2001 measurement method for nuclear electromagnetic pulse (NEMP). The test is divided into two parts: filter performance test and HEMP pulse current injection test. The test of HEMP pulse current injection mainly USES PCI pulse injection source, compares injection quantity with sample core wire coupling quantity, and analyzes its time domain shielding efficiency.

Through electromagnetic pulse shielding efficiency test, it is found that the shielding efficiency of composite filter electrical connector can reach the minimum requirement of 70dB.

TABLE I
TEST RESULTS OF PERFORMANCE ASSESSMENT TEST

Test item	Rquirements	Test values
Insulation resistance	≥1000MΩ	Min(4496MΩ)
Withstand voltage	Leakage current≤5mA	0mA
Mechanical life	500 times	500 times
Filtering properties	-	30MHz, Min(42.61dB)
	-	100MHz, Min(38.96dB)
	-	300MHz, Min(40.97dB)

V. CONCLUSION

With the development of model, the requirement of shielding performance of electrical connector is increasing day by day. Based on model needs, giving full play to the advantages of enterprise separated electrical connector technology, composite filter structure was designed, through the development of the products assembly and test, verify the quality of the composite filter electrical connector reliability and the effectiveness of the shielding performance, not only for subsequent product development laid a solid foundation to the filtering performance, also provides the necessary technical guarantee for the development of models.

REFERENCES

[1] Haifeng Shao, Zhichao Zheng, Wei Xu. Structural Design of six-degree-of-Freedom floating Electrical Connector. Aerospace electromechanical components.2019.4, pp.16-19.

[2] GJB 8848-2016, Test method for electromagnetic environmental effects of systems.

[3] GJB 4229-2001, Nuclear electromagnetic pulse (NEMP) measurement method.

[4] Jiemin Wang. Research and development of a new type of guide rail separation mechanism. Zhejiang University,2015.

[5] Yanmei Cui. Application of filtering Technology in Electrical Connector. Public Communication of Science & Technology.2012.3, pp.114-119.

Life Prediction and Reliability Analysis of MotorBearing Based on Vibration Signal

Helin Xu, Lin Cheng, Yuxiang Wan, Ning Qi
State Key Laboratory of Control and Simulation of Power Systems and Generation Equipment,
Tsinghua University, Beijing 100084, China

***Abstract*—As an important power equipment in the power system, the electrialc motor is an important part of the transformation of electric energy and mechanical energy. Reasonable prediction of the reliability level of the running motor, timely and effectively avoid the operational risks, can effectively ensure the safety and stable operation of the power system. This paper starts with the motor vibration signal and establishes the remaining life prediction based on SVM(Support Vector Machine). Firstly, the vibration signal is denoised by wavelet transform, and the characteristic parameters such as mean square value is extracted after signal data reconstruction. Further, combined with the characteristic value, the working state is divided, and the support vector machine regression prediction model is used to obtain the remaining life of the bearing. In the case study part, data denoising and feature extraction are performed on the bearing vibration data measured by the PRONOSTIA test bench. The trend of the selected characteristic values is used for evaluating the motor operating state. The characteristic value, running state of the equipment, and remaining life which are extracted from the training set data are input to the SVM, and then the SVM is used to predict the remaining life for the test set. Finally, failure rate of the equipment can be derived.**

***Index Terms*—Vibration signal, wavelet analysis, support vector machine, life prediction, reliability analysis**

I. INTRODUCTION

The electric motor is the link and bridge between the electric energy and the mechanical energy. However, the external environment changes, the electrical and mechanical power adjustment and the aging of the equipment components may cause the motor to malfunction during the operation. Thus ensuring the safe and reliable operation of the motor, making a prediction of remaining lifeis especially important.

According to the investigation of the cause of asynchronous motor failure initiated by the Institute of Electrical and Electronics Engineers (IEEE), the bearing failure ratio is 44% in the fault classification of the motor [1-3]. At present, motor fault detection includes fault analysis based on real-time physical signals of motor operation, feature analysis based on motor current signals and fault analysis based on vibration signals. The first two types of fault analysis need to collect physical signals of the motor during operation, such as speed, winding and bearing temperature, and phase current signal. In contrast, the motor bearing vibration signal has a good correlation with the life, and the vibration signal characteristic analysis results are more accurate.

The traditional asynchronous motor faults mostly use the physical signal of the motor to perform fault analysis. Usually, the temperature detection, stress test and voltage and current signals of each part of the motor are selected for analysis. However, the traditional fault analysis has certain shortcomings: it is difficult to do the short-term prediction and analysis of the availability and life of the equipment. For motor current characteristic analysis, it can better judge the relevant faults on the stator and rotor side of the motor, such as rotor broken strip, short circuit/open circuit, etc., but the correlation between current signal and bearing signal is small, it is difficult to quantitatively describe the relationship between the two and pass the signal. The fault analysis based on the vibration signal can effectively identify the working state of the motor bearing. By extracting the variation characteristics of the vibration signal, the bearing life and the probability of failure in a short time can be effectively predicted.

Traditional life predictions are usually based on establishing a statistical life model or building a life model based on theoretical mechanics. At present, the life prediction model based on information technology and neural network has become a new means of life prediction. Some related literature proposes a regression model based on time domain statistical parameters. Haitao Liao et al. completed the proportional hazard assessment and logarithmic regression prediction scheme for the remaining life of rolling bearings based on the proportional hazards model and the logistic regression model[4]. BP neural network[5] and ANN algorithm[6] are also applied to the field of life prediction, respectively. However, the above model has certain disadvantages for the correlation prediction of remaining life and various other algorithms.

The prediction results of the Logistic regression model fluctuate greatly. The neural network algorithm has a high degree of dependence on training data and low computational efficiency. In this paper, the SVM model is used to predict the remaining life of the bearing. The SVM considers the principle of structural risk minimization of the system and has a stronger generalization ability than traditional artificial intelligence methods (such as neural networks).

Therefore, this paper uses the vibration signal characteristic analysis to analyze the motor fault state. For the problem that traditional life data is difficult to obtain, this paper uses the full-life data of the accelerated test. Fisrt, the vibration signal is wavelet transformed, the characteristic values are extracted from the recombined data, thenmake a evaluation of motor working state, establish the residual life prediction model based on SVM, and the failure rate of the motor equipment is further analyzed and predicted.

II. NOISEREDUCTIONPROCESSINGOFMOTORBEARINGVIBRATIONSIGNAL

Signal denoising is an important part of data preprocessing. Common methods for equipment failure analysis include Fourier transform, wavelet analysis, and local mean decomposition and so on. Wavelet analysis is widely used in signal processing because it can perform multi-scale refinement analysis of telescopic translation of wavelet transform kernel functions with locality in both time domain and frequency domain[7]. In this paper, the vibration analysis of the motor is processed by wavelet analysis.

Assume that a function $\psi(t)$ which is square integrable, ie. $\psi(t) \in L^2(R)$. If the Fourier transform $\hat{\psi}(\omega)$ satisfies the condition:

$$C_{\psi} = \int_{-\infty}^{+\infty} \frac{|\hat{\psi}(\omega)|}{|\omega|} < +\infty \tag{1}$$

Then $\psi(t)$ can be called a basic wavelet or mother wavelet function. and the above conditionis an admissible condition.

It can be inferred from the definition and the formula (1) that the mother wavelet function $\psi(t)$ satisfies $\hat{\psi}(0)=0$, ie.

$$\int_{-\infty}^{+\infty} \psi(t)dt = 0 \tag{2}$$

$\psi(t)$ is a bandpass filter.

After the mother wavelet function $\psi(t)$ is stretched and translated, a wavelet sequence can be obtained:

$$\psi_{a,b}(t) = \frac{1}{\sqrt{|a|}} \psi\left(\frac{t-b}{a}\right) \tag{3}$$

And in formula (3), $a,b \in R, a \neq 0$. Usually a is the scaling factor and b is the translation factor.

For any function $f(t) \in L^2(R)$, the continuous wavelet transform is:

$$W_f(a,b) = \frac{1}{\sqrt{|a|}} \int_{-\infty}^{+\infty} f(t)\psi^*\left(\frac{t-b}{a}\right) \tag{4}$$

When the mother wavelet $\psi(t)$ satisfies the admissibility condition (Equation 1), the signal $f(t)$ can be reconstructed:

$$f(t) = \frac{1}{C\psi} \int_{-\infty}^{+\infty} \int_{-\infty}^{+\infty} \frac{1}{a^2} W_f(a,b)\psi\left(\frac{t-b}{a}\right) dadb \tag{5}$$

The time-frequency window of the wavelet transform can be adjusted by the scaling factor a and the translation factor b. The translation factor b can change the position of the window on the time axis, and the scaling factor a affects the position of the window on the frequency axis. When using wavelet transform to process signals, firstly select the appropriate wavelet function to decompose the signal, then perform threshold analysis on the decomposed parameters, and finally use the processed parameters to reconstruct the signal.

III. MOTOROPERATINGSTATEIDENTIFICATION

Rolling bearings, as a key component of typical mechanical equipment, are subject to degradation during their operation. Usually, the degradation process is not obvious in the early stage, and the bearing fault will not appear until after running for a while. It is important to analyze the data collected by the sensors installed on the surface of the equipment for the health status of the bearing. The bearing health information can be visually judged based on the relevant feature information extracted from the original data to determine the health state of the device.

A. StateDivisionof Power Equipment

The operating state of power equipment are generally divided into four kinds normal, attentitive, abnormal, and serious[8].

Normal: This state indicates that the status of each device is stable and it can operate normally.

Attentive: A single (or multiple) characteristic parameters of a device has a tendency to approach the limit, but it doesn't exceed the limit.

Abnormal: The characteristic parameters of the equipment has approached or slightly exceeded the standard limit. The equipment should be closely monitored and scheduled for power outage maintenance.

Serious: The characteristic parameters of the equipment is seriously exceeding the standard limit, and should be immediately shut down for maintenance.

It can be seen from the above definition that the normal, attention, and abnormal states are common states of the power equipment during the work process, and the state transition is caused by the aging of the power equipment in the work process. A critical state indicates that the device is not working properly, that is, the device is already in a fault state.

B. Motor Vibration Signal Feature Quantity Extraction

In signal analysis processing, values that characterize the time-frequency variation of a signal and the law of its distribution are often referred to as features.

In general, the statistical features that signals can extract in the time domain include variance, root mean square, crest factor and so on.

The frequency domain features include center frequency, mean square frequency, and frequency variance.

The definition of each feature and the calculation formula are as follows:

Variance: The variance describes the extent to which the data deviates from its mean. It is obtained by summing the squares of the difference between the signal parameters and the mean.

$$\sigma^2 = \sum_{j=1}^{n}(X_j - \bar{X})^2 \tag{6}$$

Root mean square: The root mean square reflects the change of the signal sample X_j around the zero point, which can represent the average energy of the signal.

$$X_{RMS} = \sqrt{\frac{1}{n}\sum_{j=1}^{n} X_j^2} \tag{7}$$

Peak Factor: The peak factor is the ratio of the peak value to the root mean square of the signal. It is an indicator of the magnitude of the signal waveform impact and can indicate the trend of the peak value of the signal waveform.

$$X_{peak} = \max(X) - \min(X) \tag{8}$$

$$C_f = \frac{X_{peak}}{X_{RMS}} \tag{9}$$

Waveform factor:

The waveform factor is the ratio of the root mean square to the absolute mean, which characterizes the trend of the signal waveform.

$$S = \frac{X_{RMS}}{\frac{1}{n}\sum_{j=1}^{n} |X_j|} \tag{10}$$

Center frequency:

The center frequency can reflect the center position of the power spectrum of the sample signal. When the energy of each frequency component in the signal changes, the center position also shifts. P_i in the following equation is the amplitude of the signal at the frequency f_i.

$$FC = \frac{\sum_{i=1}^{n} f_i p_i}{\sum_{i=1}^{n} p_i} \tag{11}$$

Finally, this paper chooses RMS as the characteristic parameter. The root mean square RMS can be used to detect the vibration level of the whole system. It is a widely used characteristic index in the fault diagnosis of mechanical systems, which can better track the overall noise level of the system, so the rotating machinery The imbalance in the fault is very effective.

IV. MOTOR LIFE PREDICTION MODEL BASED ON SUPPORT VECTOR MACHINE

A. Basic principles of SVM

Support Vector Machine(SVM)was proposed by Cortes and Vapnik[9] to solve the problem of data analysis and pattern recognition. The main applications of SVM can be divided into two categories: classification and regression.

Support Vector Machine is a machine learning algorithm based on statistical theory. Its basic model is defined as the linear classifier with the largest interval in the feature space. SVM is widely used in the fields of classification prediction, pattern recognition and so on. SVM tends to find an optimal classification hyperplane that meets the classification requirements, so that the hyperplane can maximize the blank area on both sides of the hyperplane while ensuring classification accuracy. Theoretically, support vector machines can achieve optimal classification of linearly separable data.

Taking two types of data classification as an example, given a set of training samples (x_i, y_i) , $i = 1, 2, \cdots, m$, $x \in R^n$, $y \in \{\pm 1\}$, hyperplane is defined as (w · x) + b = 0. In order for the classification which correctly classify all samples and the classification interval, it is required to satisfy the following constraints:

$$y_i[(w \cdot x_i) + b] \geq 1 \tag{12}$$

Where $i = 1,2,\cdots,m$. The classification interval can be calculated as $2/\|\mathbf{w}\|$, so the problem of constructing the optimal hyperplane is transformed into the constraint:

$$\min \phi(\mathbf{w}) = \frac{1}{2}(\mathbf{w}' \cdot \mathbf{w}) \tag{13}$$

To solve this constraint optimization problem, the Lagrange function is introduced as follow:

$$L(\mathbf{w}, b, a) = \frac{1}{2}\|\mathbf{w}\| - a(\mathbf{y}((\mathbf{w} \cdot \mathbf{x}) + b) - 1) \tag{14}$$

The optimal classification hyperplane can be solved as $(w^* \cdot x_i) + b^* = 0$, the optimal weight vector w^* and the optimal bias b^* can be calculated as follow:

$$\mathbf{w}^* = \sum_{j=1}^{m} a_j^* y_j x_j \tag{15}$$

$$b^* = y_i - \sum_{j=1}^{m} y_j a_j^* (x_j \cdot x_i) \tag{16}$$

In the formula 15 and 16, the subscript $j \in \{a_j^* > 0\}$. The optimal classification function is:

$$f(x) = \text{sgn}\{(\mathbf{w}^* \cdot \mathbf{x}) + b^*\}$$
$$= \text{sgn}\{(\sum_{j=1}^{m} a_j^* y_j (x_j \cdot x_i) + b^*\} \quad (17)$$

Wherein equation 17, $\mathbf{x} \in R^n$. When x is transformed from the input space R^n to the feature space H, ie.

$$\mathbf{x} \rightarrow \phi(\mathbf{x}) = (\phi_1(\mathbf{x}), \phi_2(\mathbf{x}), \cdots, \phi_m(\mathbf{x}))^T \quad (18)$$

By replacing the input vector x with the eigenvector, the optimal classification function can be obtained as:

$$f(x) = \text{sgn}\{(\mathbf{w} \cdot \phi(\mathbf{x})) + b\}$$
$$= \text{sgn}\{(\sum_{j=1}^{m} a_j y_j \phi(\mathbf{x}_i) \cdot \phi(\mathbf{x}) + b\} \quad (19)$$

Defined $K(x_i, x) = \phi(\mathbf{x}_i) \cdot \phi(\mathbf{x})$ as a kernel function. This paper uses the Radial Basis Function (RBF) as the kernel function.

B. *Using SVM for life prediction*

As shown in Fig. 1, after the SVM model is established, firstly, combined with the vibration information of the bearing, wavelet transform is performed on the vibration signal to achieve signal denoising, and then the feature of bearing signal is extracted, and the feature is set into a label, and then input into the SVM for the remaining life prediction.

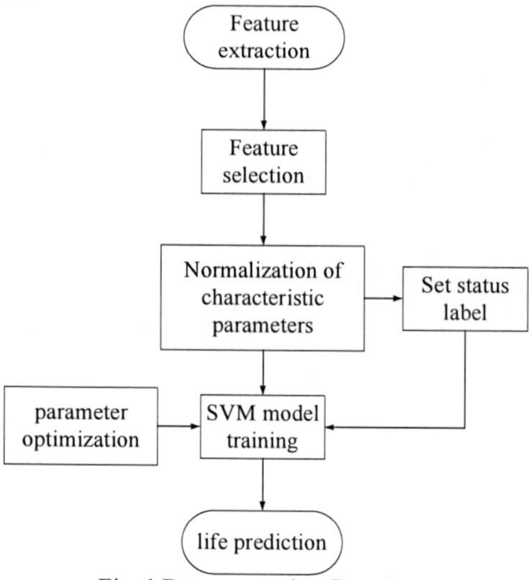

Fig. 1 Data processing flow chart

Firstly, the characteristic parameters are normalized. In this paper, RMS is selected as the characteristic parameter, and the linear normalization function is used to normalize the feature quantity. The normalized mapping is as follows:

$$y = \frac{x - x_{min}}{x_{max} - x_{min}} \quad (20)$$

$y \in [0,1]$.

Then, the RMS, working state and remaining life corresponding to each sample are input into the SVM as a set of input data, and the SVM is trained by the training set. Then through the test set to analyze the pros and cons of the model.

To use SVM for life prediction, we firstly determine the type of kernel function chosen for the SVM model. This paper uses the Radial Basis Function (RBF) function as the kernel function. There are two basic parameters in the model that need to be determined, the penalty factor C and the RBF parameter gamma.

In this paper, the mean squared value (Mse) of the error between the signal prediction result and the actual result is selected as the error parameter indicator training model.

$$Mse = \frac{\sum_{i=1}^{n} (Y_{obs,i} - Y_{model,i})^2}{n} \quad (21)$$

Y_{obs} is the desired target value (true value), Y_{model} is the actual output value predicted by the model, *n* is the number of samples predicted by the model.

C. *Equipment failure rate calculation*

The lifetime T of the component is a non-negative continuous random variable which obeys a certain probability distribution. The cumulative distribution function of T is defined as:

$$F(t) = P(T \le t) \quad (22)$$

The probability density function is defined as:

$$f(t) = \lim_{\Delta t \to 0} \frac{1}{\Delta t} P(t < T < t + \Delta t) \quad (23)$$

and the reliability of the component $R(t)$ is defined as the probability that the component will not fail before time t under given environmental conditions.

$$R(t) = 1 - F(t) \quad (24)$$

The failure rate of the component $\lambda(t)$ is the conditional probability density that the component will work normally before time t, and the unit time will fail after time t. By definition, it can be known as follow:

$$\lambda(t) = \frac{f(t)}{1 - F(t)} \quad (25)$$

V. CASE STUDY

In normal production practice, motor bearings usually have a long life cycle, and the remaining life prediction is difficult to perform. In order to obtain bearing life data, it is necessary to accelerate the research experiment on the design life of the rolling bearing. This paper uses the rolling bearing life cycle degradation test data provided by the French FEMTO-ST research institute for analysis[10], and its data acquisition platform (PRONOSTIA) is shown in Figure 2. The PRONOSTIA test rig is an experimental system for rolling bearing testing and wear detection, through which the test data for different wear states of the bearing can be obtained. Under the conditions of different running loads and rotating speeds, the accelerated running state of the rolling bearing under different conditions is monitored separately. Each degenerate bearing can complete the entire decay process in a few hours to achieve the full life test of the rolling bearing.

The experiment sets up information on the two types of sensor acquisition bearings during the accelerated life test operation: acceleration sensor and temperature sensor. This experiment uses two acceleration sensors to collect vibration information from the horizontal and vertical directions.

Fig. 2 PRONOSTIA test rig

The test bench is equipped with a vibration accelerometer model Dytran 3035B with a sampling frequency of 25.6 kHz, a maximum usage range of 50 g and a sensitivity of 100 mV/g.

TABLE I

BEARING VIBRATION TEST DATA

Working condition	Load (KN)	Rotor speed (RPM)	data (group)
Working condition 1	4	1800	7
Working condition 2	4.2	1650	7
Working condition 3	5	1500	3

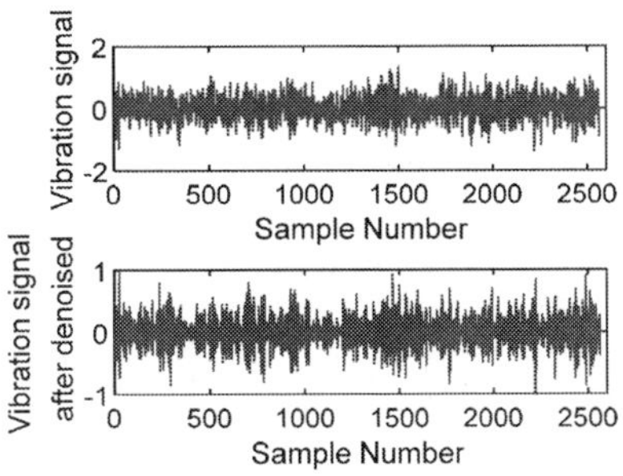

Fig. 3 Original data and wavelet denoising data

The vibration signal of the rolling bearing was collected under different speeds and loads. The sampling frequency was 25.6 kHz. During the whole life cycle of the rolling bearing, a vibration signal sample was collected every 10 s. The sample duration was 0.1 s. The data collected is shown in Table 1. The data before and after the noise reduction processing is shown in Figure 3.

It can be seen from Fig. 3 that it can be observed that after the noise reduction, the curve burrs are reduced, and the peaks and valleys of the data are clearly distinguished, and the variation trend of the vibration amplitude can be more clearly seen.

Further, it is necessary to extract the data feature amount, and FIG. 4 compares the extracted different feature values. Generally, when the motor bearing is in the normal and attention state, the vibration amplitude is small, and in the abnormal state, the vibration amplitude is significantly increased. It can be seen from Fig. 4 that the variation of the variance and the mean square value in the first 2000 samples is small, and when the sample number is higher than 2000, a significant increase begins to occur, indicating that the remaining life of the bearing is low. This is in line with the actual working conditions of the bearing. Compared with the trend of the variance, the variation of the mean square value is more obvious, and it can reflect the change of the working condition of the equipment. In Figure 5, according to the interval of the mean square value, it can be The motor equipment is divided into a normal state (0-0.1), a caution state (0.1-0.3), and an abnormal state (0.3-1). However, the variation of other signals such as the margin factor is large, and the correlation with the remaining life of the bearing is weak. Finally, the mean square value of the selected signal is used as the characteristic parameter for the next step.

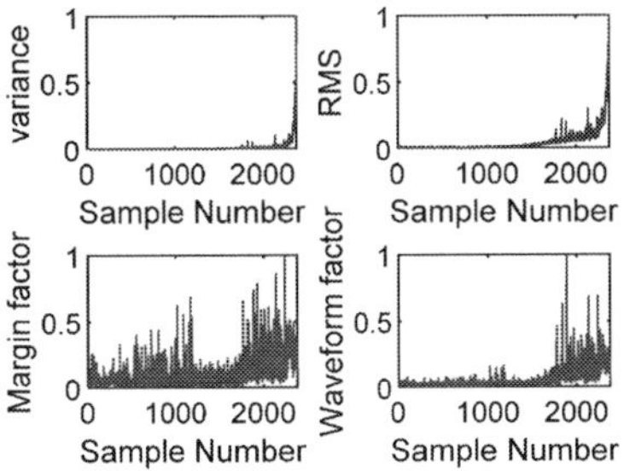

Fig. 4 Correlation analysis diagram of characteristic quantity and life

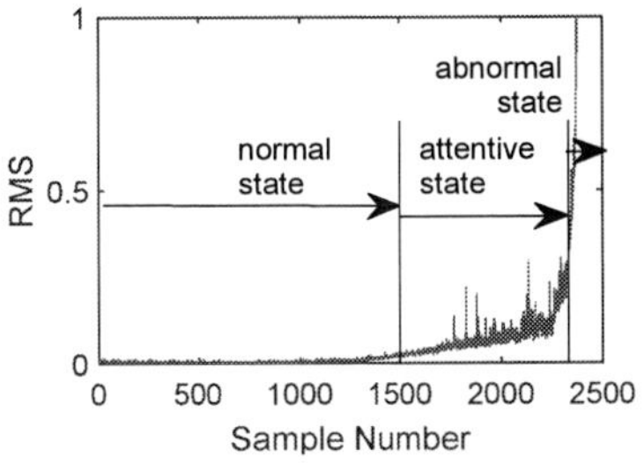

Fig. 5 Set status label

The obtained feature parameters are classified into states, and the feature quantity, state and remaining life are input into the SVM prediction model as data samples, and the kernel function selects the RBF function.

There are two key parameters C and g in the model, C is the penalty coefficient, that is, for the tolerance latitude, g is the parameter of the RBF function, which represents the distribution of the data after mapping to the new feature space. C and g can get an optimal solution through the cross-validation algorithm. In this experiment, the final penalty coefficient C was 512 and g was 32.

As shown in Fig. 6, under the optimal c and g parameters, the SVM model has higher prediction accuracy, and its mean square error is MSE = 0.0024. Compared with BP neural network, the MSE is 0.0044 with high precision. Under actual operating conditions, the remaining life of the bearing can be effectively predicted by first judging its working state and then combining the values of the characteristic parameters.

According to formula (22-24), in the case of predicting the life data, the time-varying failure rate of the equipment for a period of time can be calculated. As can be seen from Fig. 7, the failure rate changes relatively smoothly, and the average failure rate is calculated as hour.

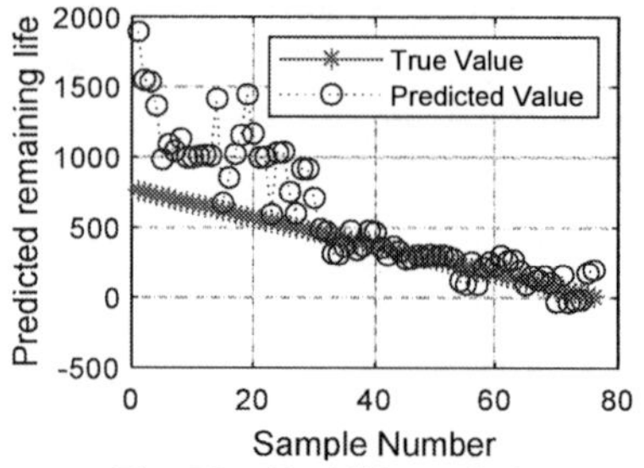

Fig. 6 Residual life prediction

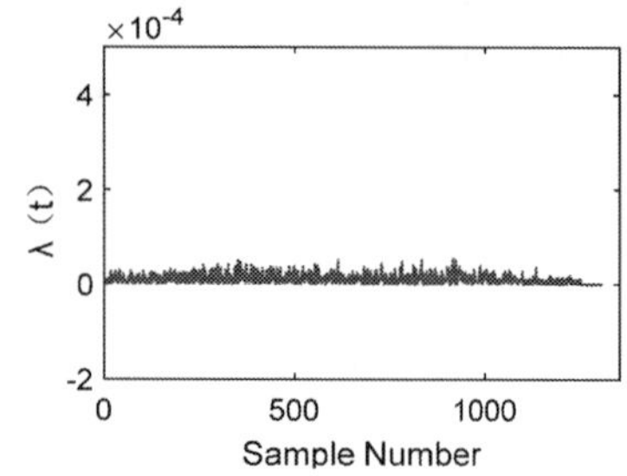

Fig. 7 Failure rate calculation

VI. CONCLUSION

This paper mainly studies the calculation of the remaining life of the motor bearing and the failure rate of the equipment. By using accelerated test data to collect data, long-term testing of bearing components and the uncertainty of test datacan be avoided. The study starts from the vibration signal analysis of the motor bearing, with the time domain and frequency domain parameters. The bearing life data is analyzed as follows. The signal is denoised by wavelet transform. After the signal data is reconstructed, the characteristic parameters such as the RMS are extracted as the evaluation index of the motor running state. According to the different values of the characteristic parameters, the bearing condition is divided into various states, and the remaining life of the bearing is obtained by using the support vector machine regression prediction model. The final result shows that by dividing the running state of the motor and combining the characteristic parameter of motor bearing vibration signal to calculate the equipment life and the failure rate, the prediction accuracy can be effectively improved so that the operation and maintenance planning can be facilitated in practice.

REFERENCES

[1] J. P. Llinares, J. A. Daviu, J. R. Folch, et al. Eccentricity diagnosis in inverter-fed induction motors via the analytic wavelet transform of transient currents. The XIX International Conference on Electrical Machines (ICEM 2010), Rome, 2010, pp. 1-6.

[2] IEEE recommended practice for the design of reliable industrial and commercial power systems, IEEE Std. 493, 1997.

[3] P. F. Allbrecht, J. C. Appiarius, R. M. Coy, et al. Assessment of the reliability of motors in utility applications-updated. IEEE Transactions on Energy Conversion, 1986, 1(1): 39-46.

[4] H. Liao, W. Zhao and H. Guo. Predicting remaining useful life of an individual unit using proportional hazards model and logistic regression model[C]. Annual Reliability and Maintainability Symposium, 2006, pp. 127-132.

[5] N. Gebraeel, M. Lawley, R. Liu, et al.. Residual life predictions from vibration-based degradation signals: a neural network approach. IEEE Transactions on Industrial Electronics, 2004, 51(3): 694-700.

[6] Z. Tian. A neural network approach for remaining useful life prediction utilizing both failure and suspension data. Annual Reliability and Maintainability Symposium (RAMS), (San Jose, CA), 2010, pp. 1-6.

[7] G. G. Yen and K. Lin. Wavelet packet feature extraction for vibration monitoring. IEEE Transactions on Industrial Electronics, 2000, 47(3): 650-667.

[8] IEEE guide for the interpretation of gases generated in oil-immersed transformers. IEEE Std C57. 104TM-2008, Sept 2008.

[9] C. Cortes, V. Vapnik. Support-vector networks. Machine learning, 1995, 20(3):273-297

[10]P. Nectoux, R. Gouriveau, K. Medjaher, et al. Pronostia: an experimental platform for bearings accelerated degradation tests. IEEE International Conference on Prognostics and Health Management (PHM 2012), Denver, United States, 2012, pp.1-8

7th International Conference on Reliability of
Electrical Products and Electrical Contacts,
November 04-06, 2019

Effects of Installation and Winding Distribution on False Detection in Open Type Residual Current Devices

Wei Chen, Guichu Wu, Zhichao Hu
Key Laboratory of Low-voltage Apparatus Intellectual Technology of Zhejiang,
Wenzhou University, Wenzhou 325027, China
E-mail: chenwei1989@wzu.edu.cn, Tel: 86-577-88373126

Abstract—**Installation of residual current devices can effectively prevent electric fire accidents and electric shock hazards. False residual currents (FRCs) have been a fatal issue for the abnormal tripping of residual circuit breakers under heavy current conditions. Analytic method is utilized to illustrate the mechanism of the FRCs. The effects of the installation and the winding distribution are analyzed using the analytic model. The results show that the FRCs are sensitive to the position of supply conductors and the non-uniform winding distribution. Experimental tests are carried out to validate the analytic results with errors less than 5%.**

Index Terms— **Analytic method, false residual currents, residual current sensors, winding distribution.**

I. INTRODUCTION

According to the fire statistics in 2018 from the fire department of China, electric fire accidents rank first among all kinds of fire accidents, accounting for 34.6 percent of the total number. The installation of residual current devices (RCDs) can effectively prevent most electric fire accidents caused by arc short faults in circuits. The research on the reliability of the RCDs has always been a popular research interest. The mechanisms of different types of RCDs malfunction were anatomized under various operation conditions [1]. Two techniques, including phase detection to eliminate sensitivity to capacitive leakage and a two-stage time delay to reduce vulnerability to transients, were proposed to reduce the vulnerability to nuisance tripping [2]. Several monitoring systems for RCDs were developed to improve the automation by reducing control complexity [3], to improve the efficiency by setting up a direct current into three-phase mains with a fixed-set-point of protection [4], and for electric shock fault diagnose based on local mean decomposition and support vector machine [5].

According to IEC standards IEC60947-2, the circuit breakers are supposed to be immune to the nuisance tripping under 6 times the rated current. However, under the condition of practical operation, heavy currents often lead to a malfunction [1], [6]. The main reasons for malfunctions include external magnetic field interferences to magnetic cores, improper grounding, improper insulation impedance of zero lines, and false residual current (FRC). The FRC, which is the induced current by false detection of residual current sensors (RCSs) when there is no residual current in the circuits, is one of the most important nuisance tripping sources for the RCDs. For RCSs with ring cores made of a wound magnetic ribbon, researchers had analyzed contribution of the anomalies, such as spiral shape effect, conductor eccentricity, and lamination effect [7], [8]. It was found out that air gaps between the magnetic layers develop a shielding effect responsible of the core high sensibility to primary conductor eccentricity. However, few researches were found to study FRCs of open type RCSs, which are quite popular taking advantages of convenient installation. For RCSs with iron cores, the mechanism of the FRCs is different because the cores are made of silicon steel laminations unlike the wound magnetic ribbon. The FRCs of open type RCSs in three-phase applications can be greater than 100mA when the rated operative residual current is 1A. Thus, it is of great significance to study mechanism and impact factors of open type RCSs.

This paper is focused on the effect of the installation and the winding distribution on FRCs in open type RCSs. Analytic method is implemented to illustrate the mechanism of the FRCs and find out the different sources of the FRCs and more specifically analyze the contributions of the installation and the winding distribution effects. Experimental tests are carried out to validate the analytic results.

II. ANALYTICAL MODEL

In order to illustrate the mechanism of FRCs, analytical method is applied to calculate the value of FRCs. The diagram for the analytical calculation, along with the physical structure of the iron core and the windings, is shown in Fig. 1. The open type RCS is composed with two semi-ring cores wounded by two series secondary windings.

Most parts of the cores are wounded by windings, while some parts near the air gap are not covered. This winding distribution is a specific type of non-uniform windings. The windings are simplified as layers placed inside and outside of the iron core. The angular positions of the winding edges are modeled with same angle for corresponding inside and outside layers. In the calculation, the tiny air gap between two cores is neglected. Moreover, the currents are treated as vectors at the center of conductors neglecting the effect of current distribution.

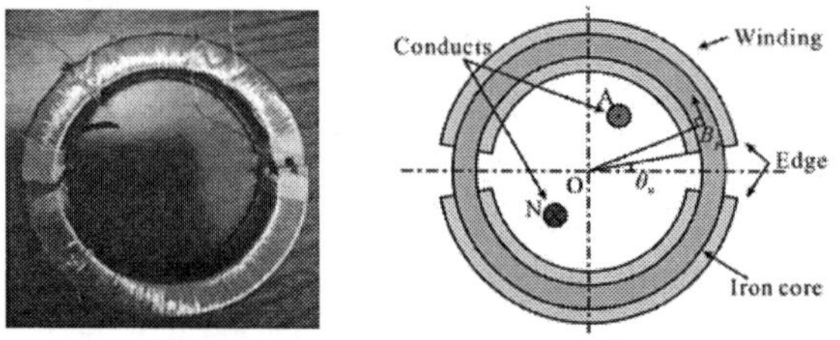

(a) (b)

Fig. 1 (a). Physical structure of the iron core and the wingdings. (b). Diagram for the analytic calculation.

The electro-magnetic calculation is carried out in cylindrical coordinates. The coordinates of the center of phase A and phase N conductors are (ρ_A, θ_A) and (ρ_N, θ_N), respectively. According to Biot-Savart Law, the magnitude of the flux density in the normal direction of cross section at arbitrary point P in the iron core can be calculated by Eqn. (1).

$$B_P = \sum_{i=A,N} \frac{\mu I_i(t)}{2\pi R_i}\cos\alpha_i \tag{1}$$

$$I_A(t) = -I_N(t) = \sqrt{2}I_{\mathrm{rms}}\sin(2\pi f t) \tag{2}$$

$$\cos\alpha_i = \frac{R_i^2 + r^2 - \rho_i^2}{2R_i r} \tag{3}$$

$$R_i = \sqrt{\rho_i^2 + r^2 - 2\rho_i r\cos(\theta - \theta_i)} \tag{4}$$

where μ is the permeability of the iron core, $I_A(t)$ and $I_N(t)$ are the current values of phase A and N at time t, I_{rms} is the root mean square (RMS) of the currents, and f is the frequency of load currents. α_i is the angle between the normal vector of the cross section and the vector of the flux density produced by the current of phase i. R_i is the distance between point P and the center of phase i.

The induced voltage can be achieved by the Faraday's Law.

$$u(t) = -\frac{\mathrm{d}\Phi}{\mathrm{d}t} = \frac{\int n_w(\theta)\int B_P \cdot \mathrm{d}s\mathrm{d}\theta}{\mathrm{d}t} = \sum_{i=A,N} u_i(t) \tag{5}$$

where n_w is the turn density of the windings. ds=Ldr where L is the depth of the iron core. By substituting Eqn. (1)-(4), the induced voltage by phase i can be derived as

$$u_i(t) = \frac{\mu L}{2\pi}\frac{\mathrm{d}I_i(t)}{\mathrm{d}t}\iint n_w \frac{r - \rho_i\cos(\theta-\theta_i)}{\rho_i^2 + r^2 - 2\rho_i r\cos(\theta-\theta_i)}\mathrm{d}r\mathrm{d}\theta \tag{6}$$

By assuming the windings are uniformly wounded around the iron core, n_w can be written as

$$n_w = \begin{cases} \dfrac{N_w}{2\pi - 4\theta_u} & \left(\begin{matrix}\theta_u \le \theta \le \pi - \theta_u \\ \pi + \theta_u \le \theta \le 2\pi - \theta_u\end{matrix}\right) \\ 0 & \text{else} \end{cases} \tag{7}$$

where N_w is the total turn number and θ_u is the angular position of the winding edges. Thus, Eqn. (6) can be simplified as

$$u_i(t) = \frac{n_w \mu L}{2\pi}\frac{\mathrm{d}I_i(t)}{\mathrm{d}t} \cdot \int_{R_1}^{R_2}\left[\frac{1}{2r} + \frac{1}{r}\arctan\left(\frac{r+\rho_i}{r-\rho_i}\tan\frac{\theta-\theta_i}{2}\right)\right]_{\theta_1}^{\theta_2}\mathrm{d}r \tag{8}$$

where R_1 and R_2 are the inner and outer radius of the iron core. θ_1 and θ_2, which are only used to simplify the formula, are the lower and upper limits of integral.

According to Eqn. (8), the value of the induced voltage u_i is relative to the positions of the conductors. The FRC can easily be derived by dividing $u(t)$ by the sampling resistance. Only when one of the following two conditions is achieved, (1) the iron core and the phases are centered (ρ_A=ρ_N, θ_A=π+θ_N) and (2) the iron core is fully wounded with uniform windings (θ_u=0), which cannot be easily achieved in practical application of open type RCSs, there would be no FRC. Otherwise, there would be always FRCs, whose magnitude is relative to the magnitude of load currents in circuits, the winding distribution, and the positions of the conductors. The calculation for three-phase application can be expanded by taking another two phases into consideration as Eqn. (9).

$$u(t) = \sum_{i=A,B,C,N} u_i(t) = \frac{n_w \mu L}{2\pi}\sum_{i=A,B,C,N}\left\{\frac{\mathrm{d}I_i(t)}{\mathrm{d}t}\int_{R_1}^{R_2}\left[\frac{1}{2r} + \frac{1}{r}\arctan\left(\frac{r+\rho_i}{r-\rho_i}\tan\frac{\theta-\theta_i}{2}\right)\right]_{\theta_1}^{\theta_2}\mathrm{d}r\right\} \tag{9}$$

$$\begin{cases} I_A(t) = \sqrt{2}I_{\mathrm{rms}}\sin(2\pi f t) \\ I_B(t) = \sqrt{2}I_{\mathrm{rms}}\sin(2\pi f t - 2\pi/3) \\ I_C(t) = \sqrt{2}I_{\mathrm{rms}}\sin(2\pi f t + 2\pi/3) \\ I_N(t) = -I_A(t) - I_B(t) - I_C(t) \end{cases} \tag{10}$$

Assuming a similar condition like condition (1) mentioned above in single-phase application is achieved, the three phases are arranged in symmetrical distribution to a specific point P_0 which is centered to the iron core with phase N. Since θ_u does not equal to zero, the resultant contribution to the induced voltage by the three phases cannot be simplified to a resultant current at P_0 according to Eqn. (8). Moreover, the rotating magnetic field caused by the three phases also leads to a FRC. Indeed, the FRC for the three-phase application of open type RCSs is inevitable.

III. MATHEMATIC AND EXPERIMENT RESULTS

An open type RCS was implemented to discuss the effects of the installation of the supply conductors and the non-uniform winding distribution on FRCs. The design specification of the RCS is listed in Table I.

TABLE I

DESIGN SPECIFICATION OF THE OPEN TYPE RCS

Parameter	Symbol	Value
Inner radius of the iron core	R_1	32mm
Outer radius of the iron core	R_2	36.5mm
Depth of the iron core	L	15mm
Diameter of load lines	D_l	11.2mm
Total turn number of windings	N_w	2000
Angular position of winding edges	θ_u	5°
Load current	I_{rms}	0-100A
Residual current	I_r	0-1A
RMS of the induced voltage	u_{rms}	517mV (I_r=1A)

A. *Effect of Installation and Winding Distribution*

Compared to the load currents of phase *A*, *B* and *C*, the RMS of the current of phase *N* is commonly rather small than others under both balanced and unbalanced operations. Since the effect of installation is proportional to the currents with specific positions according to Eqn. (5), (8), only positions of phase *A*, *B* and *C* are considered. To take the unbalanced currents into account, the three phases are arranged in equilateral triangle distribution as shown in Fig. 2. The coordinate of the center of the three phases is defined as (r_0, θ_0). When θ_0 equal to 0, θ_A is 90° in Fig. 1. Since the line diameter is 11.2mm, the minimum value of the distance d between two conductors set to 6.5mm according to Eqn. (11). The maximum value of r_0 is set to 20mm according to inner space of the iron core. The FRC calculation is carried out under the load current I_{rms}=100A, and the results of RMS are normalized to 20mA.

$$d_{min} = D_l / \sqrt{3} = 6.47\text{mm} \tag{11}$$

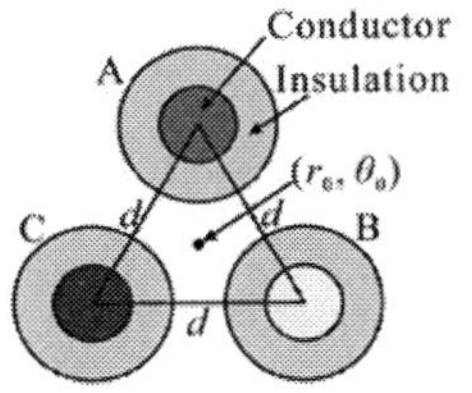

Fig. 2 Arrangement of the three phases.

Fig. 3, Fig. 4 and Fig. 5 show the effect of the installation of the supply conductors. It can be seen in Fig. 3 that the RMS values of the FRC changes with the angular positions when d=6.5mm and r_0=0. Instead of a 120° period, the period of the FRC is 60° while extremum points appear in every 30° as consequences of symmetric structure of the iron core and the non-uniform windings of upper and lower parts. The minimum value is 20.91mA, while the maximum is 26.51mA. It seems that the FRC is barely sensitive to the angular positions with a maximum change rate 1.27.

In Fig. 4, the FRCs gradually increase with larger distances at different angular positions. The effect of the angular position is greater with a bigger value of the distance. It is found out that the FRCs can be suppressed by holding conductors close together. In this way, the minimum value is decided by the diameter of load lines. The change rate of FRCs becomes greater as the distance increases, which indicate that the FRC is quite sensitive to the distance between conductors.

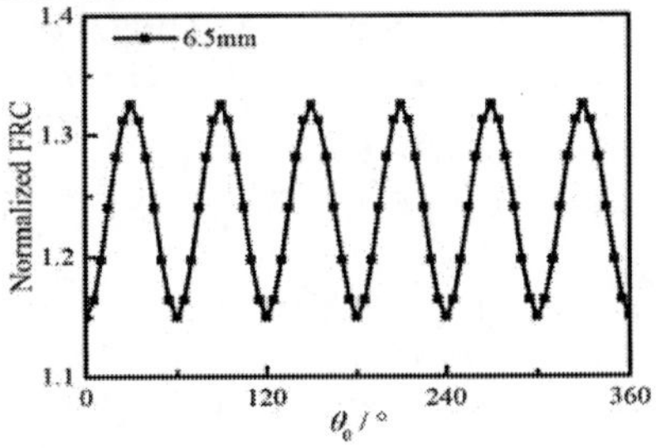

Fig. 3 Influence of the angular position θ_0 on FRCs when d=6.5mm and r_0=0.

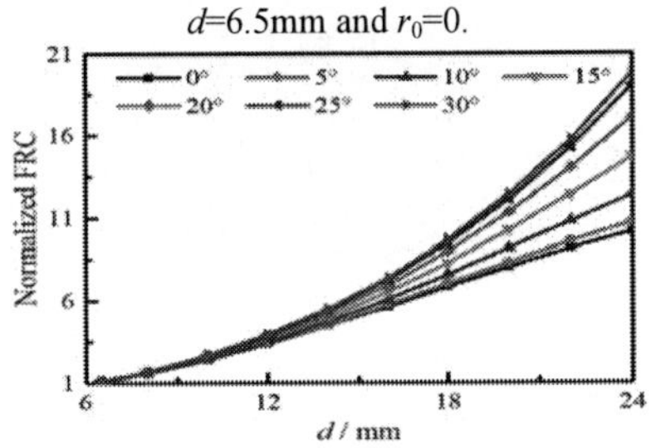

Fig. 4 Influence of the distance d between conductors on FRCs at different angular positions θ_0 values when r_0=0.

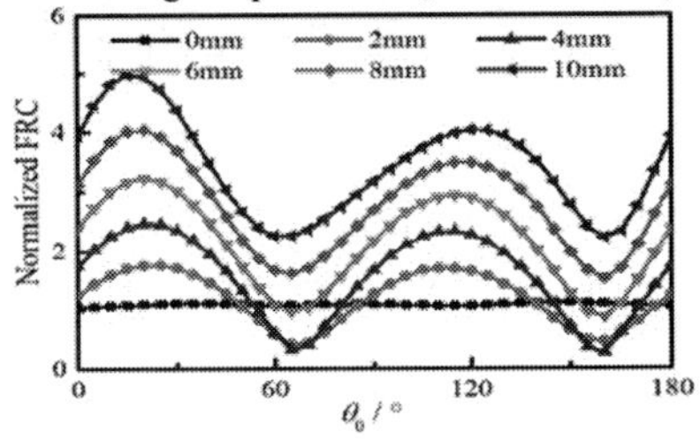

Fig. 5 Variation of FRCs responding to the angular positions θ_0 at different r_0 values when d=6.5mm.

Fig. 5 shows the joint effect of the conductor distribution on the FRCs. For a specific r_0 value, which is greater than zero, the period of the FRC responding to the angular positions is no longer 60°. The minimum values at different r_0 values (0-8mm) are 20.91mA, 8.28mA, 5.20mA, 17.44mA, 30.50mA, and 44.26mA, respectively. It is interesting to find that the minimum value of the FRC is found to be 5.20mA at the position where r_0=4mm and θ_0=160°.

Fig. 6 presents the effect of the non-uniform winding distribution on FRCs. It seems that the FRC is proportional to variable *th* with change rates in the range from 4.30mA/° to 4.58mA/°. Covering the iron core with windings as completely as possible can make significant contribution to suppressing the FRCs.

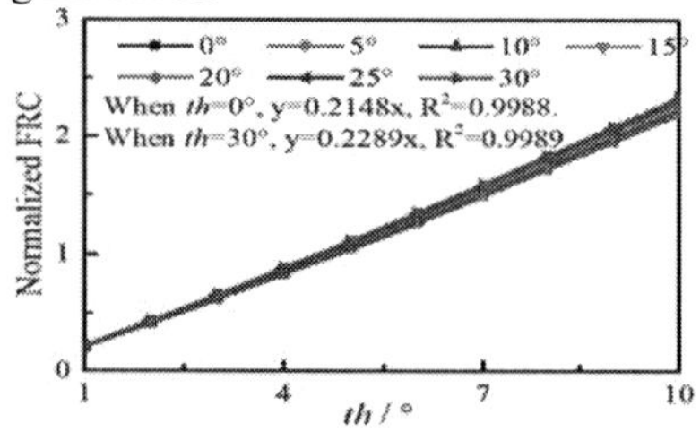

Fig. 6 Influence of non-uniform winding distribution on FRCs at different angular positions θ_0 when r_0=0 and d=6.5mm.

B. Experimental Validation

In the process of the practical installation, the conductors can be easily hold close together to fulfill the condition of d=6.5mm as far as possible. However, it is hard to positioning the conductors at precise values of r_0 and θ_0. A relative precise position can be achieved by filling the space inside the ring core with specific shapes of polyfoams, shown in Fig. 7.

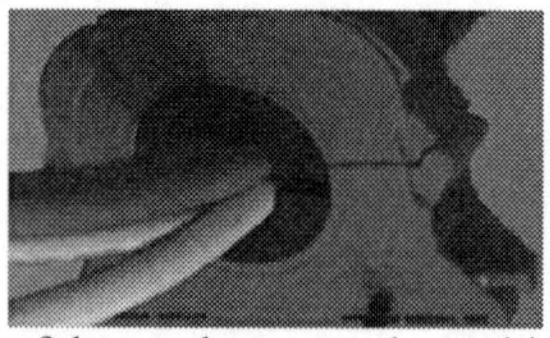

Fig. 7 Installation of the conductors to the position r_0=0mm, θ_0=0°

To validate the analytical results, five positions were selected for the experimental tests. The analytical and experimental results were achieved as the minimum values at five positions by rotating the combined conductors. Five RCSs with same design parameters were tests, and the average values of the five RCSs were compared to the analytical results, listed in Table II.

TABLE II
COMPARISON OF ANALYTICAL AND EXPERIMENTAL RESULTS

Position	Analytical result / mA	Experimental result / mA	Error / %
r_0=0mm, θ_0=0°	20.9	21.8	4.3
r_0=20mm, θ_0=0°	129.4	132.6	2.5
r_0=20mm, θ_0=90°	87.9	89.5	1.8
r_0=20mm, θ_0=180°	129.4	135.4	4.6
r_0=20mm, θ_0=270°	87.9	90.3	2.7

The errors between the analytical and experimental results, which are the results from the positioning uncertainty and the idealization of the RCS structure in analytical calculation, are less than 5%. The differences between the experimental results at symmetric positions may come from the asymmetry of the windings.

IV. CONCLUSION

This paper studies the mechanism and the impact factors of FRCs in open type RCSs using analytical method. It is found that both the installation of supply conductors and the non-uniform winding distribution make contribution to the FRCs. A closely combined conductor installation at the center of the iron core is suggested to suppress the FRCs. The analytical model is validated by experimental tests with errors less than 5%. Further work will focus on factors of unbalanced loads, on-line correction, and compensation algorithm with non-uniform windings

ACKNOWLEDGMENT

This work was supported by the National Natural Science Foundation of China (No. 51607123) and the Fund of Wenzhou Municipal Science and Technology Bureau, China (No. ZG2017002).

REFERENCES

[1] Y. Xia, S. Du, C. Li, J, Su, J, Zhang, and L. Zhang, "Development tendency of residual current protection technology and device in China", *Transactions of the Chinese Society of Agricultural Engineering*, vol. 26, pp. 151-155, 2010.

[2] P. V. Brennan, "Residual current device with high immunity to nuisance tripping", IEE Proceedings G - Circuits, Devices and Systems, vol. 140, no. 2, pp. 140-144, 2002.

[3] J. Diao, and H. Hu, "Study on Residual Current Monitoring System for Detection", *Applied Mechanics & Materials*, vol. 536, pp. 1101-1104, 2014.

[4] B. Utegulov, A. B. Utegulov, and A. B. Uakhitova, "Development of method to improve efficiency of residual current device under 1000 V on excavators of mining enterprises", *Journal of Mining Science*, vol. 52, no. 2, pp. 325–331, 2016.

[5] X. Han, S. Du, J. Su, and G. Liu, "Electric shock fault diagnosis of low-voltage residual current operated protective device", *Ieej Transactions on Electrical & Electronic Engineering*, vol. 13, no. 3, pp. 180-186,2017.

[6] Z. Erdei, M. Horgos, C. Lung, A. Pop-Vadean, and R. Muresan, "Frequency behavior of the residual current devices", *IOP Conference Series: Materials Science and Engineering*, vol. 163, 012053, 2017.

[7] B. Colin, A. Kedous-Lebouc, C. Chillet, and P. Mas, "Wound magnetic core consequences on false residual currents", *Compel International Journal of Computations & Mathematics in Electrical*, vol. 27, no. 1, pp. 246-255, 2008.

[8] B. Colin, C. Chillet, A. Kedous-Lebouc, and P. Mas, "Effects of magnetic core geometry on false detection in residual current sensor", *Journal of Magnetism & Magnetic Materials*, vol. 304, no. 2, pp. e804-e806, 2006.

7th International Conference on Reliability of
Electrical Products and Electrical Contacts,
November 04-06, 2019

Vibration Simulation and Analysis of Automotive Electrical Connector Based on ABAQUS

Guoping Wang[1], Yanyan Luo[1,2]
[1]State Key Laboratory of Reliability and Intelligence of Electrical Equipment, Hebei University of Technology, Tianjin, 300130
[2]Electrical Apparatus Institute of Hebei Province, Tianjin, 300130
E-mail: wgpplq@163.com Tel: 16622810887

Abstract—**Electrical connector is a kind of basic component that connects components, devices and systems through electrical signals. It can realize the transmission of electrical signals between electrical equipment and electronic equipment, so that the circuit can achieve predetermined functions. Automotive electrical connectors have a great impact on the reliability of various electrical systems used in automobiles, as a basic element used to connect the car electrical system, subjected to the vibration of the automobile running engine, The vibration that may occur when driving on roads of different roughness, will also be a leading to the connector of vibration excitation source. In this paper, using ABAQUS finite element simulation software for a certain type of automobile electrical connector under the vibration to simulation and analysis, further research for the data from the simulation and analysis, the vibration is important factor affecting the automobile electrical connector reliability, and different vibration levels have different impact on the reliability of the auto electrical connector. This conclusion can also provide some references for the design and optimization of automotive electrical connectors.**

Index Terms— **vibration, electrical connector, finite element analysis, reliability, ABAQUS**

I. INTRODUCTION

The statistical data show that the electric and electronic system faults account for a very high proportion of the vehicle faults in the process of running, and the tendency is increasing year by year [1]. As the basic component of the electrical system, electrical connectors have an important influence on the performance of on-board electrical system and even the quality and performance of the whole vehicle. Vibration is an important cause of degradation or even failure of automobile electrical connector. Therefore, the simulation analysis of automotive electrical connector under vibration is of great significance.

Many scholars at home and abroad have studied the degradation and failure mechanism of electrical connectors under vibration. Yang qiang et al.[2] established a physical model of fatigue failure of contact parts of electrical connectors based on the fracture mechanics theory. Luo yanyan et al.[3] analyzed the degradation mechanism of contact performance of electrical connectors in ambient vibration by conducting vibration test of electrical connector. Flowers et al.[4,5] studied the fretting corrosion and wear of electrical connectors caused by axial vibration. In this paper, the ABAQUS finite element simulation software is used to simulate and analyze the automobile electrical connector under vibration situation, and the specific mechanism and mode of the influence on the reliability of the automobile electrical connector under vibration condition can be inferred. It can also be used as a reference for the actual test, providing a reasonable solution for the physical test. The conclusions obtained through simulation analysis can provide certain theoretical basis for the design and production of electrical connectors and the next step of optimization and upgrading, and help researchers to improve the component material, structure composition, appearance design and other parameters of the same or similar type of automobile electrical connectors, in order to enhance the overall performance and reliable stability of automobile electric connectors.

II. IDENTIFY AND CREATE MODELS

The selected type of automobile electrical connector is subdivided, the core components to be studied are determined, and the corresponding three-dimensional model is established. The corresponding dynamic model is established on the basis of vibration condition.

A. Structure of Automotive Electrical Connector

The components of automobile connectors consist of the following four types: contact parts, insulators, shells and other accessories, as shown in the following figure.

The correct combination and collocation of these four types of components can make the automobile electrical connector act as a bridge of circuit, so that each original independent system and device in the automobile are connected and interact with each other, forming a whole and ensuring the normal and stable operation of the automotive electrical system.

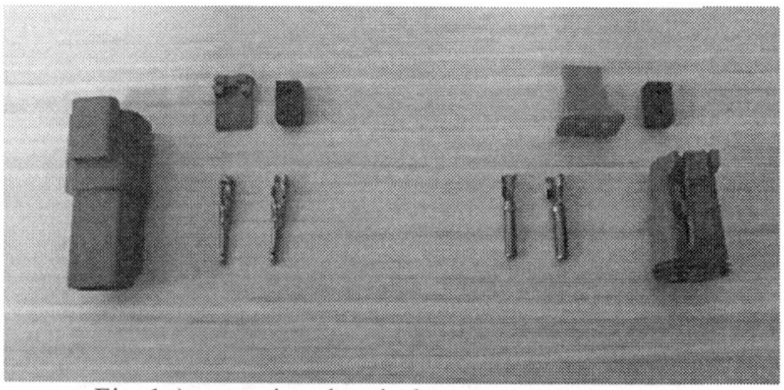

Fig. 1 Automotive electrical connector components

Fig. 2 Complete assembly of automotive electrical connector

B. 3d model

Contactor plays a core role in automobile electrical connector. Because the current signal in the automobile is circulated or blocked, it depends on different states such as intercalation or separation between metal contacts of the automobile electrical connector. Among them, the materials used in the positive metal contacts are usually phosphorous bronze or brass, which are usually called pins or inserts according to their different appearance shapes. Negative metal contacts are commonly referred to as sockets and come in many varieties. The reliable contact of electrical connector is realized by the stable contact force between the contact parts (pins and sockets) [6]. When vibration occurs, pins and sockets will be affected by the vibration stress. Therefore, only metal connection devices need to be considered in the simulation, and other parts, such as shell accessories, shall not be considered. The pins numbered 1060-16-0122 and the sockets numbered 1062-16-0122 were used in the simulation. The three-dimensional model established according to the real objects is shown in figure 3.

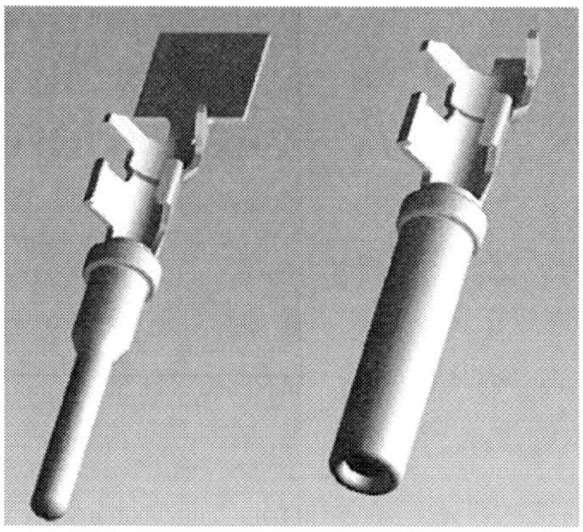

Fig. 3 3d model of pin and socket

C. Dynamical model

Then the vibration simulation work begins. Before the design of vibration simulation scheme, the vibration force model of automobile electrical connector is supposed to be established. In the actual process, due to the action of many factors, the force under the vibration of automobile electrical connector is more complex. In order to facilitate the analysis, the vibration and stress state of automobile electrical connectors can be simplified. All vibrations can be converted into two types of directions that along the axial and vertical axes, because all kinds of forces can be basically decomposed into the above two cases, and the two directions of forces can also be combined into the effects of forces in other directions. Therefore, the dynamic model shown in Fig. 4[7] can be established.

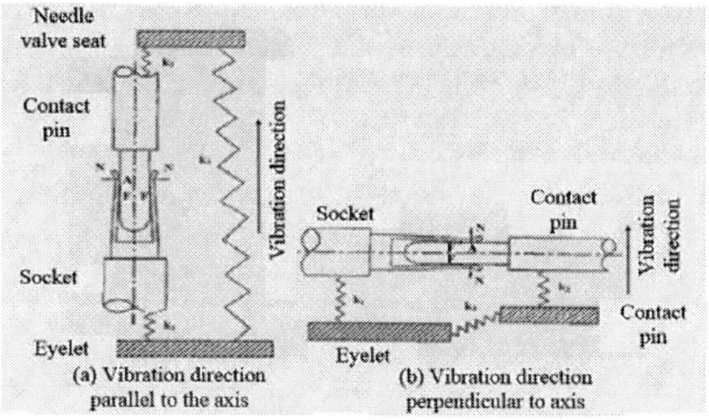

Fig. 4 dynamic model of electrical connector

III. THE SIMULATION SCHEME

A. Determination of Simulation Parameters

Table 1 shows the specific characteristics of contact parts of electrical connector to be studied.

TABLE 1

CHARACTERISTICS OF SIMULATED OBJECTS

character	specific parameter
Crimping type	F type pressure welding
Typical rated current(A)	7.5,13,25
Terminal and connector types	Pin,Socket
Diameter of joint pin(mm)	1,1.5,2.5
Diameter of joint pin(in)	1,1.5,2.5
Contact plating	Au,PdNi,Sn,Ni
Plating material for the terminal end connection area	Au,Sn,Ni
Termination method	Pressure welding
Operating temperature range	-55—125℃[-67—257° F]

According to the analysis of the characteristics of metal contact parts, the corresponding material properties can be determined to facilitate the input of relevant parameters in ABAQUS software. The material properties of metal contact parts of automotive electrical connector are shown in table 2.

TABLE 2

MATERIAL PROPERTIES OF METAL CONTACT PARTS USED IN AUTOMOTIVE ELECTRICAL CONNECTORS

property	parameter
material type	brass
density/kg·m^{-3}	8500
elasticity modulus /GPa	106
Poisson's ratio	0.324

B. *model rigging*

After importing the model of the insert pin and the socket into ABAQUS, the assembly operation is carried out according to the simulation needs. After the assembly is completed, the effect diagram is shown in Fig.5.

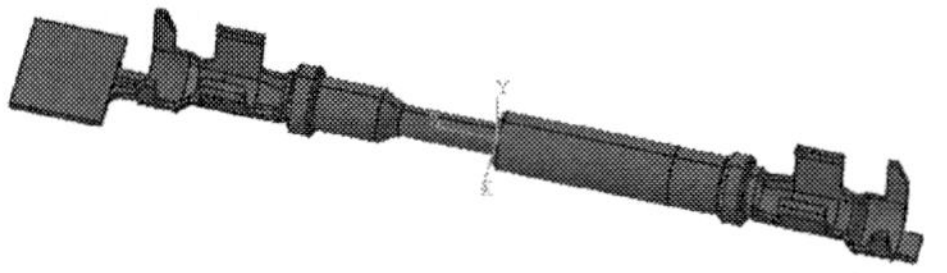

Fig. 5 assembly diagram of automobile electrical connector parts

Socket and pin for assembly parts size is relatively small, and the model is more complex, there are a lot of chamfers and many irregular shape structures, so the parts would be more difficult in mesh, the grid quality is relatively low. In addition, if the assembly diagram shown above is directly simulated, the calculation process will be very complicated and take too long, so the parts will be further modified to improve the simulation efficiency without affecting the calculation results. The other end of the contact part of pin and socket model used in the simulation has a complex structure and irregular shape, which will have a great impact on the speed of the simulation. Moreover, this part has nothing to do with the research, so the jumble structure at both ends can be replaced by a simple rigid body, which will greatly reduce the calculation amount. Or remove the structure at both ends and keep the contact parts, so as to improve the simulation efficiency and get more intuitive simulation results. In this paper, the second scheme is selected for optimization, namely, the redundant and irrelevant structure is directly removed (Fig. 6).

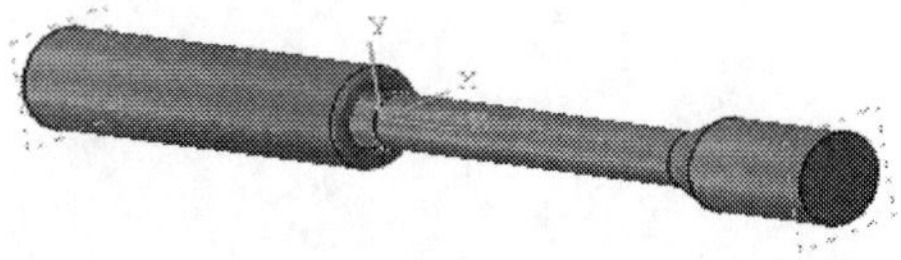

Fig. 6 assembly diagram after optimization

C. *Design simulation scheme*

A lot of research work is based on contact resistance as monitoring quantity to explore the reliability of electrical connector under vibration stress. For products with high reliability and long life, the performance degradation process is very slow, the monitoring value of contact resistance fluctuates, and the growth trend of contact resistance value is not obvious [8-11] .The impact of vibration on the stability of contact parts can also be intuitively demonstrated by the value of contact pressure during vibration. Therefore, a simulation scheme is adopted to observe the contact pressure between pin and socket under vibration. FIG. 7 is the grid division diagram of pin and socket.

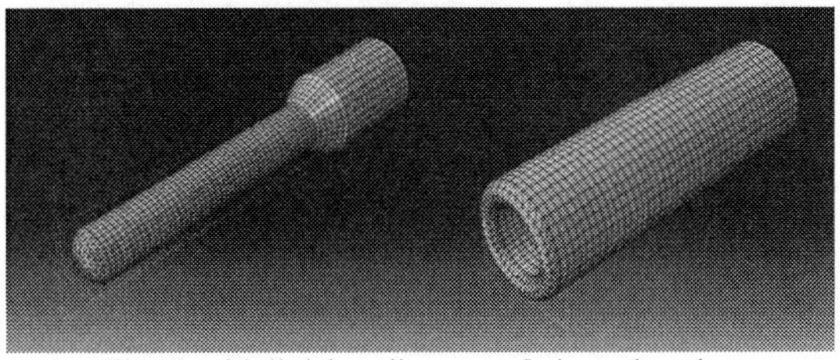

Fig. 7 grid division diagram of pin and socket

Experiments conditions with acceleration of 2g and frequency of 25Hz were selected for simulation, the following display effects can be obtained: a Mises stress cloud diagram (Fig.8), a reaction force cloud diagram (Fig.9), and a logarithmic strain cloud diagram (Fig.10).In addition, the field output view of spatial displacement and spatial velocity of the model can also be obtained through simulation, and the time history and resonance and other processes can be demonstrated through animation for the vibration in the required time, so as to obtain more detailed and intuitive simulation results.

Fig. 8 Cloud diagram of Mises stress

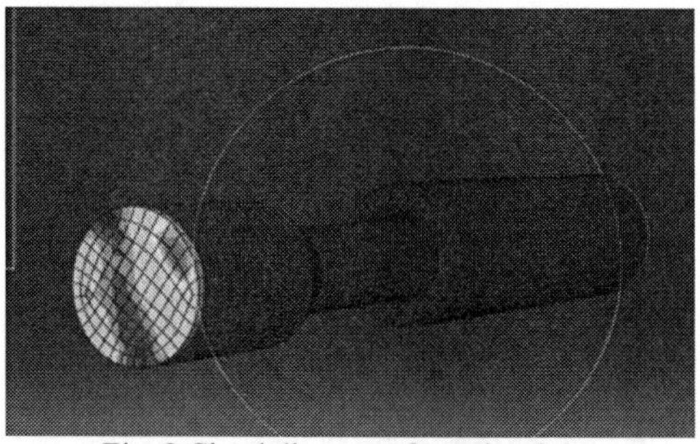

Fig. 9 Cloud diagram of reaction force

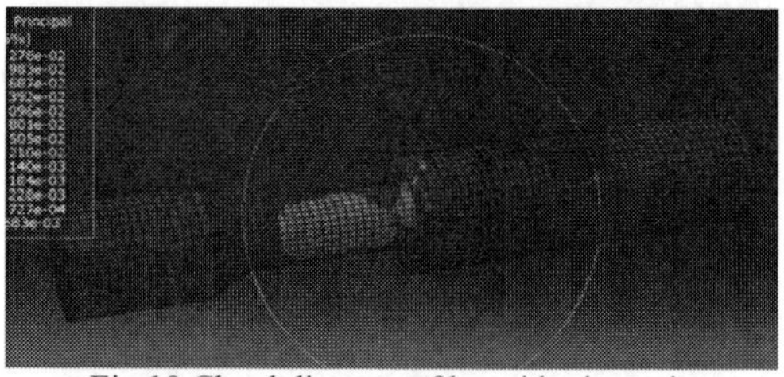

Fig.10 Cloud diagram of logarithmic strain

Output the process variable XY data to the simulation results, the curves of external work done, pseudo-strain energy and others are drawn, as shown below.

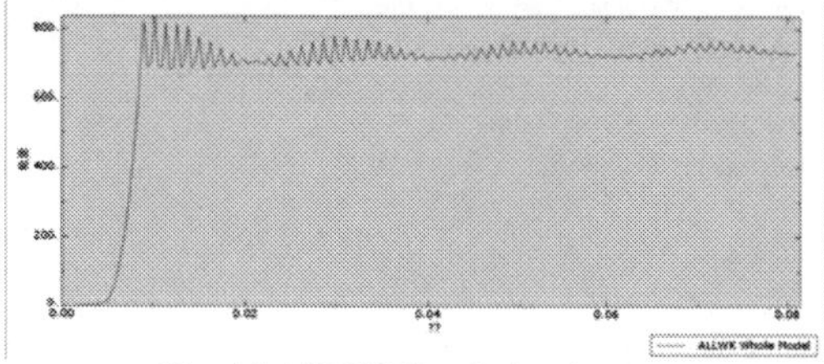

Fig. 11 ALLWK(work done) curve

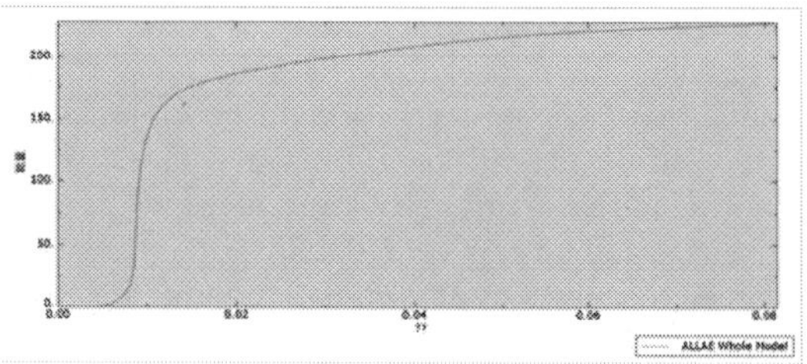

Fig. 12 ALLAE(pseudo strain energy) curve

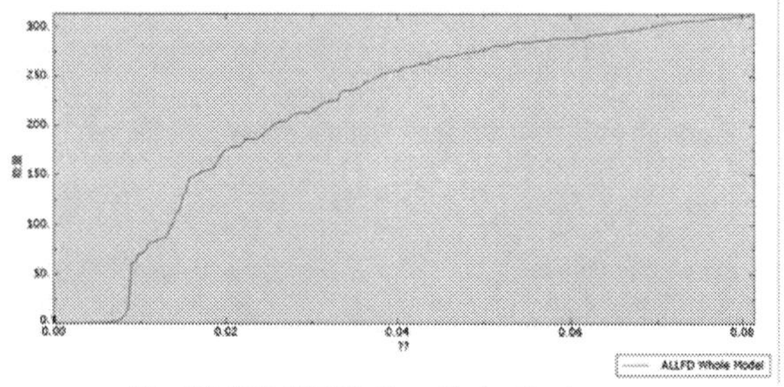

Fig. 13 ALLFD(friction dissipation) curve

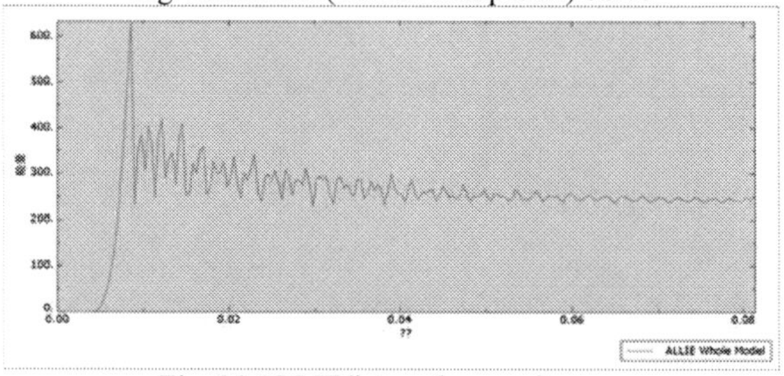

Fig. 14 ALLIE(internal energy) curve

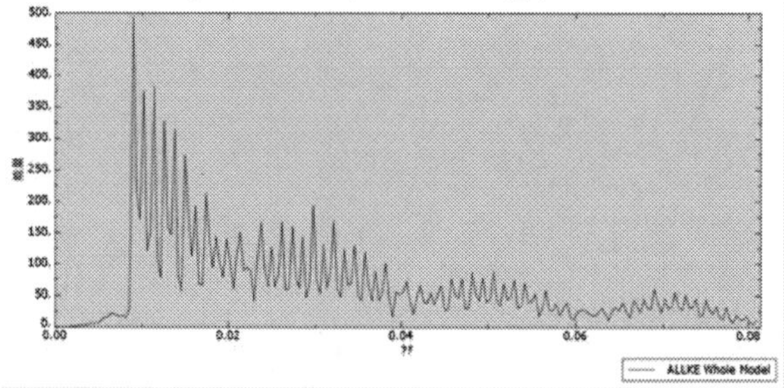

Fig. 15 ALLKE(kinetic energy) curve

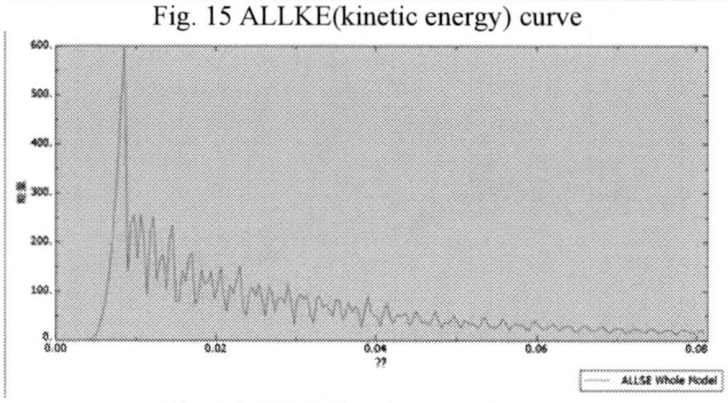

Fig. 16 ALLSE(strain energy) curve

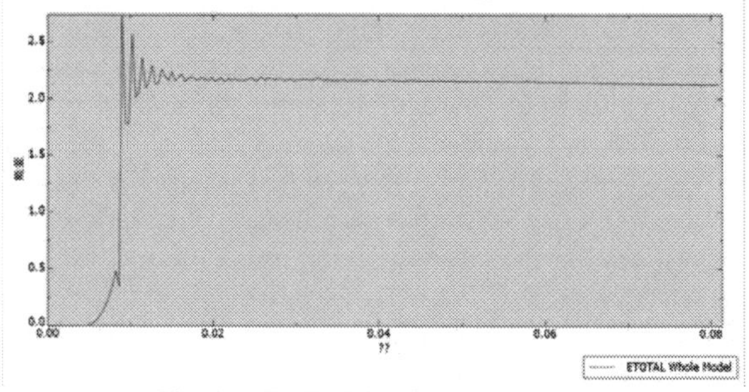

Fig. 17 ETOTAL(total energy) curve

Different parameter are also set in the test to achieve the goal of comparative study. The vibration simulation scheme is shown in table 3.

Table 3 vibration simulation scheme of automotive electrical connector

No.	direction of vibration	frequency/Hz	amplitude/ (m/s^2)
1	axial	25	2g
2	axial	25	10g
3	axial	25	16g
4	axial	100	4g
5	axial	100	10g
6	axial	200	4g
7	axial	200	10g
8	axial	400	4g
9	axial	400	10g

IV. CONCLUSION

In this paper, by using ABAQUS finite element simulation software, the force simulation analysis of automobile electrical connector under vibration is carried out, and several sets of simulation data are obtained. It can be seen from the stress cloud diagram that under the vibration, the vibration pressure at the bottom of the pin and the contact area between the pin and the socket is large, and the reliability of the parts is low. Considering the short interruption and collision phenomenon caused by vertical axial vibration, as well as the analysis of axial vibration in this simulation, different degrees of wear will be generated at the contact point, which will greatly influence the contact resistance at the contact point of plug and socket. Transient phenomenon can seriously affect the value of the contact resistance, because the current flows through certain points in the contact surface of two conductors, the effective contact points will be reduced during the transient process, and the contact resistance value will be increased. Vibration friction, on the other hand, has a great influence on the film resistance, which will damage the coating on the contact surface and reduce the overall reliability and stability of connectors. For different simulation conditions, it can be seen that the peak of contact pressure fluctuation basically remains unchanged with the change of frequency, and will increase with the increase of vibration amplitude. The larger the vibration amplitude and frequency are, the larger the stress variation range of contact parts of automobile electrical connector will be, and the shorter the fatigue life will be. Among them, the impact of vibration amplitude on the fatigue life of contact parts of automobile electrical connector will be greater.

Through software simulation, test results of multiple groups of different parameters can be obtained according to requirements. Compared with the direct test of the research object entity, simulation saves costs, reduces operational difficulty and greatly increases the feasibility of the test. The obtained data are intuitive and specific. The simulation results can be used as a reference to study the reliability of automotive electrical connectors, and can also provide a basis for the design, manufacture, optimization and upgrading of automotive electrical connectors.

REFERENCES

[1] Yu Wang. Working process and troubleshooting of battery electric vehicle charging system[J]. Automobile Maintenance, 2019(01):8-12.

[2] Qiang Yang, Congcong Wen, Zhili Sun, Mengjun Zhang. Reliability analysis of contact fatigue life of aviation electrical connector [J]. Acta Aeronautica et Astronautica Sinica, 2018, 39(10): 222123.

[3] Yanyan Luo, Le Zhang, Fanbin Meng, Jie Hao. Degradation mechanism of electrical connector contact performance under vibration environment [J]. China Mechanical Engineering,2018,29(16):1952-1957.

[4] YANG H, FLOWERS G T. Fretting in electrical connectors induced by axial vibration[J]. IEEE Transactions on Components Packaging & Manufacturing Technology, 2015, 5(3):328-336.

[5] ZHANG F, FLOWERS G T. Fretting corrosion in electric connector induced by axial vibration[C]//Electrical Contacts. Piscataway, NJ: IEEE Press, 2015:1-8.

[6] Yanyan Luo, Xuyang Liu, et al . Study on thermal fatigue failure mechanism of aviation electrical connector [J]. Acta Armamentarii, 2016,7.

[7] Jun Pan. Modeling and evaluation of vibration reliability of aerospace electrical connector[D]. Zhejiang University, 2002.

[8] Ruijin Lin, Wenhua Chen, Juan Liu, Liang Gao, Jun Pan. Feasibility study on accelerating performance degradation test of aerospace electrical connector [J]. Chinese Journal of Engineering Design, 2010, 17（4）: 317-320.

[9] FU R, CHOE S Y B, JACKSON R L, et al. Vibration induced changes in the contact resistance of high power electrical connectors for hybrid vehicles[J]. IEEE Transactions on Components Packaging and Manufacturing Technology, 2012,2(2) : 185-193.

[10] MCBRIDE J W. The relationship between surface wear and contact resistance during the fretting of in-vivoelectrical contacts[J].IEEE Transactions on Components and Packaging Technologies, 2008, 31(3): 592-600.

[11] Yilin Zhou, Peng Wang, Shichao Ge, Fang Li. Study on long-term storage of dust contamination of aerospace electrical connectors[J].Transactions of China Electrotechnical Society, 2014, 29(7):269-276.

Research on Adaptive Control Strategy of Stable Holding of Intelligent Electromagnetic Switch

Binxin Zhang, Zhihong Xu
Fujian Province Key Laboratory of New Energy Generation and Power Conversion, College of Electrical Engineering and Automation, Fuzhou University, Fuzhou 350108 Fujian Province China
E-mail: 277596318@qq.com Tel: 13164802540

***Abstract*—In order to solve the contradiction between energy-saving operation and reliability of intelligent electromagnetic switch, and keep stable holding when the switch operating conditions change, this paper proposes an adaptive control strategy based on a double closed loop control system: The coil current is used as inner loop feedback for energy-saving operation control of low current holding of electromagnetic switch, the contact signal is introduced to calculate the amplitude and slope quickly, and feedback the contact state as the outer loop; Two coil current control modes, normal and abnormal, are designed. Normal control realizes energy-saving operation of the switch, the abnormal control realizes the stable holding of the switch under overload, short circuit and other extremely large current levels, the outer loop feedback discriminates the contact load condition, the control mode of inner loop coil current is judged based on it. The ampere-turns at core saturation is deduced by constructing equivalent magnetic circuit of core, combined with strong excitation control and switching action time, the coil current adjustment scheme is determined to achieve fast switching between the normal state and the abnormal state control mode. Relevant simulations and experiments verify the effectiveness of the control strategy and have a universal significance for improving the reliability of intelligent electromagnetic switches.**

***Index Terms*—double closed loop, adaptive, magnetic circuit, electromagnetic switch, reliability**

I. INTRODUCTION

Electromagnetic switch is a kind of electric appliance which is widely used in power distribution system. With the continuous development of smart grid, new energy and other power industry, the research on intelligent control of traditional electromagnetic switch is also deepening [1]. At present, the intelligent electromagnetic switch combines the switch itself with the intelligent control module, and optimizes the control in the whole cycle by introducing the closed-loop technology. In literature [2-3], PWM closed-loop chopper technology of electromagnetic switch is proposed to overcome the defect of uncontrolled coil current under open-loop control, and the current required is adjusted and controlled through current feedback to reduce core collision energy. In literature [4], an intelligent control scheme based on step-chopper cascade mode is proposed, which can flexibly change the voltage/current and improve the flexibility and reliability of contactor closed-loop control.

In order to realize energy-saving operation of the electromagnetic switch, the coil should be converted to constant current control during the holding process to maintain fluctuation within a small value range [5]. Most of the relevant literatures have carried out research on energy conservation and reduction of small noise. Literature [6] proposed multivariable energy feedback control ideas, automatic access to contact the current conditions of critical holding current, closed loop duty ratio control law is derived, effectively reduced the coil current ripple and harmonic holding stage, inhibition of iron core vibration assignment, reduce the high frequency noise. PID control of coil current can improve the stability of closed-loop control, have good adaptive robustness, reduce contact bounce, and also realize energy-saving operation of holding process [7].

However the holding process of control strategies in the implementation of energy-saving running at the same time, due to the coil current in a small range of values lead to essentially unchanged electromagnetic suction, makes the electromagnetic switch in contact condition changes may not be able to reliable holding [8], such as overload, short circuit fault, short-term tolerance experiment when the contact current exceeds more than rated current, If the coil current is still maintained at a low value, the contact will be accidentally dislodged due to the sudden increase in the electric repulsion, that is to bring the contradiction between the energy-saving operation of the electromagnetic switch and the stable suction, which is especially important in the large-capacity electromagnetic switch.

In order to solve the above contradiction, this paper proposes an adaptive control strategy based on the double-closed-loop control system with contact state feedback: Energy-saving operation control with low current holding of electromagnetic switch with coil current feedback as inner loop. The contact signal is introduced to calculate the amplitude and slope quickly, and the contact state feedback is used as the outer ring. Different from the simple energy saving operation control scheme, the external loop feedback of this strategy identifies the contact load condition, and as a given current control mode of the inner loop, it realizes the adaptive control of stable holding process. By constructing the equivalent magnetic circuit of the iron core, the ampere-turns number when the iron core is saturated is deduced. By constructing the core equivalent magnetic circuit to derive the number of ampere-turns when the core is saturated, the coil current adjustment scheme is determined combined with the strong excitation control and switching action time and the ampere-turns. The realization of the control strategy requires the design of two kinds of coil current control modes: normal state and abnormal state. The normal state control switch energy-saving operation, the abnormal state control realizes the stable holding of the switch under overload, short circuit and other extra large current levels. In this paper, relevant theoretical analysis is made on the control strategy. Taking the single-pole intelligent contactor [11] designed by the research group as the control object, relevant experiments verify the effectiveness of the control strategy, breaking the limitation of keeping the given value of current unchanged in the holding process, and it is of general significance to improve the reliability of the operation of intelligent electromagnetic switches..

II. HYSTERESIS COMPARISON CONTROL

A. Principle of hysteresis comparison control

The driving circuit topology of the coil current is composed of the modified Buck circuit. The coil current, coil voltage and contact current signals are collected into the dsPIC control unit through the sampling circuit. Its overall control module structure block diagram is shown in Fig 1. The required control signals of the module are coil current and contact current, and the coil voltage signal is used as the starting and closing action signal of the module to form the voltage loss and under-voltage protection functions of the electromagnetic switch.

The actual coil current is used as the feedback signal, and the signal is filtered by the sliding filter algorithm during sampling. The hysteresis comparison tracking control is used to control the coil current by PWM chopping. The basic idea is to compare the actual current i_{coil} with the given value i_r, and the error is defined as:

$$e = i_{coil} - i_r \qquad (1)$$

When $e < -\varepsilon$, PWM outputs high level, and the input voltage is applied to both ends of the coil, the coil current increases. When it reaches $e > \varepsilon$, PWM output is at a low level. The voltage of the coil is 0, the coil current is in a natural freewheeling state, and the current decreases. When $-\varepsilon < e < \varepsilon$, the duty cycle is not updated, and the coil current is basically maintained around the given value. The Editor will type the final page number on the face of each page.

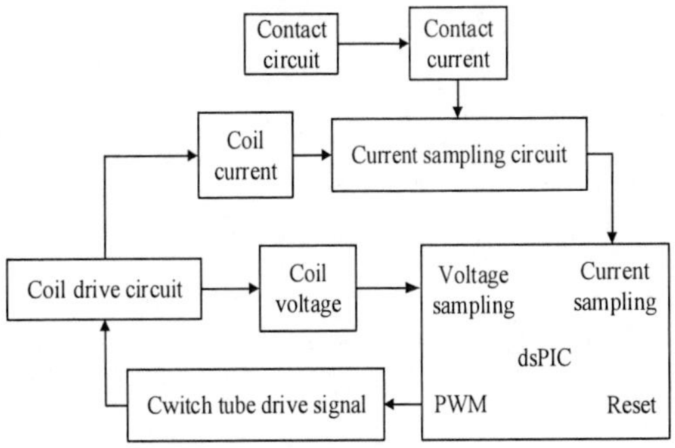

Fig 1 Block diagram of the control module

B. Experimental verification of hysteresis comparison control

The experiment set up the switch between the given values of different currents, recorded the changes of coil current waveform, and verified the feasibility of hysteresis comparison control. Fig 2 shows the waveform of coil current and voltage at both ends of the coil under different given values of current. It can be seen from the experimental waveform that the current ripple of the coil is small and basically stable near the given value of current in the maintenance stage. It has a good closed-loop control effect for different given values of current, with fast response speed. Moreover, when switching between different given values of current, the control system still runs stably with strong robustness.

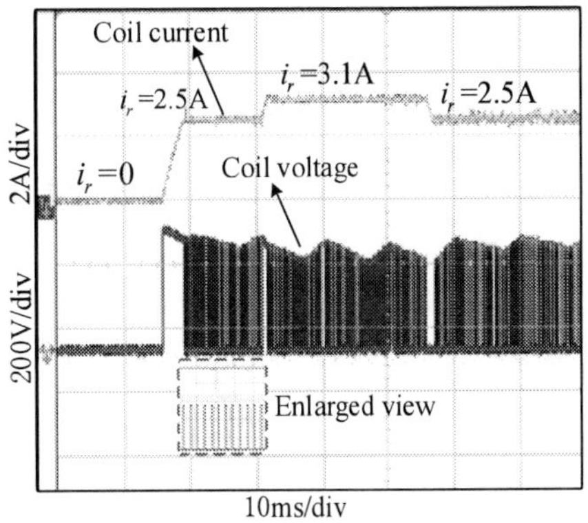

Fig. 2 Closed-loop control effect of different current given values

The adaptive control strategy changes the control idea that the given value of current remains unchanged during the holding process of electromagnetic switch, and realizes fast switching of coil current between the given value of different current. The well-designed hysteresis comparison controller has the characteristics of real-time control, fast response and strong robustness, which provides a favorable foundation for the implementation of the whole control strategy.

III. DOUBLE CLOSED LOOP CONTROL STRATEGY

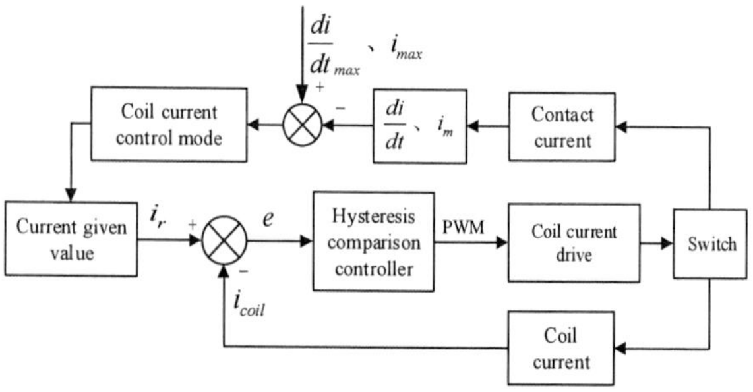

Fig. 3 Structure diagram of double closed-loop control system

The inner loop of the double closed-loop control system takes the actual coil current as feedback, and adopts hysteresis comparison control, while the outer loop takes the calculated contact current slope and amplitude signal as feedback, and the given value of the inner loop current is controlled by the outer loop, Fig3 shows the structure of the double closed-loop control system, $\frac{di}{dt}_{max}$ is the maximum slope of normal current in the contact circuit calculated theoretically, i_{max} is the maximum amplitude of the current, $\frac{di}{dt}$ and i_m are respectively the slope and amplitude of contact current obtained by actual calculation. During the electromagnetic switch holding process, the contact current signal is continuously detected by the Hall current sensor, and the slope and amplitude are quickly calculated. The selected sensor model is BJHCS-BS3.3 series open-loop Hall current sensor, and its input-output relationship is:

$$V = 1.65 + 1.25 * \frac{i_a}{I_n} \tag{2}$$

i_a is the contact current, I_n is the rating value of the current sensor, and V is the output voltage value of the current sensor. Assume that the contact current is:

$$i_a = I_m \sin(wt+\theta) \tag{3}$$

Then the current slope is:

$$\frac{di}{dt} = wI_m \cos(wt+\theta) \tag{4}$$

By substituting formula (4) into equation (2), we can get:

$$\frac{dV}{dt} = 1.25 * \frac{\frac{di_a}{dt}}{I_n} = 1.25 * \frac{wI_m \cos(wt+\theta)}{I_n} \tag{5}$$

According to equations (2) and (5), the output voltage signal and current of the current sensor are also sinusoidal signals, and the slope calculated is also sinusoidal signal and is proportional to I_m. Within half a cycle, when $wt+\theta=0^\circ$ or 180°, the absolute value of slope is the maximum, while the output signal of the sensor is the minimum; when $wt+\theta=90^\circ$, the absolute value of slope is the minimum, while the output signal of the sensor is the maximum.

The outer loop control simultaneously compares the slope and the amplitude. The advantage is that if the slope is judged only, the slope is small when the current phase angle is nearby 90°, and the slope calculation value is less than $\frac{di}{dt}_{max}$ in a period of time. If only by the slope detection, the judgment time is long. While the current reaches the maximum value, the magnitude of the contact current is judged by the calculated amplitude, and the coil current given value can be quickly adjusted by comparing it with i_{max}. If the current phase Angle is near 0° or 180°, the situation changes, if only relying on the amplitude calculation, the accurate judgment of the contact current cannot be completed. At this time, by comparing the calculated slope value with $\frac{di}{dt}_{max}$, it can quickly determine whether the given value of the coil current needs to be adjusted.

IV. ADAPTIVE CONTROL STRATEGY OF STABLE HOLDING

A. Normal and abnormal control

The realization of the control strategy requires the design of two kinds of coil current control modes: normal state and abnormal state. The normal state control energy-saving operation of switch, the abnormal state control realizes the stable holding of the switch under overload, short circuit and other extra large current levels.

In the normal control mode, the holding current given value is set to a small value, the electromagnetic switch is reliably closed after the holding process, the air gap is stabilized at a minimum value, and the electromagnetic suction is inversely proportional to the air gap. Therefore, when the other conditions are the same, the holding process requires only a small current to be able to generate a sufficiently large electromagnetic attraction [9]. In literature [6], the critical current value is obtained by extracting the characteristic quantity at the time of iron core separation, so as to maximize the energy-saving operation effect. In order to ensure the reliable absorption of contactor, the given value of coil holding current in normal control can be set to slightly higher than the critical current value.

The abnormal state refers to conditions such as overload and short circuit in the contact circuit, short-time withstand current capability test in accordance with national standards, and other high current conditions, and the non-protective electromagnetic switch in this case should not automatically bounce off. The time for other protective appliances in the system to cut off the fault should be given, and the equipment can continue to be used normally after the fault is removed.

The parameters required for the abnormal control mode are strong excitation current, strong excitation time, and ampere-turns at critical saturation of the core. Strong excitation control is mostly used in the closing process of the electromagnetic switch, which makes the electromagnetic switch contact move quickly and is conducive to reducing the motion time dispersion and inhibiting the bounce [10]. The time of strong excitation control is determined by the electromagnetic switch closing time. The purpose is to ensure that the contact is separated for a short distance due to the instantaneous increase of electric repulsion, and the electromagnetic suction provided by the applied strong excitation current can still pull the contact back reliably. The critical saturation point of the iron core is the knee point on the magnetization curve, the corresponding B and H are recorded as B_0 and H_0. When the iron core works at this point, if the magnetic induction intensity continues to increase, the iron core enters a saturated state, and the core magnetic conductivity decreases significantly, and the increase in magnetic field strength also decreases, and the utilization rate of the core will decrease. Therefore, the core is most suitable for working at the knee point.

The equivalent magnetic circuit model of electromagnetic mechanism must be established to calculate the current under given air gap δ and air gap flux Φ_δ. Taking the double E-type electromagnetic mechanism as an example, the simplified model and the equivalent magnetic circuit are as shown in Fig4. When the armature is in the closed position, the air gap is small, and magnetic circuit estimation can be carried out by only counting the core magneto resistance without magnetic leakage [9]. And the electromagnetic mechanism is symmetrical, so only half of the magnetic circuit calculation needs to be calculated.

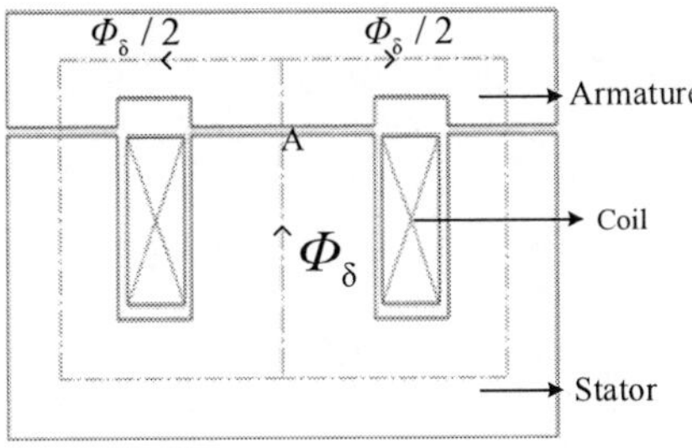

(a) Simplified model of double E electromagnetic mechanism

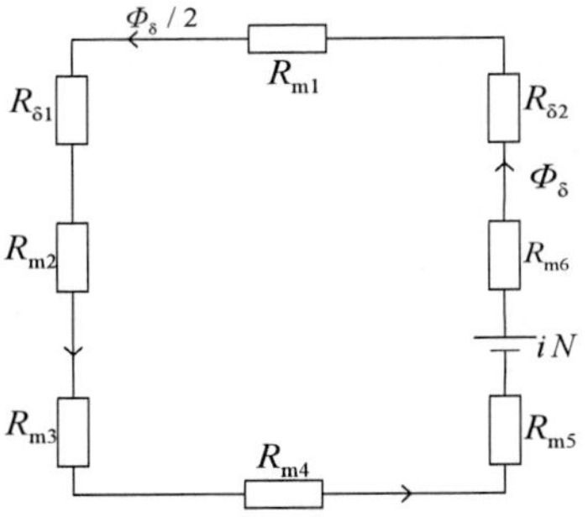

(b) Equivalent magnetic circuit of double E electromagnetic mechanism

Fig. 4 Simplified model and equivalent magnetic circuit of double E electromagnetic mechanism

After the establishment of the equivalent magnetic circuit model of the stingy gap, the working air gap reluctance is calculated by analytic method. The calculation formula of air gap reluctance between two parallel plane magnetic poles [9] is:

$$R_\delta = \frac{BA}{H\delta} \tag{6}$$

Where A is the cross-sectional area of the core, δ is the length of the air gap, B and H respectively take the B_0 and H_0, and make the air gap flux $\Phi_\delta = B_0 A_2$ at A, and A_2 is the end area of the middle part of the static iron core, The core flux density of each segment is calculated by $B = \frac{\Phi}{A}$, and the magnetic field strength H is detected by the magnetization curve. According to the second law of the magnetic path Kirchhoff:

$$\sum_{k=1}^{n} H_k l_k = \sum_{j=1}^{m} (iN)_j \tag{7}$$

The equivalent magnetic circuit equation can be obtained by expanding equation (7):

$$i = \frac{\Phi_\delta R_{\delta 1} + (\Phi_\delta / 2) R_{\delta 2} + \sum_{i=1}^{6} H_i l_i}{N} \tag{8}$$

N is the number of coil turns, H_i and l_i are the magnetic induction intensity and core length of each section. After substituting (6) and the calculated data into equation (8), the current i can be obtained. The current is the coil current value when the end iron core is working at the knee point of the magnetization curve. This point is in the critical saturation state of the iron core, and the utilization rate of the iron core is high.

B. Adaptive adjustment scheme of coil current

The adaptive adjustment scheme of coil current in the whole holding process is based on hysteresis comparison tracking control, and the double closed loop system is used as feedback to realize adaptive switching between normal and abnormal state control. The switching process has time for detection and adjustment. It is required to avoid the contact being disengaged when the coil current is adjusted to a safe value. The complete working process is shown in Fig 5.

When the electromagnetic switch enters the holding process, the contact current signal is continuously detected, and the magnitude of the current is determined by the amplitude and the slope, and the coil current is adjusted in time. The difficulty lies in how to quickly increase the small current value during energy-saving operation to a safe current value that can generate enough suction force when the abnormal current is generated. If the adjustment time is too long, the contact will be disengaged before the coil current adjustment is completed, and the control strategy will be invalid. Another advantage of strong excitation control is that it can save energy and make the maintaining current quickly increase to the safe current value, and then reduce the given current value and keep it until the contact current returns to the normal range, and then turn to normal control. Therefore, it is very important to strengthen the excitation control when abnormal current is detected.

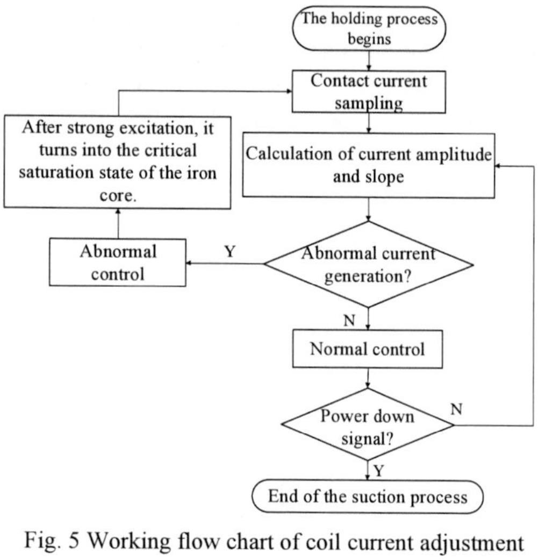

Fig. 5 Working flow chart of coil current adjustment

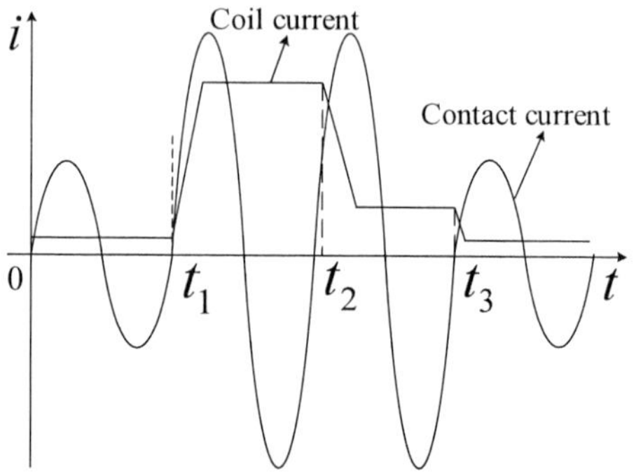

Fig. 6 Schematic diagram of coil current adjustment

Fig 6 is a schematic diagram of adaptive adjustment of coil current. The contact current suddenly increases at time t_1. At this time, the control scheme firstly uses the strong excitation control to quickly adjust the coil current to the safe current value. The time period t_1~t_2 is the strong excitation control time, which is determined by the switch closing time. The strong excitation control ends at t_2 time, the coil current given value is reduced to the coil current value when the core is critically saturated, The contact current returns to normal at time t_3, and it is converted to normal control to reduce the given value of current and maintain energy saving operation.

V. EXPERIMENTAL VERIFICATION

To verify the effectiveness of the control strategy, dsPIC33FJ16GS502 is adopted as the control core to design the hardware control module. And set up an experimental platform, with the single-stage intelligent contactor designed by the research group as the control object, the coil control voltage is AC220V. The process of sudden increase of contact current and normal state is simulated, and the effectiveness of the stable adaptive control strategy is verified. The waveform of coil current and the contact current during the electromagnetic switch holding process are recorded.

In Fig 7 (a), the contact current suddenly increases at time t_4, and the coil current starts to enter into abnormal control at time t_5. The measured detection time t_4~t_5 is only 0.2ms, that is, in the case of abnormal current generation, the detection time of the control strategy is only 0.2ms. In Fig 7 (b), i_1 is the coil current value of the energy-saving operation during normal control, i_2 is the coil current value of the strong excitation control, i_3 is the calculated coil current value that makes the iron core in the critical saturation state, and t_6 is the strong excitation control. The time is consistent with the pre-measured contactor action time. The time from i_1 to i_3 is 0.6ms after the excitation of the strong excitation control. When the contact current suddenly increases, the time of the control strategy from detecting the abnormal current to adjusting the coil current to the safe current value is about 0.8ms. In Fi 8, t is the moment when the contact current returns to normal, and the coil current control mode is switched to the normal state control to maintain the energy-saving operation state. The experimental results show that the control strategy can quickly and accurately determine the normal and abnormal currents. After the discrimination is completed, the coil current can be adjusted quickly. Especially when the normal control is changed to the abnormal state, the whole process only needs about 0.8ms. Effectively respond to the sudden occurrence of extremely large currents and achieve stable holding.

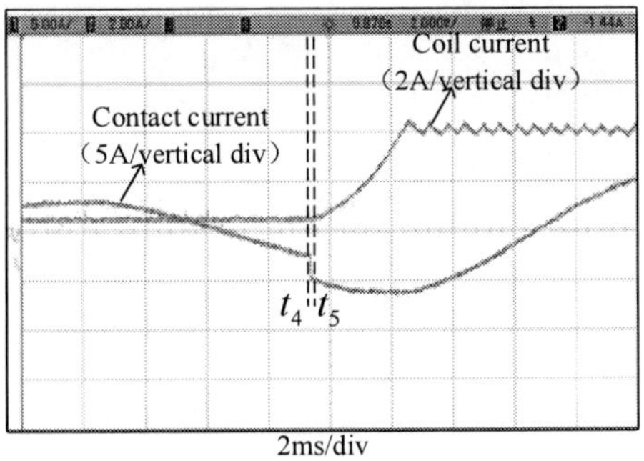

2ms/div

(a) Ascending process

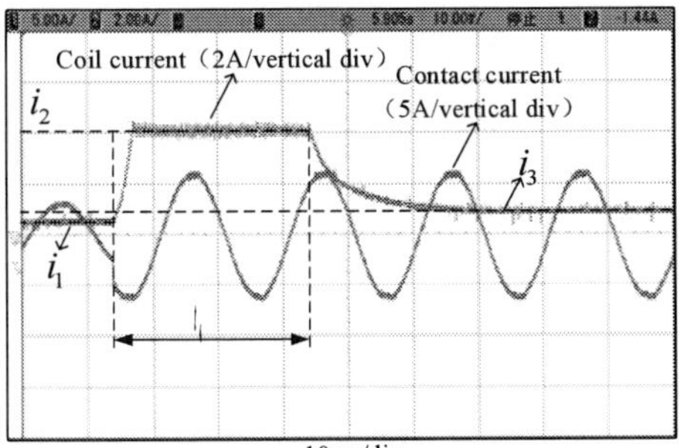

10ms/div

(b) Adjustment process

Fig. 7 Abnormal control process

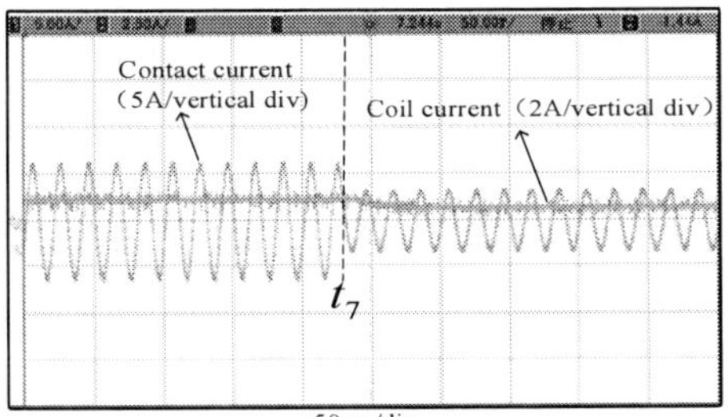

50ms/div

Fig. 8 Normal control process

VI. CONCLUSION

Adaptive control strategy of stable holding of intelligent electromagnetic based on hysteresis comparison tracking control technology, set up the double closed loop control system including contact state feedback, according to the electromagnetic switch ontology with specific design parameters, establish the key parameters of coil adjustment scheme, the control scheme of constant coil current in the holding process of intelligent electromagnetic switch is changed. And the electromagnetic switch can distinguish the current of contact in real time, and switch the coil current control mode quickly, so as to realize adaptive and stable holding of intelligent electromagnetic switch, realize the energy-saving operation of the electromagnetic switch while ensuring its reliable operation, it is of general significance to improve intelligent control and reliability of electromagnetic switch.

ACKNOWLEDGMENT

Project Supported by Funding program for leading talents in scientific and technological innovation of Fujian Province; Research Development Fund of Ningde Normal University (2016FZ14).

REFERENCES

[1] Zeng Yunwen. Principle and Application of Intelligent Low Voltage Apparatus [J]. Beijing Chemical Industry Press, 2015

[2] Tang Longfei, Xu Zhihong. Intelligent AC contactor self-correction control technology [J]. Proceedings of the Chinese Society of Electrical Engineering, 2015, 35(6): 1516-1523

[3] P. M. dos Santos Diasde Moraes and A. J. Perin, "An electronic control unit for reducing contact bounce in electromagnetic contactors," IEEE Trans. Ind. Electron., vol. 55, no. 2, pp. 861–870, Feb. 2008.

[4] Zhuang jierong, xu zhihong. Design of contactor control module based on boost chopper cascade [J]. Chinese journal of electrical engineering, 2016,36(15):4281-4291.

[5] Zhang haidong. Design and performance optimization of intelligent ac-dc vacuum contactor [D]. East China university of science and technology, 2017

[6] Zhuang jierong, xu zhihong. Study on multivariable feedback holding control strategy of electromagnetic contactor [J]. Chinese journal of electrical engineering, 2019,39(05):1516-1526.

[7] Tang longfei, xu zhihong. PID tuning of contactor slope controller [J]. Journal of nanchang university (engineering edition), 2017,39(04):404-408.

[8] Ji guoce, su xiuping, zhang youzi, qiao yan-hua. Research on electrodynamics of magnetic latching

relay [J]. Electric appliance and energy efficiency management technology, 2017(23):6-9.

[9] Xu zhihong. Theoretical basis of electrical appliances [J]. Beijing machinery industry press, 2014

[10] Luo haihai, xu zhihong. Analysis and design of digital control of ac contactor [J]. Journal of fuzhou university: natural science edition, 2015(5):636-641.

[11] Lin wengui, xu zhihong. Study on dynamic characteristics of the breaking process of a new single-pole electromagnetic switch [J]. Chinese journal of electrical engineering, 2017,37(06):1819-1828.

First Author, Binxin Zhang (1996-), is currently pursuing the M.S degree in the College of Electrical Engineering and Automation, Fuzhou University, China. His research interests is in the Electrical Appliances and Intelligent Technology.

Corresponding Author, Zhihong Xu (1963-), received her B.S, M.S and Ph.D. degrees from Fuzhou University, China, all with electrical engineering major. Since 1983, she works as a teacher in College of Electrical Engineering and Automation, Fuzhou University. And currently, she is a professor and a doctor tutor. She has involved in teach and research. Her research interests is in the Electrical Appliances and Intelligent Technology

7th International Conference on Reliability of
Electrical Products and Electrical Contacts,
November 04-06, 2019

Investigation of the Contact Welding Failure Phenomena in the Electrical Endurance Experiments

Wanbin Ren, Xu Zhang, Yide Cai, Zhe Zheng
School of Electrical Engineering and Automation, Harbin Institute of Technology, Harbin, 150001, China
E-mail: renwanbin@hit.edu.cn

Abstract—**Contact welding failure phenomena, always occurred in the electrical endurance test, can be the enormous obstacle for electromechanical relays with long electrical life and high reliability. Contact welding correlates with the mechanical switching process (including bounce, breaking velocity and contact force and so on) and electrical erosion of material closely. In this paper, the degradation process of static contact force, contact resistance and sliding distance of contacts under resistive load and inrush load in the electrical endurance experiments is compared explicitly. Combining with the SEM pictures of the failed contacts, the physical mechanism of contact welding is proposed. The in-situ simulation experiment method and conclusions are useful for the fault prediction of relays the optimization of contact materials.**

Index Terms— **Electromagnetic relay, Contact welding, electrical performance simulation, Failure reproduction, Failure analysis**

I. INTRODUCTION

Contact welding failure is commonly referred to the melting or semi-melting state of contacts, which could not break away with the elastic restoring force [1]. Contact welding could be divided into the static welding and the dynamic welding. The root reason of dynamic welding is arcing occurred in contact making or breaking. Ever published results and field data believe that the contact dynamic welding is the fatal and uncertain failure of electromagnetic relay [2,3]. Compared with other electromagnetic devices, the flexible spring structure of electromagnetic relay always leads to the obvious contact bounce, which could further generate the strong welding. In addition, the degradation of physical and chemical properties of contact materials used in electromagnetic relays are possible another reason of welding failure during the electrical endurance tests. Specially, either the inrush duty or the hermetically sealed housing could accelerate the electrical performance degradation of contact material and aggravate the probability of contact welding failure.

It is challengeable to reveal the contact welding phenomena and associate failure mechanisms of electromagnetic relay. Firstly, the limited space of real relay brings much difficulty for measuring the welding force. Secondly, the contact switching process included the strong coupled mechanical, electrical and thermal field, causes the modeling and solving with the use of traditional theoretical analysis method and finite element simulation technology is impracticable. So, the model switch concept is presented and adopted as the main experimental research and verification method [4-8]. The influence of mechanical parameters of switching devices and manufacturing process and methods of contact material in erosion performance evaluation could be investigated with such kind of model switch.

In order to guarantee the mechanical operation process provided by model switch similar with the practical switching device, an innovative test rig which allows for simulating contact mechanical operation and collecting electrical performance parameters during switching is presented in this paper. With the use of test rig, the multidimensional data (including bounce energy, contact resistance, static contact force, break arc energy), which could characterize the degradation process of relay and contact material, is collected and analyzed explicitly during the electrical endurance test.

In two previous papers by the present authors, the in situ observation and measurement test rig for electromagnetic relays and contactors is described in detail [9,10], and the degradation of electrical performance parameters of contact (including contact resistance, break arc energy, bounce energy and so on) is recorded explicitly and analyzed [11,12]. In this paper, the influences of contact gap and resistive, capacitive and lamp load on contact dynamic welding failure are investigated and compared. The possible physical mechanisms of contact welding failure are proposed.

II. EXPERIMENTAL DETAILS

In general, there are three main purposes and requirements of electrical performance simulation test for contact material, i.e.:

- The movement of contact should be similar with the original relay product utmost.
- Variable mechanical parameters (such as contact gap, free travel and actuation travel of pushing rod, pushing position of rod, over travel, etc.) to simulate different contact structure configurations.
- Synchronization of data with electromagnet actuation to allow real measurement of electrical performance parameters between two contacts (including break arc energy, bounce energy, welding force, contact resistance, contact temperature, etc.).

A schematic diagram of the test rig is shown in Fig.1. The horizontal actuation of the moving electrode is realized by a micro electromagnet connected with an insulated pushing rod. The movable contact is attached to the free end of the leaf spring (beryllium bronze strip). Mechanical parameters can be adjusted by multi-dimensional linear translation stage. The stationary contact is connected with the force sensor by the stationary strip. The optical module allows in situ observation of the contact surface morphology and associated sliding distance of making contacts. All the signals include contact voltage, contact current, coil current, image and dynamic force are acquired and uploaded to PC and processed by software specifically programmed for this purpose.

TABLE I

EXPERIMENTAL CONDITIONS

Environment	Ambient temperature
Operating Frequency	1.5s on/1.5s off
Contact Voltage/Current	DC28V/18A
Inrush Current	90A
Initial Contact Force	1.69N
Initial Contact Gap	0.3mm/0.4mm/0.6mm
Inrush Opening force	0.3N
Load Type	Resistive/Capacitive/Lamp

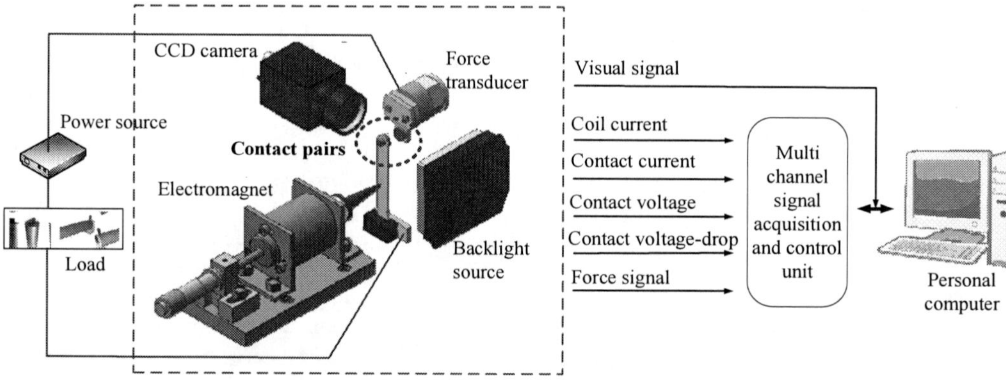

Fig. 1 Schematic of test rig

III. RESULTS AND DISCUSSION

A. *Effect of Contact Gap*

The variations in contact resistance of contact pair as a function of operation cycles for contact gap of 0.3mm, 0.4mm and 0.6mm are shown in Fig.2(a), (b) and (c), respectively. The electrical lifetime of contacts, which is defined as the operation cycles corresponding to the contacts occurred welding failure, is 9,975 times, 30,460 times and 51,954 times respectively for the contact gap of 0.3mm, 0.4mm and 0.6mm. There is a slight decrease in the contact resistance during electrical endurance experiment for these three cases, and there is a sharp upward trend before welding failure.

The variations in static force of contact pair as a function of operation cycles for contact gap of 0.3mm, 0.4mm and 0.6mm are shown in Fig.3(a), (b) and (c), respectively. The initial value is almost same as 1.69 N. After an initial rapid increment, the force remains going up with local fluctuation. Before welding failure, the raising trend is remarkable.

Fig.4 shows the initial contact status and the final contact status of contact pair. Taking the lower edge of static contact as the horizontal axis x and the contact interface as the vertical axis y, and then the cross-over point O is selected as the origin. For calculation, point C, is defined as the center of contact zone. So, OC_1 and OC_2 represent the initial and the final contact position within the contact surface separately. The coordinate difference between OC_1 and OC_2 is the measurement value of sliding distance.

The images of contact making process were recorded

every 1000 cycles during electrical endurance experiment. Fig.5 shows the variations in sliding distance of making contacts as a function of operation cycles for contact gap of 0.3mm, 0.4mm and 0.6mm respectively.

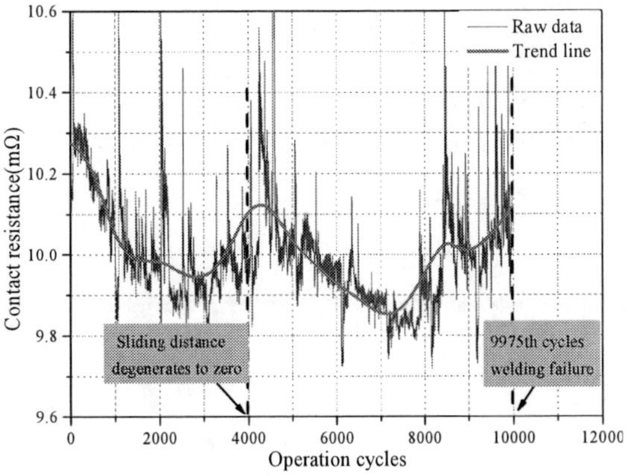

(a)

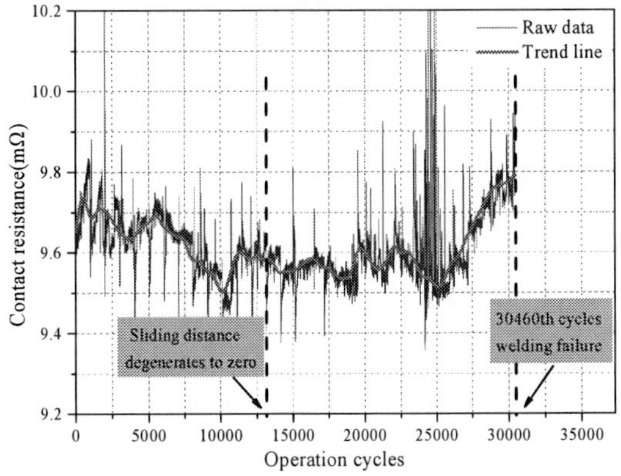

(b)

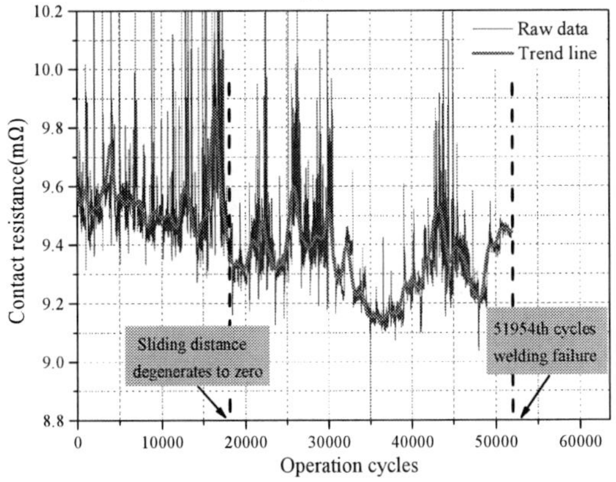

(c)

Fig. 2 Variations in contact resistance of contact pair as a function of operation cycles for different contact gap (E=28V, I=18A, I_{rush}=90A, C=2mF). (a) Contact gap is 0.3mm; (b) Contact gap is 0.4mm; (c) Contact gap is 0.6mm

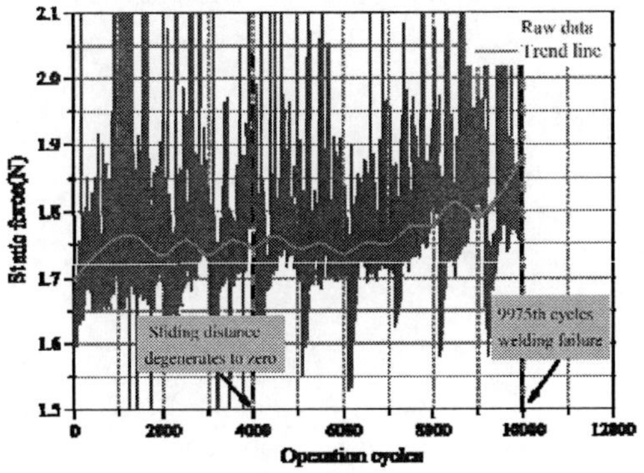

(a)

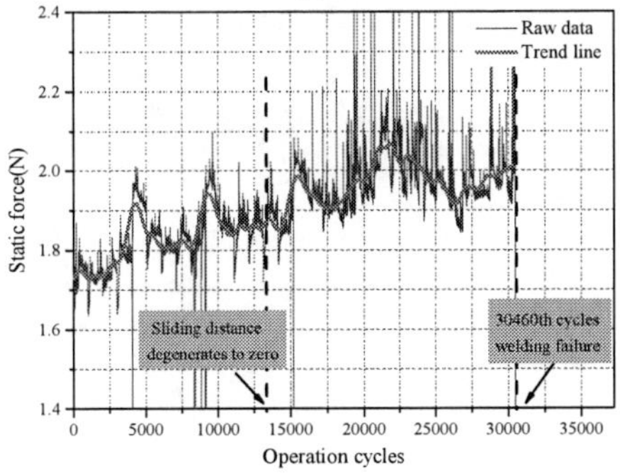

(b)

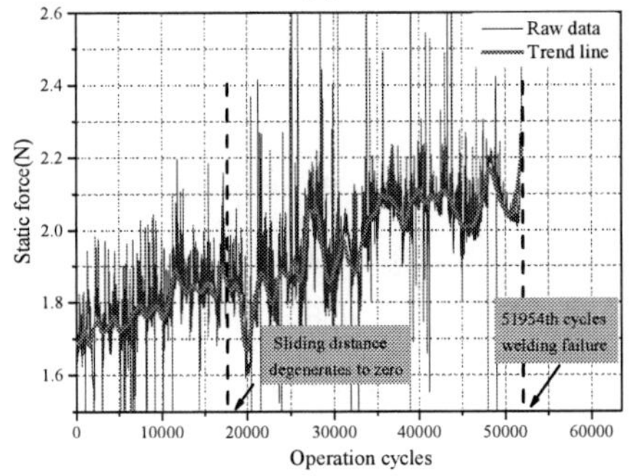

(c)

Fig. 3 Variations in static force of contact pair as a function of operation cycles for different contact gap (E=28V, I=18A, I_{rush}=90A, C=2mF) (a) Contact gap is 0.3mm; (b) Contact gap is 0.4mm; (c) Contact gap is 0.6mm

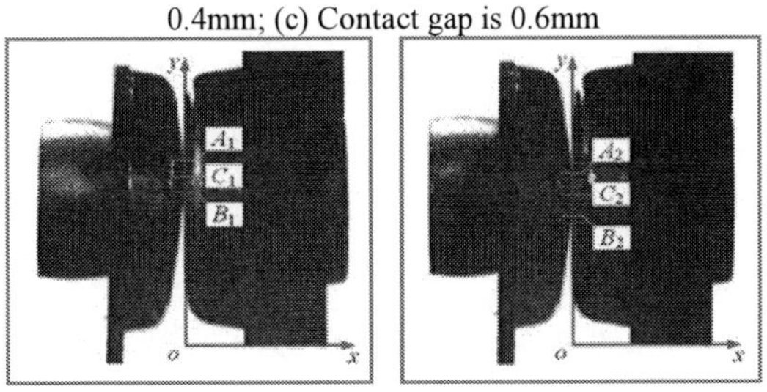

(a) (b)

Fig. 4 Pictures of contact pair obtained from CCD camera. (a) Initial contact status; (b) Final contact status

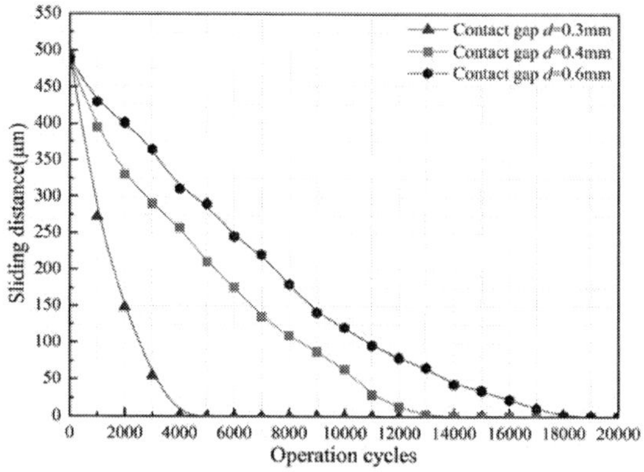

Fig. 5 The degradation curves of sliding distance of contact pairs during electrical endurance experiment

It is found that the initial sliding distance keeps almost same as 480μm in spite of different contact gap conditions. The critical operation cycles corresponding to the sliding distance reduced to zero is about 4000, 13000 and 18000 for the contact gap of 0.3mm, 0.4mm, 0.6mm. It should be noted that the degradation rate of sliding distance tends to slow down with the increase of contact gap, and the critical operation cycles are extended correspondingly. It indicates the disappearance of sliding distance is the prelude of contact welding failure. The electrical lifetime could be predicted directly with the help of sliding behavior information.

B. Effect of load type

It is known that contact breaking common resistive load results in the strong arc and associated material erosion, while contact making capacitive load or lamp load could produce the inrush current and more serious contact erosion. For simplicity, contact switching lamp load is equivalent to the combination of making capacitive load and breaking resistive load. In this experiment, the contact voltage is set as 28V, and the load resistance is 1.56Ω and the load capacitance is 2.5mF. So the steady contact current is 18A and the peak inrush current is 90A. The contact gap is set as 0.6mm.

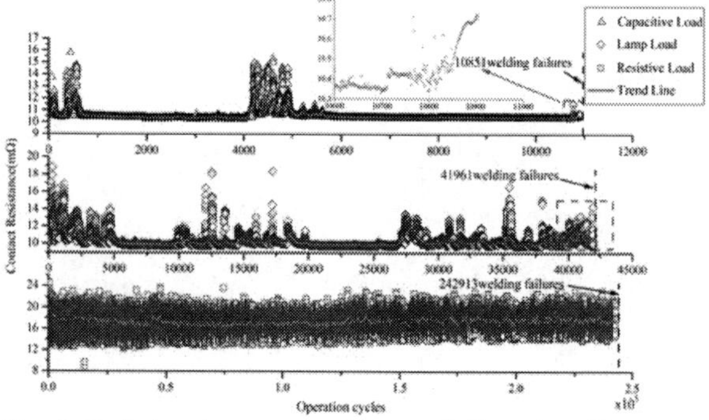

Fig. 6 Variations in contact resistance of silver tin oxide contact material as a function of operation cycles for different load types

Fig.6 shows the variations in contact resistance of silver tin oxide contact material as a function of operation cycles for different load types. The electrical lifetime of contacts is 242,913 times, 10,851 times and 41,961 times for resistive load, capacitive load and lamp load respectively. For capacitive and lamp loads, the contact resistance keeps a small value (below 11mΩ) for a long time, while it fluctuates greatly in the range of 12-24mΩ under the resistive load. However, the contact resistance increases sharply in the end of experiment for the inrush current load condition.

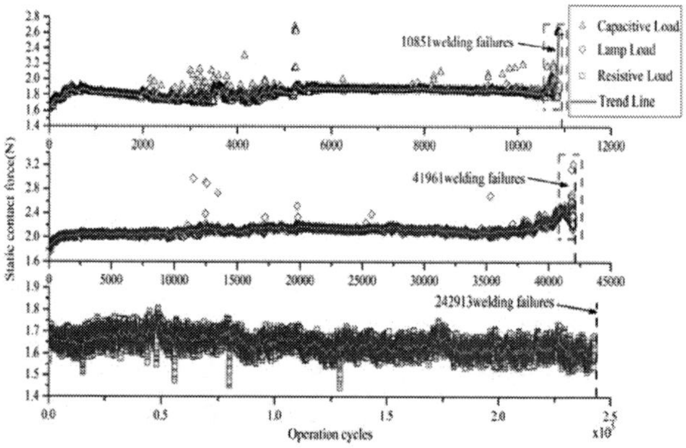

Fig. 7 Variations in static contact force of silver tin oxide contact material as a function of operation cycles for different load types

The variations in static contact force of silver tin oxide contact material as a function of operation cycles for different load types are shown in Fig.7. For capacitive and lamp loads, the static contact force increases significantly at the early stage due to the strong material transfer caused by the inrush current during the making process, and rises sharply before the contact welding failure occurs. But, there is no obvious change in the initial stage of experiment under the resistive load condition and tends to decrease with the increase of operation cycles. It is mainly attributed to the severe electrical erosion, such as surface metal evaporation and splashing occurred in contact breaking. By comparison, the capacitive load could result in the strongest contact welding strength and great possibilities. Just as above mentioned, the breaking arc could inhibit the contact dynamic welding phenomena, so the anti-welding ability of contact material in the lamp load condition is superior to the resistive load condition, but inferior to the capacitive load.

IV. SURFACE CHARACTERIZATION AND FAILURE MECHANISMS

Fig.8 shows the surface morphologies of welded contact pairs after electrical endurance experiments in the capacitive load. The arc erosion is mainly occurred at the center of the contact surface, which accounts for about half of the whole contact surface. There is an obvious fracture cross section and delamination layer in the pit center, which corresponding to the final welding zone.

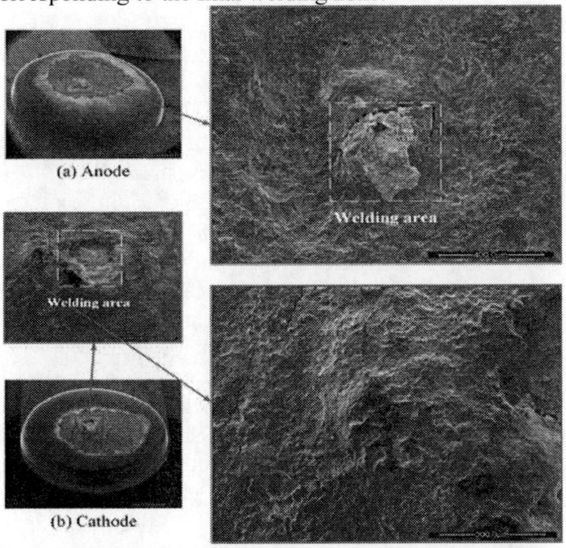

Fig. 8 SEM pictures of contact surfaces after electrical endurance test (Capacitive load)

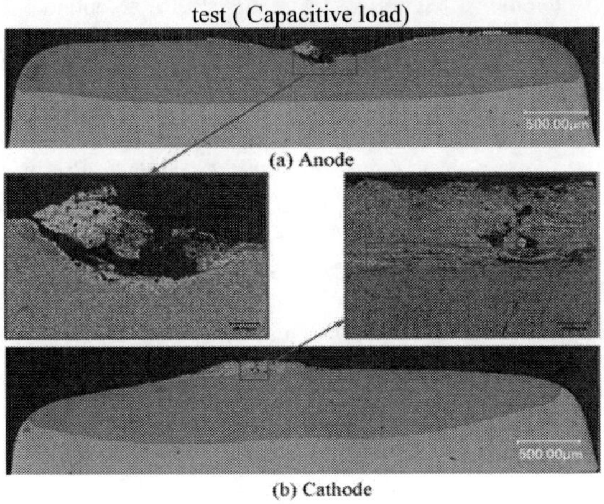

Fig. 9 Cross-section pictures of the contacts

As shown in Fig.9, the material on anode surface transfers to the cathode surface, forming a large pip on the anode surface and a clear crater is observed on the cathode surface. Material transfer is a gradual accumulation process, so the crater on the cathode surface presents a stacked and layered structure.

Metal melting caused by arc leads to the weakening of anti-welding ability of contacts. When contact bounce at making process, there are some small welding joints on the contacts. Fig.10 shows the force analysis of the contact making process with bounce. At the early stage of experiment, the anti-welding ability of contact material is excellent and the resultant force of the contact after impact can be expressed as $F=F_{impact}-F_{spring}$. However, when the weak welding occurs, as shown in Fig.10(b), the resultant force is rewritten as $F'=F_{impact}'-F_{spring}-F_{weld}$, F is smaller than F', and the traces of metal fracture begin to appear in the electrical erosion area of the contact.

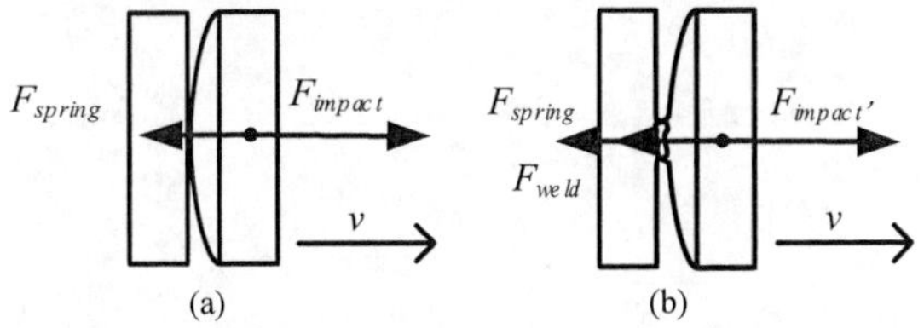

Fig. 10 Force analysis of contact pair. (a) Initial stage; (b) Final stage

These weak welding phenomena occur randomly at the later stage of the experiment. The anode arc caused by the bounce in making process leads the material transfer from anode to cathode. With the material consecutive accumulation on the cathode, the raised part of the surface frequently become the burning point of the bounce arc (as shown in Fig. 11(b)). Fig.12 shows the degradation process of contact surface. With the accumulation of materials, the contact gap decreases gradually and the static contact force rises slowly, as shown in Fig.7. The arc accelerates the oxidation of silver on the contact surface, which increases the contact resistance and agglomerates tin dioxide particles. This leads to the anti-welding ability of the material weak and the welding phenomenon occurs frequently. When a large number of metal materials are heated and melted by bounce arc during contact making process, and the height of this bounce is not enough to make the formed molten metal bridge broken. After contact bounce, the molten metal bridge cooling solidifies to form a strong nugget (as shown in the central part of Fig.8), and the contact welding failure occurs.

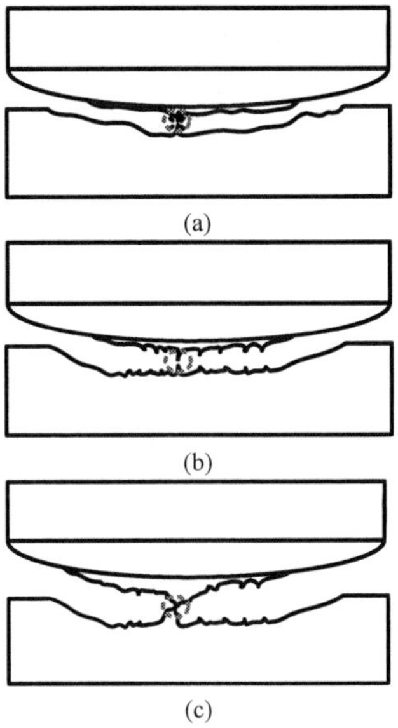

Fig. 11 Contact welding failure process. (a) Initial stage; (b) Middle stage; (c) Final stage

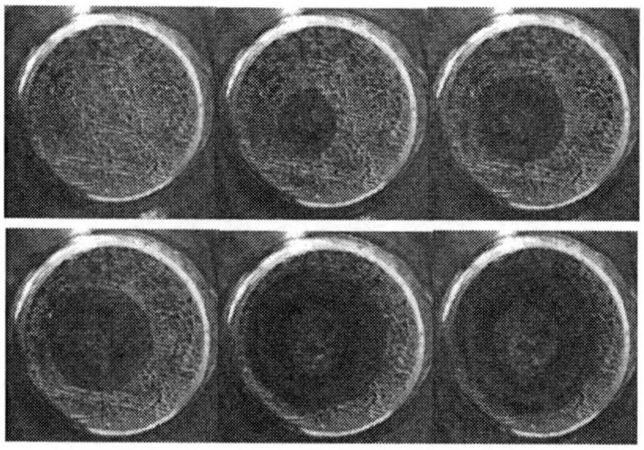

Fig. 12 The degradation process of contact surface

V. CONCLUSION

In this paper, the contact welding failure of silver tin oxide contact material is studied by using designed model switch during the electrical endurance test. It is found that increasing the contact gap is important to restrain the degeneration of the contact sliding distance and prolong the contact life. The time for contact welding failure increases from 10,851 to 41,961 and 242,913 for electric load type of capacitance, lamp and resistance, meanwhile the contact resistance and static contact force increase sharply under capacitive and lamp load conditions before welding failure. By analyzing the SEM images of welded contact surface, it is confirmed that melting, splashing, mass transfer and fracture of materials are the main reasons for the reduction of contact area, the increase of static contact force and the contact welding failure.

ACKNOWLEDGMENT

The authors express their gratitude for the kind support provided by The National Natural Science Foundation of China (Contract Number 51377029 and 51777039).

REFERENCES

[1] Ning Yuantao, Zhao Zhihuai. Silver. Central South University Press, 2005. (In Chinese)

[2] Zhuan-Ke CHEN, Gerald J. WITTER. Electrical contacts for automotive applications: A Review. IEICE TRANS. ELECTRON, 2004, E87-C(8):1248-1254.

[3] Wang Shujuan, Yu Qiong, Zhai Guofu. Discrimination Method of Contact Failure Mechanisms for Electromagnetic Apparatus. Transactions of China Electrotechnical Society, 2010, 25(8):38-44. (In Chinese)

[4] L. Morin, N. Ben Jemaa, D. Jeannot, et al. Make arc erosion and welding in the automotive area. Proceddings of the 45th IEEE Holm conference on electrical contacts, 1999:9-16.

[5] Zhuan-Ke Chen, G. Witter. Dynamic Welding of Silver Contacts under different mechanical bounce condition. Proceeding of 45th IEEE Holm conference on electrical contacts, 1999:1-8.

[6] Wanbin Ren, Jianbing Jin, Yinghua Fu, et al. A novel test rig for in situ real time measurement of welding force and impact force of contacts within electromagnetic relay. Proceedings of the 60th IEEE Holm conference on electrical contacts, 2014:389-395.

[7] Wanbin Ren, Jianbin Jin, Dan Li, et al. Design and Application of a Novel Test Rig for Simulating and Evaluating Electric Arc and Electrical Contact Characteristics of Contact Materials. Electrical Engineering Materials. 2014, (4):28-32+37. (In Chinese)

[8] Clemens Schrank, Alaxander R. Neuhaus. The influence of different atmospheres on arc width, arc modility, and contact welding investigated for low power switches. Proceeding of 53rd IEEE Holm conference on electrical contacts, 2007:130-133.

[9] Jianmin Wei, Yuan He, Wanbin Ren, et al. Preliminary Study on the Dynamic Welding Characteristics of Contacts within Relay. Electrical and Energy Management Technology. 2016, (1):22-26+70. (In Chinese)

[10] Wanbin Ren, Yinwei Du, Da Mansi. A Test Rig for Simulating the Electrical Performance of Contact Materials Used in AC Contactor. Electrical and Energy Management Technology. 2016, (7):12-16. (In Chinese)

[11] Wanbin Ren, Jianmin Wei, Xu Zhang, et al. Priliminary study on switching characteristics of silver tin oxide type contacts for capacitive load. Proceedings of the 63rd IEEE Holm conference on electrical contacts. 2017,63-68.

[12] Wanbin Ren, Tengyu Wang, Xu Zhang, et al. Research on the Rolling and Sliding Behavior of Making Contact and Associated Welding Mechanism for Low-Current Switching Devices. IEEE Transactions on Components, Packaging and Manufacturing Technology. 2019, 9(1):18-27.

Study on the Effect of Different Sn/In Ratio on the Properties of $AgSnO_2In_2O_3$ Electrical Contact Material

Jie Li, Xiaofang Yan, Xiaoping Bai, Yangfang Chen, Linyun Song,
Xiangfen Lu, Changlin Yang, Xiufang Zhang
Fuda Alloy Materials Co., Ltd., Wenzhou, Zhejiang, 325025,China
E-mail: lijie821016@163.com Tel: 86-18357800054 Fax: 86-577-86909166

***Abstract*—$AgSnO_2In_2O_3$ electric contact material has high anti material transfer and excellent anti welding properties. It is widely used in high voltage DC relay of electric vehicles., automobile relay, magnetic retaining relay of intelligent meter, and other fields. In this paper, the effect of different Sn/In ratios (1.2, 1.8, 2.4, 3.0) on mechanical, physical and electrical properties of $AgSnO_2In_2O_3$ electrical contact materials were investigated. It is concluded that with the increase of Sn/In ratios, the tensile strength, hardness and resistivity of $AgSnO_2In_2O_3$ materials increased gradually, while the density and elongation decreased gradually. When the Sn/In ratio is 2.4, the material has the lowest arc energy, the shortest arc time, the lowest welding power and the best electric life in Weibull distribution 95% confidence interval under the condition of simulating electrical performance of DC inductive load (24V, 15A, 1mH, 1s on 1s off. When the ratio of Sn/In is less than 2.4, the number of oxides was less and the anti-weldability of the material was poorer. When the ratio of Sn/In is more than 2.4, the number of oxides was larger, the contact resistance during the electrical performance test results in the increase of contact temperature and obvious material transfer phenomenon took place in contact working face, which leads to failure. It is expected to provide important reference for the development and design of high performance $AgSnO_2In_2O_3$ electrical contact materials.**

Keywords—Electrical contact material, $AgSnO_2In_2O_3$, Sn/In ratio, Welding resistance

I. INTRODUCTION

Tin oxide has good brittleness and thermal stability, therefore it is difficult to decompose when it is subjected to arc. Tin oxide can remain on the contact surface even after multiple arc action. When the arc is extinguished, the molten metal on the contact surface cools and solidifies rapidly due to the decrease of temperature, which may lead to the welding phenomenon of the contact. However, the existence of brittle SnO_2 particles makes the welding force decreases greatly, which is beneficial to breaking off, therefore the silver tin oxide electrical contact material exhibits excellent and stable welding resistance [1-2]. Meanwhile, $AgSnO_2In_2O_3$ has been widely used in high voltage DC relay, automobile relay, intelligent meter magnetic retaining relay, sealed power relay and other fields because of its high internal oxidation rate promoted by the addition of indium and excellent arc burning resistance and ani welding resistance.

Many scholars have studied $AgSnO_2In_2O_3$ electrical contact materials [3-8]. Literature [3] studied the effect of different In content on the mechanical and electrical properties of $AgSnO_2In_2O_3$ electrical contact material, and it was concluded that when In content was 5.5%, the anti welding performance of the electrical contact material showed the best. Literature [5] investigated the internal oxidation mechanism of AgSn6In3, and grain size played little important in the dynamics of internal oxidation microstructures. Literature [6] studied the effect of Cu on internal oxidation mechanism of AgSnIn. However, the effects of different Sn/In ratios on the mechanical and electrical properties of electrical contact materials have not been reported in the literature systematically.

In this paper, the effects of different Sn/In ratios on the electrical contact properties of $AgSnO_2In_2O_3$ are investigated. It is expected to provide important reference for the development and design of high performance $AgSnO_2In_2O_3$ electrical contact materials.

II. MATERIALS AND TEST METHODS

A. Materials

The different Sn/In ratios (1.2, 1.8, 2.4, 3.0) of $AgSnO_2In_2O_3$ electrical contact materials were prepared by internal oxidation process. The specific material composition is shown in Table 1, and the content of additives was 1%.

TABLE 1

COMPOSITION OF DIFFERENT SN/IN RATIO MATERIALS

Serial number	Sn/In Ratio	Component content (wt.%)				Note
		Ag	Sn	In	Additives	
1	1.2	90	4	3.3	1	
2	1.8	88	5.67	3.15	1	
3	2.4	86	7.32	3.05	1	
4	3.0	84	9	3	1	

B. Electrical Performance Testing Equipment, Parameters and Analysis Method

The above wire was made into rivets by cold heading machine. The specifications of movable and static contacts were both R3x0.5(0.25)+1.5x1.2SR15. Then the electrical performance simulated test was carried out on the self-made electrical contact material performance simulated test device. The device were mainly composed of industrial control computer, software, chassis and contact action simulated device. The schematic diagram is shown in Figure 1. The parameters such as arc energy, arc time and welding force can be obtained by simulating the action of contacts, which could meet the test requirements of electrical performance simulation, providing important reference for the development and design of electrical contact materials.

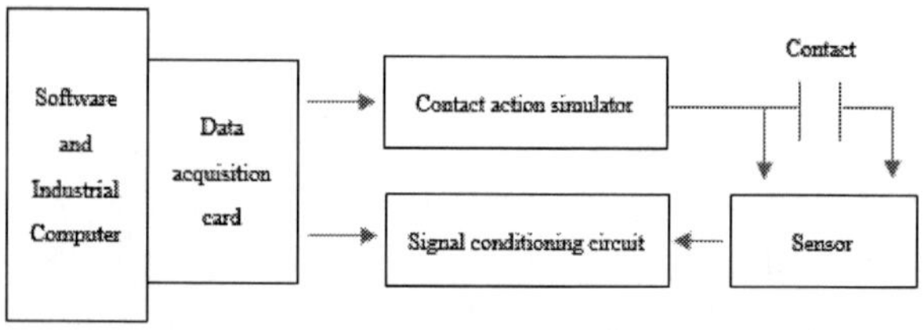

Fig. 1 Structural schematic diagram of electrical performance simulated device

Fig. 2 shows the schematic diagram of the contact action device. The displacement control ruler controls the relative distance between the static and moving contacts. Then the power amplifier circuit receives the analog voltage from the data acquisition card to amplify and drive the electromagnetic exciter to complete the contact action. After that, the electromagnetic exciter receives the current signal from the power amplifier to drive the contacts to move.

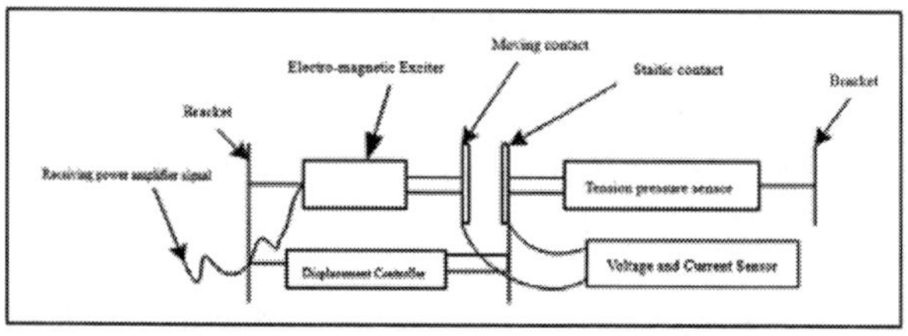

Fig. 2 Schematic diagram of contact action device

When the contacts were separated under the pulling force of the electromagnetic exciter, the tension pressure sensor which was installed on the static contact can collect the welding force. Meanwhile, the peak signal of the tension pressure sensor can be saved through the peak holding circuit by controlling the slow motion of the electromagnetic exciter, and then transmitted to the computer through the data acquisition card to obtain the welding force.

The occurrence and ending of arc can be judged by voltage sensor and current sensor together. In this interval, arc time can be obtained by counting with timer. In the arc time, the arc energy can be obtained by the product of contact voltage and current.

The contacts of the four materials were tested by simulating electrical properties, and five groups were tested seperately. The test condition is shown in Table 2. Scanning electron microscopy (SEM) was used to observe the surface morphology of the contact and to analyze the micro-area composition.

TABLE 2

SPECIFIC TEST PARAMETERS FOR ELECTRICAL PERFORMANCE

Load Type	Voltage (V)	Current (A)	On-Off Frequency	Inductance	Number of times (times)	Failure determination
Inductive load	24V	15A	1s on 1s off	1mH	until failure	Welding force exceeds 40g for five consecutive times

III. TEST RESULTS AND ANALYSIS

In this paper, different Sn/In ratios (1.2, 1.8, 2.4, 3.0) of $AgSnO_2In_2O_3$ electrical contact materials have been prepared. Table 3 shows the effects of different Sn/In ratios on the mechanical and physical properties of $AgSnO_2In_2O_3$ contact materials. It can be seen that as the increase of Sn/In ratios, hardness, tensile strength and electrical resistivity increased gradually, while the elongation and density decreased.

As the increase of Sn/In ratio, the silver content decreased, the oxide content increases and the strengthening effect of oxide particles increased, therefore the hardness and tensile strength increased gradually and the elongation decreased gradually. The silver content decreased gradually, and the resistivity of oxide is higher than that of silver, so the resistivity increased gradually. The density of the oxide is higher than the density of the oxide (the density of Ag, SnO_2, In_2O_3 are 10.5g/cm^3, 6.95 g/cm^3 and 7.18 g/cm^3, respectively), therefore, as the increase of Sn/In ratio, the density decreased gradually.

TABLE 3

EFFECT OF SN/IN RATIO ON MECHANICAL AND PHYSICAL PROPERTIES OF $AgSnO_2In_2O_3$ ELECTRICAL CONTACT MATERIALS

Number	Sn/In Ratio	Hardness				Tensile Strength (MPa)	Elongation (%)	Electrical Resistivity (μΩ·cm)	Density (g/cm³)	Note
		Data 1	Data 2	Data 3	Average value					
1	1.2	94.2	93.5	92.8	93.5	300	27	2.14	9.9	
2	1.8	99.6	97.0	99.3	98.6	316	25	2.23	9.82	
3	2.4	101	98.9	102	100.6	335	23	2.36	9.76	
4	3.0	103	100	104	102.3	347	21	2.54	9.54	

Fig. 3 shows the microstructures of different Sn/In ratios of electrical contact materials (200x). It can be seen that the number of oxide particles increased as the increase of Sn/In ratios. When Sn/In=3.0, the number of oxide particles was the largest, and the size of oxide particles was bigger than the other three materials. The reason is that As the Sn/In ratio decreased, especially when Sn/In ratio=3.0, the rate of internal oxidation was the lowest in the process of internal oxidation, which made the size of oxide particles grow up.

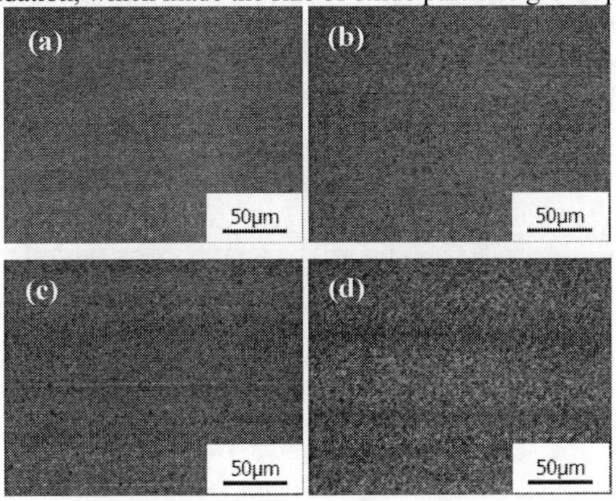

Fig. 3 Microstructure of Different Sn/In of Electrical Contact Materials (200x)(a)Sn/In=1.2 (b)Sn/In=1.8 (c)Sn/In=2.4 (d)Sn/In=3.0

Different Sn/In ratio of electrical contact materials were made into rivet, and then simulated electrical performance tests were carried out on self-made simulated electrical performance test equipment. The materials with different Sn/In ratios were tested in five groups. Fig. 4 and Table 4 are the weibull curve electrical life diagram and 95% confidence interval electrical life of different Sn/In ratio of electrical contact materials. It can be seen that when Sn/In ratio =2.4, the electrical life was the lowest. As the increase of Sn/In ratio, the 95% confidence interval number of electrical life times increased first and then decreased, and reached maximum when Sn/In ratio=2.4 (the maximum was 104,400 times).

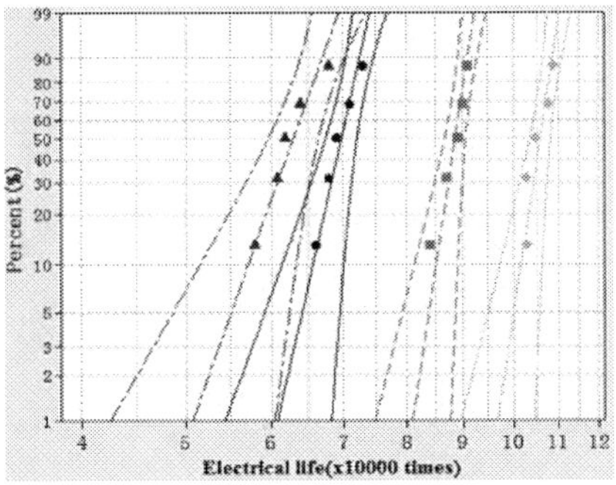

Fig. 4 Weibull Curves of Electrical Life of Different Sn/In Specific Electrical Contact Materials

TABLE 4

ELECTRICAL LIFE TIMES OF DIFFERENT SN/IN ELECTRICAL CONTACT MATERIALS (95% CONFIDENCE INTERVAL)

Sn/In Ratio	1.2	1.8	2.4	3.0
95% confidence interval electrical life times (x 10,000 times)	7.31	9.14	10.94	6.79

At the same time, the arc energy, arc time, welding force and contact resistance of different Sn/In ratio electrical contact materials were monitored by simulated electrical performance device. The average arc energy is shown in Table 5. It can be seen that as the increase of Sn/In ratio, arc energy, arc time, welding force and contact resistance decreased first and then increased. When Sn/In ratio =2.4, arc energy, arc time, welding force and contact resistance were the smallest, the number were 1547 mJ, 15ms, 12g and 14m, respectively.

TABLE 5

ARC ENERGY, ARC TIME, WELDING FORCE AND CONTACT RESISTANCE OF DIFFERENT SN/IN SPECIFIC ELECTRICAL CONTACT MATERIALS

Number	Sn/In ratio	Average Arc Energy (mJ)	Average arcing time (ms)	Average Welding Force (g)	Average Contact Resistance (mΩ)	Note
1	1.2	2135	25	21	15	
2	1.8	1825	24	17	18	
3	2.4	1547	15	12	14	
4	3.0	1698	18	23	25	

Fig. 5 shows the surface morphology of different Sn/In ratios of electrical contact materials after testing. It can be seen that when Sn/In ratio=1.2, contacts life time was 71,000 times and the movable and static contacts were burned obviously. What's more, the "roll-up" was formed by arc erosion and pressure, which was the main reason of contact failure, as shown in Fig. 5(a). When Sn/In ratio=1.8, contacts life time was almost 90,000 times, and obvious silver bags appeared at the edge of static contact, as shown in figure 5(d). When Sn/In ratio=2.4, contacts life time was 105,000 times, and obvious silver bags appeared at the edge of moving contact, as shown in figure 5€. When Sn/In ratio =3.0, contacts life time was 64,000 times, phenomenon of material transfer occurred obviously, which was from static point to moving point, as shown in Fig. 5 (g) and (h).

When Sn/In ratio =1.2, due to the low content of oxide particles (10% oxide content) and the poor weldability of the material, electrical life times was low. As the increase of Sn/In ratio, the content of oxide increased (12% and 14% respectively when Sn/In ratio =1.8 and 2.4), the weldability of the material increased, and the number of electrical life times reached the maximum when Sn/In ratio =2.4. While Sn/In ratio =3.0, the oxide content was 16%, and the contact resistance increased rapidly (the average contact resistance reaches 25 mΩ), which led to serious heating of contacts and material transfer phenomenon.

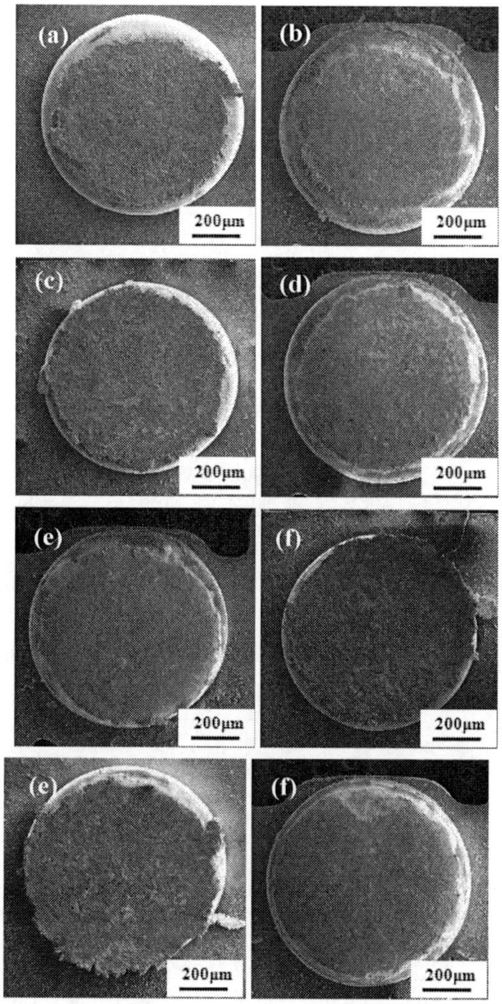

Fig. 5 Surface Morphology of Different Sn/In Specific Electrical Contact Materials after Testing (Scanning Electron Microscope)

(a) Sn/In ratio =1.2, 71000 times, moving contact
(b) Sn/In ratio =1.2, 71000 times, static contact
(c) Sn/In ratio =1.8, 90000 times, moving contact
(d) Sn/In ratio =1.8, 90000 times, static contact
(e) Sn/In ratio =2.4, 105000 times, moving contact
(f) Sn/In ratio =2.4, 105000 times, static contact
(g) Sn/In ratio =3, 64000 times, moving contact
(h) Sn/In ratio =2.4, 64000 times, static contact

IV. CONCLUSION

(1) As the increase of Sn/In ratio, the tensile strength, hardness and electrical resistivity of the material increased gradually, while the density and elongation decreased gradually.

(2) When the Sn/In ratio is 2.4, the material has the lowest arc energy, the shortest arc time, the lowest welding force and the longest electric life in the 95% confidence interval of Weibull distribution under the condition of simulated electrical performance of DC inductive load (24V, 15A, 1mH, 1s through 1s off).

(3) When the Sn/In ratio is less than 2.4, the number of oxides is small and the anti-fusion welding performance of materials is poor; when the Sn/In ratio is more than 2.4, the number of oxides is large. The contact resistance during the electrical performance test results in the increase of contact temperature, and the obvious material transfer phenomenon occurs in the contact working face leading to failure.

REFERENCES

[1] Y. C. Zhu, H. T. Wang, J. Zhao. The preparation methods and research progress of nano-$AgSnO_2$ electrical contact materials in low voltage electrical appliances[J]. Low voltage electrical apparatus ,2015(4):1-5.

[2] Y. C. Liu, M. Xie, J. M. Zhang, J. K. Yan, J. H. Du, G. Y. Gan, J. H. Yi. The summary of preparation methods of silver tin oxide electrical contact materials[J]. Material Report, 2013(10): 60-64.

[3] J. Li, W. Weng, X. P. Bai, X.f. Yan, H. Wang, L. Q. Liu, L. Zhou. Study on the effect of different indium content on arc erosion performance of AgSnO2 contacts under simulated automobile relay conditions [J]. Electrical appliances and energy efficiency management technology, 2016(3): 22-26.

[4] J. Li, X. F. Yan, X. P. Bai, L.Q. Liu, S. H. Li, W. Weng. Effect of different In contents on hardness and microstructure of AgSnIn alloy during internal oxidation[J], The Institute of Electronics, Information and Communication Engineers Technical Report, 2013[C], 113(298): 95-98.

[5] A. Verma, T.R. Anantharaman. Internal oxidation of rapidly solidified solver-tin-indium alloy powders, Journal of Materials Science [J], 1992(27): 5623-5628.

[6] G. Schimmel, B. Kempf, M. Rettenmayr. Exudation of Ag and Cu In Internal lyoxidized Ag-Sn-In-(Cu) Alloys. Material Letters [J], 2009:1521-1524.

[7] X. Yang, Q. Y. Han, C. C. Liu. Cause Analysis and Counter measure of Contact Wear of Automotive Relay[J]. Journal of Hubei Automotive Industries Institute, 2004(18): 9-12.

[8] J. Li, X.F. Yan, X.P. Bai, F. Lu, L. Q. Liu, W. Weng, S.H. Li. Effect of AgSn Alloy Powder Size on Preoxidation Microstructure [J]. Electrical materials, 2013(3): 10-13.

7th International Conference on Reliability of Electrical Products and Electrical Contacts, November 04-06, 2019

A Study of Passive Intermodulation in Degraded Coaxial Connectors

Lingyu Bi[1], Jinchun Gao[1], Qiuyan Jin[1], Gang Xie[1], Xiaoming Li[2]
[1]Beijing University of Posts and Telecommunications, Beijing 100876, China
[2]The 54th Research Institute of CETC, Shijiazhuang, Hebei 050081, China
E-mail: gjc@bupt.edu.cn

***Abstract*—Coaxial connectors generally have slight nonlinear characteristics. The nonlinearity of connectors can cause passive intermodulation (PIM) interference. The connectors will degrade continuously during use, which will aggravate the PIM interference and affect the transmission quality of communication systems. In this paper, a nonlinear behavior model and a prediction model of third-order intermodulation product power of pristine connectors are obtained first. The contact resistance is selected as the index to quantify the degradation degree of the connectors, then the prediction model of third-order intermodulation product power for connectors with various degrees of degradation is developed for the first time. A series of PIM tests are conducted to verify the correctness of the model. This paper provides a theoretical basis for predicting the PIM of degraded coaxial connectors.**

***Index Terms*—Coaxial connector, degradation, nonlinear characteristics, passive intermodulation.**

I. INTRODUCTION

Passive intermodulation (PIM) refers to the generation of harmonics in the output signal when two or more frequencies are input into a passive device. These harmonics may fall into the receiving frequency bands, which has a non-negligible negative impact on communication system quality. Coaxial connectors generally have nonlinear characteristics even though they are pristine. The nonlinearity of connectors can cause PIM interference. Besides, coaxial connectors will degrade due to the harsh work environment, which will make their nonlinear characteristics more serious and aggravate the PIM interference. Therefore, the PIM interference and coaxial connector degradation have attracted widespread attention and research interest. Henrie *et al.* [1], [2] developed a circuit model enabling estimation of PIM interference in coaxial connectors in high-frequency networks. Jin *et al.* [3], [4] used microscopic surface analysis and macroscopic nonlinear models to provide explanations for PIM characteristic. Kozlov *et al.* [5] investigated the PIM generated by analog and digital signals on transmission lines with distributes nonlinearities. Chen *et al.* [6] proposed a novel PIM prediction method considering random contact behavior for coaxial connects. In addition, Ji *et al.* [7], [8] studied the impact of the degradation of coaxial connector on its high-frequency behaviors. Significant conclusions on PIM and coaxial connector degradation are well summarized by these studies, but less is known about the nonlinear characteristics and PIM of coaxial connectors with various degrees of degradation.

In this paper, a nonlinear behavior model and a prediction model of third-order intermodulation product power of pristine connectors are obtained first. On this basis, a new polynomial behavior model is developed for the first time to describe the nonlinear characteristics of various levels of degraded connectors. Then the prediction model of third-order intermodulation product power of degraded connectors is derived. A series of experiments were conducted to verify the correctness of the model. The details of this work and some conclusions are described in the following sections.

II. PIM ANALYSIS ON PRISTINE CONNECTORS

A. Model Establishment

The nonlinearity of coaxial connectors arises from a variety of complex influencing factors, such as the skin effect and the magnetic hysteresis effect. Accordingly, it is very difficult to develop an accurate physical model taking all these factors into account. An alternative approach is to employ an empirical "current-voltage" polynomial model to describe the nonlinear behavior of coaxial connectors, as shown in (1).

$$i_{out} = \sum_{n=1}^{M} a_n v^n \tag{1}$$

where i_{out} is the current of the output signal through the connectors, v is the input signal voltage, and a_n (n=1, 2, ..., M) are the coefficients of polynomial model. M represents the number of terms retained in the polynomial model.

The frequencies of odd harmonics are relatively closer to the fundamental frequency than those of even harmonics, then only odd terms need to be retained. The first term, a_1v, is the linear term which can be ignored, then the model (1) can be simplified to (2).

$$i^*_{out} = \sum_{n=1}^{M} a_{2n+1} v^{2n+1} \quad (2)$$

where i^*_{out} is the nonlinear output signal current, a_{2n+1} (n=1, 2,..., M) are the coefficients of polynomial model.

Two-tone PIM test is a standard PIM test method. As a result, the two-tone continuous wave (CW) signal used in two-tone PIM test is taken into consideration. The voltage v_1 of this signal is represented in (3).

$$v_1 = V[\cos(\omega_1 t) + \cos(\omega_2 t)] \quad (3)$$

where V is the voltage amplitude of the carriers, ω_1 and ω_2 are the angular frequencies of the carriers, and t is the independent variable represented for time.

The nonlinear output signal current $i_{out,1}$ can be calculated by substituting (3) into (2):

$$i_{out,1} = \sum_{n=1}^{M} a_{2n+1} V^{2n+1} [\cos(\omega_1 t) + \cos(\omega_2 t)]^{2n+1} \quad (4)$$

According to the binomial theorem,

$$[\cos(\omega_1 t) + \cos(\omega_2 t)]^{2n+1} = \sum_{k=0}^{2n+1} C_{2n+1}^{k} \cos^{2n+1-k}(\omega_1 t)\cos^{k}(\omega_2 t) \quad (5)$$

The third-order PIM product typically has the greatest power among all harmonics and it is most likely to fall into the receiver band, so it is mainly considered in this paper. Only when $2n+1-k \geq 2$ and k is odd simultaneously, $cos^{2n+1-k}(\omega_1 t)cos^{k}(\omega_2 t)$ can produce the third-order PIM term whose frequency is $(2\omega_1\text{-}\omega_2)$. Extracting the terms that meet the requirements above in (5) and expressing them as $A_{n,1}$:

$$A_{n,1} = \sum_{k=1}^{n} C_{2n+1}^{2k-1} \cos^{2n+2-2k}(\omega_1 t)\cos^{2k-1}(\omega_2 t) \quad (6)$$

According to the product-to-sum identity of trigonometric functions,

$$\cos(\omega_1 t)\cos(\omega_2 t) = \frac{1}{2}[\cos(\omega_1 + \omega_2)t + \cos(\omega_1 - \omega_2)t] \quad (7)$$

For $\cos^{2n+2-2k}(\omega_1 t)\cos^{2k-1}(\omega_2 t)$, the term whose frequency is $(2\omega_1\text{-}\omega_2)$ can obtained by picking $(n\text{-}k)$ negative $(\omega_1 t)$ in $\cos^{2n+2-2k}(\omega_1 t)$ and picking k negative $(\omega_2 t)$ in $\cos^{2k-1}(\omega_2 t)$. The product-to-sum identity of trigonometric function is applied for $2n$ times, then the coefficient $b_{n,1}$ of the term whose frequency is $(2\omega_1\text{-}\omega_2)$ in (6) can be calculated as:

$$b_{n,1} = \frac{1}{4^n} \sum_{k=1}^{n} C_{2n+1}^{2k-1} C_{2n+2-2k}^{n-k} C_{2k-1}^{k} \quad (8)$$

Accordingly, the third-order PIM term P in $i_{out,1}$ can be expressed as:

$$P = \left(\sum_{n=1}^{M} \frac{a_{2n+1} V^{2n+1}}{4^n} \sum_{k=1}^{n} C_{2n+1}^{2k-1} C_{2n+2-2k}^{n-k} C_{2k-1}^{k}\right)\cos[(2\omega_1 - \omega_2)t] \quad (9)$$

B. Coefficient Obtainment

There is a question that should be considered is how many terms should be retained for providing an adequate model of the nonlinear behavior. Various investigators have taken different approaches. A polynomial model was retained to the forty-ninth order in an earlier work by Henrie *et al.* [1]. However, that would seem excessive for the current study. The differences of retaining the polynomial model to the third order, the fifth order and the seventh order were discussed by Jin *et al.* [3]. Based upon a series of tests, it was found that retaining terms up to the seventh order is sufficient to adequately capture the nonlinear behavior in the present study. Accordingly, the model as shown in (10) will be used for this current study.

$$i^{\#}_{out} = a_3 v^3 + a_5 v^5 + a_7 v^7 \quad (10)$$

where $i^{\#}_{out}$ is the nonlinear output signal current.

Let M equal to 3 in (9), then the third-order PIM term P_1 can be expressed as:

$$P_1 = \left(\frac{3}{4}a_3 V^3 + \frac{25}{8}a_5 V^5 + \frac{735}{64}a_7 V^7\right)\cos[(2\omega_1 - \omega_2)t] \quad (11)$$

The coefficients of the polynomial model can be obtained by curve fitting of the two-tone PIM test results and a series of calculations. A series of two-tone PIM tests are conducted to measure the third-order PIM product power using an *rFlight* NTPIM-900B PIM distortion analyzer. Five pristine male-to-female and female-to-female N-type connector pairs from the same factory are selected to be the devices under test (DUTs) in the experiments. The photographs of connector samples are shown in Fig. 1.

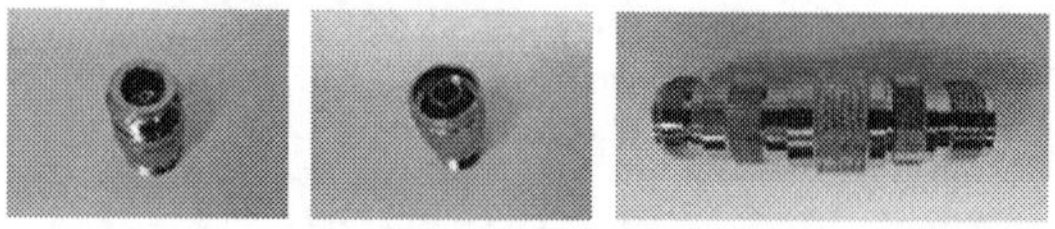

(a) (b) (c)

Fig. 1 Photographs of (a) a female-to-female connector, (b) a male-to-female connector, and (c) a pair of N-type coaxial connector.

The input powers of the two carriers are configured to increase from 35dBm to 44dBm simultaneously. The frequencies of the two carriers are f_1=935MHz and f_2=960MHz, respectively. The measured third-order PIM product is at the frequency of f_{IM3}=910MHz. Based on the observations, the nonlinearity of a connector is stationary in 900MHz frequency band. The individual differences between five samples are less than 3dB at any input power. This modest variation in the individual performance of these DUTs is assumed to be insignificant and the average result of the five samples is taken to be the standard experimental result. The input power is converted into voltage and the standard result of the output third-order PIM product power is converted into current, then the output third-order PIM product current is fitted, as shown in Fig. 2.

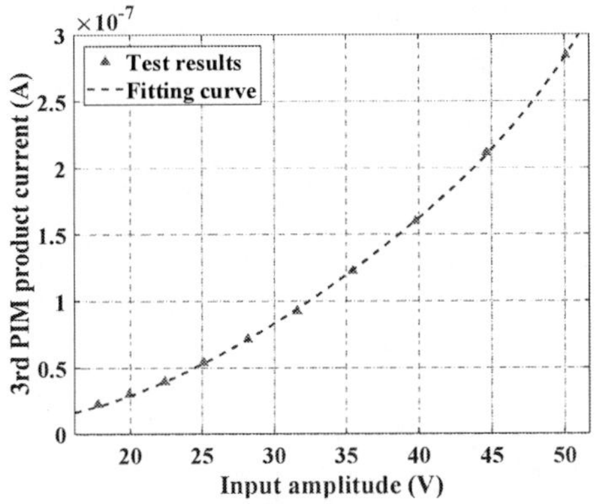

Fig. 2 Test results and fitting curve.

The equation of the resulting curve is:

$$I_{IM3} = 4.177\times10^{-12}V^3 - 1.494\times10^{-15}V^5 + 2.905\times10^{-19}V^7 \quad (12)$$

where I_{IM3} is the current amplitude of the third-order PIM product, V is the voltage amplitude of the carriers.

It can be seen in Fig. 2 that the fitting is quite good. By retaining terms up to seventh order, the chosen polynomial model retains enough terms to adequately capture the nonlinear behavior.

By comparing (11) and (12), the coefficients of the polynomial model can be obtained as:

$$\begin{cases} a_3 = 5.569\times10^{-12} \\ a_5 = -4.781\times10^{-16} \\ a_7 = 2.530\times10^{-20} \end{cases} \quad (13)$$

Then the coefficients are substituted into (10) and the polynomial model describing the nonlinear behavior of the sample coaxial connectors can be expressed as:

$$i_{out}^{\#} = 5.569\times10^{-12}v^3 - 4.781\times10^{-16}v^5 + 2.530\times10^{-20}v^7 \quad (14)$$

III. PIM ANALYSIS ON DEGRADED CONNECTORS

Due to the harsh work environment in mobile communication base stations, maritime communication, and satellite communication, coaxial connectors will degrade to various degrees. A series of accelerated degradation tests are designed and performed to produce degraded connectors in order to investigate the nonlinear behavior of coaxial connectors of various degradation degrees. In addition to the five pairs of connectors used in the above, ten pairs of pristine connectors are selected as samples. These fifteen pairs of connectors are from the same factory.

The accelerated degradation tests are performed using nitric acid vapor. The concentration of the nitric acid is 69%. During the accelerated degradation tests, only the pin of the male-to-female N-type connector is contaminated by the acid, the receptacle of the male-to-female connector is protected with a rubber casing and anticorrosion tape. Then the degraded male-to-female connector is connected to a pristine female-to-female connector. This connector pair can be used to investigate the degradation due to the corrosion between the pin and receptacle. Besides, it can prevent corrosion from directly contacting with test instrument. In order to produce connector pairs with various degrees of degradation, these fifteen pairs of connector are divided into five groups of three. The duration of the accelerated degradation tests of these five group is set to one hour, two hours, four hours, six hours and eight hours, respectively.

In this paper, the contact resistance is selected to quantify the level of connector degradation. The contact resistance of these fifteen connector pairs is measured before and after degradation using a Shuanghe DM-100A digital μΩ & μV meter. The contact resistance of pristine connector pairs is similar, and the average contact resistance is calculated to be 1.02mΩ, which is taken to be standard contact resistance R_0. Due to the randomness of the formation of corrosion film, contact resistance does not rise monotonically as the duration of the accelerated degradation tests increases, but there is a slight upward trend. The ratio of the contact resistance of degraded and pristine connectors is taken to quantify the level of degradation. Based on the nonlinear behaviour model (10), a nonlinear behavior model is developed for the first time to describe the nonlinearity of various levels of degraded connectors:

$$i_d = a_3 v^3 \times \left(\frac{R}{R_0}\right)^{3r} + a_5 v^5 \times \left(\frac{R}{R_0}\right)^{5r} + a_7 v^7 \times \left(\frac{R}{R_0}\right)^{7r} \quad (15)$$

where i_d is the output nonlinear current through degraded connectors, R is the contact resistance of degraded connectors, R_0 is the standard contact resistance of pristine connectors, and r is a correction factor. It should be noted that when R=R_0 (the connector is pristine), this model (15) is the same as the model of pristine connectors (10).

Then the third-order PIM product power of degraded connectors P_d can be expressed as:

$$P_d = \frac{3}{4}a_3V^3 \times \left(\frac{R}{R_0}\right)^{3r} + \frac{25}{8}a_5V^5 \times \left(\frac{R}{R_0}\right)^{5r} + \frac{735}{64}a_7V^7 \times \left(\frac{R}{R_0}\right)^{7r} \quad (16)$$

The third-order PIM product power of degraded connectors is obtained by a series of two-tone PIM tests. In this paper, the test results of connector samples when the input power is 43dBm are used to obtain the value of r, and the results at other input powers are used to verify the correctness of the model. The curve of model (16) and the test results of degraded connectors when the input power is 43dBm are shown in Fig. 3.

The correction factor r of the model curve shown in Fig. 3 is fitted to 0.502. In order to verify the correctness of this factor r and the model, the test results of a sample with relatively high contact resistance, the results of a sample with relatively low contact resistance, and the standard results of pristine connector samples, and their corresponding model curves when the input powers are from 35dBm to 44dBm are shown in Fig. 4.

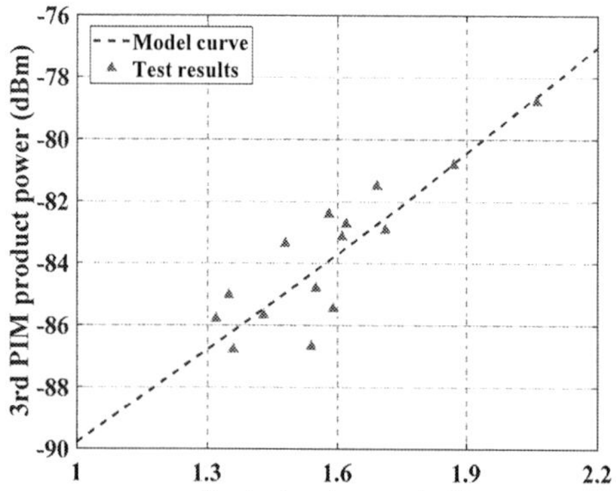

Fig. 3 Model curve and test results of degraded connector samples.

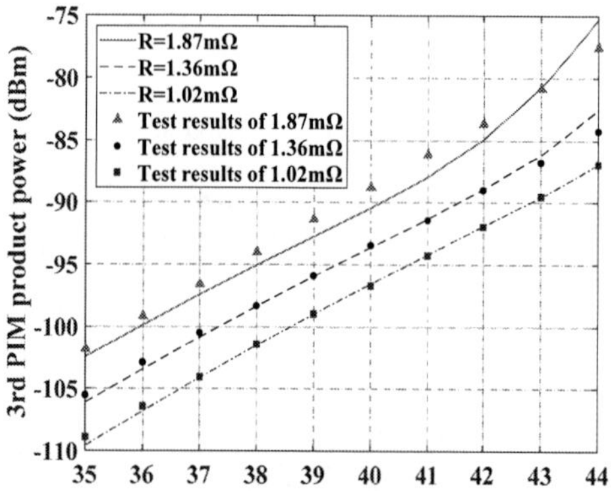

Fig. 4. Model curves and test results versus input power for different contact resistance.

It can be seen from inspection of Fig. 4 that the predictions of pristine connector and low contact resistance sample are quite good, and the prediction of relatively high contact resistance sample have a difference which is less than 2dB. On the whole, when the input powers are from 35dBm to 44dBm, the correctness of the PIM prediction model of degraded connectors is verified. The model curves in Fig. 4 indicate that when the contact resistance is relatively low, the third-order PIM product power increases linearly with the increase of input power. However, when the contact resistance is relatively high, the third-order PIM product power will show nonlinear growth trend with input power.

In order to evaluate the impact of connector degradation on PIM interference. The curves of the third-order PIM product power versus contact resistance according to model (16) when the input power is 35dBm, 38dBm, 41dBm and 44dBm are presented in Fig. 5.

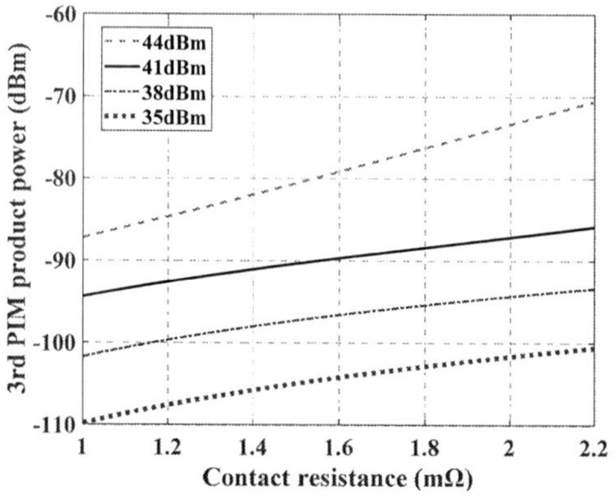

Fig. 5 Model curves versus contact resistance for different input power.

It can be observed in Fig. 5 that the third-order PIM product power increases with the increase of contact resistance and input power. When the input power is relatively low, the growth rate of PIM power versus contact resistance is low, the impact of connector degradation on PIM is relatively small. When the input power is relatively high, the growth rate of PIM power versus contact resistance is high, the impact of connector degradation on PIM becomes greater.

IV. CONCLUSION

The objective of this work is to explore the nonlinear characteristics and develop a model to predict the PIM product power of pristine and degraded coaxial connectors. In this work, a nonlinear behavior model and a prediction model of third-order PIM product power of pristine connectors are obtained first. Then the prediction model of third-order PIM product power for connectors with various degrees of degradation is developed. The correctness of the model is verified by a series of two-tone PIM tests. It is found that the degradation of coaxial connectors could make the third-order PIM product power increase, when the input power is relatively high, the impact of connector degradation on PIM becomes greater.

ACKNOWLEDGMENT

This work was supported in part by the National Natural Science Foundation of China (No. 51877010), in part by the Open Fund of State Key Laboratory of Information Photonics and Optical Communications, Beijing University of Posts and Telecommunications (BUPT), and in part by the Fundamental Research Funds for the Central Universities, BUPT (No. 2019PTB-014).

REFERENCES

[1] J. Henrie, A. Christianson, and W. J. Chappell, "Prediction of passive intermodulation from coaxial connectors in microwave networks", IEEE Transactions

on Microwave Theory and Techniques, vol. 56, no. 1, pp. 209-216, Jan. 2008.
[2] J. Henrie, A. Christianson, and W. J. Chappell, "Linear–nonlinear interaction and passive intermodulation distortion", IEEE Transactions on Microwave Theory and Techniques, vol. 58, no. 5, pp. 1230-1237, May. 2010.
[3] Q. Jin, J. Gao, G. Xie, G. T. Flowers, and R. Ji, "A study of the passive intermodulation induced by nonlinear characteristics of RF connectors", in 62nd IEEE Holm Conference on Electrical Contacts, pp. 1-8, Oct. 2016.
[4] Q. Jin, J. Gao, G. T. Flowers, Y. Wu, and G. Xie, "Modeling of passive intermodulation with electrical contacts in coaxial connectors", IEEE Transactions on Microwave Theory and Techniques, vol. 66, no. 9, pp. 4007-4016, Sept. 2018.
[5] D. S. Kozlov, A. P. Shitvov, A. G. Schuchinsky, and M. B. Steer, "Passive Intermodulation of Analog and Digital Signals on Transmission Lines with Distributed Nonlinearities: Modelling and Characterization", IEEE Transactions on Microwave Theory and Techniques, vol. 64, no. 5, pp. 1383-1395, May. 2016.
[6] X. Chen, Y. He, S. Yang, W. Cui, Y. Zhang, D. J. Pommerenke, and J. Fan, "Analytic passive intermodulation behavior on the coaxial connector using Monte Carlo approximation", IEEE Transactions on Electromagnetic Compatibility, vol. 60, no. 5, pp. 1207-1214, Oct. 2018.
[7] R. Ji, J. Gao, G. T. Flowers, G. Xie, Z. Cheng and Q. Jin, "The Effect of Electrical Connector Degradation on High-Frequency Signal Transmission", IEEE Transactions on Components, Packaging and Manufacturing Technology, vol. 7, no. 7, pp. 1163-1172, Jul. 2017.
[8] R. Ji, G. T. Flowers, J. Gao, Z. Cheng and G. Xie, "High-Frequency Characterization and Modeling of Coaxial Connectors With Degraded Contact Surfaces", IEEE Transactions on Components, Packaging and Manufacturing Technology, vol. 8, no. 3, pp. 447-455, Mar. 2018.

7th International Conference on Reliability of Electrical Products and Electrical Contacts, November 04-06, 2019

The Analysis and Improvement of the Problem on the Excessive Power Consumption of Miniature Circuit Breaker

Yanbao Chen, Changliu Jiang, Lei Yi
Xiamen HongFa Electroacoustic CO., Ltd., Xiamen, China, 361021
E-mail: 1001314@hongfa.cn Tel: 86-0592-6106688 Fax: 86-0592-6106688

Abstract---**With the development of electric system, higher reliability of the electrical products has been proposed, and meanwhile more performance index of the products has been cares by users. For miniature circuit breaker (MCB) as an example, the requirement of power consumption after electrical life experience has been demand, except for the mechanical life times, electrical life times, short circuit characteristics which were cared usually. In this paper, the failure case about a type of MCB with the problem of excessive power consumption has been introduced. By means of infrared thermal imaging analysis technology, segmented parameter test method, SEM-EDS analysis, the failure site and probable reasons were clarified, and this problem of excessive power consumption has been significantly improved by the improvement steps.**

Index Terms— **Miniature Circuit Breaker, Reliability, Power Consumption, Improvement**

I. INTRODUCTION

Low-voltage apparatus usually refers to electrical appliances that play the role of switch, control, detection, display and alarm in low-voltage distribution system and control system. Miniature circuit breaker is a kind of small capacity plastic shell circuit breaker with very compact structure, which is Mainly used to protect wires, cables and low-voltage circuit breakers as control lighting, also can be a wire protection switch. According to the definition of GB/T 10963.1, mini-circuit breaker refers to "ac circuit breaker used for ac 50Hz or 60Hz, rated voltage 440V and below, rated current 125A and below, rated short-circuit breaking capacity not exceeding 25000A".

With the development of the electric power industry, people have put forward higher requirements for the reliability of electrical products, and more and more attention has been paid to product performance indicators.

in recent years abroad a certain electric power company requirements hongfa paragraph 1P+N miniature circuit breaker should not only satisfy the requirement of the rated frequency tripping performance, at the same time, the power consumption of the test after the product has certain requirements; reduce the power consumption of the circuit breaker in the process of using can make the products of lower power consumption, so as to achieve the goal of energy saving.

This article is based on the client's requirements, to groping test of the small circuit breakers, found its tripping performance can meet the requirements, but after test power consumption can not meet the requirements. therefore using infrared thermal imaging analysis technology, segmented parameter test method, SEM-EDS analysis, the failure site and probable reasons were clarified, and this problem of excessive power consumption has been significantly improved by the improvement steps.

II. FAILURE ANALYSIS PROCESS AND RESULTS

A. Failure performance

Three small 1P+N circuit breakers (numbered 1 #~3 #) were randomly selected to perform rated tripping performance tests according to customer load conditions. At the same time, 10 minutes power consumption performance tests were carried out for the products after the tests according to customer conditions. results: the three products tripping performance testing can meet the requirements, but power consumption test after test can not meet the requirements, power test results description as shown in table 1.

TABLE I

Description of power consumption test results after test

Product number	Description of test results
1#	Power supply to 7min, product trip, power dissipation not exceeding standard
2#	test after 10min , the power consumption result is qualified
3#	Power supply to 2min, product trip, power dissipation exceeding standard

B. Identify the failure site

According to the test principle of power consumption, power consumption $P=I^2R$, Where I is the current of the coil (fixed value), R is the contact resistance of the inlet and outlet terminals, so it is speculated that the large P may be caused by the large contact resistance of a certain part.

When the contact resistance of this component is large, it can be intuitively shown as high temperature and high pressure drop. Therefore, the analysis method of infrared thermal imaging temperature measurement (method A) and segmental parameter test (method B) are adopted to identify the failure site. Identify the failure site and describe the analysis process as follows:

Method A: Infrared thermal imaging analysis method

The structure of this miniature circuit breaker is analyzed and it is concluded that the temperature rise of the operating mechanism may be relatively low during the long time (10 minutes) power consumption test, but if the operating mechanism is opened, the miniature circuit breaker will not work properly; but if it is not opened, there will be heat conduction in the process of infrared temperature measurement, and the test error is relatively large. For this reason, the method of partial shell opening is adopted, that is, the operation mechanism does not open the shell, and the other parts of the shell opening are used for testing.

Fig. 1 is the infrared thermal imaging distribution of the products tested after 10 minutes. It can be seen that the temperature of coil position, contact touch position, static contact welding position, moving contact soft connection line position (limited to L pole, N pole without soft connection line) and other components is higher than that of other components.

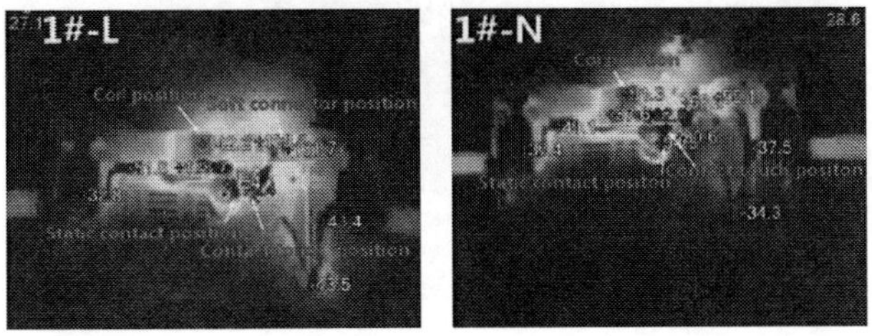

Fig. 1 1 # Product Infrared Thermal Imaging Distribution Map

According to the distribution of infrared thermal imaging in Fig. 1, the positions with higher temperatures are compared and analyzed. Fig. 2 is the schematic diagram of the analysis results, from which the following phenomena can be found:

(a) The overall temperature of L pole is higher than that of N pole.

(b) The temperature of the contact position of the L-pole or the N-pole is obviously higher than that of other positions, and the temperature of the position is 3-L pole > 1-L pole > 2-L pole, which is consistent with the power consumption test.

In conclusion, it can be inferred that the failure of L pole and the contact position may be the failure location.

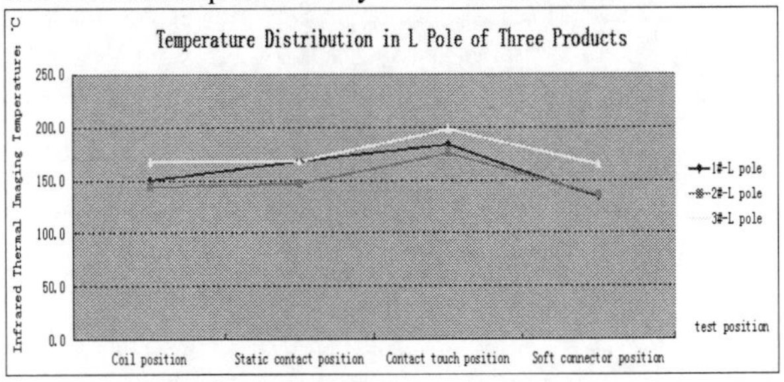

(a) Temperature distribution in L pole of three prducts

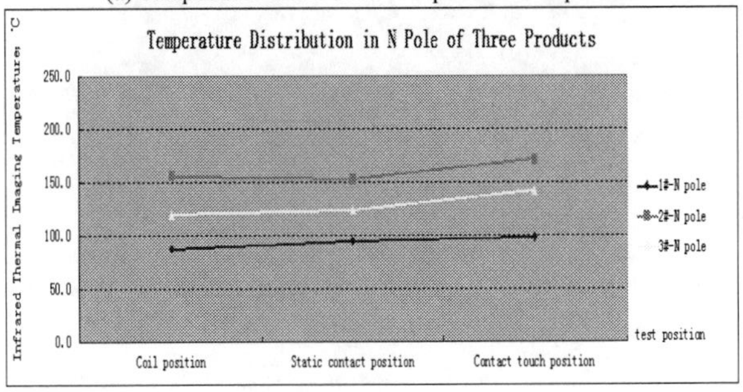

(b) Temperature distribution in N pole of three prducts

Fig. 2 Infrared Temperature Contrast Map of Three Products

Method B: Segmented parameter test method

Combining with the structure characteristics of circuit breaker, in the process of power consumption test, synchronously use high precision desktop multimeter to test the voltage drop values ,such as outlet terminal to bimetal sheet (L pole), bimetal to moving contact, moving contact to static contact, static contact to coil terminal, coil terminal to incoming terminal. And in the process of test. Two initial products were tested synchronously to facilitate the analysis of voltage drop.

FIG.3 is the schematic diagram of numerical analysis of voltage drop test at each part. It can be seen that the voltage drop between the moving contact and the static contact (i.e., the voltage drop at the contact touch position) is significantly higher than that of the untested product, and there is no significant change in the contact voltage drop at the other positions. Therefore, The failure position is further defined as the contact touch position.

C. Failure Cause Analysis

The analysis of part 2.2 clarifies the failure position, i.e. contact touch position;The analysis of this part shows that the abnormality may be related to the mechanical abnormality of contact or the abnormal contact surface.

Therefore, the analysis is focused on these two aspects.

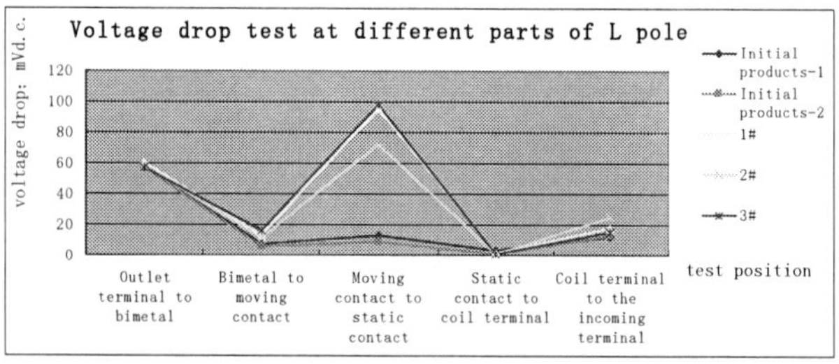

(a) Value of voltage drop test at different parts of L pole of 5 products

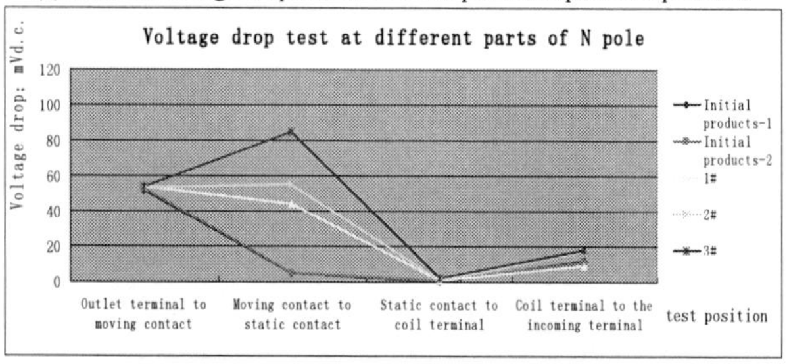

(b) Value of voltage drop test at different parts of L pole of 5 products

Fig. 3 Voltage drop Test Value of Five Product Parts

(1) Analysis of mechanical parameters related to contacts

The contact parameters (final pressure, tripping force, tripping trip) of the three products after groping test, as shown in Table 2. Can be seen that the values of the contact parameters are relatively large, so it is speculated that the power consumption of the contact touch position be large may not due to abnormal mechanical parameters.

TABLE II

Test Value of Relevant Parameters of Contact Points of Three Products after groping Test

Sample number	test positon	Final pressure (N)	Tripping force (N)	Tripping trip (mm)
1#	L pole	4.8	1.195	0.79
	N pole	4.6	1.252	0.77
2#	L pole	4.3	1.433	0.84
	N pole	4.7	1.197	0.85
3#	L pole	4.5	1.406	0.78
	N pole	4.5	1.305	0.89

(2) *Contact surface analysis*

Firstly,Surface Analysis of Moving Contacts:

Scanning electron microscopy (SEM) is a commonly used analysis equipment in the field of modern material analysis. It has very powerful functions and can clearly observe the surface morphology of products. Fig.4 shows the surface morphology of the moving contacts observed by the SEM equipment under BSD conditions. From it, black small foreign bodies with more distribution on the surface of the 3# L pole and small number on the surface of the 1# L pole are observed. while almost no foreign bodies are found on the other contacts, which is consistent with the power consumption test.

Scanning electron microscopy (SEM) and X-ray energy dispersive spectrometer (EDS) are generally used in combination. EDS can be used to determine the elements existing on the surface of the product and the corresponding percentage. EDS Magnification analysis of the small black spot foreign body found in Figure 4 shows that it mainly contains C, N, O elements. Meanwhile, EDS Magnification analysis of spatter around the contact shows that its main components are C, N and O, which are close to the foreign body components of small black spots on the contact. The spatters around the contacts were larger, and the spatters were analyzed by FT-IR. The spatters were divided into PA, according to the material information of this product (the shell material is PA), it is speculated that the black foreign body on the moving contact surface comes from the shell.

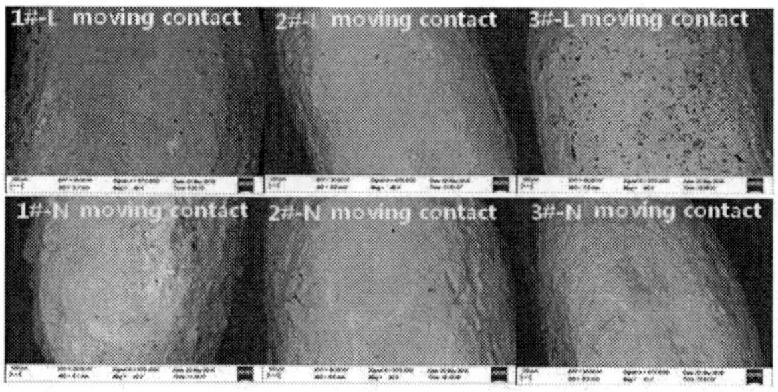

Fig. 4 SEM Analysis of Contact Surface of Three Products

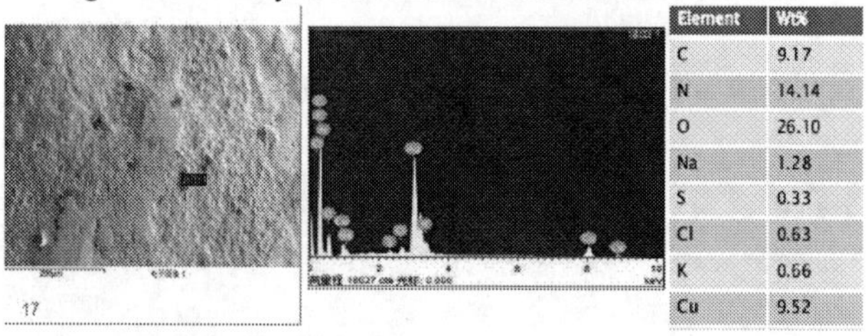

(a) EDS Analysis of Black Spot Foreign Body on the Surface of Moving Contact

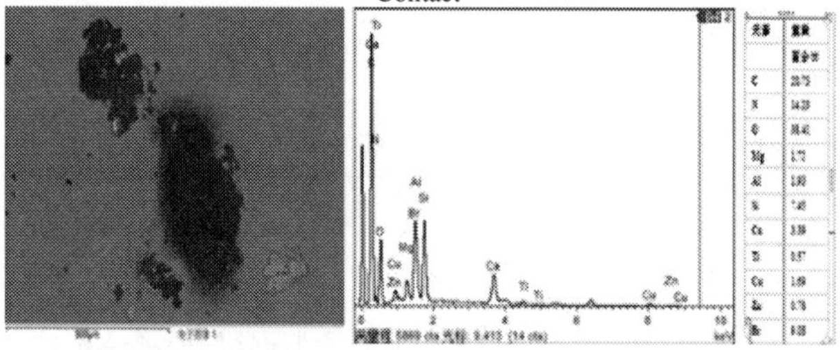

(b) EDS analysis of spatters around contacts

Fig. 5 Component Analysis of Spatters on the Surface and around position of 3 # L Pole Moving Contact

Secondly, Surface Analysis of Static Contacts:

Scanning electron microscopy (SEM) was used to observe the surface morphology of static contacts under the same conditions. It was found that the static contacts were generally grey and partially white, as shown in Fig. 6.

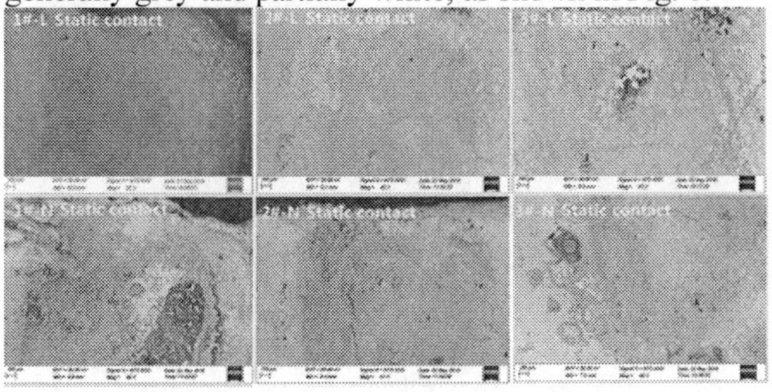

Fig. 6 SEM analysis of surface conditions of three static contacts

Fig. 7 is the analysis of different color areas by EDS. The results show that the main components of white area are Ag, the main components of gray area are Cu and O, and the main components of black area are also Cu and O, but the content of C is slightly higher.

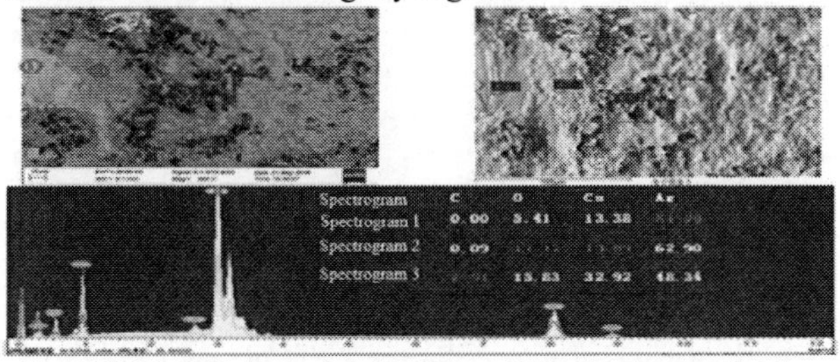

Fig. 7 SEM-EDS Analysis of Different Color Regions on Static Contact Surface

Cu element was detected on the surface of the static contact. The material of the static contact of this circuit breaker is AgC and the material of the moving contact is Cu plated Ag. It is speculated that Cu element on the surface of the static contact may come from the substrate of the moving contact. The contact consumption is analyzed. The result is shown in Figure 8. After the test, the silver plating layer on the surface of the movable contact of the product has been exhausted, and the copper layer is exposed, which is consistent with the speculation; At the same time, it was found that the static contact surface was covered with a black layer (CuO was analyzed by EDS), which was consistent with the grey layer observed on the contact surface.

(3) Other aspects of analysis

During the analysis of the failed product after the groping test, it was found that the 3#L extremely soft connecting line was severely broken, the 1#L extremely soft connecting line was slightly broken, and the 2#L pole was almost unbroken; which is consistent with the situation of early tripping of products. It is speculated that it may not be the main cause of high power consumption of products, but it may be the cause of early tripping of products, and it should also be improve it.

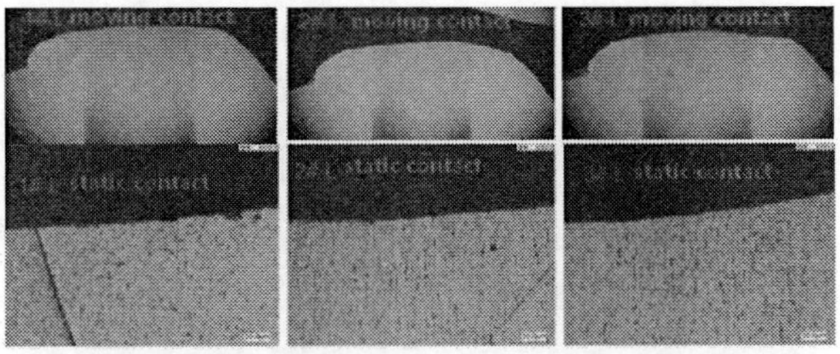

(a) Consumption of L Pole moving and Static Contacts

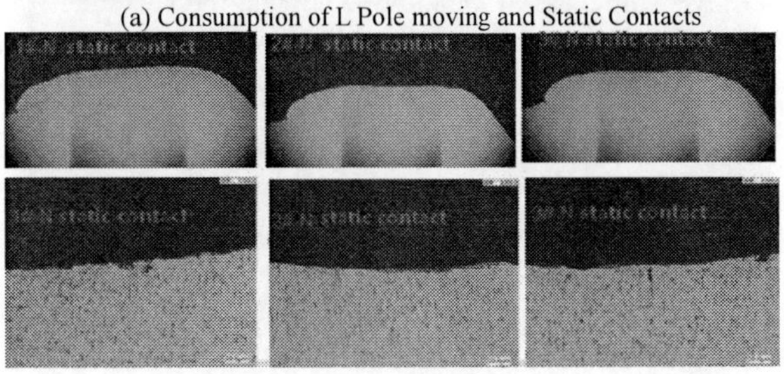

(b) Consumption of N Pole moving and Static Contacts

Fig. 8 Analysis of Surface Consumption of Contact Points of Three Products

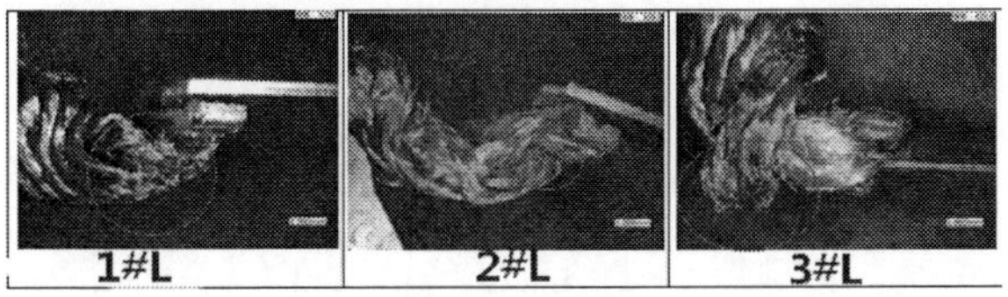

Fig. 9 Analysis of L pole Soft Connection Wire Breakage in Three Products

(4) Summary of Failure Cause Analysis

Firstly, through infrared thermal imaging and segmented parameter test method, it is clear that the failure part is the contact touch position.

Secondly, t Through SEM-EDS analysis, the possible causes of the large power consumption of the contact position are the small black foreign matter on the contact surface (from the shell) and the CuO on the static contact surface (when the silver plating layer of the moving contact is exhausted, the copper layer is exposed).

In addition, the disconnection of the soft connection wire of the L-pole moving contact may not be the direct cause of high power consumption, but it will lead to the early tripping of the products, which is also not allowed, and should be improved.

III. EFFECTIVENESS EVALUATION OF IMPROVEMENT PROGRAMS

A. Improvement program

From the second point of failure analysis, it is inferred that the high power consumption of this product may be related to more splashes produced by the shell, splashing to the contact surface; the silver layer of the moving contact is exhausted and the copper layer is exposed; at the same time, the phenomenon of early tripping in the process of power consumption may be related to the breaking of the soft connection wire of the contact. Based on the above analysis results, a program for improving the program was developed to verify:

(a) Reduction of shell spatter: changes in shell material and moving contact position.

(b) The moving contact exposes the copper layer: the silver layer thickness of the moving contact increases.

(c) Soft connection wire breakage: copper stranded parallel wire is replaced by copper braided wire.

B. Effectiveness evaluation

Make the product according to the above improvement program (numbered A1~A3). The power consumption of the product was tested, and the surface condition of the product's moving contact, the CuO content of the static contact surface and the breakage of the soft connection line were observed.

(1) Power consumption test after test

The improved product is tested by tripping test and power consumption test under the same conditions, and the results are shown in FIG. 10. After the target times tripping test, the power is qualified, and no early tripping phenomenon is found in the power testing process;The tripping performance test is increased to 1.5 times synchronously, and the results are still qualified. From this numerical value, the improvement program has obvious effect on the power consumption after the test.

(2) Observation of Black Spots on the Surface of Product-Moving Contact after Test

In order to further evaluate the improvement effect, the surface morphology of the product's moving contacts after 1.5 times the number of targets was observed by scanning electron microscopy. Fig.11 shows the surface topography of the moving contact. It is found that the number of black spots on the moving contact surface of the product is significantly reduced; From this aspect, it is proved that the modification of shell material and moving contact position has obvious effect on reducing the number of black foreign matter on moving contact surface.

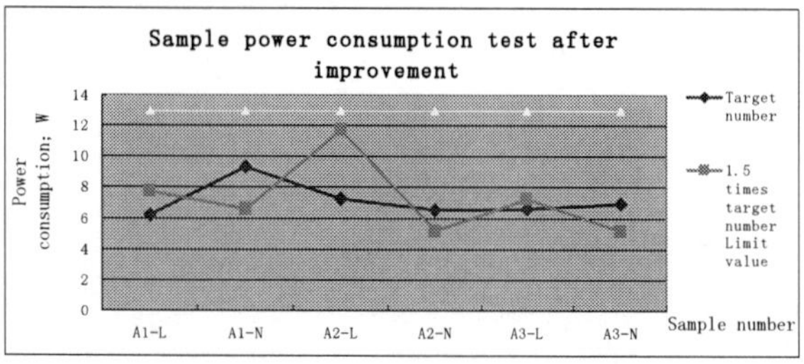

Fig. 10 Improved power consumption test

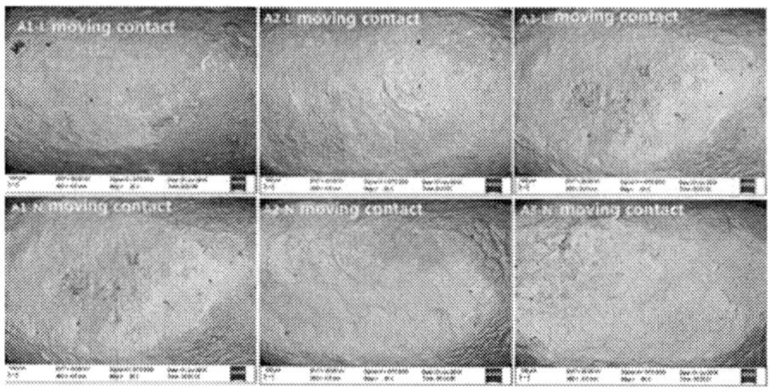

Fig. 11 Analysis of the number of black spots on the surface of the product contact after improvement

(3) Observation of CuO on the Surface of Product-Static Contact after Test

From the analysis of the second point, it is found that the existence of CuO on the surface of the static contact has a certain influence on the power consumption; For this reason, an improvement program is adopted in which the thickness of the silver plating layer on the surface of the movable contact is increased to reduce the content of CuO on the surface of the static contact. Fig.12 is the schematic diagram of the CuO content on the surface of the sample's static contact after the improvement under SEM. It is found that the content of CuO on the surface of the static contact of the improved product is significantly reduced. It is speculated that the scheme of increasing the silver plating layer of the movable contact has a significant effect on reducing the CuO content on the surface of the static contact.

(4) Observation on the Breakage of Soft Connection Wire of Moving Contact after Improvement

According to the analysis of point 2, it is speculated that the broken soft connection wire may lead to the early tripping of the product. Therefore, the soft connection wire of moving contact is changed into copper braided wire. The premature tripping phenomenon is not found in the improved product test;In order to further evaluate the improvement effect, the disconnection of the soft connection line of the tested product was observed. As shown in FIG. 13, after improvement, the disconnection of products is significantly reduced. The result shows that changing copper twisted wire to copper braided wire is effective.

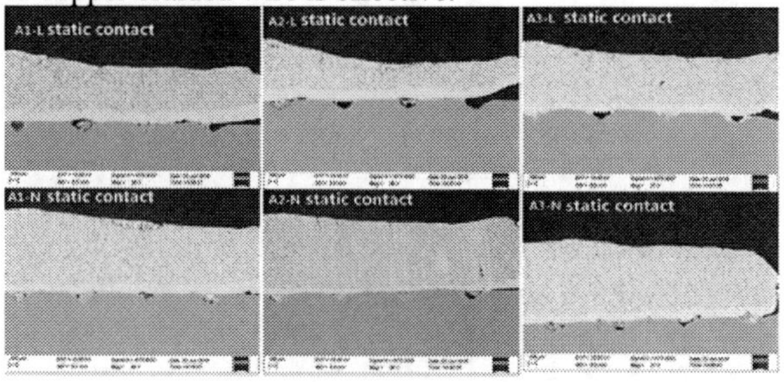

Fig. 12 CuO Content on the Surface of Static Contact after Improvement

Fig. 13 Observation on the Breakage of Soft Connection Wire after Improvement

III. CONCLUDE

Firstly, in this paper, the failure part is identified by infrared thermal imaging analysis and segmented parameter test method.

Secondly, through scanning electron microscope, X-ray energy spectrum analyzer, stereo microscope observation, FT-IR analysis, metallographic analysis and other analytical techniques, It is speculated that the high power consumption and early tripping of the product are related to the shell material, the silver-plated layer thickness of the moving contact and the broken soft connection wire.

Thirdly, By making the improvement program into a real product and testing and verifying it, the power consumption data are tested, and the improvement effect is confirmed one by one from the abnormal points found in the process of failure analysis (large number of black spots on the surface of moving contacts, a layer of CuO on the surface of static contacts, and serious breakage of the L-extremely soft connection line of the product after testing). As a result, comprehensively confirmed that the improvement program is effective;

Lastly, Subsequent implementation of the improvement plan into actual production, and regular sampling of mass production products for testing, the results show that the power consumption is good, further confirming the effectiveness of the improvement program.

REFERENCE

[1] Jinyang Dong. Basic concepts and functional characteristics of intelligent circuit breakers [J]. Rural electrification, 2019.

[2] Haofeng Cheng. Analysis of Reliability Test Scheme for Small Circuit Breakers [J]. Electrical Appliances and Energy Efficiency Management Technology, 2018.

7th International Conference on Reliability of
Electrical Products and Electrical Contacts,
November 04-06, 2019

Research of Interruption Performance of Miniature DC Circuit Breaker Based on Magnetic Properties and Position of Permanent Magnet

Jinsheng Chen, Changchun Chi, Jia Liu
School of Electrical Engineering, Shanghai Dian Ji University, Shanghai, 201306

***Abstract*—With the rapid development of DC transmission technology,the role of DC circuit breaker continues to rise in high and low voltage DC grids,whether the DC circuit breaker can reliably cut off the circuit has become the focus of research in the field of electrical appliances. Aiming at the arc can not be extinguished easily during the breaking of the DC breaker, this paper mainly takes the miniature DC circuit breaker arc-extinguishing process as the research object. Firstly, the arc motion process is analyzed, then further study the influence of the magnetic properties strength of the permanent magnet in different position on the arc electrodynamicsforce in the miniature DC circuit breaker and simulate it with Ansoft Maxwell software, The simulation results show that the miniatureDC circuit breaker has the best arc extinguishing effect when the weak magnetic permanent magnet is at the corner of the iron sheet. This paper provides an important reference for improving the reliability of miniature DC circuit breakers.**

***Index Terms*—miniature DCcircuitbreaker, arc electrodynamicsforce, permanent magnet, reliability**

I. INTRODUCTION

Low-voltage circuit breakers include frame-type circuit breakers, flow-limiting circuit breakers, leakage protection circuit breakers, and DC fast circuit breakers.The miniature DC circuit breaker belongs to the plastic shell circuit breaker and is a low-voltage circuit breaker that is widely used in daily life.At the same time,it serves as an electrical device for the protection line and undertakes a simple circuit breaker switch. Withtheincrease of industrial manufacturing capability, more and more attention is paid to the power life of miniature DC circuit breakers.

At present, our industrial equipment and technical level capacity is insufficient, the manufacturing of circuit breaker shell hardness and plasticity and circuit breaker reliability and other aspects still need to be improved. In order to improve the reliability of the circuit breaker, a method to change the magnetic strength and position of the permanent magnet inside the circuit breaker is proposed to improve the reliability of the circuit breaker and shorten the arc time.

II. RESEARCH THEORY OF ARC OF MINIATURE DC CIRCUIT BREAKER

A. Arc generation and endanger

This phenomenon can be seen in daily life: when the current in the line is greater than 1 ampere, the line is cut off. If the voltage at both ends of the switch has a certain value, the process of seeing the switch disconnect is often accompanied by a bar spark as shown in Figure 1. The bar spark that appears here is an arc. The study found that the generation of arcs is a relatively complex process. Due to the moment of separation between the moving contacts and the static contacts, there is a certain number of voltages between the two, which can generally reach ten volts and add smaller gaps. After the electrons are excited by the field force, they are still affected by the force, generate acceleration and move at high speed to form a higher energy kinetic energy. The electrons containing kinetic energy collide with other particles to start the chain reaction and gradually stimulate more electrons. Start their own chain reaction to form an electronic channel, which is an arc. Although the circuit is disconnected, due to the appearance of electronic channels, circuits still exist.

The appearance of arc will cause unpredictable losses. For example, due to the long arc duration, when there is a large current on the line, it will not only burn home appliances, but even endanger the safety of life property, especially the industry that is exposed to flammable and explosive items; In the past, when a certain line of the power grid system failed, the operating unions engaged in the electricity industry often had to manually open the switch and work in Gaodianya. When the operator under high current conditions was troubleshooting the line failure, he would make a slight operation mistake. Will be injured. Even electrocution; Common fault problems such as short-circuit ground failure, aging circuit breaker equipment, electrical equipment inspection oversight, etc. are very easy to generate arc, so it is necessary to carefully check all parts of the line electrical components to avoid disasters; In the same way, the oil industry must also pay attention to the generation of arc to curb and extinguish in time to avoid major casualties.

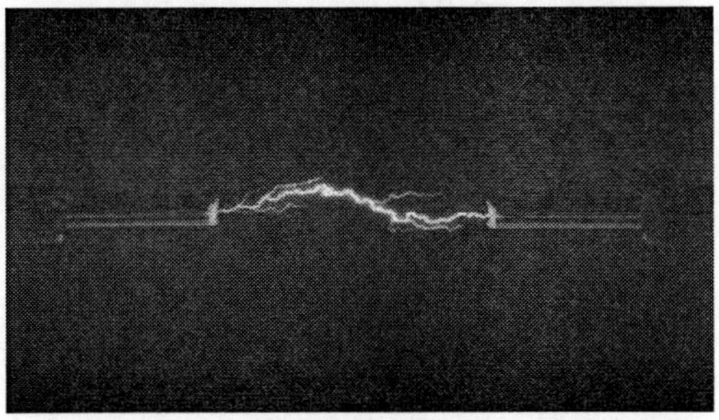

Fig. 1 Bar spark

III. RESEARCH THEORY OF ARC OF MINIATURE DC CIRCUIT BREAKER

A. Properties and Extinction Principle of Miniature DC Arc

The extinguishing principle of the AC arc is to cut off the circuit immediately when the current passes through the zero point twice in a cycle. After the current has passed through the zero point, the changes in the medium and voltage in the arc gap are shown in Fig.2.Fig.2U_{jf} is the recovery process of the medium, that is, when the medium is restored from conductivity to normal non-conductive state, it will increase the voltage between the arc gaps until the maximum voltage can be maintained in the insulation state. U_{hf} is the voltage recovery process, that is, the voltage recovery process at both ends of the break gap after the arc is extinguished. It can be seen from the figure that the medium and voltage changes in the arc gap and the arc gap are simultaneous, and the value of$U_{jf}-U_{hf}$ is negative, and the arc will re-ignite; $U_{jf}-U_{hf}$is positive, the arc extinguishes. Therefore, as long as the circuit breaker device can meet the requirements set above the specific voltage value, it can be judged that the circuit breaker device has the ability to safely cut off the AC line. If the circuit breaker equipment does not meet the requirements and does not meet the arc extinguishing principle, although the line is cut off at the zero point, the arc will re-ignite, which will endanger the safety of the equipment of the entire line.

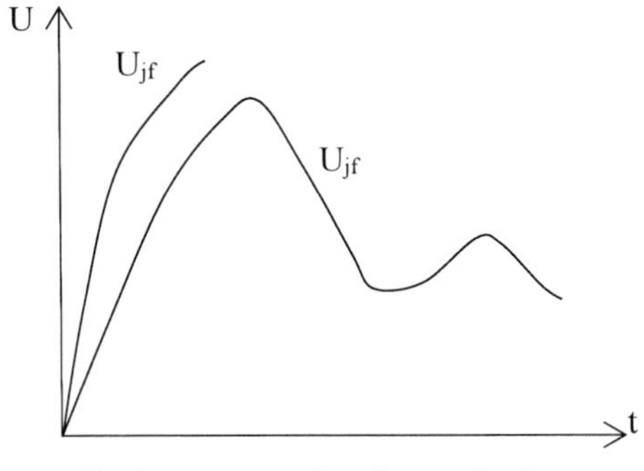

Fig. 2 Recovery of medium and voltage

Since the DC current does not pass the zero moment, cutting off the DC line is more complicated. In order to accurately describe the static voltage-ampere characteristics of the DC arc, it is not only necessary to base on empirical formulas, but also to perform multiple tests to draw more numerical points. In order to quickly and safely extinguish the DC arc to lay a solid theoretical foundation. The simplified DC circuit shown in Fig.3 shows that the electromotive force L of the power supply indicates that the inductance R is the resistor CB in the circuit representing the switch.

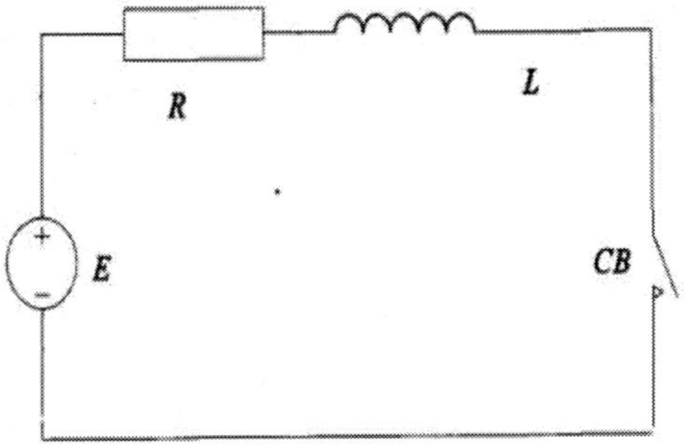

Fig. 3 Simplified DC circuit

When the line is cut, an arc is generated on the moving and static contacts, and the voltage equation of the line is:

$$E = L\frac{di_h}{dt} + R \times I_h + U_h \quad (2.1)$$

When switching equipment is actually used, people hope that they can safely and reliably remove the fault line and use the switch device for the longest time. This requires that the static and dynamic contacts be as good as possible, but when cutting off the faulty DC line, In order to achieve the principle of Arc extinction, the above requirements can not be met at the same time.

Due to the thermal inertia of the arc and the presence of energy storage elements in the line, the arc extinguishing time will be extended. From the moving contact and the static contact to the arc extinguishing, the moment experienced represents the arc time, so the formula(2.2) is transformed and the time integral is made on both sides of the equation, so that the integral time interval is(0, t) The following formula:

$$\int_0^t U_h = \int_0^t EI_h dt - \int_0^t RI^2 dt + \frac{LI^2{}_0}{2} \quad (2.2)$$

It can be seen that in the case of a DC power supply and a certain line resistance, the energy of the arc has a great relationship with the inductance. The greater the inductance coefficient in the line, the more energy the inductor stores, and the greater the arc energy, that is, the more difficult the arc is, so the energy storage characteristics of the inductor increase the arc extinction time.

The basic reference principle of this paper is to apply a resistor to the DC arc extinguishing system. When the $RI_h + U_h > E$ is applied, the arc will not continue to burn and then extinguish. Obviously, increasing the arc resistance R is not advisable. Therefore, measures are taken to improve the arc voltammetry characteristics by applying magnetic field magnetic blowing room to improve the arc voltammetry characteristics.

IV. SIMULATION OF ARC ELECTRIC DYNAMICS OF MINIATURE CIRCUIT BREAKERS UNDER DIFFERENT SCHEMES

A. The establishment of simulation arc model for micro DC circuit breaker

Place the permanent magnet at the corner of the iron sheet, as shown in Fig 4. The more complex model operation in Ansoft software is more complex. Therefore, using the modeling tool UG, the corner permanent magnet model is introduced into Ansoft software after it is completed in UG, and the material properties can be set to continue the numerical calculation. Experimental data are shown in table 2.

The structure of the micro DC circuit breaker is shown in Fig4. In this paper, Ansoft electromagnetic simulation software is used to solve the electromagnetic force. At the same time, only the influence of the magnetic field on the arc is considered. Other factors such as temperature and airflow are no longer considered. Parallel magnetic fields are added to the periphery of the simulation model to simulate the natural boundary conditions.The DC arc can be approximated as a cylindrical conductor. This article simplifies the arc into a copper pillar conductor. The arc motion process [3] can be divided into two phases, the first phase is from the formation of the arc to the entry into the arc extinguishing chamber, and the second phase is the complete entry of the arc into the arc extinguishing chamber.Fig 5 shows the main four areas of the arc motion. The area is the arc formed between the contacts after the dynamic and static contacts are opened. This position is defined as the area-arc. In zone one, the range of arc movement is small and can be regarded as always being subjected to a downward force; the arc jumps into the arcing plate into zone two defined as the zone two arcs, in which the arc is inclined and always receives The direction of the Lorentz force is inclined downward. The direction of the force changes with the movement of the arc. Before the arc enters the arc chute, the direction of the force of the arc tends to change slowly, and the final direction is almost stable in one direction. The directional stability zone is defined as the zone three arc; after the arc enters the arc chute, it enters zone four, which is defined as the zone four arc.

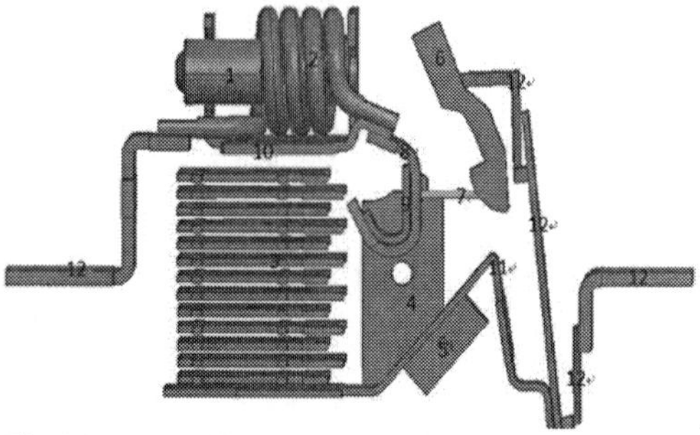

Fig.4 Structure diagram of miniature DC circuit breaker

Note: In the figure, 1 iron core 2 coil 3 arc suppression gate 4 enamels 5 magnets 6 contacts 7 arc 8 static contacts 9 corner iron plate 10 magnetic yoke 11 arc plate 12 connecting rods

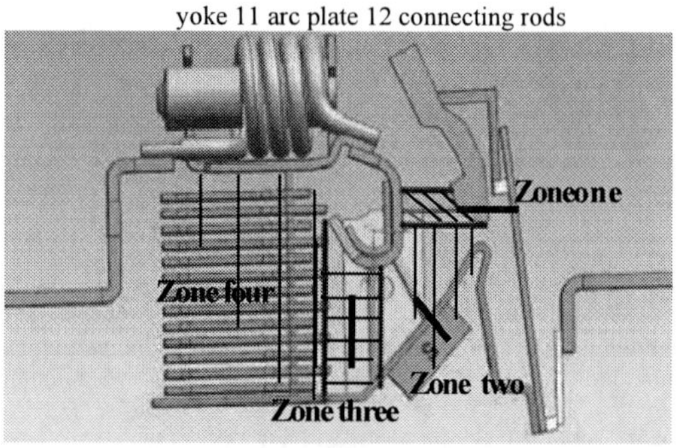

Fig. 5 Arc motion area chart

B. Electrodynamic simulation of a permanent magnet under an arc plate

After establishing the circuit breaker arc model, the corresponding parameters can be entered into the Ansoft electromagnetic simulation software for numerical calculation. The original model of the miniature DC circuit breaker sample(set to flow rated current of 63A) is that the arc plate material is iron, the permanent magnet is below the arc plate and the magnetism is weak magnetic. The following will study the magnetic properties of the permanent magnet in the case of Arc plate material being iron, and simulate the arc electric power in the simulation software[7] The data are analyzed and compared, and all simulation results are studied and analyzed, and preliminary conclusions are obtained.

Table 1 shows the Electrodynamic data of different magnetic permanent magnet arc simulation. The simulation results show that the arc is mainly subjected to arc electrodynamics in four typical regions. From the table, it can be seen that the arc electric force in the absence of a permanent magnet is significantly smaller than the arc electric force in the presence of a permanent magnet; With the continuous strengthening of permanent magnet magnetism, the arc electric power in the area is gradually increasing. However, no matter how the magnetic strength of the permanent magnet changes, there is little influence on the electric power of the arc in the area

TABLEI
ELECTRODYNAMIC DATA OF DIFFERENT MAGNETIC PERMANENT MAGNET ARC SIMULATION

Arc electric power (10^{-5}N)	Zone one	Zone two	Zone Three	Zone Four
Strong mpm	301.58	566.6	-881.55	-1385
Medium mpm	230.52	467	-566.7	-1369
Weak mpm	170.6	285	-328.16	-1369
No permanent magnet	81.39	91	-170.05	-844.1

mpm = magnetic permanent magnet

.

C. Electrodynamic simulation of the permanent magnet at the corner of the iron sheet

Place the permanent magnet at the corner of the iron sheet, as shown in Fig.4. The more complex model operation in Ansoft software is more complex. Therefore, using the modeling tool UG, the corner permanent magnet model is introduced into Ansoft software after it is completed in UG, and the material properties can be set to continue the numerical calculation. Experimental data are shown in table 2.

TABLE II
ELECTRODYNAMIC DATA OF DIFFERENT MAGNETIC PERMANENT MAGNET ARC SIMULATION

Arc electric power (10^{-5}N)	Zone one	Zone two	Zone Three	Zone Four
Strong mpm	1528	1617	-2369	-1398
Medium mpm	1010	1067	-1583	-1420
Weak mpm	686	709	-1033	-1401
No permanent magnet	81.39	91	-170.05	-844.1

mpm = magnetic permanent magnet

From the table, it can be seen that the different magnetic permanent magnets placed at the corner of the iron sheet have a significant effect on the arc electric power of the region one,two,three, but the arc electric power enhancement effect on the region 4 is not as good as the first three regions. Fig.6 is derived from the consolidation of tables 1 and 2. It can be clearly seen from the figure that when the strong magnetic permanent magnet is at the corner of the iron sheet, the arc electric power is best enhanced, and the time of Arc entry into the arc extinguishing gate can be better improved and the arc extinguishing time can be improved, thus improving the breaker reliability.

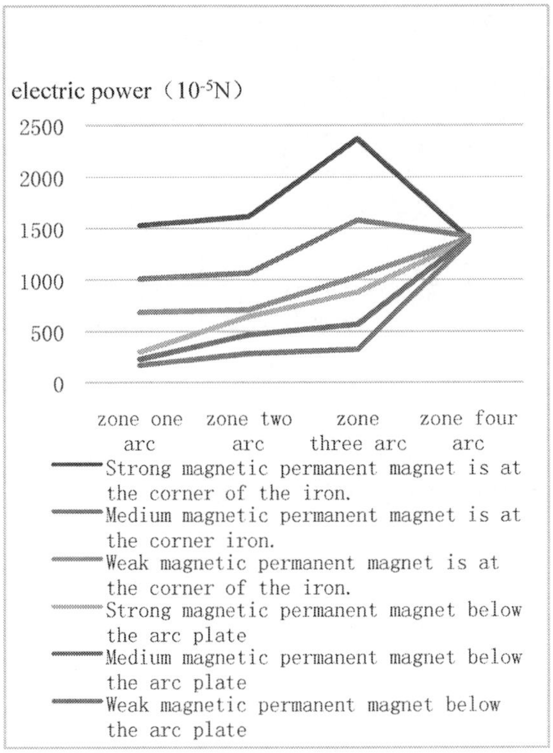

Fig. 6 Electric power comparison chart

V. CONCLUSION

Through the study of the arc motion process of the miniature DC circuit breaker, the simulation arc model of the miniature DC circuit breaker is established. First, the arc is regarded as a copper cylinder. According to the arc motion process and force direction, the arc motion trajectory is divided into four regions. And define the typical position of Arc motion in each area. In order to find out the external factors that affect the arc electric power, the effect of the position of different magnetic permanent magnets on the arc electric power is designed, and the arc electric power of each scheme is numerically calculated by using Ansoft electromagnetic simulation software, and the scheme is analyzed and compared. The simulation results show that the effect of placing the permanent magnet at the corner of the iron sheet is better, that is, when the permanent magnet magnetism is a weak magnetic permanent magnet, the arc electric power at each position is equivalent to that of the strong magnetic permanent magnet under the original model.

Electric power.

REFERENCES

[1] G. O. Young, “Synthetic structure of industrial plastics (Book style with paper title and editor)” in *Plastics*, 2nd ed. vol.3, J. Peters, Ed. New York: McGraw-Hill, 1964, pp. 15–64

[2] Switching of the vacuum-arc discharge direct current[J] .E. F. Prozorov, K. N. Ul’yanov, V. A. Fedorov. High Temperature .2014 (2)

[3] Bifurcation theory of ac electric arcing[J] .Thomas Christen, Emanuel Peinke. Journal of Physics D: Applied Physics .2012 (6)

[4] Quenching of an electric arc in a vacuum gap with a uniform transverse magnetic field[J] .D. F. Alferov, M. R. Ahmetgareev, D. V. Yevsin, V. P. Ivanov. Plasma Physics Reports .2010 (13)

[5] Modeling of breakdown during the post-arc phase of a vacuum circuit breaker[J] .PSarrailh, LGarrigues,J P Boeuf, G J M Hagelaar. Plasma Sources Science and Technology .2010 (6)

[6] Design and Experimental Study of a Novel Fault Current Limiter[J] . Zhao Chun, Lu Jia Zheng, Jiang Zheng Long, Fang Zhen, Li Bo. Advanced Materials Research .2010 (139)

[7] Simulation and experimental research on series vacuum arc of vacuum circuit breaker with double-break. Liao M,GeG, DuanX,et al. Discharges and Electrical Insulation in Vacuum (ISDEIV),2014 International Symposium on . 2014

[8] Experimental Investigation into the Synergy of Vacuum Circuit Breaker with Double-Break. Ge G, LiaoM, DuanX, et al. IEEE Transactions on Plasma Science . 2016

Research on Reliability in High Power Density Motor Driver

Feng Niu[1*], Ximeng Zhang[1], Shihui Yang[2], Wenjing Xu[3], Dakang Sun[4], Wu Bao[5], Kui Li[1]
[1]State Key Laboratory of Reliability and Intelligence of Electrical Equipment, Hebei University of Technology, Tianjin 300130, China
[2]Global Energy Interconnection Research Institute Co., Ltd., Beijing 102209, China
[3]Binhai Power Supply Company, State Grid Tianjin Electric Power Co., Ltd., Tianjin 300450, China
[4]Tianjin Power Transmission and Transfer Engineering Co., Ltd., Tianjin 300011, China
[5]Yingda Business Service Co., Ltd., Tianjin 300300, China
Email: niu.feng.hebut@gmail.com

***Abstract* —With the rapid development of motor drive system, motor drivers with more compact and higher power density design are needed for applications with limited board space. However, the high power density design can lead to heat dissipation, which may decrease the reliability of motor driver. In order to analyze the heat dissipation of high power density motor driver, firstly, the simplified topology of high power density motor drive system is established. Secondly, based the simplified high power density motor drive system, the power loss model of heat source is carried out. Finally, thermal simulation is conducted based on theoretical analysis. The simulations are presented to verify the correctness of theoretical analysis and lay theoretical foundation for analysis of heat dissipation in high power density motor driver.**

***Index Terms*—high power density motor driver, power loss, thermal simulation.**

I. INTRODUCTION

Motor drives are widely used in automotive electrical equipment, defense and aerospace, which makes the design of motor drive system receiving more attention. With the miniaturization and high power density of electronic devices, its structural design is facing problems such as heat dissipation, electromagnetic compatibility, insulation and so on [1]-[3]. Thermal failure caused by poor heat dissipation is the main failure mode of electronic equipment. It seriously affects the reliability of high power density motor drive system.

During the product design process, the thermal distribution in equipment can be obtained by thermal simulation. Analysis of thermal simulation can reduce the experimental cost, shorten the product development cycle and improve the reliability of high power density motor drive system. For thermal analysis, the calculation of device power loss and the thermal simulation of the system are two important issues.

IGBT power calculation is the key for device-level thermal simulation, which affects the reliability of electronic equipment. In view of this situation, some scholars have studied the power losses of IGBT in chips. R. Wu has proposed an improved method to describe power losses in IGBT converters [3]. A. Bhalla has studied the effect of IGBT switching dynamics on loss calculations in high speed applications [3]. Boyu Wang has studies a novel power loss calculation method for IGBTs in power converters via chaotic SPWM control [3].

Thermal simulation is the basis for thermal analysis of electrical equipment. There are various kinds of software for thermal simulation. Ma Jianzhuang has conducted thermal simulation of amplifier and heat dissipation measurement using FloTHERM [3]. Nampoothiri has introduced the Peltier cooling method for sealed electronic packaging unit and carried out thermal simulation with FloTHERM [3].

In this paper, based on the simplified high power density motor drive system, the power loss model of heat source is carried out. Then, the thermal simulation of overall PCB board is conducted. This paper provides a reference for thermal analysis of motor driver.

II. THE POWER LOSS MODEL OF INVERTER

A. Topology of High Power Density Motor Drive System

A typical high power density motor drive system mainly consists of rectifier, inverter, controller, encoder, motor and so on, which are shown in Fig. 1.

In order to make the study of heat dissipation more convenient, the structure of high power density motor drive system is simplified. The main heat source of motor drive system is switch devices. Therefore, the power circuit associated with switch devices is retained as much as possible, and the control circuits and signal circuits are removed without affecting the thermal analysis. The simplified system topology shown in Fig. 2 is used for the thermal analysis in this paper.

B. Mathematical Model of Power Loss

High switching frequency of inverter in motor driver can cause serious thermal problems, so the power loss calculation of inverter is very important for the thermal design of high power density motor drive system. The inverter is generally composed of six IGBT modules, each of which consists of an IGBT and an anti-parallel diode, and both of them are periodically in a switching state and an off state. The loss is mainly generated by the IGBT and the anti-parallel diode, which includes conduction loss and switching loss. The total loss in a control cycle is the sum of these losses. So, the total loss power formula of IGBT is shown as

$$P_{T-Tr} = P_{DC-Tr} + P_{SW-Tr} \tag{1}$$

where $P_{T\text{-}Tr}$, $P_{DC\text{-}Tr}$ and $P_{SW\text{-}Tr}$ are the total loss power, conduction loss and switching loss of IGBT, respectively. The loss power of the anti-parallel diode is shown as

$$P_{T-\text{Dio}} = P_{DC-\text{Dio}} + P_{SW-\text{Dio}} \tag{2}$$

where $P_{T\text{-}Dio}$, $P_{DC\text{-}Dio}$ and $P_{SW\text{-}Dio}$ are the total loss power, conduction loss and switching loss of anti-parallel diode, respectively.

The on-state voltage drop V_T and current i_T of IGBT and diode are approximately linear, and the expression is shown as

$$V_T(i_T) = V_{T0} + Ir_T \tag{3}$$

where V_{T0} is threshold voltage, r_T is on-state internal resistance, and I is on-state current. The energy loss of a

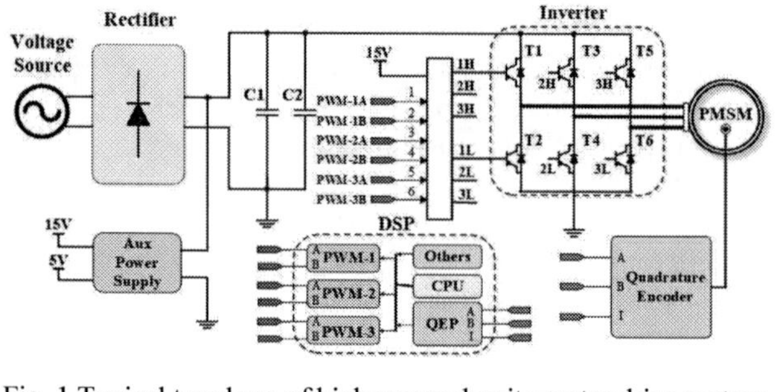

Fig. 1 Typical topology of high power density motor drive system.

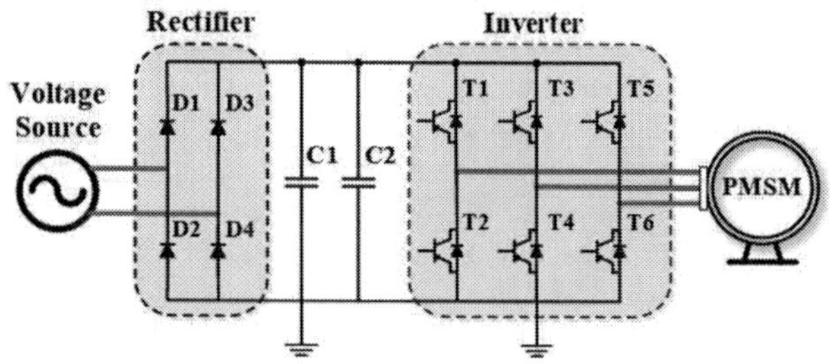

Fig. 2 Simplified topology of high power density motor drive system.

device during one carrier cycle is shown as

$$E = V_T I D T_C \tag{4}$$

where D is the conduction duty cycle and T_C is carrier cycle. I and D can be expressed as

$$\begin{cases} I = I_m \sin(\omega t) \\ D = \dfrac{1 + M\sin(\omega t + \theta)}{2} \end{cases} \tag{5}$$

where I_m is the current amplitude, and M is modulation degree. According to the principle of constant energy, (4) can be transformed into the form of differential equations, and the power is evenly distributed over entire period.

$$\begin{cases} dt = \dfrac{T}{2\pi} d\omega t \\ P = \dfrac{1}{T}\sum E \end{cases} \tag{6}$$

According to (4)-(6), the on-state loss of IGBT can be obtained as

$$P_{DC-Tr} = (\frac{1}{8} + \frac{M}{3\pi}) r_{T-Tr} I_m^2 + (\frac{1}{2\pi} + \frac{\pi}{8}\cos\theta) V_{T0-Tr} I_m \tag{7}$$

where $r_{T\text{-}Tr}$ is the on-state internal resistance of IGBT, $\cos\theta$ is the power factor, and $V_{T0\text{-}Tr}$ is the threshold voltage of IGBT. The on-state loss of anti-parallel diode is obtained as

$$P_{DC-Dio} = (\frac{1}{8} - \frac{M}{3\pi}) r_{T-Dio} I_m^2 + (\frac{1}{2\pi} - \frac{\pi}{8}\cos\theta) V_{T0-Dio} I_m \tag{8}$$

where $r_{T\text{-}Dio}$ is the on-state internal resistance of anti-parallel diode, $V_{T0\text{-}Dio}$ is the threshold voltage of anti-parallel diode. The switching loss of IGBT is shown as

$$P_{SW-Tr} = \frac{f_s}{2\pi}(E_{on} + E_{off})(1 + \cos\theta) \tag{9}$$

where f_s is the switching frequency, E_{on} and E_{off} are switch-on loss and switch-off loss of IGBT, respectively. The switching loss of the anti-parallel diode is shown as

$$P_{SW-Dio} = \frac{f_s}{2\pi} E_{rr}(1 + \cos\theta) \tag{10}$$

where E_{rr} is the switching loss of anti-parallel diode. The total loss power of IGBT module is expressed as

$$P_T = P_{T-Tr} + P_{T-\text{Dio}} \tag{11}$$

where P_T is the total power loss of IGBT module. The temperature rise of IGBT module is shown as

$$\Delta T = P_T R_T \tag{12}$$

where ΔT is the temperature rise of IGBT module, R_T is the thermal resistance of IGBT module.

C. Verification of Mathematical Model

According to power loss mathematical model of PS21765 IGBT, modulation degrees, switching frequencies and current amplitudes are major factors affecting thermal change. In order to verify the correctness of power loss mathematical model established above, this paper takes

PS21765 IGBT as an example for theoretical calculation. The theoretical calculation results are compared with simulation results obtained by the power module simulation software Melcosim. When V_{CC}=100V and cosθ=0.8, comparison results under different modulation degrees, switching frequencies and current amplitudes are shown in Table I.

The comparison results shown in Table I clearly show that the relative error between calculation results and simulation results is below 5% under different operation conditions, which verifies the correctness of established power loss mathematical model. And power loss mathematical model can provide a basis for heat dissipation design of high power density motor driver.

III. THERMAL SIMULATION

A. Establishment of Thermal Analysis Model

Thermal simulation model is build based on the experimental setup, and the PCB board of high power density motor driver is shown in Fig. 3. The motor driver consists of rectifier, inverter, DSP controller, encoder and protection circuits.

The high power density motor driver has power module, rectifier module, inverter module, data transmission module and various protection circuits. In order to improve the calculation efficiency, the auxiliary circuits with less power loss are ignored during model generation process. The simplified thermal model is shown in Fig. 4.

B. Simulation Results and Analysis

Thermal simulation and analysis of the high power density motor driver is carried out. Based on the results of Table I, two typical conditions are applied. The simulation result of thermal distribution under M=0.9, f_s=10kHz and I_m=1A is shown in Fig. 5(a). The simulation result of thermal distribution under M=0.9, f_s=10kHz and I_m=4A is shown in Fig. 5(b).

It can be seen from Fig. 5 that the heat source is mainly concentrated on the inverter. This phenomenon is caused by the high switching frequency of the inverter, which is consistent with the result analyzed in part B of Section II. And the thermal growth of inverter leads to that of surrounding device. Therefore, it is necessary to dissipate inverter heat so that the overall heat reach an acceptable range.

In order to further analyze the factors affecting the thermal change, the thermal simulations of inverters under different current amplitudes and switching frequencies are carried out. The simulation result is shown in Fig. 6.

TABLE I

COMPARISON OF SIMULATION AND CALCULATION RESULTS

M	f_s	I_m	Symbol	Simulation Results	Calculation Results	Relative Error
0.9	10k Hz	1A	P_{DC-Tr}/W	0.40	0.406	1.5%
			P_{SW-Tr}/W	0.32	0.325	1.6%
			P_{DC-Dio}/W	0.09	0.092	2.2%
			P_{SW-Dio}/W	0.05	0.051	2.9%
			$\Delta T/K$	1.40	1.38	1.4%
0.7	10k Hz	1A	P_{DC-Tr}/W	0.37	0.383	3.5%
			P_{SW-Tr}/W	0.32	0.325	1.6%
			P_{DC-Dio}/W	0.12	0.124	3.3%
			P_{SW-Dio}/W	0.05	0.051	2.9%
			$\Delta T/K$	1.45	1.45	0
0.9	5k Hz	1A	P_{DC-Tr}/W	0.40	0.406	1.5%
			P_{SW-Tr}/W	0.16	0.162	1.3%
			P_{DC-Dio}/W	0.09	0.092	2.2%
			P_{SW-Dio}/W	0.02	0.020	0
			$\Delta T/K$	1.10	1.07	2.7%
0.9	10k Hz	4A	P_{DC-Tr}/W	2.26	2.29	1.3%
			P_{SW-Tr}/W	0.97	0.985	1.5%
			P_{DC-Dio}/W	0.53	0.532	0.4%
			P_{SW-Dio}/W	0.11	0.11	0
			$\Delta T/K$	6.14	6.184	0.7%

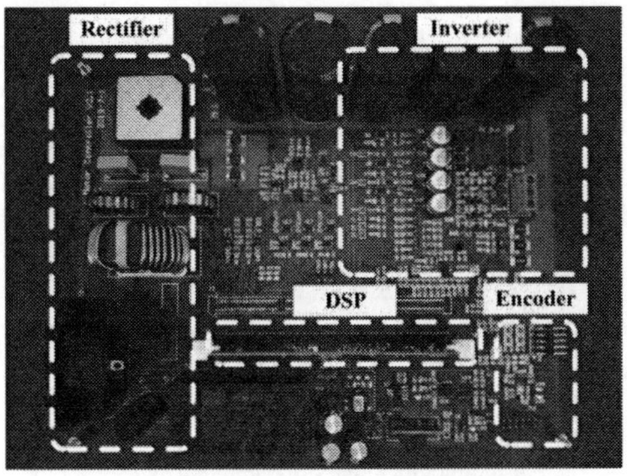

Fig. 3 PCB board of high power density motor driver.

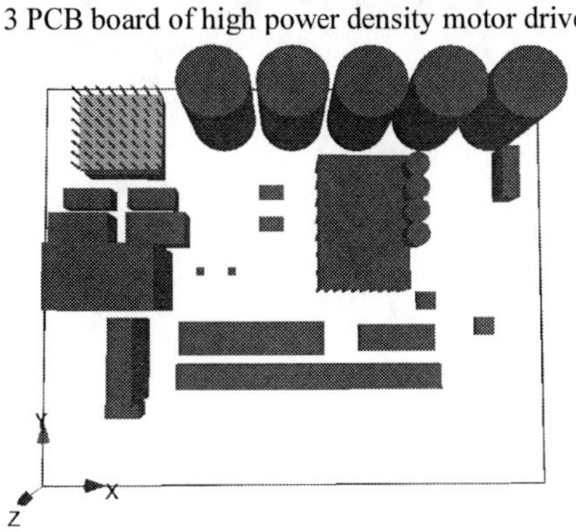

Fig. 4 The simplified thermal simulation model.

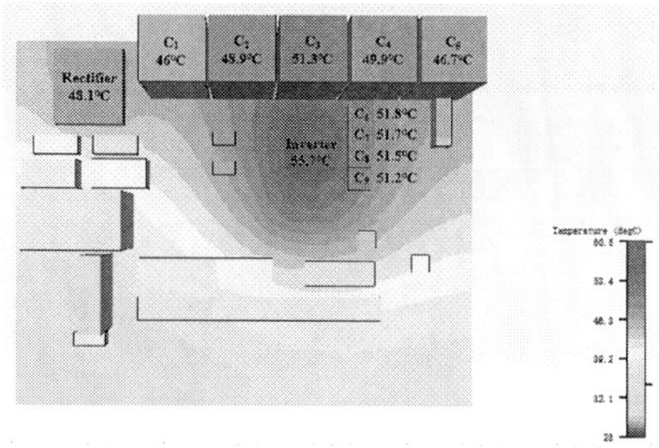

(a) Thermal distribution under M=0.9, f_s=10kHz and I_m=1A.

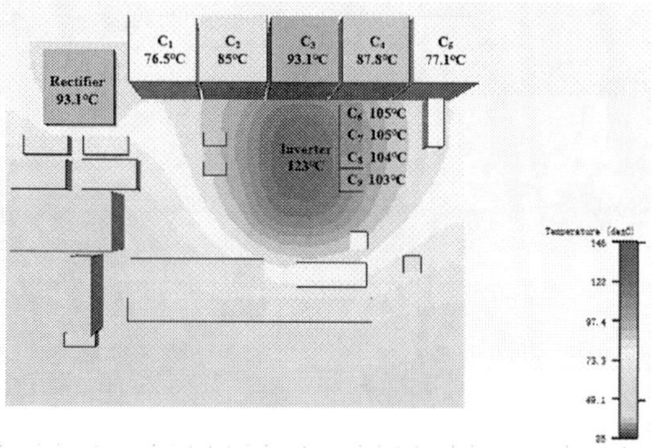

(b) Thermal distribution under M=0.9, f_s=10kHz and I_m=4A

Fig. 5 Thermal distribution under different current amplitudes.

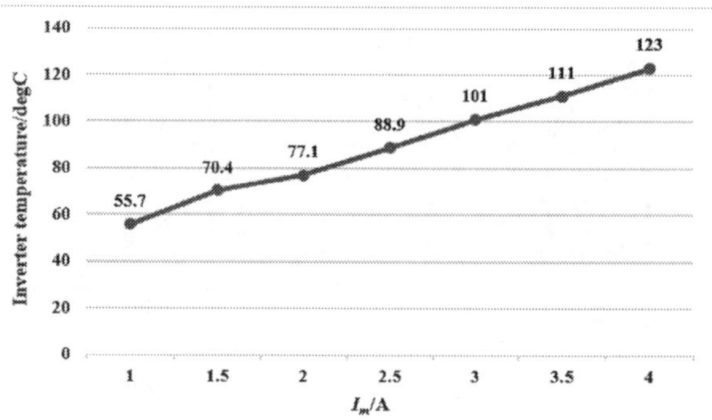

(a) Inverter temperature under different current amplitudes

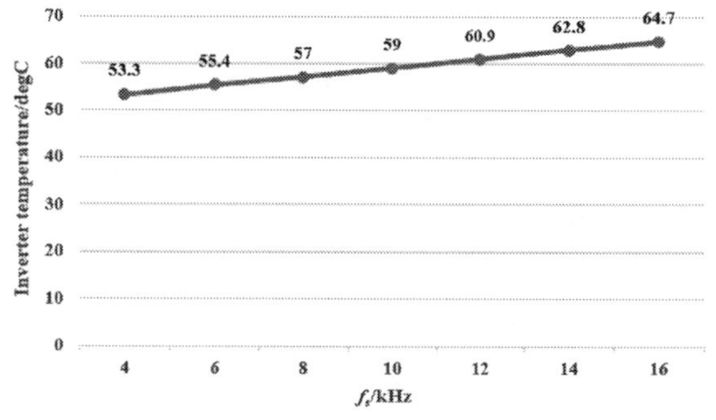

(b) Inverter temperature under different switching frequencies

Fig. 6 Inverter temperature under different current amplitudes and switching frequencies.

It can be obviously seen from Fig. 6 that the increase of current amplitude and switching frequency promotes the increase of inverter heat, which is consistent with the conclusion obtained in part C of Section II.

It can be concluded that the simulation results are highly consistent with the results of theoretical analysis, which can effectively verify their correctness.

IV. CONCLUSION

This paper presents the power loss model of IGBT module and its anti-parallel diode, taking PS21765 as an example. The power loss model provides a theoretical basis for the loss calculation of other devices. In addition, the high power density motor driver system is designed and thermal simulation analysis of system are carried out. Thermal simulation analysis provides a basis for the design and optimization of products, and greatly improve the reliability of products.

ACKNOWLEDGMENT

This work is supported in part by the National Natural Science Foundation of China under Grant 51707174, in part by Excellent Youth Science Foundation of Hebei province under Grant E2019202092, in part by Research Projects of Tianjin Sino-German University of Applied Sciences under Grant zdkt2018-004.

REFERENCES

[1] Yinhan Gao, et al, "Automotive EMC prediction technology based on fuzzy reasoning ," Journal of Jilin University (Engineering Edition), vol. 36, no. 3, pp. 399-403, 2011.

[2] F. Niu, S. Cao, X. Huang, J. Zhang, K. Li and Y. Fang, "Analysis of EMI in Motor System Driven by PWM Inverter," 2018 1st Workshop on Wide Bandgap Power Devices and Applications in Asia (WiPDA Asia), Xi'an, China, 2018, pp. 66-70.

[3] Y. Tang, B. Wang and M. Chen, "Temperature characteris-tic and electric-thermal model of IGBT switching tran-sient," Transactions of China Electrotechnical Society, vol. 27, no. 12, pp. 146-153, 2012 (in Chinese).

[4] R. Wu et al., "A Power Loss Calculation Method of IGBT Three-Phase SPWM Converter," 2012 Second International Conference on Intelligent System Design and Engineering Application, Sanya, Hainan, 2012, pp. 1180-1183.

[5] A. Bhalla, J. Gladish and G. Dolny, "Effect of IGBT switching dynamics on loss calculations in high speed applications," in IEEE Electron Device Letters, vol. 20, no. 1, pp. 51-53, Jan. 1999.

[6] Boyu Wang, H. Li, Xiaojie You and Trillion Zheng, "A novel power loss calculation method for IGBTs in power converters via Chaotic SPWM control," 2014

International Power Electronics Conference (IPEC-Hiroshima 2014 - ECCE ASIA), Hiroshima, 2014, pp. 2893-2898.

[7] Jianzhuang Ma, "Thermal simulation of amplifier unit based on Flotherm," 2016 IEEE International Conference on Microwave and Millimeter Wave Technology (ICMMT), 2016: 865-867.

[8] Nampoothiri, SM; Sebastian, MS; Kumar, PCS. "Implementation of Peltier Cooling in Hermetically Sealed Electronic Packaging Unit for Sub-sea Vessel," Defence Science Journal, vol. 68, no. 3, pp. 326-332, 2018.

7th International Conference on Reliability of
Electrical Products and Electrical Contacts,
November 04-06, 2019

First-principle Study of the Influence of La-dopedon the Thermal Properties of $AgSnO_2$Contact Material

Ling Chen, Jingqin Wang, Shaoqi Sun
State Key Laboratory of Reliability and Intelligence of Electrical Equipment,
Hebei University of Technology, Tianjin 300130,China
E-mail:15620459603@163.comTel:86-15620459603

Abstract—**According to the influence of La atom doping on the thermal properties of $AgSnO_2$ contact materials, the theoretical calculations are carried out by density functional theory, first principle and CASTEP software. The formation energy, phonon spectrum, phonon state density and partial wave state density and related thermodynamic parameters of the SnO_2 crystal before and after doping are obtained., and theoretical analysis of each calculation result and curve. The results show that the doped system has good forming ability. Combined with the phonon spectrum curve, when the doping concentration is 25%, the phonon spectrum does not show a virtual frequency, and the crystal can exist stably. Through the analysis of density of states and the density of partial wave states, La atoms and O atoms have a strong coupling effect, which effectively stimulates the activity of O atoms, which increases the number of molecules participating in motion, that is, the heat capacity is significantly improved compared with the undoped system.The doping of La makes the entropy, free energy and enthalpy curveof the SnO_2 crystal become steep, that is, the chaos of the system increases, the free energy of the crystal decreases, and the absorbed heat increases, which improves the recovery ability of the crystal.**

Index Terms—**first principle, La-doped SnO_2, vibration property, thermodynamic property**

I. INTRODUCTION

$AgSnO_2$ material is a new type of electrical switch contact material with corrosion resistance, wear resistance and long service life [1], but the defect of $AgSnO_2$ material, such as large contact resistance, high temperature, and difficult processing, limit its use. The main reason is that SnO_2 is a wide band gap semiconductor material,nearly insulated, which makes the resistance of the material increase and the temperature rise is high, which hinders the conduction and thermal conductivity [2-3]. Studies have shown that the introduction of impurities, defects or stoichiometric deviations in the crystals may improve the electrical and thermal properties of the material.

At present, a lot of research work focuses on the electronic structure, band structure, charge population and mechanical properties of $AgSnO_2$ contact materials, but lacks of research on its lattice dynamics. Zhang Xiaojun and other research results show that the interaction between phonons and electrons determines the conductance, superconductivity and thermal conductivity of the solid material[4]. Therefore, the physicochemical properties closely related to thermal properties need to be further explored, including the special stability of SnO_2 crystals, thermal properties (such as the heat capacity of the crystal), transport properties (such as heat conduction, sound propagation) and temperature effects (such as thermal expansion)[5]. The phonon spectrum is the basis of lattice dynamics, reflecting the vibration situation of various vibration modes inside the material, which can directly reflect the interaction between atoms. It is also the basic of the thermodynamic properties of solid materials such as molar heat capacity, Debye temperature and thermal expansion coefficient. The lattice heat capacity (hereinafter referred to as heat capacity) is an important thermodynamic parameter for studying the above process, and characterizes the flow of thermal energy, which can be directly calculated by phonon spectrum[6].

In this paper, the first principle method based on Density Functional Theory (DFT) is used to calculate the physical parameters of different concentrations of La-doped SnO_2 contact materials[7-8], and the formation energy is obtained. The difficulty of formation. The phonon spectrum is calculated, and the complete phonon spectrum curve of the crystal is obtained and used to judge the stability of the crystal structure. Then the rare earth element, La doping, is analyzed from the interaction between the microscopic atoms to improve the thermal properties of SnO_2. The morphological density of the crystal is used to obtain the curve of the heat capacity of the crystal with temperature, and analyzed the effect of doping on the thermal conductivity of the crystal

II. THEORETICAL MODEL AND CALCULATION METHOD

A. Theoretical model

The ideal rutile structure belongs to the 136 P4/MNM space group. In this paper, each SnO_2 unit cell contains 2 Sn atoms and 4 O atoms. The Sn atoms are at the apex and body center of the crystal lattice. The crystal and molecular structure are shown in the figure. 1. Five La doping concentrations are set, which were 0%, 12.5%, 16.67%, 25%, and 50%, respectively. The respective doping concentrations and their corresponding supercell correspondences are shown in Table 1.

Table.1 Correspondence relationship between doping concentration and the super cell

super cell	doping concentration/%
1×1×1	50%
1×1×2	25%
1×1×3	16. 67%
1×2×2	12. 5%
1×1×1	0%

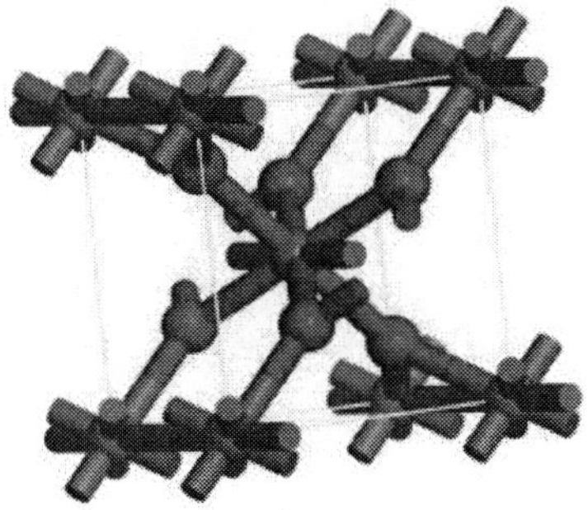

Fig.1model of primitive cell of SnO_2

B. Calculation method

The optimization of the unit cell and the calculation of the phonon spectrum are carried out in the CASTEP module in Materials Studio software. The inverse space Norm-conserving method based on density functional theory (DFT) and the generalized gradient approximation method for the exchange correlation function (GGA+PW91), the GGA approximation method overcomes the shortcomings of describing the real system in the case of severe density changes, and improves the calculation result of the exchange correlation energy, thereby improving the accuracy of the density functional method calculation. The interaction between valence electrons and core electrons is described by the projection-enhanced plane wave (PAW) method[9-10]. TheBrillouin area adopts the 5×5×8 Monkorst-Park scheme, and the plane wave truncation can select 750 eV. The optimization uses the BFGS algorithm. The convergence criterion between atoms is 0.3 eV/nm, and the maximum internal stress is set to 0.05 GPa.

Firstly, the geometric structure of the SnO_2 crystal was optimized by the CASTEP module to achieve a stable structure, and then the phonon spectrum, phonon density and thermodynamic properties of the crystal are calculated

III. CALCULATIONRESULTSANDANALYSIS

A. Difficulties in the formation of doping systems

Before comparing the effects of different doping concentrations on the thermal properties of SnO_2, it is necessary to discuss the difficulty of doping structure formation, which will determine whether the corresponding doping samples can be obtained experimentally. Therefore, the calculation of the formation of each doping model is carried out in this paper. The formula is as follows[11]:

$$E_{\Delta} = E_{SnO_2:\ La} - E_{SnO_2} - nE_{La} + mE_{Sn} \quad (1)$$

In the formula, $E_{SnO_2:\ La}$ and E_{SnO_2} represent the total energy of the SnO_2 system before and after La doping, E_{La} and E_{Sn} represent the ground state energy of La and Sn single atoms, and n and m represent the number of doped La atoms and the number of replaced Sn atoms, respectively.The physical meaning of formula (1) refers to the energy released by the formation of crystals from the elemental state before and after doping. It can be used to characterize the difficulty of crystal formation. When the formation energy is negative, the absolute value is larger., the crystal is to synthesize easily. If it is positive, it means that it is not easy to form[12].

The energy of each isolated atom is listed in Table 2. The calculation results of the main physical parameters of each model are listed in Table 3. Combined with Equation 1, the formation energy of four different doping concentrations of crystals is obtained. It can be seen that the results are all negative values, indicating that each doping system can all be formed. When the doping concentration is 50%, the absolute value of the formation energy is the largest, that is to say, its formation ability is the strongest.

Table.2 The energy of an isolated atom

Element	Sn	O	La
Energy/eV	−90. 8599	−423. 8746	−35. 6086

Table.3 Physical parameters of all compute models

	Pure SnO_2	SnO_2:La (12. 5%)	SnO_2:La (16. 67 %)	SnO_2:La (25%)	SnO_2:La (50%)
Total energy/eV	−1925. 03636	−7646. 56085	−5721. 66791	−3796. 97228	−1872. 20790
Formation energy/eV		−1. 66671	−1. 80683	−2. 15086	−2. 42286

I. Analysis of vibration properties of SnO_2 crystal

The phonon spectrum reflects the vibration of each vibration mode inside the material, which has important significance for the study of material stability. For any particular structure, lattice dynamics requires that all normal vibration modes have a finite real value. For any Brillian wave, the phonon frequency cannot be imaginary, ie, the phonon is stable[13]. Once the system produces a virtual frequency phonon, it indicates that for this vibration mode, the ions cannot be at the minimum point of the system energy and will be replaced by the lower energy structure, which destroys the symmetry of the original crystal structure, resulting in the structural phase change .This is because the vibration frequency tends to zero, which means that the vibration is slower and slower, and the corresponding elastic restoring force also tends to zero; if the ion according to the vibration mode of the phonon does not have a displacement equal to zero, there will be no restoring force to make the ion Go back to the balance position.

In order to further analyze the causes of the structural changes of SnO_2 crystals at different La doping concentrations, by calculating the lattice vibration spectra of pure SnO_2 crystals at different La doping concentrations, it can be found that different doping concentrations change the frequency of phonons, If a virtual frequency occurs, it indicates that the structure is not stable. Figure 2 shows the calculation results of five kinds of doping concentration phonon spectra. From the figure, we can see that the concentration N = 12.5%, 16.67%, 50%, and the phonon spectrum shows a virtual frequency, indicating that the structure will not be existence stably after formation. When N=25%, the frequency of any wave vector in the Brillouin zone is not imaginary, indicating that it has phonon stability. That is to say, the crystal structure with a doping concentration of 25% is more stable than the crystals of other doping concentrations.

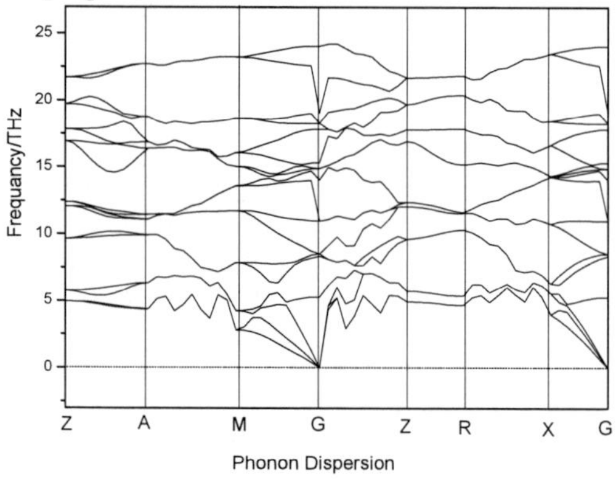

(a)

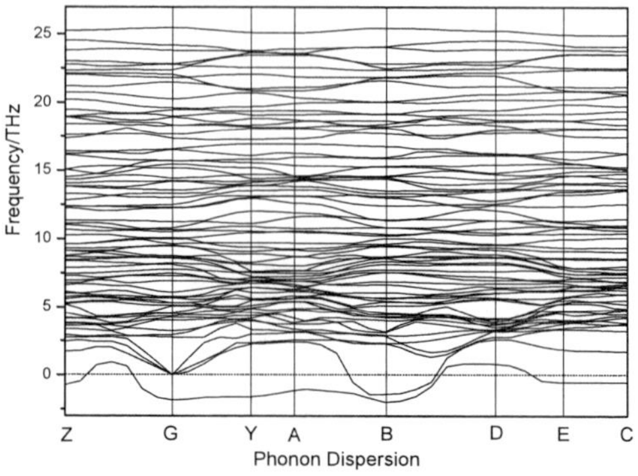

(b)

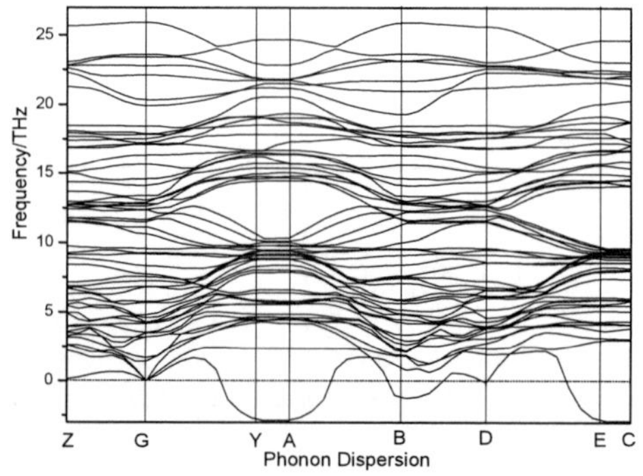

(c)

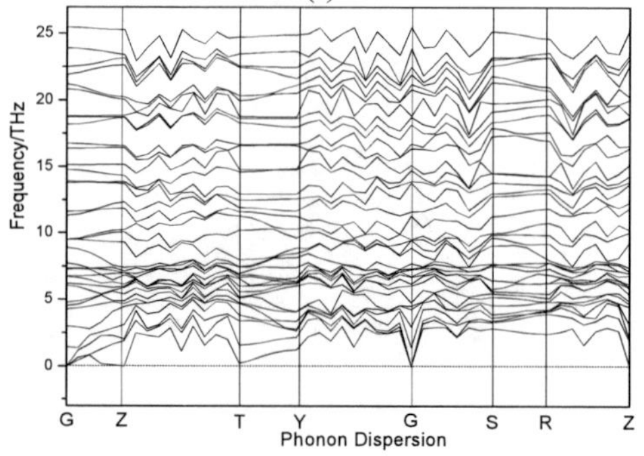

(d)

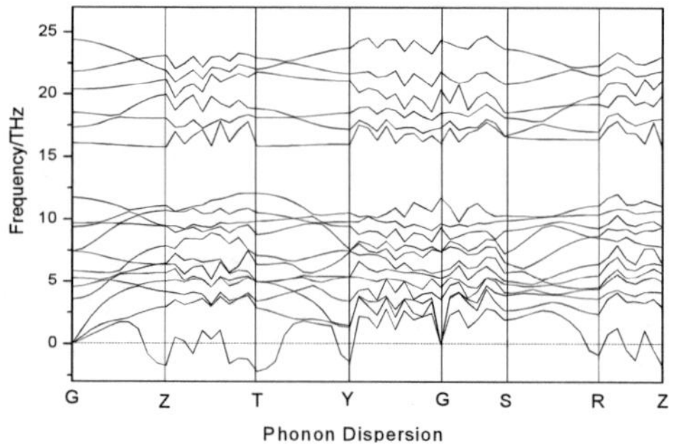

(e)

Fig.2 The diagram of Phonon dispersion (a)pure SnO_2 (b)SnO_2:La{12.5%}(c)SnO_2:La{16.67%} (d)SnO_2:La{25%} (e)SnO_2:La{50%}

Taking the crystals with doping concentration of 0% and 25% as an example, the phonon density of state and the partial density of state of the vortex are analyzed (see Figure 3). The vibration mode in the SnO_2:La{25%} crystal mainly appears at 1.3-26.2 THz of the frequency band, in which the calculation results show that the phonon state density peaks at 7.1 THz. In addition, according to the phonon spectrum, the contribution of different types of atoms in the crystal to the density of states is calculated. It is found that the density of the oxygen atoms is mainly distributed between 2.5-10 THz and 16-26 THz. The partial density of state of Sn atom and La atom is close to 0-10 THz. Compared with the phonon state density of pure SnO_2 crystal, the doping of La atom mainly changes the vibration mode of O atom. The vibration mode of the O atom in the low frequency band is enhanced, and the vibration mode in the high frequency band is lowered, which embodies a strong coupling effect between the La element and the O element.

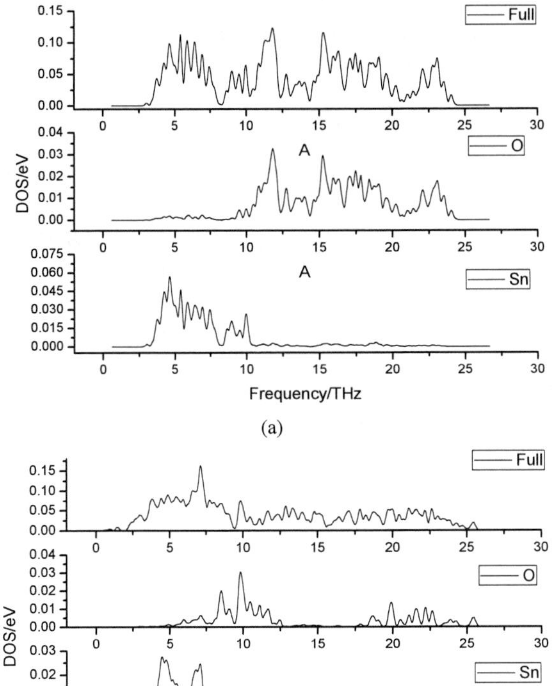

(a)

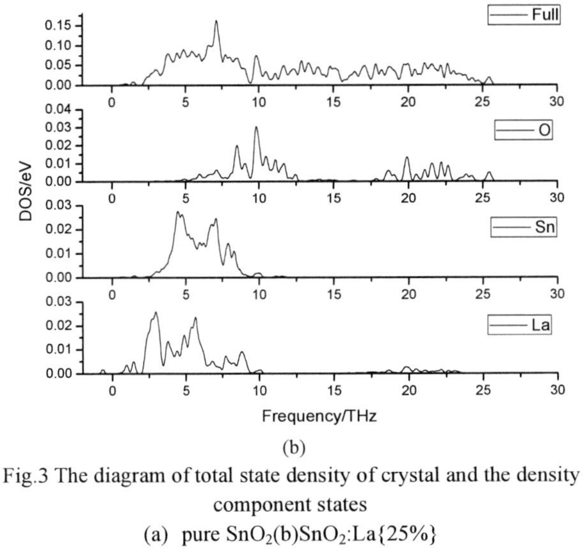

(b)

Fig.3 The diagram of total state density of crystal and the density component states

(a) pure SnO_2(b)SnO_2:La{25%}

IV. ANALYSISOFTHERMODYNAMICPROPERTIESOF SnO_2CRYSTALS

Entropy, enthalpy and free energy are important parameters reflecting the thermodynamic properties of materials. On the basis of harmonic approximation, we only use crystals with doping concentrations of 0% and 25% as examples. Using the obtained phonon spectrum, the phonon free energy, the phonon entropy, and the phonon enthalpy can be obtained, as shown in figure.4. Figure (a) shows that the entropy increases monotonously with increasing temperature. Because the temperature increases, the more intense the movement of atoms in the system, the chaotic degree of the system increases. Entropy is the scale of the disorder of molecular thermal motion in the system [14], so the temperature will increase and the entropy will increase. Figure (b) is a plot of phonon free energy decreasing with increasing temperature, and its reduction is the driving force of crystal phase transition [15], the formula is [16]:

$$F = U^* - TS \tag{2}$$

In the formula: U^* is the internal energy of the system, T is the temperature of the system, and S is the entropy. When the temperature rises, the energy in the system increases, and the entropy of the system increases, but the rate of increase is greater than the rate of increase, so the free energy of the crystal decreases with increasing temperature. Figure (c) shows the relationship between enthalpy and temperature. It can be seen that the enthalpy of the SnO_2 crystal increases with increasing temperature. The formula is:

$$H = U^* + PV \tag{3}$$

In the formula: P is the system pressure and V is the system volume. The physical meaning of enthalpy is that the system is equal to the heat absorbed by the crystal under isobaric conditions.It can be seen from the formula (3) that as the temperature increases, the internal energy of the system increases, and the crystal thermally expands, and PV increases. Therefore, the enthalpy of the SnO_2 crystal increases with an increase in temperature.

Analysis of Fig. 4 shows that the entropy, free energy, and enthalpy curve of the SnO_2 crystal become steep after the La element is doped. It shows that under the same conditions, compared with the undoped system, the chaos of the system increases, the crystal free energy decreases, and the absorbed heat increases, which indicates that the doped crystal is easier to form than the undoped crystal, and It can be judged that the recovery ability of the $AgSnO_2$ contact material after doping the La element in a high temperature environment is better than that of the undoped crystal.

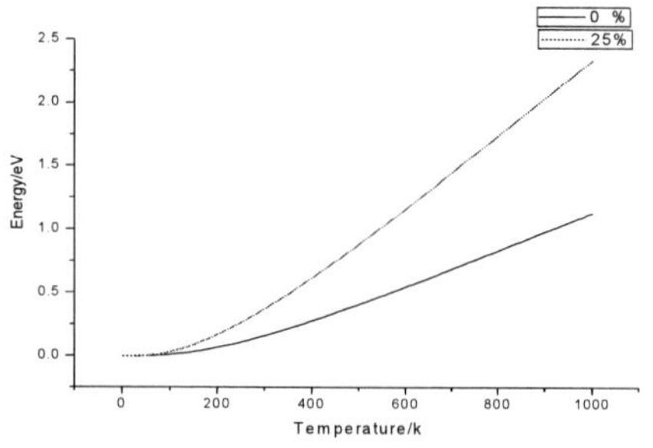

(a)

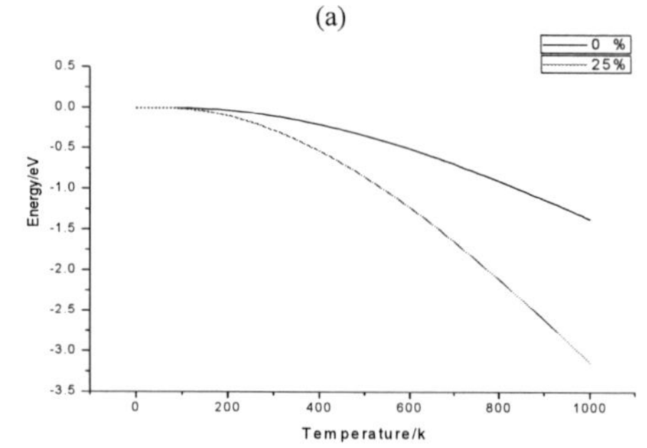

(b)

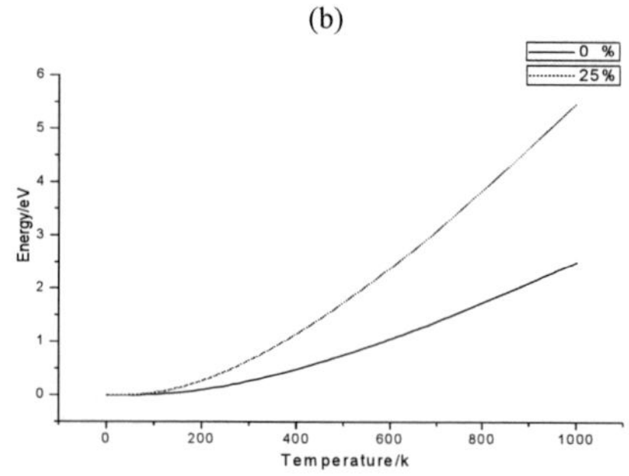

(c)

Fig.4 The thermodynamic function of SnO_2 crystal varies with temperature

(a)entropy (b) free energy (c) enthalpy

V. HEATCAPACITYANDTHERMALCONDUCTIVITYANALYSIS

A. Heat capacity analysis

The curve of the heat capacity of SnO_2 crystal with temperature is calculated by using the phonon partial wave state density, as shown in Fig. 5. It can be seen that in the range of 0-300K, the heat capacity of the SnO_2 crystal before and after doping increases almost linearly, and the growth rate slows down between 300-700K. After 700K, the curve is basically horizontal, that is, the heat capacity tends to a certain value. .It is because the change in heat capacity is related to the state of motion of the molecule.At the beginning, as the temperature increases, the molecules involved in the movement increase, and the heat capacity increases. When the temperature rises to a certain extent, the molecules participating in the movement tend to be saturated, and the heat capacity does not rise with the increase of temperature,and gradually approach a constant value [17].Therefore, it can be explained that in the temperature range of 0-300K, the heat capacity increases rapidly, and when it exceeds 300K, the heat capacity growth becomes slow and finally saturates.

Comparing the difference of crystal heat capacity before and after doping, it can be seen that at the same temperature, the heat capacity of the crystal after doping is significantly larger than that of the undoped crystal, and the change speed is faster at low temperature. This indicates that the doping of the La element increases the activity of the molecule, that is, the number of molecules participating in the movement increases. At the same time, combined with the phonon partial wave state density map, it also shows that the doping of La element greatly activates the activity of O element, which increases the heat capacity of the crystal.

B. Thermal conductivity analysis

The thermal conductivity of a solid depends mainly on the mean free path of the phonon and the relationship between the heat capacity per unit volume and the temperature. The formula is [18]:

$$\lambda = \frac{1}{3} C_v \bar{\upsilon} l \qquad (4)$$

Where $\bar{\upsilon}$ represents the average rate of directional diffusion of phonons, but both theory and experiment have shown that temperature has no significant effect on it and can be omitted.It can be seen from Fig. 5 that the heat capacity of the crystal after doping is significantly larger than that of the undoped crystal, and after doping, the mean free path of the phonon is reduced under the same condition because the crystal lattice is near the defect,the elasticity of lattice is different from the complete crystal, then the phonon will also be scattered after it hits the defect. The above two factors indicate that doping has a significant effect on the thermal conductivity of the crystal.

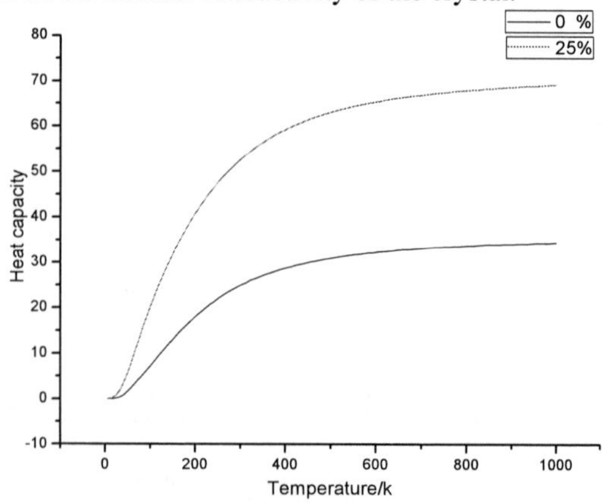

Fig.5 The relation between phonon heat capacity and temperature

REFERENCES

[1] Jingqin Wang, Yancai Zhu, Haitao Wang, JunZhao. Effect of Additive Bi on $AgSnO_2$ Contact Materials[J]. Transactions of China Electrotechnical Society,2011,26(01):29-33.

[2] Zhiyong Liu. Calculation and research of nano-doped $AgSnO_2$ electrical contact materials[D]. Tianjin University, 2007.

[3] Chunping Wu, Danqing Yi, Canhui Xu, Yimin Zhou, Yan. Research Status and Development Trend of Silver-based Alloys[J]. Electrical Materials, 2012, 02: 1-8.

[4] Xiaojun Zhang, Anxiang Wang, Bin Gao, Changle Chen. Study on the phonon spectrum and vibration properties of metal ruthenium[J].Materials Review, 2015, 29(04):136-140.

[5] Dove M T. Introduction to Lattice Dynamics[M]. Cam-bridge: Cambridge University Press,1993.

[6] Wencan Jiang, Hua Chen, Weibin Zhang. First-principles study of phonon spectrum and specific heat capacity of TATB crystal[J].Acta PhysicaSinica, 2016, 65(12): 220-228.

[7] Ying Wang. Development and application of new theoretical methods for complex molecular systems[D]. East China Normal University, 2018.

[8] Xin Mu. First-principles study of electron spin polarization of some materials[D]. University of Science and Technology of China, 2011.

[9] Torrent M, Jollet F, Bottin F. Implementation of the Projector Augmented-wave Method in the ABINIT Code: Applicationtothe Study of Iron under Pressure[J]. Comput.Mater.Sci.2008,42(2): 337-351.

[10] Kresse G, Joubert D. From Ultrasoft Pseudopotentials to the Projector Augmented-wave Method[J]. Phys. Rev. B,1999,59(3) :1758-1775.

[11] Cui X Y, Medvedeva J E, Delley B, et al. Role of Embedded Clustering in Dilute Magnetic Semiconductors: Cr doped GaN[J].Phys. Rev.Lett, 2005,95 (25) :6404-6405.

[12] G. Ghosh, M. Asta. First-principles calculation of structural energetics of Al-TM (TM=Ti, Zr, Hf) intermetallics[J]. Acta Materialia, 2005,53(11): 3225- 3252.

[13] Born M, Huang K. Dynamical Theory of Crystal Lattices[M]. Oxford University Press, 1998.

[14] Su Hui, Gao Xuan, Hu Baowen, Yuan Zhouxiang, Li Wenxing. Study on Entropy Change Law Based on Particle Discrete Element Rock Model[J]. International Journal of Hydroelectric Energy, 2018,36(06):106-109.

[15] Wen Xu. Preparation and growth mechanism of zinc oxide crystal materials[D]. Xi'an University of Science and Technology, 2008.

[16] He Cuiyun. Phase diagram determination and thermodynamic study of Al-Cu-Mn, Al-Cu-Si, Al-Mg-Ni and Ni-Ti-Si systems[D]. Central South University, 2008.

[17] He Weizhong, Fang Zhijie. First-principles study of phonon spectrum and thermodynamic properties of $LiNiPO_4$[J].Journal of Guangxi University of Science and Technology,2014,25(04):14-18.

[18] Cao Quanxi, Lei Tianming, Huang Yunxia, et al. The basis of solid physics[M]. Xidian University Press, 2008.

Ling Chen was born in Baoding City, Hebei Province in March 1993. Now he is a master of electrical engineering at Hebei University of Technology.

Jingqin Wang was born in Hengshui District, Hebei Province, in 1964. The author received the B.S., M.S. and Ph.D. degrees in electrical engineering from Hebei University of Technology, Tianjin, P.R.China, in 1984, 1986 and 1997 respectively.

Since 1998, she has been a Professor. And she became Doctoral Tutor of Electrical Engineering College, Hebei University of Technology in 2003. She currently holds 21 patents and has written more than 110 journal articles.

Prof. Wang is the Secretary General of Electrical Products Reliability Association of China Electro Technical Society (CES). She was a recipient of the National Science and Technology Progress Award in 2000, 2002, 2008, Science and Technology Progress Award of Hebei Province in 1991, 2005, 2013.

She is currently deputy director of the Institute of Electrical Appliances of Hebei University of Technology.She is an expert on special allowances of the State Council, a national candidate for hundreds of millions of the talents project of the new century, and an outstanding expert of Hebei Province. Vice Chairman and Member of the Arc-electricity Contact Committee of China Electrotechnical Society, Member of the Low-voltage Electrical Appliances Committee of China Electrotechnical Society.

Shaoqi Sun was born Xingtai City, Hebei Province in March 1995. Now she is a master of electrical engineering at Hebei University of Technology.

7th International Conference on Reliability of
Electrical Products and Electrical Contacts,
November 04-06, 2019

Quality Consistency Detection Method of Permanent Magnet Synchronous Motor Based on No-load Current

Xuerong Ye*, Liqin Wu, Qisen Sun, Yanmuzi Yang
Harbin Institute of Technology, Harbin,150001
E-mail: xuelai1981@163.com Tel:13946177562

Abstract—**Permanent magnet synchronous motor (PMSM), as an electromechanical product, has many parts, complex technology and outstanding quality consistency problems. The dynamic eccentricity of the rotor is affected by both the stator and the rotor, which will directly affect the air gap, vibration, noise and reliability of the motor. At present, manufacturers lack the detection method of rotor dynamic eccentricity consistency. Based on the no-load current, this paper presents a method of rotor dynamic eccentricity consistency detection for all kinds of motors with strong applicability. Firstly, the relationship between no-load current and dynamic eccentric displacement of rotor is analyzed, and the current spectrum characteristics strongly related to dynamic eccentricity are extracted. Then, the fitting function between different eccentric displacement and characteristic harmonic content of no-load current is obtained by least square method, and the quantitative estimation of dynamic eccentricity is realized. Through Monte Carlo simulation, the influence of the decentralization of motor structural parameters on the consistency detection of motor rotor dynamic eccentricity is analyzed. Finally, a permanent magnet synchronous motor is taken as an example to test and analyze the quality consistency, and to verify the effectiveness of the proposed method**

Index Terms—**Rotor Dynamic Eccentricity, Quality Consistency, Permanent Magnet Synchronous Motor, On-line Fault Diagnosis**

I. INTRODUCTION

Motor is an important component of each joint of the manipulator, and its working characteristics directly determine the performance and reliability of the manipulator. In recent years, the development of the manipulator towards miniaturization, low loss and high precision has put forward higher requirements for the loss, volume and consistency of the motor [1-2]. The application of permanent magnet synchronous motor (PMSM) is helpful to solve the above problems to a certain extent, and its consistency detection has attracted wide attention [3-5].

As a common synchronous motor, the rotor eccentricity diagnosis of permanent magnet synchronous motor (PMSM) is complex. It is a method to use the end-jump of the shaft as the static rotation accuracy value. The biggest problem of measuring the end-jump of the shaft is limited to the static rotation eccentricity, but not suitable for the detection of dynamic eccentricity. In order to study the dynamic eccentricity of rotor, scholars have studied the relationship between dynamic eccentricity and air gap magnetic field, unbalanced magnetic pull force and cogging torque, but these are not easy to obtain in actual measurement. Usually, the dynamic eccentricity is analyzed theoretically by simulation. Some scholars have solved the problem of rotor dynamic eccentricity diagnosis to a certain extent by combining motor current information with position information, but they can not detect the consistency of dynamic eccentricity displacement of batch rotor before the motor leaves the factory, and can not locate the key structural parameters that cause dynamic eccentricity, and then reduce the rotor dynamic eccentricity by improving the technology. The impact.

In this paper, a permanent magnet synchronous motor (PMSM) used in a manipulator joint is taken as an example. A finite element model for solving the motor body is established based on Ansoft/Maxwell, and a SVPWM control system model of PMSM is established based on Maxwell and Simulink combined simulation. Under the stable operation of the motor under no-load, different dynamic eccentric displacements and no-load of the motor are simulated. Based on the relationship between the characteristic frequency amplitude of current and the fitting function obtained by the least square method, the on-line diagnosis of the dynamic eccentricity displacement of the rotor before the motor leaves the factory is realized, and the consistency of the dynamic eccentricity of the batch rotor is detected. On this basis, the key structural parameters that aggravate the dynamic eccentricity are positioned by Monte Carlo simulation. The corresponding motor structure lays the foundation for improving motor quality consistency.

II. MOTIVATION

The production process of permanent magnet synchronous motor (PMSM) is complex. When the stator and rotor are assembled, it is difficult to ensure that the stator and rotor axes are completely aligned, so the motor and rotor appear different degrees of eccentricity. The factory usually does not have the equipment to measure the eccentric displacement of the motor, so it is impossible to measure the dynamic eccentric displacement of the motor rotor, so it is impossible to detect the consistency of the dynamic eccentric displacement of the motor rotor. In the case of motor rotor dynamic eccentricity, the dispersion of motor structure size even aggravates the impact of rotor dynamic eccentricity, and at the same time increases the dispersion of rotor dynamic eccentricity, thereby reducing the consistency of mass motor quality.

In order to ensure the consistency of qualified rate and motor quality, online diagnosis and consistency detection of motor eccentricity are needed before the motor leaves the factory, and key structural parameters of the motor are optimized to improve the consistency of motor quality. On the basis of studying the fault mechanism of dynamic eccentricity of permanent magnet synchronous motor (PMSM) rotor and the influence of different degrees of dynamic eccentricity on no-load current of motor, this paper studies the method of extracting dynamic eccentricity fault characteristics of PMSM rotor on-line and predicting eccentricity displacement, so as to solve the consistency detection of dynamic eccentricity of batch motor rotor. Through Monte Carlo simulation, the influence of structural parameters on eccentricity is obtained, and the key structural parameters affecting the motor quality consistency are obtained, which lays a foundation for further optimizing the key motor technology and improving the motor quality consistency.

III. FRAMEWORK OF METHODOLOGY

Taking a 10-pole 12-slot permanent magnet synchronous motor as an example, this paper studies the on-line diagnosis of dynamic eccentricity of motor rotor. Maxwell finite element method is used to calculate the effect of dynamic eccentricity displacement on no-load current of motor. Combined with Fourier decomposition theory, signal processing of no-load current of motor is carried out to extract dynamic eccentricity. Characteristic frequencies are simulated for different dynamic eccentricity displacements. Based on least square method, the function between dynamic eccentricity displacement and eccentricity characteristic frequency is fitted. Thus, the diagnosis of dynamic eccentricity displacement of PMSM under no-load state is realized, and the consistency detection of dynamic eccentricity of a group of rotors is carried out. By Monte Carlo simulation, the influence of the structure parameters of the motor on the dynamic eccentricity of the rotor is obtained, and the key process parameters affecting the quality consistency of the motor are obtained, which lays a foundation for further improving the quality consistency of the motor. The block diagram of the overall scheme is shown in Figure 1.

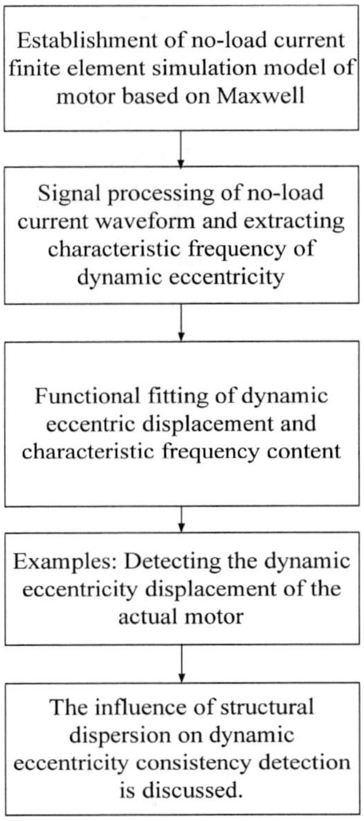

Fig. 1 Overall schematic block diagram

IV. CONSISTENCY DETECTION OF ROTOR DYNAMIC ECCENTRICITY

A. Normal no-load current simulation

In this paper, a 10-pole 12-slot surface mounted permanent magnet synchronous motor (SMPM) is simulated and analyzed. The speed is set to 2000 rpm, and it runs in no-load state. The sampling time of current is 0.06s, and the sampling frequency is 20,000 Hz.

The basic parameters of the motor are shown in Table 1.

According to the actual structure of permanent magnet synchronous motor (PMSM), a two-dimensional simulation and analysis model of the motor body is established based on Maxwell. The self-inductance and mutual inductance waveforms of the motor are obtained through the simulation of Maxwell model.

$$L_s = \frac{L_{aa} + L_{bb} + L_{cc}}{3}$$

$$M_s = \frac{L_{ab} + L_{bc} + L_{ba} + L_{bc} + L_{ca} + L_{cb}}{6}$$
$$L_{phase-average} = L_s + 2M_s \tag{1}$$

$$L_d = L_q = \frac{3}{2} L_{phase-average}$$
$$L_0 = L_s - 2M_s \tag{2}$$

The average self-inductance, average mutual inductance and average phase inductance of the motor are calculated according to formula (1). Then the DQ inductance is calculated according to formula (2). The calculated DQ inductance is input into the PMSM module of the double closed-loop control system model of Simulink motor, and the torque is set to 0. The no-load current waveform is simulated. Simulink simulation model block diagram is shown in Figure 2.

TABLE I

BASIC PARAMETERS OF PERMANENT MAGNET SYNCHRONOUS MOTOR

parameters	value
Rated torque/Nm	8
Rated speed/(r/min)	2000
pole	10
Number of parallel branches	1
Magnetization modeStator	Matched magnetization
Outer Diameter/mm	135
Stator inner diameter/mm	95
Stator core length/mm	55
Winding connection mode	Three-phase satellite
Slot number	connection
	12

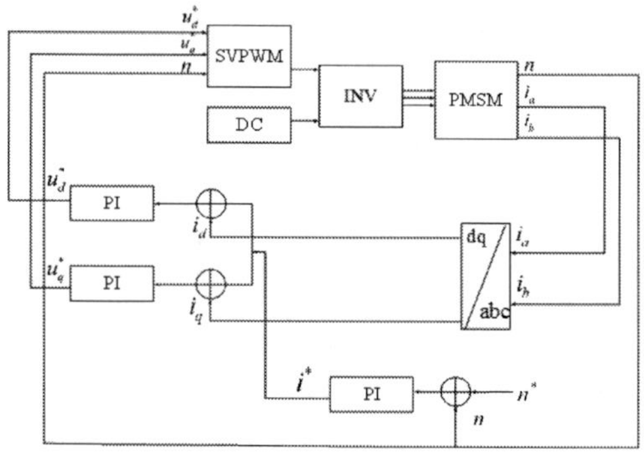

Fig. 2 Model block diagram of double closed-loop control system for Simulink motor

When the motor is in normal no-load state, the phase currents and their Fourier decomposition results are shown in Fig. 3 and Fig. 4.

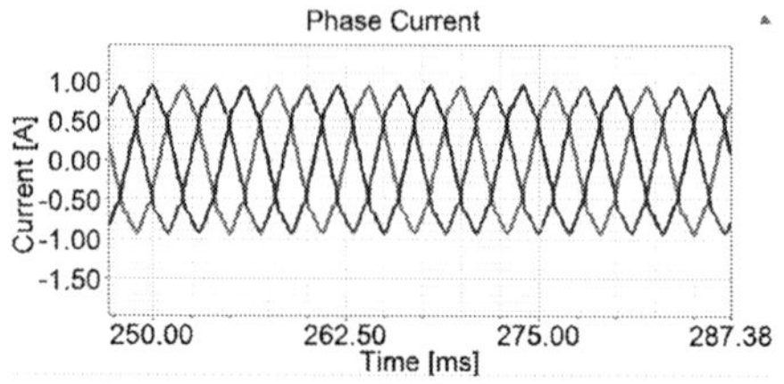

Fig. 3 Normal operation no-load current

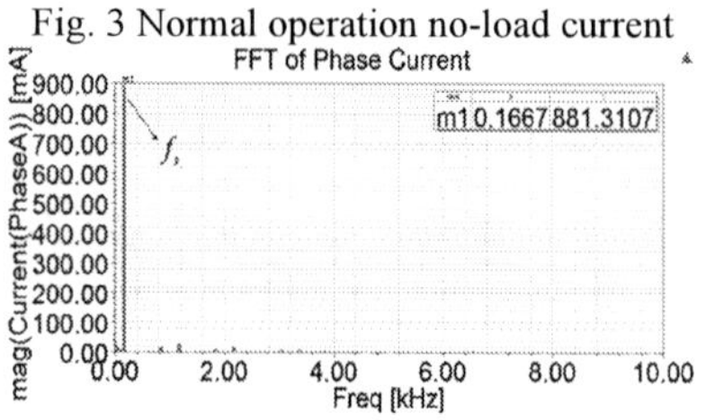

Fig. 4 Normal operation no-load current FFT

It can be seen from the figure that when the motor is in normal no-load state, the phase current only contains fundamental and sub-harmonics, that is, fundamental and 5, 7, 11, 13 harmonics.

B. Relation between Frequency Characteristics of No-load Current and Dynamic Eccentricity

1) Frequency characteristics of dynamic eccentric no-load current

Dynamic eccentricity is caused by the bending of the rotor shaft, bearing wear, mechanical resonance at the limit speed, etc. The center of the rotor is not the center of rotation, and the position of the minimum air gap changes with the rotation of the rotor [11]. Because the air gap is not uniform due to the eccentricity of the motor, the magnetic momentum of the permanent magnet acting on the air gap at the corresponding position is different, and the period of the air gap permeability change is the circumference of the whole air gap, so it will inevitably affect the size of the air gap magnetic density, and the harmonic magnetic field in the air gap will change accordingly, which will not only cause the change of the slot torque, but also cause the change of the slot magnetic field. Causes the motor performance and the loss change.

When the rotor is eccentric, the air gap permeability changes. Assuming that the stator and rotor surfaces are smooth, for dynamic eccentricity, the air gap permeability can be expressed as

$$P_s(\theta,t) = P_0 + \sum P_n \cos n(\omega_r t - \theta) \tag{3}$$

In the formula, P_0 is the average air gap permeability, P_n is the magnitude of the second permeability, ω_r is the angular velocity of the motor and θ is the mechanical angle are used.

The expression of characteristic frequency induced by stator current is as follows.

$$f_s = \left[(kZ \pm n_d)\frac{1-s}{p} \pm n_s \right] f \qquad (4)$$

In the formula, f_s is the eccentric characteristic frequency needed to be monitored, f is the fundamental frequency of the power supply, k is the arbitrary integer (usually 1), Z is the number of slots in the rotor, n_d is the static eccentric frequency and $n_d = 1, 2, 3...$ is the dynamic eccentric frequency are obtained when $n_d = 0$ the eccentric series is eccentric. n_s is the time harmonic series in the stator power supply, $n_s = \pm 1, \pm 2, \pm 3, ...$, the p is pole logarithm of the motor, and s is the slip rate.

2) Dynamic eccentricity modeling

The frequency of stator current of permanent magnet synchronous motor is the frequency of the switching state of the inverter when the motor is in normal operation, which can be calculated according to formula (5):

$$f_e = np / 60 \qquad (5)$$

In the formula, p it is the polar logarithm and n is the rotational speed.

Formula (5) shows that the fundamental frequency of stator current corresponding to 2000 rpm is 166.67 Hz. Formula (4) shows that the characteristic frequencies of dynamic eccentricity are 200 Hz and 233 Hz. In this paper, 233Hz is taken as the characteristic frequency of dynamic eccentricity.

On the basis of normal motor simulation, the coordinates of the rotor center are modified to simulate the dynamic eccentricity of the rotor, and the no-load current waveform and the results of Fourier decomposition of the no-load current are obtained. The no-load current with eccentric displacement of 0.24 mm is shown in Fig. 5, and the result of Fourier decomposition is shown in Fig. 6. The no-load current and Fourier decomposition results of the motor with eccentric displacement of 0.32mm are shown in fig. 7 and 8.

As can be seen from the figure, when the motor has dynamic eccentricity, the fundamental wave amplitude of no-load current is larger than that of normal, and obvious harmonic components appear at 233 Hz ($1.4 f_e$)frequency and 566 Hz($3 f_e$) harmonic.

When the eccentric displacement increases to 0.32mm, the harmonic components at the fundamental, 233Hz and 566Hz frequencies also increase.

The eccentric displacement of electromotor is studied. A batch of simulation models are set up. The displacement of rotor is 5 values of equal interval between 0 mm and 0.32 mm, respectively. The harmonic contents of no-load current and no-load current under different dynamic eccentric displacements are obtained by simulation.

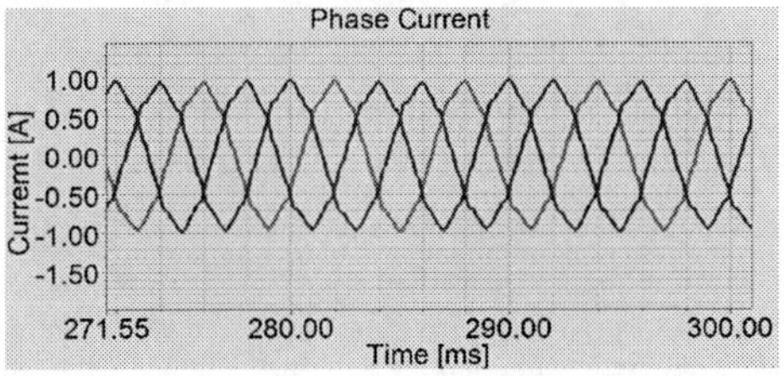

Fig.5 No-load current with eccentric displacement of 0.24mm

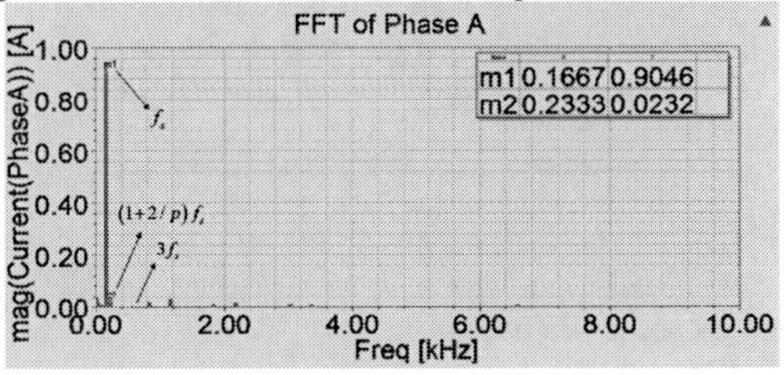

Fig.6 Fourier decomposition of no-load current with eccentric displacement of 0.24 mm

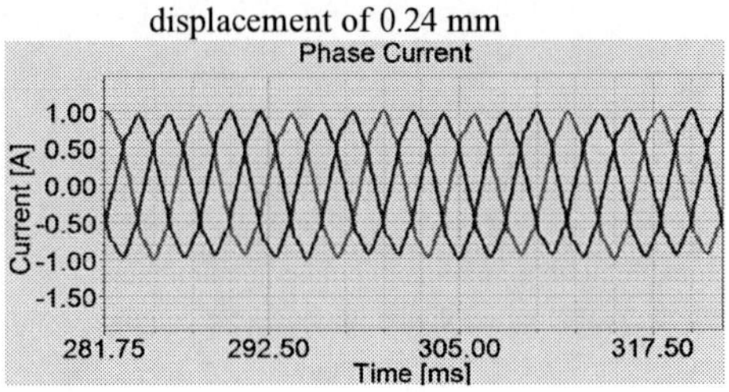

Fig.7 No-load current of 0.32mm eccentric displacement of motor

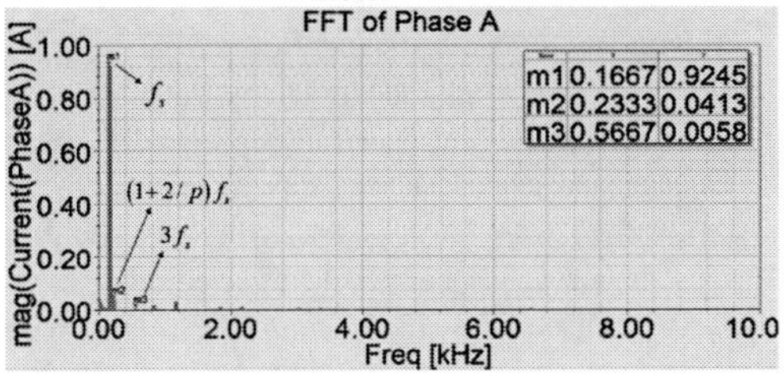

Fig. 8 Fourier decomposition of no-load current with eccentric

TABLE II

THE HARMONIC CONTENT CORRESPONDING TO DIFFERENT ECCENTRIC DISPLACEMENTS

harmonic content /mA Eccentric displacement /mm	166.7Hz	233Hz	833Hz	1167Hz
0	881.3	0	18.8097	29.1264
0.08	883.9634	3.7228	18.7163	29.1667
0.16	892.136	10.8508	18.3018	29.3151
0.24	904.6	23.2	18.9	29.4
0.32	924.5	41.3	17.1	29.7

For the no-load current of the motor whose fundamental

frequency is 166.7Hz, it normally contains sub-harmonics, so in the table above, 833Hz ($5f_s$) and 1167Hz ($7f_s$) outside the fundamental wave are normal harmonics, and the characteristic harmonics caused by eccentricity are 233Hz ($1.4f_e$), which are used as the eigenvalues of detecting dynamic eccentricity. It can be seen from the above table that with the increase of eccentric displacement of the motor, the amplitude of no-load current increases, and the harmonic content at 233Hz increases.

According to the least square method, the harmonic amplitudes of 233Hz under different eccentric displacements are fitted, and the fitting function is obtained as shown in equation (6):

$$f(x) = -1.458\times10^{\wedge(-4)}x^2 + 0.01339x + 0.01394 \quad (6)$$

Fitted waveforms of harmonic amplitudes of different eccentric displacements and no-load current 233Hz are obtained as shown in Fig. 9.

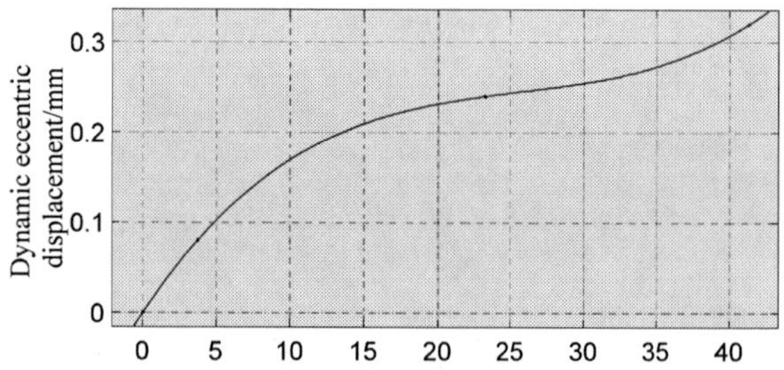

Fig. 9 Fitted waveforms of harmonic amplitudes in different eccentric displacements and no-load currents of 233Hz

C. Dynamic eccentricity consistency detection

1) Examples of dynamic eccentricity detection

In this section, taking permanent magnet synchronous motor as an example, a method of motor eccentricity consistency detection is proposed, which is suitable for all motors with no-load current and dynamic eccentricity characteristic harmonics. It can diagnose motor eccentricity online at the stage of motor copying, and characterize motor quality consistency through dynamic eccentricity.

A finite element simulation model is built with the actual structure size of a motor, and dynamic eccentricity detection is carried out. The no-load current waveform and FFT characteristic frequency are extracted by simulation, as shown in the figure.

According to the fitting function (6), the dynamic eccentric displacement of this example is 0.2923 mm.

2) Effect of Structure Dispersion on Dynamic Eccentricity Consistency Detection

In this section, the influence of motor structure size dispersion on dynamic eccentricity consistency detection is analyzed and discussed. The simulation studies the motor model with eccentric displacement of 0.32mm. Considering the dispersion of the motor structure size, Monte Carlo simulation is used to obtain the characteristic harmonic distribution of the no-load current of the batch motor under the eccentric displacement. The simulation results show that the no-load current harmonic content of the motor with eccentric displacement of 0.32mm is not exactly the same, and there is a certain degree of dispersion. According to the value of harmonic content obtained by simulation, the eccentric displacement distribution of these motors is calculated by fitting function, as shown in Fig. 10.

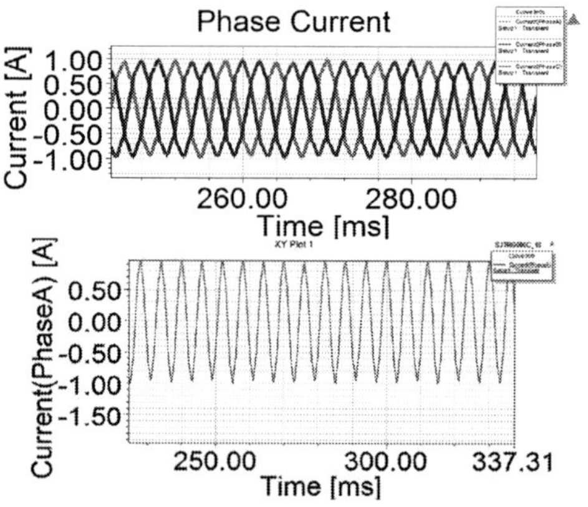

Fig. 10 Simulation waveform of no-load current for example

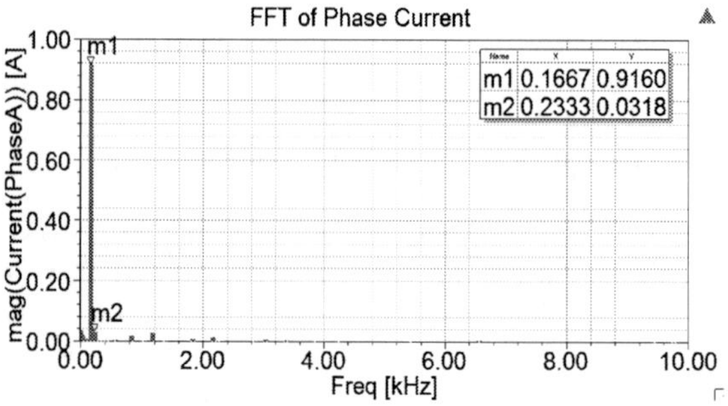

Fig. 11 Simulation waveform of no-load current for example FFT

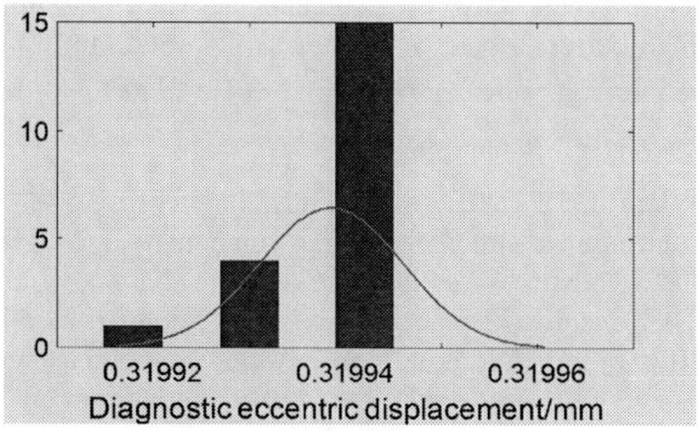

Fig. 12 Distribution of Diagnostic Result of Eccentric Displacement of Batch Motor

Affected by the decentralization of motor structural parameters, the eccentric displacement of the same batch of motors with the same eccentric displacement is dispersed, which is diagnosed by harmonic of no-load current. It shows that the size of motor structure has an effect on the effect of motor eccentricity reflected on harmonic. The dispersion of some structures may aggravate the effect of rotor dynamic eccentricity, and some junctions. The decentralization of the mechanism may reduce the effect of rotor dynamic eccentricity, and further illustrate that the consistency of motor structure size affects the consistency of motor quality. Therefore, according to this method, the quality consistency of batch motor can be evaluated while the dynamic eccentricity displacement of batch motor is diagnosed.

V. CONCLUSION

On the basis of studying the fault mechanism and fault characteristics of PMSM's dynamic eccentricity, the relationship between dynamic eccentricity and characteristic harmonics of motor's no-load current is analyzed by simulation of motor's no-load current with maxwell. The harmonic amplitude of each dynamic eccentricity displacement and characteristic frequency of no-load current at 233Hz is obtained by least square method. The fitting function between the values can detect the displacement of the motor's dynamic eccentricity under no-load steady-state operation, and then realize the dynamic eccentricity consistency detection of the batch rotor. On this basis, the influence of the motor structure dispersion on the motor's dynamic eccentricity consistency detection is analyzed and discussed.

1) Modeling the no-load current and extracting the characteristic frequencies strongly related to the dynamic eccentricity of the motor rotor.

2) Based on the least square method, the fitting function curve of harmonic amplitude on the frequency of dynamic eccentricity displacement and no-load current 233Hz is obtained, which realizes on-line diagnosis of dynamic eccentricity displacement of electric motor under no-load condition, and is verified by an example.

3) The method to characterize motor quality consistency based on motor dynamic eccentricity consistency is obtained, and the influence of motor structure dispersion on motor rotor dynamic eccentricity detection is discussed.

ACKNOWLEDGMENT

National Key R&D Program of China (2017YFB1300800) and National Natural Science Foundation of China (61671172)

REFERENCES

[1] Haijun Wang, Jianwei Leng. Summary On Development Of Permanent Magnet Synchronous Motor, The 30th Chinese Control and Decision Conference, 2018, 689-693.

[2] Cao Wenping, Mecro B C, Atkinson G J, et al. Overview of electric motor technologies used for more electric aircraft(MEA)[J]. IEEE Transactions on Industrial Electronics, 2012, 59(9):3523-3531.

[3] Pillay P, Krishnan R. Application characteristics of permanent magnet synchronous and brushless DC motors for servo drives[J]. IEEE Transactions on Industry Applications,1991, 27(5):986-996.

[4] Li Bingqiang,Lin Hui. Novel high-precision speed regulation system for permanent magnet synchronous motor[J]. Proceedings of the CSEE, 2009, 29(15):61- 66.

[5] Chem Lizhou,Robust design[M]. Beijing: China Machine Press,2000:1-21(in Chinese).

[6] Liu Fei, Liang Lin, Xu Guanghua et al. Detection method of electrode rotation eccentricity based on current information [J]. Journal of Electrical Technology, 2014 (7), 181-186.

[7] Kong Han, Liu Jinglin. Study on the influence of rotor eccentricity of permanent magnet servo motor on motor performance [J]. Journal of Motor and Control, 2016.01.008, 52-59.

[8] Li Ming, Wang Wei. The effect of static eccentricity of rotor on the torque waveform of permanent magnet synchronous motor in electric vehicle [J]. Micromotor [J], 2016.04.007.23-24.

[9] Huang Xin, Fang Chao, Tan Gengrui, Du Xiaobin. Study on the Performance of Permanent Magnet Synchronous Motor with Dynamic Eccentricity of Rotor [J]. Explosion-proof Motor, 2017 (5). 10-12.

[10] Bashir Mahdi Ebrahimi, Jawad Faiz. Configuration Impacts on Eccentricity Fault Detection in Permanent Magnet Synchronous Motors. IEEE TRANSACTIONS ON MAGNETICS, 2012,2,903-906.

[11] Zhao Xiangyang et al. Fault model simulation research based on stator current method to detect dynamic eccentricity of brushless DC motor rotor. Journal of Electrical Engineering of China [J], 2011, 12, 25, 124-130.

Xuerong Ye (M'11) received the B.S., M.S. and Ph.D. degrees in Electrical Engineering from Harbin Institute of Technology, Harbin, China, in 2003, 2005, and 2009 respectively. He is currently an Associate Professor of the Department of Electrical Engineering, Harbin Institute of Technology. His research interests include the failure analysis and reliability design for electronic devices and systems.

Liqin Wu was born in 1993. She received the B.S degree in Electrical Engineering and Its Automation from Northeast Agricultural University, Harbin, China, in 2015, received the M.S. degree in Electrical Engineering from Harbin Engineering University, Harbin, China, in 2018. She is currently working towards the Ph.D. degree at Harbin Institute of Technology. Her research area is motor quality consistency optimization design.

Qisen Sun was born in 1995. He received the B.S. degree in Electrical Engineering from Harbin Institute of Technology, Harbin, China, in 2019. He is currently working towards the M.S. degree at Harbin Institute of Technology.

Yanmuzi Yang was born in 1993. She received the B.S. degree in Electrical Engineering and Automation from Northeast Forestry University, Harbin, China, in 2015. She is currently an assistant engineer at institute of reliability in electrical apparatus and electronics. She is response for reliability prediction, taguchi robust design optimization and software development.

Study on $AgSnO_2$ Contact Material for the Electric Vehicles' Power Switch

Xiaofang Yan, Xiaoping Bai, Jie Li, Yangfang Chen, Yangdeng Jin
Fuda Alloy Materials Co., Ltd., Wenzhou, Zhejiang, 325025
E-mail: sophyan@chian-fuda.com Tel: 86-577-86909177

***Abstract*—This paper states the common failures of several popular silver metal oxides in EV power switches at the conditions of DC 40V-60V, 10A-1000A. A new $AgSnO_2$ has been introduced, the properties of Electrical life and electric arc have been improved by doping to modify the properties and changing the oxidation parameters to. The results show that the material has good welding resistance and low arc by comparing the welding force, arc duration and energy with several popular silver metal oxides in the simulation device at 2000A and 20A, which meets the demands of the electric vehicles' power switches.**

***Index Terms*—Electric Vehicle, Power switch, Eelectrical contact material, $AgSnO_2$**

I. INTRODUCTION

Energy crisis and environmental pollution are increasing. In terms of energy consumption and environmental pollution, the impact of automobiles can not be ignored. The development of Environmentally friendly electric vehicles with high efficiency, energy saving, low noise and zero emission has become an inevitable trend in the development of automotive industry at home and abroad. All countries in the world have set goals for the development of electric vehicles. China will produce and sell 5 million electric vehicles in 2020. The sales share of electric vehicles will reach 7%-10% in 2020, 15-20% in 2025 and more than 50% in 2030.

The power switch can automatically control and switch, and supply power to the battery management system to ensure the normal operation of the battery management system in the running and charging of the electric vehicle. The power voltage is about DC 40V-60V. Electric vehicles with frequent start-up, acceleration and deceleration will lead to large current. Therefore, the power switch of electric vehicle needs to withstand a current range from several amperes to more than 1000 amperes. General electrical life: under 2A-10A current needs to meet the life cycles of more than 100,000 about 300 A needs several hundred. breaking capacity test: It is necessary to cut off the current several dozen life cycles under 1000A-2000A, and the switch can be breaking normally. For the contact material used in power switch, it not only has good electrical conductivity, but also has good wear resistance, better welding resistance, low hardness, small arc and so on. This paper introduces the contact material used in power switch of electric vehicle.

AgMeO material is used in power switch of electric vehicle because of its good electrical conductivity, not easy to be oxidized and material stability. According to the feedback from the market, the common AgMeO materials have the following advantages and disadvantages:

A. $AgSnO_2$ material

$AgSnO_2$ material has good welding resistance and wear resistance, and the tendency of forming arc pits under the action of arc is very weak[2]. Therefore, it is widely used in automobile relay function management system, such as steering lights, car seats. In the electric vehicle switch, the $AgSnO_2$ material 1 on the market has good electrical performance at current below 500A, but it is easy to welding at current close to 1000A. Most contact material manufacturers improve their performance by increasing oxide content, which results in high bulk resistance, high temperature, high hardness and even affects the noise requirements of automobiles， welding still occurs at 1000A.

B. AgZnO material

The thermal stability of ZnO is higher than that of CdO, and its melting point is 1795 ° C. It is generally considered that AgZnO material has excellent resistance to welding, arc corrosion and low and stable resistance [3]. The material can meet the requirement of 1000A about 60 cycles in the switch of electric vehicle, and the arc time is obviously shorter than that of $AgSnO_2$ material, but the welding occurs around 300A. Contact manufacturers try to improve the interruption performance by adding brittle materials to reduce the strength of the interface. The effect is not significant, and the arc time increases sharply.

C. AgCuO material

Copper oxide has high stability, good bonding with silver matrix interface, the material has good welding resistance, and can meet the needs of 1000A or larger. However, due to the decomposition of CuO under the action of arc, the weak conductivity of Cu_2O is produced. It is easy to form oxide film on the contact surface, which leads to larger film resistance, and leads to the risk of temperature rise or non-conduction.

Given the above, the contact materials on the market have potential quality hazards in the use of power switches for electric vehicles. Contact manufacturers are carrying out upgrading research in order to meet the high reliability and quality requirements of power switches for electric vehicles. This paper introduces a kind of silver tin oxide material which meets the market demand.

II. $AgSnO_2$ CONTACT MATERIAL FOR POWER SWITCHES

This paper mainly introduces a common contact material for low-speed power supply switchgear. The voltage is 50V-60V. Its minimum service current is 2A. The other current classes are about 20A, 100A, 200A, 300A. The cut-off life current is 1000A-2000A.

A. Introduction of Material Preparation and Physical Properties

Composition of material: Ag content is about wt.88%, the remainder is MeO. The MeO are mainly tin oxide and indium oxide as reinforcing phases.

Material preparation: Ag, Sn and In additives were first alloyed to form silver alloy material, then the alloy was oxidized to be $AgSnO_2$, pressing and extrusion and then obtained the silver tin oxide material with uniform distribution and high density. By doping, oxygen vacancies are generated to increase the carrier concentration and improve the conductivity of materials. The oxide particles are coarsened by step oxidation, and the uniform distribution structure is adopted to ensure the material's life stability.

B. Mechanical Properties of Materials

The content of silver and indium oxide in the improved material is the same as that in the original material. The physical properties and metallographic structure of the improved material are compared with those of the original material in Tables I and Fig. 1.

TABLE I
COMPARISON OF PHYSICAL AND MECHANICAL PROPERTIES

Name	Density g/cm³	Resistivity μ Ω • cm	Elongation %	Hardness HV0.3
The improved material	≥9.78	2.20-2.30	≥20	85-95
The original material	≥9.80	2.45-2.60	≥18	110-120

Compared with physical properties, the improved material has low resistance and hardness.

Compared with the metallographic structure in Fig. 1, the oxidized particles of the improved material are thicker than those of the original material.

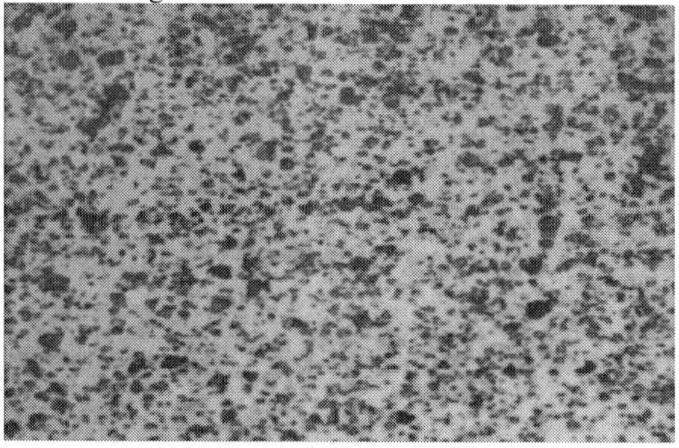

The improved material 1000X

The original material 1000X

Fig. 1 microstructure

C. Analog Electrical Performance

Rivet contacts were made, Specifications are as follows: R 3X0.5(0.3)+1.5X1.5,F 3X0.5(0.3)+1.75X1, R 6X1.85(0.6)+3X1.7 and F6X1.9(0.6)+3X3.5.

a) 2 0 A Electrical Life Simulated Test

test condition:

Specifications: R 3 X 0.5(0.3)+1.5 X 1.5 and F 3 X 0.5(0.3)+1.75 X 1

Load: 40V 20A DC Resistance

Contact pressure: 30g

Contact spacing: 1.5mm

Frequency: 1s on 1s off

The surface structures of contact were obtained by SEM, there are many serious cracks on the surface of the original material.

As shown in Figure 3, the electrical life of the improved material has been significantly improved: 95% of the improved material is 163, 668 cycles, 92, 397 cycles of the original material.

At low current, the welding force of the improved material is slightly better than that of the original material.

■ Surface morphology

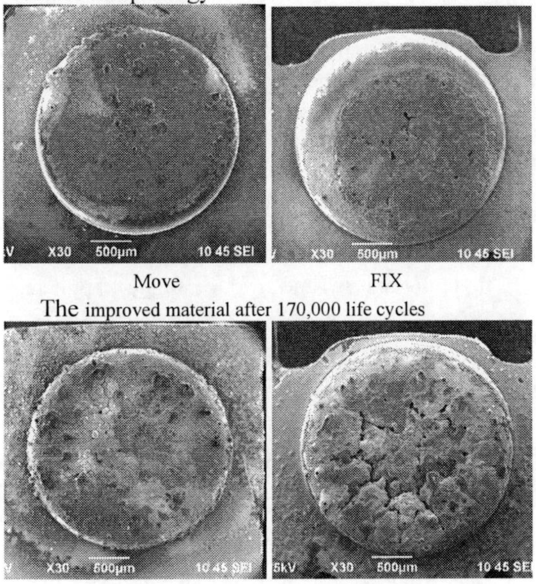

Fig. 2 Surface morphology after life test

■ Electrical life and welding force

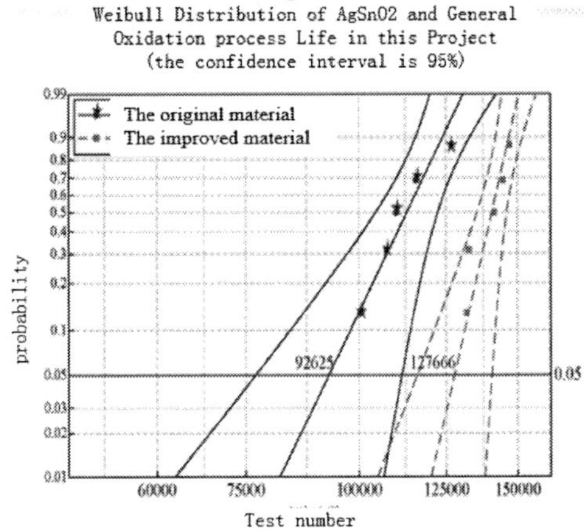

Fig. 3 Weibull Curve of Electrical Life

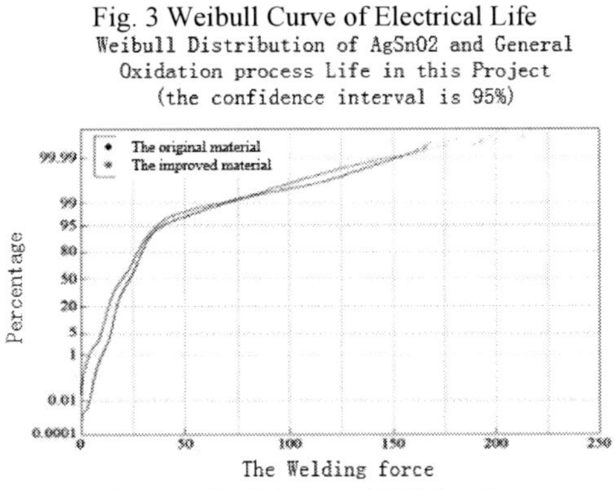

Fig. 4 Weibull Curve of Welding force

b) The welding force of 2000A high current simulating test

Test materials: AgCuO10, the improved $AgSnO_2$ and the original $AgSnO_2$.

Using capacitive discharge,2000A, pulse width about 10ms.

Each material test five groups, 10 closing-breaking operations for each group , and each operation's welding force was measured by a sensor when the contact was broken.

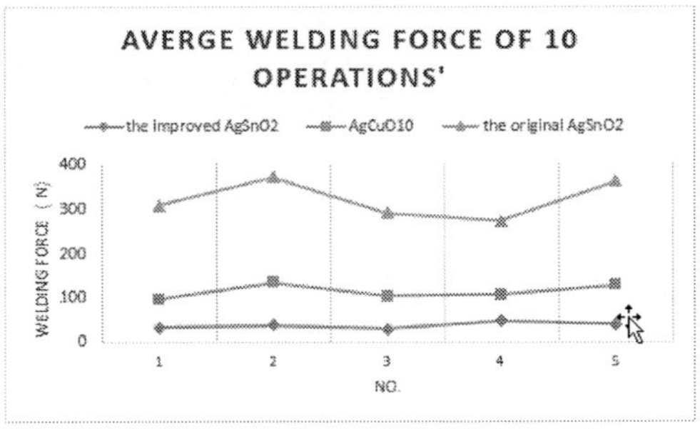

Fig. 5 Average Welding Force at 2000A

Under high current about 2000A, the material improvement effect is good, and the welding force is less than that of AgCuO10 material.

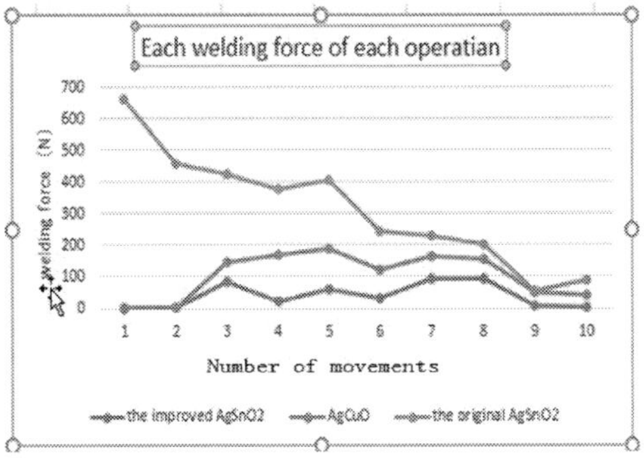

Fig. 6 Each Welding Force at 2000A

In the first 10 operations of the same contact spot contact, the welding force decreases with the increase of the number of operations.

III. RESULTS AND ANALYSIS

1) Low material resistance reduces material contact resistance and improves temperature rise of power switch in electric vehicle.

2) Coarse oxide particles obtained by gradient high temperature oxidation process not only improve the welding resistance of materials, but also reduce the hardness of materials and ensure the noise requirements for new energy vehicles.

3) The electrical performance data of 40V 20A DC simulation test: the surface of material is smooth after

170,000 cycles life test, and it is not easy to form cracks on the surface corroded by arc. Therefore, it is better to improve the life cycles and stability of material. This is mainly due to the addition of additives to improve the wettability of oxide and silver matrix, which is not easy to form cracks and reduce secondary arc generation.

4) The data of welding force at 2000A high current show that the improved $AgSnO_2$ material in this project has low welding force, and its welding resistance is much lower than that of original silver tin oxide material and AgCuO 10 material with good welding resistance. In this paper introduced $AgSnO_2$material, the coarsening of oxide particles improves the welding resistance of materials, and the material contains brittle materials to improve the breaking ability of contacts. By comparing the welding force of AgCuO10 with that of AgCuO10 under 2000 A current, the improved $AgSnO_2$ material introduced in this paper can meet the 1000A-2000A high current interruption requirements of electric vehicles.

IV. CONCLUSION

Silver content is 88%. The reinforcement phase is mainly tin oxide and indium oxide. A small amount of additives are added to improve wettability and resistance. Ag, Sn and In additives are first alloyed to form silver alloy materials, then oxidized by alloys and gradient oxidation to obtain coarse oxide particles. Then through upsetting and extrusion deformation, wire materials are obtained and rivet contacts of required specifications are prepared. The prepared materials is introduced in this paper have good electrical conductivity, low hardness, coarse oxide particles, high density and uniform distribution of structure.

According to the test data of DV 40V 20A and 2000A, the material has better resistance to welding than AgCuO 10. The material has low resistance and hardness, and good wettability. It can meet the requirements of electric vehicle power switch, especially improve the resistance to welding, and ensure the requirement of 1000A-2000A high current impact.

The $AgSnO_2$ material is introduced in this paper has been used in large quantities in the market. The material used in the client can meet the electrical performance requirements of the electric vehicle power switch from small current to high current. The arcing time of this $AgSnO_2$ material is better than that of $AgSnO_2$ and AgCuO materials, but not as good as that of AgZnO materials through HD cameras' data. So the material can also be better optimized in reducing arc time.

The importance of the work or suggest applications and extensions.

REFERENCES

[1] Panoramic Map of China's Electric Vehicle Industry in 2019, Lithium Power Distribution, 2019.5.15

[2] Wansheng Zhang. Guidelines for the application of AgSnO 2 contact materials in low voltage power engineering switchgear. Electrical alloys, No. 4, 1995

[3] Chunping Wu. Thermodynamics and Kinetics of Internal Oxidation in AgZnO Electrical Contact Materials. Electrical Materials 2006 NO.1

[4] Qiying Tao, "Contact Resistance and Arc Erosion Morphology of AgCuO Electrical Contact Material)" in *RARE METAL,MATERIALS AND ENGINEERING* ,5nd ed. Vol44, 20154, pp. 1119–1122

[5] J. Li, X. F. Yan, X. P. Bai, L.Q. Liu, S. H. Li, W. Weng. Effect of different In contents on hardness and microstructure of AgSnIn alloy during internal oxidation[J], The Institute of Electronics, Information and Communication Engineers Technical Report, 2013[C], 113(298): 95-98.

Yan Xiaofang, female, senior engineer, undergraduate, Central South University. Engaged in research and development of electrical contact materials

7th International Conference on Reliability of
Electrical Products and Electrical Contacts,
November 04-06, 2019

Optimization of Heat Dissipation Design for High-power SiC SSPC Based on Icepak Thermal Simulation

Hongyu Zhang[1], Kangyao Lai[2], Shuang Si[1], Yan Zhu[1], Kaixin Zhang[1], Shujuan Wang[1]
[1]Harbin Institute of Technology, Harbin, 150001
[2]Beijing Keytone Electronic Relay General Factory Co., Ltd.,100054
E-mail: 1092383004@qq.com Tel: 86-15663633662

***Abstract*—With the increase of power level, the research of high-power and high-reliability SiC SSPC has become a hot spot in the industry. The heat generated by SSPC work will also increase greatly due to the increase of current level. As the power core device of SiC SSPC, overheating damage of SiC MOSFET is one of the main causes of its failure. The SiC MOSFET in the die package mode can effectively improve the heat dissipation performance of the SSPC under high current operation and can significantly reduce the size of the SSPC. However, there are few studies on the actual heat dissipation and heat dissipation performance optimization of die-packaged SSPC. This paper takes 20A DC high-power SiC SSPC working in high temperature environment as the research object. Firstly, temperature field simulation analysis of die-packaged SiC SSPC is carried out based on the actual working conditions. Then, the electrical characteristics of the SiC MOSFET power part of SSPC operating under different ambient temperature and load conditions are analyzed. Finally, using the DOE experimental design algorithm, and considering the junction temperature and switching characteristics of the SiC MOSFET and the process level of the heat sink, the structure of the SiC MOSFET's heat sink is parametrically analyzed and getting the heat sink optimized design scheme, and verify the correctness of the optimization scheme through temperature field simulation analysis.**

***Index Terms*—high-power SiC SSPC, Die-packaged SiC MOSFET, thermal simulation, optimized design**

I. INTRODUCTION

As a smart terminal device that integrates traditional devices such as high-power relays and circuit breakers, solid-state power controllers (SSPCs) are the core components of all-electric aircraft power distribution systems [1]. However, with the increasing power levels of aircraft, traditional Si devices have not been able to meet their high-power density and small volume requirements [2]. Wide bandgap semiconductor devices such as SiC MOSFETs perform well due to their ability to withstand high voltages [3,4,], high on-current, good temperature performance, and low conduction loss [5,6], among others, which are especially suitable for high-voltage and high-power solid-state power controllers [7,8]. As the power level of SiC SSPC becomes higher and higher, the probability of SSPC failure due to overheating damage of its power core device SiC MOSFET is also greatly improved [9]. Therefore, high-reliability heat dissipation design of high-power SiC SSPC is of great significance.

In practical applications, although the on-resistance of SiC MOSFETs is significantly reduced compared to conventional Si MOSFETs, as the SSPC current level increases, the amount of heat generated during operation increases significantly [10]. Under the temperature gradient, the parameters of the power device will change significantly, which will seriously affect the driving characteristics of the SSPC and the switching characteristics of the MOSFET [11,12]. In paper [13], the influence of temperature difference of MOSFT device on MOSFET switching characteristics is studied. It is found that the effect of temperature on the dynamic uneven flow of MOSFET parallel module is positively correlated. The higher the temperature, the greater the difference of uneven current. In paper [14], the thermal simulation analysis of aerospace thick film SSPC was carried out, and the thermal optimization design of SSPC was carried out through the change of basic process [15].

In summary, the thermal simulation analysis and heat dissipation optimization design of high-power SiC SSPC in the form of die package are less, and the research on the temperature of the core device SiC MOSFET and the switching characteristics of SSPC are not perfect. Therefore, this paper uses a 270V/240Adc high-power and high-power density SiC SSPC research object to simulate the temperature field of SSPC using die-packaging process. Then using simulation software to analyze the electrical characteristics of

SSPC under different working temperature and load conditions. Finally, the heat dissipation performance of the SSPC is optimized by optimizing the design of the heat sink structure.

II. SIC SSPC THERMAL SIMULATION ANALYSIS

A. Single Channel Thermal Simulation Analysis

The SSPC developed in this paper is divided into 12 channels, each channel has a conduction current of 20A, and its power loop is composed of two SiC MOSFET dies in parallel, the model is CREE3C9000-10010A.

According to the analysis, the main heating device of the SSPC is the power MOSFETs, and the heat generated by other devices during operation can be ignored within the error tolerance. The 3-D finite element analysis model of the wire-bonding module is established in the finite element analysis software ANSYS, including a SiC MOSFET chip, wire-bonding, solid surfaces, leadframe, a heat sink, Direct Bonding Copper (DBC), and so on. Figure 1 shows the various parts of the 3-D model.

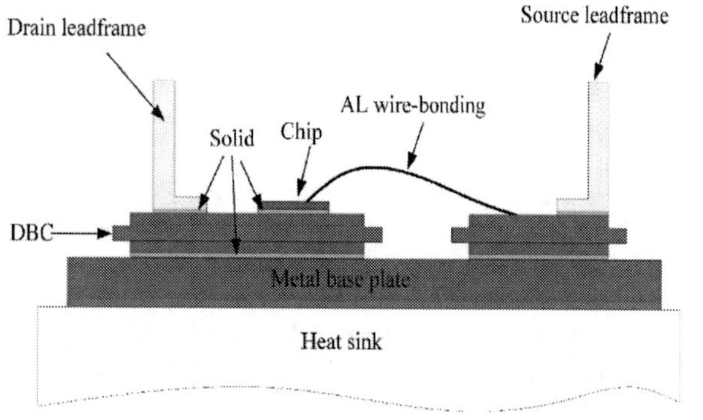

Fig. 1 The composition of each part of the 3-D model.

The circuit model of SSPC is built in the EDA simulation software Saber, and the simulation shows that the on-current of each MOSFET is 10A under the rated working condition. According to the chip manual, the on-resistance of the selected SiC MOSFET is 10mΩ, and the power of each MOSFET is calculated to be 1W. The established 3-D finite element model is imported into the thermal simulation software ICEPAK, through attribute setting, network division, simulation time setting, simulation condition setting, etc. The temperature field distribution of the SiC MOSFET in the single-channel SSPC is shown in Figure 2. It can be seen that the maximum temperature of the SiC MOSFET at steady state is 99.37°C.

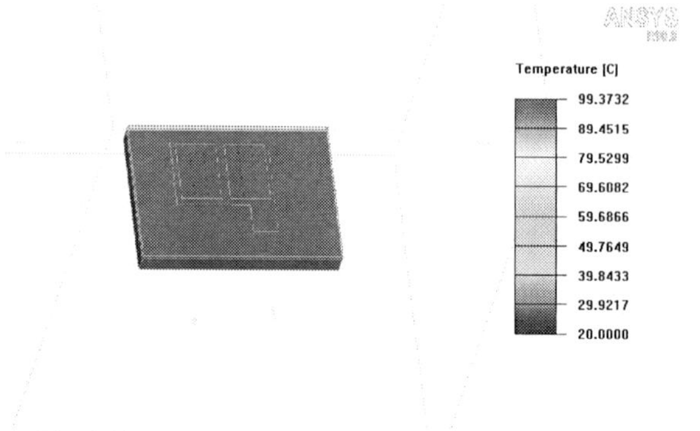

Fig. 2 SiC MOSFET temperature field distribution cloud.

B. SiC SSPC Overall Thermal Simulation Analysis

The multi-channel high-power SSPC model developed in this paper is shown in Figure 3. The model size is 20 × 10 × 3cm. To facilitate heat dissipation and uniform temperature distribution, the 12-channel power MOSFETs are uniformly and symmetrically packaged on the metal backplane of the SSPC. The temperature field distribution of the SSPC is obtained by using ICEPAK simulation, figure 4 shows the SSPC temperature distribution cloud map. It can be found that due to the arrangement of the power MOSFET, the middle MOSFET has a higher temperature of about 89.75°C, and the MOSFET temperature on both sides is lower, and the temperature difference between the two is about 8°C.

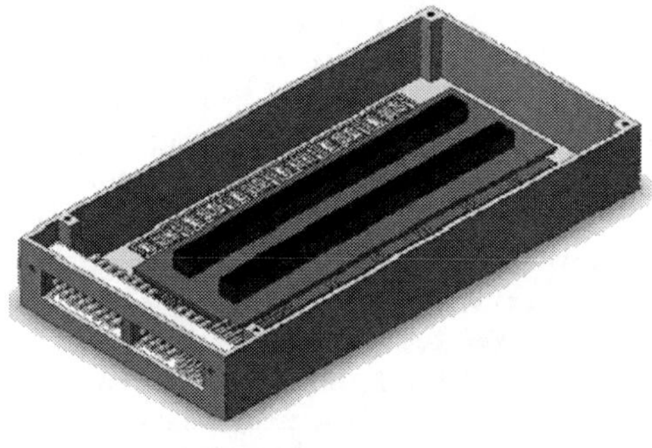

Fig. 3 SiC SSPC machine 3D model.

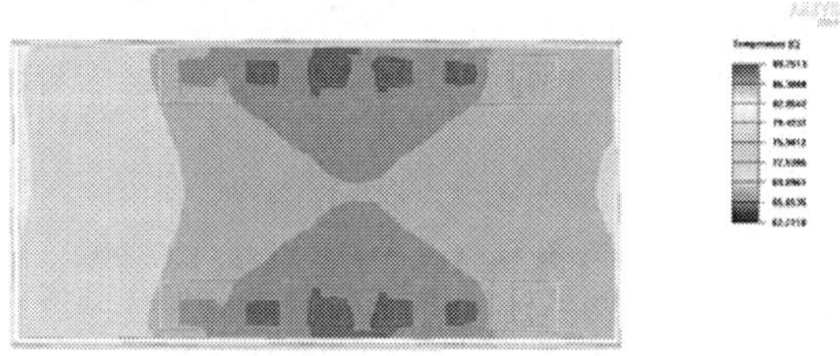

Fig. 4 SSPC internal temperature field distribution cloud map.

III. ELECTROTHERMAL SIMULATION ANALYSIS OF SSPC SWITCH CHARACTERISTICS

The SSPC studied in this paper has 12 channels. When the SSPC is turned on and off, the consistency of the MOSFETs switching characteristics is very important. If the switching time is highly dispersed, may cause multi-channel current unevenness. The conduction current of the first conducting MOS tube may be much larger than its rated current and damaged, which lead to SSPC failure. The characteristic parameters of the MOSFET, such as the threshold voltage, change with temperature, causing the switching characteristics to change, resulting in uneven shunting of the SSPC, which threatens the operational reliability of the SSPC. Therefore, the dynamic switching characteristics of SSPC under different temperature and different load conditions are analyzed by Saber software simulation.

A. Resistive Load

The SSPC is easier to analyze under the working resistive load condition. Based on the circuit simulation model built in Saber, the MOSFET model is a non-ideal model considering the parasitic inductance and parasitic capacitance of each part of the switching loop and power loop, as shown in Figure 5. According to the technical indicators, the operating temperature range of this SSPC is -55°C ~ 105°C, Figure 5 simulation shows SSPC steady state temperature is 90 °C. The MOSFET turn-on time and turn-off time were obtained by setting the operating temperature to 70°C, 80°C, 90°C and 105 °C respectively, as shown in Table 2. As the operating temperature increases, the threshold voltage of the MOSFET gradually decreases, and the turn-on time of the MOS transistor gradually increases. When the temperature is gradually increased from 70°C to 105°C, the turn-on time of the MOSFET is reduced by 0.5 ms, and the turn-off time is increased by 2.4 ms. It can be seen that under resistive load, the temperature has an influence on the switching characteristics of MOSFET, and the influence on the shutdown characteristic is particularly obvious.

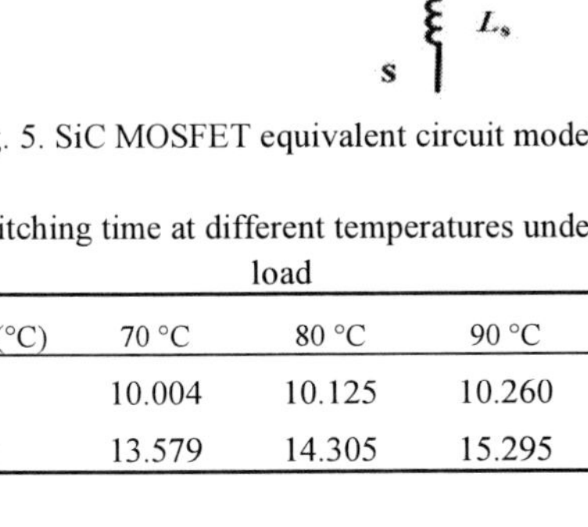

Fig. 5. SiC MOSFET equivalent circuit model.

Table.1 Switching time at different temperatures under resistive load

Temperature(°C)	70 °C	80 °C	90 °C	105 °C
T_{on}(ms)	10.004	10.125	10.260	10.504
T_{off}(ms)	13.579	14.305	15.295	15.996

B. Capacitive Load

When the SSPC is working with a capacitive load, the formula I=Cdu/dt shows that the larger the voltage change rate is, the larger the capacitance value is, and the larger the inrush current is when it is turned on. When the inrush current exceeds the SSPC protection threshold, the SSPC typically triggers overcurrent protection, causing false protection, so the SSPC's capacitive load capacity is limited. The SSPC developed in this paper adopts the method of increasing the bypass to greatly improve the capacity of the SSPC, and can achieve a total turn-on 10000μF without tripping. As shown in Figure 6, the bypass consists of a power MOSFET and a power resistor. The bypass MOSFET is turned on first, and the load capacitor is charged by the power resistor. Generally, the ms level can be charged to the power supply voltage by more than 90%. At this time, the main circuit MOSFET is turned on, and the instantaneous current through the main circuit MOSFET is greatly reduced, the circuit does not suffer from false protection.

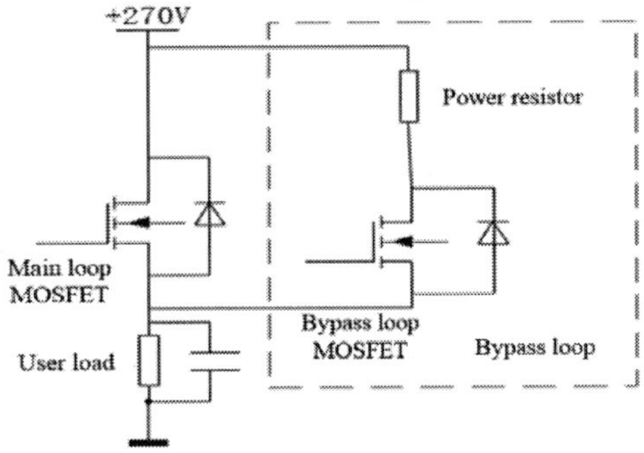

Fig. 6 Anti-"false short circuit" protection circuit design

Set the operating temperature to 70°C, 80°C, 90°C, 105°C, using the simulation software to get the MOSFET turn-on time and turn-off time, as shown in Table 2. According to the simulation results obtained in Saber, under the capacitive load condition, the switching characteristics of SSPC are also affected by the operating temperature. As the temperature increases, the turn-on time of MOSFT gradually decreases, and the turn-off time gradually increases. The turn-on time and turn-off time are 11.004ms and 14.579ms at 70°C. When the temperature rises to 105°C, the turn-on time is reduced to 10.704ms, and the turn-off time is raised to 16.496ms. It can be seen that under capacitive loading, temperature also has a significant effect on the switching characteristics of the MOSFET.

Table. 2 Switching time at different temperatures under capacitive load

Temperature(°C)	70 °C	80 °C	90 °C	105 °C
T_{on}(ms)	11.004	11.125	10.960	10.704
T_{off}(ms)	14.579	15.105	15.695	16.496

C. Inductance Load

Under inductive load, it is known from the formula *U*=L*di*/*dt* that the inductive load circuit is prone to overshoot voltage, and the value of the overshoot voltage is related to the value of the inductive load and the rate of current change. If a transient overcharge voltage is applied to the SiC MOSFET, the power transistor voltage breakdown may occur. When the MOSFET is turned on, the overshoot voltage generated by the inductive load is opposite to the bus voltage. The voltage across the MOSFET is small and generally does not cause breakdown. However, when the MOSFET is turned off, the voltage overshoot generated by the inductive load is the same as the bus voltage, which is likely to cause breakdown of the power MOSFET. The SSPC designed in this paper adds a reverse suppression diode and a bleeder diode to the power loop in order to improve the inductive load capability and avoid the danger of MOSFET overvoltage breakdown. The operating temperature was set to 70°C, 80°C, 90°C, 105°C using the simulation software to obtain the MOSFET turn-on time and turn-off time, as shown in Table 3. According to the simulation results obtained in Saber, the switching characteristics of SSPC are also affected by the operating temperature under inductive load conditions. As the temperature increases, the turn-on time decreases gradually, the turn-off time gradually increases, and the turn-off characteristics are more affected by temperature.

Table. 3 Switching time at different temperatures under inductance load

Temperature(°C)	70 °C	80 °C	90 °C	105 °C
T_{on}(ms)	11.104	11.125	10.880	10.404
T_{off}(ms)	15.579	15.805	16.495	16.952

D. Simulation Result Analysis

By analyzing the simulation results of SSPC with resistive load, capacitive load and inductive load at different temperatures, it can be seen that the temperature change has an effect on the switching characteristics of SSPC. With the increase of its operating temperature, the SiC MOSFET the turn-on time is gradually reduced, and the turn-off time is gradually increased. When SSPC working, power MOSFETs of different channels may have temperature differences due to layout, which will affect the consistency of switching characteristics of different channels, resulting in multi-channel current sharing problem. The following is an optimized design of the SSPC heat sink structure to improve the heat dissipation capability of the SSPC, reduce the temperature of the whole machine, and reduce the difference in MOSFET temperature distribution between the channels, and improve the consistency of the switching characteristics between the channels.

IV. SSPC HEAT DISSIPATION OPTIMIZATION DESIGN

A. Analysis of Influence of Process Parameters on Radiator Heat Dissipation Performance

The solid state power controller developed in this paper is a high-voltage and high-power solid-state power controller. The large amount of heat generated during operation may cause thermal damage to the power tube. Therefore, a fin heat sink is installed on the bottom plate of the SSPC to improve its heat dissipation. performance. Commonly used fin heat sinks are made of aluminum alloy and copper. After considering the heat dissipation performance, cost and quality of the heat sink, select the heat sink of the aluminum alloy material. The main geometric parameters of the heat sink are the count of the fins, the thickness of the fins, the height of the fins, and the thickness, length and width of the base. Since the length and width of the base are limited by the size of the SSPC backplane. Therefore, taking the SSPC temperature as the objective function, and the number of fins, thickness, height and base thickness of the heat sink are analyzed by parametric simulation.

1) Effect of the thickness of the heat sink base

According to the heat dissipation path of the MOSFET, the heat generated by the power MOSFET is first conducted through heat conduction with the base, and then convective heat exchange and radiation heat exchange are performed through the fins and the air. Keeping the other dimensions of the heat sink unchanged, the single parameter change method was used to simulate the influence of the thickness change of the base on the heat dissipation performance of the SSPC. The thickness of the pedestal was set to 2 mm, 2.5 mm, 3 mm, 3.5 mm, 4 mm, and 4.5 mm, respectively. The temperature of the SSPC under different base thickness was simulated in ICEPAK as shown in Fig. 7. It can be seen from Fig. 7 that when the thickness of the pedestal is less than 3.5 mm, the thickness of the base has little effect on the heat dissipation performance of the heat sink. When the thickness exceeds 3.5 mm, the heat dissipation performance of the heat sink is degraded due to the significant increase in the thermal resistance of the base.

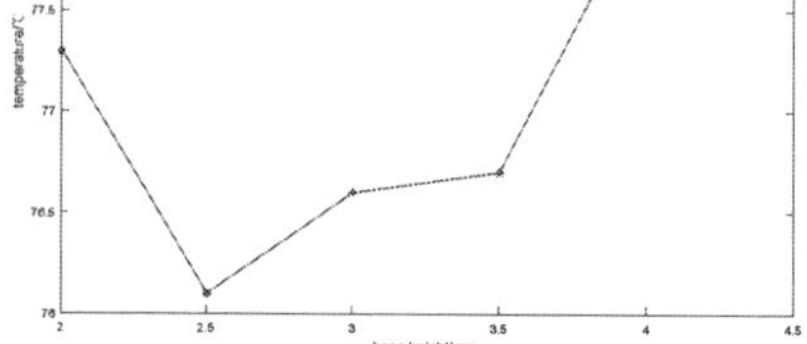

Fig. 7 Effect of pedestal thickness on temperature.

(2) Effect of the number of radiator fins

The number of fins has a significant influence on the heat

dissipation performance of the heat sink, as is shown in Fig 8, As the number of radiator fins increases, the distance between the fins decreases, increasing the contact area between the fins and the air, and the temperature of the heat source is continuously lowered. Therefore, it is possible to increase the number of fins to increase the thermal performance. At the same time, attention should be paid to the quality of the heat sink, and the number of heat sink fins should be determined reasonably considering the heat dissipation performance and product quality.

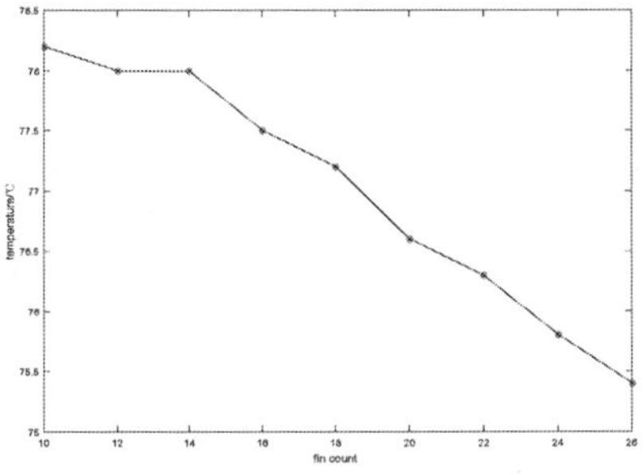

Fig. 8 Effect of the number of radiator fins.

(3) Effect of radiator fin height

The height of the heat sink fin has a significant influence on the heat dissipation performance of the heat sink. As the height of the fin increases, the heat generated by the power MOSFET is more easily dissipated to the surrounding space through the fins, but limited by the installation position and the product volume, the height of the fins of the radiator should not be too high. The parametric simulation results of the rib height are shown in Fig. 9. As the height of the fin increases, the temperature of the MOS tube decreases continuously. When the height of the fin increases to 12 mm, the temperature of the MOSFET becomes inconspicuous due to the height of the rib. In summary, under the premise of considering product quality and volume, increasing the height of the radiator fins within a certain range can increase the heat dissipation area of the radiator and improve the heat dissipation performance.

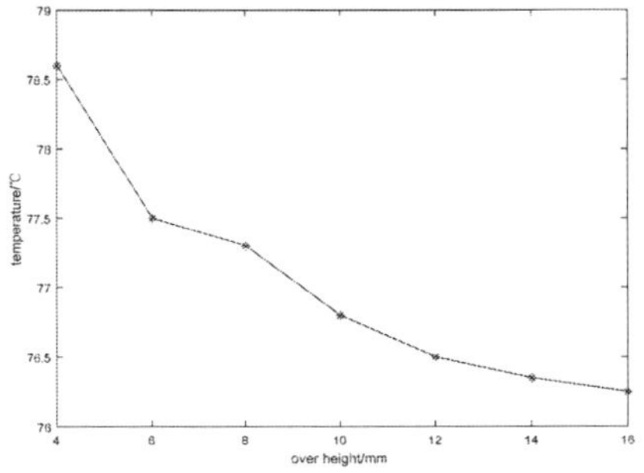

Fig. 9 Effect of radiator fin height.

(4) Effect of fin thickness

The height and width of the heat sink fins are much larger than the thickness of the fins. Therefore, it is considered that the heat dissipation of the heat sink mainly depends on the longitudinal heat conduction of the fins, so the thickness of the fins does not have much influence on the heat dissipation performance. The simulation results for the fins are shown in Fig. 10. As the thickness of the fin increases, the temperature of the power MOSFET begins to decrease slightly, and then the temperature increases. This is because the increase in fin thickness does not increase the contact area between the fin and the air. Instead, it will reduce the fin spacing and affect the efficiency of the heat sink.

B. The Optimization Design of the Heat Sink

According to the above analysis, the thickness of the heat sink base, the number and height of the fins have a great influence on the heat dissipation performance, and the thickness of the fins has little influence on the heat dissipation performance. Therefore, using the parametric simulation function of the thermodynamic simulation software ICEPAK, the base thickness, the number of fins and the height of fins are used as variable parameters, and the parametric simulation analysis is carried out according to the scheme of Table 4, for a total of 27 sets of simulations. Considering the heat dissipation performance, product volume and heat sink manufacturing process, the final optimized design scheme is determined to have a base thickness of 3 mm, a number of ribs of 22, a rib height of 10 mm, and a rib thickness of 1.5 mm. The optimized simulation results are shown in Fig. 11. The maximum temperature of SSPC is 71.1°C, which is 7°C lower than before optimization, and the overall temperature difference of SSPC is reduced. The temperature difference between the MOSFET in the middle of the bottom plate and the MOSFET on both sides is reduced to 2°C, which reduces the temperature difference to multi-channel switching characteristics. The consistency of the effect is conducive to the realization of multi-channel current sharing.

Table. 4 Parametric design orthogonal table

sequence	Base thickness/mm	Thin height/mm	Fin count
1	2.5	10	20
2	3	12	22
3	3.5	14	24

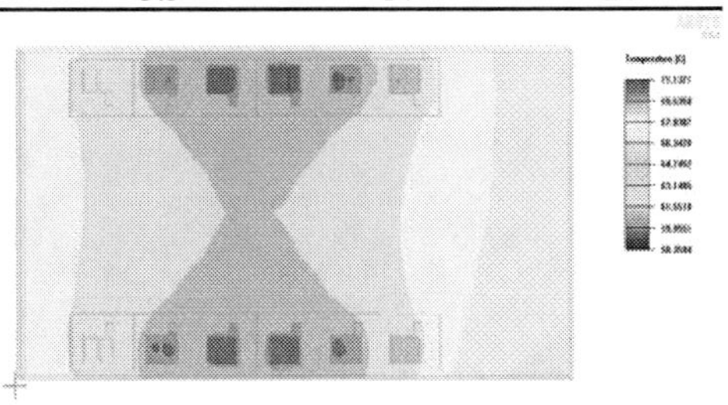

Fig. 11 Optimized SSPC temperature distribution cloud map

V.CONCLUSION

This paper optimizes the thermal design of a multi-channel high-power SiC SSPC. The switching characteristics of SiC MOSFETs with different temperatures and different loads were analyzed by establishing an electrothermal simulation model. The relationship between temperature and SiC MOSFET turn-on time and turn-off time was obtained. Based on ICEPAK simulation, the influence of the key size parameters of the heat sink on the heat dissipation performance is analyzed. Through the parametric simulation of the height of the base, the number of fins and the height of the fins, the optimal structure of the heat sink is determined by considering the heat dissipation effect of SSPC and the quality and processing technology of the heat sink. Compared with the SSPC before the optimized design, the product temperature is reduced by about 7°C, and the temperature distribution is more uniform, which significantly improves the working reliability of the product.

REFERENCES

[1] A. Garrigós, J. M. Blanes, R. Gutiérrez, J. Borrell, E. Maset, D. Ramirez, S. Cardoso, Silicon Carbide and Magnetorresistive Technologies for Solid State Power Controllers. ESPC 2016, 12004 (2017) 1-6.

[2] Ashutosh Sharma, Soon Jae Lee, Young Joo Jang, Jae Pil Jung, SiC based technology for high power electronics and packaging applications. J. Microelectron. Packag. Soc., 21(2014), 71-78.

[3] J. Hayes, K. George, P. Killeen, B. McPherson, K. J. Olejniczak, T. R. McNutt, Bidirectional, SiC Module-based Solid-State Circuit Breakers for 270 VDC MEA/AEA Systems. 2016 IEEE 4th Workshop on Wide Bandgap Power Devices and Applications, (2016), 70-77.

[4] Xiaohu Feng, Arthur V Radun, SiC based Solid State Power Controller. IEEE Applied Power Electronics Conference and Exposition, (2008) 1855-1860.

[5] Yu Zhu. Overview of foreign solid state power controllers [J]. Electromechanical components， 2014,34(5):49-60.

[6] D. Tournier, H. Morel, and D. Planson.Comparison of high voltage and high temperature performances of wide bandgap semiconductors for vertical power devices[J]. Diamond Related Mater, 2010, 19(1): 1-6.

[7] Feng, X., Radun, A. V. SiC based Solid State Power Controller[C]. IEEE APEC. 2008: 1855-1860.

[8] H. Matsunami. Current SiC Technology for Power Electronic Devices [J]. Microelectronic Engineering, 2006, (83): 2–4.

[9] S. R. Goldman, M. Glass. SSPC Advancements Enhance VehiclePower System Designs [C]. COTS Journal, 2019: 18-24.

[10] JingJue Tao. SiC MOSFET applied technology research [D]. Nanjing: Transactions of Nanjing University of Aeronautics & Astronautics, 2013.

[11] R. Wang, D. Boroyevich, P. Ning, Z. Wang, F. Wang, P. Mattavelli, K. Ngo, and K. Rajashekara.high-temperature SiC three-phase ac-dc converter design for 100 °C ambient temperature[C]. IEEE Trans. Power Electron, 2013, 28(1): 555–572.

[12] Guo, Y. B., Bhat, K. P., Aravamudhan, A., Hopkins D. C., Hazelmeyer, D. R. High current and thermal transient design of a SiC SSPC for aircraft application[C]. IEEE APEC, 2011: 1-9.

[13] Wang Z, Zhang J, Wu X, et al. Analysis of stray inductance on SiC MOSFET switching performance[C]// Energy Conversion Congress and Exposion. IEEE, 2014:2838-2843.

[14] Yu Zhang, MiaoMiao Guo, HuaMing Zhang. Optimization design of thick film SSPC for aerospace based on thermal simulation [M]. Beijing：Space electronics, 2016.

[15] J. Microelectron. Packag. Soc., 21(2014), 71-78. ohanna Mütinga, Bhagyalakshmi Kakarlab, Ulrike Grossner. Comprehensive and Detailed Study on the Modeling of Commercial SiC Power MOSFET Devices Using TCAD [C]. European Conference on Silicon Carbide & Related Materials. 2016: 12-18.

Study on the Influence of Single Stress on the Dynamic Characteristics of Electromagnetic Mechanism during the Process of Electromagnetic Relay Being Turned on

Liuliu Wang[1], Fang Yao[1], Xiaopeng Wang[1], Fa Zhao[2]
[1]State Key Laboratory of Reliability and Intelligence of Electrical Equipment (Ministry of Education, Hebei University of Technology), Tianjin 300131;
[2]Shougang Jingtang Iron and Steel Joint Co., Ltd., Tangshan City 063200

***Abstract*—The single stress of power supply amplitude, frequency and distortion has different effects on the dynamic characteristics of the electromagnetic relay and the stability of the on-state. Studying the influence law of power supply variation on the dynamic characteristics of relays is of great significance for the design, optimization and rational selection of electromagnetic relays, and is one of the important contents of reliability research. In this paper, the static and dynamic mathematical model of the electromagnetic mechanism is established by using the AC electromagnetic relay prototype for small industrial control. The equation of state equation is established and the dynamic characteristics of the electromagnetic mechanism is simulated. According to the simulation results, the influence of the fluctuation of the power supply amplitude, frequency and distortion degree on the single stress of the relay on-time characteristic is studied, and the simulation characteristics of the electromagnetic mechanism can not be reliably absorbed under the influence of two stresses and three stresses.**

***Index Terms*— Power Quality, Electromagnetic Relay, Harmonic Content Rate, Time Characteristics**

I. INTRODUCTION

Electromagnetic relays are important basic devices and play an important role in automatic control systems, electronic communication systems, and power grid terminal distribution systems. The electromechanical performance of the relay itself, the working environment in which it is placed, the applied power excitation and the load carried by the contacts are all important factors that affect its performance. The action characteristic of the relay closing process is a comprehensive reflection of its electromagnetic attraction, spring reaction force, contact state, etc. [1-3]. Among them, cores, coils, springs, contacts, and other electromechanical parts are depleted parts that will degrade over time: when these electromechanical parts degrade slowly, the power supply excitation is the main factor determining the size of the electromagnetic attraction and whether the suction reaction is well matched. It is also the decisive factor of the action characteristics [4-6]. The time characteristic is an important part of the action characteristics, which reflects the duration of the relay action process [8-9]. Previous studies have shown that the faster the pull-in time, the faster the final speed of the moving contact, the more severe the contact collision, and the more serious the electromechanical wear of the contact; as far as the connection process of the relay is concerned, the uncertainty of the bounce phenomenon occurs, the bounce time is long or short, which is directly related to the suction-reaction coordination, which is directly related to the reaction of the suction force. When the key linkage components such as the iron core and the spring degrade slowly, the closing phase angle, amplitude, frequency and distortion of the power supply are the essential reasons [10- 13].

At present, the proportion of new energy power generation has increased year by year. More and more electromagnetic relays for control, power distribution or communication are used in microgrids whose power quality may be difficult to guarantee. This puts higher requirements for electromagnetic relays to withstand power quality fluctuations. Requirements [11-12]. The armature drives the movable contact to perform the function of switching the load current. The time characteristic has a decisive influence on the operating performance of the electromagnetic relay. Therefore, this paper takes electromagnetic mechanism of electromagnetic relay as an object to study the influence of power quality on its time characteristic [14-17].

This paper establishes the physical model, electromagnetic model and dynamic model of electromagnetic relay, simulates and tests the correctness of the model under sinusoidal excitation, simulates the electromagnetic and dynamic characteristics under simulated distorted excitation, and obtains the time characteristics from them, and then studies the influence of power quality on the time characteristics.

II. DYNAMIC SIMULATION MODELING OF ELECTROMAGNETIC RELAY

The electromagnetic mechanism of electromagnetic relay is mainly composed of coil, yoke iron, stationary iron core, armature and magnetic ring. Relay coils are electrically magnetized, and most of the flux passes through ferromagnetic medium with high magnetic density, which generates electromagnetic attraction at the armature end to reduce the air gap. The suction force is less than the reaction force, and it is in the process of stirring; when the suction force is greater than the reaction force, the armature is sucked into the motion process; when the armature and the stationary core are closed steadily, the motion process stops. In the closing process of electromagnetic relay, the coil circuit follows the voltage balance equation, the electromagnetic mechanism follows Maxwell equation, and the power follows Darumbell equation. In addition, the system also follows the energy conservation of electricity, heat and machinery. Solid modeling, static modeling, simulation and dynamic modeling are the necessary links of dynamic simulation.

A. Solid modeling

The electromagnetic mechanism of the relay under study is U-shaped snap-on type, the material of coil and magnetic ring is copper, the coil resistance is 7950Ω, the inductance is 2.875H, the number of turns is 18500; the moving iron core, the static iron core and the yoke iron material are all DT4E, and its conductivity is 1 ×107simens/m, density 7850kg/m3. The physical model of the electromagnetic mechanism is shown in Figure 1, and the geometric parameters of each component are shown in Table 1.

The reaction spring is located on the outer side of the armature shaft (Figure 1). Theoretically, the counter torque Tf is proportional to the armature angular displacement α, and the measured reaction force characteristics are shown in Fig. 2.

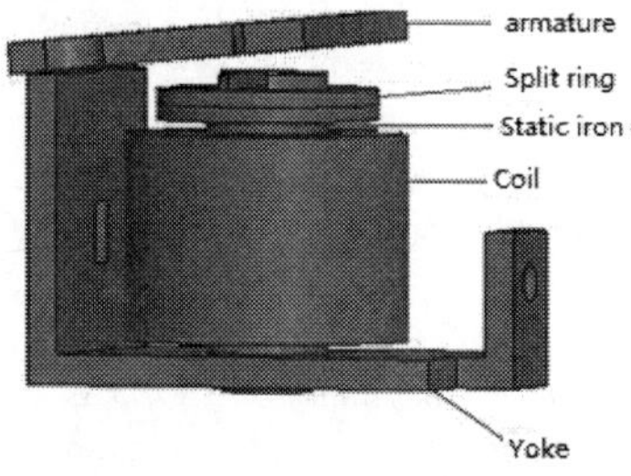

Fig. 1 Solid model of electromagnetic mechanism of electromagnetic relay

Tab.1 Geometrical parameters of electromagnetic mechanism components of electromagnetic relay

parameter	size (mm	parameter	size (mm)
Armature thickness	2	Coil height	13.6
Armature length	24	Coil inner diameter	4.1
Armature width	21.6	Coil outer diameter	10
Yoke width	17.4	Core height	20.3
Yoke thickness	2	Core diameter	1.3
Yoke bottom length	27.6	Iron core outer diameter	4
Split ring thickness	1	Air gap between armature and iron core	0.1

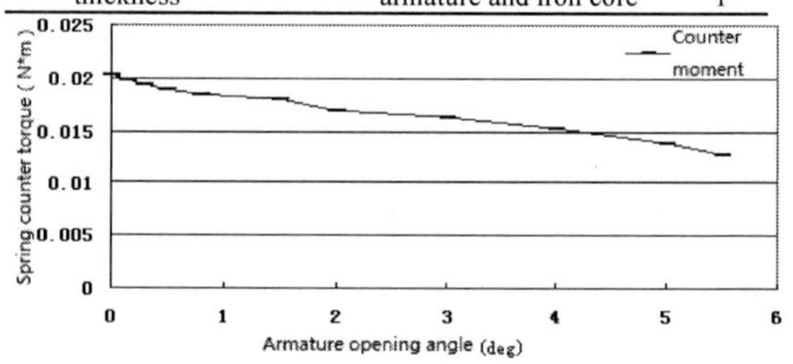

Fig. 2 Measured reaction torque characteristic curve

B. Static feature modeling and simulation

Static characteristics refer to the relationship between electromagnetic suction moment and air gap, regardless of the time-varying characteristics of each variable when the armature moves infinitely slowly to a certain air gap. Coil current I can be calculated from given coil voltage U without time-varying characteristics, as shown in formula (1):

$$I = \frac{U}{2\pi f N^2 (\Lambda_\delta + \Lambda_{g\delta})} \tag{1}$$

n the formula, N is the number of coil turns, Λ_δ is air gap permeability ($= \frac{\mu_0 A}{l\alpha}$) , $\Lambda_{g\delta}$ is leakage permeance。

At the air gap δ of the axis of the iron core column, the electromagnetic suction is calculated according to formula (2):

$$F = \frac{1}{2}(IN)^2 \mu_0 \frac{A}{\delta^2} \tag{2}$$

In the formula, μ_0 is the vacuum permeability and the area of the magnetic extreme surface at the air gap are expressed by A.

Constant magnetic flux, no magnetic leakage, neglecting the magnetic resistance of ferromagnetic materials, excluding iron core, non-working air gap reluctance and magnetic edge effect of air gap flux, the electromagnetic moment of the armature is approximately calculated according to formula (3):

$$T = \frac{1}{2}(IN)^2 \mu_0 \frac{A}{l\alpha^2} \tag{3}$$

In the formula, l is the distance between the armature axis and the core column; the armature opening angle α is less than 5.5, so the air gap δ is very small; L is satisfied with the armature opening angle alpha and the air gap δ. When $T = T_f$、 α=5.5°, The armature is at the critical point of the touch and motion state. At this time, the trigger current I_c can be calculated from equation (3) and FIG. 2 to be about 0.02A.

Given the coil voltage u, the static characteristics (I, F and T) at different air gaps can be calculated. Figure 3 shows the characteristics of electromagnetic moment when the coil voltage RMS is 198V, 220V and 235.4V.

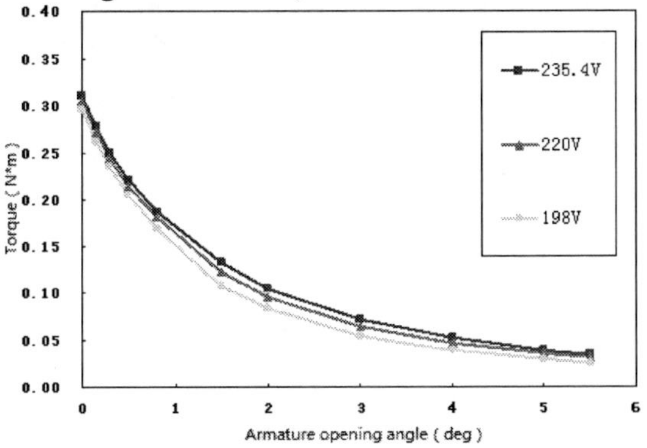

Fig. 3 Static electromagnetic torque characteristics

Figure 3 shows that the higher the voltage is, the larger the static electromagnetic torque is. The comparison between Figure 2 and Figure 3 shows that the static electromagnetic torque characteristic curve of the relay prototype is higher than the anti-torque characteristic curve. When the grid voltage fluctuates within the standard range, the prototype can absorb reliably.

C. *Dynamic feature modeling and simulation*

Regardless of the thermal energy consumption of the relay, the coil resistance R is considered as a constant and the voltage balance equation is shown in formula (4).

$$u = Ri + \frac{d\Psi}{dt} \tag{4}$$

In the formula, ψ is the flux, u is the coil voltage and I is the coil current. Before the armature movement, the contact process lasts for a short time, the magnetic conductor is unsaturated, the flux linkage is proportional to the current i, the inductance L is constant, and the current I is the superposition of sinusoidal wave and attenuation exponential wave; during the movement between the armature movement and reliable absorption, the magnetic conductor may approach saturation, the inductance L is no longer constant, and the current I may distort and appear spike when the value is large.

The flux linkage is approximated by equation (5):

$$\psi = iN^2 \mu_0 \frac{\pi r^2}{l\alpha} \tag{5}$$

In the formula, R is the radius of the polar surface of the static iron core. At the maximum tension angle, the flux is proportional to the current; when the tension angle changes, the flux is not only related to the current i, but also increases with the decrease of the tension angle A.

The dynamic equation of the armature movement process is:

$$T - T_f = J\frac{d^2 a}{dt^2} \tag{6}$$

In the formula, J is the moment of inertia of the armature and the moment of inertia of the rotating structure of mass m is $\frac{1}{3}ml^2$。

D. Equation of state

The dynamic process of the relay electromagnetic system is determined by equations (4)~(6). The equations are related to each other and form the equation of state for describing the dynamic pull-in process, as shown in equation (7):

$$\begin{cases} \frac{dt}{dt} = 1 \\ \frac{d\psi}{dt} = u(t) - Ri(t) \\ \frac{d\alpha}{dt} = \xi\omega \\ \frac{d\omega}{dt} = \xi\frac{T - T_f}{J} \\ \psi(t_0) = \psi_0, \omega(t_0) = \omega_0, \alpha(t_0) = \alpha_0 \end{cases} \tag{7}$$

Where ξ is the armature state coefficient, taking 0 or 1, ξ=0 means that it is in the touch process, ξ=1 means it is in the motion process; ψ_0、 ω_0、 α_0 is the Initial value of flux linkage, angular velocity, and opening angle。

According to the dynamic and static mathematical model of the electromagnetic mechanism suction process and the state equation, the characteristic simulation of the dynamic pull-in process can be realized.

III. EFFECT OF AMPLITUDE ON TIME CHARACTERISTICS

The sample coils of electromagnetic relays need to apply a sinusoidal voltage of 50 Hz, the rated voltage Ue=220V, and the rated voltage of 85%~105% to enable the relays to absorb reliably in a specified time. This requires that the amplitude fluctuation of the supply voltage should be within the range of the product power supply. According to the operation specifications of the power grid, the supply voltage can vary in the range of - 10% - 7% rated voltage, while the voltage of the supply coil is 90% - 107% rated voltage, which meets the requirements of the power supply environment of the relay products. Thus, as far as the power supply amplitude is concerned, the supply and demand of electromagnetic relay products and power grids are in harmony. However, the voltage amplitude has an important influence on the electromagnetic torque, action time and impact speed of armature. Too small electromagnetic torque may prolong the engagement time and increase the final speed. The dynamic and static core will suffer severe mechanical wear due to severe collision. In microgrid environment, the coil voltage amplitude of electromagnetic relay varies greatly, which may exceed the allowable absorption voltage range. Therefore, it is necessary to study the influence of coil voltage amplitude to provide scientific guidance for the design and selection of electromagnetic relay in microgrid.

A. *Coil current characteristics*

1) Coil current characteristic simulation

Fig. 4 is a typical test waveform (Um=311V) of the coil current during the process of the electromagnetic relay being turned on. In the figure, tm1 and tm2 are the movement times when the closing phase angles are 0° and 90°, respectively.

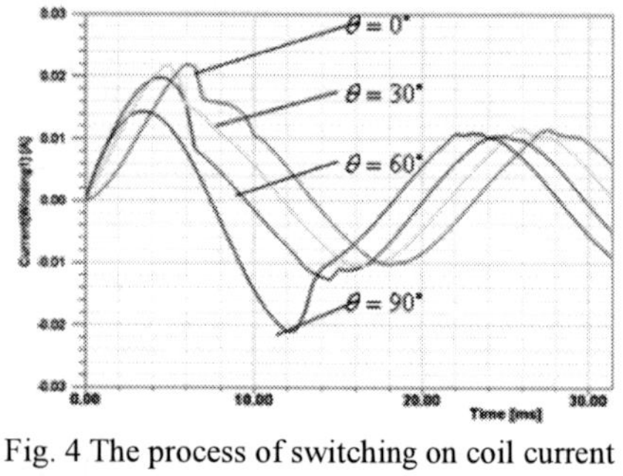

Fig. 4 The process of switching on coil current

It can be seen from Fig. 4: 1) The closing phase angle is between 0° and 90°, and the first peak of the coil current is monotonously reduced; 2) The coil current does not appear cusp during the actuation.

2) Coil current characteristic analysis

From the circuit balance equation, the coil loop satisfies the energy balance equation:

$$\int_0^{t_c} uidt = \int_0^{t_c} i^2 Rdt + \int_0^{\psi} id\psi \tag{8}$$

It can be seen that part of the energy supplied by the power supply is used for the coil loop resistance heating, and part is used to establish the magnetic field.

From the coil energization time 0s to the actuation time tc, the resistance R is a constant 7950Ω; the touch time is very short, it is considered that the magnetic conductor is not saturated before the touch, the flux linkage and the current are in a proportional relationship, the inductance L is a constant 2.875H; the coil loop impedance Z=8001.09 ∠6.48°, the time constant $\tau = \frac{1}{2765.22}$ s。 The coil current wave before the touch can be obtained from the voltage balance equation

$$i(t) = \frac{U_m}{8001.09}[\sin(314t + \theta - 6.48^{\circ}) - \sin(\theta - 6.48^{\circ})e^{-2765.22t}]$$

$$0 \le t \le t_c \tag{9}$$

It can be seen that the amplitude of the coil voltage and the closing phase angle of the front arm are the main factors affecting the coil current, wherein the closing phase angle determines the shape of the current waveform.

With the movement of armature, air gap decreases, and coil current begins to be affected by air gap at the same time, and the smaller the air gap, the greater the influence; moreover, when the current value is larger after touching, the magnetic conductor gradually saturates, and the power supply energy is more used to heat the resistance of coil loop, and the coil current wave appears a pinnacle.

B. *Torque and displacement characteristics*

Fig. 5 is a typical test waveform (Um=311V) of the electromagnetic moment characteristic of the armature of the electromagnetic relay when it is turned on. In the figure, tc1, tc2, and tC3 are the actuation times when the closing phase angles are 180°, 150°, and 120°, respectively.

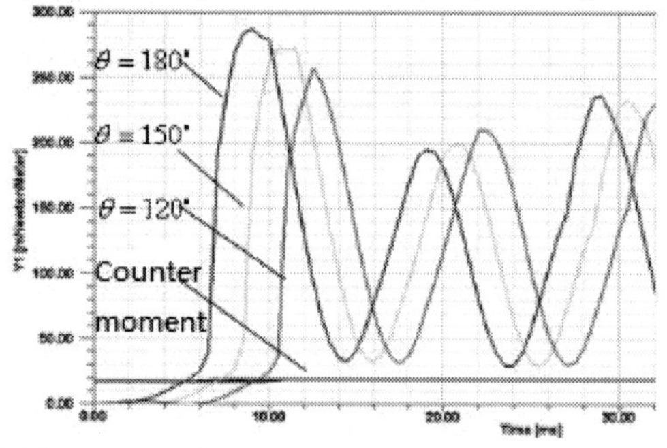

Fig. 5 Electromagnetic torque and counter torque characteristics

In Figure 5, the armature begins to move at t1, and the armature is reliably attracted at time t2. T1-0, t2-t1, and t2+t1 are the contact time tc of the armature, the movement time tm, and the suction time tx, respectively, when the closing phase angle is 180°.

Fig. 6 is a typical test waveform (Um=311V) of the electromagnetic moment characteristic of the armature of the electromagnetic relay when it is turned on.

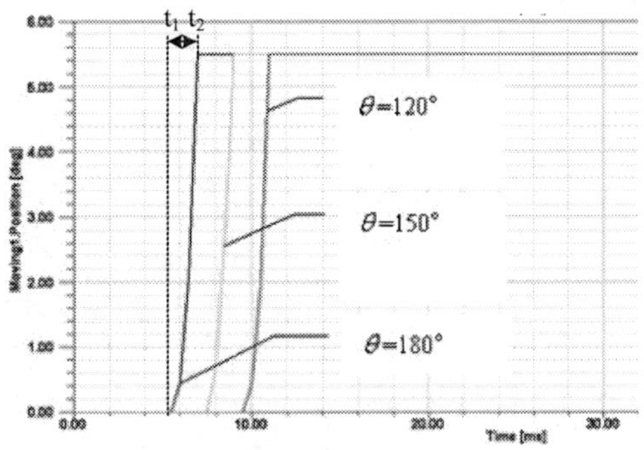

Fig. 6 Armature displacement characteristics

C. *Time characteristic*

The pull-in time tx of the armature is the sum of the touch time tc and the exercise time tm, and the exercise time ratio δ is the specific gravity of the exercise time tm in the pull-in time tx, as shown in the formula (10).

$$\delta = \frac{t_m}{t_x} \tag{10}$$

These time characteristic parameters are affected by closing phase angle theta and voltage amplitude Um. From the displacement curve of armature, the time characteristic of different amplitude and different closing phase angle can be obtained. The dynamic simulation of the position characteristics with the RMS of 198V, 210V, 220V and 235.4V excitation and different closing phase angles (30 degrees per interval) is carried out, and the time parameters are extracted. The time characteristic curve is shown in Figure 7.

It can be seen from Fig. 7 that: 1) the larger the voltage amplitude, the shorter the touch time and the pull-in time; the touch, motion and pull-in time of the amplitude 235.4V are the shortest around the closing phase angle of 90°. 2) Between 30°~60° closing phase angles, the larger the voltage amplitude, the shorter the movement time; the closing phase angle is below 60°, 150°~180°, and the movement time is basically not affected by the amplitude.. 3) The larger the voltage amplitude, the greater the influence of the movement time on the phase angle of the closing.

D. *Angular velocity characteristic*

The collision speed when the static and dynamic iron core is closed is an important performance parameter, and the energy lost to the static and dynamic iron core during the collision causes the mechanical life to be degraded. The amount of kinetic energy loss ΔE when the moving and moving iron core collides is calculated according to formula (11):

$$\Delta E = (1-e^2)\frac{mv^2}{2} \tag{11}$$

Where e is the material collision recovery coefficient, m is the motion system mass, and v is the motion speed at the time of the collision.

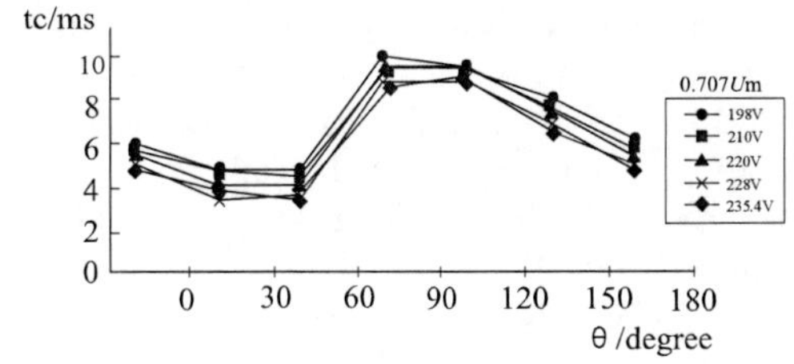

(a) tc-Um,θ characteristics

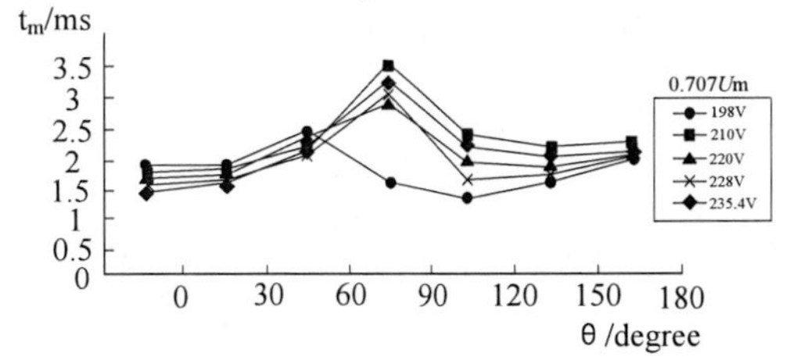

(b) t_m-Um,θ characteristics

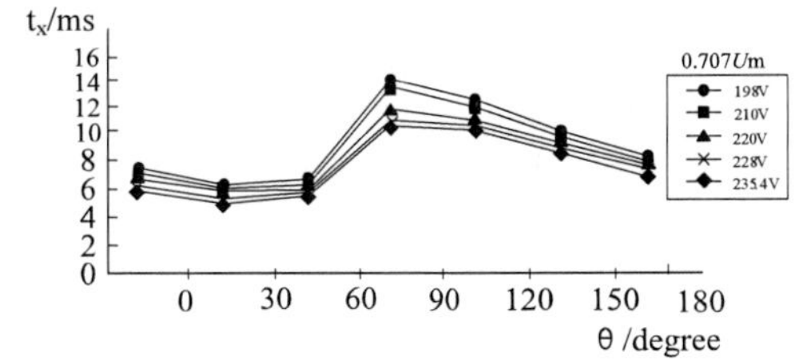

(c) t_x-Um,θ characteristics

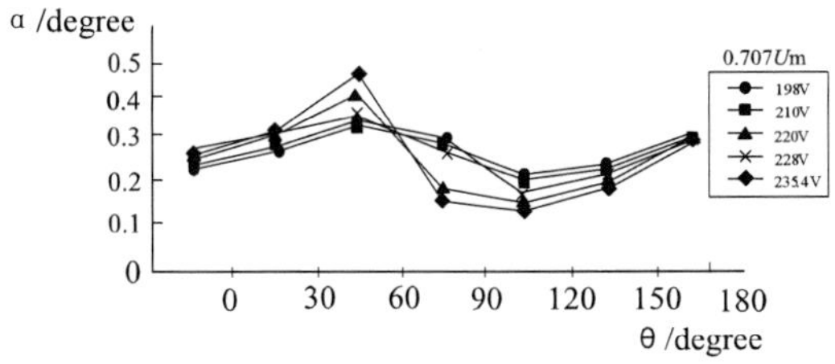

(d) α-Um,θ characteristics

Fig. 7 Time characteristics of armature in switching on process

In the elastic collision, the recovery coefficient is 1, the core has no mechanical energy loss; the non-sexual collision has a recovery coefficient less than l, part of the energy is converted into internal energy, acting on the core to cause strain, and part of the armature is rebounded or vibrated; if the recovery coefficient is 0 The static and dynamic iron cores are glued together immediately after contact, without any bounce or chattering, and the collision kinetic energy is all converted into the internal energy of the iron core strain. The smaller the recovery coefficient, the greater the amount of kinetic energy loss, the more severe the core face deformation and the lower the mechanical life. Therefore, the magnitude of the collision speed reflects the degree of mechanical wear of the electromagnetic mechanism to a certain extent, and mastering the law of the final velocity characteristic has a guiding role in the study of the equivalent test method for the mechanical life of the electromagnetic mechanism.

The dynamic characteristics of the 192V, 210V, 220V, 228V and 235.4V excitation and different closing phase angles (30° interval) are simulated dynamically, and the collision speed is extracted. The relationship between the collision speed and the closing phase angle is shown in Fig. 8. The relationship between the collision speed and the time parameter is shown in Fig. 8.

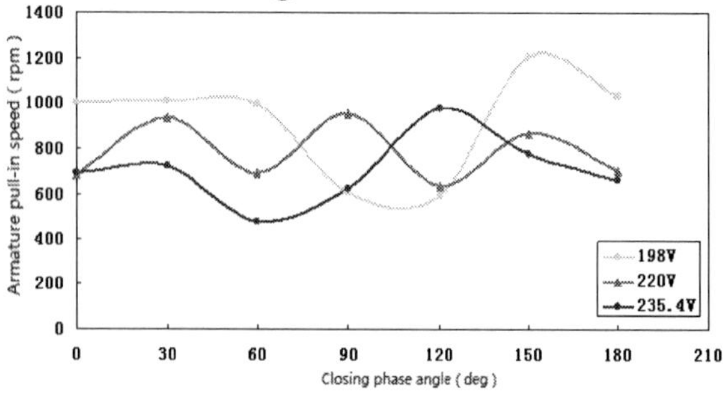

Fig. 8 Motion characteristics of armature in switching on process

It can be seen from Fig. 8 that: 1) within the range of 90°~120° closing phase angle, the collision speed is the slowest when the effective value is 198V; 2) 0°~75° and 135°~180° within the range of other closing phase angles, voltage The smaller the collision, the faster the collision.

E. Average angular acceleration characteristic

The angular acceleration of the armature is linear with the electromagnetic attraction and the spring reaction force. The angular velocity of the armature is equal to the integral of the rotational angular acceleration for the movement time tm. Since the electromagnetic attraction is a parameter that is affected by the closing phase angle and changes with time during the movement, the angular acceleration and angular velocity of the rotation change with the movement time. Therefore, the angular velocity of the static and dynamic iron core may be different when the closing phase angle is different. Define the average angular acceleration ζ, which reflects the relationship between velocity characteristics and motion time characteristics, as shown in equation (12):

$$\zeta = \frac{\omega_m}{t_m} \tag{12}$$

Figure 9 shows the relationship between collision speed and motion time for different closing phase angles.

It can be seen from Fig. 9 that: 1) Within the range of 0°~75°, 150°~180° closing phase angle, the smaller the coil voltage, the larger the average angular acceleration; 2) within the range of 75°~150° closing phase angle, The larger the coil voltage, the larger the average angular acceleration.

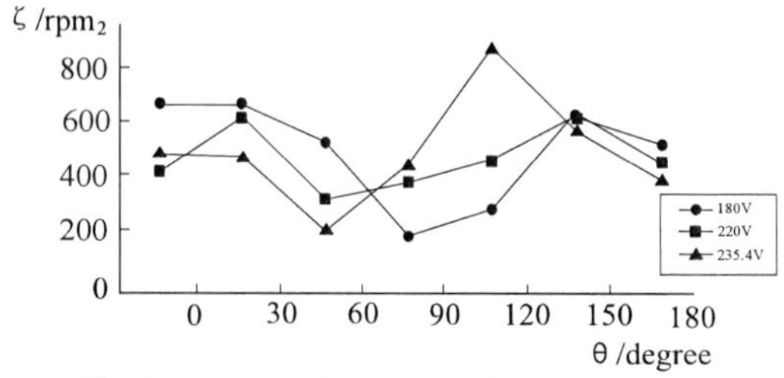

Fig. 9 Mean angular acceleration uniqueness

IV. EFFECT OF FREQUENCY ON TIME CHARACTRISTICS

The national standard GB/T 15945-2008 "Frequency deviation of power quality power system" stipulates that 50Hz is the standard frequency (power frequency) of power system in China. It also stipulates that the normal frequency standard of power grid voltage is 50Hz±0.2Hz. When the system capacity is small, it can be relaxed to 50Hz±0.5Hz. Considering the actual working frequency of the electromagnetic relay sample is 50 Hz or 60 Hz, the influence of 45-60 Hz frequency on the time characteristics of the electromagnetic relay is mainly studied.

A. Effect of Frequency on Time Characteristics

Table 1 shows that the coil excitation effective values are 198V, 220V and 235.4V, respectively, and the closing initial phase angle is 0°. The frequency of the touch time is 45, 49.5, 50, 50.5 and 60 Hz, respectively.

Tab.1 Frequency characteristics of actuation time

U/V \ f/Hz	45	49.5	50	50.5	60
	6.2	6	6	6	5.8
	5.6	5.3	5.3	5.3	5
	5.5	5	5	4.9	4.7

It can be seen from Table 1 that the touch time is almost unaffected in the standard frequency range of 49.5~50.5 Hz, but within the range of 45-60 Hz, the touch time is slightly shortened with increasing frequency.

B. Effect of harmonics on speed characteristics

Tables 2 and 10 show the effective values of coil voltage of 198V, 220V and 235.4V respectively, and the initial phase angle of closing is 0 degrees. At frequencies of 45, 49.5, 50, 50.5 and 60 Hz respectively, the terminal velocity of armature is obtained.

Tab.2 Frequency characteristics of armature end velocity

f/Hz U/V	45	49.5	50	50.5	60
	778.2	1055.8	1004.1	1096.5	1147.9
	1272	667.7	682.8	727.2	1058.9
	953	1513.7	688.1	573.7	901.6

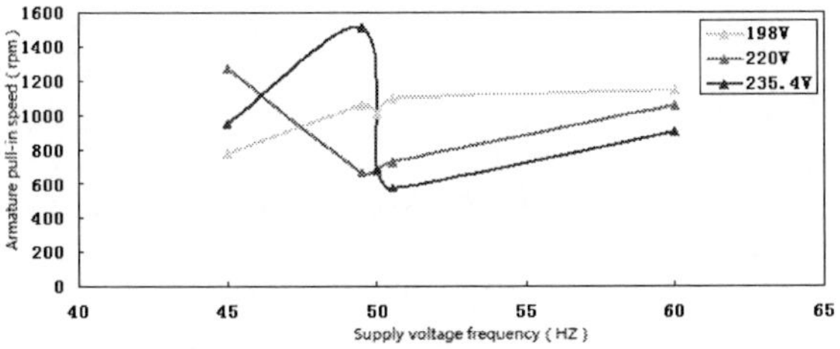

Fig. 10 Frequency characteristics of armature end velocity

It can be seen from Table 2 and Figure 10 that in the standard frequency range of 49.5-50.5 Hz, the final velocity of armature under 220V RMS excitation is low and basically stable at 680 rpm, which is the optimum working frequency and effective value for restraining the mechanical wear caused by core collision.

C. Effect of frequency on minimum electromagnetic torque characteristics

When the armature closes, the minimum value of electromagnetic moment must be greater than the counterforce moment to ensure that the armature absorbs reliably without flutter. Therefore, it is significant to study the characteristics of minimum electromagnetic moment. Table 3 shows that the effective coil voltage values are l98V, 220V and 235.4V, respectively, and the initial phase angle of closing is 0 degrees. The minimum electromagnetic moment at frequencies of 45, 49.5, 50, 50.5 and 60 Hz, respectively.

Tab.3 Frequency characteristics of the minimum electromagnetic torque

f/Hz U/V	45	49.5	50	50.5	60
	26	28.1	25.9	24.9	23.3
	32.7	30.5	29.3	30.4	25.1
	34.1	33.8	33.6	33.1	28.5

It can be seen from Table 3: (1) Under the given amplitude, the higher the frequency, the smaller the minimum electromagnetic torque, which is disadvantageous for suppressing the armature chattering; (2) The 198V RMS, 60Hz frequency power supply excitation, the minimum electromagnetic torque 23.3mN·m is only greater than the back moment of 1.1mN·m when closed, and the safety margin is very small.

V. THE EFFECT OF HARMONICS ON TIME CHARACTERISTICS

The actual grid voltage has different degrees of distortion, and the distorted voltage wave contains high-frequency harmonic components. The harmonic frequency is an integer multiple of the fundamental frequency, which suppresses the coil current and electromagnetic torque, and thus affects the dynamic process of the armature pull-in.

A. Distortion rate and harmonic content

The distortion rate of sinusoidal waveform (THD) is usually used to indicate the degree of deviation of the distortion waveform from the sinusoidal waveform, and the harmonic inclusion rate (HRU) is used to indicate the proportion of a certain harmonic in the distortion wave. They are defined as:

$$\text{THD}=\sqrt{\sum_{n=2}^{\infty}U_n^2}\Big/U_L\times 100\% \tag{13}$$

$$\text{HRU}=U_n/U_l\times 100\% \tag{14}$$

In the formula, U1 is the rated effective value of the fundamental wave voltage, n is the harmonic order, and Un is the effective value of the nth harmonic voltage.

When the Shaoshan I type electric locomotive is running in the Shiyang section of the Shi (Shijiazhuang) Tai (Taiyuan) line, the harmonic content of the section of the grid voltage is shown in Table 4. It can be seen from Table 4 that the 3rd, 5th, and 7th harmonics are the main harmonic components. Ignore the minor harmonic components and construct an analog distortion grid voltage u' with an effective value of 220V:

$$u' = 298.532\sin(100\pi+\theta)+74.006\sin(300\pi+\theta)$$
$$+39.556\sin(500\pi+\theta)+25.244\sin(700\pi+\theta)$$

Tab.4 Each harmonic content of the grid voltage in shi-tai section

n	2	3	4	5	6
	0.3136	24.79	0.1724	13.25	0.061
n	7	8	9	10	11
	8.456	5.305	3.337	2.099	1.422

According to formula (12), the actual grid voltage distortion rate listed in Table 4 is 30.12%, and the grid voltage distortion rate of the construction voltage u' is

29.35%, which is basically consistent. Therefore, u' can be used as a power source to simulate the dynamic characteristics of the electromagnetic relay. The simulation results can be approximated as an estimate of the dynamic characteristics of the actual distortion wave. The dynamic characteristics of the relay that simulates the distortion wave are simulated and compared with the dynamic characteristics of the relay with the same amplitude sine wave.

B. Influence of harmonics on current and time characteristics

The current simulation waveform is shown in Figure 11 under the action of a standard sine wave change and a distorted sine wave with an effective value of 220V, a closing phase angle of θ = 0°.

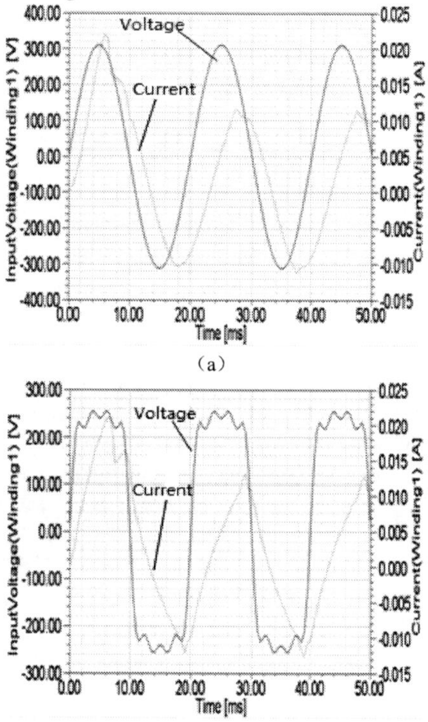

Fig. 11 Effect of harmonics on current characteristics

As can be seen from Fig. 9, the peak value of the 220V positive excitation voltage is about 250V, the current reaches the maximum peak of 0.022A at 6.2ms, the peak of the 220V distortion sinusoidal voltage of the distortion rate is about 250V, and the current reaches the maximum peak of 0.022A at 7ms. It is explained that the harmonics slow down the current growth rate and prolong the time when the current reaches the peak value, thereby prolonging the contact time and the pull-in time of the armature, and the time characteristic of the electromagnetic relay is deteriorated.

The coil current simulation waveform is shown in Fig. 12 under the action of a distorted sine wave with an effective value of 220V when the closing phase angle is θ=30°, 60°, and 90°.

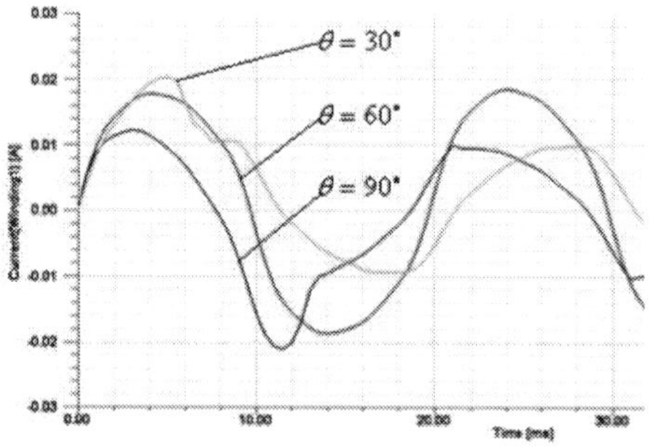

Fig. 12 Coil current characteristics under distorted excitation

It can be seen from Fig. 12 that: (1) When θ=30°, the first peak current of the current characteristic exceeds 0.02A of the touch current; (2) When θ=60°, all the peak currents of the current characteristics are less than 0.02A; (3) When θ = 90°, the first valley current of the current characteristic exceeds 0.02A. According to the trigger criterion, the armature actuation time is the shortest when θ=30°, the armature cannot be sucked when θ=60°, and the touch time is longer than 10 ms when θ=90°. Further torque and speed simulations confirm this conclusion. Table 5 lists the effects of distortion excitation u', actuation, movement, and pull-in time for different closing phase angles.

Tab.5 The time characteristic under distortion excitation

θ/degre€	0	30	60	90	120	150	180
tc/	5.	4.	>	10	9.	8	5
ms	6	2	50	.8	8		.6
tm/	2.	2.	>	2.	1.	1	2
ms	1	3	50	2	5	.6	.1
tx/	7.	6.	>	13	1	9	7
ms	7	5	50		1.3	.6	.7

The time characteristics of Table 5 (excluding the case where θ=60° is not touched) are compared with the time characteristics of the 220V sinusoidal excitation (shown in Figure 6), and the average touch, motion, and pull-in time are extended by 0.76ms, 0.1ms, and 0.87ms, respectively. It shows that the distortion makes the time characteristic of the electromagnetic relay prolonged, and even cannot be sucked reliably.

C. Effect of harmonics on torque and speed characteristics

The simulated electromagnetic torque simulation waveform of the 220V RMS sine wave and the distortion positive strong wave under the action of the closing phase angle θ=120°, 150°, 180° is shown in Fig. 13.

From Figure 13, it can be seen that the waveform top of electromagnetic attraction moment of electromagnetic relay under distortion excitation is sharper, and the first peak value is larger and the valley value is smaller than that under standard positive excitation. The sharp top of the electromagnetic moment means that the average suction moment decreases, while the first peak value increases the collision velocity and the valley value is small, which means that the safety margin of the armature is small when it closes steadily. Table 6 and Table 7 show the comparison of minimum electromagnetic moment and collision velocity of relay armature at different closing phase angles.

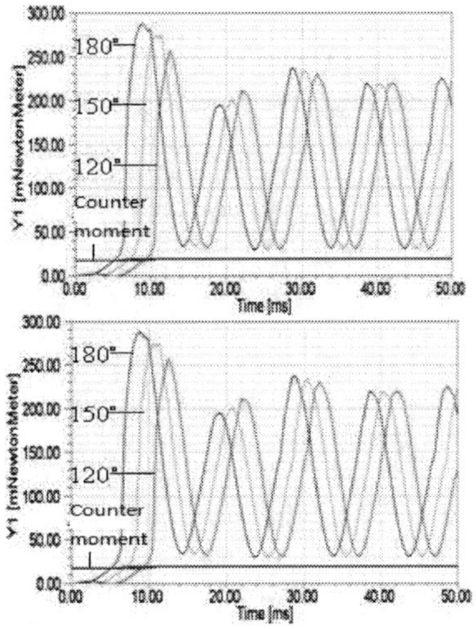

Fig. 13 Effect of harmonics under the closing phase angle

Tab.6 Comparison of Tmin characteristics of electromagnetic torque

θ	0°	30°	90°	120°	150°	180°
Tmin/ mN· m	2 9.3	3 0.1	3 0.4	3 0.5	3 1.3	2 9.3
Tmin/ mN· m	2 5.7	3 2	2 9.9	2 1.9	2 2	2 5.7

Tab.7 Comparison of collision velocity characteristics

θ	0	30	90	120	150	180
ω/rp m	6 82.8	9 37.3	9 52	63 4.1	86 8.3	70 0.3
ω/rp m	7 41.1	1 102. 8	9 32. 3	10 31.3	80 0.9	74 4.9

The minimum electromagnetic moment and velocity in Tables 6 and 7 are averaged respectively. The mean values of T min and T'min are 30.2 mN m and 26.2 mN m, and the mean values of W and are 795.8 rpm and 892.2 rpm, respectively. Explanation: (1) Distortion reduces the minimum moment, which is closer to the closed counter moment of 20.2mN.m. If the distortion rate increases and the minimum electromagnetic moment is less than the counter moment, the armature may be unstable or broken; (2) Distortion increases the collision speed, intensifies the collision between armature and stationary core, and accelerates the mechanical wear.

VI. EFFECT OF TIME CHARACTERISTICS UNDER NON-SINUSOIDAL EXCITATION

When the magnitude, frequency and distortion rate of the power supply are simultaneously changed, the dynamic characteristics of the electromagnetic relay may be greatly affected or even reliably closed. For example, the armature displacement characteristic in the case of the effective value 198V frequency 60 Hz shown in FIG. It can be seen that the 180° phase angle can be reliably sucked. When the 120° phase angle is sucked for a period of time, the armature jumps back to the off position, while at the 150° phase angle, it cannot be sucked.

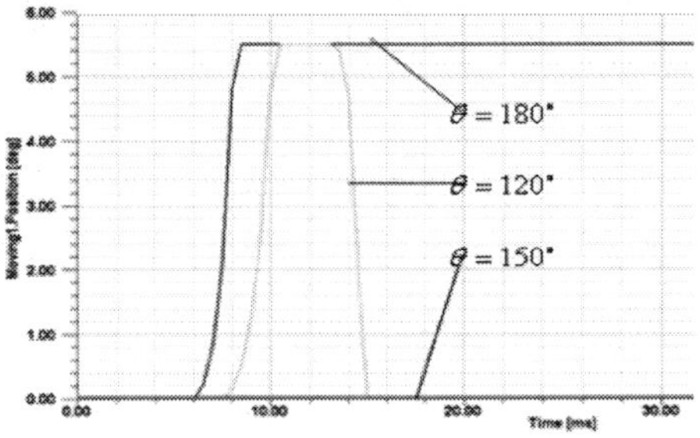

Fig. 14 Armature displacement curve

For another example, the distortion excitation u' effective value is reduced to 198V and the armature displacement characteristic is increased to 60 Hz as shown in Fig. 15.

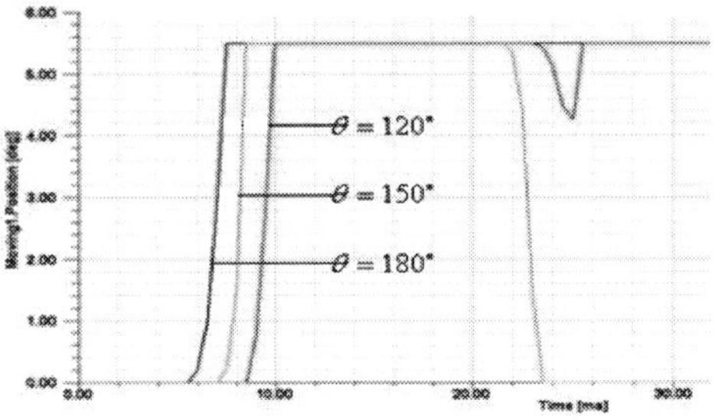

Fig. 15 Armature displacement curve

Fig. 15 shows that: 1) when θ is 180 degrees, the relay can suck in normally; 2) when θ is 120 degrees, the armature will jump back at 23.8ms after suction for a period of time, until the re-suction well reaches a stable closed state at 25ms; 3) when θ is 150 degrees, the armature will return to the breaking state at 21.5ms, but will not close again at 23.5ms and 25ms.

VII. CONCLUSION

In this paper, the electromagnetic and dynamic equations of the relay rotating electromagnetic mechanism are derived. The influences of the power supply amplitude, frequency and distortion rate on the dynamic characteristics of the electromagnetic relay electromagnetic mechanism are mainly studied. The main conclusions are as follows:

1) The higher the voltage, the shorter the touch time and the pull-in time, and the longer the exercise time ratio is affected by the closing phase angle; the smaller the voltage in the 90°~120° phase angle range, the slowest the armature end speed, 0° In the range of ~75° and 135°~180° closing phase angles, the lower the voltage, the faster the end of the armature.

2) The touching time decreases slightly with the increase of frequency; only 220V RMS excitation takes 49.5-50.5Hz as the optimal operating frequency range, in which the terminal velocity of armature is low and basically stable at 680rpm; the higher the frequency, the smaller the minimum electromagnetic moment.

3) Harmonics make the current growth rate slow down and the time when the current reaches the peak is prolonged; the distortion makes the time characteristic of the electromagnetic relay prolonged, and even cannot be reliably sucked; the distortion causes the minimum torque to decrease and the collision speed to increase.

4) Considering the simultaneous changes of the power amplitude, frequency and distortion rate, the dynamic characteristics of the relay may be greatly affected, and the armature may not even be reliably closed.

Further research work includes:

1) Design an orthogonal test scheme to study the direction of deterioration of the dynamic characteristics of the relay electromagnetic mechanism under the influence of three stresses, and find the weak link of the reliability of the relay sample.

2) The kinetic study is extended to the contact system to fully study the dynamic characteristics of the relay prototype.

3) Study the dynamic process of the breaking of the electromagnetic mechanism of the relay prototype, and find the weak link of the reliability of the relay prototype.

REFERENCES

[1] Guansheng Zhang. The basis of electrical theory [M]. Beijing: China Machine Press, 1997.

[2] Chen peng, Lu jianguo, Yaofang, et al. Research on dynamic contact resistance measurement and failure prediction of relay contacts[J]. Advanced Technology of Electrical Engineering and Energy,2005(03):27-30.

[3] Song Dongdong, Ding Laiwei, Dong Biao, et al. Experiment analysis and research on the arc process of different topology on loadtap-changer[J]. Advanced Technology of Electrical Engineering and Energy,1-10[2019-02-01]

[4] GB/T 12325-2008, Power quality-Deviation of supply voltage[S].

[5] Guo Fengyi, Liu Shuai, Wang Zhiyong, et al. R esearch on transient temperature field of electrical sliding contact in pantograph and catenary system[J]. Advanced Technology of Electrical Engineering and Energy,2017,36(03):29-34.

[6] Fei Hongjun, Zhang Guansheng. Dynamic Calculation and Analysis for EMC Body [M]. Beijing: China Machine Press, 1997.

[7] GB/T 12325-2008, Power quality-Frequency deviation for power system[S].

[8] M. Wada, H. Yoshimoto and Y. Kitaide. Dynamic analysis and simulation of electromagnetic contactors with AC solenoids [A] IEEE 2002 28th Annual Conference of the Industrial Electronics Society [C]. Sevilla, 2002, 2745-2751

[9]Xiao Xiangning. Analysis and Control of Power Quality [M]. Beijing: China Electric Power Press, 2004.

[10] Xu Zhihong, Zhang Peiming. Intelligent Control Technology of AC Contactor [A] 2005 IEEE/PES Transmission & Distribution Conference & Exposition [C]. Asia and Pacific, Dalian, 2002, 1-5

[11] M. Wada, H. Yoshimoto and Y. Kitaide. Dynamic analysis and simulation of electromagnetic contactors with AC solenoids [A] IEEE 2002 28th Annual Conference of the Industrial Electronics Society [C]. Sevilla, 2002, 2745-2751

[12] Guo Fengyi, Li Peng, Li Bin, et al. Simulation and experimental research on electromagnetic buffer of electromagnetic actuator[J]. Electrician Advanced Technology of Electrical Engineering and Energy, 2010, 29(03): 68-71+80

[13] Yang Wenying, Guo Jiuwei, Wang ru, et al. Establishing and Calculating Methods of Electromagnetic-Thermal Coupling Model of Relay's Electromagnetic Mechanism [J]. TRANSACTIONS OF CHINA ELECTRO-TECHNICAL SOCIETY, 2017, 32(13): 169-177.

[14] Liu Guojin, Duan Wenle, Li Feng. Calculation of Electromagnetic System of Magnetic atching Relay Based on ANSYS based on ANSYS [J]. Electrotechnics Electric,2016(06):16-19+23.

[15] Liu Xiangjun, Xu Xiong, Lan Dashou. Three-dimensional dynamic characteristic testing, and data processing analysis for electromagnetic mechanism [J] Chinese Journal of Scientific Instrument, 2014, 35(10): 2208-2215.

[16] Y. Kawase, S. Tatsuoka, T. Yamaguchi, et al. 3-D finite element analysis of operating characteristics of AC electromagnetic contactors [J]. IEEE Transactions on Magnetics,1994, 30(5): 3244-3247.

[17] Li Jia. Study of operating characteristics and analyze the specific faliure of the clap-type relay electromagnetic system [D]. Tianjin: Hebei University of Technology, 2013

7th International Conference on Reliability of
Electrical Products and Electrical Contacts,
November 04-06, 2019

Analysis on Contact Resistance for Nickel-plated Connector

Chaoqun Lv, Jianglong Jiang, Chong Pang, Tianlan Liu
Hangzhou Aerospace Electronic Technology Co.; Ltd., Hangzhou, 310051, China
E-mail: lvchaoqun@sina.com.cn Tel: 86-571-88359149 Fax: 86-571-88020250

Abstract — **with theoretical analysis on contact resistance between contacting conductors, this paper developed a mathematical model of contact resistance based on Holm theory and discusses factors that affected contact resistance. By testing the nickel-plated bronze connectors with different phosphorus content, we drew a conclusion that the phosphorous content in nickel cladding determined contact resistance value.**

Index Terms— **Contact resistance, Resistivity, Nickel-plated, Phosphorous content.**

I. INTRODUCTION

When the current passes through a pair of contacting conductors, the voltage drop occurs at and near the contacting interface between the conductors. The resistance that causes the voltage drop is the contact resistance between conductors. Contact resistance is one of the most important performance indexes of electric contacting components. For example, electric transmission efficiency, contact reliability, and working life of the electric contacting components are all reflected by the change of contact resistance. In most medium and small power contact devices, contact functions are often accomplished by contacts coated with metal coatings (such as gold, silver, tin, nickel, etc.). Then the contact resistance of the device is actually the one between the metal coatings. In this paper, the contact resistance of the outer conductor of copper-based nickel-plated coaxial connector is analyzed, and the main reasons affecting the contact resistance are studied.

II. THE FORMATION PRINCIPLE OF CONTACT RESISTANCE

There are three forms of contact between conductors: point contact, line contact, and surface contact. However, all solid surfaces are uneven at microscopic view, with convex peaks and valleys. When the two conductors contact each other, the contact area is consisting of contacting points between the peaks, rather than a continuous line or surface (Fig. 1).

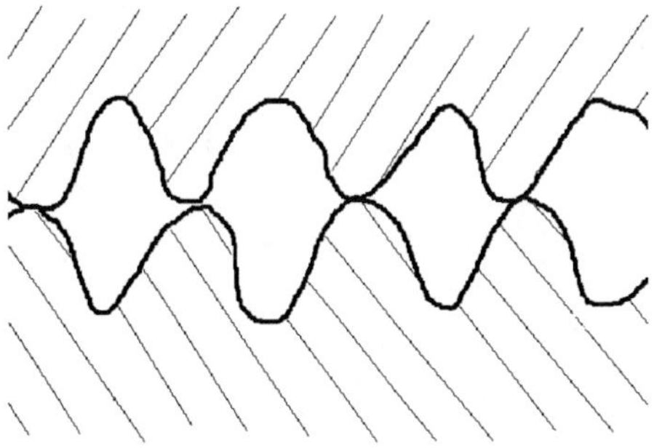

Fig. 1 Microscopic contact state between conductors

When the two contacting conductors are powered up, the current can only flow from one conductor to the other from a small number of contacting points. Compared with the ideal smooth plane contact, the rough surface contact has longer current line and much smaller current crossing section. These result in additional resistance between conductors - shrinkage resistance.

In addition, there are poorly conductive films between contacting conductors such as inorganic films and inorganic contaminated films or adsorption films, which create additional resistance between conductors - film resistance.

A large number of experiments and studies have proved that the contact resistance of conductive elements is composed of shrinkage resistance and film resistance. When the metal conductor is coated, the conducting material changes from the base material to the coating material. Although the contact resistance is still composed of shrinkage resistance and film resistance, the composition, hardness and surface state of the coating material become the related factors to the contact resistance.

III. MATHEMATICAL MODEL AND INFLUENCING FACTORS OF CONTACT RESISTANCE

Assuming that there are n single contact points between the two conductors and each contact point is spherical contact. Under the action of positive pressure between conductors, the spherical contact point is deformed slightly. A small plane is formed on the single conductor contact, on which the two conductors are bonded together. The single contact point model is shown in Fig. 2.

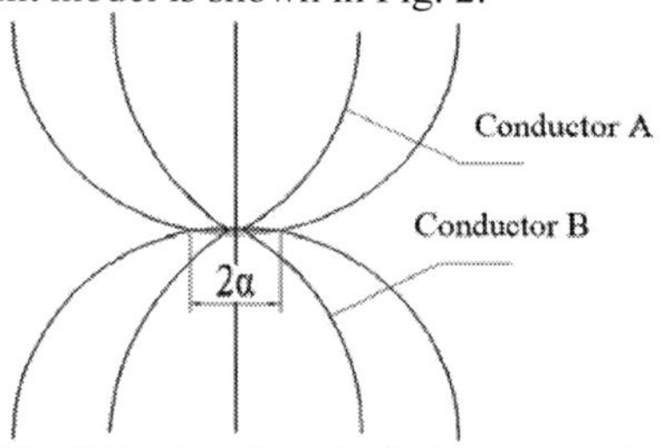

Fig. 2 Single point spherical contact model

If the film resistance is not considered, the shrinkage resistance is just the single point contact resistance. According to the Holm spherical contact theory, the formula for calculating the single point contact resistance is as following:

$$R_s = \frac{\rho_1+\rho_2}{4\alpha} \quad (1)$$

In formula (1), ρ_1 and ρ_2 are the resistivity of conductors A and B respectively, and α is the radius of contact point.

Generally, the deformation state between the connector contacts is elastic without plastic deformation. According to hertz's elastic deformation theory, the formula for calculating the contact radius is as following:

$$\alpha = \sqrt[3]{\frac{3F}{4n}\left(\frac{1-\mu_1^2}{E_1}+\frac{1-\mu_2^2}{E_2}\right)\left(\frac{1}{r_1}+\frac{1}{r_2}\right)^{-1}} \quad (2)$$

In formula (2), F represents positive pressure between contact conductors; μ_1 and μ_2 represent Poisson's ratio of conductors; E_1 and E_2 represent the Young's elastic modulus of these two conductors; r_1 and r_2 represent the curvature radius of spherical contacts.

For copper-based nickel-plated conductors, the materials in contact with each other are nickel. The electrical resistivity, Poisson's ratio and Yang elastic modulus of both conductors are the same. When the manufacturing process of both conductors is the same, their curvature radiuses are approximately equal. Then $\mu_1 = \mu_2 = \mu$, $E_1=E_2=E$, $\rho_1 = \rho_2 = \rho$, $r_1 = r_2 = r$.

Combining formulas (1) and formula (2), the formula for calculating the single point contact resistance is as following:

$$R_s = 0.55\rho\cdot\sqrt[3]{\frac{E\cdot n}{F\cdot r}(1-\mu^2)^{-1}} \quad (3)$$

When there are n contact points between the two conductors, the total contact resistance equal to the parallel value of n single point contact resistance. The formula for calculating contact resistance is as following:

$$R = 0.55\rho\cdot\sqrt[3]{\frac{E}{n^2\cdot F\cdot r}(1-\mu^2)^{-1}} \quad (4)$$

In formula (4), the contact resistance is related to the resistivity of the material, the hardness of the material, the deformation coefficient of the conductor, the pressure between conductors, the surface roughness, and the shape of the contact points. For copper based nickel plated contact parts, the Young's elastic modulus and Poisson's ratio of conductors are constant value. Then the contact resistance is proportional to the resistivity and inversely proportional to the cubic root of the positive pressure and contact point radius. Among the factors influencing the contact resistance, Coating resistivity of the conductor is the most prominent one.

IV. CONTACT RESISTANCE TEST OF NICKEL PLATED CONTACT PARTS

Copper alloy is often used as external conductor in the design of coaxial electrical connector. Its surface is nickel plated: either electro nickel-plating or chemical nickel-plating. Nickel plated copper has been widely used in many fields because of its excellent comprehensive physical and chemical properties, such as uniform coating, high hardness, wear resistance, corrosion resistance, gloss and adhesion.

The nickel coating obtained by electroplating nickel is pure nickel, while the nickel coating of chemical nickel plating is nickel-phosphorus alloy. In the process of chemical nickel plating, hypophosphite is use as reductant. When nickel atoms in the bath are reduced and deposited on the surface of the work piece, some of the secondary phosphate is reduced to simple phosphorus and enters the nickel coating, forming amorphous Ni-P alloy sheet structure. According to the different phosphorus content, there are three kinds of chemical nickel plating: low phosphorus nickel plating, medium phosphorus nickel plating and high phosphorus nickel plating. With the increase of phosphorus content, the resistance of nickel coating also increases. The relationship between phosphorus content and resistivity of nickel plated layer is shown in Table I.

We made the outer conductor contact pair (including pin and Jack) of coaxial connector shown in Fig. 3 as the test pieces. The material of test pieces is copper alloy. All test pieces are from the same batch. They are made of the same batch of copper alloy materials and machined under the same conditions, with the same hardness, surface roughness, separation force and diameter. These parts are separated into three groups and treated with electro nickel plating, medium phosphorus nickel plating and high phosphorus nickel plating respectively. The phosphorus content of nickel coating on the surface of each conductors group is different. The parameters of these test pieces are shown in Table III.

Taking five pairs of pin and socket from each group,

inserting pin into socket. Under the same environmental conditions, each contact pair is measured with a contact resistance tester, and the same sample is measured three times at different point. The test results are shown in TableIII.

The data in Table I and Table III show that with the increase of phosphorus content in nickel plating layer, the resistivity increases gradually, and the value of measured contact resistance increases. For the contact parts with high phosphorus content, the contact resistance values measured between different sample individuals and different points of the same sample become discrete and the contact stability decreases.

Fig. 3 Nickel plating contact pair for external conductors of coaxial connectors

Table I Nickel-phosphorus coating resistivity

kind	electro nickel-plating	low phosphorus nickel plating	medium phosphorus nickel plating	high phosphorus nickel plating
phosphorus content	0%	1%—4%	5%—8%	9%—12%
resistivity (Ω.m)	8×10^{-8}	25×10^{-8}	60×10^{-8}	75×10^{-8}

Table II Parameters of test parts

Group	Pin diameter (mm)	separating force (N)	roughness	Plating	quantity
1	$6.1^{0}_{-0.02}$	1.0~1.2	$R_a0.8$	electro	5
2	$6.1^{0}_{-0.02}$	1.0~1.2	$R_a0.8$	medium phosphorus	5
3	$6.1^{0}_{-0.02}$	1.0~1.2	$R_a0.8$	high phosphorus	5

Table III Test value of contact resistance (m Ω)

kind	electro nickel-plating					medium phosphorus nickel plating					high phosphorus nickel plating				
times \ number	1	2	3	4	5	1	2	3	4	5	1	2	3	4	5
1	2.0	1.3	1.6	1.3	1.7	5.8	2.9	3.5	4.7	5.7	8.6	11.6	12.5	10.5	9.8
2	1.9	1.3	1.6	1.4	1.7	6.5	7.9	6.9	3.6	4.2	6.6	10.8	8.3	11.4	6.5
3	2.0	1.4	1.6	1.3	1.7	4.6	5.7	5.0	2.8	4.9	14.8	10.4	12.7	12.3	6.0
single average	1.97	1.33	1.60	1.33	1.70	5.63	5.50	5.13	3.70	4.93	10.00	10.93	11.17	11.40	7.43
average	1.59					4.98					10.19				

V. CONCLUSION

In this paper, the microscopic surface contact structure of conductors and the generation principle of conductor contact resistance were analyzed. Based on the Holm spherical contact theory, we established the mathematical model of the contact resistance for copper-based nickel plating contact pair, and confirmed that the coating resistivity is the main reason that affects the contact resistance. We had made copper-based nickel plating test parts with different phosphorus content, that are outer conductors of coaxial connector. The effect of phosphorus content in nickel layer on contact resistance was verified by experimental method. The test results show that the higher the phosphorus content in the nickel plating layer of the contact parts is, the greater the contact resistance is.

In conclusion, the main factor affecting the resistance of contact pairs with copper-based nickel plating is the phosphorus content in the nickel layer. For the outer conductor of coaxial connector, reducing the phosphorus content in nickel layer can effectively reduce the contact resistance and improve the electrical continuity between contact parts.

REFERENCES

[1] Fengyi Guo, Zhonghua Chen. "Electric contact theory and its application technology" electric Power Publishing House, Beijing, 2008.

[2] Jun Xu, Kun Li. "Study on resistance of electric contact" Electeical Materials, No.1, 2011.

[3] Haiquan Zhang. "Study on contact resistance between contacts of electrical switches" Journal of Henan Institute of Education, Vol.17, No.2, 2008.

[4] Yongguo Du, Weijun Zhang, Junsui Hu. "Research on electrical contact material" Electrical materials, No.3, 2005.

[5] Yuan Yu, Guiying Xu, Huang Hong. "Study on Microstructure and Properties of Electroless Ni-P alloy coating" Journal of Liaoning normal University, Vol.21, No.1, 1998.

Chaoqun Lv (1970): This author became a Master of Engineering in 2007, a senior engineer in 2011. The major field of study is Electrical connection Technology and Application.

Research on Effectiveness Evaluation Model and Analytical Algorithms of Electronic Jamming System

Jingde Huang[1], Jiaxiang Yu[2], Benfu Jiang[1]
[1]Zhuhai College of Jilin University, Zhuhai, 519041, China
[2]Dalian Naval Academy, Dalian, 116018, China
E-mail: jdh925@sina.com Tel: 86-756-7626130 Fax: 86-756-7626130

Abstract—**This paper established a kind of electronic jamming system for damage efficiency evaluation model when targets jamming. Real-time simulation of the error caused by the electronic jamming system, fast calculation and real-time description of the impact of the electronic jamming system on the target damage, avoiding the shortcomings of the traditional statistical simulation method to calculate the air defense damage probability that requires multiple simulation statistics, optimization of the damage probability calculation model, fast calculation speed, calculation results which has the characteristics of high reliability, high precision and satisfying the requirement of simulation calculation, also can evaluate and simulate the damage effect of air defense weapon system in real time. It provides a theoretical basis for the real-time evaluation of the work efficiency of electronic jamming system. Effectively solves the defects of presetting damage effect in the past equipment simulation training, and has practical guiding significance in engineering.**

***Index Terms*—Electronic jamming system, Work efficiency, Damage probability, Analytical algorithm**

I. INTRODUCTION

With the rapid development of science and technology, the new air defense weapon system has the remarkable characteristics of functional integration, complex structure, short reaction time and high automation, and has become one of the indispensable components in the future air defense system. The electronic jamming system is the main electronic equipment that affects the damage probability of air attack. and interception accuracy, its performance directly affects the working accuracy of air defense weapon system units. Effectiveness of electronic jamming system is closely related to target type and regional environment, and is also affected by our weapon unit configuration system. When evaluating the effectiveness of electronic jamming system, it is necessary to evaluate the effectiveness of the system in real time. At present, the traditional numerical simulation method is difficult to describe the actual performance of electronic jamming system quickly. Because of the above reasons, In this paper, an analytical algorithm model for air target damage caused by electronic jamming is presented. It not only achieves fast calculation, but also describes the working efficiency of electronic jamming system to air targets in real time. It has engineering practice opinions.

II. DAMAGE EFFECTIVENESS MODEL UNDER IDEAL CONDITIONS

It is well known that when a target is located in the flying cone, it is likely to be damaged; otherwise, the target can not be damaged. The size of the flying cone is expressed by the angle φ_1 and φ_2 of the projectile axis. Approximately available: $\varphi_1 \approx \varphi_0$-15°, $\varphi_2 \approx \varphi_0$+15°, φ_0=tg$^{-1}(V_g/V_{re})$, which V_{re} is the storage speed of the advance point; V_g is the additional speed of the explosion.

Fragments of each weight can be considered uniformly distributed in the flying cone. The fragment flow density $\lambda_i(R)$ of the i weighted fragment at the distance of R meter from the explosion point is as follows:

$$\lambda_i(R) = \frac{N_i}{S} = \frac{N_i}{2\pi R^2(\cos\varphi_1 - \cos\varphi_2)}$$

Which N_i is number of fragments in the heavyweight i ;

S is the surface area of the flying cone away from the explosion point R : $S = 2\pi R^2(\cos\varphi_1 - \cos\varphi_2)$.

The flying orbit of fragments can be approximately taken as a straight line in a relatively short distance. Without considering the bending of fragment trajectory caused by gravity, the flying speed and flying time of fragment from the explosion point can be obtained by the linear motion equation of mass center.

$$V_b = V_{b0} e^{-\frac{R}{C}}$$

$$t = \frac{C}{V_{bo}}(e^{\frac{R}{C}} - 1)$$

Which C is equal to $q^{\frac{1}{3}} / 0.00374H(y)$, q is fragment weight(Kg) .

Then relative speed of fragments to targets $V_\rho = \sqrt{V_b^{\,2} + V_t^2 - 2V_b V_t \cos\alpha}$, α is the angle between the speed of storage V_b for fragments and the target speed V_t .

When fragments hit the target, the damage to the target can be divided into two situations: one is that the fragment hits the key part of the target and causes perforation to damage the target; the other is that the flammable part of the target hits and causes combustion to damage the target.

When the fragment hits the target, whether perforation or not is a random event. The probability is related to the fragment weight q (Kg), the relative speed V_ρ (m/s) when the fragment meets the target, the material thickness h (mm) and the material strength . The piercing probability P_p can be approximately calculated as:

$$P_p = \begin{cases} 1 - e^{-(0.07E-0.235)} & \text{E} \geq 3.3 \\ 0 & \text{E} < 3.3 \end{cases}$$

$$E = \frac{1}{9.81 \times 10^2} \frac{q^{\frac{1}{3}} V_\rho^2}{h}$$

When fragments hit flammable parts of the target, combustion probability P_f is as follows:

$$P_f = \begin{cases} 1 - e^{-0.6\times10^{-2} q^{\frac{2}{3}} (V_\rho - 400) H(y)} & V_\rho \geq 400\text{m/s} \\ 0 & V_\rho < 400\text{m/s} \end{cases}$$

Finally, the target law of fragment damage is as follows:

$$\mathrm{K}(X) = \begin{cases} 1 - e^{-\sum_{i=1}^{n} \lambda_i \left[P_p(i) \left(S_0 + k q_i^{\frac{1}{3}} \right) + S_f P_f(i) \right]} & X \in \Omega \\ 0 & X \notin \Omega \end{cases}$$

which $\mathrm{q_i}$ is average weight(g) for the fragments in the heavyweight i .

III. DAMAGE EFFECTIVENESS MODEL UNDER ELECTRONIC JAMMING CONDITIONS

A. Damage effectiveness model

When the air defense weapon unit is subjected to electronic interference, it will inevitably affect the damage accuracy. Generally speaking, the fragment dispersion error can be considered to consist of three sets of errors which obey the three-dimensional normal distribution. The probability of fragment hit after the implementation of electronic jamming is as follows:

$$P_{k1} = \int_{-\infty}^{\infty} \int_{-\infty}^{\infty} \int_{-\infty}^{\infty} \frac{1}{\sqrt{(2\pi)^3 |K_X|}} e^{-\frac{1}{2}(X-M)^T K_X^{-1} (X-M)} \mathrm{K}(X) dX$$

$$K_X = K_{\mathrm{I}} + K_{\mathrm{II}} + K_{\mathrm{III}}$$

The first set of errors includes disturbance errors caused by interference $\Delta\beta_{\mathrm{s}}$, $\Delta\varphi_{\mathrm{s}}$, ΔN_{s} ,and dispersion center error caused by dispersion of action time; co-variance matrix K_I is as follows:

$$K_I = K_{\beta s} + K_{\varphi s} + K_{Ns} + K_{\Delta t} + K_x + K_y + K_z$$

The second set of errors includes errors in calculating relative advance coordinates $\Delta\beta$, $\Delta\varphi$, ΔN ; co-variance matrix K_{II} is as follows:

$$K_{II} = K_\beta + K_\varphi + K_N$$

The third set of errors includes errors in calculating environmental corrections ΔV_0 , $\Delta\rho$, ΔW_{d} , ΔW_{z} ; co-variance matrix K_{III} is as follows:

$$K_{III} = K_{V0} + K_\rho + K_{Wd} + K_{Wz}$$

Mathematical expectations of three sets of errors is as follows:

$$M = M_\beta + M_\varphi + M_N$$

According to Damage Target Law, fragment coordinates is obtained from fragment speed V_{b0} away from the explosion point R and flight time t, the expression is as follows:

$$\begin{cases} y_1 = R \sin\varphi \cos\beta \\ y_2 = R \sin\varphi \sin\beta \\ y_3 = R \cos\varphi \end{cases}$$

$$\begin{cases} x_1 = y_1 - V_t \cdot t \cdot \sin\gamma \\ x_2 = y_2 \\ x_3 = y_3 - V_t \cdot t \cdot \cos\gamma \end{cases}$$

Calculating t , the average weight of fragments q is equal to 40(g).

$$\frac{D(y_1, y_2, y_3)}{D(R, \varphi, \beta)} = R^2 \sin\beta$$

$$J(R, \varphi, \beta) = \frac{D(x_1, x_2, x_3)}{D(y_1, y_2, y_3)} = 1 - \frac{V_t}{V_{b0}} e^{\frac{R}{C}} \cos\alpha$$

The integral interval is as follows:

$$R = 0 \sim \infty, \varphi = \varphi_1 \sim \varphi_2, \beta = -\pi \sim \pi$$

Then the probability of damage after disturbance is as follows:

$$P_{k1} = \int_0^\infty \int_{\varphi_1}^{\varphi_2} \int_{-\pi}^{\pi} \varphi(R, \varphi, \beta) \mathrm{K}(R, \varphi, \beta) R^2 \left[1 - \frac{V_t}{V_{b0}} e^{\frac{R}{C}} \cos\alpha \right] \sin\varphi dR d\varphi d\beta$$

The integral region of variable φ is from φ_1 to φ_2 , Because of φ_1-$\varphi_2 \approx 30^{\mathrm{o}}$, The range of change is not large, The integral function K and J hardly changes with the change of φ , replacing variable φ with average divergence angle φ which is equal to $(\varphi_2 + \varphi_1)/2$,then:

$$P_{k1} = (\cos\varphi_1 - \cos\varphi_2) \int_0^{R_0} \int_{-\pi}^{\pi} \varphi(R, \varphi_0, \beta) \mathrm{K}(R, \varphi_0, \beta) J(R, \varphi_0, \beta) R^2 dR d\beta$$

Because $K(R,\varphi_0,\beta)$ and $J(R,\varphi_0,\beta)$ are the functions of $\cos\alpha$ which is β 's even function, R is divided into n intervals, β is divided into w intervals, then:

$$P_{k1}=(\cos\phi_1-\cos\phi_2)\sum_{i=1}^{n}\frac{R_0}{2n}\cdot\sum_{k=1}^{m}A_k$$
$$\cdot\left\{\sum_{l=1}^{w}\frac{\pi}{2w}\cdot\sum_{j=1}^{m}A_j\cdot[\phi(R^*,\phi_0,\beta^*)+\phi(R^*,\phi_0,-\beta^*)]\cdot R^{*2}\left(1-\frac{V_t}{V_{b0}}e^{\frac{R^*}{C}}\cos\alpha\right)K(R^*,\phi_0,\beta^*)\right\}$$

$$R^*=\frac{2i-1+\xi_k}{2n}R_0$$

$$\beta^*=\frac{2l-1+\xi_j}{2w}\beta_0$$

Which m is number of nodes integrating for Gauss method, A_k and A_j are both quadrature coefficient of Gauss method, ξ_k and ξ_j are both quadrature node for Gauss method.

B. Analytical algorithm

The calculation process of $K(R^*,\varphi_0,\beta^*)$ is as follows:

$$(1)\ V_{b0}=\sqrt{V_g^2+V_{re}^2}$$

$$(2)\ t=\frac{C}{V_{b0}}(e^{\frac{R^*}{C}}-1)\qquad C=\frac{\bar{q}^{\frac{1}{3}}}{0.0374H(y)}\qquad \bar{q}=40(\mathrm{g})$$

$$(3)\ \cos\gamma=-\sin\theta\sin\lambda+\cos\theta\cos\lambda\cos Q_t$$
$$\sin\gamma=\sqrt{1-\cos^2\gamma}$$
$$\cos\alpha=-(\sin\varphi_0\cos\beta^*\sin\gamma+\cos\varphi_0\cos\gamma)$$

$$(4)\ V_b=V_{b0}e^{-\frac{R^*}{C}}$$

$$(5)\ V_\rho=\sqrt{V_b^2+V_t^2-2V_bV_t\cos\alpha}$$

$$(6)\ E_i=\frac{1}{9.8\times10^3}\frac{q_i^{\frac{1}{3}}V_\rho^2}{h}$$

$$(7)\ P_\rho(i)=\begin{cases}1-e^{-(0.07E_i+0.235)} & E_i\geq3.36\\ 0 & E_i<3.36\end{cases}$$

$$(8)\ P_f(i)=\begin{cases}1-e^{-(0.6\times10^{-4}q_i^{\frac{2}{3}}(V_\rho-400)H(y)} & \mathrm{V}_\rho\geq400\\ 0 & \mathrm{V}_\rho<400\end{cases}$$

$$(9)\ K(X)=\begin{cases}1-e^{-\frac{1}{2\pi R^{*2}(\cos\phi_1-\cos\phi_2)}\sum_{i=1}^{5}N_i\left[P_\rho(i)(A_h+kq_i^{\frac{1}{3}})+A_tP_f(i)\right]} & X\in\Omega\\ 0 & X\notin\Omega\end{cases}$$

The calculation process of $\varphi(R^*,\varphi_0,\beta^*)$ is as follows:

$$\varphi(R^*,\varphi_0,\beta^*)=\varphi(x_1,x_2,x_3)=\frac{1}{\sqrt{(2\pi)^3|K_x|}}e^{-\frac{1}{2}(X-M_{\text{II}})^TK_x^{-1}(X-M_{\text{II}})}$$
$$M_{\text{II}}=(m_1,m_2,m_3)^T$$
$$X=(x_1,x_2,x_3)^T$$
$$K_x=K_{\text{I}}+K_{\text{II}}+K_{\text{III}}$$
$$\begin{cases}x_1=R^*\cdot\sin\varphi_0\cdot\cos\beta^*-V_t\cdot t\cdot\sin\gamma\\ x_2=R^*\cdot\sin\varphi_0\cdot\sin\beta^*\\ x_3=R^*\cdot\cos\varphi_0-V_t\cdot t\cdot\cos\gamma\end{cases}$$

IV. THE EXAMPLE ANALYSIS

The altitude h of an aerial target is 800 m, the shortcut d_{sh} is 200 m, the horizontal flight speed V_t is 180m/s ,close to $P=0$, assuming that the horizontal distance d_p of the advance point for the implementation of electronic jamming is equal to 4000m, from the above formulas, it can be calculated that:

The first set of error co-variance matrices:

$$K_I=\begin{bmatrix}278.423 & 25.794 & 711.829\\ 25.794 & 81.892 & 79.210\\ 711.829 & 79.210 & 6123.874\end{bmatrix}$$

The second set of error co-variance matrices:

$$K_{\varphi II}=\begin{bmatrix}225.807 & -156.874 & 595.036\\ -156.874 & 1096.604 & -2.844\\ 595.036 & -2.844 & 10110.471\end{bmatrix}$$

The third set of error co-variance matrices:

$$K_{\varphi III}=\begin{bmatrix}7.535 & 1.099 & -34.221\\ 1.099 & 1.173 & -5.747\\ -34.221 & -5.747 & 578.439\end{bmatrix}$$

Mathematical expectations of systematic errors:

$$M_{\varphi II}=[-40.796\ \ 11.599\ \ -140.487]^T$$

Then the matrix of synthetic co-variance matrix is:

$$K_X=\begin{bmatrix}16812.7832 & 70.6199 & 1272.6444\\ 70.6199 & 1179.3730 & -135.3256\\ 1272.6444 & -135.3256 & 399.9038\end{bmatrix}$$

Final damage probability P_{kl} is equal to 0.006583.

V. CONCLUSION

This paper establishes an analytical algorithm model of electronic interference, which solves the disadvantage that the statistical simulation method needs multiple simulation statistics to calculate the target damage probability. It has the characteristics of simple calculation model, fast speed, high reliability and high accuracy, and can evaluate and simulate the air target damage effect in real time. It can effectively solve the shortcomings of previous simulation training such as damage effect pre-set, and has certain guiding significance for real-time damage assessment of target under disturbed conditions in the use of equipment simulation training system.

REFERENCES

[1] C. P. Pan, Analysis of Shooting Effectiveness of Weapon System [M]. BeiJing, National Defense Industry Press, 1985.6

[2] Y. M. Cheng, Principle of Evaluating Shooting Efficiency [M]. BeiJing, PLA Publishing House, 1986.9

[3] J. J. Han, W. M. LI, F. X. Liu, Queuing Model for Combat Effectiveness Analysis of Multi-Channel Air Defense Missile Weapon System [J]. Journal of Air Force Engineering University (Natural Science Edition), 2005, 6(4)

[4] Solomatine D P, Shrestha D L. AdaBoost. RT: a boosting algorithm for regression problems[C]. proceedings of the 2004 IEEE International Joint Conference on Neural Networks Budapest, Hungary, 2004

[5] Van M, Ge S S, Ren H. Finite time fault tolerant control for robot manipulators using time delay estimation and continuous nonsingular fast terminal sliding mode control [J]. IEEE Transactions on Cybernetics, 2017, 47(7):1681-1693

Study on Performance Degradation of Ship Relay under Vibration Conditions

Zhaopan Zhang[1], Yanyan Luo[1], Minmin Zhang[2], Pengfei Li[2]
[1]State Key Laboratory of Reliability and Intelligence of Electrical Equipment, Hebei University of Technology, Tianjin, 300130, China
[2]State Grid Shanxi Electric Power Company Maintenance Company, Shanxi, 030000, China
E-mail: 1414674006@qq.com Tel: 18222963840

Abstract—**The working environment of ship relays is more complicated than land. These unfavorable external environments often cause the performance of ship relays to be reduced or even failed. Therefore, the author analyzes the degradation laws of various performance parameters of ship relays under different vibration conditions were analyzed. Combined with ship vibration law and related standards, a vibration test scheme for ship relay is proposed. The software and hardware design of the ship's relay performance parameter detection system is completed and tested. Finally, the test data is processed and analyzed. The test results show that with 40-130 Hz, the contact resistance increases slowly with the increase of vibration acceleration, and the release and rebound time do not change significantly. The pick-up time increases and the fluctuation is most obvious. At the natural frequency of 160 Hz, all parameters have changed significantly and the fluctuations are very unstable.**

Index Terms—**Ship relay, Ship vibration; Performance parameter, Parameter test**

I. INTRODUCTION

The ship relay realizes the functions of automatic control and protection of electric power traction equipment and power system by controlling its own on-off state. It is one of the most widely used electromechanical components in ship electric appliances. The reliability level of ship relays has an important impact on the safe operation of the system.

During storage and use, the reliability of ship relays is affected by environmental factors such as temperature and vibration. Vibration can cause the contact performance of the relay to degrade, malfunctions and even affect the safe operation of the system seriously. Rese arches on the impact of relay reliability on domestic and foreign scholars mainly include two aspects. 1) Experimental and theoretical research, mainly through the basic theory or the application of external conditions to study the relay degradation process. G. Wang et al. used the principles of electrostatics and dynamics to analyze the mechanism of electrostatic adsorption of the excess particles of the relay and the process of contact charging [1]. Li Lingling et al. used rough set theory to establish life decision rules and predict relay life [2]. Wang Jia et al. used PCA to process the column vector of the sequence information matrix to construct a function describing the feature quantity of the relay's comprehensive performance reliability, and obtained the relay comprehensive performance degradation model [3]. W. Ren et al. studied the influence of vibration environment on the vibration resistance of relay contact springs from the theoretical and experimental perspectives [4]. Kazuaki Miyanaga et al. discussed how to reduce the influence of needle dust on contact resistance when designing relays [5]. Fan Weiwei et al. briefly described the working environment and classification methods of ship relays, introduced the relevant standards of ship relays, and put forward the content countermeasures for the characteristics of ship relays [6]. 2) In terms of simulation and model research, Z. Guofu et al. used Fokker-Planck equation and Monte-Carlo simulation to analyze the influence of model parameters and system behavior on the reliability of ship relays [7]. Niels Lambrecht et al. studied the relay electromagnetic contact bounce, and verified that the MTL and contact bounce combination model can be used to optimize the design of the load box and the device under test [8]. Zhao Han et al. proposed to modify the reed size parameters and upgrade the reed material optimization scheme to alleviate the problem of releasing the jump back of the decoupling power relay [9].

At present, there are few studies on the sensitive performance parameters of ship relays under vibration conditions [10-11]. This paper mainly discusses the variation of performance parameters of ship relays under different vibration frequencies and acceleration conditions.

II. SHIP RELAY VIBRATION TEST METHOD

A. *Test sample*

The test sample selected in this paper is a small DC ship

relay of a certain type, and some of its performance parameters are shown in Table I.

TABLE I
SHIP RELAY TEST SAMPLE PART PERFORMANCE PARAMETERS

Dimensions/mm	38*21.5*28
Contact resistance / mΩ	50
Contact load / Resistive	1A, 24VDC
Mechanical life / Times	$1*10^7$
Electrical life / Times	$1*10^5$
Ambient temperature / ℃	-40～+70
Pull-in voltage / V	DC≤70%
Release voltage / V	DC≤10%
Pick up time / ms	25
Release time / ms	20

B. *Test plan*

According to the provisions of GB/T2423 "Environmental Testing of Electrical and Electronic Products" [12], the environmental conditions of the test are set as follows: the temperature is 15 °C ~ 35 °C, the relative humidity is 45% ~ 75%, and the atmospheric pressure is 86 kPa ~ 106 kPa. The load condition is set to 1A current.

In this paper, the vibration stress is applied to the sample in the form of a sinusoidal displacement load. The displacement equation is:

$$S = A \cdot \sin(2\pi ft + \theta) \quad (1)$$

The acceleration equation is:

$$a = -4A \cdot \pi^2 \cdot f^2 \cdot \sin(2\pi ft + \theta) \quad (2)$$

Refer to GB/T3738-2008 "Basic Requirements for Ship Low-Voltage Electrical Appliances" and GJB 3952-2000 "General Requirements for Ship Electrical Safety" [13-14] and other related standards and the natural frequency of the test sample (160Hz). The frequency range of the ship relay vibration test is set to 40Hz to 160Hz. The vibration acceleration is 2g~14g, where g=9.8m/s^2. The specific vibration test schemes formulated in this paper are shown in Table II.

During the test, the contact parameters such as contact resistance, pick-up time, release time, rebound time, pull-in voltage, and release voltage of the ship relay are regularly monitored.

C. *Test device*

The ship relay vibration test device is mainly composed of a vibration table, a driving unit, a signal adjusting unit, a data collecting unit and an industrial computer, as shown in Fig. 1. The driving unit mainly completes the timing connection and control breaking of the relay sample group; the signal conditioning unit is mainly responsible for the test monitoring of the contact pressure drop, so that it satisfies the requirements of the accuracy and range of the data acquisition module; the data acquisition unit controls the output of the conditioning unit The signal is entered into the industrial computer.

TABLE II
SHIP RELAY VIBRATION TEST PROGRAM

Vibration frequency / Hz	Vibration acceleration / (m/s^2)	Number of actions / Times	Test group
40		10^5	1-7
70		10^5	8-14
100	2g, 4g, 6g, 8g, 10g, 12g, 14g	10^5	15-21
130		10^5	22-28
160		10^5	29-35

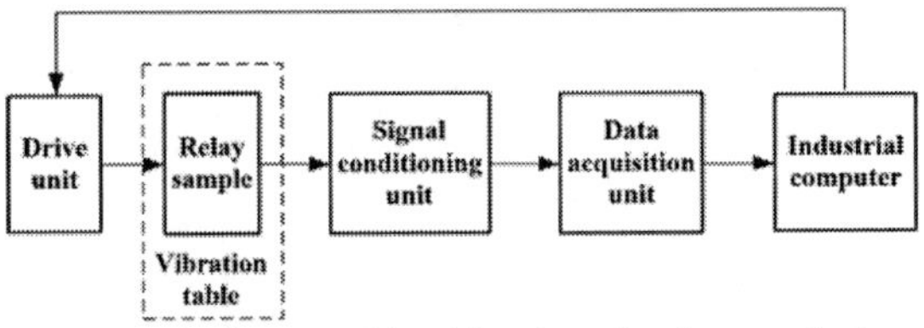

Fig. 1 Block diagram of the ship relay vibration test device

The simulation of the vibration excitation conditions in the test is mainly realized by the vibration table and its matched power amplifier, signal generator and dynamic signal test system. In this paper, the JZK-40 mode excitation small vibration table is used to simulate the highest vibration acceleration of 48.5g, the amplitude is ±10mm, and the vertical direction is sinusoidal motion.

III. ANALYSIS ON THE CHANGE RULE OF PERFORMANCE PARAMETERS OF SHIP RELAY

A. *Analysis of the Change Law of Contact Resistance of Ship relay*

In the 35 sets of tests conducted in this paper, although the contact resistance of the sample fluctuated to varying degrees, it did not reach the limit of failure (50 mΩ), and its variation curve is shown in Fig. 2.

It can be seen from Fig. 2 that under the vibration condition of 40~160Hz, when the vibration frequency is the same, the contact resistance of the sample increases slowly with the increase of the vibration acceleration; when the vibration acceleration is equal, the sample touches as the vibration frequency becomes larger. The resistance increases.

According to the basic theory of electrical contact, the magnitude of the contact pressure determines the size of the contact resistance:

$$R_j = \frac{K}{(0.102F)^m} \tag{3}$$

Where, R_j is the contact resistance, F is the contact pressure, N; K is the correlation coefficient determined by factors such as the surface condition of the electrical material; m is the coefficient related to the form of the contact surface.

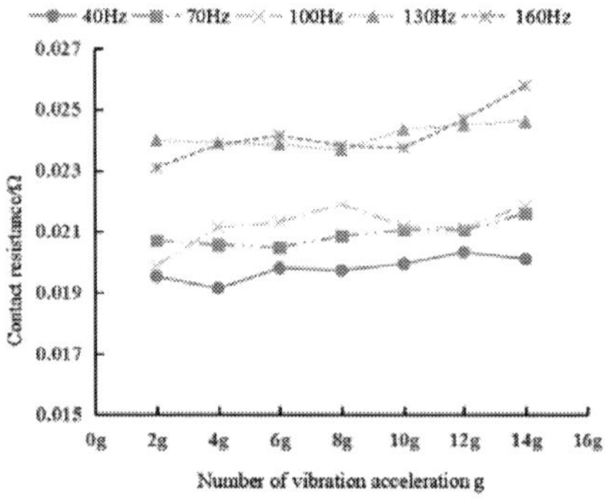

Fig. 2 Curve of contact resistance of relay sample under different vibration conditions

The formula (3) shows that the contact pressure is reduced to cause the contact resistance to become large.

The contact pressure of the contact under vibration conditions is related to F_0、$F_{ИН}$、N: [15]

$$F = F_0 - |F_{ИН} + N| \tag{4}$$

The maximum value of the contact inertia force $F_{ИН} = m_k a$, m_k is the mass of the contact; and the elastic dynamic reaction force N is:

$$N = \frac{125}{64}\pi^3 \frac{EJA}{l^3}[V^2(\frac{5}{4}\pi) - S(\frac{5}{4}\pi)U(\frac{5}{4}\pi)] \tag{5}$$

In the formula, E is the elastic modulus of the material; J is the moment of inertia of the cross section of the reed; l is the length of the reed; S(x), T(x), U(x), V(x) are Cray The Love function is determined by equation (6); A is an unknown constant, which is determined by equation (7).

In the formula, $r^4 = f_0^2 \frac{\gamma S l^4}{EJg}$ is the characteristic value of the system, γ is the material density of the reed, and S is the cross-sectional area of the reed.

$$\begin{cases} S(r\xi) = \frac{1}{2}(chr\xi + \cos r\xi) \\ T(r\xi) = \frac{1}{2}(shr\xi + \sin r\xi) \\ U(r\xi) = \frac{1}{2}(chr\xi - \cos r\xi) \\ V(r\xi) = \frac{1}{2}(shr\xi - \sin r\xi) \end{cases} \tag{6}$$

In the formula (7), f_0 is a natural vibration frequency; Δ is a logarithmic vibration attenuation coefficient of the reed; and $\xi = x/l$ is a dimensionless coordinate.

$$A = \frac{\pi}{\Delta}\frac{a}{f_0^2}\frac{\int_0^1 f(\xi)d\xi}{\int_0^1 [f(\xi)]^2 d\xi} \tag{7}$$

$$f(\xi) = V(\frac{5}{4}\pi)U(\frac{5}{4}\pi\xi) - U(\frac{5}{4}\pi)V(\frac{5}{4}\pi\xi) \tag{8}$$

It can be known from equations (4) to (8) that when the vibration acceleration increases, the maximum value of the inertia force of the contact and the elastic dynamic reaction force N increase, and the contact pressure decreases, which leads to a slow contact resistance increase.

In addition, as the vibration frequency of the sample increases, the number of vibrations increases, and the contact spring material of the relay gradually exhibits stress relaxation. The contact pressure becomes smaller, causing the contact resistance to increase. At the same time, the contact wear also causes the contact resistance to increase.

In summary, the increase of the vibration frequency and the vibration acceleration will cause the contact resistance to increase, and the fluctuation of the contact resistance at the natural frequency of 160 Hz is the largest, reaching 27 mΩ.

B. Analysis of the Change Law of Ship relay Pick-up Time

The pick-up time refers to the time required for the relay coil to be energized until the movable contact first hits the static contact. In Fig. 3, 0~t1 is the pick-up time.

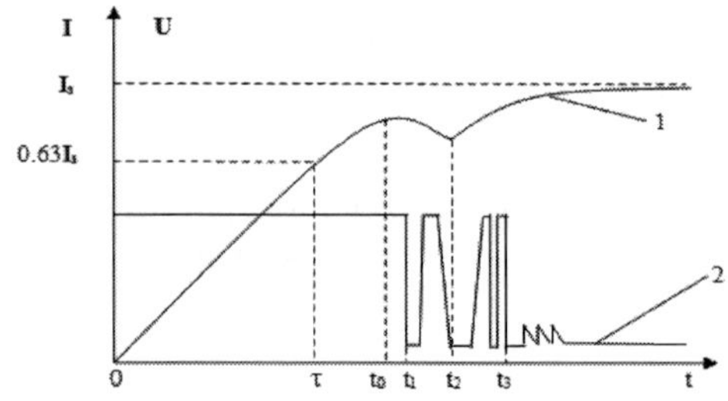

1-coil current waveform 2-contact voltage waveform

t_0-touch end t_1-contact closure t_2-armature closure t_3-bounce end

Fig. 3 Dynamic pull-in process characteristic curve of ship relay

According to the relay coil current and the contact voltage waveform monitored during the test, the variation curve of the maximum value and fluctuation of the sample pick-up time is calculated in Fig. 4.

From Fig. 4 can be seen:

1) When the vibration frequency is the same, as the vibration acceleration increases, the maximum value of the sample pick-up time increases and the fluctuation is gradually increased. Related studies have shown that long-term vibration can cause magnetic degradation of the core material, and under the same working conditions, the electromagnetic suction is reduced, resulting in an increase in the pick-up time.

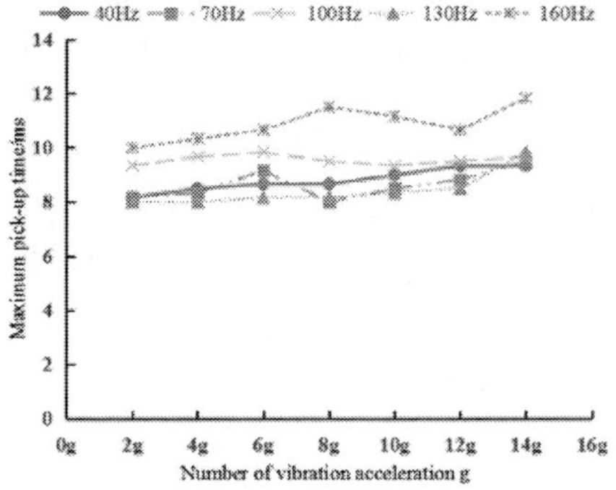

(a) Maximum

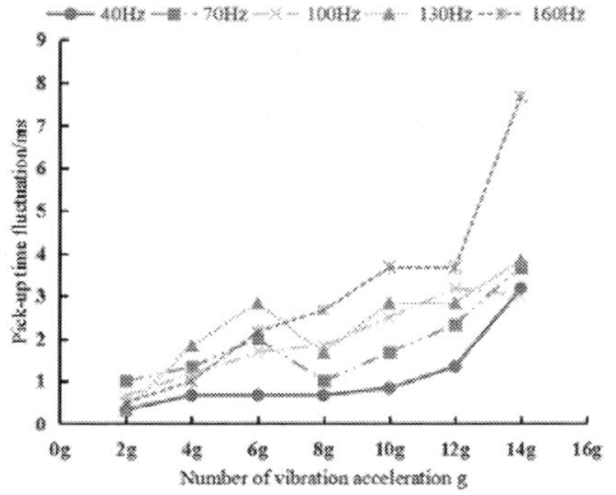

(b) Fluctuation

Fig. 4 Variation curve of the pick-up time of relay samples under different vibration conditions

2) When the vibration acceleration amplitude is equal, the vibration frequency is in the range of 40~130Hz, the fluctuation of the pick-up time is small, and the maximum fluctuation range is basically maintained between 3.166 and 3.834ms. At 160 Hz, the maximum fluctuation range of the pick-up time is 7.666ms. It can be inferred that the mechanical vibration of high frequency or high vibration acceleration may cause the bounce time to be too long when the contact is closed, and the electrical wear is aggravated, resulting in a sharp fluctuation of the pick-up time.

C. Analysis of the Change Law of Ship relay Release Time

The release time refers to the time interval between when the relay is de-energized, and when the relay moving contact and the moving and closing static contact are separated for the first time. The release time of the test sample under different vibration conditions is shown in Fig. 5.

1) When the vibration frequency is the same, the release time does not change significantly as the vibration acceleration increases.

2) When the vibration acceleration is the same, when the vibration frequency is 40~130Hz, the release time is relatively close. When the natural frequency is 160Hz, the release time of the sample is about 3.60ms, which is about 0.6ms away from the release time at other frequencies. From this, it can be inferred that the spring force of the contact spring is slightly reduced due to the high frequency vibration, and the release time is increased.

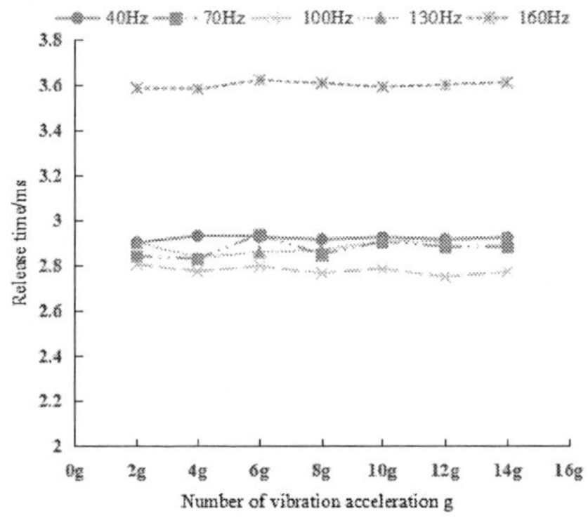

Fig. 5 Change curve of relay test release time under different vibration conditions

D. Analysis of the Change Law of the Rebound time of Ship relay

The rebound time is the time interval between the start of the first contact of the movable contact and the movable contact, and the time when the two are fully closed. The rebound time of the curve test sample under different vibration conditions is shown in Fig. 6.

It can be seen from Fig. 6:

1) When the vibration frequency is equal, the vibration frequency is 40~130Hz, and the rebound time does not change significantly. When the natural frequency is 160Hz, the rebound time is firstly reduced and then increased. During the release process of the relay, there is a rebound phenomenon in the contact. During the rebound process, the movable contact and the static contact may re-engage, causing secondary arcing, so the rebound frequency is unstable at the natural frequency.

2) When the vibration acceleration is the same, the rebound time is relatively close at 40~130Hz, and the rebound time fluctuates greatly when the natural frequency is 160Hz, about 0.29ms.

E. Analysis of the Change Law of Ship relay Pull-in and Release Voltage

The pull-in voltage refers to the minimum voltage required on the coil when the applied voltage at both ends of the relay coil increases gradually, which can completely disconnect the moving contact from the dynamic contact and the static contact, and make the moving contact and the dynamic contact completely closed.

The release voltage refers to the maximum value of the voltage required to completely disconnect the movable contact from the movable and static contact when the two ends of the coil are gradually reduced by the rated value, and the dynamic disconnection contact is completely closed. The pull-in and release voltages of the test specimens under different vibration conditions are shown in Fig. 7.

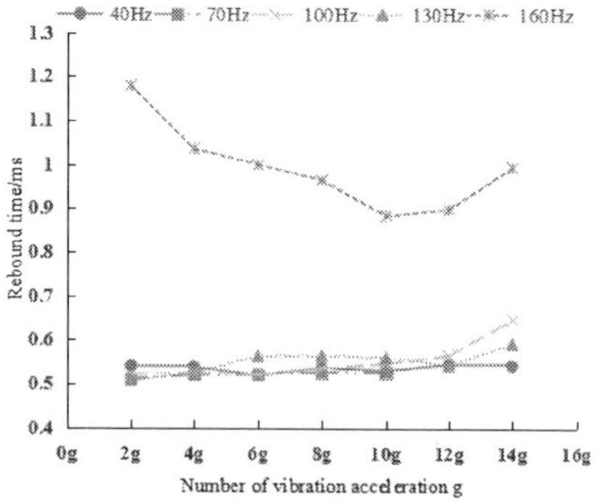

Fig. 6 Curve of rebound time of relay sample under different vibration conditions

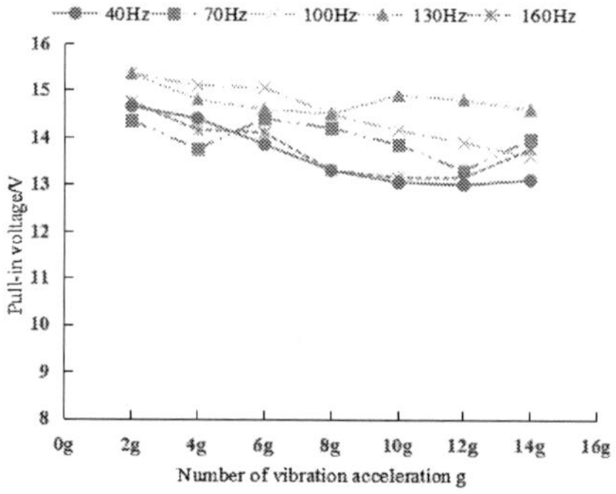

(a) pull-in voltage

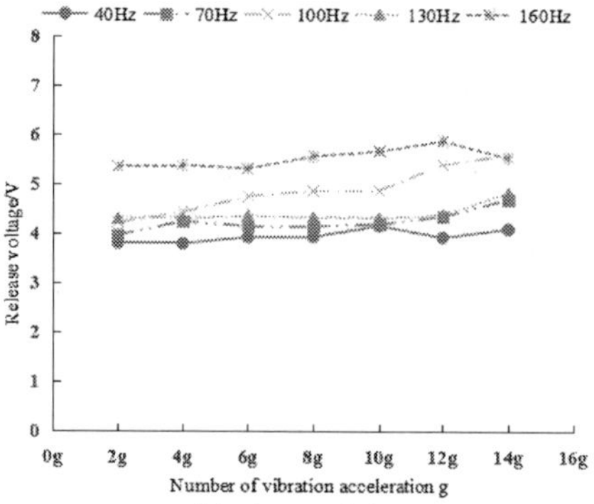

(b) release voltage

Fig. 7 Curve of the pull-in and release voltage of relay samples under different vibration conditions

IV. CONCLUSION

Based on the analysis of the performance parameters and operational characteristics of ship electrical relays, this paper studies the degradation law of the performance parameters of ship relays under different vibration conditions. The results show:

(1) Under the same vibration frequency, as the vibration amplitude or vibration acceleration increases, the pull-in voltage gradually decreases, the release voltage gradually increases, and the fluctuation of the pick-up time increases most obviously.

(2) At the natural frequency of 160 Hz, all parameters have changed significantly and the fluctuations are not very stable.

In the variation of the performance parameters of the ship relay caused by vibration, the pick-up time is a relatively sensitive parameter. Further study of the variation of the suction and reaction characteristics of ship relays under vibration conditions may reveal the correlation between the ship relay system and the performance parameters of the components in the contact system.

ACKNOWLEDGMENT

This work was supported by the Hebei Province Electrical Product Reliability Technology 2011 Collaborative Innovation Center Funded Project.

REFERENCES

[1] G. Wang, S. Wang and K. Li. A study on the activation condition of vibration tests for Particle Impact Noise Detection of space relay remainders[C].2011 6th IEEE Conference on Industrial Electronics and Applications, Beijing, 2011, pp. 2610-2614.

[2] Lingling Li, Shiai Zhang, Zhigang Li, et al. The Life Prediction Method of Relay Based on Rough Set Theory and Relay's Initial Life Information[J]. TRANSACTIONS OF CHINA ELECTROTECHNIC- AL SOCIETY, 2016, 31(18): 46-53.

[3] J. Wang, F. Yao and Z. Li. Study on acquiring key performance parameters and comprehensive performance degradation model of relays[C]. 26th International Conference on Electrical Contacts (ICEC 2012), Beijing, 2012, pp. 306-310.

[4] W. Ren, H. Liang, Y. Chen, et all. Mechanical and Electrical Characteristics of the Ship relay under Vibration and Shock Environment[C]. 2009 Proceedings of the 55th IEEE Holm Conference on Electrical Contacts, Vancouver, British Columbia, Canada, 2009, pp. 42-48.

[5] K. Miyanaga, et al. A Study on Growth of Dust of Needle-like Crystal from a Flame Retarder of Ship relay Housing[C]. 2018 IEEE Holm Conference on Electrical Contacts, Albuquerque, NM, 2018, pp. 516-520.

[6] Fan Weiwei, Wu Shihua, Wang Yongling, et al. Characteristics and Research Strategy of Ship Relay[J]. Low Voltage Apparatus, 2011, (14): 17-20.

[7] Z. Guofu, C. Yinghua and R. Wanbin. Analyzing Method of Random Vibration Characteristic for Armature System of Hermetically Sealed Ship relay[C]. Electrical Contacts - 2007 Proceedings of the 53rd IEEE Holm Conference on Electrical

Contacts, Pittsburgh, PA, 2007, pp. 183-187.
[8] N. Lambrecht, H. Pues, D. De Zutter and D. V. Ginste. Modeling of Contact Bounce in a Transient Electromagnetic Compatibility Test for the Analysis and Optimization of Nonlinear Devices[J]. in IEEE Transactions on Electromagnetic Compatibility, vol. 59, no. 2, pp. 541-544, April 2017.
[9] Han Zhao, Haidan Yu, Xu Yang, et al. Research on Optimization Techniques for Contact Release Rebound of Clapping Power Relay Under AC Load[J]. 2014(22):10-15.
[10] Yubin Jiao, Haoye Zhen, Wanbin Ren, et al. Effect of Vibration Environment on Characteristics Parameters of Ship relay[J]. Low Voltage Apparatus, 2011(3):8-12.
[11] Xuerong Ye, Yigang Lin, Xiaoyi Huang, et al. Research on Storage Degradation Mechanism of Aerospace Electromagnetic [J]. TRANSACTIONS OF CHINA ELECTROTECHNICAL SOCIETY, 2017, 32(11): 173-179.
[12] Standardization Administration of the People's Republic of China. GB/T2423 Electrical and Electronic Products Environmental Test[S]. Beijing: China Standard Press, 2008: 6-7.
[13] Standardization Administration of the People's Republic of China. GB/T3738-2008 Basic Requirements for Ship Low Voltage Electrical Appliances [S]. Beijing: China Standard Press, 2009: 24-25.
[14] The General Reserve Department of PLA.GJB 3952-2000 General Requirements for Ship Electrical Safety[S]. Beijing: China Military Standards Press, 2000: 4-5.
[15] Yijin Luo. Small sealed ship relay [M]. Rongfang Wang, translated. Beijing: People's Posts and Telecommunications Press,1979.

Zhaopan Zhang received his B.Sc. degree from Hebei University of Technology City College in 2017. He is now a M. Sc. candidate in Hebei University of Technology. His research interests include electrical reliability and testing technology.

Yanyan Luo received her B.Sc., M.Sc. and Ph.D. degrees all from Hebei University of Technology in 1993, 1996 and 2000, respectively. She is now a professor and Ph.D. in Hebei University of Technology. Her main research interests include electrical reliability.

Research on Limit Life Test and Analysis System of Electromagnetic Relay Based on Combined Load

Jie Deng, Jiaming Lai, Guofu Zhai
Harbin Institute of Technology, Harbin, 150001, China
E-mail: ljmllp1208@163.com Tel:86-451-86413193 Fax: 86-451-86413192

Abstract—**The existing electromagnetic relay life test system can only carry out reliability test under single load type and fixed load grade. For the actual application conditions of relays, the reliability can only be evaluated by means of load equivalence or reduction. Obviously, this method can not accurately and adequately verify the limit life index of relay, so as to bury a huge hidden danger for the reliable use of load control system. In order to solve this problem, firstly, through the design of programmable load box, the arbitrary combination of resistive, inductive and surge load types and step-by-step adjustment of load parameters are realized, which can simulate the actual application load for life test. Secondly, the method of extracting characteristic parameters of actual load waveform is studied, and real-time acquisition is carried out in the process of life experiment. The system can provide reliable data for limit life evaluation, failure analysis and reliability optimization of electromagnetic relay under actual load conditions.**

Index Terms— **Limit life test, Actual load conditions, Electromagnetic relay.**

I. INTRODUCTION

Electromagnetic relays are widely used in load control systems [1]. As a key component of control system, its performance directly affects the reliability of the whole spaceflight system [2]. However, although many researchers have devoted a lot of efforts to the optimal design of relays [3]–[6], the relay's quality reliability is still the worst among all electronic components [7]–[9]. Therefore, it is particularly important to study electromagnetic relay.

One of the reasons that lead to high failure rate and poor reliability of electromagnetic relays can not be ignored is that the load capacity of electromagnetic relays does not match the actual operating conditions. The test circuit with the typical application load of the target relay is built in the existing electromagnetic relay life test device mainly [10]. Its load type is single and the load grade is fixed. Therefore, only rated load life test and fixed multiple overload test can be carried out, and the life reliability under other load conditions can be estimated by means of load equivalent or reduction. Such experimental results can easily lead to the acceleration of the failure process of relays due to load mismatch [11], [12]. Therefore, it is urgent to study the limit life test and analysis system of electromagnetic relay under different load conditions, to provide a test platform for quantitative and accurate evaluation of the load capacity of electromagnetic relay, so as to give the use boundary of electromagnetic relay load.

The traditional relay life test device judges the failure of relay by monitoring the on-off state of contacts, and records the action times and failure times of relay during the test process. On this basis, a programmable load and high-speed data acquisition and processing unit is designed, which can collect the dynamic waveforms of relay signals when different types of loads are switched off in real time, and calculate the relay characteristic parameters such as pick-up time, release time, arc time and bounce time [13]. It can provide reliable data for limit life evaluation, failure analysis and reliability optimization of electromagnetic relay under actual load conditions.

II. OVERALL RESEARCH SCHEME

In the life test system designed in this paper, ARM (LPC2292) is used as the main controller, and the logic timing of data acquisition is controlled by FPGA (EP1C3T144). The overall block diagram is shown in Fig. 1, including high-power load power supply, programmable load, signal conditioning unit, signal acquisition and parameter calculation unit, main control unit and PC. Distributed control is adopted in the system and data communication is carried out between units through isolated CAN bus. It can realize the control and management of coil driving, signal conditioning and acquisition, parameter calculation and transmission of relays at three stations.

Before testing, test conditions are set on the upper computer and sent to the main control unit. Then the test parameters such as coil voltage, contact voltage and load current are transmitted to all data acquisition units through CAN bus. Based on this, the amplification factor of signal conditioning unit is set to make the dynamic waveform amplitude of the relay to be collected within a reasonable range. At the same time, the load type and load level are set by the load regulation system.

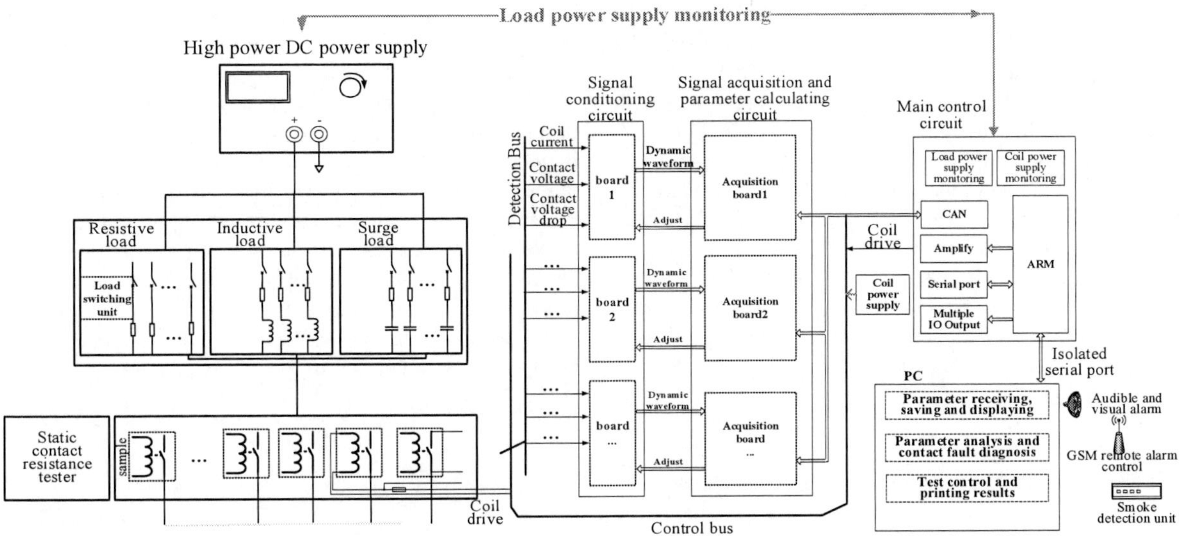

Fig. 1 System structure block diagram.

When the test is started, the relay is driven by the coil driving circuit to complete the action of suction and release. At the same time, the electrical signal is regulated by the signal conditioning circuit and the data is collected through the acquisition board, then the parameters are calculated by the parameter calculation unit. Before the next action is started, the results of calculation are transmitted to the main control unit through CAN bus. Then they are sorted out by the main control unit and sent to the upper computer for display. After termination or completion of the test, the upper computer software can be used to print out the test results.

III. SYSTEM HARDWARE DESIGN

A. Main Circuit Design

The necessary test conditions such as load and power supply in relay life test are provided by the main circuit, as shown in Fig. 2. The connection and disconnection of relay coils are controlled by the main controller ARM through the dry spring relay K1. K2 is used to select different coil current amplification multiples to meet the coil current acquisition requirements of different types of relays.

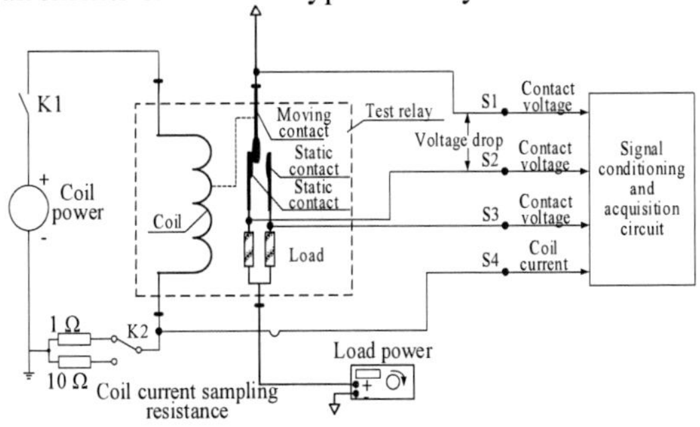

Fig. 2 Main loop block diagram of conversion contact.

B. Data Acquisition and Processing Unit Design

In this paper, a multi-channel synchronous high-speed acquisition circuit is designed to collect the output signals such as contact voltage and coil current. The schematic diagram is shown in Fig. 3. The selected 12-bit A/D converter model is AD9220, and the sampling rate is 1 MHz. The high-speed and accurate acquisition of relay output signal is achieved.

The parameter calculating unit is mainly processed by high performance ARM single chip computer. On the one hand, according to the command of the main control unit, the signal acquisition circuit is controlled to complete the functions of acquisition start, data read and write, acquisition stop; on the other hand, according to the collected dynamic waveform data, the parameters such as pick-up time, release time and arc time are calculated and sent to the main control unit through the isolated CAN bus.

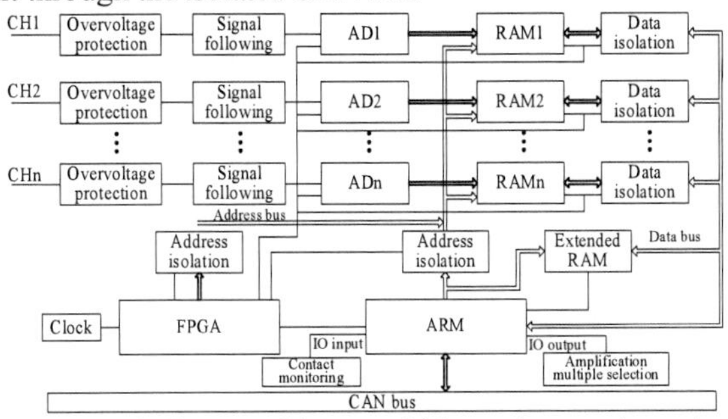

Fig. 3 Block diagram of data acquisition and processing unit.

C. Programmable Load Box Design

A programmable load box is designed, which includes three basic load types: resistive load, inductive load and surge load. And they can be combined according to certain rules. At the same time, the adjusting step of load is small enough and the adjusting range is wide enough to test the electrical life of relay under different test conditions.

Resistive load is composed of several resistors with resistance values of 1.4 ohms, 2.8 ohms, 5.6 ohms, 14 ohms and 28 ohms in parallel. The load current can be adjusted with 1A as step length in the range of 0 ~ 80A at 28V DC by switching switches. In addition, the function of parallel sliding rheostat is to compensate the error of load current.

The inductive load is composed of four inductors with inductance values of 5mH, 10mH, 20mH and 40mH respectively. Arbitrary inductance values with 5mH as step length in the range of 5mH to 75mH can be provided.

The charging and discharging process of capacitors is used to control the on-off of MOS transistors, thus changing the load circuit and generating surge current. By adjusting the sliding rheostat, the surge pulse width can be changed. In the surge load designed in this paper, it can be adjusted in the range of 0 ~ 200ms, and the surge current can be changed by switching from KA1 to KA8.

The design block diagram of the load box is shown in Fig. 4. The combination of three types of loads is realized by switching four switches: KA, KA9, KA18 and KA19.

IV. SYSTEM SOFTWARE DESIGN

A. *Lower Computer Software Design*

In the software of the lower computer, the ARM is programmed in C language. The software flow chart is shown in Fig. 5. Its main function is to broadcast the test conditions set by the upper computer to the parameter calculation units through the CAN bus. At the same time, it is responsible for synchronizing the coil charging and power off, dynamic waveform acquisition, electrical parameters calculation and other operations of each unit during the test, and sending all the parameters of the test samples to the upper computer through serial port.

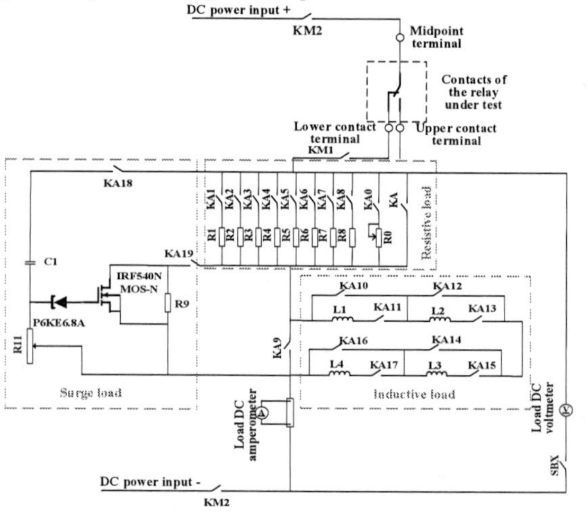

Fig. 4. Principle diagram of programmable load box.

In this paper, the duration of dynamic waveform acquisition is 25ms and the sampling rate is 1MHz in both the suction and release processes. Four groups of floating-point one-dimensional arrays with length of 25K are defined for this program, and the collected data of four dynamic waveforms are stored separately. Based on the dynamic data collected and the definition of relay time parameters by the National Military Standard, the characteristic parameters such as pick-up time, release time, super-path time, arc time and bounce time are calculated. In this paper, the software algorithm for extracting characteristic parameters is determined by researching and verifying a large number of experimental data.

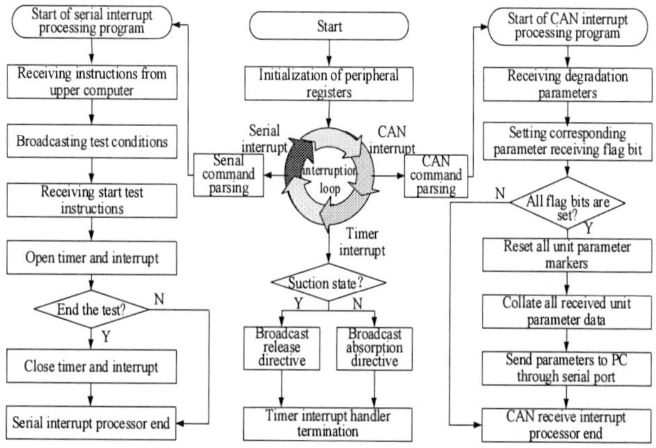

Fig. 5. Software flow chart of main control unit.

Taking arc time as an example, according to the definition of arc time of relay, the arc time is solved by analyzing and calculating the data of contact voltage waveform collected. The software algorithm searches backward from the time of suction (release) to find that if the voltage values of 10 consecutive data are less than the threshold voltage, it is considered to be the time of the end of the arc. Similarly, the starting point of the arc can be found by looking forward. Then, the exact solution of arc time is obtained by making the difference between the arc ending time and the arc starting point.

B. *Upper Computer Software Design*

The upper computer software of the system is written in the integrated development environment of VC++ and object-oriented technology. The functions of setting test conditions, managing electrical parameters, identifying failure mechanism and evaluating load capacity are completed. Various transformations of electrical parameters are carried out′ by using MATLAB, and mathematical features are extracted from them.

Before the life test is started, the test parameters are set by the upper computer, including test condition parameters, fault handling parameters and management parameters. The parameters of coil voltage, coil resistance, load voltage, load current, connection time, disconnection time, monitoring time and other test conditions need to be sent from the upper computer to the lower computer main control unit through serial port, and the program flow of each parameter calculation unit is set. The working state of the system is set in the fault processing parameters, including the fault limit, whether to stop when the fault occurs, etc. Management parameters include relay type, sample number, contact number, test batch, test personnel, test time, test temperature and humidity, etc. After the test parameters are set up, the test parameters sent by the lower computer are received, updated and managed by the upper computer in real time. According to the characteristics of the test parameters, the contact status is determined and the subsequent load capacity evaluation and analysis are carried out. The whole test flow chart is shown in Fig. 6.

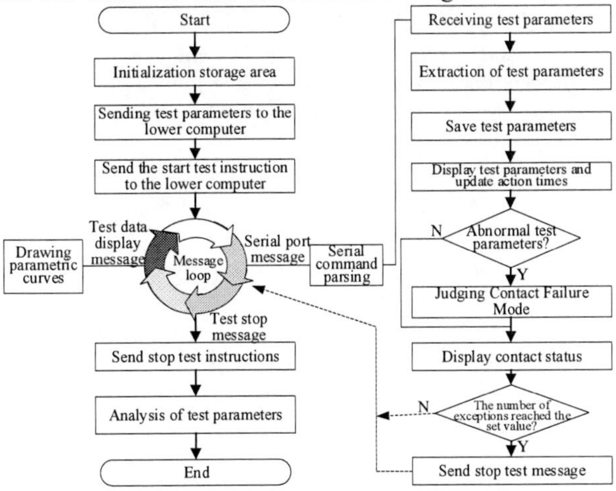

Fig. 6 Software flow chart of upper computer.

V. TEST VERIFICATION

The output characteristics of a certain type of aerospace relay with rated load 5A are tested under the practical application condition of load current 10A and series inductance 5mH. The results are compared with the waveforms measured by DSOX3024T oscilloscope to verify the accuracy of signal acquisition and characteristic parameter calculation.

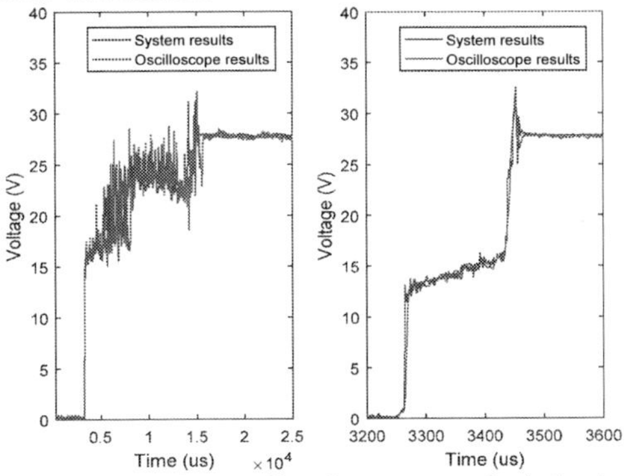

Fig. 7 Voltage waveforms of break contacts under inductive (left) and resistive (right) loads.

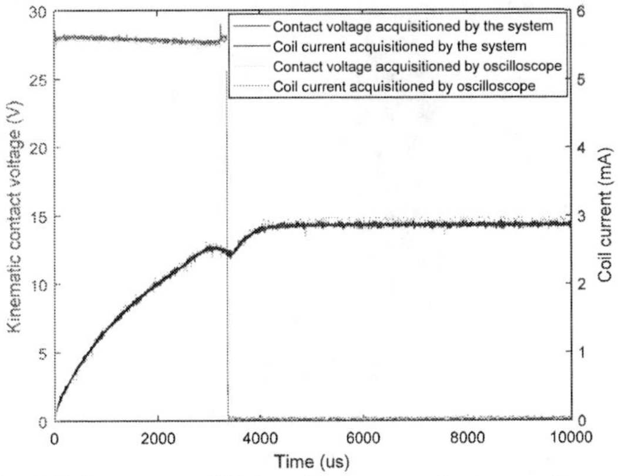

Fig. 8 Coil current and kinematic contact voltage waveforms.

From the results of waveform comparison, it can be clearly seen that the waveform collected by the system is basically consistent with the waveform collected by the oscilloscope. Then the arc time obtained by the system parameter calculation software is compared with the result of the oscilloscope display. The result is shown in Table 1.

TABLE I

ACCURACY VERIFICATION OF PARAMETER CALCULATING SOFTWARE

Load Type		Arc Time	Error
inductive load	calculated value	10.588 ms	0.16%
	actual value	10.571 ms	
resistive load	calculated value	185 us	1.6%
	actual value	182 us	
surge load	calculated value	121 us	2.4%
	actual value	124 us	

Table 1 shows that the error of parameter calculation is within 5%, which fully meets the accuracy requirement. It proves that the experimental data measured by this system are completely accurate and reliable. In addition, the degradation trend of life characteristic parameters of electromagnetic relays is given in each limit life process, as shown in Fig. 9, Fig. 10 and Fig. 11. It provides an important reference for failure reason analysis and life prediction of relay.

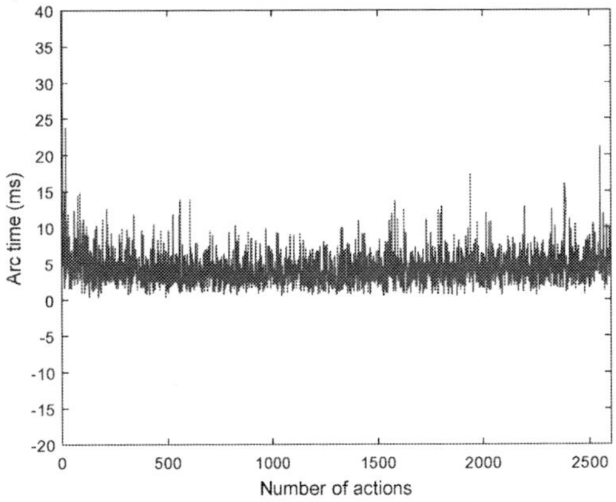

Fig. 9 Trend chart of arc time change.

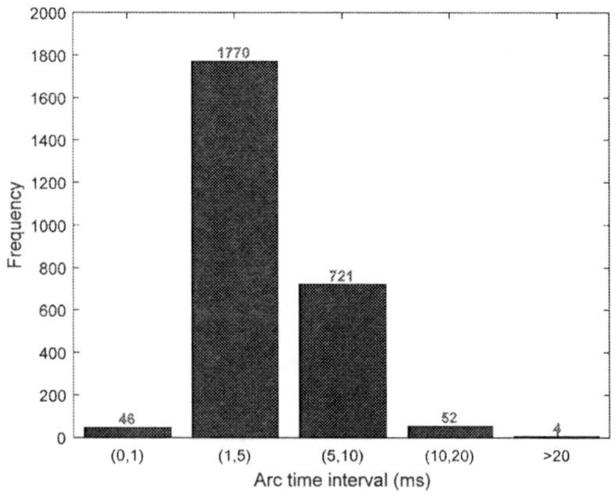

Fig. 10 Histogram of arc time distribution.

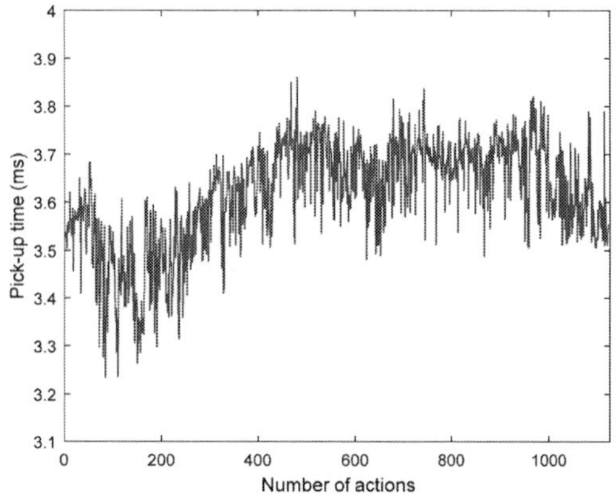

Fig. 11 Trend chart of pick-up time.

VI. CONCLUSION

In this paper, a test and analysis system of electromagnetic relay based on combined load is designed, which can obtain the quantitative limit life test results under the actual load conditions of the relay. The system makes up for the shortcomings of single load type and fixed load grade existing in the existing life test system. It can eliminate the risk of accelerated failure of relay due to the mismatch between equivalent or reduction and actual load in the existing reliability evaluation methods of electrical life. It has important research significance and high application value.

1) A programmable load box is designed based on three load conditions: resistive load, inductive load and surge load.
2) The software algorithm for extracting characteristic parameters of dynamic acquisition waveform is studied. The experimental results show that the calculation error of the characteristic value can be guaranteed within 5%.
3) The waveform acquisition and limit life test of the relay prototype under actual load conditions are carried out, and the acquisition accuracy of the system is verified by comparing with the measured data of the oscilloscope.

ACKNOWLEDGMENT

This work was supported by the National Natural Science Foundation of China [grant numbers 51707044]; and the China Postdoctoral Science Foundation [grant number 2018M632377].

REFERENCES

[1] L. Xin, "Study on the related parameters of electromagnetic relay contacts", Hebei University of Technology, 2012

[2] L. H. Ming, R. W. Bin, Y. X. Rong and Z. G. Fu, "Research on the Reliability Tolerance Analysis Method of Electromagnetic Relay in Aerospace" in *Chinese Journal of Aeronautics*, vol. 18, no. 1, 2005, pp. 65-71

[3] W. Yang, "Finite element analysis of electromagnetic interference of inner structures of twin-type relay" in *Transactions of China Electrotechnical Society*, vol. 22, no. 8, 2007, pp. 179-184

[4] T. Xu, "Optimization design of anti-surge ability of crystal relays under overload condition", Harbin Institute of Technology, 2018

[5] W. J. Xin, "Optimization and anti interference design on the electromagnetic system of magnetic latching relay", Hebei University of Technology, 2016

[6] D. Jie, "Research on aerospace electromagnetic relay robust design", Harbin Institute of Technology, 2010

[7] Y. Li, W. J. Xian and C. Na, "A preliminary study on the development of key spaceflight components at home and abroad" in *Aerospace Standardization*, no. 1, 2013, pp. 26-29

[8] S. X. Na and K. X. Jian, "Quality and reliability analysis of domestic electronic components in recent years" in *Electronic Product Reliability and Environmental Testing*, no. 4, 1997

[9] Y. Fang and Z. Fa, "Study on the operational reliability of AC relay based on the impact from electric energy quality" in *International Conference on Electrical Contacts*, 2012

[10] Y. Qiong, "Research on reliability evaluation and life test methods for space relays", Harbin Institute of Technology, 2011

[11] M. Yue, "Research on failure mechanism and life prediction method for aerospace relays", Harbin Institute of Technology, 2013

[12] J. Li, M. Shi and Z. Liu, "The study of failure mechanism of contact resistance enhancement of relay contact" in *Electronic Product Reliability & Environmental Testing*, 2009

[13] L. H. Min, Z. Q. Sen and Z. G. Fu, "Research and application of testing and analyzing system for sealed relay's time parameters" in *IEEE Holm Conference on Electrical Contacts & the International Conference on Electrical Contacts*, 2004

7th International Conference on Reliability of
Electrical Products and Electrical Contacts,
November 04-06, 2019

Reliability Study of Closing Process for Operating Mechanisms of MCCB

Nairui Yin[1,2], Xinyi Xie[2], Hongwu Liu[2], Ruiliang Guan[2]
[1]State key laboratory of electrical insulation and power equipment, Xi'an Jiaotong University, Xi'an, Shaanxi Province 710049, China
[2]Changshu Switchgear Mfg. Co., Ltd., (Former Changshu Switchgear Plant) & Jiangsu Key Laboratory of Smart Grid Distribution and Utilization Technology Research, Changshu, Jiangsu, 215500, China
E-mail: doveynr@qq.com

***Abstract*—According to fundamental of operating mechanisms analysis of slow closing operation is used to evaluate closing reliability for MCCB. Based on characteristics of operating mechanisms, key parameters of driving moment for closing operating are extracted. And optimization of key parameters can improve closing reliability of operating mechanisms.**

***Index Terms*— MCCB, Operating mechanism, Reliability**

I. INTRODUCTION

Operating mechanism is the core unit of low-voltage circuit breaker. By receiving and executing the tripping signal, the state of operating mechanism is switched and the contacts are operated to break or close the circuit. The driving energy of operating mechanism includes the energy of main springs and contacts springs, which is related to pressure of contacts and over-travel. The operating process contains opening, closing and tripping processes. For opening and tripping process the main and contacting springs release energy simultaneously and the circuit breaker is switched from closing state to opening or tripping state. For closing process the main springs release the energy and overcome energy of contacts spring to realize the state switch of circuit breaker from the open state to the close state.

If the circuit breaker isn't in place for the open state, the operating mechanism is between the open and close states stably. And the pressure between contacts is greatly less than theoretical design value, which is disadvantage to temperature rise. To improve reliability of the open state, the rate of main spring energy to contacts spring energy for closing process should be increased. Meanwhile the energy difference of main spring and contact spring is absorbed by locating part of the operating mechanism and it will increase stress of operating mechanism and decrease mechanical life of the circuit breaker. In this paper acting principle of operating mechanism is studied and the influences of operating handle to the opening torque are analyzed in different positions. A method for the operating mechanism is introduced to evaluate reliability of the opening process.

II. PRINCIPLE OF CLOSE OPERATION

The open state of circuit breaker is shown in Fig. 1a. Here EO_1 is operating handle, E is hanging point of the main spring, O_1 is rotation axis of handle, AO_2 is the jump pin, A is hinged point of upper link and the jump pin, and O_2 is rotation axis of the jump pin. AB is upper link, B is hinged point of upper and down links. BC is down rod, C is hinged point of down link and spindle. CD is spindle and D is rotation axis of spindle.

In the closing process the operating force is applied on the handle and the handle is driven to closing indication direction. When the handle moves across the critical position, the main spring release the energy and drive the operating mechanism to the close position. Finally, the operating mechanism overcome the resistance force of the contacts spring and stay in the close position. The whole closing process can be separated into following four phases:

A. Operating force drives the handle from the closing indication position to the critical position of four-links system

The schematic configuration of circuit breaker in the open state is shown in Fig. 1a). In the open state the main spring applies the clockwise torque to the handle, which keeps the handle in the opening indication position. Meanwhile the main spring apply the anti-clockwise torque to the upper link and make the moving contact in the open state. Initially the operating force drives the handle start to move, energy is gradually stored in the main spring and the four-links system is still static. When the handle moves across the critical position of four-links system, the torque direction changes and the main spring drive the four-links system to the open direction.

B. The main spring moves cross the critical position of the handle

As shown in Fig. 1b), the handle rotates anti-clockwise and move cross the critical position of the handle. Torque applying on the handle changes in the opposite direction, and the main spring start to drive the handle to the closing indication direction.

C. Operating mechanism make the contacts close

The force of main spring to the handle is shown in Fig 1.c). The four-links system is driven to the closing direction by main spring. When the moving and static contacts are contacted, the contact spring generates resistance force and the main spring should overcome it.

D. the operating mechanism moves and is limited in the close position

As shown in Fig. 1d), operating mechanism continued to move to the close position after the moving contact is limited by the static contact. Finally, the contact spring absorbs the energy and position of the four-links system is limited by the limited part. The operating mechanism is in the close state stably.

According above analysis of operating mechanism motion, the main spring both drives the handle and four-links system after the mechanism move across position in Fig. C. Then it's difficult to get analytic expression of operating mechanism motion.

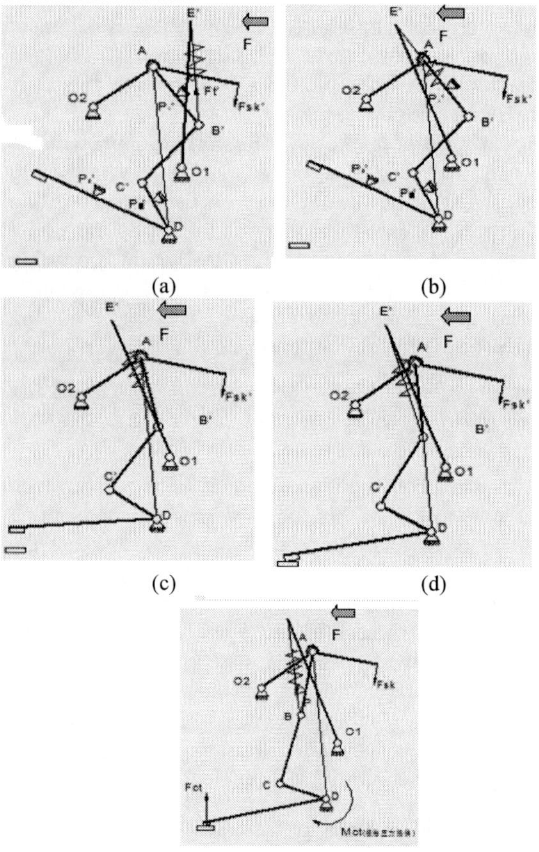

Fig. 1 Schematic diagram of operating mechanism in the close process

III. THE CLOSE TORQUE AND ENERGY ANALYSIS

The closing process shouldn't be influenced by manual operation. It means even when speed of operating handle is very slow, reliability of the close operation should be insured. The operating torque is provided by motor mechanism or manual operation. For both operating methods the handle moves with relatively low speed and the whole operating process will last from several to dozens of seconds. Although the operating mechanism moves fast from the opening indication position to the closing indication position and it lasts several milliseconds. To simplify analysis of four-links system, the handle is assumed to be static when the four-links system is in moving process. There are two limiting positions of the handle:

1) The handle is in the closing indication position.
2) The handle is in the critical position of four-links system, where the four-links system starts to operate. The second condition is more rigorous than the first one. The actual condition of handle is between these two conditions.

When the hinge point E of the main spring is fixed, the driving torque applying on the four-links system can be calculated. The force diagram can be represented in Fig.2.

1) The length of the main spring can be calculated as:

$$l_{B'E} = \sqrt{l_{EA} * l_{EA} + l_{AB'} * l_{AB'} - 2 * l_{EA} * l_{AB'} * \cos \angle EAB'} \tag{1}$$

$$Ft_{close} = Kt * (l_{B'P} - l) \tag{2}$$

2) The component force of main spring on down link can be written as:

$$F_{down} = \frac{Ft_{close}}{\sin(\angle AB'C')} * \sin(\angle AB'E) \tag{3}$$

3) The arm of force on the spindle can be written as:

$$l = l_{CD} * \sin(\angle B'C'D) \tag{4}$$

4) The driving torque for closing operation can be written as:

$$M_{close} = F_{down} * l \tag{5}$$

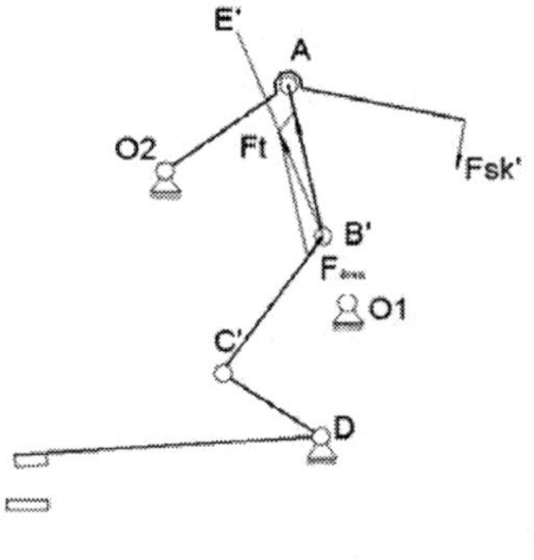

Fig. 2 Force diagram of operating mechanism in the critical close position

According to two limiting positions of the handle, the torque curves applying on the operating mechanism by the handle can be plotted in Fig. 3.

Whether the circuit breaker can be operated to the close position successfully or not is dependent to the relations of driving and resistant torques, which are provided by the main spring and contact spring. While the driving torque is always larger than the resistance torque, the operating mechanism can be operated reliably.

Driving torque for the closing process is affected by parameters of operating mechanism and position of the handle. For certain structure of operating mechanism, when position of the handle is nearer to the closing indication position, the energy stored in the main spring is bigger. And it's easier to realize the close operation.

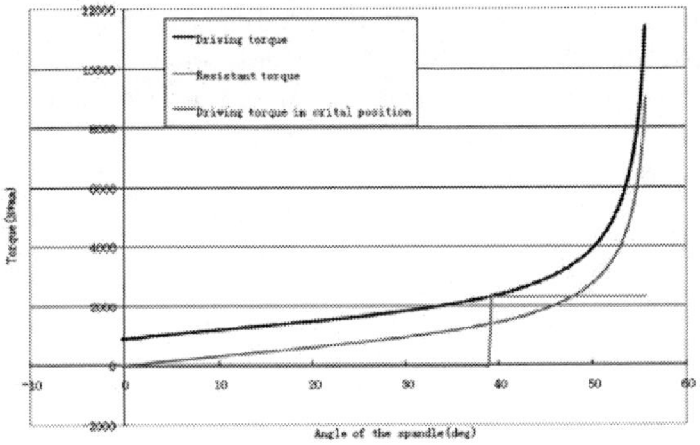

Fig. 3 Curve of driving and resistant torque varying with different handle positions

IV. CONCLUSION

Based on the motion analysis of the handle and operating mechanism for the closing process of MCCB, the torque and energy can be used to evaluate reliability of the closing operation. By optimizing the position of the handle where the handle start to move, the reliability of operating mechanism can be improved.

REFERENCES

[1] Liu Hongwu, Gu Jianqing, Wang Yunfeng, Xie Xinyi Analysis on Circuit Breaker Operation Based on Elastic Potential Energy Release Route [J] Low Voltage Apparatus 2009(11) 1-3

[2] Zheng Wenwei, Wu Kejian mechanical principle[M] 1997

[3] Liu Hongwu, Guan Ruiliang, Wang Cheng Design on Main Body of Intelligent MCCB [J] Low Voltage Apparatus 2008(5) 1-4

Nairui Yin was born in Jiangsu, China, in 1980. He received the M.S. degrees in Mechanics from Peking University, Beijing, China, in 2005. Now he is Ph.D candidate in electrical engineering of Xi'an Jiaotong University. His research interests focus on simulation of low voltage apparatus.

7th International Conference on Reliability of
Electrical Products and Electrical Contacts,
November 04-06, 2019

Degradation Performance Analysis on Tantalum Capacitor

Jianmeng Liu, Jingying Zhao, Ke Zhang
State Key Laboratory of Reliability and Intelligence of Electrical Equipment
Hebei University of Technology, Tianjin, 300130, China
E-mail: zhaojy931@hebut.edu.cn Tel: 86-22-26378968 Fax: 86-22-26549256

Abstract—**The performance of tantalum capacitor is important for the safe running in the system. Aiming at the degradation parameters of tantalum capacitor such as capacitance, dissipation factor and leakage current, test stresses with temperature and humidity are selected and test plan is designed. The parameters trend with 95 °C and 70% RH was obtained within 3200h and degradation mechanism is analyzed. The trend fitting method is put forward to. The degradation trend model for each parameter is determined, which is verified with the degradation trend at 95 °C and 85% RH. After lifetime distribution function and the maximum likelihood estimation are introduced, the average pseudo-lifetime model using each degradation parameter are developed. The results show that the failure of tantalum capacitor may be obviously expressed on the capacitance of tantalum capacitor firstly.**

Index Terms—**Tantalum capacitor, Pseudo-lifetime, Degradation trend model, Degradation parameters, the maximum likelihood estimation**

I. INTRODUCTION

Tantalum capacitor with high stability and reliability are widely used in all kinds of fields. The performance of tantalum capacitor directly influences the safe running of the whole system. [1-3]

Now tantalum capacitor has 100,000–1,000,000 cycles. More degradation information can be obtained with higher stresses. Kotz *et al.* [4] analyzed the degradation performance of double-layer electrochemical capacitors at 2.5V/30°C, 3.3V/30°C and 2.5V/70°C. Their experimental results showed that tantalum capacitor will only fail for a short time under extreme conditions of 70°C or 3.5V. Kobayashi *et al.* [5] applied "10°C law of temperature" for electrolytic capacitors to state that a 10°C increase under 70°C can reduce the lifetime by half. J.Virkki *et al.*[6] found no failure capacitors with 85°C /85RH during 2500h. However, after ripple voltage was added, failures could occur in a relatively shorter time.

Many researchers have monitored and analyzed important degradation parameters such as capacitance, leakage current and dissipation factor. Zednicek *et al.* [7] confirmed that the maximum leakage current of tantalum capacitor could reach three orders of magnitude at 125°C. Teverovsky *et al.* [8] derived the changing rate of leakage current in various regimes based on the degradation data. The mechanism of parameter failure and catastrophic failure were described. LI Bo *et al.* [9] obtained the changing trends of capacitance, leakage current and dissipation factor from 25 °C to 205 °C. The capacitance was approximately linear with the increasing temperature and $\Delta C/C$ <12%. The leakage current increased by 2-3 times for every increasing 60°C. The dissipation factor increased with fluctuation. Peter *et al.* [10] proposed that 85% RH had different effects on MnO_2 and polymer tantalum capacitor.

The failure mechanism and degradation model of tantalum capacitor can be explored by degradation analysis. Dehbi *et al.* [11] showed that the damaged oxide layer of tantalum capacitor at high temperature resulted in the change of leakage current. Verchiani *et al.* [12] established thermal model by use of defect generation rate based on the Poole-Frenkel equation to predict the lifetime and breakdown voltage of tantalum capacitor. Jiaoying *et al.* [13] proposed a two-parameter life prediction model of capacitance and leakage current based on grey theory. The prediction accuracy of leakage current and capacitance are as high as 93.779% and 99.983% respectively.

In this paper, the chip tantalum capacitor is chosen as research object. The degeneration parameters are selected and the test design are carried out. The failure mechanism and variation trend of degradation parameters are analyzed. Based on data information, the polynomial fitting method is put forward to and the optimization fitting model is established. The lifetime distribution is researched and the key degradation parameter are found out, which can predict the change of the performance and provide an effective means for performance monitoring and replacement warning.

II. DEGRADATION TEST DESIGN

The chip tantalum electrolytic capacitor with conductive

polymer-PEDOT as the cathode is taken as the research object. The capacitance, dissipation factor and leakage current of tantalum capacitor are selected as the degradation performance parameters of tantalum capacitor.

The rated voltage and capacitance of tantalum capacitor tested are 6.3V and 330μF, respectively. With the same failure mechanism, the stress level of 95 ° C and 70% RH is chosen. The failure criterion is as follows: capacitance goes below 264μF or exceeds 396μF (a deviation of ±20%); dissipation factor goes above 0.1; Leakage current goes above 208μA.

The experimental setup is shown in Fig.1 [10]. The Agilent N6702A provides DC source with 6.3V; The Agilent 4263B LCR measures capacitance and dissipation factor; The Agilent 4339B measures leakage current. 16 samples were placed in ESPEC PRA-3AP. Then, the samples and DC source were switched by use of Agilent 34980A.

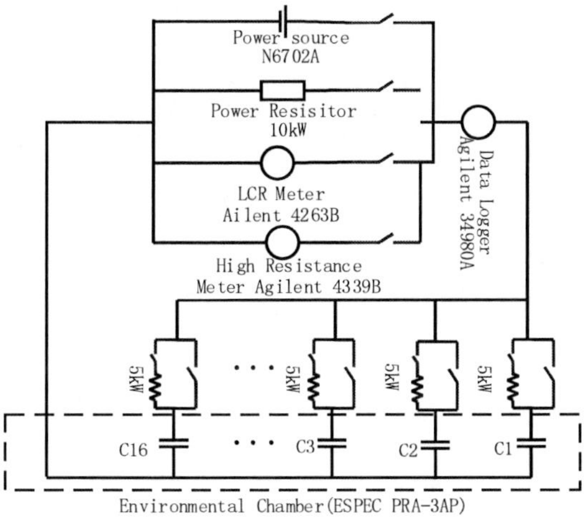

Fig. 1 Experimental principle diagram

During the test, the samples are connected in series with a 10kΩ resistor. With 70% RH, temperature is reduced as 25°C and the data is measured each time with different data acquisition rates in different intervals. Then each capacitor is fully discharged through a 5 kΩ resistor. Before 3200h, no samples failed at 95 ° C and 70% RH.

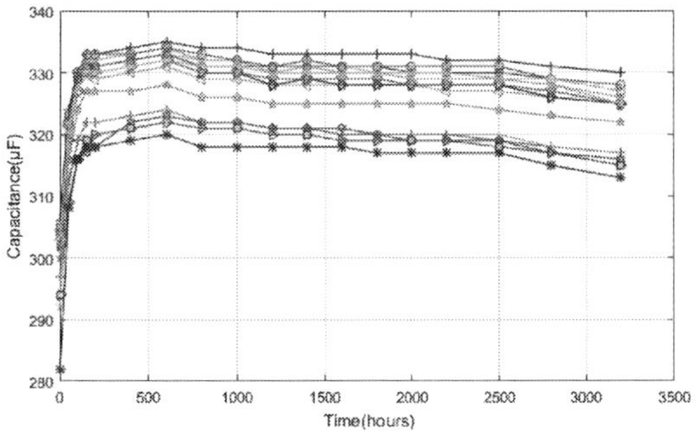

Fig. 2 Capacitance with 95 ° C and 70% RH

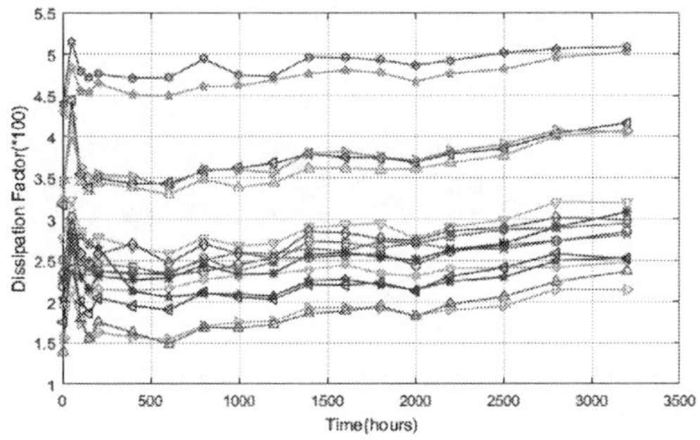

Fig. 3 Dissipation factor with 95 ° C and 70% RH

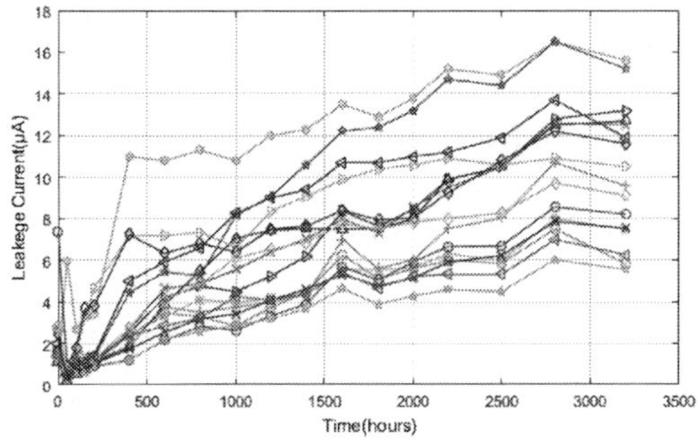

Fig. 4 Leakage current with 95 ° C and 70% RH

III. DEGRADATION MECHANISM ANALYSIS

A. Degradation trend Analysis

There are different degradation trend and degradation mechanism in different degradation regimes.

For capacitance in Fig.2, at the beginning between 0 and 150h, the average of capacitance is 299μF, which is less about 9.4% than nominal capacitance. The average of the capacitance sharply increases 28μF. And then, the increase growth rate of capacitance slows down. At 600h, the capacitor reaches the rated capacitance and then the capacitance decreases.

For dissipation factor in Fig.3, dissipation factor increases drastically with 27.4% and an average rate of 1.45E-4/h between 0 and 50h. Dissipation factor has a peak at 50h. Then, dissipation factor decreases rapidly with an average rate of 1.16E-5/h. After 600h, dissipation factor increases gradually.

For leakage current in Fig.4, leakage current show decreasing trend with 1.27μA. At 50h, leakage current reaches the minimum value of 0.91μA. After 50h, leakage current slowly increases with a gentle rate. The average changing range is 9.51μA between 50h-1600h and 2.37μA between 1600h-3200h.

B. Degradation Mechanism Analysis

The physical anatomy of tantalum capacitor is shown in Fig. 5. Capacitance *C* and dissipation factor can be calculated by *Eqs*. (1) and (2)[15].

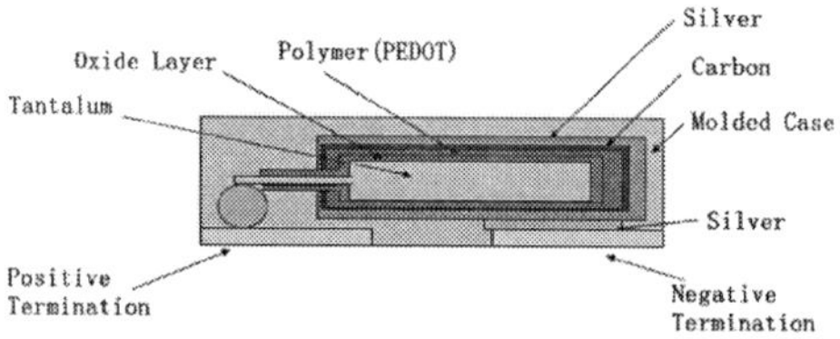

Fig. 5 Physical anatomy of a tantalum capacitor

$$C = \frac{\varepsilon_0 S}{d} \tag{1}$$

$$tan\delta = \frac{ESR}{X_C} = \frac{ESR}{\omega C_P} \tag{2}$$

Where, $\mathcal{E}_0$ is the dielectric constant of Ta_2O_5; S is the area of plate; d is the thickness of medium; ESR is equivalent series resistance; X_c is capacitive reactance; ω is the frequency.

The external part of tantalum capacitor is made of silicone-doped epoxy resin with strong moisture-proof characteristics. Due to the differences in thermal expansion rate between the lead and the epoxy encapsulation layer, a small gap which gas can enter by is formed in tantalum capacitor molding process.

With a high-humidity environment, moisture quickly diffuses into the interior of the capacitor in the early regime. The PEDOT expansion with high temperature and high humidity enlarges the effective contacting area between cathode and dielectric [17]. In addition, moisture can fill some gaps. Moisture, tantalum and PEDOT may form many tiny capacitors, which can also increase the capacitance [18]. So the capacitance increases rapidly before the water is saturated

In addition, because more moisture diffuses into the PEDOT, the de-doping causes a loss of conductivity in cathode layer and an increase of *ESR* [10], which result in a sudden increase in dissipation factor and a sudden decrease in leakage current at the beginning.

After the moisture reaches saturation, *ESR* increases slowly. The capacitance goes the adjustment regime and dissipation factor decreases with a peak at 50h.

It has been reported that mechanical stress has little effect on capacitance [19], so the physical changes caused by thermal stress are negligible. It is known from *Eq*. (1) that the capacitance degradation is caused by a decrease in dielectric constant.

With high temperature and humidity, amorphous Ta_2O_5 may transform into conductive crystals, but this process is extremely slow. So, a limited increase in leakage current is caused by this reason [10]. According to the space-charge theory, because of an oxygen vacancy defect between the dielectric layer Ta_2O_5 and the electrode, the positively charged oxygen vacancies may migrate into the dielectric to form a space charge. With external electric field, the space charge transfer forms a space limitation current, which may be the main cause of leakage current [16]. In addition, resistance degradation occurs and ESR increases.

With self-healing characteristics of tantalum capacitor, fluctuation can be seen in the same regime. But the self-healing ability weakens with the degradation to result in the failure.

IV. RESEARCH ON FITTING METHOD OF PERFORMANCE DEGRADATION

A. Basic Principles of Polynomial Fitting

The stable degradation of capacitance, dissipation factor and leakage current begin at 600h, 600h and 50h, respectively.

The trend of capacitance, dissipation factor and leakage current is nonlinear, so suitable polynomials fitting curves for the degradation quantity are selected. The polynomial fitting curve y is

$$y = f(x) = a_0 + a_1 x + a_2 x + L + a_k x^k \tag{3}$$

Where a_i is the coefficient of the polynomial and k is the highest power of polynomials.

The least square method [20] is introduced to minimize R:

$$R = \sum_{i=1}^{n} (y_i - f(x_i))^2 \tag{4}$$

First, a_i are derived by R:

$$\left.\begin{aligned} & a_0 + a_1 \sum_{i=1}^{n} X_i + a_2 \sum_{i=1}^{n} X_i^2 + L \\ & + a_n \sum_{i=1}^{n} X_i^n = \sum_{i=1}^{n} y_i \\ & a_0 \sum_{i=1}^{n} X_i + a_1 \sum_{i=1}^{n} X_i^2 + a_2 \sum_{i=1}^{n} X_i^3 + L \\ & + a_n \sum_{i=1}^{n} X_i^{n+1} = \sum_{i=1}^{n} x_i y_i \\ & M \\ & a_0 \sum_{i=1}^{n} X_i^k + a_1 \sum_{i=1}^{n} X_i^{k+1} + a_2 \sum_{i=1}^{n} X_i^{k+2} + L \\ & + a_n \sum_{i=1}^{n} X_i^{2k} = \sum_{i=1}^{n} x_i^k y_i \end{aligned}\right\} \tag{5}$$

Matrix model is

$$\begin{bmatrix} 1 & \sum_{i=1}^{n} X_i & L & \sum_{i=1}^{n} X_i^k \\ \sum_{i=1}^{n} X_i & \sum_{i=1}^{n} X_i^2 & L & \sum_{i=1}^{n} X_i^{k+1} \\ M & M & M & M \\ \sum_{i=1}^{n} X_i^k & \sum_{i=1}^{n} X_i^{k+1} & L & \sum_{i=1}^{n} X_i^{2k} \end{bmatrix} \begin{bmatrix} a_0 \\ a_1 \\ M \\ a_k \end{bmatrix} = \begin{bmatrix} \sum_{i=1}^{n} y_i \\ \sum_{i=1}^{n} y_i x_i \\ M \\ \sum_{i=1}^{n} y_i x_i^k \end{bmatrix} \tag{6}$$

According to matrix rules, *Eq*. (6) can be simplified.

$$
\begin{bmatrix} 1 & x_1 & L & x_1^k \\ 1 & x_2 & L & x_2^k \\ M & M & M & M \\ 1 & x_n & L & x_n^k \end{bmatrix} \begin{bmatrix} a_0 \\ a_1 \\ M \\ a_k \end{bmatrix} = \begin{bmatrix} y_1 \\ y_2 \\ M \\ y_k \end{bmatrix} \tag{7}
$$

Express the above formula in the form of letters, which can be obtained:

$$\mathbf{XA} = \mathbf{Y} \tag{8}$$

A is the coefficient matrix sought, then

$$A = \frac{X^T Y}{X^T X} \tag{9}$$

Find the various terms of A to get the coefficients of $y = f(x)$. The pseudo-lifetime for each parameter can be obtained by

$$T = f^{-1}(F_i) \tag{10}$$

where F_i is failure threshold of three degradation parameters.

B. Parameter Fitting Result Analysis

First, the appropriate degradation model is selected through degradation quantity of three degradation parameters. A confidence of 0.95 and the precision control of 1E-5 are set.

From Fig.2 and Fig.3, capacitance and dissipation factor degenerate nonlinearly during 600h-3200h, so quadratic and cubic polynomial fitting methods are selected.

$$f(x) = a_1 + a_2 t + a_3 t^2 \tag{11}$$

$$f(x) = a_1 + a_2 t + a_3 t^2 + a_4 t^3 \tag{12}$$

From Fig.4, leakage current degradation quantity is characterized by a smooth increase, so the linear fit is more fitting with the trend of the data.

$$f(x) = a_1 + a_2 t \tag{13}$$

The fitting result and evaluation are shown in Table I, and the fitting curve are shown in Figs. 6-8.

TABLE I
FIT AND EVALUATION COEFFICIENTS

Parameter	Model	Fit coefficients				Evaluation coefficients	
		a_1	a_2	a_3	a_4	*RMSE*	R^2
capacitance	$f(x)=a_1+a_2t+a_3t^2$	1.774	-4.24E-4	5.78E-7		0.3440	0.9567
	$f(x)=a_1+a_2t+a_3t^2+a_4t^3$	-2.367	7.24E-3	-3.64E-6	7.06E-10	0.2271	0.9835
dissipation factor	$f(x)=a_1+a_2t+a_3t^2$	0.09071	4.24E-5	3.62E-8		0.0577	0.8840
	$f(x)=a_1+a_2t+a_3t^2+a_4t^3$	-0.0892 3	3.75E-4	-1.47E-7	3.07E-11	0.0603	0.8880
leakage current	$f(x)=a_1+a_2t$	1.09	3.01E-3			0.7881	0.9378

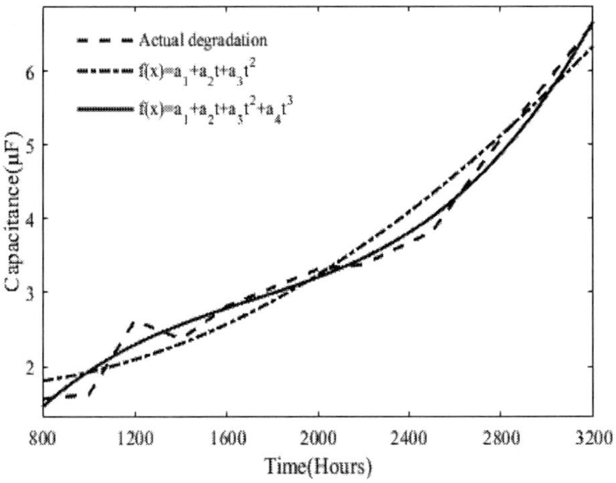

Fig. 6 Capacitance quadratic and cubic polynomial fitting

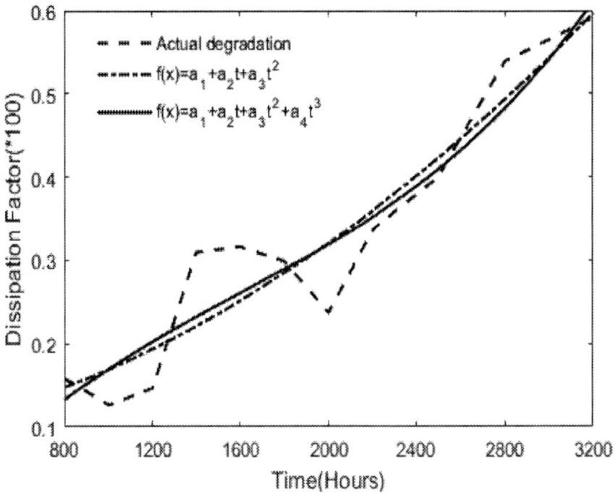

Fig. 7 Quadratic and cubic polynomial fitting model of dissipation factor

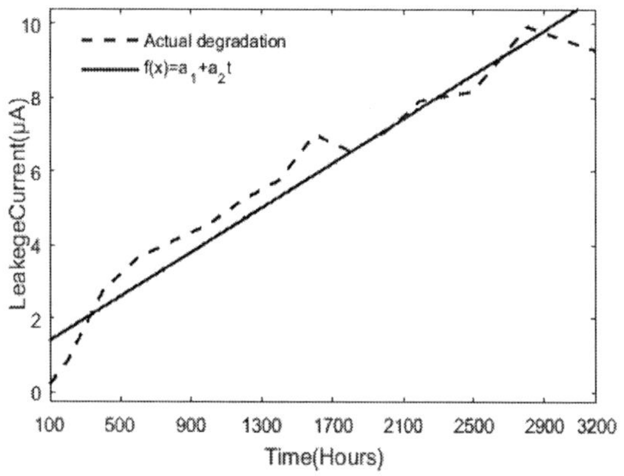

Fig. 8 Leakage current linear fitting

From Table I, according to RMSE and R_2, the cubic polynomial fitting method for capacitance is more suitable, and more in line with the increasing rate in the late regime of degradation with the error of 0.2311 from Fig. 6. The quadratic polynomial model for dissipation factor is adopted by smaller RMSE and R_2. And from Fig. 7, the actual degradation process of dissipation factor has waves due to the self-healing of the tantalum capacitor. The maximum error is only 0.7340. The linear function for leakage current has the maximum error of 0.9336 from Fig. 8.

C. Fitting Method Verification

In order to verify the fitting methods, 5 sets of tantalum capacitors with 95°C and 85% RH are measured. The data of capacitance, dissipation factor and leakage current are shown in Figs. 9-11.

From Figs. 9-11, the capacitance, dissipation factor and leakage current begin to degrade after 400 h, 400 h and 50 h with 95 ° C and 85% RH, respectively.

The degradation quantity of capacitance, dissipation factor and leakage current are fitted by *Eqs.* (11)-(13) respectively. The fitting curves are shown in Fig.12-14. With 95 ° C and 85% RH, the fitting curves are more relevant to the degraded data.

V. LIFE PREDICTION METHOD

Tantalum capacitor has self-healing characteristics, but there is a loss in each operation to result in permanent failure. Pseudo-lifetime of degradation parameters of each sample can be calculated by *Eq.* (10). In order to determine the best fitting distribution, the Weibull distribution, the Normal Distribution and the Exponential Distribution were tested for 16 samples with Kolmoglrov-Smirnov. With significance level α=0.05, the probability distributions for degradation parameters are listed in Table II.

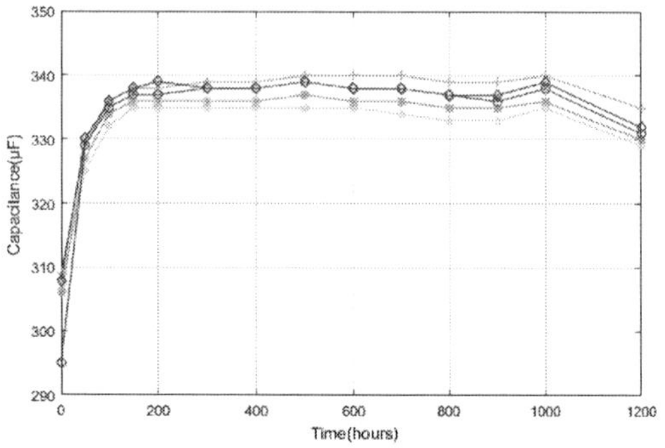

Fig. 9 Capacitance at 95 ° C and 85% RH

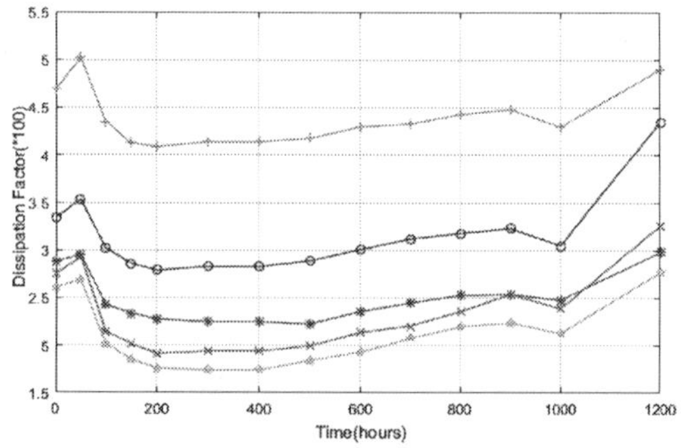

Fig. 10 Dissipation factor at 95 ° C and 85% RH

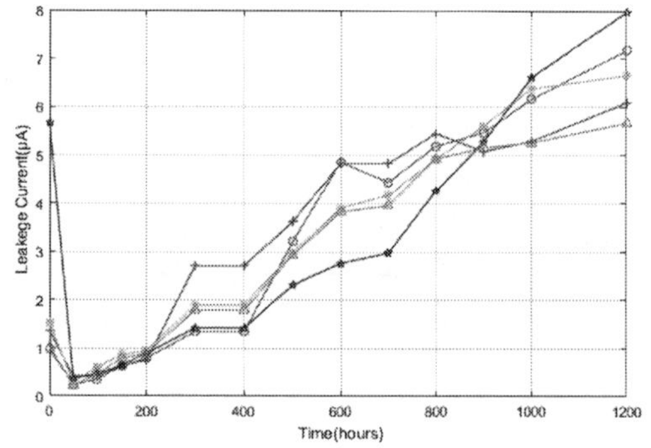

Fig. 11 Leakage current at 95 ° C and 85% RH

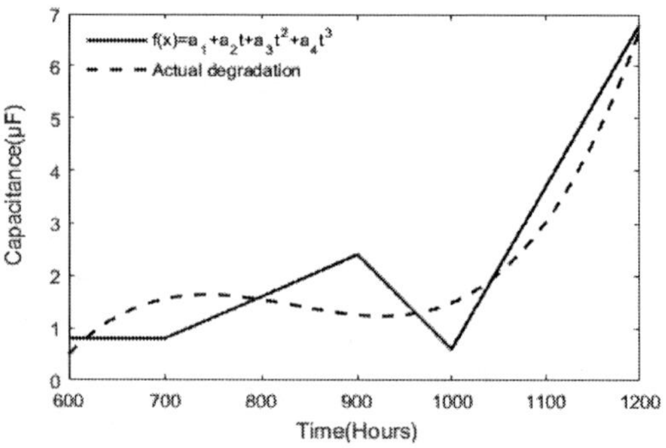

Fig. 12 Cubic polynomial fitting model of capacitance at 95 ° C and 85% RH

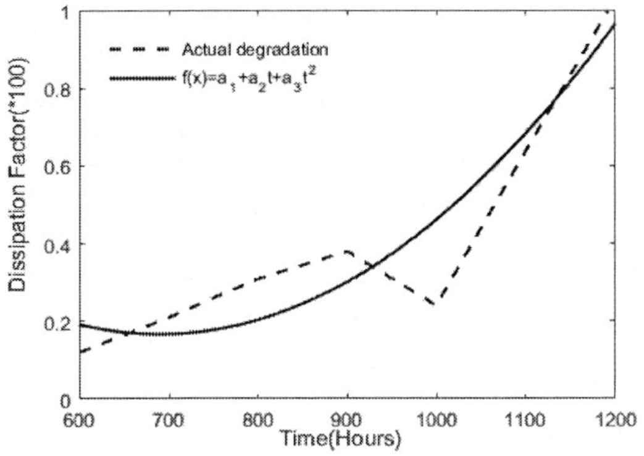

Fig. 13 Quadratic polynomial fitting model of dissipation factor at 95 ° C and 85% RH

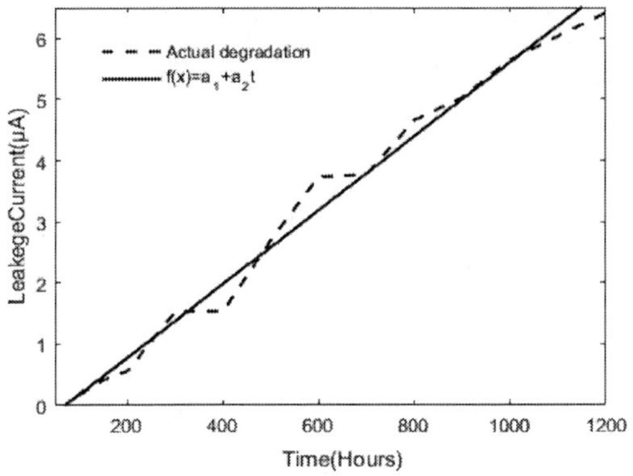

Fig. 14 Linear fitting model of leakage current at 95 ° C and 85% RH

TABLE II

PROBABILITY DISTRIBUTION FOR PSEUDO-LIFE

Parameter	Exponential	Normal	Weibull
Capacitance	Disobey	0.659	Disobey
Dissipation factor	Disobey	0.914	0.865
Leakage current	Disobey	0.755	Disobey

From Table II, Normal Distribution is the best. The unknown parameters of the distribution are obtained by the maximum likelihood estimation method, shown in Table III. The lifetime of tantalum capacitor predicted by capacitance, dissipation factor and leakage current are 6085 h, 15970 h, 68786 h, respectively. Degradation on capacitance mostly restricts the performance of the tantalum capacitor to become a key factor.

TABLE III

ESTIMATED LIFETIME WITH NORMAL DISTRIBUTION

Parameter	Average lifetime	Standard deviation
Capacitance	6085	471
Dissipation factor	15970	1137
Leakage current	68786	4688

VI. CONCLUSION

(1) With the double stresses of temperature and humidity, the degradation experiment of tantalum capacitor is designed and the degradation trends of the degradation parameters such as capacitance, dissipation factor and leakage current are acquired and analyzed.

(2) For stable degradation at the stress level of 95 °C and 70% RH, the fitting model of degradation parameters such as capacitance, dissipation factor, and leakage current are established as cubic polynomial fitting model, quadratic polynomial model and linear model, respectively. In addition, the fitting models are verified by the degradation trends of degradation parameters with 95 °C and 85% RH.

(3) The pseudo-lifetime Normal Distribution models of each degradation parameter are built. By the maximum likelihood estimation, the unknown parameters of the distribution are obtained. The result shows that capacitance has an important effect on the degradation to become a key parameter for stable degradation regime.

ACKNOWLEDGMENT

We would like to thank the Center for Advanced Life Cycle Engineering (CALCE) at the University of Maryland and China Scholarship Council (CSC) that support the research activities.

REFERENCES

[1] Kotz R, Ruch P W, Cericola D. Aging and failure mode of electrochemical double layer capacitors during accelerated constant load tests[J]. Journal of Power Sources, 2010, 195(3): 923-928.

[2] Kobayashi Y. Acceleration Coefficient of the Molded Electric Double-Layer Capacitor[J]. 42nd Electronic Components & Technology Conference :1992 Proceedings, 1992: 617-623.

[3] Virkki J, Seppala T, Frisk L, et al. Accelerated testing for failures of tantalum capacitor[J]. Microelectronics Reliability, 2010, 50(2): 217-219.

[4] Zednicek T, Sikula J, Leibovitz H. A study of field crystallization in tantalum capacitor and its effect on DCL and reliability[J]. Carts Usa, 2009.

[5] Teverovsky A. Degradation of Leakage Currents and Reliability Prediction for Tantalum capacitor[J]. Annual Reliability and Maintainability Symposium 2016 Proceedings, 2016.

[6] Bo L, Ya Z, Jian-Jun X, et al. Parameters Variation Mechanism of Solid Electrolytic Tantalum capacitor in Very High Temperatures[J]. Transactions of Beijing Institute of Technology, 2009, 29(10): 921-923.

[7] Peter A, Azarian M H, Pecht M. Reliability of Manganese Dioxide and Conductive Polymer Tantalum capacitor under Temperature Humidity Bias Testing[J], 2015, 2015(1): 000713-000719.

[8] Dehbi A, Wondrak W, Ousten Y, et al. High

temperature reliability testing of aluminum and tantalum electrolytic capacitors[J]. Microelectronics Reliability, 2002, 42(6): 835-840.

[9] Verchiani M, Bouyssou E, Fiannaca G, et al. Reliability study of TaON capacitors: From leakage current characterization to ESD robustness prediction[J]. Microelectronics Reliability, 2008, 48(8-9): 1412-1416.

[10] Huang J Y, Gao C, Cui W, et al. Lifetime prediction for tantalum capacitor with multiple degradation measures and particle swarm optimization based grey model[J]. Journal of Central South University Of Technology, 2012, 19(5): 1302-1310.

[11] Yue T, Mei X, Tang L. Piecewise least squares polynomial curve fitting algorithm for tested pump performance data[J]. Journal of Drainage & Irrigation Machinery Engineering, 2017, 35(9): 744-748.

[12] Ren W, Ren Q Q, Han L, et al. Piecewise Polynomial Fitting with Trend Item Removal and Its Application in a Cab Vibration Test[J]. Journal of Sensors, 2018.

[13] Havashinejadian E, Danaee I, Eskandari H, et al. Investigation on Trend Removal in Time Domain Analysis of Electrochemical Noise Data Using Polynomial Fitting and Moving Average Removal Methods[J]. Journal of Electrochemical Science And Technology, 2017, 8(2): 115-123.

[14] Yoon J S, Kim B I. Characteristics and production of tantalum powders for solid-electrolyte capacitors[J]. Journal of Power Sources, 2007, 164(2): 959-963.

[15] Gournay P. Capacitance and dissipation factor measurements under high voltage at BNM-LCIE[J]. 2000 Conference on Precision Electromagnetic Measurements Digest, 2000: 419-420.

[16] Manceau J P, Bruyere S, Jeannot S, et al. Leakage current variation with time in Ta2O5 MIM and MIS capacitors[J]. 2006 Ieee International Integrated Reliability Workshop, Final Report, 2006: 129-+.

[17] Freeman Y, Luzinov I, Burtovyy R, et al. Capacitance Stability in Polymer Tantalum capacitor with PEDOT Counter Electrodes[J]. Ecs Journal of Solid State Science And Technology, 2017, 6(7): N104-N110.

[18] Teverovsky A A, Teverovsky A A. Effect of moisture on characteristics of surface mount solid tantalum capacitor[J]. Carts, 2003.

[19] Teverovsky A. Effect of mechanical stresses on characteristics of chip tantalum capacitor[J]. Ieee Transactions on Device and Materials Reliability, 2007, 7(3): 399-406.

[20] Yugang S, Long C, Zhihui W, et al. A Load Identification Method for Inductive Power Transfer System Based on the Least Squares Algorithm[J]. Transactions of China Electrotechnical Societ, 2015, 30(5): 9-14.

Jianmeng Liu received the B.S. degree from the School of Electrical Engineering and Automation, Shijiazhuang University, Hebei, China, in 2017. He is currently studying towards the M.S. degree at the School of Electrical Engineering, Hebei University of Technology, Tianjin, China. His research focuses on the tantalum capacitor.

Jingying Zhao received the M.S. and Ph.D. degrees from the school of Electrical Engineering, Hebei University of Technology, Tianjin, China, in 2000 and 2004, respectively. She is currently a professor in the School of Electrical Engineering, Hebei University of Technology, Tianjin, China. She had an academic exchange for one year in University of Maryland, USA in 2018. Her research directions are electrical reliability and detection technology, and wireless power transfer.

7th International Conference on Reliability of
Electrical Products and Electrical Contacts,
November 04-06, 2019

Research on Material Identification Technology of Sealed Relay Remainder Material Based on Decision Tree

Huizhen Yan[1], Xiaohang Cao[3], Zixin Wang[2], Guotao Wang[1,2]
[1]Harbin Institute of Technology, Harbin 150001;
[2]Heilongjiang University, Harbin 150008
[3]Guizhou Space Appliance Co., Guiyang 550000
E-mail: heuyhzhen@163.com Tel: 86-18804633042

***Abstract*—PIND is one of most important tests for sealed electronic components. At present, this test can only detect the presence or absence of remainder and cannot infer the material information of remainders. The material information can provide reference for the subsequent processing decision of remainders, it is of great significance to trace the process steps in which the remainders generated. Currently, the accuracy of the material identification detection is less than 70%, which needs further improvement. Machine learning is used for remainder detection in this paper, which improves the utilization of data information. Based on the orthogonal design theory, the experimental scheme is designed, and the signal data set of the remainder material is established. The filtering and segmentation algorithm are designed to extract the effective signal. Multi-feature combinations of frequency domain and time domain are designed as input parameters. Classification model of remainder material signals is established based on decision tree algorithm. The trained classification model can achieve 85% accuracy of metal and non-metal classification for unlabeled test sets. High-precision identification of the remainder material is successfully realized.**

***Index Terms*— remainder; sealed relay; identification of remainder material; decision tree**

I. INTRODUCTION

Sealed relays are commonly used components in the aerospace field. They are an important part of various subsystems in spacecraft. Their reliability is directly related to the operational reliability of the spacecraft. One of the most important factors affecting the reliability of sealed relays is the internal remainder problem. The internals remainder of the sealed relay are copper wires, solder particles, aluminum chips, wire skins, etc. that are accidentally sealed in the relay during the production process. When the sealed relay is operated under conditions of overweight, weight loss or sudden impact, it is easy to cause the internal remainder to be freed and randomly move inside the sealed relay. If the remainder moves to the internal contacts or component parts, it will cause the performance reduction and local failures of some equipment, even cause burning of the system which result in serious aerospace accidents[1]. Remainder lead to a decline in the performance of the sealed relay or functional failure. And it is urgent to control and solve the problem of sealed relay remainder.

There are two main ways to control and solve the problem of remainder. The first is performing a PIND test and screening out the qualified sealed relay; The second is improving the production process to reduce the sealed relay containing remainder[2]. For the first way, the GJB has clearly stated that sealed relays must perform the PIND test before leaving the factory. At present, the remainder automatic detection equipment which can accurately detect the presence or absence of remainder has gradually matured and widely used. But this way can only get qualified relays and can't solve the remainder problem fundamentally. For the second way, it is necessary to know the source of producing remainder, that is, it is necessary to know the material information of the remainder.

There are two ways to obtain material information of the remainder. The first is opening the relay and taking out the remainder directly by physical means. Then obtaining the material information of the remainder by using various analysis methods. The second is to analyze the impact signal of the remainder and obtain the material information of the remainder indirectly according to the characteristics of the remainder signal. The first way has high accuracy and the acquired information of remainder is comprehensive. However, the process of opening the relay is complicated and inefficient. And it is difficult to ensure that no remainder be introduced in this process; The second way obtains relatively little information, but it is efficient and does not need to damage the relays. It belongs to non-destructive testing. At the same time, the remainder of some materials is not harmful to the sealed relay. The indirect identification method can filter out these parts and continue to use them[3]. In contrast, the indirect method works better, but the indirect method of the current application whose accuracy rate is less than 70% needs to be further improved.

In this paper, an indirect identification method for remainder material based on decision tree is proposed. Based on PIND test, the remainder signal is collected and analyzed to select and screen the signal characteristics. Based on the decision tree algorithm, this paper builds an identification classifier of remainder material and uses the established material identification data set to train and optimize the classifier model. Finally, this paper uses the test sample set to verify the accuracy of the optimized model.

II. THE ESTABLISHMENT OF DATA SET

A. *Remainder signal acquisition*

According to the materials of the common remainder in the sealed relay, this paper selects six kinds of remainders including copper wire, solder particle, aluminum particle, hot glue particle, PVC wire sheaths particle and silicone wire sheaths particle, among which three non-metal remainder and three metal remainder are used. According to the sensor sensitivity test, the quality of the silicone wire sheaths particle is designed to be 0.6~1.6mg, and the quality of the rest is 0.02~0.2mg. Then this paper designs the remainder signal acquisition scheme according to the orthogonal design theory and collects the remainder signal according to sealed relay remainder detection standard in the GJB by using DZJC-III remainder automatic detection system[4].

B. *Remainder signal filtering and segmentation*

The remainder signals collected by the DZJC-III remainder automatic detection system are continuous signals include much noise. And each of the remainder signals contains a plurality of remainder pulse signals. Therefore, the remainder signal needs to be filtered and segmented. The DZJC-III remainder automatic detection system focuses on whether there are reminders, and few considers for identification of remainder material relatively in the process of processing the remainder signal. Therefore, some the algorithms used in the DZJC-III remainder automatic detection system need to be adjusted appropriately to meet the requirements for identification of remainder material.

The filtering algorithm used in the DZJC-III remainder automatic detection system uses band-pass filtering. And this filter allows only the sound signal whose frequency is in the most sensitive frequency band of the sound sensor to pass. This causes some the characteristic information of the remainder signal to be distorted, so the filtering algorithm is re-adjusted to minimize the noise under the premise that the characteristics of the remainder signal are not distorted.

The segmentation algorithm used in the DZJC-III remainder automatic detection system uses only short-time energy threshold. This makes it difficult to ensure signal integrity. Moreover, this algorithm doesn't consider the case where multiple remainder pulse signals are adjacent to each other, so that multiple adjacent remainder pulse signals are segmented into one signal. Therefore, the remainder signal segmentation algorithm is re-adjusted so that it can better segment the remainder signal[5].

III. THE CHARACTERISTICS OF REMAINDER SIGNAL

A. *remainder signal*

The remainder signal is generated by the impact of the activated remainder particles with the internal mechanism or the inner wall of the sealed relay. Each impact within the relay corresponds to a spike pulse that lasts for a period[6]. The typical remainder signal is shown in the Fig. 1.

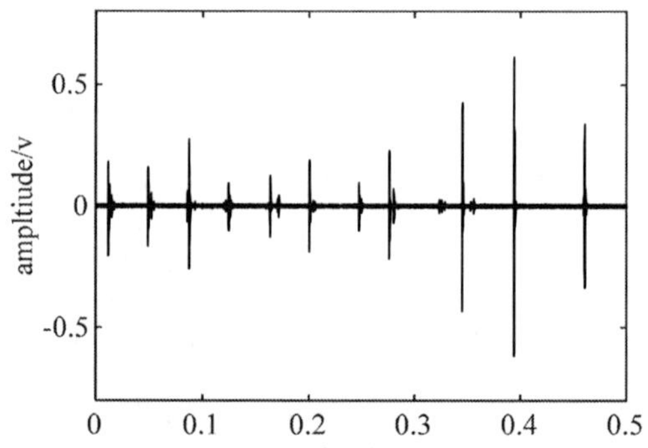

Fig. 1 Remainder sign

Due to the different hardness and other characteristics of different materials, the pulse signals generated by the remainder of different materials are different. The typical metallic and non-metallic remainder pulse signals are shown in Fig. 2 and Fig. 3.

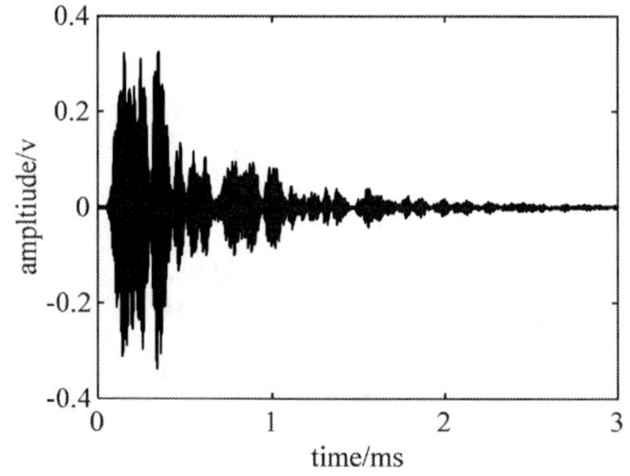

Fig. 2 non-metallic remainder pulse signal

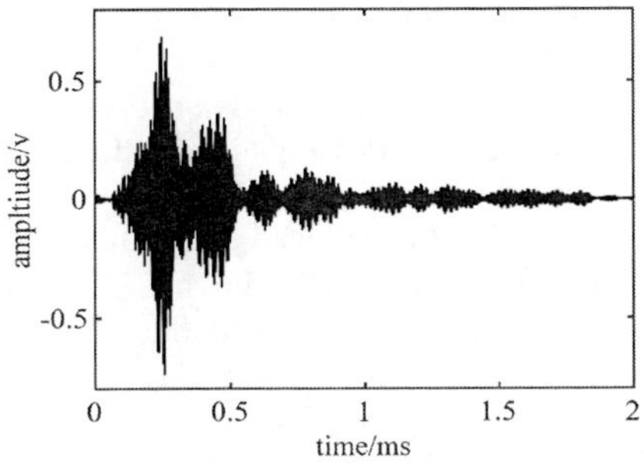

Fig. 3 metallic remainder pulse signal

B. Feature selection and feature vector calculation

From the perspective of acoustic emission signal recognition, the identification of the remainder material is to infer the nature of the acoustic emission source based on the characteristics of the acoustic signal[7]. Therefore, according to the principle of acoustic emission, the time domain and frequency domain characteristics of the remainder pulse signal are selected. In addition, the experimental conditions of vibration frequency are added as characteristics. Finally, 15 features including fre (vibration frequency), s (pulse area), dczy (degree of lateral symmetry), Tp (percentage of pulse rise), Tl (duration), MD (energy density), ZB (pulse ratio) , bf (crest factor), dcsx (degree of longitudinal symmetry), dp (area ratio), zerorate (zero-crossing rate), var (variance), mainHz (spectral centroid), MSF (cepstrum coefficient) and MSFcha (cepst coefficient difference) are selected. Then, the remainder pulse signal is converted into a feature vector according to the above features.

C. Feature screening

Feature screening refers to selecting a representative subset from the original feature set, which has great significance for many problems in the field of machine learning. Effective features can reduce the noise interference of the model and can effectively improve the classification effect and efficiency of the model[8]. Typically, feature selection is considered in two perspectives. The first is whether the feature is divergent. If the sample doesn't have a difference in a feature, this feature won't have a good classification effect. The second is the correlation between the feature and the target, and it is preferable to select the feature with high relevance to the target[9]. This paper uses the univariate feature selection method to screen the features. This method separately calculates a certain statistical indicator of each feature. Then this method judges the importance of the feature according to the indicator and screens out the features with low importance.

First, this paper uses the correlation coefficient as screening indicator, and only retains one of the features with high correlation. The correlation between features is shown in Fig. 4.

It can be seen from Fig. 4 that ZB and TL and zerorate are positively correlated with each other, mainHz and MSF are positively correlated, bf and dp are highly correlated, MD and s are highly correlated. Therefore, the five characteristics of ZB, TL, dp, s, and mainHz are discarded, and the other features are retained.

Then this paper uses the f_classif method provided by the sklearn library to do the next features screening. f_classif is the F value of the variance analysis, which is a commonly used indicator for screening features. The principle of f_classif is to calculate the variance of each feature and perform a significance test by comparing the sizes of the individual variances[10]. The larger the F value, the more significant the feature is and the stronger the predictive power. After running this method, a set of scores for each feature based on the f_classif method is returned. And then the feature can be filtered based on this score. The f_classif score of the feature is shown in Fig. 5.

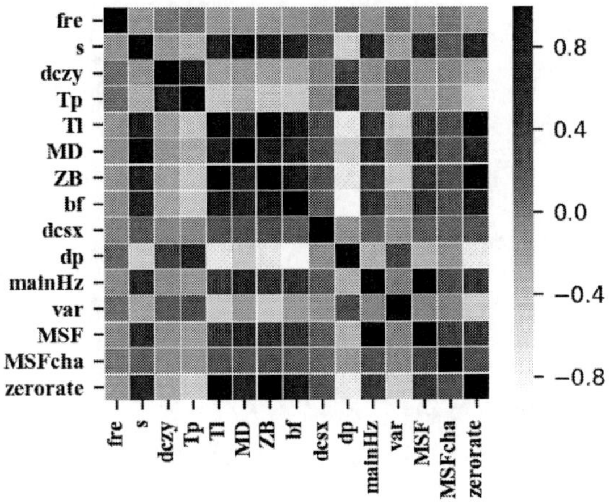

Fig. 4 the correlation between features

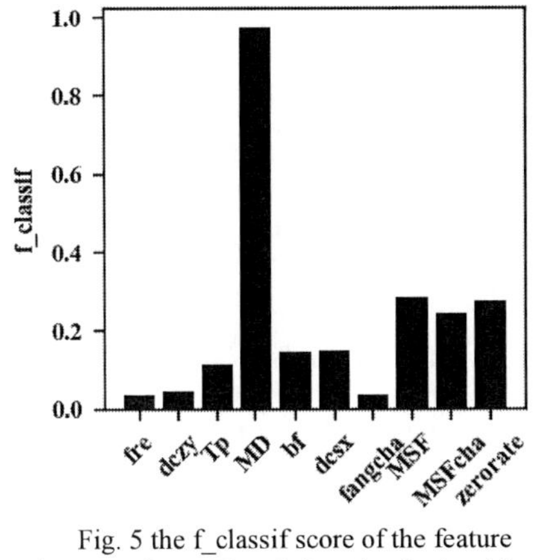

Fig. 5 the f_classif score of the feature

It can be seen from Fig. 5 that the f_classif scores of fre and var are very low. So, these two features are discarded, and the other features are reserved for the training of the decision tree.

IV. IDENTIFICATION OF REMAINDER MATERIAL BASED ON DECISION TREE ALGORITHM

A. Decision tree algorithm

1) Decision tree generation

The decision tree algorithm is an instance-based inductive learning method that can extract a tree classification model from a given out-of-order training sample.

The first step in the decision tree generation is to select the partitioning feature. The ideal partition feature selection can keep the purity of the decision tree branch nodes higher and higher with the decision trees growing. There are many different quantitative evaluation criteria to evaluate the improvement of branch node purity. And different quantitative evaluation criteria can derive different decision tree algorithms.

Entropy is one of the most commonly used indicators for measuring the purity of a sample set[11]. If the proportion of the kth sample in the current sample set D is $P_k(k = 1, 2, ..., n)$, the entropy of the sample set D is

$$Ent(D) = -\sum_{k=1}^{n} p_k \log_2 p_k \tag{1}$$

The smaller the value of Ent(D), the higher the purity of sample set 'D'. If sample set 'D' generates 'v' branches according to the feature 'a', the entropy of sample set 'D' after dividing can be calculated. And consider the influence of the number of samples in each branch node, the "information gain" generated by the dividing step is

$$Gain_{Ent}(D,a) = Ent(D) - \sum_{v=1}^{v} \frac{|D^v|}{|D|} Ent(D^v) \tag{2}$$

The larger the "information gain", the greater the "purity improvement" of the sample set 'D' can be obtained by using feature 'a' for partitioning.

The Gini coefficient was originally used to measure the income gap of a country or region. It was introduced into data processing as a measure of data inequality. The more chaotic the categories contained in the data, the larger the Gini coefficient. The Gini coefficient of sample set 'D' is

$$Gini(D) = \sum_{k=1}^{n} \sum_{k' \neq k} p_k p_{k'} = 1 - \sum_{k=1}^{n} p_k^2 \tag{3}$$

Gini(D) reflects the probability of category inconsistency between two sample which is randomly selected from sample set 'D'. Therefore, the smaller the Gini(D) is, the higher the purity of the sample set 'D' is. Like the entropy information gain, the Gini information gain is

$$Gain_{Gini}(D,a) = Gini(D) - \sum_{v=1}^{v} \frac{|D^v|}{|D|} Gini(D^v) \tag{4}$$

After the partitioning feature is selected, the recursive child nodes can be generated recursively according to the selected features, so that the decision tree can grow continuously until the data set cannot be divided.

2) Decision tree pruning

The process of simplifying a complex decision tree is called pruning, with the goal of removing some nodes to mitigate overfitting. Decision tree pruning has two ways. The first is to do pruning while constructing a decision tree. Before building a decision tree that completely categorizes the training set, stop the tree construction based on a threshold. The second is to do pruning after building a complete decision tree. The pruning process is to replace the subtree with a leaf node and judge whether the accuracy of the decision tree is increased. If the accuracy is increased, the pruning can be accepted[12].

3) Continuous value processing

Decision trees are generally based on discrete features, while some of features of the remainder pulse signals are continuous values. This requires discretizing the continuous features to applicate in the decision tree. The easiest way to discretize is the dichotomy. Selecting the segmentation point 't' divides the continuous feature 'a' into positive and negative attribute values, so that the effect of the feature 'a' can be evaluated based on the segmentation point 't' for division. Then select the optimal segmentation point to discretize the feature 'a'. And then the feature 'a' can be handled completely in terms of discrete features. For example, for continuous feature 'a', the entropy information gain formula should be changed to

$$\begin{aligned} Gain_{Ent}(D,a) &= \max_{t \in a} Gain(D,a,t) \\ &= Ent(D) - \max_{t \in a} \sum_{\lambda=\{+,-\}} \frac{|D_t^\lambda|}{|D|} Ent(D_t^\lambda) \end{aligned} \tag{5}$$

B. Evaluation index

When doing the classification tasks in machine learning, the evaluation index should be used to evaluate the effect of the model. The most common is accuracy, but sometimes the accuracy does not meet all requirements. For a two-class problem, one prediction may produce 4 different results as shown in Table 1.

Table 1 Two-class confusion matrix

Predicted codition	True condition	
	Positive	Negative
Positive	True positive(TP)	False positive(FP)
Negative	False negative(FN)	True negative(TN)

Among them, TP and TN are all correct classifications. FP is the number of negative classes predicted to be positive classes. FN is the number of positive classes predicted to be negative classes. The commonly used index to evaluate the effect of the model has the Precision P, the Recall R and the F1 measure. And their calculation formula is shown in Equations 6-8.

$$P = \frac{TP}{TP + FP} \quad (6)$$

$$R = \frac{TP}{TP + FN} \quad (7)$$

$$F1 = \frac{2 * P * R}{P + R} \quad (8)$$

When evaluating a model, the most important index is the precision and the recall. However, the precision and the recall are contradictory. They often cannot have good scores at the same time. Therefore, this paper uses the F1 measure to evaluate the quality of the model.

C. *Training decision tree model*

Since the remainder of different materials produces different numbers of pulse signals under the same test conditions, the data is unbalanced. So, this paper uses the under-sampling method to extract 2000 samples from each of the six materials data sets to form the training data set. Then the total data set is divided into three sets of training set, test set and verification set according to the proportion of 60%, 20% and 20%. The training set is used to train the decision tree model. The test set is a separate set of samples left during the model training process to adjust the hyperparameters of the model and to provide a preliminary assessment of the model's capabilities. The verification set is used to evaluate the generalization capabilities of the final model.

Use decision tree classification model in sklearn library and select default parameters to generate the identification classifier of remainder. Then train the identification classifier of remainder material on the training set and use the trained identification classifier of remainder material to test on the test set. The test results are shown in Table 2.

Table 2 test result by using default parameter

Remainder material	Precision	Recall	F1-score
Non-metal	0.81	0.80	0.81
Metal	0.79	0.80	0.80

And the test set accuracy rate is 79.5%. The training set is tested using the trained identification classifier of remainder material, and the result shows that the accuracy of the classification on the training set is 100%. Combined with the prediction results of the test set, it can be seen that the decision tree model generated by the default parameters has low bias and high variance. This indicates that the classifier is heavily over-fitting. So, further adjustments to the decision tree parameters are required.

V. PARAMETER ADJUSTMENT AND RESULTS

A. *Decision tree parameter*

In order to solve the over-fitting problem of the identification classifier of remainder material, the generation parameters of the decision tree model, that is the hyper-parameters, can be adjusted to limit the complexity of the decision tree, so that the decision tree generation can stop early and avoid over-fitting. And the decision tree model can be optimized to improve the accuracy of decision tree prediction. The decision tree model has many hyperparameters, but not all parameters need to be adjusted. The hyperparameters that need to be adjusted mainly include the max_depth, the max_leaf_nodes, the min_samples_split, and the min_impurity_decrease.

B. *The result of parameter adjusting*

First, the max_depth is adjusted. The depth of the material identification classifier generated by the default parameters is 21. Use the max_depth of the difference to generate the decision tree and get the F1-score. Finally, the optimal max_depth is approximately 3~10. The curve of the F1-score with the max_depth is shown in Fig. 6.

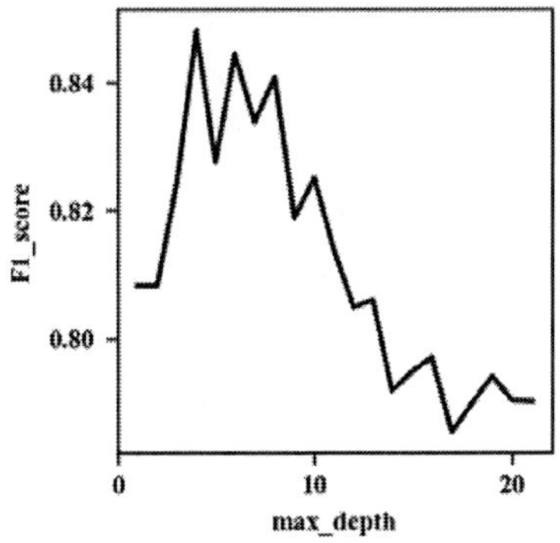

Fig. 6 The curve of the F1-score with the max_depth

Then the max_leaf_nodes is adjusted. The leaf node number of the material identification classifier generated by the default parameters is 843. Use the max_leaf_nodes of the difference to generate a decision tree and get the F1-score. Finally, the optimal max_leaf_nodes is approximately 20~90. The curve of the F1-score with the max_leaf_nodes is shown in Fig. 7.

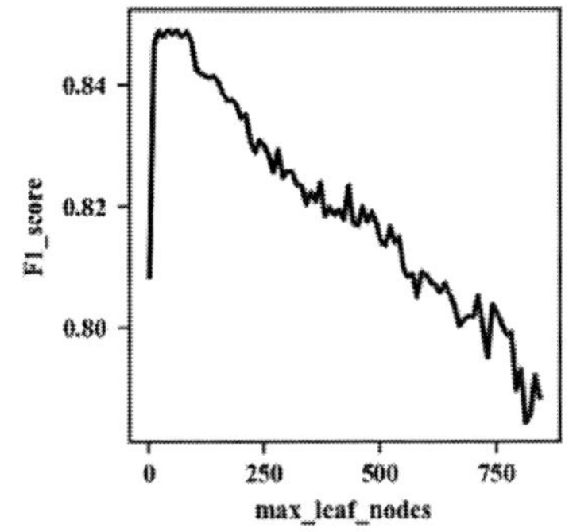

Fig. 7 The curve of the F1-score with the max_leaf_nodes

The min_samples_split and the min_impurity_decrease also use similar methods to get the optimal parameters roughly in the range of 150~200 and 1e-4~1e-3 respectively. Since the influence of various parameters on the decision tree model is not independent of each other, the next step requires several parameters to be adjusted together to get the best results. And perhaps, the final parameters may not be in the optimal range of separate adjusting. Therefore, specific values of these four parameters found by using grid-search and cross-validation, and other parameters use the default values. The parameters are still optimized by gradually narrowing the parameter range. Finally, the optimal parameters values are max_depth=9, max_leaf_nodes=36, min_samples_split=2, and min_impurity_decrease=1e-4. Use the optimized parameter generating the identification classifier of remainder material and test on the test set. The results are shown in Table 3. And the accuracy of the material identification classifier on the test set is 85%. At this time, the accuracy of the material identification classifier on the training set is 86.3%. This shows that the deviation and variance are no longer high. So, it is not necessary to continue to adjust the parameters.

Then the trained material identification classifier is tested on the verification set. The results are shown in Table 4. And the accuracy of the material identification classifier on the verification set is 84.9%

Table 3 test set test results after optimizing

Remainder material	Precision	Recall	F1-score
Non-metal	0.85	0.86	0.85
Metal	0.85	0.84	0.85

Table 4 verification set test results after optimizing

Remainder material	Precision	Recall	F1-score
Non-metal	0.85	0.85	0.85
Metal	0.85	0.84	0.84

C. Discussion

In this paper, a material identification method based on decision tree algorithm is proposed for the problem of low accuracy of material identification of remainder. And the experimental results show that the recognition accuracy of this method for unknown samples is 84.9%, which proves that the method is effective for material identification. The remainder material can be identified by using this method, which is helpful for finding the process links of the problem, thereby improving the probability of the process to reduce the occurrence of remainder.

VI. CONCLUSIONS

In this paper, a method for identifying the remainder material of sealed relay based on decision tree algorithm is proposed. After analyzing the remainder signal, the decision tree is trained and optimized by using eight characteristics: degree of lateral symmetry, energy density, degree of longitudinal symmetry, zero-crossing rate and so on. And determine the decision tree parameters as max_depth=9, max_leaf_nodes=36, min_samples_split=2, and min_impurity_decrease=1e-4. Finally, a material recognition classifier with an accuracy of 84.9% is obtained. Its identification accuracy is high, which proves that the decision tree algorithm can be used to realize the identification of remainder material. However, the method can only distinguish whether the remainder is metal or non-metal, and the identification accuracy of the specific material is not high. So, the material identification needs further study.

ACKNOWLEDGMENT

The authors gratefully acknowledge the financial supports for this research from the National Natural Science Foundation of China (Nos. 51607059, 51077022 and 61271347); Natural Science Foundation of Heilongjiang Province (QC2017059); Postdoctoral Fund in Heilongjiang Province (LBH-Z16169); Talent Innovation Special Project of Heilongjiang Province (HDRCCX-201604); Science and Technology Innovative Research Team in Higher Educational Institutions of Heilongjiang Province (No.2012TD007); Heilongjiang University Youth Science Fund Project (QL201505).

REFERENCES

[1] Guotao Wang, Qiang Wang, Han Xiao, et al., "Summary of Detection Technology for Sealed Electronic Components", Electromechanical Components, vol. 37, no 1, pp. 55-63, 2017.

[2] Zhonglai Gao, Honghui Yu, Wensheng Liu, et al., "Analysis on Effective Prevention and Control of Product Excess", Electronics World, no 4, pp. 47-48, 2019.

[3] Shikun Zhou., "Relay screening and the hazards of excess", Quality and Reliability, no 5, pp. 33-34, 40, 1994.

[4] Dejian Su, Guotao Wang, Yanhui Lou, et al., "Research on vibration test conditions of aerospace relay excess detection based on curve fitting theory", Electrical Energy Management Technology, no 7, pp. 27-31, 44, 2017.

[5] Leizhen Gao, Huizhen Yan, Guotao Wang, et al., Design of Pulse Extraction Method Based on PIND Excessive Material Testing Equipment", Electrical Energy Management Technology, no 10, pp. 21-26, 73, 2019.

[6] Guangcheng Ma, Guoxing Yi, Qiyong Wen, et al., "Particle Impact Noise Detection in Sealed Relays Based on Neural Network" in Electrical Contacts, 2003. Proceedings of the Forty-ninth IEEE Holm Conference on, 2003.

[7] Haibin Fu., "Research on Surface Material Recognition of Objects Based on Auditory Feature Analysis", Shijiazhuang Tiedao University, 2018.

[8] Canfei sun, Youren wang, Guodong sun., "A Multi-criteria Fusion Feature Selection Algorithm

for Fault Diagnosis of Helicopter Planetary Gear Train", Chinese Journal of Aeronautics, 2019.

[9] Huang Dong, Xiaosha Cai, Changdong Wang., "Unsupervised Feature Selection with Multi-subspace Randomization and Collaboration", Knowledge-based Systems, 2019.

[10] Fernando jiménez, Horacio pérez-sánchez, José palma, et al., "A Methodology for Evaluating Multi-objective Evolutionary Feature Selection for Classification in the Context of Virtual Screening", Soft Computing, vol. 23, no 18, 2019

[11] Min Zhang, Zhaori Bi, Xinping Fu, et al., "A Parsimonious Approach for Screening Moderate-to-profound Hearing Loss in a Community-dwelling Geriatric Population Based on a Decision Tree Analysis.", Bmc Geriatrics, vol. 19, no 1, 2019.

[12] Ching yee yong, Kim mey chew, Rubita sudirman., "Human Wrist Motion Classification Using Decision Tree and Principle Component Analysis", Materials Today: Proceedings, vol. 16, 2019.

7th International Conference on Reliability of
Electrical Products and Electrical Contacts,
November 04-06, 2019

A Method of Improving Signal Integrity of Solder Joints

Kaixuan Song, Jinchun Gao, Ziren Wang, Babar Ali, Hafiz Muhammad Bilal, Gang Xie
Beijing University of Posts and Telecommunications, Beijing 100876, China
E-mail: gjc@bupt.edu.cn

Abstract—**Solder joints are a common electrical connection in the RF circuit, and the characteristic impedance discontinuity of solder joints increases the energy loss of the signal in the circuit. In this paper, the solder joints of the RF connector and microstrip line component were investigated. Using transmission line theory, the reasons for the characteristic impedance discontinuity of the solder joint were discussed, and the compensation schemes were proposed. Based on the actual structure of the component, a 3D electromagnetic field model was established to evaluate transmission loss and signal reflection. In the simulation, time-domain-reflectometry (TDR) was used to evaluate the characteristic impedance of solder joints. Finally, the experiments were completed. The electromagnetic field model results are in good agreements with experimental results, which indicate that the compensation scheme has an obvious effect on the impedance compensation of solder joints.**

Index Terms— **Solder joint, Impedance discontinuity, Anti-pad, Compensation**

I. INTRODUCTION

Solder joints play a critical role in RF circuits. With the increment of the signal frequency, the signal energy loss caused by impedance discontinuity of solder joints has attracted more attention. Consequently, systematic schemes to improve signal integrity for solder joints have gained substantial value.

Chang [1] studied the effect of solder joint materials on mechanical properties. He proved that shear fracture tends to occur in the IMC layer at room temperature. Liu [2] proposed the transmission line electrical model of solder joints. This work simplified the physical model for the damaged solder joint. Manfredi [3] developed a 3-D model for cracking solder joint, which simulated the effect of solder joint cracking on impedance and improved the model and future applications. Keat [4] showed the solder joint reliability under shock loading condition. The modeling data suggested that the maximum principal stress at the solder joint interface is a good failure criterion. Wang [5] provided two compensation schemes for impedance discontinuity caused by the solder joint, which improved the signal integrity and transmission performance of solder joints. Rong [6] conducted a series of simulation on signal integrity issues caused by discontinuity of SMA connector to PCB transition structure. This work provides optimized compensation schemes. Yu [7] proposed a compensation scheme of adding an anti-pad in the reference formation, which improved signal integrity. Xu [8] established the corresponding analytical structure for the discontinuities in the flip-chip connection. This work can be employed to improve the model parameters and make the structure's optimization more effective. Huang [9] established an electromagnetic simulation model for solder joints and analyzed the influence of solder joint size on return loss.

There are many problems of impedance mismatch caused by solder joints in electrical connections. However, few people are concerned about the compensation schemes of solder joints. In the current study, the reasons for characteristic impedance discontinuity were discussed. Then the compensation schemes were proposed, which are divided into the following three types: optimization of solder joint size, optimization of the dielectric layer structure and the optimization of the ground plane structure. Based on different schemes, electromagnetic field models for RF connector and microstrip line component with solder joints were developed using the electromagnetic simulation software. The *S*-parameters and TDR were obtained from an electromagnetic field model to analyze high-frequency performance. The experimental measurements show good agreements with electromagnetic simulation, which prove that compensation schemes can effectively improve the quality of electrical connection and signal integrity.

II. ELECTROMAGNETIC NUMERICAL MODEL DEVELOPMENT AND SIMULATION ANALYSIS

A. Simulation Setup

As shown in Fig.1, the model of component consists of SMP coaxial connectors and micro strip line. The insulation medium of the microstrip line is Rogers 4350B, which has a dielectric constant of 3.48 and a thickness of 0.254mm. The micro strip line conductor is made of copper, of which width is 0.58mm. The solder joint connects the inner conductor of SMP coaxial connectors to the top signal line of micro stripline, and four conductive through holes connect the outer conductor of SMP to the ground plane of micro strip line. The excitation is a waveguide port. The boundary of the model is set as an open boundary. The frequency ranges 0 to 18GHz. In order to understand the effect of solder joints in communication and give compensation schemes, an electromagnetic numerical field model was established.

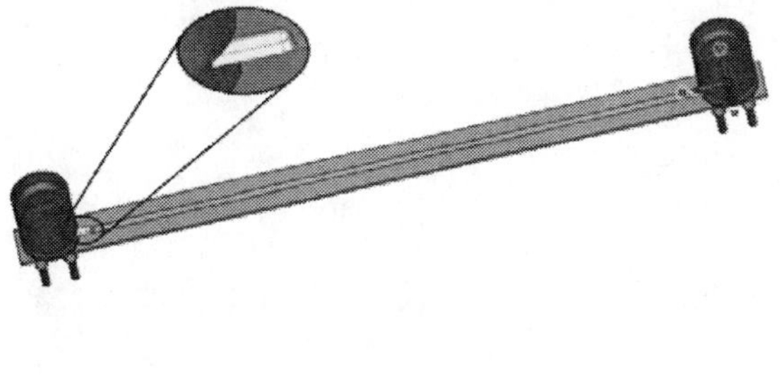

Fig. 1 3D model of RF connector and micro strip line

B. Size of Solder Joint

For the size of the solder joint, the model of the component was simulated. The length of the solder joint was set as the variable L to characterize the solder joint size. The relationships between characteristic impedance and time are shown in Fig.2. With the variable L decreasing from 1.9mm to 0.9mm, the characteristic impedance is closer to 50Ω, which has a minimum value of 46.25Ω 46.75Ω 47.5Ω in order. The relationship between S-parameters and frequency are shown in Fig 3. With the variable L decreasing from 1.9mm to 0.9mm, S_{11} decreases and S_{21} increases in the frequency range from 0 to 18GHz. The smaller of the solder joint size, the better of the performance. However, in order to ensure effective mechanical connection and electrical connection, the size of the solder joint cannot be reduced without limitation. As a result, the reduction in the solder joint size is not a good optimization to improve signal integrity.

C. Structure of Dielectric Substrate

The empirical Eq. (1) for the characteristic impedance of microstrip lines is shown as follows.

$$Z_0 = \frac{87}{\sqrt{1.41+\varepsilon}} \ln\left(\frac{5.98H}{0.8w+t}\right) \tag{1}$$

where w is the width of the microstrip line, H is the thickness of a dielectric layer, t is the thickness of microstrip line conductor, ε is the dielectric constant of the dielectric layer between these two conductors.

Inspection of Eq. (1) shows that with the thickness of dielectric substrate h increasing, the characteristic impedance Z_0 increases. In the simulation, the thickness of the dielectric substrate at the non-solder-joint is 0.254 mm, and the difference in thickness of the dielectric substrate between the solder joint and the non-solder-joint is set as variable Δh. The relationships between characteristic impedance and time are shown in Fig.4. With the variable Δh increasing from 0 to 0.2mm, the characteristic impedance increases from 46.25Ω to 54.25Ω at T=0.125ns. Comparison of the lines in Fig.5(a) and Fig.5(b) provides an insight into the effects of the dielectric substrate structure on signal transmission performance. When Δh=0.08mm, S-parameters of the model are best. Consequently, the optimization in dielectric substrate structure can increase the characteristic impedance to approach 50Ω, which can improve transmission and matching performance. However, in an engineering application, it is difficult and much costing to use this method.

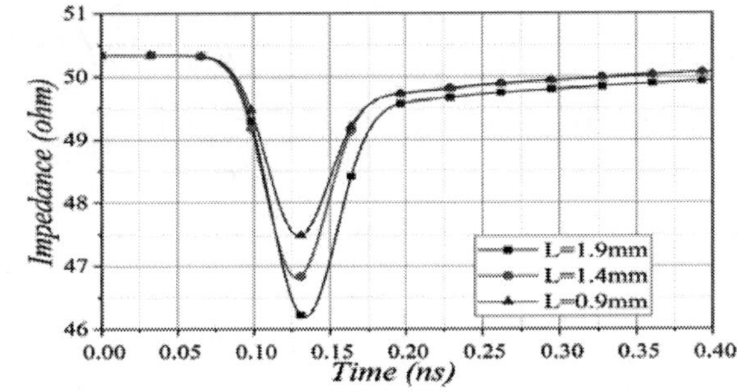

Fig. 2 TDR under the different size of solder joint

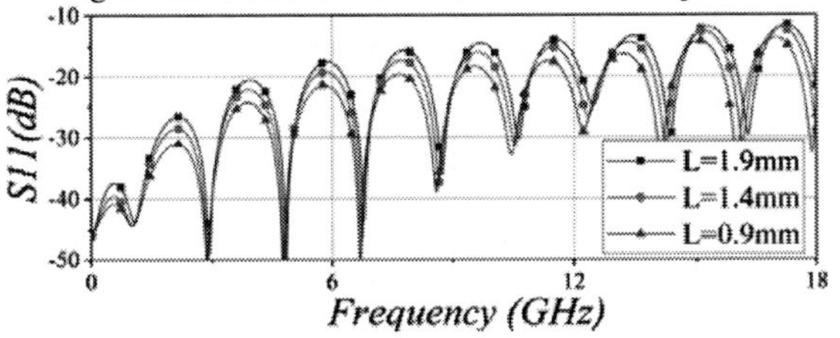

(a)

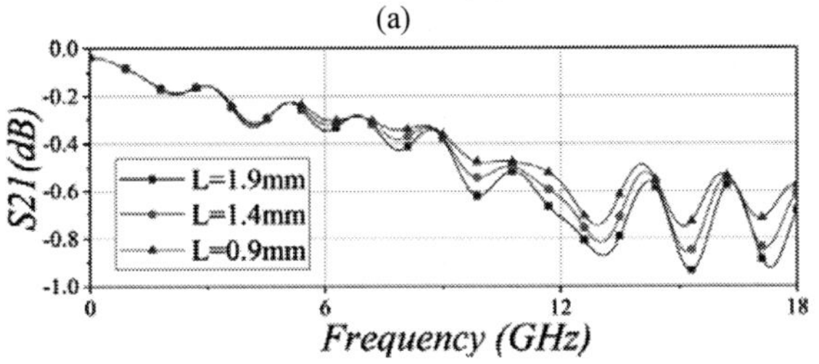

(b)

Fig. 3 S-parameters of components under different sizes of solder joint (a) S_{11} (b) S_{21}

D. Anti-pad on Ground

Based on transmission line theory, the characteristic impedance Z_0 can be obtained as shown below:

$$Z_0 = \sqrt{\frac{R + j\omega L}{G + j\omega C}} \tag{2}$$

where L is unit length inductance, representing the total inductance of the two conductors. C is unit length capacitance, caused by the close proximity of the two conductors.

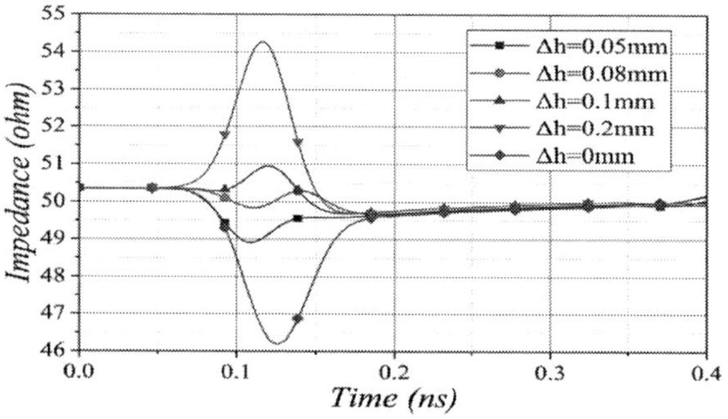

Fig.4 TDR under different variable Δh

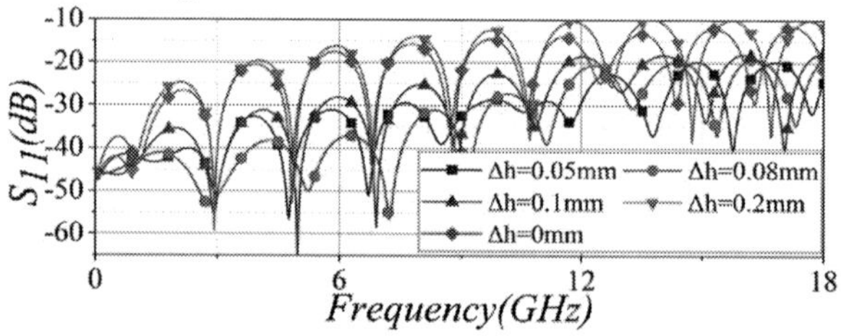

(a)

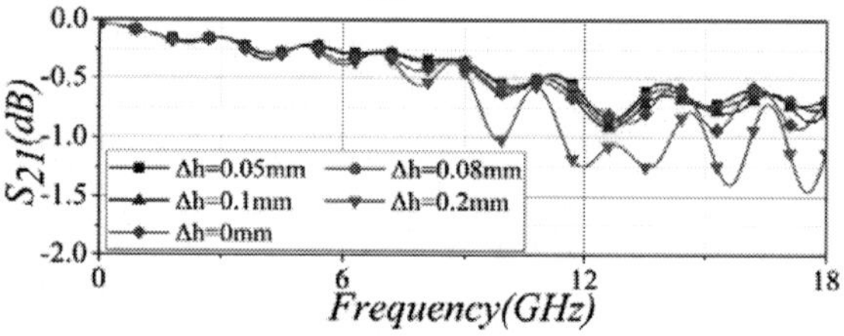

(b)

Fig. 5 S-parameters of components under different variable Δh (a) S_{11} (b) S_{21}

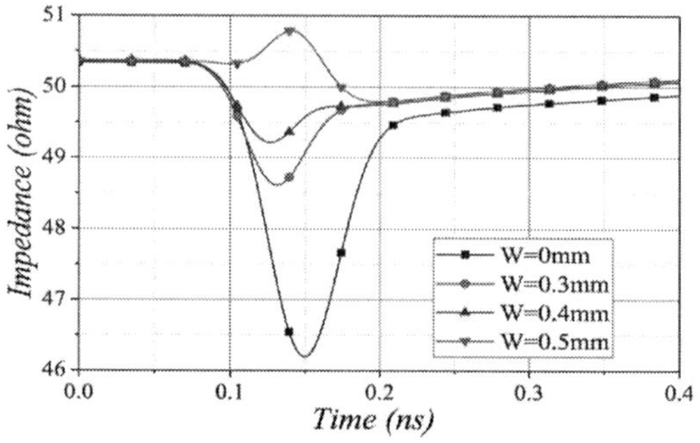

Fig.6 TDR under different variable W

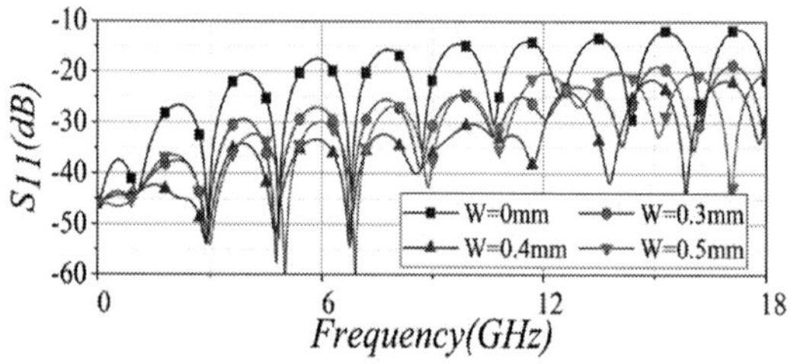

(a)

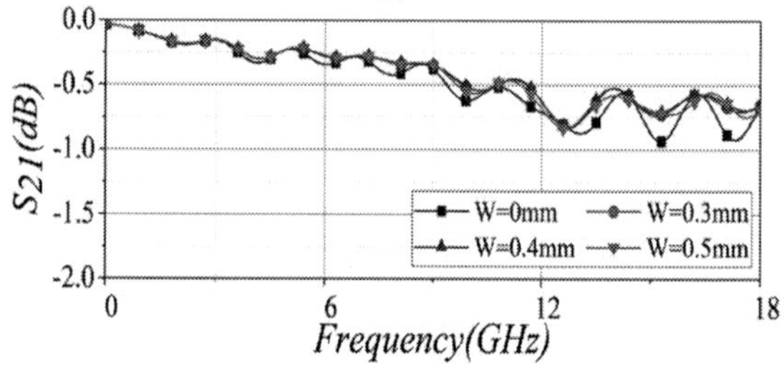

(b)

Fig. 7 S-parameters of components under different variable W. (a) S_{11} (b) S_{21}

As shown in Eq. (2), it can be seen that with C decreasing, the characteristic impedance Z_0 increases. In order to reduce the variable C, anti-pads are added on the ground plane. In the simulation, the shape of the anti-pad is a rectangle, of which width is set as the variable W. The relationships between characteristic impedance and time are shown in Fig.6. With the variable W increasing from 0 to 0.5mm, the characteristic impedance increases from 46.25Ω to 50.75Ω at T=0.125ns. Comparison of the lines in Fig 8(a) and Fig 8(b) provides insight into the effects of the anti-pad on signal transmission performance. When W=0.4mm, the values of S_{11} of the compensation scheme are reduced by more than 10dB in the most frequency range, which means the reflection of electromagnetic waves at the input port is significantly reduced. The values of S_{21} of the compensation scheme are significantly improved in the high-frequency range. Accordingly, this optimization is effective to solve the problem of the characteristic impedance discontinuity. In addition, considering the two aspects of processing difficulty and performance improvement, the optimization of the ground structure is better than the optimization of the dielectric substrate structure.

III. EXPERIMENTAL INVESTIGATION

A. *Experimental Setup*

For the optimization of adding anti-pad on the ground, experimental testing was accomplished. The insulation medium of the micro strip line is Rogers 4350B, which has a dielectric constant of 3.48 and a thickness of 0.254mm. The micro strip line conductor is made of copper, of which width is 0.58mm. S-parameters are measured using a vector network analyzer (VNA). In addition, the frequency ranges from 10MHz to 18GHz and the number of sampling points is 200.

B. *Results and Discussion*

There are four types of PCB in experimental testing. The relationships between S-parameters and frequency are shown in Fig.8.

Comparison of Fig.7 and Fig.8 shows that the measurement S_{11} is greater than the simulated S_{11} and the measurement S_{21} is lower than the simulated S_{21}, which is due to the difference of solder joint in experimental testing and the exclusion of material loss in simulation.

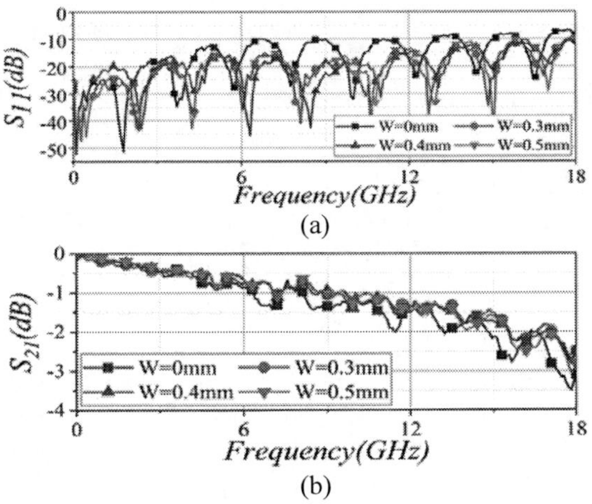

Fig. 8 Measurement S-parameters under different variable W (a) S_{11} (b) S_{21}

As shown in Fig.8, when W=0mm, the transmission and matching performance is poor. When the frequency is greater than 6GHz, the values of S_{11} start to be higher than -10dB and the maximum value is about -7.5dB at 17GHz. With regard to the S_{21}, the minimum value is about -4.5dB. The S-parameters of W=0.3mm, 0.4mm, 0.5mm is similar. When W=0.4mm, the S-parameters are best. Compared with the W=0mm, the values of S_{11} is reduced by about 5dB and the minimum value of S_{21} is increased by 0.5 dB. The experimental testing shows that the optimization scheme of adding anti-pad on the ground can solve the impedance mismatch problem and ensure the high-quality electrical connection of solder joints.

IV. CONCLUSION

In this paper, the effect of solder joints on the electrical connection's quality was studied. The characteristic impedance discontinuity of solder joints increases signal return loss, which results in poor signal integrity. Using transmission line theory, three schemes were proposed for compensating the characteristic impedance discontinuity. In order to evaluate the performance of the schemes, electromagnetic numerical simulation models were developed.

For the optimization of the solder joint, the smaller the size, the better the performance. For the optimization of dielectric substrate structure, when the variable $\Delta h=0.08mm$, the characteristic impedance is nearly 50Ω and the performance is the best. For the optimization of ground structure, when the anti-pad width W=0.4mm, the characteristic impedance is nearly 50Ω and the performance is the best.

Synthetically analyzing three compensation schemes, the compensation scheme of changing grounding structure is the easiest to produce and also has good performance. Based on this compensation scheme, the experimental measurements were conducted. The experimental results show good agreements with electromagnetic simulation results, which prove that compensation schemes can effectively improve the quality of electrical connection and signal integrity.

ACKNOWLEDGMENT

This work was supported in part by the National Natural Science Foundation of China (No. 51877010), in part by the Open Fund of State Key Laboratory of Information Photonics and Optical Communications, Beijing University of Posts and Telecommunications (BUPT), and in part by the Fundamental Research Funds for the Central Universities, BUPT (No.2019PTB-014).

REFERENCES

[1] C. Chang, K. Lin, "The microstructure and shear behavior of Zn–25Sn–XTi solder joints with Ni substrate," Journal of Materials Science: Materials in Electronics, vol.30, no.14, pp.13090-13098, 2019.

[2] Z. Liu, Y. Sun, "A solder joint crack-Characteristic impedance model based on transmission line theory," 10th International Conference on Reliability, Maintainability and Safety (ICRMS), pp.237-241, 2014.

[3] P. Manfredi, M. H. Azarian and F. G. Canavero, "Numerical simulation of impedance discontinuities resulting from degradation of interconnections on printed circuit boards," 2011 IEEE 15th Workshop on Signal Propagation on Interconnects (SPI), pp.93-96, 2011.

[4] L. W. Keat, L. Y. Hsiang, A. Munigayah and T. T. We, "Nonlinear dynamic behavior of thin PCB board for solder joint reliability study under shock loading," 2005 International Symposium on Electronics Materials and Packaging, pp.268-274, 2005.

[5] Z. Wang, J. Gao, H. M. Bilal, J. Luo and X. Li, "Impendence Compensation of the Welding Area of the RF Connector and Micro Strip Line," The 10th International Conference on Communications, Circuits and Systems, pp.190-194, 2018.

[6] B. Ben, S. Hu, X. Li, T. Long, "Study of Signal Integrity of Transient Structure from SMA Connector to PCB," 10th National Symposium on Signal and Intelligent Information Processing and Application, pp.16-21, 2016.

[7] W. Yu, X. Li, B. Wu, F. Wu, Y. Qian, "Study of Impedance Compensation of Micro Strip Line," Instrument Technique and Sensor, no.14, pp.88-91,2015.

[8] Y. Xu, E. Ping, M. Wang and H. Zheng, "Analysis of Discontinuity in Flip-Chip Interconnection for High-Speed Circuit," Journal of Microwaves, vol.34, no.05, pp.79-83, 2018.

[9] C. Huang, D. Zhou, Z. Wu, "Study on the Relationships between Solder Joint Process Parameters and Reliability of Plastic Ball Grid Array Component," Act Electronic Sonica, vol.33, no. 5, pp.788-792, 2005.

7th International Conference on Reliability of
Electrical Products and Electrical Contacts,
November 04-06, 2019

The Static Welding Phenomena of Electrical Contact Materials

Heng Wang[1], Xiaoping Bai[1], Wanbin Ren[2]
[1]Fuda Alloy Materials Co., Ltd., Wenzhou, 325025, China
[2]School of Electrical Engineering and Automation, Harbin Institute of Technology, Harbin 150001, China
E-mail: wh@china-fuda.com Tel: 86-577-86809706 Fax: 86-577-55888720

Abstract— **This paper provides a review of studies on the static welding phenomena of electrical contact materials, including the analysis of influential factors on static welding and the summary of experiment and theoretical investigation on static welding. Finally, suggestions are given for further studies aim at decreasing the static welding force.**

Index Terms— **Electrical contact materials, Static welding, Electric relay, Circuit breaker**

I. INTRODUCTION

Low voltage distribution system has full range selective protection, it provides safer and more stability electric, this hopes the distribution switch in this system has higher short time withstand current value. It is an important way to improve the short-time withstand current of switching device to analyze the mechanism of static welding in the process of electrical contact and to produce electrical contacts with low welding force.

Electrical contact materials are widely used in electric relays and circuit breakers as core components of electrical switch and instruments and meters [1-3]. The main reason of the electrical equipment fault is the welding of electrical contact materials [4]. Electrical contact welding is divided into two types: dynamic welding and static welding [5]. The welding is connected with contact current, voltage, pressure and arcing time from its appearance to its completion [6], these connections are some function relationships. These functional relationships have been studied at home and abroad, especially in dynamic welding. For example Zhenbiao Li [7] studied on the dynamic welding mechanism of electromagnetic relay contact materials, he proposed that the occurrence of dynamic welding of the contact depends on the condensation of the molten metal, and dynamic welding will occur when the contact turns into condensed metal during the closing process; Xiangjun Liu [8] put forward the mathematical model of contact dynamic welding, which derived the formula for calculating contact dynamic welding force. At present, there are few researches on static welding of electrical contact materials, the relevant data are mostly obtained by probability statistics method [9, 10]. So, the study on static welding of electrical contact materials has important guiding significance for how to select electric relays and circuit breakers.

II. INFLUENCE FACTORS OF STATIC WELDING OF ELECTRICAL CONTACT MATERIALS

In a fixed contact connection or a closed contact with large enough contact force, the fusion welding of the conductive spot and the metal near it due to the heating of the contact resistance is called static welding [5]. The occurrence of static welding of electrical contact materials is related to many factors, including current, choice of contact materials, manufacturing process, etc.

A. Current

There is such a relationship between static welding and current: when a current pass a pair of closed contacts, the current increases gradually from zero, when the current reaches a certain value, the thin layer in the spot a on the contact inner surface of the two contacts is just beginning to melt, and the contact resistance decreased, if turn the current off at this moment, it's easy to separate the two contact, slight traces of melting may be observed on the contact surface, then the current called start melting current. If the current increases further and is more than start melting current 20-30%, the spot a and the metal nearby it will melt in large area and the contact will start to weld. At this time, a certain pulling force must be applied to separate the two contacts. The current when the contact starts to weld is called start welding current. If the current increases further, the melting zone nearby spot a is developing in depth, making the welding stronger and the welding force increases until reaches the tensile strength.

The start melting current of the contacts and the time for the current to pass through the contacts are shown in Fig. 1 [5]. Fig. 1 shows the test results of the start melting current i corresponding to a pair of surface contact copper contacts with contact area of 50 times 15 square millimeters at different electrification time t. You can see from the curve that when the current passes through the contacts for a very short time (t is less than 1 second in the conditions shown in Fig 1), the start melting current value is very large, and the smaller t is, the value of i increases more rapidly. When the electrification time t is greater than 1 second, the start melting current no longer changes, which shows up no relation to t. The reason for this is that the volume of spot a and the melting zone nearby it is very small (the size of spot a is within a few tenths of a millimeter) and its thermal time constant is very small (milliseconds). When the electrification time reaches 4 times of the thermal time constant, the temperature is close to the stable state. Therefore, for the melting area of spot a, even if the electrification time is very short (e.g., within 1 second), it has already reached a stable state. Therefore, when t is more than 1 second, the start melting current has no relation to the electrification time.

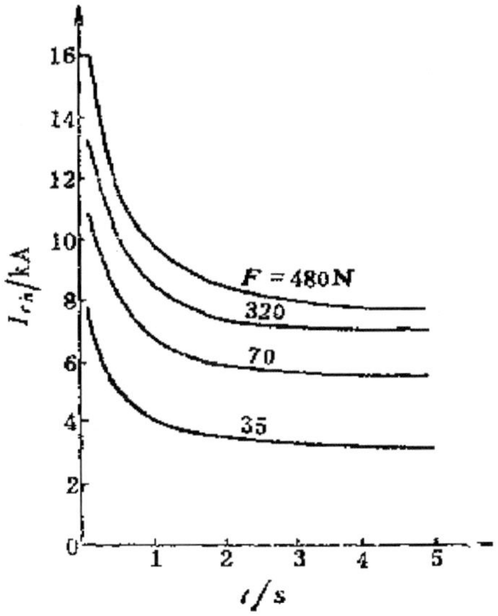

Fig. 1 the relationship between the start melting current and the electrification time of the copper contacts [5]

B. Physical Parameters

The physical parameters of contact materials such as melting point, specific heat, density, thermal conductivity, resistivity, etc. have direct influence on its static welding. Zhenbiao Li pointed out that for a kind of contact material, the more heat the K_{wt} required by current heating to reach its melting point, and the better static welding resistance it will be. He gave the K_{wt} values of some materials as shown in Table 1. Therefore, the order of the static welding resistance ability is as follows: Ag→Cu→W→Pt→Ni→Fe→Sn.

C. Hardness

M. Kaplan et al. [12] proposed that the K_{wt} of static welding criterion of electrical contact materials is determined by hardness H_0. The higher the hardness H_0 is, the smaller the K_{wt} is. The higher the static welding force is, the worse static welding resistance is. The specific data are shown in Table 2.

TABLE I

K_{WT} VALUES [11]

Material	K_{wt}
Ag	26.6
Cu	20.4
W	4.38
Pt	1.77
Ni	1.5
Fe	1.1
Sn	0.406

TABLE II

THE RELATIONSHIP BETWEEN K_{WT} AND H_0 [12]

Material	H_0(N/mm^2)	K_{wt}
Ag	250	1.07
Au	200	1.15
Cu	350	0.88
Al	270	0.67
Cd	160	0.48
Pt	400	0.34
Zn	330	0.33
Ni	700	0.21
Fe	620	0.2
Co	1250	0.12
W	3500	0.05

D. Tensile Strength

P. g. Slade proposed [13] static welding force F_w of electrical contact materials is the product of tensile strength Γ and welding area A_w. The larger Γ is the larger F_w is, the static welding resistance is worse. At the same time he listed the tensile strength of several materials, as shown in Table 3.

TABLE III

Γ VALUES [13]

Material	Γ(10^8Nm^{-2})
Cu (as-cast)	1.2-1.7
Cu (as-extruded)	2.0-4.0
Cu wire (hard state)	4.0-4.6
Cu wire (as-annealed)	2.8-3.1
Ag wire	2.3-3.5
W wire	15-35

E. Alloying Elements

By adding alloying elements into the electrical contact materials, the principle of segregation is used to make the electrical contacts to become brittle in the area of static welding, thus reducing the static welding force. For example, Wansheng Zhang [14] added Ni to CuW alloys, H. R. Geng et Al. [15] added Al to CuCr alloys, and K. Ozawa [16] added Bi, Se and other elements that could reduce the melting point to CuCrFe alloys. B. J. Ding et al. [17] added different content of brittle C to CuCr alloys. The parameters of the alloys are shown in Table 4. Proved by tests that the static welding force is the lowest when C content is 1.8%.

TABLE IV

PHYSICAL PARAMETERS OF CuCr ALLOYS WITH DIFFERENT C CONTENTS [17]

Cu/Cr	C(wt%)	Brinell Hardness	Ultimate Strength (MPa)	Conductivity ($10^3\Omega$/mm)
70/30	1.8	114-129	120	19.8-22.2
60/40	2.38	132-141	110	16.3-17.1
50/50	0.28	101-107	290	18.9-20.1
50/50	0	80-90	380	16-17.5

F. Manufacturing Technology

The manufacturing technology of electrical contact materials is usually divided into melting method, oxidation method and powder metallurgy method, among them the static welding force is lower within the powder metallurgy method. Sujia Fu [18] used two different processes to prepare CuCr electrical contact materials, one was infiltration process and the other was sintering process. Tensile Strength of the electrical contact materials prepared by infiltration process was 350 MPa, by sintering process was 280 MPa. Sujia Fu believes that the static welding resistance ability of electrical contact materials which was prepared by infiltration process is strong, the reason may be that its tensile strength was low, its tissues were easily stretched to fracture in practical applications, at the same time, more metal droplets were produced by arc erosion, which caused serious burning damage. The electrical contact materials which were prepared by infiltration process had good static welding resistance ability and could meet practical application. Cr droplets could also absorb gas well during arc erosion, make sure the contacts were not severely eroded.

III. THEORETICAL CALCULATION FORMULA FOR STATIC WELDING OF ELECTRICAL CONTACT MATERIALS

P. G. Slade thinks that [13], when electrical contact materials occur static welding, there is an area here, this area is mostly like a spheroid. Assuming that the radius of the spheroid is equal to the radius of welding, the energy produced by the current is used for the heating of the spheroid. Under this assumption, the static welding force of electrical contact materials F_w is calculated as formula (1):

$$F_w = KW_c^{2/3} \tag{1}$$

In formula (1), W_c is the energy produced by current, as shown in formula (2):

$$W_c = \int_{t_c} V_c I dt \tag{2}$$

In formula (2), t_c is the contact time and V_c is the pressure drop. In formula (1), K is shown in formula (3):

$$K = \Gamma\pi\left\{\frac{3}{4\pi\delta\left[C_v(T_m - T_b) + C_L\right]}\right\}^{2/3} \tag{3}$$

In formula (3) Γ is tensile strength, δ is density, C_v is specific heat, C_L is latent heat, T_m is melting temperature, T_b is initial temperature.

A. Tslaf believes [19] that the static welding process of electrical contact materials is a temperature rise process, and the temperature rise can be calculated by calculating the pressure drop. The static welding force of electrical contact materials depends on ηw, as shown in formula (4), the larger the value of η_w is the smaller the static welding force is.

$$\eta_w = \int_{\theta_0}^{\theta_m} \frac{\lambda(\theta)d\theta}{\sqrt{\int_{\theta_0}^{\theta_m} \rho_d(\theta)\lambda d\theta}} \tag{4}$$

In formula (4), θ_m is melting point, θ_0 is environment temperature, λ is thermal conductivity, ρ_d is resistivity.

M. Kaplan thinks [12] that the static welding force of electrical contact materials can be calculated by using the thermal state equation, and its size depends on K_{wt} as shown in formula (5). The larger the value is, the smaller the static welding force is.

$$K_{wt} = \frac{1}{H}\sqrt{\int_{\theta_0}^{\theta_m} \frac{\rho_m C_p(\theta)}{\rho_d(\theta)} d\theta} \tag{5}$$

In formula (5), H is hardness, θ_m is melting point, θ_0 is environmental temperature, ρ_m is density, C_p is specific heat capacity, ρ_d is resistivity.

Zhenbiao Li [11] believes that the electrostatic welding force is influenced by the paired manner of electrical contact materials. The static welding is different with different paired manner. The static welding force is determined by K_w, the larger K_w is, the smaller static welding force is, when electrical contact material is symmetrically matched, K_w is shown in formula (6).

$$K_w' = \frac{\theta_m\sqrt{C_p\rho_m\lambda}}{\rho_d}\frac{1}{\pi\sigma}\sqrt{\frac{F_c}{\pi H_c} + \left(\frac{3}{2}\cdot\frac{F_c R}{E}\right)^{2/3}} \tag{6}$$

In formula (6), θ_m is melting point, C_p is specific heat capacity, ρ_m is density, ρ_d is resistivity, λ is thermal conductivity, σ is welding strength, F_c is closing force, H_c is hardness, R is spherical radius, E is elastic modulus.

When the electrical contact materials is asymmetrical contact pair, k_w' is shown in formula (7).

$$K_w' = \frac{\theta_m\left[\lambda_1\sqrt{\lambda_2 C_{p1}\rho_{m1}} + \lambda_2\sqrt{\lambda_1 C_{p2}\rho_{m2}}\right]}{\sqrt{\lambda_1\lambda_2}(\rho_{1d} + \rho_{2d})}\frac{1}{\pi\sigma}\sqrt{\frac{F_c}{\pi H_c} + \left[\frac{3}{4}\cdot F_c R\left(\frac{1}{E_1} + \frac{1}{E_2}\right)\right]^{2/3}} \tag{7}$$

In formula (7), 1 is the moving contact parameter and 2 is the static contact parameter.

In this way, Zhenbiao Li also improved the theoretical formula of A. Tslaf [20], when electrical contact material is symmetrically matched, η_w is shown in formula (8).

$$\eta_w = \int_0^{T_0} \frac{\lambda_1 dT_1}{\sqrt{2\int_T^{T_0} \rho_1\lambda_1 dT + 2\int_{T_0}^{T_m} \rho_2\lambda_2 dT}} \quad (8)$$

When the electrical contact materials is asymmetrical contact pair, η_w is shown in formula (9).

$$\eta_w = \int_0^{T_m} \frac{\lambda(T_1)dT_1}{\sqrt{\int_{T_1}^{T_m} \rho_d(T_2)\lambda(T_2)dT_2}} \quad (9)$$

In formulas (8) and (9), 1 is the moving contact parameter and 2 is the static contact parameter. At the same time, Zhenbiao Li believes that the heating process of static welding of electrical contact materials is divided into two stages. The first stage is pre-heating stage, the contact material does not occur any phase transition in this stage. The second stage is the heating stage, in this stage the current density in the contact spot area is evenly distributed, the contact surface melts and the electrical contacts occur phase transition.

IV. THE TEST METHOD FOR STATIC WELDING OF ELECTRICAL CONTACT MATERIALS

J. Ambier et al. [21] studied on the static welding between 5-10 KA of $AgSnO_2$ electrical contact materials with different oxide weights and particle sizes. The characteristics diagram of the testing device is shown in Fig 2.

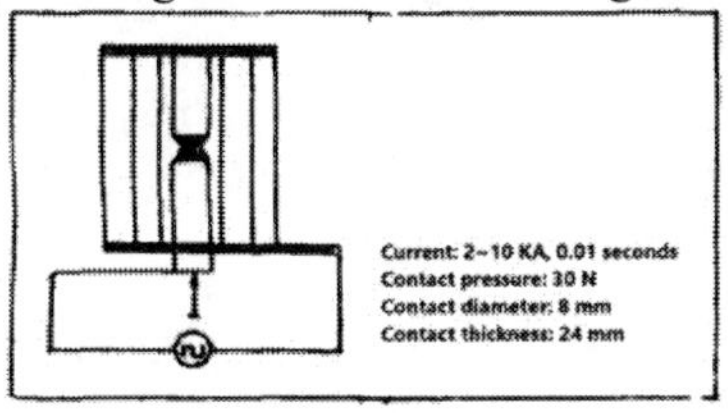

Fig. 2 Characteristics diagram of static welding force testing device [21]

Test method: the contact pressure is 30 N, record the changes of voltage, current and contact pressure when 50Hz half-wave current is switched on. After the test, the contact resistance and the force F_s required to pull the contact are recorded, and the force F_s is the welding force. The results are shown in Fig 3, it can be seen that the static welding force of $AgSnO_2$ electrical contact materials decrease with the increase of oxide weight and size. The static welding force data of $AgSnO_2$ electrical contact materials with Ag content of 92% and particle size of 10 μm and Ag content of 86% and particle size of 3 μm are better than other materials.

Our company uses XTS-12D pulse current test device to test the static welding force of pure silver solid contacts with different hardness. The test device is shown in Fig 4 [22]. Test method: the fixed contact components were installed respectively on the upper and lower of the fixtures, then turned on the power and started stepping motor to drive the shaft put a prescriptive pressure on the fixtures, after pressure holding for a while applied a prescriptive current to the contacts. After impact, the stepping motor is started to drive the lever to move upward, at this time, the tensile force value displayed on the digital display device connected with the sensor is the static welding force value. In this test, the impulse voltage is 1.5 KV, the impulse current is 3.21 KA, the contact pressure is 3.92-15.68 N, the diameter of the contact is 6 mm, and the thickness of the contact is 1.5 mm.

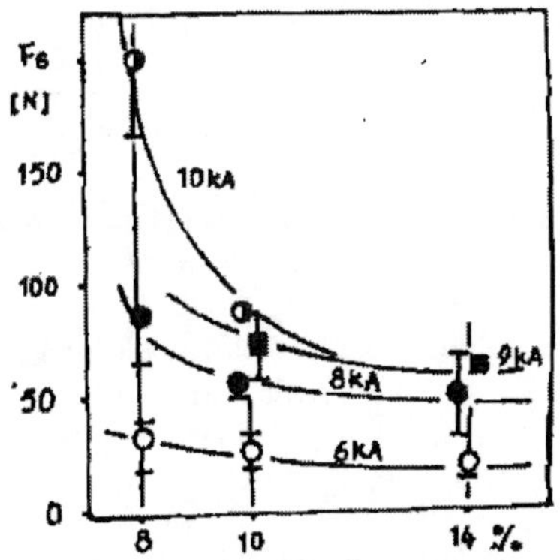

Fig. 3 Relationship between static welding force and oxide content [21]

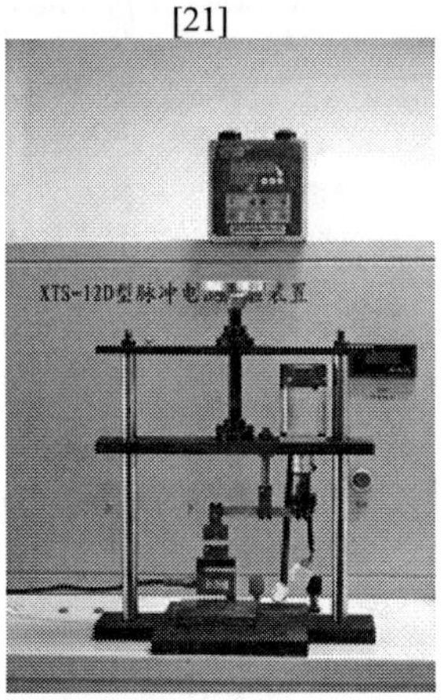

Fig. 4 The static welding force testing device for electrical contact materials of Fuda

The curve of static welding force of pure silver solid contacts with different hardness is shown in Fig 5. You can see, with the increase of the pressure P and the hardness HV decreases, the static welding force all appears the decreasing trend. When $P < 9.90$ N the decreasing trend is obvious, when $P > 9.90$ N the decreasing trend is becoming less and less obvious, when $P = 13.89$ N and $P = 15.68$ N the static welding force of contacts with the same hardness changes little.

V. CONCLUDING REMARKS

To sum up, the purpose of studying static welding of electrical contact materials is to find a measure to reduce the harm caused by static welding on electrical appliances. According to the above, the method of reducing static welding can be obtained:

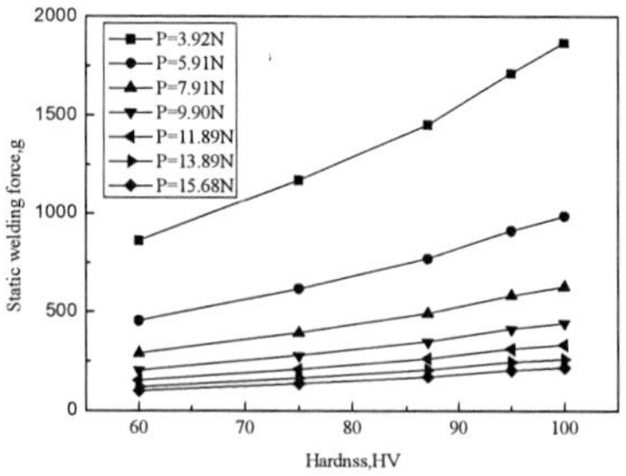

Fig. 5 The curve of static welding force of pure silver solid contacts with different hardness

1) Static welding force of electrical contact material is inversely proportional to melting point, specific heat, density and thermal conductivity, and directly proportional to hardness and tensile strength, so electrical contact material should use materials with high melting point, low hardness and tensile strength as possible;

2) The choice of the theoretical calculation formula is the direct evidence to judge whether the electrical contact material occurs static welding, and the theoretical calculation formula can also play a guiding role in the test;

3) The static welding testing device for electrical contact materials which was developed by Fuda through independent research and development is simple and fast in operation, it is the first choice device to test the static welding force of electrical contact materials.

REFERENCES

[1] Saibei Wang, Ming Xie, Manmen Liu, et al. Research progress of AgNi contact materials [J]. Rare metal materials and engineering, 2013, 42(4): 875-880.

[2] Heng Wang, Suhua Li, Liqiang Liu, et al. Research review on CuW electrical contact materials [J]. Electrical engineering materials, 2014, 5: 11-17.

[3] Yonggen Wang, Xiaoqing Cao, Yuping Ni, et al. Application of contact materials in low voltage apparatus [J]. Low voltage apparatus, 2011, 10: 58-61.

[4] Yanchuan Li. Transient thermal analysis of low-voltage electric apparatus contact and its application in anti-welding [J]. Electrotechnics Electric, 2012, 10: 25-27.

[5] Zhenbiao Li, Guansheng Zhang, Qingsheng Qin. Static welding resistance of electric contact materials [J]. Proceedings of the CSEE, 1994, 14(1): 34-39.

[6] Wanbin Ren, Qiong Yu, Guofu Zhai. Failure Analysis of Electrical Contacts for Electromagnetic Relay with Switched Type Contacts [J]. Electrical engineering materials, 2011, 1: 14-23.

[7] Zhenbiao Li, Ling Jin, Liang Huang, et al. Mechanism analysis on dynamic welding of electromagnetic relay contacts [J]. Low voltage apparatus, 2007, 5: 1-3.

[8] Xiangjun Liu, Hongjun Fei. A new mathematical model of dynamic welding for electric contacts [J]. Transactions of China electrotechnical society, 2002, 17(1): 81-84.

[9] H. Yamasaki, T. Ishii. An estimation of closing current of electrical contacts for power switches[C]. Proc 30th IEEE Holm Conf. on Electrical Contacts, 1984: 281-288.

[10] C. H. Leung, P. C. Wingert. Microstructure effects on dynamic welding of Ag-W contacts[C]. Proc 33rd IEEE Holm Conf. on Electrical Contacts, 1987: 133-136.

[11] Zhenbiao Li, Guansheng Zhang. Research on the criterion of static welding of electric contact [J]. High voltage apparatus, 1991,1: 11-16.

[12] M. Kaplan, A. Tslaf. Criteria for the weldability of contact material in adiabatic transient conditions[J]. IEEE Trans. on CHMT, 1984, 17(1): 33-38.

[13] P. G. Slade. Electrical Contacts[M]. Marcel Dekker, Inc., New York-basel, 1999: 513- 519.

[14] Tiansheng Zhang. Silver saving of electrical contact and industry development [J]. Electrician alloy, 1995, 3: 8-11.

[15] H. R. Geng, Y. Liu, C. Z. Chen, et al. Laser surface remelting of Cu-Cr-Fe contact material[J]. Materials Science and Technology, 2000, 5: 564- 567.

[16] K. Ozawa. Sintered CuCrFe alloy for vacuum circuit breaker contact[C]. Proc International Conf. on Electrical Contacts, Electronmechanical Components and Their Applications, Nagoya, 1986: 823- 830.

[17] B. J. Ding, H. Q. Li, X. T. Wang, et al. Residual carbon in CuCr contact materials[J]. IEEE Trans. on CHMT, 1990, 13(2): 414- 416.

[18] Sujia Fu. Microstructures and interrupting behaviors of CuCr contacts made by P/M manufacture processes [J]. Electrical engineering materials, 2003, 2: 3-9.

[19] A. Tslaf. A thermophysical criterion for the weldability of electrical contact material in a steady-state regime [J]. IEEE Trans. on CHMT, 1982, 5(1): 147- 152.

[20] Z. B. Li, G. S. Zhang. The study of the criterion for dynamic welding of electrical contact[C]. Proc 16th International Conf. on Electrical Contacts, 1992: 34-40.

[21] J. Ambier. Research on the 5-10 KA appearance of static welding of AgSnO2 electric contact [J]. Electrician alloy collection, 1989, Z1: 96-101.

[22] Wei Weng, Suhua Li, Heng Wang, et al. Testing device for static welding force of electric contact materials and its testing method [P]. Chinese patent: ZL 201310212917.3.

7th International Conference on Reliability of
Electrical Products and Electrical Contacts,
November 04-06, 2019

Research on Cogging Torque Reduction of Hub Motor for Electric Bicycle

Zhijun Zou, Changchun Chi, Huaying Li
School of Electrical Engineering, Shanghai Dianji University, Shanghai 201306, China
E-mail: 237583812@qq.com Tel: 17076860423

Abstract—**To improve the reliability and efficiency of the hub motor for electric bicycle, the basic expression of cogging torque is given based on the energy method and Fourier series analysis method, and the factors affecting the cogging torque are analyzed. the cogging torque of a 54 slot and 48 pole table stick radial permanent magnet hub motor for electric bicycle was calculated by Ansoft finite element software. Finally, a method to weaken the cogging torque is proposed: optimizing the size of the auxiliary cogging of stator teeth by response surface method, which use the multiple quadratic regression equation fitting the functional relationship between factors and response values and the analysis of regression equation to find the optimal process parameters. The simulation results show that this method effectively reduces the cogging torque of the hub motor, and after optimization, the peak-to-peak value of it decreases from 4.0091N.m to 2.1594N.m, down by 46%, which improves the reliability of the hub motor.**

Index Terms— **Hub motor, Finite element analysis, Response surface method, Cogging torque weakening**

I. INTRODUCTION

With the deepening of the concept of green environment and the rapid development of science and technology, the new energy vehicle industry has risen rapidly, which has spawned a series of new vehicles such as new energy vehicles, electric motorcycles and electric bicycles. As the core driving component of electric bicycles, the hub motor is of great significance. Cogging torque is an important indicator of the performance of permanent magnet hub motors. Reducing the cogging torque is important for improving the reliability and efficiency of the hub motor and riding comfort.

Many researchers have studied the weakening of the cogging torque of the hub motor and obtained some research results. According to the references 1, in the non-ideal state, the permanent magnet hub motor has cogging torque under the condition of stator ellipse and permanent magnet offset; In the references 2, the model of the vehicle hub motor with the auxiliary slot is established and the cogging torque is optimized. In the references 3, the influence of different pole slot matching on cogging torque is studied, and the optimization strategy of rotor tooth opening auxiliary groove is proposed. The influence of different auxiliary groove type and size on the positioning torque of permanent magnet motor is studied in references 4. In the references 5, the cogging torque corresponding to different slots is analyzed, and a method is proposed to determine the optimal auxiliary tooth width and the auxiliary tooth height.

In this paper, a 54-slot 48-pole surface-mounted radial permanent magnet hub motor for an electric bicycle is analyzed. Under the condition of opening two auxiliary rectangular grooves, considering the influence of the groove width, the groove depth and the angle of the groove center line on the cogging torque, the optimal auxiliary groove size is found in combination with the response surface method to weaken the cogging torque and improve Reliability and efficiency of the hub motor.

II. MECHANISM ANALYSIS OF COGGING TORQUE GENERATION

The cogging torque is a tangential component of the force between the permanent magnet magnetic field and the cogging, and its direction always faces the direction in which the magnetic energy product becomes small. According to the virtual displacement theory, the cogging torque is the negative partial derivative of the air gap magnetic field energy storage to the rotor position angle when the stator winding is not energized [8], which is defined as:

$$T_{\mathrm{cog}}=-\frac{\partial W}{\partial \alpha} \tag{1}$$

In the equation (1), α is the initial position of the stator, that is, the angle θ between the center line of the stator teeth and the center line of the permanent magnet pole, and $\theta=0$ is defined as the center line of the permanent magnet pole [9], as shown in Figure 1.

The magnetic field energy can be approximated as the energy in the air gap and the permanent magnet [6], which can be described as:

$$W = W_{gap} + W_{pm} = \frac{1}{2\mu}\int_V B^2 dV \tag{2}$$

The magnetic field density B in equation (2) and the position α of the rotor have the following relationship:

$$B(\theta,\alpha) = B_r(\theta)\frac{h_m(\theta)}{h_m(\theta)+G(\theta,\alpha)} \tag{3}$$

In the equation (3), $B_r(\theta)$ is a permanent magnet remanence, $h_m(\theta)$ is a length of the permanent magnet in the magnetization direction, and $G(\theta,\alpha)$ is an effective length of the air gap. Substituting equation (3) into equation (2), the magnetic field energy can be written as below:

$$W = \frac{1}{2\mu}\int_V B_r^2(\theta)\left(\frac{h_m(\theta)}{h_m(\theta)+G(\theta,\alpha)}\right)^2 dV \tag{4}$$

By performing Fourier decomposition on $B_r(\theta)$ and $\left(\frac{h_m(\theta)}{h_m(\theta)+G(\theta,\alpha)}\right)^2$ in equation (4), the magnetic field energy can be obtained and substituted into equation (1) to get the expression of cogging torque.

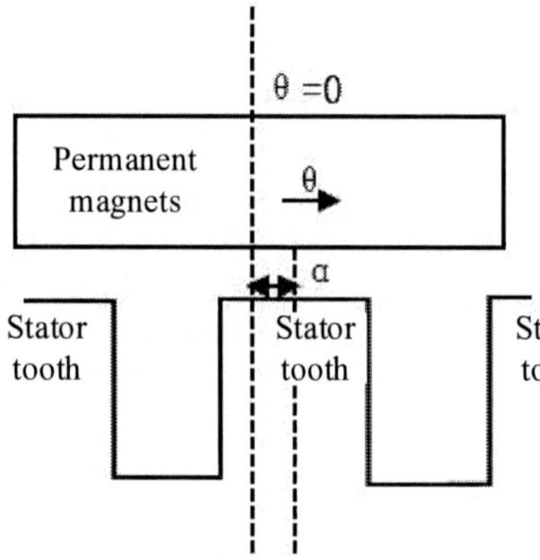

Fig. 1 Relative position diagram of permanent magnet and stator

(1) Fourier decomposition of $B_r(\theta)$

The distribution of $B_r(\theta)$ is shown in Figure 2, and its Fourier decomposition is obtained in the interval $\left[\frac{-\pi}{2P},\frac{\pi}{2P}\right]$:

$$B_r^2(\theta) = \alpha_P B_r^2 + \sum_{n=1}^{\infty} B_r^2 \sin(n\alpha_P\pi)cos(2np\theta) \tag{5}$$

Where α_P, B_r and p are the permanent magnet magnetic pole arc coefficient, permanent magnet remanence density and pole pair.

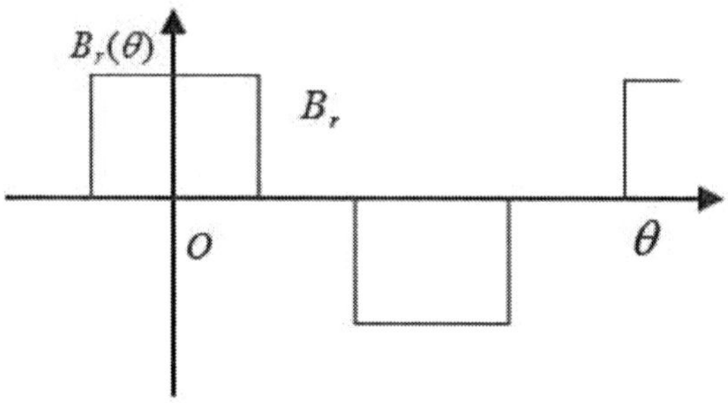

Fig. 2 The distribution of $B_r(\theta)$

(2) Fourier decomposition of $\left(\frac{h_m(\theta)}{h_m(\theta)+G(\theta,\alpha)}\right)^2$

In the interval $\left[\frac{-\pi}{Z},\frac{\pi}{Z}\right]$, its Fourier decomposition is obtained:

$$\left(\frac{h_m(\theta)}{h_m(\theta)+G(\theta,\alpha)}\right)^2 = G_0 + \sum_{n=1}^{\infty} G_n cos(nz(\theta+\alpha)) \tag{6}$$

(3) Cogging torque expression

Substituting equations (5) and (6) into equations (2) and (1), and considering the orthogonality of trigonometric functions, when the frequencies of two sine or cosine functions are not equal, the integral of their product is 0 in the range of 2π, so that only the item that makes $nz/2p$ an integer is left, and the cogging torque expression is sorted as:

$$T_{cog}(\alpha) = \frac{nzL_{Fe}}{4\mu_0}(R_2^2 - R_1^2)\sum_{n=1}^{\infty} nG_n B_{r(\frac{nz}{2p})} \sin(nz\alpha) \tag{7}$$

Where,

$B_r(\theta)$ ----the distribution of permanent magnet remanence in the circumferential direction;

$G(\theta,\alpha)$ ----The circumferential effective distribution of the effective air gap length at the angle between the magnetic pole center line and the tooth center line;

h_m ----Permanent magnet body magnetization direction length;

L_{Fe} ----Armature core length;

α ----The center line of the magnetic pole is at an angle to the center line of the tooth;

P ----Number of pole pairs;

Z ----Number of slots;

R_1 ----Armature outer diameter;

R_2 ----Inner diameter of the stator yoke;

III. ESTABLISHMENT OF MOTOR MODEL

A. Motor model

In this paper, Ansoft software is used to model and finite element analysis of the 54-slot 48-pole electric bicycle hub motor. The main parameters of the motor are shown in Table I.

In order to improve the speed of the finite element analysis, the 1/6 model of the motor was simulated. The analytical model of the motor is shown in Figure 3.

TABLE I
MAIN PARAMETERS OF THE MOTOR

Quantity	Parameter
Number of stator slots	54
Stator outer diameter	204 mm
Stator inner diameter	160 mm
Stator core length	30 mm
Stator punching material	DW310-35
Winding method	star connection scheme
Wire diameter	0.78 mm
Magnetic pole pair	24
Rotor outer diameter	226 mm
Rotor inner diameter	205 mm
Rotor core length	30 mm
Permanent magnet brand	N38M
Polar arc coefficient	1
Magnetic steel width	3.5 mm

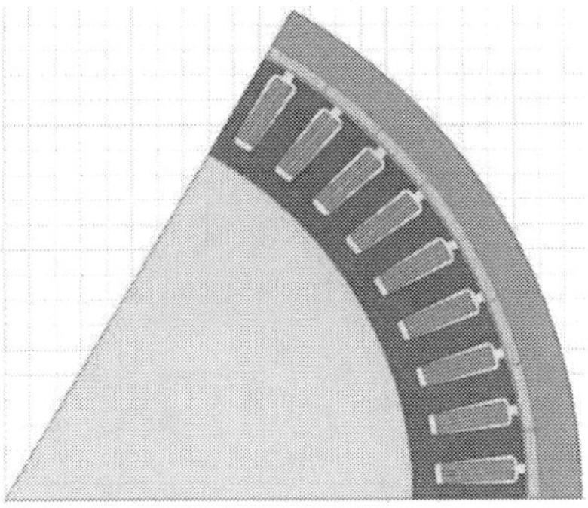

Fig. 3 1/6 analysis model of the hub motor

B. Stator tooth slotting

Among the three auxiliary grooves of rectangular groove, triangular groove and semi-circular groove, the rectangular groove has the best effect of suppressing cogging torque [4]. The auxiliary slot itself generates harmonics. In order to reduce the positioning torque, the harmonics generated by the auxiliary groove should be reversed from the harmonics generated by the original stator, that is, the auxiliary grooves are symmetrically arranged along the center line of the stator teeth. Therefore, the method adopted in this paper is to analyze the cogging torque by opening two auxiliary rectangular grooves in the stator teeth, as shown in Fig. 4, which is the width of the auxiliary groove, which is the depth of the auxiliary groove, and is the adjacent auxiliary groove. Center line angle.

IV. OPTIMIZED DESIGN

The response surface method (RSM) is a statistical method that uses a multivariate quadratic regression equation to fit the relationship between the factor and the response value, and analyzes the regression equation to reveal the interaction between the multivariate factors to find the optimal parameters.

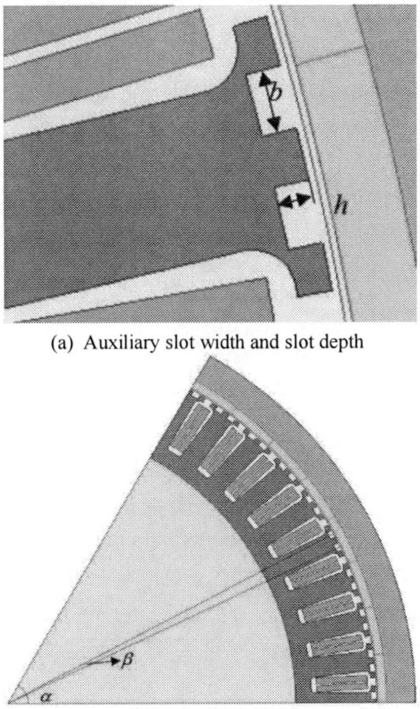

(a) Auxiliary slot width and slot depth

(b) Auxiliary groove center line angle

Fig. 4 Auxiliary tank parameters of the hub motor

RSM design methods include: center combination design (CCD), BOX-Behnken design (BBD), secondary saturated D-optimal design, and uniform design. In this paper, the wheel-electric motor, due to the influence of nonlinear factors, the relationship between the independent variable and the response is unknown, and the independent variables are interactive, so the second-order response model is used to obtain the appropriate response function.

In this paper, using the BBD method, with the help of Design-Expert, the software processes the slot width, slot depth and slot center angle of the auxiliary slot to find the optimal auxiliary groove size.

Second-order model approximation:

$$y(x) = \beta_0 + \sum_{i=1}^{k} \beta_i x_i + \sum_{i=1}^{k} \beta_{ii} x_i^2 + \sum_{i=1}^{k} \beta_{ij} x_i x_j + \varepsilon \quad (8)$$

Where β_i is the linear effect of x_i, β_{ii} is the quadratic effect of x_i, and β_{ij} is the interaction of $x_i x_j$.

The range of values of the arguments in this paper: $1 \le b \le 3$, $0.2 \le h \le 1.5$, $1.5 \le \beta \le 3$.

The three independent variables are represented by x_1, x_2, x_3, where that is β and the cogging torque is represented by y. The second-order regression equation is obtained by Design Expert software design:

$$\begin{aligned} y = & 10.551120 - 0.31194x_1 - 2.52695x_2 - 6.02616x_3 \\ & -0.19369x_1x_2 + 0.14047x_1x_3 - 0.79544x_2x_3 \\ & +0.075182x_1^2 + 2.87197x_2^2 + 1.37059x_3^2 \end{aligned} \tag{9}$$

It is solved by the second-order regression model equation, as shown in Figure 5 and Figure 6.

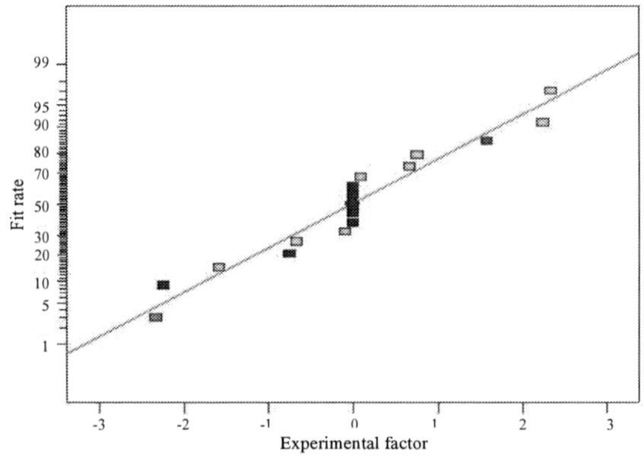

Fig. 5 Rankit diagram of the second-order regression model

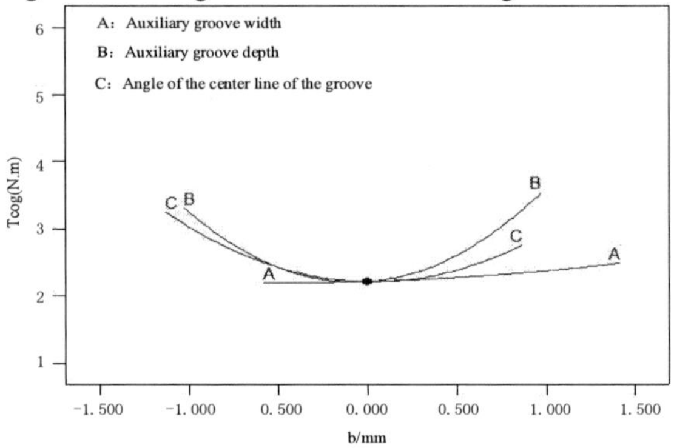

Fig. 6 Regression model equation curve

It can be seen from Figure 5 that the relationship between the order residual and the expected value is close to a linear relationship, and it can be seen that the regression model of the permanent magnet wheel motor is suitable and effective. At the same time, as can be seen from Figure 6, the size of the auxiliary groove width has the least effect on the cogging torque, and the change is extremely gentle, and the auxiliary groove depth has the largest variation to the cogging torque, and the groove center line has a similar angle, so it can pass Changing the groove depth and the center angle of the groove causes a significant change in cogging torque.

At the same time, a three-dimensional map of the interaction between the three variables can be obtained, and one of the independent variables is fixed, and the three-dimensional map of the influence of the interaction of the other two independent variables on the cogging torque is obtained, as shown in Figure 7 to Figure 9.

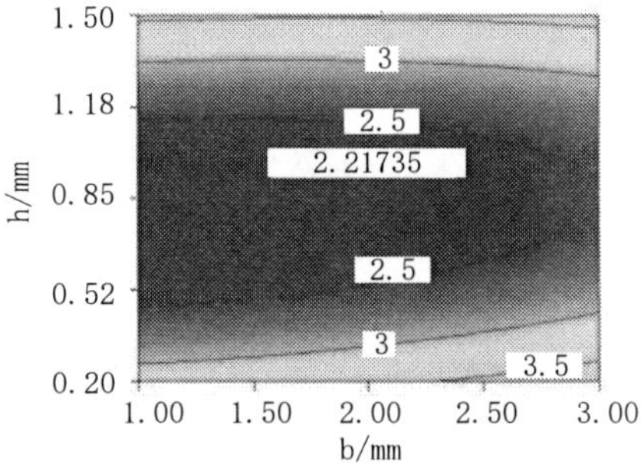

(a) Contour map

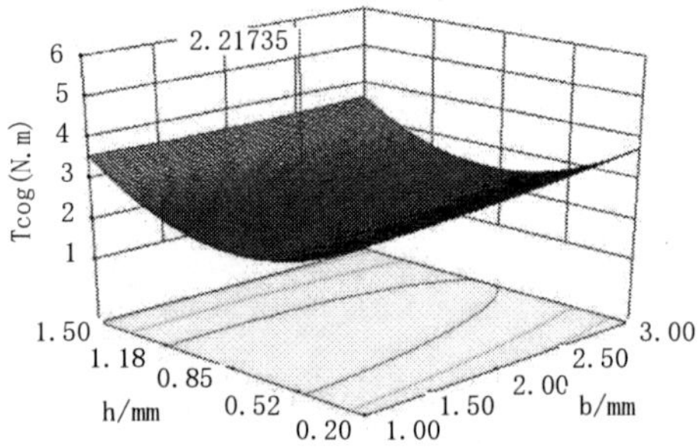

(b) Three-dimensional response map

Fig. 7 Interaction of groove width and groove height on cogging torque

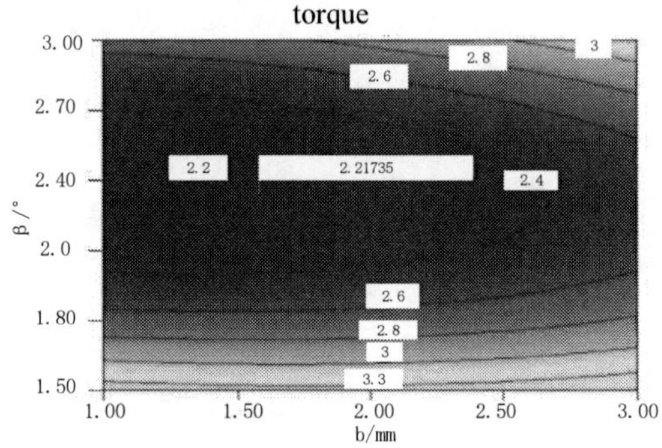

(a) Contour map

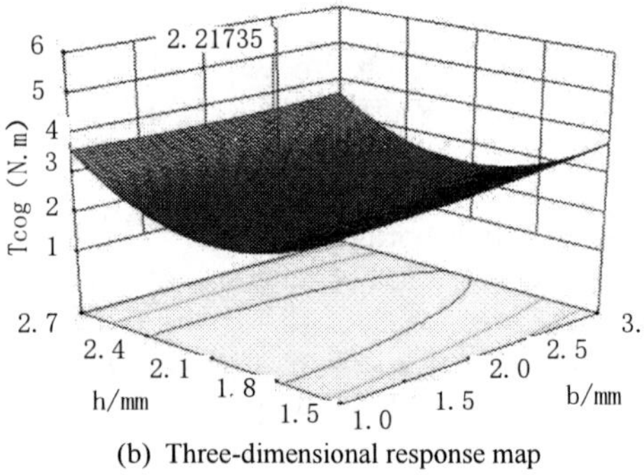

(b) Three-dimensional response map

Fig. 8 Interaction between slot width and slot centerline angle on cogging torque

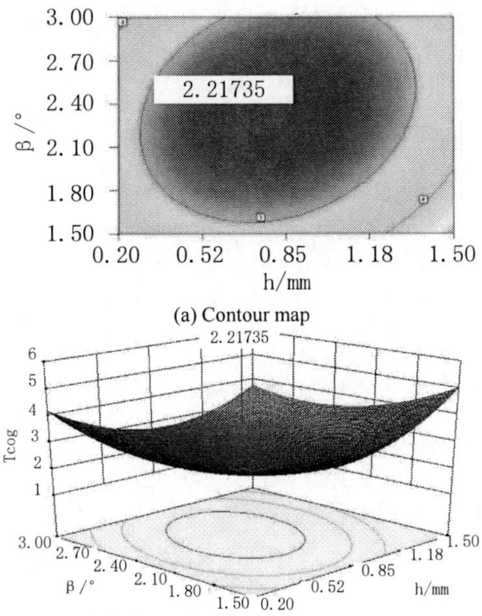

(a) Contour map

(b) Three-dimensional response map

Fig. 9 Interaction between slot height and slot centerline angle on cogging torque

It can be seen from Figure 7 to Figure 9 that the auxiliary groove width has little influence on the variation of the cogging torque, and the influence of the groove depth and the groove center line on the variation of the cogging torque is significant, and the permanent magnet wheel motor is verified. The rationality of the regression model also reflects the rationality of the size of the auxiliary groove.

Using the Design-Expert software to solve the second-order regression model, the optimal auxiliary slot size for the response surface optimization is (x_1, x_2, x_3) = (1. 58,0.87,2.35), and the cogging torque of the response function is y=2. 21735 Ngm .

The optimal solution b=1. 58 mm , h=0. 87 mm , $\beta = 2.35°$ is obtained by the response surface method, and the finite element simulation is shown in Figure 10.

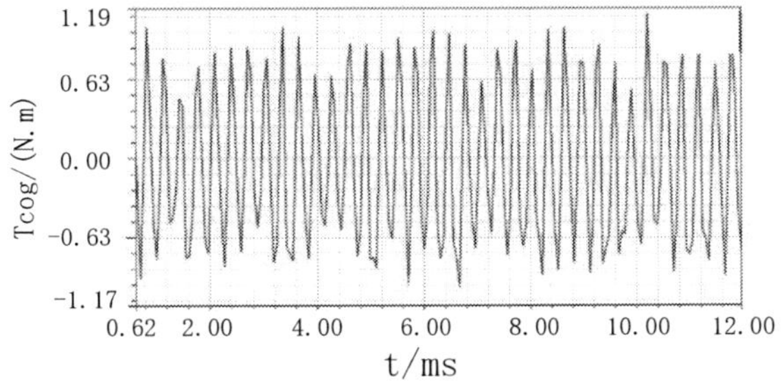

Fig. 10 Simulation results of cogging torque

The finite element simulation shows that the cogging torque varies with different auxiliary groove sizes as shown in Figure 11. As can be seen from Figure 11, the change in the size of the auxiliary groove to the cogging torque. The cogging torque changes in a parabolic manner as the width of the auxiliary groove increases. The cogging torque is minimized when the auxiliary groove depth is 0.9 mm and the groove center angle is 2.5°. Similar to the response surface method, the correctness of the method is verified.

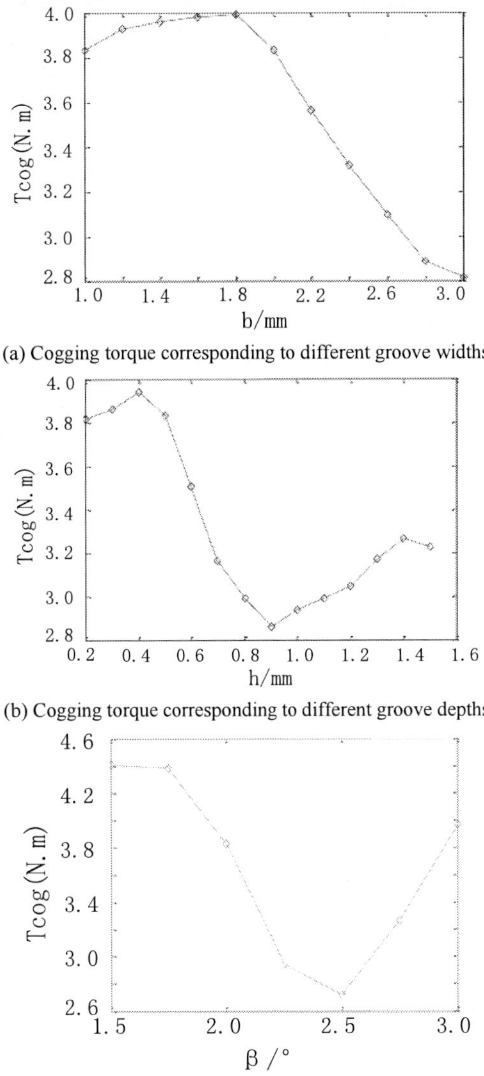

(a) Cogging torque corresponding to different groove widths

(b) Cogging torque corresponding to different groove depths

(c) Cogging torque corresponding to the angle between different centerlines

Fig. 11 Curve of cogging torque as a function of auxiliary groove size

As shown in Figure 12, the opening of two auxiliary parallel rectangular grooves effectively reduces the cogging torque of the hub motor, and optimizes the cogging torque peak-to-peak value of the auxiliary groove from 4.0091 N•m to 2.1594 N•m. The slot torque has dropped by 46%.

By comparing the simulation results of Ansoft finite element software with the results of response surface optimization, the peak-to-peak values of the cogging torque of the permanent magnet motor are basically the same, which verifies the feasibility and effectiveness of the surface response method.

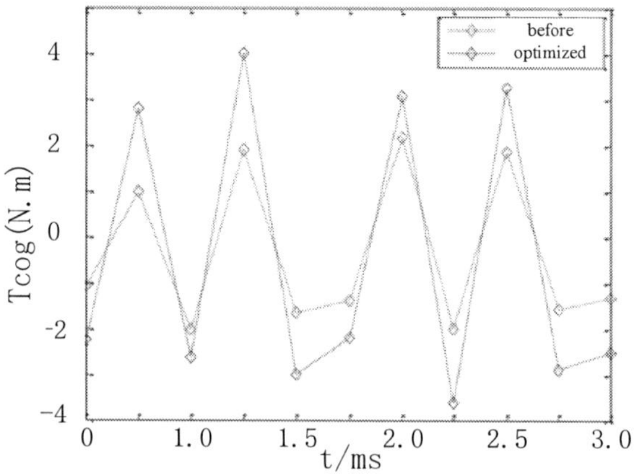

Fig. 12 Cogging torque curve before and after optimization

V. CONCLUSION

Aiming at the problem of selecting the size of the auxiliary slot when the permanent magnet brushless hub motor opens the auxiliary parallel rectangular groove, a new method of optimizing the size of the auxiliary groove by the response surface method is proposed. The new method is simple and effective, and the operation precision is high. It can ensure the running relationship between multiple variables at the same time, and the applicability is strong.

By comparing the finite element simulation results with the response surface optimization results, the peak-to-peak value of the cogging torque is basically the same, which effectively verifies the reliability and superiority of the response surface method to optimize the size of the auxiliary groove of the permanent magnet hub motor. From the cogging torque simulation result map and the cogging torque waveform diagram before and after optimization, it can be seen that opening the two auxiliary slots effectively reduces the cogging torque of the hub motor. The peak-to-peak value of the cogging torque of the auxiliary groove before and after optimization is reduced by 46%, which improves the reliability and efficiency of the hub motor for electric vehicles.

REFERENCES

[1] Shukang Cheng, Hailong Gong, Feng Chai, Hongwei Gao. Research on cogging torque of permanent magnet hub motor [J]. Proceeding of the CSEE, 2009, 29(30): 47-51.

[2] Jinge Yang, Zhaoxiang Deng, Yi Zhou, Heshan Zhang, Tao Tan. Analytical Modeling and Cogging Torque Reduction of Permanent Magnet Hub Motors for Vehicles [J]. Journal of Xi'An JiaoTong Universuty, 2018, 52(01):84-91+114.

[3] Baishan Mei, Dong Wang, Xiangjian Zhang. Research on Optimizing Rotor Weakening Cogging Torque of Permanent Magnet Synchronous Motor [J]. Small & Special Electrical Machines, 2018,46(10):38-41.

[4] Jiakuan Xia, Bing Yu. Stator tooth opening auxiliary slot suppresses the positioning torque of permanent magnet motor [J]. Small & Special Electrical Machines, 2010, 38(01):13-14+23.

[5] Qingling He, Xiaohua Bao. Reducing cogging torque in permanent-magnet synchronous motors by auxiliary teeth method, IEEE transactions on magnetics, vol. 55, no. 7, july 2019.

[6] Xiuhe Wang, Yubo Yang, Tingting Ding,etc. Research on Cogging Torque Reduction Method of Solid Rotor Permanent Magnet Synchronous Motor Based on Polar Arc Coefficient Selection [J]. Proceeding of the CSEE, 2005(15): 146- 149.

[7] Chuanlin Lin, Zhen Lin. A Summary of the Influence of Structural Parameters of Permanent Magnet Motors on Cogging Torque [J]. Electrical Engineering, 2018, 19(02): 6-10+15.

[8] Xiuhe Wang. Permanent Magnet Motor [M].BeiJing: China Electric Power Press, 2007.

[9] Junjie Zhou, Chengzhi Fan, Yunyue Ye. Mechanical & Electrical Engineering Magazine,2009(2) :79- 82.

[10] Silun Peng. Research on Torque Optimization Method of Hub Motor[D]. Jilin University,2014.

[11] HWANG K Y, LIN H, RHYU S H etc. A study on the novel co-efficient modeling for a skewed permanent magnet and overhang structure for optimal design of brushless DC motor[J]. IEEE Transactions on Magnetics 2012 48(5):1918-1923.

[12] Karim Abbaszadeh, MostafaJafari. Optimizing cogging torque re-duction in slot opening shift method for BLDC motor by R SM[C]/ /Power Electronics, Drive Systems and Technologies Conference. IEEE,2011:62- 66.

7th International Conference on Reliability of
Electrical Products and Electrical Contacts,
November 04-06, 2019

A Discriminant Method of Accelerated Degradation Mechanism Consistency Based on Wiener Process

Shuang Si, Bokai Zheng, Hongyu Zhang, Zhu Yan, Xuerong Ye*, Shujuan Wang
School of Electrical Engineering and Automation, Harbin Institute of Technology, Harbin, Heilongjiang Province 150001
TEL: +8615663633661 E-mail: 1169295848@qq.com

***Abstract*—Accelerated degradation test methods provide an effective and feasible means for quickly assessing product reliability or life indicators, and thus become an important research direction in the field of reliability. Discriminating products' failure mechanism consistency under normal conditions and acceleration conditions is a key link to ensure the effectiveness of accelerated degradation tests. In order to solve the problems of the existing methods for discriminating the failure mechanism consistency, such as time-consuming and labor-intensive operation, unclear physical meaning, poor resistance to test interference and unconsidered individual product differences, in this paper we proposea discriminant method of accelerated degradation mechanism consistency based on Wiener process.**

Firstly, based on the Wiener process degradation modeling method, the relationship between the stresses and the drift parameters when the failure mechanism is invariant is derived. Then, considering the influence of individual differences on the drift parameters, the test samples are constructed by using the theoretical and estimated values of drift parameters under the same stress, and based on the reasonable assumption that the test samples obey the normal distribution, the failure mechanism consistency discrimination is based on the t-test method. Finally, taking the accelerated degradation test data of a certain type of resistors as an example, the above method is applied to discriminate the failure mechanism consistency, and the effectiveness of the method is verified.

***Index Terms*—Wiener process, Accelerated degradation test, Individual differences, Failure mechanism consistency discrimination, t-test**

I. INTRODUCTION

With the development of science and technology, products are usually characterized by high reliability and long life [1]. In order to quickly stimulate the potential failure mode of products, obtain product degradation data in a short period of time, and then evaluate product reliability and life indexes, accelerated degradation tests (ADT) of products are required [2]. Accelerated degradation tests can be divided into constant stress accelerated degradation test (CSADT), step stress accelerated degradation test (SSADT) and sequential stress accelerated degradation test. The constant stress accelerated degradation test method is the most widely used and most studied test method. Temperature can accelerate the physical and chemical reactions inside the product and accelerate the process of product degradation, so it is widely used as an accelerated stress in accelerated degradation tests [3-6]. However, the product may introduce a new failure mechanism under excessive accelerated stress, so that the reliability index obtained under the accelerated conditions of the test cannot be directly extrapolated to normal stress. Therefore, research on discriminant methods of accelerated degradation mechanism consistency is needed.

At present, the domestic and international accelerated degradation mechanism consistency discrimination methods are mainly divided into four categories: the first is the accelerated model parameter invariant method [3-4]. the principle is on the assumption that the failure activation energy is unchanged, based on the Arrhenius equation is used to calculate the relationship between the degradation rate of the product and the negative reciprocal of the temperature to determine the consistency of the failure mechanism of the acceleration model. Although this method has clear physical meaning, it does not consider the influence of the difference of product individual degradation process on the discriminant result. The second is the degradation trajectory consistency method. This type of methods is mainly divided into rank correlation coefficient method and grey prediction method. The rank correlation coefficient method [5] considers that if the failure mechanism of the product under different stresses is consistent, the corresponding degradation curves are similar in shape, that is, the amount of degradation of the stress S_1 is large in the same time interval, and the degradation amount of the stress S_2should also be large. The orders of the data sizes in the two stress degradation sequences are basically the same. The grey prediction method [6-9] uses the gray model to predict the degradation data, and determines the consistency of the failure mechanism based on the residual size of the real data and the prediction data. This method can be used in the baseline test before theaccelerated test. However, because the sample size of the baseline test is small and the test data is limited, the error of the judgment result is large. The third is the life distribution parameter consistency method. The method assumes that the acceleration factor between any two stresses in the accelerated degradation test is a constant independent of reliability, but only related to the stress level, and then derives that the equal coefficient of variation corresponding to the life distribution under different stresses is a sufficient condition of the consistency of the product failure mechanism, such as the consistency test of the shape parameters of the Willbu life distribution product [10], the lognormal distribution consistency test [11-13]. The hypothesis of this method is originally to make the acceleration factor easy to be applied in practical engineering, but it lacks clear physical meaning. The fourth is experimental observation method, which mainly includes direct observation method, chemical analysis method, microscopic observation method [14-15], etc. Such methods mainly use scanning electron microscopy (SEM) and other tools to analyze the physical and chemical changes of the product failure process, and then determine the consistency of the failure mechanism. Although this type of method is more direct, it has the disadvantages of difficulty in operation, large workload, and high cost.

The Wiener process can be used to describe the degradation process of many typical products and has good computational analysis properties, so it is widely used in product degradation modeling. In order to solve the existing problems of methods for discriminating the failure mechanism consistency, this paper, based on the Wiener process, considering the product individual differences, proposes a discriminant method of accelerated degradation mechanism consistency for constant temperature stress accelerated degradation test. Firstly, the relationship between the accelerated stress and the drift parameter in the Wiener process degradation model is deduced when the failure mechanism is unchanged. Then, considering the individual differences, the test samples are constructed by using the theoretical and estimated values of drift parameters under the same stress, and the failure mechanism consistency discrimination is based on the t-test method. Finally, the method is applied to the accelerated degradation test data of a certain type of resistors, and the failure mechanism change interval is given.

II. DISCRIMINANT PRINCIPLE OF ACCELERATED DEGRADATION MECHANISM CONSISTENCY

A. Degeneration Modeling and Parameter Estimation Based on Wiener Process

When the one-dimensional Wiener process is used to describe the products' degradation process, the amount of degradation $\{X(t), t \geq 0\}$ can be described as the form shown in equation (1).

$$X(t) = \mu t + \sigma W(t) \tag{1}$$

Where, σ is the diffusion coefficient of the degradation stochastic process and describes the impact of operating and environmental conditions on products' degradation process, so it is assumed not to change with stress, σ>0; μ is the drift parameter and commonly known as degradation rate. $W(t)$ is a standard Brownian motion and $E[W(t)] = 0, E[W(t_1)W(t_2)] = \min(t_1, t_2)$.

It is assumed that n products are carried out in a CSADT under s temperature stresses.For the product i under the temperature stress T_k, the amount of degradation at the initial time t_{i0} is X_{i0}=0, and the amount of degradation of the products are measured respectively at time $t_{i1k}, \cdots, t_{imk}$, and the measured value $X_{i1k}, \cdots, X_{imk}$ are obtained. $\Delta x_{ijk} = X_{ijk} - X_{i(j-1)k}$ is the amount of degradation of product i at $t_{i(j-1)k}, t_{ijk}$, and Δx_{ijk} can be expressed:

$$\Delta x_{ijk} \sim N(\mu_{ik}\Delta t_{ijk}, \sigma_{ik}^2 \Delta t_{ijk}) \tag{2}$$

Where, $\Delta t_{ijk} = t_{ijk} - t_{i(j-1)k}, i = 1, 2, \cdots, n, j = 1, 2, \cdots, m,$ $k = 1, 2, \cdots, s$.

The likelihood function obtained from the degradation data of test product i under stress T_k is:

$$L(\mu_{ik}, \sigma_{ik}^2) = \prod_{j=1}^{m} \frac{1}{\sqrt{2\sigma_{ik}^2 \pi \Delta t_{ijk}}} \exp\left[-\frac{(\Delta x_{ijk} - \mu_{ik}\Delta t_{ijk})}{2\sigma_{ik}^2 \Delta t_{ijk}}\right] \tag{3}$$

The maximum likelihood estimated value of the parameter can be obtained from equation (3) as:

$$\hat{\mu}_{ik} = \frac{X_{imk}}{t_{imk}} \tag{4}$$

B. Stress-drift parameter Relationship to Ensure a Consistent Mechanism

The degradation process $Y(t)$ of the product can be subject to the following drift Brownian motion model:

In the temperature ADTs, the relationship between the stress level and the degradation rate is usually described using the Arrhenius equation as shown in (5).

$$\frac{\partial X}{\partial t} = Ae^{-\frac{Q}{KT}} \tag{5}$$

Where, $\partial X / \partial t$ is the degradation rate of product at temperature T, X is the degradation sensitive parameter, t is the degradation time; A is the constant; Q is the failure activation energy, the unit is J/mol; T is the absolute temperature, the unit is K; K is the molar gas Constant, 8.314 J/mol•K. Integrate equation (5) to get:

$$X = Ate^{-\frac{Q}{KT}} + X_0 \tag{6}$$

Perform the logarithm on both sides of equation (6) and organize it:

$$\ln t = \ln\frac{X - X_0}{A} + \frac{Q}{KT} \tag{7}$$

The temperature stresses of the ADT are $T_1 < \cdots < T_k < \cdots < T_s$, assuming that the failure mechanism of the products under the two minimum acceleration stresses T_1 and T_2 in the test do not change, then we can get:

$$T_1 : \ln t = \ln\frac{X_{T_1} - X_{0,T_1}}{A} + \frac{Q}{KT_1} \tag{8}$$

$$T_2 : \ln t = \ln\frac{X_{T_2} - X_{0,T_2}}{A} + \frac{Q}{KT_2} \tag{9}$$

When the degradation time t is equal, the equations (8) and (9) are combined:

$$Q = K\frac{T_1T_2}{T_1 - T_2}\ln\frac{X_{T_1} - X_{0,T_1}}{X_{T_2} - X_{0,T_2}} \tag{10}$$

If the failure mechanism does not change, the failure activation energy of the products under this stress does not change. Therefore, it is assumed that the failure activation energy of the products does not change under the temperature stress T_k, and the equivalent equation (11) is obtained.

$$Q = K\frac{T_1T_k}{T_1 - T_k}\ln\frac{X_{T_1} - X_{0,T_1}}{X_{T_k} - X_{0,T_k}} \tag{11}$$

From equations (10) and (11):

$$T_k = \frac{T_1T_2\ln a}{T_2\ln a + (T_1 - T_2)\ln b} \tag{12}$$

Where, $a = \frac{X_{T_1} - X_{0,T_1}}{X_{T_2} - X_{0,T_2}}, b = \frac{X_{T_1} - X_{0,T_1}}{X_{T_k} - X_{0,T_k}}$.

In the Wiener process, the drift parameter μ represents the product degradation rate. From equation (12), when the failure mechanism is constant, the relationship between the temperature stress and the corresponding drift parameter is obtained:

$$T_k = \frac{T_1T_2\ln\frac{\mu_2}{\mu_1}}{T_2\ln\frac{\mu_2}{\mu_k} + T_1\ln\frac{\mu_k}{\mu_1}} \tag{13}$$

Since the drift parameters μ_1 and μ_2 corresponding to the temperature stresses T_1 and T_2 are unknown, the estimated values $\hat{\mu}_1$、$\hat{\mu}_2$ can be used instead of the true values. From the equation (13), when the failure mechanism is constant, the theoretical value of the drift parameter μ_k under the temperature stress T_k can be obtained:

$$\mu_k = \exp\left(\frac{\left(\frac{1}{T_2} - \frac{1}{T_k}\right)\ln\hat{\mu}_1 - \left(\frac{1}{T_1} - \frac{1}{T_k}\right)\ln\hat{\mu}_2}{\frac{1}{T_2} - \frac{1}{T_1}}\right) \tag{14}$$

Considering the individual differences between products and products, the degradation process of different products is different, so the estimated values of drift parameters obtained by equation (4) are not consistent, and the theoretical values of drift parameters are also inconsistent. Therefore, from the equation (14), when the failure mechanism is constant, the theoretical value of the ith drift parameter under the temperature stress T_k is as shown in the equation (15).

$$\mu_{ik} = \exp\left(\frac{\left(\frac{1}{T_2} - \frac{1}{T_k}\right)\ln\hat{\mu}_{i_1,1} - \left(\frac{1}{T_1} - \frac{1}{T_k}\right)\ln\hat{\mu}_{i_2,2}}{\frac{1}{T_2} - \frac{1}{T_1}}\right) \tag{15}$$

$$i_1 = 1,2,\cdots,n, i_2 = 1,2,\cdots,n$$

C. Hypothesis Testing

It is assumed that the estimated values and the theoretical values of drift parameter are both from the normal distribution and their standard deviations are equal. We take the theoretical values and estimated values of the drift parameters of different product individuals under the same stress as test samples, and t-test is performed. If the two population samples do not have significant differences, then the failure mechanism of the products under this stress is considered to be consistent, otherwise, inconsistent.

Assume that the theoretical values of the drift parameters $\mu_{1,k}$, $\mu_{2,k}$,$\cdots$, $\mu_{n,k}$ under the temperature stress T_k are the samples from the population $X \sim N(\alpha_1, \delta^2)$, and the estimated values of the drift parameters $\hat{\mu}_{1,k}, \hat{\mu}_{2,k}, \ldots, \hat{\mu}_{m,k}$ under the temperature stress T_k are the samples from the population $Y \sim N(\alpha_2, \delta^2)$. The null hypothesis is $H_0 : \alpha_1 = \alpha_2$, and the alternative hypothesis is $H_1 : \alpha_1 \neq \alpha_2$. Establish the following t statistic:

$$t = \sqrt{\frac{nm}{n+m}} \bullet \frac{\bar{X} - \bar{Y}}{S} \tag{16}$$

Where,

$$\bar{X} = \frac{1}{n}\sum_{i=1}^{n}\mu_{ik} \tag{17}$$

$$\bar{Y} = \frac{1}{m}\sum_{i=1}^{m}\hat{\mu}_{ik} \tag{18}$$

$$S = \sqrt{\frac{(n-1)S_1^2 + (m-1)S_2^2}{n+m-2}} \tag{19}$$

$$S_1^2 = \frac{1}{n-1}\sum_{i=1}^{n}\left(\mu_{ik} - \bar{X}\right)^2 \qquad (20)$$

$$S_2^2 = \frac{1}{m-1}\sum_{i=1}^{m}\left(\hat{\mu}_{ik} - \bar{Y}\right)^2 \qquad (21)$$

Since $\sqrt{\frac{nm}{n+m}} \cdot \frac{\bar{X}-\bar{Y}}{S} \sim t(n+m-2)$, when the level of significance is β, if $\sqrt{\frac{nm}{n+m}} \cdot \frac{|\bar{X}-\bar{Y}|}{S} < t_{1-\beta/2}(n+m-2)$, the null hypothesis is accepted, that is, the failure mechanism of the products under the temperature stress T_k is unchanged; if $\sqrt{\frac{nm}{n+m}} \cdot \frac{|\bar{X}-\bar{Y}|}{S} \geq t_{1-\beta/2}(n+m-2)$, the null hypothesis is rejected, that is, the failure mechanism of the products under the temperature stress T_k has changed.

III. CASE STUDY

In this paper, based on the accelerated degradation test data of a certain type of resistors, the failure mechanism consistency of the product is determined.

A. ADT Description

This type of resistor is widely used in weapon equipment. In the long-term storage state, the main failure cause of this type of resistor is the parameter drift failure caused by the continuous degradation of the resistance value. This ADT selects the temperature as the accelerated stress and uses constant stress loading method.

20 resistors of this type were extracted and the ADTs were carried out under 5 sets of accelerated stresses T_1=90°C, T_2=120°C, T_3=130°C, T_4=175°C, T_5=190°C, and 4 resistors were placed under each group of stress. The resistance values of the resistors under various stresses were measured and collected every 24 hours. The test degradation data increment can be obtained by subtracting the initial value of the product from the degradation data under the same product, as shown in Figure 1.

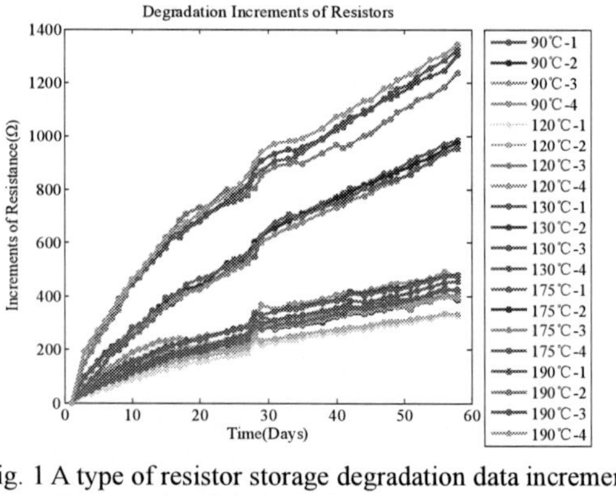

Fig. 1 A type of resistor storage degradation data increments

B. Wiener Process Modeling and Parameter Estimation

According to the degradation curve shown in Figure 1, this type of resistor exhibits linear degradation and is not strictly monotonically increasing, so it is considered to use the Wiener process for degradation modeling.The estimated values of the drift parameters for each product are obtained by equation (4), as shown in Table 1. According to the technical manual of this type of resistor, its maximum working environment is 150 °C. Therefore, it is feasible to assume that the failure mechanism of this type of resistor is consistent at T_1=90°C and T_2=120°C. According to equation (15), the theoretical values of the drift parameters under various stresses are shown in Table 2.

Table 1 The estimated values of the drift parameters

Ite m	T_1	T_2	T_3	T_4	T_5
1	7.578	5.931	7.745	17.940	24.074
	2	4	3	5	8
2	7.032	6.068	8.741	17.758	22.490
	1	1	9	8	0
3	7.149	7.344	8.291	17.291	23.712
	4	2	1	3	3
4	8.650	7.171	8.648	17.390	24.470
	5	0	3	2	6

Table 2 The theoretical values of the drift parameters

number	T_3	T_4	T_5
1	7.5108	9.1219	10.7888
2	7.6764	9.3619	10.0410
3	7.2754	8.0099	9.9347
4	8.0530	7.6060	9.4817
5	7.6359	9.6062	10.3443
6	7.8053	9.8745	10.6335
7	8.4406	8.8336	9.9514
8	8.2132	7.3823	9.4321
9	7.6080	9.4944	10.2149
10	7.7765	9.7562	10.4954
11	8.4037	8.6435	9.7145
12	8.1774	8.2031	9.2106
13	8.2961	9.3862	9.9741
14	8.4553	9.5834	10.1721
15	7.9920	8.7588	9.4436
16	8.7782	7.4270	9.0880

C. Failure Mechanism Consistency Discriminant

It can be seen from the above section that the sample size of the drift parameter estimation under each stress is 4, and the sample size of the theoretical value is 16. When the significance level is 0.05, the rejection boundary in the *t* distribution table is $t_{0.975}(18) = 2.101$. Perform t-test on samples under each stress and the results are shown in Table 3. It can be seen from the table that the failure mechanism of this type of resistor is consistent under the temperature stress of 90°C, 120°C and 130°C. However, under the temperature stress of 175°C and 190°C, the failure mechanism changes, that is, the failure mechanism change interval is 130°C to 175°C.

Table 3 *t* statistic test results

Item	T_3	T_4	T_5
t statistic	1.4892	19.9257	42.4945
H_0	Accept	Reject	Reject

IV. CONCLUSION

Aiming at the problems of time-consuming and laborious, unclear physical meaning, and product individual differences unconsidered in the existing method of discriminating failure mechanism, this paper proposes a discriminant method of accelerated degradation mechanism consistency based on Wiener process, and obtains the following conclusions:

(1) Based on the Wiener process and the Arrhenius equation, the maximum likelihood estimated value of the drift parameter in the degradation model is given. Under the premise that the failure mechanism is unchanged, the relationship between the stress and the drift parameter is deduced, and the theoretical value of the drift parameters under each stress is given. It provides a data foundation for failure mechanism consistency discriminant.

(2) This paper considers that there are differences in the degradation process of the product individuals, so the estimated values and the theoretical values of the drift parameters of different product individuals are not completely consistent. The two are used as test samples, and the failure mechanism consistency discriminant is performed by t-test.

(3) Applying the proposed method to the accelerated degradation test data of a certain type of resistor, the failure mechanism change interval is 130°C to 175°C.

ACKNOWLEDGMENT

The authors gratefully acknowledge the financial supports for this research from National Key R&D Program of China (2017YFB1300800) and National Natural Science Foundation of China (61671172).

REFERENCES

[1] Liao C M, Tseng S. T., "Optimal design for step-stress accelerated degradation tests," IEEE Transactions on Reliability, vol. 55, no 1, pp. 59-66, 2006.

[2] Meeker W. Q., Escobar L. A., Lu C. J., "Accelerated Degradation Tests: Modeling and Analysis," Technometrics, vol. 40, no 2, pp. 89-99, 1998.

[3] Guo Chunsheng, Xie Xuesong, Ma Weidong, et al., A Failure Mechanism Identification Method in Accelerated Testing, Chinese Journal of Semiconductors, vol. 26, (Nov.) 2011, pp2439-2444.

[4] Wang Qiancheng, Chen Yunxia, Deng Fengli, et al., "Approach of Determining Accelerated Degradation Mechanism Consistency's Boundary for Accelerometers", Journal of Beijing University of Aeronautics and Astronautics, vol. 38, (Nov.) 2012, pp1512-1516.

[5] Feng Jin, "Consistent test of accelerated storage degradation failure mechanism based on rank correlation coefficient", Journal of Aerospace Power, vol. 26, (Nov.) 2011, pp2439-2444.

[6] Yao Jun, Wang Huan, et al., "Failure mechanism consistency test method based on grey theory," Journal of Beijing University of Aeronautics and Astronautics, vol. 39, no 6, 2013, pp735-744.

[7] Pan Xiaoxi, Kang Rui, "Accelerated test mechanism consistency test method based on grey prediction", Journal of Beijing University of Aeronautics and Astronautics, vol. 39, no 6, 2013, pp788-797.

[8] Li Xiaogang, Wang Yahui, "Using Non-Isometric Gray Theory to Determine Consistency of Failure Mechanism", Journal of Beijing University of Aeronautics and Astronautics, vol. 40, no 7, 2014, pp900-904.

[9] Yunxia, Chen, Hongxia, Wang Yashun, et al., "Consistency analysis of accelerated degradation mechanism based on gray theory", Journal of Aerospace Power, vol. 25, (Feb.) 2014, pp322-331.

[10] Lin Fengchun, Wang Qiancheng, Chen Yunxia, et al., "Pseudo-life-based Test Method of Mechanism Consistency Boundary for Accelerated Degradation Testing", Journal of Beijing University of Aeronautics and Astronautics, vol. 38, (Feb.) 2012, pp233-238.

[11] Zhou Yuanquan，Weng Zhaoxi, Ye Xitao, "Study on Accelerated Factor and Condition for Constant Failure Mechanism (I)- The Case for Lifetime is a Random Variable", Systems Engineering and Electronics, vol. 1, 1996, pp55-67.

[12] Wang Haowei, Xu Tingxue, Wang Weiya, "Test Method of Failure Mechanism Consistency Based on Degradation Model", Acta Aeronautica et Astronautica Sinica, vol. 36, (Mar.) 2015, pp889-897.

[13] Ma Xiaobing, Wang Jinzhong, "Reliability assessment using constant-stress accelerated degradation data based on pseudo life distribution", System Engineering and Electronics, vol. 33, no 1, 2011, pp. 228-232.

[14] Bao Yiwang, Su Shengbiao, Wang Yimin, et al., "High Temperature Creep and Failure Mechanism of Ceramics Containing Titaniferous Compound",

Journal of the Chinese Ceramic Society, vol. 30, (Jun.) 2002, pp300-304.
[15] Wu Hongbing, Lin Zhen, "Design Research of Certain Capacitor Accelerated Storage Life Testing", Environmental Apaptability & Reliability, vol. 25, (May.) 2007, pp17-21.

7th International Conference on Reliability of
Electrical Products and Electrical Contacts,
November 04-06, 2019

Electrical Life Prediction Method of AC Contactor Based on Fuzzy Neural Network

Yingmin You[1,2], JinQin Wang[1*], Guichu Wu[2], Liang Shu[2], Ziran Wu[2]
[1]State Key Laboratory for Reliability and Intelligence of Electrical Equipment, Hebei University of Technology ,Tianjin 300130,China
[2]The Engineering Technology Research Center of Low-voltage Apparatus of Zhejiang province, Wenzhou University,Wenzhou,325035, China

Abstract—**The paper studies the electrical life test device with residual electrical life prediction function, which can predict the residual electrical life of AC contactor online. Firstly, the life cycle database of AC contactor under AC4 condition is established. The audio frequency of AC contactor is collected, the spectrum characteristic data is analyzed, the arc energy is collected and calculated when the contactor is broken, and the quality loss data of each contactor is measured. Secondly, the residual electrical life prediction model of AC contactor is established by using the method of fuzzy neural network. After initialization of input data and training of neural network, the residual electrical life of this type of AC contactor can be predicted online. The method can improve the efficiency of electrical life test of AC contactor, reliability and safety of AC contactor, and it has important practical significance for shortening product design cycle.**

Index Terms—**AC contactor, Audio, Fuzzy neural network, Electrical life, Prediction**

I INTRODUCTION

AC contactor is a widely used automatic on-off control device. It is mainly used in frequently switching on or off AC circuit. Its electrical life index is one of the most critical performance indexes, which directly affects the operation quality and level of low-voltage distribution system and automatic control system. The research of AC contactor electrical life test device and residual electrical life prediction method has been a hot spot in the field of low voltage electrical appliances.

The research on electrical life test devices at home and abroad mainly includes: The electrical life test system of AC contactor under vibration condition based on LabVIEW is introduced in [1]. The key technology of AC contactor electrical life test device is studied in [2]-[3] .The life test system of low voltage electrical appliances such as control and protection switches, miniature circuit breakers, vacuum switches, switching reactor/capacitor circuit breakers are respectively studied in [4]-[7] .The main research on the method of electric life prediction is as follows: BP neural network and Gamma process respectively are introduced in [8]-[10].In[8], the input parameters of BP neural network are the absorption time and three-phase accumulative arc energy of AC contactor. In [10], the Gamma process model is established and the residual life is predicted based on the simulation data of AC contactor. The extraction of failure characteristics of AC contactor electrical life prediction under mechanical vibration is introduced in [11]. The method of switch contact electrical life prediction is summarized in [12]. The method of relay bivariate life prediction based on overrun time and suction time modeling is introduced in [13].According to the research, it has not been found at home and abroad that the change of the absorbed audio frequency of AC contactor can be used as the judgment basis of the electric life prediction.

Firstly, the paper introduces the electrical life test device, which is used to collect audio data when AC contactor is sucked in. The characteristics of the absorbed audio frequency spectrum under different electrical life times are analyzed. It is concluded that the absorbed audio frequency spectrum of AC contactor changes obviouslyunder different electrical life conditions. Secondly, the audio characteristics and the accumulated arc energy of contacts are used as input parameters of the electric life prediction model. By establishing and initializing the fuzzy neural network model, the training data are learned. Finally, the residual electrical life prediction function of AC contactor is realized.

II DESIGNOF ELECTRICAL LIFE TESTING DEVICE

The functional block diagram of the multi-loop AC contactor electrical life test device is shown in Figure 1The main controller of the device can communicate with 16 sub-controllers at the same time. Each sub-controller controls an AC contactor of one specification for electrical life test. The sub-controller has the function of electric parameter acquisition. It can collect AC voltage, AC current and frequency signals, and calculate the breaking arc energy of AC contactor contacts. The main controller communicates with the sub-controller through Modbus fieldbus. The main controller has an Ethernet communication interface and a Web server function. It can transfer the test data to the server for operation, and support online query, remote control, infrared control and other functions.

The physical diagram of the test device is shown in Figure 2. Many kinds of AC contactors can be tested at the same time. Using the recording device shown in Figure 3, the audio when the AC contactor is absorbed can be collected. The effective audio interception, filtering, frequency domain transformation and eigenvalue extraction can be processed by the audio processing program in the server.

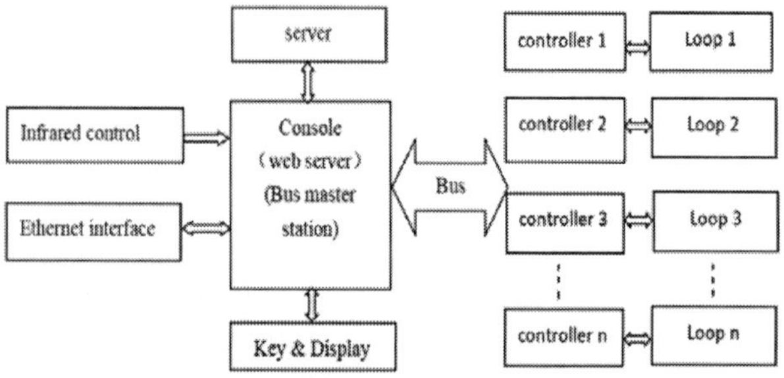

Fig. 1 Principle block diagram of multi-loop AC contactor electrical life test device

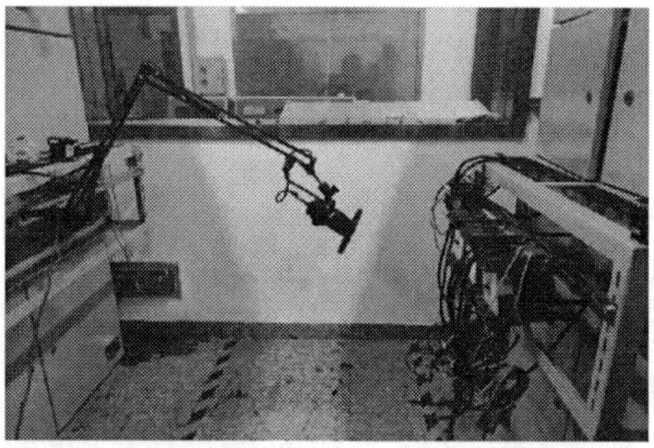

Fig. 2 Diagram of multi-loop electrical life test device

Fig. 3 Audio acquisition device for electrical life of AC contactor

III AUDIO FEATURE EXTRATIONFOR AC CONTACTS CLOSED

CJX2-40 AC contactor is selected for AC4 electrical life test. Its test parameters are shown in Table 1. Three samples are taken for comparative test. In the experiment, the distance between the fixed recording microphone and the tested AC contactor is 40 centimeters and the gain of the audio power amplifier is fixed at 50 times. Sample 1 is used to collect audio data and arc energy data in the whole life cycle. Under AC4 condition, sample 1 fails when the number of electric lifetimes is 20067, and phase B contacts can not be connected due to arc ablation.

Table.1 Electrical Life Test of AC Contactors
Table of parameters

Parameter	value
MODEL	CJX2-40
TEST TYPES	AC4
RATED CURRENT	40A
RATED VOLTAGE	AC380V
POWER FACTOR	0.35

A. Method of Extracting Audio Features

The process of audio preprocessing for AC contactor suction is as follows: Firstly, separated frame, secondly windowed and thirdly filtering. The feature extraction of audio signal is a key step. Whether the extracted feature parameters can reflect the essential features of the original audio information determines the accuracy of recognition [14-16].

In the frequency domain of audio signal, there are many peaks, called resonance peaks, which can reflect the characteristics of audio signal. In this paper, Mel frequency cepstrum coefficient method is used to extract the characteristics of audio in different life times of AC contactor.

Let the original audio signal be $X(n)$, $X(n)$ is transformed into $X(\omega)$ after Fourier transform. $X(\omega)$ can be expressed as:

$$X(\omega)=|X(\omega)|e^{-j\arg[X(\omega)]} \quad (1)$$

The logarithm of the two sides of the formula (1) is obtained.

$$\ln|X(\omega)|=\ln|X(\omega)|\text{-}j\arg[X(\omega)] \quad (2)$$

For formula (2), only the real part is taken, and then the FT^{-1} transformation is obtained formula (3).

$$C(n)=FT^{-1}[\ln|X(\omega)|] \quad (3)$$

$C(n)$ is called the cepstrum of $X(n)$.

B. Audio Characteristic Comparison of AC Contactors

After the audio data are intercepted and filtered, the time domain signal is converted into frequency domain signal by Fourier transform. The data of sample 1 under different electrical life are compared. As shown in Fig. 5, the audio frequency spectra of the new sample 1 under no-load, 1000 times, 10000 times, 20000 times and after sample failure are given respectively. In the early stage of electrical life test, the absorbed audio of AC contactor is clear and crisp. As the test proceeds, the absorbed audio becomes dull due to the erosion of contacts. Therefore, the frequency spectrum changes obviously in the low frequency band. As can be seen from Fig. 5, the spectrum characteristics of AC contactors vary significantly in different electrical life states. When the electrical life of the contactor reaches 20000 times, it belongs to the later period of electrical life. And the decibels of the absorbed audio at 600HZ, 700HZ and 900HZ are higher than 10000 times, 1000 times and no load in turn.

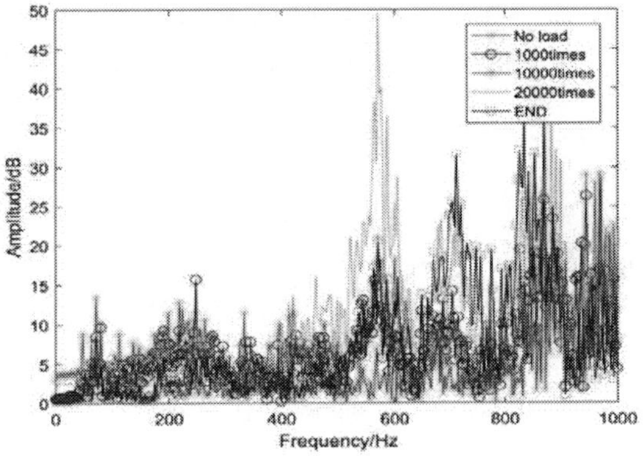

Fig. 4 Frequency spectrum comparison of AC contactor in different states

Mel cepstrum coefficient method is used to extract eigenvalues and save them in the following array format:

$$X = [x_0, x_1, x_2, \cdots x_{24}]^T$$

Among them, x_0 is the number of times the electrical life has been executed, and $x_1 \cdots x_{24}$ represents 24 features of this audio.

IV PRINCIPLEOF FUZZY NEURAL NETWORKAND GENETIC ALGORITHMS

In this paper, a self-organizing fuzzy neural network model based on genetic algorithm (SOFNNGA) is used to predict the residual electrical life of AC contactors.

A. Establishment of Electrical Life Prediction Model Based on Fuzzy Neural Network

The structure of fuzzy neural network includes three parts: input layer, hidden layer and output layer. It is a kind of multi-layer feed for ward neural network. Forward transmission of input signal and reverse transmission of error signal are the main characteristics of the whole network signal transmission. In the process of forward transmission, the input signal is input by the input layer, then processed by the fuzzy rules of the hidden layer, and finally output from the output layer. SOFNNGA is composed of five layers of fuzzy neural network, as shown in Fig.5.The first layer is the input layer, the second to fourth layers are the EBF layer, the normalization layer and the weighting layer, and the fifth layer is the output layer.

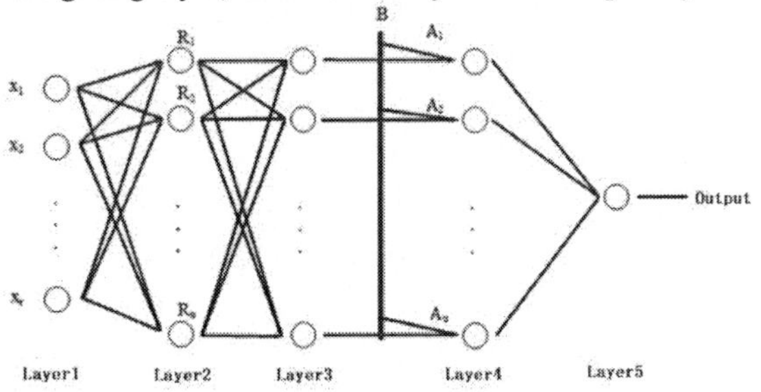

Fig. 5 Network Structure of Fuzzy Neural Network

In the input layer, the $X_i(i = 1,2,3,\cdots r)$ vector represents a neuron.

The EBF layer corresponds to the premise (IF) part of the fuzzy rules, and its structure is shown in Figure 6.Each neuron in EBF layer consists of two parts: central subordinate vector c_i and width subordinate vector σ_i.Each input vector in the input layer enters the neuron in the EBF layer, which corresponds to the central and width membership vectors c_i and σ_i of the fuzzy rules, the output value ϕ_j of the jth EBF layer neuron is calculated according to formula (4).

$$\phi_j = \exp[-\sum_{i=1}^{r} \frac{(x_i - c_{ij})^2}{2\sigma_{ij}^2}] \quad (4)$$

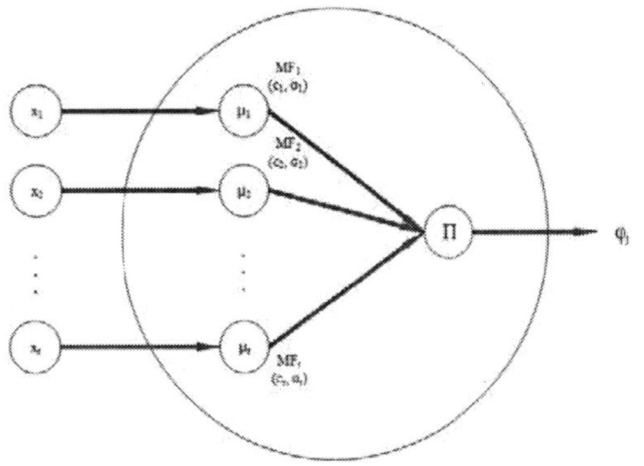

Fig. 6 EBF layer structure of the jth neuron

After introducing the premise (IF) part of the fuzzy rules into the EBF layer, the output signal of the EBF layer enters the normalized layer. The output ψ_j of the normalized layer can be obtained by formula (5):

$$\psi_j = \frac{\phi_j}{\sum_{k=1}^{u}\phi_k} = \frac{\exp[-\sum_{i=1}^{r}\frac{(x_i - c_{ij})^2}{2\sigma_{ij}^2}]}{\sum_{k=1}^{u}\exp[-\sum_{i=1}^{r}\frac{(x_i - c_{ij})^2}{2\sigma_{ij}^2}]}, j = 1,2,...,u \quad (5)$$

The input of the weighted layer consists of the output value of the normalized layer and the weighted deviation. For TS model, column vector $B = [1, x_1, x_2, ..., x_r]^T$ is used as the weighted deviation and row vector $A = [a_{j0}, a_{j1}, a_{j2}, ..., a_{jr}]$ is used as a set of parameter fuzzy rules of corresponding result (THEN).The weighted deviation can be obtained by formula (6).

$$\omega_{2j} = AB = a_{j0} + a_{j1}x_1 + ... + a_{jr}x_r \quad (6)$$

The output of the weighted layer is $f_j = \omega_{2j}\psi_j$, The output layer accumulates the outputs of all the weighted layers of neurons and gets formula (7):

$$y(x) = \sum_{j=1}^{u} f_j = \frac{\sum_{j=1}^{u}\omega_{2j}\exp[-\sum_{i=1}^{r}\frac{(x_i - c_{ij})^2}{2\sigma_{ij}^2}]}{\sum_{k=1}^{u}\exp[-\sum_{i=1}^{r}\frac{(x_i - c_{ij})^2}{2\sigma_{ij}^2}]} \quad (7)$$

B. The Principle of Genetic Algorithms

The genetic algorithm can make the whole neural network get an optimal structure of EBF layer. In this paper, the genetic algorithm of standard roulette selection is adopted. The standard roulette selection method divides the roulette range according to the proportion according to the fitness value of each individual. The higher the fitness value, the larger the proportion obtained, the higher the probability of being selected. Therefore, the standard roulette selection can continuously improve the proportion of the better individuals in the group.

Through gene crossover, offspring are generated based on two strings of parent and parent. Let the parent string be $Father = a_1a_2...a_{u_0}$ and the parent string be $Mother = b_1b_2...b_{u_0}$,the optimum individual for continuous development is $EW = c_1c_2...c_{u_0}$. According to formula (8), the progeny genes are generated by cross-manipulation, Setting the progeny gene to $Child = d_1d_2...d_{u_0}$.

$$d_i = \begin{cases} a_i, & a_i = b_i \\ c_i, \ a_i \neq b_i \ and \ p \geq 0.5 \\ \overline{c_i}, a_i \neq b_i \ and \ p < 0.5 \end{cases} \quad (8)$$

Where P is a random number. When the genes of the father and the mother at the same location are the same, the genes of the offspring at the same location depend on the father; when the genes of the father and the mother at the same location are different, the genes of the offspring at the same location depend on the random number P and the genes of the best individual in evolution. In this way, the offspring genes are derived from the paternal and maternal genes and from the evolving best individuals, enabling some relatively superior genes to be passed on to the offspring.

V EXPERIMENTS AND ANALYSIS OF RESIDUAL ELECTRIC LIFE PREDICTION

The audio processing program is used to extract the characteristic data of the absorbed audio of the AC contactor, and as the input variable of the fuzzy neural network, 1000 data of sample 2 are trained. The initial learning rate η is set to 0.7.After learning the parameters, the data of sample 2 are predicted and the predicted results are output. The predicted data are shown in Table 2. The error rate curve is shown in figure 7.

VI CONCLUSION

The electrical life test equipment with residual electrical life prediction function based on fuzzy neural network is studied in this paper. Based on the analysis of the audio characteristics of AC contactor, the prediction function of residual electrical life is realized by using the model of neural network. This research can monitor the use of AC contactor on-line. It is of great practical significance to improve the reliability and safety of electrical appliances and shorten the design cycle of AC contactor products.

Table 2 Prediction and Errors

Prediction results	Actual electrical life	Error
1702	1591	0.07
2880	2527	0.14
4047	3550	0.14
4536	4200	0.08
5529	5120	0.08
6810	6950	0.02
8757	7750	0.13
9105	8277	0.10
10739	9503	0.13
11390	10450	0.09
11422	11309	0.01
14392	12850	0.12
14528	13578	0.07
18411	16150	0.14
18819	17109	0.10

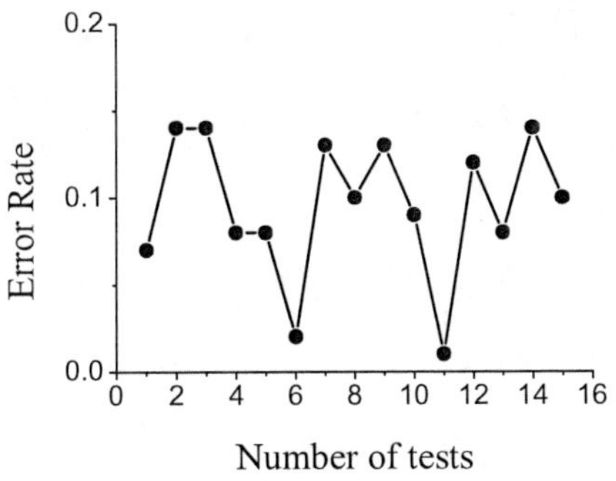

Fig. 7 Error Rate of Residual Electric Life Prediction

REFERENCE

[1] Du T H,AN J P,Sun S G,Jin S H, Hao L L, Ji X L. Electric Life Test System of AC Contactor Under Vibration Condition Based on LabView[J]. Instrument Technique and Sensor, 2018(08): 113-117.

[2] Li K, Zhou C Z, Huang S P. Research on the Electrical Life Test Device of AC Contactors [J]. Electrical Appliances and Energy Efficiency Management TechnologySurgery, 2017 (01): 58-61+67.

[3] Li Y H. Research on electrical life test system and key technology of contactor [D]. Shenyang University of Technology, 2016.

[4] Wang H Y. Design of Electrical Life Test Device for Control and Protection Switch and Research on Life Prediction Method[D]. Shenyang University of Technology,2018.

[5] Luo Y L. Research and design of electrical life testing system for miniature circuit breakers based on SIMATIC S7-1200 [D]. Lanzhou Jiaotong University, 2016.

[6] Zhang L P, Dong H B, Wu Z C, Wang J. Research on on-line monitoring system of electric life of vacuum switch [J]Software, 2012,33(07): 9-10+17.

[7] Wang S J, Chen Y L, Mai R H, Cui P Y. Residual Electric Life Early Warning System for Circuit Breakers for Switching Reactors/Capacitors [J]. Electrical Automation, 2017,39(05): 111-114.

[8] LI K,LI X B,ZHENG S M,HE J C,WU Y. Residual Elect-rical Life Prediction for AC Contactor Based on BPN eur-al Network[J]. Transactions of China Eleclro-Technical Society,2017,32(15):120-127.

[9] Zhang Q. Study on electrical lifetime prediction of contactor's contacts based on Neural Network [D].Heibei: Hebei University of Technology,2015.

[10] LiKui, Li Zhengguang, DuanYu, Zheng Shumei etc. Simulation residual electrical life prediction of AC contactor based on the Gamma process[J].Electrical Measurement & Instrumentation, 2018, 55(16): 105- 111.

[11] Sun S G, JI X L,Du T H,Hao L L,Wang R X. Failure feature extraction for electrical life prediction of AC contactor under mechanical vibration[J]. Chinese Journal of Scientific Instrument, 2019,40(03):114-125.

[12] Wei M F, Li Z B, Song X L, Wu X X. Analysis of Electrical Life Prediction Method for Switch Contacts [J]. Low Voltage Electrical Appliances, 2006 (01): 11-15.

[13] Zhai G F,Wang S J,XuF,Liu M K, Resarch on Double-variable life forecasting based on Model-Building of Super-Path time and Pick-up time for relays[J]. Proceedings of the CSEE, 2002(07): 76-80.

[14] Fu T J. Research on The Pick-up Algorithm of Phonetic Enigenvalue Based on The wavelet Transform[D]. Liaoning: Shenyang Ligong University, 2015.

[15] Alena Galilee, ChrysiStefanidou, Joseph P McCleery. Atypical speech versus non-speech detection and discrimination in 4- to 6- yr old children with autism spectrum disorder: An ERP study.[J]. PLoS ONE, 2017, 12(7).

[16] Li W X. Research of Explosion-proof Motor Fault Monitoring Based on Audio Recognition[D]. Northeast Petroleum University,2015.

[17] ZhangQ. Study on electrical lifetime prediction of contactor's contacts based on Neural Network [D].Heibei: Hebei University of Technology,2015.

[18] Zhang D M,Lin H P,Lin Z Y,Xu M, Lv Z Y. Energy management of energy saving elevator based on neural network predictive control[J]. Chinese Journal of Scientific Instrument, 2017, 38(12): 3137-3142.

[19] Meng B, Liu Xj Wang X L. Human body action recognition based on quaternion spatial temporal convolutional neural network[J]. Chinese Journal of Scientific Instrument,2017,38(11):2643-2650.

[20] Chugoku Electric Power Co. Inc.; Patent Issued for Remaining Life Estimation Method For Estimating Remaining Life Of High-Chromium Steel Pipe (USPTO 10,295,456)[J]. Energy Weekly News, 2019.

7th International Conference on Reliability of
Electrical Products and Electrical Contacts,
November 04-06, 2019

Rapid Control Prototype Verification System for Electromagnetic Switch Based on CompactRIO

Jianxiong Zhuang [1], Longfei Tang [1,2]
[1]College of Electrical Engineering and Automation, Fuzhou University, Fuzhou, 350108, China
[2]Fujian Key Laboratory of New Energy Generation and Power Conversion, Fuzhou, 350108, China
E-mail: zjxfzu@qq.com Tel: 13123296007

Abstract—**The electromagnetic switch is an electric appliance that controls a load by energizing a coil to generate an electromagnetic force, and is widely used in a power application. Rapid control prototype verification system for electromagnetic switch based on CompactRIO is introduced in this paper. The LabVIEW program of FPGA, RT controller and host PC are written in the system. The data acquisition realizes synchronous data acquisition of multiple signals, and uses the shared variable technology to transmit the collected data to the upper PC for analysis and storage. The intelligent control realizes the control of starting, holding and breaking. The starting process is controlled by on/off mode; the holding process is controlled by PID coil current closed loop control, which uses digital technology to adjust the PWM duty cycle dynamically; the breaking process realizes demagnetizing quickly by using a three-state control circuit. The reliability of the system is studied by means of experimental tests. The system provides technical support for electromagnetic switch monitoring and intelligent control, which has theoretical and practical significance for shortening product development cycle, reducing development cost and improving switch operation reliability.**

Index Terms—**CompactRIO, Data acquisition, Electromagnetic switch, Intelligent control, Rapid control prototype verification system**

I. INTRODUCTION

An electromagnetic switch is an electric appliance that energizes a coil to generate an electromagnetic force to control a load, and is widely used [1]. The excitation voltage of the traditional AC electromagnetic switch changes periodically, so that the magnetic flux and electromagnetic force also change periodically. When the force of electromagnetic mechanism is less than the spring reaction force, the iron core will vibrate and emit noise [2]. Generally, the AC electromagnetic mechanism reduces the vibration by adding a magnetic separation ring so that the synthetic force is always greater than the spring reaction force to reduce the noise. In recent years, the intelligent control technology of electromagnetic switches has developed rapidly. By introducing various control schemes on the traditional electromagnetic switches, the working process of switch can be controlled effectively, and the working performance is improved.

Coil current closed loop control technology: by taking the coil current as feedback, the PWM adjusts the period and duty cycle of the high-frequency square wave voltage of the coil to perform closed loop control [3], [4]. Coil voltage closed loop control technology: the PWM adjusts the duty cycle to control the excitation voltage of the coil by taking the average value of the coil voltage as feedback [5]. Displacement closed loop control technology: in order to construct the displacement closed loop control of the position sensorless the displacement estimation technique is used to estimate the core displacement based on the coil current closed loop control [6], [7]. Slope closed loop control scheme: using the slope as outer loop to control the current inner loop to reduce the contact bounce during the starting process [8]. Through the above intelligent control scheme, it can be seen that the electromagnetic switch with intelligent control makes the excitation from the traditional power frequency to the high frequency square wave, and the coil current in the high frequency operation mode generates the current spike and the inherent ripple. Compared with the power frequency noise, the high-frequency noise is higher. And we need to take some measures to suppress it.

Rapid control prototype verification system for electromagnetic switch based on CompactRIO is introduced in this paper. The system combines data acquisition with intelligent control. The control strategy of electromagnetic switch can be placed in the system for prototype verification quickly. At the same time, the system has the function of displaying and storing the collected data online, which saves the connection of the oscilloscope. The data acquisition realizes synchronous data acquisition of multiple signals. Setting the FPGA scan interface mode, and then the collected data is transmitted to the RTOS by using the FIFO data transmission method. Finally, the data is uploaded to the upper PC for waveform display and TDMS store by using the shared variable technology. The intelligent control realizes the process control of starting, holding and breaking. The starting process realizes starting quickly by using on/off mode. The holding process adopts digital PID coil current closed loop control. By setting reasonable PID parameters, the high-frequency noise can be suppressed effectively. The breaking process uses a three-state coil drive topology to add the coil a negative voltage, which achieves demagnetizing rapidly. The system provides technical support for monitoring and intelligent control of electromagnetic switches, which has theoretical and practical significance for shortening product development cycle, reducing costs and improving the reliability of switch operation.

II. CLOSED LOOP CONTROL STRATEGY

The coil current is the most basic electrical parameter reflecting the excitation state of the electromagnetic switch. The coil current closed loop control technology is used in this paper. Starting process on/off controls, holding process PID controls and breaking process uses the three-state topology. Finally, the control strategy is applied to the system.

A. PID control principle

PID algorithm has the advantages of simple structure, easy implementation, strong robustness, and is widely used in industrial control field [9].The PID control schematic is shown in Fig.1. It consists of a proportional unit, an integral unit, and a differential unit. The expected value $r(t)$ is compared with the measured actual value of the controlled target. After the PID algorithm is applied, the output signal $u(t)$ controls the controlled target, and the result $y(t)$ is obtained, thereby performing the correction system response and reducing the uncertainty of the error $e(t)$.

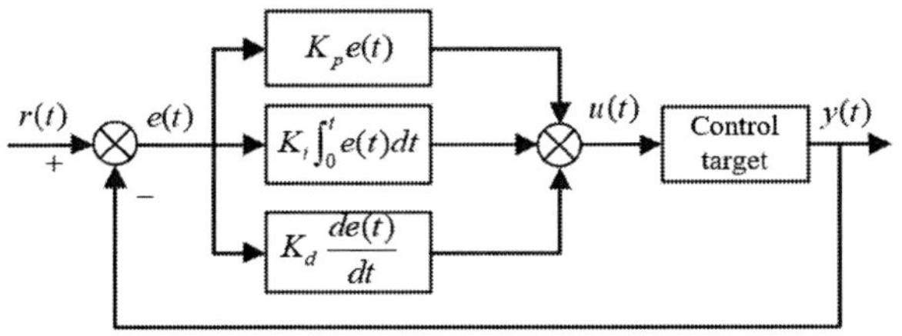

Fig. 1 PID control schematic

PID algorithm formula:

$$u(t) = K_pe(t) + K_i\int_0^t e(t)dt + K_d\frac{de(t)}{dt} \quad (2.1)$$

$$K_i\int_0^t e(t)dt = K_p\frac{1}{T_I}\int_0^t e(t)dt \quad (2.2)$$

$$K_d\frac{de(t)}{dt} = K_p\frac{T_D de(t)}{dt} \quad (2.3)$$

K_p, K_i, K_d are proportional factor, integral factor and differential factor. T_I is the integral time constant, and T_D is the differential time constant.

Proportional control is the basis of PID control. The characteristic of proportional adjustment is that the output is proportional to the input and has the function of timely adjustment. The excessive proportional coefficient leads to the poor dynamic quality factor, which makes the system unstable. The characteristic of integral control is the elimination of the static difference, but may increase the overshoot. The larger integral time constant, the slower integral speed and the weaker integral action. Differential control speeds up system response and reduces overshoot, reducing system tuning time and improving system dynamic performance.

B. Digital PID coil current closed loop construction

The key subVI of the digital PID coil current closed loop control program is shown in Fig.2: (a) is the digital PID (FPGA) subVI. The subVI has output range, PID gains, process variable, reset, setpoint, and output; (b) is the digital PWM subVI. The subVI connects the FPGA I/O node. By setting a reasonable underlying clock, the PWM can enable updating the period and duty cycle dynamically, and control the excitation state of the coil flexibly.

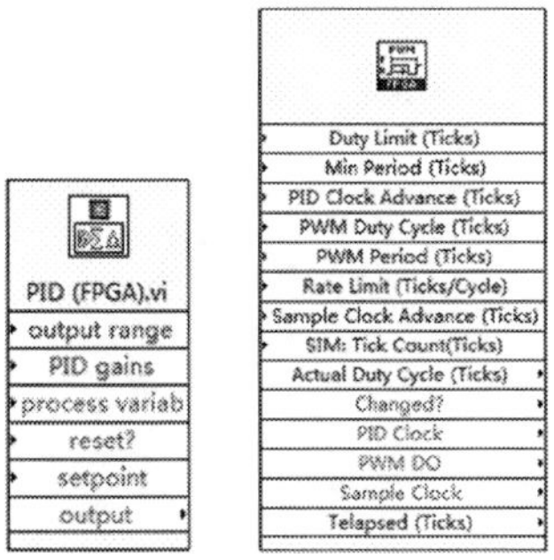

(a) PID (b) PWM

Fig. 2 Digital closed loop control subVI

C. Closed loop control program

A closed loop control program is built in LabVIEW (Fig.3). Starting process on/off mode. The AI0 channel of module 1 is the real-time sampling current. When the sampling current is greater than the starting current reference, the PWM duty ratio is 0%; when the sampling current is less than the starting current reference, the PWM duty ratio is 100%. The holding process realizes PID coil current closed loop control. The sampling current as the system feedback is compared with the set holding current reference. Their error is applied by the PID algorithm, and then the output of PID is used as the PWM duty cycle controls circuit switches. A three-state control topology is selected during the breaking process. The control program is placed in the while loop, and an excellent control effect is achieved after setting a reasonable timing clock and PID parameters.

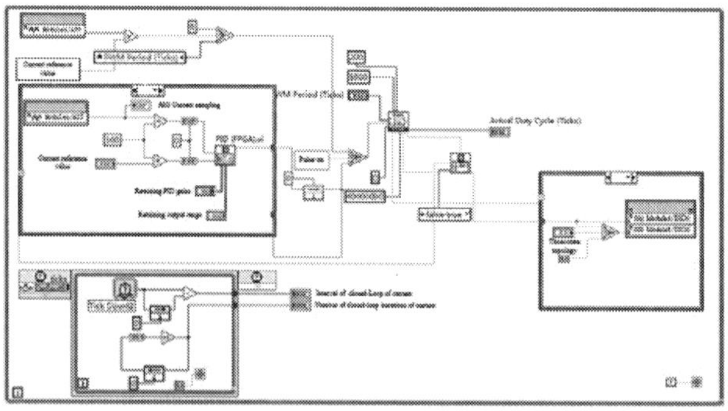

Fig. 3 Closed loop control program

III. RAPID CONTROL PROTOTYPE VERIFICATION SYSTEM

Control system development is a complex process that requires both hardware and software. The traditional control system needs a long development cycle and requires many human resources, which affects the product development cycle seriously. The rapid control prototype verification system can make the control theory to control the actual object quickly, and has the functions of online testing and fast storage.

A. Rapid control prototype verification system structure

The system overall structure is shown in Fig.4.

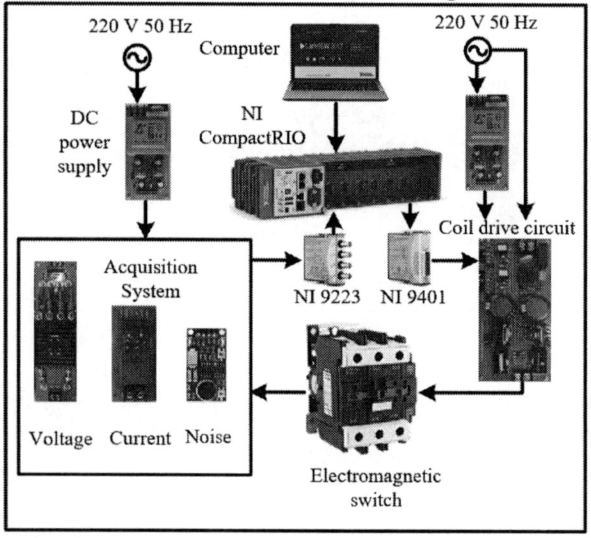

Fig. 4 System Overall structure

The host PC is a computer pre-installed with NI LabVIEW 2017, NI LabVIEW Real-Time Module, NI LabVIEW FPGA Module, NI-RIO and so on. NI cRIO-9039Sync is used as the controller core. It is equipped with C series hot-swappable modules NI 9223 and NI 9401. And they are connected with a coil drive circuit and data acquisition with switching power supply to realize online real-time data acquisition and intelligent control.

B. System hardware

The NI cRIO-9039Sync is an open, compact and rugged embedded controller with real-time processor and reconfigurable FPGA. It consists of:

- Xilinx Kintex-7 FPGA 7K325T
- E3845 1.91GHz quad core System-On-Chip
- 8 slots for modules

The NI 9223 analog input card has the following parameters:

- 4-channel analog input, 1MS/s/ch, simultaneous
- Measure range ±10V,16-bit resolution
- Operating temperature range from -40℃ to 70℃

The NI 9401 analog output card has the following parameters:

- 8 DIO channels, 5V/TTL, bidirectional
- Operating temperature range from -40℃ to 70℃

Coil current acquisition module has the following parameters:

- LEM current transducer LA25-NP
- Current measurement range from -36A to 36A

Coil voltage acquisition module has the following parameters:

- LEM voltage transducer CV3-1000
- Voltage measurement range from -1000V to 1000V
- The highest measurement frequency is 500kHz
- Voltage ratio is 1000:10

Noise acquisition module has the following parameters:

- The audio integrated power amplifier LM386
- Determine the strength of the sound

The three-state coil drive topology is shown in Fig5.

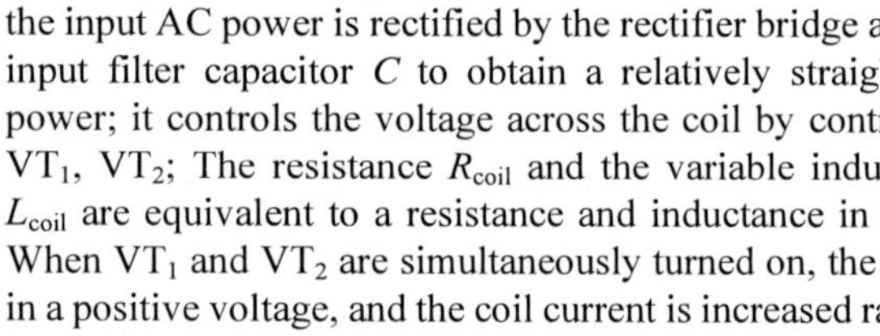

Fig. 5 Three-state coil drive topology

The working principle of the three-state coil drive circuit: the input AC power is rectified by the rectifier bridge and the input filter capacitor C to obtain a relatively straight DC power; it controls the voltage across the coil by controlling VT_1, VT_2; The resistance R_{coil} and the variable inductance L_{coil} are equivalent to a resistance and inductance in series. When VT_1 and VT_2 are simultaneously turned on, the coil is in a positive voltage, and the coil current is increased rapidly. When VT_1 and VT_2 are simultaneously turned off, the coil current cannot be immediately reduced to zero due to inductance, and the coil current flow path is VD_1, R_{coil}, L_{coil}, and VD_2, which the energy is fed back to the input filter capacitor *C*. And the coil is in a negative voltage, so that the coil current is decreased rapidly. When VT_2 is turned on and VT_1 is turned off, the coil current continues to flow through VD_1, and the coil is in a zero state.

C. System software

As shown in Fig.6, the created system project, the program of FPGA, RT controller and host PC are written in LabVIEW.

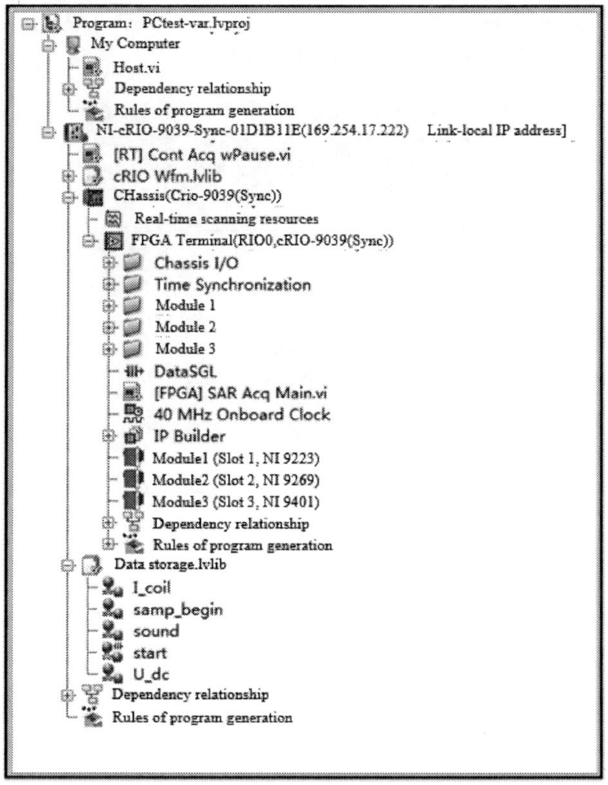

Fig. 6 System project

FPGA.vi is the underlying development of FPGA. It mainly used for data acquisition and prototype verification design. Reconfigurable FPGA has the advantages of high speed, parallelism and so on. In the LabVIEW FPGA Module, the acquired data is stored in the FIFO before being transferred to the RT controller. When FPGA.vi is running, the FPGA I/O node performs data acquisition, and then writes the acquired data into the FIFO by using the write FIFO.

The front panel of the RT.vi is shown in Fig.7. The main function of RT.vi is online parameter adjustment and error display for data acquisition, closed loop control and process control. The time it takes for a general operating system (for example, Microsoft Windows) to complete an operation is unpredictable. In contrast, each operation in the RTOS has a known maximum execution time. The RT FIFO is similar to a fixed-size queue, and the first value written to the FIFO queue is the first value that can be read from the FIFO queue. The RT FIFO limits the size of the shared data and pre-allocates the memory to ensure determinism in program execution. Designing applications that run on the RTOS by using the LabVIEW Real-Time Module to improve the performance and reliability of your application.

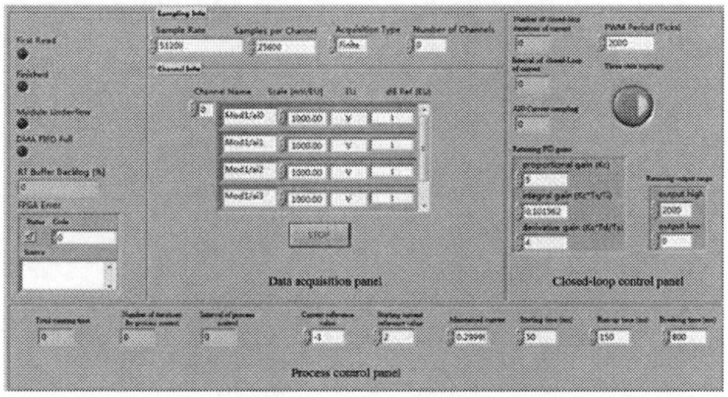

Fig. 7 The front panel of the RT.vi

The main function of Host.vi is to display the acquired data in waveform display and fast storage in TDMS. As shown in Fig.8, using shared variable technology to read and write shared variables on a PC with a network-published shared variable. The RTOS publishes the latest value in the shared variable data set to the computer, and transfers the data to the host computer by calling the released shared variable. Finally, the data is stored in the programmed TDMS program to achieve fast data storage and waveform display.

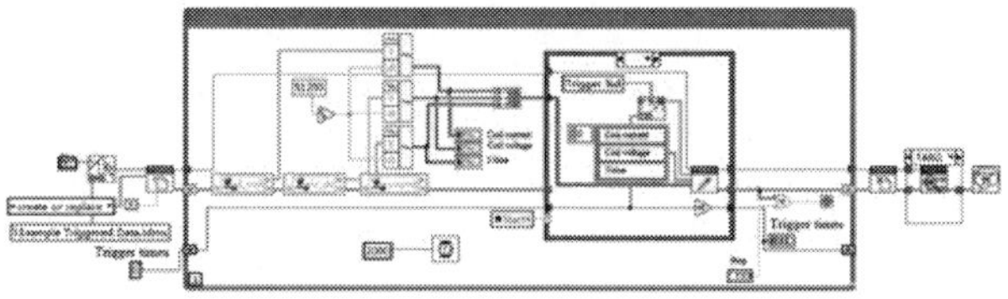

Fig. 8 Waveform display and TDMS

IV. EXPERIMENTAL VERIFICATION AND RESULT ANALYSIS

A. PID parameter setting

The prototype selected for the experiment is CJX2-50 AC contactor. As shown in Fig.9 and Fig.10, the noise waveforms before and after the PID parameter setting are adjusted. Before t_1, it is environmental noise, t_1-t_2 is the noise of the starting process, t_2-t_3 is holding process noise, t_3-t_4 is the noise of the breaking process, and after t_4 is the noise after breaking. It can be seen from the figures that before the setting, the noise intensity of the contactor is significantly higher than the ambient noise intensity, and after the setting, the contactor keeps the process noise intensity and the ambient noise intensity no difference basically.

The setting of PID parameters takes into account the switching operation frequency of the control topology and the role of the proportional unit, the integral unit, and the differential unit. Finally, the switching tube tends to a constant duty cycle to reduce the current ripple and achieve holding silent.

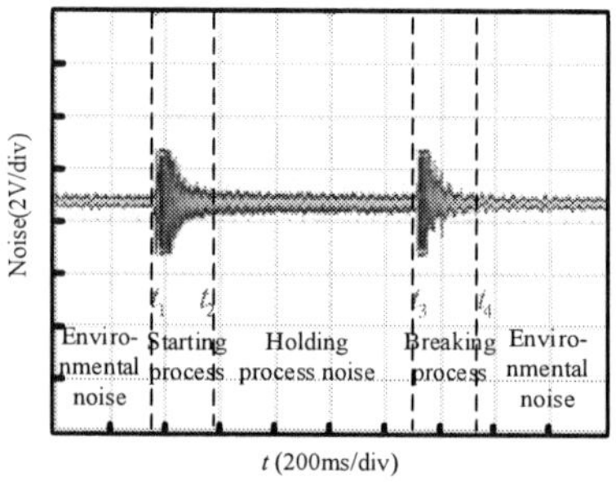

Fig. 9 Pre-setting noise waveform

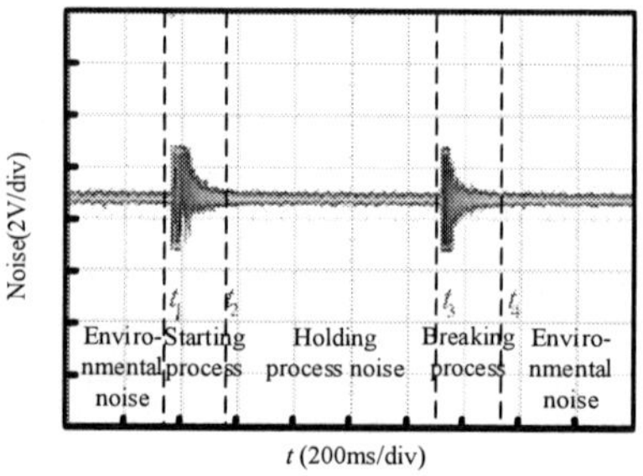

Fig. 10 Post-setting noise waveform

B. *Rapid control prototype verification system overall test*

The system can verify the control strategy quickly and save the connection of oscilloscope. The experiment performs the whole process current closed loop control, and the operating frequency is set to 20 kHz. As shown in Fig. 11 and Fig. 12, the upper PC waveform display and the oscilloscope waveform display. The starting moment is set to 50ms (t0), starting time is set to 150ms (t0-t1), starting current reference is set to 1A, then turn to small current PID coil current closed loop control, the holding current reference is set to 0.3A, holding time 600ms (t1-t2), the breaking moment is set to 800ms (t2), the breaking process adds negative voltage to the coil through the three-state coil drive topology to achieve breaking rapidly. By comparison, the correctness and reliability of the data acquisition and intelligent control of the developed rapid control prototype verification system can be verified.

V. CONCLUSION

Rapid control prototype verification system based on CompactRIO is developed in this paper. The whole system integrates multi-channel data acquisition and intelligent control. The following conclusions are drawn:

1) Under the current closed loop control, by setting a reasonable PID parameter, the digital PWM controls the excitation state of the electromagnetic switch, so that the switch can remain silent.

2) The system realizes online real-time data acquisition, saving the connection of oscilloscope during the process of debugging the electromagnetic switch, saving time and cost.

3) Different control strategies can be placed in the system for test verification quickly and accelerating product development cycle.

4) The system is universal for all kinds of electromagnetic switches, and can be used as a test system for new products to improve the reliability.

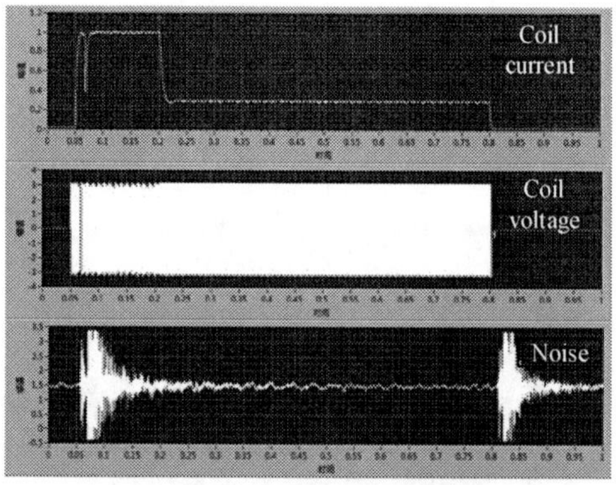

Fig. 11 Host PC waveform display

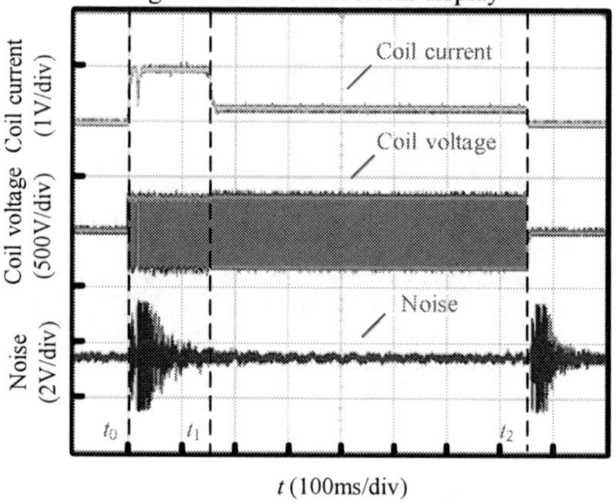

Fig. 12 Oscilloscope waveform display

ACKNOWLEDGMENT

This work was supported in part by the Foundation of the Department of Science and Technology of Fujian Province under Grant 2017J05076, and in part by the National Natural Science Foundation of China under Grant 51707039.

REFERENCES

[1] Xu Zhihong. Basic Theory of Electrical Appliances [M]. Beijing: Mechanical Industry Press. 2014

[2] Zhao Jing. Analysis on the Noise of AC Contactor [J]. Low voltage appliances, 2018(15):4-7.

[3] Tang Longfei, Xu Zhihong. Design of an AC Contactor Control Module Started by Closed Loop Chopping [J]. Proceedings of the CSEE , 2013,33(18): 132-139+5.

[4] Xu Zhihong, Tang Longfei. Design of an AC Contactor Control Module Started by Closed Loop Chopping [J]. Proceedings of the CSEE, 2015, 35(11):2870-2878.

[5] Ji Liang, Chen Degui, Liu Yingyi, et al. Thermal analysis of contactors with voltage feedback system[J] . Journal of Xi'an Jiaotong University,2010, 44(8): 90-95.

[6] A. G. Espinosa, J. R. Ruiz and X. A. Morera, "A Sensorless Method for Controlling the Closure of a Contactor," in IEEE Transactions on Magnetics, vol. 43, no. 10, pp. 3896-3903, Oct. 2007.

[7] A. G. Espinosa, J. R. Ruiz, J. Cusido and X. A. Morera, "Sensorless Control and Fault Diagnosis of Electromechanical Contactors," in IEEE Transactions on Industrial Electronics, vol. 55, no. 10, pp. 3742-3750, Oct. 2008.

[8] Tang Longfei, Xu Zhihong. A Slope Closed loop Control Technology of AC Contactors [J]. Proceedings of the CSEE, 2017, 37(03):956-965.

[9] Lou Bin, Chen Chen, Shen Yanxin. Design of PID Temperature Control System Based on LabVIEW [J]. China Computer&Communication, 2018(22):107-109.

First Author, Jianxiong Zhuang is currently pursuing the M.S. degree in the College of Electrical Engineering and Automation, Fuzhou University, Fuzhou, China. His current research interests include electrical appliances and intelligent technology.

Corresponding Author, Longfei Tang received the B.Sc. degrees in electrical engineering and automation and the Ph.D. degree from Fuzhou University, Fuzhou, China, in 2009 and 2015, respectively.

He is an Associate Professor of the College of Electrical Engineering and Automation with Fuzhou University, Fuzhou, China. His current research interests include intelligent control of electrical appliances and power system analysis and optimization.

7th International Conference on Reliability of
Electrical Products and Electrical Contacts,
November 04-06, 2019

Study on Electrical Properties for Doped $AgSnO_2$ at Different Current Levels under DC 24V

Haitao Wang, Menglin Yang, Wei Liu, Pengtao Ju,
State Key Laboratory of Reliability and Intelligence of Electrical Equipment, (School of Electrical Engineering), Hebei University of Technology, Tianjin 300130, China

***Abstract*—$AgSnO_2$ contact materials are widely used in automotive relays due to their good resistance to arc erosion and soldering, as well as their high electrical lifetime. In this paper, the working environment of the automotive relay was simulated by the test system, and the electrical contact properties of the doped $AgSnO_2$ contact materials at different current levels were studied. $AgSnO_2$ contact material was prepared by powder metallurgy technology, Bi_2O_3, La_2O_3 and TiO_2 were selected as additives. The JF04C electrical contact material test system was utilized to test the electrical contact properties of the four materials at different current levels. Considering the increase in power demand of automotive electrical systems in recent years, the test voltage is set to 42V. Based on the test data obtained, the effect of the current level on the electrical contact performance was analyzed. The results showed that the contact resistance of the four materials decreases and the arc energy increases as the current level increases, and additives can effectively improve the electrical properties of $AgSnO_2$ contact materials. Combining with the microstructure analysis results, the applicable current levels of $AgSnO_2$, $AgSnO_2$/ Bi_2O_3 and $AgSnO_2$/ La_2O_3 were found.**

***Index Terms*—Car relay, Contact resistance, Arc energy, Surface topography, Electrical contact materials.**

I. INTRODUCTION

Relays in automotive electrical systems are devices that act as switches, controls, and protection, and have a crucial influence on the normal operation of automotive electrical systems. Contact material is the most critical material used in automotive relays, and its performance directly affects the reliability of the relay and even affects the safety of the vehicle. In addition, the failure of automotive relays usually occurs in the contact area because of its high operating frequency, so it is of great significance to study the electrical properties of contact materials [1]-[3]. In recent years, with the increase of on-board smart devices, the demand for automotive electrical systems is also increasing. Therefore, the 14-volt conventional power supply is difficult to meet the growing power demand of smart cars, and the development of power supply systems from 14-volt to 42-volt is an inevitable trend. Compared to the traditional 14V power supply, the 42V power supply has a significant advantage [4], [5]. In the 14V power supply condition, increasing the power results in an increase in the current, and an increase in the current means that the cross-sectional area of the wire and cable also becomes larger. Current can be effectively reduced through the 42V power system, which reduces the cross-sectional and weight of the wires and cables, and also reduces space and wire costs. Considering this situation, this paper mainly studied the effect of current grade in the electrical contact performance of doped $AgSnO_2$ contact materials at 42V voltage. Additive type and material ratio were determined, and $AgSnO_2$ contact material was prepared by powder metallurgy method. After the electrical contact performance test, the contact resistance and arc energy data of the contact materials at the four current levels were obtained. According to the test results and analysis, the contact materials with better performance at each current level can be found, which is helpful for the application of $AgSnO_2$ contact materials in vehicle relays.

II. EXPERIMENTAL SETUP

Powder metallurgy was used to prepare contact materials in this paper [7]. Powder metallurgy is a traditional and important preparation method for $AgSnO_2$ contact materials. The method of powder metallurgy is used to press the material into the desired compact, which can reduce the processing steps, save a large amount of raw materials, and reduce the production cost. Moreover, the material is sintered in a vacuum in order to prevent oxidation and contamination of the material, so this method can produce a high-purity material [8]. The compositions and proportion of $AgSnO_2$ contact materials prepared with Bi_2O_3, La_2O_3, and TiO_2 as additives in this paper are shown in Table 1[9], [10].

According to the composition and proportion of the $AgSnO_2$ contact materials shown in Table 1, the required composition and proportion of the composite powders was weighed using an electronic balance. Then the vacuum drying box was used to dry the oxide powder. The powder was heated to 120 degrees in a vacuum and incubated for 30 minutes. The dry composite powder was placed in a ball mill and dry ground. After pressing, sintering and other processes, it meets the test requirements of the sample.

TABLE I

COMPOSITIONS AND PROPORTION OF $AgSnO_2$ CONTACT MATERIALS

Contact material composition	Quality proportion
Ag: SnO_2	88:12
Ag: SnO_2: Bi_2O_3	88:10.5:1.5
Ag: SnO_2: La_2O_3	88:9.5:2.5
Ag: SnO_2: TiO_2	88:9.5:2.5

In this paper, the test system of JF04C electrical contact material was used to test the electrical contact properties of the prepared $AgSnO_2$ contact material. Contact resistance, arc energy, arc duration and welding force under experimental conditions were collected by the test system in real time. The working environment of the electrical equipment was simulated by setting parameters such as voltage, current, contact mode and contact pressure of the experimental device. However, there are two main differences between the simulation experiment and the actual working environment of the on-board relay: First of all, the contacts were not working in a vacuum or insulating gas in simulation experiments. The second is that the contact action in the simulation experiment was not intermittent, so the heat generated by the arc is not radiated in time. Both of these reduce the life of the contact and shorten the test cycle of the sample. Four current levels of 10A, 20A, 30A and 40A were selected for the experiment. The experimental parameters of the JF04C electrical contact material test system was set as follows: the contact mode was surface contact, the contact pressure of the test system was set to 86cN, and the contact spacing was set to 2.0mm, the test load was set to resistive, the contact on-off cycle was set to 800ms, the on-time and off-time were each 400ms, and the number of electrical contacts was set to 25,000 times.

III. EXPERIMENTAL RESULTS

A. Contact Resistance

The contact resistance was measured after each 100 times normal make-and-break operations, and 250 contact resistance values were obtained for each pair of contacts. The average value of 250 contact resistance values were calculated and recorded as the average contact resistance. The average contact resistance of the four contact materials is shown in Fig. 1.

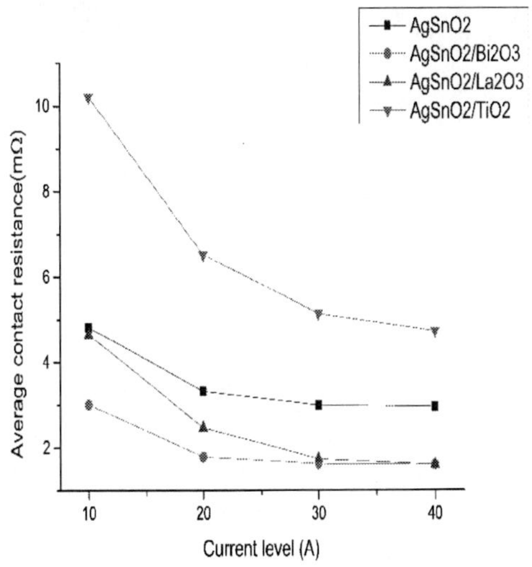

Fig. 1 Average contact resistance.

It can be seen from Fig. 1 that the contact resistance of the four contact materials decreases as the current level increases when the current level changes from 10A to 40A, and the resistance is the lowest at the current level of 40A. The average contact resistance of $AgSnO_2$, $AgSnO_2$/ Bi_2O_3 and $AgSnO_2$/ La_2O_3 is relatively small compared to $AgSnO_2$/ TiO_2 materials. It is worth mentioning that the average contact resistance of $AgSnO_2$/ Bi_2O_3 and $AgSnO_2$/ La_2O_3 is less than 2.00mΩ when the current level is at 30A and 40A. For $AgSnO_2$/ TiO_2 contact materials, the average contact resistance at all four current levels is large. It can also be seen from Fig. 1 that the average contact resistance of the $AgSnO_2$/ Bi_2O_3 contact material is the smallest at the same current level.

B. Arc Energy

After 25,000 contact operations, 25000 arc energy values were obtained for each pair of contacts, and the average value of 25000 arc energy values were calculated as the average arc energy. The average arc energy of the four contact materials is shown in Fig.2.

From Fig.2, it can be seen that the arc energy is large at DC 42V and gradually increases with the increase in the current level. When the current level increases from 10A to 30A, the average arcing energy growth of the four contact materials is relatively flat. However, the average arc energy increases significantly at 40A. In addition, the average arcing energy of $AgSnO_2$/ Bi_2O_3 and $AgSnO_2$/ La_2O_3 is lower than $AgSnO_2$, whereas $AgSnO_2$/ TiO_2 is higher than $AgSnO_2$. It shows that adding a small amount of Bi_2O_3 and La_2O_3 additives will reduce the arc energy [11].

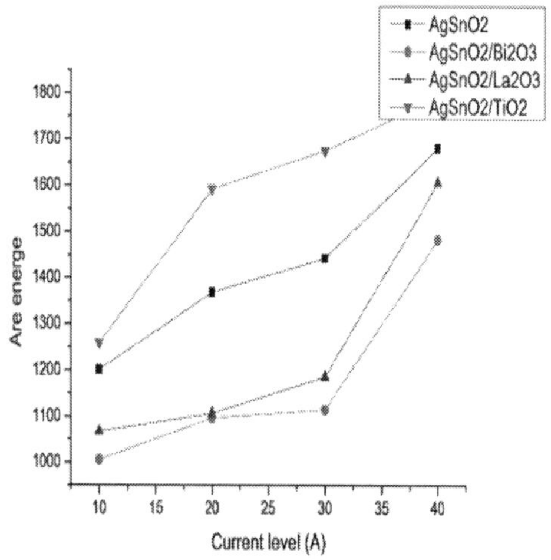

Fig. 2 Average arc energy.

C. Surface Morphology

After 25,000 electrical contact performance tests, the surface of the four contact materials with a magnification of 1000 times is shown in Figure 3, Figure 4, Figure 5, and Figure 6 respectively.

When the test voltage is DC 42V, the surface of the four contact materials shows the state of the liquid metal flow and the shape of the mountain package formed after solidification with holes. At the same time, black non-conductive oxide agglomeration and precipitation appear on the contact surface. From the aspect of surface morphology and oxide aggregation, the surface of $AgSnO_2$/ Bi_2O_3 in the four types of contact materials is relatively flat and no large holes appear.

IV. ANALYSIS AND DISCUSSION

A. Contact Resistance

Contact materials with low contact resistance and stability are often selected for application in automotive relays [21]. Because the lower contact resistance means lower Joule heating, it also means that the contact welding is less likely.

From Fig.2, it can be seen that the arc energy is large at DC 42V and gradually increases with the increase in the current level. When the current level increases from 10A to 30A, the average arcing energy growth of the four contact materials is relatively flat. However, the average arc energy increases significantly at 40A. In addition, the average arcing energy of $AgSnO_2$/ Bi_2O_3 and $AgSnO_2$/ La_2O_3 is lower than $AgSnO_2$, whereas $AgSnO_2$/ TiO_2 is higher than $AgSnO_2$. It shows that adding a small amount of Bi_2O_3 and La_2O_3 additives will reduce the arc energy [11].

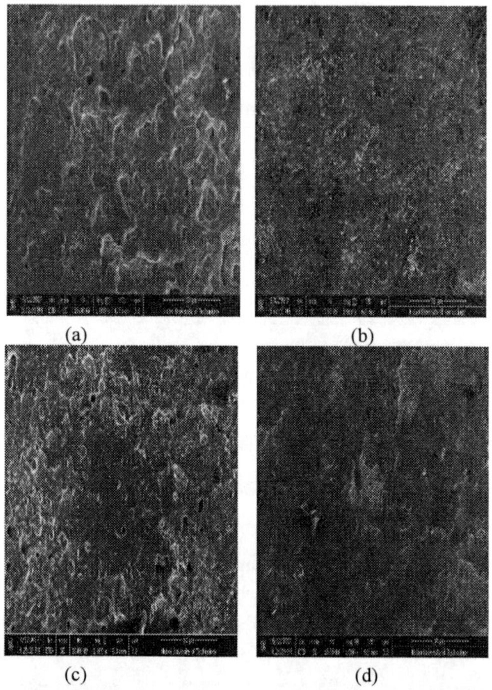

Fig. 3 Surface morphology of $AgSnO_2$. (a) 10A. (b) 20A. (c) 30A. (d) 40A.

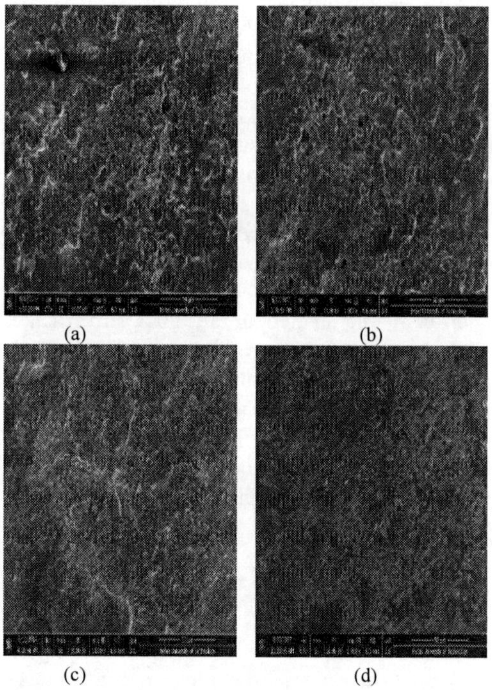

Fig. 4 Surface morphology of $AgSnO_2$/Bi_2O_3. (a) 10A. (b) 20A. (c) 30A. (d) 40A.

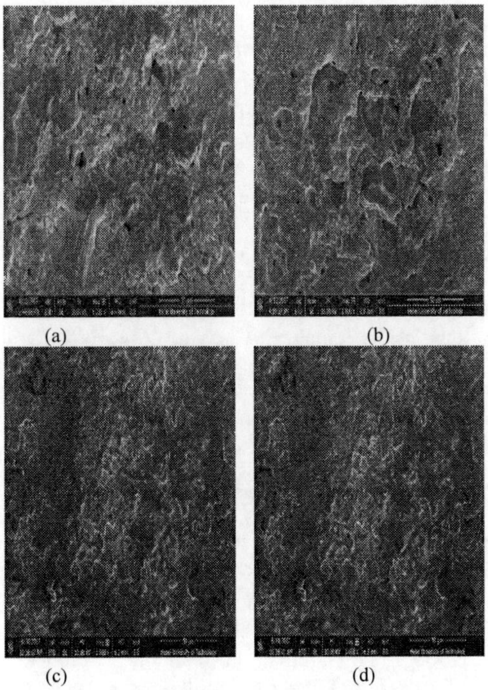

Fig. 5 Surface morphology of $AgSnO_2/La_2O_3$.(a) 10A. (b) 20A. (c) 30A. (d) 40A.

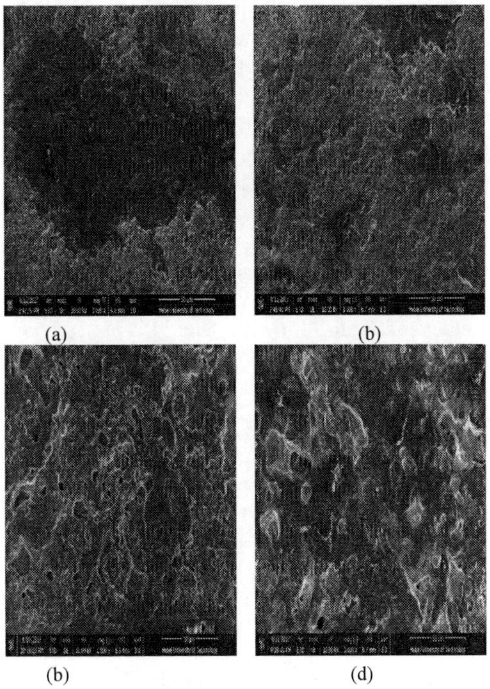

Fig. 6 Surface morphology of $AgSnO_2/TiO_2$. (a) 10A. (b) 20A . (c) 30A. (d) 40A.

As shown in Fig. 1, compared with the DC14V of the relay voltage of the conventional car, the contact resistance of the four contact materials under the condition of DC42V is significantly increased [6], and the higher the current level, the smaller the contact resistance. Aggregation of oxides on contact surfaces is the cause of the increase in resistance of DC42V. The arc energy at high voltage is higher than at low voltage, and so liquid metal splashing and flow also was more serious, which enhance the aggregation of SnO_2 particles on the contact surface. This phenomenon leads to an increase in contact resistance [12]. The decrease in contact resistance with increasing current could be explained by the tunneling effect. Increasing current enhances the arc energy and so the breakdown and softening effects on the contact surface film is also further strengthened. Compared with the aggregation of SnO_2 particles caused by the increase in current, the effect of large current on the softening and breakdown of surface film is more obvious. With the breakdown and softening of the surface film, more and more electrons pass through the surface film through the "tunneling effect" [13], which reduces the surface film resistance. Consequently, we can conclude that the contact resistance will become smaller with the increase in current under the condition of DC 42V.

B. Arc Energy

A large amount of Joule heats generated by the arc discharge raises the contact temperature, resulting in formation of a weld pool on the contact surface and evaporating part of the material [21]. At the same time, the arc will also bring electromagnetic force, plasma force, etc. Due to these forces, the contact material is prone to liquid splashing, resulting in a large loss of contact material [16]. These phenomena will cause deterioration of the contact surface condition, and even affect the reliability of the relay operation, and should be avoided as much as possible. Therefore, the effect of arc discharge should be reduced as much as possible.

Arc energy is utilized to characterize contact arcs. The arcing energy is defined as

$$\int_0^t u\, i\, dt \qquad (1)$$

t is the arc duration of the contact, u is the arcing voltage, and i is the arcing current. The arc voltage u in the equation will increase with arc current and contact resistance, which in turn will result in an increase in arc energy. Therefore, it can be concluded that as the current level increases in the test, the arc discharge energy of the four contact materials will increase, and according to Figure 2, the result is indeed the case. In addition, it can be seen from Fig. 2 that the average arc energy of $AgSnO_2$/ Bi_2O_3 and $AgSnO_2$/ La_2O_3 is significantly lower than that of $AgSnO_2$, which is the positive influence of the additive. Although the average arc energy of $AgSnO_2$/ TiO_2 is higher than that of $AgSnO_2$, according to the curves of $AgSnO_2$/ Bi_2O_3 and $AgSnO_2$/

La_2O_3, we can believe that choosing the right additive can reduce the arc energy [17]-[19].

C. Surface Morphology

From Fig. 3(a), Fig. 4(a) and Fig. 5(a) we can refer to the state of liquid metal flow and the formation of solidified hillocks. The reason for this morphology is that the surface temperature rapidly rises above the melting point of Ag under the action of the arc heat, and the melted silver flows under the mechanical force and converges together. After the silver melts, the surface structure of the contact changes, the molten SnO_2 particles floats to the surface, and the melted silver also sputters under the action of the arc force, both of which lead to agglomeration and precipitation of SnO_2 [14], [20]. Therefore, from Fig. 3(a), Fig. 3(c), Fig. 4(b) and Fig. 5(b), it can be seen that black non-conductive oxide agglomeration and precipitation appear on the contact surface, from Fig. 3(b), Fig. 5(c), Fig .6(a) and Fig .6(b) show that there is a large area of black oxide on the contact surface. In addition, from Fig .3(c), Fig .4(b), Fig .5(b), and Fig .7(d), we can see that there are holes in the contact surface. As the temperature rises, the solubility of the material to the gas increases, and the silver in the molten state absorbs a large amount of gas, mainly oxygen, from the outside. After the arc was extinguished, the melting zone cooled and solidified due to heat loss, but the absorbed gas was not completely discharged. Because of the presence of residual gas, there is a large degree of gas supersaturation at the solid-liquid phase interface when the melt zone cools and solidifies. The greater the degree of gas supersaturation, the easier it is to generate bubbles. In the repeated action of the high temperature of the arc, the bubbles grow up and overflow the surface of the gas to form holes [15].

According to the surface microstructure, it can be concluded that $AgSnO_2$ has better arc erosion resistance at the current level of 10A, and $AgSnO_2$/ Bi_2O_3 has better arc erosion resistance at each current level. $AgSnO_2$/ La_2O_3 has better arc erosion resistance at the current level of 10A and 20A.

V. CONCLUSION

Four $AgSnO_2$ contact materials were prepared by powder metallurgy, and the electrical properties were tested at 10A, 20A, 30A and 40A current levels. According to the test data, the influence of the current level on the electrical contact performance was analyzed, and combined with the results of the microstructure analysis, the applicable current level of each electrical material under DC 42V was found.

1) As the current level increases, the contact resistance of the four contact materials decreases and the arc energy increases. The $AgSnO_2$/ Bi_2O_3 contact material performs better at all current levels.
2) According to the results of electrical contact performance test and microstructure analysis, the applicable current level of $AgSnO_2$ is 10A, the applicable current level of $AgSnO_2$/ Bi_2O_3 is 10A, 20A, 30A and 40A, and the applicable current level of $AgSnO_2$/ La_2O_3 is 10A and 20A.

This work was supported by the National Natural Science Foundation of China (51777057), by Natural Science Foundation of Hebei Province (E2016202106), by Science and Technology Research Project of Hebei Higher Education(ZD2016078).

REFERENCES

[1] Sallais, N. B. Jemaa, E. Carvou, "An arc study at high DC current levels in automotive applications," IEEE Trans. Compon. Packag. Technol, vol.30, no. 3, pp. 540-545, Sep. 2013.

[2] H. Leung and A. Lee "Electric Contact Materials and Their Erosion in Automotive DC Relays," in Proc. IEEE Holm Conf. Elect. Contact, 1991, pp. 114-121.

[3] N. B. Jemaa, L. Nedelec, S. Benhenda, "Break arc duration and contact erosion in automotive application," IEEE Trans. Comp. Packag. Manuf. Technol. A, vol. 19, pp. 82, no. 1, Mar. 1996.

[4] L. Doublet, N. B. jemaa, D. Jeannot, F. Hauner, "Make Arc Erosion and Welding Tendancy under 42V DC in Automotive Area," in Proc. 49th IEEE Holm Conf. Elect. Contacts, Oct 2003, pp. 158-162.

[5] L. Doublet, N. B. Jemaa, F. Hauner, D. Jeannot, "Electrical arc phenomena and its interaction on contact material at 42V DC for automotive applications," in Proc 50th Holm Conf. Elect. Contacts, Seattle, 2004, 8-14.

[6] Sakaguchi, K. Takahashi, T. Yamamoto, "Performance Investigation of Contact Material in 42V DC Automotive Relay,"in Proc.21 ICEC, Zuerich, CH, 2002, pp. 65-69.

[7] X.H.Chen,C.C.Jia, X. B. Liu, "Applications of powder metallurgy technology to manufacture of silver based contact materials,"Powder. Metall, vol. 19, no. 4, pp. 41-46, Apr. 2009.

[8] N. Setoudeh, M. H. Paydar, M. Sajjadnejad, "Effect of high energy ball milling on the reduction of nickel oxide by zinc powder,". J Alloys Compd, vol. 623, pp. 117–120.

[9] H. T. Wang, J. Q. Wang, J. Du, "Influence of Rare Earth on the Wetting Ability of AgSnO2 Contact Material," Rare. Metal. Mat. Eng, vol. 43, no. 8, pp. 1846-1849, Aug. 2014.

[10] H.A.Francisco, M. Myers, "The effect of various silver tin oxide materials on contact performance under motor load (a.c.)," in Proc. 43th Holm Conf. Elect. Contacts, 1997, pp. 254-263.

[11] H. T. Wang, J. Q. Wang, W. Ming, "Testing results analysis of contact materials' electrical contact performance," *J Zhejiang. Univ. Sci. A*, vol. 8, no. 3,

PP. 459-463, Aug. 2007.

[12] N. B. Jemaa, L. Morin, "Transition from the Anodic Arc Phase to the Cathodic Metallic Arc Phase in Vacuum at Low DC Electrical Level," *IEEE Trans. CPT*, vol. 25, no. 4, pp. 651-655, Dec. 2002.

[13] J. G. Simmons, "Generalized formula for the electric tunnel effect between similar electrodes separated by a thin insulating film," J. Appl. Phys, vol. 34, no. 6, pp. 1793–1803, 1963.

[14] M. Lindmayer, "Modeling of contact heating and erosion under arc influence," in *Proc. ICEC*, Saint Malo, France, 2008, pp. 37-42.

[15] J. Swingler, J. W. McBride, "The erosion and arc characteristics of Ag/CdO and Ag/SnO_2 contact materials under dc break conditions," *IEEE Trans. Comp. Packag. Manufact. Technol. A*, vol. 19, no. 3, pp. 404-415, Sept. 1996.

[16] W. Rieder, A. R. Neuhaus, "Contact welding influenced by anode arc and cathode arc, respectively," in *Proc. 45th Holm Conf. Elect. Contacts*, 2004, pp. 378-381.

[17] D. Jeannot, J. Pinard, P. Ramoni, "Physical and chemical properties of metal oxide additions to Ag-SnO_2 contact material and predictions electrical performance," *IEEE Trans. Compon. Packag. Manuf. Technol. A*, vol. 17, no. 1, pp. 17-23, Mar.1994.

[18] Y. C. Zhu, J. Q. Wang,"Preparation and Study on Performance for Silver Rare-earth Alloy Electrical Contact Materials,"in *Proc. 56th IEEE Holm Conf. Elect. Contacts /25th ICEC*, 2010, PP. 163-166.

[19] X. M. Liu, S. L. Wu, K. Paul, "Effects of coating process on the characteristics of AgSnO2 contact materials," *Mater. Chem. Phys*, vol. 98, no. 2-3, pp. 477-480, Aug. 2006.

[20] T. Takagi, H. Inoue, "Distribution of Arc Duration and Material Wear Due to Arc for Ag, Cu, and Pd Contacts," *IEEE Trans. Comp. Hybrids. and Manuf. Tech*, vol. 2, no. 1, pp. 20-24, Mar. 1979.

[21] Z. K. Chen, H. Mizukoshi, K. Sawa, "Contact Resistance Characteristics of Ag Material in Breaking Low-Load DC Arcs," *IEEE Trans. Comp. Hybrids Manf. Tech*, vol. 16, no. 1, pp. 211-219, Mar.1994.

[22] P. G. Slade, "Electrical Contacts Principles and Applications," New York, USA: Markel Dekker Inc, 1999. pp. 438-445.

Statistical Analysis of Contact Voltage Drop Trend of Railway Signal Relay

Zhengyuan Zhao, Wei Liu, Wentian Luo, Qingshi Li, Yanhua Xia, Yannan Wu, Guoqing Guo
Shenyang Railway Signal Co., Ltd., Shenyang 110025, China
E-mail: 13644062882@126.com Tel: 86-24-62071172 Fax: 86-24-62136267

Abstract—**Contact voltage drop refers to the voltage drop between a pair of closed contacts measured from both ends of the contact assembly, which reflects the contact reliability of relay contacts from the side. Relevant standards stipulate that all contacts of the test should be monitored during 40% of the "on" period and 40% of the "off" period of each cycle of the test, and the contact voltage drop of the closed contacts and the voltage between the disconnected contacts should be monitored. Through on-line monitoring of 20,000 times of contact voltage drop of 50 railway signal relays under the condition of 24 V DC and 10 mA resistive load, it is found that the contact voltage drop curves before and after the relays show three trends: smooth and stable, first fluctuating and then stable, and always fluctuating. Then, the electrical characteristics, mechanical characteristics, contact resistance, SEM and EDS tests of the relays with these three trends are analyzed, and the trend of contact voltage drop is studied.**

Index Terms—**Contact pressure drop, Change trend, Reliability**

I. INTRODUCTION

Railway signal relay is the most important basic safety component in the centralized electric control of railway station. Its reliability and safety in operation is the necessary condition to ensure various automatic control equipment, which directly affects the safety of railway train operation. Usually during the relay's continuous operation, due to the influence of external working environment such as temperature, humidity and vibration, the contact surface of the relay is oxidized, carbonized, vulcanized or worn. Thus, the contact voltage drop of the relay contacts increases and the contact resistance increases, which leads to the decrease of the contact reliability of the relay.

Railway signal relay is the most important basic safety component in the centralized electric control of railway station. Its reliability and safety in operation is the necessary condition to ensure various automatic control equipment, which directly affects the safety of railway train operation. Usually during the relay's continuous operation, due to the influence of external working environment such as temperature, humidity and vibration, the contact surface of the relay is oxidized, carbonized, vulcanized or worn. Thus, the contact voltage drop of the relay contacts increases and the contact resistance increases, which leads to the decrease of the contact reliability of the relay.

II. CHANGE TREND OF CONTACT PRESSURE DROP CURVE

Fifty relays are monitored on-line for 20,000 times. The specific test conditions are as follows:

1)Contact load: DC 24V, 10mA resistive load;
2)Test times: 20000;
3)Operating frequency: 2400 times per hour;
4)Contact pressure drop limit value: 0.1V;
5)Load factor: 0.5

After the test, the data statistics show that the contact voltage drop of the above relay before and after contacts presents three trends: always smooth and stable, first fluctuating and then stable, always fluctuating and fluctuating. The specific situation is shown in Table 1 and Table 2

From the on-line test of contact voltage drop of relays, it can be seen that some contact voltage drop values have been in a stable state, some of them fluctuated up and down first and then remained in a stable state, and some of them have been in a fluctuant state. This shows that there is a certain randomness and discreteness in contact voltage drop values of these relays in the process of continuous operation.During each action, the contact area will also change. For example, the contact area will change microscopically due to the influence of mechanical characteristics. The contact voltage drop will also change microscopically, and then the shrinkage resistance and film resistance will change microscopically, which will lead to the deterioration of contact reliability.

TABLE 1 CONTACT PRESSURE DROP TREND STATISTICS

Project	Front contact	Rear contact
Always smooth and stable	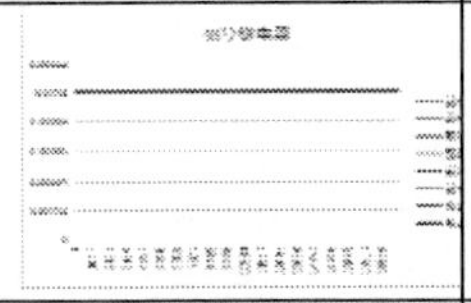	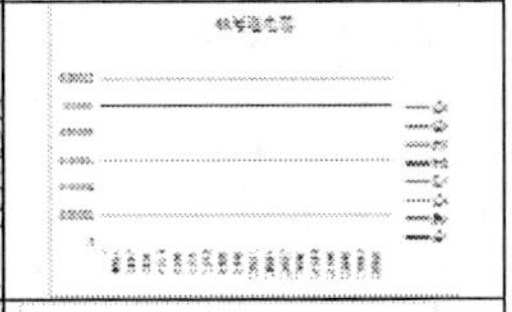
Fluctuate first and then stabilize	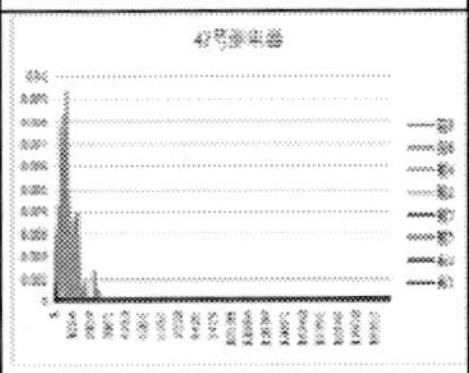	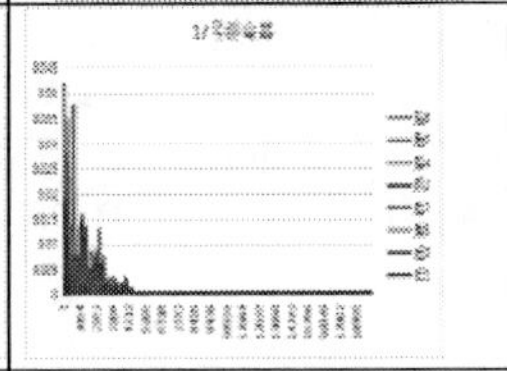
Always fluctuate and fluctuate	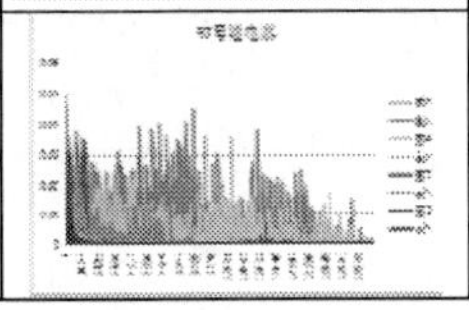	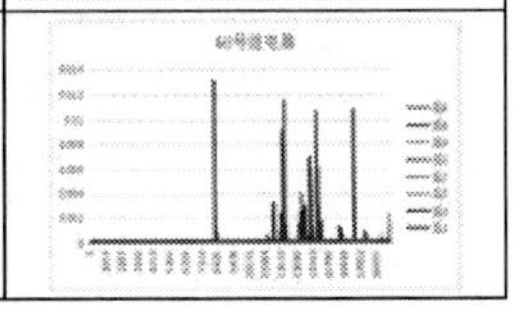

TABLE 2 TREND STATISTICS OF CONTACT PRESSURE DROP CURVES

Project	Number of front contacts	Front Contact Proportion	Number of rear contacts	Rear Contact Proportion
Always smooth and stable	30	60.0%	34	68.0%
Fluctuate first and then stabilize	16	32.0%	16	32.0%
Always fluctuate and fluctuate	4	8.0%	0	0.0%
Total	50	100.0%	50	100.0%

III. TEST RESERACH AND ANLYSIS

In order to study the three trends of contact voltage drop of relay, the electrical characteristics, mechanical characteristics, contact resistance, SEM and EDS of relay were analyzed.

A. Electrical Characteristic Testing

The electrical characteristics of 50 relays are tested one by one. The electrical characteristics parameters include working value, release value, reverse working value and coil resistance value [2] [3]. The statistical results of the test values are shown in Table 3:

B. Mechanical Characteristic Testing

The mechanical characteristics of 50 relays are tested one by one. The mechanical characteristics parameters include contact pressure, contact clearance, bracket clearance, contact homogeneity, etc. [4]. The statistical results of the test values are shown in Table 4

TABLE 3 STATISTICAL TABLE OF ELECTRICAL CHARACTERISTIC TESTING OF RELAYS

Project	Work value (front and back)	Release value (before and after)	Reverse Operating Value (Front and Back)	Front coil resistance value	Rear coil resistance value
Number of test benches	50	50	50	50	50
Qualified proportion	100%	100%	100%	100%	100%

TABLE 4 STATISTICAL INFORMATION TABLE FOR MECHANICAL CHARACTERISTIC TESTING

Test item points	Contact pressure	Contact clearance	Bracket clearance (mm)					
			Ordinary front contact <0.35	Ordinary rear contact <0.35	Strengthen Front Contact <0.1	Strengthen Front Contact >0.3	Strengthen rear Contact <0.1	Strengthen rear Contact >0.3
Qualified Number	46	50	50	42	49	38	49	39

Test item points	Contact homogeneity (mm)					
	Kinematics (ordinary)	Dynamic breaking (ordinary)	Kinematics (strengthen)	Dynamic breaking (strengthen)	Kinematics (complete machine)	Dynamic breaking (complete machine)
Qualified Number	49	50	32	39	50	50

From the above data, it can be seen that the clearance of bracket and contact homogeneity are two indicators that exceed the standard seriously, followed by contact pressure. For bracket clearance, the unqualified number of brackets with clearance greater than 0.3mm before strengthening is 12, accounting for 24.0%; for contact homogeneity, the unqualified number of dynamic contact (strengthening) is 18, the unqualified number is 36.0%; for contact pressure, the unqualified number is 4, accounting for 8% (other test points are less unqualified). In this case, no statistics will be made. Statistical analysis was made on relays with three changing trends: gap between brackets, contact homogeneity and unqualified contact pressure, and contact pressure drop. The results are shown in Table 5:

TABLE 5 COMPARISONS BETWEEN UNQUALIFIED MECHANICAL PARAMETERS AND CONTACT PRESSURE DROP TRENDS

Project	Bracket clearance Unqualified Number	Contact homogeneity Unqualified Number	Contact pressure Unqualified Number
Always smooth and stable	3	3	0
Fluctuate first and then stabilize	2	7	2
Always fluctuate and fluctuate	7	8	2
Total	12	18	4

It can be seen from the table that all three trends include relays with unqualified bracket clearance, contact homogeneity and contact pressure. Although the gap between the brackets does not directly affect the contact voltage drop like the contact pressure, the relay is a combination of mechanical, electrical, magnetic and force products, which will indirectly affect the contact voltage drop of the relay. Relays are generally affected by local temperature, humidity and vibration environment in the field. The components such as base, contact plate unit, armature, yoke iron and steel wire clamp inevitably have relatively small movement. In addition, they also have certain influence on the closing and separating process of dynamic and static contacts, resulting in contact parts. At the same time, slight deformation of contact may occur in the course of continuous movement. Mechanical parts are formed by mechanical external forces in the process of processing. Because most of the mechanical parts are made of metal materials and have certain rigidity, they will be deformed by stress release after a period of time. In addition, fatigue deformation will occur when mechanical parts are subjected to stress for a long time in use. For example, the gap between brackets becomes larger, which indicates that the gap between brackets and contacts becomes larger, resulting in excessive virtual travel, resulting in smaller sweep range or less contact spots during contact between front and back contacts, thus affecting contact points. Pressure drop. For contact homogeneity, it stipulates the homogeneity between ordinary contacts, reinforced contacts, ordinary contacts and reinforced contacts. It is the error of contact of relay groups at the same time. The large error means that the contact pressure or gap is deviated, which leads to the change of contact pressure drop and affects contact reliability.

C. *Contact resistance test*

Using GOM-802 programmable DC micro-Eurometer, the contact resistance of 50 relays which have completed 20,000 on-line monitoring of contact voltage drop is tested one by one. The test results show that 47 of the 50 relays are all qualified, which meets the requirements of GB/T 7417-2010 "AX Series Relays for Railway Signals" (P The contact resistance of the contacts is not more than 0.05_, and the contact resistance of the strengthened contacts is not more than 0.1_. The contact resistance of the other three relays exceeds the standard or is infinite. Statistical analysis was carried out on relays with qualified and unqualified contact resistance and contact voltage drop. The results are shown in Table 6:

It can be seen from the table that qualified relays with contact resistance exist in all three changing trends, but they account for a large proportion in the steady and smooth trend, and they account for a small proportion in the continuous fluctuation trend, and there is no obvious positive proportion relationship; while three relays with unqualified contact resistance, one of them is in the trend of fluctuation first and then stability. The other two stations are in the trend of continuous fluctuation, and the regularity is not obvious. It can be seen that there is a certain relationship between contact resistance and contact voltage drop, but the regularity is not strong. Through investigation, the inconsistency of load voltage and current applied to relay contacts by using DC micro-Euclidean resistance meter and on-line monitoring of contact voltage drop is one of the reasons for the weak regularity of contact resistance and contact voltage drop.

TABLE 6 CONTRAST TABLE OF CONTACT RESISTANCE AND CONTACT VOLTAGE DROP TRENDS

Project	Contact Resistance Qualified Relay	Contact Resistance Unqualified Relay
Always smooth and stable	28	0
Fluctuate first and then stabilize	13	1
Always fluctuate and fluctuate	6	2
Total	47	3

D. *SEM and EDS analysis*

Based on the results of contact resistance test and on-line monitoring of contact voltage drop of relays, we selected three representative relays with qualified contact resistance, over-standard contact resistance and infinite contact resistance from 50 relays for SEM and EDS analysis. The detailed analysis results are shown in Table 7:

It can be seen from the table that the contact surface with qualified contact resistance is clean and has slight striking marks. Energy spectrum analysis shows that the contact surface contains a small amount of impurities composed of C, O and other elements. The contact surface with exceeded contact resistance is clean and has slight ablation striking marks. Energy spectrum analysis shows that the contact surface contains a small amount of C, N, O. Impurities consisting of elements such as P, C, O, S, P, etc. The contact surface with infinite contact resistance has obvious ablation and strike marks, and there are prominent impurities around the contact area. Energy spectrum analysis shows that the contact surface contains a small amount of impurities consisting of elements such as C, O, S and P.

TABLE 7 SEM AND EDS ANALYSIS OF REPRESENTATIVE CONTACT SURFACES

<table>
<tr><th>Project</th><th>Microscopic morphology characteristics</th><th>Microstructure analysis</th></tr>
<tr><td>Qualified Contact Resistance</td><td></td><td><table><tr><th>Element</th><th>Weight percentage</th><th>Atomic percentage</th></tr><tr><td>C K</td><td>12.99</td><td>47.93</td></tr><tr><td>O K</td><td>6.62</td><td>18.33</td></tr><tr><td>Mg K</td><td>0.25</td><td>0.45</td></tr><tr><td>Fe K</td><td>0.63</td><td>0.49</td></tr><tr><td>Ag L</td><td>79.15</td><td>32.51</td></tr><tr><td>Total</td><td>100.00</td><td></td></tr></table></td></tr>
<tr><td>Contact resistance exceeding standard</td><td></td><td><table><tr><th>Element</th><th>Weight percentage</th><th>Atomic percentage</th></tr><tr><td>C K</td><td>4.01</td><td>10.89</td></tr><tr><td>N K</td><td>8.76</td><td>20.42</td></tr><tr><td>O K</td><td>22.78</td><td>46.46</td></tr><tr><td>P K</td><td>3.38</td><td>3.56</td></tr><tr><td>Fe K</td><td>0.72</td><td>0.42</td></tr><tr><td>Ag L</td><td>60.36</td><td>18.26</td></tr><tr><td>Total</td><td>100.00</td><td></td></tr></table></td></tr>
<tr><td>Contact resistance is infinite</td><td></td><td><table><tr><th>Element</th><th>Weight percentage</th><th>Atomic percentage</th></tr><tr><td>C K</td><td>5.72</td><td>15.78</td></tr><tr><td>N K</td><td>7.20</td><td>17.01</td></tr><tr><td>O K</td><td>21.29</td><td>44.06</td></tr><tr><td>Mg K</td><td>0.20</td><td>0.27</td></tr><tr><td>Si K</td><td>0.25</td><td>0.30</td></tr><tr><td>P K</td><td>3.01</td><td>3.22</td></tr><tr><td>Fe K</td><td>0.79</td><td>0.47</td></tr><tr><td>Ag L</td><td>61.55</td><td>18.90</td></tr><tr><td>Total</td><td>100.00</td><td></td></tr></table></td></tr>
</table>

It is found that the surface morphology and element composition of the contacts are different from each other by means of SEM (scanning electron microscopy) and EDS (energy dispersive X-ray spectrometer). Surface morphology features such as bumps, pits, scattered impurities and adhering foreign bodies can be clearly seen on some contacts. During the long-term operation of the relay, the relay is accompanied by them. Due to a series of mechanical, chemical, thermal and electrical effects, the surface morphology of contacts deteriorates gradually, and the chemical reactions of contact materials become more and more serious, such as bumps and pits, the surface of contacts becomes more rough under microscopic conditions, and the area of contact area (contact spot) becomes smaller gradually, which hinders the surface current of contacts. Through this, the shrinkage resistance will increase. At the same time, under the influence of heat, electricity, temperature and humidity, the surface of these bumps and pits will be oxidized, sulfided and chlorinated, forming a compound film on the contact surface. Because of the low current passing through the contact surface and insufficient contact pressure, the film has not been successfully broken down. The contact film resistance increases. When the surface shrinkage resistance and film resistance of a contact increase, the contact voltage drop will increase, which will affect the contact reliability of the relay. Similarly, scattered impurities accumulate continuously and extend to the surrounding area. When some or a small amount of impurities appear in the contact area, the contact spot will also decrease and the shrinkage resistance will increase. At the same time, because of the accumulation of impurities, the contact film will become thicker, the membrane resistance will become larger, and the contact voltage drop will also become larger, which will affect the contact point. Contact reliability.

IV. CONCLUSION

The change trend of contact voltage drop of railway signal relay reflects the randomness and contingency of contact reliability from the side, and these characteristics are related to the electrical characteristics, mechanical characteristics, contact resistance, contact surface morphological characteristics and composition of the relay itself.

1) Electrical characteristic parameters are the necessary conditions to ensure the normal suction and release of the relay, and also the prerequisite to meet the real-time acquisition of the contact voltage drop of the relay
2) The three trends include relays with qualified mechanical characteristics and relays with unqualified mechanical characteristics, but the proportion is different and no obvious rule is found.
3) There is a certain relationship between the contact resistance and the contact voltage drop of the relay. There is no obvious regularity between the two because of the different conditions of voltage and current applied in the test.
4) Surface morphology and composition distribution of relay contacts have a certain impact on contact pressure drop acquisition. Especially, foreign bodies consisting of C, O, S and P elements on contact surface destroy contact surface with a series of mechanical, chemical, thermal and electrical effects, affecting contact pressure drop.

REFERENCES

[1] Liu Wei.Zhou dasan Development of AN Series Relays [J]. Railway Signalling & Communication, Volume 39, No. 2, 2003

[2] GB / T 7417-2010, Railway signal AX series relay [S]

[3] GB / T 6902-2010, Railway signal relay test method [S]

[4] Hu Yaohua. Signal relay and maintenance (on the book) [M]. Beijing: China Railway Publishing House, 1998: 9.

[5] Xu Fuchun et al. SEM and XPS study on contact surface of electromagnetic relay [J]. Journal of Xiamen University (Natural Science Edition) July 2001 Vol.40 No.4

7th International Conference on Reliability of
Electrical Products and Electrical Contacts,
November 04-06, 2019

Degradation Modeling and Reliability Evaluation of Key Assembly Parameters of Electromagnetic Relays

Hao Chen, Xuerong Ye*, Yanmuzi Yang, Guofu Zhai
Harbin Institute of Technology, Harbin, 150001, China
E-mail: hao@hit.edu.cn Tel: 86-451-86413193 Fax: 86-451-86413192

Abstract—**The degraded reliability of in-service electronic components has become the main reason for the failure of weapons. Electromagnetic relays are the least reliable components in electronic systems. It is therefore important imperative to evaluate the reliability of in-service electromagnetic relays. Most existing research on the degraded reliability of relays uses the performance parameters of the whole machine to evaluate the performance degradation. Although such traditional methods for conducting reliability evaluation and life prediction using the performance parameters of the whole machine have shown to play a role in relay applications, they have no substantial effect on optimizing the relays themselves and improving the service life. The root cause of this is that reliable life evaluation models based on the performance parameters of the whole machine cannot reflect the reasons for the failure of in-service relays and the out of tolerance values of electrical parameters. Therefore, it is impossible for these traditional methods to fundamentally locate the causes of the poor reliability of relays, and they cannot provide guidance for the design of reliable relays. This paper first analyzes the degradation and failure mechanism of a contact spring system for electromagnetic relay under cyclic loading. The performance degradation of the contact spring system is then modelled and analysed using stochastic uncertainty theory. Finally, based on the contact gap degradation model, this paper conducts a reliable life evaluation of the electromagnetic relay by considering the degradation of the key assembly parameters of the contact spring system. The research results lay a foundation for the design of reliable electromagnetic relays.**

Index Terms— **Electromagnetic relay, Gap degradation, Degradation modeling, Reliability assessment.**

I. INTRODUCTION

Relays are a basic component with important functions such as circuit regulation, circuit protection and circuit conversion. They have the advantages of good versatility, high stability, long life, small size, high conversion depth, strong anti-interference ability and low price. Relays have been extensively applied to the industrial control circuits of home appliances, automatic control, communication and aerospace, as well as mechatronic products, remote telemetry [1-3].

In the field of weaponry, the life of weapons has been greatly extended in recent years, increasing attention has been paid to the reliability evaluation of modern weapons, especially the degradation and failure of some components. The degradation of weapons is usually simulated by a variety of mechanisms, and electronic components are the main elements that cause such degradation. The reliability of in-service electronic components has become a major cause of weaponry failure. Relay failure has become a serious problem for electronic components, and research on the reliability of electromagnetic relays is increasingly an important issue [4-6].

Although the problem of the dispersion of the reliability of relays can be solved to a certain extent by improving the processing or assembly precision, there is limited research on the dispersion of the reliability of relays due to various parts, complex assembly processes and different degrees of performance degradation. The reasons are that on one hand there is a lack of degradation data and degradation models of in-service relays, and on the other hand there are no methods for evaluating reliable life that consider the performance degradation of in-service relays [7]-[8].

In this paper, an electromagnetic relay with permanent magnet is taken as the research object, Firstly, the sensitive parameters of the contact spring system are selected for analysis of the degradation mechanism. In addition, an assembly parameter measuring device and experimental method for the contact spring system are designed so as to conduct a performance degradation experiment of the contact spring system under different working conditions. After that, the degradation model is established using a stochastic process method and the experimental data collected. Finally, a finite element calculation model considering the degradation of the spring is determined, in order to conduct a reliable life evaluation of the electromagnetic relay.

II. DEGRADATION MODELING AND RELIABILITY EVALUATION OF THE ELECTROMAGNETIC RELAY

A. Research object introduction and analysis

The research object is a typical differential polarized electromagnetic relay with double permanent magnets, with 1/2 crystal cover and four sets of conversion contacts. The contact form is a spring-contact structure, and each set of conversion contacts consists of one movable contact and two stationary contacts. The physical diagram of the relay is shown in Fig. 2-1.

a) sealed relay b) shell relay

Fig. 1 Electromagnetic relay

The main performance parameters of this relay can be seen in Table 1, where it is shown that the rated load is 28 V/2 A, and the rated working voltage of the coil is 27V.

Table1

Main indicator of relay

Indicator type	Indicator	Indicator type	Indicator
Rated load	28V/2A	Rated voltage	27V
Coil resistance	1000Ω	Operate voltage	11.5~14.5V

B. Analysis of the degradation mechanism of key assembly parameters of the contact spring system for the electromagnetic relay

During the operation of this type of electromagnetic relay, the electrical erosion of the contact caused by arcs directly causes the performance degradation and the failure of the relay. The melting and solidification process on the contact surface during the cumulative electric erosion process will lead to changes in the key assembly parameters of the contact spring system, e.g. contact gap, etc. The process of contact gap degradation caused by arc erosion is shown in Fig. 3.

As shown in Fig. 3, the arc burning phenomenon of the electromagnetic relay during the breaking and turning-on process causes the relay contact material to melt and form a molten product. After the arc is extinguished, the molten product will be concentrated around the contacts, resulting in material transfer on the contacts. As the relay continues to operate, the material transfer becomes more intense. When the burning reaches a certain level, the heights of the contacts are reduced from the original x_1 and x_2 to x_1' and x_2'. At the same time, the physical wear of the electromagnetic relay (mechanical wear and electrical wear) will also cause degradation in the contact height by x_1'' and x_2''. The above process will cause a macroscopic increase in the contact gap of the key assembly parameters of the contact spring system to degrade (increase by $x_1'+x_1''$ and $x_2'+x_2''$), resulting in performance degradation or even failure of the relay.

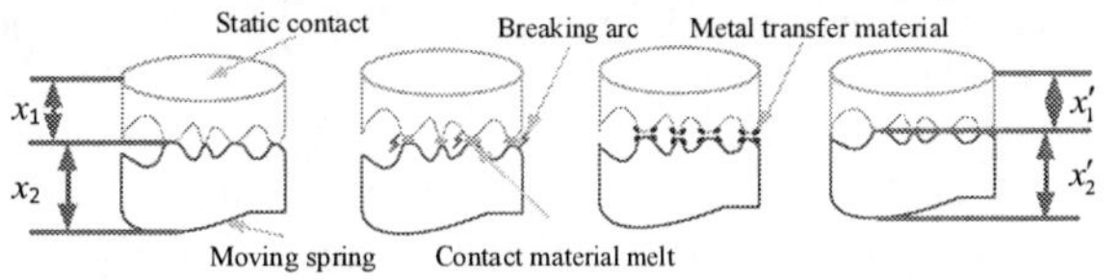

Fig. 2 Contact gap change caused by arc erosion

C. Degradation experiment of key assembly parameters of the contact spring system for the electromagnetic relay

The relay used in this research is an aerospace relay. Its size is smaller than many measuring tools, and the internal structure is occluded, so that direct measurement of the assembly parameters is difficult, and obtaining degradation data is not easy. In this paper, a new method for the direct measurement of the assembly parameters of the relay is designed using laser displacement sensors. The whole measurement scheme is designed by focusing on the goal of obtaining as much effective data as possible for the assembly parameters of the contact spring system under different working conditions. The principles of the experiment are shown in Fig. 4.

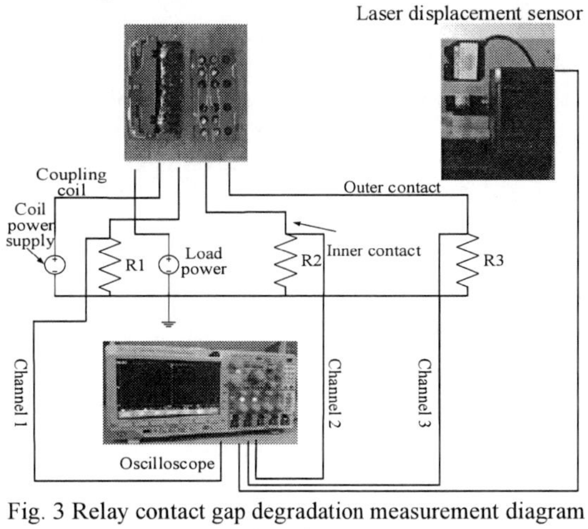

Fig. 3 Relay contact gap degradation measurement diagram

The controller LK-HD500 transmits the signal sensed by the laser displacement sensor to the oscilloscope to visually display the distance as a waveform. The inner and outer contact pins connected to the spring monitored by the laser displacement sensor are mounted with sampling resistors, and the common contact pin is connected to the load power supply. In this way, the oscilloscope can be used to simultaneously monitor the contact transition state and the spring displacement. In addition, the power supply and the sampling resistors are connected between the two ends of the trigger coil, and the coil waveform can be obtained to analyze the performance parameters of the relay, such as pull-in voltage, pick-up time, and release time.

In order to make the experimental conditions as close to actual working conditions as possible, this paper randomly selected 8 relays from the batch products for the life experiment. The environmental temperature and humidity of the life experiment are set according to GJB-65B, and the load is set according to the rated load requirement for the product. During the life experiment, the contact gap measurement device described above is used for data acquisition. The data is collected every 2,000 times within 50,000 times, and every 4,000 times after that. The ten sets of data collected each time are averaged to obtain a final value. The experimental results are shown in Fig. 4.

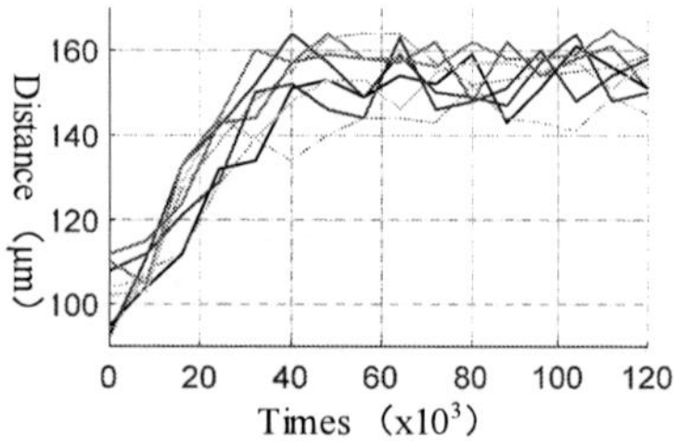

Fig. 4 Degradation of contact gap of electromagnetic relay

D. Degradation modeling of key assembly parameters of the contact spring system for the electromagnetic relay

The measurement of the contact gap using the laser displacement sensor can accurately obtain the degradation process of the assembly parameters. This feature severely limits the selectivity of the stochastic process for degradation modeling. On the other hand, the above-mentioned contact spring system has been manually adjusted, which causes a difference in the degradation process among the springs. This paper attempts to add the distributions to the shape parameter and scale parameter of the 1D Wiener process, to make the established degradation model to be as close to actual conditions as possible, thereby achieving more accurate and reliable life evaluation.

The 1D Wiener process is expressed as:

$$X(t) = \mu t + \sigma \cdot W(t) \tag{1}$$

where $W(t)$ represents the standard Wiener process, μ quantifies the rate at which the mean shift of the degraded parameter $X(t)$ leaves the degradation origin (also known as the shift parameter or shape parameter), σ represents the variance of the possible distribution of the degradation parameter $X(t)$ around the mean at a certain point in time t (also known as the scale parameter, or diffusion parameter).

In the 1D Wiener process, the parameters μ and σ default to constants. In actual production, the same batch of products often have significant process dispersion, which can be fully verified in the operating voltage of the same batch of samples. Therefore, the Wiener process cannot correctly describe such degradation process, and it is necessary to introduce dispersion in the parameters μ and σ.

Let μ and σ be two random variables which satisfy the following conditions:

$$\omega = \sigma^{-2} \sim \mathrm{Gam}(\delta, \gamma), \mu|\omega \sim N(\nu, \frac{\eta}{\omega}) \tag{2}$$

Usually, the Wiener process with random parameters is also a nonlinear process. For the time parameter, linearization is required. The time function $\Lambda(t)$ is introduced, let $\Lambda(0)=0$ with $\Lambda(t)$ as a monotonically increasing function. Then the degradation process can be expressed as:

$$X(t) = \mu\Lambda(t) + \sigma \cdot W(\Lambda(t)) \tag{3}$$

In the Wiener process with random parameters, the two random variables μ and σ are made to obey the specific conjugate distribution for the convenience of calculation, which draws on the Bayesian linear regression analysis. Specifically, if i=1,2,..,n is the number of measurements, j=1,2,..,N is the sample number, t_{ij} represents the measurement time, the degradation data X_{ij} measured for a group of equal time interval and $X_{i0}=0$, then $\Delta X_{ij} = X_{ij} - X_{i(j-1)}$ represents the degradation increment of the j th sample between $t_{i(j-1)}$ and t_{ij}. The time function is $\Lambda(t)$, let $\Lambda(0)=0$ and $\Lambda(t)$ is a monotone increasing function. $\Delta\Lambda(t_{ij}) = \Lambda(t_{ij}) - \Lambda(t_{i(j-1)})$ represents the time increment function of the j th sample.

$$L(\mu_j, \omega_j, \delta, \gamma, \nu, \eta) = \prod_{i=1}^{n}\prod_{j=1}^{N} \frac{\omega_j^{1/2}}{\sqrt{2\pi\Delta\Lambda(t_{ij})}} \exp(\frac{-\omega_j(\Delta X_{ij} - \mu_j \Delta\Lambda(t_{ij}))^2}{2\Delta\Lambda(t_{ij})}) \cdot$$

$$\prod_{j=1}^{N} \frac{\omega_j^{1/2}}{\sqrt{2\pi\eta}} \exp(\frac{-\omega_j(\mu_j - \nu)^2}{2\eta}) \frac{\gamma^{\delta}\omega_j^{\delta-1}}{\Gamma(\delta)} \exp(-\gamma\omega_j) \tag{4}$$

The maximum likelihood function A is given by:

$$\psi(\delta) - \ln\delta = \frac{1}{N}\sum_{j=1}^{N} \ln\omega_j + \ln N - \ln\sum_{j=1}^{N}\omega_j \tag{5}$$

In Eq. (3), the function $\psi(\cdot)$ is the logarithmic derivative of the Gamma function $\Gamma(x)$.

In the solution of the maximum likelihood function of the Wiener process with random parameters, the analytical solutions of each parameter contain implicit parameters, and the results cannot be directly obtained. In this paper, the EM algorithm is used to iterate and obtain a set of numerical solutions that satisfy the accuracy requirements. When the difference between the two iterations is less than a pre-set value, the EM algorithm obtains the final numerical solution of the parameters.

E. Reliable life evaluation based on the degradation of key assembly parameters of the contact spring system

Section 2.4 demonstrated the 1D degradation trajectory modeling of the over-travel gap. If a failure threshold l is specifed, then it is assumed that the degradation trajectory fails once it reaches the threshold for the first time. It is obvious that this hypothesis is true for the reaction force of the contact spring system. In this case, the time (the number of actions) for first reaching the failure threshold is expressed as t, and during the Wiener degradation process, t is subject to the Inverse Gaussian distribution, with its probability density function given by:

$$f(t)=\frac{l}{\sqrt{2\pi\sigma^2(\Lambda(t))^3}}\exp[-\frac{(l-\mu\Lambda(t))^2}{2\sigma^2\Lambda(t)}] \quad (10)$$

The cumulative distribution function is given by:

$$F(t)=\Phi(\frac{\mu\Lambda(t)-l}{\sigma\sqrt{\Lambda(t)}})+\exp(\frac{2\mu l}{\sigma^2})\Phi(\frac{-l-\mu\Lambda(t)}{\sigma\sqrt{\Lambda(t)}}) \quad (11)$$

where $\Phi(\cdot)$ is the probability density function of the standard normal distribution,

$$\Phi(x)=\frac{1}{\sqrt{2\pi}}\int_{-\infty}^{x}e^{\frac{t^2}{2}}dt \quad (12)$$

where μ and σ are the drift parameter and diffusion parameter of the Wiener process, respectively, which can be calculated from the results δ,γ,ν,η of the parameter estimation in Section 2.4.

According to the contact gap degradation model of the electromagnetic relay, we have:

$$\begin{cases}\hat{\mu}_x=0.7339\\ \hat{\sigma}_x=25.8156\end{cases} \quad (13)$$

The failure threshold l represents the condition where the relay is picked up and released after 100,000 times, and the release voltage does not exceed 16V. For the contact spring system, the condition for judging failure is equivalent to when the reaction force of the contact spring system does not exceed 0.62N. Thus, the reliability function of the contact spring system based on single factor degradation can be obtained:

$$R(t)=1-\Phi(\frac{\mu\Lambda(t)-l}{\sigma\sqrt{\Lambda(t)}})+\exp(\frac{2\mu l}{\sigma^2})\Phi(\frac{-l-\mu\Lambda(t)}{\sigma\sqrt{\Lambda(t)}}) \quad (14)$$

The reliability function of the contact spring system considering the single-factor degradation of the gap is given by:

$$R_x(t)=1-\Phi(\frac{0.7339\Lambda_2(t)-48}{25.8156\sqrt{\Lambda_2(t)}})+ \exp(\frac{70.4544}{666.4452})\Phi(\frac{-48-0.7339\Lambda_2(t)}{25.8156\sqrt{\Lambda_2(t)}}) \quad (15)$$

where $\Lambda_1(t)$ is the best linearization function chosen in Section 2.4. The reliability curve that considers the over travel and the single-factor degradation of the gap is shown in Fig. 5. For $R(t)=50\%$, the pseudo-fault number of the contact spring system considering gap degradation is 81,367 times.

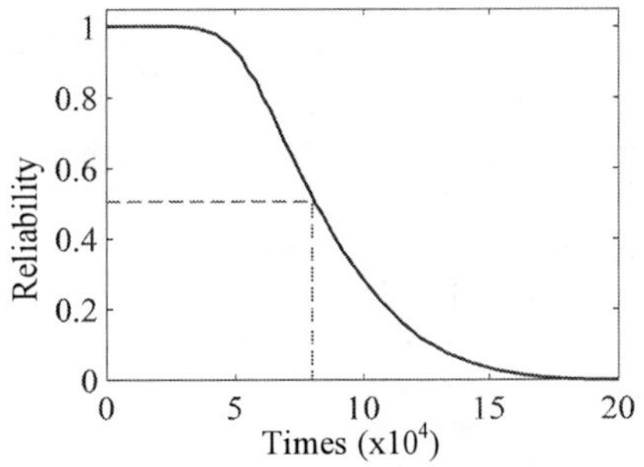

Fig. 5. Relay reliability curve with contact gap degradation

III. CONCLUSION

The degraded reliability of in-service electromagnetic relays is the main cause of equipment failure. Reasonable evaluation of the reliability of in-service electromagnetic relays has become the focus of many studies for improving the overall reliability of equipment. In this paper, the degradation and failure mechanism of the contact spring system is analyzed experimentally. Degradation model of the assembly parameters of the contact spring system with random parameters was established. Based on the degradation model of the assembly parameters, a reliable life evaluation model is established for the relay. The main conclusions are summarized as follows:

(1) With the electric ablation and wear during the working process of the researched relay, large pits or even burn-through will occur on the movable spring. As the material moves on the stationary contact, the surface morphology of the contact gradually changes from convex sphere to concave plane. The change to the macroscopic surface morphology of the movable and stationary contacts causes the contact gap to gradually increase, further resulting in the degradation or even failure of the relay performance.

(2) A method is proposed for measuring the assembly parameters of the contact spring system using a laser displacement sensor. The data obtained by the experimental platform was used to analyze the degradation of assembly parameters of the contact spring system. To address the rich random information in the degradation data, a Wiener degradation modeling method with random parameters is proposed. The degradation trajectory model of the contact gap under different working conditions is established, laying a foundation for the reliable life evaluation of batched relays.

(3) The relay reliability function with single-factor degradation of gap has been established. The pseudo-fault number of the contact spring system with the gap degradation is 81367 times.

REFERENCES

[1] Johler W. The Design Challenges Involved in Miniaturization of Electromechanical Relays[C]. Proceedings of the fifty-second holm conference on IEEE. 2006, pp. 151-152.

[2] P. Zhou, D. Lin, Y. Xiao, N. Lambert, and M. A. Rahman, "Temperature-Dependent Demagnetization Model of Permanent Magnets for Finite Element Analysis," IEEE Trans. Magn., vol. 48, no. 2, pp. 1031-1034, Feb. 2012.

[3] Y. Jiaxin, W. Ruichao, C. Hao, C. Feng, and L. Huimin, "A Novel Design of the Rotary Electromagnetic Actuator and the Analysis of Critical Demagnetization State for Its Permanent Magnet," IEEE Trans. Magn., vol. 53, no. 11, pp. 1-6, Nov. 2017.

[4] Gebraeel, Nagi Z, Lawley, Mark A. A neural network degradation model for com-puting and updating residual life distributions[J]. IEEE Transactions on Auto-mation Science and Engineering, 2008, pp, 154-163.

[5] Wang X, Xu D. An Inverse Gaussian Process Model for Degradation Data[J]. Technometrics, 2010, 52(2), pp, 188-197.

[6] Weiwen Peng, Yan-Feng Li, "Bayesian Degradation Analysis with Inverse Gauss-ian Process Models Under Time-Varying Degradation Rates" [J]. IEEE Trans-actions on Reliability, 2017, pp, 66(1).

[7] Zhai Guofu, Wang Qiya, Ren Wanbin. Research on Electromagnetic Relay's Dy-namic Characteristics Disturbed by Uniform Static Magnetic Field[J]. Journal of Zhejiang University Science A, 2008, 9(4), pp, 577-582.

[8] Fan WeiWei, Zhai Guofu, Wu Shihua. The Inverse Design Method for Reaction System of Electromagnetic Relay[C]. Proceedings of International Conference on Electrical Machines and Systems, 2008, pp, 4349-4353.

Arc Fault Detection Based on Wavelet Energy Entropy in Aviation Power System

Ze Li[1], Deshuan Tong[1], Ruihua Cui[1,2]
[1]Hebei University of Technology, Tianjin, 300130
[2]Electrical Apparatus Institute of Hebei Province, Tianjin, 300130

***Abstract*—Aiming at the problems of complex environment, high real-time requirements and vulnerability to interference in the detection of aviation AC arc faults in this paper, the wavelet energy entropy is used as the characteristic quantity of the analysis. Starting from the theory of wavelet packet transform. The current signal is decomposed and reconstructed by selecting the appropriate wavelet packet order and decomposition layer number. The wavelet energy entropy is used to detect the arc fault under linear load and nonlinear with the information entropy theory; the test results show that the proposed method is more anti-interference than the traditional time domain analysis and makes up for the Fourier transform for time-frequency analysis of non-stationary signal, combines the advantages of information entropy on the statistical characteristics of uncertain events and complex systems. On the basis of satisfying the comprehensiveness and reliability of detection, it also shortens the detection time. There is a large promotion on the real-time detection.**

***Index Terms*— Arc fault, Wavelet energy entropy, Wavelet packet transform, Information entropy**

I. INTRODUCTION

With the rapid development of the aviation industry, the aviation electrical system is becoming more and more complex [1], coupled with the narrow space, the complex line, and susceptible to flight conditions. The occurrence of faults is random and rapid. In the event that the arc fault cannot be detected in time. The high temperature arc will be generated when arc fault occurs which will cause serious damage to the power lines and surrounding equipment of the aircraft, seriously affecting the safety of the aircraft operation.

The series fault arc of the aviation electrical system has the characteristics of short duration and low current intensity. Moreover, arc faults are usually latent, intermittent and transient [2]-[3],which brings a lot of difficulties to the detection of aviation arc faults. Related researches can be traced back to the 1990s. Domestic and foreign scholars first collected current signals from the most intuitive time domain, and proposed a method to detect arcs by measuring changes in current peaks[4]. In recent years, studies based on the time-domain characteristics of series AC arcs have included the use of the mean of the current signal, the rate of change of the arc current[5] to detect arc faults. Although the time domain signal acquisition is simple, the detection is intuitive and effective, the anti-interference is poor, and it is susceptible to interference from other signals under complicated aviation conditions. The threshold needs to be manually set, and the randomness of the detection is relatively large. In order to avoid the lack of detection in the time domain, researchers began to use the Fourier transform to transform the time domain into the frequency domain, but the arc current is a distinct non-stationary signal, and the Fourier transform[6]cannot reflect time-frequency local characteristics when processing non-stationary signal. The appearance of wavelet transform can better analyze the spectrum, but its frequency resolution is poor in the high frequency band and the time resolution is poor in the low frequency band. Arc currents contain a lot of high frequency noise. The wavelet packet transform can divide the frequency band, and can adaptively select the corresponding frequency band according to different characteristics of the signal to improve the time-frequency resolution. In addition, with the development of artificial intelligence, time-frequency characteristics combined with some complex computer algorithms are widely used, including neural network[7], support vector machine[8] and so on. Although statistics and calculations on a large amount of data can be realized, problems such as long calculation time and need for offline training samples cannot be avoided, and the real-time detection is not high enough.

In this paper, the theory of wavelet packet transform combined with information entropy is used, and the wavelet energy entropy is used as the feature quantity to analyze the arc fault under various loads such as linear and nonlinear. It not only improves the time-frequency characteristics of detection, but also exerts the advantage of the statistical characteristics of information entropy in processing large amounts of data. Improve the real-time and reliability of arc fault detection.

II. AVIATION ARC FAULT TEST

A. Arc fault test platform

This article performs a point contact test based on the standard UL1699 proposed by the United States in 1999. The point contact test simulates an arc fault caused by aging of the line and poor contact in an aeronautical arc fault. The circuit schematic shown in Fig. 1 is given. In the test, the output voltage of the aviation power supply was 115V, and the power supply frequency was 400Hz. For a more comprehensive simulation of aeronautical arc faults under different loads, the load used in this test is linear and non-linear. Linear loads include pure resistance (57.5Ω), RL (57.5Ω+5mH), RC (57.5Ω+47μF), and non-linear load auto transformer rectifier units (ATRU).

B. Analysis of arc fault waveform

The sampling frequency of the test was 409.6 kHz, and a total of 20 cycles from normal to fault were selected. This test uses current transformers and DSP to collect current under various loads. The current at the sampling point is divided by the maximum value and normalized to any unit (a.u.). The current waveforms obtained under different loads are shown in Fig. 2~ 5.

The following conclusions can be drawn by analyzing the current waveform of each load in Fig. 2~ 5:

1) For linear loads, the current waveform is a smooth sine wave before the arc fault occurs. When an arc fault occurs, there will be a region where the current

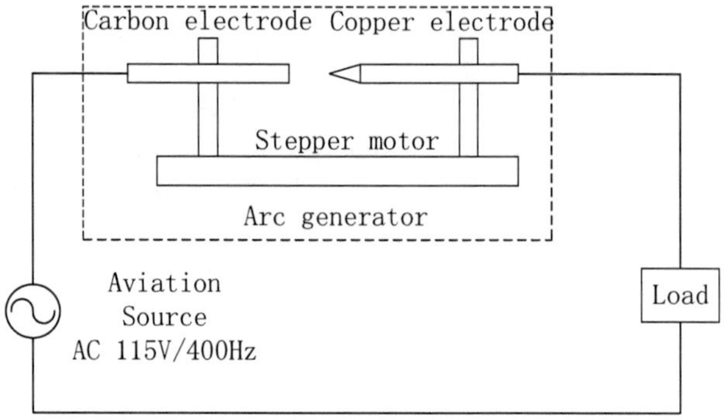

Fig. 1 Schematic diagram of contact test circuit.

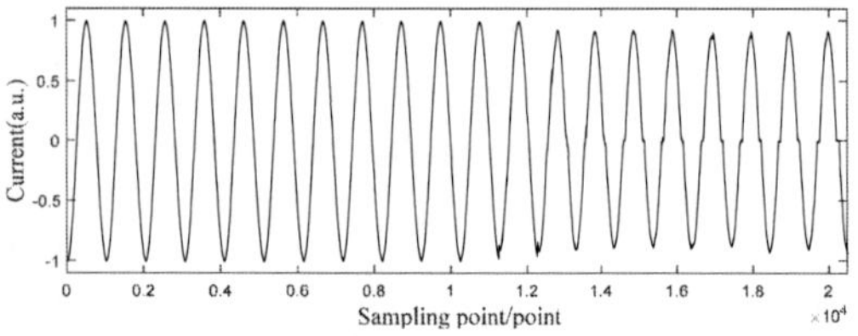

Fig. 2 The current waveform of pure resistance (57.5Ω).

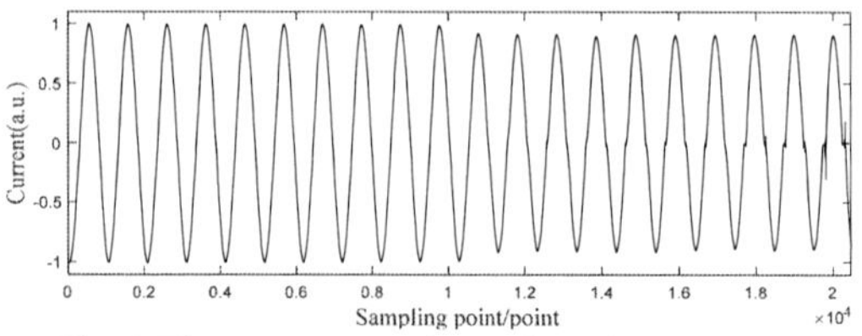

Fig. 3 The current waveform of RL (57.5Ω+5mH).

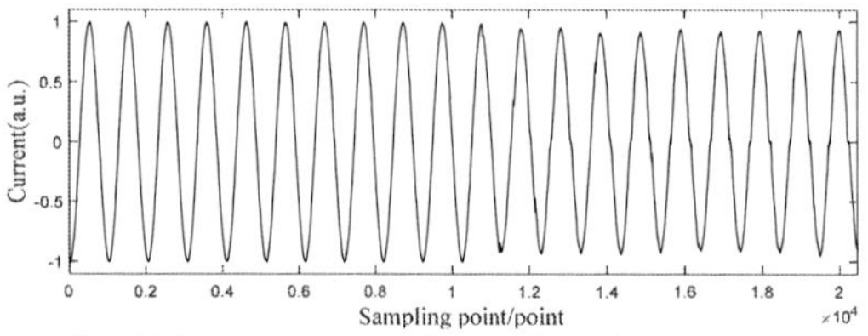

Fig. 4 The current waveform of RC (57.5Ω+47μF).

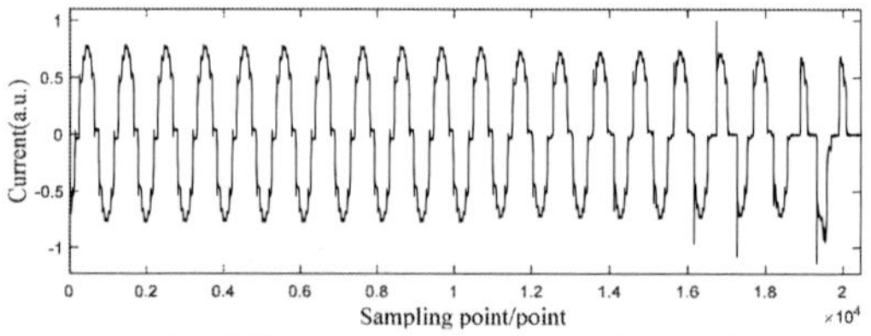

Fig. 5 The current waveform of ATRU.

is close to zero when the current crosses zero. This area is called "current zero zone" because there will be a process of extinguishing and then resetting before and after the current crosses zero.

2) When an arc fault occurs, the high frequency component of the current increases significantly and the current amplitude decreases significantly.

3) For the non-linear load ATRU, there is high-frequency noise before and after the arc fault occurs. Because the ATRU has a "zero-happiness phenomenon" when it works normally. However, its high frequency noise will increase significantly and the amplitude of the current will also decrease when an arc fault occurs.

In practice, the high-frequency component of the current is not only caused by an arc fault, but also by other loads or power quality to produce interference similar to the characteristic harmonics of the arc current. Therefore, simply using the current and voltage in the time domain as the characteristic quantity for discriminating the arc fault often leads to misjudgment. The use of Fourier decomposition of the current signal is also insufficient to accurately determine the occurrence of an arc fault due to the influence of harmonics.

Wavelet analysis and wavelet packet analysis are generally used when non-stationary signals are processed in some projects. Compared with wavelet analysis, wavelet packet analysis can make the signal analysis more precise. The time-frequency plane can be divided more carefully. The resolution of the high-frequency part of the signal is better than the wavelet analysis. It can be adaptively selected the best wavelet basis function according to the characteristics of the signal for better analysis of the signal. However, the wavelet packet transform will greatly increase the amount of information that needs to be processed, increasing the complexity of the system and reducing the real-time and reliability of the detection. To this end, the theory of wavelet energy entropy is introduced to give full play to the advantages of the statistical characteristics of information entropy theory in dealing with complex signals. The wavelet energy entropy is used to realize the accurate and reliable identification of arc faults based on the wavelet packet transform theory, the concept of entropy, and the theory of wavelet energy entropy.

III. PRINCIPLE ANALYSIS OF WAVELET ENERGY ENTROPY

A. *Wavelet packet decomposition*

The wavelet packet transform can decompose the low-frequency part of the signal or decompose the high-frequency part and the decomposition has neither redundancy nor omission, so it can better perform signals containing a large amount of medium and high frequency information in term of time-frequency localization. The wavelet packet decomposition tree diagram is shown in Fig.6.

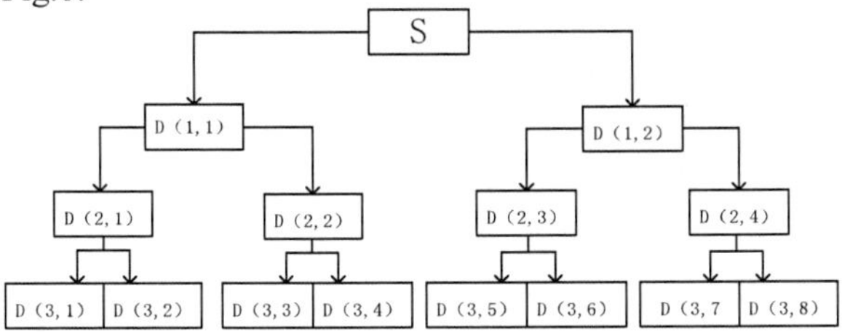

Fig. 6 Diagram of wavelet packet decomposition tree

In Fig. 6, "S" is the original current signal to be decomposed, node $D(i,m)$ is the coefficient of group "m" of decomposition at layer "i", i=1,2,⋯,n; m=1,2,⋯,j,where "n" is the layer of decomposition, $j=2^i$.

B. *Shannon information entropy*

Shannon's information entropy theory indicates that information entropy H can be used to describe the average uncertainty of multiple values of a random variable and reflect the complexity of the system, sequence uncertainty and so on. Setting a random event X that has different values of $U_1, U_2, \cdots, U_N$ and the corresponding probability is $P_1, P_2, \cdots, P_N$. Information entropy represents the average uncertainty of event X. The equation is shown below:

$$H(X) = -\sum_{j=1}^{N} P_j \log(P_j) \tag{1}$$

C. *Wavelet energy entropy*

Set E(i,m) be the wavelet energy of the signal current $x(t)$. where "i" represents the number of wavelet packet decomposition layers, "m" represents the scale of decomposition. m=1,2,⋯, j. The equation is shown below:

$$E(i,m) = \sum_{m=1}^{j} \left|D(i,m)\right|^2 \tag{2}$$

Wavelet energy entropy can be obtained according to the theory of information entropy. Wavelet energy entropy can be expressed as below:

$$p_m = E(i,m)/E \tag{3}$$

$$E = \sum_{m=1}^{j} E(i,\mathrm{m}) \tag{4}$$

$$Wee = -\sum_{m=1}^{j} p_m \log(p_m) \tag{5}$$

IV. ARC FAULT DETECTION BASED ON WAVELET ENERGY ENTROPY

The wavelet packet decomposition theory is introduced above, which can divide the frequency band part into multiple layers. According to different characteristics of the signal to be analyzed, the corresponding frequency band can be adaptively selected to match the signal spectrum, thereby improving the time-frequency resolution. In order to better distinguish between arc faults and normal cycles, the data is decomposed and reconstructed by db4 wavelet, in which the frequency band of the approximate reconstructed signal "a_j" of the wavelet contains $0\sim f_s/2^{(i+1)}$.where "f_s" is signal sampling frequency, "i" is wavelet packet decomposition layer[9]. The more decomposition layers of wavelet packet decomposition, the more frequency bands are decomposed, and the narrower the frequency included in each frequency segment. The sampling frequency is 409.6kHz, according to the sampling theorem, the Nyquist sampling frequency is 204.8kHz. The selected number of decomposition layers is 4 layers, and the selected frequency band is 0~12.8kHz. The feature extraction steps for wavelet energy entropy are as follows:

1) The current signal of each cycle is taken as the signal to be decomposed, and the normal and fault cycles are 20 cycles in total.
2) Decompose and reconstruct the current signal of each cycle with db4 wavelet whose decomposition layers is 4 layers.
3) The energy spectrum of the reconstructed signal for each period is obtained according to formula (2).
4) According to formula (4), the energy values of the reconstructed signals at each wavelet level are added, and the probability of the energy at each layer scale

in the total energy E is obtained.

5) According to formula (5), the wavelet energy entropy is obtained after each period decomposition and reconstruction.

The wavelet energy entropy curves of 20 cycles from normal to fault under different loads are shown in fig.7 ~ 10.

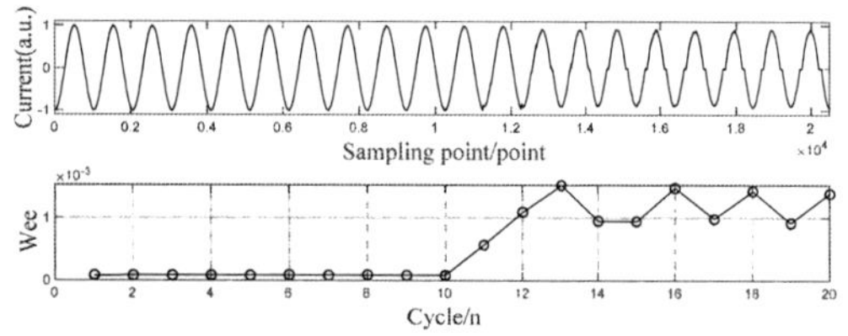

Fig. 7 Wavelet energy entropy curve of pure resistance (57.5Ω).

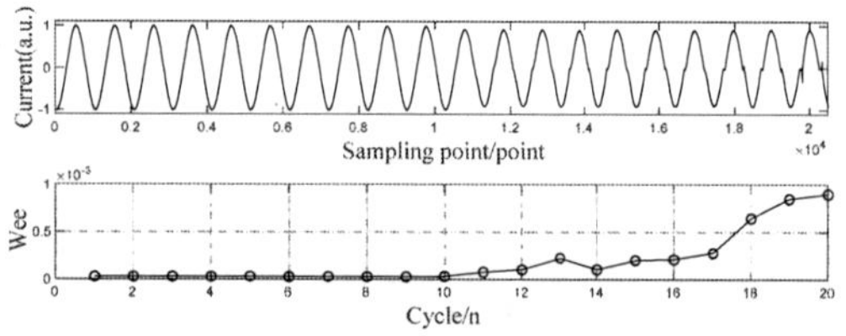

Fig. 8 Wavelet energy entropy curve of RL (57.5Ω+5mH).

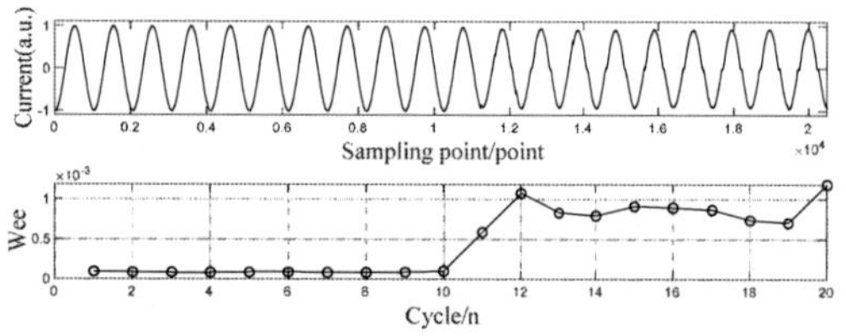

Fig. 9 Wavelet energy entropy curve of RC (57.5Ω+47μF).

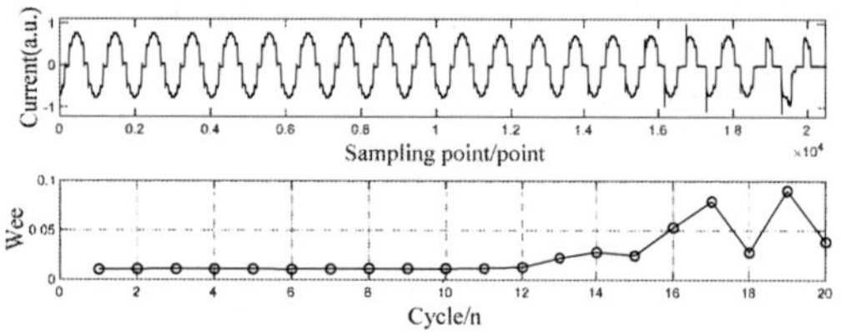

Fig. 10 Wavelet energy entropy curve of ATRU.

Through the analysis of the wavelet energy entropy curve under each load, it can be seen that before the arc fault occurs, the wavelet energy entropy value is near zero and remains basically stable, showing a horizontal straight line. When an arc fault occurs, the wavelet energy entropy value of the fault period is significantly larger than the entropy value of the normal period, and the variation range is large. For the normal cycle of linear load, the entropy value is about $2\times10^{-5}\sim9\times10^{-5}$, which is close to zero. The entropy value is greater than 1×10^{-4}, which is ten times that of normal when the arc fault occurs. For the first twelve cycles of nonlinear load, the entropy value is about $1\times10^{-2}\sim1.2\times10^{-2}$ and after the occurrence of arc fault, the entropy value is about $2.2\times10^{-2}\sim9.9\times10^{-2}$, which is 2~10 times of the normal value. Therefore, it can be used as a basis for discriminating whether an arc fault has occurred. In the time domain, the problem of misjudgment caused by current and voltage as characteristic quantity easily influenced by harmonics from other causes is solved and the reliability of detection is increased. Combined with the advantages of information entropy on complex systems, the detection time is reduced and the detection of arc faults is more accurate. Combined with the advantages of information entropy on complex systems, the detection time is reduced and the detection of arc faults is more accurate.

V. CONCLUSION

This paper introduces wavelet packet transform and combines the theory of information entropy. Wavelet energy entropy is used to detect the arc fault, which is based on the experiment. The experimental results show that the wavelet packet transform is a good complement to the shortcomings of the Fourier transform. The appropriate frequency segment and the wavelet energy entropy analysis method can be used to characterize the difference between before and after the arc fault. The detection method of wavelet energy entropy is more accurate in identifying arc faults and has strong anti-interference ability. It has better real-time performance than complex computer algorithms. This method provides a good research direction for the detection of aviation arc fault.

REFERENCES

[1] X Xiong. "Research on Test Apparatus and Diagnostic Technology of Aviation Arc Fault," Dalian University of Technology, 2018.

[2] R.H. Cui, S.S. Li, and L.K. Geng. "Application of Three Order Cumulant in the Detection of Aviation Series Fault Arc," Electric Drive, 2018, 48 (08): 88-92.

[3] Y.Q. Luo, T.J. He. "Research on new fault arc detection technology," Guangdong Public Security Technology, 2018, 26 (04): 60-62.

[4] J. Jiang, et al., "Series Arc Detection and Complex Load Recognition Based on Principal Component Analysis and Support Vector Machine," in IEEE Access, vol. 7, pp. 47221-47229, 2019.

[5] Y.Wang, Q.Q.Wei, L.J.Ge, et al. "Series AC arc fault detection method based on high frequency component of arc current," Electric Power Automation Equipment, 2017, 37 (07): 191-197.

[6] J.X.Cai. "Based on the five time harmonic component probability distribution of arc fault identification method of research," Shenyang University of Technology, 2017.

[7] Qiongfang Yu,Gaolu Huang,Yi Yang. Low voltage AC series arc fault detection method based on

parallel deep convolutional neural network[J]. IOP Conference Series: Materials Science and Engineering,2019,490(7).
[8] J. Jiang,et al., "Series Arc Detection and Complex Load Recognition Based on Principal Component Analysis and Support Vector Machine," in IEEE Access, vol. 7, pp. 47221-47229, 2019.
[9] R.H.Cui,W.D.Hu,L,K,Geng. "Arc Fault Detection Method Based on Singularity of the Wavelet Reconstruction Signal in Aviation Power System," Electric Drive, 2018,48(06):69-72.
[10] Y.J.Zhang,L.Wang,Z.D.Yin. "HHT - Based Feature Extraction Method for Aeronautical DC Serial Arc," Acta Aeronautica ET Astronautica Sinica, 2019,40(1):522404-522404.
[11] L.P.Huang,C.W.Wu,J.Wang. "Fault pattern recognition of rolling bearing using wavelet package analysis and BP neural network," Electronic Measurement Technology, 2016,39(04):164-168.
[12] C.Jiang. "Fault detection of distribution network system based on wavelet energy chirp,"Practical Electronics, 2013(19):38-40.

Study on the Effect of Ag Layer Thickness of Composite Contacts on Electric Life

Changliu Jiang, Lei Yi, Yanbao Chen, Jinliang Zhang
Xiamen Hongfa Electroacoustic Co., Ltd., Xiamen, China, 361021

***Abstract*—As one of the most critical parts of relay, contact has a significant impact on the electric life. In order to save cost, Ag/Cu composite contacts, even Ag/Cu/Ag three composite contacts, are often used by relay manufacturers. The silver layer thickness of Ag/Cu composite contact often fluctuates due to the influence of upsetting process. In this paper, the failure analysis was carried out with one type automobile relay after electrical life testing, and the electrical life results of the relays using welding-contact and single-contact were also consulted. The influence of silver layer thickness at the edge of composite contact on the electrical life was confirmed. By improving the shape and thickness of the silver layer, the electrical life of relay was significantly promoted.**

***Index Terms*—Relay, Failure, Reliability, Improvement**

I. INTRODUCTION

Electromagnetic relay is widely used in automotive, electric power, household appliances, industrial control as an automatic control electric switch through the closure and disconnection of contacts. At the moment of contacts closure or disconnection, the arc between contacts makes the contacts wear, spatter, welding etc, which will cause the failure of conducting (high resistance) and release. According to the statistics of historical failure, more than 75% of failure occurs in the contact system. Contact is the most critical part of relay, a lot of research work on contact materials, manufacturing technology, contact performance evaluation device etc, has been done by scholars and enterprise technicians at home or abroad, which plays an important role in improving the reliability of relay products [1-2].

In order to ensure good conductivity and thermal conductivity, precious metal (such as silver alloy) is usually chosen as contact material of relay; and relay manufacturers often use Ag/Cu composite contacts, even Ag/Cu/Ag triple composite contacts for cost saving. However, the thickness of silver layer of Ag/Cu composite contacts, especially the thickness of silver layer at the edge of contacts, usually fluctuates due to the influence of contact upsetting process [3]. Through the failure analysis and a series of test with one type automobile relay, the influence mechanism that the silver layer thickness of composite contact affect the electrical life was discussed, and the improvement schemes were given in this paper.

II. FAILURE INFORMATION

A. Research Object

The research object is one type automobile clapping electromagnetic relay. Its X-Ray image is shown in Fig.1. The main parameters and indicators are shown in Table I.

Fig. 1 X-Ray image of research object.

TABLE I
MAIN CHARACTERISTICS OF RESEARCH OBJECT

Characteristics	Values
Dimensions	26.5mm×26.5mm×25.2mm
Contact form	One set of Normally Open
Sealing	Dust-proof type
Rated load	70A switching capability
Working temperature	Max 125℃

B. Electrical Life Failure

Three lots of samples (10 samples each lot) were selected to do the electrical life test with the conditions show in the Table II.2-parameters Weibull is used as the life distribution, and the results are shown in Table III and Figure 2. The number of electrical life is about 20,000~100,000, and it shows good lifetime consistency of three lots because the B10 life and the shape parameters of Weibull distribution are close to each other. The failure performance in three tests above-mentioned is contact instantaneous adhesion.

TABLE II

TEST CONDITIONSFFOR ELECTRICAL ENDURANCE

Characteristics	Specific conditions
Ambient temperature	-40~125℃
Load type	DC Inductive load, 0.16 mH
Load	Inrush 150A,Static 50A
Cycle frequency	2s ON 4s OFF
Life requirements	100,000 cycles
Failure criteria	Once detected malfunction are defined as failure
Remarks	Movable contacts connected to load positive poles

TABLE III

POINT ESTIMATIONSOF WEIBULL PARAMETERS FOR GROPE TESTS

	Shape parameter (β)	B10 life
1st test	2.82	31244
2nd test	4.01	52340
3rd test	4.72	58787

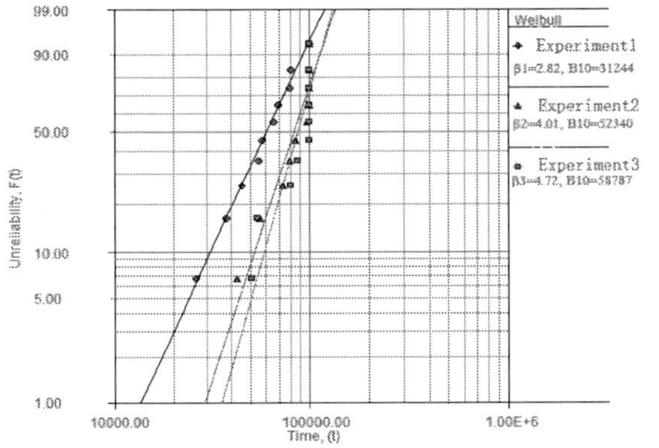

Fig. 2 Electrical life test results of three lots of samples.

III. FAILURE ANALYSIS

A. *Contact Morphology Analysis*

As shown in Table IV, the contact morphology of samples with different life times is observed. All samples with different life time show the consumption of movable contacts due to the connection of the movable contact with the positive poles in the DC load. The movable contacts with lower life time show unilateral consumption and warping phenomena. However, the samples with higher life time show warping on both sides. In the end of life time, the copper layer is even with the silver layer. for 100,000 life-span samples, the welding force may be a little lower and the edge copper layer was slightly warped.

B. *Component of Welding Position Analysis*

A thin silver layer was found at the weld location of the failure contact section by SEM-EDS analysis, but the content of Cu in these areas was high, as shown in Figure 3.

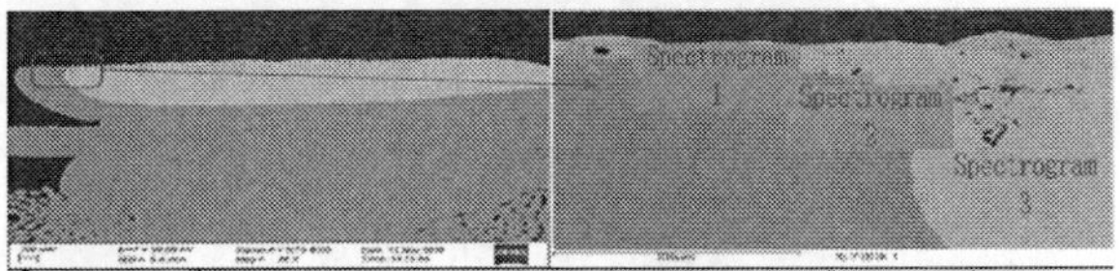

Spectrogram	C	O	Cu	Ag	In	Sn
Spectrogram 1	1.16	18.70	26.54	34.29	7.72	11.59
Spectrogram 2		1.63	9.13	87.03	1.45	0.76
Spectrogram 3		6.59		83.46	4.00	5.95

Fig. 3 Component analysis of contact welding position.

C. *Electrical Life Process Analysis*

The consumption of silver layer and the warping of copper layer in the test process were monitored by X-Ray. And the result was shown in Table V. Comparing with 1#sample and 2#sample, the initial contact position and contact morphology after 20,000 cycles are similar. But the movable contact of 1# sample unilaterally consumed and warped after 40,000 cycles, and it soon failed. For 2# sample both sides of the movable contact consumed and warped, and the warping speed is obviously increased in the last 10,000 cycles compared with the pictures of 80,000 times and 89501 times.

D. *Summary of Failure Analysis*

Based on the above analysis, contacts were constantly consumed and warped during electrical life. Because of the thin silver layer, copper layer may be exposure at the edge of the movable contact, which will increase the welding force. The increasing of welding force will further aggravated contact warping, and the phenomenon of copper-exposure will be more obvious. It is a positively feedback. Ultimately, the sample failed when the contact welding force was greater than the counter-force of movable spring.

The difference of electrical life times is mainly due to the behavior of contact. If the contact unilaterally consumed and warped, the life time was low, both sides of contact consumed and warped, the life time was higher.

IV. DISCUSSION

According to the conclusion of failure analysis, the potential improvement directions are put forward:

①Replace composite contacts with single contacts (Avoiding copper-exposure). ②Replace upsetting process with soldering process (Eliminate contact warping). ③Improvement of the thickness of contact composite layer (Delaying copper-exposure). ④Replace the contact material (Reduce contact consumption). Due to the limitation of engineering conditions, the improvement scheme② was validated by products with similar structure and parameter specifications

TABLE IV

CONTACT MORPHOLOGY OF TTYPICAL FAILURE SAMPLES

	Life time 43433	Life time81700	Life time100000
Contact morphology	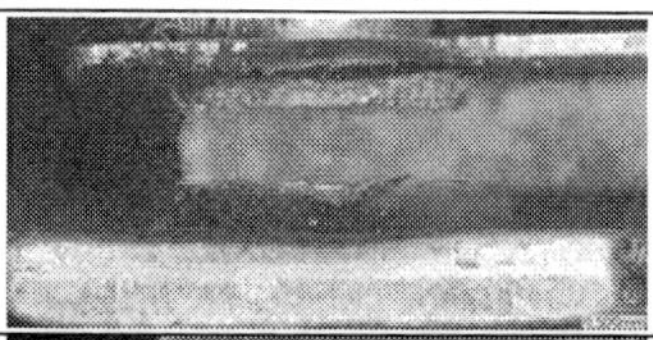		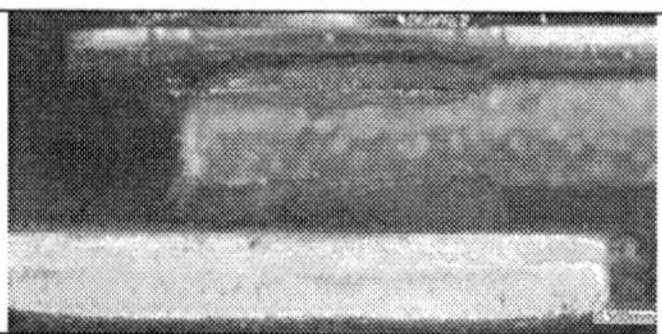
Movable contact surface	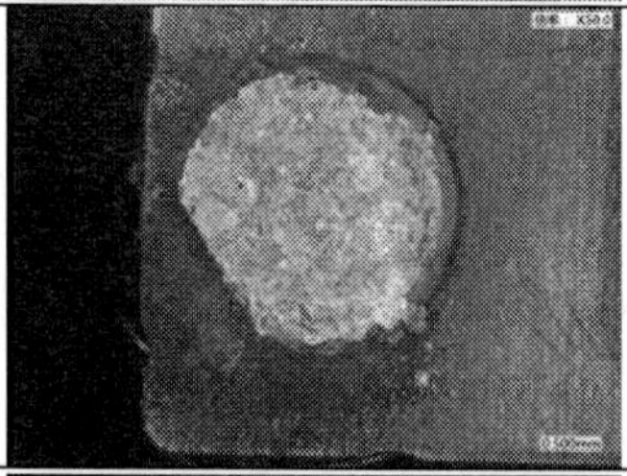	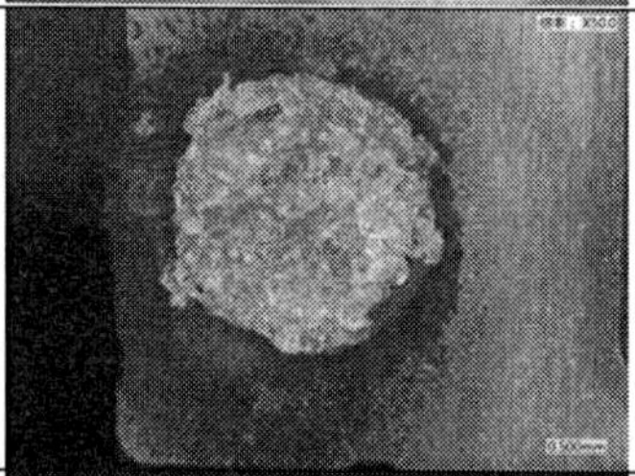	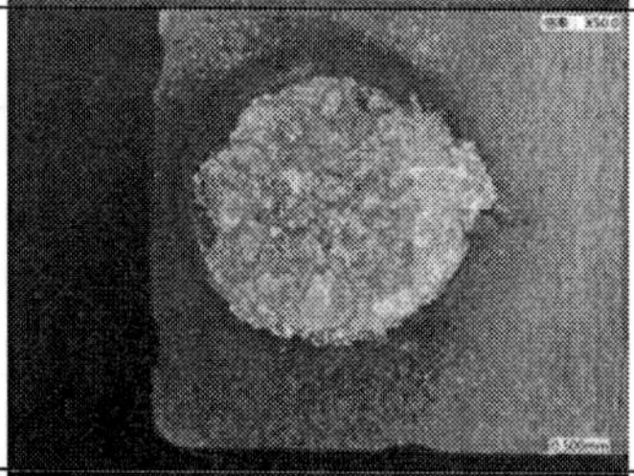
Movable contact section	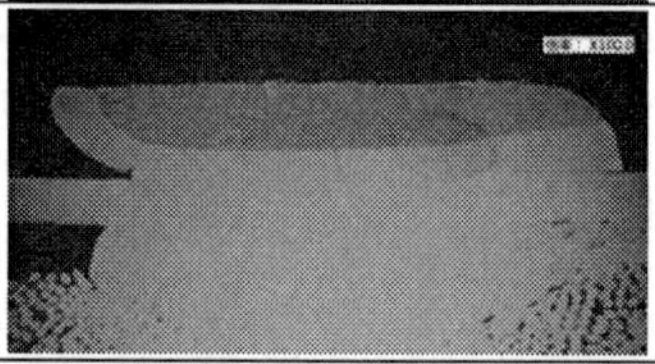	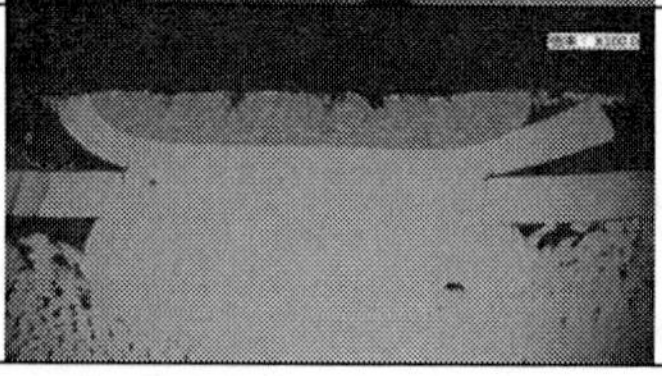	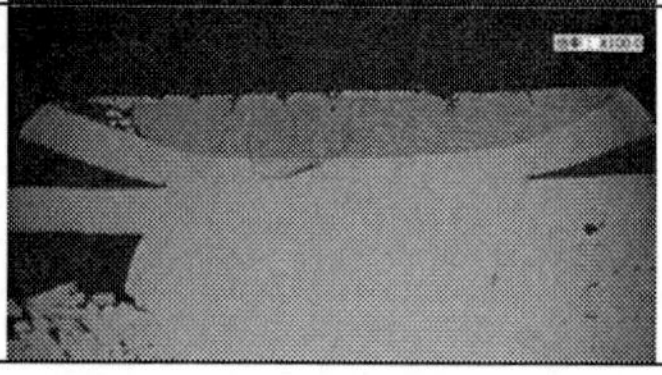

TABLE V

CONTACT MORPHOLOGY MONITORED BY X-RAY

Life time	0	20000	40000	6000	80000	Failure Time
Sample1# Failure Number 54976		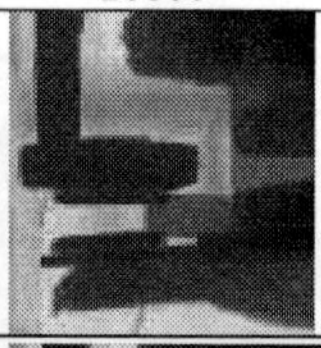		/	/	
Sample2# Failure Number 89501	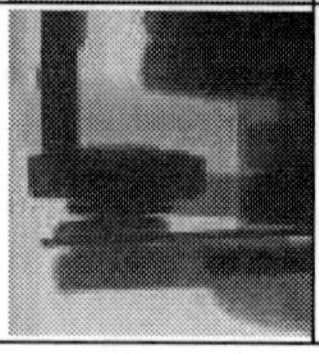				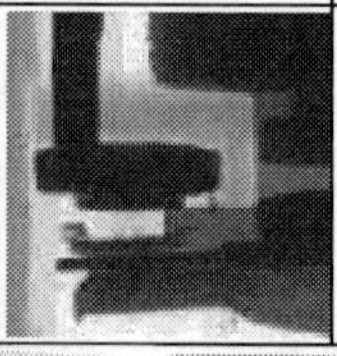	

A. Test results of scheme ① and scheme ②

Five samples of each scheme were tested. No failure occurred in 150,000 cycles, so the test was terminated. The life times are obviously increased compared with the results of composite contacts. The contact morphology after the test was shown in Figure 4, it can be seen that the single contact is slightly warped, and the soldering contact has no warping phenomenon at all.

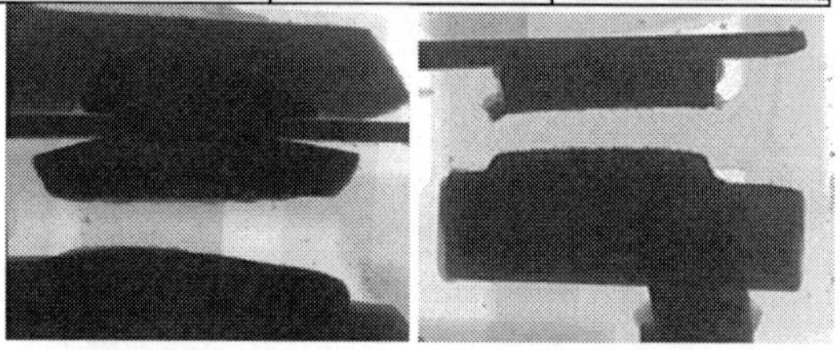

Fig. 4 The contact morphology after the test. (Left-single contact right-soldering contact)

B. Test results of scheme ③

Improvement scheme of contact composite layer thickness is shown in Fig.5. The shape of composite layer was changed and the edge silver thickness of contact increase.

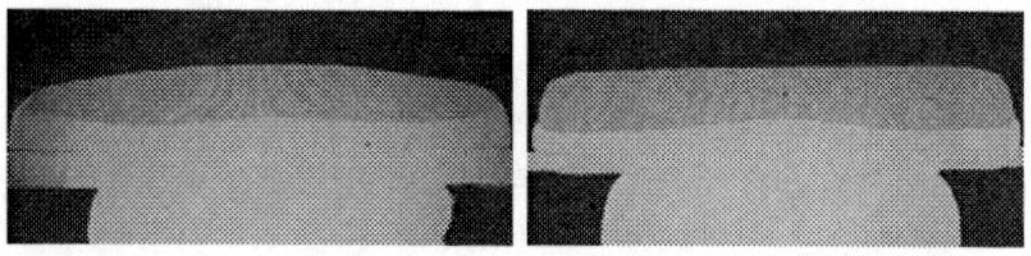

Fig. 5 Improvement scheme of contact composite layer. (Left-Before improvement right-After improvement)

10 samples were tested (9 samples failed), The numbers of electrical life times are between 120,000 and 170,000, which are bigger than composite contacts. The phenomenon of copper-exposed and warping still existed at the edge of contact, but it is delayed comparing with the contact section morphology of samples before and after improvement.

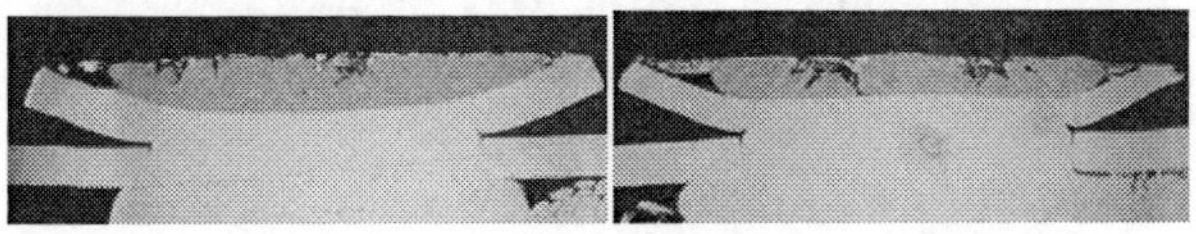

Fig. 6 The section morphology of contact after the test.. (Left-Before improvement,100,000cycles right-After improvement, about 140,000cycles)

C. Test results of scheme ④

According to the test data from the device for evaluating the consumption performance of contact materials, a new kind of contact material with good performance was chosen to assemble the relay samples using the regular process. Ten samples were tested to failure, the numbers of electrical life times are between 50,000 and 110,000. The improvement was insufficient, and the contact morphology after the test was similar.

D. Summary of improvement scheme

Integrating the above improvement schemes and test results, the improvement schemes of single contact and soldering contact can completely solve the problem of electrical life of the product, but it cost much. By changing the shape of the contact composite layer (increasing the edge thickness of contact) can also significantly improve the performance of the product. and its cost have not risen much. The life time of new material with good consumption performance increases slightly, the improvement scheme is insufficient. The specific improvement effect is shown in Table VI.

TABLE VI

TEST RESULTS BEFORE AND AFTER IMPROVEMENT

	Shape parameter (β)	B10 life
Before improvement-1st test	2.82	31244
Before improvement-2nd test	4.01	52340
Before improvement-3rd test	4.72	58787
After improvement-scheme①	5samples each scheme,no failure occurred in 150,000 cycles	
After improvement-scheme②		
After improvement-scheme③	11.72	124037
After improvement-scheme④	3.96	62805

V. CONCLUSION

Ag/Cu composite contacts are used to replace single contacts in a lot of relay products. Although the theoretically thickness of silver layer is sufficient to meet the requirements of electrical life. The silver layer thickness of Ag/Cu composite contact maybe fluctuates due to the influence of upsetting process. The interaction mechanism between contact consumption, copper-exposure, increasing of welding force and contact warping was clarified through multiple electrical life testing and failure analysis of the research object. Base on the failure analysis, different improvement schemes were implemented and test results were confirmed. Finally, the scheme of changing the shape of composite layer (Increasing the edge thickness of contact) was proved that it can significantly promote the electrical life, and no remarkable rising in cost, which provide an idea for the solution of similar problems.

REFERENCES

[1] Z.K.Chen, A Correlation of Silver Tin Indium Oxide-Copper Composite Rivet Interface Bond Quality and Switching Endurance Life in DC Relays[A]. Proceedings of the 26th International Conference on Electrical contacts and the 4th International Conference on Reliability of Electrical Products & Electrical Contacts[C]. China Electrotechnical Society(CES), 2012:6.

[2] Rieder W., Electrical Contacts[M]. USA: IEEE, 2005.

[3] Liao Danpei, Zhan Yanran. Thickness Distribution of the Ag Layer for the Upsetted Ag- Cu Composite Contact [J]Journal of Netshape Forming Engineering, 2014,6(05):113-118.

Effect of Mo,C Co-doping on the Electrical Properties of $AgSnO_2$ Contact

Zhe Zhang [1],Jingqin Wang[1,2]
[1]Hebei University of Technology, Tianjin, 300130
[2]Electrical Apparatus Institute of Hebei Province, Tianjin, 300130

***Abstract*—In order to study the electrical properties of Mo C co-doped SnO_2 contact materials, We calculate the band structure, density of states and number of charge distribution based on density functional theory using the CASTEP module in the Materials Studio software. The results show that the structure of the co-doped SnO_2 still belongs to a direct bandgap semiconductor. The 2s state of C and 4d state of Moinserts into the valence band, which moves in the direction of the high-energy level and passes through the Fermi energy level.The 4d state of Mo atom insertsintothe conduction band, which moves to the lower energy level, making the forbidden band width decrease.The layout analysis shows that, when co-doping occurs, the layout value of charge overlap between atoms increases, the carrier concentration increases, and the degree of charge transfer between atoms increases.In conclusion, compared with single doping, co-doping can improve the conductivity of $AgSnO_2$, providing a theoretical basis for the development of contact materials.**

***Index Terms*—Contact materials, $AgSnO_2$, The first principle,Co-doped, Electrical properties**

I. INTRODUCTION

In recent years, $AgSnO_2$ has been widely used for its excellent resistance to arc erosion and fusion welding. However, as SnO_2 is a wide-bandgap semiconductor with poor electrical conductivity, the overall contact resistance of $AgSnO_2$ materials will increase and the temperature rise will be too high[1-2]. Many scholars have found that doping technology can effectively improve the conductivity of SnO_2 materials, and has been a breakthrough in this field. On the basis of the first principle, Lu yao et al. calculated and analyzed the photoelectric properties of SnO_2 at different doping concentrations of Fe[3]; Based on the first principle of density functional theory, Peng caiyun et al. analyzed the electronic structure and optical properties of SnO_2 with different doping ratios of C,and results show that the conductivity of doped SnO_2 materials increases with the increase of doping ratio[4]. Based on the first principle, he haiying et al. analyzed the electronic structure of SnO_2 co-doped with mg-f and found that the stability and conductivity of SnO_2 were improved after doping [5]. At present, most scholars focus on the study of the properties of Mo and C single-doping SnO_2, and there are few studies on Mo and C co-doping SnO_2.

Based on the first principle of density functional theory [6-8], this paper calculated the Mo-C co-doped SnO_2, and electrical properties such as energy band structure, state density and charge layout were analyzed, and compared with the intrinsic and Mo and C single-doped SnO_2, providing theoretical basis for the development of $AgSnO_2$ electrical contact materials.

II. CELL MODEL AND CALCULATION METHOD

A. Cell Mode

SnO_2 is rutile structure, belongs to body centroid tetragonal system, and the lattice constant is:a=b=0.4737nm, c=0.3816nm, $\alpha=\beta=90°$ .In this paper, the 1×2×3 SnO_2 super cell model was constructed. as shown in figure 1 (a), the super cell has 24 O atoms and 12 Sn atoms, and the body center contains 6 Sn atoms.This experiment by using alternative methods of atom, the dopant atoms instead of Sn and O atoms in the cell.In the case of a single doped Mo element, two Mo atoms are used to replace the two Sn atoms in the body center, as shown in figure 1 (b). When a single C element is doped, four C atoms are substituted for four O atoms in the body center, as shown in figure 1 (C).When Mo and C are co-doped, one Mo atom and two C atoms are used to replace one Sn atom and two O atoms in the body center successively.The doping ratio of both single doping and co-doping is 16.67%, which is more conducive to verifying the influence of Mo and C co-doping on the conductivity of $AgSnO_2$.

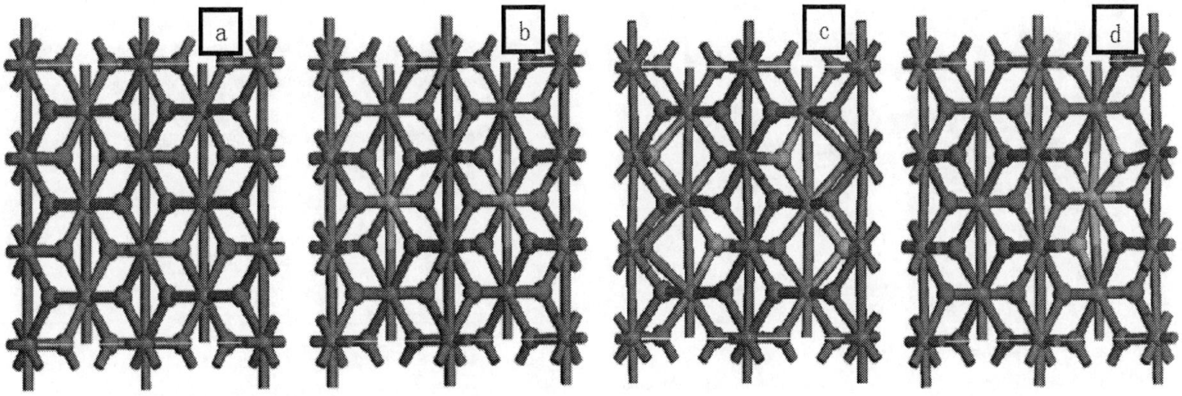

Fig.1 Intrinsic SnO_2(a),Mo doped SnO_2(b),C doped SnO_2(c) and Mo,C co-doped SnO_2(d) 1×2×3 supercell structures

B. Cell Model and Calculation Method

In this paper, using the CASTEP module of Materials Studio software and based on the first principle of density functional theory, using the PBE of GGA to deal with the exchange correlation functional, and the calculation process is carried out in reciprocal space[10].The Ecutoff was set as 340eV， and the k spatial grid point of brillouin region was set as4×2×2，The convergence accuracy was 1×10^{-5}eV/atom， and the self-consistent accuracy is2.0×10^{-6}eV/atom.The structure of crystal cell was optimized geometrically, then the stable structure was calculated, and the calculated results were analyzed. The selected valence electron configuration are:Sn： $5s^25p^2$,O： $2s^22p^4$,Mo： $4d^55s^1$,C： $2s^22p^2$.

III. CALCULATION RESULTS AND ANALYSIS

3.1 Band Structure

The energy band structures of intrinsic SnO_2, Mo single doping, C single doping and Mo-C co-doping are shown in figure 2 successively.It can be seen from figure 2 (a) that both the minimum conduction band value and the maximum valence band value of SnO_2 occur at the high symmetric point G, so SnO_2 is a direct bandgap semiconductor material.The calculated value of the intrinsic SnO_2 band gap is 1.079eV, which is obviously smaller than the experimental value [11]3.6eV. Because the generalized gradient approximation in the calculation module has limitations, this paper mainly compares the band gaps of different doping systems, so it will not affect the analysis results.

Band structure of the single doped Mo atoms as shown in figure 2 (b), because of doping after conduction band minimum and maximum valence band is still in the G point of brillouin area, so after Mo single doped SnO_2 still belongs to the direct band gap structure.Compared with the undoped, the single doped band becomes tighter, the inter-band fluctuation is smoother, and the conduction band width is narrower.New bands appear in the valence states of -65~-60 eV and -35~-40 eV. Compared with the intrinsic SnO2, the conduction and valence bands as a whole move towards lower energy levels, and the Fermi level is in the conduction band.The band gap value after Mo doping is 1.628eV, and the band gap width increases, which is very close to the band gap value obtained in reference [12], which can verify the correctness of the experiment.

Figure 2 (c) shows the band structure after single doping of c, in which the valence top and conduction band bottom are both in G point, so it is still a direct band gap structure after single doping.Compared with the band structure diagram of intrinsic SnO_2, the doped band becomes tighter, the valence band width increases, and new valence states appear in the region of -20~ -22eV, and new bands are introduced at the bottom of the conduction band and the top of the valence state.Due to the introduction of element C, the bottom of the conduction band moves towards the low energy direction, increasing the interaction between atoms and enhancing the metallic properties of materials.After doping, the band gap width decreases to 0.671eV, so the energy required for carrier to transition from valence band to conduction band decreases, so single doping of C atom can improve the conductivity.

It can be seen from figure 2 (d) that the co-doping is still a direct bandgap structure.Doping causes the energy levels to become denser and smoother around the Fermi level (at 0eV).The calculated band gap width is 0.653eV, which is smaller than that of undoped and single doped. This is because the co-doping leads the band to move to a lower level, and the bottom of the band is closer to the Fermi level, which increases the probability of carrier transition and the material's electrical conductivity.

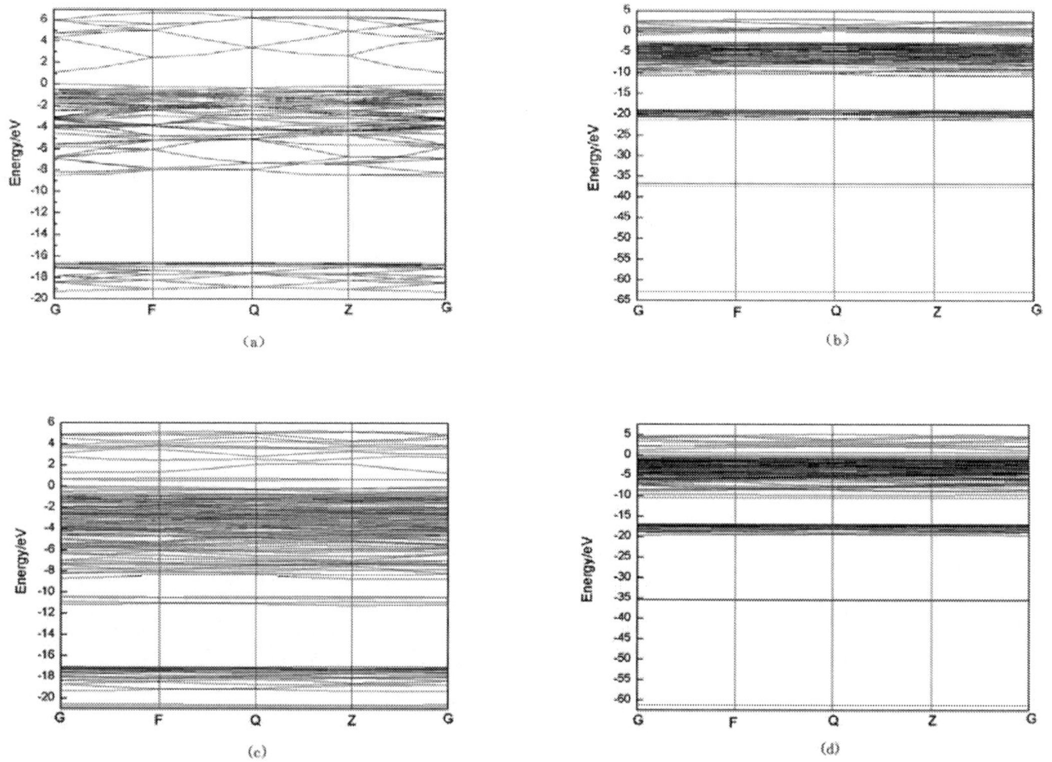

Fig.2 Intrinsic SnO_2(a),Mo doped SnO_2(b),C doped SnO_2(c) and Mo,C co-doped SnO_2(d) 1×2×3 band structures

C. Density of States

The total state density and partial wave state density of the intrinsic SnO_2 (a), Mo single-doping (b), C single-doping (C) and mo-c co-doping (d) are shown in figure 3.

It can be seen from figure 3 (a) that the intrinsic SnO_2 in the conduction band region of 0~7.5eV is mainly contributed by the Sn-5s state, Sn-5p state and a small number of O-2pstate.There are two peaks in the valence band region, the upper valence band is located at -10~0eV, mainly contributing to the Sn-5s states, Sn-5pstateand O-2p state. The valence band is between -20 and -15 ev, mainly composed of the Sn-5s state, Sn-5p state and O-2s state.

After the single doping of Mo, it can be seen from figure 3 (b) that the conduction band has a new peak and moves to the Fermi energy level under the contribution of Mo-4d state, Sn-5s state, O-5p state and O-2p state.In the region of -1.7~0eV, the conduction band passes through the Fermi energy level, which is mainly contributed by the Mo-4d state. In the valence band, the contribution of Mo atoms is mainly in the -12.5~-1.7eV region, resulting in a new peak value in the valence band. Due to the contributions of the Mo-4p state and Mo-5s state, new energy bands appear in the -40~-35 eV region and the -65~-60 eV region, making the valence band as a whole wider.

After single doping of C, it can be seen from figure 3 (C) that the valence state as a whole moves towards the Fermi energy level, and the valence state passes through the Fermi energy level and enters the conduction band. In the region of 0~1.25eV, the 2p state of C atom is the main component of the valence band, and the contribution of 5s state of Sn atom, 5p state of O atom and 2p state of O atom.At -10~0eV, the valence state is close to the Fermi energy level, which is mainly contributed by the C-2p state, Sn-5s and Sn-5p state, and O-2p state.In the region of 1.25~5.25eV, the conduction band is closer to the Fermi energy level, which is mainly contributed by the 2s and 2p states of C atom, 5s and 5p states of Sn atom, and 2p states of O atom.

After the co-doping of mo-c, it can be seen from figure 3 (d) that the valence state moves towards the Fermi energy level and passes through the Fermi energy level to enter the conduction band, which is mainly composed of the 4d state of Mo atom and the 2p state of C atom.At -12.5~0eV, the valence band is close to the Fermi energy level, which is mainly contributed Mo-5s state,Mo-4p state, C-2s state,C-2p state, Sn-5s state and Sn-5p state and 2p states of O atom.The width of valence states increases as a whole, due to the emergence of new valence bands in the -65~-60eV region with contribution of the Mo-5s state and in the -37.5~-32.5eV region with the Mo-4p state.Two new peaks appear in the conduction band. The first peak is in the region of 0~3eV, and the second peak is in the region of 3~ 7.5ev. This is mainly due to the contribution of Mo-4d state, Mo-2s state,C-2p state, Sn-5s state,Sn-5p stateandO-2p state,After co-doping, under the joint action of Mo atom and C atom, the energy band is more concentrated at the Fermi energy level, the band gap value is smaller, and the conductivity is improved correspondingly.

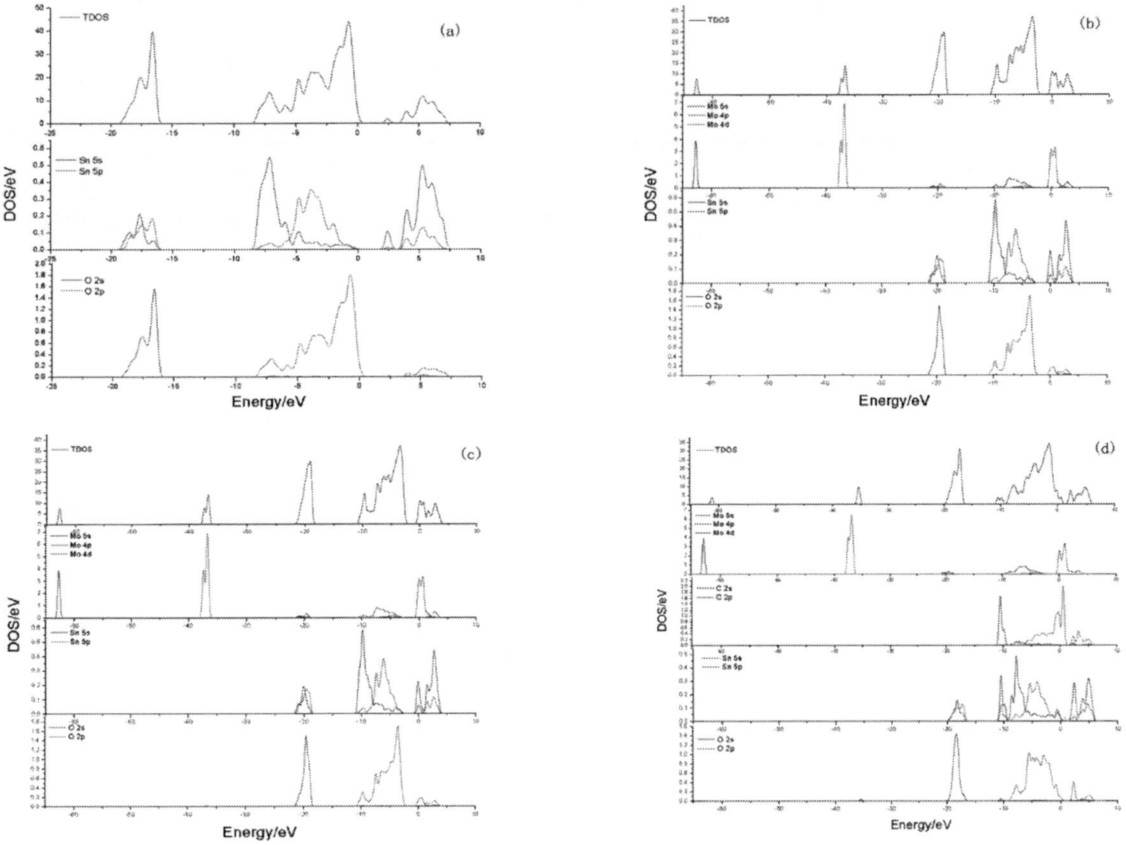

Fig.3 Intrinsic SnO_2(a),Mo doped SnO_2(b),C doped SnO_2(c) and Mo,C co-doped SnO_2(d)state densities

D. ChargeLayoutAnalysis

For intrinsic SnO_2, the average charge arrangement and overlap sets of single and co-doped atoms are shown in table 1.For intrinsic SnO_2, the average charge arrangement of Sn atom and O atom is 1.90e and -0.95e respectively, and Sn with positive charge loses electrons and O with negative charge gains electrons.The average charge distribution of both Sn and O atoms decreases with single doping, so the ability of Sn atoms to lose electrons and O atoms to gain electrons decreases.After co-doping with mo-c, the average charge population of Sn atom and O atom decreases more significantly, that is, the electron loss capacity of Sn atom and the electron gain capacity of O atom are significantly lower than those of undoped and single doping.When Mo atoms are introduced into the doping system, it is found that the electron overlap between Mo-O is greater than that between Sn-O, indicating that the charge density increases and the carrier concentration increases, so it is more conducive to electron transfer.toCompared with Sn-O bond and Mo-O bond, Sn-C bond and Mo-C bond have a larger charge population, which indicates that after impurity atoms enter SnO_2, electron shell overlap between atoms is intensified and electron transfer between atoms is intensified, so the conductivity is further improved.

Table 1 Mulliken bond population and intrinsic charge of SnO_2 and doped SnO_2 after optimization

Model	Atom charge				Bond population			
	Sn	O	Mo	C	Sn-O	Mo-O	Sn-C	Mo-C
SnO_2	1.90	-0.95			0.53			
Mo-SnO_2	1.81	-0.81	1.26		0.34	0.43		
C-SnO_2	1.77	-0.90		-0.76	0.32		0.62	
Mo-C-SnO_2	1.76	-0.79	1.18	-0.63	0.31	0.42	0.61	0.51

IV. CONCLUSION

This paperestablishedthe SnO_2 supercell model of 1×2×3. Based on the first principle of density functional theory, the geometric optimization of SnO_2 with single doping of tail-plug, Mo and C and co-doping was carried out, and the energy band structure diagram, state density and charge layout number of the doped system after optimization were calculated.The following conclusions are obtained: both single doping C and co-doping Mo-C can reduce the band gap of SnO_2, and the co-doping band gap decreases to a greater extent and the band is closer.The band gap of Mo single doping increases. After co-doping, under the contribution of 4d state of Mo atom, the conductance band near the Fermi energy level is more dense and approaches to the low energy level. In the valence band near the Fermi level, under the action of the 2p state of C atom, the top of the valence band passes through the Fermi level into the conduction band, the gap width decreases, and the energy required for carrier transition decreases.According to the layout charge analysis, after Mo atom and C atom are co-doped, the electron overlapping layout value between atoms increases, carrier concentration increases, and electron transfer between atoms intensifies.In conclusion, Mo-C co-doping has better electrical conductivity than undoped and single-doped. The theoretical analysis in this paper has certain guiding significance for the study of improving the conductivity of $AgSnO_2$.

REFERENCES

[1] W. song, F. zuoxin and W. saibei,et al. "Present Research and Future Development of Silver-based Electrical Contact Material,"[J]. Precious Metals,vol:5,no.2,pp:79-83,2013.

[2] Z. yancai,W.jingqin,L. qiang, et al. "Influence of rare earth oxide on anti-welding performance of AgSnO2 electrical contact materials,"[J]. Journal of Hebei University of Technology.vol:43,no.3,pp:16-20,2014.

[3] L.yao, W. jipei, Z. changwen, et al. "First-principles calculation on electronic structure and optical propertiesof iron-doped SnO_2,"[J]. Acta. Phys.Sin.vol:60,no.11,pp:414-417,2011.

[4] P. caiyun, L. bocheng, X. tong, et al. "First-principle study of C-doped SnO2 at different concentrations,"[J].Journal of Atomic and Molecular Physics.vol:35,no. 3,pp:401-406,2018.

[5] H. haiying, Z. zhaojun, C. yali, et al. "First-principles study on acceptor-donor Mg-F co-doped SnO_2,"[J]. Journal of Atomic and Molecular Physics.vol:36,no.5,pp:861-865,2019.

[6] G.Tingkun and Q.Yuanhua. "First- principles Simula-tion on Pressure-dependent Local Structure Change of AsS melt," Journal of Molecular Liquids, vol. 22,no.4,pp. 466-471, 2016.

[7] K. huiling, W. jingqin, Z. ying, et al. "Simulation Analysis of the Effect of Sr-F Co-doping on the Electrical Properties of $AgSnO_2$,"[J]. Precious Metals.vol:39,no.2,pp:34-38,2018.

[8] Khuili M, Fazouan N, Makarim H A E, et al. "First principle study of structural, electronic, optical and electrical properties of Ga doped ZnO with GGA andmBJapproximations,"Journal of Physics: Conference series, vol. 758,no.1,pp.1742-6596, 2016.

[9] Z. Ying,W.Jingqin,K. Kuiling. "Simulation and Experimental Study on the Properties of Fe, Y Co-Doped$AgSnO_2$ Contact Materials," IEEJ Transactions on Electrical and Electronic Engineering.vol.14,pp:990-995.

[10] L. Chuanyan, N.Jin, L. Zhiqing, et al. "First principles Calculationson the Electronic Structure and Bonding Nature of TaN(111)/TiN(111) Interface," Journal ofAlloys and Compounds, vol:71,no.7,pp: 326~332,2017.

[11] C yuhong, F. yujie, L. junfeng, et al. "Preparation and characterization on Sb dopedTi base SnO_2 electro catalytic electrodes,"[J]. Functional Materials.vol:36,no.2,pp:234-237,2005.

[12] X. chunhui, Y.ping, L. junfeng. "Study on Photoelectric Characteristics of Mo-doped SnO2 with First-Principles,"[J]. Semiconductor Photoelectric.vol:40,no.4,pp:534- 595,2019.

[13] H. haiying. "First-principles study on the doping of Sno, with II A elements and its film preparation, [D]. Shenzhen University, Shenzhen,China, 2015.

[14] X. shuai, Y.ping, L. junfeng, "Aluminum and Nitrogen Co-doping Effects on the Electrical Structure and OpticalProperties of SnO_2,"[J]. Electronic Sci.vol:31,no.12,pp:47-51,2018.

[15] D. chao, L. wei, L. juyan. "First principle study of electronic structure of Sb, S Co-doped SnO_2,"[J]. Acta. Phys.Sin.vol:67,no.21,pp:439-448,2008.

[16] Godinho K G,WalshA,Watson G W."Energetic and Electronic Structure Analysis of Intrinsic Defects inSnO_2,"[J]. The Journal of Physical Chemistry,vol:113,no.1,pp:439-448,2008

[17] H YanJun,ZJun,ZLin,et al. "Structure Phase Transition and Elastic Properties of Hafnium:First-principles study"[J]. Philosophical Magazine Letters,vol:91,pp:61-69,2011.

[18] J. yanming, Z. fengji, L. zhiqiang, et al. "First-Principle Study on the Band Gap andOptical Absorption Spectra of Be Doping ZnO,"[J]. Journal of Inner Mongolia Normal University.vol:44,no.3,pp:359-363,2015.

[19] ETIN K,ZUNGERA."Origins of Coexistence of Conductivity and Transparency in SnO_2"[J].Physical ReviewLetters,vol:88,no.9,pp:095501-095504,2002

[20] Z. jinkui, D. shenghua, Q. hui, et al. "First principle study on the electronic structure and p-type conductivity of ZnO,"[J]. Acta.Phys.Sin.vol:56,no.9,pp:5371-5375,2007.

7th International Conference on Reliability of
Electrical Products and Electrical Contacts,
November 04-06, 2019

Correlation between Load Current Mode and Electrical Contact Resistance of a Closed Pair of Contacts

Chuwan Xiao[1], Teng Wang[1], Dazhao Yu[1], Ming Li[2], Sihuan Wang[1], Wanbin Ren[3]
[1]Naval Aviation University Yantai 264001 China
[2]AVIC China Aero-poly Technology Establishment Beijing 100000 China
[3]Harbin Institute of Technology Harbin 150001 China

Abstract—**The electrical contact resistance of closed contact pair is dependent on contact material physical characteristics, contact type (sphere-flat or flat-flat), contact surface status (clean or contaminated), but also contact current and mechanical load during measuring. The relationships between contact resistance and load current and load force with the use of DC mode and non-constant current mode measurement method are compared in this paper. The variations in thermoelectric voltage of contact pairs as a function of time with constant force load are presented.**

Index Terms—**Contact resistance, Measurement, Load current, Delta mode, Thermoelectric voltage**

I. INTRODUCTION

The electrical contact, being an essential part of the electric circuit, plays an important role in electrical interconnections, electrical switches, electronic packaging and so on [1]. The static contact is the electric junctions designed for infrequent separation and connection, and intended to perform their function only when contacting members are stationary relative to each other. This definition includes crimped, welded, brazed, riveted, or soldered joints; friction connections such as pin and socket connectors or taper pins, twisted-wire splices; and connections made with screws, or bolts and nuts between electrical wiring and components [2].

The nature of surface roughness and non-cleanness on a microscopic scale results in the contact electrical resistance and contact thermal resistance within the circuits [3]. Generally, the contact resistance is designated as the key parameter of the circuit involved electrical junctions. The degradation of electrical contact performance is inevitable when the switches or the circuits are exposed to the harsh working environment [4-6]. Therefore, the failure modes and failure mechanisms could be determined with the use of the collected information of the contact resistance. It is meaning for improving the reliability of the modern electrical system.

The described contact resistance test methods are characterized as four-terminal resistance measuring techniques, wherein a measured and controlled test current is introduced into the sample using two terminals or connecting points, and two other points are selected on the sample across which a voltage drop is measured, as shown in Fig.1.

Two distinct levels of electrical loading are described. These levels are dry circuit and rated current. The dry circuit is a circuit in which the open-circuit voltage is less than or equal to 20mV. Current is usually low in a dry circuit, but a low-current circuit is not necessarily a dry circuit. When the applied voltage (open-circuit voltage) is too low to cause any physical changes in the contact junction, such as break-down of thin insulating films or softening of contact asperities, this circuit is said to be a dry circuit [1]. It is common practice to describe contact resistance by any of the following methods, such as contact resistance-load characteristic curves [7]- [9], frequency of failure versus load and contact resistance probability distribution plots [1].

Recently, there has been increasing demand to research the measuring method to characterize the defect of contact material products, such as the higher surface roughness, contamination and oxidation film etc. The measurement results of contact resistance correlate with the material properties, electrical current, load force, surface profile and environments closely [3]. Contact resistances are normally very small, ranging from microohms to a few milliohms in cases of practical interest. However, for contacts with worn surface or corroded or contaminated surface, the contact resistance dramatically increases into the scale of ohm or higher [10], [11]. The challenge of measuring microohm scales of contact resistance is that the value is so low level that overwhelmed by the diverse noise easily. Particularly, the thermal potentials are the main source of influencing the measured voltage signals. Either AC or DC test currents may be used, but the most general method of eliminating the effects of thermal potentials is to make forward-and-reverse-current readings and calculating resistance. Many innovative measurement methods have been reported in order to improve the accuracy of contact resistance measurements [12]-[14]. Meanwhile, the nano-scale electrical contact resistance tool (nanoECR, HYSITRON, USA), provide a powerful solution for simultaneous, in-situ electrical and mechanical measurements [15]. In a previous paper by the present authors, a new automated test equipment for measuring electrical contact resistance of real size rivets has been reported [16], [17]. The relationship between contact load and contact resistance during loading and unloading has been investigated explicitly.

In addition, besides the traditional DC mode, Delta method, Pulse-Delta method, Different conductance method and sweeping method are presented by Keithley Instrument Inc. in achieving accurate and reliable resistance measurements [18]. These methods are specially designed for contact resistance measurement, superconductor resistance measurement and resistivity measurements of conductive materials. However, to our knowledge, relative little is known about the effect of load current mode on electrical contact resistance of a closed contact pair. The measuring principle of non-constant current mode and experimental methods are described in Section 2. The relationships between electrical contact resistance and load current and load force with the use of different measurement method are compared and discussed explicitly in Section 3.

II. EXPERIMENTAL METHODS

A. Measuring principle of non-constant current mode

The traditional four-wire (four-terminals) method with constant current shown in Fig.1. The additional resistance in the test lead connections could be significantly eliminated. However, the errors due to white noise and 1/f noise will remain. Thermal potential is another dominant factor that influences the testing accuracy of contact resistance between a contact pair. Therefore, a constant thermoelectric voltage may be canceled using voltage measurements made at a positive test current and a negative test current.

The non-constant current methods, including Delta mode, Pulse Delta mode, Differential Conductance mode and Sweeping mode, are developed to measure the low voltage unaffected by the thermal potentials which varies over time. In view of the features of electrical contact resistance of static contact pairs, only Delta mode and Pulse-Delta mode are described.

When Delta starts, Delta voltage measurement outputs a reversal current and three A/D conversions are performed to yield a single Delta reading as shown in the Fig.2(a). After the 1st Delta cycle, the moving-average technique is then used in which the new A/D replaces the oldest A/D in the Delta calculation, so a Delta reading will be yielded for every subsequent A/D. The following equation can be used to calculate any Delta reading where Vn is the n-th A/D measurement.

$$U_n = \frac{V_n - 2V_{n+1} + V_{n+2}}{4}(-1)^{n-1} \tag{1}$$

For Pulse Delta, the current source (Model 6221) outputs current pulses that have a short pulse width. By default, Pulse Delta uses a 3-point repeating-average algorithm to calculate readings. Each Pulse Delta reading is calculated using A/D measurements (Model 2182A) for a low pulse, a high pulse, and another low pulse. As shown in Fig.2(b), every three pulses yields a single Pulse Delta voltage reading. The n-th Pulse Delta reading can be calculated as following

$$U_n = \frac{2V_{n\_2} - V_{n\_1} - V_{n\_3}}{4} \tag{2}$$

where V_{n_1}, V_{n_2}, V_{n_3} are the three A/Ds of the n-th cycle individually.

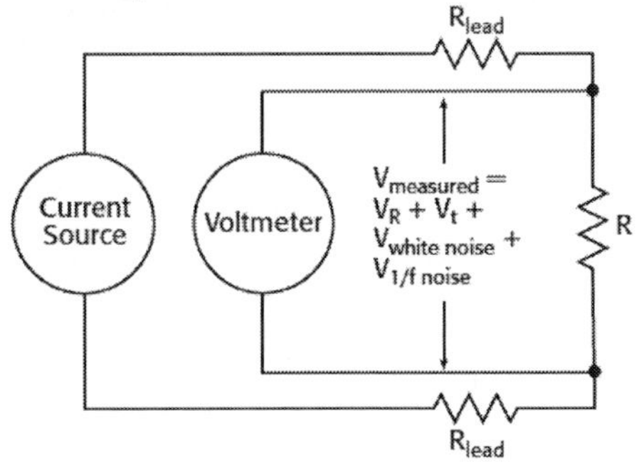

Fig. 1 Four-wire method (V_R: measured resistance voltage; V_t: thermoelectric voltage; $V_{white\ noise}$: white noise voltage in the circuit; $V_{1/f}$: low frequency noise voltage).

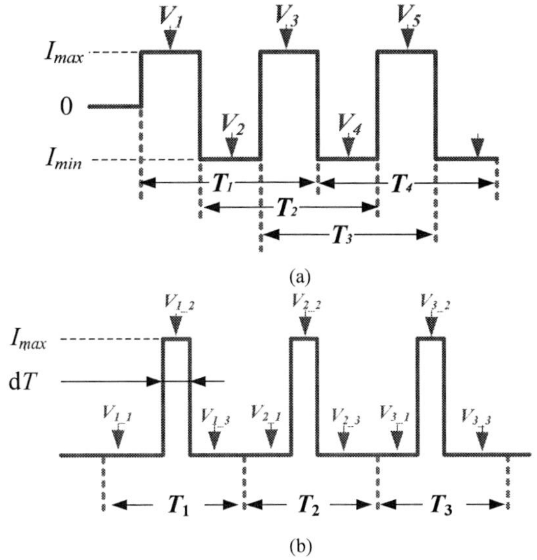

Fig. 2 Schematic plot of non-constant current mode. (a) Delta Mode. (b) Pulse-Delta Mode

B. Experimental Detail

The automated test equipment for measuring electrical contact resistance described previously is used to hold the contact and set the stationary contact force. Module 2182A Nanovoltmeter and 6221 programmable current source, with a resolution of 1pA and 1nV respectively, are applied for the measurement of contact resistance under constant current mode, Delta mode and Pulse-Delta mode. The open circuit voltage of Keithley 6221 is not allowed for less than 100mV, so a resistor of 1 ohm is connected with the contact pair in series. Configuration detail of current source Keithley 6221 are shown in Table 1. The open circuit voltage of Keithley 2182A is 1V. That is sufficient for the dry circuit experiment.

The spherical indenter (curvature radius is 1.5mm) is made of silver palladium alloy with 3 m thickness gold coating for improving electrical conductivity performance and stability. The roughness of the indenter tip was measured by a con-focal optical microscope (LEXT 3000, Olympus) and the surface roughness (SRa) is 0.4m, calculated from a scan size of 50 mx50 m. Two kinds of flat rivet specimens are selected as the contact component. One is made of copper electroplated with gold coating, and the other is silver cadmium oxide alloy. They are widely used in electrical or electronic engineering application. The indenter and flat rivet specimens are degreased using acetone, methyl alcohol and distilled water in an ultrasonic cleaner in order, dried and carefully mounted in the test rig. Keithley 6221 is interfaced to a personal computer using an Ethernet cable. The data acquisition and logging process are controlled through a PC with the help of LabVIEW software specifically programmed for this purpose. The experiment circuit is shown in Fig.3. The load current-contact resistance characteristics and the load force-contact resistance characteristics with different load current modes are investigated separately. The experiments are carried out with an air temperature of 22±1℃ and a relative humidity of 33±2%RH.

TABLE 1. Configuration details of current source Keithley 6221

	DC	Delta	Pulse-Delta
Test Current (I_{max})	10mA	10mA	10mA
Test Current (I_{min})	Non	-10mA	0
Pulse Width (dT)	Non	Non	5ms
Single Measurement Period (T_i)	Non	300ms	100ms
Filter Type	Non	Repeating filter	Repeating filter
Repeating Counts	Non	5	5

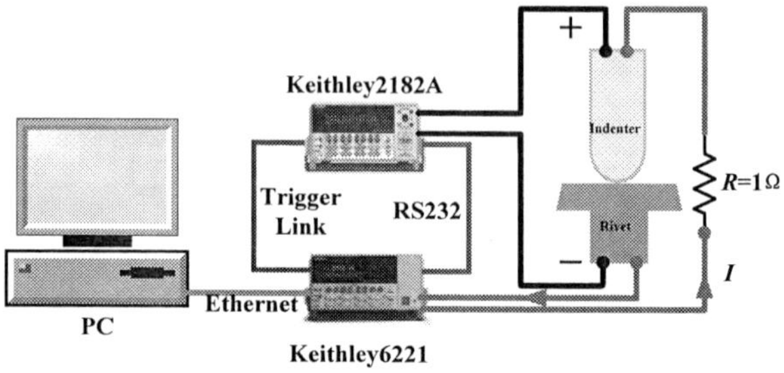

Fig. 3 Experimental circuit.

III. RESULTS AND DISCUSSION

C. Load current vs. contact resistance characteristics

The emphasis is on characterization of the conduction process for electric contacts within a current amplitude range from 5mA to a maximum 100mA. This program involves measuring contact resistance over as wide a current range as possible. The data are then examined in order to discriminate the effect of load current mode on measured contact resistance value. Fig.4(a) shows the contact resistance vs. current data for gold-plated copper contact. The load force is 0.1N. When no current is applied, the contact voltage reading is 4.6mV, we can take this value as the thermalelectric voltage. It is noticed that the contact resistance monotonically decreases from 12.8mohm to 8.245mohm with the increase of current for positive DC current mode, meanwhile the contact resistance monotonically increases from 3.7mohm to 8.245mohm with the increase of current for negative DC current mode. Because the contact voltage is dependent on the electrical current, the proportion of thermoelectric voltage in measurement reading is reduced with the increased test current. Hence, the variation in contact resistance trends to stabilization. However, the averaging results is almost constant 8.245mohm when the test current increases from 10mA to 100mA. It means the averaging method of DC mode plays a vital role in reducing the disturbance of thermoelectric voltage. It is noted that the contact resistance measurement results of Delta mode and Pulse-Delta mode are remarkably consistent with the averaging results of DC. It shows that the non-constant current mode is extremely benifical to the suppression of thermoelectric voltage and drift. Therefore, the results is more precise and accurate compared with the traditional DC mode. For Delta mode and Pulse-Delta mode, 10 consecutive contact resistance readings within 1 second are plotted in Fig.4(b). For Delta mode, the standard deviation of contact resistance reading is less than 0.632%; while for Pulse-Delta mode, the minimum standard deviation of contact resistance reading is 2.758%. By comparision, the measurement results obtained by Delta mode has the strongest robustness in terms of contact resistance.

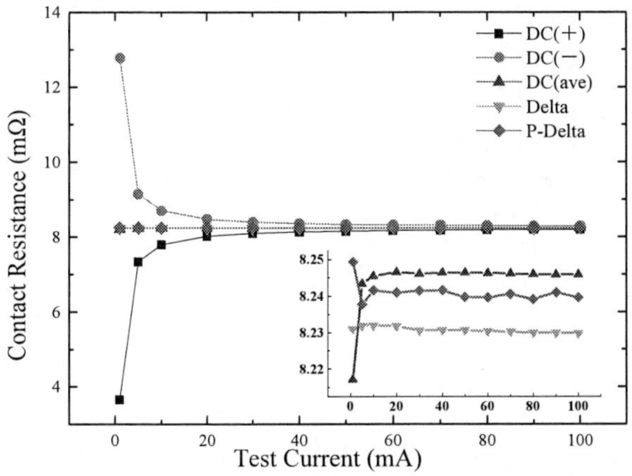

(a)

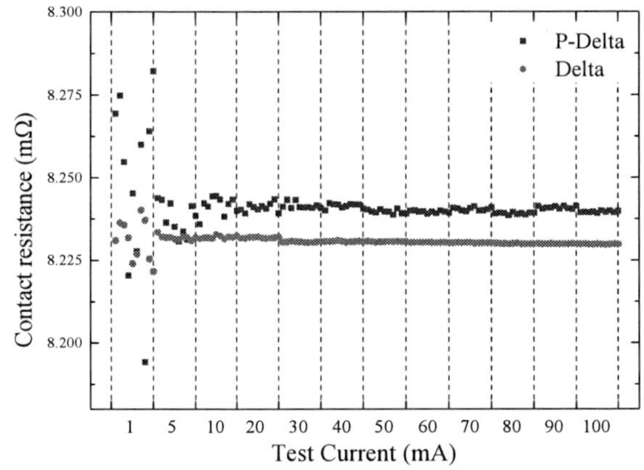

(b)

Fig. 4 The relationsip between contact resistance and test current with different load current mode (rivet material is Au-plated copper). (a) The average value of contact resistance at given test current. (b) The instantaneous value of contact resistance at given test current.

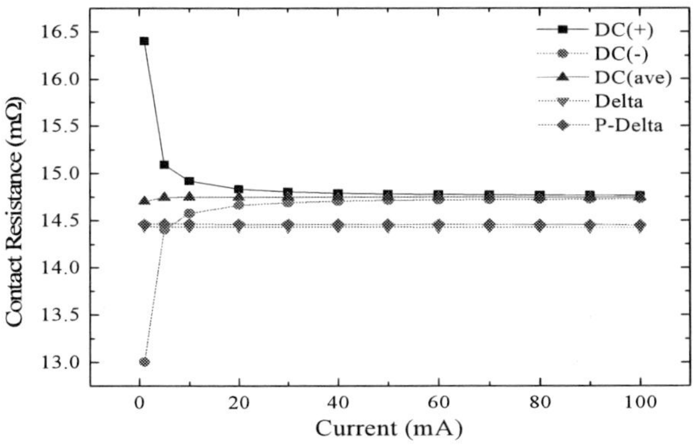

(a)

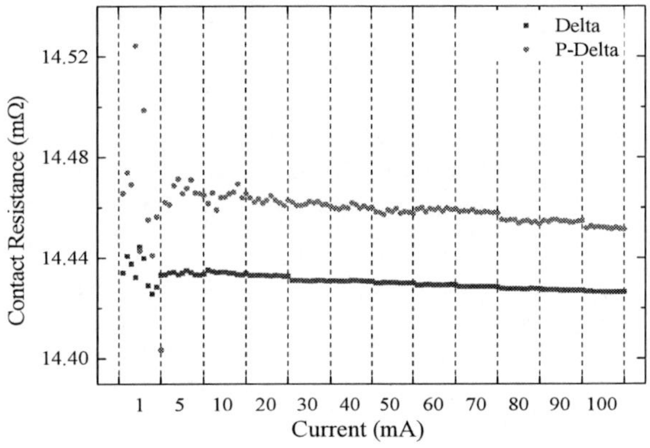

(b)

Fig. 5 The relationship between contact resistance and test current with different load current mode (rivet material is AgCdO15). (a)The average value of contact resistance at given test current. (b)The instantaneous value of contact resistance at given test current.

The similar measurement results of silver cadmium oxide alloy rivet contacts are shown in Fig.5. Although the indenter material is different from the sample material, the results indicates that Delta mode is slightly superior to the DC mode in measuring contact resistance of AgMeO material.

D. Load force vs. contact resistance characteristics

The whole load-contact resistance experiment can be described as loading stage and unloading stage. The indenter and rivet sample are brought into contact from 2cN to 50cN at a controlled loading rate. After loading force is reached the set value and keeps invariable, the pre-set current passed through the contact pair. The steady value of contact voltage drop could be recorded and saved. The indenter is unloaded at the same rate from 0.5N until they are separated. The force step is set 2cN, and the test current is 10mA.

The variation in contact resistance load depicted in Fig.6 and Fig.7 stems from a combination of several factors: Timsit [9] stated an increase in number of contacting surface asperities as the nominal surfaces are brought closer together under the influence of an increasing load; permanent flattening of the contacting asperities, which reduces the constriction resistance associated with each a-spot and thus reduces the overall contact resistance; work-hardening of the deformed contact asperities, which reduced the rate of asperity flattening etc.

Mathematical models that attempt to explain the observations of Fig.6 in terms of details of asperity deformation behaviour during compression predict a relationship between contact resistance and mechanical load. Assuming that the micro-contact deforms plastically the analytical result is plotted on the same graph using the following equation (Holm's analytical model) [3].

$$R_c = \left(\frac{\rho^2 \eta \pi H}{4F}\right)^{\frac{1}{2}} \qquad (3)$$

In which, R_c is the contact resistance is the resistivity of contact material; H is the harness of material; F is the contact force; is an empirical coefficient of order unity for clean interfaces.

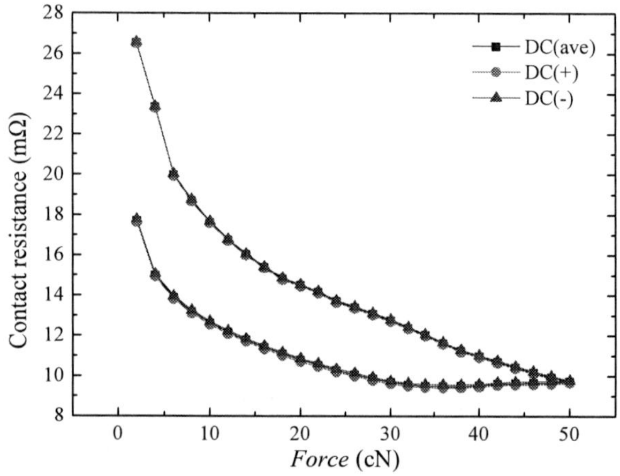

(a)

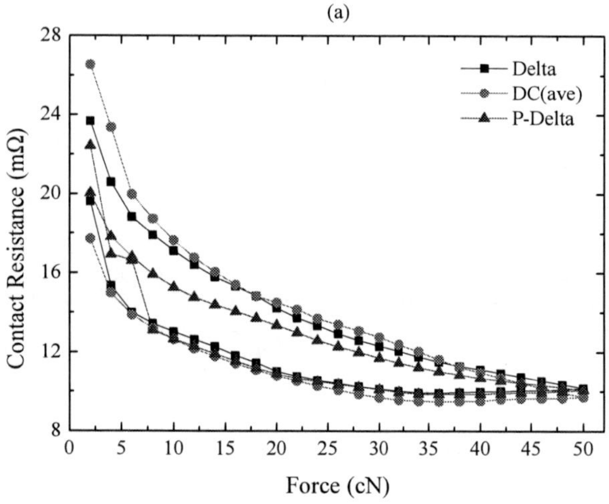

(b)

Fig. 6 Contact resistances between Au-coated indenter and Au-plated rivet as a function of applied load (test current is 10mA) (a) DC mode. (b) Results comparisons between DC mode and non-constant mode

Equations of the form (3) have been used by several workers. The general validity of that expression is consistent with much published experimental data for a variety of contact materials. However, the effect of current on contact resistance could not be taken account into Eq. (3) and any other classical analytical models.

As shown in Fig.6(a), there is no any significant difference between the measurement results obtained in positive DC mode and negative DC mode when the test current is 10mA. However, the substantial gap is found both in loading process and unloading process while the test current is reduced to 1mA (shown in Fig.7(a)). It indicates that the consistence of results is dependent on the test current amplitude, that is to say, the thermoelectrical voltage and noise are affected greatly by the test current. So, on the increasing demand of low test current, it is better to choose the non-constant current mode to obtain more accurate measurement results.

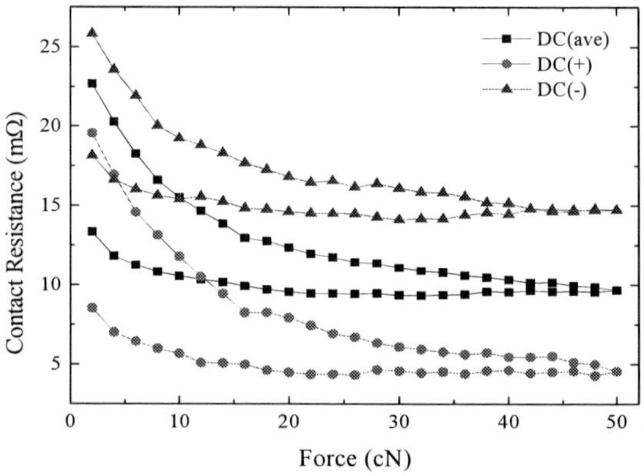

(a) DC mode

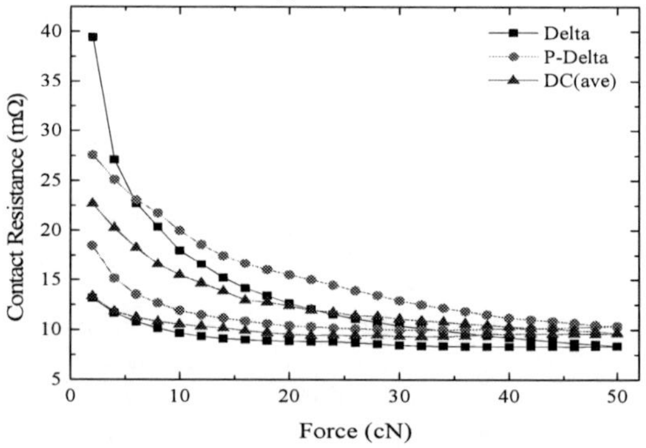

(b) Results comparisons between DC mode and non-constant mode

Fig. 7 Contact resistances between Au-coated indenter and Au-plated rivet as a function of applied load (test current is 1mA) (a) DC mode. (b) Results comparisons between DC mode and non-constant mode

Fig.8 shows the variations in thermoelectrical voltage between Au-coated indenter and different samples as a function of time. The load force is 50cN. It is noticed that the EMF of AgCdO rivet is between 6.2V and 6.8V within 65miniues, while the EMF of gold-plated copper rivet is kept between 5.3V and 6.9V. These results show that the status of thermoelectrical voltage is relatively stable for a long time. Therefore, EMF could be taken as a constant during contact resistance measurement experiment when atmosphere temperature has no change.

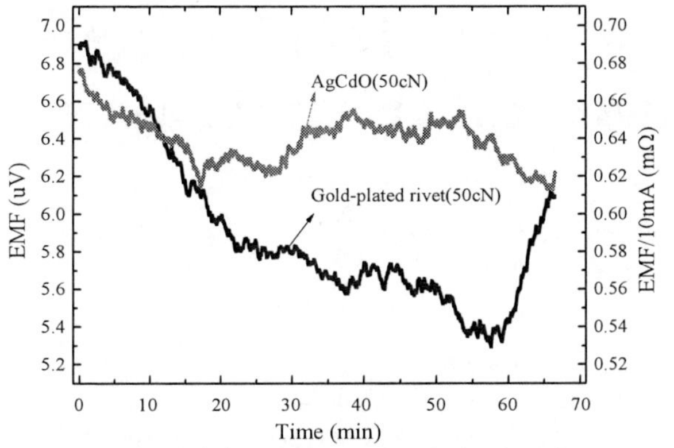

Fig. 8 The variations in thermoelectrical voltage between Au-coated indenter and different rivet as a function of time. (load force is 50cN)

IV. CONCLUSIONS

This investigation mainly aims to determine the effect of load current on contact resistance accurately. Keithley 6221 programmable current source and Keithley 2182A nanovolt meter combination are used to measure the low contact resistance under DC mode and non-constant current mode. The results show that the averaging DC method and Delta method and Pulse-Delta method are all suitable for measuring contact resistance. However, for the special low test current requirement, Delta method is remarkably superior to any other methods. The change of thermoelectrical voltage of contact pairs in a long time is within 2V.

REFERENCES

[1] P.Slade. Electrical contacts principles and applications (Second Edition). CRC Press,2014.

[2] American Society for Testing Material (ASTM) B539-02,2013.

[3] R. Holm. Electrical Contacts—Theory and application, 4th ed., Springer, New York, 1967.

[4] W. Ren, G. Zhai, L. Cui. Contact vibration characteristic of electromagnetic relay, IEICE Trans. Electron. Vol.E89-C, no.8, pp.1177-1181, August 2006.

[5] W. Ren, L. Cui, J. Chen, X. Ma, X. Zhang. Fretting behavior of Au plated copper contacts induced by high frequency vibration, Proceedings of the 58th IEEE Holm Conf. on Electrical Contacts, pp.204-210, 2012.

[6] C. Maul, J.W.Mcbride, J. Swingler. Intermittency phenomena in electrical contacts, IEEE Trans. Compon. Packag. Technol, Vol.24, no.3, pp.370-377, March 2001.

[7] N. BenJemma, J.L.Queffelec, D.Travers. Apparatus and methods for electrical contact resistance study of cleaned and corroded materials, Meas. Sci. Technol., Vol.1,no.1, pp.282-286, Jan. 1990.

[8] G. Horn: Test Method form Clenaness of Technical Contact Surfaces by an Automatic Measurement Device for Contact Resistance, Proc.8th International Conference on Electrical Contact Phenomena, pp.499-503 (in German) 1976.

[9] R.S.Timsit. Electrical contact resistance: properties of stationary interfaces, IEEE Trans. Comp. Packag. Technol., Vol.22, no.1, pp85-98, Jan. 1999.

[10] R.S.Timsit. Electrical contact resistance: properties of stationary interfaces, IEEE Trans. Comp. Packag. Technol.,Vol.22, no.1, pp85-98, Jan. 1999.

[11] M. Braunovic.Fretting in electrical/electronic connections: a review, IEICE Trans. Electron., Vol.E92-C,no.8, pp.982-991, August 2009.

[12] J. Song, C. Koch, L. Wang. Correlation between wear resistance and lifetime of electrical contacts, Advances in Tribology, pp.1-9, 2012.

[13] I.Minowa, M. Kanno. Measurement of contact resistance of electric contacts using SQUID galvanometer, Electrics and Communications in Japan(Part I: Communications), Vol.67, no.11, pp.93-103, Nov. 1984.

[14] H.Aichi, N.Tahara. Analysis on the constriction resistance of the electric contact by the contact model using the electrolyte Bath, The 20th International Conf. Electrical Contacts, 1994.

[15] Jerzy Kaczmarek. Constriction resistance measurements based on the method of third harmonic, The 19th HOLM Conf. Electrical Contacts, pp.155-158, 1973.

[16] http://www.hysitron.com/products/options-upgrades/nanoecr

[17] W. Ren, Y. Chen, S.Cao, L. Cui and H. Liang. A new automated test equipment for measuring electrical contact resistance of real size rivets, Proc. 59th IEEE Holm Conf. on Electrical Contacts, USA, pp.295-301,2013.

[18] W. Ren, Y. Chen, S. Xue, G. Horn and G. Zhai. Experimental investigation and numerical simulation on the role of sphere indenter in measuring contact resistance of flat rivets, IEICE Trans. Electron., Vol.E97-C, no.9, pp.873-879, Sep. 2014.

[19] Keithley Instruments Inc.: Low level Measurements handbook (7th Edition). 2013.

7th International Conference on Reliability of
Electrical Products and Electrical Contacts,
November 04-06, 2019

Optimization Simulation and Analysis of Dynamic Characteristics of Magnetic Latching Relay

Changchun Chi, Sai Che
School of Electrical Engineering, Shanghai Dianji University, Shanghai 201306, China
E-mail: chicc@sdju.edu.cn Tel: 13701608259

Abstract—**Magnetic latching relay has been widely used due to it's advantages of small size, low energy consumption and high stability. However, the reliability and service life of the magnetic latching relay are seriously affected due to the temperature rise, fusion welding and loss phenomenon caused by the bounce of the contact in the closing process. In order to solve this problem, the motion process of magnetic latching relay closing and disconnecting is studied and analyzed, the relevant dynamic mathematical model is established, the corresponding fuzzy control rules are designed, and the main circuit, mechanical motion module and fuzzy control optimization module are established by MATLAB Simulink. By fuzzy optimization of pulse current PWM control dynamically coil magnetic latching relay dynamic switching characteristics, greatly reduce collision speed when dynamic and static contact is closed, thus reducing the contact bounce between frequency and time, reduce caused by dynamic and static contact bounce of temperature rise and energy consumption, improve the magnetic latching relay reliability and service life, the study of magnetic latching relay development, production and processing has certain theoretical significance and practical value.**

Index Terms— **Magnetic latching relay, Closing process, Contact bounce, Fuzzy control**

As one of the most important control elements in low voltage electrical apparatus, relay plays an important role in communication, remote control, telemetry, mechatronics, automatic control and power electronics[1]. Compared with the traditional electromagnetic relay, the magnetic retention relay has a simpler structure and does not need to be energized for a long time. It only needs to pass a certain width of action and reset pulse, and the relay can realize the switching of the closed and off state, when the pulse is invalid. After that, there is still electromagnetic force to keep it in a steady state, which is convenient to control. Since the coil is not continuously energized, the heat generation of the relay is greatly reduced, a large amount of electric energy is saved compared with the conventional electromagnetic relay, and the temperature rise and the noise are small, which is less affected by the fluctuation of the power grid. Therefore, the development of intelligent magnetic holding relays will become a development trend in the future. . At present, domestic and foreign scholars have done a lot of work on magnetic holding relays, such as electrical parameter detection system and parameter optimization design of magnetic holding relay [2-3], research on arcing factors and dynamic characteristics [3-4].

Studies have shown that before the magnetic holding relay reaches the steady state during the closing process, the moving and static contacts will bounce due to the collision. The short arc generated by the long-term bounce process causes high temperature at the contact portion. Due to the large temperature gradient inside and outside the molten pool, the metal in the molten pool rapidly solidifies and crystallizes, so that the contact portion forms a fusion joint. When the welding force of the contact is greater than the breaking force of the contact, welding will occur, which seriously damages the reliability and service life of the magnetic holding relay [5]. Therefore, exploring the method of improving the dynamic characteristics of the magnetic holding relay, realizing the dynamic closing process of the magnetic holding relay, improving the service life and overall performance of the magnetic holding relay, has great theoretical significance and practicality for the research, development and processing of the magnetic holding relay. value.

The research shows that the dynamic and static contacts will bounce due to collision before the magnetic latching relay reaches steady state in the closing process. The short arc generated by long-term bouncing process causes high temperature in the contact area, resulting in welding damage to magnetic latching relay[6]. Therefore, it is of great theoretical significance and practical value to explore ways to improve the dynamic characteristics of magnetic latching relay, to optimize the dynamic closing process of magnetic latching relay, and to improve the service life and overall performance of magnetic latching relay.

I. ELECTROMAGNETIC MECHANISM OF MAGNETIC LATCHING RELAY

The electromagnetic mechanism of the rotary magnetic latching relay includes armature assembly (including permanent magnet and pole plate), iron core, yoke and coil. The schematic diagram of the electromagnetic mechanism is shown in Fig. 1. The electromagnetic energy can be converted into mechanical energy through the working air gap and armature assembly between the yoke iron and the upper and lower pole plates, thus driving the whole contact mechanism to work [3]. The permanent magnet model of magnetic latching relay is Y30BH, and the yoke iron and iron core are all made of electrical pure iron (DT4E), which are firmly combined.

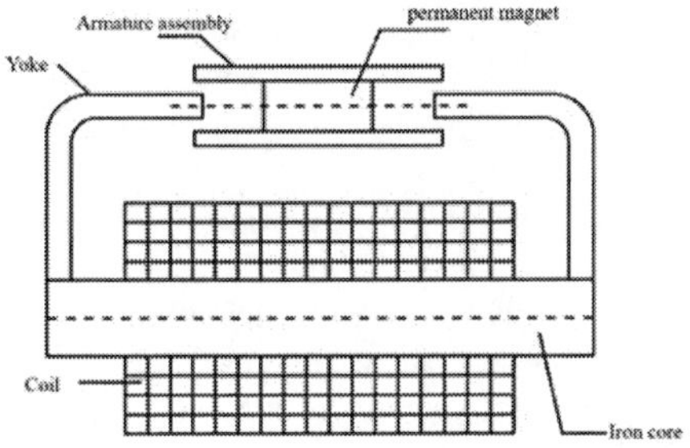

Fig. 1 Schematic diagram of electromagnetic mechanism of rotary magnetic holding relay

The rotary magnetic holding relay has no spring in the electromagnetic mechanism, and its reaction force is provided by the permanent magnet. The working principle of the magnetic holding relay is very simple: when there is no pulse current in the coil, the armature assembly is subjected to a permanent magnetic field, and a clockwise electromagnetic force is generated so that the upper magnetic pole piece and the right yoke iron are closely attracted, and the initial state is at this time. That is, the closed state. When the coil turns on the forward pulse current, the core and the two yokes internally generate a magnetic field opposite to the direction of the permanent magnet's magnetic field. And to overcome the role of the permanent magnetic field, the armature assembly is subjected to electromagnetic force to rotate counterclockwise along the center of the permanent magnet, and the push piece is driven to the left to break the normally closed contact. When the upper pole piece is rotated to complete contact with the left yoke, the coil pulse current disappears, and the armature assembly is stably maintained at the position under the action of the permanent magnet, which is referred to as the disconnected state of the magnetic holding relay. Conversely, when the coil passes the reverse pulse current, the core and the two yokes internally generate a magnetic field opposite to the direction of the permanent magnet magnetic field. When the electromagnetic force generated by the pulse current is greater than the permanent magnet electromagnetic force, the armature assembly is clockwise. Rotating electromagnetic force. When the upper pole piece is rotated until contact with the right yoke, the forward current disappears and returns to the initial state, that is, the closed state. Since the electromagnetic force generated by the permanent magnetic field still exists, the armature assembly is stably maintained at this position, which is the bistable state of the magnetic holding relay.

II. SIMULATION AND OPTIMIZATION OF DYNAMIC CHARACTERISTICS

A. Establishment of Dynamic Mathematical Model of 2.1 Magnetic RelayFormat for the paper should be as follows:

In the dynamic process of closing and closing of electromagnetic mechanism of magnetic latching relay, many factors are involved, such as electromagnetic, thermal energy change and mechanical movement. The establishment of mathematical model needs to be concise and complete. Therefore, it is necessary to add voltage balance equation to the electromagnetic system, Maxwell equation to the magnetic field, Darumbel equation to the mechanical motion and thermal balance equation to the thermodynamics [7]. These interrelated equations constitute the differential equations describing the dynamic process of the mechanism. The equations are as follows:

$$U = \mathrm{i}(\mathrm{t})R + \frac{d\psi(\mathrm{t})}{dt} \qquad (1)$$

$$T - T_{\mathrm{f}} = J\frac{d\omega}{dt} \qquad (2)$$

$$\omega(t) = \frac{d\alpha(t)}{dt} \qquad (3)$$

The initial condition is: $\psi|_{t=0} = \psi_0, \omega|_{t=0} = 0, \alpha|_{t=0} = \alpha_0$

B. Fuzzy Controller Design

From the resultant moment curve and dynamic mathematical model of armature assembly, it can be seen that the resultant moment of armature assembly in the closing process is related to the number of amperes and turns of coil, the rotation angular velocity of armature assembly and the angle at which it is located. Therefore, the input of the fuzzy control rules is the rotation angle and rotation speed of armature assembly, and the output is the duty cycle D of PWM. The table of the fuzzy control rules is shown in Table 1. XS, S, M, L and XL are small, small, medium, large and large respectively.

The ambiguous conditional statements in Table 1 are as follows: IF is XS and is XS then D is XL

That is to say, when the rotating angle of armature assembly is very small and the rotating angular velocity is also very small, the duty cycle of output PWM should be very large. At this time, the coil is fed into a large pulse current, the resultant moment of armature assembly is increased, and the rotating speed of armature assembly is increased, so as to achieve the purpose of fast closure and improve the reliability of magnetic latching relay On the contrary, when the duty cycle of PWM is very small, the angular velocity of armature assembly before the collision of dynamic and static contacts is reduced, so as to reduce the bounce between contacts.

TABLE I

FUZZY CONTROL RULE TABLE

α	ω				
	XS	S	M	L	XL
XS	XL	XL	L	L	M
S	XL	L	L	M	S
M	L	L	M	S	S
L	L	M	S	S	XS
XL	M	S	S	XS	XS

C. Dynamic System Simulation and Analysis

In the simulink, the main circuit, the mechanical motion module and the fuzzy control module are built to constitute the dynamic system, as shown in Figure 2. The voltage at both ends of the coil of magnetic latching relay is changed in real time by applying different duty ratios of PWM through fuzzy control after voltage-reducing rectification filtering of 220V AC power supply, thus realizing the regulation of dynamic characteristics. The output is the rotation angle and angular velocity of armature assembly. When the output angle reaches - 7 degrees, the simulation of motion system is completed.

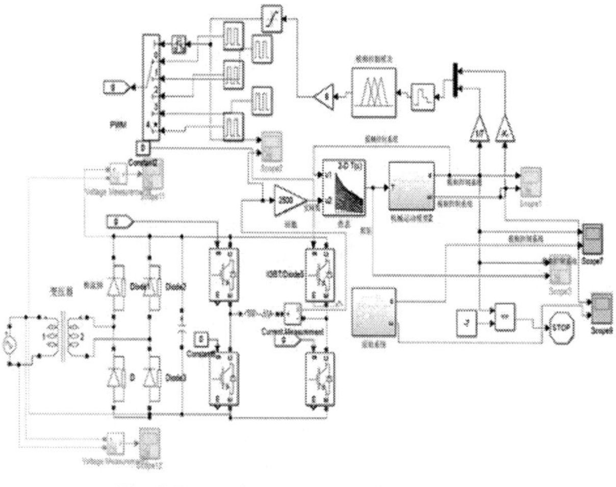

Fig. 2 Dynamic system simulation model

In the model, the output of the original system and the fuzzy control system are compared and simulated. The simulation results of angle and angular velocity are shown in figs. 3 and 4.

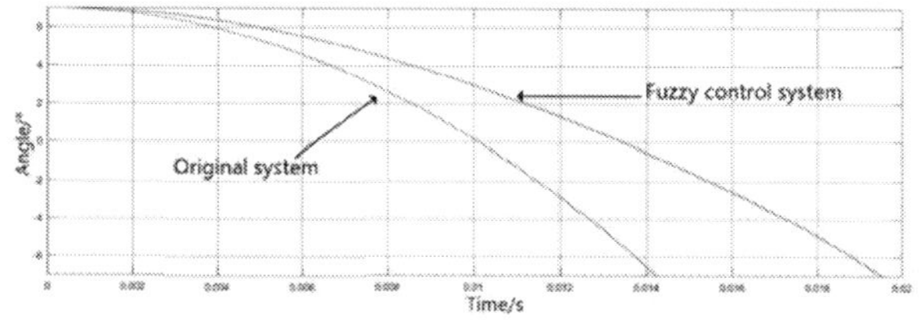

Fig. 3 angle comparison simulation diagram

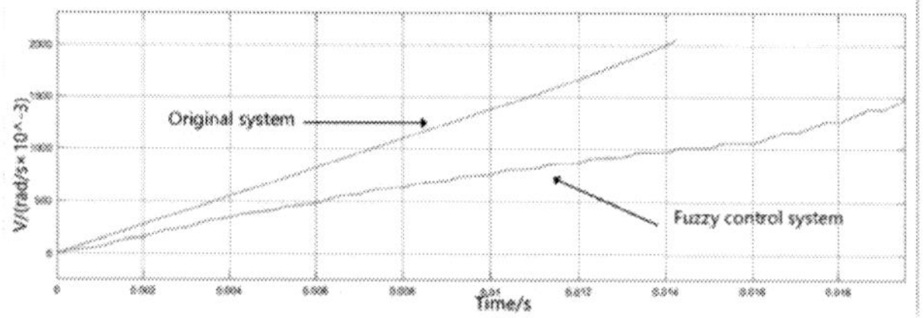

Fig. 4 angular velocity comparison simulation diagram

The simulation results of Fig. 3 and Fig. 4 show that after the fuzzy control optimization of the system, the time of the whole closing process is controlled within 20ms, which meets the requirements of reliable closing time. And when the armature assembly rotates at the end of the closing, the angular velocity is -7 degrees, the angular velocity is significantly smaller than the original system angular velocity, which will greatly reduce the bounce between the dynamic and static contacts, improve the service life of the magnetic latching relay, and reduce the energy consumption. Improvements in dynamic characteristics play an important role.

III. CONCLUSION

In this paper, the dynamic characteristics of the magnetic latching relay are analyzed, and the dynamic mathematical model of the magnetic latching relay is established. The dynamic system simulation model is established by using MATLAB, and the fuzzy PWM control method is used to optimize the closing characteristics, and the motion curve of the armature assembly during the closing process is simulated. It can be seen from the simulation results that the fuzzy PWM control method can effectively improve the dynamic characteristics of the magnetic latching relay, thereby reducing the contact bounce phenomenon and improving the reliability and service life of the magnetic latching relay.

REFERENCES

[1] De-sheng Li, Ben-dong Liu. Research on Microelectromagnetic Relays[J]. Frontiers of Mechanical Engineering in China, 2006, 1(1): 111-114.

[2] Pandey S, Garg A. Performance testing and reliablity of 2 pole magnetic latching relays for smart meters[C]// IET International Conference on Renewable Power Generation. London: IEEE, 2017:1-5.

[3] SU Xiu-ping,DU Shi-ping,QIAO Yan-hua, PANG Xiao-meng.Design of robustness parameters of magnetic holding relays[J].Journal of Hebei University of Technology,2017,46(05):17-22.

[4] Zhou Z, Lv Z, Guo K, et al. Research on the Test System for Electrical Parameters of Relay Based on STM32[C]// Fifth International Conference on Instrumentation & Measurement. Qinhuangdao: IEEE, 2016: 1812-1815.

[5] LI Junfeng, SU Xiuping, ZHENG Xinfang, ZHAO Jingying. Analysis of contact bounce based on contact dynamic contact pressure[J]. Transactions of Electrical Engineering, 2015, 30(09): 138-144.

[6] Kai B, Xue Z, Guofu Z. Simulation of Arc Dwelling Behavior During Bridge-Type Contacts Opening Process for High-Power Relay[J]. IEEE Transactions on Components, Packaging and Manufacturing Technology, 2018, 8(6):975-981.

[7] Lucio Boccardo,Luigi Orsina. A semilinear system of Schrödinger–Maxwell equations[J]. Nonlinear Analysis,2019.

First A. CHI Changchun and the other authors is CHE Sai .Both authors Research directions are smart appliances.

7th International Conference on Reliability of
Electrical Products and Electrical Contacts,
November 04-06, 2019

Long-life Reliability Optimization Design of High-power DC Electromagnetic Relay Considering Thermal Degradation

Jie Deng, Hongliang Xu, Guofu Zhai
Harbin Institute of Technology, Harbin, 150001, China
E-mail:m18846441684@163.comTel:86-451-86413193 Fax:86-451-86413192

Abstract—**As a key component in load control circuits, high-power electromagnetic relay (EMR) has been widely used in aviation and weaponry. However, due to the absence of arc-extinguishing structure in the relay, the arc-burning heat is severe under high-power DC load. Under the influence of high temperature, the properties of magnetic material and reed material will generate thermal degradation inevitably, resulting in electromagnetic force and mechanical force declining in different degrees. For products with poor design, the decline of the pull-in and release capacity will lead to the failure of the relay directly, or the failure of the life such as ablative bonding of contact. Therefore, it is important to ensure the reliable life of the suction-reaction force with sufficient thermal degradation margin in the design and optimization process of high-power relays. In this paper, the failure mechanism of electrical life is first analyzed through the thermal simulation and test under the 25A DC relay. Then the thermal degradation characteristics of magnetic material and reed material is taken into account. And the action characteristics of the relay at high temperature is improved by optimizing the suction reaction characteristics, thereby improving the electrical life of the high-power DC relay. Finally, the correctness of the optimization scheme is verifiedthroughthe actual manufacture and test of the EMR.**

Index Terms—**Failure mechanism analysis, Electrical life optimization, High-power electro-magnetic relay**

I. INTRODUCTION

As a key electromechanical component, electro-magnetic relays are widely used in electronic systems such as automatic control and communication[1, 2].The application reliability of the relay directly affects whether the electronic system can operate normally[3].However, statistics show that electro-magnetic relays are still the least reliable of all electronic components [4].Because there is no arc-extinguishing structure in the relay, the arc cannot be quickly extinguished by external force, and the arc can only be extinguished by the opening of the self-contact [5, 6].The arcing time is directly related to the ablation of the contacts, which in turn affects the electrical life of the relay.

Especially for DC high-power electromagnetic relays, the arc ablate the contacts more severely. Moreover, the high internal temperature of the relay caused by high-power arc combustion inevitably causes thermal degradation of the properties of the magnetic material and the reed material [7]. On the one hand, the coil resistance increases with increasing temperature, and the performance of the permanent magnet material decreases with increasing temperature. On the other hand, the reed stiffness decreases with increasing temperature, which can cause contact pressure and mechanical force to drop. Degradation of suction and reaction characteristics will inevitably reduce the ability of the relay to pull and release. Therefore, for a relay product with insufficient thermal degradation design margin, the armature action speed decreases and the arcing time increases rapidly as the pull-in or release capacity decreases under the influence of high temperature. The increase in arcing energy will cause the internal temperature of the relay to continue to rise, forming a vicious circle. It can be seen that the rational design of the suction and reaction characteristics is an important factor to ensure the reliability of the electrical life of the relay.

Domestic and foreign scholars have also carried out a lot of research on the electrical life and performance optimization of electromechanical components such as relays. Zhang Feifei, Li Zhigang et al. proposed a method for determining the electrical contact performance evaluation index of relays under different categories to estimate the life of the contact relay. Yang Wenying et al. analyzed and studied the mechanism affecting the rated life of electromagnetic relays based on the large difference between the rated life of electromagnetic relays.

In this paper, a certain type of balanced force military high-power DC electromagnetic relay is taken as an example. Firstly, the failure mechanism is used to determine the mechanism of electrical life failure. Secondly, considering the influence of high temperature on the characteristics of suction and reaction, the long-life reliability optimization design is carried out. Finally, the correctness of the optimization scheme is verified by manufacturing the prototype and electrical life test.

II. FAILURE MECHANISM ANALYSIS

A.Electrical life test study

Five relay prototypes were selected to perform 28V/25A DC resistive load electrical life test at room temperature of 25 °C, and its rated life was 50,000 times. The 5 prototypes all failed within 14000~16000 times. The failure mode was that the moving contact was bonded and the relay could not be released.

After the electrical life test, the sample was opened and the internal structure was observed. It was found that the ablation of the static contact group was normal and the reed did not show significant deformation. The moving contact group is severely ablated, as shown in Figure 1. And the reed has undergone severe deformation under the influence of high temperature, and even breaks, as shown in Figure 2.

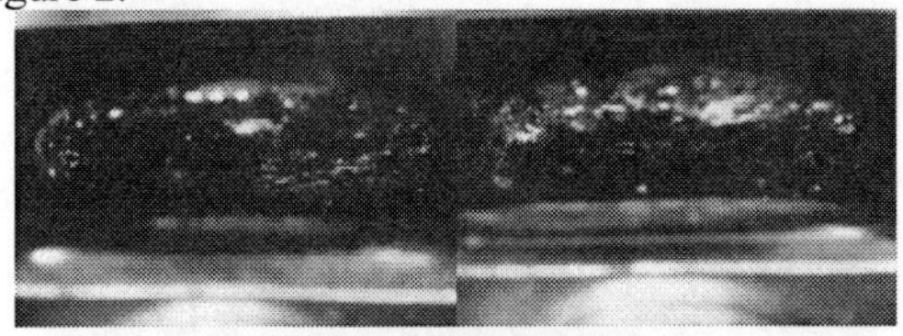

Fig. 1 Activating contact ablation

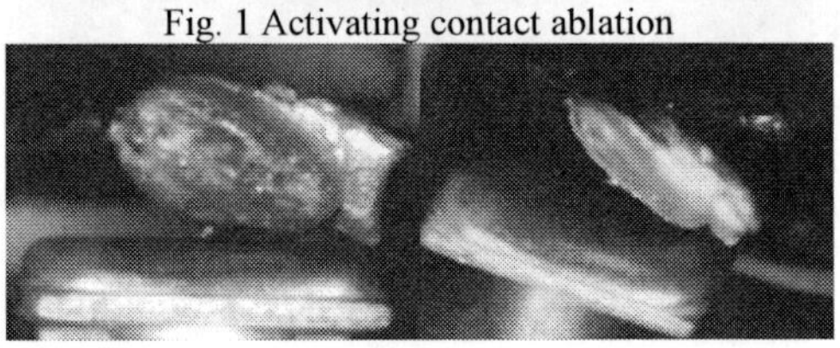

Fig. 2 Dynamic reed deformation and fracture

During the electrical life test, after the temperature rise of the prototype was stabilized, the oscilloscope is used to collect the typical waveform of the breaking arc of the moving contact during the release process, as shown in FIG.3It can be seen that the arcing time has reached 7-8ms.

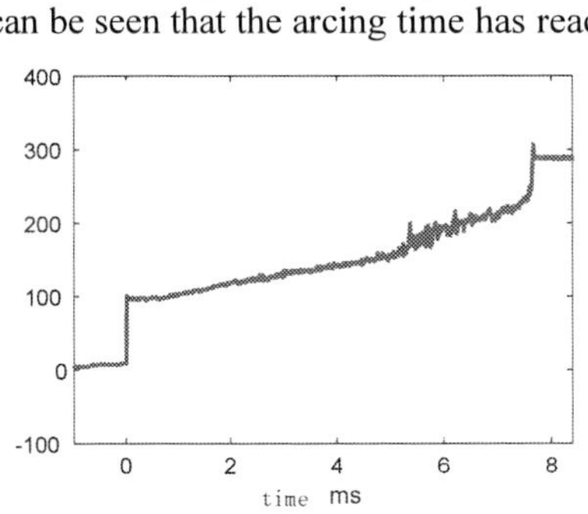

Fig. 3 The moving contact breaks the arcing waveform

B. Electrical life failure analysis

The finite element model of the relay thermal simulation was established, and the ambient temperature was set at 25 °C. Under the condition of 28V/25A load, the simulation results are shown in Fig. 4. The maximum temperature of the case is 337°C, which is consistent with the measured results. The internal contacts and reeds reached a temperature of 481°C.

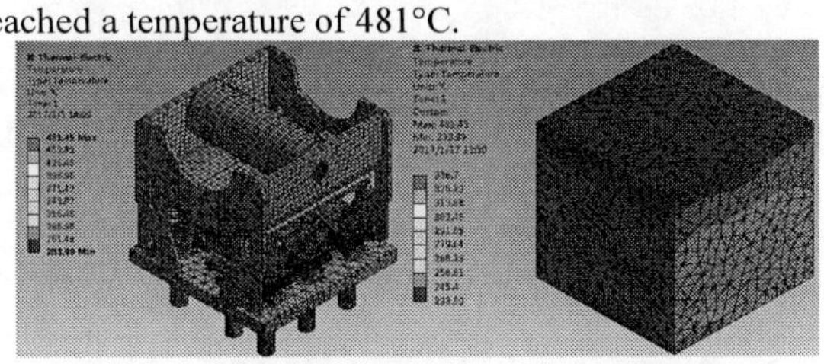

Fig. 4 Relay thermal simulation results

At the same time, the finite element simulation model of the relay electromagnetic system is established, and the electromagnetic suction characteristic curve is obtained, as shown in Fig. 5. A relay dynamics simulation model is established to obtain a mechanical reaction force characteristic curve, as shown in Fig. 6.

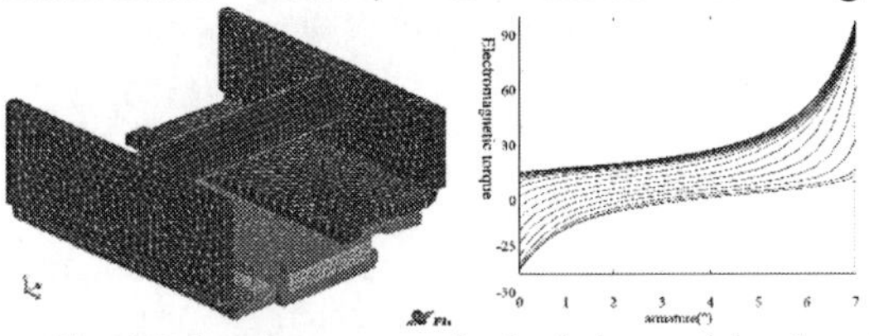

Fig. 5 Relay electromagnetic simulation model and results

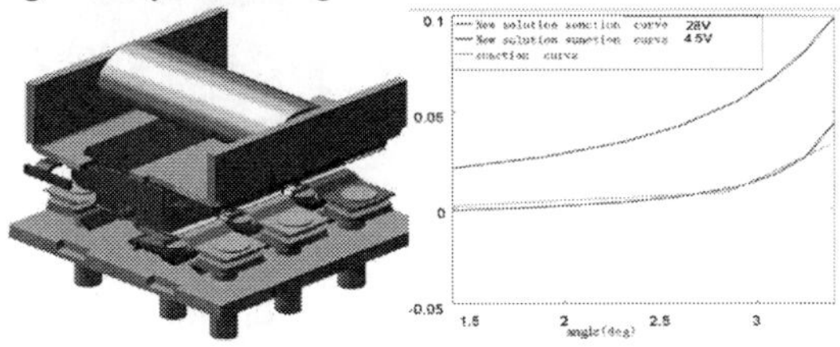

Fig. 6 Simulation model of relay dynamics and characteristics of suction and reaction force

It can be seen from the characteristics of the suction reaction force that the electromagnetic attraction curve with the release voltage of 4.5V has a significant intersection with the reaction force curve. Only when the suction characteristic is lower than the reaction force can the relay be released to the initial position, so the current matching characteristics may cause the armature to release slowly, that is, the release ability is poor.

On this basis, the decrease of the reaction force curve caused by the reduction of the reed stiffness further reduces the release voltage and release capability of the relay, further increases the arcing time, and the internal temperature continues to rise, thereby forming a vicious circle. Eventually, the relay will not be released or the contact will be severely ablated and will fail, which will greatly reduce the reliability of its electrical life.

Based on the above analysis, it is determined that the release capacity and insufficient high temperature degradation margin are the mechanisms that cause the electrical life of this type of relay to fail. Therefore, the lifting release capability is the goal of this paper's optimization design.

III. LONG LIFE OPTIMIZATION DESIGN

A. Optimization ideas

In order to ensure the vibration resistance of the relay, it is necessary to have sufficient armature retention. Therefore, while improving the release ability, it is necessary to ensure that the armature has sufficient suction retention. These two factors are inherently contradictory. To this end, this paper proposes the following optimization ideas:

(1) By eliminating the magnetic saturation problem and parameter optimization, the electromagnetic force is absorbed as much as possible;

(2) Determine the upper limit that the reaction force can be raised according to the requirements of the vibration resistance to the holding force;

(3)Through the optimization of the reed parameters, the ability to resist high temperature deformation is improved, and the reed stiffness is determined;

(4) In order to eliminate the intersection of the suction and reaction curves, optimize the parameters of the spring system and increase the release voltage and its thermal degradation margin.;

(5) Verify the correctness of the solution through the simulation and the physical verification.

B.Optimization plan.

A. Electromagnetic system optimization

（1）Magnetic saturation problem optimization

Through the electromagnetic simulation model, the weak point of magnetic saturation in the relay electromagnetic system is determined. By increasing the cross-sectional area of the magnetic saturation position andeliminating magnetic saturation, the electro-magnetic force can be effectively increased.

The magnetic flux simulation cloud diagram of the relay in the pull-in state is shown in Fig. 7. It can be seen that the iron core is magnetically saturated. According to the characteristics of the electromagnetic structure, this paper proposes an optimization scheme for increasing the cross-sectional area of the square core. At the same time, the coil parameters were changed from 260 Ω、3200 circles to 520 Ω and 4500 circles ,and the simulation model and magnetic flux cloud diagram are shown in Fig. 8.

The electromagnetic force curve before and after optimization is shown in Fig. 9. It can be seen that the electromagnetic force under the release voltage does not change, and the pull-in electromagnetic force at the 28V operating voltage increases by 56%. It shows that the optimization scheme effectively solves the magnetic saturation problem.

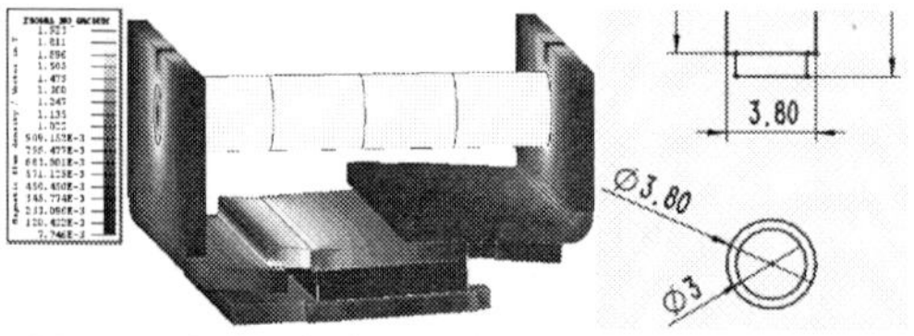

Fig. 7 Magnetic flux before optimization and Core parameters beforeoptimization

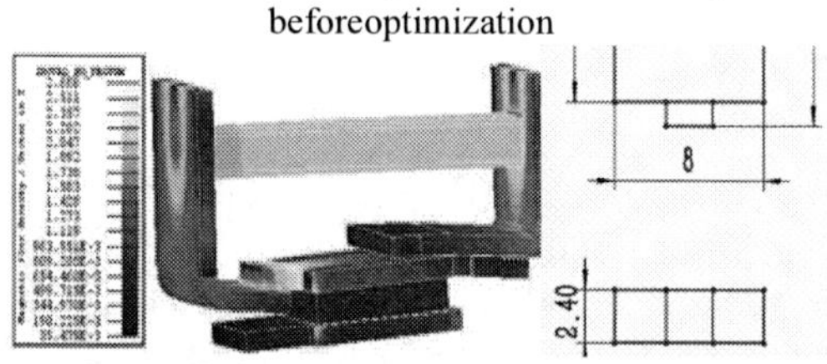

Fig. 8 Optimized flux cloud map and Optimized core parameters

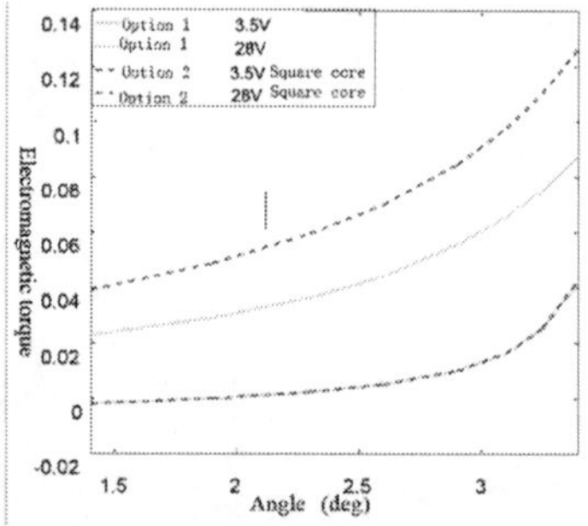

Fig. 9 Electromagnetic force curve before and after optimization

(2)Key parameter determination and optimization

On the basis of solving the magnetic saturation problem, the electromagnetic force is further improved by determining the parameters in the electromagnetic system that have significant influence on the attracting electromagnetic force and optimizing the parameters.

According to the magnetic circuit theory, 11 parameters were initially screened for single factor significance analysis. The parameters and their range of variation are shown in Table 1. The influence of each parameter change on the pull-in electromagnetic force is calculated by an electromagnetic simulation model, and the result is shown in fig.10.

According to the extreme value of the electro-magnetic force change, the significant order is determined, and the magnetic gap is determined as the key parameter.

The magnetic flux is optimized for the purpose of improving the electromagnetic force. Six values are selected at equal intervals in the range of 0.02~0.07mm, and the electromagnetic force curve under the release voltage is simulated and analyzed, as shown in Fig. 11.

TABLE I

ELECTROMAGNETIC SYSTEM DESIGN PARAMETERS

Serial number	Design Parameters	Range of parameter values
1	The length of the end of pull-in armature	-1.6~0.4
2	The length of the tail of pull-in armature	-0.8~1.6
3	The length of release armature	-0.8~1.6
4	The length of suction yoke	-0.4~1.6
5	The length of release yoke	-0.8~1.6
6	The width of the end of pull-in armature	-1.6~0
7	The width of the tail of pull-in armature	-1.6~0.8
8	The width of release armature	-3.2~0
9	The width of suction yoke	-1.6~0
10	The width of release yoke	-2.4~0
11	Release the gap between the yoke and the tail of the action armature	0.02~0.2

(Note: The width in the design parameters is the one-sided width in mm)

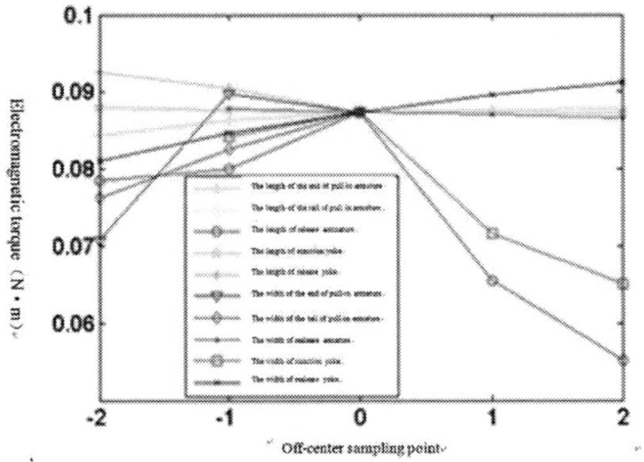

Fig. 10 Effect of parameter changes on the pull-in electromagnetic force

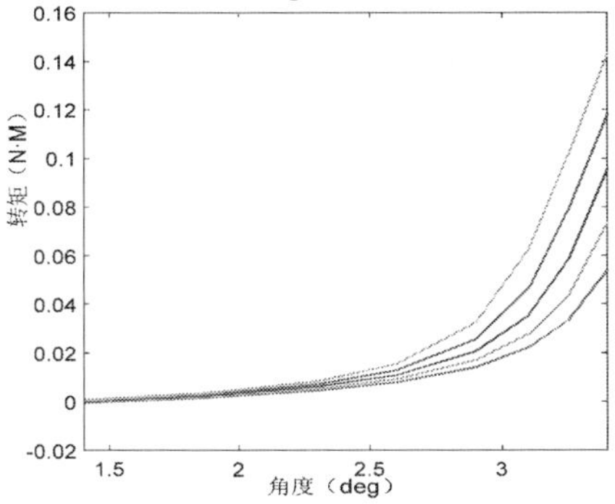

Fig. 11 Effect of magnetic gap on electromagnetic force

Considering the requirements of contact pressure and suction retention force, an optimization scheme of 0.05 mm is selected as the magnetic gap, and the original scheme is 0.09 mm.The suction curve before and after the simulation is optimized is shown in Fig. 12.

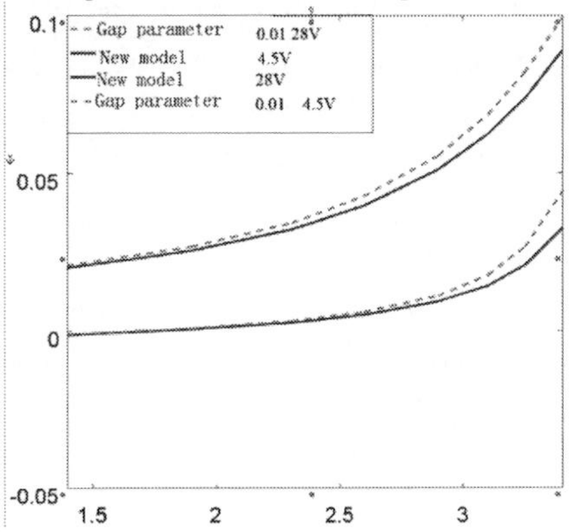

Fig. 12 Electromagnetic force curve before and after magnetic gap optimization

B. Spring system optimization

(1) Dynamic reed parameter optimization

The structural schematic diagram of the moving reed parts is shown in Fig. 13. By reducing the bending height of the moving spring and reducing the bending slope, the deformation resistance of the moving spring at high temperature is improved. The optimization scheme is shown in Table 2.

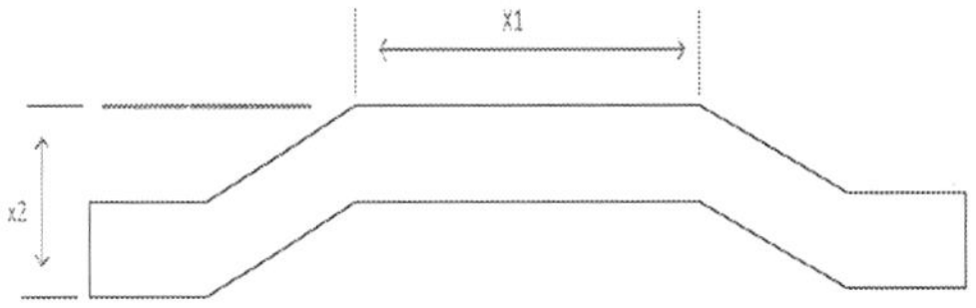

Fig. 13 Schematic diagram of moving reed parts

TABLE II

ELECTROMAGNETIC SYSTEM DESIGN PARAMETERS

Serial number	X1	X2
Before optimization	11	1.1
After optimization	7	0.9

(2) Optimization of suction and reaction coordination characteristics

Improve the release capability of the relay while ensuring that the suction retention force meets the requirements.See Table 3 for the parameters of the contact spring system before and after optimization.

(3) Simulation verification

The optimized suction and force matching

characteristics are shown in Fig. 14. It can be seen that the reaction force value has been significantly improved compared with that before optimization, and the problem of crossover force absorption has also been solved.

TABLE III

COMPARISON OF PARAMETERS BEFORE AND AFTER OPTIMIZATION OF THE SPRING SYSTEM

	overstroke	contact pressure	contact gap	retentivity
Before optimization	0.072mm	0.72N	0.83mm	3.1N
After optimization	0.092mm	0.92N	0.8mm	4.0N

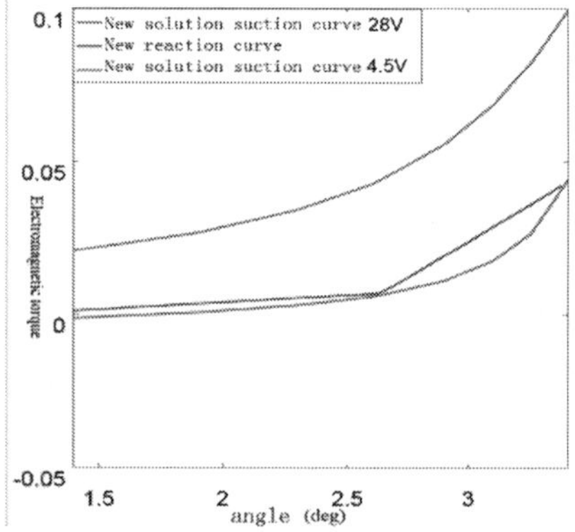

Fig. 14 The reaction fit curve of the new scheme

IV. PROTOTYPE VERIFICATION

The prototype was made according to the optimized drawings and the electrical life test was carried out under the same load conditions. Use the oscilloscope to capture the typical waveform of the split arc, as shown in Figure 15. It can be seen that the arcing time can be shortened to within 2 ms.

Secondly, the prototype is tested for arcing characteristics of the whole life process, and the test data is shown in Table 4. During the subsequent limit life test, the first failure occurred in 66,492 times, and no dead failure occurred at 80,000 times. The test data is shown in table 4.

V. CONCLUSION

The suction and release capacity and the degradation margin under the influence of arcing heat are the most important factors determining the electrical life of high-power DC electromagnetic relays. In this paper, the failure mechanism analysis and long life optimization design are carried out for 25A DC relay.

(1)Combined with thermal simulation and simulation of suction and reaction characteristics, it is determined that the lack of release ability is the mechanism leading to electrical life failure;

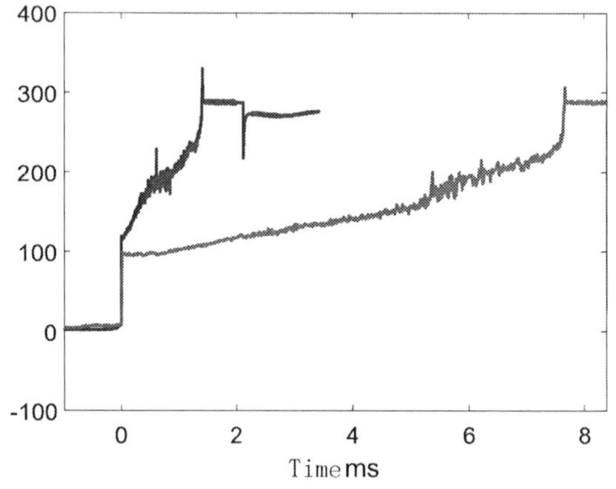

Fig. 15 Optimized release process dynamics test results

TABLE IV

ELECTRICAL LIFE TEST DATA

Prototype	Static separation arc			Movement separation arc		
Contact	1#	2#	3#	1#	2#	3#
0	1.28	1.44	1.47	870	900	900
5000	1.16	1.17	1.22	600	730	830
10000	1.82	1.77	1.69	930	930	980
20000	1.77	1.63	1.64	920	1.07	970
30000	1.76	1.83	1.92	960	960	950
40000	1.82	1.57	1.64	990	1.03	1.11
50000	1.50	1.46	1.51	970	990	890

TABLE V

ULTIMATE LIFE TEST DATA

Prototype	Static separation arc			Movement separation arc		
Contact	1#	2#	3#	1#	2#	3#
50000	1.59	1.46	1.52	1.01	1.06	1.19
60000	2.31	2.13	1.49	960	960	960
70000	2.14	2.02	1.01	1.26	1.25	1.41
80000	2.36	2.21	1.07	1.17	1.70	1.68

(2)It is determined that the iron core is the weak point that causes the magnetic circuit to be saturated, and the magnetic flux cross-sectional area is improved by designing the square iron core, which effectively solves the magnetic saturation and increases the attracting electromagnetic force by 56%;

(3)It is determined that the key parameter affecting the electromagnetic force in the electromagnetic system is the magnetic gap, and the electromagnetic force is further increased by 44% through parameter optimization;

(4)Through the optimization of the parameters of the moving reed and the spring system, the reaction force value is increased by 28% and the crossover of the suction reaction curve is eliminated;

(5)Through the manufacture and testing of the relay prototype, it was verified that the optimization scheme can increase the electrical life to more than 50,000 times.

ACKNOWLEDGMENT

This work was supported by the National Natural Science Foundation of China [grant numbers 51707044]; and the China Postdoctoral Science Foundation [grant number 2018M632377].

REFERENCES

[1] Chen, Hongke, Chen, Yanbao. ect."Study on relaibility improvement of one type power relay", ICREPEC 2014,November 16,2014-November 18,2014.

[2] Zhao, Jingying, Lu, Jianguo. ect."Study on reliability test of protective relays in power system", ICREPEC 2009,October 18,2009-October 21,2009.

[3] X. bin, Y. W. ying, X. L. wei. ect,Optimized design of rated life of electromagnetic relay. Journal of Harbin Institude of Technology,2019.

[4] Z.F.fei, L.Z. gang.ect, Performance evaluation index of contact relay and its correlation with lifetime.5th International Conference on Reliability of Electrical Products and Electrical Contacts,2014.

[5] W.Z.ran, Y.Y.min.ect, Study on arc characteristics of AC contactor breaking process based on statistical method. .5th International Conference on Reliability of Electrical Products and Electrical Contacts,2014.

[6] Z.G.fu,Z.xue.ect, Summary of research on Dchigh power relay arc. Journal of electrotechnics, 2017.

[7] L.R.yao, Y.W.ying. ect, Numerical algorithm for temperature field of high voltage Dcrelay coil. Journal of electrotechnics,2018.

Study on Calculation of Armature Actuation Time for Railway Relay Based on Electromagnetic Force

Wenhua Li[1], Zhipeng Jiao[1], zhengyuan Zhao[2], Jing Xu[2], Dayong Tong[2]
[1]State Key Laboratory of Electrical Equipment Reliability and Intelligence，Hebei University of Technology, Tianjin 300130, China.
[2]Shenyang Railway Signal Co., Ltd., Shenyang, Liaoning 110025, China.

Abstract—**The stability and reliability of communication systems is determined by the electromagnetic relays. As one of important principles, the calculation of armature actuation time is meaningful to real-time monitoring. The electromagnetic relay selected as the research object, the contributions of this paper are that the electromagnetic system structure and principle of the railway signal relay were introduced, and the electromagnetic relay electrical parameter test was conducted. The current and voltage of electromagnetic relays were collected. The collected signal was filtered by wavelet analysis to obtain a smooth curve. The dynamic characteristics of the relay were analyzed. The calculation of electromagnetic force and the mechanical characteristic curve of the relay were combined. A calculation method of the armature actuation time based on the electromagnetic force was proposed. Then, according to the definition of the time parameter, the armature actuation time was calculated, and the absolute error satisfied the expected requirement.**

Index Terms—**Electromagnetic relay, Time parameters, Armature actuation time, Electromagnetic force**

I. INTRODUCTION

According to GB/T 7417-2010 "AX series relays" and other standards for electromagnetic relays, it can be seen that mechanical parameters are one of the important indicators to evaluate the performance of a particular type of electromagnetic relay. However, the direct measurement method is unrecoverable for the relay, so it is especially important to indirectly describe the mechanical parameter characteristics of the contact without damaging the relay. Therefore, the time parameters of the relay are more collected and calculated to reflect its mechanical reliability [1].

Regarding the calculation of relay time parameters, relevant theoretical analysis and experimental research were carried out by researchers from Harbin Institute of Technology, Xu Zhifu of Fuzhou University, Xu Zhihong of Fuzhou University, and Yang Shaojun of Harbin University of Science and Technology, and achieved certain results. For example, Yan Guofu research team developed a comprehensive test and analysis system for electromagnetic relay time parameters, Xu Zhihong research team developed the system of AC contactor dynamic characteristics simulation analysis system, Yang Shaojun research team proposed the contact reliability measurement of aerospace electromagnetic relay method. In addition, there are theoretical methods based on the single-chip CPLD micro-electromagnetic relay time parameter test method, which lays a theoretical basis and experimental basis for the calculation of electromagnetic relay time parameters [2-13]. The traditional touch time calculation method mainly uses the least squares method and Newton iteration method to calculate, which has the limitation of large calculation amount and low calculation speed. Therefore, this paper proposes a method of calculating the touch time based on the electromagnetic suction principle.

The research in this paper is mainly for electromagnetic relays. The structure of this paper is as follow: the introductory part is described as this section. In Section 2, the test conditions for the electrical parameters of electromagnetic relays is introduced. The contact voltage, coil current, coil voltage and other electrical parameters were collected by analog acquisition card P CI-1747 and PCI-1713, and then the curve was performed waveform smoothing.The Section 3 is evolved with introduction of the electromagnetic system structure and working principle of electromagnetic relay. According to the analysis of the dynamic characteristics of the relay, a calculation method of the touch time based on the electromagnetic suction principle was proposed. Based on the definition of the time parameters, the calculation about the armature actuation timewas conducted in Section 4. The conclusion was summarized in the Section 5.

II. TESTFORTHEELECTROMAGNETICRELAY

A. *Experimental*

Randomly select three relays as samples in the batch of qualified products and them were numbered 1, 2 and 3. And the parameters of the experimental conditions and electromagnetic relay are shown in Table 1.

B. *Signal acquisition and processing*

According to the wavelet decomposition theory [15],

after wavelet decomposition, the components of the noisy signal are usually concentrated in the larger wavelet coefficients. However, the noise components are mainly distributed in the whole wavelet domain. The significance of the threshold function is denoising, which can achieve the maximum removal of the wavelet coefficients of the noise signal and the original effective signal as much as possible while ensuring the wavelet coefficients of the effective signal.

Table 1. The parameters of the experimental conditions and samples.

Parameter	Value
Contact material	Silver cadmium oxide
Experimental environment	Temperature：+20~+65℃；Humidity：≤90%
Working voltage	220V(AC)
Working current	5A(AC)
Operating frequency	1200 times per hour
Load properties	Resistive load

The wavelet decomposition and reconstruction process is as follows:

(1) The discrete signal $f(n)$ is obtained by discretizing the original noise-containing signal by discrete sampling. The wavelet transform coefficient $\omega_f(j,k)$ is as follow:

$$\omega_f(j,k)=2^{-\frac{j}{2}}\sum_{n=0}^{N-1} f(n)\varphi(2^{-j}n-k) \tag{1}$$

(2) The key part of wavelet decomposition is to choose the appropriate db5 wavelet basis function. Using the wavelet basis function, the noisy signal can be decomposed, and j approximate components and j detail components at the j scale can be obtained. The orthogonal wavelet decomposition formula used to calculate the noisy signal $f(n)$ is as Formula (2):

$$\begin{cases} c_k^{j-1}=\sum_n c_n^j h_{n-2k}^* \\ d_k^{j-1}=\sum_n c_n^j g_{n-2k}^* \end{cases} \tag{2}$$

where, c^{j-1} is approximating the wavelet coefficients; n is the number of discrete samples; d^{j-1} is the detail wavelet coefficient; h^* and g^* is a set of orthogonal image filter banks.

(3) After wavelet multi-scale decomposition, the noisy signal retains all low-frequency wavelet coefficients. For the high frequency coefficient, the threshold is first set, and then the amplitude of the high frequency wavelet coefficients at each scale below the threshold is set to zero. Finally, different threshold functions are used to shrink all of the remaining coefficients above the threshold to obtain estimated wavelet coefficients for each scale.

(4) Wavelet reconstruction is actually the inverse process of wavelet decomposition. Therefore, the estimated wavelet coefficients and inverse wavelet transform are used to obtain the estimated value of the reconstructed signal. The reconstructed wavelet coefficients are as follows:

$$c_k^j=\sum_n c_n^{j-1}h_{k-2n}^*+\sum_n d_n^{j-1}g_{k-2n}^* \tag{3}$$

In the actual calculation, $f(n)\approx f_j$ corresponding to the value point is assumed. For a certain positive number $m(0\le m\le j)$, the signal is decomposed from the j level to the horizontal $j-m$, that is, $\{c_k^j\}$ is known from $\{c_k^{j-1}\}$ and $\{d_k^{j-1}\}$, $j=n-1,\cdots,n-m$.

After wavelet decomposition, the coefficients of some layers are reconstructed using a reconstruction filter to achieve the purpose of noise reduction.

With j fixed, $\{c_k^{j-1}\}$ and $\{d_k^{j-1}\}$ can quickly reconstruct the data $\{c_k^j\}$ to achieve the expected reconfiguration of $f(n)$, the reconstruction process is shown in Figure 1.

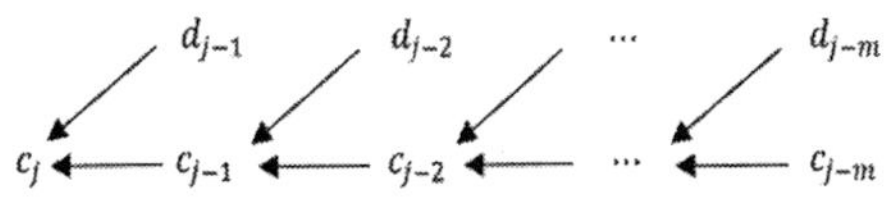

Fig. 1 The process of reconstruction.

The test system relies on the digital output of the PCL-720 control card to control the on/off of the solid state relay, thereby enabling the on/off operation of the relay coil. The PCI-1747 and PCI-1713 analog acquisition cards are used to collect the contact voltage. Signals such as coil current and coil voltage.

The original signal is wavelet decomposed and reconstructed, and then the decomposed detail signal is soft threshold denoised. The reconstructed filtered signal is shown in Figure 2.

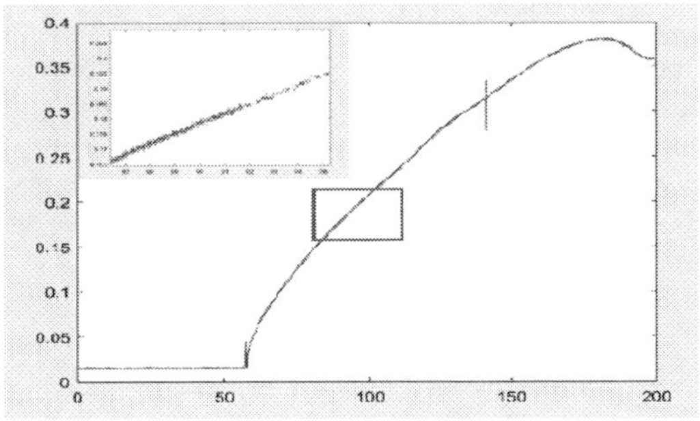

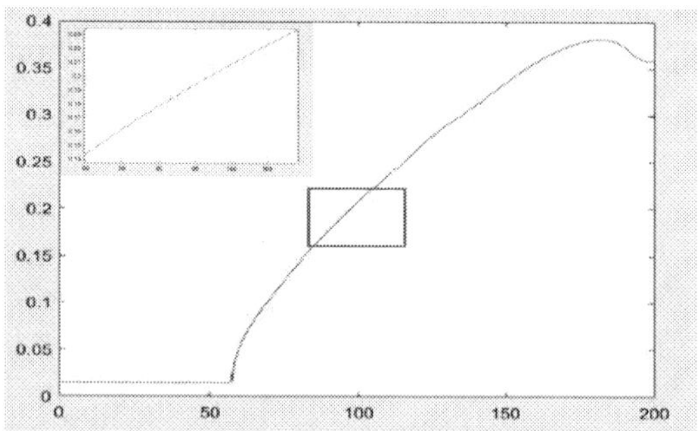

Fig. 2 Comparison of current waveform processing: before (up) and after (below).

III. CALCULATIONMETHODFORTHEAR MATUREACTUATIONTIME

A. Structure and working principle of the electromagnetic system

As a research object, the structure of a DC electrodeless relay is shown in Figure 3. A stepless relay consists of two parts: an electromagnetic system and a contact system. Among them, the electromagnetic system includes a coil, a core, a ferritic iron, and an armature.

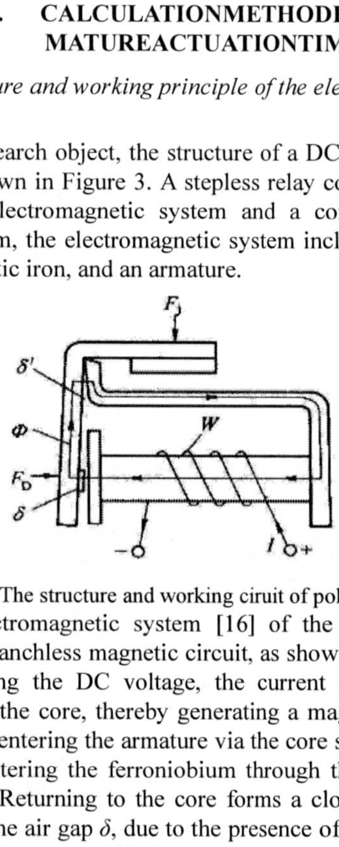

Fig. 3 The structure and working ciruit of poleless relay.

The electromagnetic system [16] of the electrodeless relay is a branchless magnetic circuit, as shown in Figure 3. After passing the DC voltage, the current I in the coil magnetizes the core, thereby generating a magnetic flux Φ in the core, entering the armature via the core shoe-air gap δ, and then entering the ferroniobium through the air gap δ', and finally Returning to the core forms a closed magnetic circuit. At the air gap δ, due to the presence of the magnetic flux Φ, the iron core generates an electromagnetic attraction forceF_D acting on the armature. When the electromagnetic suction force F_D is greater than the mechanical force of the armature action, the armature starts to move, and at the same time, the armature is moved by the tie rod. The contact movement is gradually separated from the dynamic breaking contact until the moving contact and the moving and closing static contact are completely attracted.

B. Mechanical characteristics

The mechanical force of the relay is affected by many

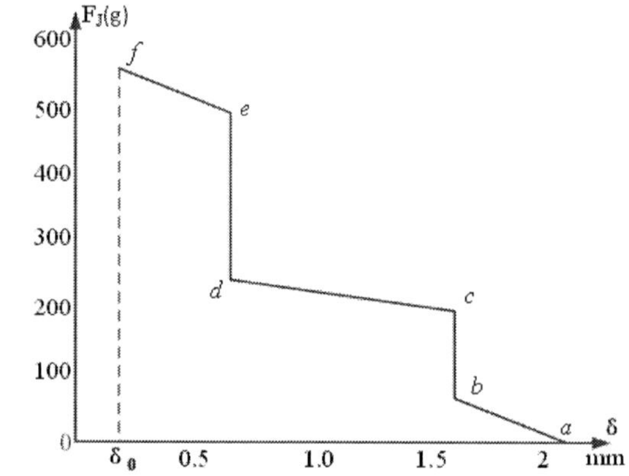

Fig. 4 Mechanical characteristic curve of poleless relay.

factors: the number of contact pieces, the number of heavy hammers, and the stroke of the armature. During the entire movement of the armature, the mechanical force is not constant, but varies within a certain range. The relationship between the mechanical force Fj and the change of the armature with the working air gap δ between the cores is called the mechanical characteristic, and its curve is shown in Figure 4 [17].

where F_j is the mechanical force during the armature moves, andδindicates the working air gap between the armature and the core.

C. Definition of the armature actuation time

According to GJB65B-1999 general specifications for relay reliability indicators, high-speed data acquisition cards are used to high-speed sampling of the electrical parameters (coil current, coil voltage and contact voltage) of a set of conversion contacts of the sample. The coil current during the electromagnetic relay pull-in process is shown in Figure 5, and the time parameter definition is given accordingly [18].

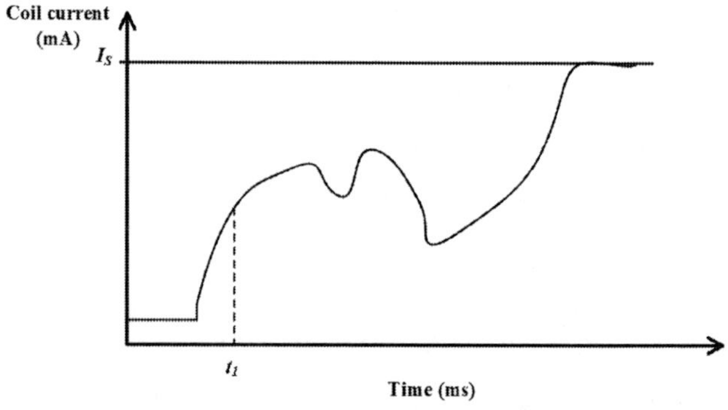

Fig. 5 Schematic of the armature actuation time.

where the time t_1 is when the current exceeds a certain threshold, and the armature just starts to act under the action of electromagnetic attraction.

The touch phase as follows: after the coil is energized, the coil current does not change abruptly, but gradually increases in accordance with an exponential law, and a magnetic flux Φ is generated in the electromagnetic circuit. While the coil current increases, the electromagnetic attraction of the electromagnetic system to the armature is also gradually increasing, but at this stage, the electromagnetic suction force is smaller than the reaction force provided by the comparison mechanism, and the armature and the contacts do not operate. The comparison mechanism is the reaction system of the electromagnetic relay. The typical electromagnetic relay reaction system mainly includes: the reaction force spring and the reed. The reaction system of the signal relay selected in this paper mainly includes: the reed and the heavy hammer on the armature.

According to the actuation phase, the actuation time is defined as the time (0-t_1) from the energization of the excitation loop coil to the action of the armature of the relay.

D. *Electromagnetic characteristics*

The electromagnetic attraction acting on the magnetized ferromagnetic object is proportional to the total area of the magnetic flux passing through the magnetic pole and the square of the magnetic induction in the air gap. It is considered that the magnetic induction intensity $\boldsymbol{B}$ in the air gap δ of the electromagnetic relay is evenly distributed along the surface of the magnetic pole. According to Maxwell's formula, the basic formula of electromagnetic attraction is as follows:

$$F = \frac{B^2 \cdot S}{2\mu_0} \tag{4}$$

where $\boldsymbol{F}$ is the electromagnetic force (*J/cm*); $\boldsymbol{B}$ is the magnetic induction (*Wb/cm*^{2}); S is the total surface area of the magnetic pole (*cm*^{2}); and the air permeability is 1.25×10^{-8}*H/cm.*

In order to obtain a practical formula, the unit of $\boldsymbol{B}$ is that the magnetic induction intensity is converted into Gauss by the unit, and the unit of $\boldsymbol{F}$ is the electromagnetic force converted into kilograms by unit, and the following formula can be obtained:

$$F = \left(\frac{\Phi}{5000}\right)^2 \cdot \frac{1}{S} \tag{5}$$

In order to calculate the relationship between magnetic flux, magnetomotive force and magnetoresistance, a magnetic circuit equivalent model is established, as shown in Figure 6 According to the structure of the electromagnet model, the following assumptions are made:

(1) the magnetic flux leakage effec is not considered;

(2) The electromagnet mounting shaft is a non-magnetic material, and the model is established according to the air permeability.

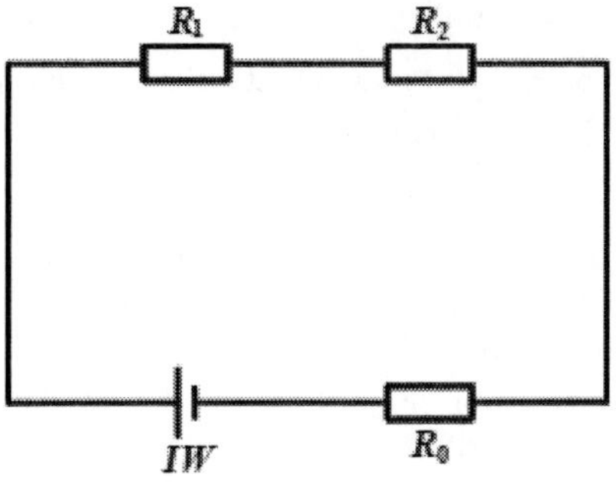

Fig. 6 The equivalent model of magnetic circuit.

where, *IW* is the magnetomotive force generated by the coil; R0 is the air gap reluctance; R_1 is the core magnetoresistance; R_2 is the armature magnetoresistance. According to the model, the following Formula (6) is obtained.

$$\Phi_0 = IW\left(G_0 + \frac{1}{R_1} + \frac{1}{R_2}\right)\times10^8 \tag{6}$$

The air gap permeability is calculated as follow:

$$G_0 = \mu_0 \frac{S_1 \cdot S_2}{\delta\left(S_1 + S_2\right)} \tag{7}$$

where, $S_1 = \pi R_1^2$ (*cm*^{2}) is the inner cylindrical core area. $S_2 = \pi\left(R_2^2 - R_1^2\right)$ (*cm*^{2}) is the end ring area andδ (*cm*^{2}) is the air gap length.

According to Kirchhoff's second law, considering that the air gap reluctance is much larger than the core magnetoresistance and the armature magnetoresistance in actual work, which can be roughly assumed that most of the magnetomotive force is consumed in the air gap, hence, the Formula (8) is as follow:

$$\Phi_0 = IWG_0\times10^8 \tag{8}$$

However, in the actual magnetic circuit, the core and the armature still consume a small portion of the magnetomotive force, and there are also some leakage fluxes. Therefore, the magnetic flux in the actual magnetic circuit is usually smaller than the estimated value. According to the literature [19], the actual value is selected to decrease by 5%.

$$\Phi_0{}' = IWG_0\times10^8\times\left(1-5\%\right) \tag{9}$$

Combining equations (5) and (6) (7), the formula for calculating the suction force of the electromagnet can be obtained as Formula (10):

$$F = 1.77\cdot\frac{\left(IW\right)^2\cdot R_1^2\cdot\left(R_2^2 - R_1^2\right)}{\delta^2 R_2^2}\times10^{-7} \tag{10}$$

IV CALCULATIONRESULTOFTHEARMATUREACTUATIONTIME

According to the specifications of the selected electromagnetic relay, R_2 is12*mm*, and R_1 is9*mm*, and δ is 3*mm*. It can be seen from the mechanical characteristic curve that the mechanical force *Fj* is 550 g before the armature starts moving.

Under the action of the magnetic flux Φ, when the electromagnetic attraction generated between the iron core and the armature just overcomes the mechanical force Fj, the armature is about to start to move. According to the Formulas (4)-(11), the coil current value at the critical point at this time can be obtained as 4.978 mA. In the coil current change graph, the time corresponding to the calculated current value is found, when the armature starts to operate. By definition, the touch time can be calculated. In order to verify the accuracy of the calculation results of this method, the time parameters of the same relay are collected and compared with the oscilloscope. The calculation results and relative errors are shown in Table 2. The calculation results in Table 2 show that the calculation result of the relay touch time selected in this paper is 0.56±0.03 (5.7%) ms.

It can be seen from Table 2 that the relative error between the calculation results of the proposed method and the oscilloscope acquisition value does not exceed 4%, which satisfies the expected requirements, which can prove the rationality of the proposed electromagnetic relay actuation time calculation method based on the electromagnetic suction principle. feasibility.

Table 2. The calculation of the armature actuation time and absolute error.

Relay number	Number of groups	Armature actuation time (ms)		
		Calculation value	Actual value	Absolute error
1	1	0.56	0.52	0.04
	2	0.56	0.52	0.04
	3	0.60	0.57	0.03
2	1	0.59	0.55	0.04
	2	0.54	0.52	0.02
	3	0.57	0.55	0.02
3	1	0.52	0.56	-0.04
	2	0.56	0.58	-0.02
	3	0.50	0.52	-0.02

V CONCLUSION

In this paper, the contact voltage, coil current and coil voltage data collected by the electromagnetic relay electrical parameter test are filtered, and an ideal smooth curve is obtained, which facilitates the calculation of the touch time. After analyzing the principle of electromagnetic force and the mechanical characteristic curve of the relay, this paper proposes a method of calculating the touch time based on the principle of electromagnetic suction. The electromagnetic relay is selected as the research object, and the calculated result is compared with the oscilloscope acquisition result. The error is not more than 4 %, meet the expected requirements, verify the rationality and feasibility of the proposed method.

As one of the main parameters of relay reliability, it is necessary to analyze the relationship between time parameters and reliability. The relay life test is carried out, and the attenuation trend of the relay time parameter in the life cycle is extracted, and the fitting function is selected from the fitting function selection library according to the square of the fitting residual using the classical regression function fitting. The significance of the fitting function in practical engineering application is that the relationship between the cycle life and the time parameter can be obtained.

ACKNOWLEDGMENT

This work is funded by the Natural Science Foundation of Hebei Province (E2016202206).

REFERENCES

[1] Lu Jianguo, Wang Jingqin, Lu Bin. Electrical equipment reliability work overview and development prospects [J]. Low-voltage electrical appliances, 2014 (2): 1-7.

[2] Tong Weiming, Zhai Guofu. Low-voltage electrical relay and its control system [M]. Harbin: Harbin Institute of Technology Press. 2003: 83.

[3] Yixu Song, Jing Hu. A method for data stream processing based on curve fitting[C]. 2010 2nd International Conference on Signal Processing Systems. Jul, 2010: 542-546.

[4] Xu Guangrui. Research on Reliability Test System of DC Electromagnetic Relay [D]. Harbin: Harbin Institute of Technology, 2013.

[5] Zhang Qingsen, Chen Xingwen, Yan Guofu. Test and Analysis Method of Electromagnetic Relay Touch Time, Overtravel Time and Free Motion Time[J]. Electromechanical Components. 2003, 23(3): 3-7.

[6] Li Hongyi. Detection of time constant of electromagnetic relay coil [D]. Tianjin: Hebei University of Technology. 2012.

[7] Zhai Guofu, Research on Integrated Test and Analysis System for Time Parameters of Electromagnetic Relay [J], Low Voltage Electrical Appliances, 2003 (02): 48-52.

[8] Zhou Wei, the influence of electrical and mechanical parameters on DC arc of relay [J], China Journal of

Electrical Engineering, 2006, 26 (19): 151-155.

[9] Lu Jianguo, Reliability Theory of Low Voltage Protective Appliances and Its Application [M], Beijing, Machinery Industry Press, 2004.

[10] Xuerong Ye, Yue Ma, Hang Meng. Degradation failure model of electromagnetic relay [C]. The 26th international conference on electrical contacts. 2012: 116-123.

[11] Yang Zhang, Regan Zane, Aleksandar Prodic. Online calibration of MOSFET on-state resistance for precise current sensing[J]. Power Electronics Letters, IEEE. 2004, 2(3): 100-103.

[12] Gabriel Eirea, Seth R.Sanders. High Precision Load Current Sensing using On-Line Calibration of Trace Resistance in VRM Applications[C]. The 37th IEEE Power Electronics Specialists Conference. 2006: 1-6.

[13] Bo Zhiqian, Zhang Baohui, Dong Xinzhou, etc. Development of Intelligent Protection and Intelligent Relay Network [J]. Power System Protection and Control, 2013, 41 (2): 1-5.

[14] Lu Jianguo, Zhang Naikuan, Li Kui. Testing and Testing of Low Voltage Electrical Appliances [M]. Beijing: China Electric Power Publishing House, 2007.30-50.

[15] Lu Jun, Li Xia, Wang Chongma, Yu Qingyang, Gao Lin, Wu Litian. Signal Processing and Fault Detection of MSMA Vibration Sensor Based on Wavelet Analysis [J]. Journal of Electrical Technology, 2015, 30 (10): 354-360.

[16] Zhang Yadong, Zhang Weijie, Yang Shengkuan. Mechanical properties and fabrication methods of electromagnetic driving coils [J]. High Voltage Technology, 2014, 40 (04): 1186-1193.

[17] Zhou Xue, Shi Jinfeng, Zhai Guofu. Measurement and analysis of static suction and reaction characteristics of electromagnetic relays [J]. Electromechanical components, 2005, 25 (4): 6-10.

[18] Rong Mingzhe. Simulation analysis and experimental study on the action characteristics of the moving contacts of permanent magnet contactors[J]. Journal of Electrical Engineering of China, 2005, 25(1):109-113.

[19] Li Xin, Measurement and Research of Contact Related Parameters of Electromagnetic Relay [D]: [Master's Degree Thesis], Hebei University of Technology, 2013.

[20] General Specification for GJB65B Electromagnetic Relays with Reliability Index [S]. 1999.

The Effect of Different WC Particle Size on Arc Erosion of AgWC12C3 Static Contact Material

Xun Luo
Shanghai Liangxin Electrical Appliances Co., Ltd., Shanghai, 200000, China
E-mail: luoxun@sh-liangxin.com Tel: 18116397230

Abstract—**In this paper, AgWC12C3 contact materials with different particle size WC powders were prepared by uniform mixing and compression molding by the same process method Among them, 2 WC particles are 3 times the size of 1 # WC particles) and matched with the movable contact AgW50. It is applied to the molded case circuit breaker product (1600A) for electric life verification, and then the physical properties of the contact material are compared respectively. Microscopic analysis and theoretical calculations, contact arc erosion mechanism, arc moving influence factor and other related methods were used to analyze the effects of different WC particle sizes on AgWC12C3 static contact arc erosion. Finally, it is concluded that under the premise of the same quality, the finer the tungsten carbide particles, the larger the surface area occupied by the WC particles on the contact working surface, and the more effective the solution viscosity during the arc burning process, so it is more effective. Prevent the splashing and loss of silver and increase the number of times of electricity.**

Index Terms— **Particle size, Arc erosion, Electric life**

I. INTRODUCTION

The electrical contact is a contact component in the switchgear, instrumentation, etc., and is responsible for the task of connecting, carrying and breaking current. Its performance directly affects the reliable operation and service life of the switchgear. Commonly used contact materials are AgC, AgMeO, AgW, etc. The quality of electrical contact materials directly affects the performance of the product. Its AgWC12C3 electrical contact material has excellent characteristics such as good electrical and thermal conductivity, anti-welding and arc erosion resistance. It is often used as a static contact in conjunction with the AgW50 moving contact in MCCB circuit breakers, thus improving the AgWC12C3 contact material. Performance is a major concern of current processes.

Among AgWC12C3 contact materials, pure silver is mainly responsible for carrying current because of its good conductivity, while WC is often used as a second phase particle to compensate for the soft hardness, low melting point and non-wear resistance of pure silver due to its high melting point, high hardness and oxidation resistance. Shortcomings such as splashing can improve the physical and electrical properties of contact materials, such as mechanical strength, resistance to arc burning, resistance to fusion welding, resistance to material transfer, etc.

So how do you maximize the role of WC in the contact material? WC is usually evenly distributed in the contact material in the form of particles. In order to verify the influence of WC powder particle size on the material properties of the contact material, the two different particle size WC powders are used to make AgWC12C3 contact materials, through physical and chemical tests and product life. The test analyzes the effect of different WC particle sizes on the physical and electrical properties of the contact material.

II. PRODUCT PROCESS

Two kinds of coarse and fine WC powders with different milling time are prepared in this process. They are mixed according to the mass ratio m (Ag): m (WC): m (C) = 85:12:3. The deviation of each element content can not exceed 1%. It is made by powder metallurgy process. (1 AgWC12C3 contacts are made of fine WC particles and 2 AgWC12C3 contacts are made of coarse WC particles). The technological process of making contacts is shown in the following figure:

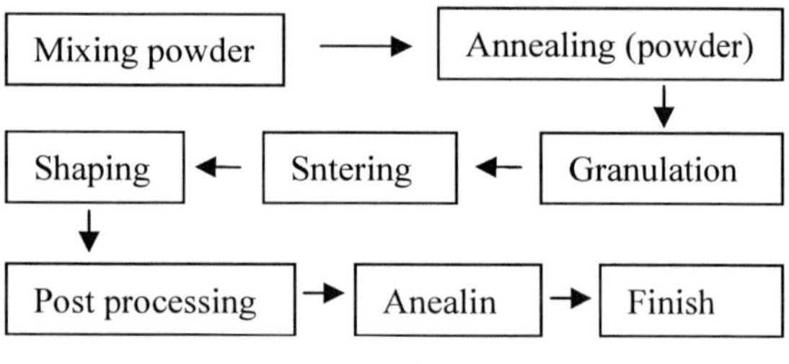

III. CONTACT MATERIAL TESTING

The effects of different WC particle sizes on the physical properties of AgWC12C3 contact materials were analyzed by comparing the hardness, density, electrical conductivity and metallographic analysis of the two contact materials.

In order to obtain accurate test data, in addition to the

difference in WC particle size between the two contact materials to be tested, the remaining element content and process parameters are guaranteed to be consistent. Considering the test error, 5 samples were taken for each test, and 3 samples were taken for each sample and averaged.

A. Hardness Test

The Vickers hardness test method is used for the hardness test of contact materials. In order to avoid the difference of surface hardness due to cold work hardening, the samples were longitudinally split and hot-inlaid at 130 C. After polishing, the hardness of the core of the samples was tested by applying a force of 1kg.

Table 1 is the hardness test results of AgWC12C3 contact material with 1 # fine WC particles and AgWC12C3 contact material with 2 # coarse WC particles. From the test results, it can be seen that the hardness value of 1 # contact is nearly 10% higher than that of 2 #. Therefore, it can be inferred that fine WC particles can improve the hardness value of contact material and increase the wear resistance of contact.

Table 1

Hardness Comparison of Fine WC Particle Contact and Coarse WC Particle Contact

	Hardness test results（HV1）	
Sample	1#	2#
1	58.7	53.6
2	57.5	52.7
3	58.1	54.1
4	57.9	53.9
5	56.9	53.8
Average value	57.8	53.6

B. Density Test

In order to avoid the error caused by AgWC12C3 welding silver layer, it is necessary to remove the silver layer of contact material before conducting density test. The density test was carried out by Archimedes drainage method. The liquid medium impregnated with the sample was distilled water. The results are as follows:

$$\rho_S = \frac{M_{SA} \times \rho_{IL}}{M_{SA} - M_{IL}}$$

In the formula:

ρ_S —Density of Samples at 27 C, g/cm^3

M_{SA} —The quality of the sample in air，g

ρ_{IL} —The Density of Distilled Water at 27C，0. 996 51 g/cm^3

M_{IL} —Quality of Samples in Distilled Water，g

Table 2 shows the density data of fine WC particle contacts and coarse WC particle A contacts. The experimental results show that the density of WC particle contacts has little effect.

Table 2

Comparisons of contact densities between fine WC particles and coarse WC particles

	Density test results（g/cm3）	
Sample	1#	2#
1	9.698	9.799
2	9.755	9.689
3	9.765	9.900
4	9.899	9.742
5	9.699	9.649
Averge value	9.763	9.755

C. Conductivity Test

The electrical conductivity of contact materials is measured by eddy current method and alternating current method. The bridge balance principle is measured. To avoid oxide formation on sample surface Error of test data, so wipe sample table with alcohol before test measure after the face.

Table 3 is the experimental data of conductivity of fine WC particle AgWC12C3 contact material and coarse WC particle AgWC12C3 contact material. The experimental results show that the conductivity of coarse WC particle is 20% higher than that of fine WC particle. Therefore, it can be inferred that the contact material of fine WC particle should be AgWC12C3 contact material of coarse WC particle. As a static contact point, it is more conducive to reducing the contact resistance of the product, and the temperature rise of the product after its lifetime plays a certain role in helping.

Table 3

Comparison of electrical conductivity between fine WC particle contact and coarse WC particle contact

	Test results of conductivity（Ms/m）	
Sample	1#	2#
1	33.0	39.2
2	33.2	39.1
3	32.6	38.9
4	33.4	39.4
5	32.9	38.6
Average value	33.02	39.04

D. Metallographic Analysis

The microstructures of AgWC12C3 contacts with coarse WC particles and AgWC12C3 contacts with fine WC particles were compared by metallographic examination.

Detection and analysis: The working faces of two contact materials were polished with diamond suspension and then placed under Olympus optical metallographic microscope with large X 1000 times for microscopic observation. As can be seen from Fig. 1 and Fig. 2, tungsten carbide can be dispersed well in silver-based materials by using the same mixing process, no matter the contact materials of coarse WC particles or fine WC particles, which can help to verify the electric life of products. In addition, under the same field of view, it can be clearly seen that the proportion of coarse WC particles to silver-based contact materials is less than that of fine WC particles to silver-based contact materials. According to the calculation formula of surface area, inference is made.

The area ratio of coarse WC particles to silver-based contact materials is smaller than that of fine WC particles under the same working area. This inference can be verified by small tests. The number of WC particles in the working area of 1.57 cm long and 1.23 cm wide is calculated in Fig. 1 and Fig. 2 respectively. Through calculation, the number of fine WC particles in the same area is obviously more than that of coarse WC particles.

In addition, the contact material surface was corroded by hydrogen peroxide, and then the microstructure of AgWC12C3 surface was observed by magnifying X1000 times. It is obvious from metallographic figures 3 and 4 that the silver grain size of fine WC particle contact is very small (average grain size is 3-5 micron), while that of coarse WC particle contact is relatively large (average grain size is 6-10 micron). The main reason for the difference of silver grain size is that AgWC12C3 contact material is sintered at high temperature. As the area ratio of fine WC particles is larger than that of coarse WC particles, it is equivalent to dividing silver into several parts. When silver is recrystallized at high temperature, WC particles can effectively hinder the migration of silver grain boundaries, prevent grain growth, and make AgWC12C3 of fine WC particles obtain fine and uniform grain size.

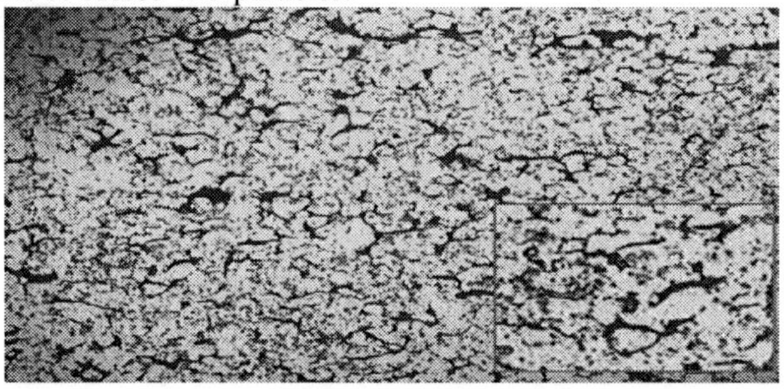

Fig. 1 Metallographic structure of fine WC particle AgWC12C3 contact material

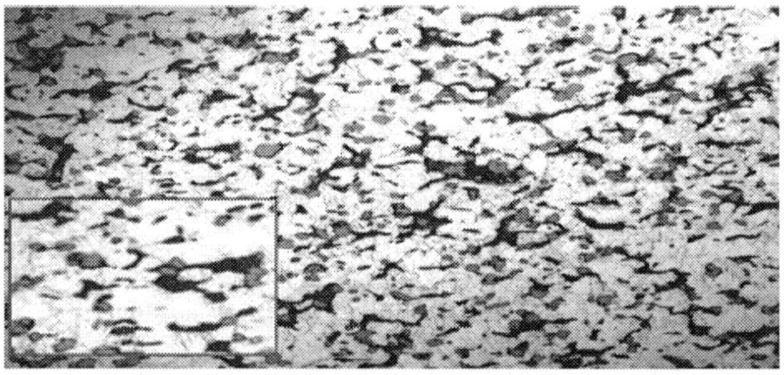

Fig. 2 Metallographic structure of coarse WC particle AgWC12C3 contact material

Area	Number of the sross WC particles	Number of the tiny WC particles
Length:1.57cm Width:1.57cm	≈ 27	> 27 obviously

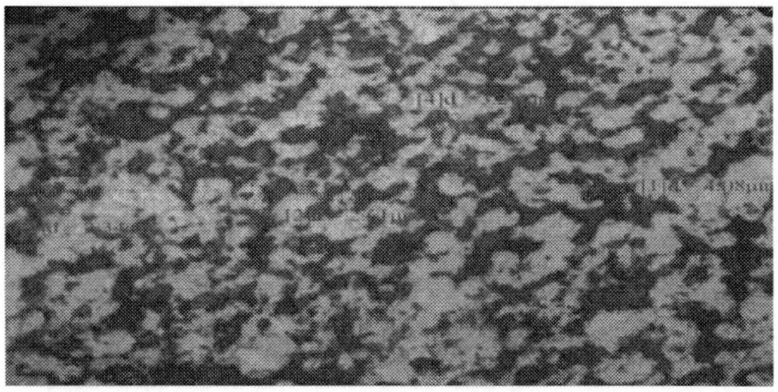

Fig. 3 Metallographic structure of fine WC particles AgWC12C3 after corrosion

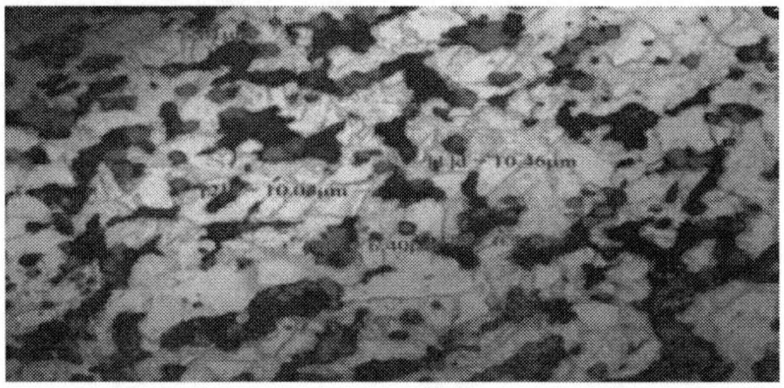

Fig. 4 Metallographic structure of AgWC12C3 coarse WC particles after corrosion

Sample	Silver crystal size comparison (μm)	
	1# the tiny particles (0.7~1 μm)	1# the sross particles (0.7~1 μm)
1	3.21	6.61
	4.08	10.46
	2.61	6.50
	2.34	10.03

IV. TYPE TEST

Through the analysis of physical and chemical experiments, the physical properties of AgWC12 contact material with coarse WC particles are quite different from that of AgWC12C3 contact material with fine WC particles. If the two contact materials are used in products, is there a great difference in the resistance to arc burning? In order to verify the effect of WC particle size on electrical performance, AgWC12C3 contact material was used as static contact and AgW50 as dynamic contact in MCCB plastic case circuit breaker. The electrical life test, contact resistance test and post-life temperature rise test were carried out. The effect of WC particle on electrical performance of contact material was analyzed through the test results.

A. Electric Life Test of Products

Two groups of dynamic and static contacts are prepared to be used in two plastic case circuit breakers for life verification. The test conditions are 415V voltage and 1600A current for life test. Among them, the static contact point of 1# product is fine WC particle AgWC12C3 contact material matched with the dynamic contact point AgW50, and the static contact point of 2# product is coarse WC particle AgWC12C3 contact material matched with the dynamic contact point AgW50. in order to prevent AgWC12C3 from ablating completely after electrical life test, the surface morphology and material loss of AgWC12C3 contact material were observed after 700 electrical life tests.

B. Analysis of Contact Surface Morphology after Electric Life Test

The AgWC12C3 static contacts after electric life test were cleaned by ultrasonic, and the surface morphology of contact materials after arc ablation was observed. From Fig. 5, it can be clearly seen that the surface of fine WC particle static contact material is fairly flat in the contact surface of dynamic and static contacts. The surface of fine WC particle static contact material is observed by enlarging the SEM by X40. In Fig. 7, there are many micro-holes formed on the static contact surface after electric life. The formation of micropore [1] is due to the formation of skeleton of refractory WC under the action of high temperature arc, in which porous silver evaporates or oxides decompose to escape as gas. Compared with the static contact of fine WC particles, the surface of coarse WC particles contact material in Fig. 6 is very rough due to severe ablation, and there are more solidification state left by splashing after melting at high arc temperature near the contact surface. By observing the contact surface of Fig. 8 under the magnification of 40X by SEM, it can be clearly seen that there are many pits and cracks on the contact surface caused by material spalling during the life test.

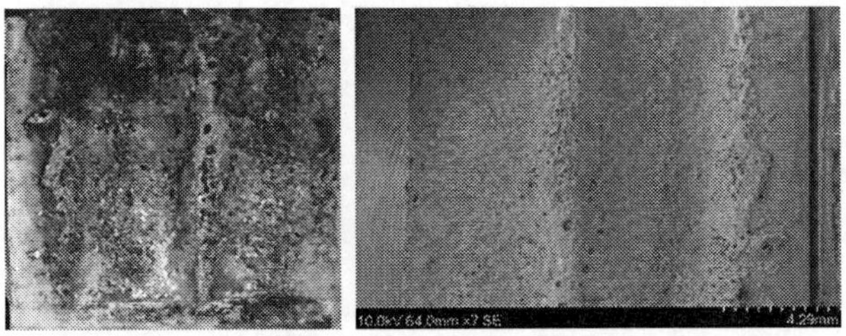

Fig. 5 Macroscopic Surface Morphology of Fine WC Particles AgWC12C3 after Electric Life

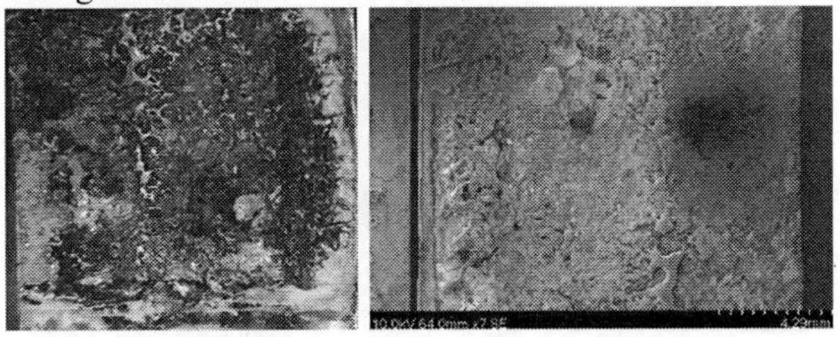

Fig. 6 Macroscopic Surface Morphology of AgWC12C3 Coarse WC Particles after Electric Life

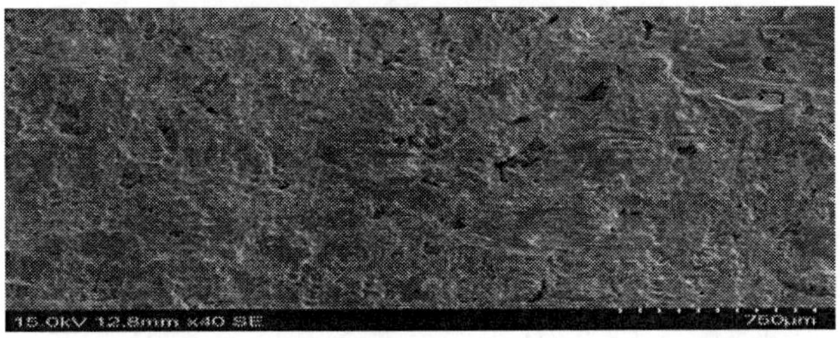

Fig. 7 Surface Microstructure of Fine WC Particles AgWC12C3 after Electric Life

Fig. 8 Surface Microstructure of AgWC12C3 Coarse WC Particles after Electric Life

In addition, from the analysis of material loss in the process of electric life, it can be seen in Figure 9-10 that both fine WC particle static contact and coarse WC particle static contact will produce a certain amount of material migration, splash and loss after 700 electric life, but the material migration and loss of coarse WC particle static contact is more serious than that of fine WC particle contact in the process of electric life test. Fig. 9 (a, b) is the contact area between the static and dynamic contact points of fine WC particles and the sputtering area of materials microstructure and EDS scanning component analysis showed that there was no significant difference in Ag and W contents between the contact area and the sputtering area. The results show that the static contact of fine WC particles is uniform even though material migration and splashing occur in the process of electrical life, indicating that fine WC particles can effectively increase the viscosity of liquid contact materials and prevent material splashing loss. Compared with the static contact of fine WC particles, the static contact of coarse WC particles appears a large number of layers of tungsten carbide and pure silver in the whole working face after the electrical life test. Tungsten carbide gathers under pure silver. Through EDS scanning, there are a large number of solid silver blocks left by pure silver sputtering in the sputtering area as shown in figs. 10 (a, b).

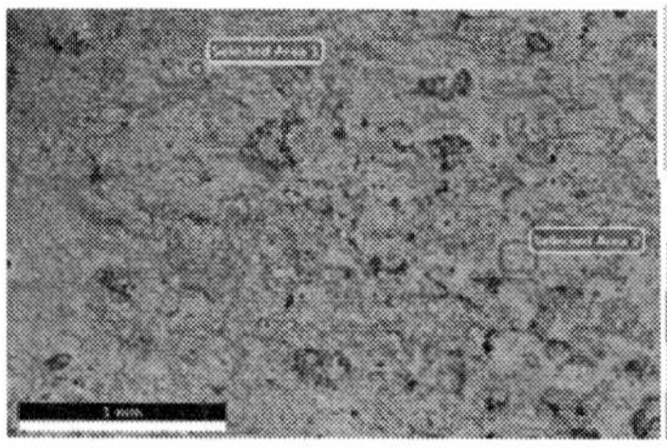
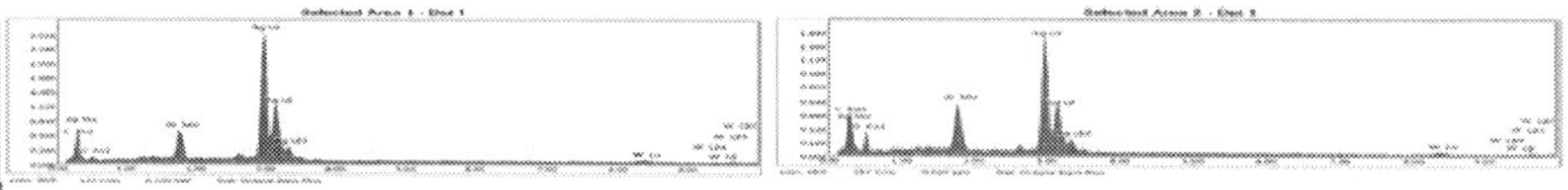

Element	Weight %	Atomic %	Net Int.	Error %
C K	5.51	31.28	154.56	7.42
O K	3.22	13.73	38.31	16.56
W M	10.47	3.88	257.86	7.36
AgL	80.80	51.10	1740.19	2.52

Element	Weight %	Atomic %	Net Int.	Error %
C K	8.89	35.63	464.03	7.91
O K	10.43	31.38	295.55	12.62
W M	16.26	4.25	849.84	6.26
AgL	64.42	28.73	2821.89	3.15

Fig 9-a Fine WC Particles AgWC12C3 Contact Area Scanning Results

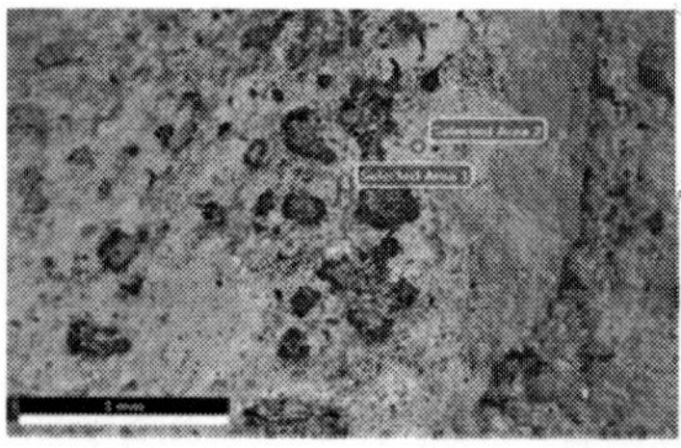
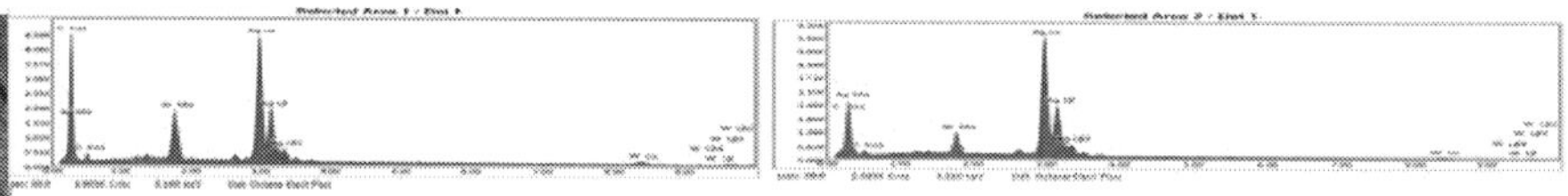

Element	Weight %	Atomic %	Net Int.	Error %
C K	24.05	70.75	1569.39	5.79
O K	3.28	7.25	97.67	15.54
W M	13.37	2.57	821.97	4.45
AgL	59.30	19.43	3018.42	2.16

Element	Weight %	Atomic %	Net Int.	Error %
C K	10.77	46.45	712.49	5.94
O K	4.48	14.52	121.73	13.48
W M	8.45	2.38	482.57	5.17
AgL	76.30	36.65	3801.34	2.02

Fig 9-b Scanning Results of Sputtering Zone of Fine WC Particles AgWC12C3

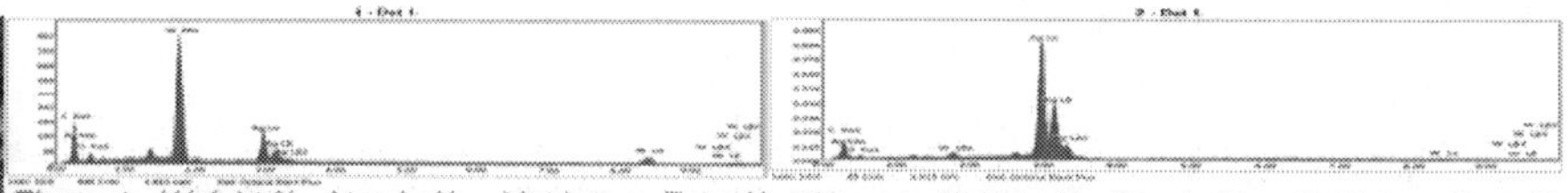

Element	Weight %	Atomic %	Net Int.	Error %
C K	19.23	67.51	272.57	10.42
O K	4.31	11.36	68.98	16.67
W M	54.20	12.43	1312.15	3.58
AgL	22.26	8.70	379.16	7.92

Element	Weight %	Atomic %	Net Int.	Error %
C K	3.53	22.18	105.65	8.91
O K	2.72	12.84	28.08	22.51
W M	2.15	0.88	48.68	32.30
AgL	91.60	64.09	1882.84	2.50

Fig 10-a Coarse WC Particles AgWC12C3 Contact Area Scanning Results

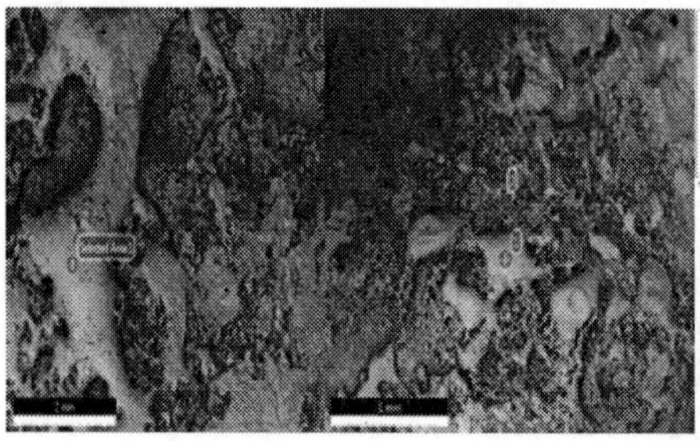
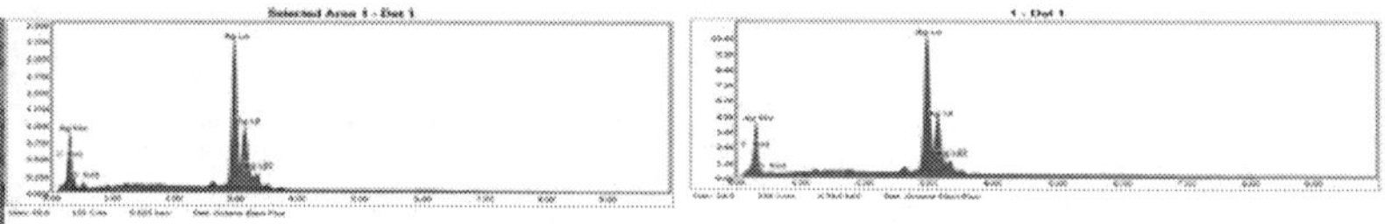

Element	Weight %	Atomic %	Net Int.	Error %
C K	5.80	29.87	447.19	6.28
O K	4.90	18.94	127.21	16.76
AgL	89.30	51.19	4588.52	2.40

Element	Weight %	Atomic %	Net Int.	Error %
C K	5.22	30.04	1354.66	5.04
O K	2.52	10.88	215.52	15.06
AgL	92.25	59.07	15388.49	1.83

Fig 10-b Scanning Results of Sputtering Zone of Coarse WC Particles AgWC12C3

C. Contact Resistance and Temperature Rise of Products after Electric Life Test

In order to verify the influence of WC particles on the contact resistance of the product, the contact resistance of the two products and the temperature rise after the life are verified. From the test results in the following table, it can be inferred that the coarse WC particles can improve the conductivity of the contact material. Reducing the contact resistance of the circuit breaker improves the temperature rise of the product (see Table 4, Table 5).

Table 4

Comparison of contact resistance of two AgWC12C3 static contact products

Product	Contact resistance result（uΩ） 1#（Fine WC particles）	2#（Coarse WC particles）
Phase A	29.3	26.0
Phase B	29.5	24.0
Phase C	29.0	23.0

Table 5

Comparison of temperature rise of two AgWC12C3 static contact products after life

Product	Product temperature rise after power life（℃） 1#（Fine WC particles）		2#（Coarse WC particles）	
Direction	Enter	Out	Enter	Out
Phase A	71.2	72.8	63.5	63.7
Phase B	74.5	72.7	72.4	72.7
Phase C	73.8	67.8	76.6	66.5
Handle	37.8		31.4	
Shell	52.4		47.7	

D. Type test results analysis

From the surface morphology of the two contact materials after electrical life, it can be inferred that the WC particles have a great influence on the electrical properties of the contact materials. The main analysis is:

From the microstructure analysis, the role of the WC particles in the AgWC12C3 contact material is to form a skeleton at the high temperature of the arc to prevent liquid silver from splashing and migrating. According to the research, the connection between the two particles through the liquid phase bridge F[2] is affected by the liquid phase volume (v), the interparticle contact angle (Φ), the particle spacing (r), and the liquid capillary pressure (Δ P). :F= 2 π vrcos Φ - π r2 △P, you can also change this formula to: F=f(D), where D is the spacing between particles, affected by particle volume V0, liquid volume V, when other conditions are fixed, F As the D decreases, the finer the particles are, the smaller the D value is, and the larger the F value is, the easier it is to make the two WC particles close together. Therefore, the finer the WC particles, the easier it is to form a skeleton. It can effectively prevent the splash of liquid silver and reduce the loss of materials. Compared with the fine WC particles, the coarse WC particles have a smaller F force value and the ability to protect the contacts is smaller than the fine WC particles, so the arc-resistant burning resistance of the coarse WC particle static contacts is smaller than that of the fine WC particles.

Because the gravity of WC solid particles is greater than the buoyancy of liquid, WC is in the state of subsidence. According to Stokes'formula of subsidence velocity of particles in liquid:

$$U_t = \frac{gd^2}{18\nu}\left(\frac{\rho^s - \rho}{\rho}\right)$$

In the formula:

ν — fluid kinematic viscosity; m2 / s

d —spherical solid particle diameter; m

g —gravity acceleration; m2/s

ρ —luid density; Kg / m3

ρ^s —solid particle density; Kg / m3

U_t —settlement speed; m/s

According to the formula, when the other conditions of the two contact materials are fixed, the settling velocity of WC particles in Ag solution increases with the increase of WC particles. Therefore, it can be seen from the SEM images that there are obvious stratification of Ag and WC on the surface of the static contact of coarse WC particles. WC is concentrated under the silver layer, which results in silver splashing under the contact pressure, but it can be seen from the SEM images that the surface of the static contact of coarse WC particles has obvious stratification. On the contrary, the static contact point of fine WC particles has a relatively uniform distribution of surface elements in the SEM image, which plays a role in protecting silver loss due to the small settling speed of fine WC particles in Ag solution.

V. CONCLUTION

1). Fine WC particles in the AgWC12C3 contact material can improve the hardness and arc ablation resistance of the contact, prevent the contact from being deformed during the electrical life process and the past splash of the material to improve the electrical life of the product.

2.) The coarse WC particles in the AgWC12C3 contact material can improve the electrical conductivity of the contacts due to improved contact resistance and temperature rise of the product.

REFERENCE

[1] Wan Jiangwen. Rong Mingzhe. Wang Qiping. Arc erosion and pore and crack generation mechanism of silver-based contacts. Xi'an Journal of Electrical Engineering, 1997.

[2] Feng Wei. Ruan Daocheng. Wang Zhengyun. Yang Lirong. Effect of Forming Pressure and Powder Particle Size on Sintering Properties of Tungsten-Copper Composites. Powder Metallurgy Materials Science and Process, 2000

7th International Conference on Reliability of
Electrical Products and Electrical Contacts,
November 04-06, 2019

Arc Fault Feature Extraction Method Based on Maximum Overlapping Discrete Wavelet Packet

Ruihua Cui[1,2], Yingnan Li[1,2]
[1]State Key Laboratory of Reliability and Intelligence of Electrical Equipment, Hebei University of Technology, Tianjin, 300130, China
[2]Key Laboratory of Electromagnetic Field and Electrical Apparatus Reliability of Hebei Province, Hebei University of Technology, Tianjin, 300130, China
E-mail: 632739522@qq.com Tel: 13463676065

***Abstract*—Air arc faults are a type of electrical fault that occurs in aircraft and are difficult to be detected by thermal protection circuit breakers and solid-state power controllers that are commonly assembled in aircraft. Once the arc fault continues to occur, the high temperature released will quickly ignite the combustible material near the fault point, causing the aircraft to catch fire, some systems in the aircraft fail, and even cause a fire that causes the aircraft to crash out of control. Accurate detection of arc faults in avionics systems is particularly important. Based on the Hilbert spectrum's time-frequency analysis capability, this paper focuses on the characteristics of both traditional wavelet packet transform and maximum overlap discrete wavelet packet transform. Due to better time-frequency resolution and time-frequency aggregation, the maximum overlap discrete wavelet packet transform is used as a method to extract the characteristics of the loop current signal. According to the feature extraction results, the feature quantity extracted by the method can accurately distinguish the normal operation, transient arc fault and steady arc fault in the line.**

***Index Terms*— Aeronautical arc fault, Hilbert spectrum, Time-frequency aggregation, Maximum overlap discrete wavelet packet transform, Feature extraction**

I. INTRODUCTION

The latest annual fire inspection of the Ministry of Public Security has carried out statistics on fires in China since 2014. Statistics show that in recent years, China has received a total of 395,000 fire alarms, of which the number of electrical fires accounted for 27.4% of the total number of fires. The loss of personal property is huge[1]. Studies have shown that only 20V voltage can make the arc with high combustion temperature up to 2000 °C ~ 4000 °C continuous and stable combustion. When only the thermal protection device such as the traditional thermal protection circuit breaker is installed in the line, the arc fault's risk of fire is particularly important.

For aircraft that have been put into operation in the market, regardless of the length of operation, the insulation and aging damage of wires or harnesses are common inside the fuselage, and the resulting arc fault will be the EWIS harness itself, various types of pipelines and structural components caused damage. Especially in some civil aircraft models that have not been independently certified for EWIS, the arc fault in the aircraft is more hidden due to the selection of wires with no anti-arc marking ability and older models[2].

In the aspect of arc detection, due to the 115V and 400Hz constant-speed constant-frequency three-phase AC power supply system widely used in aviation AC power supply systems, the arc faults appearing in the aviation AC power supply system have their special features in addition to the characteristics of general arc faults, the arc faults appearing in the aviation AC power supply system also have their own particularities, such as short arc duration and complex arc waveform, brings certain difficulties to the detection of series arc faults.

The most important thing in arc fault detection technology is to extract features that can effectively distinguish between normal and arc faults. Features include but are not limited to, physical characteristics when arc fault occurs and line current and voltage waveform characteristics when arc fault occurs.

In recent years, in addition to the series arc detection technology of arc physics phenomenon or the simulation of series arc fault in the detection of series arc faults, the other detection techniques mostly analyze the above-mentioned time-domain characteristics and frequency. Domain characteristics and time-frequency domain characteristics are used to detect arc faults. The electrical noise generated during the arc fault causes the waveform distortion in the time domain of the current and voltage signals in the line. For the characteristics in the time domain: the literature [3] extracts the correlation coefficient of the current signal in the line to detect the arc fault. The signal waveform changes caused by the literature [4] can calculate the presence or absence of the series arc in the AC electrical device and the DC electrical device by calculating the algebraic derivative of the line current; the literature [5] improves the current collection mode and analyzes the acquisition. The fourth-order cumulant kurtosis value of the high-frequency residual flux-coupled signal results in a uniform arc discrimination threshold. When an arc fault occurs, the loop current and voltage signals also produce spectral energy increase and decrease in a specific frequency band, taking into account the characteristics of such frequency domain: Scholars form Xi'an Jiaotong University in their published patent [6] proposed to use the regularity of the frequency spectrum and the phase angle position of the high-frequency current signal to detect the occurrence of arc fault; in [7], after analyzing the frequency domain characteristics of the arc under resistive load, the frequency domain harmonic factor is selected. The rate of change is used to detect the arc fault; foreign scholars apply a CZT transform with higher spectral resolution than the traditional DFT transform to periodically window the periodic arc fault current signal, and analyze the current after the CZT refinement in each window. Signal 2, 4, and 6 harmonic levels, combined with a variety of features to detect arc faults[8].

It can be seen that in the research of arc fault detection by domestic and foreign scholars, the traditional method of analyzing the zero current phenomena of the loop current in the event of an arc fault, the change of the current zero-crossing or the low-frequency harmonic factor of the extracted current is also known. Mostly, and mostly used in the field of civil arc detection. When an arc fault occurs, the non-stationary characteristics exhibited by the current and voltage signals also reflect the local information of the signal in the time-frequency domain. The time-frequency domain analysis method has been paid more and more attention and application in the field of fault detection due to its focus on detecting the abrupt changes in the signal. Traditional time-frequency domain analysis methods include DFT-based short-time Fourier transform, Mallat multi-resolution wavelet transform, empirical mode decomposition (EMD), and HMD-modified Hilbert-Huang transform (HHT). However, the above methods have certain limitations, such as a global constant time-frequency window size or a calculated modal aliasing problem of time-frequency components, so the time-frequency domain analysis method combines artificial neural network and intelligent classification. Pattern recognition methods such as algorithms are designed to improve the accuracy of arc fault detection.

Considering the many problems analyzed above, this paper applies an improved wavelet transform, Maximal overlap discrete wavelet transform (MODWT), to extract the feature of the collected loop current signal. Through the characteristics of MODWT's approximation coefficient obtained by decomposing the signal and the translation invariance of the detail coefficient and the same time resolution, the information of each band of the extracted signal maintains a good time-frequency resolution, which provides the feature quantity for the intelligent recognition algorithm. support.

II. ARC FAULT CURRENT ANALYSIS OF AVIATION AC SYSTEM

Referring to the UL1699 standard published in the United States[9], a point contact series arc fault generating device is constructed. The schematic diagram is shown in Fig. 1(a), and Fig. 1(b) shows the phenomenon when an arc fault occurs. The loop current waveform signal of three typical loads is obtained by using the arc generating and waveform collecting device constructed in Fig. 1(a), and the waveform includes two states of normal operation and arc fault occurrence.

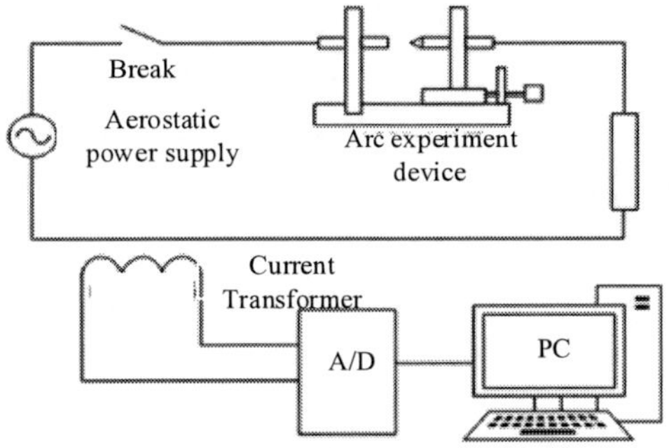

(a) Schematic diagram of point contact series arc fault test

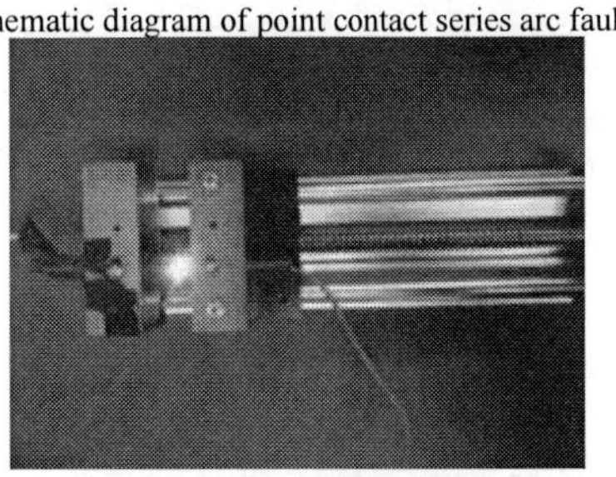

(b) Series arc fault combustion

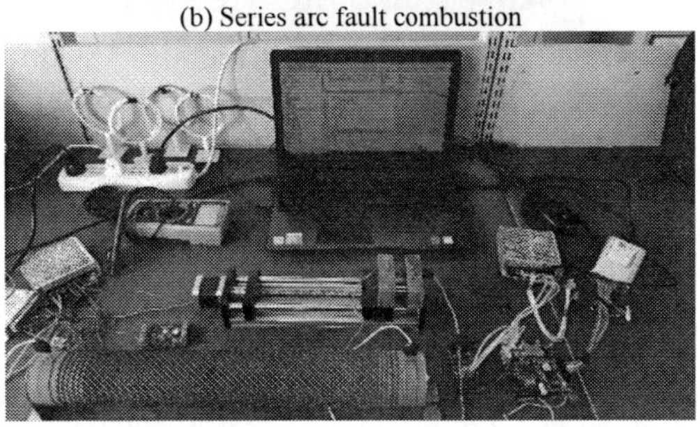

(c) Point contact arc fault data acquisition environment

Fig. 1 Point-contact series arc generator and arc combustion diagram and environment of test.

The waveforms of the three loads are shown in Fig 2. The second half of Fig 2(a) to Fig 2(c) shows the current waveform when a series arc fault occurs.

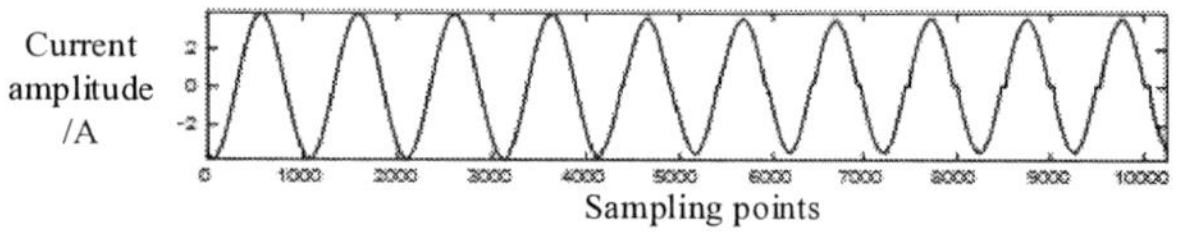

(a) Resistive load loop current waveform

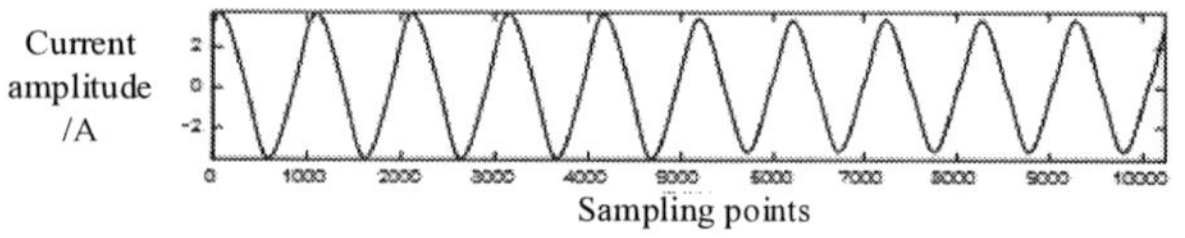

(b) Resistance inductive load loop current waveform

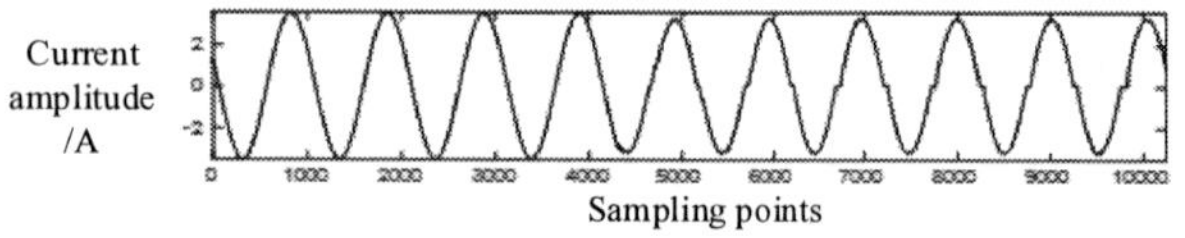

(c) Resistive capacitive loop current waveform

Fig. 2 Loop current waveforms during normal operation and arc fault at four load conditions.

It can be seen that in the case of resistive load and resistive-capacitive load, there is a significant "zero rest" phenomenon when the arc current crosses zero when the arc fault occurs, and the voltage in the resistance-inductive load loop rises quickly due to the rise in the arc gap. The voltage appears early, which leads to the phenomenon of "zero rest" is not so obvious. It is not conducive to the general series arc fault detection method to accurately determine the fault of the line connected with such load.

III. ARC FAULT FEATURE EXTRACTION BASED ON MODWPT

A. Discrete wavelet transform

Discrete wavelet transform (DWT) is based on the "multi-resolution analysis" method created by Mallat et al. It is a fast algorithm in the wavelet transform[10]. The principle is to use the wavelet base with orthogonal properties to decompose the discrete signal $f(n)$ into the form of equation (1):

$$f=\sum_k c_{j,k}2^{\frac{-j}{2}}\phi(2^{-j}n-k)+\sum_k d_{j,k}2^{\frac{-j}{2}}\psi(2^{-j}n-k) \quad (1)$$

Where: $\varphi(2^{-j}n-k)$ is a scaling function; $\psi(2^{-j}n-k)$ is a wavelet function; j is the current decomposition layer number; k is the current sampling point number; $c_{j,k}$ is the jth decomposition layer number The scale factor under; $d_{j,k}$ is the detail coefficient under the jth decomposition layer, and has:

$$c_{j,k}=\sum_{n=-\infty}^{\infty}c_{j-1}(n)g_l(n-2k) \quad (2)$$

$$d_{j,k}=\sum_{n=-\infty}^{\infty}c_{j-1}(n)h_l(n-2k) \quad (3)$$

Where: g_l, h_l are two filters of the two-scale difference equation. It is equivalent to a set of low-pass and high-pass filters that are used repeatedly to achieve a stepwise decomposition of the original discrete signal $f(n)$: a low-frequency approximation component of the signal is generated by g_l, and a high-frequency detail component of the signal is generated by h_l. If the sampling frequency of the original signal is Fs, after the j-layer decomposition, the frequency band of the approximate signal is $[0, {}^{Fs}/2^{j+1}]$, and the frequency band of the detail signal is $[Fs/2^{j+1}, Fs/2^j]$.

B. Maximum overlapping discrete wavelet packet transform

Walden pointed out in his published paper that DWT has the following three limitations in the decomposition process [11]:

Performing a local DWT requires a signal having a length that is a multiple of an integer power of two, and if a complete DWT is performed, the signal length must be an integer power of two;

Cyclic displacement of the decomposed signal will cause the approximation coefficient and detail coefficient of the DWT to change, and the coefficients after the DWT cannot be obtained with the same equal cyclic displacement as the signal;

The increase in the number of DWT decomposition layers causes the resulting approximation coefficients and detail coefficients to be halved in turn, affecting the statistical properties of the coefficients.

In response to the above limitations, MODWT has been modified in the traditional DWT decomposition process[12]. For DWT original scale filter and wavelet filter, a set of its special scale filter ($\tilde{g}_l$) and wavelet filter ($\tilde{h}_l$) are redefined. The two sets of filters have the following relationship:

$$\tilde{g}_l=g_l/\sqrt{2} \quad (4)$$

$$\tilde{h}_l=h_l/\sqrt{2} \quad (5)$$

Again, the filter also satisfies:

$$\sum_{l=0}^{L-1}\tilde{g}_l^2=1/2,$$

$$\sum_{l=0}^{L-1}\tilde{g}_l\,\tilde{g}_{l+2n}=\sum_{l=-\infty}^{+\infty}\tilde{g}_l\,\tilde{g}_{l+2n}=0 \quad (6)$$

$$\tilde{h}_l=(-1)^l\,\tilde{g}_{L-l-1} \quad (7)$$

Due to the down sampling in the DWT decomposition process, MODWT chooses to construct 2^{j-1}-1 zeros in the filter coefficients $\{\tilde{g}_l\}$ and $\{\tilde{h}_l\}$ when the number of decomposition layers is j. New filter: for the paper should be as follows:

$$\tilde{g}_0, 0, \text{L}, \tilde{g}_1, 0, \text{L}, \tilde{g}_{L-2}, 0, \text{L}, 0, \tilde{g}_{L-1} \tag{8}$$

$$\tilde{h}_0, 0, \text{L}, \tilde{h}_1, 0, \text{L}, \tilde{h}_{L-2}, 0, \text{L}, 0, \tilde{h}_{L-1} \tag{9}$$

According to the new filter coefficient, the MODWT approximation coefficient and detail coefficient of the decomposition layer number j are recalculated by the Mallat algorithm:

$$c_{j,k} = \sum_{n=-\infty}^{\infty} c_{j-1}(n)\tilde{g}_l(n-2k) \tag{10}$$

$$d_{j,k} = \sum_{n=-\infty}^{\infty} c_{j-1}(n)\tilde{h}_l(n-2k) \tag{11}$$

The j-layer MODWT coefficients obtained by the above process transformation are the same as the traditional DWT in the frequency band, and are also $[0, Fs/2^{j+1}]$ and $[Fs/2^{j+1}, Fs/2^j]$. But the difference is that MODWT has the translation invariance of approximation coefficient and detail coefficient, and its layers can maintain the same time-resolution when decomposed, without distortion on the phase, so the coefficients obtained after MODWT transformation have the same length N as the original signal.

By further decomposing the high-frequency detail coefficients obtained by wavelet transform, the generalized form of wavelet transform-wavelet packet transform can be obtained to compensate for the high-frequency component decomposition ability of wavelet transform. Similarly, the maximum overlap discrete wavelet packet transform (MODWPT) is a generalized form of MODWT, which not only includes all the advantages of MODWT but also further enhances the high-frequency component decomposition capability and improves the frequency domain resolution.

At this time, the coefficients decomposed by each layer of MODWPT can be uniformly represented by $W_{j,n,t}$:

$$W_{j,n,t} = \sum_{l=0}^{L-1} r_{n,l} W_{j-1,[n/2],(t-2^{j-1}l) \bmod N} \tag{12}$$

Where: $W_{j,n,t}$ are decomposition coefficients; j is the current decomposition layer number; n is the index of each coefficient frequency; t is the current sampling point; L is the length of the wavelet filter and the scale filter; $r_{n,l}$ is the wavelet Filter or scale filter, if $n \bmod 4=0$ or 3, then $r_{n,l}=\{\tilde{g}_l\}$, if $n \bmod 4=1$ or 2, then $r_{n,l}=\{\tilde{h}_l\}$.

The signal components are decomposed by MODWPT. Since the zero-phase filters of $\tilde{g}_l$ and $\tilde{h}_l$ are used in the decomposition process, the phase information of each component is preserved, so it is suitable for the basis of MODWPT. In the above, Hilbert three-dimensional time-spectrum is further constructed to calculate the instantaneous frequency of each component, and the time-frequency resolution after signal decomposition is observed.

After the Hilbert transform is performed on the equation (12), the constructed analytical signal can be expressed as:

$$s(t) = W_{j,n}(t) + jH[W_{j,n}(t)] \tag{13}$$

Where $H[W_{j,n}(t)]$ is the general form of $W_{j,n}(t)$ after Hilbert transform.

Obtaining the instantaneous amplitude function $a_{j,n}(t)$ of the nth sub-band component of the jth layer decomposition.

$$a_{j,n}(t) = \sqrt{W_{j,n}^2(t) + H^2[W_{j,n}(t)]} \tag{14}$$

And instantaneous phase function $\varphi_{j,n}(t)$

$$\phi_{j,n}(t) = \arctan\frac{H[W_{j,n}(t)]}{W_{j,n}(t)} \tag{15}$$

Accordingly, its instantaneous frequency function $f_{j,n}(t)$ can be expressed as

$$f_{j,n}(t) = \frac{1}{2\pi}\phi'_{j,n}(t) \tag{16}$$

Combining the instantaneous amplitude with the instantaneous frequency to obtain the corresponding Hilbert energy spectrum:

$$s_j(t,f) = \sum_{n=0}^{2^j-1} a_{j,n}^2(t)[f - f_{j,n}(t)] \tag{17}$$

The Hilbert energy spectrum focuses on the local time-frequency characteristics of the signal and has good time-frequency aggregation. It is very suitable for analyzing the time-frequency aggregation and time-frequency resolution of each component after time-frequency decomposition.

However, the energy dissipation phenomenon is inevitable in the sub-band components obtained by any time-frequency decomposition method, which is due to a MODWPT during decomposition may represent a single frequency component of narrowband component, we should try to increase its decomposition level J, whereby the more 2^j narrowband components are obtained. However, in the actual data acquisition work, the sampling frequency is usually not set directly according to the Nyquist sampling theorem. The actual set sampling frequency is higher than the range specified by the sampling theorem so that the excessive-high frequency band is decomposed. The narrowband component is not necessary for analysis and analysis. The more narrowband components appear in the frequency domain, the more frequent the frequency occurs between the frequency bands in which the narrowband components are located, causing the MODWPT to decompose the frequency incorrectly, causing energy leakage. To this end, Olhede and Walden recommend a minimum decomposition sub-band width of 1 / 16 of the

Nyquist frequency, that is, the number of decomposition layers is up to 4.

Using MATLAB to generate a signal containing multiple frequency components, the signal is subjected to 4- layer WPT and MODWPT decomposition, and combined with the Hilbert spectrum to investigate the time-frequency decomposition ability of the two methods. Fig 4 is a MODWPT each component Hilbert spectrum, Fig. 5 is a conventional WPT each component Hilbert spectrum.

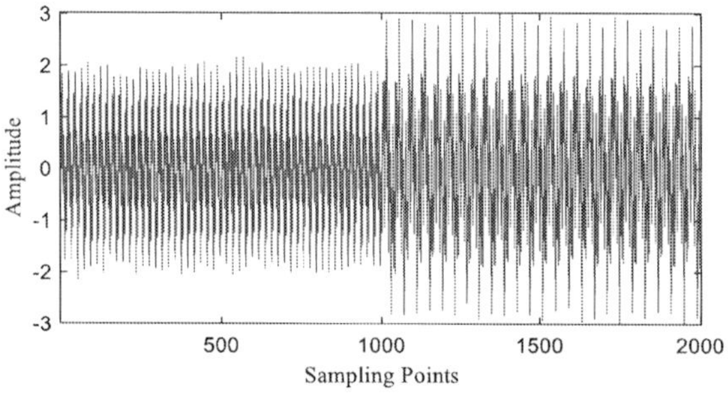

Fig. 3 The multi-frequency component signal generated by MATLAB.

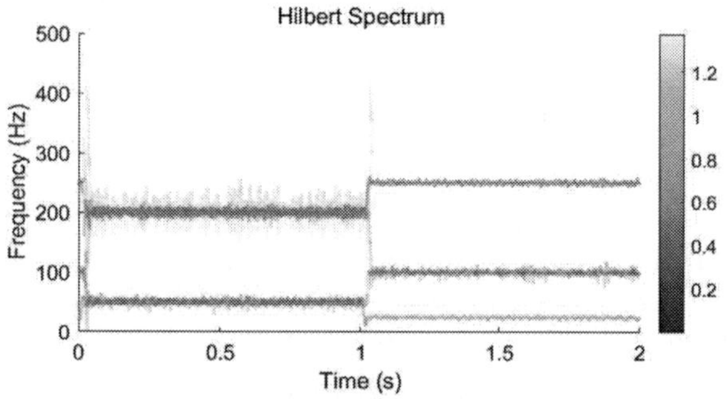

Fig. 4 MODWPT + HHT.

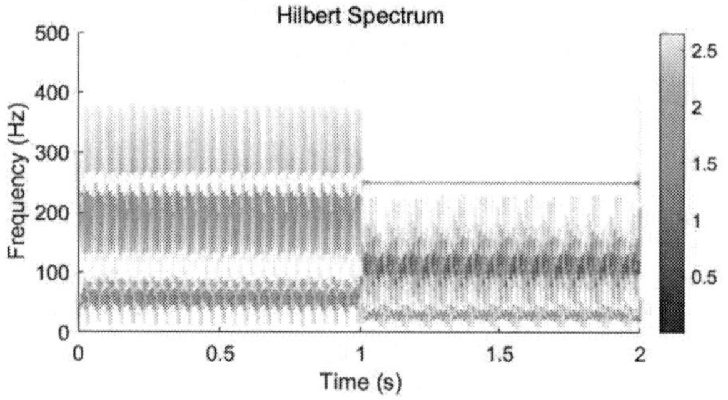

Fig. 5 WPT + HHT.

It can be seen from the comparison between Fig. 4 and Fig. 5 that the Hilbert energy spectrum composed of the components obtained by decomposing the signal by MODWPT exhibits good time-frequency aggregation. The individual frequency components distributed along the time axis are well clustered together and have good time-frequency resolution.

However, observing Fig. 5, it is found that the time-frequency aggregation of the Hilbert spectrum composed of the components decomposed by the traditional WPT is very poor, not only in the time-frequency resolution but also the single frequency component in the spectrum is divided into two different Frequency band. In ls ~ 2s period, only draws the frequency component around 250Hz while The frequency component around 100 Hz and the lowest fundamental frequency component both generate large oscillations. In 0s ~ 1s time period, all frequency components have had a large or small oscillations, while the original is 200Hz frequency component of about disappear, and further in 200Hz the frequency of occurrence of both components represent this time appear more severe energy leakage phenomenon, making the WPT decompose in 200Hz narrowband component is about to lose its physical meaning.

After the above analysis, it can be determined that the time - frequency domain decomposition ability of MODWPT is much stronger than that of the traditional WPT, and the frequency domain narrowband component which is decomposed has clear physical meaning and can be used as a feature for analyzing signals.

C. *Arc fault feature analysis and extraction*

The "zero rest" phenomenon and the decrease of the current amplitude appearing in the loop current waveform when the arc fault occurs represent the current signal is no longer a non-stationary signal. To distinguish one of the three states of normal operation, transient arc fault, and steady arc fault, the MODPWT is used to perform 3- layer decomposition processing on the collected current signal. Selecting orthogonal and tightly supported DB wavelet bases during decomposition. At the same time, since the sum of the squares of the coefficients after wavelet packet transform has the same characteristics as the total energy of the time domain waveform, the energy of each coefficient of the wavelet packet is used to quantify the characteristics obtained by the decomposition of MODWPT.

The energy E_j used is calculated as:

$$E_j = \sum_{n=1}^{N} \left| S_j(n) \right|^2 \tag{18}$$

Where: $S_j(j = 1, 2, ..., 8)$ is the reconstructed wavelet packet parameters in each frequency band under the third layer decomposition, including approximate parameters and detail parameters; N is the number of sampling points.

To unify the extracted features, the energy E_j is selected to be normalized, and the energy of each frequency band is calculated as a percentage of the total energy. Assuming:

$$E_0 = \sum_{j=1}^{8} E_j \tag{19}$$

$$E_j(\%) = \frac{E_j}{E_0}(j = 1, 2, \ldots, 8) \tag{20}$$

Since the energy at the fundamental frequency approximate parameter contained extremely high, in the latter comparison, only the energy ratio of the seven detail parameters is compared, so to observe the difference between the features extracted in the three states..

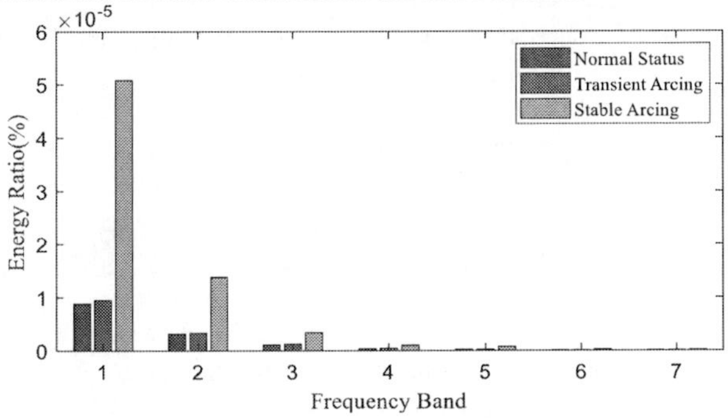

(a) Resistive load conditions

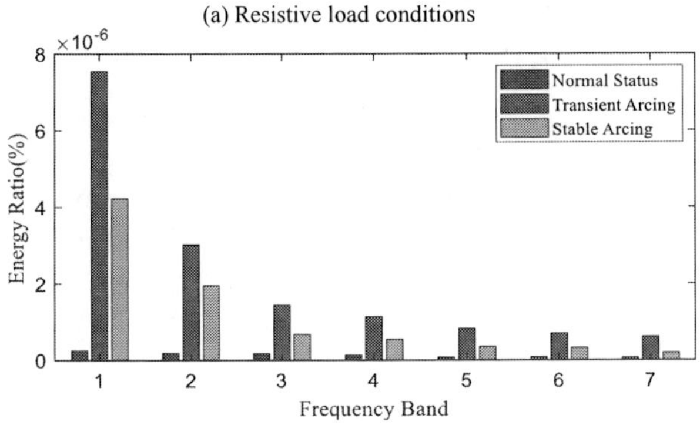

(b) Resistance inductive load conditions

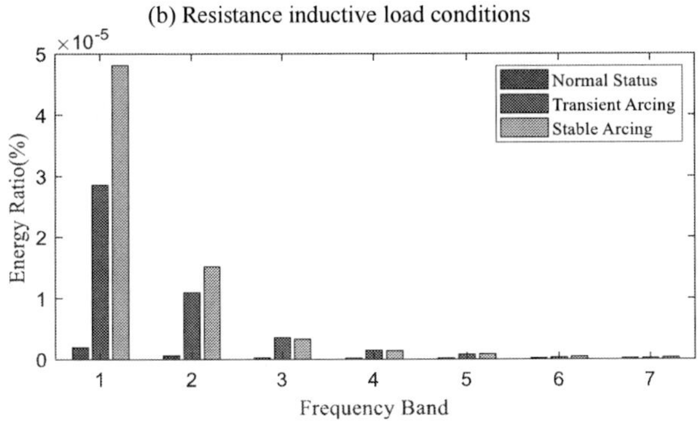

(c) Resistive capacitive load conditions

Fig. 6 MODWPT detail parameter energy ratio chart.

It can be seen from Fig. 6 that when the line is operating under different conditions, the energy of the wavelet packet detail parameter of each frequency band is different from the total energy, and the energy distribution in each frequency band is also different in the same case. In the lower frequency part, it is more energy than in the high frequency. The extracted feature value as shown in Table I ~ Table III below.

IV. CONCLUSION

In this paper, an improved wavelet packet transform (WPT) algorithm, Maximum Overlapped Discrete Wavelet Packet Decomposition (MODWPT), is proposed to compare two methods by comparing the difference between the two methods through comparing the Hilbert spectrum after decomposing the same multi-frequency component signal with the traditional wavelet packet transform. In comparison, the time-frequency resolution of MODWPT in decomposing signals is better than that of traditional WPT.

Based on MODWPT, the loop current signal collected in the simulated aviation AC arc generation experiment is analyzed. After selecting the appropriate wavelet base and the number of decomposition layers, a reliable analysis result is obtained: when the line is in different working conditions, the energy content of the sub-band detailed parameters decomposed by MODWPT is also different, and the extracted feature quantity is different. The effective area is divided into three working conditions, which can provide the basis for fault identification for intelligent recognition algorithms such as pattern recognition.

TABLE I

RESISTIVE LOAD CHARACTERISTIC VALUE

	Normal Status	Transient Arcing	Stable Arcing
E_1/E_0	8.90E-6	9.53E-6	5.08E-5
E_2/E_0	3.23E-6	3.36E-6	1.38E-5
E_3/E_0	1.16E-6	1.34E-6	3.47E-6
E_4/E_0	4.18E-7	4.84E-7	1.05E-6
E_5/E_0	2.95E-7	2.85E-7	7.66E-7
E_6/E_0	1.55E-7	1.28E-7	2.98E-7
E_7/E_0	1.41E-7	1.16E-7	1.80E-7

TABLE II

RESISTANCE INDUCTIVE LOAD CHARACTERISTIC VALUE

	Normal Status	Transient Arcing	Stable Arcing
E_1/E_0	2.54E-7	7.55E-6	4.23E-6
E_2/E_0	1.90E-7	3.02E-6	1.96E-6
E_3/E_0	1.77E-7	1.44E-6	6.77E-7
E_4/E_0	1.40E-7	1.14E-6	5.34E-7
E_5/E_0	8.02E-8	8.26E-7	3.52E-7
E_6/E_0	7.34E-8	6.96E-7	3.19E-7
E_7/E_0	7.15E-8	6.03E-7	1.92E-7

TABLE III

RESISTIVE CAPACITIVE LOAD CHARACTERISTIC VALUE

	Normal Status	Transient Arcing	Stable Arcing
E_1/E_0	2.02E-6	2.86E-5	4.81E-5
E_2/E_0	6.22E-7	1.10E-5	1.52E-5
E_3/E_0	2.65E-7	3.62E-6	3.39E-6
E_4/E_0	1.64E-7	1.45E-6	1.39E-6
E_5/E_0	1.89E-7	8.18E-7	8.38E-7
E_6/E_0	1.60E-7	3.14E-7	4.49E-7
E_7/E_0	1.72E-7	1.99E-7	3.10E-7

ACKNOWLEDGMENT

This work was supported by the Natural Science Foundation of Hebei Province of China: E2016202106.

REFERENCES

[1] Fire Department of Ministry of public security. China Fire Services. Yunnan People's Publishing House, 2015.

[2] Wang Li, Cao Lu, Yan Yangguang. Research on Arc Fault Characteristic for AC Power System in Aircraft. Low Voltage Apparatus, 2011(02): 19-23.

[3] Jinmi Lezama, Patrick Schweitzer, et al. "An embedded system for AC series arc detection by inter-period correlations of current." Electric Power Systems Research, 129, (2015): 227 - 234.

[4] Tisserand Etienne, Lezama Jinmi, et al. "Series arcing detection by algebraic derivative of the current." Electric Power Systems Research, 119, (2015): 91 - 99.

[5] Bao Guanghai, Jiang Run. Research on series arc fault detection based on asymmetrical distribution of magnetic flux. Chinese Journal of Scientific Instrument, 2019, 40(03): 54-61.

[6] Zhang Guogang, Song Zhengxiang, He Chunjun, et al. Arc fault detection method based on time frequency characteristic of high frequency current. Chinese Patent: 200910218707. 9.

[7] Wang Xiaoyuan, Gao Miao, Zhao Yushuang. Characteristic analysis of low-voltage arc fault in resistive load conditions. Electric Power Automation Equipment, 2015, 35(05): 106-110+118.

[8] Giovanni Artale, Antonio Cataliotti, et al. Arc Fault Detection Method Based on CZT Low-Frequency Harmonic Current Analysis. IEEE Transactions on Instrumentation and Measurement, 2017, 66(5): 888-896.

[9] Underwrite Laboratories Inc. UL1699, Standard for safety for arc fault circuit interrupters. 2nd Ed, April 7, 2006.

[10] Zhang Peng, Li Hongbin. A novel algorithm for harmonic analysis based on discrete wavelet transforms. Transactions of China Electrotechnical Society, 2012, 27(3): 252-259.

[11] Walden A T, Contreras Cristan A. The phase-corrected un-decimated discrete wavelet packet transform and its application to interpreting the timing of events. Proceedings of the Royal Society of London Series A Mathematical Physical and Engineering Sciences. 1998.

[12] Shan Peiwei. Time-frequency analysis system and its application. East China Normal University, 2011.

Ruihua Cui, female, born in 1962, Ph. D, professor, master tutor. She is mainly engaged in the research of electrical computer aided design and arc electric contact technology.

Analysis of Degradation Sensitive Characteristics of Switch Power Supply Based on Electro Thermal Coupling Simulation

Yifan Hu, Rui Feng, Xuerong Ye*, Sirui Liu, Guofu Zhai
School of Electrical Engineering and Automation, Harbin Institute of Technology, Harbin, Heilongjiang Province, 150001, China
E-mail: yifanhu_123@163.com Tel: +8615776610695

Abstract—**As a high reliability and long life product, the output performance parameters of switch power supply often fail to reflect its real degradation state, which causes "sudden failure" phenomenon in its working process. To address this problem, a degradation sensitive characteristic analysis method based on electro-thermal coupling simulation is proposed to excavate the real degradation sensitive characteristic parameters in the space-borne power supply accurately, which fully takes into account the electro-thermal coupling effect between the temperature and components caused by the "self-heating", and this method accurately simulates the real working state of the power supply. Firstly, the circuit simulation model of power supply is established by Saber. Secondly, the steady-state thermal field simulation model of power supply is constructed by finite element simulation analysis method. Then the electric-thermal simulation is integrated by iSIGHT to realize the automatic interaction of electric-thermal coupling simulation data. Finally, through the multi-parameter sensitivity analysis, the influence of the internal components and materials degeneration is obtained, and the sensitive parameters reflecting the degradation characteristics are determined. A case study of a certain type switch power supply fully demonstrates the effectiveness and feasibility of the proposed method. At the same time, this proposed method also greatly contributes to the degradation monitoring, fault diagnosis and reliability assessment of switch power supply.**

Index Terms— **Switch power supply, Electro-thermal coupling simulation, Multi-parameter sensitivity analysis, Degradation sensitive characteristics, Degradation state**

I. INTRODUCTION

As an important power conversion device, switching power supply is developing rapidly in the direction of high power density, high integration and high reliability. It plays an extremely important role in weapon equipment, industrial production and even in daily life [1]-[3]. Therefore, the quality and reliability of switching power supply will significantly influence the performance of the entire system. So the assessment of degradation state of switching power supply is an urgent problem to address [4]-[6]. Because switching power supply is a high reliable and long-life product, its failure life information is difficult to obtain. Meanwhile, the change of its output performance parameters is often insensitive and can not fully reflect its real degradation state. So traditional reliability analysis methods are not fully applicable to switching power supply. An effective way to measure the performance degradation state is monitoring the degradation sensitive characteristic parameters inside the power supply [7]-[8]. Multi-parameter sensitivity analysis based on the power supply simulation analysis can effectively extract the degradation sensitive feature information. Shao and Li [9] established the simulation model of switching power supply, and determined the key components according to the different influence on the output of power supply when they reached the failure threshold; Chen [10] determined the degradation sensitive information of switching power supply based on the combination of circuit simulation and sensitivity analysis, and it provided a variety of fault modes for injection and fault diagnosis. However, most of the current simulation analysis of switching power supply is carried out at a steady-state temperature, that is to say, the parameters of components do not change with temperature, and the coupling effect of temperature and power consumption is seldom considered. However, in fact, the electrothermal coupling effect can not be neglected, it will affect the simulation result a lot. In addition, it will not be able to accurately simulate the actual working state of the circuit [11]. At present, there are two main simulation methods considering the electrothermal coupling effect: direct coupling method and load transfer method [12]. On the basis of load transfer method, this paper presents an integrated simulation method of electro-thermal coupling based on iSIGHT platform. Firstly, the circuit simulation model of power supply is established by Saber, then the steady thermal field simulation model of power supply is built by finite element simulation analysis method, finally, the process of electro-thermal simulation is set up by iSIGHT. Then the automatic interaction of electrothermal coupling simulation data is realized, and the real working state of the circuit is accurately simulated. On this basis, based on multi-parameter sensitivity analysis and failure analysis of switching power supply, the degradation sensitive characteristic parameters are determined, which provide a strong support for degradation monitoring and fault diagnosis.

II. WORKING PRINCIPLE AND FAILURE ANALYSIS OF SWITCHING POWER SUPPLY

A. Working Principle of Switching Power Supply

The switching power supply studied in this paper adopts PWM switching control mode, which converts DC400V obtained by AC220V rectifier into a controllable constant current source to supply load, as shown in Fig. 1. The AC220V input from the grid side is connected with the power factor correction circuit through the input protection circuit, it is converted into DC voltage through the rectification process. And then, through the DC/DC buck circuit, it is converted into DC voltage suitable for output. The output current signal is converted into voltage signal through the sampling resistance in the constant current feedback circuit. The voltage is compared with the reference voltage. Finally, the voltage is isolated by the optocoupler chip and transmitted to the PWM controller to control the switching on and off of the MOSFET.

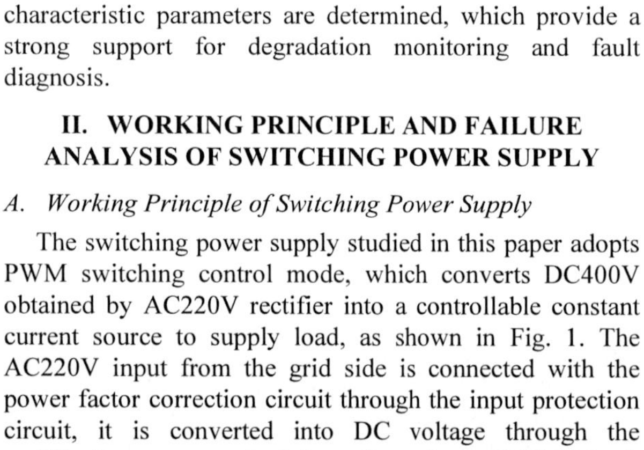

Fig. 1 Structural schematic diagram of a switching power supply

B. Failure Analysis of Switching Power Supply

As a power supply component of electronic system or equipment, the reliability of switching power supply seriously affects the operation performance of the entire system or equipment. According to relevant statistics, most of the faults of switching power supply are caused by the failure of its components [13]. Power MOSFET, aluminium electrolytic capacitor and power diode are identified as the key components which restrict the overall reliability of power supply. Therefore, the failure modes and mechanisms of the above three devices are mainly analyzed and discussed in this section.

1) Failure analysis of power MOSFET

The common failure mechanisms of power MOSFET include hot carrier effect (HCE), negative bias temperature instability (NBTI), time-dependent gate oxygen breakdown, electromigration (EM), etc. [14]. As time goes on, these slow failure processes will cause some important parameters of power MOSFET to drift, such as the increase of on-resistance R_{ds}, the decrease of transconductance g_m and the increase of threshold voltage V_{th}, which will make the performance of power MOSFET decline, and even cause power system failure. Threshold voltage will affect both transconductance and MOSFET transition characteristics. Therefore, threshold voltage is generally chosen as a physical measure of the degradation of MOSFET. It is stipulated that power MOSFET will fail when the threshold voltage exceeds 10% of the initial value. According to the inverse power rate model, the MOSFET degradation model characterized by threshold voltage V_{th} can be obtained as follows:

$$\Delta V_{th}(t) = At^n \tag{1}$$

where A represents the undetermined coefficient, t means the time, and n represents the sensitive factors of carrier species.

2) Failure Analysis of Aluminum Electrolytic Capacitor

Aluminum electrolytic capacitor mainly plays the role of energy storage and filtering in switching power supply. Its main failure modes are leakage, explosion, open circuit, breakdown, and deterioration of electrical parameters, etc. The main cause of its failure is the reduction of internal electrolyte, meanwhile, ripple current, environmental temperature, voltage and other factors can affect the electrolyte reduce speed. Generally, the aluminium electrolytic capacitor can be regarded as a series model consisting of capacitance C and equivalent series resistance ESR. The volatilization of electrolyte can lead to the increase of equivalent series resistance ESR and the decrease of capacitance C. When the capacitance C decreases to a certain extent, the basic performance of aluminium electrolytic capacitor will be lost and failure will occur [15]. When temperature is the main stress that leads to capacitance degradation, according to Arrhenius formula, the following variation rules of capacitance C and equivalent resistance ESR can be obtained:

$$ESR(t) = A_1 \cdot \exp(B_1 \cdot t) \tag{2}$$

$$C(t) = A_2 + B_2 t \tag{3}$$

where A_1, A_2, B_1, B_2 represent the undetermined coefficients, t represents the time.

(3) Failure Analysis of Power Diodes

Power Schottky Diode (SBD) works by using the contact barrier between metal and semiconductor. During the long-term operation of the diode, the PN junction produces heat, and the mechanical stress of the contact parts with different materials will be caused by the different temperature coefficients, which will lead to the fracture failure of the contact parts between the internal electrodes and the PN junction. In addition, due to the influence of voltage, current and temperature, the device performance will degrade. Reverse leakage current I_R is an important performance parameter of the diode. The bigger the reverse leakage current is, the worse the unidirectional conductivity of the diode is. Therefore, the reverse leakage current is generally chosen as the degradation characteristic parameter [16]. When considering the effects of temperature and electrical stress, the degradation model characterized by reverse leakage current of diode can be obtained from Irene model:

$$\frac{\Delta I_R}{I_R} = A\exp(V^m)\exp(-\frac{Q}{kT})dt \qquad (4)$$

where I_R represents the reverse leakage current of diode, V means the open voltage, m is a constant, A、Q、k、T represent the coefficient, degradation activation energy, Boltzmann constant, thermodynamic temperature, respectively.

III. SIMULATION ANALYSIS OF ELECTRO-THERMAL COUPLING OF SWITCHING POWER SUPPLY

A. Electrothermal Coupling Simulation Strategy

In the simulation process, the real working state of the circuit can be simulated more accurately, fully considering the electro-thermal coupling effect of the power supply. At the same time, accurate digital simulation model is an important basis to accurately establish the relationship between output response, component stress and lower characteristic parameters. It is also an important basis for multi-parameter sensitivity analysis to find out the sensitive characteristics of power degradation. Firstly, the circuit simulation model of power supply is established by Saber, then the steady-state thermal field simulation model of power supply is built by finite element simulation analysis method. Finally, the process of electric-thermal simulation is integrated by iSIGHT platform, and the automatic interaction of simulation data of electric-thermal coupling is realized. The purpose of modeling and simulation analysis is to provide a simulation environment for electro-thermal collaborative optimization design and multi-stage life cycle performance analysis [11]. The simulation strategy relationship is shown in Fig. 2.

B. Electrothermal Coupling Simulation of Switching Power Supply Based on iSIGHT Platform

The schematic diagram of a switching power supply studied in this paper is shown in Fig. 1. The simulation model of the switching power supply circuit is established by Saber according to the schematic diagram as shown in Fig. 3. Then, the thermal simulation model of switching power supply is established by ANSYS. The thermal simulation process mainly includes geometric modeling, meshing, load and boundary conditions. Because there are many components on the PCB board of power supply, in order to reduce the calculation time as much as possible under the premise of the calculation accuracy, it is necessary to simplify the structure of some components appropriately [11]. Some components with minimal power consumption can even be neglected. The material properties of the main structural components in the power supply are shown in Table 1. On the basis of establishing geometric model, the grid of switching power supply is divided by ANSYS. The cell grid is set as tetrahedron or hexahedron shape. For the parts with high power consumption or high temperature gradient, the grid is relatively dense, while the other parts are relatively sparse, and the model finally gets 243766 single meshes. The grid division of PCB board and main components of power supply is shown in Fig. 4. The simulation analysis of switching power supply is carried out under three loads: temperature 25 ℃, convection coefficient $10W/(m^2 \cdot K)$ and heat generation rate.

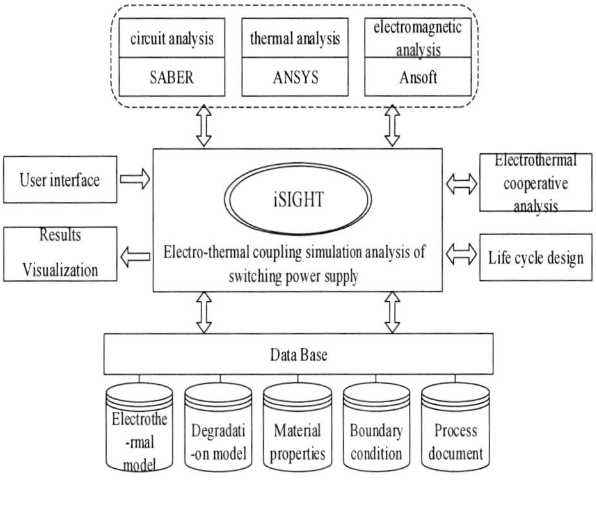

Fig. 2 Electric-thermal coupling simulation strategy of switching power supply

In the simulation process, a complete circuit network is constructed by Saber model, and then the output response of switching power supply and the power loss of components are obtained by simulation. The power consumption of components is converted into heat generation rate of heat source, which is loaded into ANSYS thermal model for steady-state thermal simulation, and the distribution of thermal field on PCB board is obtained. The working temperature of each component is extracted, and then the performance parameters of the component are obtained according to the electrothermal coupling model of the component. The circuit model in Saber is updated to continue the simulation. By this iteration calculation, the accurate values of the circuit response and steady-state temperature of the switching power supply can be obtained when the temperature difference between the two successive simulations is less than the set threshold. The leakage source voltage and driving signal waveform of power MOSFET are selected to compare with the measured waveform, as displayed in Fig. 5 and Fig. 6, respectively, and the relative error of driving voltage is 4.5%, which illustrates the validity and credibility of the simulation results.

TABLE I

MATERIAL PROPERTIES OF MAIN COMPONENTS

Component type	Category of materials	Thermal conductivity
resistor	Ceramic Matrix	31
PCB	FR4 Material	16.3
Winding, heat sink, pin	copper	398
Transformer Core	Ferrite	12
Transformer skeleton	Phenolic plastics	0.27
Semiconductor core	silicon	148
Semiconductor Encapsulation	Epoxy plastics	1.57
Thermal conductive insulating gasket	Compound material	2.45
radiator	Aluminium alloy	96.2
CBB Capacitor	Barium titanate ceramics	2.5

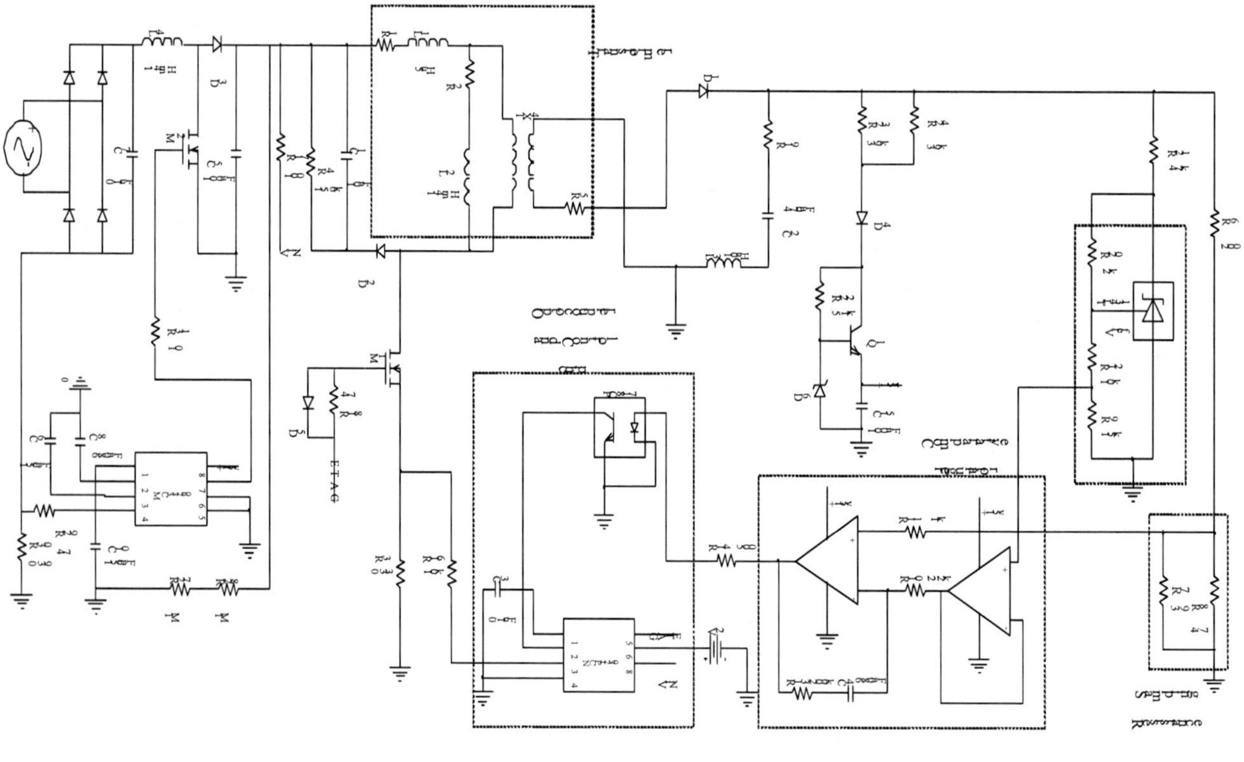

Fig. 3 Simulation Model of Switching Power Supply Circuit

Fig. 4 Mesh generation of PCB board and main components

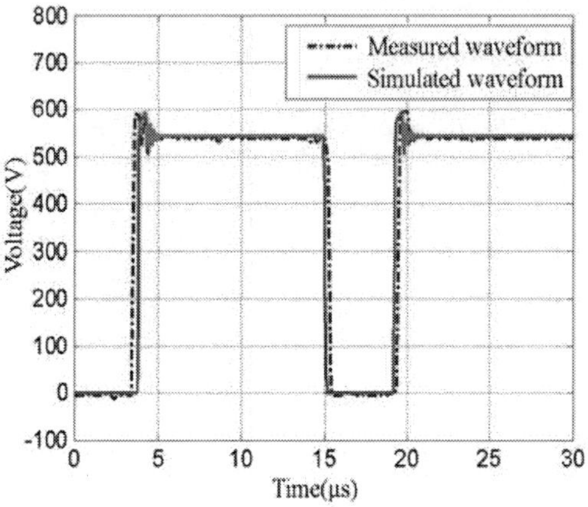

Fig. 5 Drain source voltage of MOSFET

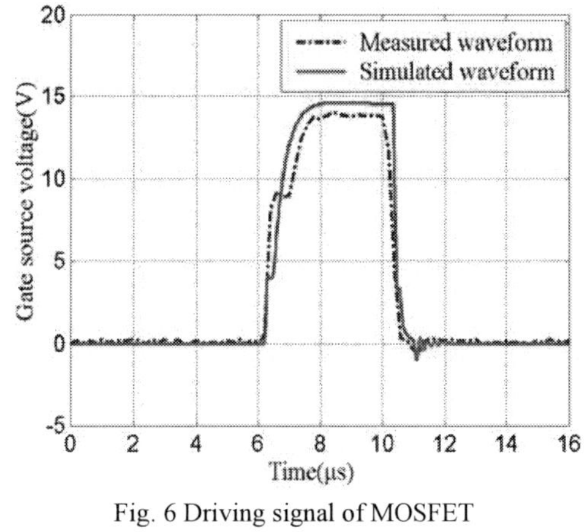

Fig. 6 Driving signal of MOSFET

Fig. 7 shows the thermal simulation results of the switching power supply under the ambient temperature of 25 ℃. The highest temperature is the power resistance of the middle part, which reaches 113.55 ℃. The maximum temperature measured by the infrared thermal imager is 116.2 ℃ as shown in Fig. 8. It can be concluded that the simulation error is pretty small to meet the actual engineering needs.

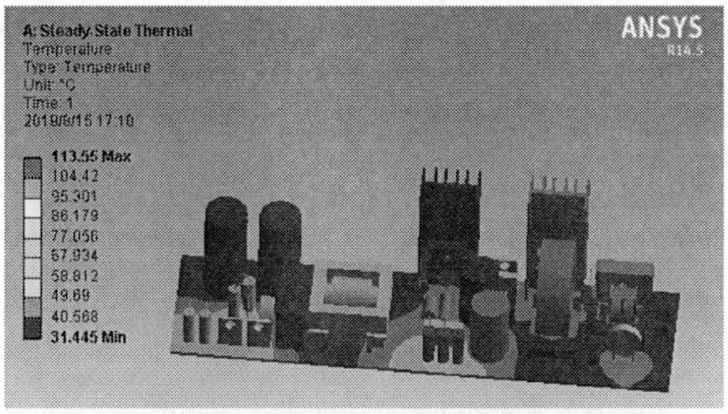

Fig. 7 The thermal simulation results

Fig. 8 Temperature contour obtained by testing

IV. MULTI-PARAMETER SENSITIVITY ANALYSIS

Sensitivity analysis is used to measure the offset of system output characteristics caused by the deviation between the parameters and the nominal values of components. It can also be used to quantify the sensitivity of circuit characteristics to the parameters of components. Sensitivity analysis includes absolute sensitivity analysis and relative sensitivity analysis. Considering the influence of components tolerance design on each output performance index of power supply, this paper adopts relative sensitivity analysis method. Relative sensitivity is the ratio of the relative change of performance parameters P to the relative change of component parameters x . Its mathematical expression is as follows:

$$D_x^P = \frac{\partial P / P}{\partial x / x} = \frac{x}{P}\frac{\partial P}{\partial x} \qquad (5)$$

According to (5), the relative sensitivity has no dimension. It can be expressed as the variation of circuit performance parameters caused by 1% variation of component parameters in the circuit [17]. The higher the D_x^P is, the greater the relative change of the power supply performance parameters caused by the relative change of the component parameters. That is to say, the higher the D_x^P is, the greater the influence of the component on the power supply characteristics is. The failure of the component is more likely to lead to the failure of the switching power supply. For the switching power supply studied in this paper, the relatively important output performance indicators including the steady-state output current I_{out} , the ripple value of the current I_r , the power efficiency E, and the start-up time T_s are constructed for sensitivity analysis. The output current fluctuation ΔI, and the dynamic adjustment time T_a are also considered when the load changes. Meanwhile, combined with the failure analysis of switching power supply, this paper selected 10 components such as aluminum electrolytic capacitor, power MOSFET et. al to carry out the multi-parameter sensitivity, respectively. Finally, the sequencing results of the sensitive components under different performance indicators were shown in Table 2.

TABLE II

SEQUENCING OF SENSITIVE COMPONENTS WITH VARIOUS PERFORMANCE INDICATORS

Number	I_{out}	T_s	I_r	E	ΔI	T_a
1	R_2	R_2	C_2	R_2	R_2	R_4
2	R_4	R_4	R_4	R_3	R_3	R_2
3	R_3	R_3	R_3	R_4	R_4	MOSFET
4	R_9	OP	R_2	MOSFET	C_2	R_3
5	C_5	C_5	OP	OP	R_9	C_2
6	C_4	MOSFET	R_9	C_2	OP	OP
7	R_{12}	R_9	MOSFET	R_9	MOSFET	C_4
8	C_2	C_4	C_4	C_4	R_{12}	R_9
9	R_1	C_2	--	R_{12}	C_5	C_5
10	C_3	R_{12}	--	C_5	C_4	R_{12}

Through the multi-parameter sensitivity analysis, we can conclude that the relative sensitivity of resistance devices are generally higher for the steady-state output current I_{out} of switching power supply, that is to say, the influence on the I_{out} is generally greater. At the same time, the corresponding sensitivity of power MOSFET and aluminium electrolytic capacitor are higher than other components through comprehensive analysis. Considering the failure mechanism of switching power supply itself, the above mentioned MOSFET and aluminium electrolytic capacitor are also the key components in the performance degradation of power supply. Therefore, the degradation sensitive parameters of switching power supply can be selected as sampling resistance, power MOSFET threshold voltage V_{th} and capacitance of aluminium electrolytic capacitor C. Subsequently, the performance degradation of switching power supply can be reflected based on the changes of the above parameters, so as to extract the early degradation characteristic information in time and make maintenance strategy to avoid "sudden" failure as much as possible.

V. CONCLUSION

A degradation sensitive characteristic analysis method based on electrothermal coupling simulation and multi-parameter sensitivity analysis is proposed in this paper to extract the real degradation sensitive parameters inside the switching power supply accurately. And the automatic interaction of electrothermal coupling simulation data is realized by using iSIGHT platform which integrates the electrothermal simulation process of switching power supply. The electrothermal coupling effect caused by "spontaneous heating" are fully considered, and the real working state of power supply is accurately simulated. On this basis, through the multi-parameter sensitivity analysis, the sensitive components which have great influence on the main output performance parameters of switching power supply are extracted and determined. Meanwhile, combined with failure mechanism analysis, the sensitive characteristic parameters which indicates power supply internal degradation should be paid more attention in the working state. So it is expected that this proposed method will serve as a potential foundation for the degradation monitoring, fault diagnosis and reliability evaluation of similar power supplies.

ACKNOWLEDGMENT

This work was supported by the National Key R&D Program of China [grant number 2017YFB1300800] and the National Natural Science Foundation of China [grant number 61671172]. In addition, we would like to thank the editor and reviewers for their valuable comments on this paper.

REFERENCES

[1] Wang Jiangang, Ruan Xinbo, Chen Junyan "Development of high power aviation modular power supply and research on key application technologies." *Transactions of China Electrotechnical Society*, 2005, 20 (12): pp. 95-100.

[2] D. Goodman, J. Hoffmeister, and J. Judkins, "Electronic prognostics for switched mode power supplies," *Microelectronics Reliability*, vol. 47, no. 12, pp. 1902-1906, Dec 2007.

[3] C. A. Gallo, F. L. Tofoli, and J. A. C. Pinto, "Two-Stage Isolated Switch-Mode Power Supply With High Efficiency and High Input Power Factor," *IEEE Transactions on Industrial Electronics*, vol. 57, no. 11, pp. 3754-3766, Nov 2010.

[4] D. Brown, P. Kalgren, and M. Roemer, "Electronic prognostics - A case study using switched-mode power supplies (SMPS)," (in English), Ieee Instrumentation & Measurement Magazine, vol. 10, no.

4, pp. 20-26, Aug 2007.
[5] Loren Nasser, Maggie Curtin. Electronics Reliability Prognosis Through Material Modeling and Simulation[C]. IEEE Aerospace Conference, 2006.
[6] Zhai Guofu, Hu Bo. et. al. "Research on Reliability Tolerance Design Technique for the Constant-Current Power Supply of LEDs Used on Street Lamp." Transactions of China Electrotechnical Society, 2011, 26(1): pp. 135-140.
[7] Liu M, Ren Z, Liu D, et al. Methodology of modeling applied to fault injection based on EDA[C]. Prognostics and Health Management Conference. IEEE, 2010:1-7.
[8] Liu M, Zeng Z, Liu D. The method for importance analysis of failure mode based on EDA simulation[C]. Prognostics and System Health Management Conference. IEEE, 2011:1-7.
[9] Shao X, Li X. A New Approach of Determining Critical Components in Electronic Systems Based on the Theory of Po F[C]. Fourth International Symposium on Computational Intelligence and Design. IEEE, 2011:266-270.
[10] Chen Liying, Ye Xuerong, Lv Mingdong, Hu Yongrun, Liao Xiaoyu, Zhai Guofu. Study of the Multiple Faults Quantitative Injection System for Switch Mode Power Supply and Its Applications[C]. ICREPEC2017.
[11] Zhou Yuege, Zheng Huiming, "Electro thermal coupling modeling for SMPS based on iSIGHT platform", *Electric Machines and Control*, 2017(10).
[12] Wünsche S., Clauß C., Schwarz P. Electro Thermal Circuit Simulation Using Simulator Coupling[J]. IEEE Transactions on Very Large Scale Integrat VLSI System, 1997, 5(3):277-282.
[13] Chen Liying, "Research on testability design of switching mode power supply considering uncertainty." [D]. 2018.
[14] M. Ershov et al., "Degradation dynamics, recovery, and characterization of negative bias temperature instability," *Microelectronics Reliability*, vol. 45, no. 1, pp. 99-105, Jan 2005.
[15] Li Xiang, Li Dailin, Ye Xuerong, Zhai Guofu, "Research on Performance Degradation Model of Aluminum Electrolytic Capacitor in LED Switching Power Supply", *Journal of Power Supply*, 2012(6): pp. 51-54.
[16] Li Xiang, "Research of degradation parameters monitoring and lifetime prognosis method for LED drivers", [D]. Harbin Institute of Technology, 2012.
[17] Haley S B. Large change response sensitivity of linear networks[J]. *IEEE Transactions on Circuits & Systems*, 1980, 27(4): pp. 305-310.

Yifan Hu was born in 1994. He received the B.S. and M.S. degrees from the College of Aerospace and Civil Engineering, Harbin Engineering University, Harbin, China, in 2016 and 2019, respectively. He is currently pursuing the Ph.D. degree with the School of Electrical Engineering and Automation, Harbin Institute of Technology, Harbin, China.

His current research interests include fault diagnosis of mechanical and electrical products, prognostics and health management, accelerated test technology, and reliability analysis.

Xuerong Ye (M'11-SM'18) received the B.S., M.S., and Ph.D. degrees in electrical engineering from Harbin Institute of Technology, Harbin, China, in 2003, 2005, and 2009, respectively.

He is currently a professor in the Department of Electrical Engineering, Harbin Institute of Technology. He has published more than 20 peer-reviewed journal papers. His research interests include the failure analysis, reliability design, and fault diagnosis of mechanical and electrical products.

Vibration Signal Analysis of Miniature Circuit Breaker Based on Empirical Mode Decomposition

Xingyu Wang, Changchun Chi, Xian Zhang
School of Electrical Engineering, Shanghai Dianji University, shanghai, 201306
E-mail: 1226480933@qq.com Tel: 18298222099

***Abstract*—Mini-circuit breaker, as a terminal electrical appliance, is one of the most important switching electrical appliances in the distribution network. If the fault occurs, it will seriously affect the personal and property safety of users. Therefore, the research on fault diagnosis of miniature circuit breakers is of great significance and value. The operating mechanism of miniature circuit breaker will form vibration wave with certain regularity and conduct along the mechanical mechanism when it is in action. In this paper, the empirical mode decomposition method is used to analyze the breaking and closing vibration signals of miniature circuit breakers, so as to extract their state characteristics and provide a reliable basis for fault detection of circuit breakers.**

***Index Terms*—Miniature circuit breaker, Fault diagnosis, Vibration signal, Empirical modal decomposition**

I. INTRODUCTION

The vibration signal of miniature circuit breaker has the characteristics of nonlinearity,nonstationarity and nonperiodicity[2]. In this paper, theempirical mode decomposition method is used to analyze the vibration signal of minicamp. Empirical Mode Decomposition (Empirical Mode Decomposition, the EMD for short) is a method of adaptive signal processing, 1998 by NordenE.Huang[3], able to complex nonlinear signal is decomposed into several Intrinsic Mode Function is relatively simple (the Intrinsic Mode Function, referred to as the fund), each IMF contains frequency components related to analysis of frequency, the most important thing is that the frequency components changes over the signal itself. In the field of fault diagnosis, this method has been widely used and achieved good results.

II. INSTANTANEOUS FREQUENCY AND EIGENMODE FUNCTION

Usually it is generally accepted that frequency is only interested in righteousness, and under the condition of global and instantaneous frequency is a kind of local basic capacity, suitable for non-stationary signal analysis. The instantaneous frequency are defined as follows: in general, for the complex signal:

$$x(t) = a(t)e^{-j\phi(t)} \tag{1}$$

or real number signal:

$$x(t) = a(t)cos\phi(t) \tag{2}$$

The instantaneous frequency is:

$$f(t) = \frac{1}{2\pi}\frac{d\phi(t)}{dt} \tag{3}$$

Most signals are more complex and changeable frequency component, contains many useless component, such as noise makes the instantaneous frequency in small circuit limits the application of vibration signal processing. If the analysis of complex vibration signals can only be conducted under the global condition, it has no significance[4].

For the above problems,N.E.huangetal. defined the necessary conditions for instantaneous frequency: a function or signal must be symmetric with respect to the local zero mean, and the number of extremum points and crossing zeros must be consistent. And thus puts forward the Intrinsic Mode Function (the Intrinsic Mode Function, referred to as the fund), and provides the necessary condition to satisfy the IMF[5]:

(1) Throughout the time sequence, the data sequence of extreme value point and the number of passing zero differ at most one.

(2) At any time in the time series, the mean value of the upper and lower envelope constructed by local maximum point and local minimum point must be zero.

Figure 1 shows a typical eigen mode function. It can be seen from the figure that the number of zero crossing points and extremum points of the signal are equal, and the envelope of maximum and minimum values is symmetric about 0, satisfying the two necessary conditions of eigen mode function.

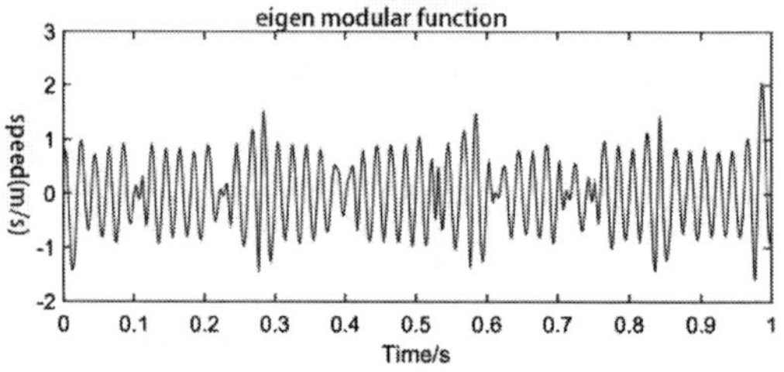

Fig. 1 A typical intrinsic mode function

III. EMPIRICAL MODAL DECOMPOSITION(EMD) METHOD

IMF conditions were obtained under ideal conditions. N.E.Huang hypothesis and others according to the problem: all of the complex signal can be decomposed into several independent of each other, linear or nonlinear IMF component; In any case, the original signal can be obtained by superimposing these IMF components on each other. On this basis, an EMD method for complex signals is proposed.

The EMD decomposition steps are as follows:

（1）. Calculate the original signal $x(t)$all the maximum points and minimum points, to the maximum and minimum points by cubic spline function fitting on the structure of the original signal envelope $X_{max}(t)$and the envelope $X_{min}(t)$.

（2）. The upper and lower envelope to calculate the mean, remember to$m_1(t)$, and the original signal $x(t)$minus the mean$m_1(t)$, get the $h_1(t)$, namely:

$$m_1(t) = \frac{[X_{max}(t) + X_{min}(t)]}{2} \tag{4}$$

$$h_1(t) = x(t) - m_1(t) \tag{5}$$

If under ideal conditions, when the $h_1(t)$are not satisfied with the IMF's conditions, the $x(t)$the first IMF component is the$h_1(t)$;

（3）. In general, $h_1(t)$ does not meet the conditions, then can be $h_1(t)$ as the original signal, the calculated according to (1), (2):

$$h_{11}(t) = h_1(t) - m_{11}(t) \tag{6}$$

Including: $m_{11}(t)$ -- $h_1(t)$ on the average of the envelope and the envelope:

If $h_{11}(t)$ is still not satisfied the IMF conditions, continued to repeat steps (1)~(3), until the first k times, meet the conditions, Get:

$$h_{1k}(k) = h_{1(k-1)}(t) - m_{1k}(t) \tag{7}$$

written:

$$c_1(t) = h_{1k}(t) \tag{8}$$

the $c_1(t)$ for signal $x(t)$ the first IMF component;

（4）. Will $c_1(t)$form$x(t)$separated, get:

$$r_1(t) = x(t) - c_1(t) \tag{9}$$

If $r_1(t)$ can also continue to decompose, will $r_1(t)$ instead of $h_1(t)$ as the original signal, repeat the above steps (1) ~ (3), until the final residual error sequence can be decomposed again can get all the residual:

$$\begin{cases} r_2(t) = r_1(t) - c_2(t) \\ \vdots \\ r_n(t) = r_{n-1} - c_n(t) \end{cases} \tag{10}$$

When $r_n(t)$ for a monotone function, can no longer decomposition, circulation end. Finally, the original signal can be expressed as:

$$\mathrm{x(t)} = r_n(t) + \sum_{i=1}^{n} c_n(t) \tag{11}$$

including: $r_n(t)$ -- the residual function; $c_n(t)$-- the IMF component;

The EMD method flowchart is shown in figure 2:

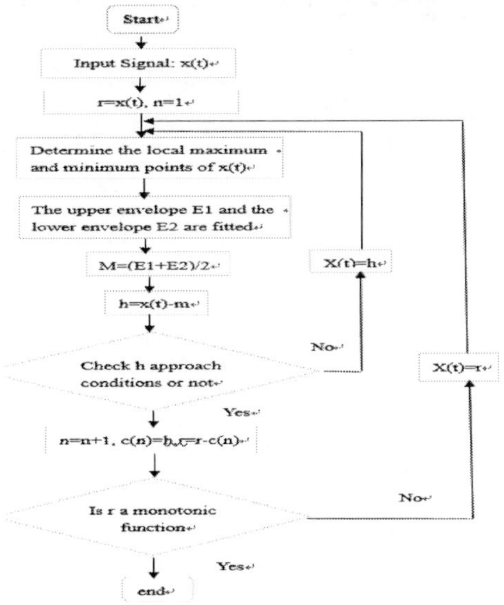

Fig. 2 EMD flowchat

The above process is called "screening", and the main purpose is to eliminate the amplitude of abnormal waves and smooth slip jitter[7]. If you do not set conditions for loop termination, the filtering becomes meaningless. In EMD algorithm, standard deviation is used as the final screening condition, and the calculation formula is:

$$SD = \sum_{t=0}^{T} \left| \frac{\left| h_{1(k-1)}(t) - h_{1k}(t) \right|^2}{h_{1(k-1)}^2(t)} \right| \tag{12}$$

When the value of SD is less than a certain set value, the "screening" process can be stopped, and the value is usually between 0.2 and 0.3[8].

Using (13) is shown in synthetic signal $x(t)$, demonstrate the EMD decomposition process, namely:

$$x(t) = sin(2\pi \times 10t) + sin(2\pi \times 50t) + sin(2\pi \times 100t), 0 \le t \le 1 \tag{13}$$

Its time domain waveform is shown in figure 3. According to equation (13), the signal is composed of three sinusoidal signals with different frequencies. The signal was decomposed according to the steps, and 3 IMF components and 1 residual component were obtained, as shown in FIG. 4. The three IMF components obtained by decomposition correspond to the sinusoidal signals of the three frequencies in equation (13) respectively, all of which have certain physical significance and correspond to the three components with frequencies of 100Hz, 50Hz and 10Hz respectively.

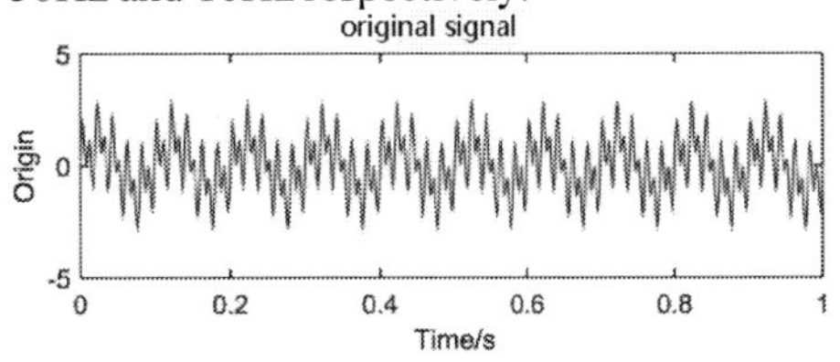

Fig.3 Simulation signal waveform

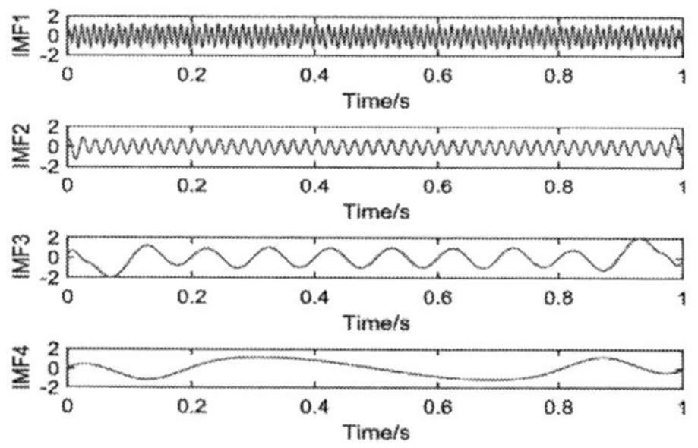

Fig. 4 EMD decomposition result of simulation signal

IV. SELECTIONOF EIGEN MODE COMPONENTS

As stated earlier, the signal after the EMD decomposition can be decomposed into several IMF component, but this component is false intrinsic mode components. The reason for this is that in the first step, the EMD decomposition of the original signal of the maximum and minimum points by cubic spline function to fit right, make a big shock in the endpoint, and form false intrinsic mode components.

Figure 5 shows the time domain waveform of a simple signal with a simple frequency structure consisting of only two sinusoidal components. EMD decomposition of this simple signal is carried out to obtain the result shown in FIG. 6. A total of 4 IMF components and a residual component are obtained by decomposition. As can be seen from FIG. 6, except for the first and second eigenmodule components (which correspond to two sinusoidal components of the signal respectively), the other three are all false IMF components, which are caused by the endpoint oscillation when calculating the upper and lower envelope of the signal, and must be removed to improve the anti-interference ability of the algorithm.

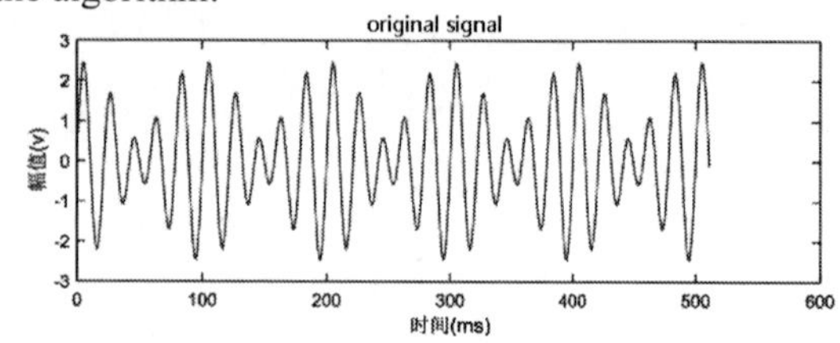

Fig. 5 Time domain waveform of a simple signal

Figure 5 is just a simple signal. In some complex actual vibration signals (such as the opening and closing vibration signals of miniature circuit breakers), the calculation of upper and lower envelope is more complex, which leads to the emergence of false eigenmode components, and these false components must be eliminated.

Since the IMF component is the expression of approximation of the original signal orthogonal, so really the IMF components must be with the original signal has good correlation, so the correlation can be as the basis, the IMF component and false reality to distinguish the IMF component, and finally merge the false the IMF component as part of the residuals. Before the algorithm run, need to the original signal and the IMF component normalized processing, finally get the IMF component beginning with the original signal correlation coefficient μ_i ($i = 1, 2,...n$), the following article statement judgment:

If $\mu_i \geq \lambda$

Keep the itha intrinsic mode components c_i

Else

out the ithc intrinsic mode components, and make$r_n = r_n + c_i$

λ in the conditional statement as a criterion, can be take as a fixed value, in addition to take:

$$\lambda = \frac{max(\mu_i)}{\eta}, i = 1,2,\cdots,n \tag{14}$$

Type of eta is a ratio greater than 1, here is 10.

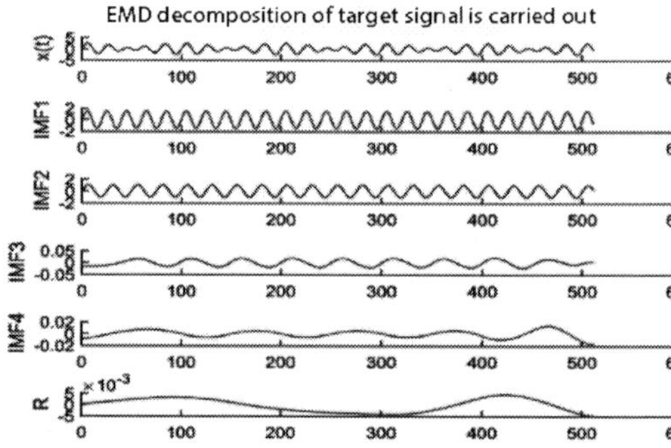

Fig. 6 IMF component and residual of thesignal

By applying the above method to the signal in FIG. 5, the correlation coefficients between the four eigenmode components and the original signal are finally obtained, as shown in table 1.

Table1 Correlation coefficient between 4 IMF components and original signal

	IMF1	IMF2	IMF3	IMF4
correlation coefficient	0.7358	0.7108	0.0487	0.0466

It can be seen that only the first two eigenmodule components have a good correlation with the original signal, while the other three IMF components have a poor correlation with the original signal. Through the above eigen component selection algorithm, only the first two IMF components are retained, and the rest are removed and added to the residual components. The final result is shown in figure 7. In the new residual component, the oscillation of the endpoint can be clearly seen.

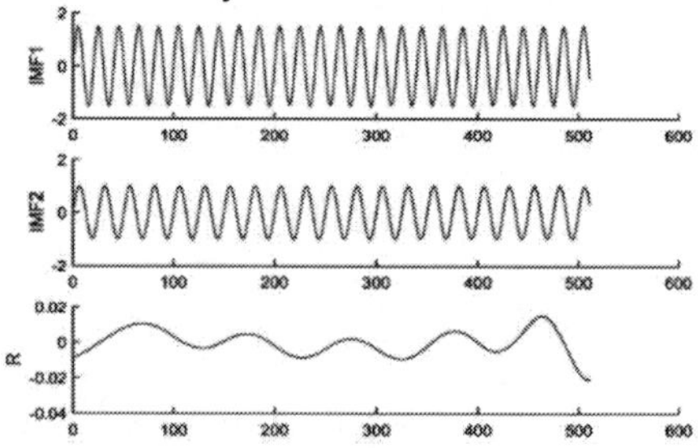

Fig. 7 Final result after eigenmode component selection algorithm

V. EMPIRICAL MODAL DECOMPOSITION AND CHARACTERISTIC ANALYSIS OF CLOSING VIBRATION SIGNAL OF MINIATURE CIRCUIT BREAKER

This paper takes ZS series miniature intelligent circuit breaker newly developed by zhengtai as the prototype, and adopts acceleration sensor to obtain the vibration signal of the three axes of circuit breaker when the circuit breaker is opening and closing. The experimental conditions are shown in FIG. 8. The 220V voltage is adjusted by the voltage regulator to make the voltage required by the circuit breaker. The vibration signal is transmitted to the upper computer through the signal acquisition device.

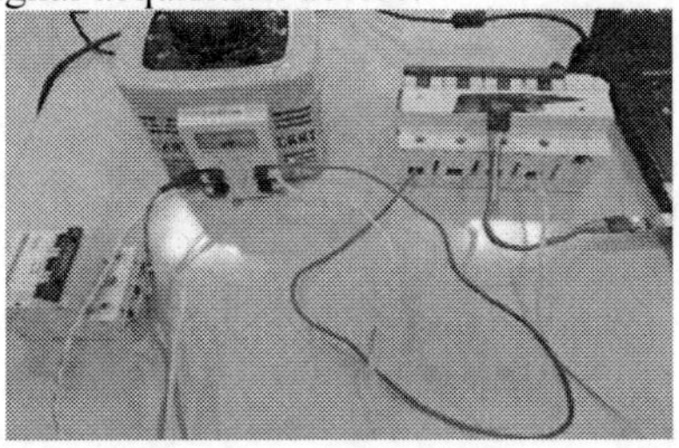

Fig. 8 Vibration signal acquisition experiment

Figure 9 shows the triaxial acceleration curve line of circuit breaker that automatically closes under normal state, and then the electric machine automatically returns to its position, and finally the tripping stops vibration after power failure. Here, vibration signal of z-axis (the top curve) is selected as EMD decomposition object.

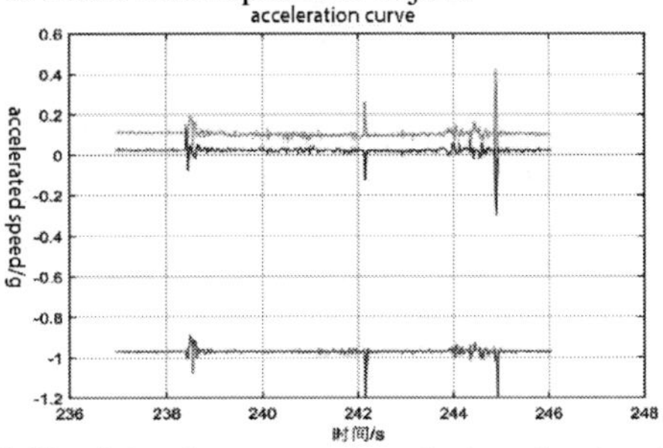

Fig. 9 Circuit breaker automatic reclosing vibration signal

First, the z-axis vibration signal in FIG. 9 is extracted separately, and its vibration curve is shown in FIG. 10.

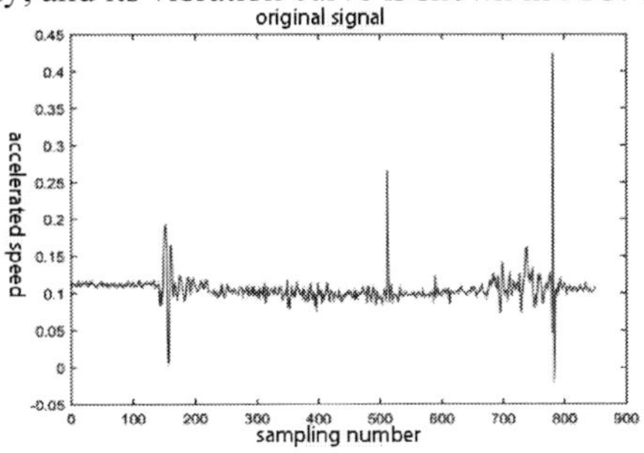

Fig. 10 Circuit breaker vibration signal and its spectrum

After analysis, its time amplitude characteristic curve is shown in FIG. 11. As can be seen from the figure, there are three stages of amplitude mutation. In this experiment, it corresponds to the closing, motor homing and tripping of miniature circuit breakers respectively. It can also be seen from FIG. 10 that the acceleration changes in these three stages are most obvious.

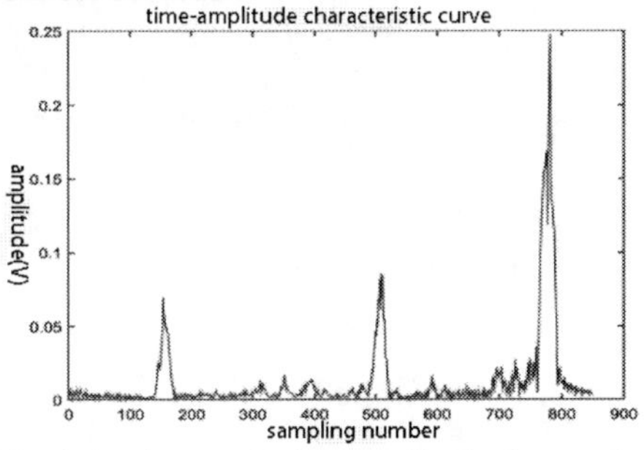

Fig. 11 Circuit breaker z-axis time-amplitude characteristic curve

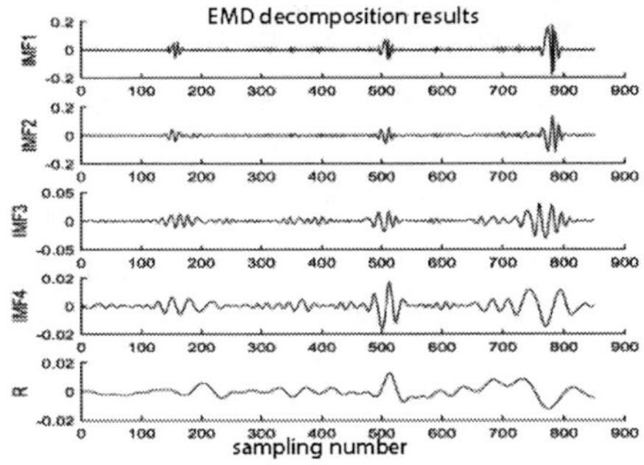

Fig. 12 Various order IMF components after vibration signal EMD decomposition

The vibration signal of miniature circuit breaker is decomposed by EMD to get several IMF components and a residual component. Since the order of the final components is not uniform, useful IMF components need to be selected for subsequent analysis. Four true IMF components and one residual component are extracted by applying the method of eliminating false IMF components proposed above, as shown in FIG. 12.

In order to verify the validity of the 4 order real IMF components, Fourier transform is adopted for spectrum analysis, and the signal is expanded in frequency order to observe its change rule, so as to obtain the amplitude and energy distribution in frequency domain. Spectrum analysis of original vibration signal of circuit breaker is shown in figure 13.

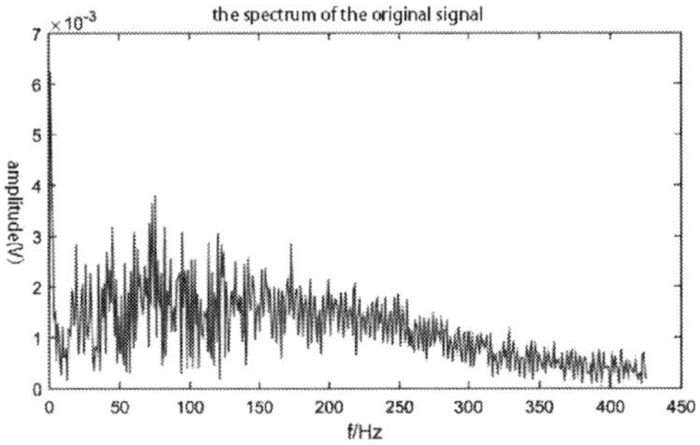

Fig. 13 Spectrum of the original vibration signal

From the spectrum of the original signal in figure 13, it can be seen that the energy of vibration signal of miniature circuit breaker mainly concentrates in the range of 20Hz~150Hz, among which the prominent part concentrates in the frequency points of 50Hz, 70Hz and 150Hz, which is mainly caused by the mechanical action collision of circuit breaker and the vibration caused by the motor rotation when the circuit breaker is opening and closing.

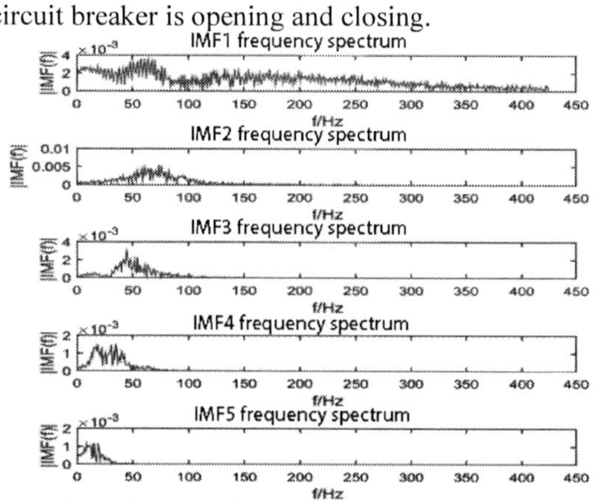

Fig. 14 Spectrum of each order IMF component

To compare the energy relationship between the original signal and the decomposed IMF components, spectrum analysis of IMF components of various orders obtained after EMD decomposition of the original vibration signal is conducted, as shown in FIG. 14, where IMF5 is the residual component of EMD decomposition. Compared with the spectrum analysis of the original signal, it can be seen that the spectrum energy of the vibration signal is mainly concentrated in the first four order components. From this, it can be concluded that the characteristics of the original signal can be obtained by analyzing the first four order IMF components of the circuit breaker.

The method of energy ratio is adopted to analyze the energy distribution of each IMF component[10], and the energy percentage of each IMF component in the original signal is shown in table 2. It can be seen from the table that the signal energy of imf1-imf4 accounts for 99.5% of the original signal energy, which further verifies the true validity of the 4-order IMF component.

Table 2 Energy share of each IMF component

IMF component	IMF1	IMF2	IMF3	IMF4	R
the energy radio	87%	8%	3%	1.5%	0.5%

VI. CONCLUSION

Miniature circuit breaker vibration signal feature extracting method was studied, the EMD decomposition method can realize the adaptive multiresolution analysis, have certain physical meaning of the component. The experimental simulation shows that the four-order IMF component decomposed by EMD contains almost all the energy of the circuit breaker vibration signal, which can correctly reflect the characteristics of the minicbreaker breaking and closing vibration signal, and can be used as the characteristic quantity of the state information of minicbreaker. It can also be applied to other kinds of fault identification, which has a good application prospect and engineering value, and further research needs to be carried out.

REFERENCES

[1] Changguang, Zhang Zhenqian, Wang Yi. Overview of vibration diagnosis for mechanical faults of high voltage circuit breakers [J]. Electrical drive automation,2013, 35(02): 41-44.

[2] Jian Huang, Xiaoguang Hu, Xin Geng. An intelligent fault diagnosis method of high voltage circuit breaker based on improved EMD energy entropy and multi-class support vector machine[J]. Electric Power Systems Research, 2011, 81(2).

[3] N.E.Huang. The empirical mode decomposition and the Hillbert spectrum for nonlinear and non-stationary time series analysis. Proceeding of Royal Society London, A, 1998(454): 903-995.

[4] Dai Haomin, Xu Aiqiang. Comparative study and improvement of instantaneous frequency calculation methods [J].Journal of Sichuan University (Natural Science Edition),2014, 51(06): 11971204.

[5] Lailing Hong, Wu Husheng, Lu Jianxin, et al. SVM recognition of rolling bearing faults based on EMD and sample entropy [J]. Coal Mine Machinery, 2011, 32 (01): 249-252.

[6] Li Ming, Li Tianrui, Chen Zhi, et al. Empirical modal decomposition of high-speed railway vibration data based on peak computing framework [J]. Computer Engineering and Application, 2016, 52 (20): 103-107+176.

[7] Liu Guizhong, Zou Shuangliang. Wavelet analysis and its application [M] Xi'an: Xi'an University of Electronic Science and Technology Press, 2001.

[8] Wu Zhe, Yang Shaop, Liu Yongqiang. Early Fault Diagnosis Method for Rotating Machinery Based on Multivariate Empirical Mode Decomposition [J]. Journal of Instruments and Instruments, 2016, 37 (02): 241-248.

[9] Hao Huan, Wang Huali, Wei Qin. Empirical mode decomposition theory and its application [J]. High-tech communications, 2016, 26 (01): 67-80.

[10] Sun Yihang, Wu Jianwen, Lian Shijun, et al. Extraction of characteristic vectors of circuit breaker vibration signals based on empirical mode decomposition energy total method [J]. Journal of Electrical Technology, 2014, 29 (03): 228-236.

Failure Analysis and Experimental Study of Railway Relay under Small Current

Xuerong Ye, Jun Tan, Yue Wang, Guofu Zhai
Reliability Institute for Electric Apparatus and Electronics
Harbin Institute of Technology, Harbin, 150001, China
E-mail: tanjun_ee@hit.edu.cn Tel: 86-451-86412976 Fax: 86-451-86412979

Abstract—**Railway Relay is one of the main electronic components in railway control systems for information detection, transfer, and power distribution, and its reliability will influence the reliability of the whole railway vehicle system. The traditional railway relay failure analysis method mainly focuses on the surface topography and pollution of the relay contacts, ignoring the structure and working principle of the relay itself. Therefore, in this paper, failure analysis and experimental research from a new perspective have been carried out on a certain railway relay which failed due to poor contact under small current. Firstly, the possible failure causes of contacts are obtained by testing basic parameters such as contact resistance and contact pressure, and analyzing the failure mechanism of poor contact with small current. Then, considering the working principle and operating environment of relays, the main causes of contact failure are further determined by static and dynamic characteristics testing of the relay and analysis of the scanning electron microscope (SEM) and X-ray energy spectroscopy (XES) results of its surface. Finally, suggestions on the optimization of railway relay are put forward from the aspects of structure and working conditions according to the failure analysis result. The proposed failure analysis process and test scheme are also applicable to the optimization and improvement of other electrical products.**

Index Terms— **Railway relay, poor contact, surface topography, working principle, failure analysis**

I. INTRODUCTION

Railway relays are widely used in the high-speed train (HST) electronic system for signal transmission, power distribution, control, circuit isolation and load transfer. With the rapid development of the HST, its safety and reliable operation have become very important. As a crucial control element in the HST electronic system, the railway relay failure endangers the safety of the HST, and even leads to accidents. Therefore, it is of great significance to study the failure analysis methods and optimization design for railway relays.

Usually the current of the HST load circuit is small, and poor contact of railway relays under small current, which reflects as the contact resistance oversteps standard, leads to 70% of the HST accidents according to feedback data in recent years. Traditional failure analysis methods are based on observing the contact surface with the naked eye, or using devices such as the optical microscope. Using this method, the intuitive failure information is obtained, but some failure causes involving contact microstructure and composition are difficult to obtain. To address these problems, some scholars have made investigations into the physical and chemical characteristics of the corrosion film between the contacts, which is caused by the diffusion of the contact region. Most of these investigations have focused on the failure mechanism of the contacts. However, the working principle and operating environment of relays are ignored. Still a complete experiment process has not been established.

Therefore, considering the structure and working principle of the relay itself, failure analysis and experimental research from a new perspective have been carried out on a certain railway relay that failed due to poor contact under small current in this paper. Suggestions on the optimization of railway relay are put forward correspondingly. The proposed failure analysis process and test scheme are also applicable to the optimization and improvement of other electrical products.

II. FAILURE ANALYSIS PROCESS

The research object of this paper is a certain type of railway relay, which is used in a automatic door-switch system of HST. The basic structure of railway relay is shown in Fig. 1. When the control loop is not excited, permanent magnet attracts left armature so the whole system remains in the state shown in Figure 1, and normal closed contact closes. Otherwise, right coil generate electromagnetic attraction making right armature rotate and normal open contact closes. There are return springs on the top of left and right armatures, which provide return force and serve fixed function.

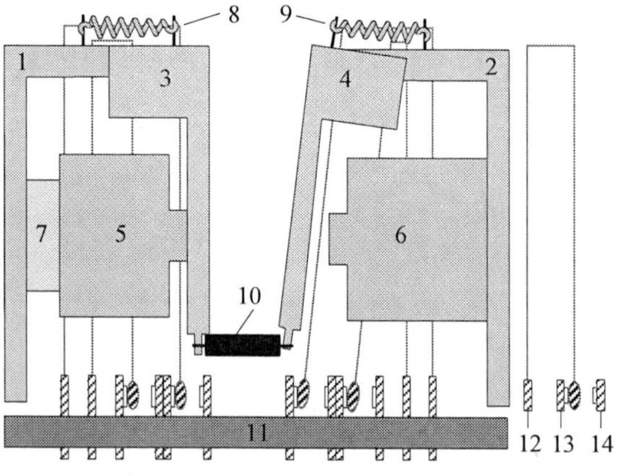

1-Left yoke, 2-Right yoke, 3-Left armature, 4-Right armature

5-Left coil, 6-Right coil, 7-Permanent magnet, 8-Left spring

9-Right spring, 10-Connecting bar, 11-Baseboard

12-Moving contact, 13-Static contact of normal closed contact

14-Static contact of normal open contact

Fig. 1 Basic structure of railway relay

The characteristic parameters of the railway relay are shown in Tab. 1.

Tab. 1 Characteristic parameters of the railway relay

Characteristic parameter	Required value
Left coil resistance	1488Ω
Right coil resistance	2182Ω
Rated control voltage	110VDC
Rated contact current	1mA
Contact resistance	≤50mΩ

First, through the contact resistance test, the poor contact is locked; then the relevant performance of the contact is tested, combined with the working principle and operating environment of the relay, the failure mechanism of the relay is analyzed, and the relay optimization suggestion is given. The failure analysis process is shown in Fig. 2.

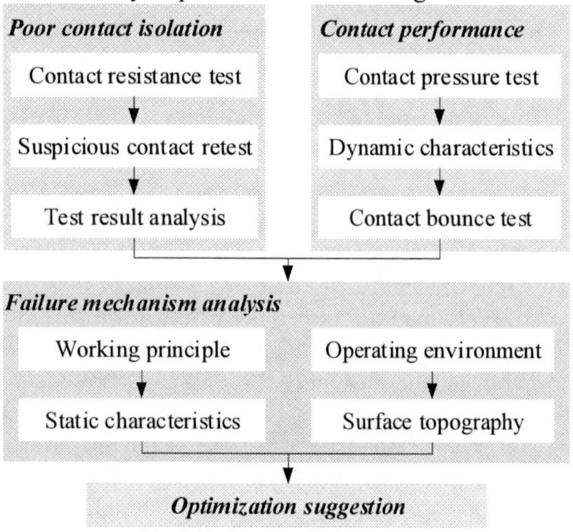

Fig. 2 Failure analysis process

III. EXPERIMENT PROCESS AND RESULTS

A. Contact resistance test

Initially researchers don't know which contact has failed, and four-line method is used to measure contact resistance. Contacts that have abnormal contact resistance are locked as poor contact. The circuit diagram of four-line method is shown in Fig. 3.

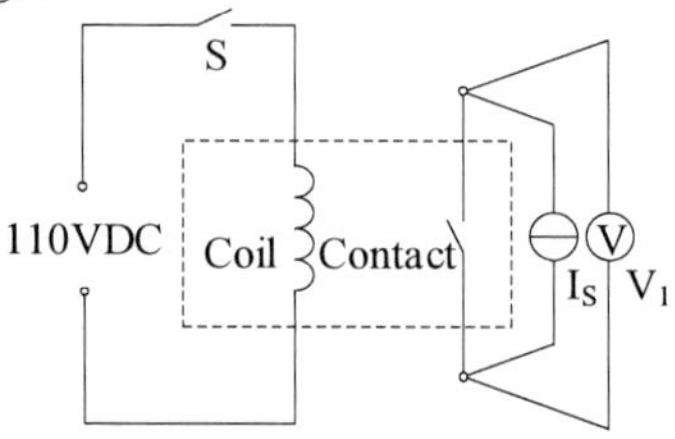

I_S-Current source, V_1-Digital nanovoltmeter

Fig. 3 Circuit diagram of four-line method

Under the contact current of 1mA, 10 times repetitive contact resistance tests' result of 8 normal open contacts is listed in Tab. 2.

Tab. 2 Contact resistance test result

Contact No.	Mean/mΩ	Standard deviation/mΩ
1	15.19	1.11
2	13.65	0.99
3	16.02	0.93
4	11.78	3.31
5	**96.48**	**26.24**
6	14.34	0.25
7	**1349.81**	**438.15**
8	14.21	0.22

From the analysis of the table above, we can see that:

1) The contact resistance of normal contacts is between 10 and 20mΩ.;
2) The contact resistance of No.5 and No.7 are larger than others;
3) The contact resistance of No.7 is over 1Ω, it is most likely to be a poor contact.

Then the contact resistance of No.2, No.5 and No.7 under different current is tested, and the result is shown in Fig. 4.

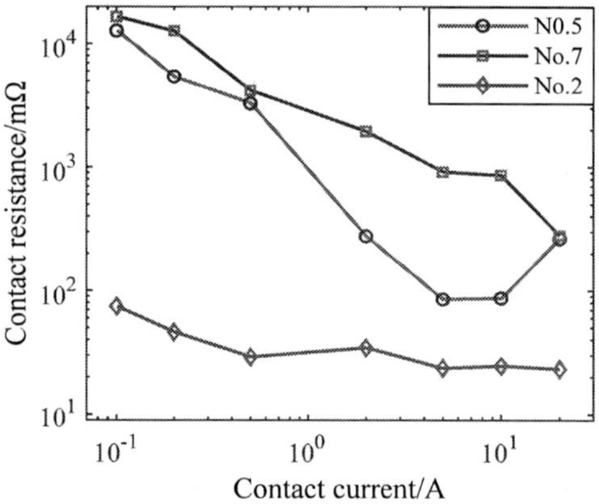

Fig. 4 Contact resistance under different current

From the figure we can conclude that:

1) As the test current decreases, the contact resistance increases correspondingly;
2) For normal contact No.2, the contact resistance tends to be stable when current is greater than a certain value;
3) For No.5 and No.7, the contact resistance is larger at low current, and the contact resistance of No.7 is larger than that of No.5. The contact resistance of No.5 decreases faster at high current.

B. Contact pressure test

The contact pressure is a adjusting parameter in the manufacturing process of the relay. Unreasonable design and deviation of the manufacturing process will result in bad contact pressure. The contact pressure is a important factor that affects the contact resistance of the contact.

A high precision dynamometer is used to conduct 10 times repetitive contact pressure tests of 8 normal open contacts, and test result is shown in Fig. 5.

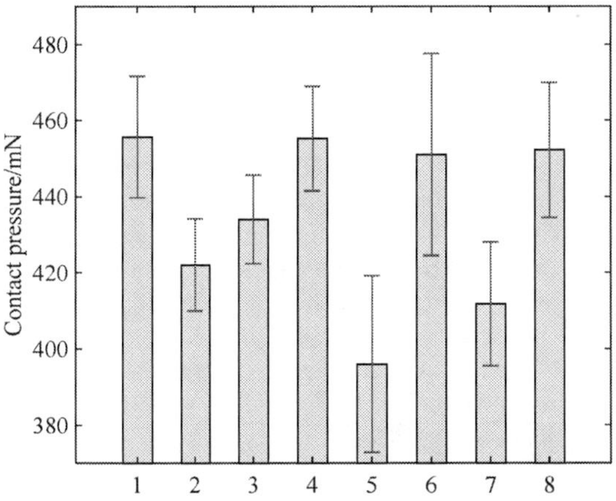

Fig. 5 Contact pressure test result

After analysis we can know:

1) The contact pressure of the normal contact is about 450mN, and the contact pressure of the fault contact is about 410mN;
2) The contact pressure of the contacts No.5 and No.7 is smaller than the normal contact.

C. Dynamic characteristic test

The dynamic characteristics of the relay refer to the dynamic change process of the coil current, the contact voltage, etc. during the energization of the coil, and include many features that reflect the performance of the relay and the contact. At the same time, when the relay is actuated, there are 8 sets of moving contact closures at the same time. The early closed contact provides a certain reaction force for the rear closed contact, which also has a great influence on the contact performance.

Therefore, by constructing the test circuit in Fig. 6, the

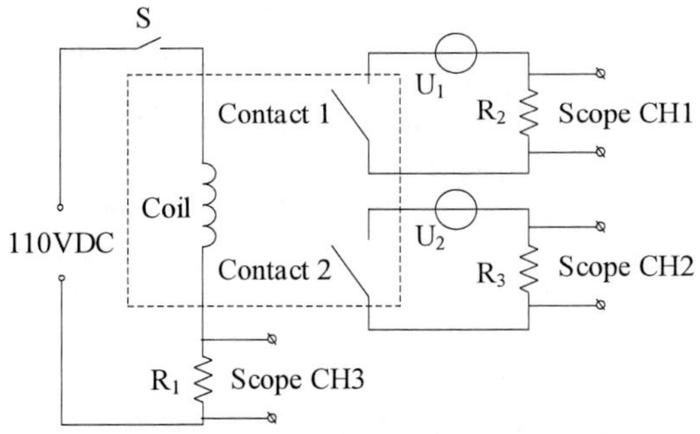

Fig. 6 Dynamic characteristic test circuit

contact voltage and coil current is monitored, and the motion consistency is analyzed.

The contact voltage and coil current waveforms are shown in Fig. 7, and the contact motion consistency test result is shown in Fig. 8.

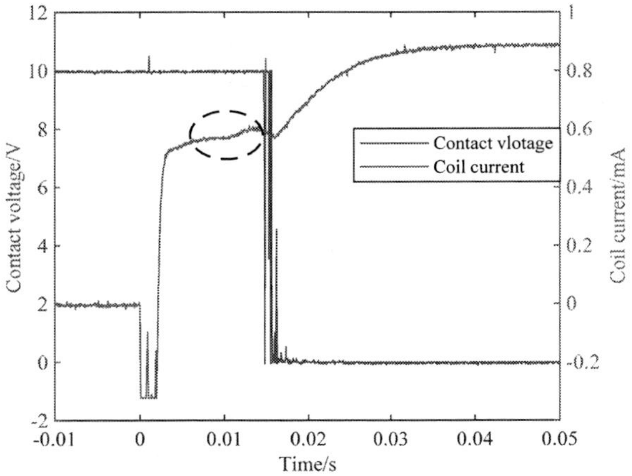

Fig. 7 Waveform of contact voltage and coil current

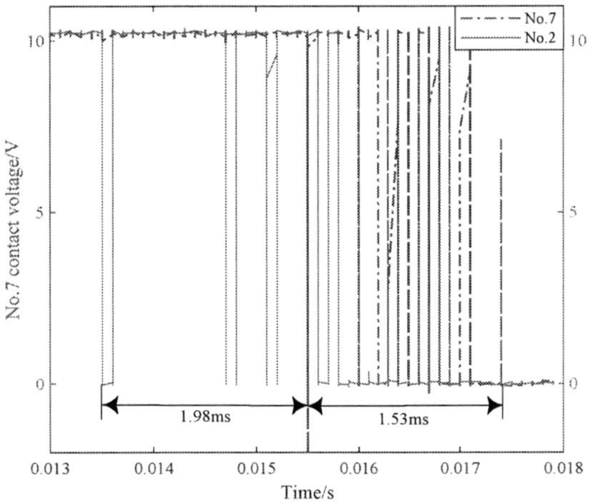

Fig. 8 Contact motion consistency test result

From the waveforms above analysis, we can see that:

1) In Fig. 7, there is a process of decreasing the rise of the coil current in the dotted line, indicating that the

movement of the armature has two steps of absorbing, that is, there is a pause in the movement of the armature.

2) In Fig. 8, the time difference between the movements of the contacts No. 2 and No. 7 driven by different armatures can reach 2ms, and No. 2 is closed earlier than No. 7.

3) In Fig. 8, the contact bounce time is about 1.5ms, and the action time difference has a great influence on the contact over-travel and contact pressure.

D. *Static characteristic test*

The reaction force of the contact-spring system and the attraction force of the electromagnetic system accomplish the switch function of the relay. The dynamic parameters such as speed, movement and release time of the relay, and the bounce of the contact, the intermediate position, etc. are all related to the cooperation of the attraction and reaction characteristics. The reaction force characteristics are determined by the requirements of the contact circuit parameters and the mechanical capability. In order to ensure the fit, it is necessary to design suitable attraction characteristics.

The test process is shown in Fig. 9.

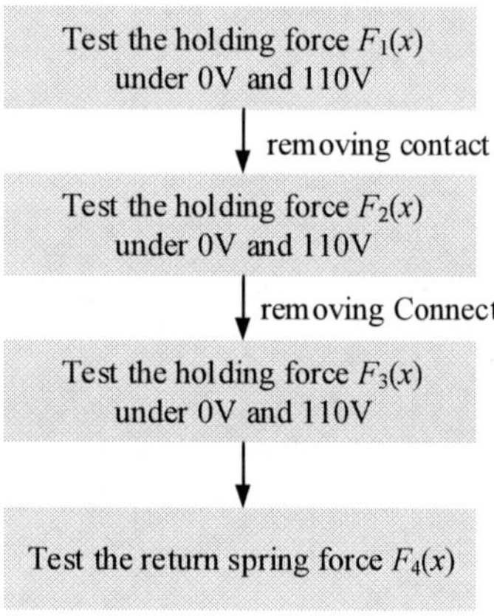

Fig. 9 Test process of static characteristic

And the attraction and reaction characteristics can be calculated according to eq. (D.1) to eq. (D.6).

$$F_{\text{Spring}}(x) = F_4(x) \tag{D.1}$$

$$F_{\text{Contact}}(x) = F_1(x)|_{U=0\text{V}/110\text{V}} - F_2(x)|_{U=0\text{V}/110\text{V}} \tag{D.2}$$

$$F_{\text{Magnet}}(x) = F_1(x)|_{U=0\text{V}} - F_{\text{Contact}}(x) - F_{\text{Spring}}(x) \tag{D.3}$$

$$F_{\text{Contact}}(x) = F_1(x)|_{U=0\text{V}/110\text{V}} - F_2(x)|_{U=0\text{V}/110\text{V}} \tag{D.4}$$

$$F_{\text{Reaction}}(x) = F_{\text{Spring}}(x) + F_{\text{Contact}}(x) \tag{D.5}$$

$$F_{\text{Attraction}}(x) = F_{\text{Magnet}}(x) + F_{\text{Coil}}(x) \tag{D.6}$$

The static characteristic of the relay is the relationship between the electromagnetic attraction and the reaction force of the contact-spring and the displacement or rotation angle of the armature. The calculated curve is shown in Fig. 10.

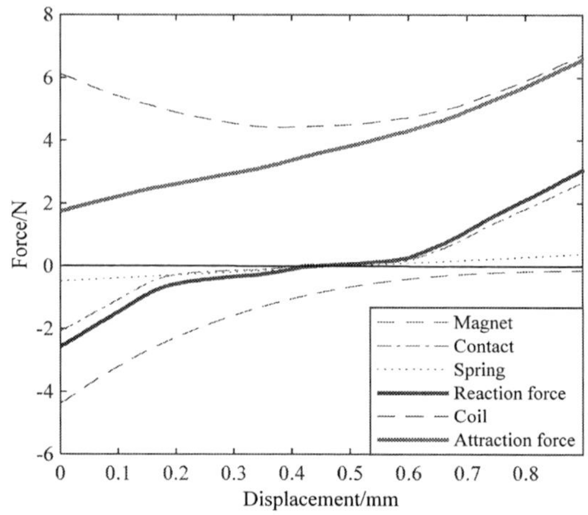

Fig. 10 Static characteristic of the relay

It can be seen from the test results that the margin between the attraction characteristic and the reaction force characteristic is large, which provides space for the optimization of the contact reaction force.

E. *Surface topography*

Scanning electron microscope and X-ray energy spectroscopy analysis are performed on the contact surfaces of the movable contacts (No.2, No.5 and No.7) and static contacts of No.7. The test point regions for energy spectrum analysis are divided into two categories: outer uncontacted area and inner contact area. The inner contact area is divided into a pollution serious area and a corresponding comparative reference with less pollution, the specific spot position is shown in Fig. 11.

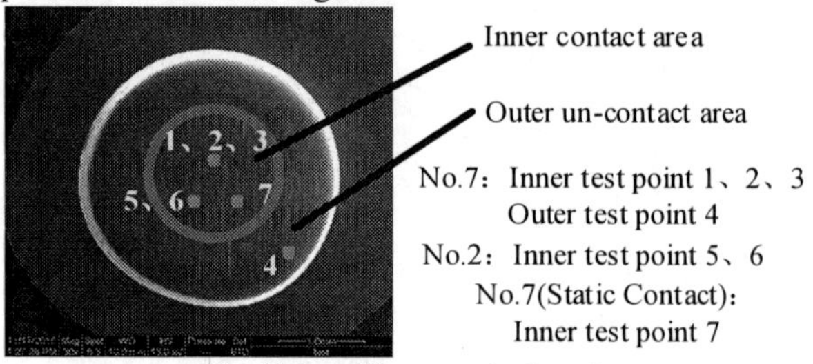

Fig. 11 Specific test point location

The results of the scanning electron microscope are shown in Fig. 12 to Fig. 15.

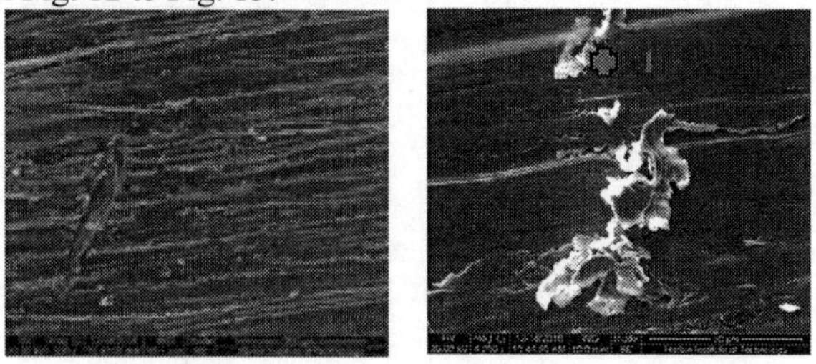

a) Contact area b) Enlarge of contact area 1

Fig. 12 Contact No.7 test result 1

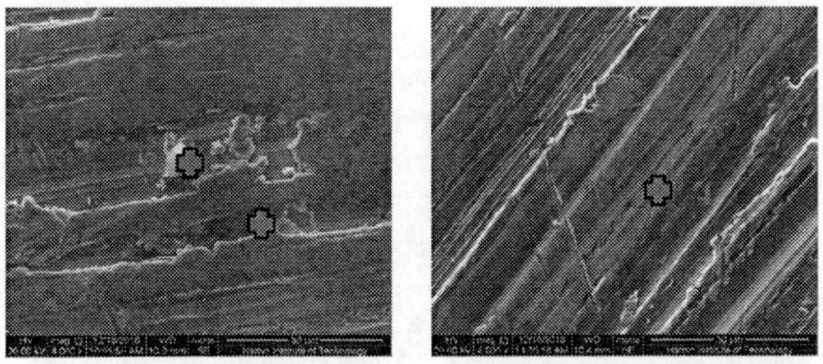

a) Enlarge of contact area 2　　　　b) Un-contact area

Fig. 13 Contact No.7 test result 2

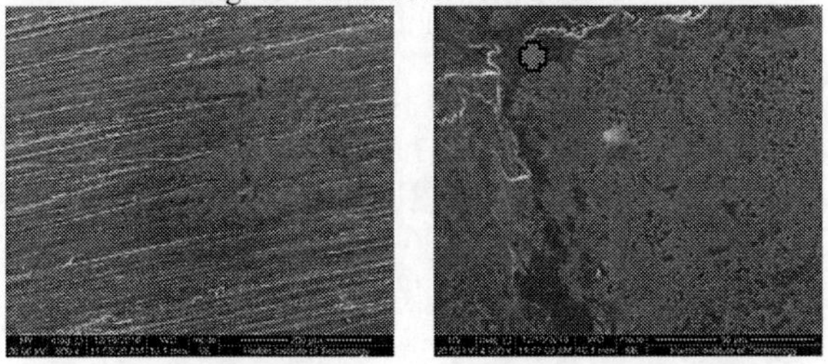

a) Contact area　　　　b) Un-contact area

Fig. 14 Contact No.5 test result

a) Contact area　　　　b) Un-contact area

Fig. 15 Contact No.2 test result

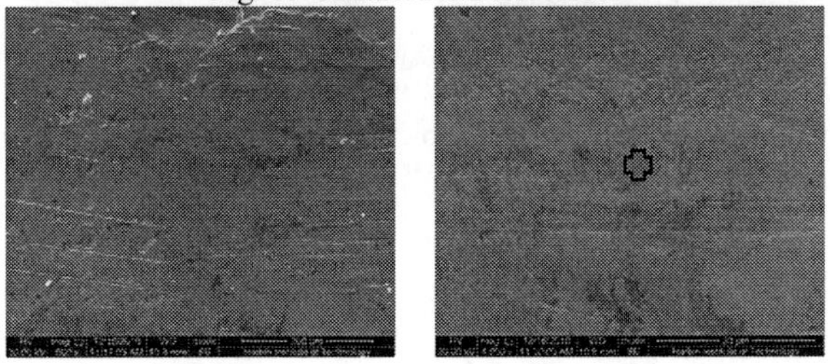

a) Contact area　　　　b) Un-contact area

Fig. 16 Static contact of No.7 test result

Analyzing the electron microscope scan image above, we can see:

1) From Fig. 13 b), the surface of the movable contact has been sanded by the sandpaper, and the un-contact area also retains the unevenness of the sandpaper after grinding;
2) From the comparison of Fig. 13 b), Fig. 14 a) and Fig. 15 a), the traces of sanding in the middle contact part are flattened during the collision with the contact, but still left after the sandpaper is polished.
3) From Fig. 12 a), Fig. 12 b), Fig. 13 a) and Fig. 14 a), Fig. 14 b), it can be seen that the surface of the movable contact corresponding to No. 7 is more worn and contaminated;
4) It can be seen from Fig. 16 a) and Fig. 16 b) that the surface of the No. 7 static contact is intact, the inner contact area is basically not distinguished, and the contaminant is also less than that of the moving contact.

The X-ray energy spectroscopy test is performed on the points indicated in Figs. 12 to Figs. 16, and the results are shown in Figs. 17 and Figs. 18.

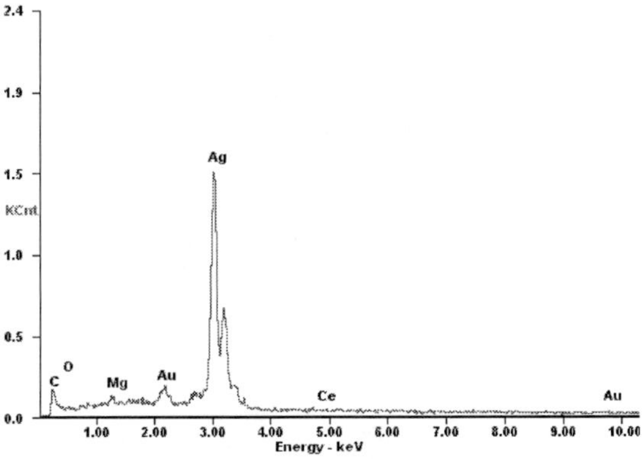

Fig. 17 X-ray energy spectroscopy test results

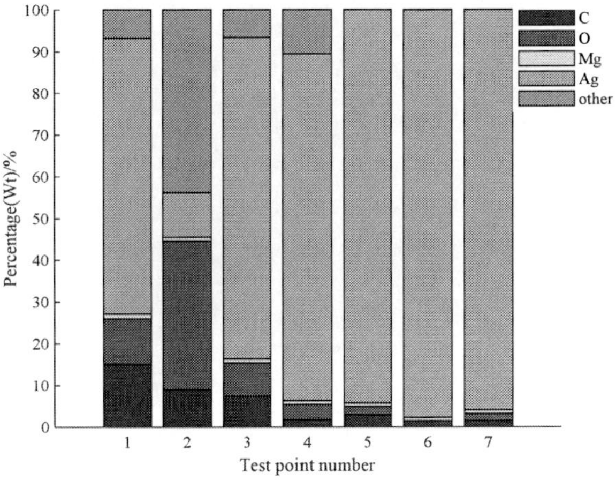

Fig. 18 Element percentage ratio

From the analysis of the X-ray energy spectroscopy test results, we can know:

1) From the analysis of the test points 1~3 of the contact No.7, C and O content are more, the corresponding pollution is more, and the total content of other pollutants is more;
2) According to test point 4, the un-contact area of the contact periphery is less polluted;
3) From the comparison of test points 5~6, the C content of contact No. 2 is between 1% and 3%, and the Ag content is relatively high, the other pollutant content is very small, and the contact pollution is less;
4) It can be seen from test point 7 of the No. 7 static

contact, surface has a small C content, and the Ag content is high, and the relative surface contaminants are less.

IV. FAILURE MECHANISM ANALYSIS AND OPTIMIZATION

A. Contact resistance increase mechanism

As shown in Fig. 19, it is the fault tree analysis (FTA) of the relay contact resistance overstepped standard.

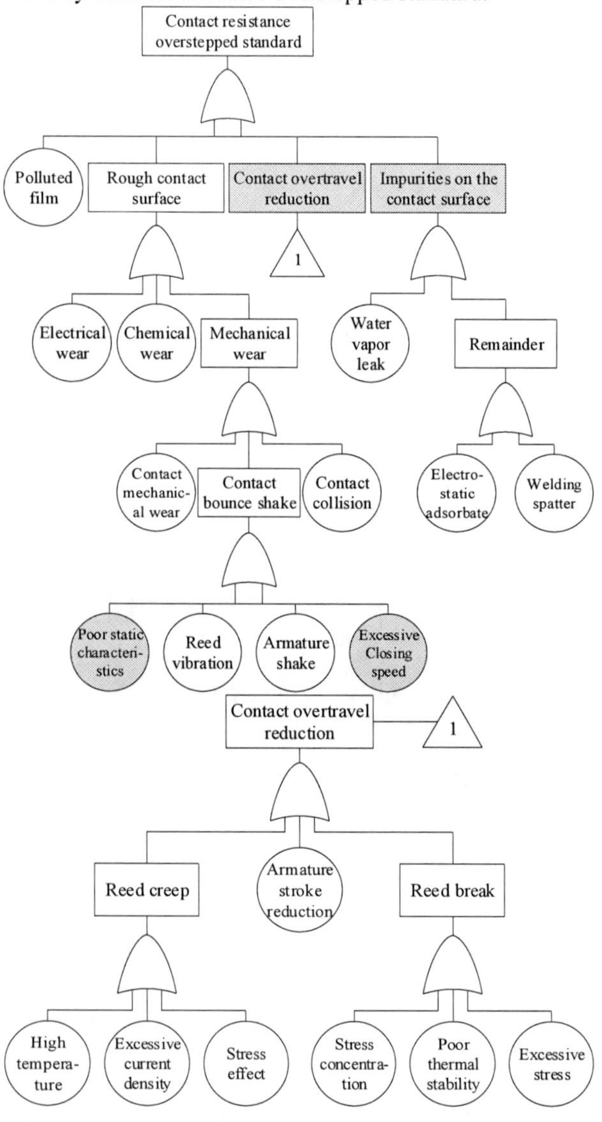

Fig. 19 FTA of the relay contact resistance overstepped standard

Combined with the results of the previous test analysis, we can see that:

1) A small contact pressure may be an innate cause of a small contact overtravel, resulting in a large contact resistance;
2) Unreasonable attraction force-reaction force collaboration and the contact closing speed is large, cause the contact bounce to be large, which is the main reason for the mechanical wear of the contact and the contact resistance overstepped standard.
3) The non-sealed working environment of the relay causes various contaminants and impurities on the contact surface, which leads to the increase of the contact resistance.

In addition, the increase or failure of the contact resistance of the contact is caused by the fretting friction of the contact and the erosion of harmful substances around the surface. The working current has a certain destructive effect on the surface of the contact surface. The larger the working current, the more obvious the melting and impacting of the contaminants, and the contact resistance is reduced.

B. Optimization suggestion

Through the above analysis, the following optimization suggestions are given to the relay:

1) Monitor the manufacturing process of the relay to ensure the consistency of the contact pressure debugging;
2) Optimizing the attraction and reaction force characteristics of the relay to reduce the contact closing speed of the relay;
3) Seal the relay or ensure the sealing of the environment in which it is used.

V. CONCLUSION

Relay failure analysis is the premise and basis for relay design and optimization. This work proposes a test scheme and failure analysis procedure for the problem of poor contact at low current, considering working principle and use environment. Still the requirements for the design, manufacturing and use of relays are put forward. This is also helpful for other products and can be widely used in the design and optimization of electromechanical products.

ACKNOWLEDGMENT

This work was supported by the National Key R&D Program of China [grant number 2017YFB1300800] and the National Natural Science Foundation of China [grant number 61671172].

REFERENCES

[1] H. Liang et al., "Structure classification of electromagnetic relays and comparison of typical magnetic system containing permanent magnet," *60th IEEE Holm Conference on Electrical Contacts.*

[2] J. Q. Liu et al., "A Reliability Assessment Method for High Speed Train Electromagnetic Relays,", *Energies*, vol. 11, no. 3, p. 15.

[3] K. Li et al., "Test and analysis of reliability for electromagnetic relay," *Electrical Contacts-2000: Proceedings of the Forty-Sixth Ieee Holm Conference on Electrical Contacts*. New York: Ieee, 2000, pp. 79-82.

[4] C. Gao et al., "Failure analysis for electromagnetic relay contacts adhesion by using XES," *2014 Prognostics and System Health Management Conference*, pp. 97-101.

[5] X. R. Ye, Q. Yu, and G. F. Zhai, "Reliability Assessment for Electromagnetic Relay Based on Time Parameters Degradation," *2010 11th International Conference on Electronic Packaging Technology & High Density Packaging*. New York: Ieee, 2010, pp. 1269-1272.

[6] M. B. Read et al., "Contact Resistance in Flat Thin Films," *Proceedings of the Fifty-Fifth Ieee Holm Conference on Electrical Contacts*. New York: Ieee, 2009, pp. 300.

[7] T. Tamait, "Effect of humidity on growth of oxide film on surface of copper contacts," *Ieice Transactions on Electronics*. vol. E90C, no. 7, pp. 1391-1397.

[8] J. Huang et al., "Internally oxidized silver contact materials- a case for the elastoplasticity of an inhomogeneous body," *Crystal Research and Technology*, vol. 44, no. 10, pp. 1147-1155.

[9] C. P. Wu et al., "Microstructure of internally oxidized layer in Ag-Sn-Cu alloy," *Corrosion Science*, vol. 50, no. 12, pp. 3508-3518.

7th International Conference on Reliability of
Electrical Products and Electrical Contacts,
November 04-06, 2019

Study of Arc Root Commutation Performance in Interrupting Process with Rate Current for MCCB

Tiansheng Zhu[1,2], Cheng Wang[2], Hongwu Liu[2], Ruiliang Guan[2]
[1]State key laboratory of Electrical Insulation and Power Equipment, Xi'an Jiaotong University, Xi'an, 710049
[2]Changshu Switchgear Mfg. Co., Ltd., (Former Changshu Switchgear Plant) & Jiangsu Key Laboratory of Smart Grid Distribution and Utilization Technology Research, Changshu, Jiangsu, 215500, China

Abstract—**Arc stagnant process can greatly influence the electrical durability of circuit breakers. When the arc stagnation time is shorter, the electrical durability of the circuit breaker is higher. So it's important to investigate how to decrease the arc stagnation time for arc moving process. In this study the arc root commutation process of flat-plate type static contact is investigated, and the effect of electric field distribution to the arc behavior is analyzed. By using high-speed CCD camera the arc root commutation process is captured and the simulation results are verified by experiments.**

Index Terms—MCCB, Interrupting process, Arc root, Commutation

I. INTRODUCTION

In the interrupting process of low-voltage circuit breaker, the arc is generated between the contacts and the arc keeps static for a certain period, which is named as arc root stagnation time ti. In waveform of arc voltage, ti is the time from contacts separating moment t0 to arc voltage suddenly jumping moment t1. The voltage jumping moment t1 can greatly influence contact erosion which depend the electric durability of the circuit breaker. The faster arc commutation speed from the contact to the arcing plane means the lower contact erosion and higher electric durability. In previous studies the parameters affecting commutation speed were studied such as: 1) magnetic field near the contacts area, 2) opening speed of the moving contact 3) contact material 4) configuration and material of arc chamber 5) surface morphology and conditions of the contact. There are few studies investigating effect of electric field distribution to the arc commutation process and arc stagnation time. In this study two types of static contacts with different structures are tested. The arc root commutation process and stagnation time are measured by experiment. Based on electric field distribution, the arc root commutation and arc moving process are analyzed. The simulation of electric field distribution of the arc can be verified by experiment results.

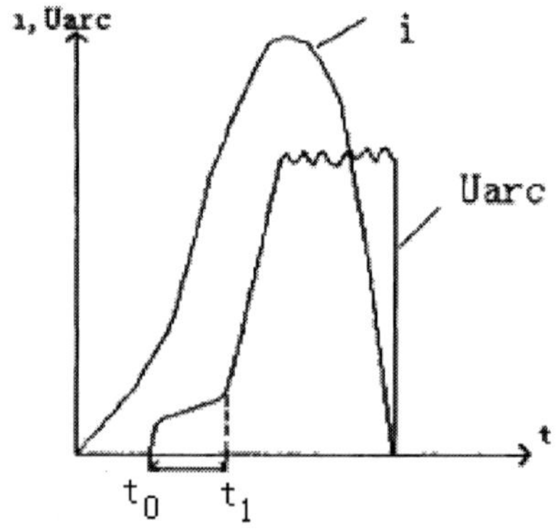

Fig. 1 Define of arc stagnation time

II. ANALYSIS OF ARC ROOT COMMUTATION PHENOMENON IN STATIC ELECTRIC FIELD

For static electric field, the free electric charge is driven by external electric field and the current is generated in conducting medium. The fundamental equations can be written as:

$$\begin{cases} \nabla \times E = 0 \\ \nabla \bullet J = 0 \\ J = \gamma E \\ \nabla^2 \varphi = 0 \\ I = \int_s J \bullet dS \end{cases} \quad (1)$$

Here: E = electric field intensity, J = current density, γ = conductivity, φ = electric potential, I = conduction current

As shown in Fig 2(a), the static contact is U type structure and the arcing plane is installed in the right of the static contact. The gap between the moving and static contacts is d1, the distance between the end of moving conducting rod and arcing plane is d2. For electric durability test the arc generates between the contacts when the moving and static contacts are separated. Because of the same electrical potential of the arcing plane and static contact, the electric field gradient between the contacts is always higher than it between the end of the moving conducting rod and the arcing plane. For U type static contact, magnetic force is used to help the arc commutate to the arcing plane. In Fig 2(b) for the flat-plane type of the static contact, when the open angle of moving rod is relatively small, it means d1<d2 and the electric field gradient between the contacts is higher than it between the end of the moving conducting rod and the arcing plane. It's disadvantage for arc commutation. When the open angle of the moving rod increases, the electric field gradient between the contacts is less than it between the end of the moving conducting rod and the arcing plane. Furthermore by considering gas blowing effect, most of the high plasma is distributed between the end of the moving conducting rod and the arcing plane. It will induce the increase of resistance between the moving conducting rod and the arcing plane, which will increase the conducting current flowing through the gap. So the arc root commutation is easier to realize from the static contact to the arcing plane.

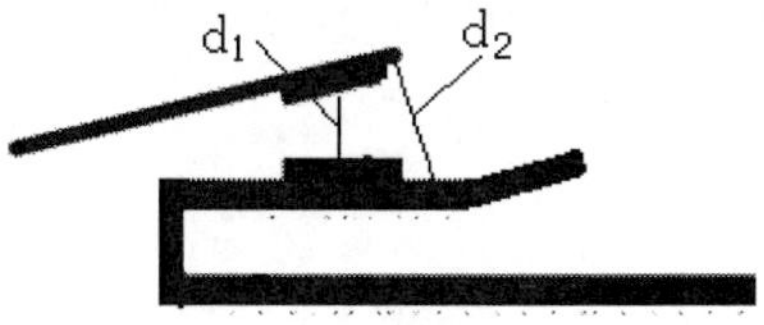

(a)

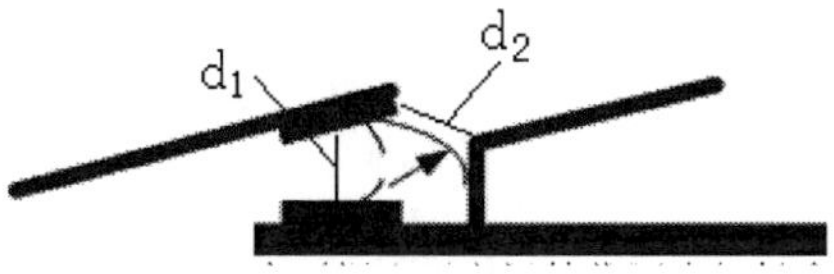

(b)

Fig. 2 Schematic diagram of contact system

III. SIMULATION OF ELECTRIC FIELD

A. Electric intensity distribution of U type contact system

As shown in Fig.3, by calculating electric intensity distribution of U type contact system, high electric intensity region can be plotted during open process of the moving rod. For U type contact system, electric intensity between the end of the moving rod and arcing plane is relatively low. So the magnetic force dominantly drives the arc to commutate.

B. Electric intensity distribution of flat-plate type contact system

Electric intensity distribution of flat-plate type contact system is plotted in Fig. 4. When the moving rod opens to a certain angle, high electric intensity region distributes between the end of the moving rod and arcing plane. Then the arc root can commutate from the gap between contacts to the arcing plane.

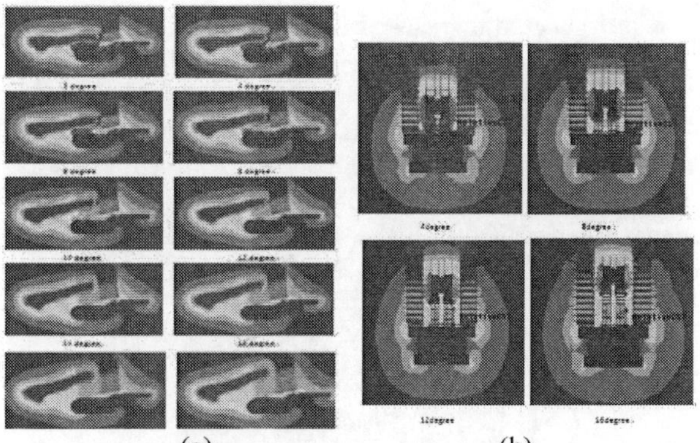

(a) (b)

Fig. 3 Electric field intensity of flat-plate type contact system

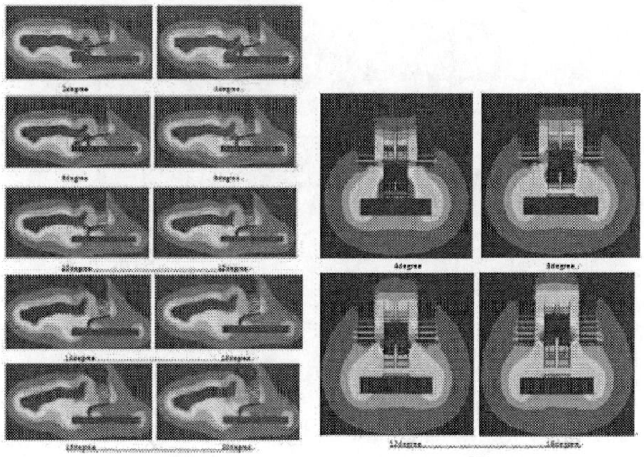

(a) (b)

Fig. 4 Electric field intensity of flat-plate type contact system

IV. COMMUTATION PROCESS OF ARC ROOT

The arc chamber with U type static contact system is represented in Fig 5(a). In this contact system, there isn't any inner arc chamber inside it. The arc chamber with flat-plate type static contact system is represented in Fig 5(b). Transparent plastic material is used for the inner arc chamber, in which the arc can be captured by high speed CCD camera.

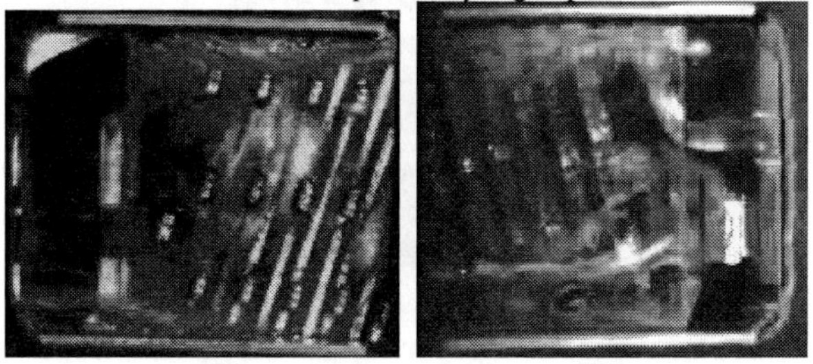

(a) (b)

Fig. 5 Physical model of contact system

A. Analysis of arc commutation process for U type contact system by high speed CCD camera

As shown in Fig.6 arc commutation process can be captured by high-speed CCD camera in electric duration test.

From arc generating between contacts to arc completely commutate to the arcing plane, the whole time is about 4ms. With the increase of angle of the moving rod, the arc ran into the metal splitters and was separated into short arcs in series. After the separating process, the short arcs re-struck in the entrance of splitters backwards. And the short arcs were generated in the leg of splitters. Finally the arc is driven into the splitters by magnetic force and the arc extinguished.

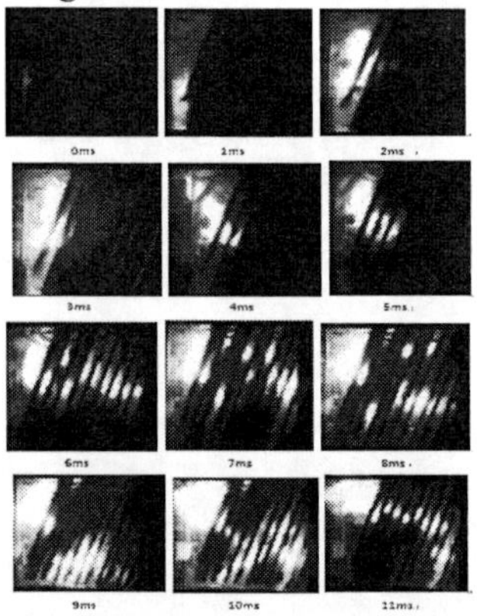

Fig. 6 Arc moving process with U type contact system

B. Analysis of arc commutation process for flat-plate type contact system by high speed CCD camera

From arc generating between contacts to arc completely commutated to the arcing plane, the whole time is about 5ms. At the time point t=6ms, the arc completed commutated to the arcing plane. And the arc was separated by splitters. By comparing U type contact system, the different phenomenon is that the arc didn't re-strike for the flat-plate contact system. The arc remained in the splitters until it extinguished finally.

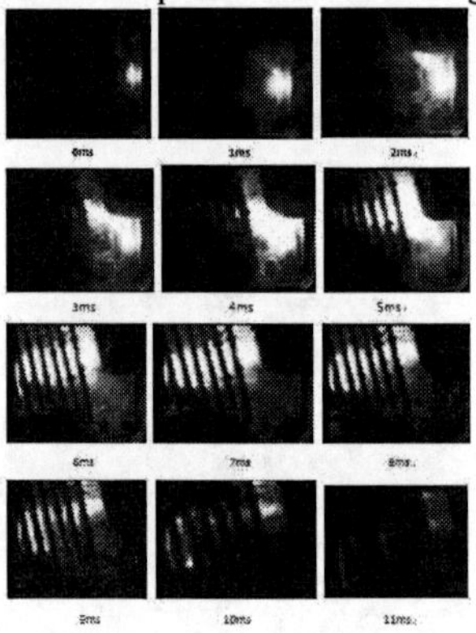

Fig.7 Arc moving process with flat-plate type contact system

V.CONCLUSION

In this study influence of electric field intensity distribution to the arc commutation is investigated. And two different types of contact system are used to analyze their arc commutation characteristics. By using high-speed camera to capture the arc moving and simulating the electric field distribution, following conclusions can be given:

1) In the open process of the moving rod, for U type contact system there are two high electric intensity regions. One is between the end of moving rod and entrance of splitters, and the other is between the sidepiece of the moving rod and leg of splitters. For flat-plate type contact system, high electric intensity regions are between the moving rod and bending area of the arcing plane, and between the sidepiece of the moving rod and leg of splitter. Electric breakdown may take place for above both contact systems.
2) By analyzing photograph of arc commutation process, the arc root commutation process is mainly influenced by magnetic field for U type contact system. For flat-plate contact system, arc commutation process is complete and obvious.
3) For U type contact system, arc re-striking phenomenon happened frequently between the moving rod and the leg of splitters. The arc moved backwards and stayed in the region near the leg of splitters for short time. For flat-plate contact system, after the arc is separated by splitters the arc always stayed in the arc chamber until it extinguished.
4) By comparing experiment results and simulation of electric intensity distribution, the conclusion can be given that the simulation results can partly predict arc root commutation path.

REFERENCES

[1] Chen Degui, interrupting arc and current limiting technology for low voltage circuit breaker[M] .

[2] Ji liang, Chen Degui, Liu Yingyi， Li Xingwen， Analysis of Influence of Two Static Conductors on the Interruption Performance of MCCB [J]Transactions of China Electrotechnical Society, 2010,25(8),46-51.

[3] Rong Mingzhe, Jia Wenhui, Wang Ruijun, investigate of characteristics of arc discharge between poles of low voltage apparatus.

First Author. Zhu Tiansheng was born in Hunan, China, in 1982. He received the B.S. and M.S. degrees in electrical engineering from Xi'an Jiaotong University, Xi'an, China, in2005 and 2008, where he is currently studying for the Ph.D. degree in electrical engineering. His research interests focus on low voltage apparatus.

7th International Conference on Reliability of
Electrical Products and Electrical Contacts,
November 04-06, 2019

Reliability Study on the Manufacturing and Test of Bimetallic Elements

Jiang Zhang, Longjiang Wang, Hengyang Wang
Shanghai Liangxin Electrical Co., Ltd., Shanghai, 201315, China
E-mail: zhangjiang@sh-liangxin.com Tel: 86-21-58628695 Fax: 86-21-23025781

Abstract—**For the problems in the unstable acting time with the delay characteristics during the manufacturing of thermomagnetic release for low-voltage circuit breaker, this article has described the principle, method and approach of the solution based on the research and analysis of the structural characteristics, manufacturing method and test approach of bimetallic element material for main parts, and raised a quick and convenient test method through theoretical computation, actual experiment and result analysis. While improving the productivity and guaranteeing the reliability of delay protection characteristics of the product, it ensures reliable operation of low-voltage circuit breaker in actual circuit.**

Index Terms— **Bimetallic element, Delay protection characteristics, Reliability, Resistance, Thermomagnetic release.**

I. INTRODUCTION

During the manufacturing of thermomagnetic release for low-voltage circuit breaker, there will be unstable acting time with delay characteristics in the batches. Such phenomenon happens mostly in case of too big or too small value of the acting time with delay characteristics, and sometimes it has gone beyond the scope of quality for the test parameters; thus during the manufacturing, some products might have unstable acting characteristics in batch production, or the parameter adjustment has narrow range and is difficult, thus influencing the production efficiency. The main reason for such phenomenon is the quality reliability problem with the bimetallic element material, and the process guarantee problem during the manufacturing of thermal release.

For such problem with quality reliability of bimetallic element material, this article has described how to develop the test approach according to the structural and manufacturing characteristics of bimetallic element, improve the test efficiency of bimetallic element while guaranteeing the test reliability of bimetallic element protection characteristics, increase the consistency and adjustability of the products in the production, improve the production efficiency on the basis of ensuring the reliability of product protection characteristics, and ensure reliable operation of the circuit breaker in actual circuit.

II. PROBLEM ANALYSIS

A. Structural characteristics of bimetallic material

Bimetallic material is a compound material, which is made by firm bonding of two or more layers of metallic alloy material with different temperature coefficient of expansion. The alloy layer with large coefficient of expansion is called active layer, and the alloy layer with small coefficient of expansion is called passive layer, and the intermediate layer (such as shunting layer) playing the role of regulating the resistance and the intermediate layer playing the role of process control (such as anti-diffusion layer: after preventing the process treatment, some metallic elements will diffuse into other layers, thus influencing the change of resistivity) will be added between active layer and passive layer.

It is in the flat and straight shape at normal temperature (about 25°C). It has thermal sensitivity, so in case of any change with the ambient temperature, it will produce positive or negative bending or turning with the change of the surrounding temperature because of different coefficients of expansion of active layer and passive layer.

In the low-voltage circuit breaker, it is an important function material for temperature test, temperature regulating and temperature compensation, and is widely used for the thermal overload protection of low-voltage circuit breaker.

B. Present situation and problems in the manufacturing method of bimetallic materials

The key process for manufacturing of bimetallic material is the compound process among the component layers.

Compound process includes fusion method, double casting method, hot rolling method, cold rolling method and explosion method and so on.

Common hot rolling method is to compound the blank in the component layers together at relatively high temperature by hot rolling with high pressure, followed by cold rolling.

The cold rolling method has the best compounding quality, that is, compounding the blank at relatively different component layers at normal temperature by cold rolling under high pressure, followed by conventional cold rolling. Thermo bimetal is generally stripy or in pieces. Such rolling method is equivalent to roll welding.

The advantage in the compounding with cold rolling is that it can produce very long strip in one time, and can realize very convenient and controlled matching of the component melting batch number with the produced bimetal. Up till now, it is universally recognized worldwide as the advanced manufacturing method of thermo bimetal and compound material……solid phase combination method at room temperature, which also belongs to the compounding by cold rolling.

Generally, bimetallic material is processed into the thickness in certain specification; finally, it is then rolled into the thickness as required by the end user. During the rolling, in case of any change with the rolling pressure on the two longitudinal sides, front and back of the stripy bimetal material, there is the problem or deviation with the welding quality in these positions during the rolling and compounding. Therefore, these positions are cut out; but compared with the intermediate position adjacent to these cut positions, its welding quality will be different. Such difference will have influence on the change of the acting characteristics of the bimetallic elements.

So, as for how to determine the size of the cut part and determine the difference in performance between the adjacent position and the intermediate position of the material, it shall be realized through certain test approach

C. Present situation and problems in the test method of bimetallic material

Since the flexivity, specific thermal deflection, modulus of elasticity and coefficient of resistance of thermo bimetal depend on the performance of thermo bimetal to a very large extent, the test of these characteristic parameters of thermo bimetal is quite important.

In the conventional test methods of the processed thermo bimetal element, except for many constant temperature bath or constant box methods, there is two-end resistance measuring method of thermo bimetal element, all in the form of spot check.

First method has relatively accurate data, but consumes too long time. This method has the related standard (GB/T 8364 - 2008 Test methods of thermal flexure of thermostat metals).

Second method has high speed, but has low data resolution. This method has the related standard (GBT 351-1995 Metallic materials—Resistivity measurement method).

But these two methods are incomplete for the test of the whole batch of materials, and easy with omission, bringing puzzlement to the batch production. This is also unbeneficial for automatic production in large scale.

III. SOLUTION

In the processing of bimetallic element materials, since the rolling method is often used, the manufacturing quality will inevitably influence the change of interface resistance, the poorer the welding quality, the bigger the interface resistance; the change of interface resistance will inevitably influence the change within the range of the delay characteristic acting time. Then how will the quality of the bimetallic element be screened, and what scheme is used for screening, thus not only guaranteeing the screening quality, but also improving the working efficiency?

According to the characteristics that the poorer the compound welding quality of bimetallic element material, the bigger the interface resistance, we can use the resistance test method. This article mainly makes the exploration with the resistance measuring method.

A. Test scheme

1) Test principle

The DC resistance with low resistance value is measured with Kelvin bridge method, usually four-wire test method for measurement of resistance at four contact points, also known as four-contact method.

Kelvin test method is used for the test of separate carrying current and voltage by electrical impedance or voltage measurement technique. The key advantage of four-wire measurement is separate current applying unit and voltage measuring unit, eliminating the impedance of wiring and contact resistance.

2) Shape of materials

Since the bimetallic element material is flat and straight in the embodiment, the shape of the material set for conventional bimetallic element is a structure of network resistance, and the brief diagram of the simulation resistance structure is shown in Figure 1.

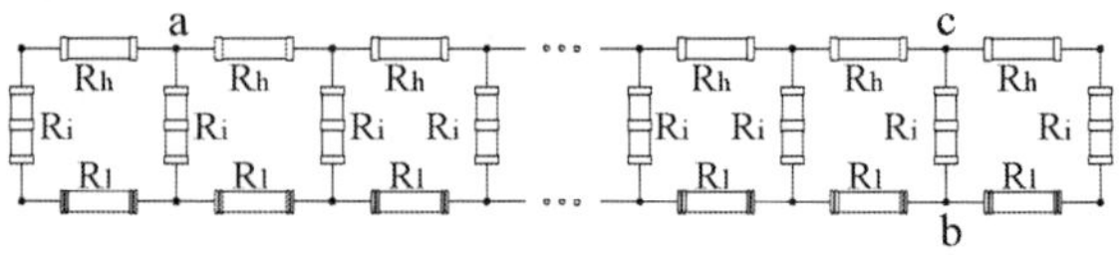

Fig. 1 Brief diagram for resistance structure simulation of bimetallic element

Rh is high expansion layer resistance, Rl is low expansion layer resistance, Ri is interface combination resistance.

3) Test position

The processing quality of bimetallic element has influence on the change of the interface resistance R high. The poorer the compounding quality, the bigger the resistance.

In the conventional test method, the test contact points have two contact means,

a) Two-point opposite and two-end test method, with points a and b shown in the brief diagram for structural simulation in Figure 1;

b) Two-end test method with two points in the same side (high expansion surface or low expansion surface), with points a and c shown in the brief diagram for the resistance structural simulation in Figure 1.

It may be seen from the figure that, different test contact means obviously correspond to different test results.

Since the processing means of bimetallic element material is rolling compound process, and the test method of two points in the same side cannot give very good feedback of the interface compounding of the bimetallic material, that is, change of resistance. Relatively speaking, the test method of two points in the opposite shall provide more reasonable feedback of the change of interface resistance of bimetallic material.

4) Theoretical computation

For argumentation about the advantages and disadvantages of the above two resistance test methods, the equivalent model of three-layer n-order resistance network is further simplified, as shown in Figure 2,

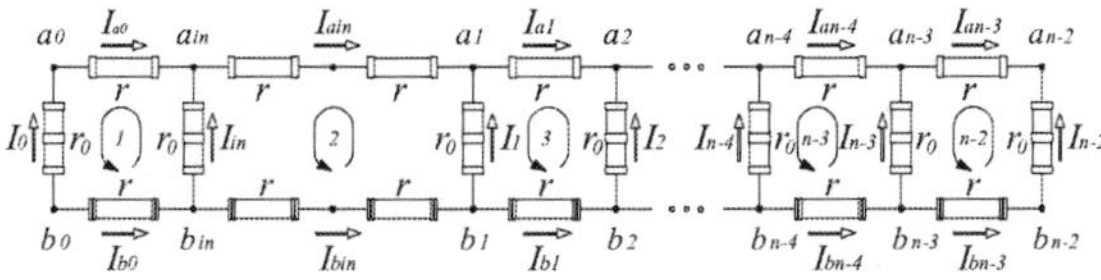

(a) Open circuit with one interface combination resistance

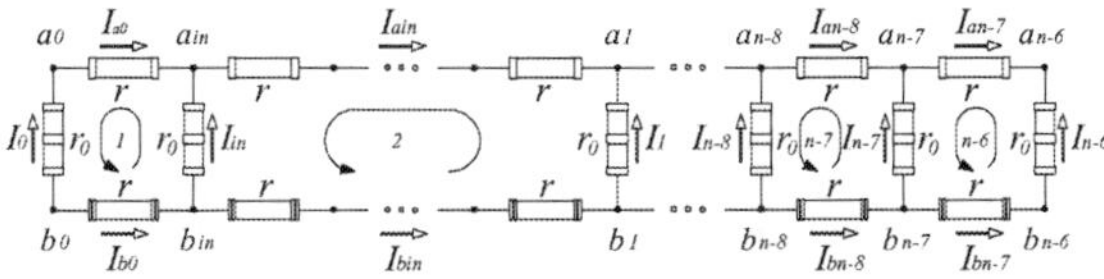

(b) Open circuit with five consecutive interface combination resistances

Fig. 2 Brief diagram for further checking computation

Suppose that Figure 2 (a) has the open circuit with one interface combination resistance, and Figure 2 (b) has the open circuit with five consecutive interface combination resistances.

The test contact points are:

(1) nodes a_{in} and b_{n-3}, two points in the opposite,

(2) nodes a_{in} and a_{n-3}, two points in the same side,

(3) nodes a_{in} and b_{n-7}, two points in the opposite,

(4) nodes a_{in} and a_{n-7}, two points in the same side.

Checking computation of the resistance values:

1. $R_a(a_{in}, b_{37})$,

2. $R_b(a_{in}, b_{33})$,

3. $R_a(a_{in}, a_{37})$,

4. $R_b(a_{in}, a_{33})$.

- For the two-end test method having two points in the opposite:

The circuit network analysis method is used. Suppose that current I is inputted between a_{in} and b_{n-3} of Figure 2(a), and current is inputted from a_{in}, and outputted from b_{n-3}, and it is possible to obtain differential equation model about current parameters (refer to Figure 3):

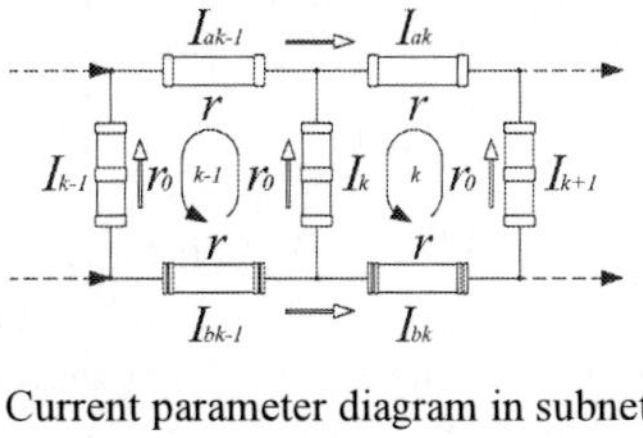

Fig. 3 Current parameter diagram in subnetwork

For network element k-1 and network element k, from Kirchhoff current law (KCL) and Kirchhoff voltage law (KVL), the formula can be inferred to obtain:

$$I_{k+1} = 2(1+h)I_k - I_{k-1}$$

From the reference [3], it can be solved to get:

$$I_k = \frac{1}{\alpha-\beta}\left[(I_2-\beta I_1)\alpha^{k-1} - (I_2-\alpha I_1)\beta^{k-1}\right],$$

$1 \le k \le n-2$,

Set $R_h = R_l = r = R_i = r_0$, n=40, the formula can be inferred to obtain:

$$I_k = \frac{\sqrt{3}}{6}\left\{\left[\left(2+\sqrt{3}\right)^{k-1} - \left(2-\sqrt{3}\right)^{k-1}\right]\times I_2 - \left[\left(2+\sqrt{3}\right)^{k-2} - \left(2-\sqrt{3}\right)^{k-2}\right]\times I_1\right\}$$

For network elements 1, 2 and 3, and network elements n-2 and n-3, since two nodes pass through two different paths, it is possible to get the voltage from Kirchhoff current law (KCL) and Kirchhoff voltage law (KVL), that is,

$$\begin{cases} U_{ain,bn-3} = -r_0 \times I_{n-3} + r\sum_{i=1}^{n-4} I_{ai} + 2r \times I_{ain} \\ U_{ain,bn-3} = -r_0 \times I_{in} + r\sum_{i=1}^{n-4} I_{bi} + 2r \times I_{bin} \end{cases}$$

$$I_{ai} + I_{bi} = I \text{ , } I_{ain} + I_{bin} = I$$

Finally, we can obtain:

$$R_{ain,bn-3} = \frac{U_{ain,bn-3}}{I} = -\frac{r_0}{2}\frac{(I_{n-3}+I_{in})}{I} + \frac{r}{2}(n-3)$$

- With the two-end test method with two points in the same side, it is possible to infer:

$$R_{ain,an-3} = \frac{U_{ain,an-3}}{I} = -\frac{r_0}{2}\frac{(I_{n-3}-I_{in})}{I} + \frac{r}{2}(n-3)$$

- It can be inferred and calculated with the above method to get:

1. Two-end test results with two points in the opposite:

$$R_a(a_{in}, b_{37}) = \frac{r_0}{2}\frac{(-0.2942 - 0.2942)I}{I} + \frac{r}{2}(40-3) = 18.794\,R\,;$$

2. Two-end test results with two points in the opposite:

$$R_b(a_{in}, b_{33}) = \frac{r_0}{2}\frac{(-0.2942 - 0.3541)I}{I} + \frac{r}{2}(40-3) = 18.824\,R\,;$$

3. Two-end test results with two points in the same side:

$$R_a(a_{in}, a_{37}) = \frac{r_0}{2}\frac{(-0.2942 + 0.2942)I}{I} + \frac{r}{2}(40-3) = 18.500\,R\,;$$

4. Two-end test results with two points in the same side:

$$R_b(a_{in}, a_{33}) = \frac{r_0}{2}\frac{(-0.2942 + 0.3541)I}{I} + \frac{r}{2}(40-3) = 18.530\,R\,.$$

From the above calculation results, it may be known that: 1. The test method with two points in the opposite will get larger resistance by comparison with the test method with two points in the same side; 2. The poorer the interlayer compound quality of bimetallic element material, the more the data value, that is, the bigger the resolution, the more beneficial for testing and screening.

On summary, the two-end test method with two points in the opposite can give more reasonable feedback of the interlayer compound quality of bimetallic material.

5) Test tools

The measurement precision depends on the tools for contact in the test to a very large extent, for example, in the meter resistance test, when the measurement position difference between two measurements is 1mm, there will be the tolerance of 0.1% for the test results. If the material less than 1m with irregular shape is tested, the test device becomes quite important. Generally speaking, Kelvin clamp is suitable for the wire test, and is not applicable for the section test or surface resistance test.

Kelvin probe is shown in Figure 4, and the needle tip is shown in Figure 5, the distance between the needle tip current end and sampling end is only 0.5mm, and the maximum diameter is only 2mm. The clamp has very small size tolerance, so it is very suitable for the surface resistance or the section resistance.

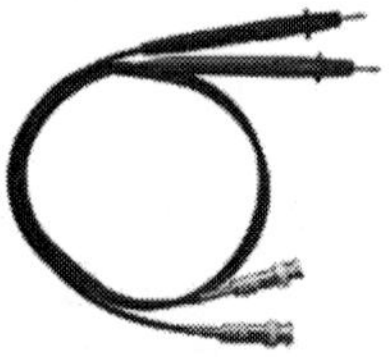

Fig. 4

Fig. 5

6) Determination of test scheme

From the analysis and comparison, the two-side and two-end test method with Kelvin probe shall be able to give more accurate feedback of the compound quality of bimetallic element material. We finally choose Kelvin probe for the test with two-end four-wire test method.

B. Test tooling

By fabrication of the dedicated test tooling, it is possible to improve the consistency and test efficiency of the test results, and avoid the interference of artificial factors.

The brief structural diagram of the dedicated test tooling is shown in Figure 6.

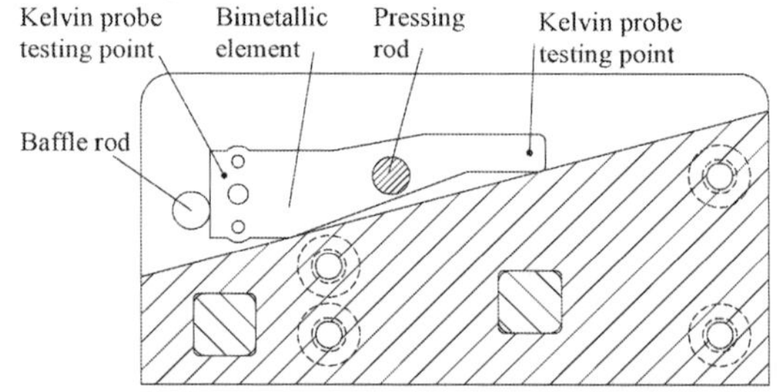

(a) Sketch for material placement and test point positions

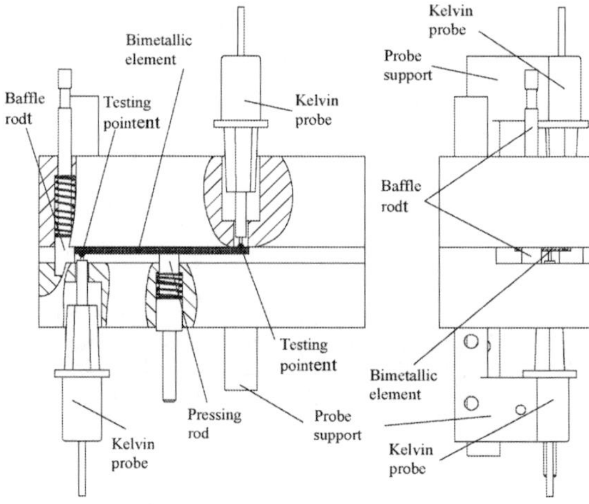

(b) Sketch for tooling structure

Fig. 6 Brief structural diagram of the dedicated test tooling

From Figure 6, it may be seen that the test points of Kelvin probe are distributed on the opposite sides at both ends of bimetallic element material. Bimetallic element material is fixed through the baffle rod and pressing rod on the dedicated test tooling.

Test process and principle: before the test, insert the baffle rod into the positioning hole, slide the bimetallic element material into the dedicated test tooling, for positioning before the baffle rod; then use the pressing rod to press the bimetallic element material, for fixing; contact Kelvin probe with bimetallic element material, for the test of the resistance value. After the test, Kelvin probe is disconnected, the pressing rod is released, then the baffle rod is released, and bimetallic element material slides off the dedicated test tooling.

The test point is positioned through the tooling, thus guaranteeing the rule of consistency for the positions of the test points for different test pieces.

IV. VERIFICATION

A. *Test requirements*

Requirements for acting characteristics of the circuit breaker in certain model: 1.05 times of the rated current does not act within 2 hours, and 1.30 times of the rated current acts within 2 hours.

The product with certain current specification shall pass the production test and verification, and the bimetallic element material complying with the adjustment range (the parameters of the acting characteristics complying with the range) has the equivalent resistance range: 3.93-4.21(mΩ).

B. *Test result*

We adopt the microhm-level intelligent DC low-resistance tester, two-side, two-end and four-wire test method with Kelvin probe, as well as the dedicated test tooling, and take 100 pieces of the sample from each for purpose of the test and comparison for bimetallic element material of this current specification produced with three bimetallic materials.

Test result:

Material A: 3.88-4.43 (mΩ); material B: 3.83-4.17 (mΩ); material C: 3.97-4.17 (mΩ).

Analysis is carried out in combination with bar chart and normal distribution curve, and the results are shown in the analysis chart of Figure 7.

C. *Result analysis*

From the analysis chart of Figure 7, it can be seen that, some test parameter values of bimetallic element material A have been beyond the range of the highest resistance value and lowest resistance value. In the production and commissioning, the acting characteristics of the product must act below 1.05 times of current and must not act under 1.30 times of current; some test parameter values of bimetallic element material B have been beyond the range of the lowest resistance value. In the production and commissioning, the acting characteristics of the product must act below 1.05 times of current; the test parameter values of bimetallic element material C are all within the reasonable range, and in the production and commissioning, the acting characteristics of the product must meet the requirements, the commissioning allowance is required, and there is very high reliability.

So it can be judged that the quality of bimetallic element material C can very well ensure the reliability of the acting characteristics of the product, and improve the production efficiency.

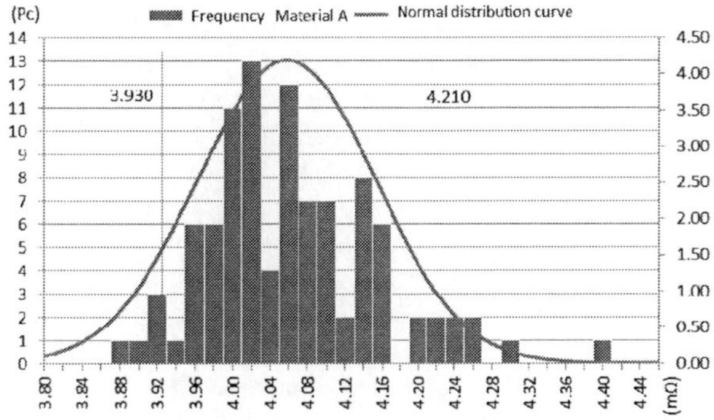

Bimetallic element material A

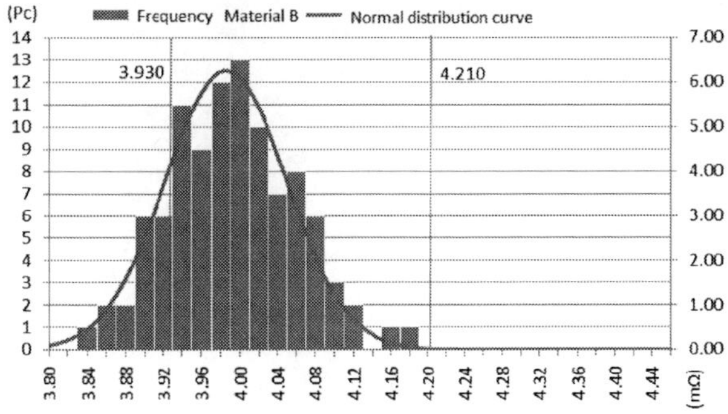

Bimetallic element material B

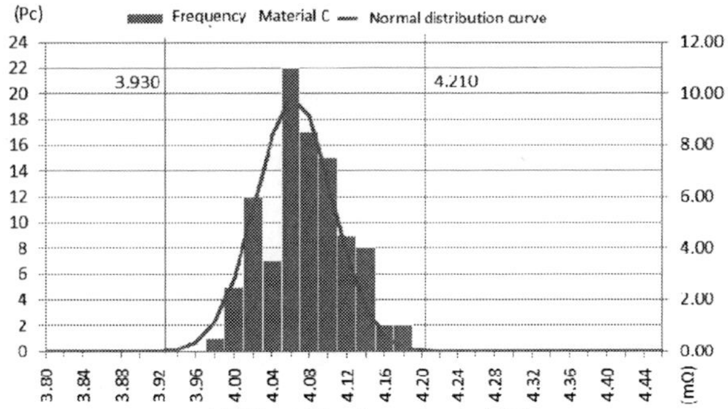

(c) Bimetallic element material C

Fig. 7 Analysis chart (microhm/pc, normal distribution curve)

D. *Production verification*

The circuit breaker product assembled and produced by using the bimetallic element material for this current specification with equivalent resistance value of 3.93-4.21 (mΩ), has passed through the production in the adjusting process with more than ten thousand products in multiple batches, on the basis of guarantee with reliable process during thermal release manufacturing, and the acting data concentrates on the intermediate range within proper range, and the delay acting characteristics are very stable and very good for adjustment. So the one-time pass rate is up to 100%.

V. CONCLUSION

The two-side, two-end and four-wire resistance test method with Kelvin probe is used; network resistance is used for theoretical computation, and the test piece will be chosen with more reasonable measurement points; scientific test tools are used, reasonable test tooling is then used, not only capable of significantly improving the test efficiency of bimetallic element material, but also capable of guaranteeing that the data fluctuation is within small range during the production and commissioning, so that the production and commissioning is easier for control. On the basis of guarantee with reliable process in the processing of thermal release, it ensures the correctness of the acting characteristics of the product, and finally improves the production efficiency to a maximal extent.

REFERENCES

[1] Test method for thermal bending of thermo bimetal: GB/T 8364-2008[S].2008.

[2] Measurement method of resistance coefficient of metallic material: GB/T 351-1995[S].2007.

[3] Tan Zhizhong. Resistance network model [M]. Xi'an: Xidian University Press, 2011.

[4] Lian Lizhi. Low-voltage electric appliance design and manufacturing [M]. Beijing: China Electric Power Press, 2003.

[5] Hope (Changzhou) Electronic Science and Technology Co., Ltd. Application of CHT3540 series in the material resistance field. 2009.

[6] Li Ziqi, Lu Quansheng, Liu Chao et al. Analysis and study on thermo bimetal element of miniature circuit breaker [J]. Electric appliance and energy efficiency management technology, 2017(11): pp.31-35.

Effect of Temperature Environment on Stress Relaxation of Spring Components within Hermetically Sealed Relay

FubiaoLuo[1,2] YanleiQin[2],Wanbin Ren[1], ShujuanWang[1]
[1]Harbin Institute of Technology, Harbin, 150001, China
[2]G&A Technology Co., Ltd., Guilin, 541002, China

Abstract—**The environmental test conditions of the temperature easily cause stress relaxation of the reed in the sealed electromagnetic relay, which in turn causes the relay contacts to fail. Firstly, this paper analyzes the mechanism of contact resilience caused by stress relaxation of relay reeds. Furthermore, the research work on the stress relaxation characteristics of reeds under normal high temperature experimental conditions, temperatureshock experimental conditions and super-stress temperature impact test conditions, and the degradation trend of relay contact static pressure was obtained. Finally, the paper analyzes the effects of initial static pressure and ambient temperature changes on the stress relaxation characteristics of the reed.**

Index Terms—**Relay, Reed, Stress relaxation, Temperature environment, Contact static pressure**

I INTRODUCTION

As an electronic control device, the sealed electromagnetic relay is a "special switch" for controlling large loads through small loads, and is widely used in the fields of national defense weapons, national economy and civil industry. Relay manufacturers have been using various solutions to reduce their failure rate, but there are still failure modes such as contact bonding, reed stress relaxation, vibration contact buckling, and excess. Among them, the reed stress relaxation is an inherent property of the material, which can make the contact pressure gradually become smaller and may cause contact bonding failure.

In this regard, research scholars believe that under long-term high temperature and stress, if the total deformation of metal parts is constant, the internal elastic strain will change into plastic deformation with time, which induces stress relaxation. Stress relaxation occurs in elastic parts that work at high temperatures and high pressures, and there are cases in elastic parts that work long-term at normal temperatures. The research results show that the essence of stress relaxation is the creep behavior of materials, so it should be based on creep theory. Some scholars believe that the relaxation process is the process of transforming the initial elastic strain into inelastic strain with time. The stress that causes the internal material to be misaligned is relaxed[1].

The reed structure in the relay is in a bent and twisted state with pre-stress. Reeds can experience varying degrees of stress relaxation during product service. The stress of the reed under the same deformation is gradually reduced, which will reduce the mechanical force, resulting in a change in the matching curve between the electromagnetic attraction and the mechanical reaction force. The probability of contact bonding of the relay increases, so the reed design must consider the effect of stress relaxation.

At present, domestic and foreign scholars have conducted in-depth research on the stress relaxation phenomenon of metal materials[2-5]. Zhu Yongqing et al. studied the stress relaxation changes of the spring materials (domestic tin bronze and beryllium bronze strips) under different initial stresses and different temperature conditions, and calculated the long-term stress relaxation amount based on the Arreheniusequation[6]. Kim et al. demonstrated the stress-strengthening mechanism of the new alloy steel material under the ultra-high temperature condition of 600-1000°C, and the relationship between stress and strain was obtained by combining the activation volume and activation energy[7]. Zhou Jianqiang et al. determined the constitutive equation of stress relaxation of aluminum alloy sheets at 182°C by uniaxial tensile test, and simulated the formation process by finite element method[8].Schedin used the finite element method to simulate the stress relaxation of the joint by using the experimental data as input, and derived the stress-strain expression of the power law form[9].

In this paper, the relay reeds are used to test the normal high temperature, temperature shock and super-stress temperature impact. Through the normalized static pressure degradation trend, the initial static pressure and ambient temperature of different contacts are analyzed.

II RELATIONSHIP BETWEEN REED STRESS RELAXATION AND RELAY CONTACT BONDING

As shown in Figure 1, the reed is an important functional part of the electromagnetic relay. Viewed from the outside, the reed is the connecting bridge between the two extraction rods of the relay, and the load current is passed through the reed to realize the communication of the two extraction rods. From the inside, the reed is the key to the contact pressure during the relay action and provides the contact pressure for the contact spring system. Therefore, the quality of the reed design directly affects the contact pressure and the suction force of the relay.

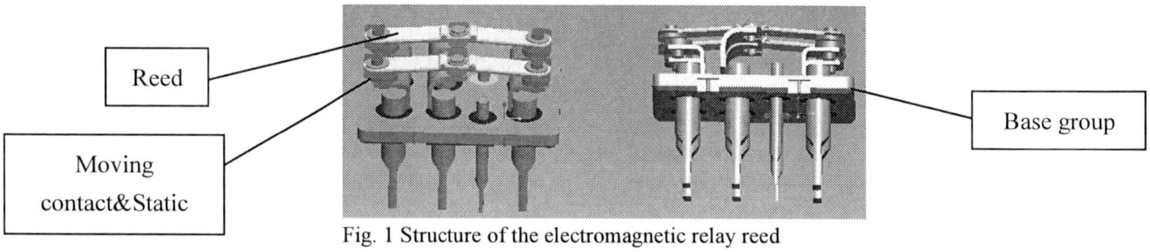

Fig. 1 Structure of the electromagnetic relay reed

Contact breaking refers to the process of opening and closing the contact between the moving contact and the stationary contact during the switching process. In this process, if the contact cannot be normally disconnected or delayed for a period of time, it is very likely to Contact bonding. The mechanism of contact bonding is mainly divided into fusion welding and cold welding. For small sealed electromagnetic relays, the failure of contact bonding caused by cold welding is very serious, but the stress relaxation of the reed makes the contact pressure gradually become smaller, resulting in The lesser the possibility of cold welding, therefore, this paper mainly studies the contact bonding caused by fusion welding.

Turning on the current is a key factor in determining the welding of the contacts. The increase in current will increase the welding strength. In severe cases, the welding force can reach or approach the tensile strength of the contact base material. At the same time, the current at which the contact begins to melt is related to the energization time of the contact. The longer the energization time, the lower the melting current of the contact begins. When the energization time exceeds 4 times the time constant, the temperature is nearly stable, and the starting melting current does not change any more, so the starting melting current can be expressed as

$$\int_{T_0}^{T_{jm}} \lambda \rho_d dT = \frac{U_j^2}{8} \qquad (1)$$

Where: T_{jm}- the center temperature of the conductive part of the contact; T_0 - the temperature outside the conductive part of the contact; λ- the electrical conductivity of the contact material; ρ_d- the resistivity of the contact material;U_j - the contact pressure drop between the contacts.

According to Wademan Franz's law, the$\lambda\rho_d$value of a pure metal material is linear with the material temperature T. Expressible as

$$\lambda \rho_d = LT \qquad (2)$$

Where, $L = 2.4 \times 10^{-8}(\frac{V}{K})^2$, This value is the Lorentz coefficient. Available from Equations (1) and (2)

$$T_{jm}^2 = \frac{U_j^2}{4L} + T_0^2 \qquad (3)$$

When T_{jm} is higher than the melting point of the contact material, the contact surface material begins to melt. If the surface energy of the contacted contact does not continue to melt until the contact is broken, bonding occurs between the contacts. If the contact adhesive force is smaller than the contact component breaking force, then the armature group of the relay will drive the contact group to break, and will not cause the contact to be bonded; if the contact adhesive force is greater than the contact component breaking force, then the relay The armature set cannot drive the contact set to break, which will cause the contacts to bond. After simplification, the key parameter T_{jm} of the contact bonding is only strongly related to the contact pressure drop U_j, and the contact pressure drop between the contacts is increased, which is more likely to cause the contact to be welded and bonded, which is the main factor.

The stress relaxation process of the material causes the internal force in the statically indeterminate structure to redistribute with time. The relaxation directly reduces the contact pressure. Therefore, the contact pressure can be expressed as a function oftime.

$$F(t_1) = F_0 - \int_{t_0}^{t_1} F(t) \qquad (4)$$

$$T_{jm}^2 = \frac{U_j^2}{4L} + T_0^2 \qquad (5)$$

When the contact pressure is within a certain range, the contact resistance between the contacts is inversely related to the contact pressure[4], which can be expressed as:

$$R_j = \frac{\sigma}{F} \qquad (6)$$

Where: σ is a constant.

In the circuit where the relay is located, when the load current I is constant, the relationship between the contact temperature and the pressure at the contact opening and closing of the contact can be expressed as:

$$T_{jm}^2 = \frac{I^2\sigma^2}{4L(F_0 - \int_{t_0}^{t_1} F(t))^2} + T_0^2 \qquad (7)$$

It can be seen that when the load is turned on and off between the contacts, the temperature of the contact position increases with the stress relaxation of the reed, and the probability of contact bonding increases; in the case of the same reed, the initial contact pressure is increased. The more obvious the stress relaxation, the greater the probability of contact bonding.

III EXPERIMENTAL STUDY ON STRESS RELAXATION CHARACTERISTICS OF REED

The experiment in this paper takes the beryllium bronze material commonly used in relay reeds as the research object, and uses the contact system of a certain type of electromagnetic relay in Fig. 1 to study the test piece. The test process uses a high-temperature baking method to accelerate the stress relaxation of the reed, and then test the contact pressure value of the contact system to verify the degree of stress relaxation of the beryllium bronze under different conditions. Finally, the experimental data and experimental phenomena of each group were analyzed using the existing stress relaxation theory.

A. *Research method*

The test method of stress relaxation is mainly used to evaluate the characteristics of the initial elastic strain transformation to inelastic strain of a material or structural member within a specified time. In order to simulate the actual use of the sample, the test is divided into three phases:

1) Stress relaxation test under normal high temperature

In the test, the samples were grouped according to the stress, and were respectively baked in a high-temperature oven at 80℃, 125℃ and 140℃, and taken out every two hours to cool under normal temperature conditions. Then measure the contact pressure and repeat the above operation until the stress is basically stable.

2) Stress relaxation test under temperature shock

In the test, the samples were grouped according to stress and placed in 80 ℃, 125 ℃ and 140 ℃ high temperature ovens for baking. After two hours, they were taken out and quickly placed in a -55℃ low temperature box. After two hours, they were taken out and returned to normal temperature. Then measure the contact pressure and repeat the above operation until the stress is basically stable.

3) Stress relaxation test with super-stress

In this test, the samples were grouped according to the stress, and a 0.8 mm gasket was placed between the contacts to simulate the super-stress state, and then placed in a high-temperature oven at 80℃, 125℃ and 140℃ for baking, and taken out after two hours. And quickly placed in a -55℃ low temperature box. After another two hours, it was taken out to return to normal temperature, and then the contact pressure was measured. Repeat the above operation until the stress is basically stable.

In this test, the dynamic contact spring group is rigidly fixed and the height of the static contact group is adjusted to form static pressure, so as to avoid spring-back during the test of the movable contact spring group. This scheme requires that the static contact spring group has better rigidity and the dynamic contact spring is not affected. The force is deformed, which ensures that the static pressure is mainly derived from the elastic deformation of the reed.

B. *Determination of static pressure value*

The material properties of beryllium bronze refer to the standard YS T323-2002 "Bronze Sheet and Strip", the specific properties are shown in Table 1:

Table 1 Beryllium bronze material properties

Material name / Material properties	Beryllium bronze (QBe2)
Material standard	YS T323-2002
Material status	Super hard (CY)
Tensile strength / MPa	≥635 (Before aging); ≥1177 (After aging)
Vickers hardness / HV	≥170 (Before aging); ≥320 (After aging)
Elastic Modulus / GPa	135.8 (After aging)
Heat treatment	Aging：320±10℃，2h，Air cooling

In order to design a suitable static pressure value, the maximum stress at the root of the reed is adjusted to 1/3 and 1/6 of the tensile strength of the material. The maximum stress at the root of the reed is 392.3MPa and 196.2MPa, and is simulated by Ansys static analysis. The stress cloud diagram and the deformation cloud diagram of the simulation reed are shown in Fig. 2 and Fig. 3.

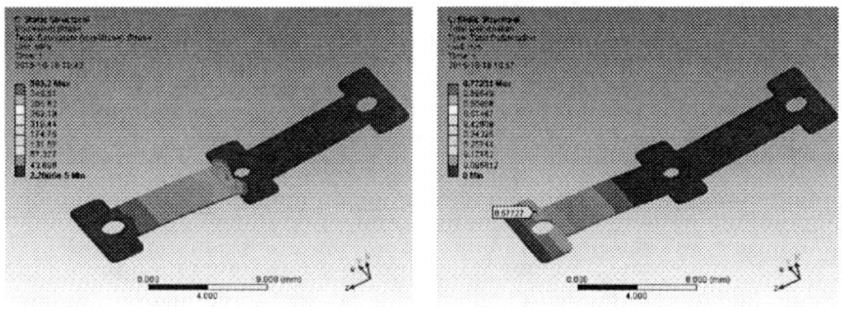

Stress analysis cloudDeformation analysis

Fig. 2 Reed stress analysis cloud image (0.76N)

According to the simulation results, the parameters of the reed corresponding stress conditions are obtained, as shown in Table 2.

C. Analysis of test results

According to the baking temperature, stress and test time points, a total of 20 sets of contact static pressure statistics for each group of 5 samples.

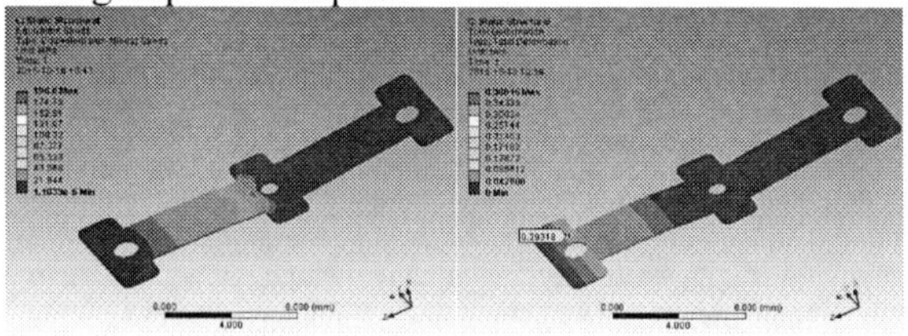

Stress analysis cloud Deformation analysis

Fig. 3 Reed stress analysis cloud image (0.76N)

1) Conventional high temperature baking

In order to facilitate the statistical static pressure of the group as the baking time changes, the average value of each row of data is taken as the statistical object to reduce the influence of the measurement error on the data. The data in Table 3 is tabulated, see Figure 4. Each chart focuses on the relationship between the static pressure drop and the baking time at different baking temperatures compared to the same static pressure and the same reed parts.

At high temperatures, under the same reed stress, the higher the ambient temperature, the greater the change in contact pressure, indicating that the reeds are more prone to slack as the temperature increases. It indicates that the internal stress of the reed increases and the relaxation is more likely to occur. According to the creep theory, the creep behavior inside the material becomes stronger as the ambient temperature increases and the stress increases, and the material is more susceptible to stress relaxation.

2) Temperature shock test

In this test, each group was placed in a -55℃ low temperature chamber immediately after baking at a high temperature, and the data after treatment are shown in Table 4. The data in Table 4 is plotted as shown in Figure 5. Each chart focuses on the relationship between the static pressure drop and the baking time at different baking temperatures compared to the same static pressure and the same reed parts.

Table 2 Reed stress and deformation calculation

Project	Contact pressure / N	Maximum stress / MPa	Maximum deformation / mm	Contact deformation / mm	Remarks
Reed parameters	0.76	392.3	0.772	0.577	Group A
	0.38	196.2	0.386	0.293	Group B

Table 3 Statistics of test results

Test group	Prototype	Testing time (h)	Static pressure average(0.1N)			Static pressure normalized by average		
			85℃	125 ℃	140 ℃	85℃	125℃	140℃
Group A	Beryllium bronze (0.38N)	0	3.78	3.71	3.70	100.00%	100.00%	100.00%
		2	3.74	3.67	3.58	99.07%	98.92%	96.62%
		4	3.65	3.60	3.46	96.56%	97.03%	93.51%
		6	3.63	3.57	3.43	96.16%	96.36%	92.70%
		10	3.63	3.56	3.40	96.03%	96.09%	91.89%
Group B	Beryllium bronze (0.76N)	0	7.67	7.52	7.63	100.00%	100.00%	100.00%
		2	7.36	7.02	7.30	96.02%	93.35%	95.67%
		4	7.21	6.89	6.98	94.00%	91.56%	91.48%
		6	7.13	6.87	6.76	92.95%	91.36%	88.60%
		10	7.10	6.81	6.69	92.63%	90.56%	87.68%

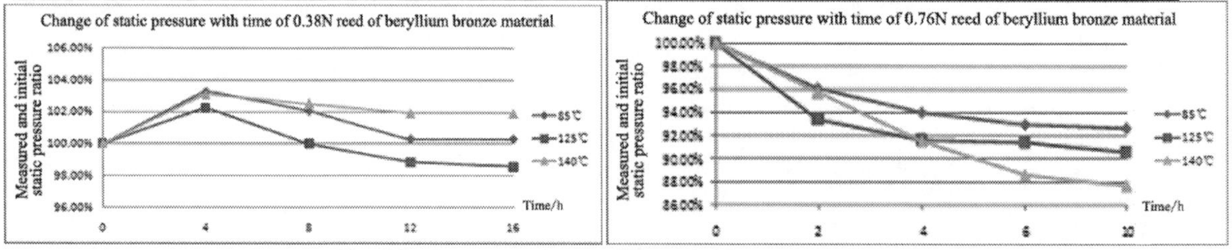

Fig. 4 Static pressure drop at different baking temperatures

Under temperature shock conditions, the contact pressure first rises and then decreases to a stable state. According to the analysis, the reed has internal stress and does not become plastically deformed. In the early stage of the test, the internal reconstitution of the material caused the initial stress to become larger. During the middle and the end of the test, the reed was plastically deformed under external stress and the stress relaxation phenomenon gradually occurred.

Table 4 Statistics of test results

Test group	Prototype	Testing time (h)	Static pressure average(0.1N)			Static pressure normalized by average		
			85℃	125 ℃	140 ℃	85℃	125℃	140℃
Group A	Beryllium bronze (0.38N)	0	3.63	3.56	3.40	100.00%	100.00%	100.00%
		4	3.75	3.64	3.51	103.31%	102.25%	103.09%
		8	3.70	3.56	3.49	102.07%	100.00%	102.50%
		12	3.64	3.52	3.47	100.28%	98.88%	101.91%
		16	3.64	3.51	3.47	100.28%	98.60%	101.91%
Group B	Berylliu m bronze (0.76N)	0	7.10	6.81	6.69	100.00%	100.00%	100.00%
		4	7.38	6.90	6.87	103.94%	101.25%	102.62%
		8	7.29	6.73	6.82	102.61%	98.83%	101.87%
		12	7.23	6.66	6.75	101.83%	97.72%	100.90%
		16	7.22	6.64	6.73	101.62%	97.50%	100.52%

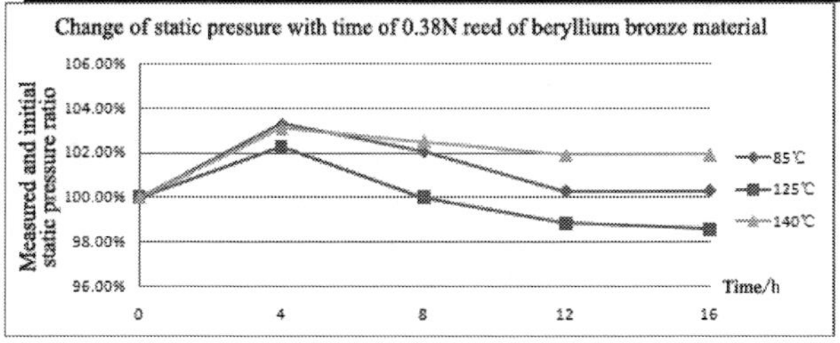

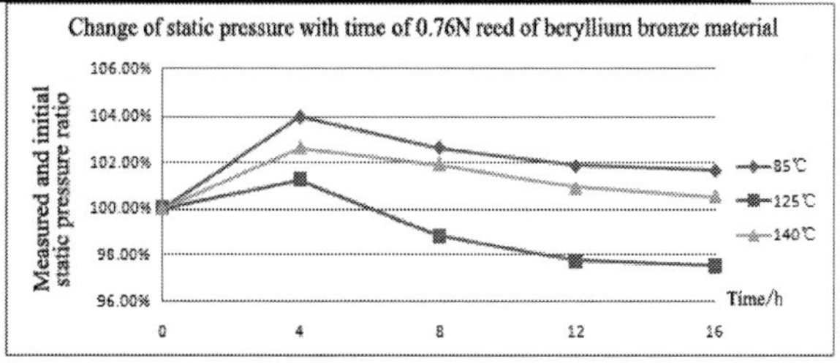

Fig. 5 Static pressure drop under different temperature impacts

3) Stress relaxation test with super-stress

In this test, the contact pressure was adjusted to 1.08 N (Group A) and 1.36 N (Group B). After the temperature impact test, the processed data is shown in Table 5, and is plotted as shown in Figure 6. Each chart focuses on the relationship between the static pressure drop and the baking time at different baking temperatures compared to the same static pressure and the same reed parts. Under the condition of excessive stress and temperature shock, the stress relaxation tendency of the reed is consistent with that under the normal temperature, but the degree of relaxation of the reed is more serious. At 140 °C, the stress attenuation increases from 13.32% to 53.39%. Therefore, under the temperature shock condition of super-stress, the internal stress of the material is greater than the dislocation stress. When the reed is creeping inside, the dislocation is more likely to occur and plastic deformation occurs. The reed cannot be recovered, resulting in a significant reduction in stress.

IV CONCLUSION

Under the action of stress relaxation, the stress of the electromagnetic relay reed is gradually reduced, resulting in a decrease in the contact pressure, and the contact is more likely to cause a bonding failure under the load life. In this paper, the stress relaxation phenomenon of beryllium bronze reeds is studied under the conditions of ambient temperature and internal stress. The stress relaxation is common in strained metal elastic parts. With the increase of temperature and internal stress, the relaxation phenomenon is more serious. Under the allowable stress condition of the reed, the stress relaxation of the reed is not serious, and the contact pressure does not change much. Under the condition of excessive stress, the stress relaxation phenomenon of the reed is very serious, and the contact pressure is even reduced by half. It has a very negative effect on the load life of the relay. In order to improve the reliability of the load life of the electromagnetic relay, the reed should be designed with a combination of factors such as structure, stress and ambient temperature to ensure that the reed maintains a stable stress state during the life of the reed, so that the contact pressure of the relay is always maintained. In a safe and reasonable range, thereby improving the reliability of the life of the relay.

Table 5 Statistics of test results

Test group	Prototype	Testing time (h)	Static pressure average(0.1N)			Static pressure normalized by average		
			85℃	125 ℃	140 ℃	85℃	125℃	140℃
Group A	Beryllium bronze (0.38N)	0	3.64	3.51	3.47	100.00%	100.00%	100.00%
		4	3.21	2.91	2.41	88.17%	82.76%	69.55%
		8	3.13	2.78	2.01	86.15%	79.06%	58.01%
		12	3.10	2.65	1.78	85.14%	75.50%	51.37%
		16	3.01	2.60	1.69	82.67%	73.93%	48.77%
Group B	Beryllium bronze (0.76N)	0	2.96	2.53	1.62	81.43%	72.08%	46.61%
		4	7.22	6.64	6.73	100.00%	100.00%	100.00%
		8	6.09	5.53	4.57	84.34%	83.28%	67.96%
		12	5.94	5.19	4.23	82.33%	78.16%	62.83%
		16	5.92	5.07	4.03	81.98%	76.36%	59.93%

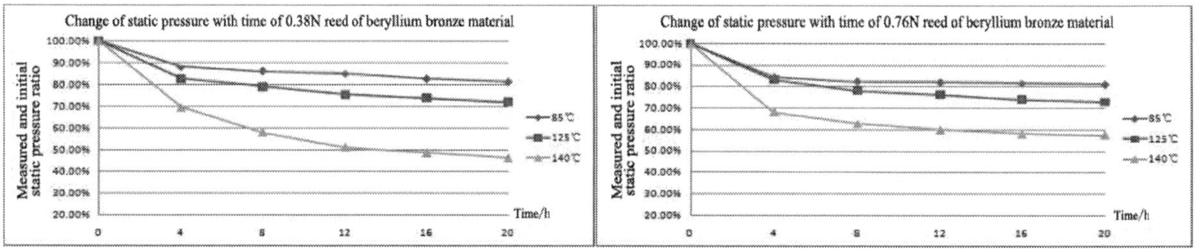

Fig. 6 The static pressure drop of super-stressed reeds under different temperature impacts

REFERENCES

[1] Mao Xinping. Stress relaxation characteristics and mechanism of high strength beryllium bronze. Central South University[D], February 2001.

[2] Drozd Z, Trojanová Z, Kúdela S. Degradation of the mechanical properties of a Mg–Li–Al composite at elevated temperatures studied by the stress relaxation technique[J]. Materials Science & Engineering A, 2007, 462(1): 234-238.

[3] Llano-Vizcaya L D, Rubio-Gonzalez C, Mesmacque G. Stress relief effect on fatigue and relaxation of compression springs[J]. Materials & Design, 2007, 28(4): 1130-1134.

[4] Li Jianming, Zhao Naiqin, Li Qunying. Relaxation Behavior of 65Mn Spring Steel under Bending Stress[J]. Heat Treatment of Metals, 2007, 32(5): 90-94.

[5] Huang Xiaotong, Wang Junxi, Zhang Xianjie. Study on the relationship between ageing creep and time effect force relaxation of aluminum alloy[J]. Aviation Manufacturing Technology, 2011, 11: 99-101.

[6] Zhu Yongqing, Lu Yiguo. Stress Relaxation Characteristics of Relay Spring Materials[J]. Low Voltage Apparatus, 2008(11): 3-5.

[7] Kim J H, Byun T S, Hoelzer D T. Stress relaxation behavior of nanocluster-strengthened ferritic alloy at high temperatures[J]. Journal of Nuclear Materials, 2012(425): 147-155.

[8] Zhou Jianqiang, Zhang Xianjie, Wang Junxi. Finite Element Simulation of Time Effect Force Relaxation Forming of 7055 Aluminum Alloy Sheet[J]. Ordnance Material Science and Engineering, 2013, 36(03): 92-95.

[9] Schedin E, Thuvander A, Henderson P, Sandberg P, Kamf A. Stress relaxation behaviour of connectors - Development of simulation techniques[C]. 42nd IEEE Holm Conference on Electrical Contacts, 1996: 142-15

The Current Closed-loop Control and Simulation of Permanent Magnet Vacuum Contactor

He Qu[1], Longfei Tang[1,2]
[1]College of Electrical Engineering and Automation, Fuzhou University, Fuzhou 350108, China
[2]Fujian Key Laboratory of New Energy Generation and Power Conversion, Fuzhou350108, China
E-mail: 541892280@qq.comTel: 18150810920

***Abstract* —Current closed-loop control technology is introduced into monostable permanent magnet (PM) contactor in this paper. There is current closed-loop control presented in detail,which adjusted coil current in real-time to control the dynamic processes directly. Full-bridge circuit is transformed to realize the controlof the coil. In addition, the simulation model of contactor with control is built. The control circuitry is designed in Multisim and the dynamic model of contactor based on magnetic circuit method is designed in LabVIEW. Connecting LabVIEW and Multisim it realizes co-simulation of dynamic model and control module of contactor. This paper analyzes the principle of control circuit and property of contactor, considering the inductance changing of circuitry and the effect of PM. In conclusion, the control module has many advantages such as compactness, high reliability, Core collision and contact bounce during pick-up and no power consumption. The experiments are performed to verify control module.**

***Index Terms*—Current closed-loop, PM, Monostable, Co-simulation.**

I. INTRODUCTION

PM operating mechanisms have attracted people's attention with the advent of high-performance PM materials and the application of PM operating mechanisms in the field of electrical appliances.The PM contactor has many merits such as low energy consumption and high reliability when compared with its electromagnetic counterparts[1]. Guo and Yang have analyzed the working principle of monostable PM contactor [2]. In addition, Fang et al. made a study onthe characteristics of the low-voltage PM operating mechanism [3].Pei and Wangchanged the duty cycle control scheme by detecting the storage capacitor voltage, which improves the energy storage efficiency and the split/close frequency of the PM contactoreffectively [4]. During the past ten years or so, researchers have made a wealth of good efforts on control strategies of PM contactor [5][6].Ni and Wang controlled the PWM output frequency through a programmable counter array in the microcontroller chip to control the contactor coil currenteffectively [8]. Compared with control strategy, it is more challenging to look into thePM actuatordesign and dynamic performance simulation for the PM actuators. Chih and Chieh designeda new type of PM operating mechanism, which has the characteristics of energy saving and no noise [7]. Lou analyzed the dynamics of a single-coil PM contactor mechanism [9].Wu proposed a new type of PM contactor with a breaking protection device, which can be forced to break when the normal working circuit loses power or fails [10]. In recent years, some scholar reported their efforts to improve the charging characteristics of storage capacitors[11][12].

The current closed-loop control technology is introduced into the control of the PM vacuum contactor in this paper. With dsPIC33FJ16GS502 as the control core, the closed-loop control of the coil current in the starting process of the PM contactor electromagnetic mechanism is realized.Through the co-simulation of Multisim and LabVIEW, the CKJ5-250/1140 PM vacuum contactor was used as the experimental object to carry out related experiments, and the advantages of the current closed-loop control scheme were analyzed and compared.

II. INTRODUCTION CONTROL STRATEGY

A. Basic working principle

The closed-loop control module of PM vacuum contactor is mainly composed of full-bridge main circuit, dsPIC and its peripheral circuits, coil current sampling circuit, switch tube drive, etc. Its structural block diagram is shown in Figure 1.

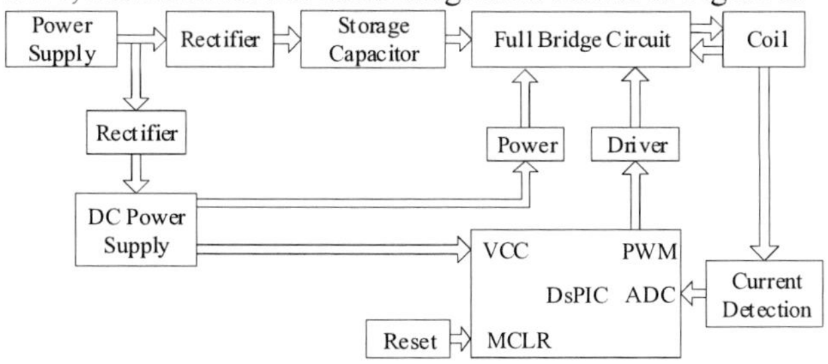

Fig. 1 Control module block diagram

The storage capacitor is charged by a smooth DC power which is obtained after the AC power is rectified and filtered. The coil obtains electric energy from the storage capacitor when the MOSFETs on the opposite arm is opened.The storage capacitor is charged and the coil current flows through the body diode of the other pair of switch tubes when the switch tube is turned off. The working process of the control module is: A plurality of stable DC voltages are obtained from the AC/DC circuit after power-on and the DC/DC circuit to provide operating power for the Hall sensor, dsPIC, MOSFETs, etc.what is exactly as shown in Figure 2. The storage capacitor obtains electric energy from a separate AC/DC switching power supply module, and supplies the contactor coil to complete the opening and closing operation. The power of MOSFETs and dsPIC chip is obtained by the isolated DC/DC converter module.

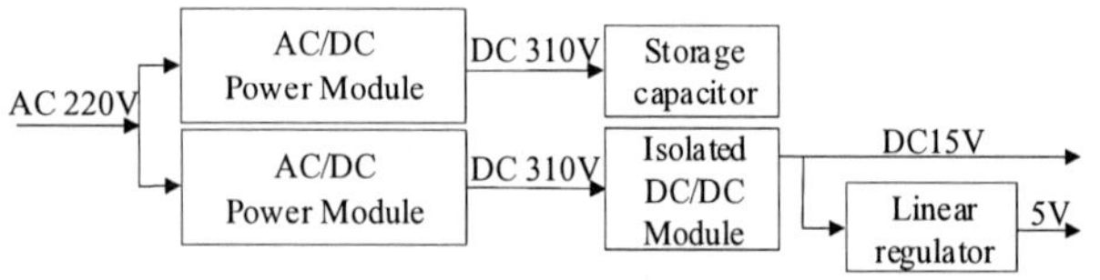

Fig. 2 Power supply block diagram

B. *The design of software*

The software system is mainly composed of initialization, high-speed PWM, high-speed ADC, high-speed analog comparator, interrupt and other modules.The flow chart of the system is shown in Figure 3.During the process of absorption, the coil current is dynamically controlled by comparing the coil current sampling with the set threshold to generate PWM1 to control the on and off of Q1 and Q4.The action process is divided into three stages, the contactor coil through a large current to make it fast absorption in the starting stage.No voltage is applied at both ends of the coil after the absorption, and the permanent magnetic force keeps the absorption.The coil is added with a reverse voltage pulse because Q2 and Q3 are switched on, and the permanent magnetic force is overcome by electromagnetic force during the breaking stage.A, B and C are three thresholds.

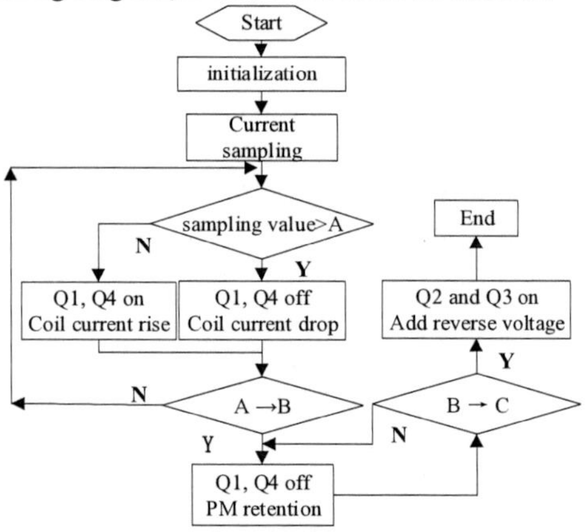

Fig. 3 Workflow diagram of the system

III. MECHATRONICS SIMULATION SYSTEM

A. *Principle of simulation system*

The electronic circuit and contactor body must be considered as a whole when intelligent control of PM vacuum contactor is implemented,theperformance index of intelligent permanent magnet vacuum contactor cannot be improved if the electronic circuit or contactor body is modeled and simulated separately.Therefore, a new closed-loop mechatronic integration simulation system is constructed in LabVIEW and Multisim software to conduct co-simulation of the PM contactor ontology and control module in this paper, what is shown in Figure 4.

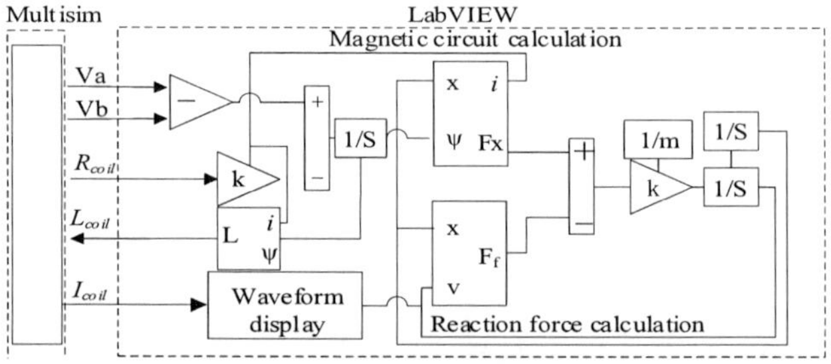

Fig.4 Mechatronics simulation system

A dynamic simulation model of PM vacuum contactor was established in LabVIEW andthe PM vacuum contactor followed the voltage balance equation (1) and d 'alembert mechanical motion equation (2) in the process of motion.

$$u_{coil} = i_{coil}R_{coil} + \frac{d\Psi}{dt} \tag{1}$$

$$F_x - F_f = m\frac{d^2x}{dt^2} \tag{2}$$

In the formula, $u_{coil}$is coil voltage, i_{coil} is coil current, R_{coil} is coil resistance, F_x is suction, and F_f is spring reaction.

Maxwell's equations are followed on magnetic fields to form the dynamic differential equations shown in (3).

$$\begin{cases} \frac{d\Psi}{dt} = u_{coil} - i_{coil}R_{coil} \\ \frac{dv}{dt} = \frac{F_x - F_f}{dt} \\ \frac{dx}{dt} = v \end{cases} \tag{3}$$

Magnetic flux loop and current loop of the double closed loop structure is established when moving core displacement x and flux Ψ are known,the inner current loop is controlled by the outer magnetic loop, and the sum of the coil current I and the electromagnetic and PM suction F_x is reversely solved through iteration.The main control circuit model is established in Multisim, what is shown in Figure 5.The interactive interface of data is composed of some key variables, and the arrow direction is used to indicate the direction of data transmission. The communication between the twosoftware is established through the data interactive interfaceand data exchange at the end of each time step.

R_{coil} is voltage-controlled resistor, L_{coil} is voltage-controlled inductance.Cis storage capacitor and V_c is the energy storage capacitor voltage;Four MOSFETs and their body diodes make up the full bridge circuit;V_a and V_b are coil voltages of contactors.FB is a current control voltage sourcewhich converts coil current changes into voltage signals and transmits them to LabVIEW.

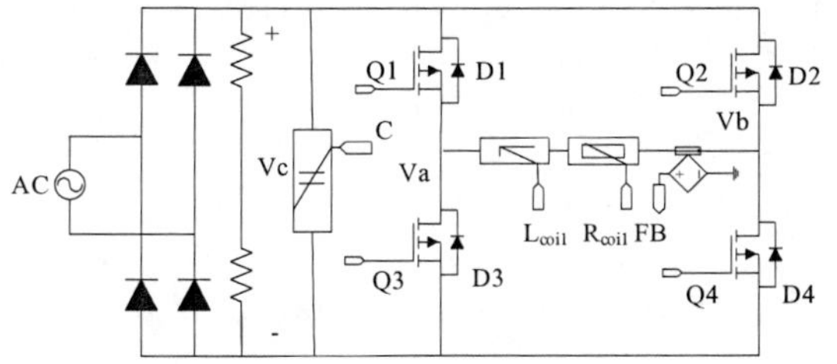

Fig. 5 Main circuit simulation model

B. The analysis ofsimulation process

The control principle of PM vacuum contactor is verified by an integrated simulation system.In the process of closing and opening, the circuit balance equation is:

$$u = iR + \frac{d\Psi}{dt} \tag{4}$$

In this formula, Ψ is the coil flux.

Some simulation parameters can be established in the front panel of LabVIEWsuch as starting and breaking voltage, coil current closed-loop value, starting and breaking time, parameters of PM contactor, etc.In this simulation, the starting and breaking voltage is 310V and the current closed-loop value is set as 3A. The results of co-simulation are shown in Figure 6.

T0-t7 period:simulation starts at time t0.MOSFET 1and 4 are conducted at time t1. At t2, the coil voltage is controlled by signal 1 which changes to a high frequency square wave due to a current loop,the current in the coil will continue to flow through D2 and D3 when MOSFETsare turned off, the voltage of the coil is $-V_c$, so the coil voltage alternates between positive and negative.The coil current is stabilized at 3Aand the air gap gradually decreases as the core begins to move.At t3, the coil current begins to fall until the core stops moving, which dueto the anti-potential of the movement generated by the movement of the core increases [14].The coil current drops to the lowest pointwhen the core closes. As the core closes, the magnetic circuit enters the saturation stage from the linear stage at t4.At time t5, the magnetic circuit tends to be saturatedand the flux stabilizes at a constant value as the coil current increases to 3A again.The starting process at time t6 ends, the current in the coil rapidly drops and continues to flow through D2 and D3 because the switch tube is in the off state.The moment t6-t7 is the holding stage, at which the coil current is 0and the iron core is kept closed by the PM.

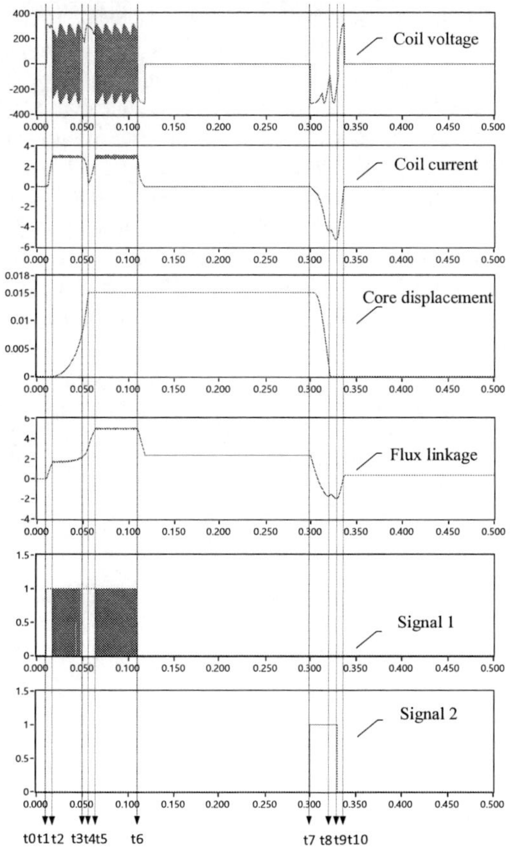

Fig. 6 Simulation waveform

T7-t10 period: the opening operation starts at t7. The coil is energized for a short time and the coil current is small relatively when opening. The current closed-loop control is not carried out in the tripping processin order to ensure the quick tripping of the PM contactor.The breaking voltage is established at both ends of the coil along with the conduction of MOSFET 2 and 3,the core starts to move in the opposite direction and the air gap gradually increases when the reverse current in the coil reaches a certain value.At t8, the moving speed of the core is the maximumwhen the core is shifted to the initial position,and the reverse current in the coil will decrease due to the movement of the back potential too.The coilcurrent decreases because the MOSFET 2 and 3 are turned off at time t9,the voltage the coil is $V_c$because of the current in the coil passes through D1 and D4 at this time,so the coil voltage will have a forward pulse after t9.

Analysis of Figure 6 showsthe flux generated by the PM changes with the air gap during the whole movement, so it is not advisable to consider the influence of the PM alone [15].In this simulation, the PM and electromagnetic influence are considered comprehensivelyand the correctness of the permanent magnet contactor current closed-loop control strategy is verified.

IV. THE ANALYSIS OF EXPERIMENT

The actual hardware control module is designed through the analysis results of mechatronic simulation system.CKJ-250/1140 PM vacuum contactor is taken as the control object, which has the merits of small volume and no maintaining power consumption.Experimental waveforms of different current closed-loop grades are shown in Figure 7, it can be seen that the experimental voltage and coil current waveforms are consistent with the variation trend of simulated voltage and current basically.The reason why the coil current decrease is not obvious during the starting process is that the strokeofPM vacuum contactor isveryshort and the core moves at a low speed.It can be seen that the mechatronics simulation system established in this paper can reflect the control law of the PM vacuum contactor, so it can be used to guide the overall design of the control module.

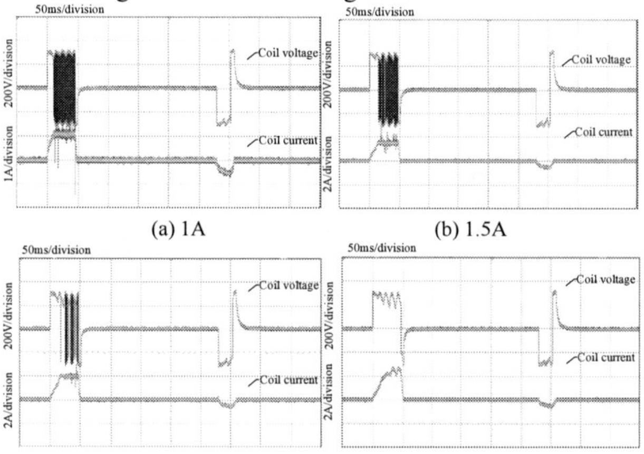

Fig. 7 Experimental waveforms of different closed loop current grades

CKJ-250/1140 PM vacuum contactors with different closed-loop current levels were tested for power consumption under operating conditions, and the current levels were 1A, 1.5a, 2A and the original control board.The power loss of one switching operation under the four states is shown in Figure 8. It can be seen from the figure that the power loss increases with the increase of the closed-loop current leveland the energy consumption of the PM contactor is reduced significantly after the closed-loop current control.

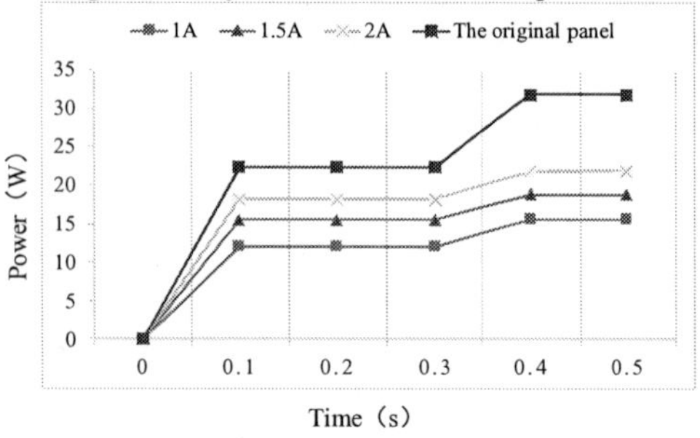

Fig. 8 The diagram power analysis

The parameters of PM vacuum contactor include coil voltage, coil current, contact speed, flux and inductance, etc., which vary complex in the process of suction. The bouncing times of the contact are used to illustrate the control effect and verify the feasibility of the control scheme, because the bouncing of the contact system can well reflect the control effect and is easy to test.

CKJ-250/1140 PM vacuum contactor was taken as the control object to record the coil voltage, current and contact signal waveform in the process of dynamic suction, holding and breaking.The waveform of each parameter under the control of AC half wave controlis shown in Figure 9(a)and the waveform of voltage, current and contact signal under the current closed-loop control is shown in Figure 9(b).

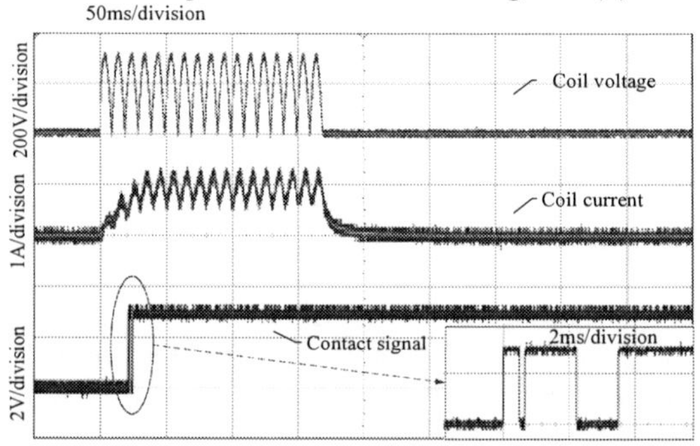

(a) The control of AC half wave

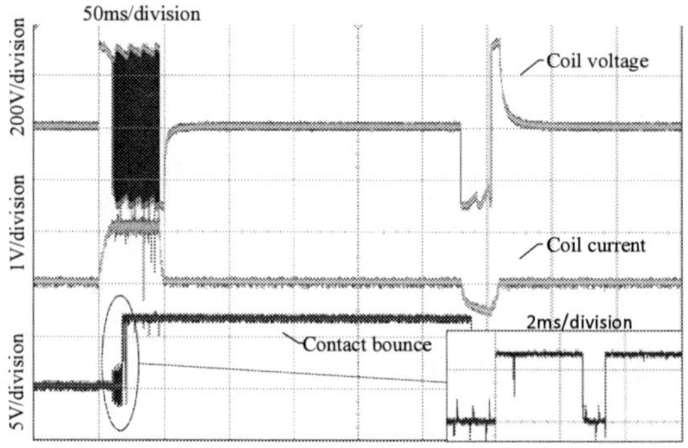

(b) The control of current closed-loop

Fig. 9 Coil voltage, current and contact signal waveforms under two control conditions

The coil voltage and current fluctuate greatly under the control of ac half-wave, and the defects include poor flexibility, high core collision energy and severe contact bounce and high energy loss.The merits of current closed-loop control include stable coil current, stable system, controllable power supply time, good flexibility, low energy loss and less contact bounce.Experiments and analysis show that the current closed-loop control reduces the energy consumption greatly, and the contradiction between the quick action of electromagnetic mechanism and the reduction of collision can be well solved, which is a more ideal control scheme compared with the ac half-wave control.

V. CONCLUSION

In this paper, the current closed-loop control scheme is applied to the control of PM vacuum contactor.Considering the influence of PM on the whole dynamic motion process, a point-by-point real-time simulation is carried out to verify the feasibility of the control scheme and provide guidance for hardware design.The rational coordination between the absorbing reaction force and permanent magnetic force in the current closed-loop scheme is realized, and the contradiction between the rapid action of the electromagnetic mechanism and the reduction of contact collision is solved, which has the merits of flexibility, high efficiency, energy saving, less contact bounce and no power consumption.

ACKNOWLEDGMENT

This work was supported in part by the Foundation of the Department of Science and Technology of Fujian Province under Grants 2017J05076, and in part by the National Natural Science Foundation of China under Grant 51707039.

REFERENCES

[1] XuZhihong. Theoretical basis of electrical appliances [M]. China Machine Press, 2014.

[2] GuoYuping,YangYiping.Research to permanent magnetic contactor principle of work with power-saving technology[J]. Manufacturing Automation, 2011, 33(10),149-151.

[3] Fang Shuhua, Lin Heyun, Ho Siulau, et al.Characteristic investigation of permanent magnet actuator for vacuum contactors operating with an intrinsically safe low voltage[J].Science China Technological Sciences,2012,55(6).

[4] Pei Jun, Wang Xianbing.Design of intelligent control module for novel permanent magnet contactor[J]. Low Voltage Apparatus, 2011(24),4-9.

[5] Wang Xianbing, Lin Heyun, Fang Shuhua, et al. Analysis of flux-weakening control and dynamic characteristic for making process of sensorless intelligent permanent magnet contactor[J].Proceedings of the CSEE,2011,31(18),93-99.

[6] Wang Xianbing,Lin Heyun,Fang Shuhuaet al. Analysis of displacement subsection PWM control and dynamic characteristic for closing process of permanent magnet contactor[J]. Proceedings of the CSEE,2010, 30(3),113-118.

[7] Chih-Yu Hung, Chieh-Tsung Chi. Actuator Design of a New AC PM Contactor with Energy-Saving and Noise-Free Characteristics[P]. Genetic and Evolutionary Computing (ICGEC), 2010 Fourth International Conference on,2010.

[8] Ni Shouchun, Wang Xianbing, Lin Heyun, et al.Study of intelligent control module for a novel permanent magnet contactor[J]. Advanced Technology of Electrical Engineering and Energy,2013,32(01),80-84.

[9] Lou Jianyong, Rong Mingzhe, Zou Hongchao, et al.Simulation on mechanism dynamic characteristics of single coil and single stable position contactor with permanent magnet[J]. Proceedings of the CSEE,2004(04),124-128.

[10] Wu Ziran, Shu Liang, Xu Chengwen, et al. A new permanent magnet AC contactor and its control circuit[J].Proceedings of the CSEE,2016, 36(13), 3667-3673+3387.

[11] Peng Jin, Wang Xianbing, Wang Xiangao, et al.Analysis of fuzzy control constant current charging characteristic for breakingand making capacitor of permanent magnet circuit breaker[J].Journal of System Simulation,2018,30(07),2648-2655+2665.

[12] Wang Xianbing, Fei Shumin, Xu Qingyang, et al. Constant current charging characteristic analysis of storage capacitor based on BP neural network PID control for permanent magnet vacuum switch[J]. Transactions of china electrotechnical society, 2015, 30(10),212-218.

[13] Xu Zhihong, Tang Longfei.Co-simulation and Digital Control Technology of the Intelligent AC Contactor[J].Proceedings of the CSEE, 2015, 35(11), 2870-2878.

[14] Fei Hongjun, Zhang Guansheng.Dynamic analysis and calculation of electromagnetic mechanism[M].China Machine Press,1993.

[15] Fang Shuhua, Lin Heyun, Liu Xiping, et al. Comparison evaluation for permanent magnet arrangements of AC permanent magnet contactor[P]. Electrical Machines and Systems, 2007. ICEMS. International Conference on,2007.

First A. Author, He Qu was born in Jiangsu Province, China, in 1996, received the B.S. degree in Taizhou Institute of Science and Technology&Nanjing University of Science and Technology, in 2018. Heis currently attending a master's degree in Electrical Engineering at Fuzhou University.

Corresponding Author, Longfei Tangwas bornin Jiangsu Province, China, in 1987, received the B.S.and Ph.D. degrees in Electrical Engineering and Its Automation from Fuzhou University, Fuzhou, China, in 2009 and 2015, respectively.

From 2016 to 2017, he was aPostdoctoral fellow at Ryerson University, Canada.He is currently an Associate Professor with theSchool of Electrical Engineering, Fuzhou University. His research interests includeintelligent control of electrical appliances and power system analysis and optimization.

7th International Conference on Reliability of
Electrical Products and Electrical Contacts,
November 04-06, 2019

Multi-feature Fusion Based on RBF Neural Network for Aviation AC Arc Fault Identification

Ruihua Cui, Chuanyu Wang
State Key Laboratory of Reliability and Intelligence of Electrical Equipment, Hebei University of Technology, Tianjin, 300130

Abstract—**Aiming at the characteristics of an aviation arc fault, such as short duration, random current distortion, and difficult detection, etc. This paper proposed a multi-feature aviation AC arc fault identification method based on radial basis (RBF) neural network. Under the condition of 115V/400Hz, we perform the series and parallel arc test separately to collect the main circuit current signal during the typical linear load and non-linear load. The kurtosis and cosine distance are used to extract the time-domain characteristics of the current signal. The fast Fourier transform (FFT) is utilized to analyze the frequency-domain features, and construct the multi-dimensional eigenvector matrix based on time-domain and frequency-domain features, input RBF neural network for arc fault recognition. The experimental results show that compared with the nearest neighbor algorithm (KNN), multi-layer perceptron (MLP) neural network and decision tree, the RBF neural network has faster recognition speed and the highest recognition accuracy (98.9%), which is suitable for aviation AC series and parallel arc fault detection.**

Index Terms— **Series and parallel arc fault, Multi-feature matrix, Radial basis (RBF) neural network**

I. INTRODUCTION

With the development of electrical technology and the emergence of multi-electric/all-electric aircraft, the number of airborne electrical equipment has increased significantly, and the aircraft power distribution system has become more complex, so the number of cables on the aircraft has also increased. Due to the limited internal space of the aircraft, the cable distribution is inevitably cross-stacked. The long-term work in high temperatures, severe cold, strong ultraviolet radiation, vibration, and other environments makes the cable easily aging and damaged, resulting in arc fault [1]. The series arc faults have the characteristics that the current value is less than the normal value and the parallel arc faults have the characteristics that the current value is less than the short-circuit current value, which causes the Thermal Circuit Breaker (TCB) and the Electrical Circuit Breaker (ECB) used in the aircraft cannot be protected in time [2]. Therefore, studying the aviation AC arc fault identification method has important practical significance for improving the safety and reliability of the aviation power distribution system.

Most scholars have realized the identification of faults by studying the time-domain, frequency-domain and time-frequency domain characteristics of arc faults. In terms of time-domain characteristics, Cui et al. [3] used statistical methods of correlation coefficient and skewness index to extract arc fault features. Zeng et al. [4] selected the root mean square and DC component deviation of the current signal as the arc fault feature characteristics. In the frequency-domain, NASA used a Fast Fourier transform (FFT) to extract high-frequency components of current signals and combined artificial neural networks to detect arc faults [5]. M. K. Khafidli et al. found that when the arc fault occurs, the amplitude of the 3-17 odd harmonics increases significantly, and the arc fault identification is realized by this feature [6]. The time-frequency domain feature extraction method is mainly based on Discrete Wavelet Transform (DWT) and Empirical Mode Decomposition (EMD) [7]-[10]. In [8], for the aeronautical arc fault, the wavelet packet is used to decompose the current, and calculated the Shannon entropy of the designated node of the decomposed signal as the feature quantity, input BP neural network for fault identification. In [10], the EMD and Wegener-Ville Distribution (WVD) was used to analyze the high-frequency characteristics of the arc fault current signal.

The above feature extraction methods, time-domain, and frequency-domain methods are relatively simple to calculate, and the calculation amount is small, which satisfies the real-time requirement of arc fault recognition. However, the detection using a single arc fault feature is susceptible to misjudgment due to changes in current and load. The time-frequency domain feature extraction methods based on DWT and EMD can well represent the arc fault information, but its algorithm is usually too complicated and has a large amount of computation, which is not suitable for the rapid judgment of arc fault. Therefore, there is still a need for an effective arc fault feature extraction methods that include many fault information.

As a relatively mature classification learning algorithm, a neural network is frequently used in the field of arc fault identification [11]-[14]. Compared with the multi-layer feedforward (BP) neural network, a radial basis (RBF) neural network has a simpler structure and faster convergence, which is suitable for the rapid identification of aviation arc faults.

Aiming at the problem that the AC series-parallel AC arc fault is difficult to detect, this paper proposes a feature extraction method based on the fusion of time-domain features and frequency domain features of current signals, which effectively reflects the changes of signal amplitude, waveform and harmonic content when the arc fault occurs, and realizes arc fault identification by using RBF neural networks. The experimental results show that the multi-feature fusion method based on RBF neural network can realize the rapid identification of aviation AC arc faults with an accuracy rate of 98.9%.

II. ARC FAULT TEST PRINCIPLE AND DATA ACQUISITION

A. Arc Fault Test Platform

Series arc test platform is built according to standard UL1699 [15] and built a parallel arc test platform with reference to standard AS5692 [16], which are simulated the aviation AC series arc fault and parallel arc fault respectively.

The series arc fault test circuit diagram and the arc generator are shown in Fig. 1 and Fig. 2. The arc fault generating device is composed of a static electrode (carbon rod), a moving electrode (copper rod) and a stepping motor. The stepper motor is used to control the uniform movement of the copper, so that the carbon rod and the copper rod are slowly disconnected to generate an arc fault.

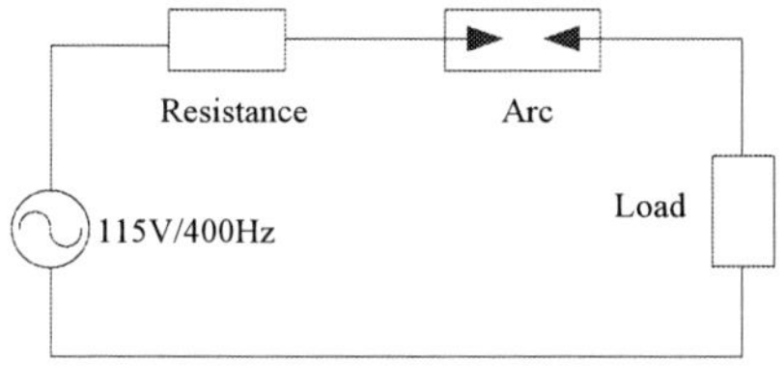

Fig. 1 Series arc fault circuit diagram

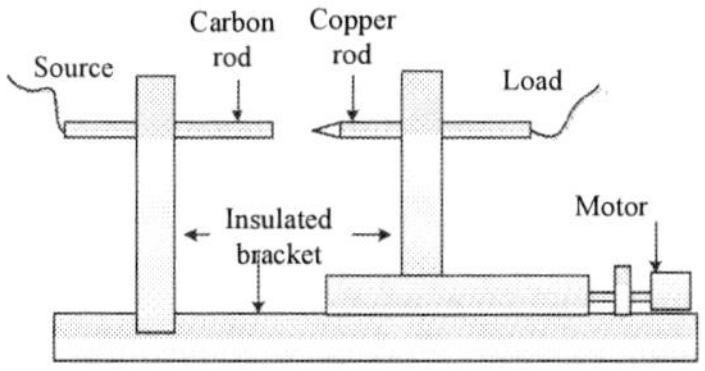

Fig. 2 Schematic diagram of the series arc fault test device

The parallel arc fault test circuit diagram and the arc generator are shown in Figures 3 and 4. The principle of the arc fault generating device is to use a blade to cut two side-by-side wires to break the wire insulation layer, and an arc fault occurs when the blade and the copper wire are not connected

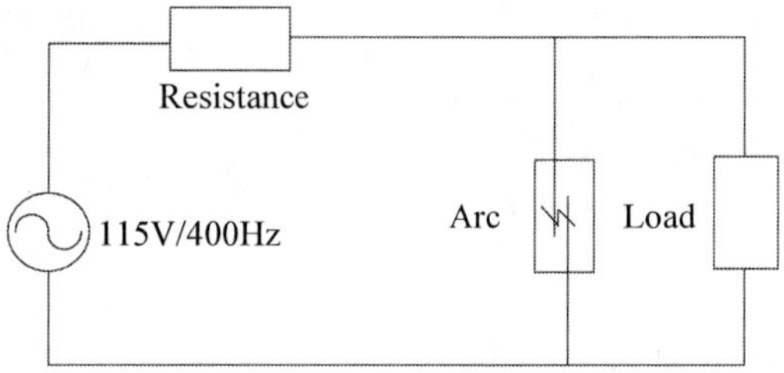

Fig. 3 Parallel arc fault circuit diagram

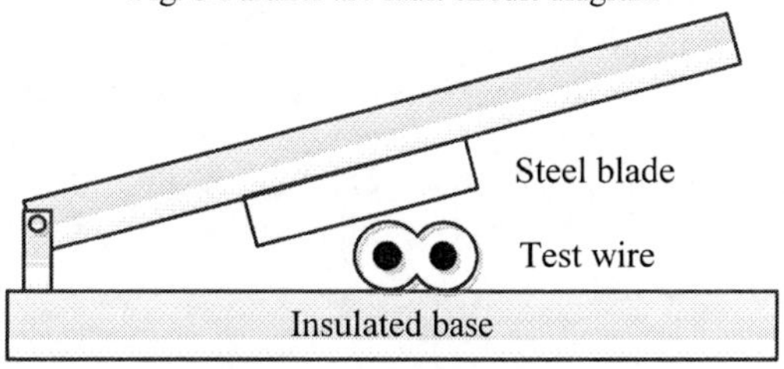

Fig. 4 Schematic diagram of parallel arc fault test device

B. Test Plan and Data Collection

115V/400Hz aviation AC power is Selected as the test power source. The series arc fault test adopts three typical linear loads of resistive, resistive and resistive capacitance, and an autotransformer (ATRU) type non-linear load. The specific load conditions are shown in Table 1. The parallel arc fault test load is dominated by the pure resistive linear load. The specific load conditions are shown in Table 2.

Table 1 Series arc fault test load

No.	Load	Type
1	resistance 7Ω	Resistive
2	resistance 57Ω	
3	resistance 7Ω+ inductance 5mH	Resistance perception
4	resistance 57Ω+ inductance 5mH	
5	resistance 57Ω+ capacitance 47μF	Resistance and capacitance
6	resistance 115Ω+ capacitance 47μF	
7	resistance 115Ω+ATRU	Nonlinearity

Table 2 Parallel arc fault test load

No.	Load	Type
1	resistance 15Ω	Resistive
2	resistance 30Ω	
3	resistance 115Ω	

The Hall current sensor and the data sampling module are used to collect the main loop current signal of the series and parallel arc fault test, which is used to extract the fault features and thereby identify the arc fault. The number of sampling points per cycle is set to 512 points, the corresponding sampling rate at the 400 Hz power frequency is 204.8 kHz, and the sampling time is set to 5 s.

III. RADIAL BASIS NEURAL NETWORK

The RBF neural network is a good forward neural network model with a global approximation. Compared with the traditional BP neural network, the RBF neural network converges faster and there is no local minimum problem. Meet the reliability and real-time requirements of aviation AC arc fault identification.

A. Network Structure

The RBF neural network generally consists of three layers: input layer, hidden layer, and output layer. The network structure diagram is shown in Figure 5. The input layer is composed of input nodes for signal transmission; the hidden layer completes the adjustment of the basis function parameters; the output layer implements a linear combination of all hidden layer node weights [17].

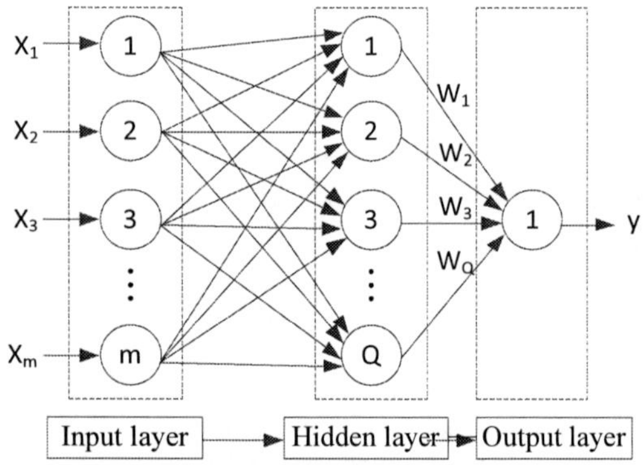

Fig. 5 RBFNN structure

B. Training and Learning

If the input of the RBF neural network is m-dimension, the expression of the input vector is as follows:

$$X = [x_1, x_2, \cdots x_m]^T \tag{1}$$

The mapping relationships used by the hidden layer are as follows:

$$Z_q = f(\|X - C_q\|) \tag{2}$$

In the formula of (2), $q = 1, 2, \cdots, Q$; the neural network input vector is *X*; *Q* is the number of hidden layer nodes; the basic function of the RBF neural network is *f(x)*; the center of the q node in the basis function is C_q; the output of the q node of the hidden layer is Z_q; the neural network input vector Euclidean distance from the center of each node is $\|X - C_q\|$.

In this paper, we choose Gaussian function as the basis function of RBF neural network, and its expression is shown in (3):

$$f(\|X - C_q\|) = \exp(-\frac{\|X - C_q\|^2}{\sigma_q^2}) \tag{3}$$

σ_q represents the standard deviation of the input vector from the center of the Gaussian function C_q.

For the entire input vector of the RBF neural network, the expected output is:

$$y = \sum_{q=1}^{Q} W_q Z_q + e \tag{4}$$

W_q is the weight vector between the node of the q hidden layer and the output layer; *e* is the fitting error.

In this paper, the orthogonal least-squares method is used to determine the center of radial basis function, and the least-squares method is used to train the output weights (see literature [18]). The objective of the training is to minimize the total error:

$$\min E = \frac{1}{2}\sum_{i=1}^{N} e_i^2 \tag{5}$$

In the formula of (5), $e_i = y_i - \sum_{q=1}^{Q} W_q Z_q$, when the input vector is $X = [x_1, x_2, \cdots x_m]^T$, the expected output is y_i.

IV. FEATURE EXTRACTION OF SERIES AND PARALLEL ARC FAULT

In aviation AC series and parallel arc fault detection, due to the instability of arc fault and the influence of load uncertainty, single feature extraction is difficult to characterize the arc fault of all loads, which makes the reliability of arc fault detection low. Considering the complexity of feature extraction method and the accuracy of arc fault identification, this paper proposes a series and parallel arc fault identification method based on the fusion of time-domain and frequency-domain features of signals, which converts the recognition of single feature into the study of arc fault with multiple feature variables. The reliability of arc fault identification is improved.

A. Time-domain Characteristics

The current signal of the aviation AC series and parallel arc test is shown in Fig. 6. The first five cycles are normal operation and the last five cycles are arc fault. Among them (a) - (d) figure is series arc test data, the corresponding load is resistance 7Ω, resistance 7Ω+ inductance 5mH, resistance 57Ω+ capacitance 47μF, resistance 115Ω+ ATRU; (e) figure is parallel arc test data, the load is resistance 15Ω.

Observe the waveform of the current signal in Figure 6. For series arc test, the current amplitude decreases when arc fault occurs under linear load, and the phenomenon of "flat shoulder" appears near the zero-crossing point of the current signal, which shows that the content of high-order harmonics increases in the frequency domain. When arc fault occurs under non-linear load, the current amplitude also decreases, but its "flat shoulder" phenomenon is not obvious compared with the normal waveform, which increases the difficulty of arc fault feature extraction and identification. For parallel arc test, when arc fault occurs, the amplitude of the current waveform increases obviously and the waveform distortion is serious.

Based on the above analysis, the kurtosis and cosine distance time-domain analysis method are used to extract fault features to reflect the waveform changes of current signals under normal and arc fault conditions. Meanwhile, FFT is used to analyze the frequency spectrum of current signals, extract their frequency domain characteristics, and construct a multi-dimensional feature based on time and frequency domain characteristics. The eigenvector matrix is input into the RBF neural network for arc fault identification.

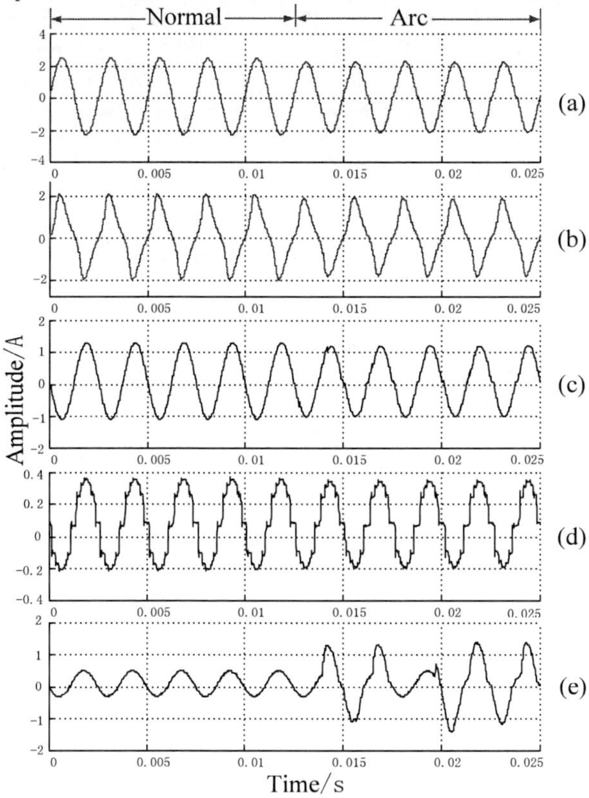

Fig. 6 Typical load current signal

For a group of random signals *x(t)*, the kurtosis formula is as follows:

$$K = \frac{E[x^4(t)] - 3\{E[x^2(t)]\}^2}{\{E[x^2(t)]\}^2} = \frac{1}{N}\sum_{i=1}^{N}\left(\frac{x_i - \bar{X}}{\sigma_x}\right)^4 - 3 \tag{6}$$

In the formula of (6), $\bar{X}$ is the mean of random signal, σ_x is the standard deviation and N is the length of signal.

The weekly kurtosis values of current signals obtained from the aviation AC series and parallel arc tests are shown in figure 7. The blue points indicate the kurtosis values of normal conditions, and the red points indicate the kurtosis values of arc faults. A load of (a)-(e) figure is consistent with Figure 6.

Observation of Figure 7 shows that the kurtosis values of different loads can well represent the arc fault information. The kurtosis values are unchanged under normal working, and will fluctuate obviously when arc fault occurs. For series and parallel pure resistance, resistance-capacitance and non-linear loads, the calculated kurtosis values show an upward trend when a fault occurs. For resistance-inductive loads, the kurtosis values decrease obviously and then increase gradually when the arc fault occurs. However, the kurtosis value in Figure 7 cannot find a uniform threshold applicable to all loads, and it is difficult to identify arc faults directly.

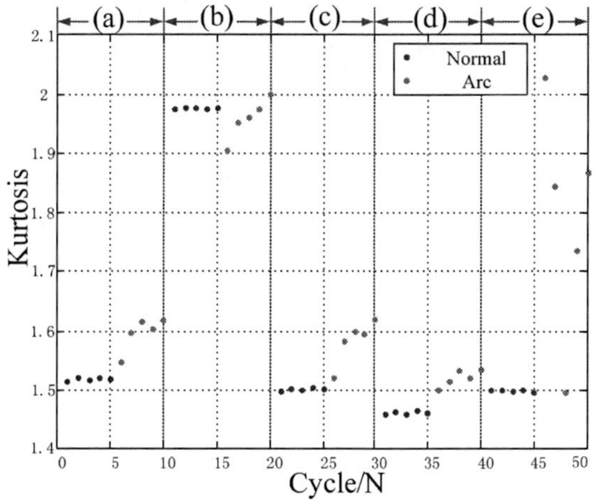

Fig. 7 Kurtosis values for different loads

Cosine distance can reflect the approximation between vectors by calculating the distance between points in two high-dimensional spaces. If the result of cosine distance is 1, they are highly similar; if the result is -1, they are not.

In two-dimensional space, the cosine formula between $a(x_1, y_1)$ and $b(x_2, y_2)$ is as follows:

$$\cos\theta = \frac{x_1x_2 + y_1y_2}{\sqrt{x_1^2 + y_1^2} \cdot \sqrt{x_2^2 + y_2^2}} \tag{7}$$

When extended to n-dimension, the angle cosine formula of two n-dimension sample points $a(x_{11}, x_{12}, \cdots, x_{1n})$ and $b(x_{21}, x_{22}, \cdots, x_{2n})$ is as follows:

$$\cos\theta = \frac{\sum_{k=1}^{n} x_{1k} \cdot x_{2k}}{\sqrt{\sum_{k=1}^{n} x_{1k}^2} \cdot \sqrt{\sum_{k=1}^{n} x_{2k}^2}} \tag{8}$$

In this paper, the first normal period is chosen as the reference period, and the cosine distance between the period after calculation and the reference period is taken as the eigenvalue, and the last four decimal points are taken as the valid values. The calculation results are shown in Fig. 8. The first five cycles are the cosine distance values under normal conditions, and the last five cycles are the cosine distance values under fault conditions. A load of (a)-(e) figure is consistent with Figure 6.

Observation figure 8 shows that for different typical loads under series and parallel arc fault test, the adjacent periodic cosine distances under normal conditions are close to 1, which indicates that the similarity between waveforms is high at this time, while when arc fault occurs, the adjacent periodic cosine distances are smaller than those under normal conditions. The above analysis shows that the method of calculating the adjacent period cosine distance as the characteristic quantity of arc fault can well reflect the similarity between waveforms and the working state of the circuit.

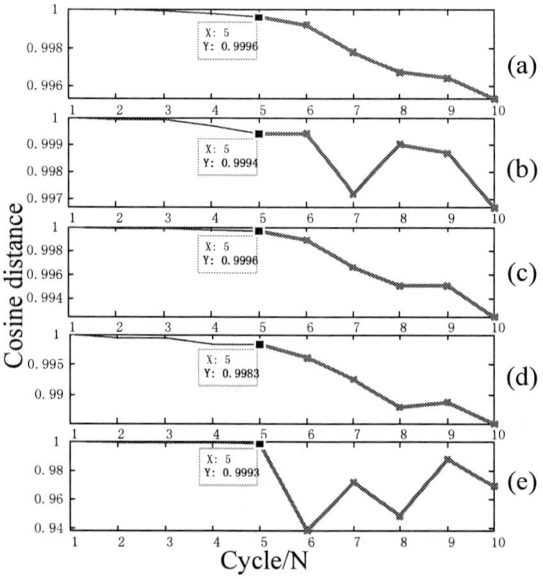

Fig. 8 Cosine Distance

However, by comparing (a)-(e) diagrams, it can be found that the minimum distance between adjacent periodic cosines is 0.9983 for non-linear ATRU loads, and there is a cross phenomenon between adjacent periodic cosines when other loads occur arc fault, which is not conducive to the selection of uniform thresholds when classifying faults.

B. *Frequency-Domain Characteristics*

As a mature method, FFT has been widely used in signal processing and other fields [19]-[20]. It can map the function relationship of signal in time-domain to frequency-domain. In this paper, FFT is used to analyze the spectrum of the current signal. The results show that the blue curve is the normal spectrum and the red curve is the spectrum of the arc fault as shown in Figure 9.

Compared with the normal and fault current spectrum in Figure 9, it can be seen that for series arc test, when the load is resistive, the spectrum amplitude changes obviously in the frequency band of 0Hz-25kHz; when the load is resistive-inductive, the spectrum amplitude changes obviously in the frequency band of 0.8kHz-20kHz; when the load is resistive-capacitive, the spectrum amplitude changes completely. There are obvious differences in the frequency range; when the load is a non-linear ATRU load, the spec--trum amplitude is different in the frequency band of 0 Hz-20 kHz; for parallel arc test, when the load is a resistive load, the spectrum amplitude of the current signal changes obviously in the frequency band of 0 Hz-25 kHz.

Based on the above analysis, 0.8 kHz-16 kHz is selected as the characteristic frequency band of series and parallel arc fault. The local magnification of this frequency band is shown in the graphs of the subgraphs in Fig. 9. The change of odd harmonic amplitude in the graphs under normal and arc fault is more significant than that of even harmonic amplitude. In order to quantify the change of odd harmonic amplitude further, the difference of odd harmonic between fault period and normal period is calculated in the characteristic frequency band of 0.8kHz-16kHz, and the difference of odd harmonic between fault period and normal period is used as the characteristic quantity to represent the information of arc fault. As shown in Fig. 10, the first five periods in the figure are normal and the last five periods are arc fault.

By comparing the odd harmonic difference of different loads under normal and fault conditions in Fig. 10, it can be found that the odd harmonic difference and the cross phenomenon exist in series arc test resistive load, which is not conducive to the identification of arc fault; for other loads, the odd harmonic difference and this characteristic can be used to distinguish arc fault clearly.

C. *Construction of Multidimensional Eigenvector Matrix*

Based on the analysis of the single feature extracted in time-domain and frequency-domain above, it can be found that the kurtosis method is not very effective in extracting the feature of resistive inductive load; the method of adjacent periodic cosine distance is not easy to find a unified threshold for all loads; the difference and square of odd harmonics in 0.8kHz-16kHz characteristic frequency band can distinguish arc faults under resistive inductive load and non-linear load, but the effect is not good for resistive load in series arc test. Therefore, in order to better extract arc fault information and improve the reliability of fault identification, this paper constructs a multi-dimensional eigenvector matrix based on the above-mentioned single eigenvalue, which combines the information of aviation series and parallel arc fault, and can represent the fault situation of all linear and non-linear loads in the test.

V. SERIES AND PARALLEL ARC FAULT IDENTIFICATION

The series and parallel arc tests were carried out for 10

typical linear and non-linear loads listed in Tables 1 and 2. Each load was repeated three times, and a total of 30 sets of current signals were collected. The characteristic matrices of 300x3 are constructed to identify arc faults by calculating the time-domain and frequency-domain characteristic quantities of the continuous current signals of five cycles in normal and arc faults.

A. RBF Neural Network Recognition

The experimental characteristic matrix is input into the RBF neural network for arc fault identification, and 70% of the random data is presupposed as training samples and 30% of the random data as testing samples. In the training process, the actual data allocation scheme is shown in Table 3. 208 groups of random data are used as training samples and 92 groups of random data as testing samples.

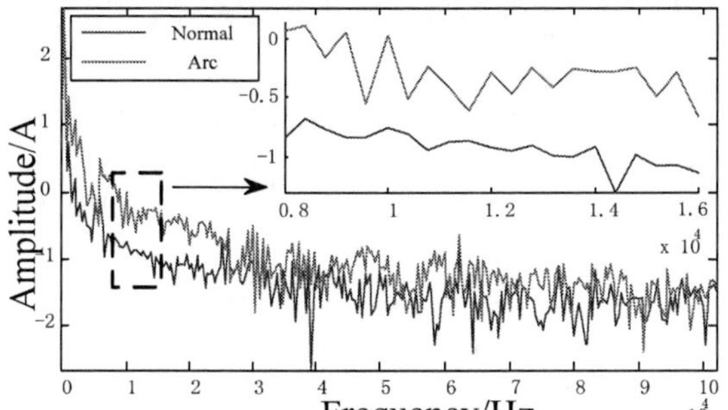

(a) Resistance 7Ω (series test)

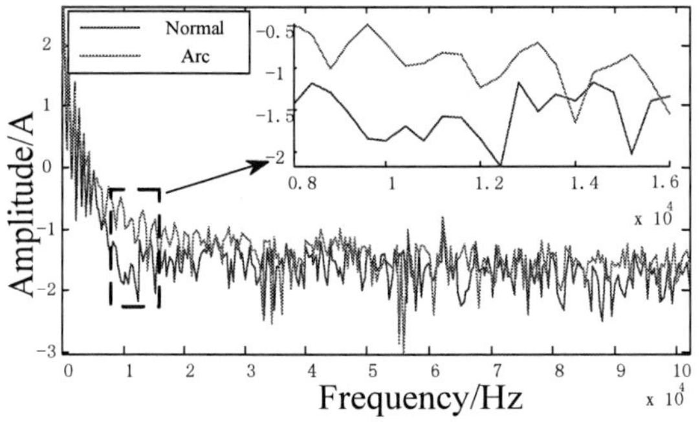

(b) Resistance 7Ω + Inductance 5 mH (series test)

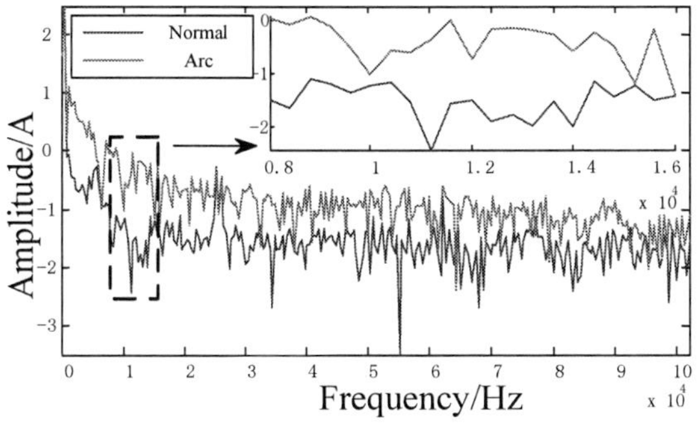

(c) Resistance 57Ω + Capacitance 47 μF (series test)

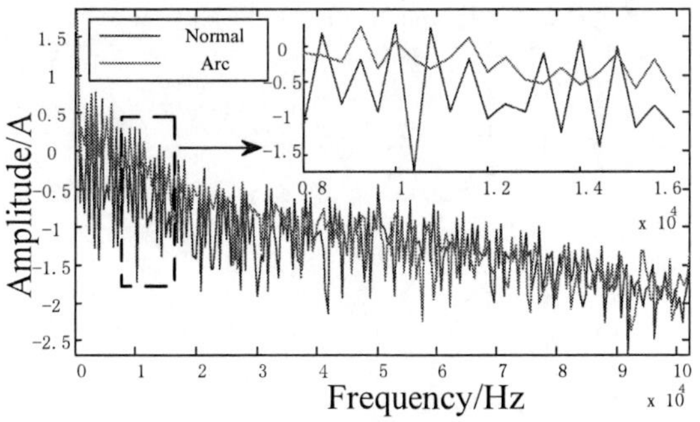

(d) Resistance 115Ω +ATRU (series test)

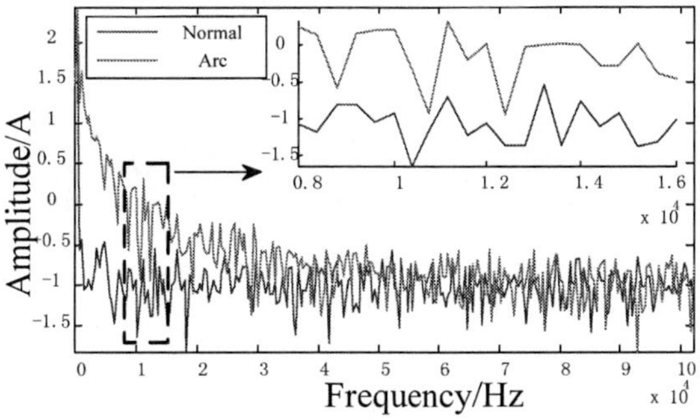

(e) Resistance 15Ω (parallel test)

Fig. 9 Spectrum of typical load current signal

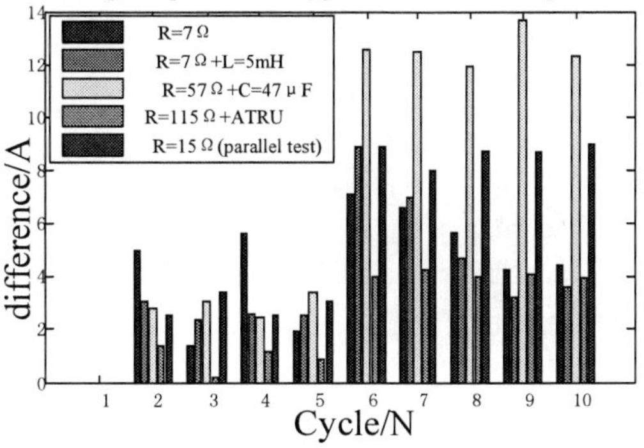

Fig. 10 Sum of 0.8 kHz-16 kHz frequency band odd harmonic difference

The classification results of arc faults are shown in Table 4. The number 0 in the table represents the normal working condition and the number 1 represents the arc faults. Table 4 shows that when RBF neural network is trained, there are two sets of data that are misjudged for 106 sets of data measured as 0 (i.e. normal condition), and the classification accuracy is 98.1%. For 102 sets of data measured as 1 (i.e. arc fault), there are three sets of data that are misjudged, and the classification accuracy is 97.1%. Therefore, for the total of 208 sets of data, the classification accuracy is 97.1%. The accuracy rate of the comprehensive classification of group training data was 97.6%. When using the above-trained model for arc fault detection, only one group of 92 groups of data containing normal and arc fault conditions has misjudged, and the classification accuracy is 98.9%, and the whole classification process takes only 0.05 seconds.

Table 3 data distribution plan

		Group	Percentage
Sample	train	208	69.3%
	test	92	30.7%
	effective	300	100.0%
	exclude	0	
	total	300	

Table 4 Classification results

Sample	Prediction / Reality	0	1	Correct
Train	0	104	2	98.1%
	1	3	99	97.1%
	overall	51.4%	48.6%	97.6%
Test	0	43	1	97.7%
	1	0	48	100%
	overall	46.7%	53.3%	98.9%

B. Comparison of Identification Methods

Three recognition methods, nearest neighbor algorithm (KNN), multi-layer perceptron neural network (MLPNN) and decision tree algorithm, are selected. The 300 X3 matrices constructed above is used as input to identify the series-parallel arc faults in aviation AC. The speed and accuracy of arc fault identification are compared with the RBF neural network. The results are shown in Table 5.

Table 5 Comparison of different recognition algorithms

Algorithms	Time/s	Correct(%)
KNN	0.56	95.3
MLP neural networks	0.04	95.3
Decision tree	0.11	98.0
RBF neural networks	0.05	98.9

From Table 5, it can be found that MLPNN, decision tree, and RBF neural network have relatively short recognition time when identifying arc faults with the same feature matrix, and can quickly realize fault recognition, and the RBF neural network has the highest recognition accuracy; KNN has the longest time and low recognition accuracy for arc faults. Considering the two factors of recognition speed and accuracy, RBF neural network has more prominent advantages and is suitable for aviation AC series-parallel arc fault identification.

VI. CONCLUSION

In this paper, the method of identifying series-parallel arc faults in the 115V/400Hz aviation AC distribution system is studied. The conclusions are as follows:

1) A multi-feature fusion feature extraction method based on time-domain and frequency-domain features is proposed, which makes up for the disadvantage that a single feature is susceptible to load changes. The kurtosis and adjacent periodic cosine distance are extracted, and the odd harmonic difference in 0.8kHz-16kHz characteristic frequency band and the multi-dimensional eigenvector matrix are constructed. The fault information of typical linear load and non-linear load in series and parallel arc test is well represented.

2) The multi-dimensional eigenvector matrix is input into the RBF neural network for arc fault identification. The results show that for typical linear and non-linear loads, the RBF neural network can identify arc fault well. The recognition accuracy is 98.9%, and the time used is 0.05s. On the whole, the multi-feature fusion method based on RBF neural network has the advantages of simple operation, good real-time performance, and high reliability. It is suitable for the identification of the aviation AC series-parallel arc fault.

ACKNOWLEDGMENT

The authors are thanks for the support of the Hebei Natural Science Foundation Project (No.2016202106).

REFERENCES

[1] Y. J. Zhang, L. Wang, Z. D. Yin, et al. "Characteristics extraction method of aviation DC serial arc fault based on HHT," J. Acta Aeronautica et Astronautica Sinica, 2019, 40(1): 522404.

[2] Y. Jin, G. H. Ma. "Research and Application of the Arc-Fault Circuit Breaker in Airplane," J. Aviation Manufacturing Technology, 2014(14): 92-94.

[3] R. H. Cui, Y. Wang, Y. N. Li. "Aviation series arc fault detection method based on correlation coefficient and bias-normal distribution index", J. Advanced Technology of Electrical Engineering and Energy. 201 9,38(01):82-88.

[4] K. Zeng, L. Xing, Y. Zhang, et al, "Characteristics analysis of AC arc fault in time and frequency domain," 2017 Prognostics and System Health Management Conference (PHM-Harbin), Harbin, 2017, pp. 1-5.

[5] J. A. Momoh and R. Button, "Design and analysis of aerospace DC arcing faults using fast fourier transformation and artificial neural network," 2003 IEEE Power Engineering Society General Meeting (IEEE Cat. No.03CH37491), Toronto, Ont., 2003, pp. 788-793 Vol. 2.

[6] M. K. Khafidli, E. Prasetyono, D. O. Anggriawan, et al."Implementation AC Series Arc Fault Recognition using Mikrokontroller Based on Fast Fourier

Transform,". 2018 International Electronics Symposium on Engineering Technology and Applications (IES-ETA), Bali, 2018, pp. 31-36.

[7] Q. W.Lu, T. Wang, Z. R. Li, et al. "Series arc fault detection method based on wavelet transform and singular value decomposition," J. Transactions of China Electrotechnical Society, 201 7,32(17):208-217.

[8] W. Dong, J. Zhang, M. Gui, et al. "The identification of aviation arc fault based on the BP neural network," CSAA/IET International Conference on Aircraft Utility Systems (AUS 2018), Guiyang, 2018, pp. 1-6.

[9] C. Chen, F. Guo, Y. Liu, et al. "Recognition of series arc fault based on the Hilbert Huang Transform," 2015 IEEE 61st Holm Conference on Electrical Contacts (Holm), San Diego, CA, 2015, pp. 324-330.

[10] J. LIU, K. ZHOU and Y. Hu, "EMD- WVD Method Based High- Frequency Current Analysis of Low Voltage Arc," 2018 Condition Monitoring and Diagnosis (CMD), Perth, WA, 2018, pp. 1-5.

[11] Y. Wang, F. Zhang, X. Zhang, et al. "Series AC Arc Fault Detection Method Based on Hybrid Time and Frequency Analysis and Fully-connected Neural Network," in IEEE Transactions on Industrial Informatics. 2018.2885945

[12] C. H.Wu, X. F. Feng, H. Tong, et al. "Research on photovoltaic fault arc detection method based on BP neural network," J. Acta Energiae Solaris Sinica, 2016,37(11):2958-2964.

[13] Z. Chen, Y. Wang, F. Niu, et al. "Fault arc detection based on neural network and D-S evidence theory," J. High Voltage Apparatus, 2019,55(03):29-36.

[14] Y. W. Liu, C. J. Wu, Y. C. Wang, "Detection of serial arc fault on low-voltage indoor power lines by using radial basis function neural network," J. International Journal of Electrical Power & Energy Systems, Volume 83,2016, Pages 149-157.

[15] UL standard for safety for arc fault circuit interrupters[S]. 2ed. ANSI UL1699, 2008.

[16] SAE Aerospace. AS5692 Arc Fault Circuit Breaker (AFCB), Aircraft, Trip-Free Single Phase 115 VAC, 400 Hz-Constant Frequency [S] . Aerospace Standard, 2004.

[17] S. L. Lei C. X. Sun, Q. Zhou, et al. "Shout-term load forecasting method based on RBF neural network and ANFIS system," J. Proceedings of the CSEE, 2005(2 2):81-85.

[18] Y. W. Liu, C. J. Wu, Y. C. Wang, "Detection of serial arc fault on low-voltage indoor power lines by using radial basis function neural network," International Journal of Electrical Power & Energy Systems,Volume 83,2016,Pages 149-157.

[19] Z. X. Geng, F. S. Zhang. "Full component correction method for power system harmonic analysis," J. Proceedings of the CSEE, 2018,38(12):3481-3487+7.

[20] H. Wen, Z. S. Teng, Y. Wang, et al. "Improved windowed interpolation FFT dynamic harmonic analysis algorithm and its application," J. Transactions of China Electrotechnical Society, 201 2,27(12):270-277.

Ruihua Cui, female, born in 1962, Ph. D, professor, master tutor. She is mainly engaged in the research of electrical computer aided design and arc electric contact technology.

Study on Lifetime of Electromagnetic Relay between Resistive Load and Inductive Load

Vincent Fang, Wei Gao
Industrial Technology Lab, Tyco Electronics (Shenzhen) Co., Ltd., China
E-mail: vincent.fang@te.com wei.gao@te.com

***Abstract*—Based on theory analysis, it is generally believed that the lifetime of electromagnetic relays under resistive load are better than that under same level current inductive load, but we found that the lifetime of some relay products the results were inverse. In this paper, the relays with different current level were selected as the study object. Through analyzed the temperature rise, morphology of the contact (after lifetime) and the product structure, it was found that the product structure greatly determines the difference of lifetime between resistive load and inductive load. And verified that by reducing the load current or adjusting the relay overtravel could reduce or even reverse the difference of lifetime between the resistive load and the inductive load. The whole study is helpful for product design, product performance evaluation and customer applications.**

***Index Terms*— Relay, Electrical lifetime, Resistive load, Inductive load, Temperature rise, Arc energy, Contact morphology.**

I. INTRODUCTION

In the product specifications of many relay manufacturers, it describes a situation that for the relays to reach same lifetime cycles, the current in inductive load is less or much less than that in resistive load (non-motor). So, what is the reason behind this difference? We all know that the difference between resistive load and inductive load at the same level current is the presence or absence of inductance. Because the inductor stores energy and the energy basically release by the arc when the contact switching off the load, the arc under inductive load is severer than that under resistive load. Thus, people generally believed that the lifetime of electromagnetic relay under resistive load is better than that under inductive load. However, is the lifetime of relays under resistive load always better than that under inductive load? Based on our past experiences, it was found that lifetime of some relay products under resistive load was worse than that under inductive load.

In order to verify the different lifetime of relays between resistive load and inductive load, in this paper, mainstream application of well-known brand relay products A08/B16/C15/D30 (Fig. 1) were selected as the study object, which contains two different structures vertical and horizontal, and the contact rated current cover typical specification from small to high level current.

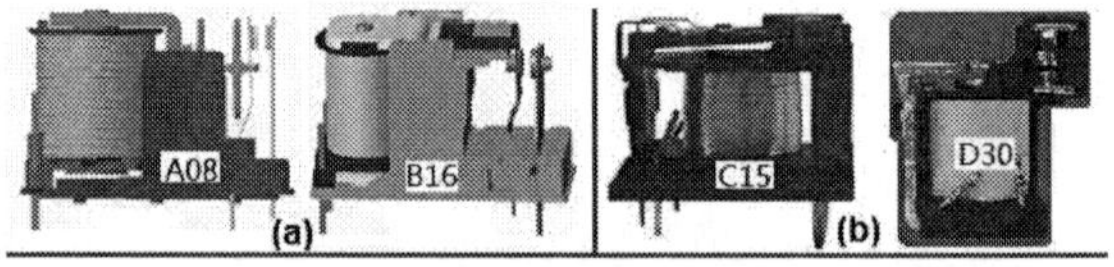

Fig. 1 (a) Vertical structure relays, with card; (b) Horizonal relays, without card

The test results (Fig. 2) showed that the lifetime of relays A08&B16 under resistive load were better than that under inductive load, while the lifetime of relays C15&D30 under resistive load were worse than that under inductive.

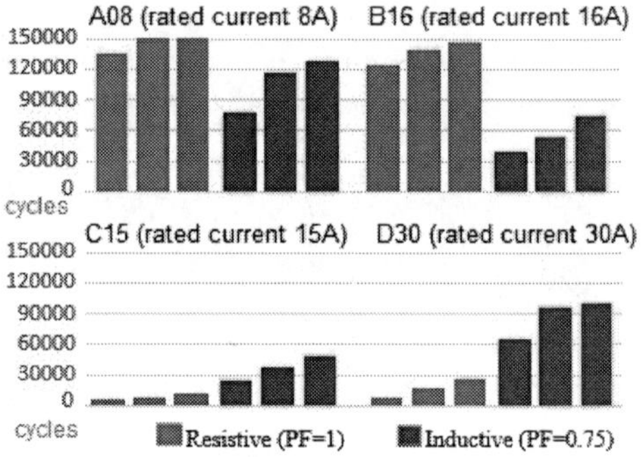

Fig. 2 Test condition: AC250V/60Hz, rated current, at 40 ℃, switching frequency was 1S on/1S off except D30 (1S:3S). Comment: failure mode is contact weld

II. METHODS AND RESULTS

The failure mode of tested samples for lifetime verification test all were contact weld. The contact weld mainly occurs at the processes of contact switching on. The mechanism is that the contact have a big resistance at initial touch, the heat generates quickly by the current and causes the metal on contact surface to melt, and result in the contact touch area increase, at this time, the contact resistance drops rapidly, and the molten metal cools rapidly and causes contact weld. During relay lifetime testing, the switching arc leads the contact material continuous loss and causes the contact resistance continuous increases or the influence of magnitude current at contact switching on will causes the contact weld. The former one analyzed the difference of arc energy between the resistive load and the inductive load (temperature rise and morphology comparison), the latter one analyzed instantaneous difference at contact switching on (load closing characteristics and product structure analysis).

The schematic of the loads and the difference of break arc energy calculated by theory were shown by Fig. 3, the difference between two loads is that the inductive load has inductance while resistive load doesn't have, and the inductance store energy (1/2) LI^2, and the energy basically release by the arc when the contact switching off the load (Base on this point, we always think the break arc energy under inductive load is stronger than that under resistive load). Considering the difference of arc energy between resistive load and inductive load could be reflected well under high level current, two groups of representative products B16 (better resistive lifetime) and D30 (better inductive lifetime) were selected to analyze what difference between two load types and what difference between the products.

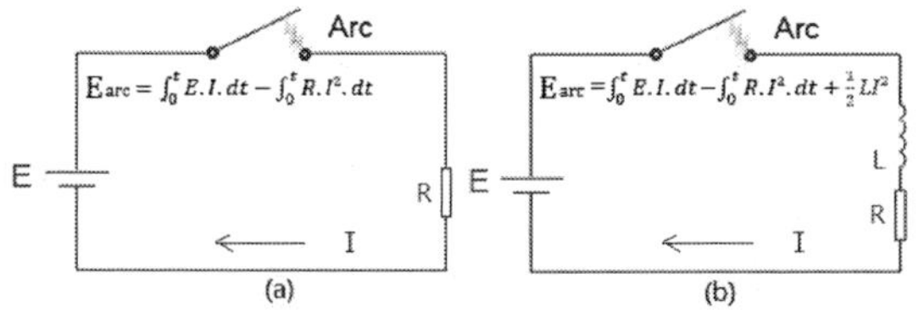

Fig. 3 Difference of break arc energy between resistive load (a) and inductive load (b)

A. Temperature rise comparison test

In order to reduce the difference of characteristic between samples, two pieces each for B16 and D30 were selected which have similar electrical and mechanical parameters, and the temperature of terminals were recording continuously during lifetime test under resistive load and inductive load (B16:250V/16A/1s:1s/40 ℃, D30: 250V/30A/1s:3s/40℃; PF=1 for resistive load, PF=0.75 for inductive load).

The installation of thermocouples and samples were shown by Fig. 4, temperature recorder YOKOGAWA GP20 recorded the temperature of movable terminal and stationary terminal. The test data was shown by Fig. 5, the temperature performance of B16 and D30 were very consistent: the average temperature of B16 terminals under resistive load were about 10℃ lowers than that under inductive load, and the average temperature of D30 terminals under resistive load were about 5℃ lower than that under inductive load (because of the different duty ratio, lower than B16 10℃). The results of temperature rise indicated that the arc energy of relay under resistive load was weaker than that under inductive load. In addition, less arc energy under resistive load is more favorable to the lifetime of relay, and it preliminarily explains that why the lifetime of B16 under resistive load was better than that under inductive load.

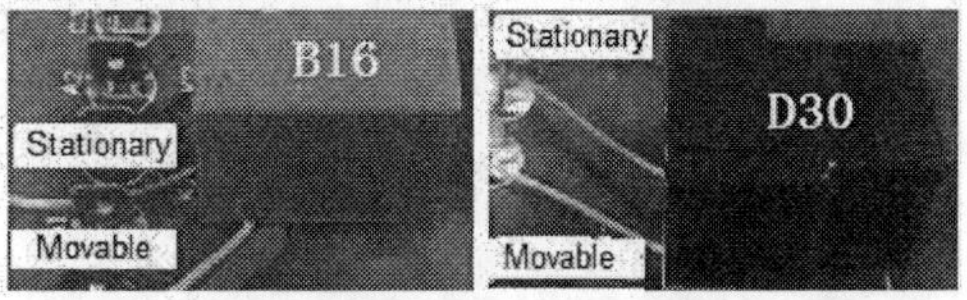

Fig. 4 Relay B16/D30 mounted on PCB, thermocouples positioned on Movable/Stationary terminal;

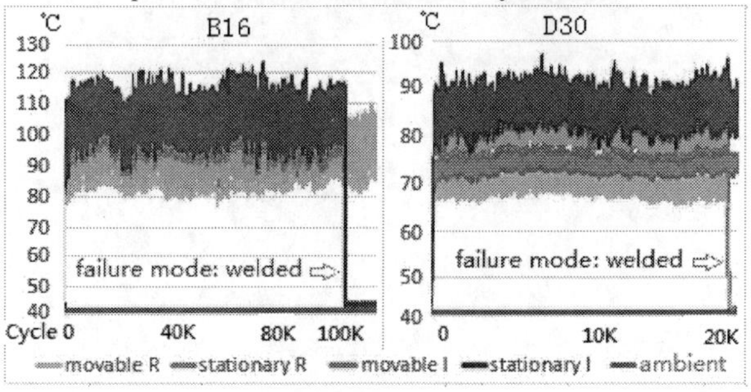

Fig. 5 Temperature graphs during lifetime test under resistive load & inductive load

B. Contact morphology analysis after lifetime test

In order to find out what difference caused to the relay contacts after lifetime test between different load types, the representative samples were selected which finished same test cycles under resistive load and inductive load, and it was found that the appearance of the contact surfaces and the surrounding area of spring were obvious difference, and the images (Fig. 6) were taken under the digital microscope (KEYENCE, VHX-5000). The color for the samples tested under inductive load were darker than that under resistive load, also the evenness of contact surfaces was worse (the erosion was severer). The darker color it reflected that the arc energy under inductive load was stronger, and more organic gases of the relay was released under higher temperature, and more carbon was decomposed by the arc, and the decomposed carbon attached to the contact surfaces and the surrounding area of the springs. Thus, the arc energy of the relay under resistive load was weaker than that under inductive load, and it was consistent with the experiment results of the temperature rise, and it is favorable to the lifetime of relay under resistive load.

C. load closing characteristics and product structure analysis

From above analysis on the morphology of contact surfaces of the samples after electrical lifetime and temperature rise of terminals during lifetime test, they mainly reflected the different intensity of break arc energy between resistive load and inductive load, and explained resistive load is favorable to the lifetime of relay, like the lifetime performance A08 and B16. But the worse lifetime under resistive load for D30 hasn't been explained yet. As the arc is not the only affecting factor to the lifetime of relay, the closing characteristics of resistive load and inductive load, as well as the structure of the products were analyzed in further.

Fig. 6 Digital microscope images of spring, movable contact & stationary contact surfaces after lifetime test

1) Closing characteristics of the load

The simulated waveform for the relay closing the circuit under resistive load and inductive load was shown by Fig. 7, for the resistive load, the phase for the current is same as the voltage, the contact will start with peak current while the contact switching on at peak voltage, and plus with big initial touch resistance, the strong energy ($E= I^2Rt$) is easy to cause the metal on contact surface to melt, and at this time, if two contacts can't slide well, it will causes the contact weld easily and causes relay failure. For the inductive load, the self-inductance opposes the change of current, hence the current can only start with zero while the contact switching on. Therefore, the closing characteristic of inductive load is more favorable for contacts lifetime performance.

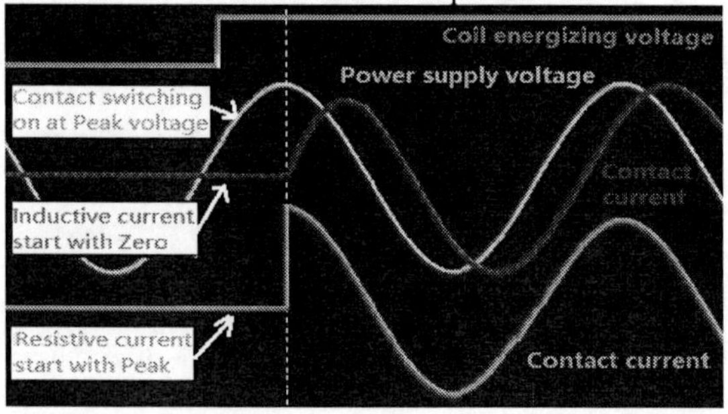

Fig. 7 Closing characteristics of Resistive & Inductive load

2) Product structure analysis

From the structure of B16 (Fig. 8 a), it belongs to the vertical structure (with card), both movable spring and stationary spring are easy to deform. The operational process is: the coil energizing and the electromagnetic force attracts the armature moving toward the core, and the other side of the armature forces the card pushing the movable spring to close the contacts. Because of the existence of overtravel (Fig. 8 a2), the movable spring drives the stationary spring to move backward (Fig. 8 a3). During the operation processes, the mechanical movement of the springs drive two contacts slide mutually in a large range, and this bidirectional slide ability is very helpful to weaken or destroy the characteristics of contact weld under resistive load at contact switching on. Therefore, the difference of arc energy plays a leading role for the lifetime of B16 relay, and the lifetime under resistive load was better than that under inductive load.

From the structure of D30 (Fig. 8 b), it belongs to the horizontal structure (without card), the movable spring was fixed on the armature (big discount to the deformation), and the stationary spring is completely unmovable. The operational process is: the coil energizing and the electromagnetic force attracts the armature moving toward the core, and forces the movable spring to close the contacts. Because of the existence of overtravel (Fig. 8 b2) and unmovable of stationary spring, the movable spring force its contact to slide over stationary contact forward with head up in a little range (Fig. 8 b3). This unidirectional slide ability is difficult to weaken or destroy the characteristics of contact weld under resistive load at contact switching on. Therefore, the closing characteristic plays a leading role for lifetime of D30 relay, and the lifetime under resistive load was worse than that under inductive load.

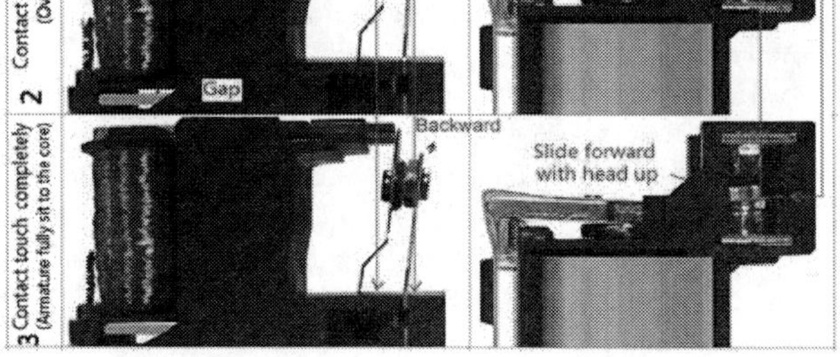

Fig. 8 B16&D30 inner structure and spring/contact movement characteristics

3) Verification

According to the analysis above about load closing characteristics and product structure, and against the bad resistive lifetime performance for the relay (D30) with vertical structure, verifications to improve lifetime of D30 were carried out as the following two aspects:

I) Reducing the contact current (to reduce current energy go through the contacts), reduce welding area and welding force of the contact, so that the unidirectional slide ability of D30 can weaken or destroy the characteristics of the contact permanent welding under resistive load at contact switching on. The lifetime test results showed by Fig. 9: (a), by decreased contact current to 50% of rated current (16A), the gap of lifetime between resistive load and inductive load was very small; (b), by decreased contact current to 33% of rated current (10A), the lifetime of relays under resistive load was better that that under inductive load.

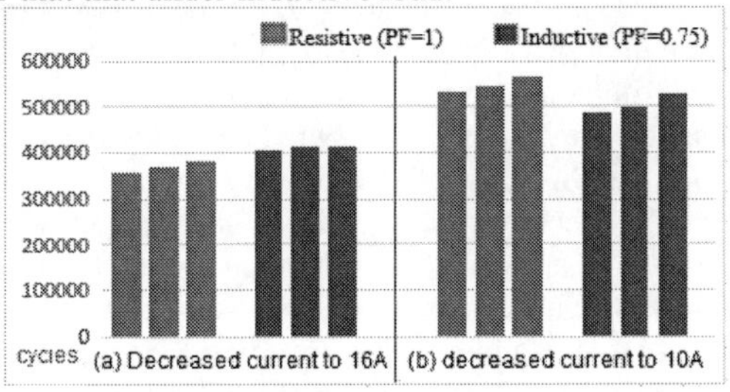

Fig. 9 (a) D30 lifetime under 250V/60Hz/16A/1s:1s/T40; (b) D30 lifetime under 250V/60Hz/10A/1s:1s/T40

II) Reducing overtravel, it means to reduce the gap between armature and core at initial touch status (Fig. 8 b2), and it increases initial touch electromagnetic force which can be calculated by formula $F=KS(NI)^2/G$ (showed by Fig. 10). it is beneficial to increase contact touch area, reduces the contact resistance, and helpful to cool the contacts, reduces the contact weld area and the welding force; and it is helpful to increase contacts slide force and slide in time to avoid contact weld. Therefore, reducing overtravel is helpful to weaken or destroy the characteristics of contact weld under resistive load at contact switching on. The verification test results shown by Fig. 11, the lifetime for the samples with overtravel (reducing) closed to lower specification (small) have a significant improvement under resistive load, and it is about twice lifetime to the samples with overtravel closed to upper specification (big), and it is consistent with the theory analysis.

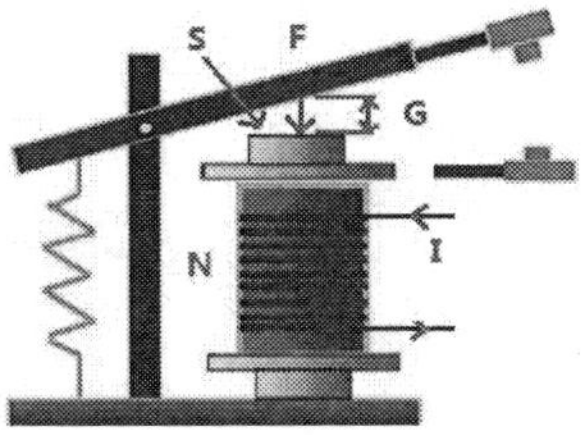

Fig. 10 Relay system

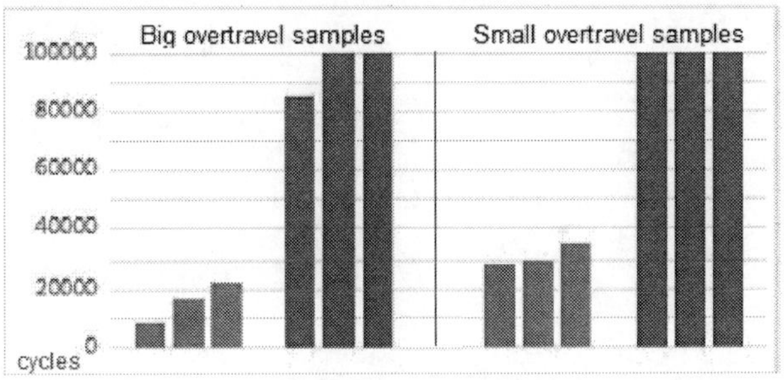

Fig. 11 Lifetime comparison, test condition: 250V/60Hz/30A/1s:3s/T40

III. CONCLUSION

1) Terminals temperature rise under inductive load were higher than that under resistive load with same level current, besides, the color of the contacts and the surrounding area of spring were darker and break arc energy was stronger under inductive load, the inductive load was more unfavorable to the lifetime of relays.

2) The relays with vertical structure (A08&B16), the contacts have a bidirectional slide ability which was helpful to weaken or destroy the characteristics of contact weld under resistive load at contact switching on. The difference of arc intensity plays a leading role to the lifetime, and lifetime under resistive load was better than that under inductive load.

3) The relays with horizonal structure (C15&D30), only the movable contact has a unidirectional slide ability which was difficult to weaken or destroy the characteristics of contact weld under resistive load at contact switching on. The closing characteristic plays a leading role to the lifetime, and lifetime under resistive load was worse than that under inductive load.

4) By reducing the contact current to reduce the welding force, it could narrow the gap of lifetime for the relay with horizonal structure (D30) between resistive load and inductive load, and even reversed the result which the lifetime under resistive was worse than that under inductive load at rated current. Besides, by reducing overtravel to increase initial touch electromagnetic force, it could have a significant improvement to the relay's lifetime under resistive load.

5) The studies in this paper is helpful for products design, product performance evaluation and customer applications.

REFERENCES

[1] M. R. Swinehart, "Arcs and Arc Erosion in high current contacts"

[2] W. Rieder, C. Veit, "Influence of Materials on the interaction of switching arcs with contacts and walls"

Research on Reliability Test of Small Capacity Auxiliary Contacts

Jing Wu, Yong Zhang
Shanghai Liangxin Electrical Co., Ltd., Shanghai, 201315

Abstract—**The auxiliary contact is used together with the low-voltage electric appliance, which is mainly used for the main circuit status indication, interlocking, fault identification, etc. Due to the difference between the low-voltage electrical protection capability and the use environment, when the auxiliary contact is under low voltage and low current load break reliability may be reduced. This article mainly uses an automated test equipment and a set of test methods to verify the auxiliary contacts to ensure reliable use under low voltage and low current loads.**

Index Terms— **Auxiliary contact, Low voltage, Low current, Reliability test**

I. INTRODUCTION

Small-capacity auxiliary contacts are usually used in appliances with control functions, which can directly reflect the separation position of the main contacts. When using the client, the customer will detect the state of the auxiliary contact within a certain period of time (μs or ms) according to the need, and determine the position of the main contact. The reliability of the auxiliary contact action is very important. Once the auxiliary contacts are not working properly, the hazard is large, and the control system cannot work normally, which will lead to major equipment safety accidents and major economic losses. The development of modern industry has placed increasing demands on the working life and working reliability of auxiliary contacts. In order to assess the performance of a new type of contact material, or to verify that the manufacturing process of the product meets the requirements, a series of performance tests, studies and comparative analysis are required on the electrical contact portion.

In this paper, the reliability of small-capacity auxiliary contacts is tested. The reliability test method is proposed and the results of test monitoring are given. The product was analyzed for failure and provided a reference for the design of small-capacity auxiliary contacts.

II. SMALL CAPACITY AUXILIARY CONTACT FAULT TYPE

The main types of faults for small-capacity auxiliary contacts are: trigger, bounce, wave, etc.:

1) Trigger failure: The small-capacity auxiliary contact has a decrease in the connection stability due to wear and aging of the material itself, changes in the use environment, etc. during use.
2) Bounce failure: In the traditional switching action, there is a case where the moving contact rebounds, which causes the micro switch to be converted from a normally open contact to a normally closed contact, and then from a normally closed contact to a normally open contact, and the cycle is switched. Until the rebound stops, at this time, the switching state signal of the auxiliary contact acquisition switch appears to be frequently switched, and the signal feed back to the control terminal is extremely inaccurate.
3) Fluctuation failure: The welding process of the auxiliary contact is not reliable, and the change of the internal resistance after the contact material wears for a long time causes the amplitude of the output signal to change

Till now, there are few researches for test methods with small-capacity auxiliary contacts for above problems. The small-capacity auxiliary contact reliability test system studied in this paper can fully find these problems, which has made it easier for researchers to find and solve problems.

III. TEST SYSTEM PERFORMANCE CHARACTERISTICS

The test conditions of the small-capacity auxiliary contact reliability test system introduced in this paper are set according to GB 14048.17-2008: the operation is convenient, simple and efficient. It is a set of test system with set judgment, automatic fault record and professional report generation. The main performance characteristics are as follows:

a) With 8 sets of test channels, the reliability test of multiple auxiliary contacts can be performed simultaneously;
b) A large number of parameters can be set by itself: main contact control voltage (0~300V), frequency (0-150Hz), auxiliary contact voltage (0-24V), current (0.5~12mA), test frequency (60~ 3600 times / h), the total number of tests (1-99999 times), etc., can meet the testing needs of a variety of small-capacity auxiliary contacts;

c) Can detect, display and save the auxiliary contact voltage waveform in real time, monitor the on-off state of the auxiliary contact, and realize the self-diagnosis of the contact failure;
d) The reliability of the auxiliary contacts can be tested in various environments in conjunction with the environmental test chamber.

IV. TEST SYSTEM DESIGN PRINCIPLE

A. Test system hardware design

The hardware structure of the test system is shown in Figure 1. The functions of each part are as follows:

1) The test system is mainly controlled by the industrial computer, and provides an AC voltage source to the control port of the test object to realize the control of the pull-in and release of the main contact, realizing the closing and opening control of the auxiliary contact.
2) The DC signal source and the high-precision program-controlled resistance load realize the accurate output of the small voltage and small current signals, can accurately determine the influence of the auxiliary contact on the auxiliary contact due to the change of the process technology and materials.
3) The oscilloscope can monitor the voltage waveform of the high-precision program-controlled load terminal in real time, collect and judge the data through the industrial computer.
4) The multimeter detects the on/off of the main contact, determines the fault category by measuring the state of the main contact of the test product when the auxiliary contact does not operate.

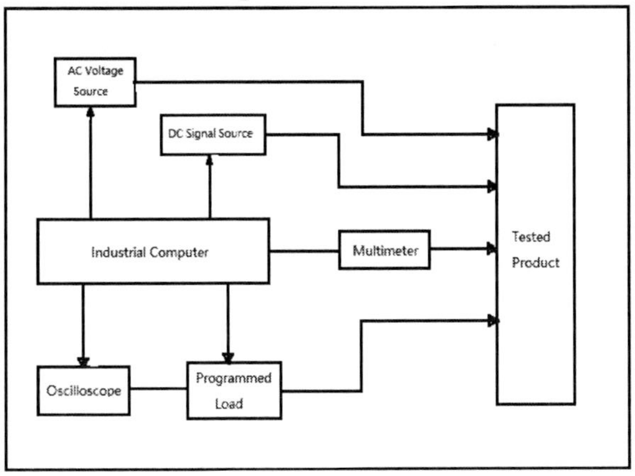

Fig. 1 Test system hardware block diagram

B. Test system software design

The test system software design can realize many functions such as automatic control of test process, high-speed signal acquisition, data processing and fault diagnosis. There are:

1) Operation control module: The industrial computer connects the AC adjustable voltage source, the DC signal source, and the high-precision program-controlled load through the serial port, and controls the input, output, and signal amplitude of the instrument through the communication port to realize the suction and release of the sample. control. The timing diagram of the contact action is shown in Figure 2.

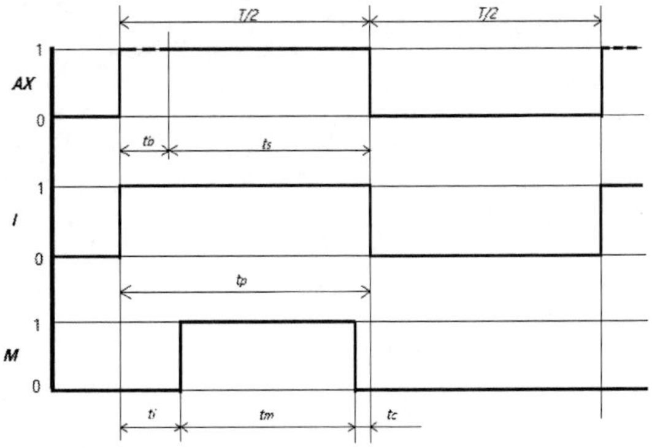

Fig. 2 Auxiliary contact action timing diagram

AX: auxiliary contact;
I: test current;
M: monitoring of voltage drop or load;
ti: Customize the allowable bounce time;
tm: contact pressure drop monitoring time;
tc: the last time without monitoring, generally 10% of T/2;
tp: the time at which the current circulates;
ts: the steady state time of the auxiliary contact being tested;
tb: bounce time before reaching steady state;

2) Parameter setting module: running parameter setting, bounce parameter setting; determining the test waveform in real time by setting the channel trigger failure rate, bounce failure rate, fluctuation failure rate, bounce width, etc. The bounce waveform exceeds the set test room and is considered to appear once. Fault, exceed the set percentage, stop working. The test parameters must be correctly set before the test. The electrical parameter setting interface is shown in Figure 3.
3) Data processing module: After the oscilloscope tests the waveform during the test, the data is uploaded to the PC, and the relevant test waveforms and values are read by the software, and then the real-time discrimination is performed according to the matching parameters, and the data is recorded at the same time.

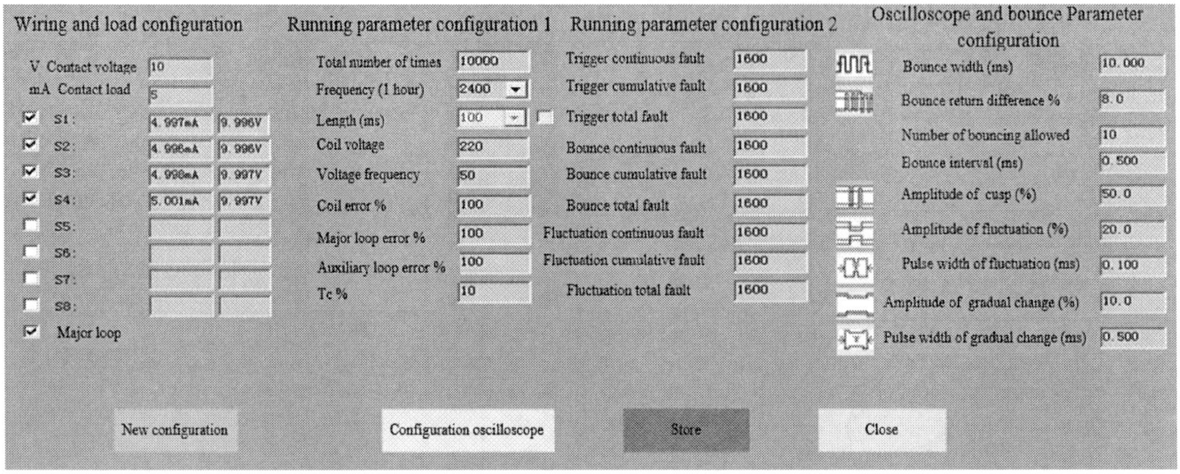

Fig. 3 Test system electrical parameter setting interface

V. TEST CASE INTRODUCTION

Take a product as an example, the contact test voltage of the auxiliary contact is set to 10V, the test current is 5mA, the coil voltage is set to 220V, 50Hz, and the test is 50,000 times. Execute the run command, the test system will display the captured test waveform in real time. As shown in Figure 4, the S3 test waveform is displayed as abnormal. The real-time information is " S3 NO 1-1 11.8-3.8_FMoff_FMon_wave1_spline", which is expressed as: S3 channel, NO often Open contact, the contact has a number of bouncing on, off, respectively, the wave artery width is 11.8ms, 3.8ms, and there is spline.

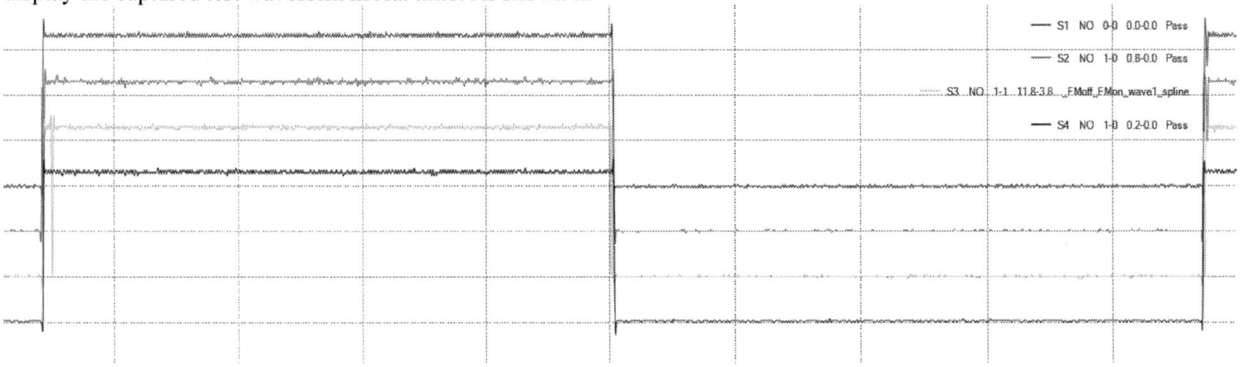

Fig. 4 The system displays the test waveform in real time.

After the end of the operation, the test system will directly display the test result pass/fail, and automatically generate a detailed fault record table, as shown in Figure 5, where the total fault is triggered 18 times, the total bounce fault is 22 times, and the total fluctuating fault is 91 times. The test result is "failed".

Print the report	Overall results	Qualified	S1		S2		S3		S4		S5		S6		S7		S8	
Input voltage (V)	10	Normally Open/Closed	NO		NO		NO		NO		EMPTY		EMPTY		EMPTY		EMPTY	
Input current	5	Turn ON/OFF	ON	OFF	ON	OFF	ON	OFF	ON	OFF	ON	OFF	ON	OFF	ON	OFF	ON	OFF
Total number of times	50000	Single-channel number of tests	50000	50000	50000	50000	50000	50000	50000	50000	-1	-1	-1	-1	-1	-1	-1	-1
Frequency (1 hour)	2400	Determination of experimental results	Qualified	Qualified	Unqualified	Qualified	Qualified	Qualified	Unqualified	Unqualified	NA	NA	NA	NA	NA	NA	NA	NA
Trigger total fault	18	Trigger continuous fault			*1													
Bounce total fault %	22	Trigger cumulative fault			*11				*4	*3								
Fluctuation total fault %	91	Bounce continuous fault																
Coil error %	0	Bounce cumulative fault			*3		*19											
Major loop error %	500	Fluctuation continuous fault					*6											
Auxiliary loop error %	0	Fluctuation cumulative fault	*1		*3		*87											

Fig. 5 System fault record table

VI. ANALYSIS AND IMPROVEMENT OF TEST RESULTS

The test results show that the total failure of the test product is 18 times, and the inspection fault waveform shows that the sample has intermittent non-sticking problems. There are many factors that cause the contact reliability to be low, and the main factors are:

1) Grinding abrasive residue: not cleaned after grinding, resulting in residual P, C, O polishing solution, carbonization during contact closure.
2) Micropores or cracks: There are a large number of pits and cracks on the surface, and they contain grease residues.
3) Electrochemical corrosion: Corrosive halo generated by electrochemical reaction at dust particles, micropores or cracks.
4) Residue of polishing liquid: After the polishing treatment, there is no pickling and cleaning procedure, which causes residual particles of polished stone.
5) Wear of the casing or bracket: the wear of the material from the casing or the bracket, the large particle impurities attached to the surface of the contact during the post-installation or use.

According to the above several factors, improve the product design: increase the contact pressure, pickle and passivate the contact, oil-impregnate the contact surface (organic coating treatment), and change the shape of the conductive loop. After the design improvement plan is completed, all parts are ultrasonically heated and cleaned to remove surface impurities, installed and tested again by the small-capacity auxiliary contact reliability test system for 50,000 times of non-connection performance test. The test results are shown in Fig. 6. The auxiliary contact triggers the total fault 2 times, the total bounce fault 5 times, and the total fluctuating fault 35 times. The number of failures is significantly reduced compared with before the improvement, indicating that the improvement scheme has a certain effect of improving the stability of the connection.

Print the report	Overall results	Qualified	S1		S2		S3		S4		S5		S6		S7		S8	
Input voltage (V)	10	Normally Open/Closed	NO		NO		NO		NO		EMPTY		EMPTY		EMPTY		EMPTY	
Input current	5	Turn ON/OFF	ON	OFF	ON	OFF	ON	OFF	ON	OFF	ON	OFF	ON	OFF	ON	OFF	ON	OFF
Total number of times	50000	Single-channel number of tests	50000	50000	50000	50000	50000	50000	50000	50000	-1	-1	-1	-1	-1	-1	-1	-1
Frequency (1 hour)	2400	Determination of experimental results	Qualified	Qualified	Unqualified	Qualified	Qualified	Qualified	Unqualified	Unqualified	NA	NA	NA	NA	NA	NA	NA	NA
Trigger total fault	2	Trigger continuous fault																
Bounce total fault %	5	Trigger cumulative fault			*2													
Fluctuation total fault %	35	Bounce continuous fault																
Coil error %	0	Bounce cumulative fault					*5											
Major loop error %	117	Fluctuation continuous fault					*4											
Auxiliary loop error %	0	Fluctuation cumulative fault	*1		*1		*32		*1									

Fig. 6 Retest after improvement

VII. CONCLUSION

This paper mainly studies the reliability test technology of small-capacity auxiliary contacts, and develops a test system based on computer control, which improves the automatic control level of small-capacity auxiliary contact test. At the same time, taking the small-capacity auxiliary contact product as an example, the actual test cases of the test system in real-time display and judgment of the test waveform are introduced, which provides ideas and basis for the reliability test plan of the small-capacity auxiliary contact in the future, thus help the product to find and solve problems during R&D and testing.

REFERENCES

[1] Rong Mingzhe. Electrical Contact Theory. Mechanical Industry Press, 2003.

[2] GB/T 14048.17-2008/IEC 60947-5-4: 2002. Low-voltage switchgear and control equipment - Part 5-4: Control circuit electrical and switch originals.

[3] Huang Shaopo, Li Kui, Wang Yang, Zhou Jungang, Huang Lixiong. Contactor Auxiliary Contact Switching Capacity Test System. Electrical Application. Infrastructure. 2018, Vol. 37, No. 5

7th International Conference on Reliability of
Electrical Products and Electrical Contacts,
November 04-06, 2019

Reliability Analysis of Arc Recognition Method Based on Cumulant Autoregressive Parameters Mahalanobis Distance

Ruihua Cui, Fengfeng Li
State Key Laboratory of Reliability and Intelligence of Electrical Equipment School of Electrical Engineering, Hebei University of Technology, Tianjin 300130

Abstract—**In order to improve the reliability of Aviation series arc fault identification, an aviation AC arc fault detection method based on the combination of autoregressive model (AR model) parameters and Mahalanobis distance was proposed. According to the characteristics of line current waveform distortion when arc fault occurs in electrical equipment and line, the accumulated AR parameter Mahalanobis distance characteristic value of arc fault current waveform was extracted to identify whether arc fault occurs in line. The factors affecting arc fault diagnosis by this method were analyzed and studied, including load variation, power supply frequency and sampling frequency variation. The results show that this method can effectively extract the characteristic difference between arc fault current and normal operation, with high reliability and easy implementation.**

Index Terms—**Higher-order cumulant, AR model, Mahalanobis distance, Fault arc, Reliability**

I. INTRODUCTION

In recent years, with the further development of electrical technology in the aviation field, the capacity of aircraft power distribution systems has been increasing, which has led to a large number of cables and structural complications. The related report [1] shows that many air crashes and aircraft faults are directly or indirectly related to the continuous arc generated on the surface of the power supply line of the electrical system. Aviation electrical safety issues have become more severe. Studying aviation AC arc fault detection technology is of great significance for ensuring the safety and reliability of distribution lines.

When detecting a fault arc, the arc can generally be divided into two types depending on where the arc occurs in the aeronautical line: a series arc and a parallel arc. Domestic and foreign scholars have studied the detection method of fault arc, and have achieved certain results. At present, there are three main research methods: diagnosis of fault arc based on arc mathematical model [2], which mainly stays in the simulation analysis stage; The characteristic detects the fault arc [3-4]; the arc is identified according to the waveform characteristics of the line voltage and current signals [5-8].

The method of discriminating arc fault based on circuit parameters is not limited by the detection location, and the data acquisition circuit is relatively simple, which has become the mainstream research direction. Fourier analysis [9], wavelet analysis [10], and empirical mode decomposition method [11] are all used in the detection of fault arcs. The combination of circuit parameters and artificial intelligence methods has also achieved certain results. In [12], the time domain signal characteristic value of current is used as one of the inputs of BP neural network; in [13], the current fractal dimension is used as the feature vector, and the support vector machine is used for classification. These methods require online training samples, which are not easy to implement in embedded systems and do not meet the requirements of real-time detection [14]. Therefore, the analysis and research of arc fault characteristics and the ability to identify arc faults quickly, accurately and reliably have high engineering practical value [15].

The autoregressive model (AR) is a time series analysis method whose parameters contain important system state information, which can be used to diagnose the state of the system. The high-order cumulant can effectively separate the stationary and cyclostationary signals, and theoretically can completely suppress Gaussian colored noise, which is especially suitable for analyzing non-Gaussian signals [16]. The Mahalanobis distance can relate the various characteristics of the sample, and can eliminate the interference of the correlation between the variables; and the calculation result of the Mahalanobis distance is not affected by the dimension [17], that is, regardless of the measurement unit of the original data. Therefore, it is very suitable for use in fault detection.

In view of the advantages of the above three methods, this paper proposes a detection method based on the cumulant AR model parameters combined with the

Mahalanobis distance to realize the diagnosis of aviation AC arc fault. Reliability analysis and experimental verification were carried out for the factors affecting the determination result of the method, including the change of load, the frequency of power supply and the variation of sampling frequency.

II. AR PARAMETER ESTIMATION BASED ON HIGHER ORDER CUMULANTS

A. Moments and Cumulatives

Higher-order statistic is higher than second-order statistic, generally including high-order moment, high-order cumulant, high-order moment spectrum, high-order cumulant, etc., which plays an important role in the field of non-Gaussian signal processing.

The *k*-th moment of the continuous random signal x(t) is:

$$m_{kx}(\tau_1,\cdots,\tau_{k-1})=E[x(t)x(t+\tau_1)\cdots x(t+\tau_{k-1})] \quad (1)$$

The k-order cumulant of the continuous random signal x(t) is:

$$c_{kx}(\tau_1,\cdots,\tau_{k-1})=cum[x(t),x(t+\tau_1),\cdots,x(t+\tau_{k-1})] \quad (2)$$

The k-th order cumulant of the stochastic process $x(t)$ describes the degree to which the *k*-th moment of the stochastic process deviates from the *k*-th moment of the Gaussian process. For a Gaussian process, its high-order cumulant is equal to zero.

Theorem [18]: If $x(t)=s(t)+y(t)+v(t)$, where $s(t)$ is a deterministic signal, $y(t)$ is a zero-mean stationary non-Gaussian process, $v(t)$ is a zero-mean Gaussian process independent of $y(t)$. when $k>2$, there are:

$$c_{kx}(\tau_1,\cdots,\tau_{k-1})=c_{ky}(\tau_1,\cdots,\tau_{k-1}) \quad (3)$$

In the formula: $c_{kx}(\tau_1,\cdots,\tau_{k-1})$ is the high-order cumulant of the signal x(t), $c_{ky}(\tau_1,\cdots,\tau_{k-1})$ is the high-order cumulant of the signal $y(t)$

The real-world signal can be seen as a stochastic process $x(t)$ consisting of a deterministic signal, a zero-mean stationary non-Gaussian process, and a zero-mean Gaussian process. Theorem knows that its high-order cumulant is unaffected by the deterministic signal and the Gaussian process.

B. AR parameter estimation based on higher order cumulants

For the discrete random sequence $x(t)$, the AR(p) model represented by the difference equation can be expressed as:

$$\sum_{l=0}^{p} a_l x(t-l)=e(t) \quad (4)$$

In the formula:p is the AR model order, a_l ($l=0,1,\ldots,p$) is the AR model parameter, and $a_0=1$,$e(t)$ is the model residual.

The regular equation corresponding to the higher order cumulant is:

$$\sum_{l=0}^{p} a_l Ckx(\tau-l,k_0,0,\cdots,0)=0 \quad (5)$$

In the formula: $\tau > 0$, k_0 is an optional parameter.Let $\tau=1,2,\cdots$, then equation (5) can be written in matrix form:

$$C(k_0)A=0 \quad (6)$$

In the formula: $A=[1\ \alpha_1\ \cdots\ \alpha_p]^T$,$C(k_0)$ is:

$$C(k_0)=\begin{pmatrix} C_{kx}(1-0,k_0,0,\cdots,0) & C_{kx}(1-1,k_0,0,\cdots,0) & \cdots & C_{kx}(1-p,k_0,0,\cdots,0) \\ C_{kx}(2-0,k_0,0,\cdots,0) & C_{kx}(2-1,k_0,0,\cdots,0) & \cdots & C_{kx}(2-p,k_0,0,\cdots,0) \\ \vdots & \vdots & \vdots & \vdots \\ C_{kx}(p+1+M-0,k_0,0,\cdots,0) & \cdots & \cdots & C_{kx}(p+1+M-p,k_0,0,\cdots,0) \end{pmatrix}$$

The choice of the parameter k_0 should ensure that the rank of $C(k_0)$ is *p*, so that *p* variables $a_1,a_2,\cdots,a_p$ can be solved by equation (6).

III. ARC RECOGNITION METHOD BASED ON MAHALANOBIS DISTANCE

A. Basic concept of Markov distance

One of the key technologies for arc fault detection is to find out the characteristic difference that can reasonably and effectively distinguish the arc fault or normal operation of the circuit, that is, to determine the similarity of the current characteristics in the two states. In statistics, two commonly used methods for comparing the similarity between two sample sets are Euclidean distance and Mahalanobis distance.

Euclidean distance has obvious shortcomings in application, limited by the dimension of the identified feature, and it is equivalent to the difference between different attributes of the sample, and the weight assigned to all components is the same. Therefore, the application of Euclidean distance has certain limitations. Sex.

The Mahalanobis distance has a unique advantage over the Euclidean distance. It represents the covariance distance of the data. Through the covariance matrix, the Mahalanobis distance assigns different weights to each component, the larger components accept smaller weights, and the smaller components accept larger weights. The calculation of the Mahalanobis distance is not affected by the dimension, ie, regardless of the unit of measurement of the original data. In this paper, the characteristic characteristics of the above-mentioned Mahalanobis distance are used to amplify the characteristic difference of the current signal, which is convenient and more intuitive to find the discriminant threshold.

B. Mahalanobis distance solving method

The extraction of eigenvalues based on Mahalanobis distance is mainly divided into two major steps: (1) solving the reference point of the Mahalanobis distance; and (2) solving the Mahalanobis distance in the real-time detection stage.

(1) Solving the reference point of the Mahalanobis distance

In the Markov distance method, the mean, standard deviation and covariance are considered simultaneously. Covariance is a quantity that describes the degree of correlation between two samples. Its value is affected by the dimension. Therefore, it needs to be de-dimensionalized, which leads to the correlation coefficient, which has the same physical meaning as the covariance, but it is A dimensionless quantity.

In this paper, the current characteristic information in the normal state is used as the parameter of the Mahalanobis distance calculation, and the characteristic parameter is the characteristic parameter matrix obtained by estimating the AR model parameters of the current time domain data through the cumulant. The feature reference correlation coefficient matrix C, the mean value and the standard deviation are obtained through the following five steps.

1) Finding the characteristic parameter matrix: sampling the current time domain data of the normal operation of the group of Y=5 groups, sampling 1000 points per group, and estimating the AR model parameters for each group of data. According to the FPE model's ordering criterion and the characteristics of the test data obtained by the trial and error method, considering the real-time requirements, the third-order AR model parameter estimation based on the third-order cumulant is finally used to extract the feature quantity, and a (5x3) order is obtained. Feature matrix $[y_{ij}]$

2) Calculating the mean value and standard deviation of the feature quantities in the feature matrix: using the feature matrix $[y_{ij}]$ obtained in step 1, the mean μ_j and standard deviation σ_j of the feature quantities of the feature matrix are obtained, which are all (1x3) order matrices;

3) Normalization: The normalized calculation of the data is performed by using the matrix obtained in the above two steps to remove the influence of the dimension. The calculation method is as shown in equation (7), and the result is a (Yx3) order matrix P. This matrix will be applied to the calculation of the correlation coefficient matrix. The calculation method is:

$$P_{ij} = \frac{y_{ij} - \mu_j}{\sigma_j} (i = 1, 2, \cdots, Y; j = 1, 2, 3) \tag{7}$$

4) Solving the correlation coefficient matrix C, the result is a (3x3) order matrix. The calculation method is as shown in equation (8).

$$C_{ij} = \frac{\sum_{a=1}^{Y} P_{ai} P_{aj}}{Y} (i = 1, 2, 3; j = 1, 2, 3) \tag{8}$$

5) Invert the correlation coefficient matrix C to obtain C^{-1}.

(2) Solving the Mahalanobis distance in the real-time detection stage

Using the parameters obtained in (1), the eigenvalues based on the Mahalanobis distance are obtained by the equation (9). When calculating the Mahalanobis distance in real time, only the value of the sample characteristic x to be tested is a variable, and the others have been found in (1).

$$D_M^2(x) = \left(\frac{x-\mu}{\sigma}\right)^T C^{-1} \left(\frac{x-\mu}{\sigma}\right) \tag{9}$$

IV. ARC SIMULATION DEVICE AND EXPERIMENT

A. Arc simulation device

The series and parallel arc fault experimental platforms were built with reference to American Standard UL1699 [19] and SAE-AS5692 [20] to simulate the series fault arc and parallel fault arc under the aviation AC system.

The schematic diagram of the series-type point contact test and the schematic diagram of the arc generator device are shown in Figures 1 and 2, which are used to simulate the fault arc caused by poor contact between two conductors and contact fracture. The main body of the circuit is a stepper motor controlled arc generator consisting of a fixed flat carbon rod electrode and a movable pointed copper rod electrode. The lateral regulator is used to slowly move the adjustment electrode gap to produce a stable arc between the electrodes. Collect loop current signals through the power supply. The test uses an aeronautical power supply with an output voltage of 115V and a frequency of 400Hz.

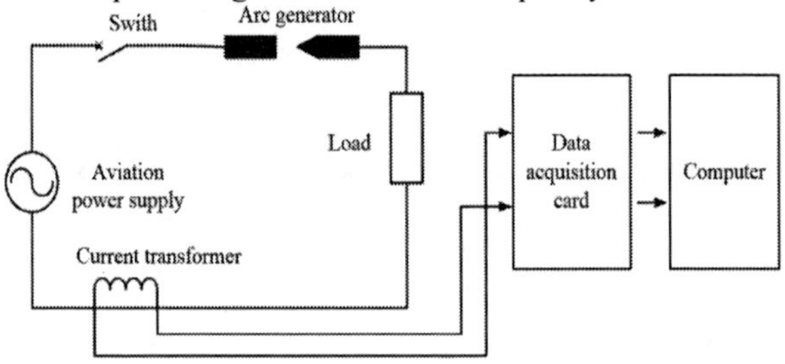

Fig. 1 Schematic diagram of series point contact test

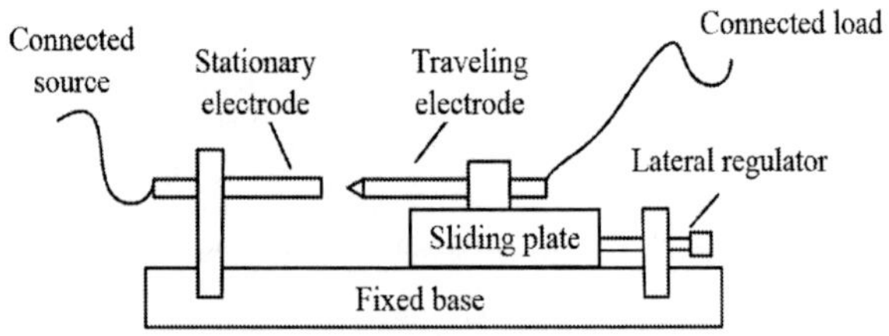

Fig.2 Schematic diagram of arc generator device

The schematic diagram of the parallel fault arc test is shown in Figure 3. It is used to simulate the phenomenon that the actual aviation cable is scratched and cut during the vibration or maintenance of the aircraft, causing a fault arc between the two wires and between the wire and the fuselage. . Points a and b in the line are the positions where the cutting process is performed before the power is turned on. Among them, the aviation power source used in the test is the same as the series point contact test. The test load is only pure resistive load, and the current limiting resistor is tested with 5Ω and 10Ω respectively.

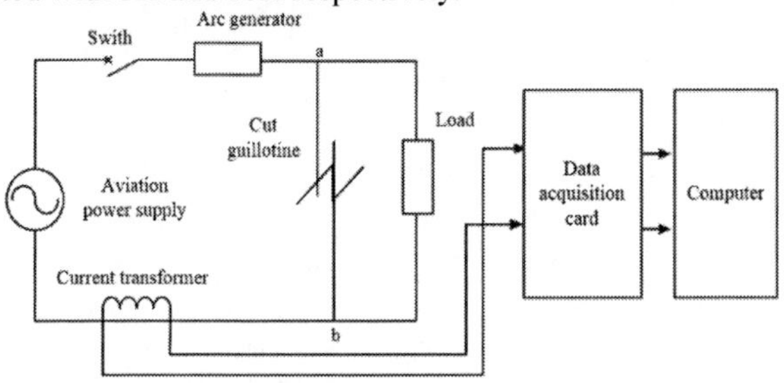

Fig. 3 Schematic diagram of parallel truncation test

B. Simulation test plan

The following tests were carried out to consider the factors affecting the diagnosis of arc faults by considering the type of load, the frequency of the power supply, and the variation of the sampling frequency. In order to find the common characteristics of the arc and obtain as many data samples as possible to avoid contingency, the same experiment was carried out under the same test conditions for 5 groups, each of which included current data during normal operation and current data with arc operation. The test scheme is shown in Table 1. The tests were carried out at a power supply frequency of 400 Hz, and the sampling frequencies were set to 100 kHz, 200 kHz, and 400 kHz, respectively. Among them, the pure power resistance 25Ω, the resistance 25Ω+5mH, the resistance capacity 30Ω+47uF were supplemented with the test of the power frequency of 360Hz and 500Hz.

Table 1 Program of arc simulation test

Test	Load nature	Load type
series connection point contact test	Linear load	25Ω
		5Ω
		100Ω+5mH
		25Ω+5mH
		30Ω+47uF
		5Ω+47 uF
	Nonlinearload	ATRU
		Transformer
Parallel cut test	Current limiting resistor	5Ω、10Ω

V. RELIABILITY ANALYSIS OF ARC RECOGNITION METHOD

A. Impact of load changes

During actual use of electrical lines and equipment, the type and size of the load typically varies. In order to study the influence of the load change on the diagnosis of arc faults by the above identification method, the characteristic data of the test data are extracted and analyzed, and the cumulant AR model parameters of the AR model parameters under normal working conditions and arc faults are calculated respectively. The results are shown in Table 2.

It can be seen from the statistical results of various loads in Table 2 that the Mahalanobis distance eigenvalues in the event of an arc fault are greater than the values of the normal smoothing of the circuit. When the circuit is normally stable, the maximum value of the Mahalanobis distance does not exceed 100; and in the event of an arc fault, the minimum value of the corresponding Mahalanobis distance is 200 or more, or even larger. The load change, the corresponding Mahalanodynamic eigenvalue does not change drastically, and it is still possible to effectively determine whether an arc fault has occurred based on the eigenvalue. It can be seen that the Mahalanobis distance can be used to identify arc faults, and the load variation in the line has little effect on the diagnosis of arc faults.

Table 2 The M value of current when load changes

Load nature	Load type	normal (maximum)	Fault (minimum)
Linear load	25Ω	64.5727	823.5151
	5Ω	87.1668	844.6580
	100Ω+5mH	54.5878	337.3593
	25Ω+5mH	66.5475	348.4607
	30Ω+47uF	61.5820	794.0312
	5Ω+47 uF	43.0508	807.8224
Nonlinear load	ATRU	25.0986	838.7359
	Transformer	57.2137	227.4720
Truncated experiment	5Ω	24.9663	455.2438
	10Ω	46.1310	398.1014

Note: Normal (max) - maximum value of the Mahalanobis distance in a normal state; failure (min) - minimum Mahalanobis distance an arc fault; Test conditions: 400Hz power frequency, 400kHz sampling frequency; each load was repeated 5 times.

B. Influence of power frequency

At present, the advanced aircraft AC power supply is developing towards the direction of the variable frequency power supply, and the frequency varies from

360 Hz to 800 Hz. And the actual aircraft operation process is affected by the environment, load changes, etc., and can not guarantee that the power frequency will remain unchanged at 400 Hz, and there will be fluctuations up and down. Therefore, in order to reliably detect arc faults, the key is that the algorithm should be able to adapt to the changes of parameters, to ensure that the algorithm is not affected by normal system fluctuations, it is necessary to analyze the impact of power frequency changes on arc fault detection. The experimental results are shown in Table 3.

Note: In order to analyze the influence of power frequency variation alone, the corresponding sampling frequency changes accordingly after the frequency is changed. The sampling rates correspond to 360 kHz, 400 kHz, and 500 kHz, respectively. The meaning of normal fault is the same as in Table 2.

Table 3 shows that the M values of the same load at different frequencies are slightly different, but the value of M is still less than 100 during normal operation and more than 200 when the arc is faulty. Due to differences between different trials, it is normal for differences between different groups. However, compared with Table 2, the overall diagnosis did not affect the diagnosis of arc faults. Therefore, if the frequency change occurs in the actual operation, the cumulative model of the AR model parameter Mahalanobis distance value can also be used for analysis without being affected by the frequency change.

Table 3 The M value of current when frequency changes

Power frequency	25Ω		25Ω+5mH		30Ω+47uF	
	normal	fault	normal	fault	normal	fault
360Hz	24.46	496.48	20.44	812.52	22.92	1195.31
400Hz	64.57	823.52	66.55	348.46	61.58	794.03
500Hz	61.96	607.88	39.45	407.59	20.66	1027.7

C. Effect of sampling frequency

In the actual application process of fault diagnosis, the sampling frequency may change. In the above experimental process, the number of sampling points of the current waveform is 1000 per cycle. If the sampling frequency is decreased, the number of sampling points of the current waveform in each cycle will decrease accordingly. Therefore, it is necessary to analyze the influence of the sampling frequency change on the method to determine the arc fault. The sampling frequency is selected as 100 kHz and 200 kHz respectively. The experimental results obtained by calculation and analysis are shown in Table 4 and Table 5.

Table 4 M value of current at sampling frequencies 100kHz

Load nature	Load type	normal (maximum)	Fault (minimum)
Linear load	25Ω	35.7688	407.9379
	5Ω	34.1069	584.5052
	100Ω+5mH	26.4350	436.8734
	25Ω+5mH	27.6239	489.7527
	30Ω+47uF	39.7042	814.3589
	5Ω+47 uF	26.5650	783.5481
Nonlinear load	ATRU	30.9363	672.7461
	Transformer	26.1840	437.5538
Truncated experiment	5Ω	16.0148	434.7966
	10Ω	28.3567	391.4802

Table 5 M value of current at sampling frequencies 200kHz

Load nature	Load type	normal (maximum)	Fault (minimum)
Linear load	25Ω	27.6043	720.9721
	5Ω	28.2969	679.6919
	100Ω+5mH	32.0993	218.4254
	25Ω+5mH	28.2335	261.1608
	30Ω+47uF	27.1903	813.6718
	5Ω+47 uF	29.4168	839.5220
Nonlinear load	ATRU	39.6118	969.1888
	Transformer	20.7545	585.6968
Truncated experiment	5Ω	23.4190	481.3416
	10Ω	39.3766	413.0330

Comparing Table 2, Table 4 and Table 5, when the

sampling frequency is changed from 400 kHz to 100 kHz and 200 kHz, the eigenvalue M will appear slightly up and down, but the variation range is small. Under normal conditions, the eigenvalue is stable less than 100. The stability is greater than 200, and there is no overlap of intervals. Due to the differences in the tests and the environmental impact of the test, it is normal for the differences between the different groups. Therefore, it can be considered that within a certain range, the change of the sampling frequency does not affect the diagnosis result of the arc fault in the line.

D. Arc fault identification strategy

Based on the above analysis, although the load, power supply frequency, and sampling frequency are different, there is still a certain Mahalanobis distance characteristic interval, which is between the normal stationary state and the Mahalanobis distance value at the time of the arc fault. Therefore, in the process of identifying the actual arc fault, the calculated Mahalanobis distance feature value can be amplified according to experience as a judgment threshold, and is applicable to any of the above cases, so that the threshold value has versatility. Here, the discriminating threshold is set to 150, that is, the calculated cumulative amount AR model parameter Mahalanobis distance characteristic value is greater than 150, that is, an arc occurs in the line. According to the US fault arc circuit breaker safety standard UL1699 [19], in the 400 Hz aeronautical AC line, when the arc fault circuit breaker detects a fault arc of 8 and a half weeks within 100 ms, the circuit breaker needs to perform a tripping action to cut off the circuit. In this paper, it is assumed that when the suspected fault arc point reaches 8, the arc fault is considered to ensure that the system can recognize the arc fault within 100ms.

VI. CONCLUSION

In this paper, the experimental examples of series-point contact and parallel-cut arc faults with different loads, different power supply frequencies and different sampling frequencies are simulated on the built-off arc fault experimental simulation platform, and the cumulative amount of AR is simulated for the current data of the simulation test. The reliability of the model parameter Mahalanobis arc identification method is summarized, and the characteristic difference between the arc fault and the normal state of the circuit is summarized. The results show that using the cumulant AR model parameter Mahalanobis distance feature identification method to diagnose arc fault can effectively reduce the influence of load variation, power frequency fluctuation and sampling frequency variation on the diagnosis results. The method proposed in this paper is highly reliable, easy to set threshold, and highly generalized.

ACKNOWLEDGMENT

The authors are thanks for the support of Hebei Natural S cience Foundation Project (No.2016202106).

REFERENCES

[1] Anonymous. Down to the wire. The Queensland Nurse, 2012; 31(1): 13-14.

[2] Yong Jing, Gui Xiaozhi, Niu Liangliang, et al. Series arc fault identification in low voltage systembased on autoregressive parameter mode[J]. Transa-ctions of China Elecrotechnical Society, 2011, 26(8):213-219.

[3] Cai Bin, Chen Degui, Wu Rui, et al. Online de-tecting and protection system for internal faults arcin switchgear[J]. Transactions of China Electrotech-nical Society, 2005, 20(10): 83-87.

[4] Kumpulainen L, Hussain, G.A, Lehtonen M, et al. Preemptive arc fault detection techniques in switchgear and controlgear[J]. Industry Applications IEEE Transactions on, 2014, 50(3): 1649-1658.

[5] Liu Yanli, Guo Fengyi, WANG Zhiyong, et al. Research on the spectral characteristics of series arc fault based on information entropy[J]. Transactions of China Electrotechnical Society, 2015, 30(12): 488-495.

[6] Zhang Guanying, Zhang Xiaoliang, Liu Hua, et al. Online detection method for series arcing faultin low voltage system[J]. Transactions of ChinaEle-ctrotechnical Society, 2016, 31(8): 109-115.

[7] Miao Xiren, Guo Yinting, Tang Jincheng, et al.Load side arc fault voltage detection and identifica-tion with morphological wavelet[J]. Transactions ofChina Electrotechnical Society, 2014, 29(3): 237-244.

[8] Liu Xiaoming, Xu Yefei, Liu Ting, et al. The ar-c fault detection based on the current signal short time zero crossing rate[J]. Transactions of China El-ectrotechnical Society, 2015, 30(13): 125-133.

[9] Ma S H, Guo J W, Bao J Q. Identification met-hod of low-voltage series arc fault based on harm-onic component relative change coefficient[J]. Appl-ied Mechanics and Materials, 2013, 331;144-147.

[10] Zhao Jingbo, Tang Yongwei, Zhang Lei. Imp-roved wavelet transform algorithm of antispectrumAliasing based on adding odd extraction before a node[J]. Electric Machines and Control, 2016,20(02):90-97.

[11] Zhang Liping, Miao Xiren, Shi Dunyi. Resear-ch on low voltage arc fault recognition method ba-sed EMD and ELM[J]. Electric Machines and Con-trol, 2016,20(09):54-60.

[12] Liu Peng, Zhang Feng, Zhang Shiwen. Resea-rch of arc fault detector based on neural networks[J]. Low Voltage Apparatus, 2013(17):1-6.

[13] Yang Kai, Zhang Rencheng, Yang Jianhong, et al. Series arc fault diagnostic method based on f-ractal dimension and support vector machine[J]. Tr-ansactions of China Electrotechnical Society,

2016,31(2):70-77.
[14] Wang Yangkun, Zhang Feng, Zhang Shiwen, et al. Research of HHT based identification methodfor low voltage[J]. Electrical & Energy Manageme-nt Technology, 2015,(21):1-7+17.
[15] Shea J J. Comparing 240 V_rms to 120 V_rms se-ries arcing faults in residential wire[C]//Proceedingsof 54th IEEE Holm Conference on Electrical Cont-acts. Pittsburgh, USA: IEEE, 2008:27-29.
[16] Jiang Lingli, Cao Yuxiang, Deng Zongqun. A-utoregressive parameters estimation based on higherorder cumulant as features combining with fuzzy c-luster analysis for fault diagnosis[J]. Journal of El-ectronic Measurement and Instrument, 2012,26(09):812-817.
[17] Zhan Jianguang, Li Hongbo, Zeng Fanjing, et al.Research on application of Mahalanobis distance infault diagnosis of analog circuits[J]. Electronic Me-asurement Technology, 2012,35(03):128-131.
[18] CHOUDHURY M A A S, SHAH S L, THORNHI-LL N F. Diagnosis of poor control-loop performan-ce using higher-order statistics[J]. Automatica, 2004,40:1719-1728.
[19] UL Inc. UL standard for safety for arc fault circuitinterrupters UL 1699[M]. Second Edition, Northbro-ok: Underwriter Laboratories Inc, 2006:16-24
[20] SAE Aerospace. AS5692 Arc Fault Circuit Breaker(AFCB), Aircraft, Trip-Free Single Phase 115VAC, 400Hz-Constant Frequency[S]. Aerospace Standard, 2004

7th International Conference on Reliability of
Electrical Products and Electrical Contacts,
November 04-06, 2019

Research on Functional Reliability Evaluation Model of Multi-unit Weapon Platform

Jingde Huang[1], Yi Huang[2], Benfu Jiang[1]
[1]Zhuhai College of Jilin University, Zhuhai, 519041, China
[2]Dalian Naval Academy, Dalian, 116018, China
E-mail: jdh925@sina.com Tel: 86-756-7626130 Fax: 86-756-7626130

Abstract—**Aiming at the actual situation of defense space, time and damage probability of multi-unit weapon platform system, the role of queuing theory in optimization analysis is studied, and the reliability evaluation model of multi-unit weapon platform system based on priority allocation criterion is established. By comparing the experimental case with the equivalent analysis method, it is proved that the evaluation model based on the priority allocation criterion is superior to the equivalent analysis method. The error caused by the equivalent method is effectively avoided, and the accuracy is significantly improved. The results also show that the evaluation model based on priority allocation criterion is beneficial to the effective allocation of different types of weapon units in the platform, and can better play the effectiveness of the whole platform system.**

Index Terms— **Multi-unit weapon platform system, Priority allocation criteria, Functional reliability, Evaluation model**

I. INTRODUCTION

Multi-unit weapon platform is an integrated and complex weapon defense system composed of different types of weapons and software modules. Due to the different performance indicators of different types of weapons, such as working time, working environment, damage probability and so on, and the overlap of defense areas of different types of weapons, it is relatively difficult to evaluate the reliability of this platform system. At present, the widely used evaluation methods are generally to analyze the reliability of various weapon equipments as a standard system, because the weapon unit of effectiveness analysis is in integer units, it can be found in the process of calculating the reliability of multi-unit weapon platform system by equivalent analysis method, the number of type i weapon units and the standard equivalent number of weapon units are not necessarily an integer. when some systems are equivalent to a system of non-integer numbers between two integers, this equivalent analysis method will produce large errors. Therefore, a scientific evaluation model for the reliability of such multi-unit weapon platforms is studied in depth.It is of great theoretical significance and practical value to optimize the application scheme of weapon unit and give full play to the working efficiency of each software and hardware module in the platform. Combining with the actual situation of multi-unit weapon platform system, this paper establishes a reliability evaluation model of multi-unit weapon platform based on priority allocation criterion, and verifies the rationality and superiority of the model by comparing with the equivalent analysis method.

II. FUNCTIONAL RELIABILITY EVALUATION MODEL BASED ON EQUIVALENT ANALYSIS METHOD

Equivalent analysis method is used to simplify each type of equipment into each unit weapon, which is same type group with the same performance index, firstly, it is assumed that a certain type of equipment in the same type group is marked as standard type b, secondly, the performance index of type i equipment is transformed into the performance of standard type b.Namely:

$$\lambda_b P_{fwb} R_{1b} = \lambda_i P_{fwi} R_{1i} \tag{1}$$

In the formula, P_{fwi} is the probability of damage to the target when using type i equipment, and R_{1i} is the probability of damage to type i equipment. When the unit weapon characteristic parameters (R_{1b}, R_{1i}, μ_b, μ_i)of standard type and the type i equipment, and the number of unit weapons n_{bi} of type i equipment are given, the equivalent unit weapon number n_{bi} of the type i equipment can be obtained by using the selected method solution (1).

The air target flow density attacked by the type I equipment is as follows:

$$\lambda_i = \frac{\lambda_{ni}}{\sum_{i=1}^{k} \rho_i} \rho_i \tag{2}$$

In the formula, λ_{ni} is the density of air target flow within the interception area of the type i equipment, usually its interception area is wider than the air target dispersion area, then λ_{ni} is equal to λ , k is the number of models of equipment in the platform system, ρ_i is the maximum density of damage target of the type i equipment:

$$\rho_i = n_i \mu_i R_{1i} \tag{3}$$

Through the equivalent calculation of various types of equipment in the platform system, the total number of equivalent unit weapons in the platform system is obtained:

$$n_{b\Sigma} = \sum_{i=1}^{k} n_{bi} + n_b \tag{4}$$

In the formula, n_b is the total number of unit weapons of standard equipment. For the same type of equipment, the probability of damage to the air target it strikes can be expressed as follows:

$$P_{fw} = 1 - \frac{\alpha^n}{n!} \Big/ \sum_{k=0}^{n} \frac{\alpha^k}{k!} \tag{5}$$

In the formula, α is equal to λ/μ, λ are the strength of air target flow, μ is the effective strike strength of the system, and n is the number of unit weapons.

The operational reliability of the platform system can be expressed as the mathematical expectation $E(M)$ of destroying the target group and the average mathematical expectation $\mu(M)$, After calculating P_{fw} from formula (5), using formula (6) and (7), the reliability of the whole platform system can be obtained.

$$E(M) = mP_{fw}R_{1b} \tag{6}$$

$$\mu(M) = \frac{E(M)}{m} = P_{fw}R_{1b} \tag{7}$$

III. EVALUATION MODEL BASED ON PRIORITY DISTRIBUTION CRITERION

For the platform system consisting of different types of equipment, one type of equipment is usually required to be deployed on the platform as the main equipment, while other types of equipment are used as auxiliary unit weapons to make up for the shortcomings of the main equipment in different defense areas. In target allocation, priority should be given to the allocation of major equipment to play a role; when all major equipment is used and air targets are attacked, the target should be allocated to auxiliary equipment. In order to establish the queue theory evaluation model under the above circumstances, the basic assumptions are as follows:

1) The number of target groups in the air is m , and the Poisson distribution with parameter λ is randomly entered into the damage area of the platform system.

2) Unit weapons adopt the principle of priority allocation of major equipment. If the target is destroyed, the unit weapons assigned to it will immediately turn to other targets. If the target is not destroyed, the unit weapons will continue to attack the target until the target is destroyed or far from the defensive area of the unit weapons. The strike time of each unit weapon against the same target obeys the exponential distribution with parameter $\mu_i (i = 1,2,\cdots,n)$.

3) There are N unit weapons in the platform system. When an air target enters the damaged area, if a unit weapon can work, it will capture the air target and attack it. If no unit weapon works, the target will break through the defense area.

Based on the above assumptions, the platform system with N unit weapons is equivalent to the vanishing stochastic system with N channels. When the number of unit weapons A_k being attacked by time t is taken as the state of a random system, the state transition of the system is shown in Figure 1.

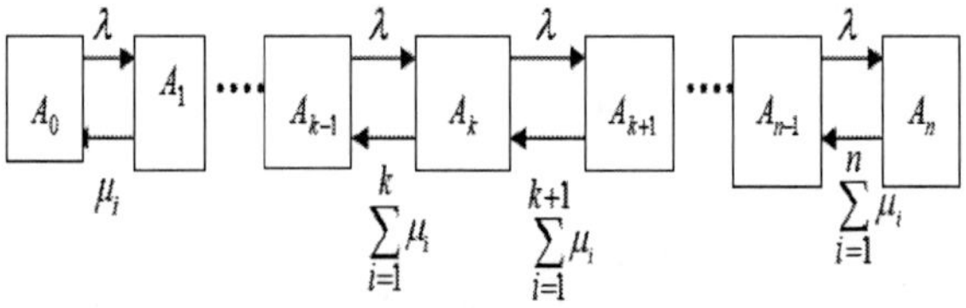

Fig. 1 The state transition of the system

The state analysis process based on queuing theory can be described as:

1) The state transition is limited to the transition from one state to its adjacent state, if the state is in $A_k (k = 1,2,\cdots,n-1)$, it can be transferred to A_{k+1} or A_{k-1}; if the state is in state A_0, it can only be transferred to state A_1; if the state is in its maximum queuing capacity A_n, it can only be transferred to A_{n-1};

2) If the process is in state A_k at the t moment, then in $(t, t+\Delta t)$ time, the probability of transition from state A_k to state A_{k+1} is $\lambda\Delta t + o(\Delta t)$, the probability from A state to B state is $\sum_{i=1}^{k} \mu_i \Delta t + o(\Delta t)$;

3) In $(t, t+\Delta t)$ time, the probability of transferring two or more states is $o(\Delta t)$.

Combining the priority allocation criterion of multi-unit weapon platform system and the actual situation of state transition, based on the above assumptions and the process of system state transition, the differential equations of equipment system state transition probability based on priority allocation criterion are established as follows:

$$\begin{cases} P_0'(t) = -\lambda P_0(t) + \mu_i P_1(t) \\ P_k'(t) = -(\lambda + \sum_{i=1}^{k} \mu_i) P_k(t) + \lambda P_{k-1}(t) + \sum_{i=1}^{k+1} \mu_i P_{k+1}(t) \\ \quad k = 1,2,\cdots,n-1 \\ P_n'(t) = -\sum_{i=1}^{n} \mu_i P_n(t) + \lambda P_{n-1}(t) \end{cases} \quad (8)$$

In the formula, $P_k(t)$ represents the probability of each state of the current system. Under steady-state conditions, the linear analytic model of equipment system state analysis based on priority assignment criterion is obtained.

$$\begin{cases} -\lambda P_0 + \mu_i P_1 = 0 \\ -(\lambda + \sum_{i=1}^{k} \mu_i) P_k + \lambda P_{k-1} + \sum_{i=1}^{k+1} \mu_i P_{k+1} = 0 \\ \quad k = 1,2,\cdots,n-1 \\ -\sum_{i=1}^{n} \mu_i P_n + \lambda P_{n-1} = 0 \end{cases} \quad (9)$$

Because of $\sum_{i=0}^{n} P_i = 1$, then the probability of system in various states is $P_i(i = 0,1,\cdots,n)$, only when the target enters the damage area and the platform system is in $A_k(k < n)$ and the unit weapon is idle, can the target be hit in time. The damage probability is as follows:

$$P_t = \sum_{i=0}^{n-1} P_i R_{1i+1} \quad (10)$$

In the formula, R_{1i+1} is the damage probability of $i+1(i = 0,1,\cdots,n-1)$ unit weapon.

Similarly, the operational reliability of the platform system can be expressed as the mathematical expectation $E(M)$ and the average mathematical expectation $\mu(M)$ of destroying the target group.

$$E(M) = mP_t \quad (11)$$

$$\mu(M) = \frac{1}{m} E(M) = P_t \quad (12)$$

IV. THE EXAMPLE ANALYSIS

A platform system consists of three units ($n_1 = 3$) with characteristics of $\mu_1 = 6$ /min and damage probability $R_{11} = 0.8$ of class I equipment, and three units($n_2 = 3$) with characteristics of $\mu_2 = 4$ /min and damage probability $R_{12} = 0.6$ of class II equipment, the two weapon systems attack at a certain point on the flight path of the target group at the same time. Target flow density $\lambda = 8$, target number is 20, calculate the reliability of the platform system.

A. Calculation results based on equivalent analysis method

If Class I equipment is of standard type, the maximum density of air targets damaged by two kinds of equipment is calculated ρ_1, ρ_2:

$$\rho_1 = n_1\mu_1 R_{11} = 3 \times 6 \times 0.8 = 14.4$$

$$\rho_2 = n_2\mu_2 R_{12} = 3 \times 4 \times 0.6 = 7.2$$

The density of the target flow attacked by two types of equipment can then be calculated:

$$\lambda_1 = \frac{\lambda_{n1}}{\sum_{i=1}^{2} \rho_1} \rho_1 = \frac{8}{14.4 + 7.2} \times 14.4 = 5.33$$

$$\lambda_2 = \lambda - \lambda_1 = 8 - 5.33 = 2.67$$

Equivalent target channel data are obtained from formula (1) as shown in Table 1, analytical data show that, the working efficiency of three unit type II equipment is close to that of one unit type I equipment. Formula (4) shows that the total number of equivalent unit weapons in the platform system is as follows:

$$n_{b\Sigma} = \sum_{i=1}^{k} n_{bi} + n_b = 1 + 2 = 3$$

TABLE I

TARGET CHANNEL DATA TABLE

n	$\lambda_1 P_{fw1} R_{11}$	$\lambda_2 P_{fw2} R_{12}$
1	1.5356	0.7322
2	2.5532	1.2711
3	3.0932	1.6071

According to $\lambda = 8$, $\mu = 4$, $n = 3$ and formula (5), the target damage probability can be calculated as $P_{fw} = 1 - 0.21 = 0.79$.

The operational reliability of the defense platform is calculated by formula (6), (7):

$$E(M) = mP_{fw} R_{11} = 11.06$$

$$\mu(M) = P_{fw} R_{11} = 0.553$$

B. Calculation results based on priority allocation criterion

The results of reliability and equivalent analysis of Platform System for Priority Allocation of Class I Equipment are shown in Table 2.

The results of Table 2 show that the evaluation model based on priority allocation criterion is superior to the equivalent analysis method, and the selection of different unit weapon allocation methods has a certain impact on the reliability of the platform system, which is consistent with the actual situation.

TABLE 2

COMPARING TABLES OF CALCULATION RESULTS OF TWO METHODS

	TARGET DAMAGE PROBABILITY	MATHEMATICAL EXPECTATIONS FOR DAMAGING TARGETS	AVERAGE MATHEMATICAL EXPECTATIONS FOR DAMAGING TARGETS
EQUIVALENT ANALYSIS METHOD	0.79	11.06	0.553
PRIORITY ALLOCATION CRITERIA	0.93	11.84	0.592

V. CONCLUSION

For the reliability of multi-unit weapon platform system, the evaluation model based on priority allocation criterion is obviously superior to the traditional equivalent analysis method, the results of case analysis also show that the evaluation model based on priority allocation criterion can better exert the work efficiency of the whole platform system by allocating unit firepower to different types of equipment in the platform system. At the same time, when using the equivalent analysis method to calculate the reliability of the platform system, the calculation results show that the number of equivalent unit weapons of the i type equipment and the standard type is not necessarily an integer, which will inevitably lead to errors in the evaluation of the platform system's work efficiency, and the evaluation model based on the priority allocation criterion can well avoid such errors. To sum up, the evaluation model based on priority allocation criterion is more scientific and reasonable for platform system composed of different types of equipment.

REFERENCES

[1] S. C. Yan. Random Theory Method for Effectiveness Analysis of Missile Weapon System[M].Beijing: National Defense Industry Press, 2001.11

[2] J. J. Han, W. M. Li, F. X. Liu. Queuing Model for Combat Effectiveness Analysis of Multi-Channel Air Defense Missile Weapon System [J]. Journal of Air Force Engineering University (Natural Science Edition), 2005, 6 (4)

[3] F. Long, J. W. Sun, J. Bai. Evaluation model of operational reliability of ship-to-air missile based on queuing theory [R]. Operational Assistant Decision Making and Military Systems Engineering, 2007,9

[4] Q. Sun, L. Zhang, S. Z. Shuan, Queuing theory-based reliability evaluation model for ground-to-air missile group [J] Aeronautical Computing Technology, 2007,37(2)

[5] D. Sun, F. C. Xing, Application of Queuing Theory in Evaluating the Performance of Air Defense Weapons[J]. Journal of Naval Engineering University,2003,15(3)

7th International Conference on Reliability of
Electrical Products and Electrical Contacts,
November 04-06, 2019

The Affecting Factors of the Electrical Insulation Performance of Polyurethane Elastomer

Hong Deng, Linhe Zhao
Hangzhou Aerospace Electronic Technology Co., Ltd., Hangzhou, 310051, China
E-mail:_cenrj2003@163.com_ Tel: 86-571-88012825 Fax: 86-571-88023684

Abstract—**In this paper, the factors affecting the electrical insulation properties of polyurethane elastomers are analyzed by the experiments of the relationship between volume resistivity and temperature. The results show that the type of polyurethane elastomer has an effect on the electrical insulation, the degree of crosslinking has an effect on the electrical insulation, and the electrical insulation decreases with the increase of temperature Increasing the thickness of polyurethane elastomer can improve its electrical insulation performance, and impurities and defects can affect its electrical insulation performance.**

Index Terms— **Polyurethane elastomer, Electrical insulation, Influence factors.**

I. BACKGROUND

In recent years, there have been a lot of problems that can not meet the requirement of product specification at high temperature (more than 85 ℃) in the sampling test of the series of electrical connector products with polyurethane elastomer as the sealing layer. As a sealing material, polyurethane elastomer not only plays the role of sealing protection, but also plays the role of insulation protection in separating the internal components of the detached electrical connector. When the internal structure or environmental factors change, the electrical insulation performance of polyurethane elastomer will be affected. Therefore, the electrical insulation stability of Polyurethane Elastomer is very important to ensure the reliability of potting products. At present, the research on the application of polyurethane elastomer mainly focuses on the mechanical properties, wear resistance, chemical resistance and heat resistance, but there are few reports on the electrical properties. Only a few related dielectric research reports can be found in China. Some researchers found that the type of Isocyanate had an effect on the electrical properties of polyurethane elastomers. [1] The change of temperature will lead to the decrease of physical cross-linking density of polyurethane elastomer and decrease the stability of its properties. [2] As conductive coating, coating thickness of acrylic polyurethane will affect the formation probability of internal conductive network[3]. In this paper, the relationship between the volume resistivity of polyurethane elastomers and the temperature is tested, and the reasons that affect the electrical insulation performance are analyzed It provides a theoretical reference for the application of polyurethane elastomer in aerospace electrical connector products.

II. TEST PART

A. *Test materials*

The polyurethane elastomers (PUE) with 12 mm* 12 mm* 2 mm were prepared by using two kinds of polyurethane sealants provided by Synthetic Material Factory of Shanxi Chemical Research Institute and Beijing Institute of Technology and Materials. The two PUE types are TDI / MOCA type (PUE1 for short) and MDI / BDO type (PUE2 for short). PUE1.1# and Pue1.2# were prepared respectively according to different chain extender coefficients. The basic properties of the two PUE are shown in Table 1.

TABLE I
BASIC PROPERTIES OF TWO KINDS OF POLYURETHANE ELASTOMERS

Parameter	PUE1 1#	PUE1 2#	PUE2
Shore A	82	85	55
Tensile strength (MPa)	15.25	17.53	10.1
Elongation at break (%)	578	425	2567
Glass conversion temperature (°C)	-48.67	-48.67	-70
Chain Extension Coefficient	0.85	0.90	/

B. *Test methods and equipment*

Test equipment: NF2511 INSULATION RESISTANCE TESTER

Test voltage: 1000V.

The specimens were tested for volume resistivity according to GB / T1410-2006"test method for volume resistivity and surface resistivity of solid insulating materials" . Each specimen was tested 3 times, averaged and recorded. The polyurethane elastomers were immersed in Acetone for 88 hours to record the weight and weight gain before and after immersion.

III. RESULTS AND DISCUSSION

A. Effect of different kinds of PUE on volume resistivity

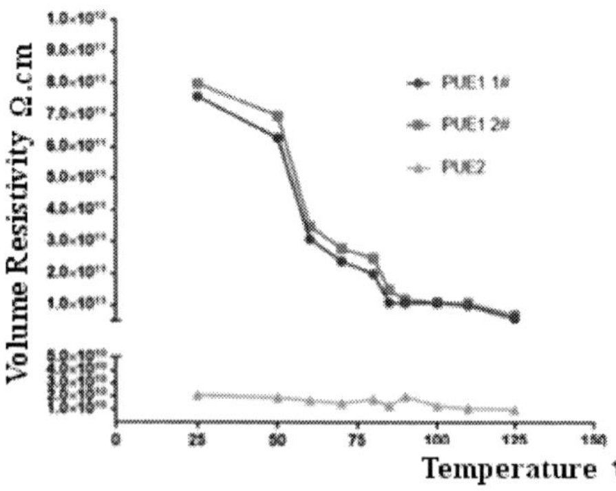

Fig. 1 Relationship between volume resistivity of PUE1 and PUE2 and temperature。

As can be seen from figure 1, the volume resistivity of PUE1(TDI / MOCA type) is an order of magnitude higher than that of PUE2(MDI / BDO type). The reason is that PUE itself is made up of blocks of soft and hard chains, which are made up of single bonds and have low intermolecular force, giving the elastomer good rubber elasticity. The hard segments are formed by the reaction of Isocyanate (TDI or MDI) and low molecular weight (MOCA or BDO) extenders, which contain strong polar groups and have large intermolecular force. The higher the molecular force of the hard segments, the higher the glass transition temperature. The glass transition temperature (- 48.67 °C) of PUE1(TDI / MOCA type) is higher than that of PUE2(MDI / BDO type) (- 70 °C). It is known that PUE1(TDI / MOCA system) has a strong intermolecular force, which restricts the transfer and orientation of carriers and polar groups in PUE1 in electric field. The degree of polarity orientation is low, thus increasing the volume resistivity.

B The effect of cross-linking degree on the volume resistivity of PUE

For Polymers, the higher the cross-linking degree, the denser the network structure and the better the solvent resistance (swelling or solubility). Pue1.1 #, pue1.2 # and PUE2 gained 43.91%, 39.72% and 31.65% respectively after being immersed in Acetone for 88 hours. It was found that the cross-linking degree of PUE2 was higher than that of PUE1, and its solvent resistance was better than PUE1. The cross-linking degree of pue1.2 # was higher than that of pue1.1 #. The interlacing degree of polymer chains in pue1.2 # is denser, which makes the network structure of polymer chains have stronger binding force to hydrogen bonds and polar groups, restrain the orientation polarization, and increase the volume resistivity.

A. Effect of temperature on volume resistivity of PUE

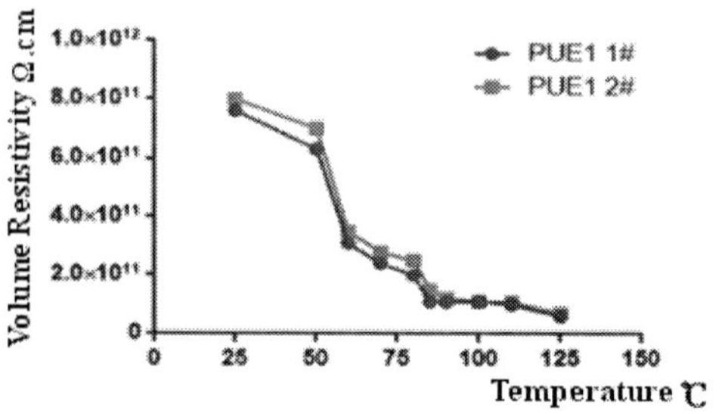

Fig. 2 Relationship between volume resistivity of PUE1 and temperature

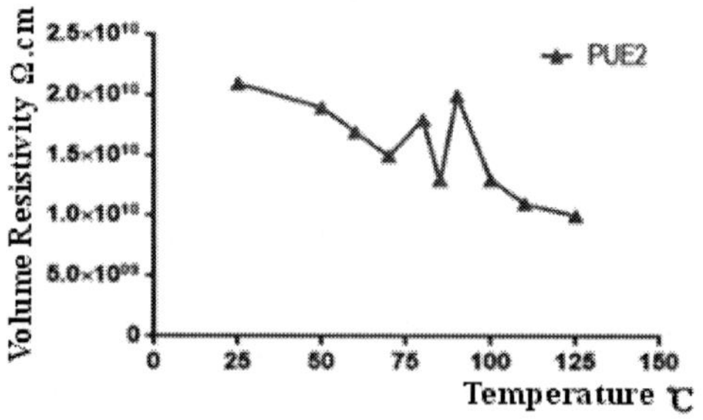

Fig. 3 Relationship between volume resistivity of PUE2 and temperature

According to Figure2 and Figure3, the volume resistivity of pue1.1 #, pue1.2 # and PUE2 decreased with the increase of temperature. The reason is that the motion of polymer molecules is temperature-dependent and the temperature and time are equivalent[5]. At low temperature, the whole polymer chain and its segments are bound, the carriers and polar groups are controlled by the polymer chain segment, the degree of polarity is low, and the volume resistivity is high. With the increase of temperature, the whole polymer chain can not move freely, but the motion of the segment is excited and starts to move freely. The carrier and Polar Group are restrained by the chain segment, which makes the degree of polar orientation increase and the volume resistivity decrease. It can also be seen from Fig. 2 that the volume resistivity of pue1.1 # and pue1.2 # (TDI / MOCA type) is the largest at room temperature, but decreases rapidly with the increase of temperature, and then decreases slowly at 85 °C ~ 90 °C. There was a rapid decrease near 120 °C. This is due to the softening of PUE1 with the increase of temperature, the rapid excitation of polymer chain segment motion, began to gradually dissociate, polar group orientation ability increased, so that the volume resistivity decreased rapidly. When the temperature rises to 80 °C ~ 90 °C, the Brownian motion of the dipole becomes more intense, the degree of polarity is affected, and the decreasing trend of the volume resistance is slowed down. At 120 °C, the more intense molecular thermal movement makes the whole polymer chain start to move, the carrier and

Polar Group are restrained by the polymer chain segment, the degree of polar orientation is increased, and the volume resistivity is further reduced. As can be seen from Fig. 3, the volume resistivity of PUE2(MDI / BDO type) also decreases with the increase of temperature, but the decreasing trend is very slow and it is not sensitive to the change of temperature. This is because the cross-linking density of PUE2(MDI / BDO type) is higher than that of PUE1, and the intermolecular entanglement of PUE2(MDI / BDO type) is denser, and the hydrogen bond content is higher. The dense network structure of polymer chain not only increases the containment ability of carriers and polar groups, but also decreases the free mobility of polymer chain The result of the interaction between them makes the temperature change has little effect on the volume resistivity.

D The influence of impurities on the electrical insulation of PUE

The trace impurities in PUE can not be ignored, especially the conductive and polar impurities. PUE is a polar material with water affinity. Even in relatively dry (relative humidity 50%) environment, polyurethane elastomer still has 0.6% water absorption rate [5] . The effects of moisture are hard to avoid. If the metal catalyst remains in the raw material or the metal impurity is brought into the product, the polar group orientation polarization degree will increase and the volume resistance will decrease

E The influence of interfacial polarization on the electrical insulation performance of PUE

If there are holes (or bubbles) in PUE or the mixing is uneven due to the large difference of relative molecular mass between polyols and chain extenders and the small mixing ratio during the production process, the cross-linking is uneven in the elastic body to form a non-uniform phase. Due to the different polarity of the inhomogeneous phase interface, the carrier will accumulate at the two-phase interface under the applied electric field, resulting in the interface polarization, and the electrical insulation performance will be reduced.

F The influence of thickness on the electrical insulation property of PUE

The volume resistance of polyurethane elastomer increases with the increase of thickness[6]. From the Formula $R=\rho d/S$ of insulation resistance, it can also be seen that R is related to the area S and thickness D of the sample, and the volume resistivity is independent of the size of the material. This is because, according to the field emission phenomenon, for an elastic body of unit area, if the thickness increases under the effect of an applied electric field, the distance of the carrier from one end to the other in the direction of the electric field increases The binding force that needs to be overcome also increases correspondingly, so that the migration velocity of the carriers under the unit field strength decreases and the insulation resistance increases.

IV. CONCLUSION

1) The type of PUE has an effect on the electrical insulation performance. The PUE of TDI / MOCA type is better than that of MDI / BDO.
2) For the same type of PUE, the structure with high cross-linking density can improve the electrical insulation performance.
3) The electrical insulation of PUE decreases with the increase of temperature. The electrical insulation performance of PUE with TDI / MOCA type decreases rapidly with the increase of temperature. The electrical insulation performance of MDI / BDO type decreases slowly with the increase of temperature.
4) Increasing the thickness of PUE can improve its electrical insulation performance.
5) Polar impurities and conductive impurities can affect the electrical insulation performance of PUE.
6) Internal defects of PUE (such as cavitation, air bubble, non-homogeneous phase) will affect its electrical insulation performance.

Therefore, in the production and use of PUE, we should fully consider the temperature, glue layer thickness, impurities and defects of these factors on electrical insulation performance. Some of the higher insulation requirements of the product to pay attention to the adaptability of PUE, according to the selection of settings.

REFERENCES

[1] K. D. Cao, P Zhang, JM Yu,CL Li, ect. “Studies on dielectric properties of polyurethane elastomers” [J],Polyurethane industry, 2013,28(5): 10-11

[2] PZ Zhao, YS Wang, JH Zhu, ect. “Temperature dependence of high elastic modulus of dielectric properties of polyurethane elastomers”[J], Polymer Materials Science and engineering, 2008, 24(4): 89-92

[3] L Chen. “Preparation and properties of Carbon Fiber/Acrylic polyurethane conductive coatings” [J],Surface Technology, 2016,45(8):110-114

[4] P He. “Structure and properties of new Polymer ”[J]. Beijing Science Press, 2009

[5] HJ Liu, LB Liu, S Liu, ect. “Handbook of polyurethane Studies on dielectric properties of polyurethane elastomers”[J], Beijing Chemical Industry Press, 2009

[6] Y Sun, WB Huang, ect. “Study on electrical insulation property of Polyurethane Pouring Sealant”[J], Polyurethane process, 2017,32(4):41-43

7th International Conference on Reliability of
Electrical Products and Electrical Contacts,
November 04-06, 2019

Series Arc Fault Recognition Based on Multi-feature Extraction and GA_SVM

Deshuan Tong[1], Ze Li[1,2], Ruihua Cui[1,2]
[1]Hebei University of Technology, Tianjin, 300130
[2]Electrical Apparatus Institute of Hebei Province, Tianjin, 300130

Abstract—**To detect the series arc fault under the condition of 115V/400Hz power supply, the even harmonic sum and kurtosis index analysis is performed on the current signal before and after the arc fault in the point contact experiment. The selected method covers the characteristics of the time and frequency domains of the signal. The even harmonic sum and kurtosis values are extracted as the features for discriminating the arc fault, and the arc fault is identified by the support vector machine optimized by genetic algorithm (GA_SVM). Compared with the recognition accuracy of a single feature, the accuracy of the recognition after combining the features into a two-dimensional matrix combination is further improved. The result shows that the correct rate reaches 98.5714%.**

Index Terms— **Series fault arc, Even harmonic sum, Kurtosis index, Support vector machine optimized by genetic algorithms**

I. INTRODUCTION

In recent years, with the continuous development of science and technology, more and more electrical equipment are used in aviation and aerospace, resulting in narrow winding in the fuselage of several tens of thousands of cables, combined with the surrounding environment of various substances cause vibrations in the line of erosion and flight process, etc., which caused a lot of line fault, most of them are caused by arc[1-4].

Therefore, the research of aviation arc fault circuit breaker is of great significance to ensure the safe operation of aviation and reduce property losses. At present, the detection of arc faults is mainly based on the physical characteristics of the arc and the analysis of current and voltage signals. In the literature [5], a Hibert fractal antenna for measuring arc electromagnetic radiation is designed. The characteristics and measurement methods of the electromagnetic radiation signal of the arc are studied. In the literature [6,7], the peak pulse index based on the collected residual current and the third and fourth-order cumulants are extracted respectively. These algorithms are simple and easy to implement but do not consider the influence of more load types on the detection results. Wavelet transform is used in the literature [8,9]. Wavelet transform can clearly describe the relationship between signal frequency distribution and time. It is a very good method to analyze non-stationary signals. The disadvantage is that sometimes it is difficult to select a wavelet basis in order to achieve the desired separation effect. In the literature [10], the experimental current signals collected are analyzed by FFT and wavelet energy entropy, and two semi-periodic detection methods are proposed by constructing the half-period into the whole period, but the analysis of nonlinear load is lacking.

In this paper, the even harmonic sum and kurtosis index of the collected experimental current signals are analyzed. After combining the analyzed features into a two-dimensional matrix, the GA_SVM recognition and detection are carried out. This method overcomes the problem that the correct rate of recognition using a single feature quantity is not ideal.

II. AVIATION ARC FAULT TEST

A. *Experimental principle and scheme*

According to the aviation standard AS5692[11] and the arc fault circuit breaker safety standard UL1699[12] design point contact experimental platform shown in Fig. 1.

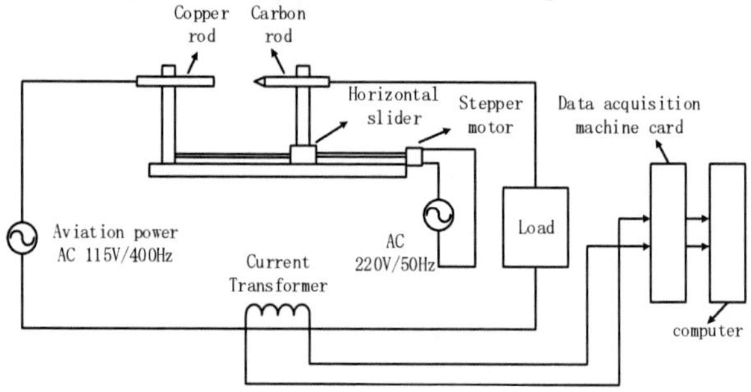

Fig. 1 Point contact experimental circuit diagram

The experiment was conducted using a variety of load loads, including six linear loads and one non-linear load. Linear loads include pure resistive (7Ω and 57Ω), resistance-inductance (7Ω + 7mH and 57Ω + 7mH), and resistance-capacitance (57Ω+470μF and 115Ω+470μF). The nonlinear load is auto transformer rectifier units (ATRU).

B. Experimental result

In the experiment, each group of experimental data intercepts 10 current signal periods (5 normal periods and 5 fault periods), 1024 points were collected for each cycle. Typical linear loads (pure resistive load 57Ω) and non-linear loads (ATRU) in the intercepted experimental current waveform are shown in Fig. 2 and Fig. 3.

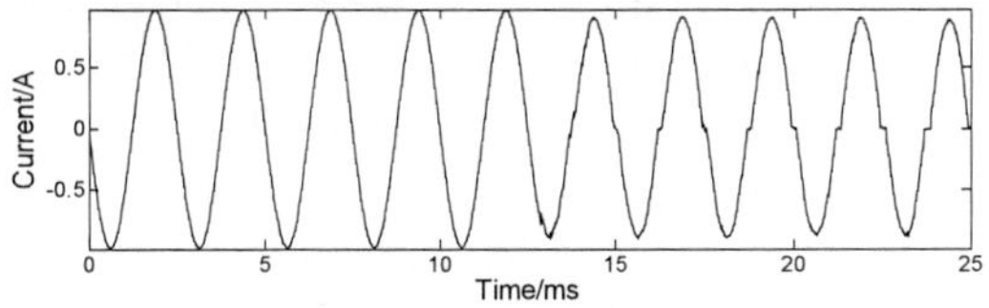

Fig. 2 Waveform of Pure Resistive Load (57Ω)

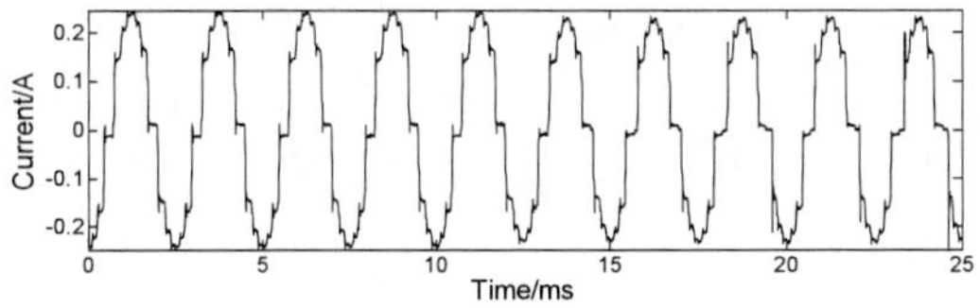

Fig. 3 Nonlinear load (ATRU) waveform

From the observation of Fig. 2 and Fig. 3, we can see that for linear loads, when the current signal is normal, the waveform is sinusoidal. After the fault occurs, the phenomenon of "zero rest" appears near the zero-crossing point of the current, the high-frequency noise content increases obviously and the current amplitude decreases; for a non-linear load, the current signal contains high-frequency noise, whether it is normal or faulty, but the waveform distortion is more obvious after the fault occurs, and the waveform amplitude is reduced. In summary, the current waveform of the linear load or the nonlinear load changes significantly after the series arc fault occurs.

III. FEATURE EXTRACTION

A. Even harmonic analysis

The essence of the Fourier transform is to transform the signal from the time domain to the frequency domain for truncation. For the infinitely long, aperiodic continuous signal $x(t)$, its Fourier transform formula is:

$$X(F)=\int_{-\infty}^{\infty} x(t)e^{-2j\pi Ft}dt \qquad (1)$$

Since the sampling point of the intercepted current signal needs to be processed, it needs to be analyzed by the Discrete Fourier Transform (DFT), and its expression is:

$$X(k)=\sum_{n=0}^{N-1} x(n)W_N^{nk} \qquad k=0,\ 1\ldots N\text{-}1 \qquad (2)$$

Among them, $x(n)$ represents the input discrete digital signal sequence, W_N is the rotation factor, and its expression is $W_N = e^{-j\frac{2\pi k}{N}}$, and $X(k)$ is the relative amplitude of the N discrete frequency points corresponding to the input sequence $x(n)$.

However, the amount of computation of the DFT is quite large, so it is improved to a Fast Fourier Transform (FFT) with a relatively small amount of computation. The FFT decomposes the DFT of the long sequence into some short-order DFT by utilizing the symmetry and periodicity of the rotation factor W_N, so that the calculation amount is changed from the original N^2 to $\frac{2}{N}\log_2 N$, which increases the calculation speed.

The experimental data were analyzed by the windowed Fourier transform method. Firstly, the window length wen is set to five periods and the step size $step$ is set to one period. The adjacent five periods of sampled data are used as data to be analyzed, and FFT is performed to obtain a corresponding logarithmic amplitude spectrum. Then move the window backward by one step to perform FFT transformation to obtain the corresponding log amplitude spectrum. And so on, until the last cycle of analysis. With the increase of frequency, the cross-spectrum of fault current signal and normal current signal increases gradually. To distinguish the harmonic characteristics between fault signal and normal signal more clearly, this paper chooses the frequency spectrum of 0～8kHz to analyze. Taking pure resistive load (57Ω) and ATRU as examples, the spectrum of 0～8kHz is intercepted as shown in Fig. 4 and Fig. 5.

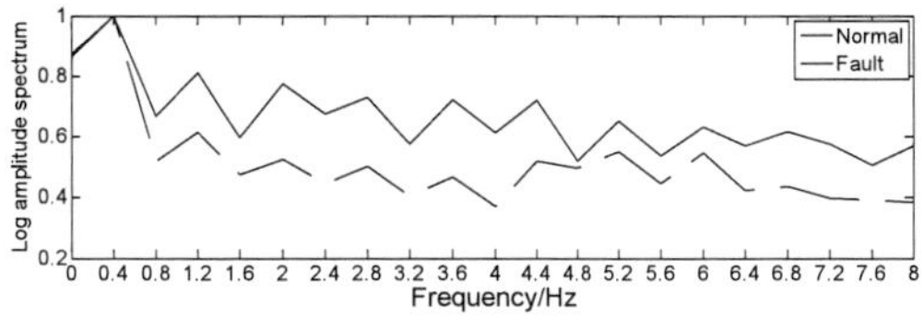

Fig. 4 Spectrum comparison diagram of pure resistive load (57Ω) 0~8kHz

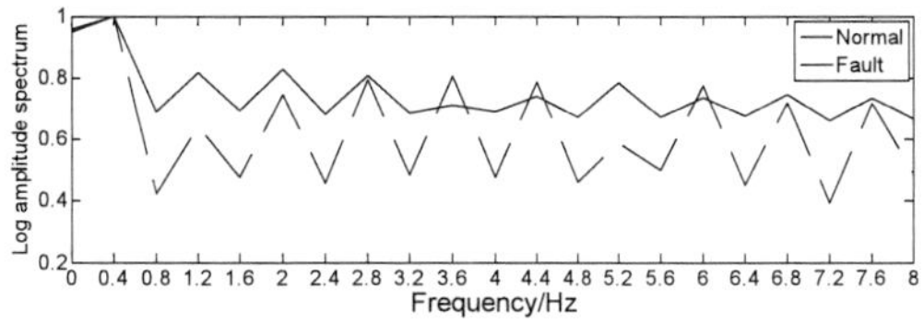

Fig. 5 Spectrum comparison diagram of nonlinear load (ATRU) 0~8kHz

By observing Fig. 4 and Fig. 5, it can be seen that for normal and fault current signals, the main component is the fundamental 400Hz component. Compared with the normal signal, the logarithmic amplitude of odd and even harmonics of pure resistive load (57Ω) increases in varying degrees, and the other linear loads are the same. However, the value of the

ATRU even harmonic of the load also rises after the arc fault occurs, but the values of the 9, 11 and 15th harmonics have dropped. Therefore, to distinguish the normal signal from the fault signal and make the difference more obvious, the sum of the logarithmic magnitudes of the even harmonics within 8 kHz is calculated to extract the feature. Taking the pure resistive load (57Ω) and the nonlinear load (ATRU) as an example, the logarithmic magnitude of the even harmonic sum is shown in Fig. 6 and Fig. 7.

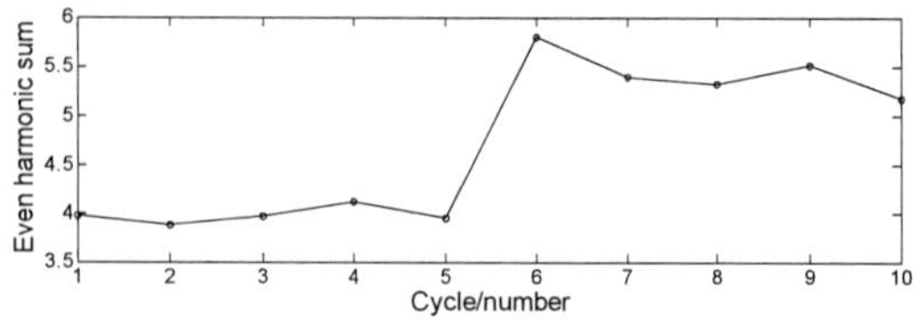

Fig. 6 Waveform diagram of pure resistive load (57Ω) even harmonic sum

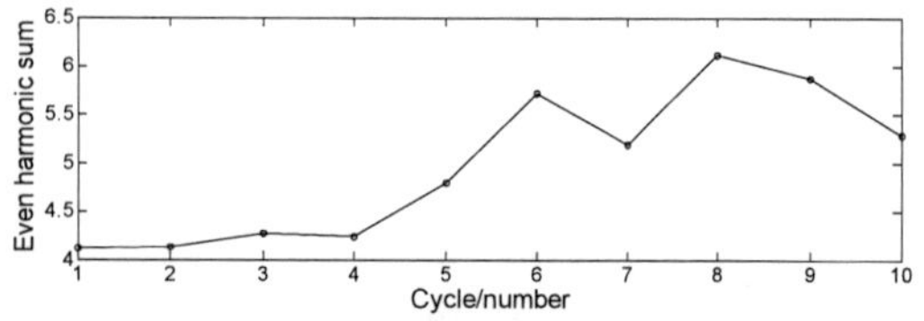

Fig. 7 Waveform diagram of the harmonic sum of the nonlinear load (ATRU)

By observing Fig. 6 and Fig. 7, it can be seen that the even harmonic sum increases after the arc fault occurs, wherein the pure resistive load (57Ω) increases by an average of 36.8%, and the nonlinear load (ATRU) increases by an average of 30.7%. The even harmonic sum of other loads increases after failure. The average of even harmonic sum of each load before and after failure is shown in TABLE Ⅰ.

TABLE I

EVEN HARMONIC SUM VALUES BEFORE AND AFTER EACH LOAD FAILURE

Load type	Load parameter	Normal even harmonics sum value	Fault even harmonics sum value
R	7Ω	3.977	5.630
	57Ω	3.975	5.438
RL	7Ω+7mH	4.184	5.284
	57Ω+7mH	3.572	5.108
RC	57Ω+470μF	4.081	5.642
	115Ω+470μF	3.697	5.079
ATRU		4.314	5.638

B. *Kurtosis index analysis*

The kurtosis index is a dimensionless parameter that is a normalized fourth-order central moment that reflects the degree of non-Gaussianness of the signal. The kurtosis is equal to 0, and the random variable is Gaussian; the kurtosis is less than 0, and the random variable is Subgauss; the kurtosis is greater than 0, and the random variable is super Gaussian[13]. The kurtosis indicator is particularly sensitive to shock signals, so the kurtosis value changes when a fault occurs causing the waveform to be distorted.

The method of calculating the kurtosis indicator for each cycle is as follows. Assuming that N sampling points are acquired in one current cycle, the kurtosis index of the current signal $i(n)$ for this period is calculated as:

$$K = \frac{1}{N-1}\sum_{n=1}^{N}[\frac{i(n)-\mu}{\alpha}]^4 \tag{3}$$

Among them, μ is the mathematical expectation of $i(n)$ and α is the standard deviation of $i(n)$.

Taking the pure resistive load (57Ω) and the nonlinear load (ATRU) as examples, the kurtosis index is calculated as shown in Fig. 8 and Fig. 9.

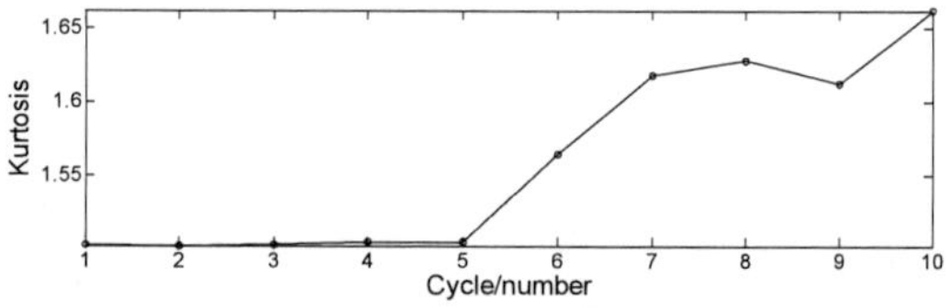

Fig. 8 Kurtosis indicator of pure resistive load (57Ω)

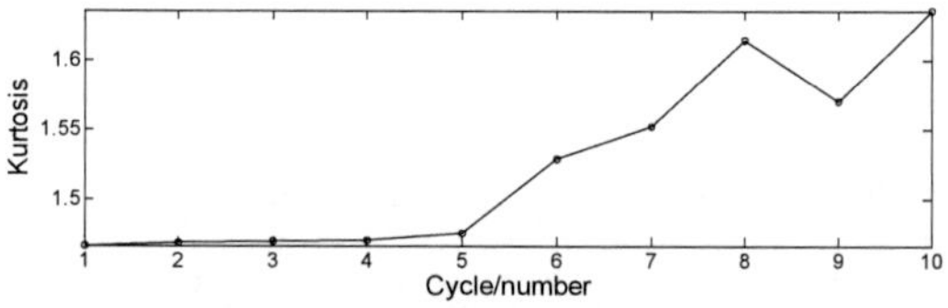

Fig. 9 Kurtosis indicator of nonlinear load (ATRU)

It can be seen by observing Fig. 8 to Fig. 9 that the kurtosis value of the current signal is stable and the volatility is small before the arc fault occurs; after the arc fault occurs, the kurtosis value increases and the volatility is large. The average value of the kurtosis before and after the arc fault of each load is as shown in TABLE Ⅱ. The kurtosis value of each load rises after the arc fault occurs, so the kurtosis index can be used as one of the indicators for judging whether or not an arc fault has occurred.

TABLE Ⅱ

SKURTOSIS VALUES BEFORE AND AFTER EACH LOAD FAILURE

Load type	Load parameter	Normal kurtosis value	Fault kurtosis value
R	7Ω	1.526	1.621
	57Ω	1.502	1.616
RL	7Ω+7mH	1.527	1.605
	57Ω+7mH	1.528	1.615
RC	57Ω+470μF	1.499	1.581
	115Ω+470μF	1.501	1.605
ATRU		1.470	1.580

IV. FAULT RECOGNITION AND DETECTION

Support Vector Machine (SVM) was first proposed by Vapnik. For non-linear samples, a support vector machine can transform non-linear samples into a new feature space, where non-linear samples can be transformed into linear separable samples[14,15]. Compared with the traditional neural network method, SVM is a novel small sample learning method with a solid theoretical foundation. It does not involve probability measure and law of large numbers. It is necessary to adjust the relevant parameters (mainly penalty parameter c and kernel function parameter g) to get a better prediction accuracy when using SVM for classification prediction.

A. SVM optimized by genetic algorithm

Genetic Algorithms (GA) is a computational model that simulates the natural evolution of Darwin's biological evolution and the evolutionary process of genetics. It is a method of searching for optimal solutions by simulating natural evolutionary processes. The steps to select the best parameters and parameters by GA are as follows.

(1) GA first needs to encode the solution to a problem. Set the range of parameters c and g and encode in binary.

(2) The individual population is initialized to generate a function of the initial population individual.

(3) Calculate the fitness value of each genetic individual, that is, calculate the recognition rate of the SVM under each parameter combination.

(4) According to the principle of genetic algorithm, an iterative loop of selection, crossover and mutation operations. Until the parameters c and g corresponding to the maximum recognition rate are obtained.

After choosing the optimum parameters c and g , SVM is used to identify, and the method of normalization adopts [0,1] interval normalization.

B. Recognition result

In this paper, the training data and the test data are respectively selected from the normal and faulty 5 groups of data of various loads, and a total of 70 sets of data.1 indicates the normal signal, 0 indicates the fault signal. The training data is brought into the GA optimized SVM for training. After the training is finished, the test set data is brought into the SVM for identification. The identification results of the even harmonic and kurtosis index test sets are shown in Fig. 10 and Fig. 11.

Looking at Fig. 10 and Fig. 11, it can be seen that 10 groups of data in the 70 sets of data of the even harmonic sum test set are misjudged, and 6 sets of data in the test set of the kurtosis index are misjudged. The correct rate of test set identification is 84.2857% and 91.4286%, respectively. The result is not very good. To further improve the correct rate of detection, the even harmonic sum and kurtosis index feature are combined into a two-dimensional matrix, and then GA_SVM training and testing are performed. The recognition result of the test set is shown in Fig. 12. It can be seen from Fig. 12 that only one group of data in 70 sets of data is misjudged and the recognition accuracy rate reaches 98.5714%. The recognition result is significantly improved compared to the single feature.

V. CONCLUSION

This paper mainly studies the detection of series arc faults based on even harmonic sum and kurtosis. When an aeronautical series arc fault occurs, the current signal will decrease in amplitude and produce "zero rest" and glitch. The analysis shows that the even harmonic sum and kurtosis index will increase to different degrees after the arc fault occurs, which can be used as the feature to detect the series arc fault. Using GA-SVM for fault identification, the recognition accuracy of a single kind of feature is compared with the accuracy of the combination of multiple feature. The results show that the correct rate of multiple feature combination recognition is greatly improved compared with the single feature, and the correct rate reaches 98.5714%.

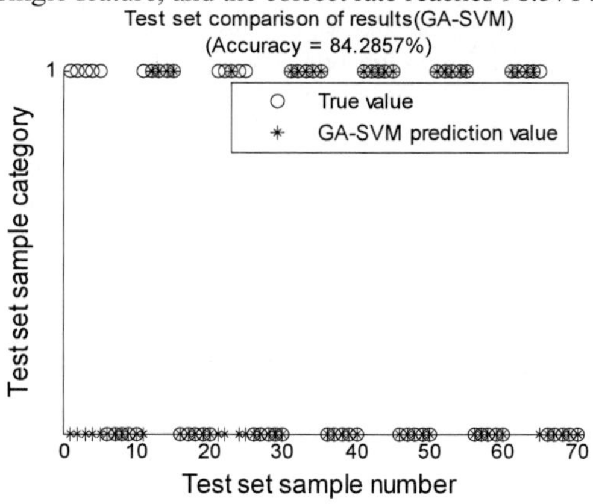

Fig. 10 Test result graph based on even harmonic sum

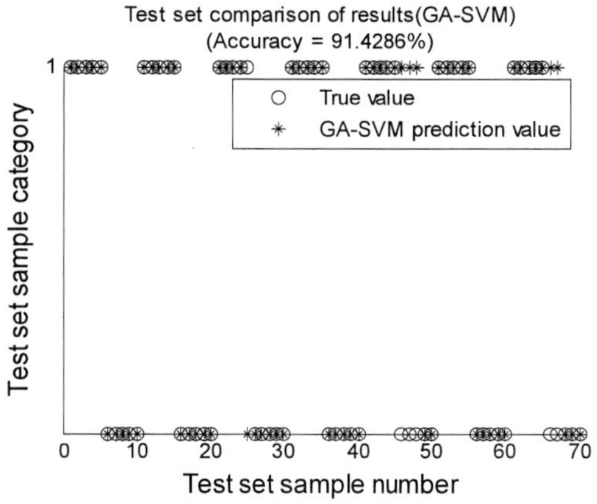

Fig. 11 Test results of the base kurtosis indicator

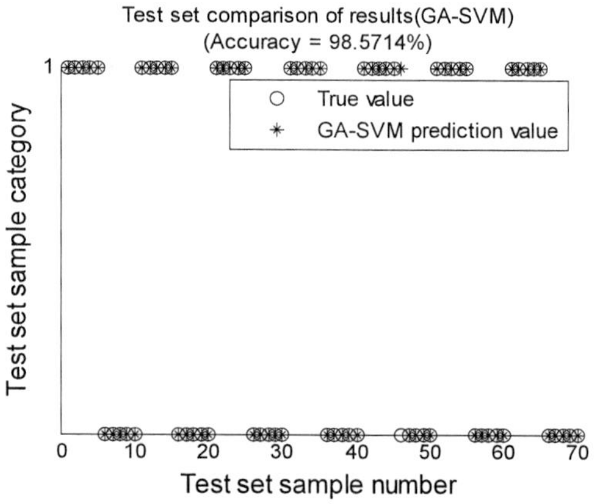

Fig. 12 Test result graph based on combined feature

REFERENCES

[1] Shaohua Ma, Jieqiu Bao,Zhiyuan Cai, et al."Research on Arc Fault Characteristics and Detection Method," International Conference on ProcessEquipment,2013, 331:133-136.

[2] Zhimin Pan, Wei Liu, Yongchao Liang, et al. "Identification of single-phase fault properties of EHV transmission lines based on kurtosis values," Journal of Electric Power Systems and Automation, 2017, 29(4): 104-109.

[3] Jun Wang, Baojun Lu, Liu Yang. "Research on Fault Arc in Aviation Electrical System," Science & Technology Innovation and Application. 2015, 18: 134-135.

[4] Yongxing Wang, Enyuan Dong, Jiyuan Cong. "Arc tracking Properties of the Aging Wires in Aircraft," ShenZhen, 2008.pp.l-5.

[5] Wei Wang, Yanfeng Zhang, Feng Niu, et al. "Analysis and quantity method of electromagnetic radiation characteristics of photovoltaic DC arc," Journal of Electric Engineering, 2019:1-9.

[6] Dejun Liu, Guanghai Bao, Huaiping Sun. "Research on series arc fault detection based on peak index and pulse index," Electrical and Energy Efficiency Management Technology.2017,16:6-9.

[7] Yanyan Gao, Jiancheng Zhang, Jianhong Yang, et al. "Research on arc fault identification method based on high frequency characteristics," Electrical and Energy Management Technology, 2014, 15: 7-9.

[8] Wei Dong, Junmin Zhang, Meijing Gui, et al."Identification of aviation fault arc based on wavelet packet decomposition," New Technology of Electrical Engineering and Energy. 2018, 37(11): 76-81.

[9] Xiaoming Liu, Yang Zhao, Yundong Cao, et al. "Series arc fault diagnosis of AC system based on wavelet transform," Transactions of China Electrotechnical Society, 2014, 29(1): 10-17.

[10] Weilin Li, Kun He, Wenjie Liu, Xiaobin Zhang, Yanjun Dong. "A fast arc fault detection method for AC solid state power controllers in MEA," Chinese Journal of Aeronautics, 2018, 31(5):1119–1129.

[11] SAE Aerospace. "AS5692 Arc Fault Circuit Breaker (AFCB)," Aircraft, Trip-Free Single Phase 115VAC, 400Hz-Constant Frequency. Aerospace Standard 2004.

[12] UL Inc. "UL standard for safety for arc fault circuit interrupters UL 1699," Second Edition, Northbrook: Underwriter Laboratories Inc, pp. 16-24, 2006.

[13] Xianchuan Yu, Dan Hu. "Theory and application of blind source separation", Beijing: Science Press, 2011

[14] Zong Meng, Yan Ji, Weiming Gu, et al. "DEMD endpoint effect suppression method based on support vector machine and window function," Acta Metrologica Sinica, 2016, 37 (2):180-184.

[15] Shuhong Cheng, Xu Gao, Bin Zhou. "Based on multi-feature extraction and SVM parameter optimization Research on vehicle type identification," Journal of Metrology. 2018, 39(3):348-352.

7th International Conference on Reliability of
Electrical Products and Electrical Contacts,
November 04-06, 2019

Multi-physics Simulation Method of Contact Resistance of Contacts Based on Fractal Theory

Ruyao Li, Wenying Yang, Zilan Qiu, Huimin Liang
Harbin Institute of Technology, Heilongjiang, 150001, China
E-mail: yangwy@hit.edu.cn Tel: 86-13796626380

Abstract—**Contact resistance Joule heat in main circuits is the main heat source of high-power contactors in the working process. As the contact resistance interacts with factors such as temperature and contact surface stress, the calculation of the contact resistance is difficult. In this paper, a mathematical model of microscopic irregular morphology of the contact surface based on fractal function was proposed, which combines the thermo-electric-force multi-field coupling model of a single micro-contact point to calculate the contact resistance of contactor working under different environments and load levels. At the same time, the steady-state temperature rise of the contactor for long-term operation was calculated based on the change in contact resistance. And the simulation method is proved to be feasible through experimental comparison.**

Index Terms— **Fractal theory, Contact resistance, Finite element method, Multi-field coupling**

I. INTRODUCTION

The contactor is a widely used switchgear. Contact resistance Joule heat in main circuits is one of its main heat sources. As the volume of the contactor is continuously reduced, the power is continuously increased, and the temperature rise caused by the Joule heat of the main circuit contacts becomes more and more obvious. Especially when used in extreme temperature environments such as aerospace, the higher temperature of the contactor in the working state will affect the coil resistance and ferromagnetic material properties, which in turn affects the electromagnetic power of the electromagnetic coil, which significantly affects the working characteristics of the device. It even causes it to fail or reduce its service life. The contact resistance value of the contact directly affects the accuracy of the heat calculation. The contact resistance is not only related to the material of the contact itself, the processing technology, but also interacting with factors such as temperature and contact surface stress. So, the calculation of the contact resistance is difficult.

There have been many studies on contact resistance. Hertz proposed a contact model that considered macroscopic elastic deformation [1]. Greenwood established a G-W model based on the statistical description of rough surfaces, pointing out that there are elastic deformation and plastic deformation during contact, and introduced the concept of plasticity index [2-3]. Holm proposed a classical method for calculating the contact resistance [4], but the number and radius of contact spots are difficult to calculate. Mandelbrot proposed the fractal concept and proposed the W-M fractal function based on the Weierstrass function [5]. Majumdar and Bhushan proposed the M-B model based on the W-M fractal function to simulate the rough contact surface, and simplified the model to a model with a rough surface in contact with a smooth rigid plane [6]. However, when calculating the deformation δ, the compression process of the Micro convex body is not considered. Wang and Konmvopoulos proposed a modified model of the M-B model, and gave the relationship between the actual contact area of the micro-contact and the contact cross-sectional area [7-8], which is widely used. Kogut analyzed the influence of thin separators, current and other factors on the contact resistance between rough surfaces [9]. The fractal method began to be used more widely in the calculation of electrical contact [10] and contact thermal resistance [11].

The contact resistance is affected by the ambient temperature and load, and needs to be predicted in advance, but contact contract resistance and internal temperature rise of the contactor in the working state in different working environments are difficult to measure. The measurement in the laboratory also faces the problem of high cost of making prototypes and long redesign cycles. Based on the fractal theory, a micro-thermal-electric-force multi-field coupling model of the contact surface is established to calculate the contact resistance of the contactor contacts under different temperatures and loads.

II. FRACTAL SURFACE MULTIPHYSICS CONTACT MODEL

The macroscopic model of the contact is the plane-to-plane contact. But in fact the microscopic contact pattern is shown in Fig. 1. Current flows through a plurality of conductive spots. The actual contact resistance is a parallel connection of a plurality of conductive spot contact resistors.

The copper contacts used in the experiment and the contact surface measured by the 3D Digital Microscope and the contour height of a vertical section on the surface are as showed in Fig. 2.

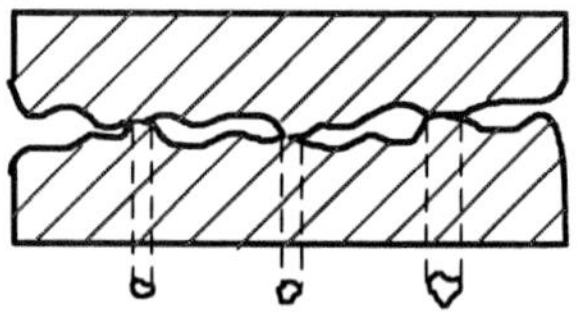

Fig. 1 Diagram of microscopic contact.

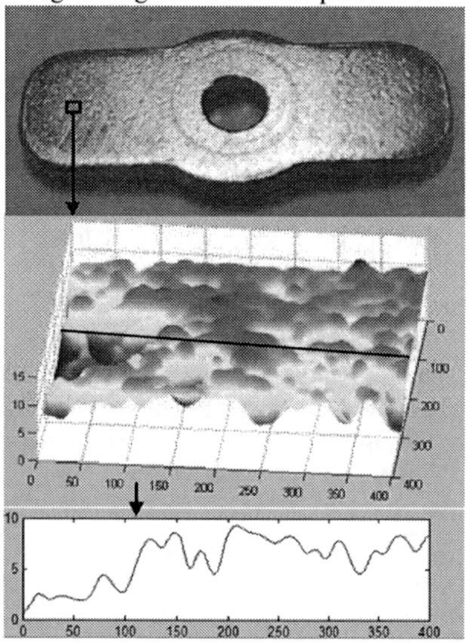

Fig. 2 Contact and its microscopic surface profile.

A. Fractal Function

W-M function was used to describe fractal surface contours with continuity and self-imitation[6].

$$Z(x) = G^{D-1} \sum_{n=n_m}^{\infty} \frac{\cos(2\pi\gamma^n x)}{\gamma^{(2-D)n}} \tag{1}$$

where D is the fractal dimension of the surface($1<D<2$), G is the fractal scale coefficient of the surface, γ^n is the Spatial frequency($\gamma>1$), $\gamma=1.5$ when the rough surface height distribution satisfies the Gaussian distribution. n_m is the ordinal of the lowest cutoff frequency, $\gamma^{n_m} = 1/L$, where L is the sample length.

B. Fractal Parameter Calculation Method

The surface fractal parameters are calculated by the structural function method. The $Z(x)$ with fractal features can make the data structure obtained by sampling satisfy:

$$S(\tau) = \left\langle [Z(x+\tau) - Z(x)]^2 \right\rangle \tag{2}$$

where τ represents any increment of the data x interval. According to (1) and the self-imitation of W-M, (3) is deduced by (2).

$$S(\tau) = CG^{2(D-1)}\tau(4-2D) \tag{3}$$

where

$$C = \frac{\Gamma(2D-3)\sin[(2D-3)\pi/2]}{(4-2D)\ln\gamma} \tag{4}$$

Draw a double logarithmic plot of $S(\tau)$ and τ. If it is a straight line, get the slope of the line k_s, and B: the intercept of the line on the log $S(\tau)$ axis. If $0 \leqslant k_s \leqslant 2$, the surface is fractal.

$$k_s = 4 - 2D \tag{5}$$

$$B = \lg CG^{2(D-1)} \tag{6}$$

The two-dimensional fractal parameters D and G are obtained according to (5) and (6). The three-dimensional fractal dimension can be approximated by the fractal dimension of the two-dimensional calculation by $D_s=D+1$

C. Multi-field Coupling Model of Single Micro-convex body

For the curve established by the W-M function[12], the contour is superimposed by the curve of the different scale ordinal n, for any scale ordinal n at $l = 1/\gamma^n$ and $-l/2 < x < l/2$

$$Z(x) = G^{D-1} l^{2-D} \cos(\pi x / L) \tag{7}$$

The contact deformation of a single micro convex body is shown in Figure 3.

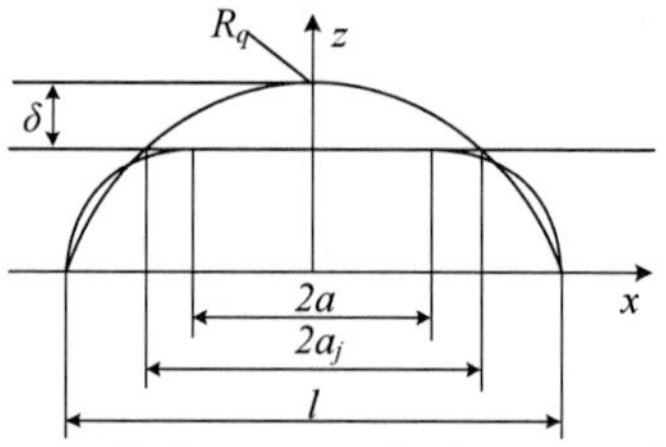

Fig. 3 Diagram of micro convex body contact deformation.

In the figure, a is the actual contact area, a_j is the cut-off area where the plane intersects the micro-convex, and the relationship between a and a_j is [7-8] $\pi a_j^2 = 2\pi a^2$. δ is the real deformation of the micro-convex. The radius of curvature of the convex tip is

$$R_q = \left| \left[\frac{d^2 Z(x)}{dx^2} \right] \right|^{-1} = \frac{l^D}{\pi^2 G^{D-1}} \tag{8}$$

With the increase of contact pressure, the deformation process of micro-convex is from elastic deformation to plastic deformation, which is divided into three stages: elastic contact, elastic-plastic contact and plastic contact [13]. The critical deformation is [14]

$$\delta_c = \left(\frac{\pi K H}{2E} \right)^2 R_q \tag{9}$$

where K=0.454+0.41υ, υ is the Poisson's ratio of the material, and E is the composite elastic modulus [3].

$$1/E = (1-\upsilon_1^2)/E_1 + (1-\upsilon_2^2)/E_2 \tag{10}$$

E_1 and E_2 are the elastic modulus of the materials on both sides. υ_1 and υ_2 are the Poisson's ratio of the materials on both sides. In this paper, the model is that the rough surface is in contact with the rigid plane. So

$$E = E_1 / (1-\upsilon_1^2) \quad (11)$$

H is the hardness-related parameter of the material, which is related to the yield strength σ_s of the material, generally taking H=2.8σ_s.

At three different stages, the force loads of the micro convex bodys are [16]

elastic contac t($0 < \delta < \delta_c$)

$$F_e(\delta) = \frac{4}{3} E R^{\frac{1}{2}} \delta^{\frac{3}{2}} \quad (12)$$

elastic-plastic contact($\delta_c < \delta < 110\delta_c$)

$$F_{ep}(\delta) = \frac{4}{3} E R^{\frac{1}{2}} \delta^{\frac{3}{2}} + \left(2\pi R \delta H - \frac{4}{3} E R^{\frac{1}{2}} \delta^{\frac{3}{2}} \right) \times \left[\frac{2(\delta-\delta_c)}{109\delta_c} - \left(\frac{\delta-\delta_c}{109\delta_c} \right)^2 \right] \quad (13)$$

plastic contact ($\delta > 110\delta_c$)

$$F_p(\delta) = 2\pi R \delta H \quad (14)$$

When the melting point is not reached, the elastic modulus of the metal decreases linearly approximately with increasing temperature [17]. When the temperature rises to ΔT, the elastic modulus is:

$$E_T = E_0(1 - 25\sigma\Delta T) \quad (15)$$

Where E_0 is the elasticity modulus of the material at a temperature rise of 0, and α is the coefficient of thermal expansion of the material. The elasticity modulus of copper at room temperature is E_0 =110GPa. the coefficient of thermal expansion of copper is $\sigma = 17.5 \times 10^{-6}$/K.

When the temperature rise is t, the resistivity of copper is

$$\rho = \rho_0(1 + 0.00393\Delta T) \quad (16)$$

where ρ_0 is the material resistivity when the temperature rise is zero.

According to Holm's formula [4], the contact resistance of a single contact spot is

$$R_j = \frac{\rho}{2a} \quad (17)$$

When the load current and the contact pressure are constant, the physical field (electric-thermal-force) coupling relationship of the contacts is:

The contact heat generates a temperature rise ΔT, and the ΔT is substituted into (15) to obtain E_T, the elastic modulus of the material after the temperature rises. E_I=E_T is substituted into (11), and the compression deformation δ is obtained from (12)(13)(14), and the value of the contact spot radius a after the temperature rise is known. From (15), the resistivity after the temperature rise can be obtained. The changed ρ and a are substituted into (17) to obtain R_j. The heating power of the contacts $P = I^2 R_j^2$ will cause a change in temperature rise.

III. CONTACT RESISTANCE CALCULATION

The contactor used in this paper has a large load current and the contact is in a sealed arc extinguishing chamber, so the film resistance is ignored and only the shrinkage resistance is considered. When there are multiple contact spots, the contact resistance is calculated as[4]

$$R_j = \frac{\rho}{\sum_{i=1}^{n_b} 2a_i} \quad (18)$$

The main content of this section is to calculate the number n_b of contact spots and the radius a_i (i = 1, 2, ... , n_b) of each spot. The calculation process is shown in Fig. 4.

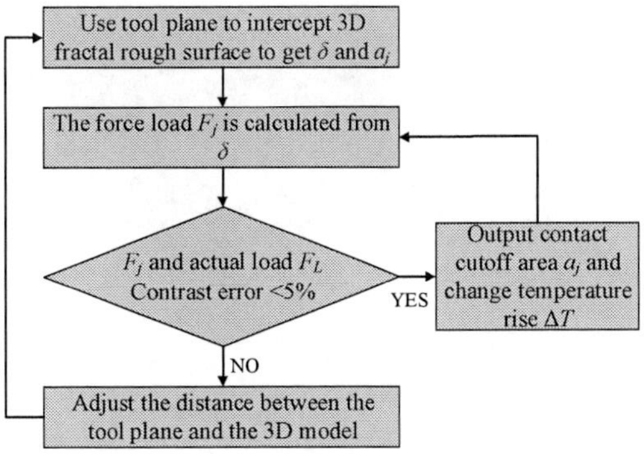

Fig. 4 Contact resistance calculation process under different temperature rises.

The specific steps are as follows:

Firstly, the three-dimensional model of the rough surface is established by the isotropic three-dimensional W-M function proposed by Yan and Komvopoulos [13].

$$Z(x,y) = L\left(\frac{G}{L}\right)^{D-2}\left(\frac{\ln\gamma}{M}\right)^{\frac{1}{2}} \sum_{m=1}^{M}\sum_{n=0}^{n_{\max}} \gamma^{(D-3)n} \times \left\{ \cos\phi_{m,n} - \cos\left[\frac{2\pi\gamma^n (x^2+y^2)^{\frac{1}{2}}}{L} \times \cos\left(\arctan\left(\frac{y}{x}\right) - \frac{\pi m}{M} \right) + \phi_{m,n} \right] \right\} \quad (19)$$

where D is the three-dimensional surface fractal dimension (2<D<3), M is the fold overlap number of the fractal surface, $\phi_{m,n}$ is the Gaussian random number, and other parameters are the same as in (1).

The contact surface used in this paper is measured by the surface profile and calculated by the structural function method. The fractal parameter is D=2.3, $G = 1.64 \times 10^{-12}$ m, taking $L = 4 \times 10^4$ m, and the rough surface is constructed as shown in Fig. 5.

The tool plane is used to simulate the ideal rigid plane to intercept the three-dimensional rough surface model, as showed in Fig. 6:

The number of micro convex bodys in contact with the rigid plane is counted, and the deformation δ and the cutoff area A_j of each micro convex body are measured.

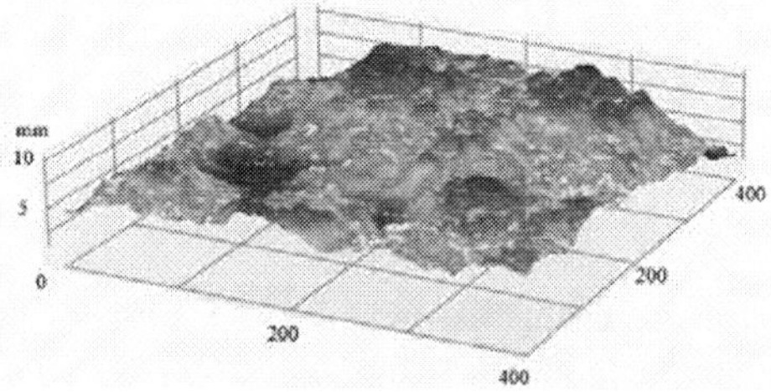

Fig. 5 Three-dimensional fractal rough surface.

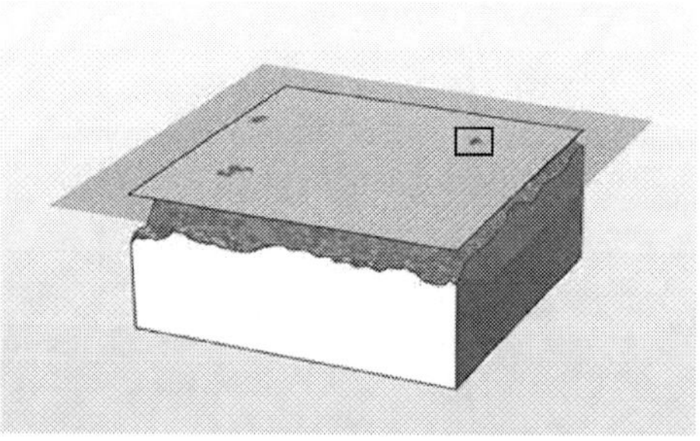

Fig. 6 Schematic of tool plane intercepting micro-convex on rough surface.

When each contact spot is equivalent to a circle, according to $A_j = \pi a_j^2$ and $\pi a_j^2 = 2\pi a^2$, the actual contact spot radius is $a = \left(A_j / 2\pi\right)^{1/2}$. The single micro-convex in the black box corresponding to Figure 6 is shown in Fig. 7.

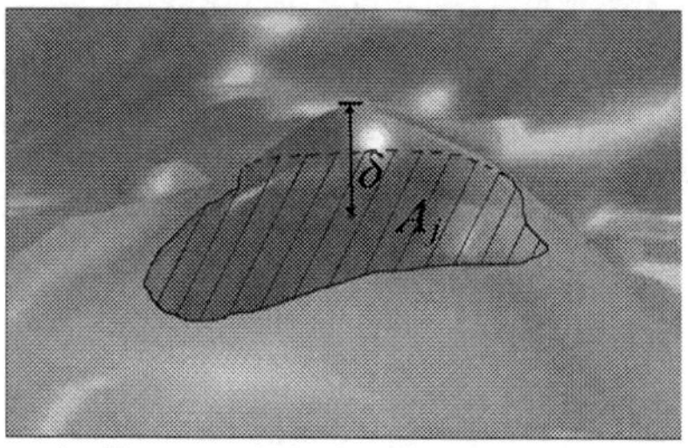

Fig. 7 Schematic diagram of single micro-convex interception data.

On the square three-dimensional model who's sampling length is L, the deformation δ of each micro convex body is obtained by the tool plane. Substituting δ into (12)(13)(14), the contact pressure of each micro convex body is obtained, and the pressure is added to obtain the contact force F_j on the surface of the area $A_L=L^2$. In this paper, the contactor dynamic contact is a plane-plane contact, and the total contact pressure F_z is evenly distributed on the visible contact surface of the area A_s. So the actual pressure on the A_L area is calculated by $F_L = F_z A_L / A_s$.

Compare F_j with F_L, and when the accuracy condition $(F_L - F_j)/F_L \leq 5\%$ is meet, the number of contact spots of the microscopic model and the contact radius of each spot are recorded. Substituting into (18), the contact resistance of the surface having the area A_L is R_{jL}. Since the parallel relationship between the sample faces is known, the contact resistance of the entire contact is $R_{jz} = R_{jL} A_s / A_L$ when the temperature rise is zero. When the contact force comparison does not meet the condition, the distance between the tool plane and the three-dimensional rough model is adjusted, so that the contact shape variable δ is changed until $(F_L - F_j)/F_L \leq 5\%$. Change Gaussian random value in (19) to generate several random three-dimensional rough planes. According to this method, the contact resistance corresponding to each plane is calculated and averaged to improve the calculation accuracy.

Add the temperature rise ΔT during the calculation, change the material properties according to (15) and (16), and adjust the distance of the tool plane to the 3D rough model. When the contact force satisfies the accuracy condition, the contact resistance at the temperature rise ΔT can be obtained. According to this method, take different temperature rise value to obtain the contact resistance of the contact at different ΔT.

IV. SIMULATION AND EXPERIMENTAL MEASUREMENT OF CONTACTOR TEMPERATURE RISE AND CONTACT RESISTANCE

The contactor used in this experiment is shown in Fig. 8. When the main circuit is connected to load current, the voltages at points A and B in the figure are measured. According to $R = U / I$, the resistance between two points can be obtained.

Since the contact surface is in the sealed arc chamber and the temperature cannot be measured, the temperature at points A and C outside the static contact is measured using a thermocouple. The thermal conductivity of copper is good, and the temperature at point A on the outside of the contact is close to the inside. And the internal temperature can be estimated from the simulation results.

Fig. 8 Experiment of contactor temperature rise and contact resistance measurement.

The FEM model of the contact part of the contactor is shown in Fig. 9.

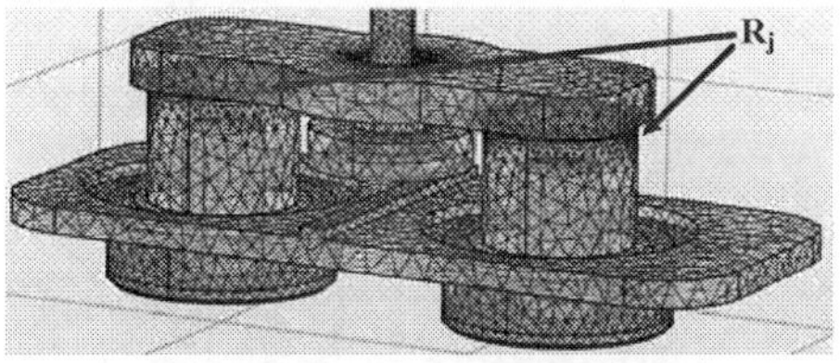

Fig. 9 Contact part FEM model.

The contact resistance calculated by the method herein is applied to the contact surface. The contact resistance is a function of temperature when the pressure is constant. It varies with temperature in the FEM model.

When the experimental environment temperature is 273K and the temperature rise is 0, the conductor resistance of the circuit composed of the moving contact and static contacts is 0.163mΩ, and the contact resistance is 0.794mΩ. The contact resistance calculated according to the method herein was 0.718 mΩ. The error is -9.6%.

When the load current is 160A, the steady state temperature simulation result of the contactor FEM model is shown in Fig. 10.

Fig. 10 Steady-state temperature rise of contactor FEM model.

The experimental and simulation data of contactor temperature rise and contact contact resistance at steady state are shown in Table I.

TABLE I

STEADY STATE SIMULATION AND EXPERIMENTAL DATA FOR CONTACTOR LOAD 160A

Data	simulation	experimant	error
Contact resistanc(mΩ)	0.655	0.616	6.3%
Temperature rise at point A(K)	93.7	84.9	9.4%
Temperature rise at point C(K)	68.3	61.1	10.5%

When the contactor is operated until the temperature reaches a steady state, the contact resistance is significantly reduced. However, the result of the contact resistance obtained by the simulation is smaller than the actual measurement when the temperature rise is zero. And the simulation result of the contact resistance is larger than the actual measured value when the steady state is reached. The contact resistance calculated by the method in this paper has a smaller tendency to change with temperature than the actual measurement.

Contact resistance simulation data of different ambient temperature and load levels are shown in Table II.

TABLE II

SIMULATED CONTACT RESISTANCE UNDER DIFFERENT AMBIENT TEMPERATURES AND LOADS

Ambient temperature(K)	120A	160A	200A
310	0.645 mΩ	0.634 mΩ	0.612 mΩ
350	0.622 mΩ	0.609 mΩ	0.598 mΩ
390	0.597 mΩ	0.586 mΩ	0.576 mΩ

As the temperature increases or the load current increases, the contact resistance of the contacts shows a significant downward trend.

V. CONCLUSION

This paper proposes a contact resistance calculation method based on fractal function and contact theory, combined with the microscopic three-dimensional irregular rough surface model of the contact and the single micro-convex multi-field coupling model. This method can be used to calculate the contact resistance of the contact in contactors at different ambient temperatures and loads. 1) By comparing with the experimental measurements, the calculation error of the contact resistance calculation method proposed in this paper is within the acceptable range. The method has certain application value. 2) When the contact pressure of the contactor is constant, the increase of the ambient temperature and the load will cause the contact resistance value to decrease. 3) The decrease in contact resistance caused by the increase of temperature and load obtained by the calculation method of this paper is less than the experimental measurement results. Further research is required for the factors of micro-convex load and deformation calculation affected by temperature in the micro-contact model.

REFERENCES

[1] Hertz H. On the contact of elastic solids[J]. J Reine AngewMath, 1882(92): 156-171.

[2] Greenwood J A, Williamson J. Contact of nominally flat surfaces[J]. Proceedings of the Royal Society of London. Series A. Mathematical and Physical Sciences. 1966, 295(1442): 300-319.

[3] Greenwood J A, Tripp J H. The elastic contact of rough spheres[J]. Applied Mechanics, 1967, 89(1): 153-159.

[4] Holm R. Electrical contact[M]. New York, USA: Springer, 1979.

[5] Mandelbrot B B. Fractals: form, chance, and dimension [M]. San Francisco: W. H. Freeman and Company, 1977.
[6] Majumdar A, Bhushan M B. Fractal model of elastic -plastic contact between rough surfaces[J]. Journal of Tribology, 1991, 113:1-11.
[7] Wang S, Komvopoulos K. A Fractal Theory of the Interfacial Temperature Distribution in the Slow Sliding Regime: Part I- Elastic Contact and Heat Transfer Analysis[J]. Journal of Tribology 1994, 116: 812-822.
[8] Wang S, Komvopoulos K. A Fractal Theory of the Interfacial Temperature Distribution in the Slow Sliding Regime: Part II- Multiple Domains, Elasto-plastic Contacts and Applications[J]. Journal of Tribology 1994, 116: 824-832.
[9] Kogut L, Komvopoulos K. Electrical contact resistance theory for conductive rough surfaces separated by a thin insulating film[J]. Journal of Applied Physics. 2004, 95(2): 576-585.
[10] Goedecke A, Jackson R L, Mock R. A fractal expansion of a three dimensional elastic-plastic multi-scale rough surface contact model[J]. Tribology International, 2012, 59(2013): 230-239.
[11] Ji Cuicui, Zhu Hua, JIANG Wei. Fractal Prediction Model of Thermal Contact Conductance of Rough Surfaces[J]. Chinese Journal of Mechanical Engineering. 2013, 26(1): 128-136.
[12] Yan W, Komvopoulos K. Contact analysis of elastic-plastic fractal surfaces[J]. Journal of Applied Physics. 1998, 84(7): 3617-3624.
[13] Morag Y, Etsion I. Elastic-Plastic contact analysis of a sphere and a rigid flat[J]. Journal of Applied Mechanics, 2002, 69(5): 657-662.
[14] Johnson K L. Contact mechanics [M]. Beijing: Higher Education Press, 1992.
[15] CHEN Yonghui, ZHANG Xueliang, WEN Shuhua, et al. Research on continuous smooth exponential model of elastic-plastic contact and normal contact stiffness of rough surface[J]. Journal of Xi'an Jiaotong University, 2016, 50(7): 58-67.

Study on the Influence of Temperature and Humidity Alternation Environment on Operation Performance of Residual Current Circuit Breaker

Guojin Liu, Xiang Li, Chenghao Yue, Xinlei Bian
Electrical Engineering College of Hebei University of Technology, Tianjin 300130, China

Abstract—**Residual current circuit breaker is used as terminal protection appliances in low-voltage distribution systems, mainly to ensure the safety of life and property of electricity users. Once they fail, it will bring great harm to the power system and people's lives and property. Its operational characteristics are easily affected by the temperature and humidity of the environment, therefore loses the leakage protection function. The temperature-humidity alternating test is designed to study the changes of the operating characteristics of the electronic residual current circuit breaker during the alternating temperature and humidity cycles. We analyze the data processing results and summarize the effects of temperature and humidity on the operation of the electronic residual current circuit breaker.**

Index Terms— **Temperature and humidity, Electronic residual current circuit breaker, Operating characteristics, Alternating cycle**

I. INTRODUCTION

Residual current circuit breaker can effectively prevent accidents, such as fires and electric shocks caused by electric leakage, and protect the lives and property of electricity users. Therefore, the reliability of the residual current circuit breaker is very important. The study found that many factors can affect the reliability of the residual current circuit breaker , and the residual current circuit breaker may malfunction, refuse to operate and operate. At present, electronic residual current circuit breakers are widely used in China [1-2]. However, with the increasing number of applications for residual current circuit breaker, the working environment of the residual current circuit breaker is becoming more and more complicated, and environmental factors are important factors for the failure of the residual current circuit breaker. Research has shown that temperature and humidity in environmental factors are important factors in the damage of electronic components. The failure caused by temperature and humidity environmental stress accounts for about 60% of all environmental stress failures[3-5]. Long-term high-humidity environment will allow water to penetrate into the interior of the residual current circuit breaker, which will cause aging and corrosion to the internal electronic components. At the same time, the insulating material adsorbing moisture will cause the electrical performance to drop, and the temperature will accelerate the process [6-7]. High temperatures change the characteristic parameters of electronic components and accelerate the corrosion process of electronic products [8-9].

In the actual operating environment, the environmental stress that lead to the failure of the residual current circuit breaker is usually complicated. Studying the influence of single environmental stress on the reliability of residual current circuit breaker has certain limitations. As the case often be, the alternating effect of temperature and humidity combined stress or simultaneous action has more impact on the residual current circuit breaker. Therefore, considering the influence of temperature and humidity on the operation performance of residual current circuit breaker, a climate test of humid heat cycle is designed, using 28 cycles of alternating wet heat cycle as test environment to detect two types of integrated and discrete electronic residual current circuit breakers. The residual current action value in the environment of high humidity and high temperature alternating cycle. Using MATLAB data fitting tool to do fusion processing of experimental data, and analyze the residual current action values of the two kinds of circuit breakers under the combined action of temperature and humidity. At last, summing up the influence of temperature and humidity on the electronic residual current circuit breaker.

II. TEMPERATURE AND HUMIDITY ALTERNATING TEST

A. Test plan

The test equipment used in this environmental test is

mainly the residual current circuit breaker detector, and the temperature regulation and humidity control box. The humidity of the environment where the residual current circuit breaker is located in the test is selected as 95% according to GB/T2423-2008 "Environmental Test Standard for Electrical and Electronic Products", and the temperature is as specified in GB/Z6829-2008 "General Requirements for Residual Current Action Protection Electrical Apparatus". The extreme temperature during the storage and transportation of the residual current circuit breaker. is selected as 55 ° C with reference to GB/T2423-2008 "Environmental Test Standard for Electrical and Electronic Products". In the test, first set the temperature in the temperature adjustment and humidity chamber to 25℃ and the humidity is 95% for 2 hours to ensure that the temperature of the residual current circuit breaker. in the test box is stable at 25℃ and the humidity is 95%.Then keep the humidity unchanged while the temperature inside the control box rises to 55℃ within 3 h and keeps it for 9 h. kept the humidity in the box constant. lowered the temperature to 25℃ within 3 h and maintained for 7 h. Finally, the temperature inside the box is kept constant. Reduce the humidity is to 50% within 1h and maintained for 2h， to ensure that the temperature of the residual current circuit breaker inside the box is stable at 25℃,and the humidity of the environment is 50%. The above is the temperature and humidity change in the temperature and humidity control tank of an experimental period [10-12].The specific changes in temperature and humidity are shown in Figure 1. The measured experimental data is processed by the data fitting tool in MATLAB. In order to ensure sufficient data for data processing and analysis, each residual current circuit breaker. measures 8 sets of data in each cycle, and measures a total of 28 cycles of data for later data processing and analysis.

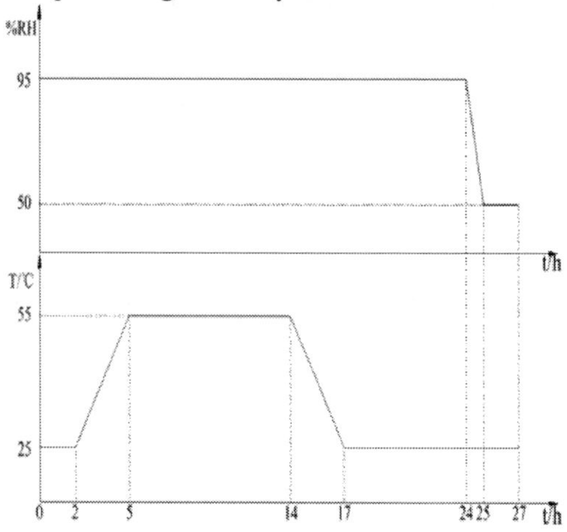

Fig. 1 Specific changes in temperature and humidity in a cycle

B. Sample selection

The test samples are integrated residual current circuit breakers and discrete of residual current circuit breakers with rated residual operating current In=0.03A and operating time t≤0.1s. When selecting the sample, the first step is to check whether the sample has mechanical damage, and then detect the action characteristics. If the unqualified product is found to be removed in time. We select randomly 3 samples from each qualified residual current circuit breaker, and then number the select samples. Integrated residual current circuit breakers No. 1, 2, and 3, and discrete residual current circuit breakers No. 4, 5, and 6.

C. Test circuit

When measuring the residual current action value, use the residual current circuit breaker detector, as shown in Figure 2, which is the block diagram of the test circuit. During the test, the wires L1 and N provide auxiliary power for the residual current circuit breaker, so that the residual current circuit breaker can operate reliably. The wires L1 and L2 apply residual current to the residual current circuit breaker, and measure the current value when the residual current circuit breaker operates.

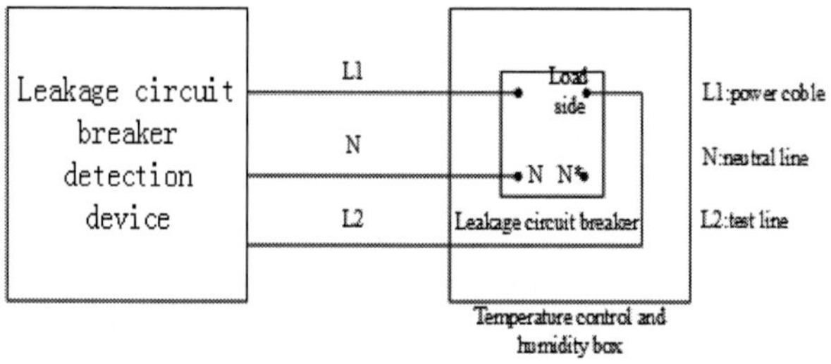

Fig. 2 Test circuit diagram

D. Test data

The experimental data is processed by data fusion, as shown in Table 1.

In order to clearly reflect the variation law of the residual operating current values of each residual current circuit breaker in Table 1, using the data fitting tool in MATLAB fits the data in Table 1. The error values (SSE) of each type fitting are shown in Table 2.

According to Table 2, the fitting error of the linear fitting is the smallest, so the data in Table 1 is linearly fitted using the MATLAB data fitting tool, as shown in Figure 3.

Analysis Table 1 and Figure 3 show that during the temperature-humidity alternating test, the residual operating current values of the two types of residual current circuit breakers were relatively stable during the first 18 cycles, and did not show a significant upward or downward trend. After 18th cycle, the residual operating current values of the two types of residual current circuit breakers all showed a linear decrease trend and the change was obvious. As the test time extended, the downward trend gradually increased, resulting in a gradual increase in the rate of decrease of the residual operating current value. It can be seen from the above analysis that the influence of temperature and humidity on the electronic residual current circuit breaker is a gradual process, and the long-term interaction of the two environmental factors will cause a permanent decrease in the residual operating current value of the electronic residual current circuit breaker. It can be seen from Fig. 3 that the residual operating current values obtained by the integrated residual current circuit breakers No. 1, No. 2 and No. 3 are close to each other during the test period, indicating that the integrated residual current circuit breaker works stably in each cycle. There is a small difference between the integrated residual current circuit breakers. however, the No. 4, No. 5 and No. 6 discrete residual current circuit breakers have different values in the residual current of the same test period, indicating that there is a large difference between each of the discrete residual current circuit breaker products.

Table 1 Change of residual operating current value under alternating temperature and humidity

cycle	*I*/mA					
	No.1	No.2	No.3	No.4	No.5	No.6
1	23.91	23.56	23.77	20.76	20.05	21.09
2	23.80	23.52	23.83	20.67	20.02	21.24
3	23.85	23.63	23.90	20.70	20.00	21.34
4	23.63	23.49	23.69	20.50	19.91	20.98
5	23.88	23.48	23.78	20.75	20.02	21.14
6	23.58	23.40	23.58	20.45	19.73	21.02
7	23.60	23.33	23.60	20.44	19.70	21.00
8	23.44	23.29	23.49	20.47	19.76	20.63
9	23.60	23.39	23.67	20.57	19.83	20.78
10	23.67	23.49	23.64	20.57	19.80	20.85
11	23.78	23.57	23.83	20.65	19.89	21.27
12	23.77	23.53	23.74	20.68	19.90	20.92
13	23.74	23.54	23.68	20.67	19.90	20.90
14	23.62	23.34	23.53	20.57	19.97	21.05
15	23.61	23.45	23.68	20.57	19.80	20.83
16	23.75	23.49	23.70	20.56	19.87	21.10

Table 1 (Continued)

cycle	*I*/mA					
	No.1	No.2	No.3	No.4	No.5	No.6
17	23.66	23.24	23.60	20.70	19.86	20.72
18	23.77	23.21	23.60	20.56	19.80	20.93
19	23.61	23.30	23.61	20.60	19.67	20.91
20	23.60	23.30	23.50	20.30	19.59	20.73
21	23.59	23.10	23.58	20.60	19.83	20.79
22	23.67	23.10	23.48	20.50	19.80	20.79
23	23.50	22.67	23.00	20.10	18.56	19.51
24	23.30	22.27	22.47	20.14	18.30	19.14
25	23.10	21.55	21.52	19.25	17.90	18.52
26	22.75	21.37	21.37	18.98	17.50	18.37
27	22.44	21.11	21.23	18.52	17.32	18.29
28	22.12	20.71	21.04	18.30	17.38	18.28

Table 2 Various types of fitting error values

Fitting type	Fitting error（SSE）					
	No.1	No.2	No.3	No.4	No.5	No.6
Linear fit	0.2043	0.3916	1.1604	0.4540	1.4191	2.2989
Exponential fitting	0.3235	0.6670	1.5050	0.6943	1.8976	2.8624
Power Fitting	0.3103	0.6041	1.4067	0.6492	1.7981	2.7094
Fourier Fitting	0.2138	0.4423	0.9048	0.4974	3.2430	4.2391
Gaussian Fitting	0.2257	0.4321	0.7926	0.4928	3.4316	4.4630

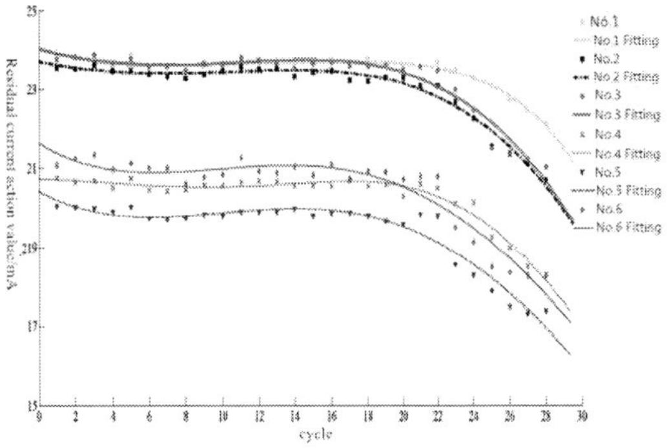

Fig. 3 Changes in residual operating current values under alternating temperature and humidity

III. ANALYSIS OF RESULTS

In the alternating temperature and humidity environment, the effects of temperature and humidity on the electronic residual current circuit breakers overlap each other. The insulation and electrical strength of the residual current circuit breaker will decrease with the increase of temperature and humidity. In addition, the temperature rise will change the characteristic parameters of the internal electronic components of the residual current circuit breaker, the zero-sequence current transformer (TA) core magnetic permeability will decrease with the increase of temperature, and the trigger current and trigger voltage of the SCR control electrode will also decrease with the increase of temperature, as shown in Figure 4 and Figure 5. The change of TA and SCR characteristic parameters have impacts on the residual current value of the residual current circuit breaker. Studies have shown that under the influence of short-term temperature, the changes of TA and SCR characteristic parameters of the residual current circuit breaker can be recovered. When the temperature is reduced to normal temperature, the characteristic parameters can recover. However, long-term temperature cycling will cause the electronic components to age, causing permanent changes in the component's characteristic parameters, which means that the zero-sequence current transformer (TA) core magnetic permeability and the SCR control electrode trigger current trigger voltage can be permanently reduced. In the temperature and humidity alternating cycle test, not only the temperature cycle, but also the influence of humidity, the higher humidity could accelerate the rate of temperature influence. Under the temperature and humidity alternating cycle, the performance of the internal electronic components of the residual current circuit breaker will be accelerated. The change of the property causes the residual operating current value of the residual current circuit breaker to be permanently reduced, and the normal power supply cannot be guaranteed.

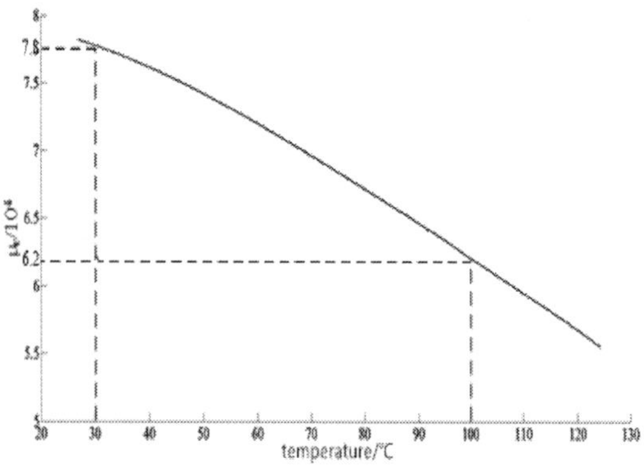

Fig. 4 TA core magnetic permeability with temperature curve

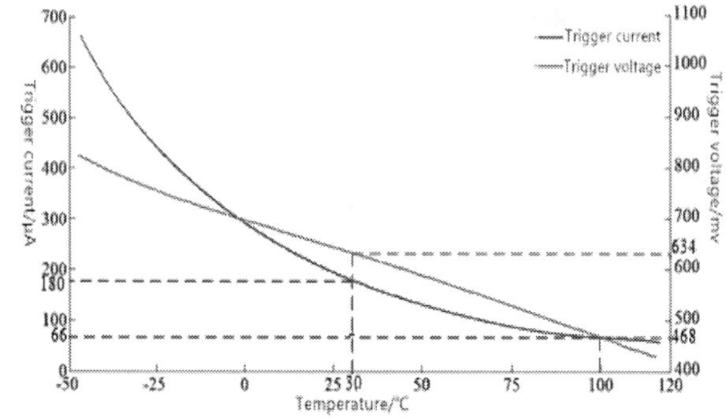

Fig. 5 SCR gate trigger current trigger voltage versus temperature curve

Influence of the internal electronic component characteristic parameter change on the residual current circuit breaker is: the decrease of the magnetic permeability of the TA core causes the magnetic induction intensity to decrease, causing the zero-sequence current value induced of the secondary side to decrease, so that the current flowing into the SCR control electrode is reduced, cause the residual operating current required for the operation of the residual current circuit breaker increases, and the trigger voltage of the SCR and the trigger current decrease to make it easier to conduct, and the residual operating current required for the operation of the residual current circuit breaker decreases. It can be seen that the change of the TA and SCR characteristic parameters has the opposite effect on the change of the residual operating current value of the residual current circuit breaker, but it is not difficult to find the SCR trigger current, the magnitude of the change of the trigger voltage is much larger than the variation of TA at the same temperature range from the Figure 4 and Figure 5. Therefore, it can be considered that the influence of the parameter change of the SCR on the residual current circuit breaker during the temperature rise is greater than the influence of the parameter change of the TA on the residual current circuit breaker, that is, the change of thyristor (SCR) characteristic parameters is the main factor for the change of residual operating current value of residual current circuit breaker . The increase in temperature can also significantly affect the corrosion process of electronic components[13-14]. Residual current circuit breakers are electronic products with printed circuit boards. The insulation material of the circuit board also decomposes organic gases at high temperatures, which not only changes its electrical characteristics, but also corrodes adjacent components. In the temperature and humidity alternating cycle experiment, not only the temperature influence but also the humidity effect. When the humidity is relatively large, the temperature has a great influence on the corrosion phenomenon and accelerates the existing corrosion phenomenon.

Humidity can significantly affect the performance of electronic products. Water vapor usually undergoes adsorption, absorption and diffusion, resulting a poor performance of the material and low strength, which leads to a decrease in mechanical properties or electrical properties of the product [15]. When the ambient humidity is high, water vapor will condense on the PCB and various electronic components. Figure 6 shows the integrated circuit board where condensation occurs. Since the packaging of the electronic components and the material of the PCB are hygroscopic, the long-term high-humidity environment causes the condensed moisture to penetrate into the PCB and the electronic components. The moisture that penetrates into the inside of the PCB will cause the ions on the board to migrate, causing the insulation strength to decrease. The moisture that penetrates into the inside of the PCB will cause the ions on the board to migrate, causing the insulation strength to decrease. The zero-sequence current in the integrated circuit will increase compared to the normal humidity, therefore, the residual operating current required for the operation of the residual current circuit breaker is reduced. The higher temperature during the experiment promotes the entry of moisture into the PCB and electronic components and accelerates the internal ion migration process.

Fig. 6 Integrated circuit board condensation phenomenon

From the above analysis, it can be inferred that the temperature characteristics of the thyristor (SCR) and the change in the dielectric strength of the electronic components are the main factors causing the change of residual operating current value of residual current circuit breaker. When the residual current circuit breaker is in an operating environment with alternating temperature and humidity for a long time, on the one hand, the trigger voltage and the trigger current of the internal SCR are reduced to make it easier to conduct, and the residual operating current required for the residual current circuit breaker to operate is reduced; On the other hand, a decrease in the dielectric strength of the internal electronic components causes an increase in the zero-sequence current in the integrated circuit, which also causes a decrease in the residual operating current value. As the operation time increases, the residual operating current value of the residual current circuit breaker can reduce permanently, so that the residual current circuit breaker cannot guarantee normal power supply.

IV. CONCLUSION

In this paper, the temperature-humidity alternating test is designed to detect the change of the residual current action value of the electronic residual current circuit breaker in the temperature and humidity alternating environment for a long time. Using the data fitting tool of MATLAB to data fusion processing, analysis of the processed data can lead to the following conclusions.

Compared with the influence of single stress of temperature and humidity on the electronic residual current circuit breaker, the temperature and humidity act together to promote each other. Humidity can accelerate the effect of temperature on the electronic residual current circuit breaker. The same, the temperature also accelerate the influence of humidity on the electronic residual current circuit breaker. That is to say, the combination of temperature and humidity can accelerate the deterioration of the residual current circuit breaker. However, the influence of temperature and humidity on the electronic residual current circuit breaker is a gradual process. When the temperature and humidity are alternating for a short time,the influence on the value of residual operating current is not obvious, but for a long time,the residual operating current value of the electronic residual current circuit breaker is a significant downward trend. As the test time increases, the rate of decrease of the residual operating current value gradually increases, which causes the residual operating current value of the electronic residual current circuit breaker to be permanently reduced, so that the residual current circuit breaker frequently trips, and normal power supply cannot be guaranteed.

REFERENCES

[1] Liu Guojin, Lu Jianguo, Li Zhigang. Test Scheme for Reliability Verification of Leakage Protector[J]. Machine Tool Electric Apparatus,2001, 28(5): 10-12.

[2] Wu Yi, Lu Jianguo, Chi Changchun. Reliability and Test Method of residual current circuit breaker [J]. Electrical Apparatus and Energy Efficiency Management Technology, 2008(11): 50-54.

[3] Liu Bin.The role of temperature and humidity stress in the failure of electrical and electronic products[J].

Electronic Technology and Software Engineering, 2017(10): 235.

[4] Lakshminarayanan V, Sriraam N. The effect of temperature on the reliability of electronic components[M]. 2014.

[5] Ma J, Xu H, Li C F, et al. Research of high precision quartz temperature sensor system based on data fusion technology[C]// International Conference on Measurement, Information and Control. 2013:1051-1054.

[6] Liu Guojin, Bian Xinlei, Ma Xiaoyan, LI Yixin, Bai Jiahang.Effect Research of Temperature on Operating Characteristics of Residual Current Circuit Breaker Based on Data Fusion Technology [j].Measurement & Control Technology, 2018, 37(04): 41-45.

[7] Zhong Xiaoming, Zhang Manyuan, Wu Hongguang. Discussion on the influence of ambient temperature on the residual current action characteristics [C]. See: Yin Tianwen. Proceedings of the Annual Conference of the Low Voltage Electrical Committee of China Electrotechnical Society. Beijing: China Electrotechnical Society, 2005. 65-66.

[8] Lei yun, Qiu Yunfeng. Research on Parameter Response of Electronic Components Based on Temperature Change[J]. Computers and Digital Engineering, 2015, 43(1): 155-158.

[9] Joshy S, Verdingovas V, Jellesen M, et al. Simulation of Electronic Circuit Sensitivity Towards Humidity Using Electrochemical Data on Water Layer[C]. Electronics Packaging and Technology Conference (EPTC), 2015 IEEE 17th. IEEE, 2015:1-5.

[10] Yan Jinglian, Wang Jie. GB/T 2423.4[S], 2008, Environmental Test for Electrical and Electronic Products Part 2: Test Methods Test Db Alternating Damp Heat (12h+12h Cycle). Beijing: China Standard Press, 2008.

[11] Qu degang, Zhang yong. Selection of Moisture and Heat Resistance of Low Voltage Electrical Products[J]. Low Voltage Apparatus, 2010(03): 54-56.

[12] Zhao Jiying,Lu Jianguo,Wang Haitao.Study on reliability test method of over-load relay. Proceedings of the 52nd IEEE Holm Conference on Electrical Contacts, 2007, 58-62.

[13] Asit Kumar Gain,Liangchi Zhang. Temperature and humidity effects on microstructure and mechanical properties of an environmentally friendly Sn–Ag–Cu material[J]. Journal of Materials Science, 2019, 54(19).

[14] Wu ningbiao. The role of temperature and humidity stress in the failure of electrical and electronic products[J]. Printed Circuit Information 2005(02): 14-20+41

[15] Peng qian. Humid heat environment and Reliability of Electronic Products[J].Electronic Product Reliability and Environmental Testing, 2003, (5): 57-60.

Index

K

L

M

N

P

Q

R

S

T

V